MASTER VISUALLY

by Jon McFarland
and Jinjer Simon

Visual®

3ds Max® 8

Wiley Publishing, Inc.

Master VISUALLY® 3ds Max® 8

Published by
Wiley Publishing, Inc.
111 River Street
Hoboken, NJ 07030-5774

Published simultaneously in Canada

Library of Congress Control Number: 2005923199

ISBN-13: 978-0-7645-7992-9

ISBN-10: 0-7645-7992-4

Manufactured in the United States of America

10 9 8 7 6 5 4 3 2 1

1K/QX/QS/QW/IN

Trademark Acknowledgments

Contact Us

For general information on our other products and services please contact our Customer Care Department within the U.S. at 800-762-2974, outside the U.S. at 317-572-3993 or fax 317-572-4002.

For technical support please visit www.wiley.com/techsupport.

WILEY

Sales

Contact Wiley
at (800) 762-2974 or
fax (317) 572-4002.

Praise for Visual Books...

"If you have to see it to believe it, this is the book for you!"

—PC World

"A master tutorial/reference — from the leaders in visual learning!"

—Infoworld

"A publishing concept whose time has come!"

—The Globe and Mail

"Just wanted to say THANK YOU to your company for providing books which make learning fast, easy, and exciting! I learn visually so your books have helped me greatly — from Windows instruction to Web development. Best wishes for continued success."

—Angela J. Barker (Springfield, MO)

"I have over the last 10–15 years purchased thousands of dollars worth of computer books but find your books the most easily read, best set out, and most helpful and easily understood books on software and computers I have ever read. Please keep up the good work."

—John Gatt (Adamstown Heights, Australia)

"You're marvelous! I am greatly in your debt."

—Patrick Baird (Lacey, WA)

"I am an avid fan of your Visual books. If I need to learn anything, I just buy one of your books and learn the topic in no time. Wonders! I have even trained my friends to give me Visual books as gifts."

—Illona Bergstrom (Aventura, FL)

"I have quite a few of your Visual books and have been very pleased with all of them. I love the way the lessons are presented!"

—Mary Jane Newman (Yorba Linda, CA)

"Like a lot of other people, I understand things best when I see them visually. Your books really make learning easy and life more fun."

—John T. Frey (Cadillac, MI)

"Your Visual books have been a great help to me. I now have a number of your books and they are all great. My friends always ask to borrow my Visual books — trouble is, I always have to ask for them back!"

—John Robson
(Brampton, Ontario, Canada)

"I write to extend my thanks and appreciation for your books. They are clear, easy to follow, and straight to the point. Keep up the good work! I bought several of your books and they are just right! No regrets! I will always buy your books because they are the best."

—Seward Kollie (Dakar, Senegal)

"What fantastic teaching books you have produced! Congratulations to you and your staff."

—Bruno Tonon (Melbourne, Australia)

"Thank you for the wonderful books you produce. It wasn't until I was an adult that I discovered how I learn — visually. Although a few publishers claim to present the materially visually, nothing compares to Visual books. I love the simple layout. Everything is easy to follow. I can just grab a book and use it at my computer, lesson by lesson. And I understand the material! You really know the way I think and learn. Thanks so much!"

—Stacey Han (Avondale, AZ)

"The Greatest. This whole series is the best computer-learning tool of any kind I've ever seen."

—Joe Orr (Brooklyn, NY)

Credits

Project Editor
Maureen Spears
Marylouise Wiack

Acquisitions Editor
Jody Lefevere

Product Development Manager
Courtney Allen

Copy Editor
Marylouise Wiack

Technical Editor
Mark Gerhard

Editorial Manager
Robyn Siesky

Manufacturing
Allan Conley
Linda Cook
Paul Gilchrist
Jennifer Guynn

Special Help
Kim Heusel
Adrienne Porter
Scott Tullis

Book Design
Kathie Rickard

Project Coordinator
Maridee Ennis

Layout
Sean Decker
Carrie Foster
Jennifer Heleine
LeAndra Hosier
Amanda Spagnuolo

Screen Artist
Jill A. Proll

Illustrators
Ronda David-Burroughs

Proofreader
Vickie Broyles

Quality Control
Amanda Briggs

Indexer
Lynnzee Elze

Vice President and Executive Group Publisher
Richard Swadley

Vice President and Publisher
Barry Pruett

Composition Director
Debbie Stailey

About the Authors

Jon McFarland is the manager of the CAD department for a Cleveland, Ohio based national owner/developer/manager of retail, office and residential properties. His responsibilities include the creation of, and supervision for, CAD drawings, 3D computer models and fly through animations of proposed facilities. He also teaches computer animation at the Virginia Marti College of Art and Design in Lakewood, Ohio.

Jon lives outside of Cleveland with his lovely wife Lucy and two, quickly growing, sons Zach and Jacob.

Jinjer Simon has been actively involved in the computer industry for the past 18 years. Her involvement includes programming, providing software technical support, training end-users, developing written and online user documentation, creating software tutorials, and developing Web sites. She is the author of several computer books, including *Excel Programming: Your visual blueprint for creating interactive spreadsheets, Excel Data Analysis: Your visual blueprint for analyzing data, charts, and PivotTables,* and *Windows CE 2 For Dummies.*

Author's Acknowledgments

Putting this text together was a fun and interesting experience, and I would like to thank Mike Roney for bringing me on board and Maureen Spears for keeping me on track. I would also like to thank my technical editor, Mark Gerhard, for lending his expertise and Marylouise Wiack for her excellent copy editing. Finally, I would like to thank my family, Lucy, Zach and Jacob for supporting me and for reminding of me what is truly important.

—Jon McFarland

PART I Explore the 3ds Max 8 Interface

1) Optimizing the 3ds Max Environment
2) Working with Objects
3) Organizing Objects

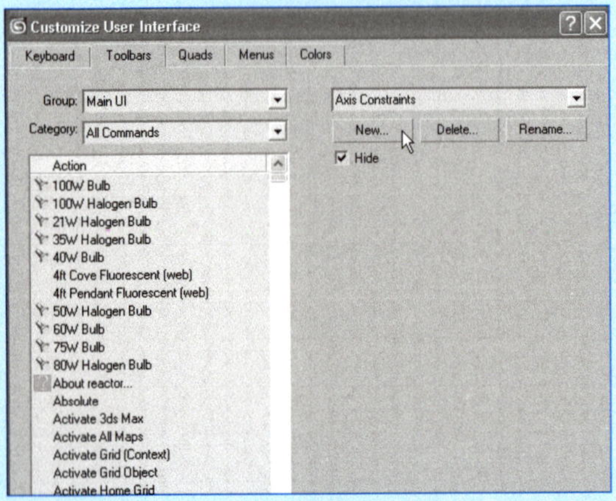

PART II Modeling Your Objects

4) Create Objects Efficiently in 3ds Max
5) Modifying 2D Objects
6) Modifying 3D Objects
7) Creating Architectural, Engineering, and Construction Objects

PART III Animating Your Scene

8) Control Animation Using Keyframes
9) Working with the Track View
10) Working with Controllers and Constraints
11) Adjusting Animation with the Curve Editor
12) Working with the Dope Sheet Editor
13) Working with Hierarchies

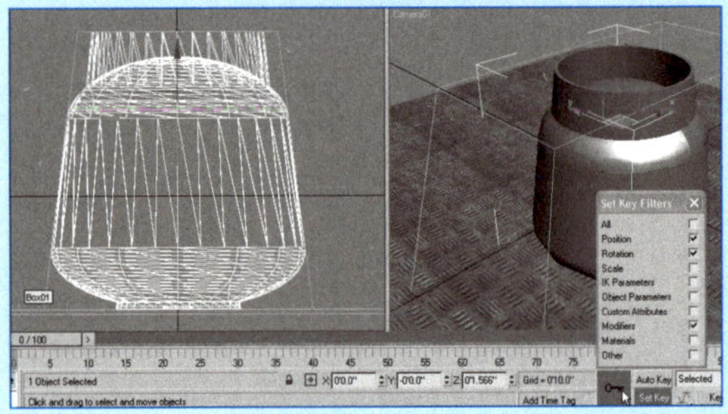

PART IV Working with Materials and Maps

14) Using the Material Editor
15) Working with the Material and Map Browser
16) Using Material and Channel Types

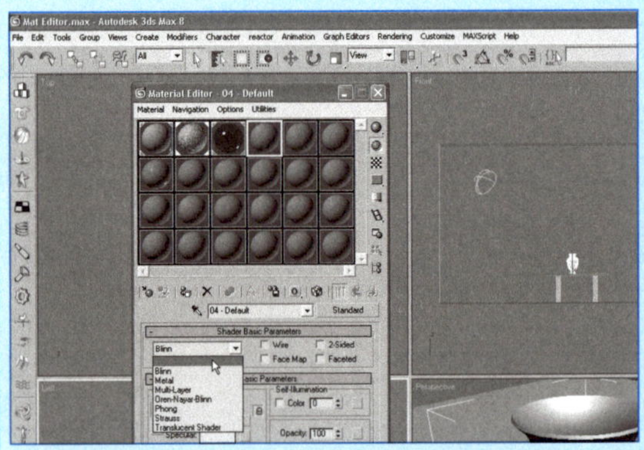

WHAT'S INSIDE

PART V Adding Lights and Cameras

PART VI Performing Quality Rendering

PART VII Apply Effects for Super Results

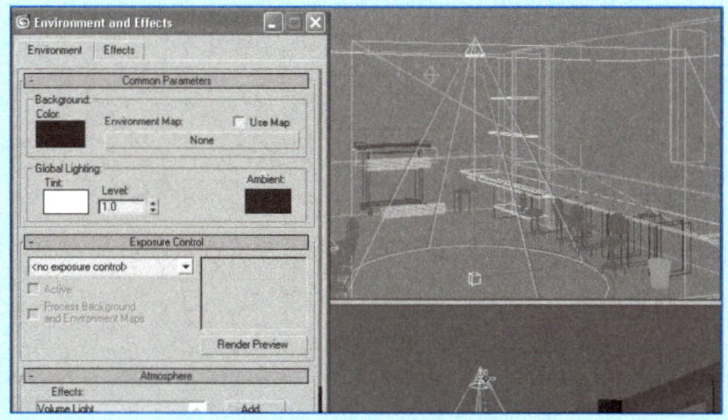

PART VIII Appendix

PART I Explore the 3ds Max 8 Interface

1 Optimizing the 3ds Max Environment

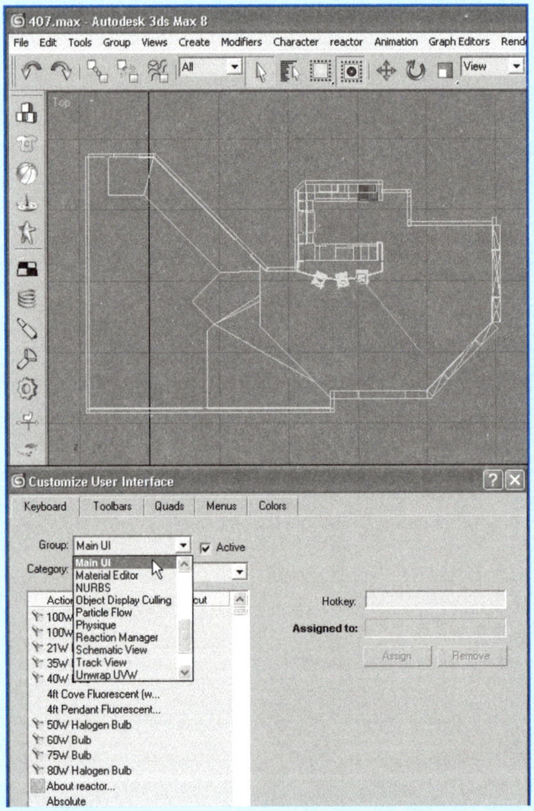

2 Working with Objects

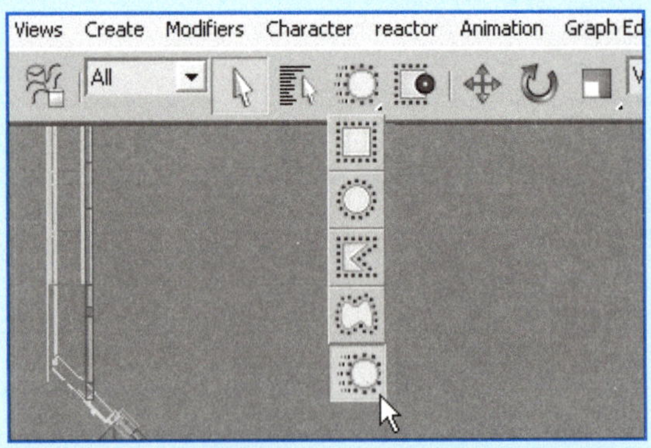

TABLE OF CONTENTS

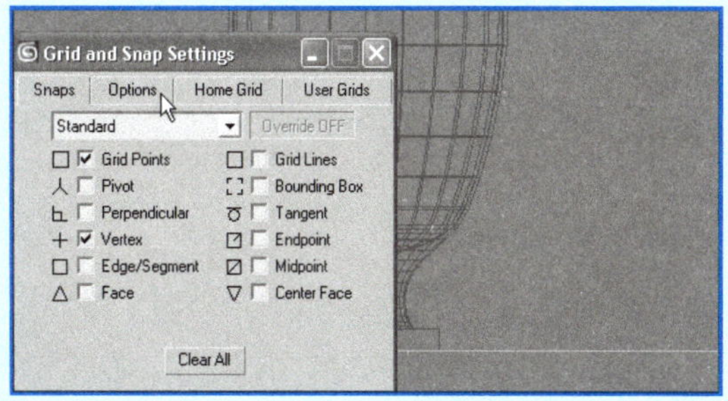

3 Organizing Objects

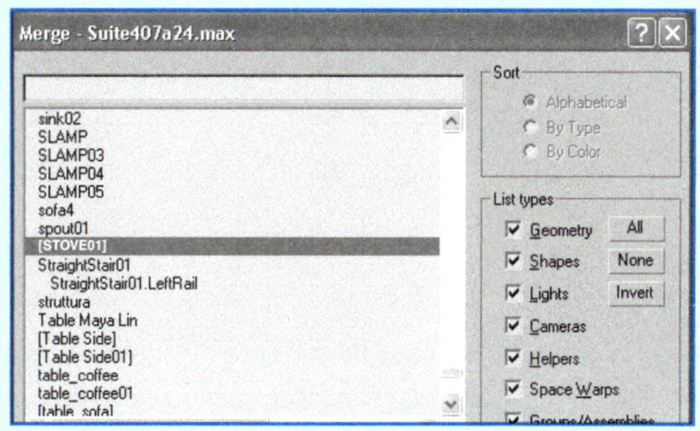

PART II Modeling Your Objects

4 Create Objects Efficiently in 3ds Max

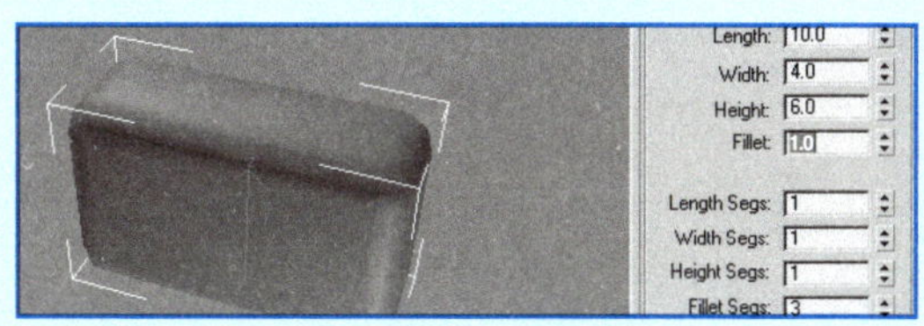

5 Modifying 2D Objects

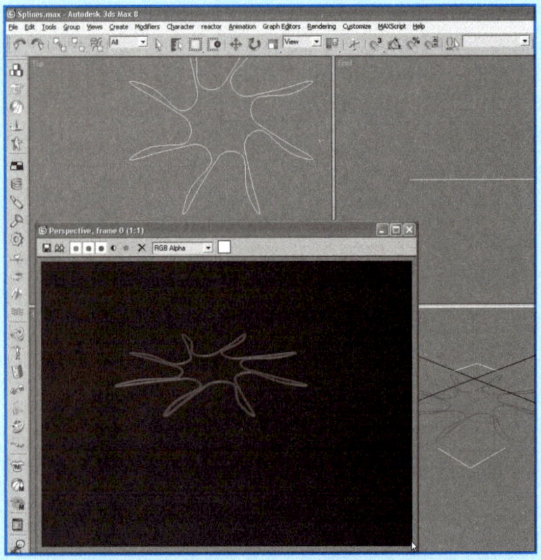

6 Modifying 3D Objects

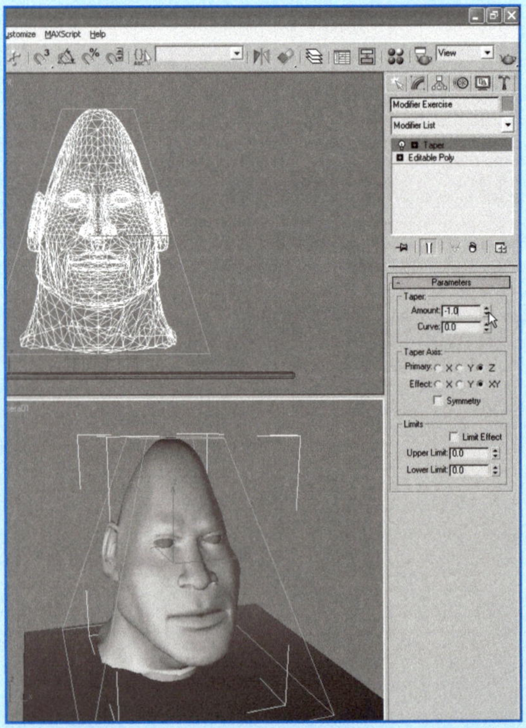

TABLE OF CONTENTS

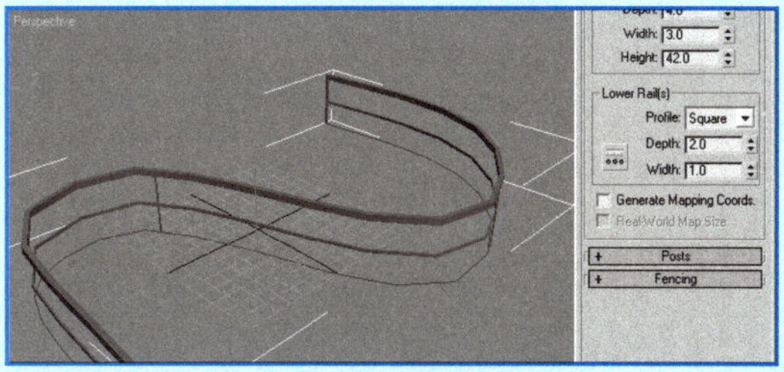

PART III Animating Your Scene

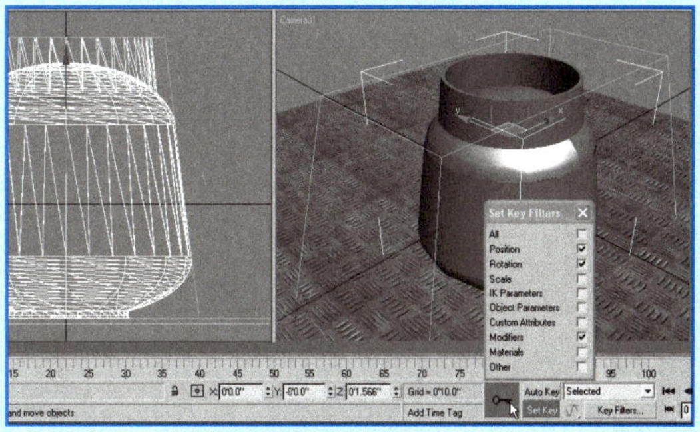

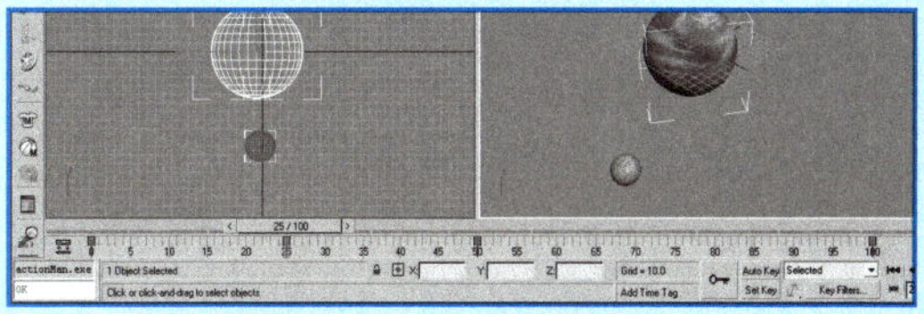

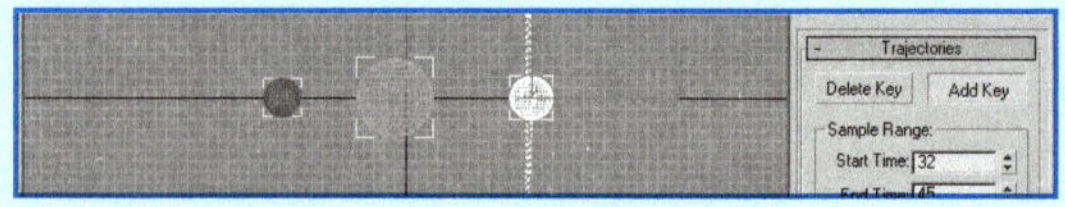

10 Working with Controllers and Constraints

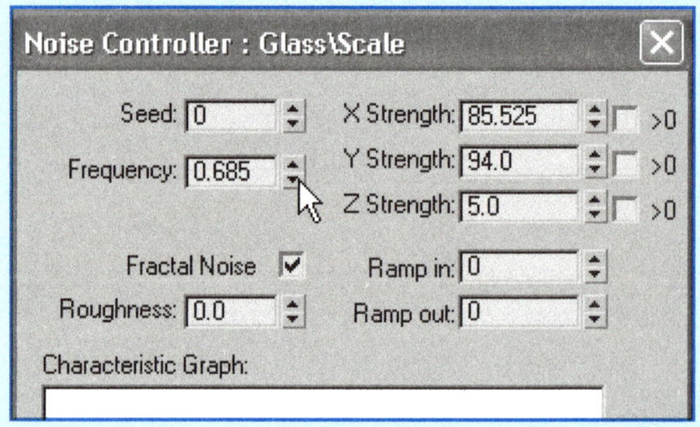

11 Adjusting Animation with the Curve Editor

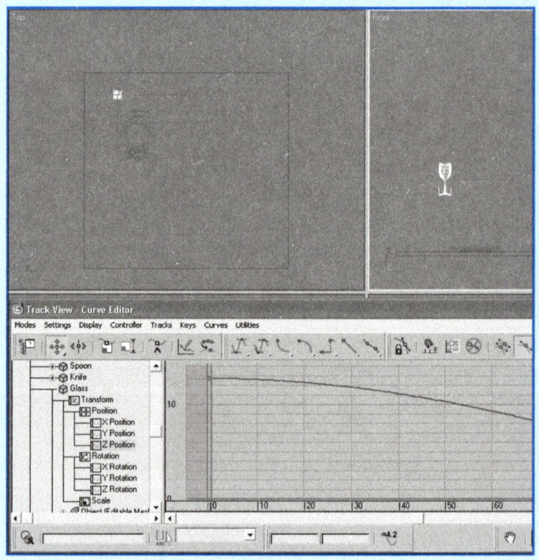

12 Working with the Dope Sheet Editor

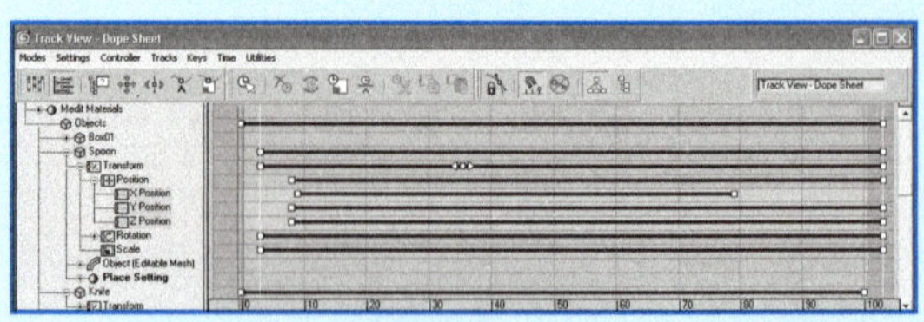

TABLE OF CONTENTS

⑬ Working with Hierarchies

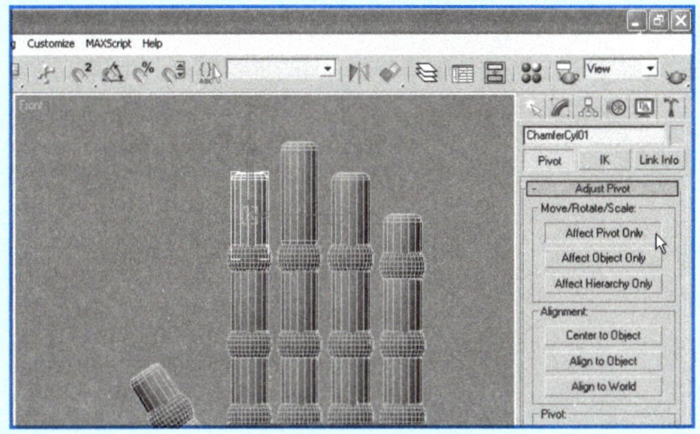

PART IV Working with Materials and Maps

⑭ Using the Material Editor

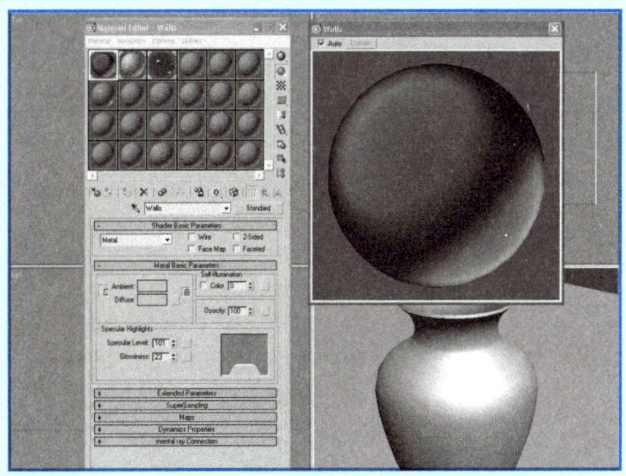

⑮ Working with the Material and Map Browser

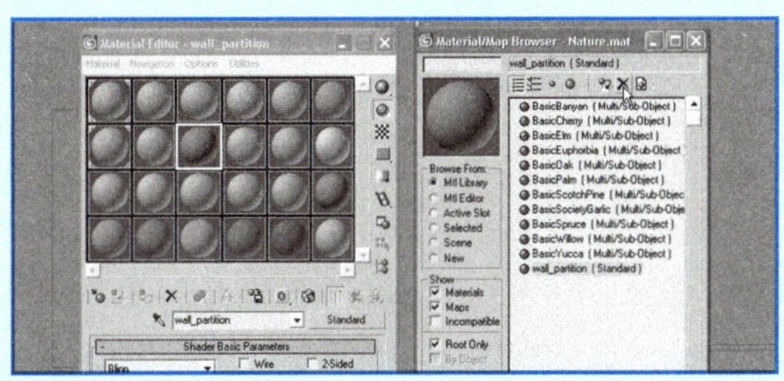

⑯ Using Material and Channel Types

PART V Adding Lights and Cameras

⑰ Using Standard Lights

⑱ Using Advanced Lighting

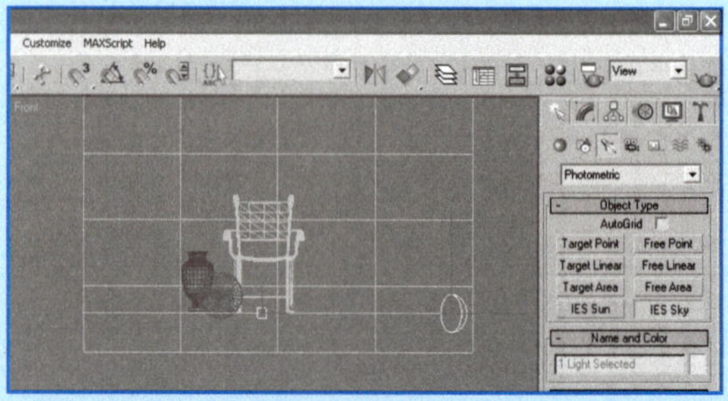

TABLE OF CONTENTS

19 Using Cameras

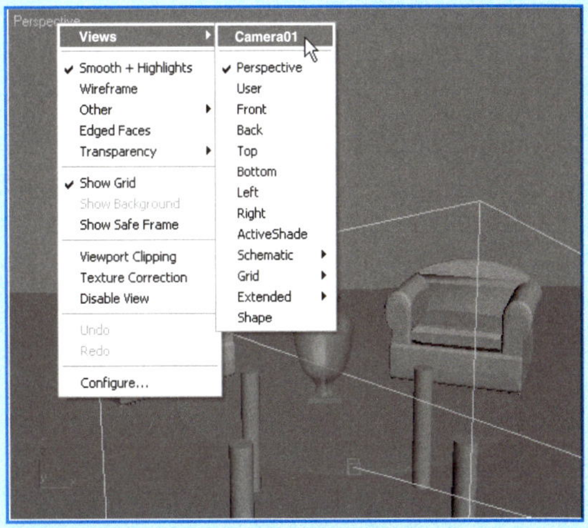

PART VI Performing Quality Rendering

20 Using the Render Tools

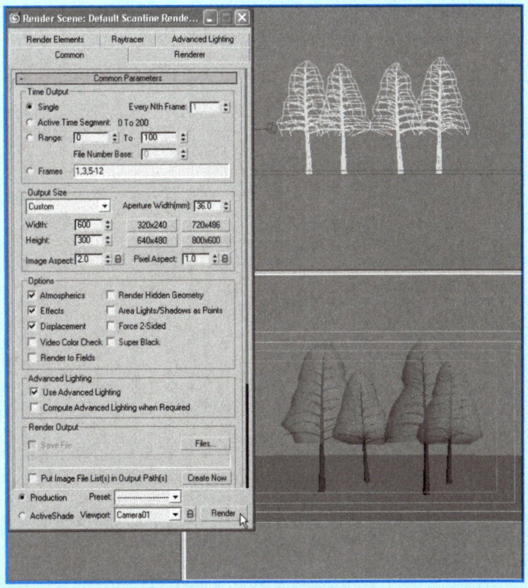

21 Using the Render Scene Dialog Box

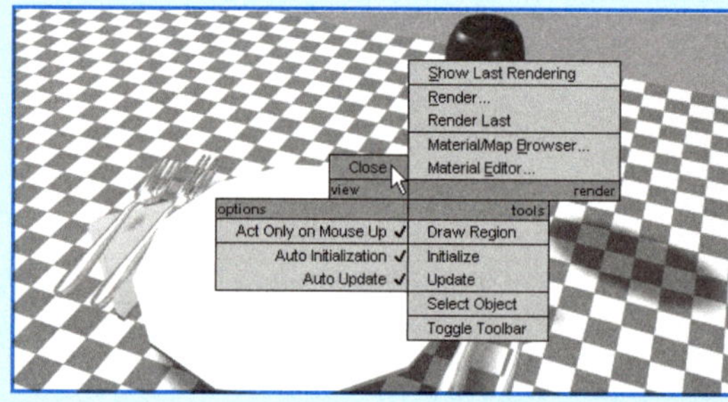

22 Apply Rendering Effects

PART VII Apply Effects for Super Results

23 Create Atmospheric Effects

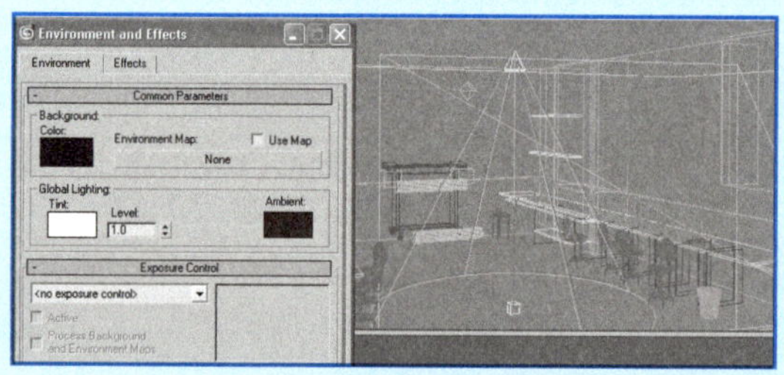

24 Working with Particle Systems

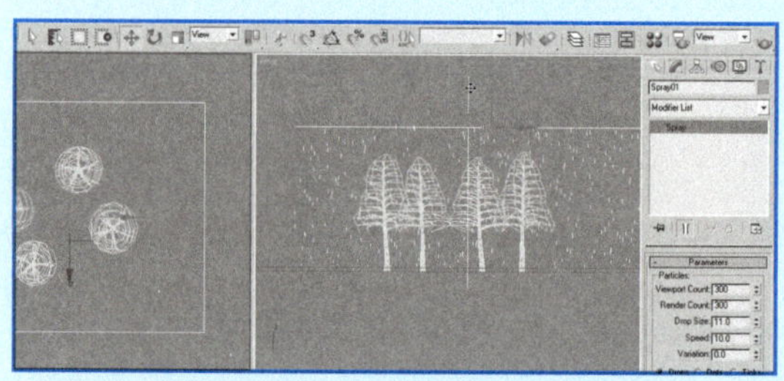

TABLE OF CONTENTS

25 Using Space Warps

26 Working with the Reactor

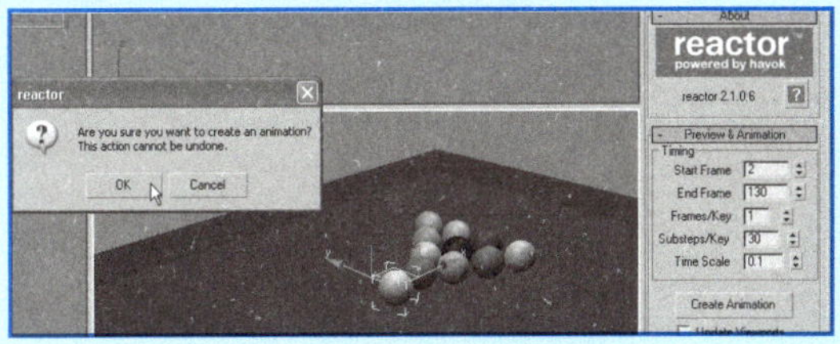

27 Controlling a Character with Character Studio

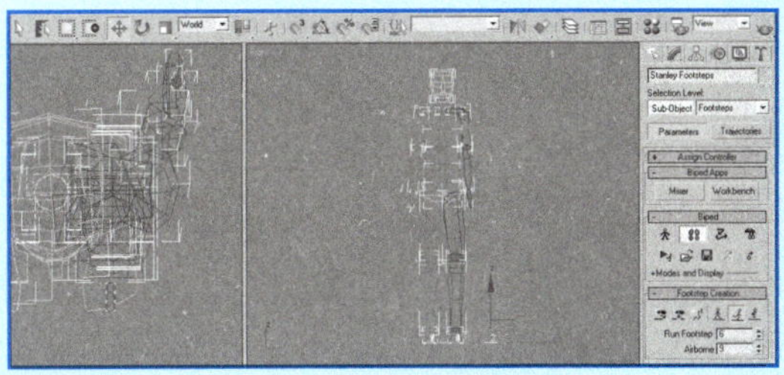

28 Adding Cloth to Your Scenes

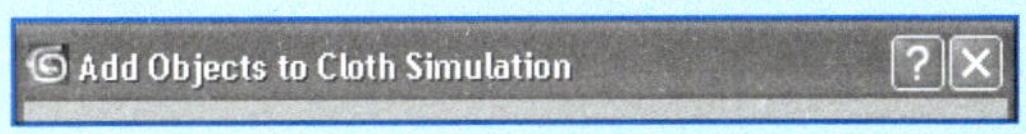

PART VIII Appendix

TABLE OF CONTENTS

How to Use this Master VISUALLY Book

Do you look at the pictures in a book or newspaper before anything else on a page? Would you rather see an image than read how to do something? Search no further. This book is for you. Opening *Master VISUALLY 3ds Max 8* allows you to read less and learn more about 3ds Max.

Who Needs This Book

This book is for a reader who has never used this particular technology or software application. It is also for more computer literate individuals who want to expand their knowledge of the different features that 3ds Max has to offer. We assume you already have a basic computer knowledge and know how to open and save files.

Book Organization

Master VISUALLY 3ds Max 8 has 29 chapters and is divided into VIII parts.

Part I, **Explore the 3ds Max 8 Interface**, gets you started with 3ds Max by showing you how set up and navigate through the viewports as well as the many ways to select, transform, adjust, display and copy objects. This section also covers organizing your scenes and transferring data between different 3ds Max files.

Part II, **Modeling Your Objects,** shows you how to efficiently create 2D and 3D objects and how to create 3D objects from 2D objects. Many of the 3ds Max modifiers and compound objects that use one of more pieces of geometry to create new shapes, and the Architectural/Engineering/Construction (AEC) objects included with 3ds Max are covered.

Part III, **Animating Your Scene,** demonstrates the techniques for creating keyframe animation and manipulating the keyframes in both the Curve Editor and Dope Sheet Track View editors. You will also gain an understanding of adding transform keys in the Motion panel and how to assign and modify object motion through the uses of controllers and constraints. Hierarchies, the passing of transforms from one object to another, are also covered in this section.

Part IV, **Working with Materials and Maps,** covers creating materials in the 3ds Max Material Editor and saving them into material libraries. The different material types, map types and navigating with the Material/Map Browser are explained and covered.

Part V, **Adding Lights and Cameras,** shows you how to create standard and advanced lighting systems and how to design lighting that is accurate to your scene's proposed time and location. You will also learn how to create and manipulate virtual camera and how to add camera effects.

Part VI, **Performing Quality Rendering,** explores the Render Scene dialog box and how it is used to define the parameters of the rendering for a scene. Selectively choosing what to render, saving render settings as presets, and adding rendering effects are also covered in this section.

Part VII, **Apply Effects for Super Results**, covers some of the more fun and interesting capabilities of 3ds Max including particle systems, space warps and the reactor simulation utility. Character animation with Character Studio and the new Cloth and Hair features of 3ds Max 8 are also addressed.

Part VIII gives you valuable information concerning the companion CD to this book. The CD contains a trial version of 3ds Max 8 as well as author files, which you can use to follow the various steps in this book.

Chapter Organization

This book consists of sections, all listed in the book's table of contents. A *section* is a set of steps that show you how to complete a specific computer task.

Each section, usually contained on two or four facing pages, has an introduction to the task at hand, a set of full-color screen shots and steps that walk you through the task, and a set of tips. This format allows you to quickly look at a topic of interest and learn it instantly.

Chapters group together three or more sections with a common theme. A chapter may also contain pages that give you the background information needed to understand the sections in a chapter.

What You Need to Use This Book

You need a PC running Windows 2000 or XP with 3ds Max 8 installed. If the Trial version is installed, the maps and materials must also be included.

HOW TO USE THIS BOOK

Using the Mouse

This book uses the following conventions to describe the actions you perform when using the mouse:

Click

Press your left mouse button once. You generally click your mouse on something to select something on the screen.

Double-click

Press your left mouse button twice. Double-clicking something on the computer screen generally opens whatever item you have double-clicked.

Right-click

Press your right mouse button. When you right-click anything on the computer screen, the program displays a contextual menu containing commands specific to the selected item.

Click and Drag, and Release the Mouse

Move your mouse pointer and hover it over an item on the screen. Press and hold down the left mouse button. Now, move the mouse to where you want to place the item and then release the button. You use this method to move an item from one area of the computer screen to another.

Scroll

Roll the mouse's scroll wheel forward or backward. This generally moves a selection highlight up or down a list and also zooms in or out of a viewport.

The Conventions in This Book

A number of typographic and layout styles have been used throughout *Master VISUALLY 3ds Max 8* to distinguish different types of information.

Bold

Bold type represents the names of commands and options that you interact with. Bold type also indicates text and numbers that you must type into a dialog box or window.

Italics

Italic words introduce a new term and are followed by a definition.

Numbered Steps

You must perform the instructions in numbered steps in order to successfully complete a section and achieve the final results.

Bulleted Steps

These steps point out various optional features. You do not have to perform these steps; they simply give additional information about a feature.

Indented Text

Indented text tells you what the program does in response to you following a numbered step. For example, if you click a certain menu command, a dialog box may appear, or a window may open. Indented text may also tell you what the final result is when you follow a set of numbered steps.

Notes

Notes give additional information. They may describe special conditions that may occur during an operation. They may warn you of a situation that you want to avoid, such as the loss of data. A note may also cross reference a related area of the book. A cross reference may guide you to another chapter, or another section within the current chapter.

Icons and Buttons

Icons and buttons are graphical representations within the text. They show you exactly what you need to click to perform a step.

You can easily identify the tips in any section by looking for the Master It icon. Master It offers additional information, including tips, hints, and tricks. You can use the Master It information to go beyond what you have learn learned in the steps.

Operating System Differences

3ds Max 8 only supports operation under a Windows 2000 or Windows XP operating system. Different Windows color schemes or styles may affect the appearance of the program or dialog boxes but do not alter the performance of 3ds Max. Many areas of this book are still accurate for recent older releases of 3ds Max; however, the newer features covered in the text will not be available.

1 Optimizing the 3ds Max Environment

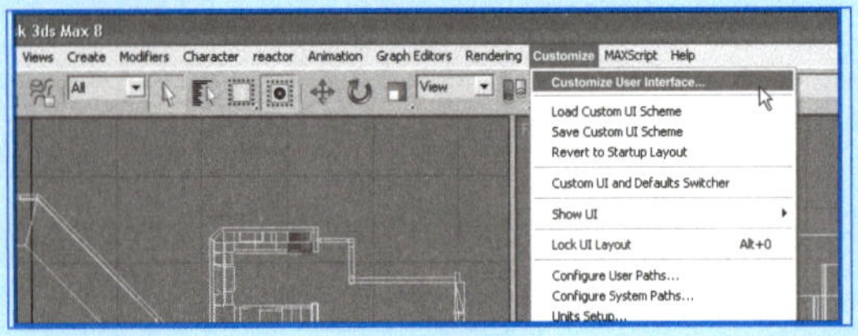

2 Working with Objects

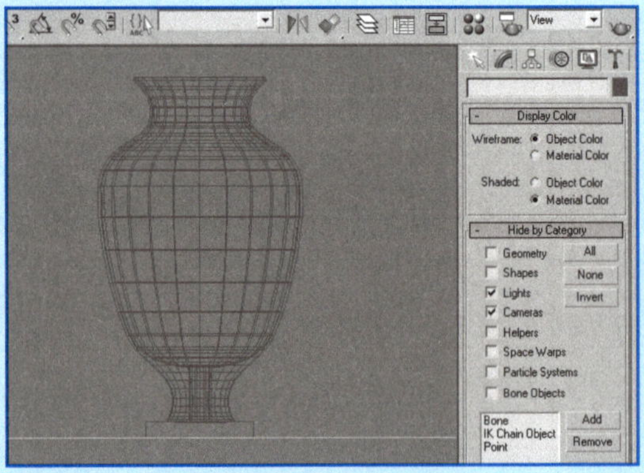

PART I
EXPLORE THE 3DS 8 MAX INTERFACE

3 Organizing Objects

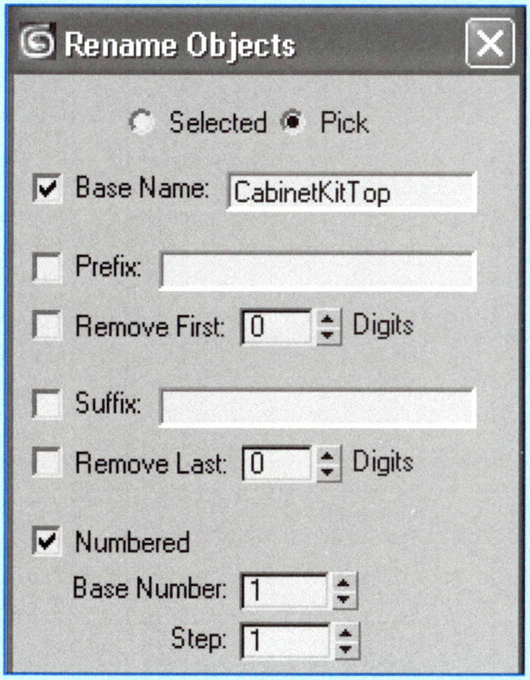

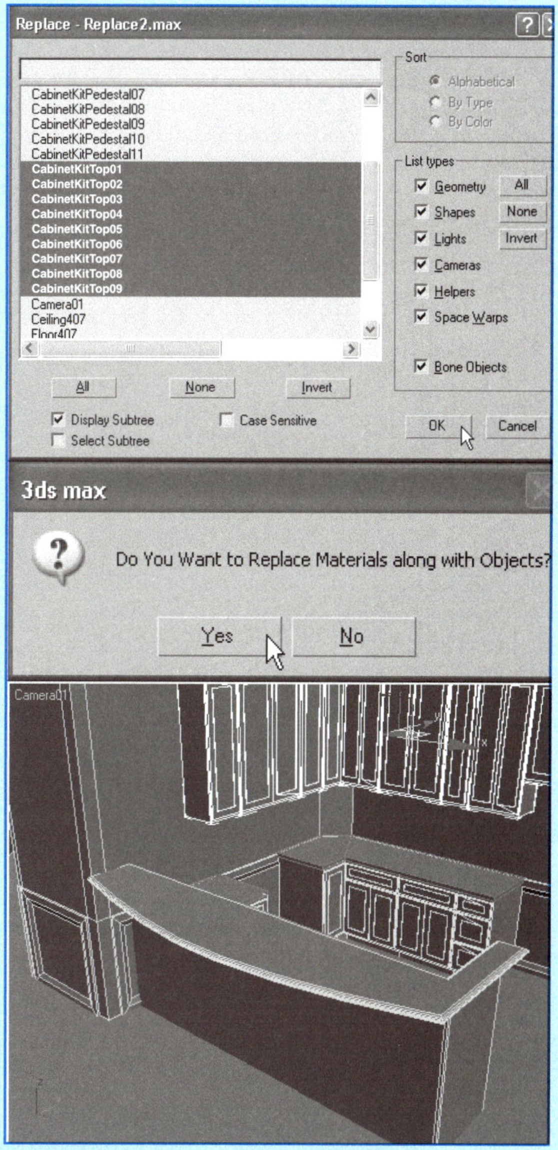

Understanding the 3ds Max Interface

You can use the 3ds Max interface to access all of the features that create and modify objects and animations. 3ds Max provides a feature-rich, customizable user interface with a Menu bar, toolbars, Timeline, Track bar, Command panels, and one or more viewports. Although 3ds Max comes with seven different toolbars, by default, only two toolbars — the Main and reactor toolbars — are visible within the 3ds Max window. The Main toolbar docks at the top of the window, and the reactor toolbar docks on the left side of the window. However, you can dock or move any toolbar to any location within the window. If you prefer, you can also allow the toolbars to float within the window.

Ⓑ Main Toolbar

Allows you to perform commonly used commands within 3ds Max.

Ⓐ Menu Bar

Has commands for creating and modifying objects and animations.

Ⓒ Reactor Toolbar

Contains buttons that perform common reactor functions, such as creating rigid and soft body collections, displaying physical properties of objects, generating simulations, and running the real-time preview utility.

Ⓓ Viewports

Show different views of your objects. You can display up to four viewports in the center of your 3ds Max window.

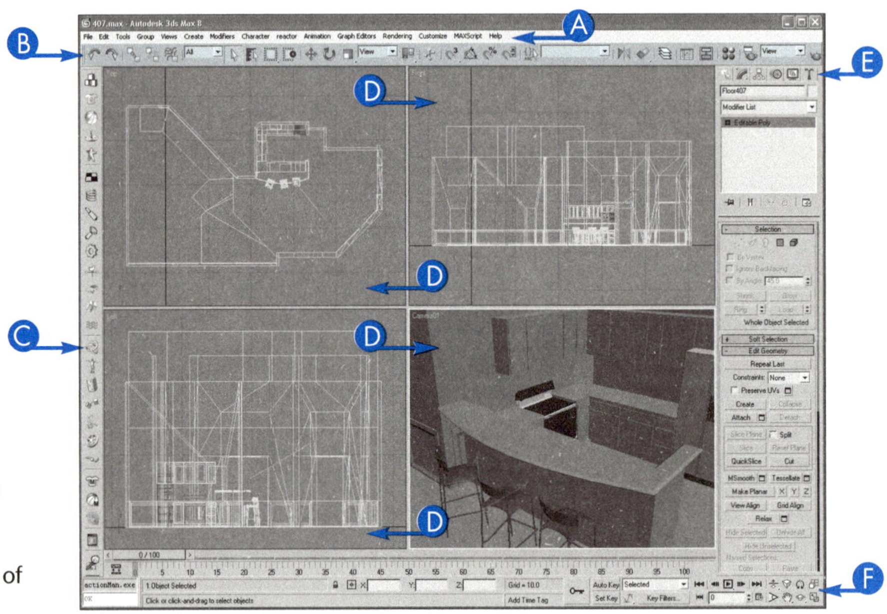

Ⓔ Command Panels

Contain six different panels with commands that allow you to model, modify, animate, and display objects.

Ⓕ Viewport Navigation Controls

Allow you to zoom, pan, and navigate within the viewports. These controls change, depending on the type of viewport selected.

A Animation Playback Controls

Allow you to review an animation in the viewports. You can play the entire animation, view individual frames, or jump to a specific frame.

B Track Bar

Displays keyframes for the selected object or objects.

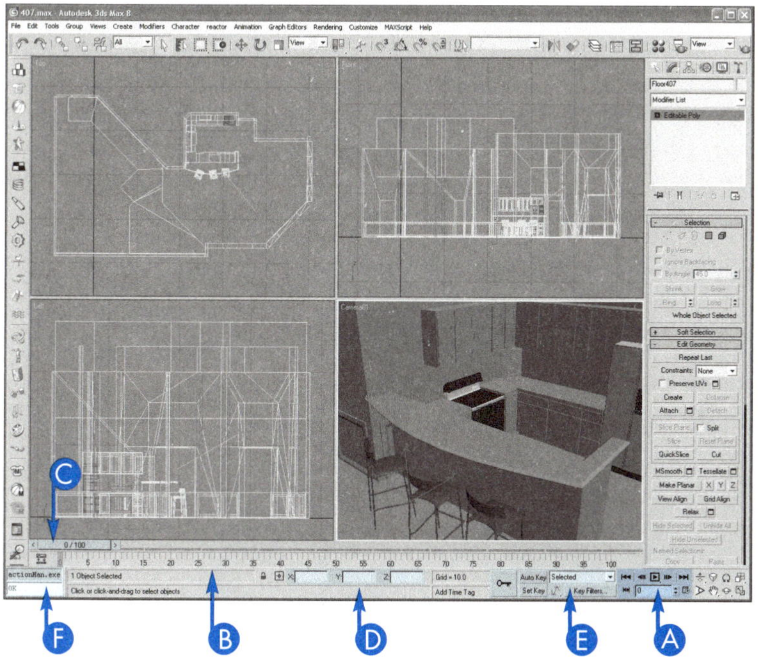

C Time Slider

Indicates the current frame displayed in the viewports. You can move the Time Slider to change the current frame.

D Coordinate Display

Indicates the position of the cursor using absolute world coordinates (X, Y, Z). When you transform an object, the display shows the object coordinates relative to its coordinates before transformation.

F MAXScript Mini-Listener

Allows you to write scripts using the MAXScript language to control 3D objects and animations.

E Animation Keying Controls

Display options that allow you to create keys for animating your objects.

Navigate within the Interface

You can customize the four different 3ds Max interface elements — toolbars, menus, panels, and viewports — to create a layout that matches your needs. For example, you can create a custom toolbar with the commands and tools that you use most frequently and dock it where it is most convenient for your workflow.

Viewports

Viewports, located in the center of the 3ds Max window, help you construct your scenes by creating and animating objects. Each viewport shows the scene from a different viewpoint, such as the top, left, or front, or through a camera or light. Viewports can also show a scene in *perspective* — with points of convergence — or *axonometric* — without points of convergence. You can specify the number of viewports display, and then assign a specific type of view to each viewport.

You can customize the appearance of the scene within each viewport independently of the other viewports. For more information, see the section "Customize the Viewport Layout."

Toolbars

Toolbars contain buttons that allow quick access to 3ds Max's commands and tools. You can create custom toolbars to fit your particular workflow or use 3ds Max's default toolbars. Although, by default, the Main toolbar is docked at the top of the window and the reactor toolbar is docked on the left side of the window, you can position toolbars wherever you want.

By default, 3ds Max hides floating toolbars, but you can view them per the instructions in the section "Create a Custom Toolbar." If you prefer, you can display only specific floating toolbars by right-clicking an empty spot on any toolbar and selecting the toolbar you want from the menu.

Ⓐ Docked Toolbar

A toolbar attached to the top, bottom, or one of the sides of the 3ds Max window.

Ⓑ Docking Toolbar in Progress

When the cursor changes from to , you can release the mouse to dock a toolbar. When you undock a toolbar, changes to indicating that the toolbar will float.

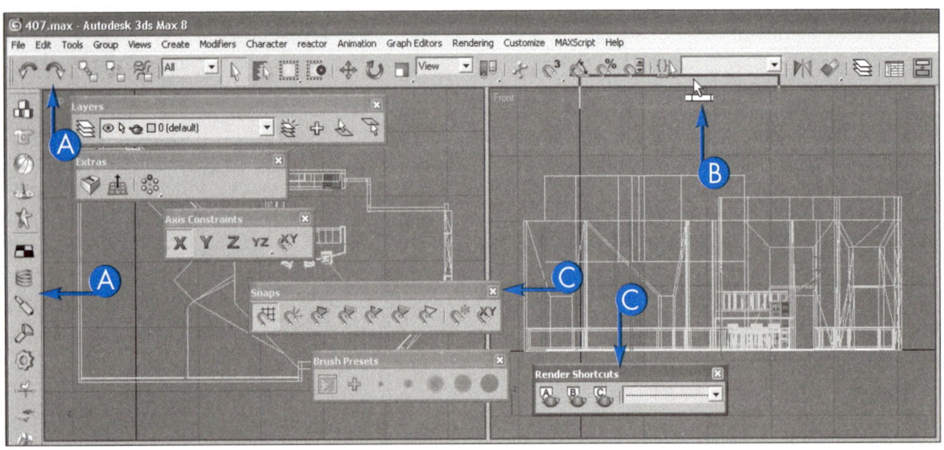

Ⓒ Floating Toolbar

Any toolbar that floats on your main screen or a second monitor. You can move, resize, or close a floating toolbar. You can reposition any floating toolbar to the edge of a viewport by dragging its edge to where you want to dock it. Likewise, you can reverse the process to undock the toolbar.

3ds Max Button Types

3ds Max has five basic button types: standard buttons, modal buttons, toggle buttons, flyout buttons, and drop-down lists that display on toolbars. You can create new toolbars and customize existing toolbars by adding and removing buttons through the Customize User Interface dialog box. See the section "Create a Custom Toolbar" for more information on working with toolbars.

A Standard Button

When you click a standard button, it immediately performs the corresponding command.

B Toggle Button

These buttons switch specific settings on or off. These settings apply to the next action, such as the next mouse-click. When you depress a toggle button, the corresponding settings are on.

C Modal Button

These buttons specify an exclusive setting for subsequent mouse actions. For example, the Select Object button selects the next object that you click. The button remains selected until you click another button.

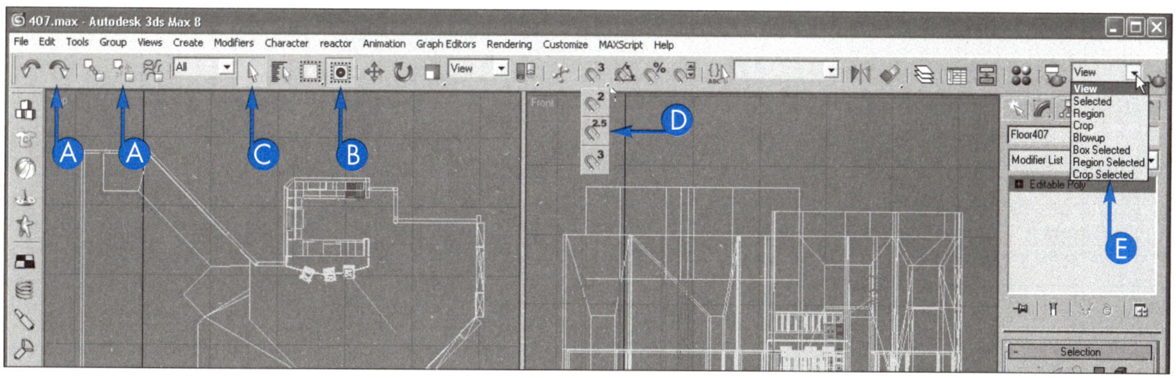

D Flyout Buttons

Conceals related buttons. A small arrow () in the lower-right corner of the button indicates a flyout. You can click and hold to display the flyout buttons, and click the button that you want.

E Drop-down List

You can click the down arrow () beside a list to select from the available options. For example, the Selection Filter drop-down list contains a list of object types that can be selected.

continued

Navigate within the Interface *(Continued)*

The Command panels and Menu bar contain the tools to create, animate, and display all possible objects in 3ds Max. You find most commands in both locations. Each has a tree structure for locating the appropriate tools.

Command Panel

You use the Command panel to create objects and specify parameters and settings for modeling and animation. The Command panel actually contains six separate panels: Create, Modify, Hierarchy, Motion, Display, and Utilities.

Each panel has different buttons and controls for setting the corresponding parameters within different rollouts. A *rollout* is a collection of related controls that are grouped together. You can expand or collapse the rollout or use the scroll bar on the right side to see the rest of the panel.

By default, 3ds Max docks the Command panel on the right side of its window, but like a toolbar, you can undock and reposition it, for example, to a different side of the window. You can also expand the panel to show more than one column of rollouts, at the cost of less viewport space, by clicking and dragging its edges.

A Create Panel

Contains controls for creating most objects in 3ds Max. Objects are grouped into seven different categories, each with its own button.

B Modify Panel

Alters an object's parameters or assigns modifiers to alter its shape or properties.

C Hierarchy Panel

Contains tools for adjusting the parent/child relationship between objects in your scene.

D Motion Panel

Contains tools for adjusting the movement of an animated object.

E Display Panel

Contains tools for adjusting how objects display globally within the scene, such as hiding or freezing an object.

F Utilities Panel

Provides access to several utility programs that are available in 3ds Max.

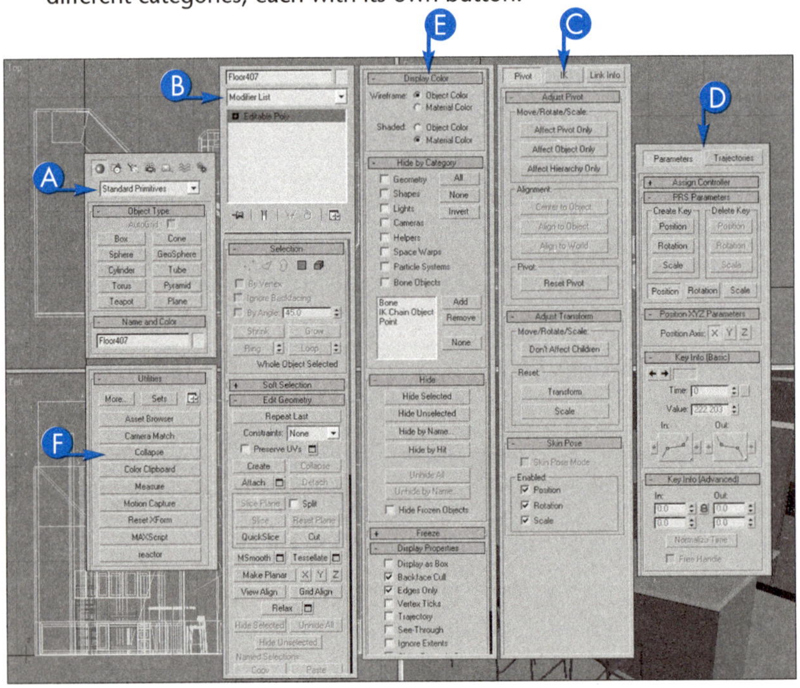

Menus

As with any Microsoft Windows–compliant program, 3ds Max provides drop-down menus on the Menu bar that access most of the program's features. You can view the menu options by clicking the corresponding menu on the Menu bar. You can customize each menu by adding and removing menu options. You can also create new custom menus that you can add to the Menu bar. See the section "Create a Custom Menu" for more information on customizing menus.

3ds Max has two other types of menus: the pop-up menu and the quad menu. Pop-up menus appear when you right-click the toolbars, rollouts, and viewport titles. Quad menus appear when you right-click objects, or in viewports. Although both types of menus display when you right-click them, you can only customize the quad menus. See the section "Create a Custom Quad Menu" for more information.

A Pop-up Menu

Contains options for customizing a feature's appearance. For example, when you right-click a toolbar, a menu appears, displaying information such as a list of all visible toolbars, as well as whether the toolbar is docked or floating.

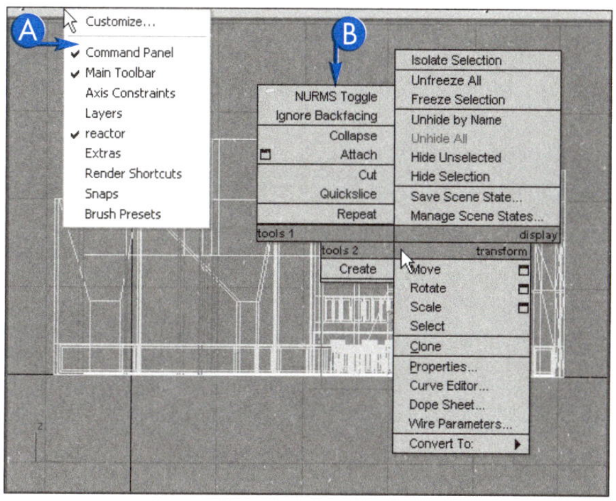

B Quad Menu

Contains between one and four smaller menus arranged in quadrants. Each smaller menu has its own Title bar. The most commonly used quad menus display when you right-click an object in a viewport. You can also access quad menus that display when you press a specific key sequence.

Create a New Keyboard Shortcut

You can create new keyboard shortcuts for commands and tools that you use often within 3ds Max. Keyboard shortcuts help you to save time when your projects require a lot of repetitive command combinations.

You can make a keyboard shortcut active for the Main user interface (UI), or for a specific program context, such as the Material Editor. If you select the Main UI, the keyboard context is available anywhere in 3ds Max. If you specify another context, then any shortcuts that you create are only available when you work with that feature. After you specify the context area, you can select the action that you want to perform and then specify the keyboard shortcut sequence.

If the keyboard sequence that you specify is already assigned to a command in the selected context, the command appears in the Assigned To field. To keep the current keyboard shortcut, you must specify a different one.

3ds Max allows you to create the same keyboard shortcut for multiple contexts. When you press a keyboard shortcut, 3ds Max checks for a context-specific shortcut first. If one does not exist, then it looks for a keyboard shortcut in the Main UI shortcuts.

Create a New Keyboard Shortcut

1. Click Customize.
2. Click Customize User Interface.

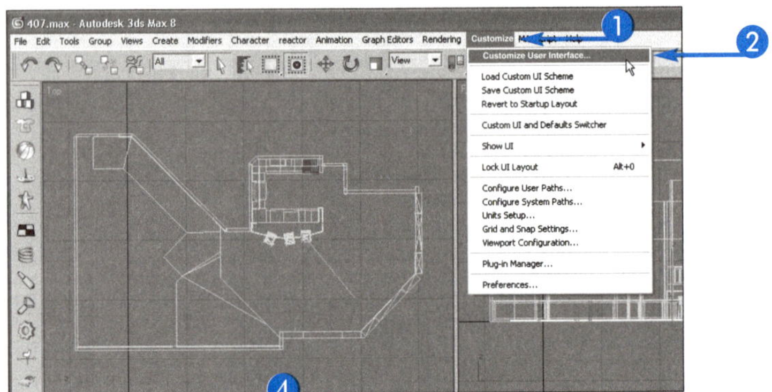

The Customize User Interface dialog box appears.

3. Click the Keyboard tab.
4. Click here and select the context for which you want your keyboard shortcut to be active.

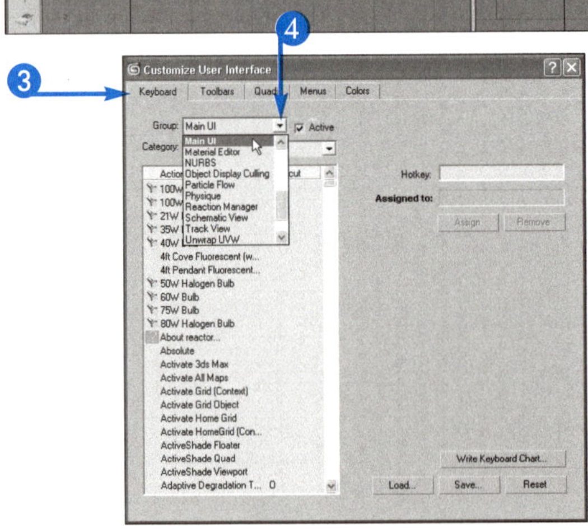

5 In the Action list, click the command or tool for which you want to assign a keyboard shortcut.

- You can select a specific category in the Category field to display only a specific group of actions.

6 Click in the Hotkey field.

7 Press the keyboard sequence that you want.

- The keys that you press appear in the Hotkey field.

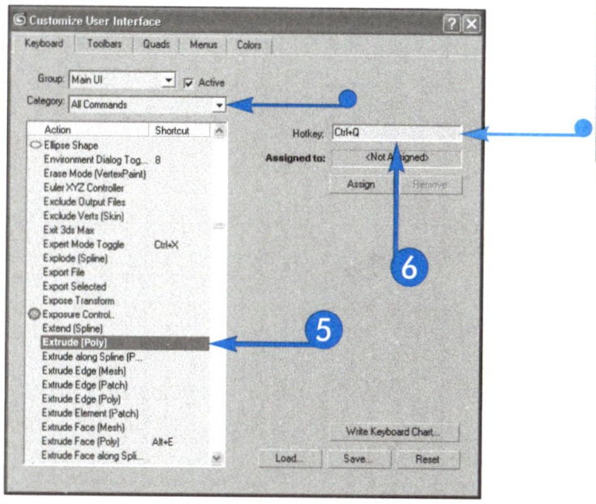

8 Click Assign.

- The assigned key sequence appears in the Shortcut column next to the corresponding command.

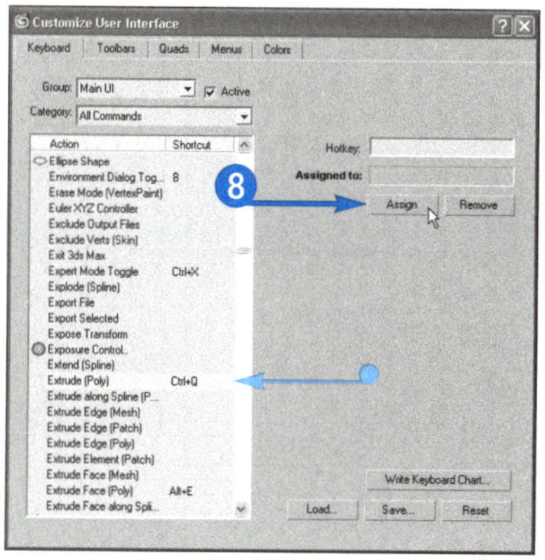

MASTER IT

My keyboard shortcut does not work. What are some possible reasons for this?

▼ 3ds Max allows you to select whether the context-specific keyboard shortcuts are active. If you do not activate context-sensitive keyboard shortcuts, you can only use the keyboard shortcuts for the Main UI. To activate the context-specific keyboard shortcuts, click the Active option (☐ changes to ☑) in the Keyboard panel of the Customize User Interface dialog box. You must also turn on the Keyboard Shortcut Override Toggle button, which is in the Extras toolbar. To display the Extras toolbar, right-click in a blank area of a toolbar and select Extras.

How do I know which keyboard shortcuts are assigned?

▼ You can create a list of current keyboard shortcuts to either view or print. To do this, click Write Keyboard Chart in the Keyboard panel of the Customize User Interface dialog box. In the Save File As dialog box that appears, give the file a name and destination, and then open it in any application that can read TXT files. You can also click Help and then click HotKey Map to display a flash-based list of common keyboard shortcuts. When you place the cursor over keys in the keyboard graphic in the lower-right corner, 3ds Max displays the associated shortcuts.

Create a Custom Toolbar

You can create a new toolbar that contains a custom set of buttons for specific commands and tools that you often use in 3ds Max. This can streamline your work flow by reducing the time it takes to access tools that you may have buried in a flyout menu. You can also add any of the 3ds Max tools and commands to your toolbars and create buttons for custom MAXScript scripts.

You create new toolbars and add buttons to toolbars using the New button on the Toolbars panel in the Customize User Interface dialog box. 3ds Max displays a blank toolbar to which you can add buttons, either from the Action list in the Toolbars panel or from another open toolbar.

By default, the Action list contains all of the available commands and tools in 3ds Max. You can reduce the list by selecting a specific group in the Group field or a specific category in the Category field. For example, if you select the Main UI in the Group field, you can select Edit in the Category field to view only the available editing commands.

Create a Custom Toolbar

Create a New Toolbar

1. Click Customize.
2. Click Customize User Interface.
   - To view all hidden toolbars, you can click Show UI, and then click Show Floating Toolbars in the dialog box that appears.

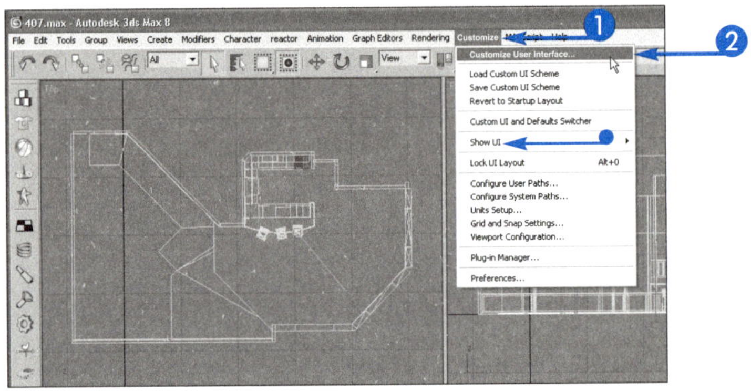

The Customize User Interface dialog box appears.

3. Click the Toolbars tab.
4. Click New.

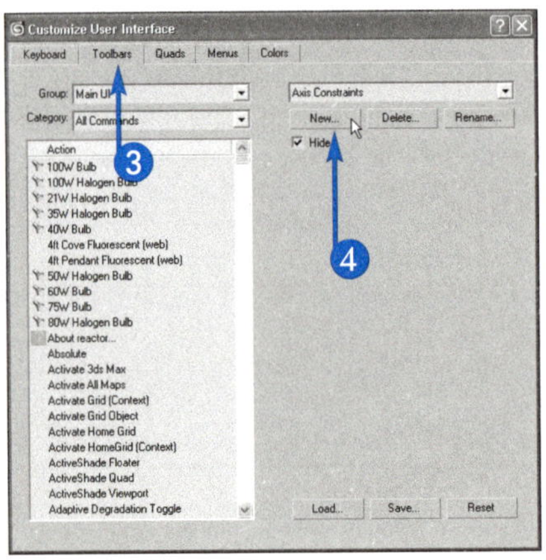

The New Toolbar dialog box appears.

5. Type a name for your new toolbar.
6. Click OK.

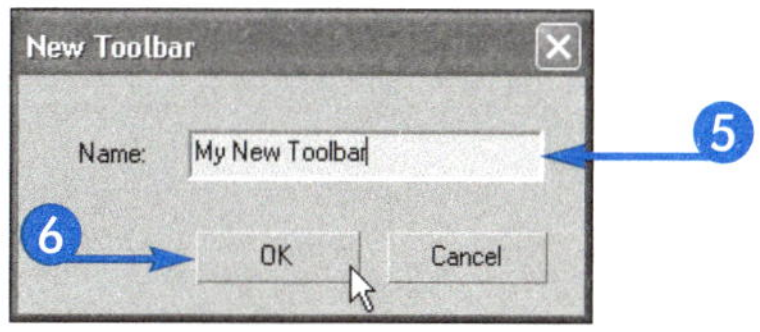

Add Buttons to a Toolbar

- 3ds Max creates a toolbar with the name you specified.

7. In the Action list, click the tool or command that you want to add to your toolbar.
8. Drag the selection to the toolbar.
9. Repeat steps 7 and 8 to add more buttons to the toolbar.

3ds Max adds the selected buttons to the toolbar.

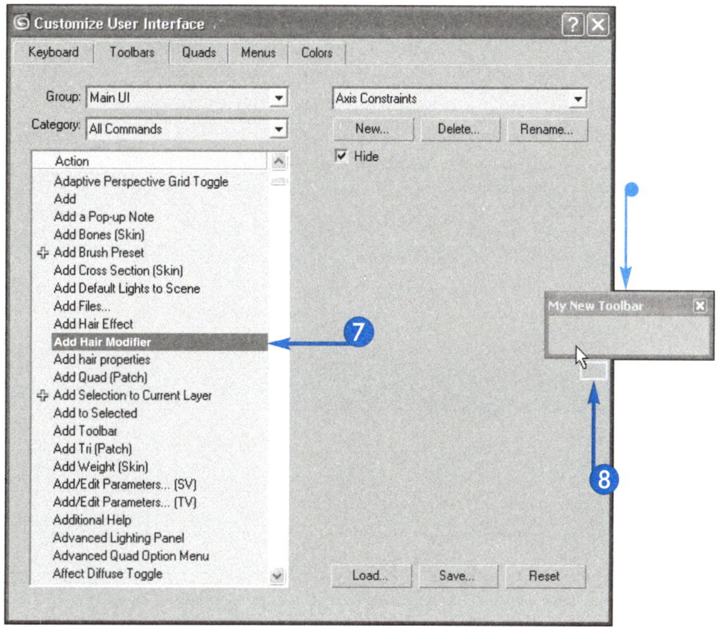

MASTER IT

How can I copy buttons from one toolbar to another?

▼ You must have both toolbars open, although you do not need to open the Customize User Interface dialog box. Press and hold the Control key, and then drag a button from the source to the destination toolbar. Release the mouse when you see a small rectangle cursor. The button now resides in both toolbars. Pressing and holding the Alt key while dragging a button moves it from one toolbar to the other.

Can I dock my custom toolbar in the 3ds Max window?

▼ Yes. Your custom toolbar can either float in the 3ds Max window or dock along the top or side of the window. To dock your toolbar, click and drag it to the location that you want, as described in the section "Navigate within the Interface." For example, to dock the toolbar at the top of the window, simply click and drag it there. Short toolbars can dock side by side or one above the other.

How do I remove unwanted buttons?

▼ You can remove buttons from any toolbar, whether it is custom or default. Right-click the button that you want to remove and then select Delete Button from the menu. A dialog box appears to confirm your selection. Click Yes to remove the button. For buttons that have a right-click function assigned to them, such as the Undo button, press and hold the Alt key and drag the button into a viewport to delete it.

Create a Custom Quad Menu

You can create custom quad menus that contain specific commands, tools, and menus that you frequently use in 3ds Max. Quad menus display when you right-click in a viewport or on an object, or when you press a specific keyboard shortcut. Quad menus are so named because they are menus that can contain up to four smaller menus, or quadrants. Each quadrant menu can have a separate label to identify the options in that menu.

You can create quad menus in the Quads panel of the Customize User Interface dialog box. You can also assign a keyboard shortcut for displaying the quad menu. After creating the quad menu set, you can place options to it from either the Action list or the Menus list. You can use the Separator object to create visual separations between related menu options.

You can specify that the quad menu display all quad menus in all quadrants at one time, or only one quadrant at a time. If you do not select the Show All Quads option, then only one quad menu displays at a time, along with the corner of each additional quad menu.

Create a Custom Quad Menu

Create a new Quad Menu

1. Click Customize.
2. Click Customize User Interface.

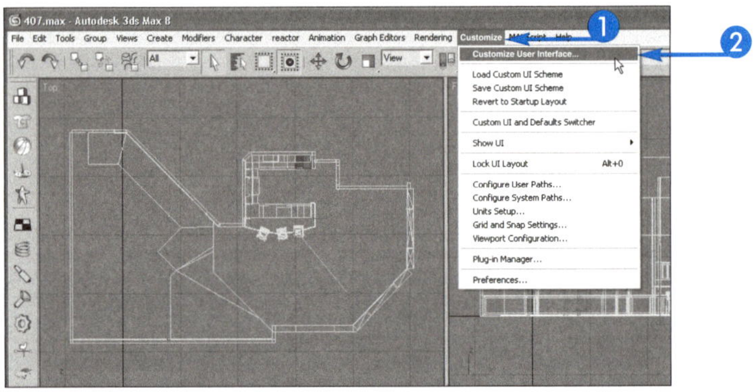

The Customize User Interface dialog box appears.

3. Click the Quads tab.
4. Click New.

The New Quad Set dialog box appears.

5. Type a name for your new quad set.
6. Click OK.

3ds Max creates a quad menu set with the name that you specified.

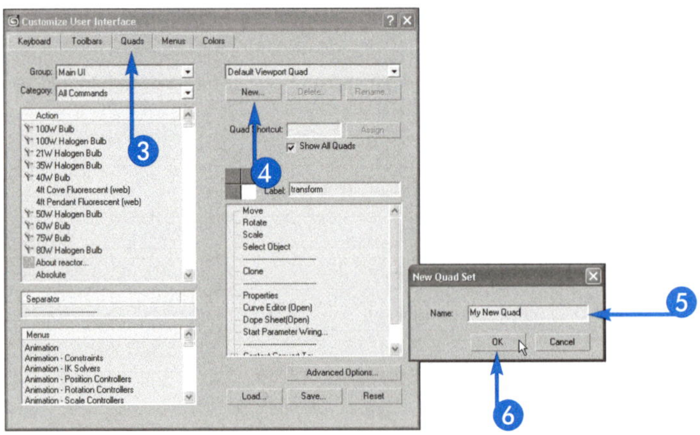

Add Quad Menu Options

7. Click here and select the quad set menu.
8. Click the quadrant where you want to place the command.
9. Type the quadrant name that you want in the Label field.
10. Click an option from the Action list or a menu from the Menus list and drag it to the Quad Menu list above the End of Menu entry.
11. Repeat steps 8 to 10 to add more menu options.

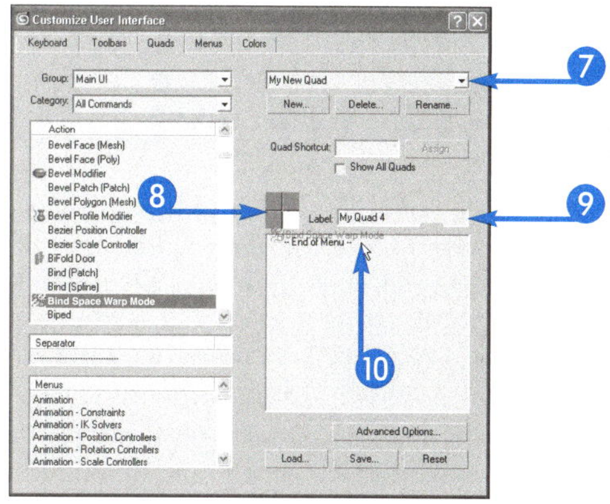

12. Click in the Quad Shortcut field.
13. Press the keyboard sequence that you want.

   The keys that you press appear in the Hotkey field.
14. Click the Show All Quads option (☐ changes to ☑).

   This displays menus in all quadrants for your custom quad menu.
15. Click Assign.

   3ds Max adds the menu options to the quad menu.

   You can now type the shortcut to display the new quad menu.

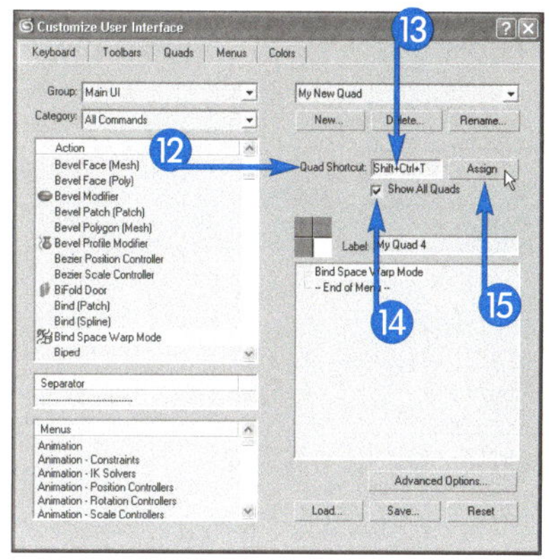

MASTER IT

How do I remove options from a quad menu?

▼ You can remove menu items from any quad menu through the Quads tab of the Customize User Interface dialog box. To remove a menu option, first select the quad set menu in the Quad Set List list box in the top-right corner of the Quads tab. Click to select the quadrant containing the menu that you want to modify. A list of the menu options for that quadrant appear in the Quad Menu window. Right-click the menu item in the Quad Menu window. In the menu that appears, click Delete Menu Item.

Can I change the appearance of my custom quad menu?

▼ Yes, you can make several changes to the appearance of the quad menus. However, your changes affect all quad menus. To make changes, click Advanced Options in the Quads tab of the Customize User Interface dialog box. In the Advanced Quad Menu Options dialog box that appears, you can change the colors of different elements of the quad menu. For example, you can change the color of the title background, select different font types and sizes, and specify the type of animation used to display the quad menus. You can add transparency to the quad menus by using the Opacity Amount field in the Advanced Options dialog box.

Create a Custom Menu

You can create new custom menus that contain your preferred tools and commands. After creating a custom menu, you can add the menu to any of the system Menu bars, or to a specific quad menu. For example, you can create a custom menu that appears in the Main Menu bar.

You can create new menus through the Menus panel of the Customize User Interface dialog box. In addition to creating new menus in this panel, you can also customize the appearance of any menu by adding, moving, or removing menu items.

You can add items to a menu by dragging them from one of the lists on the left side of the panel into the Menu window. The Action list window contains all of the commands and tools that are available in 3ds Max. You can drag the Separator onto the Menus list to create a visual separation line between menu items. The Menus list contains all of the available menus. When you add a submenu to your menu, it becomes a separate submenu.

Create a Custom Menu

Create a New Menu

1. Click Customize.
2. Click Customize User Interface.

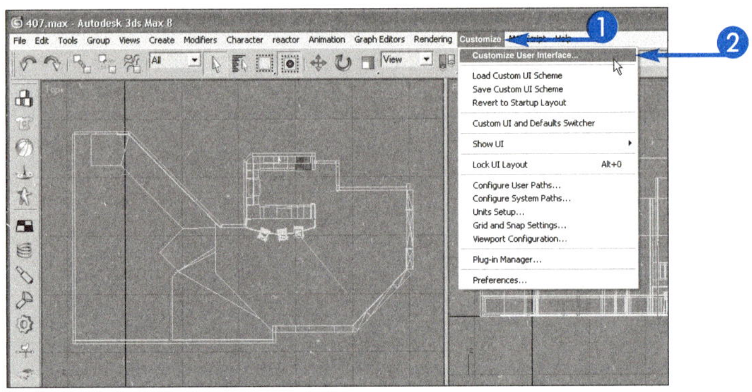

The Customize User Interface dialog box appears.

3. Click the Menus tab.
4. Click New.

The New Menu dialog box appears.

5. Type a name for your new menu.
6. Click OK.

3ds Max creates a menu with the name that you specified.

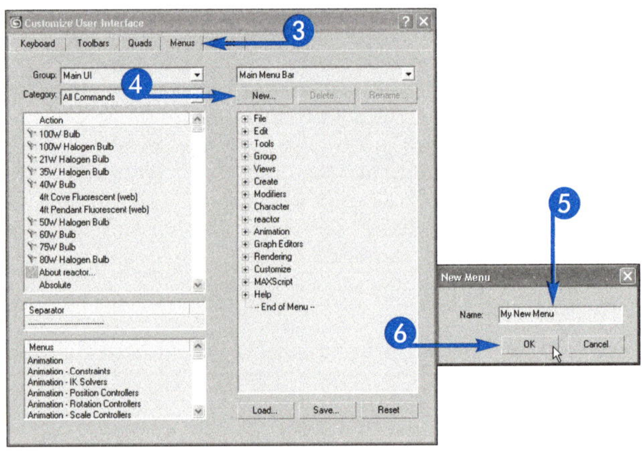

Add Menu Options

7. Click here and select the menu that you just created.
8. Click and drag an option from the Action, Separator, or Menus list to the menu that you want to customize.

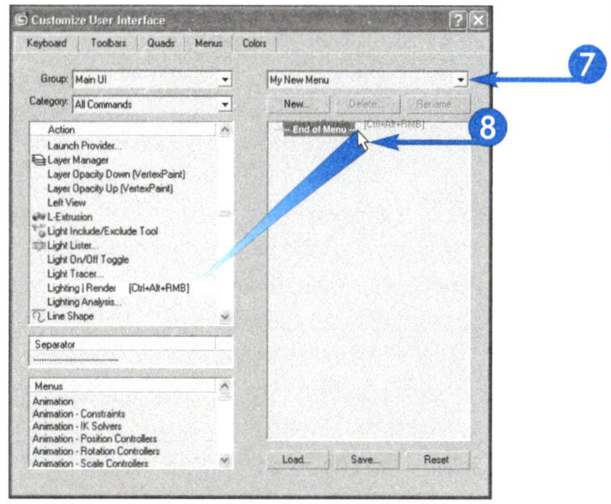

9. Repeat steps 7 and 8 to add more menu items.
   - 3ds Max adds the selected options to the menu.

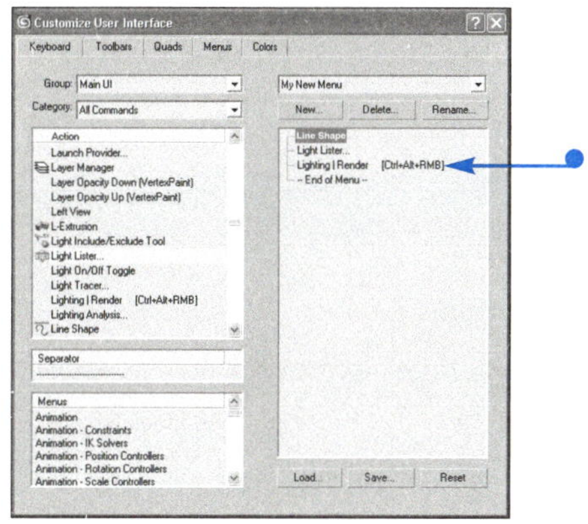

MASTER IT

How do I place my custom menu on the Main Menu bar?

▼ When you create a new menu, it appears in the Menus list in the Menus tab of the Customize User Interface dialog box. To add your new custom menu to the Main Menu bar, select Main Menu Bar from the menu. All of the menus currently on the Menu bar appear. In the Menus list on the left of the panel, click your custom menu and then drag it to the location that you want in the Menus list.

How do I delete an unwanted menu?

▼ To delete a menu from the Main Menu bar, select Main Menu Bar from the list in the Menus tab of the Customize User Interface dialog box. Right-click the menu item that you want to delete, and then select Delete Menu Item from the menu. To delete a menu entirely from 3ds Max, locate the menu in the Menus list on the left side of the Menus tab. Right-click the menu and select Delete Menu. If the selected menu is also a submenu, a dialog box appears with the option to cancel the deletion. If you delete the menu, it also disappears from any menus where it is a submenu. This action is not undoable.

Customize the Interface Colors

You can customize the appearance of your 3ds Max interface by customizing the colors of the different elements through the Colors panel of the Customize User Interface dialog box. This panel has two different lists: the Elements list and the Scheme list. The Elements list contains all of the elements within a specified user category, such as Viewports. You can select the user interface category in the Elements list. The Scheme list contains the custom colors that affect the entire user interface. For example, when you change the text color, it changes the background color of all non-menu text in all rollouts, buttons, dialog boxes, and message boxes. You must select Custom Colors in the Scheme list to customize these features.

There are two Color fields on the right side of the Colors panel. The top field displays the color of the selected element, and the bottom field displays the color of the selected scheme option. You can change the color for a selection in the Color Selector dialog box using one of the three color modes: the color spectrum on the left, which specifies the Hue, Blackness, and Whiteness; the Red, Green, and Blue fields; or the Hue, Saturation, and Value fields.

Customize the Interface Colors

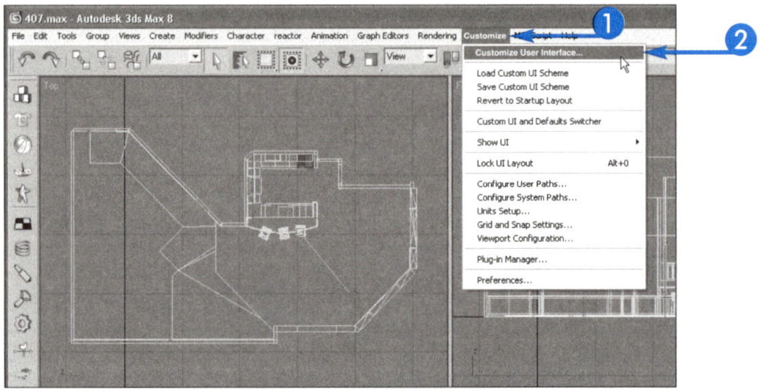

1. Click Customize.
2. Click Customize User Interface.

The Customize User Interface dialog box appears.

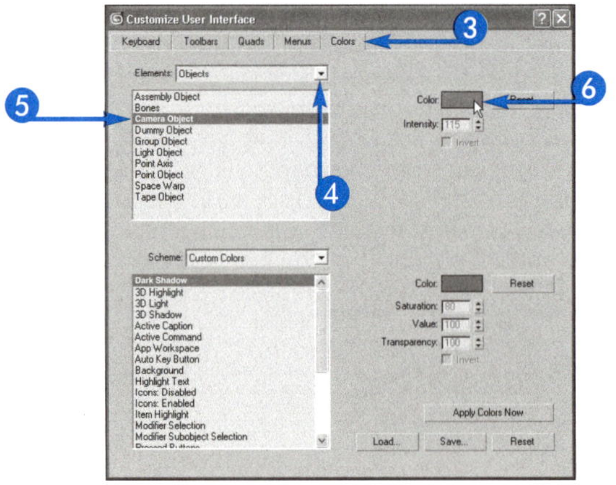

3. Click the Colors tab.
4. Click here and select the element category that you want.

   The Elements list changes to display only the elements in that category.
5. In the Elements list, click the element that you want to change.
6. Click the Color field.

The Color Selector dialog box appears.

7. Click a new color in the Color Spectrum field.
8. Click and drag the slider (◁) in the Whiteness field to adjust the amount of white in the color selection.
   - You can also click the spinners (⬍) for the Red, Green, Blue, Hue, Sat, and Value fields to specify the color that you want.
9. Click Close.
   - The new color for the selection displays in the corresponding Color field.
10. Click Apply Colors Now.

3ds Max applies all color changes that you have made to the user interface.

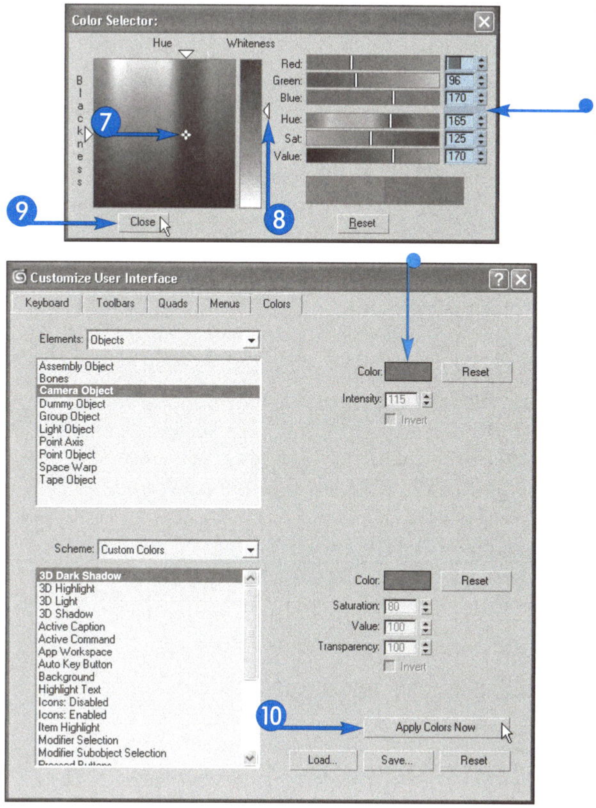

MASTER IT

How do I get rid of color changes that I have made?

▼ When you click Apply Colors Now, 3ds Max applies your color changes to the user interface. The only way to undo the color changes is to reset the interface back to the last saved version of the color settings. To do this, click Reset at the bottom of the Colors panel. See the section "Save a New User Interface" for more information on saving user interface changes. Remember that clicking the Reset button next to a Color field only resets the colors for the selected element, before you click Apply Colors Now.

Can I have multiple color schemes in 3ds Max?

▼ Yes, you can set up different color schemes and save them. When you want to switch color schemes, you simply load the corresponding color scheme file. To save a color scheme, specify the colors that you want in the Colors tab, and then click Save. In the Save Color File As dialog box, type a name for your color file. If you type an existing color filename, the new color scheme replaces the existing color scheme. To switch to a saved color scheme, click Load in the Colors tab and then select a color scheme in the Load Color File dialog box.

Save a New User Interface

You can save all of the customizations that you make to your user interface so that you can reload them at any time or transfer them to another computer. When you save your user interface, you can specify the items that you want, including the toolbar and panel layouts, color settings, menus, quad menus, keyboard shortcuts, and icon schemes.

When you save a custom user interface, you specify the name of the UI file that contains all of the user interface settings. If you want the user interface settings to load automatically when you load 3ds Max, you must save the file as MaxStartUI.ui. 3ds Max automatically searches for this file when the program loads at startup. It is recommended that you save your original MaxStartUI.ui file under another name before making any changes to it so that you can restore it to its original configuration if required.

You should not name the file DefaultUI.ui because the DefaultUI.ui file contains all of the system default settings for your user interface. If you overwrite this file, you cannot reload the default settings for a clean start if your interface becomes corrupted. See the section "Load a New User Interface" for more information.

Save a New User Interface

1. Click Customize.
2. Click Save Custom UI Scheme.

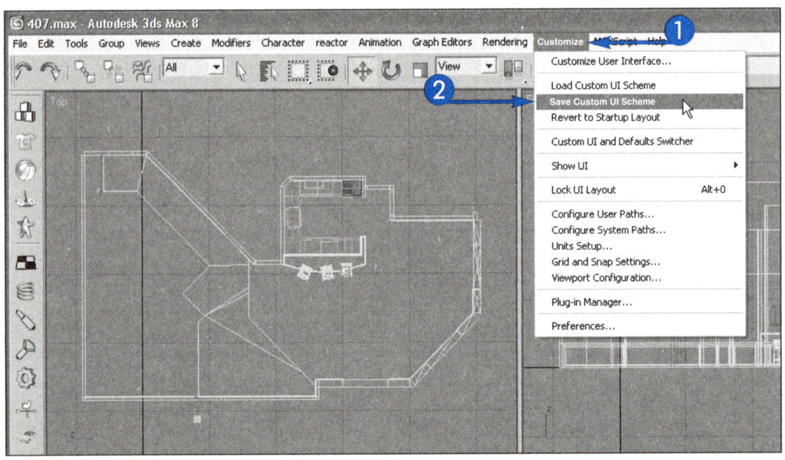

The Save Custom UI Scheme dialog box appears.

3. Type the name that you want to use to identify the user interface.
4. Click Save.

The Custom Scheme dialog box appears.

5. Click the interface options that you want to save (☐ changes to ☑).
6. Click the type of icons that you want to use when the interface is selected (○ changes to ◉).
7. Click OK.

3ds Max saves the user interface file.

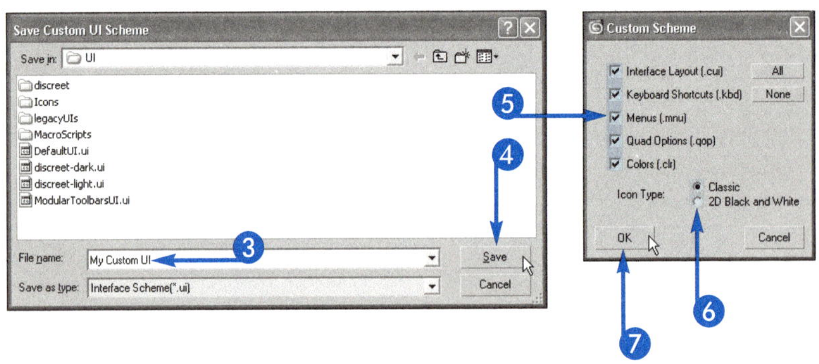

Load a New User Interface

You can load a previously created custom user interface file. When you do so, 3ds Max loads all related user interface files. For example, if you saved toolbar and panel layouts, color settings, and keyboard schemes as part of your user interface, 3ds Max loads these settings.

You use the Load Custom UI Scheme dialog box to select the type of customizations to load. For example, instead of loading all customization files related to your user interface, you may want to load only the menus. In this case, you can select Menu File (*.mnu) in the Files of type field.

3ds Max ships with some alternative UI schemes. For example, you can use ame-dark.ui or ame-light.ui if you usually work with Autodesk or Discreet video-editing products.

MASTER IT

How do I revert to the default user interface?

▼ You can reload the default settings at any time by selecting the DefaultUI.ui file. To only reload specific settings, such as menus, you can select the corresponding default file, such as DefaultUI.mnu. If you make any changes to your UI, it is safest to save it to another .ui file to preserve the DefaultUI.ui file.

Load a New User Interface

1. Click Customize.
2. Click Load Custom UI Scheme.

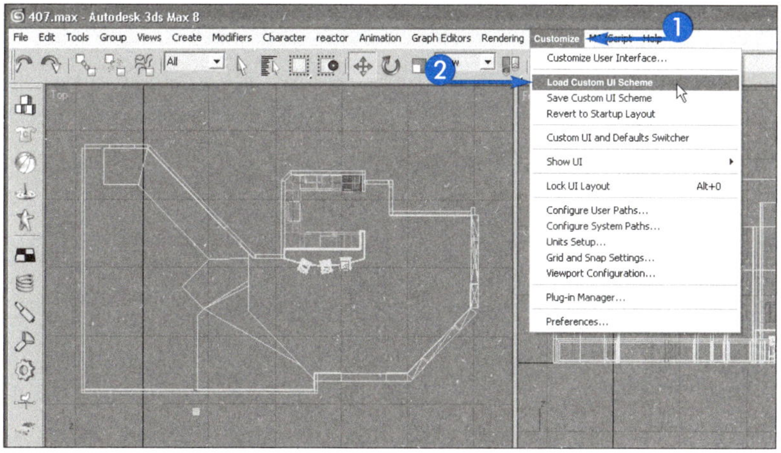

The Load Custom UI Scheme dialog box appears.

3. Click here and select the type of customizations that you want to load.
4. Click the file that you want to load.

   The selection appears in the File name field.

5. Click Open.

   3ds Max loads the selected customizations.

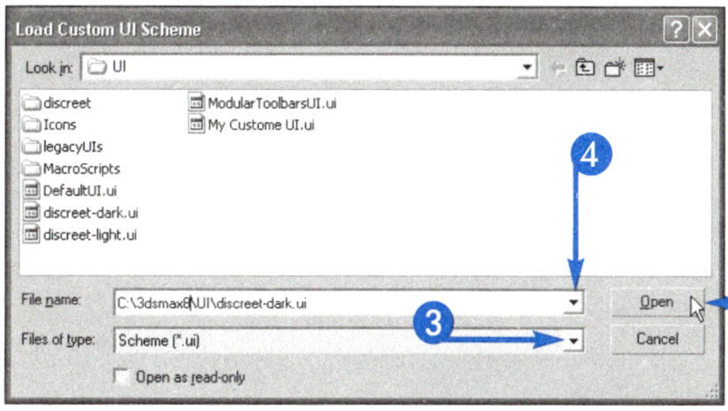

Understanding Viewports

The 3ds Max viewports act as windows into your virtual environment. You can use each of the four visible viewports to display the scene from a different point of view, such as through a camera, through a light, and in axonometric and perspective modes.

Common viewport configurations show the scene from the top, bottom, front, back, left, or right sides. These views are *axonometric* — meaning that there are no perspective points of convergence — and so lines that are parallel in your objects remain parallel in the viewport. A *User* viewport is also axonometric, but its origin is not restricted to remaining parallel to the main axes of the scene. *Perspective*, light, and camera viewports show the scene from an artist-defined point of view, or from the location and orientation of a camera, spot, or direct light that exists in the scene.

Although changes to an object in one viewport are visible in all viewports that display that object, only one viewport is current at a time. The current viewport, identified by a yellow border, is where you perform selections and transforms.

A Viewports

These are windows in your 3ds Max scene. One to four viewports can be displayed at a time to show your scene from different points of view.

B Current Viewport

This is the viewport where you make selections and apply transforms.

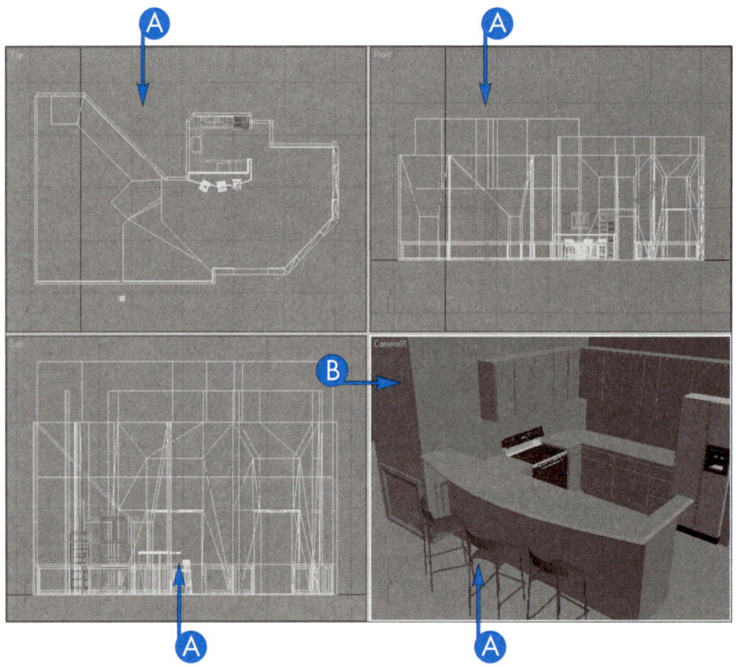

Ⓒ Viewport Label

This label displays the name of the viewport in its upper-left corner. Right-clicking the label opens a menu.

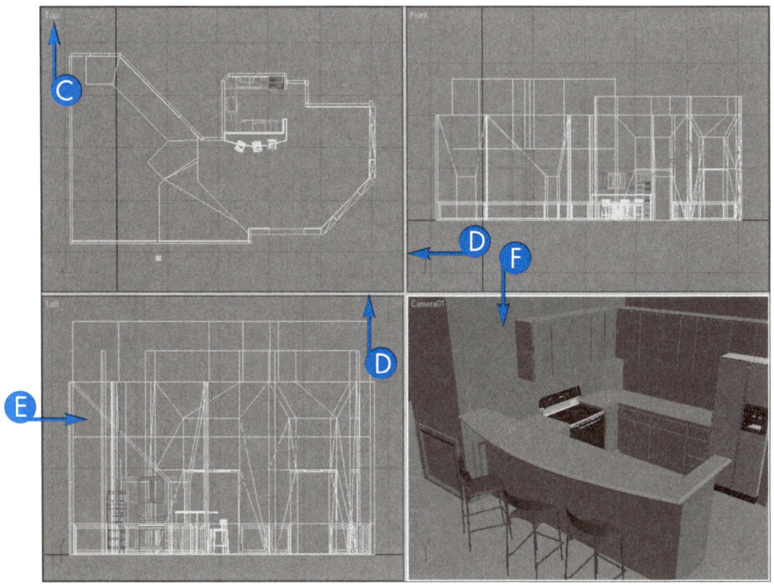

Ⓓ Viewport Border

These are resizable boundaries that define the size and shape of the viewports. A yellow border defines the current viewport, and a red border indicates that 3ds Max is in Auto Key mode.

Ⓔ User Viewport

This is an axonometric viewport with an artist-defined point of view.

Ⓕ Camera or Light Viewport

These are perspective viewports as seen through existing lights or cameras.

Understanding Viewport Rendering Options

You can display eight different visibility modes in each viewport, and you can decide which viewport mode fits your needs, depending on your workflow. Each mode shows the contents of the viewports at a distinct level of quality from best, using the Smooth + Highlights option, to worst, using the Bounding Box option.

Although it may seem odd to not show all of the viewports in the best mode possible at all times, there is a good reason for this. With quality, you have a tradeoff in speed. While Smooth + Highlights offers the closest rendition to how your scene will render, executing a pan or zoom may cause the viewport to jump from point to point, rather than resulting in a smooth transition. A pan or zoom may also cause your viewports to lag behind your commands while the system calculates the shading required to redraw them in your scene. Setting some of your viewports to display the scenes at lower quality decreases the processing time and speeds up the screen redraws.

In addition to the eight viewport rendering options, an Edged Faces option is also available in shaded viewports. A viewport that uses Edged Faces displays both the surfaces and the wireframe structure of the objects.

A Smooth

This is similar to Smooth + Highlights, without the specular highlights.

B Wireframe

Object edges display as lines. Surfaces and highlights are not shown.

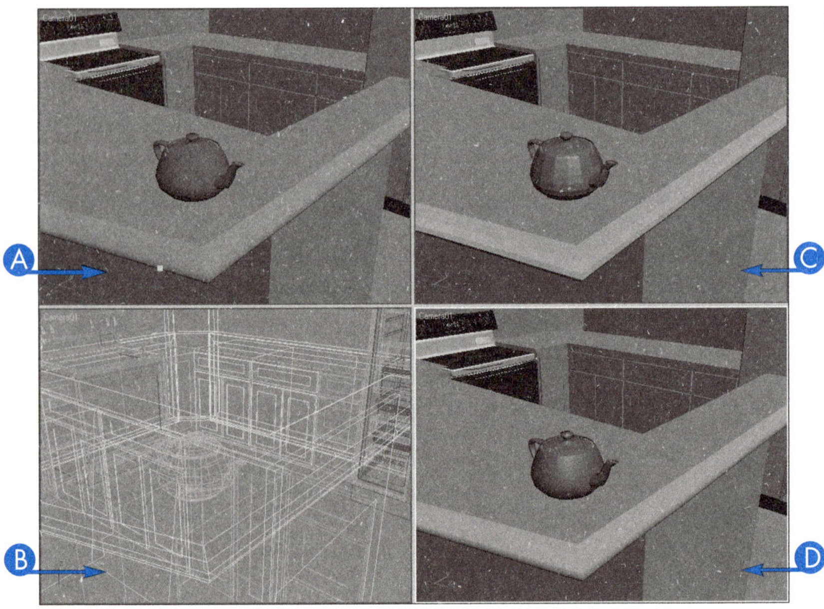

C Facets + Highlights

Highlights display in this mode, but there is no smooth shading between adjacent faces.

D Smooth + Highlights

Objects display with smooth shading between adjacent faces. Specular highlights also display in this mode.

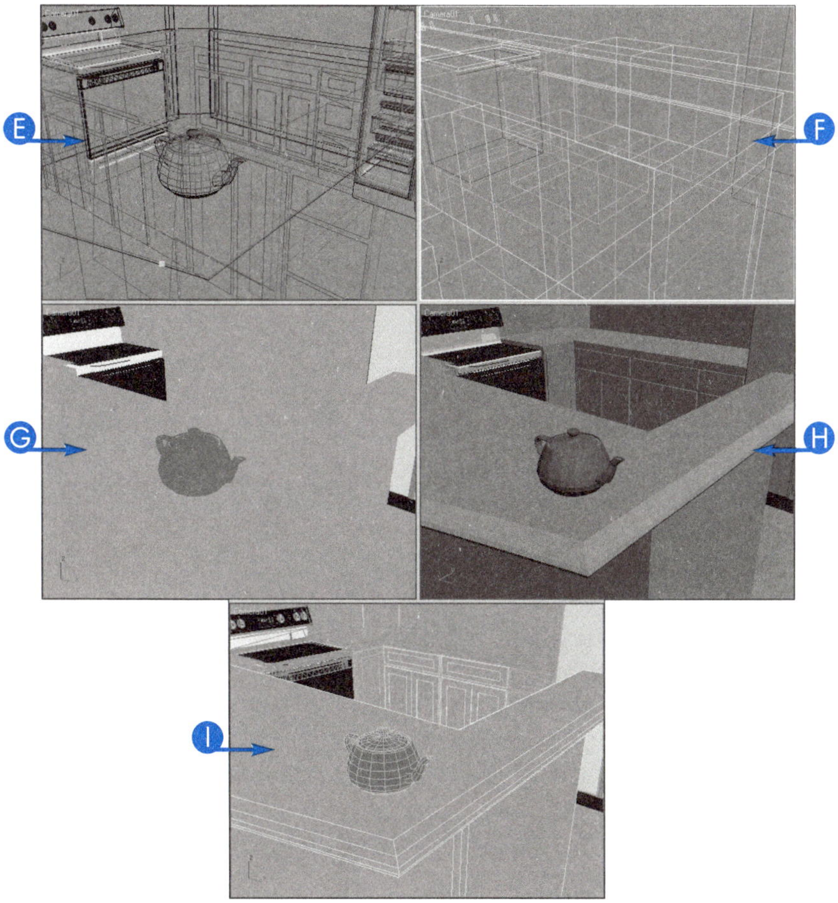

E Lit Wireframes

This is similar to Wireframe mode, but with the edge color derived from the diffuse color of the object's material.

F Bounding Box

Objects display as six-sided, wireframe boxes. This is the fastest viewport rendering option.

G Flat

Each polygon displays, ignoring the effect of lights in the scene.

H Facets

Each face appears as a flat surface, with no shading between adjacent faces and no highlights.

I Edged Faces

This displays the edges of all faces as well as the surfaces.

Set the Viewport Rendering Option

You can easily customize the viewport rendering option to meet your needs. You can do this by selecting an option from a pop-up menu or from the nested Other menu.

The viewport rendering option is assigned to a specific viewport, regardless of the viewport type. For example, if a Top viewport is currently set in Wireframe mode and you change it to Smooth + Highlights, and then change the viewport to a Left or Camera view, then it remains in Smooth + Highlights mode. It is also possible for two viewports to have the same point of view, but different rendering options.

CD FILE

The Viewports.max file is available on the CD-ROM for you to practice setting the viewport rendering options.

MASTER IT

How do I stop my viewport from temporarily changing to Bounding Box mode when I zoom or pan?

▼ Adaptive degradation is a feature that temporarily reduces the viewport quality mode so that the system can keep up with your actions. You can toggle this feature on or off in the Views menu or by pressing the O shortcut key. Turning this feature off may increase your screen's refresh time in scenes that are complex.

Set the Viewport Rendering Option

1. Right-click a viewport label.

   The viewport pop-up menu appears.

2. Click Smooth + Highlights or Wireframe to switch to either mode, or click Other for more options.

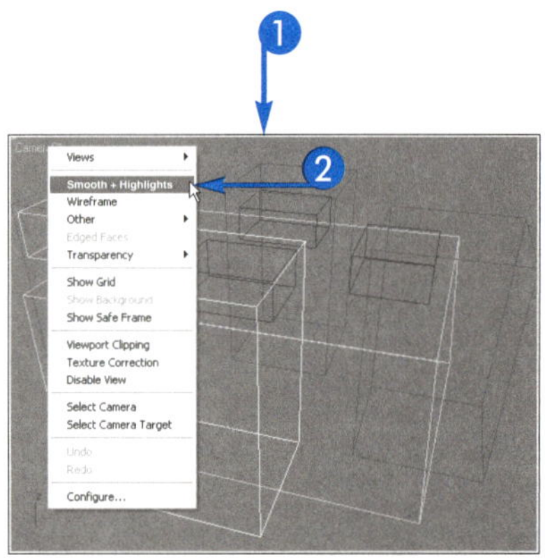

- If the viewport is in a rendered mode, you can right-click the viewport label again, and click Edged Faces.

The viewport updates to reflect your changes; if you clicked Edged Face, it updates to show the edged faces.

Resize the Viewports

The viewports are restricted in number — you can display up to four at a time — but not in size. You can resize them vertically and horizontally by moving the borders that adjacent viewports share. The viewports must remain rectangular in shape, and they must remain in equally wide columns, equally high rows, or both. For example, a 1000-pixel-wide viewport cannot have a single 600-pixel-wide viewport below it. However, it can have two or three viewports below it, as long as the total width equals 1000 pixels.

CD FILE: The Viewports.max file is available on the CD-ROM for you to practice resizing the viewports.

MASTER IT

How do I display more viewport area on my screen?

- You can run 3ds Max in Expert mode to maximize viewport area while minimizing tool display. Press and hold the Control key, and then press the X key to display only your viewports and Menu bar. If you tend to use shortcut keys and quad menus, working in Expert mode provides fast redraws and a clean interface. Many professional users run 3ds Max with a dual monitor setup with the Command panel, Track View, and Material Editor on the second monitor, and viewports on the first monitor.

Resize the Viewports

1. Place the cursor between any two viewports until it changes into a double arrow (↕).

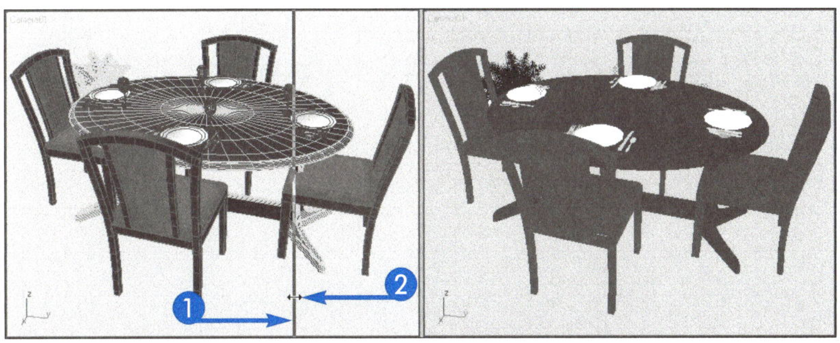

2. Click and drag to resize the viewport.
3. Place the cursor at the intersection between three or four viewports until it changes into a four-sided arrow (✣).
4. Click and drag to resize all of the viewports.
5. Right-click any border to display the Reset Layout pop-up menu.
6. Click Reset Layout.

The viewports reset to their original configuration.

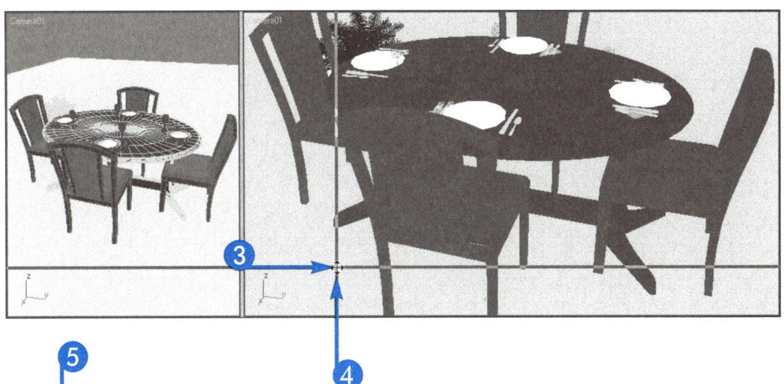

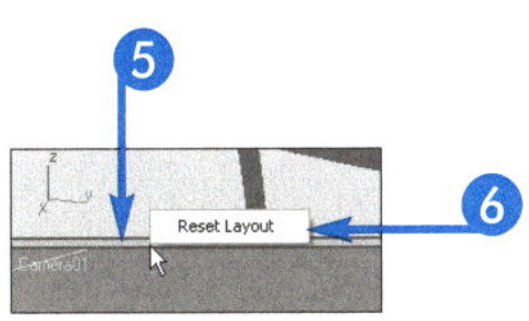

Alter a Viewport View

Viewports can display the contents of your 3ds Max scene from any viewpoint imaginable. For example, you can set one viewport to view the scene from overhead, with a second viewport from the front, and a third viewport that shows the current composition and relative locations of the objects in the scene. You can also use viewports that display your scene through a light or camera to position the light or camera for optimum effect.

You cannot animate the viewport moving over the scene. Although you can animate nearly everything in 3ds Max, viewports are one of the few exceptions. However, you can animate the location of a camera, through which the viewport is looking. Also, you can display content other than your scene in a viewport. The viewports can display a variety of tools, including the Schematic View, Asset Browser, and MAXScript Listener, as well as an ActiveShade window. These tools are available at the bottom of the menu that appears when you right-click the viewport label.

CD FILE: The Viewports2.max file is available on the CD-ROM for you to practice setting the viewport views.

Alter a Viewport View

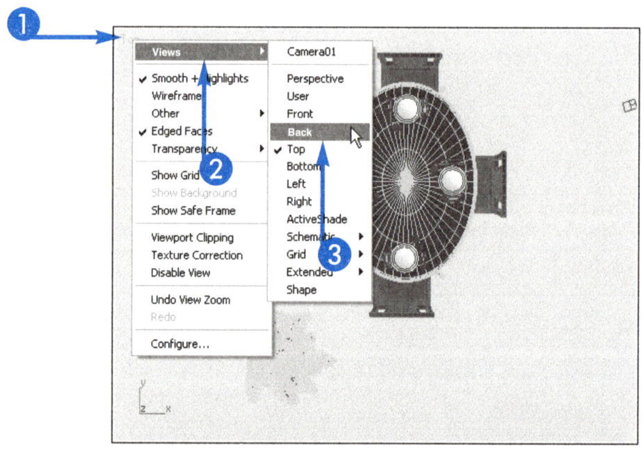

1. Right-click the Top viewport's label.

   The pop-up menu appears.
2. Click Views.
3. Click any of the options above ActiveShade.

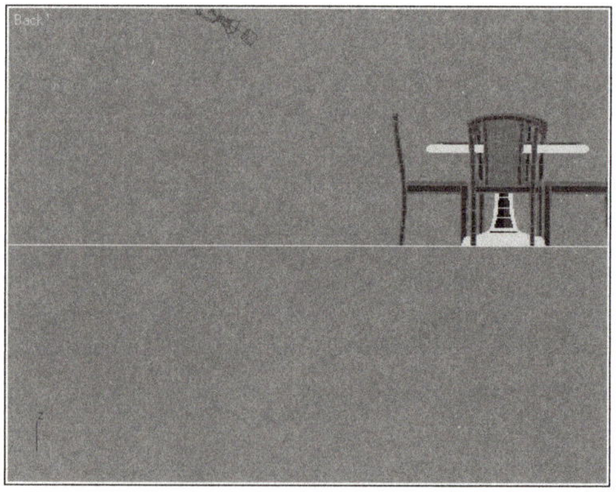

The Top viewport displays the view that you selected from the menu.

Customize the Viewport Layout

The default 3ds Max viewport layout, four equally sized viewports in a quadrant pattern, is not the best layout for every situation. You can use tools to customize your viewport layout, determining how many viewports display on your screen and which viewport rendering methods they are configured to display. You can also set the current view type for each viewport. See the sections "Resize the Viewports" and "Set the Viewport Rendering Option" for more on changing sizes and rendering modes. Note that changes that you make in the Viewport Configuration dialog box apply only to your current scene. To apply settings to all new scenes, save them in an empty file named maxstart.max in the /scenes folder under the 3ds Max root folder. You can reinstate the default 3ds Max configuration, along with other customized settings, by deleting or renaming maxstart.max and then resetting 3ds Max.

MASTER IT

If I output to video, will what I see in the viewports be what I see on TV?

▼ For the most part. Televisions vary in how they display their content. To view what is ultimately shown, open the Render Scene dialog box and set the Output Size to 720x480 for NTSC, or 768x576 for PAL. In the viewport that you render, right-click the label, and then click Show Safe Frame.

Customize the Viewport Layout

1. Click Customize.
2. Click Viewport Configuration.

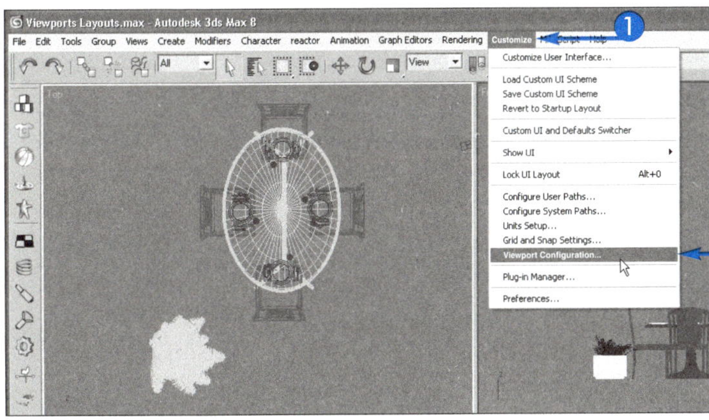

The Viewport Configuration dialog box appears.

3. Click the Layout tab.
4. Click the viewport layout that you want.
5. Click in a viewport image, and then select the current view type.
6. Click OK.

The selected view type is reflected in the graphic.

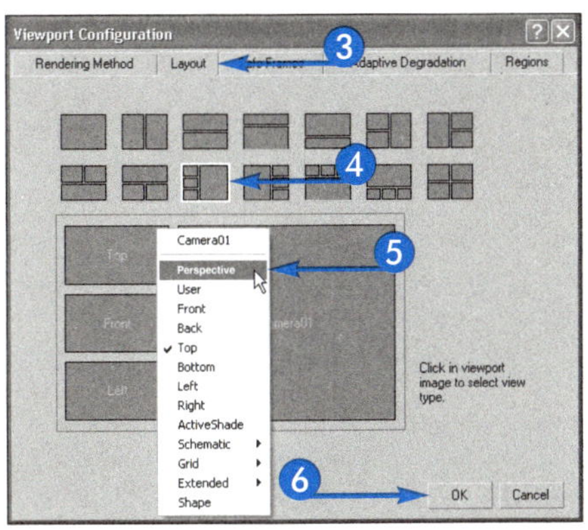

Zoom in a Viewport

During the modeling and animation process, you must see your objects clearly. You cannot modify or accurately transform objects that appear too small on the screen, and objects that are off the screen are extremely difficult to modify.

3ds Max contains several tools that enable you to zoom in and out of your viewports. They are located in the Viewport Controls area in the bottom-right corner of the user interface. Several pairs of these viewport control tools are similar in that they either affect the current viewport or all viewports. For example, the Zoom Extents tool zooms the current viewport to display all visible objects, while the Zoom Extents All button zooms all viewports to display all visible objects.

The dark blue Zoom Extents tools apply to all of the objects in the scene, while the light blue tools, which are in the flyout menus, apply only to selected objects. You can also zoom in or out in a viewport with a mouse that has a scroll wheel.

CD FILE: The Viewport Zoom.max file is available on the CD-ROM for you to practice using the Zoom tools.

Zoom in a Viewport

1. Click Zoom ().
2. Click and drag in the Top viewport.

   The viewport zooms in or out as you drag the cursor down or up.
3. Click the Zoom Extents button ().

   The current viewport zooms out to show all visible objects.
4. Click the Zoom Extents All button ().

   All non-camera viewports expand to show all visible objects in the scene.

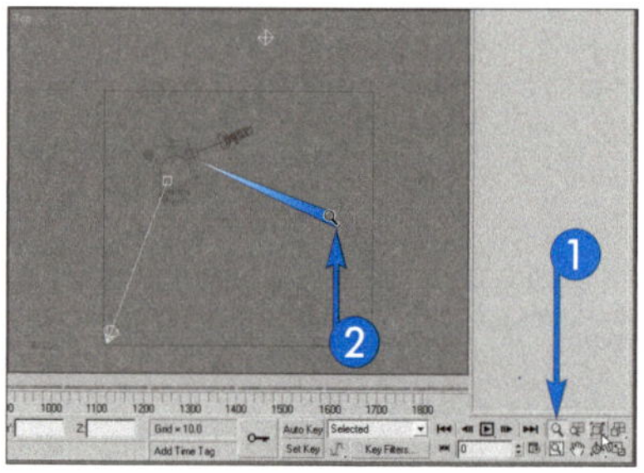

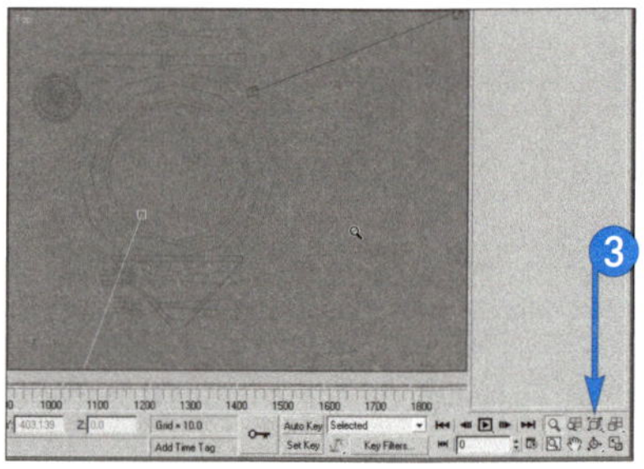

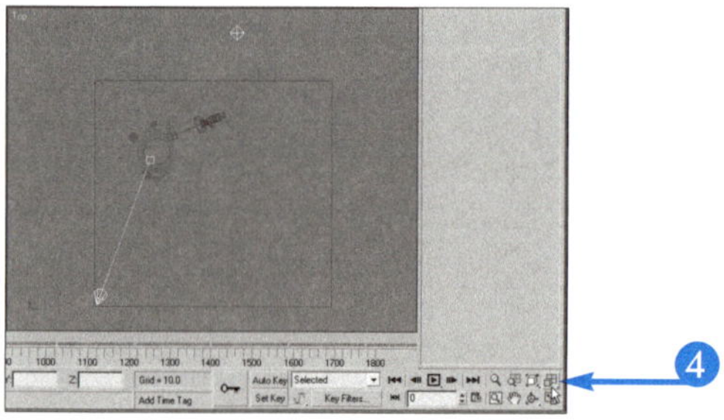

5 Click the Select Object button (![icon]) in the Main toolbar.

6 Click an object in the scene.

The object highlights to indicate that it is selected.

7 Click the Zoom Extents Selected button (![icon]).

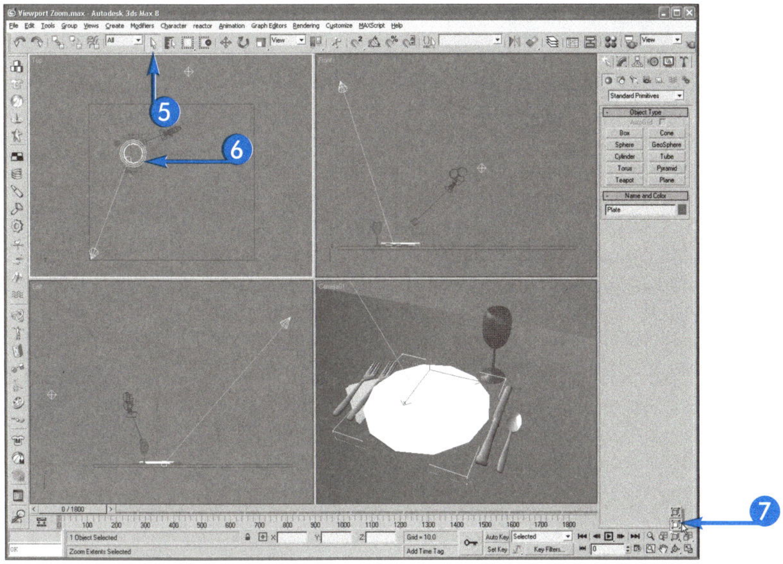

The current viewport zooms to show the limits of the selected object.

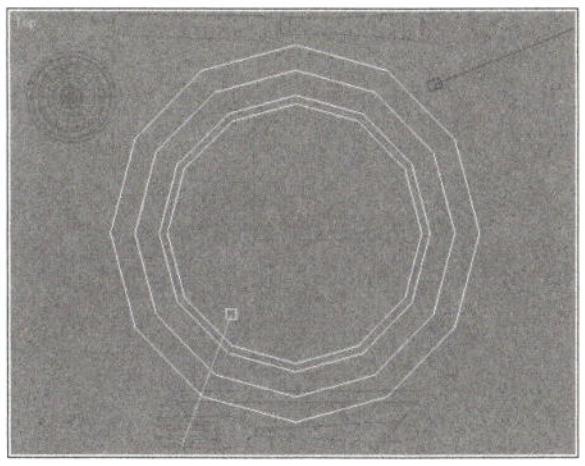

MASTER IT

Can I select a specific area to zoom into?

Yes. The Zoom Region tool (![icon]) allows you to designate a rectangular area that can fit into the viewport. To use it, click ![icon] from the Viewport Controls area. Click, drag, and then release to define the area that you want to zoom into. 3ds Max takes the longest axis of your rectangle and fits its contents into the viewport. In a Perspective viewport, where Zoom Region does not usually work as expected, 3ds Max may hide the button under the Field-of-View flyout.

When I roll the mouse wheel, the zoom occurs from the center of the viewport. Can I change this?

Yes. You can change the mouse wheel feature of the Zoom tool to zoom in and out, based on the location of the cursor. To set this mode, click Customize and then click Preferences. Click the Preferences tab and, in the Mouse Control area, click one or both of the Zoom About Mouse Point options (☐ changes to ☑).

Are there keyboard shortcuts to zoom in and zoom out of viewports?

Yes. You can press [to zoom into the viewport. You can press] to zoom out. The keyboard shortcut for Zoom Extents is Z.

Rotate a Viewport

When you look at an object from the top or side, you may not see its true shape or configuration. For example, when seen from the top, a 2D circle and a 3D cylinder both appear as multi-sided polygons. You can fix this problem by rotating the viewport. The Arc Rotate tools, located in the Viewport Controls area, provide a Trackball gizmo to specify how the tool operates when you orient the viewport to best reflect the scene.

In Arc Rotate mode, you can drag outside the Trackball circle to rotate the viewport around its center and perpendicular to its borders. When you drag inside the Trackball circle, you remove any constraints that restrict the viewport orientation. You can drag any of the Trackball handles to restrict the rotation to either a left-right or up-down orientation.

In Arc Rotate Selected mode, the center of the selected object or objects is used as the center point of the viewport rotation. Using the Arc Rotate mode in a Top or Front viewport changes it into an axonometric User viewport.

CD FILE The Viewport Arc Rotate.max file is available on the CD-ROM for you to practice using the Arc Rotate tool.

Rotate a Viewport

1. Right-click in the Perspective viewport to make it active.
2. Click the Arc Rotate button ( ).
   - The cursor changes from to .
3. Click and drag outside the Trackball.

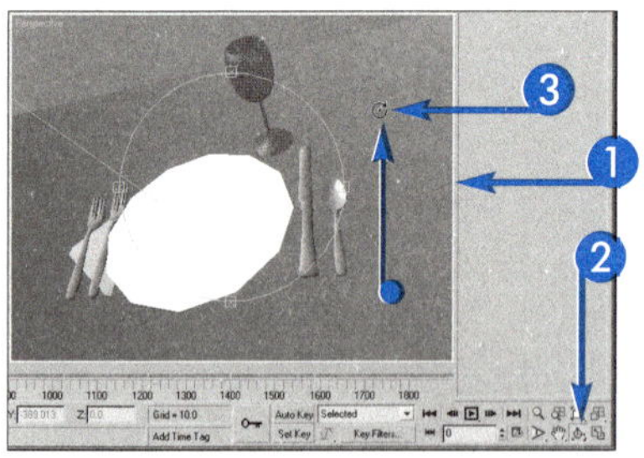

The viewport rotates around its center point.

4. Click and drag inside the Trackball.
   - The cursor changes from to and the viewport rotates freely.

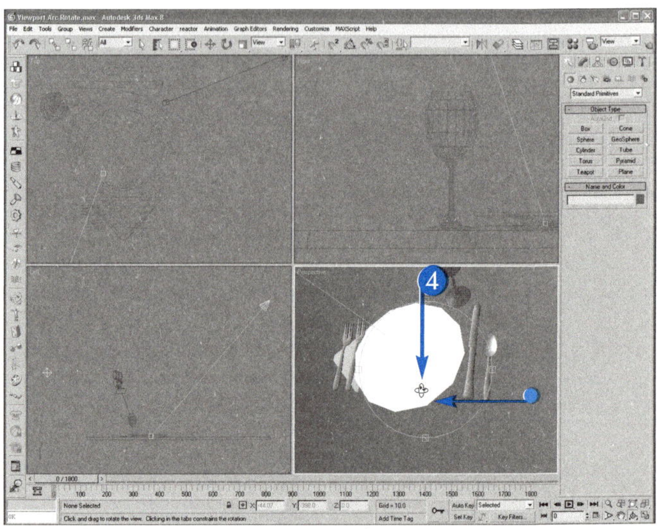

5. Click the Select Object button () in the Main toolbar.
6. Click an object in the Perspective viewport.

   A bounding box appears around the object to indicate that it is selected.
7. Click the Arc Rotate Selected button ().
8. Click and drag inside the Trackball.

   The viewport rotates with the selected object as the center point.
9. Right-click to end the command.

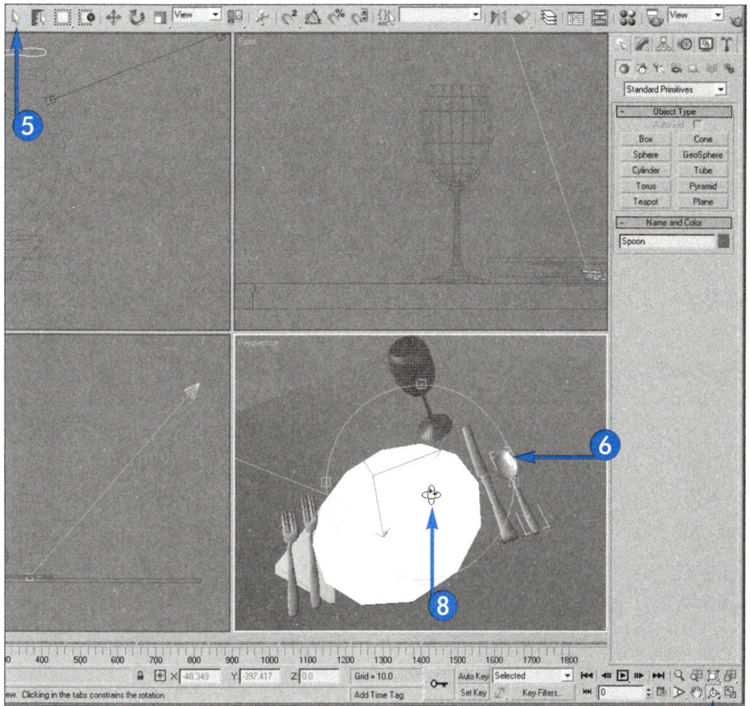

- You can click the Arc Rotate SubObject button () to rotate only the SubObject of your object.

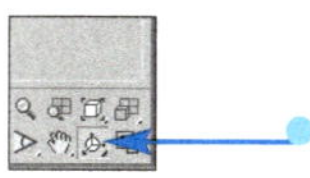

MASTER IT

Can I use a shortcut key to activate the Arc Rotate tool?

▼ Yes. Pressing and holding the Alt key while dragging with the middle mouse button or scroll wheel button has the same effect as clicking the Arc Rotate button (). Using in this manner allows you to rotate the viewport transparently without leaving the command or action that you are currently performing. However, this method does not use the Trackball gizmo. Pressing Ctrl + R also activates the Arc Rotate gizmo.

How can I control the angle at which the Arc Rotate tool rotates my viewport?

▼ When dragging outside the Trackball, the Arc Rotate tool matches the Angle value that was set when the Angle Snap Toggle was active. To set the Angle value, right-click the Angle Snap Toggle in the Main toolbar to open the Grid and Snap Settings dialog box. Type a value in the Angle (deg.) field and then close the dialog box. Click the Angle Snap Toggle button to activate it.

Using the Field-of-View Tool

In a Perspective viewport, you can use the Field-of-View tool to establish what you can view by setting the width extents of the viewport. Similarly, in a camera viewport, the Field-of-View tool determines the angle of the camera's viewing cone. You can also adjust a camera's field of view by selecting it, opening the Modify tab in the Command panel, and changing the FOV field in the Parameters rollout.

The Field-of-View tool is in the Viewport Controls area and, when a Perspective viewport is active, in the flyout menu with the Zoom Region tool.

The FOV.max file is available on the CD-ROM for you to practice using the Field-of-View tool.

Can I set a specific value for the field of view in a Perspective viewport?

- Yes. You can do so in a Perspective viewport in the Viewport Configuration dialog box. Right-click the Field-of-View tool to open the Viewport Configuration dialog box, and then click the Rendering Method tab. Type a value in the Field of View field to change the current value. Note that you cannot use the Field-of-View tool to zoom because very low field-of-view gives strange performance problems when you attempt to zoom, pan, or move objects in the viewport.

Using the Field-of-View Tool

1. Right-click in the Perspective viewport to make it active.
2. Click the Field-of-View button ( ).

   The cursor changes from to .
3. Click and drag in the viewport.

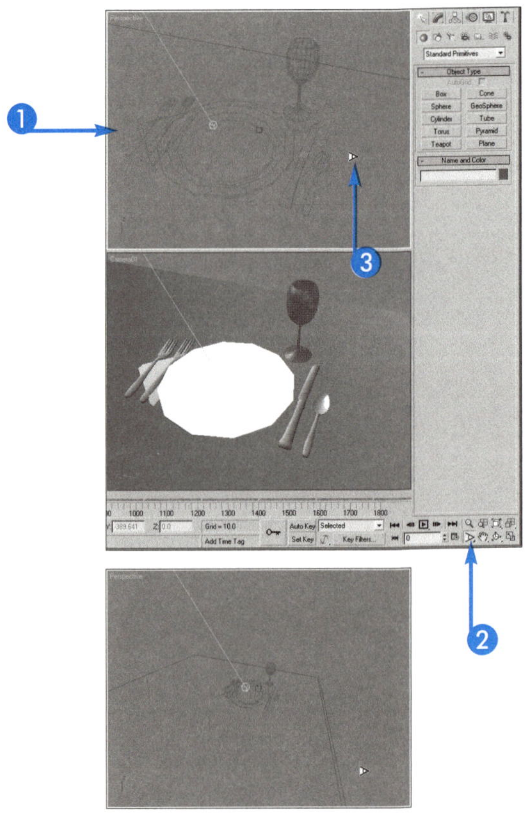

The viewport's field of view increases or decreases accordingly.

Using the Maximize Viewport Toggle

Screen space is always at a premium in computer graphics, and with toolbars, menus, and panels crowding the screen, the leftover space is dedicated to viewports. Subdividing that remaining space can often leave you three or four small viewports that are difficult to use in some situations. You can use the Maximize Viewport Toggle button, located in the bottom-right corner of the Viewport Controls, to replace all existing viewports with a larger version of the current viewport.

CD FILE: The FOV.max file is available on the CD-ROM for you to practice using the Maximize Viewport Toggle.

MASTER IT

Can I change the viewport view while a viewport is maximized?

- Yes, but the new viewport view replaces the existing view when the multi-viewport configuration is restored. For example, in the previous exercise, if you change the Camera01 viewport to a Top view after step 3, and click again, a Top view appears in both the upper-right and lower-left viewports. See the section "Alter a Viewport View" for more information.

Using the Maximize Viewport Toggle

1. Right-click in a viewport to make it active.
2. Click the Maximize Viewport Toggle button ().

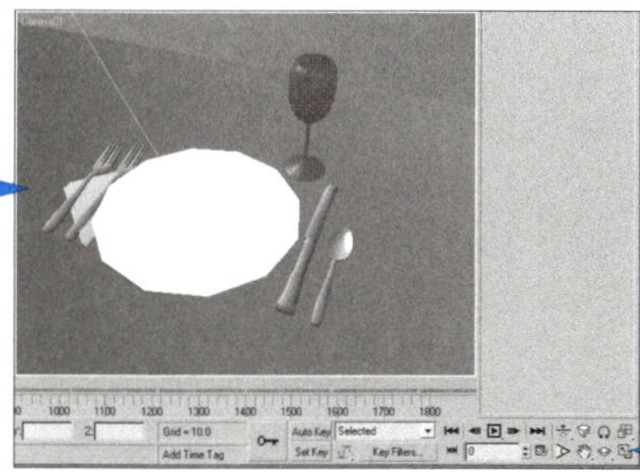

The four viewports are replaced with one large viewport.

3. Click again.

3ds Max restores the four-viewport configuration.

Navigate with the Pan View and Walk Through Tools

3ds Max scenes tend to be linear and spread out across the virtual landscape. Therefore, you may find navigating your scene using only the Zoom and Arc Rotate tools time consuming, and replicating zoom factors, when viewing similar objects for comparison, difficult at best. The Pan View tool increases your navigation toolset by adding the ability to shift the viewport laterally without changing the zoom factor, and is similar to the Hand tool you find in Adobe Photoshop.

Using the Walk Through tool, you can travel through a scene using the keyboard similar to moving in a video game. The main controls for the Walk Through tool's movement directions are the W, A, S, and D keys on the left side of your keyboard, and the arrow keys on the right; both sets of keys perform the same functions. The arrow keys in the numeric keypad do not function with this tool. For a full list of the Walk Through tool's keyboard commands, see "Using Walkthrough Navigation" in the 3ds Max User Reference.

The Walk Through tools are only available in Camera and Perspective viewports.

The FOV.max file is available on the CD-ROM for you to practice using the Pan and Walk Through tools.

Navigate with the Pan View and Walk Through Tools

Using the Pan View Tool

1. Right-click in a viewport to make it active.
2. Click the Pan View button ( ).

   The cursor changes from ( ) to ( ).
3. Click and drag in the viewport.

   The viewport shifts without changing the zoom factor.
4. Right-click to exit the command.

Note: *Pressing and holding the middle mouse button or scroll wheel allows you to access a transparent Pan View tool that you can use without exiting other commands.*

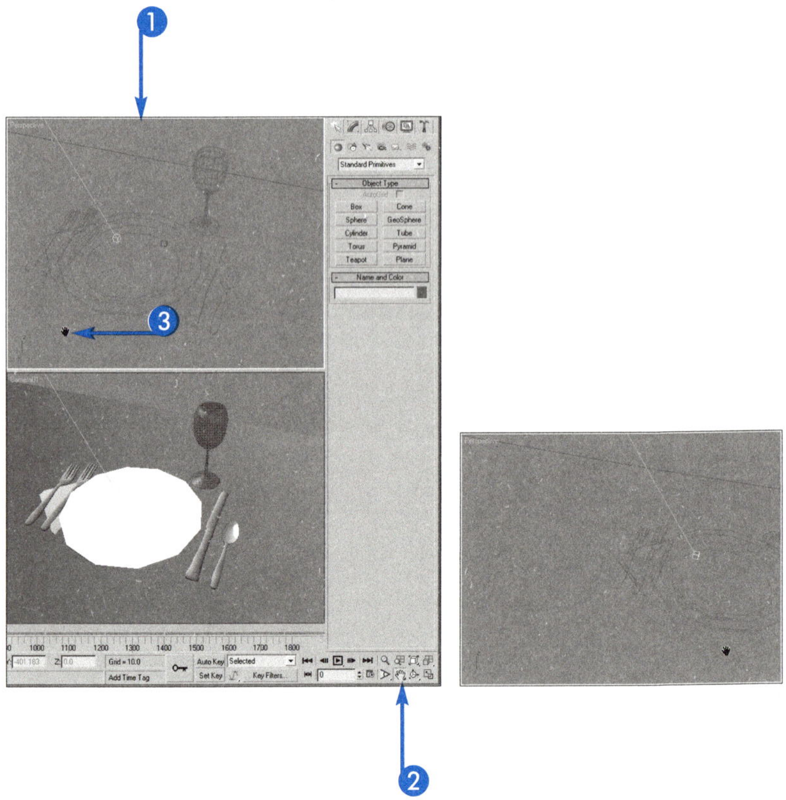

Using the Walk Through Tool

5 Right-click in a Camera or Perspective viewport.

6 Click and hold , and then select the Walk Through button () from the flyout menu.

The cursor changes from to .

7 Hold down the Up arrow or W key.

The cursor changes from to and the viewport zooms forward.

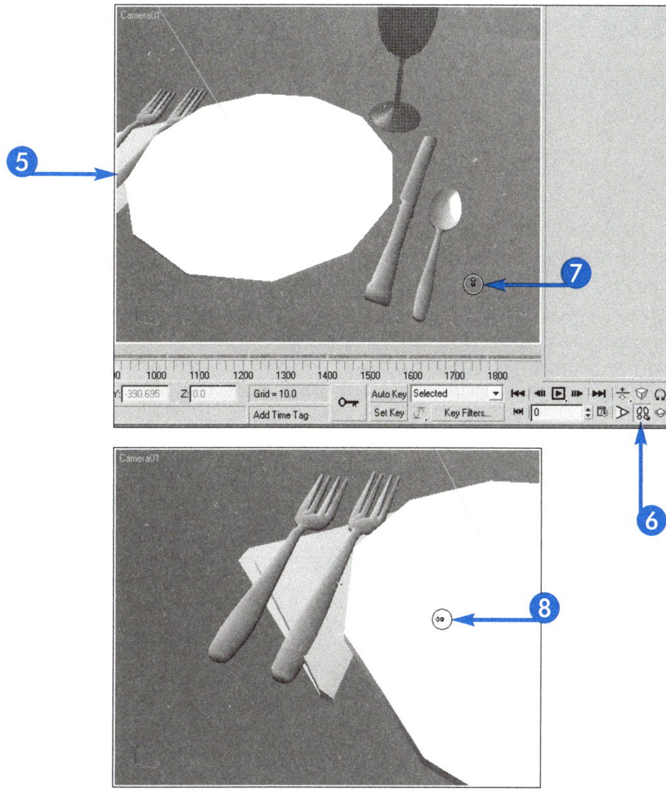

8 Press and hold the Left arrow or A key.

The cursor changes from to and the viewport rotates to the left.

9 Right-click to exit the command.

The viewport walks through your scene.

MASTER IT

How can I get back to my previous view after I use the Pan View tool? Undo does not work.

- The Pan View () or Zoom tools do not change anything in your scene — only your view — so the Undo tool has nothing to undo. Instead, click Views and then click Undo View Change, or press Shift + Z. You can repeat this several times to step backward or forward, using Redo View Change or Shift + Y. Undo View Change does not work after changing the view in a Camera viewport where a change in a scene object has occurred. In this case, click Undo or press Control + Z. Undo View Change also does not restore the view after you use the Walk Through tool () in a Perspective viewport.

How can I slow down the Walk Through tool's movements?

- The Walk Through tool's progress can often be too fast or too slow for your particular needs. These movements are controlled by adjusting the step size for the tool's forward, backward, or sideways actions. With the Walk Through tool active, press the [key repeatedly to slow the movement down, or press the] key to speed it up. Press the Alt + [keys to reset the step size to the program's default.

Add a Viewport Background Image

You can easily add background images to any or all of your 3ds Max viewports. Viewport background images usually have one of two purposes: The first is to match the rendering background image and to assist you when placing objects in your scene that exist in front of a background plate. The second purpose is to assist the modeling process. When the latter is the case, the background image, usually a sketch or a photograph, is used as a reference for the creation of a 3D model of the object that appears in the image.

It is a common practice to place a front and side image of the object to be created in the corresponding viewports to help model it in all dimensions. Viewport background image files can be from almost any digital image format, including JPG, TIF, and TGA and can also be animated file formats such as AVI or MOV files. Each viewport in 3ds Max can contain a different background image.

Add a Viewport Background Image

1. Click Views.
2. Click Viewport Background.

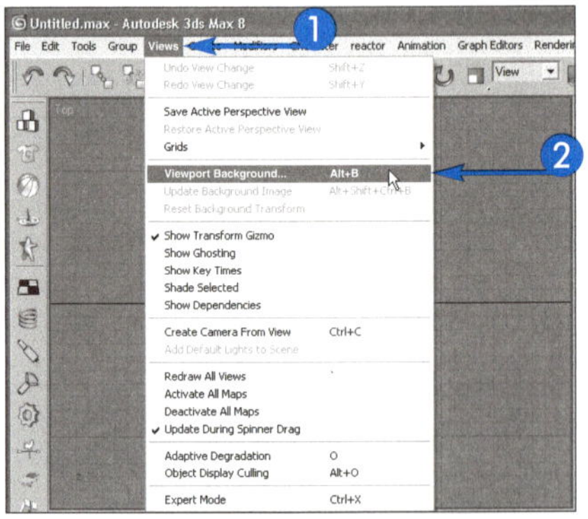

The Viewport Background dialog box appears.

3. Click Files.

The Select Background Image dialog box appears.

4. Navigate to the folder containing the image.
5. Click the image.
6. Click Open.

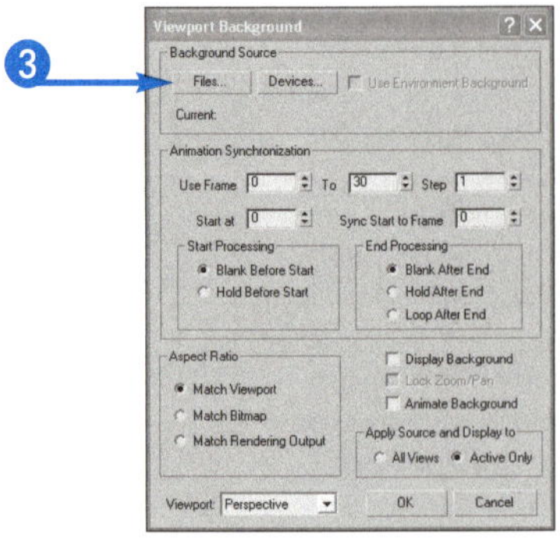

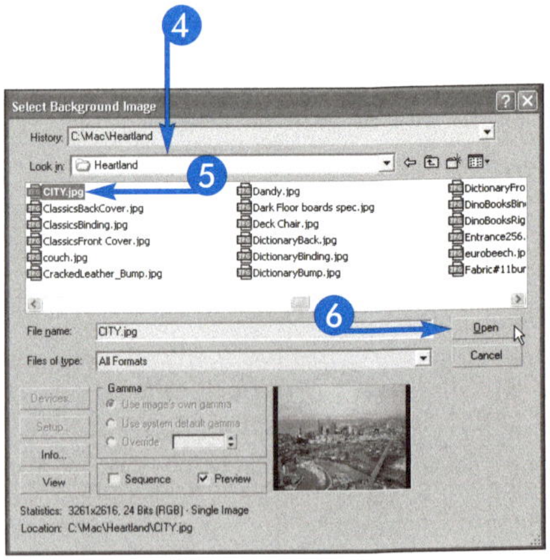

The filename appears in the Background Source section of the Viewport Background dialog box.

7. Click the Display Background option (☐ changes to ☑).

8. Click OK.

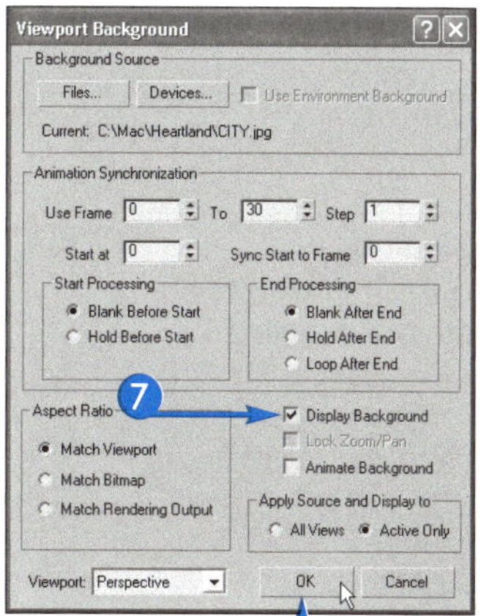

The image appears in the viewport.

Why does the background image appear in my viewport but not in my rendered scene?

▼ The viewport background image is a different object than the environment background image. To set the environment background image, click Rendering in the Main menu, and then click Environment. Click the Environment Map button, click Bitmap in the Material/Map Browser that opens, and then navigate to the appropriate background image in the Select Bitmap Image File dialog box. To synchronize the viewport background image to the environment background image, select the Use Environment Background option (☐ changes to ☑) in the Viewport Background dialog box.

Why is my viewport background image squashed and distorted?

▼ The viewport background image's aspect ratio — the length in pixels divided by the width in pixels — is different from the aspect ratio of the viewport. As a result, the image is squashing or stretching itself to completely fill the available area of the viewport. To constrain the background image to its correct aspect ratio, follow steps 1 and 2 to open the Viewport Background dialog box, and then select Match Bitmap in the Aspect Ratio area (○ changes to ◉).

Select Objects

You must select objects to modify, transform, or delete them. The most common selection methods are the Select Object button in the Main toolbar and the Select option in the quad menu. Once activated, you can click to select any visible object in the viewports. You can use the Ctrl button to add objects to the selection or to deselect currently selected objects. You can use the Alt key to remove a selected object from the selection or use a blank area of a viewport to deselect all objects.

You can select objects by name in the Select Objects dialog box. By default, the list of objects sorts alphabetically, but you can also sort by object type, color, and size. If you only want specific object types, such as 3D Geometry, then you can omit other object types from the list.

You must often select objects along with their hierarchical parents, or select another object's coordinate system. In all cases, the Select Objects dialog box reflects the requirements of the tool that you are using. The H shortcut key quickly displays the appropriate Select Objects dialog box.

CD FILE: The Select.max file is available on the CD-ROM for you to practice selecting objects.

Select Objects

Select by Name

1. Click Edit.
2. Click Select By.
3. Click Name.

   You can also click the Select by Name button ( ) in the Main toolbar or press the H shortcut key.

4. In the Select Object dialog box, click the name of the object that you want to select.

   To select multiple objects, you can press and hold Ctrl or Shift while you click objects in the list.

5. Click Select.

   The objects that you selected are highlighted in the viewports.

Select with the Select Object tool

1. Click the Select Object button ( ).
2. Place the cursor over an object.

   - The cursor changes from ( ) to ( ) and a tooltip displays the object name.

3. Click the object.

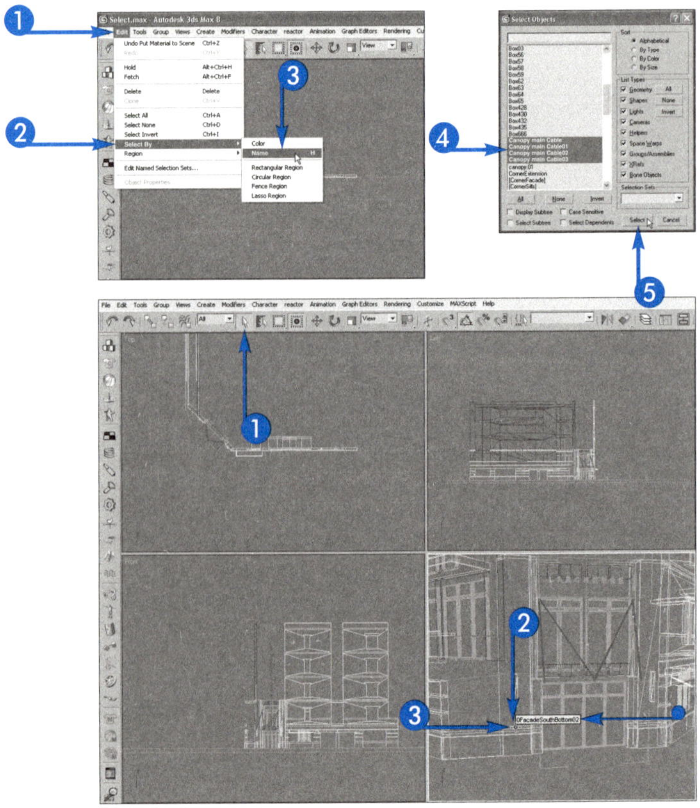

- The object highlights to indicate that it is selected.

4 Press and hold the Ctrl key.

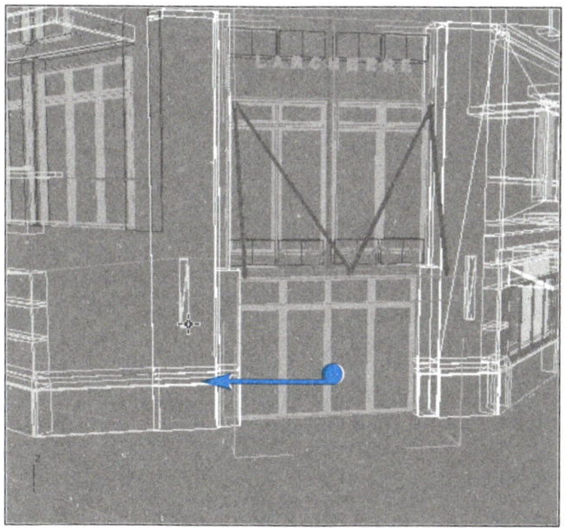

5 Click another object.

The second object is selected.

To remove an object, you can press and hold the Alt key, and then click a selected object.

You can click a blank area of the viewport to deselect all objects.

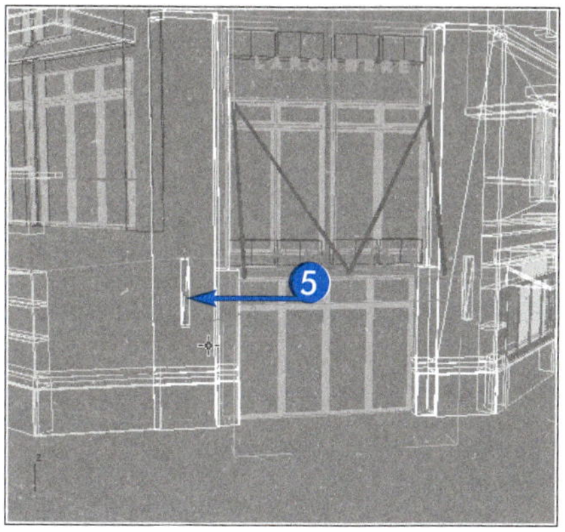

MASTER IT

Why do my objects have object names?

Objects have unique names so that both the user and the program can locate them and distinguish them from each other. When you create an object, 3ds Max automatically names the object with the object type, such as Sphere or Deflector, followed by a number. Each subsequent object is given the same name, followed by the next sequentially higher number. When you select one object, you can change its name in the Name field of the Name and Color rollout in the Create panel, at the top of the Modify panel or in the Object Properties dialog box. For more information on renaming multiple objects, see Chapter 3.

How can I select an object that is clustered with several other objects? When I click it, I always select the wrong one.

A logical and standard naming convention for your objects is the key to quickly selecting the objects by name. If several objects are co-located in the same place, and the naming convention does not distinguish them, then temporarily hide the objects that are getting in your way. Organizing objects by layer can also assist you to select or hide objects that you need. See the section "Hide and Unhide Objects" for information on hiding scene objects. Be aware that 3ds Max allows you to give multiple objects the same name. For information on changing objects' names and organizing layers, see Chapter 3.

continued

Select Objects

(Continued)

The Region selection tools allow you to select the objects in a specific viewport area by drawing a boundary around the objects. The selection types include: Rectangular Selection Region, Circular Selection Region, Fence Selection Region, Lasso Selection Region, and Paint Selection Region.

With the Select Object tool active, click and drag a blank area of a viewport to start a region selection. To select objects with the Fence Selection Region, click with the mouse in a pattern around the objects. You create a curvaceous selection Region by clicking and dragging around the target objects with the Lasso Selection Region active.

When the Window/Crossing button is set to Window, the objects must be completely within the boundary to be selected. When you set the button to Crossing, the objects that cross the boundary are also selected.

The Paint Selection Region uses a paintbrush analogy to select objects. You drag the cursor over the objects in your scene to add them to the selection set. You can enlarge or reduce the Selection Brush size in the General tab of the Preference Settings dialog box.

CD FILE — The Select.max file is available on the CD-ROM for you to practice selecting objects.

Select Objects *(continued)*

Select by Rectangular Region

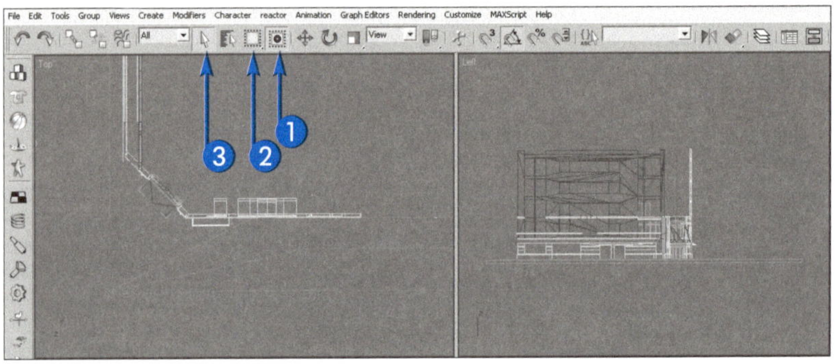

1. Set the Window/Crossing button to Window ( ).
2. Click here and select the Rectangular Selection Region button ( ) from the Selection Region flyout menu.

   You can click the Circular Selection Region button ( ) for circular selections.
3. Click Select Objects ( ).

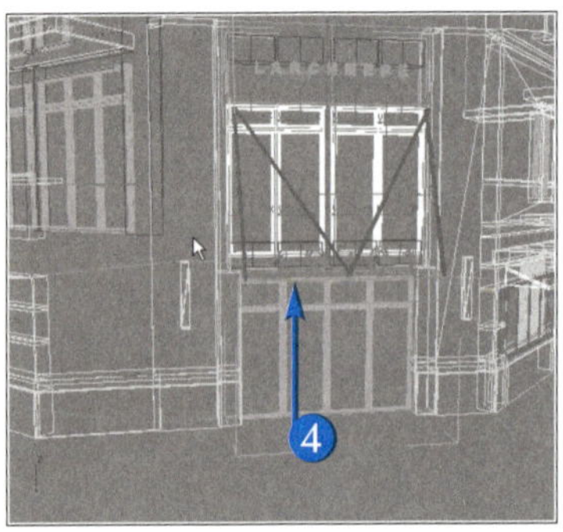

4. Click and drag to create a Rectangular Region.

   As you drag the cursor, a rectangular marquee defines the region that you are selecting.
5. Release the mouse button.

   The objects completely within the region are selected.

Select by Painting

1 Click and hold here to display the Selection Region flyout menu.

2 Click the Region Paint button ( ).

3 Click here to change to a Crossing selection .

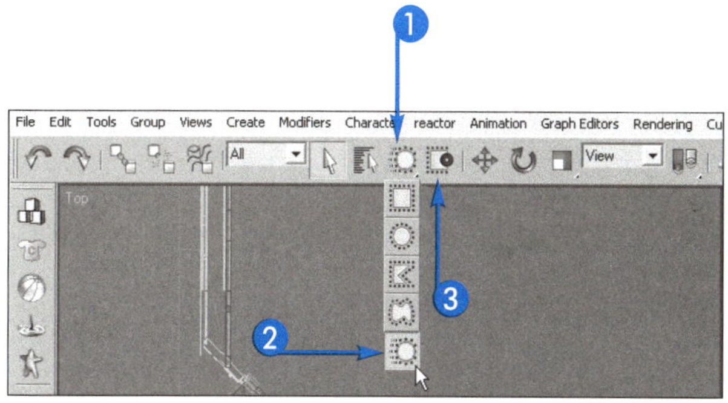

4 Using the left mouse button, click and drag across the objects that you want to select.

The cursor changes to .

The objects that the cursor passes over are selected.

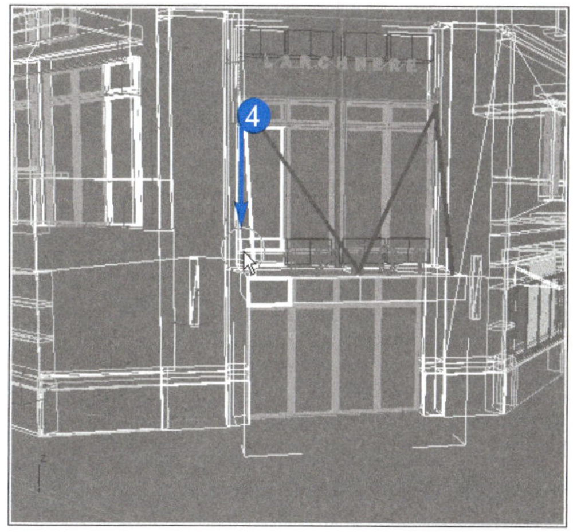

MASTER IT

How do I select objects in an oddly shaped region?

▼ The Lasso Region ( ) and Fence Region ( ) selection tools create odd-shaped selection boundaries. For example, you can use either tool to select the objects that make up a serpentine wall weaving its way through a scene. Drag a freehand boundary around the wall with , and then release the mouse to initiate the selection. Be careful not to overlap any loops you create with the Lasso boundary, as this may make the selection unpredictable. When you use , each click of the mouse adds a line to the polygon that defines the selection boundary. Clicking the point that initiated the fence closes the boundary and initiates the selection.

How do I add or remove objects from a selection?

▼ There are as many ways to edit a selection as there are to create one. When you make a selection with a 3ds Max tool, you may not be able to select all of the objects that you want at once. To add more objects to a selection, press and hold Ctrl while selecting additional objects. The Ctrl key acts as a toggle; objects that are already selected are deselected with Ctrl held down. You can also add or remove objects in the Select Objects dialog box — opened with or the H shortcut key — by holding Ctrl while clicking additional object names. Objects are removed from the selection by holding down the Alt key and clicking them.

Set Object Properties

An object's properties determine how it appears in a scene, renders, and reacts to lights and effects. You adjust an object's properties in the Object Properties dialog box. You can open the dialog box by selecting an object, via the Object Properties command in the Edit menu. Alternatively, you can open it via a quad menu. The Object Properties dialog box also displays read-only information that pertains to the object, such as its location, number of faces, and whether it is a member of a group.

The controls for displaying and rendering an object are in the General tab of the Object Properties dialog box. The options in the Rendering Control area determine how the objects render and how they react to lights. For example, a shadow-casting light does not cast a shadow from an object when you select the Cast Shadows option and does not cast a shadow onto an object when you deselect the Receive Shadows option. You can also find the options in the Display Properties in the Display panel in the Command panel area.

CD FILE The Properties.max file is available on the CD-ROM for you to practice setting an object's properties.

Set Object Properties

1. Select an object.
2. Right-click and then select Properties.

The Object Properties dialog box appears.

3. Click the See-Through option (☐ changes to ☑).

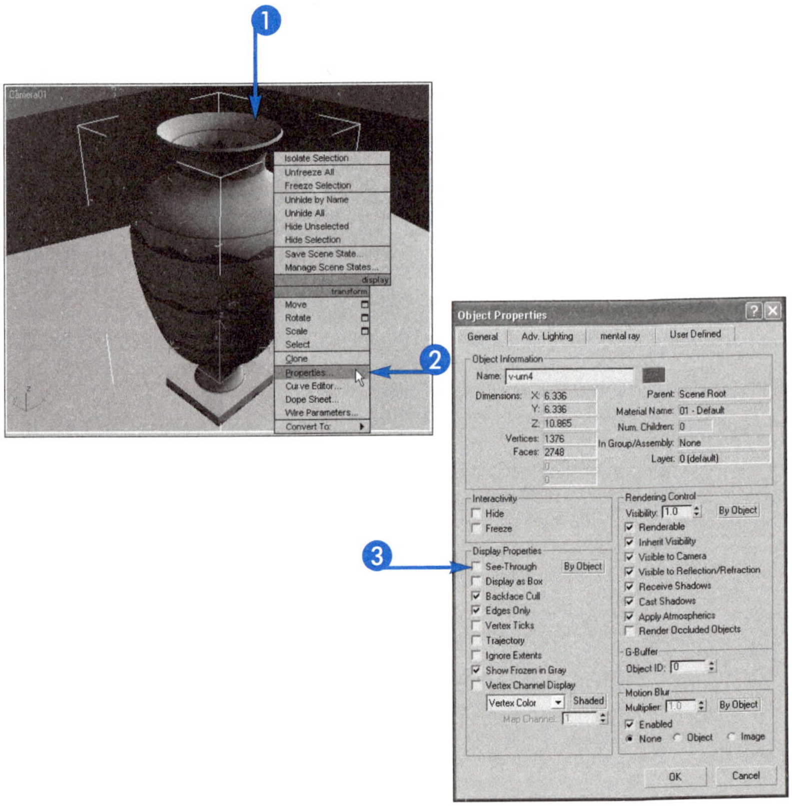

4. Click to deselect the Backface Cull option (☑ changes to ☐).
5. Click to deselect the Renderable option (☑ changes to ☐).
6. Click OK.

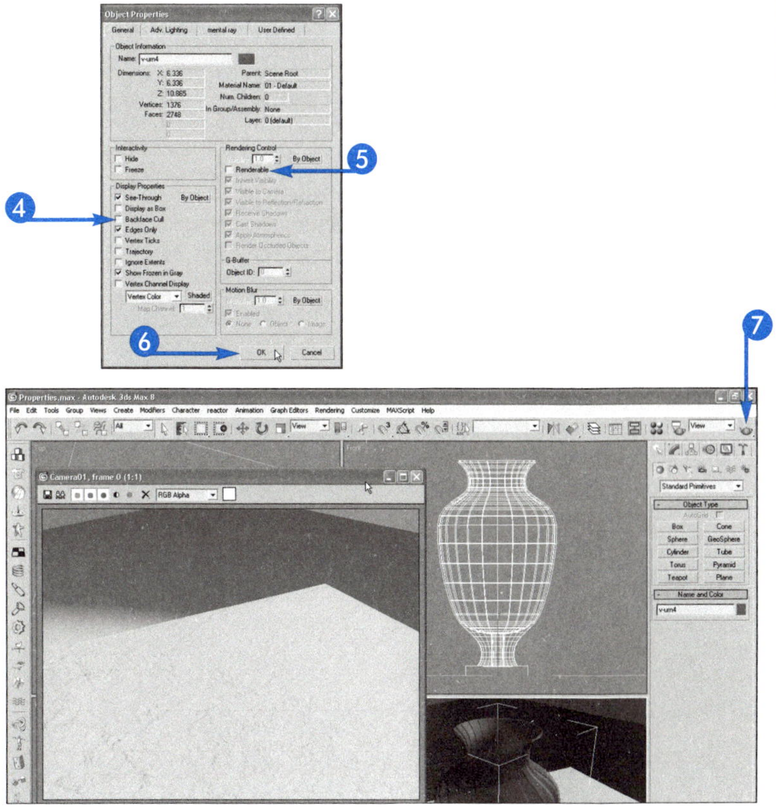

The dialog box closes.

The edges in the back of the object appear in the wireframe viewports, and the object is transparent in rendered viewports.

7. Click the Quick Render button ( ).

The object does not render in the scene.

MASTER IT

What do the By Object buttons do in the Object Properties dialog box?

▼ The By Object buttons specify whether the Object Properties dialog box sets and displays the property options specifically for selected objects. This is the default setting. When you click By Object, the active state becomes By Layer. When By Layer is active, the properties of the object are determined by the settings for the object's layer. Layer properties are set in the Layer Manager dialog box. By Object or By Layer are selected in several places in the Object Properties dialog box. For more information about layers, see Chapter 3.

Can I change the properties of several objects at one time?

▼ Yes, the Object Properties dialog box opens, regardless of the number of objects that are currently selected. When more than one object is selected, "Multiple Selected" appears in the name field, and you cannot change the objects' names. Changing any of the options shown changes that option for all of the selected objects. Values in the Object Information section display as gray with a value of zero, rather than displaying the object data. When the objects have different option settings, those options appear as gray, but you can change them to be either checked or unchecked.

Hide and Unhide Objects

You can hide objects when you want to only display other objects that may be obscured in your viewports. Hiding objects also improves your system performance when you work in a complex scene, because 3ds Max does not redraw hidden objects as you make changes, or pan and zoom the viewports. Hidden objects remain hidden in all viewports until you unhide them.

You can hide objects by current selection, name, category, or hit, or you can hide only the objects that are currently unselected. The Hide Selection and Hide Unselected options are in the quad menu when an object is selected, and all of the methods for hiding objects are in the Display panel in the Command panel area.

Use Hide by Hit to select objects individually, and hide them by selecting them directly; the other selection methods do not work with Hide by Hit. You can select individual objects to unhide via the Unhide by Name button in the Display panel, and then select the objects that you want to unhide in the Unhide Objects dialog box that appears.

CD FILE

The Properties.max file is available on the CD-ROM for you to practice hiding objects.

Hide and Unhide Objects

Hide by Hit

1. Click the Display button ( ).

   The Display Panel appears.

   If the Hide rollout is not expanded, then click the plus sign ( ) to expand it.

2. Click Hide by Hit.
3. Click the objects that you want to hide.

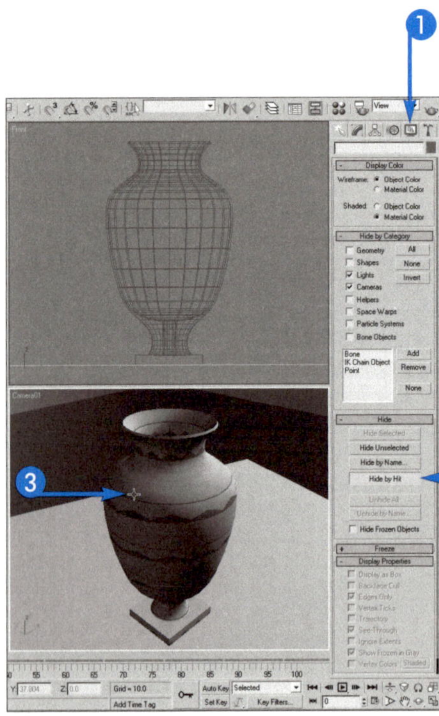

The objects that you selected are hidden in all viewports.

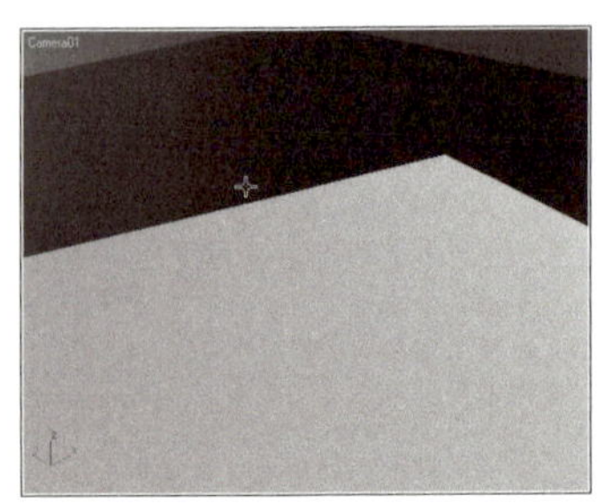

Unhide by Name

1. Follow steps 1 to 3 in the subsection "Hide by Hit" on the previous page.
2. Click Unhide by Name.

   The Unhide Objects dialog box appears.
3. Select the objects that you want to unhide.

   You can press and hold Ctrl or Shift to select multiple objects.
4. Click Unhide.

   The dialog box closes, and the objects that you selected are unhidden.

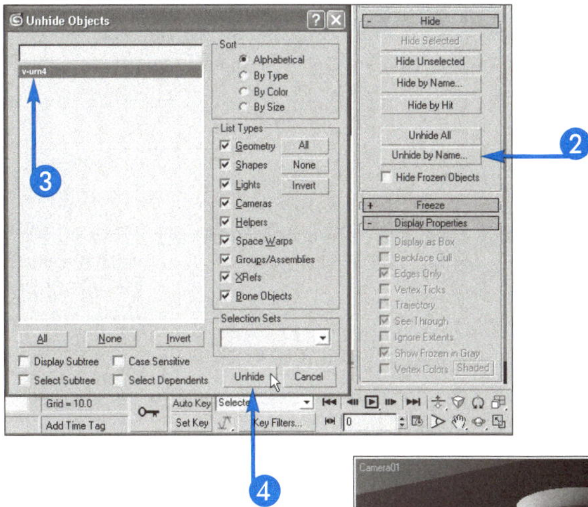

What if I want to hide a specific type of object?

When you are working on the modeling aspect of a project, the lights, cameras, and particle systems are often irrelevant to the process and clutter the screen. If you want to hide objects of a specific type, then you can use the Hide by Category rollout in the Display panel. In the list of category options, you can hide a specific object type by selecting the check box next to the category name. For example, to hide all lights in your scene, click the Lights option (☐ changes to ☑). You can redisplay the hidden objects by clicking the same check box again to deselect it (☑ changes to ☐). Objects that are hidden by category are not listed in the Unhide Objects dialog box.

I am constantly hiding and unhiding the same objects between renderings. How can I do this faster?

There are two possible ways. First, you can tell 3ds Max to render objects, even when they are hidden. Do this by clicking the Render Hidden Geometry option (☐ changes to ☑) in the Common tab or the Render Scene dialog box. For more about rendering, see Chapter 21. A second solution is to add the objects that you are constantly hiding and unhiding to a named selection set. You can then quickly select these objects using the Named Selection Sets menu in the Main toolbar, or the Selection Sets menu in the Select Objects dialog box. You can also use Layers to hide and unhide objects.

Freeze and Unfreeze Objects

In a cluttered scene, selecting the correct objects can often be complicated. Hiding objects may not always be the appropriate solution, especially when you need to move one object relative to another object. This is where freezing objects is a good idea.

Frozen objects are visible in the viewports, but you cannot select them using any selection method. For example, you may have modeled a bouquet of flowers and need to arrange each flower individually in the vase. In the Top viewport, you may inadvertently select the vase, and all objects above and below it, when you try to pick a flower. When you freeze the vase and other objects, they become grayed out in the viewports and you cannot select them. See the section "Select Objects" for more information.

You can freeze objects that are selected, unselected, by name, or by hit, and you can unfreeze objects by name, by hit, or all at once. You can freeze or unfreeze entire layers using the Layer Manager. For more information, see Chapter 3. Frozen objects still render and do not lose any of their object properties or animation.

CD FILE — The Properties.max file is available on the CD-ROM for you to practice hiding objects.

Freeze and Unfreeze Objects

Freeze by Hit

1 Click ▣.

The Display Panel appears.

If the Freeze rollout is not expanded, then you can click the plus sign (+).

2 Click Freeze by Hit.

3 Click the objects that you want to freeze.

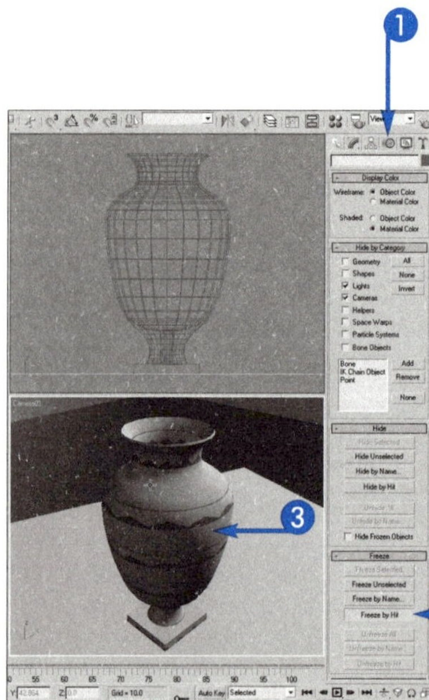

The objects that you selected are grayed out and frozen in all viewports.

Continue selecting objects that you want to freeze.

-k Freeze by Hit.

ımmand discontinues.

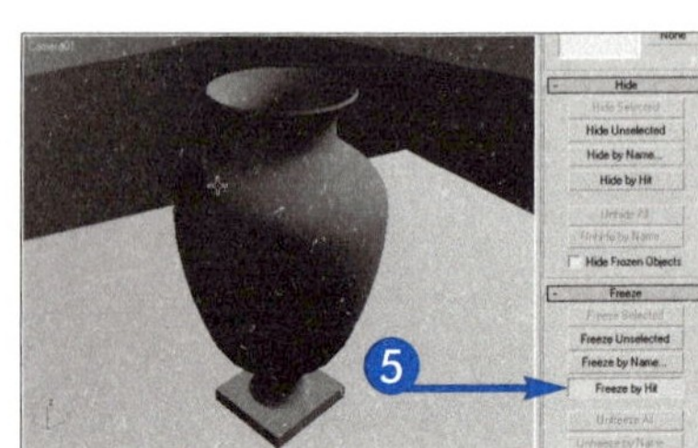

Unfreeze by Name

1. Follow steps 1 to 3 in the subsection "Freeze by Hit" on the previous page.
2. Click Unfreeze by Name.

   The Unfreeze Objects dialog box appears.
3. Select the objects that you want to unfreeze.

   You can press and hold Ctrl or Shift to select multiple objects.
4. Click Unfreeze.

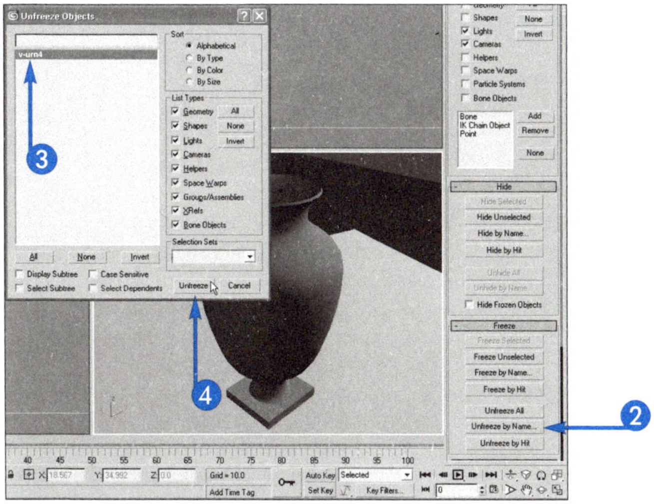

The dialog box closes, and the objects that you selected are unfrozen.

MASTER IT

My frozen objects are gray and lost against the background. Can I change the frozen color?

Yes. There are two ways to change the color of frozen objects. First, in the Customize User Interface dialog box, open the Colors tab. Select Geometry in the Elements drop-down list, and then select Geometry from the Elements field. Click the Color swatch, change the color in the Color Selector that opens, and then close the Color Selector. Close the Customize User Interface dialog box. Current and future frozen objects have the color that you chose. You can also deselect the Show Frozen in Gray option (☐ changes to ☑) in the Object Properties dialog box. Frozen objects retain their colors in the viewports, but they appear identical to unfrozen objects.

Can I freeze members of a group or a named selection set?

If an object is a member of a group, you cannot freeze that object, even when the group is open. However, you can freeze an entire group. Named selection sets are a list of objects that are selected as if you picked them in a viewport. You can hide or freeze objects that are members of a selection set. When you select a named selection set, a dialog box appears asking if the hidden or frozen objects should be unhidden or unfrozen. Click Yes to unhide or unfreeze, and then select them. Click No to leave the objects hidden or frozen, but still selected. For information on groups and named selection sets, see Chapter 3.

Understanding the Transform Gizmos

Each one of the transform tools — Move, Rotate, and Scale — includes a distinct gizmo. A *gizmo* is a tool that visually shows the axis or axes in which the transform takes place. For example, selecting an object and then activating the Move transform causes the Move Transform gizmo to appear. Dragging the X-axis handle causes that line in the gizmo to turn yellow and restricts the object's movement to the X-axis. Dragging the small box, called a center box handle, between the X- and Y-axes, or any other combination, restricts the movement to the plane for those axes. You find similar line or box features in the Rotate and Scale Transform gizmos.

3ds Max color-codes each axis for easy identification, with the X-axis in red, the Y-axis in green, and the Z-axis in blue. This color-coding is common among several software packages, and is easily remembered with the phrase "RGB=XYZ". The X keyboard shortcut toggles the transform gizmos on and off. To change the size of your transform gizmos, you can use the = keyboard shortcut to increase the size and the – key to decrease it. See the sections "Using the Move Tool," "Using the Rotate Tool," and "Using the Scale Tool" for more information about the Move, Rotate, and Scale tools and their gizmos.

Move Transform Gizmo

The Move Transform gizmo represents each visible axis in a viewport with an arrow. When you select an axis, you can only move along that specific axis. To move along two axes simultaneously, you must click the location where the two perpendicular lines meet, or click the yellow planes in the gizmo.

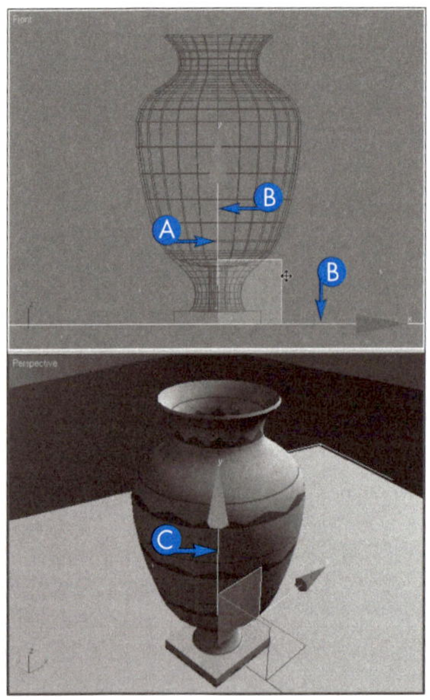

A Move Transform Gizmo

When you select an axis handle, you can only move the object along that axis.

B Perpendicular Axes

To move an object simultaneously along two perpendicular axes, select a center-box handle where two axes meet.

C Move Gizmo – Perspective View

In a Perspective, User, or Camera viewport, the Move Transform gizmo displays all three axes. You can move along one axis, or select two perpendicular axes to move along them simultaneously.

Rotate Transform Gizmo

The Rotate Transform gizmo places three perpendicular rings around the selected object and a fourth ring parallel to the viewport. The colored rings rotate your object along any of the axes when you drag over the appropriately colored ring. Dragging the gray outer ring rotates the object parallel to the viewport. To freely rotate between all axes at once, click and drag anywhere between the different axis rings. As you rotate the object along an axis, a transparent arc is highlighted to indicate the amount and direction of rotation about the axis. A text readout indicates the amount of the rotation.

A Rotate Transform Gizmo

Axis handles only move the object along that axis.

B Rotation Arc

A highlighted arc indicates how much you have rotated the selected object.

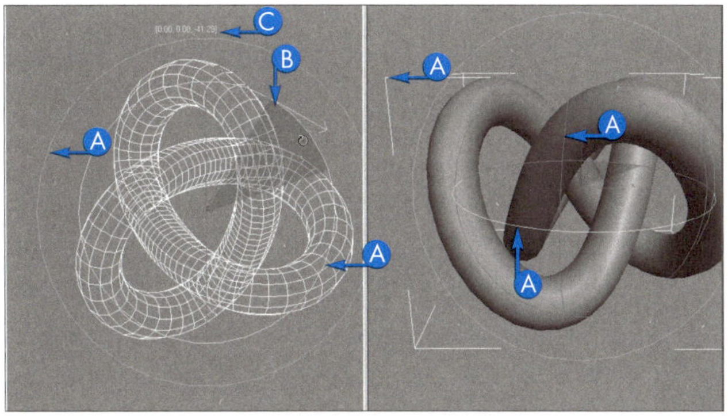

C Offset Values

Indicate the amount of the current rotation. The offset values display in the order X, Y, Z. The values display relative to the object's orientation prior to the rotation and are not absolute values.

A Scale Gizmo

Drag over an axis line to select the axis along which you want to scale the object.

B Uniform Scale Triangle

Select this triangle to uniformly scale along all axes.

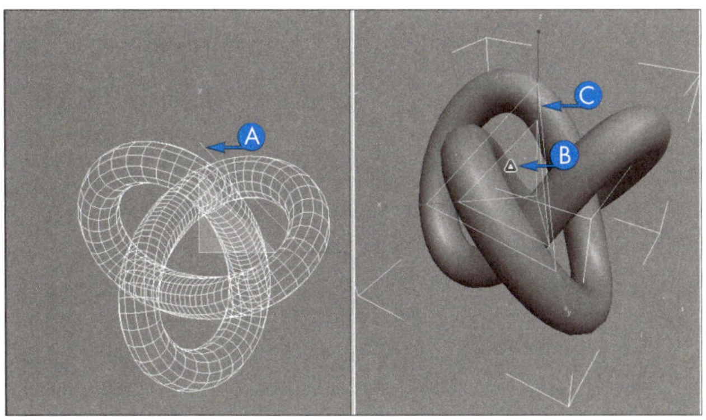

C Plane Handle

Select this polygon to scale along the two adjoining axes.

Scale Transform Gizmo

The Scale Transform gizmo has three right triangles, each parallel with the XY, XZ, or YZ plane. The Scale Transform gizmo's center is at a point shared by one corner of each triangle. Both short edges of each triangle are shared with another triangle. Round-tipped axis lines, similar to the axis lines in the Move Transform gizmo, project from the center of the gizmo and extend beyond the edges of the triangles. You scale objects differently, depending on where you move the gizmo. When you click and drag, the center triangle scales the object uniformly along all three axes. Selecting the double edge of an outer triangle, called a plane handle, only scales the object along the two adjoining axes. To scale one axis, click and drag one of the axis lines.

Using the Move Tool

Before you can move an object in your scene, with either the Move Transform gizmo or the Transform Type-Ins, you must activate the Move tool. The Move tool's gizmo allows for free movement of objects in one or two axes. You simply drag an axis line to move the object along that axis, or click inside one of the boxes at the gizmo's center, to move the object in two axes. You do not need to select an object before activating the Move tool — the Move tool also acts as a selection tool — but you should select the objects using another selection method. Selecting with the Move tool may result in moving the object before you intend and altering its initial location.

With the Transform Type-Ins, you can enter precise coordinate values, either absolute or offset, that you want the objects to move. You enter each axis value in a separate field and 3ds Max applies it as soon as you leave the field. See the sections "Understanding the Transform Gizmos" and "Using the Transform Type-Ins" for more information.

CD FILE: The Transform.max file is available on the CD-ROM for you to practice using the Move tool.

Using the Move Tool

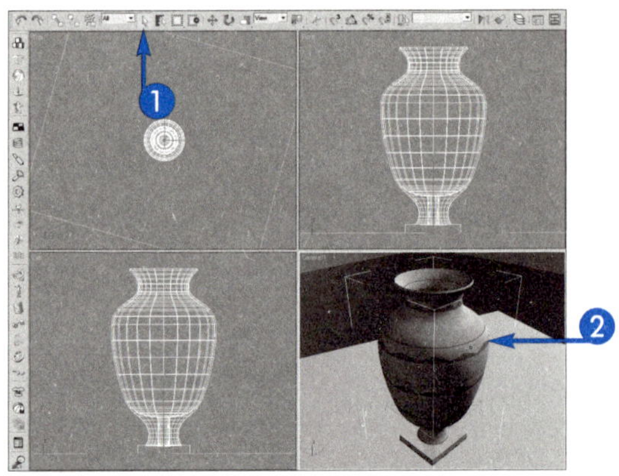

1. Click the Select Object button ( ).
2. Click the object that you want to move.

   The selected object highlights.

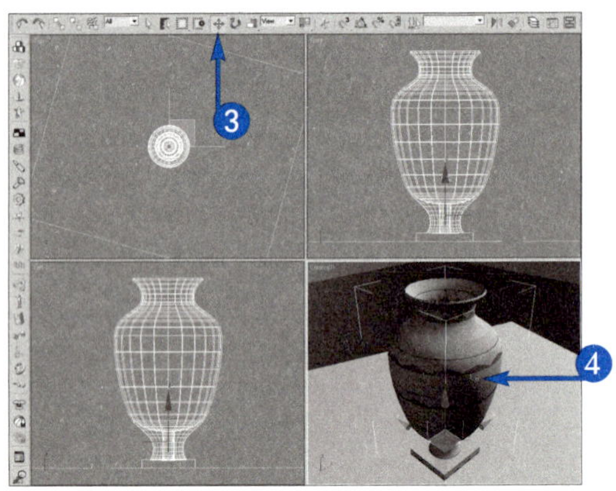

3. Click the Select and Move button ( ).

   The axis tripod changes to the Move Transform gizmo.

4. Move the cursor over the gizmo.

   The cursor changes from ↖ to ✥.

5 Move the cursor over an axis line.

The axis line highlights.

6 Click and drag the object along the selected axis.

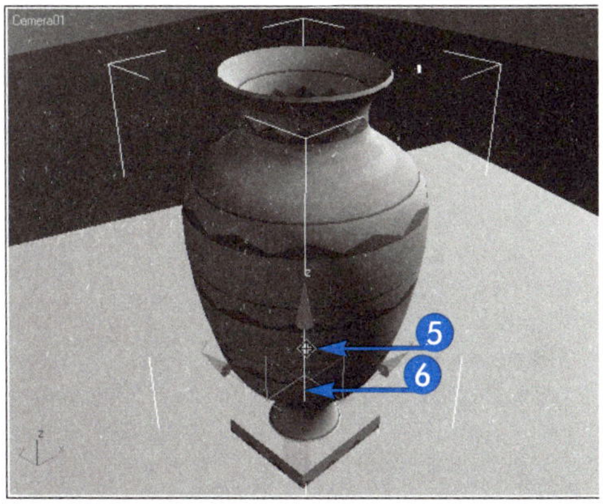

The object moves within your scene.

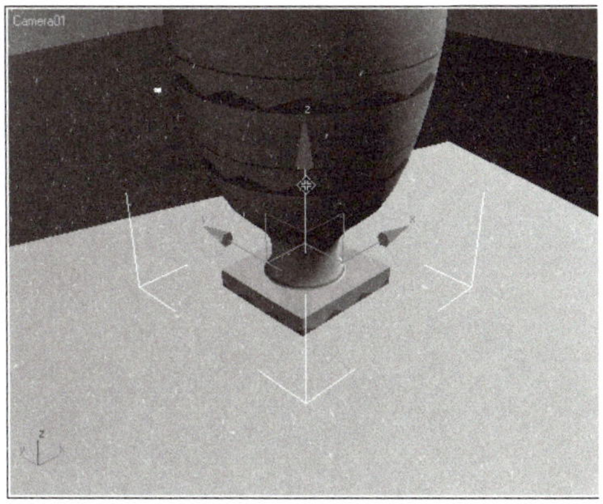

MASTER IT

Can I change the size of the gizmo?

- The size of the Transform gizmo does not change when you change the size of the viewport. You can change the size of the gizmo by clicking the equals key on your keyboard to make it larger, or the the minus key to make it smaller. These are the keys in the top row of the keyboard, not in the keyboard's numeric keypad. When you change the gizmo size, you change its size in all viewports and for all Transform gizmos.

Why can I not move in two axes when I drag the object?

- When the Select and Move tool () is active, you do not need to drag any of its axis handles to move the object freely; you can just drag the object itself. Once you use an axis handle, is locked in that axis or those axes, until you select another axis, even when you are dragging on the object directly. To exit one axis restriction and activate another, just click a different axis handle to activate it. You can also use the keyboard shortcuts F5, F6, and F7 to restrict movements to the X-, Y-, or Z-axis, repectively. F8 cycles through the three different plane restrictions: XY, XZ, and YZ.

Using the Rotate Tool

You can use the Rotate tool to rotate the selected objects around any of the three axes, X, Y, or Z. When the Rotate tool is active, the Rotate Transform gizmo appears at the pivot point of the selected object. You can use this gizmo to restrict the rotation around a specific axis by dragging one of the colored axis rings; to rotate the object freely, drag anywhere inside the three rings. When you drag any axis ring, a sweeping arc appears, as well as rotation coordinates, to give you feedback pertaining to the current rotation activity.

Use the Transform Type-Ins to manually enter specific rotation values into fields dedicated to each rotation axis. Type values in a field, and then leave the field to apply the rotation value to the object. Transform Type-Ins are available from the quad menu, or by right-clicking the transform icons on the Main toolbar.

See the section "Understanding the Transform Gizmos" for more information about the Rotate Transform gizmo. See the section "Using the Transform Type-Ins" to specify an exact amount when you rotate an object.

CD FILE: The Transform.max file is available on the CD-ROM for you to practice using the Rotate tool.

Using the Rotate Tool

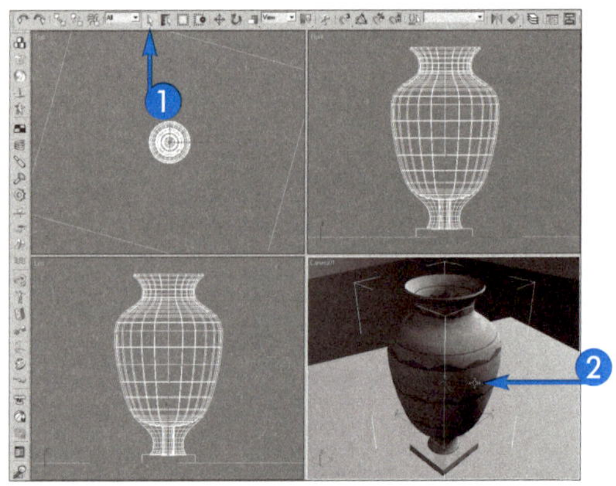

1. Click .
2. Click the object that you want to rotate.

   The selected object highlights.

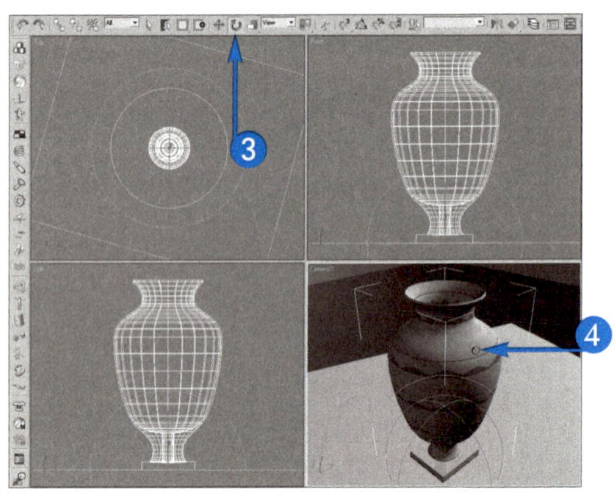

3. Click the Select and Rotate button ( ).

   The axis tripod changes to the Rotate Transform gizmo.

4. Move the cursor over the object.

   The cursor changes from to .

5 Move the cursor over an axis ring.

The axis ring highlights.

6 Click and drag over the axis ring.

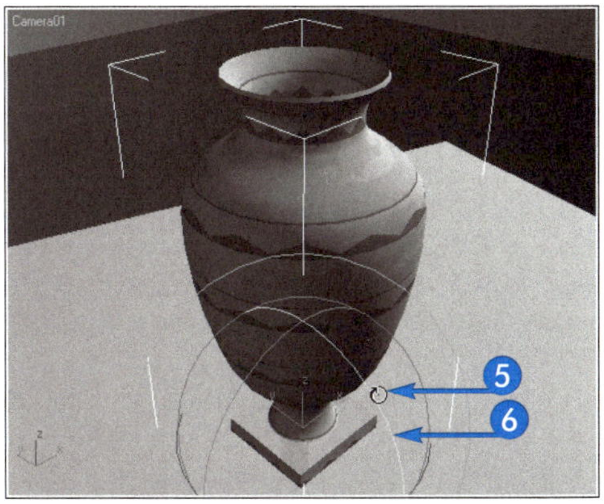

The object rotates in the corresponding axis, and an arc appears along with coordinates.

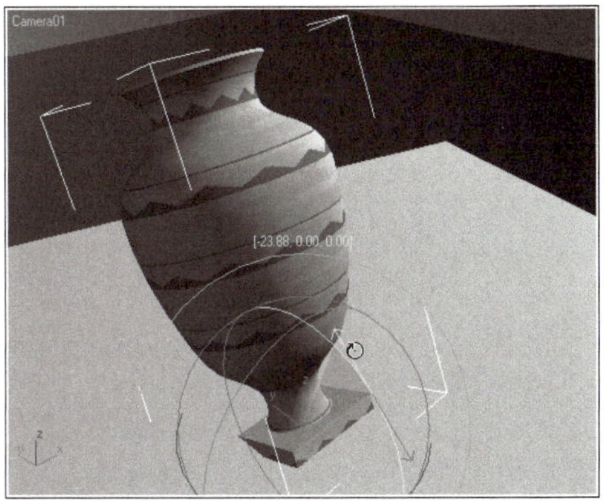

MASTER IT

Can I make the object rotate faster with less mouse movement?

- Yes. If you seem to be dragging the mouse too far on the screen to achieve the desired mouse movement, then you can adjust the Rotation Increment value. This value represents the amount the object rotates when you move the cursor one pixel on the screen. You can increase the default value of .5 to a value that reduces the mouse movement needed to generate the same amount of rotation. Reducing the value makes the object rotate more slowly. To change this value, click Customize in the Main menu, and then click Preferences. Click the Gizmos tab of the Preference Settings dialog box that appears. The Rotation Increment field is in the bottom-right corner of the Move/Rotate Transforms area.

Why does my gizmo not appear when I click a transform tool?

- The Transform gizmo has been turned off. You can turn it on by clicking Views in the Main toolbar, and then clicking Show Transform Gizmo, or by pressing the X shortcut key.

When I click in my viewport with the Rotate tool active, I lose my selection. Why?

- Unlike the Select and Move tool ( ), you must click within the gizmo's area to rotate the object manually. The Rotate tool is also a selection tool. When you click outside the Transform gizmo, even if you are clicking the currently selected object, 3ds Max thinks you are trying to make a new selection and tries to select the next object.

Using the Scale Tool

You can use the Scale tool to apply a scale multiplier to resize an object. 3ds Max allows you to scale an object uniformly along all axes, or along just one or two axes. You can scale an object using the Scale Transform gizmo or the Transform Type-Ins.

You can scale your objects uniformly or non-uniformly, using either the Select and Uniform Scale tool or the Select and Non-Uniform Scale tool. Improvements in the Transform gizmo have made these buttons redundant, but they remain for legacy purposes. The Scale Transform gizmo allows you to easily scale your object with the proportions that you choose. The gizmo displays a line for each axis and three triangles. Drag the center portion of the gizmo to scale the object equally along all axes. Dragging an outer edge of a triangle scales the object in two axes, and dragging an axis handle scales the object along only one axis.

See the section "Understanding the Transform Gizmos" for more information on the Scale Transform gizmo. See the section "Using the Transform Type-Ins" to specify an exact amount to scale an object.

CD FILE: The Transform.max file is available on the CD-ROM for you to practice using the Scale tool.

Using the Scale Tool

1. Click .
2. Click the object that you want to scale.

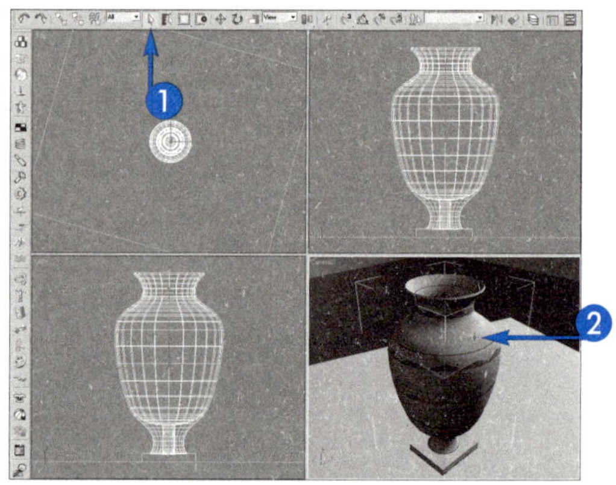

The selected object highlights.

3. Click the Select and Uniform Scale button ( ) or the Select and Non-Uniform Scale button ( ).

The axis tripod changes to the Scale Transform gizmo.

4. Move the cursor over the middle of the gizmo.

The cursor changes from to , and the gizmo center highlights.

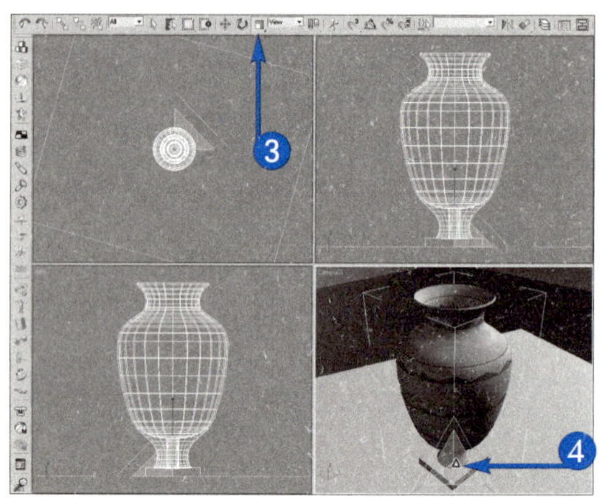

5 Click and drag the cursor over the middle of the gizmo.

The object scales uniformly.

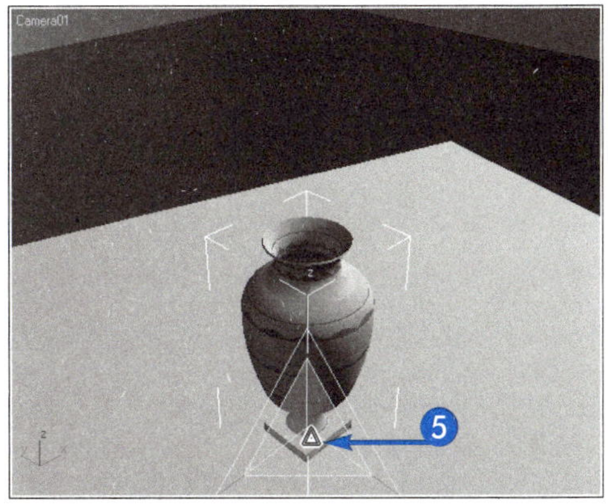

6 Click and drag over one axis handle.

The axis highlights, and the cursor changes to [icon].

The object scales along a single axis.

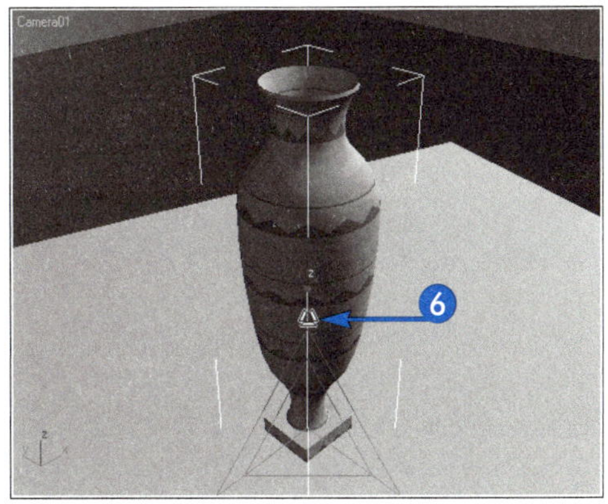

MASTER IT

What happens if I use the Select and Squash button to resize my object?

▼ The Select and Squash button ([icon]), located in the Scale flyout menu, scales your object so that it maintains a constant volume. When you scale your object to be larger in two axes, the third axis is scaled down automatically. Similarily, when you scale an object down in one axis, it scales up in the other two to compensate. The Select and Squash tool changes the cursor to [icon] to indicate that it is active. In addition to the obvious choice of using the Select and Squash tool to simulate soft balls bouncing, it is also a great tool to use when creating cartoonish effects on characters.

Why does the Radius value of a sphere remain the same after I have scaled it?

▼ In the order of operations that 3ds Max follows, when placing objects on the screen, the transforms are last. Transforms are only applied after parameters are set, modifiers are applied, and the effect of space warps are calculated. This means that the sphere's radius is first determined, and then the scale factor is applied to it. As a result, a sphere with a radius of 4.0 and a uniform scale of 100 percent may appear the same as a sphere of 8.0 and a uniform scale of 50 percent, although they are different. This may affect operations such as parameter wiring or linking, which look at the actual parameter values, or pass the parameters to other objects.

Using the Manipulate Tool

Several objects, including spotlights and most primitives with a Radius parameter, contain a manipulator. Manipulators are visual tools, which you can drag the mouse over to modify an object's parameters.

While the transform tools must be the only tools active when you use them, the Manipulate tool can remain active constantly, regardless of any other active commands. You can use the Manipulate tool to change a sphere's Radius value or a spotlight's Hotspot, Falloff, or Roll Angle values without opening the Modify panel or closing an active transform. The Manipulate tool is often used when wiring object parameters so that one object's parameter changes affect another object's parameters.

The Manipulate.max file is available on the CD-ROM for you to practice using the Manipulate tool.

MASTER IT

Can I add manipulators to an object?

No, but you can create a Manipulator object and wire its parameters to the parameters of the object that you want to modify. For example, you can wire the Value amount in a manipulator to the Height and Radius of a cone so that increasing the values of the manipulator causes the cone to become taller and wider. You can find manipulators in the Command panel by clicking Create, then clicking Helpers, and then clicking Manipulators.

Using the Manipulate Tool

1. Select an object with a manipulator.
2. Click the Select and Manipulate button ( ).

   The manipulator becomes visible.
3. Position the cursor over the manipulator.
   - The manipulator highlights, and a tooltip appears, showing the manipulator and its value.
4. Click and drag the manipulator.
   - 3ds Max updates the parameter that is associated with the manipulator.

Isolate Objects

To complete a task, you may need to hide some objects, so that you can see the current object, and then unhide to restore the scene to its previous condition. You can simplify this procedure by using the Isolate Selection tool to display selected objects while all others are hidden. You access this tool through the Tools menu, the quad menu, or the Alt+Q shortcut keys. A dialog box appears to remind you that objects are isolated. The Exit Isolation Mode button unhides all objects that were hidden with the Isolate Selection tool. Objects that were hidden before using the Isolate Selection tool remain hidden.

CD FILE: The Isolate.max file is available on the CD-ROM for you to practice isolating objects.

MASTER IT

Can I unhide certain objects after using the Isolate Selection tool?

Yes, you can use either of the methods — Unhide by Name or Unhide All — discussed in the "Hide and Unhide Objects" section to unhide objects that were hidden with the Isolate Selection tool. When you are in Isolation mode, select Unhide by Name from the quad menu to open the Unhide Objects dialog box. Select the objects that you want to unhide and then click Unhide to reveal them.

Isolate Objects

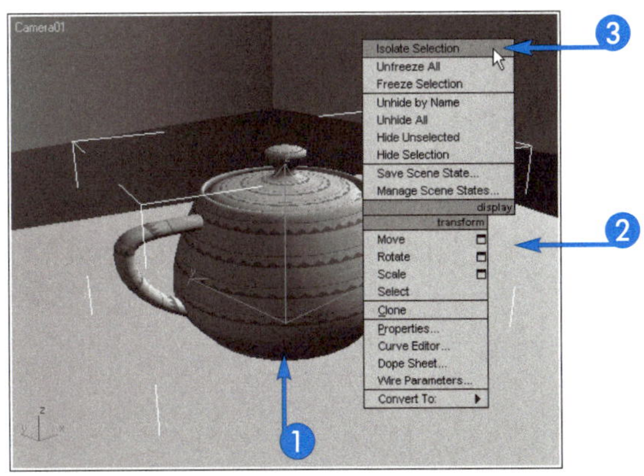

1. Select an object.
2. Right-click to open the quad menu.
3. Click Isolate Selection.

   All objects are hidden, except for those that you selected.

   You can now zoom, pan, and modify the object.

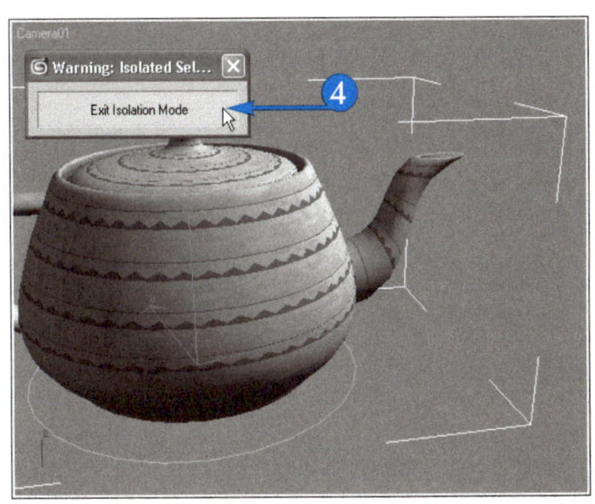

4. Click Exit Isolation Mode.

   The hidden objects are once again visible, but the viewport changes are retained.

Using the Transform Type-Ins

You can use the Transform Type-Ins at the bottom of the 3ds Max interface to precisely transform your objects. There are separate fields for each axis, and each reflects the current coordinates for the active transform.

You can view and modify values in two different modes, Absolute and Offset, with the Transform Type-Ins using the Absolute/Offset Mode button to toggle between the modes. Using Absolute mode, you enter the exact coordinates or amount that you want your object to move or rotate, or the percentage of the original size to scale your object. In Offset mode, you enter values that are relative to the current values. For example, in Absolute mode, when you enter 50 in the X field with the Rotate transform active, the object rotates 50 degrees in the X-axis from its original orientation. Entering 50 in the same field in Offset mode rotates the object an additional 50 degrees from its current position.

Transform Type-Ins, as a dialog box, are also available from the quad menu by pressing the settings boxes to the right of the Move, Rotate, and Scale entries, or by right-clicking the transform icons on the Main toolbar.

The Transform.max file is available on the CD-ROM for you to practice using the Transform Type-Ins.

Using the Transform Type-Ins

Move an Object in Absolute Mode

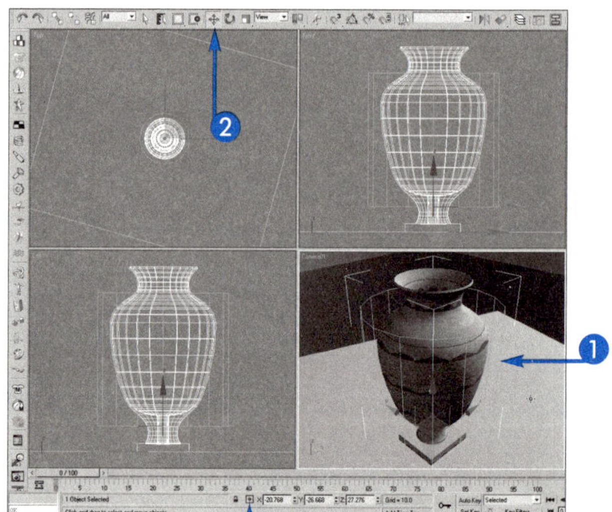

1. Select the object that you want to transform.
2. Click .
3. Click the Absolute/Offset button to toggle to Absolute ( ), if required.

   The values of the axes in the Transform Type-In tool change to show the object's current location.

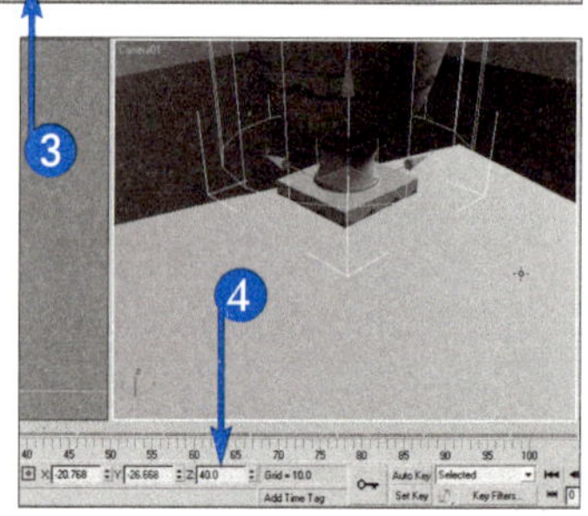

4. Type a positive value in the Z-axis field.

   This example uses 40.

5. Press Enter.

   The object moves until its pivot point is at the units you typed in the Z-axis.

Move an Object in Offset Mode

6 Click the Absolute/Offset button ( ).

changes to , and the fields reset to 0.0.

7 Type a negative value in the Z-axis field.

This example uses –60.

8 Press Enter.

The object moves the units you typed downward on the Z-axis.

In this example, the object moves 60 units downward to a total of –20 on the Z-axis, and the field resets to 0.0.

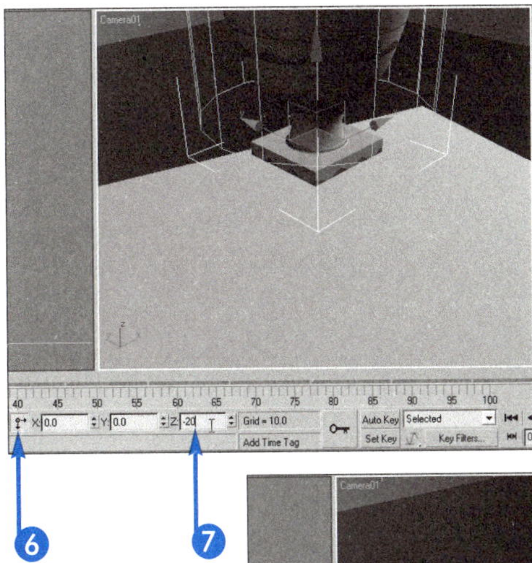

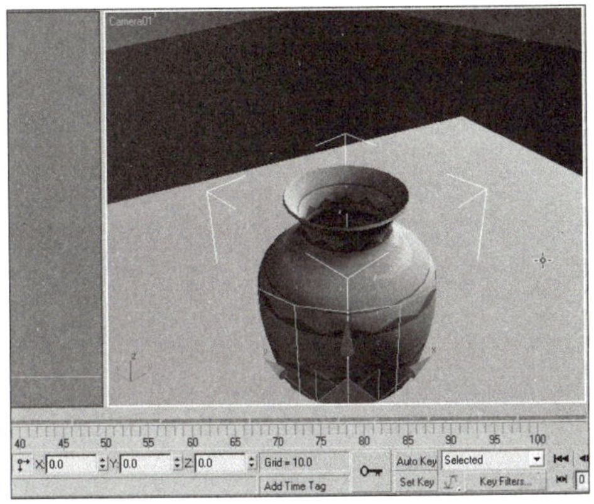

MASTER IT

Is the Transform Type-In tool in the Status bar the same as the Transform Type-In dialog box?

▼ Yes, they perform the same function. Some 3ds Max users work in Expert mode, a condition where many of the tools, including the Status bar, are not visible. This provides much more viewport area, but you must use the shortcut buttons and dialog boxes in lieu of the more commonly used toolbars and panels. With a transform active, click Tools in the Menu bar; then click Transform Type-In, or right-click the transform button, to open the appropriate Transform Type-In dialog box. In this dialog box, both the Absolute and Offset values are available in separate sections, allowing for more flexible input.

What type of values can I enter to transform the object?

▼ The type of value that you specify depends upon which transform you are using. When you move an object, you can type values for each axis to control the unit distance that the object moves along each axis. When you rotate an object, the value that you type determines the degrees that the object rotates on the corresponding axis. When you scale an object, you enter percentages. If the Select and Uniform Scale transform is active, then only the X field is available. Any value that you enter here is automatically copied to the Y and Z fields. To enter different values in each field, use the Select and Non-Uniform Scale transform.

Using Reference Coordinate Systems

3ds Max has several reference coordinate systems to move, rotate, and scale transforms. A coordinate system is the position and orientation structure that identifies how and where objects transform, with the root being the *origin*, around which all objects move, rotate, or scale.

One main coordinate system in 3ds Max, the World coordinate system, has the X, Y, and Z directions always fixed in this system, regardless of the viewport or current tool. These axes display in the small tripod in the lower-left corner of each viewport. By default, the Perspective and Camera viewports use the World coordinate system, and you may notice that the Move Transform gizmo is always oriented the same as the axis tripod. The common viewports — Top, Bottom, Left, Right, Front, and Back — generally use the View coordinate system. With this system, the X-axis always orients to the left and right of the viewport, and the Y-axis always orients to the top and bottom. This provides a standard tool between viewports. You can change Reference coordinate systems by making a selection from the drop-down list in the middle of the Main toolbar.

Each object has its own specific coordinate system — called its Local coordinate system — that is oriented to its major axes when it was created. Using this system, and the Transform gizmos, you can move or rotate an object relative to its original axis. For example, imagine a jet plane model that has been randomly rotated around all three axes. Without changing its orientation, you can move it forward, in the direction the nose is currently pointing, by using the Local coordinate system. As a result, one axis points toward the nose, regardless of the plane's orientation in your scene.

Other reference coordinate systems are available that are oriented to the screen, a parent object, a grid, or any other object in the scene.

See the sections "Using the Move Tool," "Using the Rotate Tool," and "Using the Scale Tool" for more information about the transforms. In the following figures, Allow Multiple Gizmos mode was activated by clicking Edit, then clicking Preferences, and then clicking Gizmos.

View Coordinate System

When they are active, the current Top, Left, and Front viewports show the axes oriented with the X to the right and the Y toward the top. The Perspective viewport shows the World coordinate system.

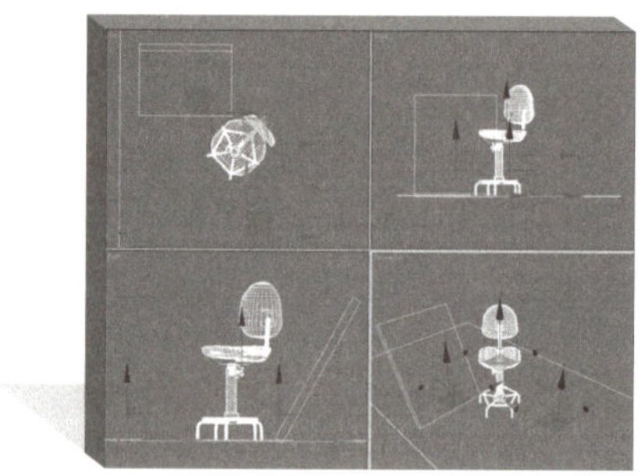

Screen Coordinate System

X- and Y-axes remain parallel to the active viewport borders, regardless of the orientation of the objects.

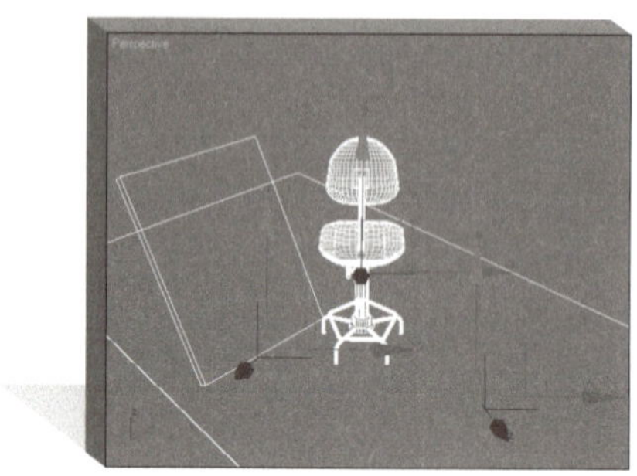

World Coordinate System

Axes remain oriented to the World coordinate system, regardless of the current viewport.

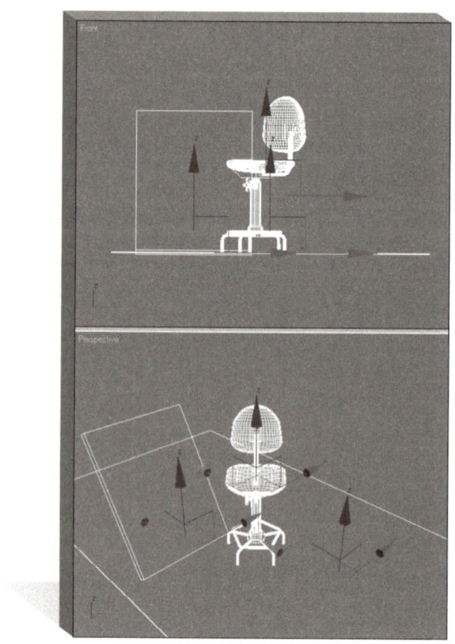

Local Coordinate System

Axes remain oriented to the object, regardless of the object's orientation in the scene.

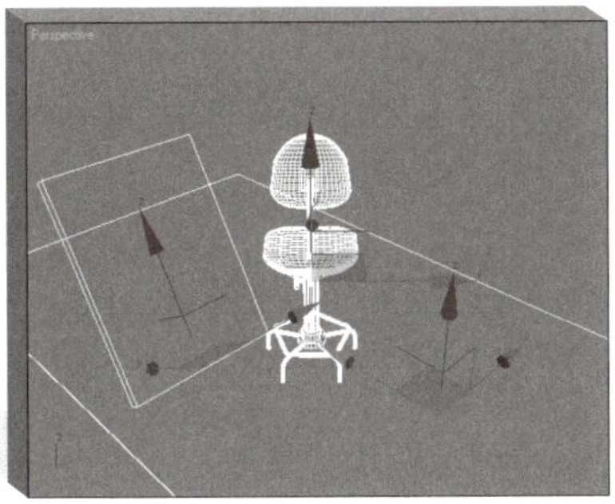

Parent Coordinate System

Axes for the selected objects are oriented to the local coordinate system of the parent to which the object is linked. In this example, the chair is linked to the canted box. No gizmo appears for a child object when the parent is selected because you cannot move the parent independent of the child.

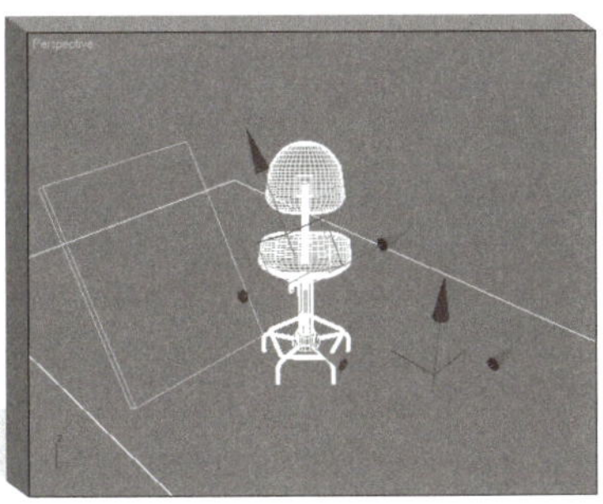

Pick Coordinate System

Axes for the selected object are oriented to the local coordinate system of any object that is picked by the user. In this example, the floor is picked by the chair.

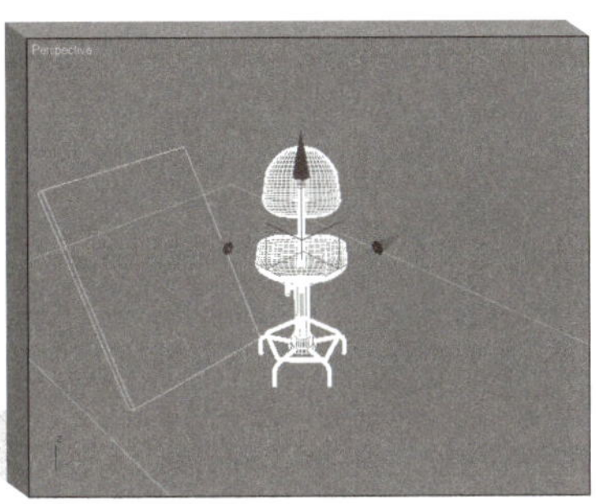

Gimbal Coordinate System

For use with the Euler rotation controller. This coordinate system does not restrict its axes to remain perpendicular to each other.

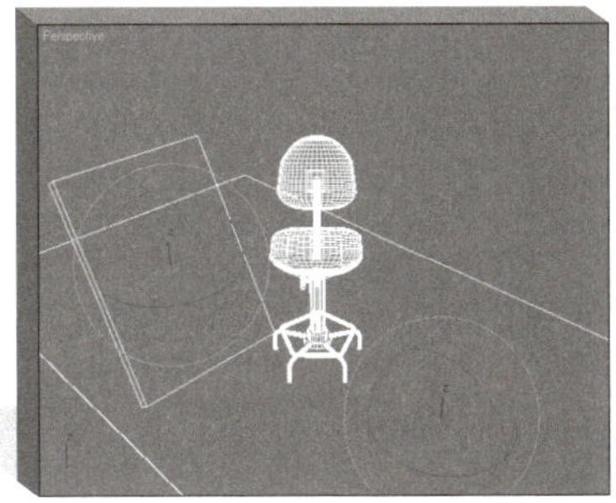

Grid Coordinate System

Uses the coordinate system from the active grid in the scene.

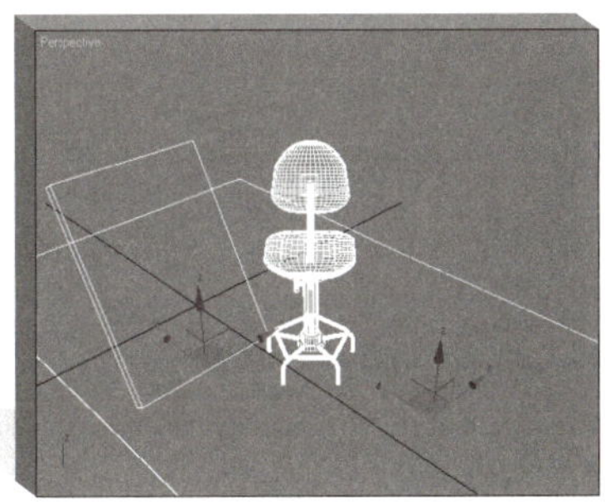

Using the Snap Tools

The Snap tools make it faster and easier to create, move, rotate, and scale objects. The snaps cause your cursor to jump, or snap, to an object feature, such as an endpoint or vertex, when the cursor is close to it. You activate snaps via the Snaps Toggle button on the Main toolbar. You can also display a Snaps toolbar. There can be up to twelve tools functioning at one time, and these are turned on in the Snaps tab of the Grid and Snap Settings dialog box.

In addition to the Snaps Toggle, there is also an Angle, Percent, and Spinner Snap Toggle. With the Angle Snap Toggle active, your rotation transforms jump in specific angular increments. The Percent Snap Toggle causes the scale transform to jump in specific percentage increments. Angle and percent snap increments are set in the Options tab of the Grid and Snap Settings dialog box. Spinner Snaps cause the spinner values to jump at a set increment, which you set in the General tab of the Preference Settings dialog box.

The Transform.max file is available on the CD-ROM for you to practice using the Snap tools.

Using the Snap Tools

Set Snap Settings

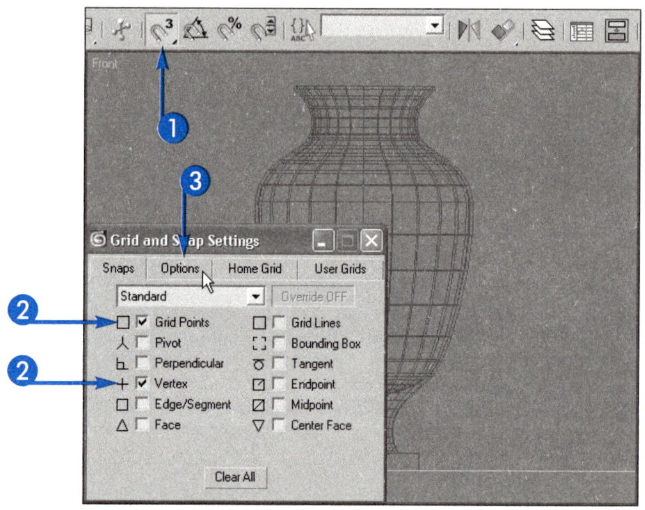

1. Right-click the Snap Toggle button ( ).

   The Snaps tab of the Grid and Snap Settings dialog box appears.

2. Click the Grid Points and Vertex options (☐ changes to ☑).

3. Click the Options tab.

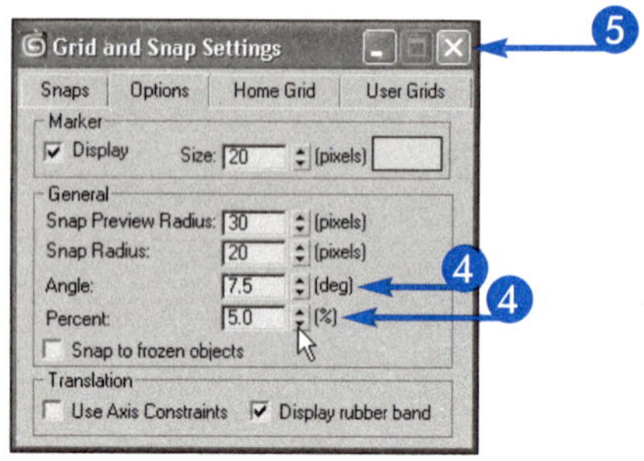

4. Type values in the Angle field, and the Percent field.

   This example uses an Angle value of 7.5 and a Percent value of 5.0.

5. Click the Close button ( ).

   The dialog box closes.

Move an Object with Snaps

6. Click , and then click .
7. Select an object.
8. Place your cursor over a vertex on the object.

   A snap marker appears over the vertex.
9. Click and drag to a grid intersection or a vertex from another object.

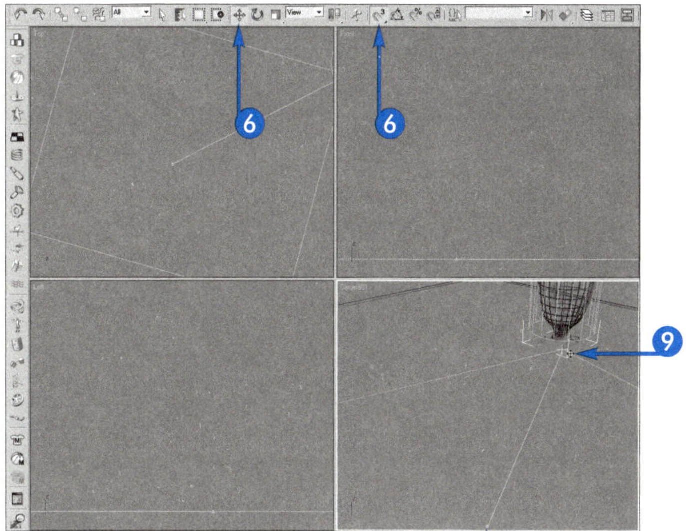

- The object moves precisely to the location specified in Step 4.

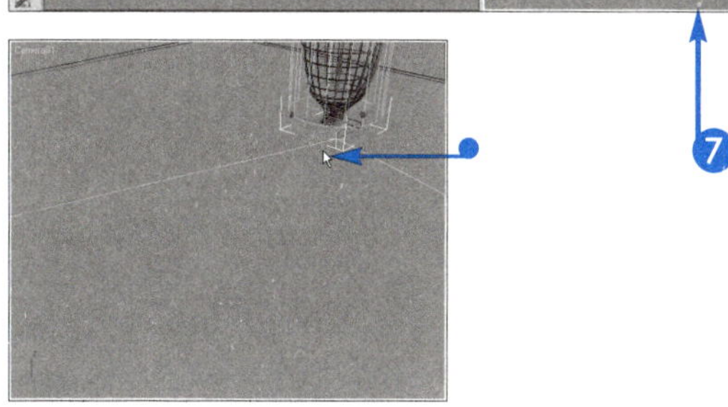

MASTER IT

What are the blue objects that I see when the snaps are turned on?

When the Snaps toggle is turned on, so are the snap markers. The snap markers are the visual indicators that appear when you move your cursor over the features, such as midpoints or grid points, for which the active snap is searching. The size and color of the snap markers are set in the Options tab of the Grid and Snap Settings dialog box. Deselecting the Display option (☑ changes to ☐) turns the snap markers off altogether. The Snap Radius Preview, in the same tab, determines how close to the feature, in pixels, your cursor must be to display the marker. The Snap Radius determines how close the cursor must be to snap to that feature.

What is the difference between the three buttons in the Snaps flyout menu?

When you expand the Snaps flyout menu, three buttons appear: the 3D Snap Toggle ( ), the 2.5D Snap Toggle ( ), and the 2D Snap Toggle ( ). These buttons control the actual locations to which the cursor is snapped, as opposed to the visual locations. The allows objects to snap directly to any points in 3D space. The snaps to the location where a projection of an object or feature meets the construction grid. The limits the snapping to the current construction grid and objects that are coplanar to that grid.

Using the Align Tool

You can use the Align tool to align an object to another object on one or more axes. In reality, the bounding box — an implied box that completely encompasses an object — of the first object is aligned to the bounding box of the second object. The object you move into alignment is the Current Object, and the object to which it is aligned is the Target Object.

At the top of the Align Selection dialog box are X-, Y-, and Z-Position options, which you use to specify the axes upon which your two objects align.

In the center of the Align Selection dialog box, you can select the points that you want to use for each object. You can select one of four options: Minimum, Center, Pivot Point, or Maximum. Minimum aligns the point on the bounding box with the lowest X-, Y-, or Z-axis value. Center aligns to the center point of the bounding box, and Pivot Point aligns the Pivot Point of the object. Maximum aligns the point with the highest X-, Y-, or Z-axis value.

The Align.max file is available on the CD-ROM for you to practice using the Align tool.

Using the Align Tool

1. Select the object that you want to align.
2. Click the Align button ().
3. Click an object to which you want to align the first object.

   The objects automatically align on all axes at the pivot point.

   The Align Selection dialog box appears.
4. Click to deselect the axes to which you do not want to align your object (☑ changes to ☐).

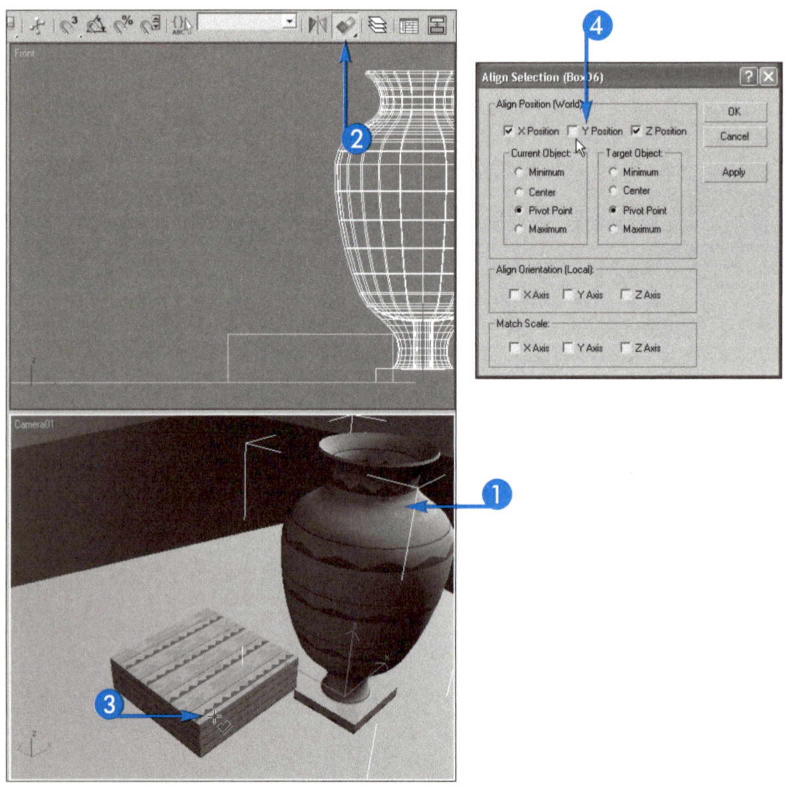

- The objects align only on the selected axes.

5 Click an alignment point for the first (Current) object (○ changes to ◉).

6 Click an alignment point for the second (Target) object (○ changes to ◉).

7 Click OK.

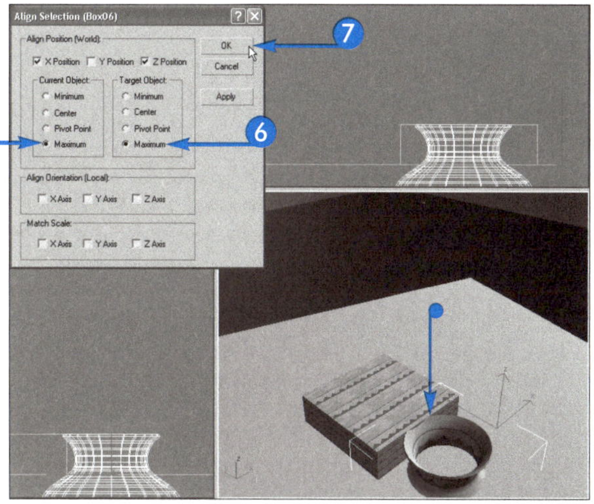

The Align Selection dialog box closes.

The objects align, based upon your selections.

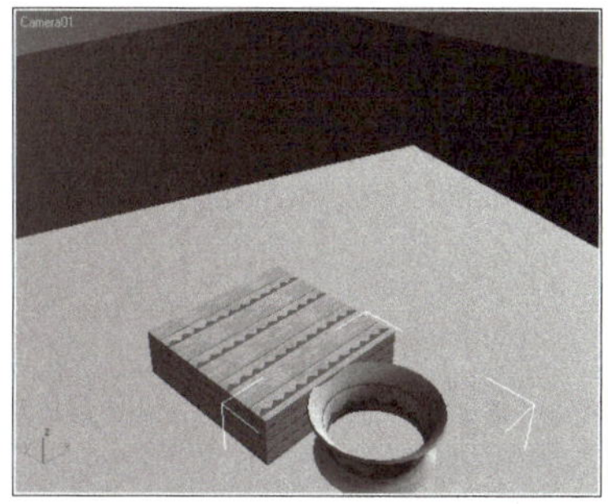

Can I align two objects without a dialog box?

▼ Yes. You can align two objects based on their pivot points using the Quick Align tool. To do this, select one object and then click the Quick Align button (■) from the Align button flyout menu, or press Shift + A. Click the object to which you want to align the first object. Both objects align, based on their pivot points on all axes.

What is the difference between the OK and Apply buttons?

▼ OK is used when the axes are aligned properly and you are done with the dialog box. You click Apply when some of the axes are aligned properly, but you want to align another axis in a different way. Align leaves the dialog box open.

Can I match the scaling of the first object to that of the second object during alignment?

▼ Yes. If you previously scaled one of the objects, then you can scale the other object to match the first by using the fields in the Match Scale section of the Align Selection dialog box. First, select the axis where you want to match the scale. Keep in mind that 3ds Max matches the scaling of the two objects but does not make them the same size. For example, if you scaled one object by 50 percent, then the other object is also scaled by 50 percent. If you have not scaled either object, then there are no changes to apply.

Clone an Object

3ds Max uses the term *clone* to describe a duplicate made from an existing object. There are three types of clones: copy, instance, and reference. A copy is a separate and distinct clone of the original; a change to one does not affect the other. An instance is another occurrence of the original in which all parameters and modifiers that affect one affect the other, regardless of whether the changes are made to the original or the clone. A reference is similar to an instance in that any parameter or modifier changes applied to one affect them all. However, the difference is that modifiers applied to the top of the Modifier Stack of a reference clone affect only that clone.

For information on modifiers, see Chapters 5 and 6. For more information about the Modifier Stack, see Chapter 6.

There are several ways to create clones in 3ds Max. The most common involves the Shift key and the Move transform. This method opens a Clone Options dialog box where you choose the type of clone, number of copies, and base name for the clones.

CD FILE: The Transform.max file is available on the CD-ROM for you to practice cloning objects.

Clone an Object

1. Select the object that you want to clone.
2. Click [Move icon].
3. Hold down the Shift key.
4. Click and drag the object, and then release the mouse button.

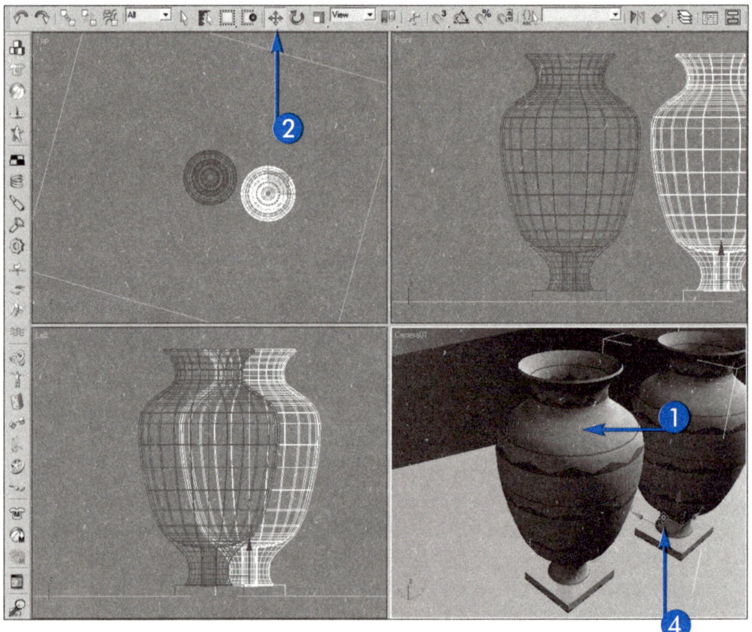

The clone displays, and the Clone Options dialog box appears.

5. Accept the defaults and click OK.

3ds Max creates and selects the clone.

6. Repeat steps 1, 3, and 4 to create other clones.

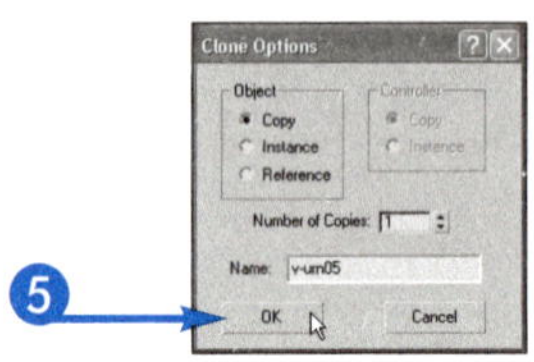

7. Click the Instance option (○ changes to ◉).
8. Type **2** in the Number of Copies field.
9. Click OK.

   3ds Max creates and selects the clones.

10. Click the Modify Panel button ().
11. Change the object parameters.

    The original and instances change, but the copy does not.

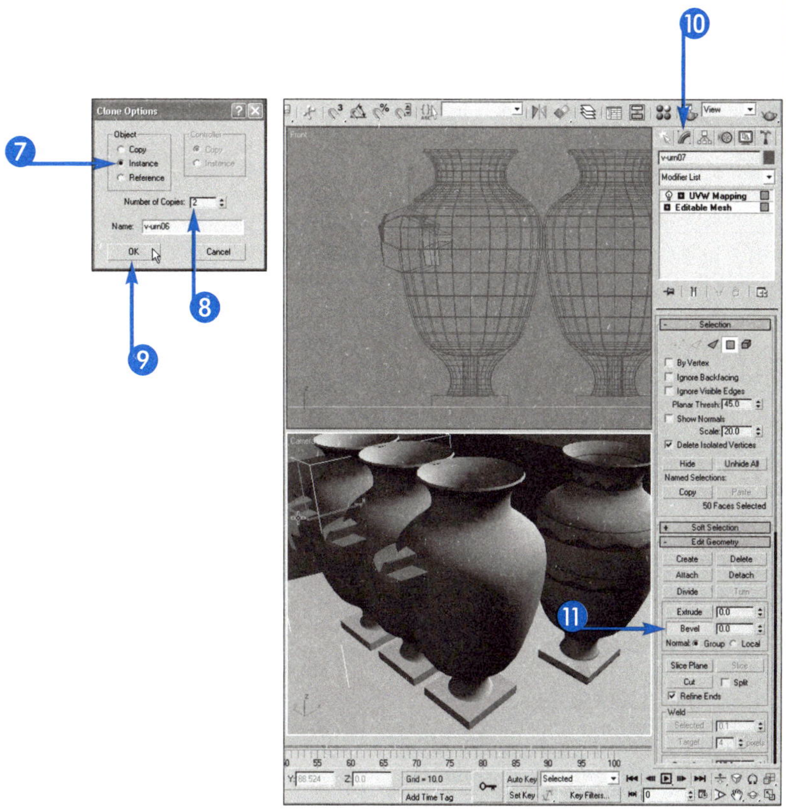

Why do all instances not rotate when I rotate one of them?

Instances and references share parameters and modifiers with each other, but not transforms. This is generally a good thing, because you may not want all instances to move when you move one of them. However, there is a way around this. Select one of the instances, apply an XForm modifier to it, and then use a transform on one of your objects. This modifier works with the transforms but applies the effect through the Modifier Stack so that it is passed to all of the instanced objects. For more information on modifiers, see Chapter 6.

How does the Number of Copies option space the clones?

When you press and hold the Shift key and use a transform to generate a clone, the increment between the original and the first clone is maintained between each subsequent clone. For example, press and hold the Shift key while rotating an object 30 degrees and select 11 copies. This creates 12 objects — 11 plus the original — that are oriented equally around a 360-degree pattern. To move, rotate, and create clones at the same time, you need to use the Array tool. See the section "Create Clones with the Array Tool" for more information.

Using the Mirror Tool

You can use the Mirror tool to mirror the orientation of an object, or a group of objects, around the object's pivot point and perpendicular to the World coordinate system. When you mirror an object, the object rotates 180 degrees around one or two selected axes.

The Mirror dialog box allows you to specify the axes and cloning for the mirrored object. After you specify the axis around which you want to mirror the selected object, you can mirror the object around any of the three axes or one of the three combinations of axes. As you select the different mirror options, the viewports show a preview of how 3ds Max mirrors the object.

To move the object as you mirror it, you can specify an Offset value. The Offset value indicates the distance of the mirrored object's pivot point from the pivot point of the original object.

By default, the Mirror option mirrors the object by altering the original. To create a copy of the original, you can select the Copy, Instance, or Reference option.

CD FILE The Mirror.max file is available on the CD-ROM for you to practice using the Mirror tool.

Using the Mirror Tool

Mirror the Object

1. Select the object that you want to mirror.
2. Click the Mirror button ( ).

   The Mirror dialog box appears.
3. Click the axis around which you want to mirror the object (○ changes to ◉).
4. Click OK.

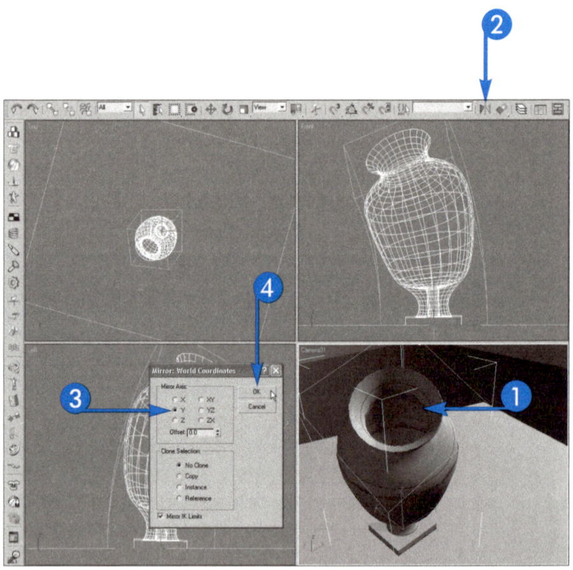

The Mirror dialog box closes.

3ds Max mirrors the object.

Mirror a Copy

1. Repeat steps 1 and 2 on the previous page.
2. Click the axis around which you want to mirror the object (○ changes to ◉).
3. Click to select a Clone option (○ changes to ◉).
4. Type an Offset value to separate the two objects.
5. Click OK.

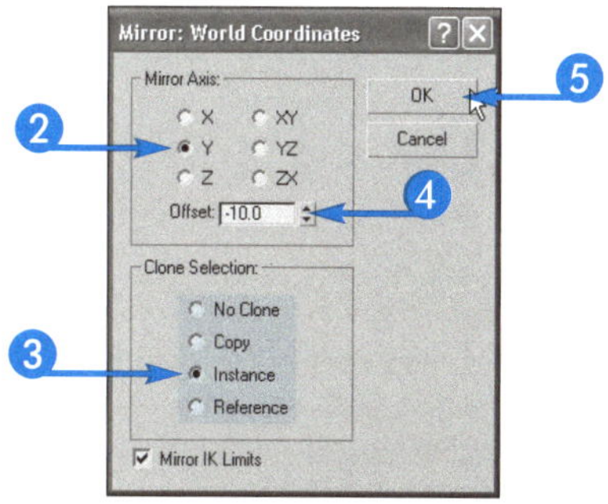

The Mirror dialog box closes.

3ds Max creates a clone of the object that is a mirror of the original.

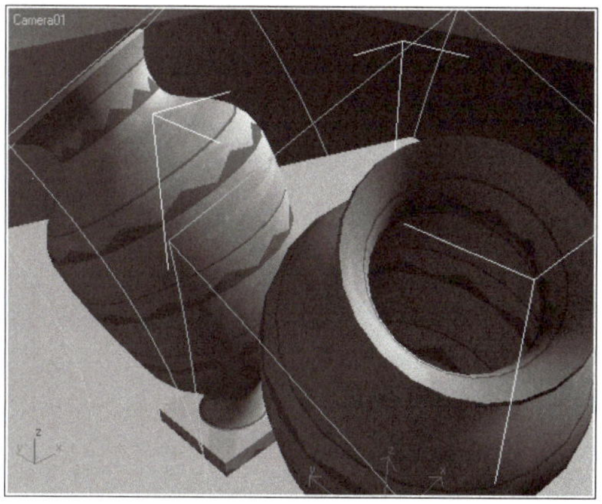

MASTER IT

What is the difference between the Mirror tool and the Mirror modifier?

▼ Both the Mirror tool and the Mirror modifier are identical in how they mirror and offset an object. The significant difference is in how the clones or copies are created. The Mirror tool creates a second cloned object that is a copy, instance, or reference to the original; you now have two objects in the scene. The Mirror modifier's Copy option creates a mirrored version of the object, but they are both non-contiguous pieces of the same object; there is still only one object in the scene. For information about modifying 3D objects, see Chapter 6.

Can I mirror multiple objects or groups?

▼ Yes, you can mirror both multiple object selections and groups. With multiple objects selected, each object mirrors around its own pivot point when you select Use Pivot Point Center (icon) in the Main toolbar. When you select Use Selection Center (icon), the object mirrors around the point equidistant from all of the objects' pivot points. This point is called the selection center. When you mirror groups, they mirror around the group's pivot point, which is the selection center if the objects were ungrouped and selected.

Create Clones with the Array Tool

An array is a structured, usually rectangular, arrangement of objects in rows and columns. Using the Array tool, you can quickly and easily create and position buildings in a city, cars in a dealership, or invading troops on a series of tiered platforms.

Arrays come in three types: 1D, 2D, and 3D. When creating a 1D array, you can move, rotate, and scale objects in one or all axes. A 2D array creates copies of the 1D array at a specified offset distance and direction. A 3D array creates copies of the 2D array at a specified offset distance and direction. You can be creative with the Array tool, but generally a 1D array makes a row of objects, a 2D array makes a field of objects, and a 3D array turns the field into a column. The clones that you create can be copies, instances, or references.

You can access the Array tool on the Extras toolbar by right-clicking a blank area of the main toolbar and then selecting the Extras command on the contextual menu. See the section "Clone an Object" for more information.

CD FILE: The Array.max file is available on the CD-ROM for you to practice using the Array tool.

Create Clones with the Array Tool

Create a 1D Array

1. Select the object that you want to array.
2. Click the Array button ( ).

   The Array dialog box appears.
3. Type Move, Rotate, or Scale values.
4. Type the number of clones that you want to create.
5. Click Preview.

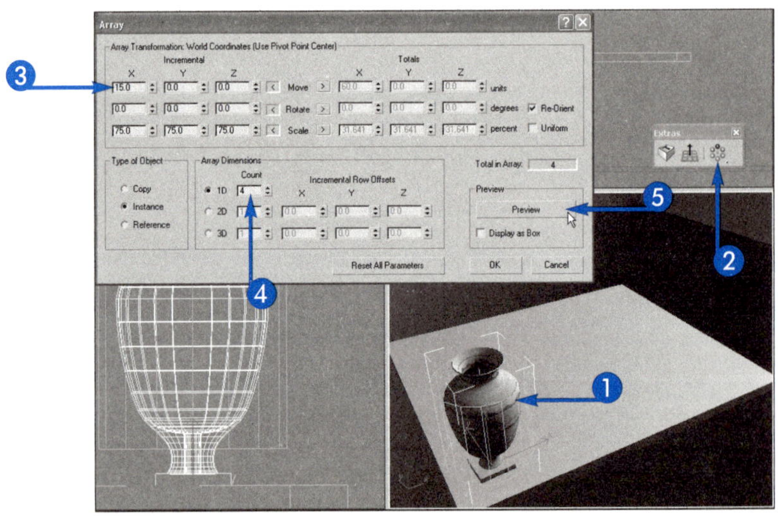

- 3ds Max previews the array.
- You can click OK to create the array, or change the parameters.

This exercise does neither.

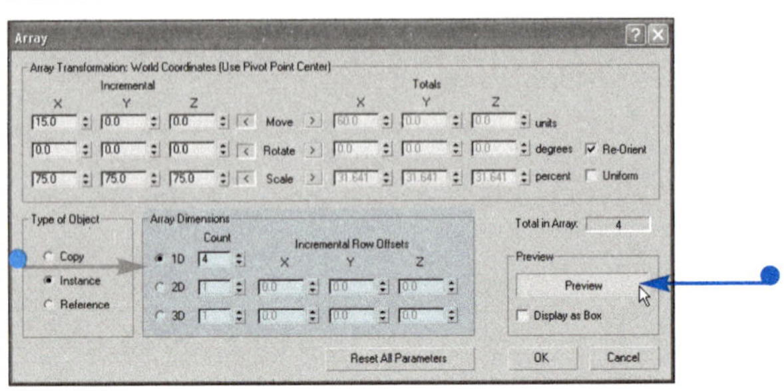

Create a 3D Array

6. Click Preview to deactivate the Preview.

   The array disappears.

7. Click the 3D option in the Array Dimensions section (○ changes to ◉).

8. Type 2D and 3D counts.

9. Type 2D and 3D row offsets.

10. Repeat step 6 to activate Preview.

- 3ds Max previews the array.

11. Click OK to accept the array.

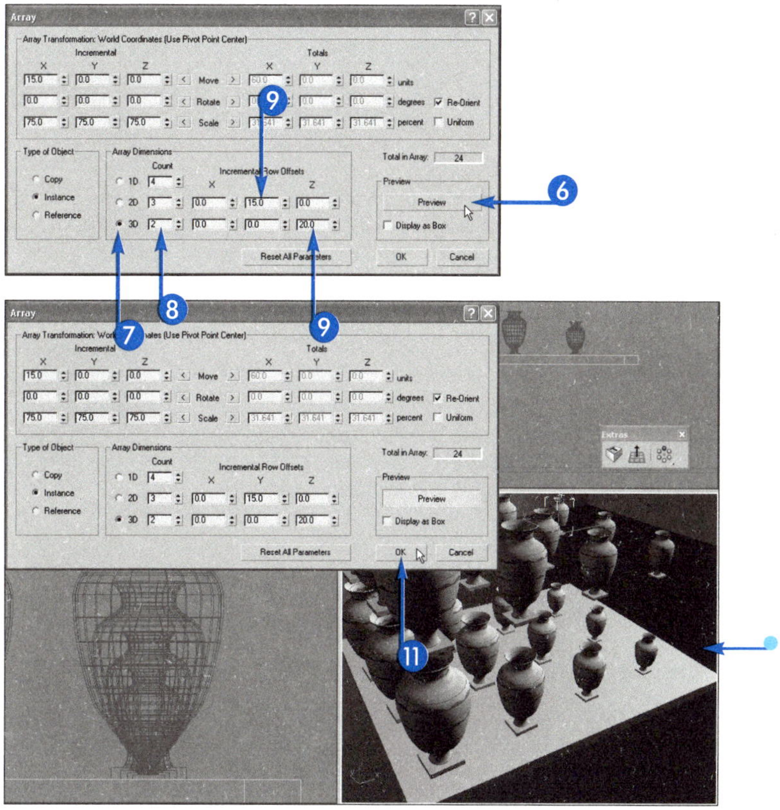

MASTER IT

Why does my system lock up or slow down when I create an array?

▼ Your system may not have enough memory. For example, if you create an object with 5,000 faces (the simple vase in our example has 1,024), and you create an array with a 1D, 2D, and 3D Count of 10, then this generates 1,000 objects, and your scene contains 5,000,000 faces. If each object is a copy, rather than an instance, then 3ds Max needs to maintain the data structure for each object separately. If you then add some modifiers to each object, then the scene taxes even the fastest computer system. Keep your arrays and your objects as simple as possible to avoid this problem.

I entered 90 in all three scale fields, and 10 in the 1D Count field. Why does my object not disappear on the last clone?

▼ With each iteration of a clone, 3ds Max applies the transforms relative to the previous object in the array. With 10 in the X Move field, the second object moves 10 units from the first, and the third moves 10 units from the second. With 90 in the Scale fields, the second object is 90 percent the size of the first, and the third is 90 percent the size of the second and 81 percent the size of the first. The fourth is 72.9 percent of the first, the fifth is 65.61 percent, and so on. As a result, regardless of the count, the scale never reaches zero when you use incremental values.

Using the Snapshot Tool

The Snapshot tool creates a series of clones of animated objects that are based on their state at any point in time. For example, you can create a series of fence posts in a serpentine pattern or a trail of ants leading to a picnic by building one object, animating it, and then creating clones of that object with the Snapshot tool. You can create a single clone, or any number of clones, that can be spread out over a user-specified range in the animation.

The types of objects that you create can be copies, instances, references, or mesh objects. Mesh objects do not have any parametric or modifier controls that the original may have.

The Snapshot tool is located on the Extras toolbar. Right-click an empty area on any toolbar and choose Extras from the pop-up menu to display the Extras toolbar. The Snapshot tool is located in the Array flyout menu. See the section "Clone an Object" for more information on the different clone types.

CD FILE — The Snapshot.max file is available on the CD-ROM for you to practice using the Snapshot tool.

Using the Snapshot Tool

1. Select the object that you want to clone.
2. Click the Snapshot button ( ).

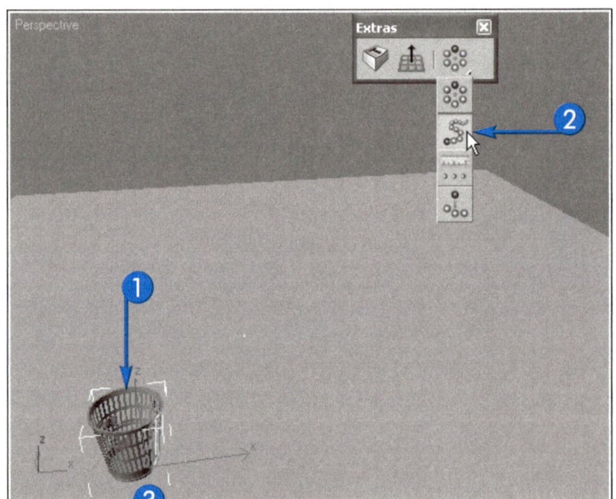

The Snapshot dialog box appears.

3. Click the Range option (○ changes to ◉).
4. Type a value in the Copies field.

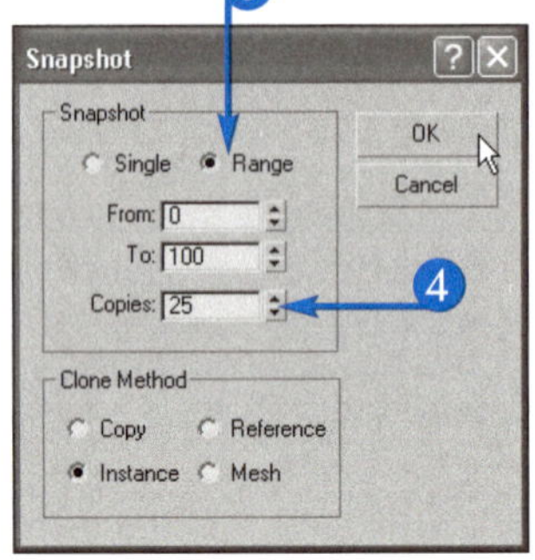

5 Click the Instance option (○ changes to ◉).

6 Click OK.

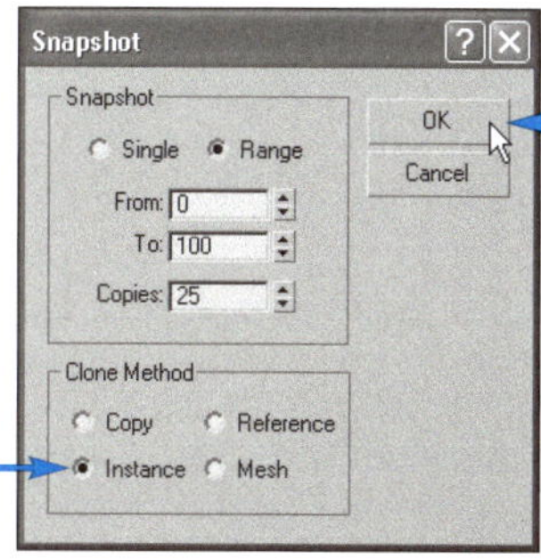

3ds Max creates 25 clones of the original at 4-frame intervals (100 frames per 25 clones).

The Snapshot dialog box closes.

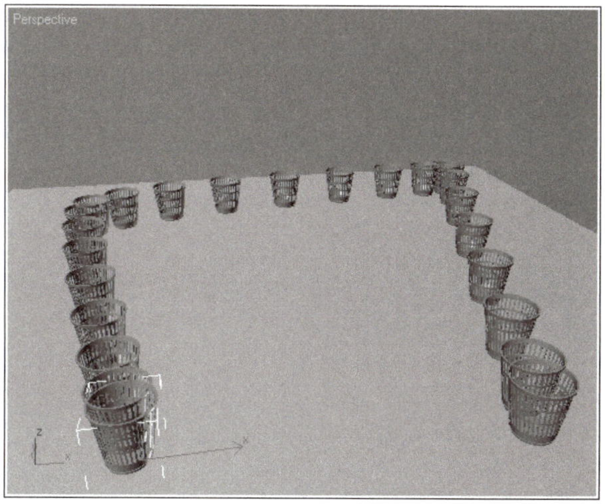

Can I space my objects out evenly?

▼ Yes. The Snapshot tool spaces the objects out by their position in space at any particular time. To space the objects out evenly with the Snapshot tool, you need to make the object movement consistent and even throughout the animation. Find the object's Position track in the Function Curve editor, and then assign a Bezier Position controller, if necessary. Select the Position keys, and then right-click. Click Advanced in the Key Info dialog box that appears. Turn on Constant Velocity and click the Normalize Time button. The clones are now spaced evenly when you use the Snapshot tool. For information about controllers and the Curve Editor, see Chapters 10 and 11.

Rename Objects

You can name all of the objects in your scene for easy identification and selection. When you create an object, 3ds Max assigns a default name that consists of the object type and number. For example, if you use the Sphere object to create a character's eyes, 3ds Max names them Sphere01 and Sphere02. You give them more descriptive and useful names, such as EyeLeft and EyeRight. This is important because three months into a project, you may have no idea what Box257 is, while ShelfDenBottom is self-explanatory.

You can rename each object individually by specifying a new name in the Name field of the Name and Color rollout. However, this is tedious if you must create numerous objects. With the Rename Objects tool, you can create a naming scheme that 3ds Max applies to your objects. You can rename only objects that are selected when you access the tool, or objects that you select from a list in the Pick Objects to Rename dialog box.

When you specify the new object names, you have four options: Base Name, Prefix, Suffix, and Numbered. You can use any combination of these options to rename the objects.

CD FILE The Rename.max file is available on the CD-ROM for you to practice renaming objects.

Rename Objects

1. Click Tools.
2. Click Rename Objects.

   The Rename Objects dialog box appears.

3. Click the Pick option (○ changes to ◉).

   - To rename currently selected objects in the scene, you can click the Selected option (○ changes to ◉).

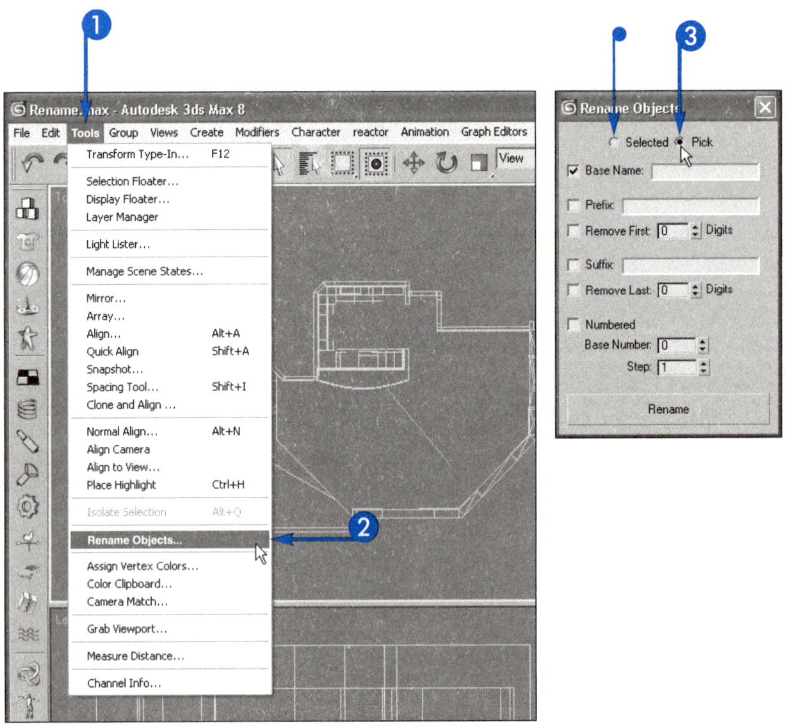

The Pick Objects to Rename dialog box appears.

4. Select the objects that you want to rename.
5. Click Use.

   The Pick Objects to Rename dialog box closes.

   - If necessary, you can click the Base Name option (☐ changes to ☑) in the Rename Objects dialog box.

6. Type the name that you want to apply to all objects.
7. Click the Numbered option (☐ changes to ☑).
8. Type the number that you want your objects to start using in the Base Number field.
9. Click Rename.

   3ds Max renames the selected objects.

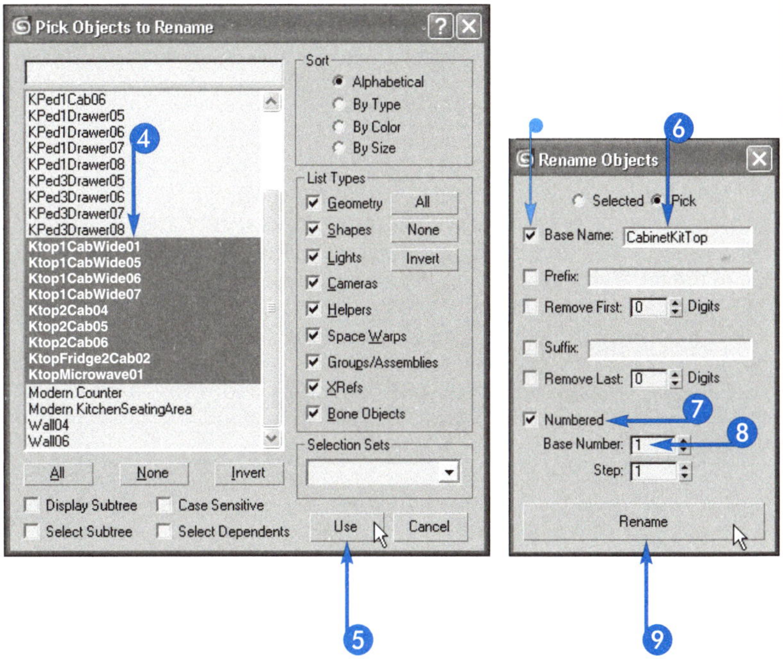

Why does 3ds Max shorten the base name that I typed in step 6?

▼ The Remove First or Remove Last option (☐ changes to ☑) shortens the name of the selected objects by the number of specified digits. For example, if you select the Remove Last option and then type **2** in the Digits field, all object names shorten by two characters; if you type a base name of **Table**, then the base name becomes Tab. These features are effective when you are renumbering sequential objects, but you should avoid using the Remove First and Remove Last options when you use the Base Name option. Remove First and Remove Last work best when you want to replace a prefix or suffix in existing object names.

How do I rename objects using the viewport?

▼ If you click the Selected option (○ changes to ◉) in the Rename Objects dialog box, then you can rename objects after selecting them in the viewport. You can use any of the selection methods to pick the objects. For more information about selecting objects, see Chapter 2.

How do I verify that 3ds Max renamed my objects correctly?

▼ You can view a list of objects in your scene by clicking the Select by Name button ( ), or pressing the H shortcut key. This opens the Select Objects dialog box and displays a list of all unhidden objects and object groups in your scene. You can use this list of objects to verify that 3ds Max correctly renamed your objects.

Create a Selection Set

You can use selection sets to create collections of items that you want to select simultaneously within your scene. For example, if you have a scene that contains several tables and chairs, you can create a selection set for all the table and chair sets in the scene. Selection sets are just lists of objects that you need to select repetitively; objects can be members of multiple sets. Although the objects are clustered together in the selection set, they remain separate objects that you can select and modify individually. For more information about selecting objects, see Chapter 2.

The Named Selection Sets dialog box provides all of the options for creating and modifying your selection sets. You can create or remove selection sets, and you can add things to or remove things from objects, or transfer between sets in this dialog box. Although you do not need to select objects prior to opening the Named Selection Set dialog box, you can easily add selected objects to selection sets.

You can pick your selection set from either the Named Selection Sets dialog box or from the Named Selection Sets list box in the Main toolbar.

CD FILE: The SelectionSet.max file is available on the CD-ROM for you to practice creating selection sets.

Create a Selection Set

1. Select objects for your selection set.
2. Click the Edit Named Selection Sets button ( ).

   The Named Selection Sets dialog box appears.
3. Click the Create New Set button ( ).

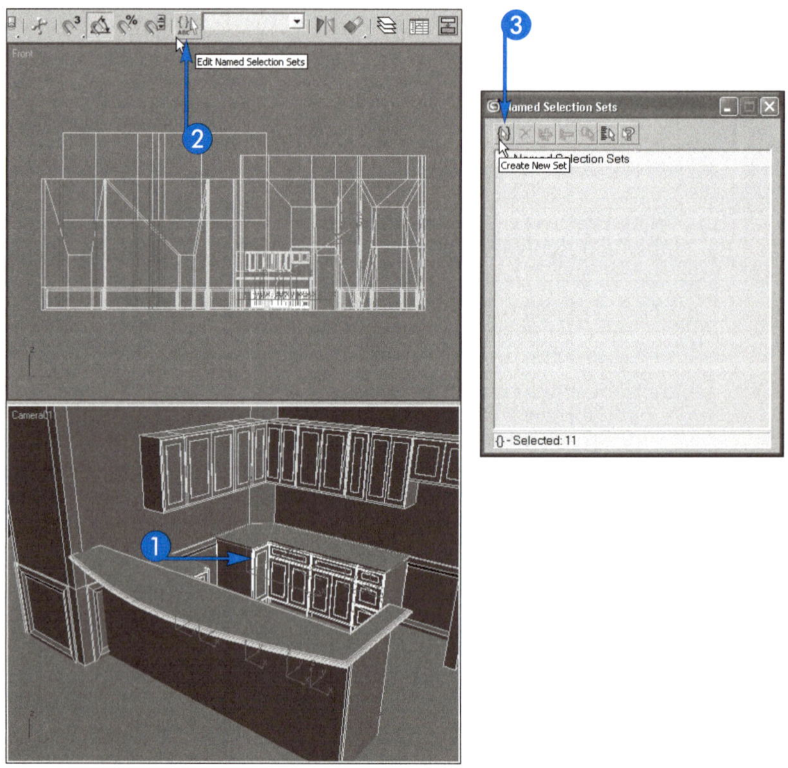

3ds Max creates a new set with the default name, New Set, highlighted.

4 Type a name for the selection set.

5 Click the Plus sign (+) to expand the selection set.

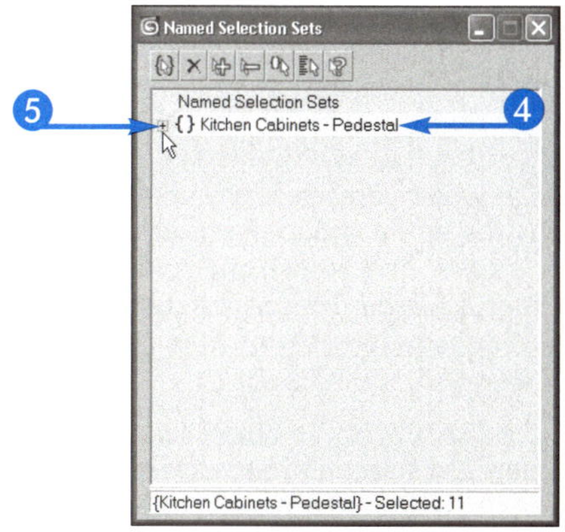

The selection set's contents appear.

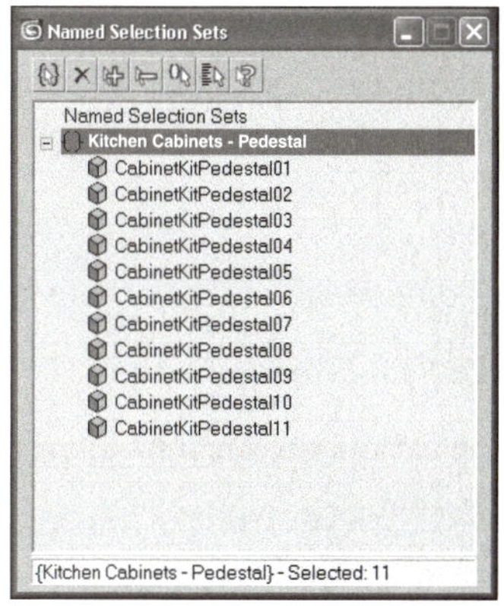

MASTER IT

How do I add more objects to an existing selection set?

- First, simply select the objects that you want to add. Then display the Named Selection Sets dialog box using steps 1 to 3 in this section, or click the Edit Named Selection Sets button ( ) in the Main toolbar. Click the selection set to which you want to add more objects, and click Add Selected Objects ( ). You can also add objects to a selection list by using the objects' names. In the Named Selection Sets dialog box, click Select Objects By Name ( ). In the Select Objects dialog box, click the objects that you want to add from the list.

How do I select a selection set?

- You can use the Named Selection Set field in the Main toolbar by clicking ( ) and selecting the set. To select the objects in a selection set in the Named Selection Sets dialog box, double-click a set in the list that appears.

Why are there more objects selected in my scene than there are in my selection set?

- Selecting objects with a selection set yields the same result as picking them from within a viewport. If a member of a selection set becomes a member of a group, then selecting the selection set member selects the group as well. See the section "Group and Ungroup Objects" for more information on groups.

Group and Ungroup Objects

You can combine objects to form one group object that 3ds Max treats as a single object. As a result, when you select any object in the group, 3ds Max selects the entire group. For example, you can group a bicycle's tire, rim, wheel, and spokes. Groups that are members of larger groups are called *nested* groups. Groups have unique names, assigned in the Group dialog box, for easy selection and editing.

You can use any of the object selection methods discussed in Chapter 2 to select a group object. The group's name appears in bold in the Name field of the Name and Color rollout in the Command panel. This distinguishes grouped objects from ungrouped objects. In the Select Objects dialog box, group names appear with brackets around them. For example, a group named Table appears as [Table].

To work with the group members individually, you can permanently ungroup the group or temporarily *open* it. *Exploding* a group ungroups the objects, as well as any nested groups.

Note that it is often unwise to use groups in character animation because they create a hidden object that becomes the parent of the group's hierarchy. For this reason, consider setting up your own hierarchies with characters.

CD FILE: The Group.max file is available on the CD-ROM for you to practice creating groups.

Group and Ungroup Objects

Create an Object Group

1. Select the objects that you want to group.
2. Click Group.
3. Click Group.

   The Group dialog box appears.

4. Type a name for the group in the Group name field.
5. Click OK.

   3ds Max creates a group containing the selected objects.

   The name of the group displays in the Name field of the Name and Color rollout.

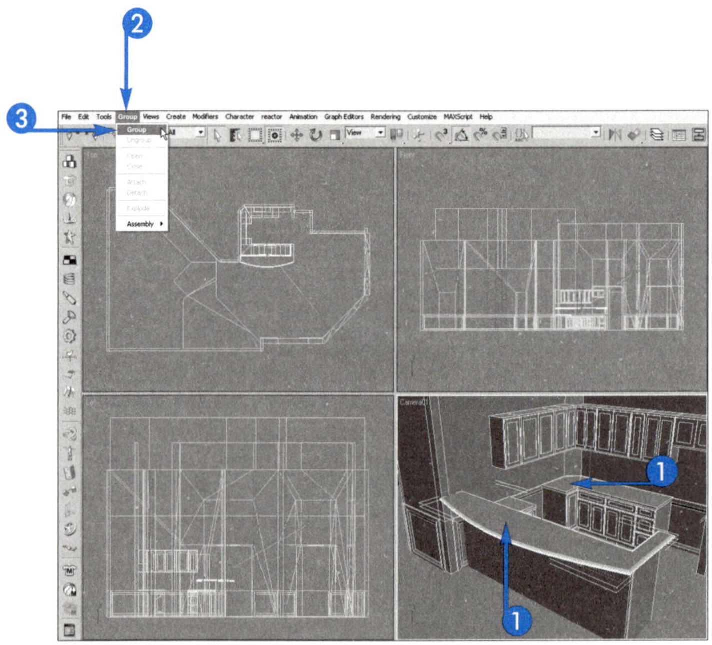

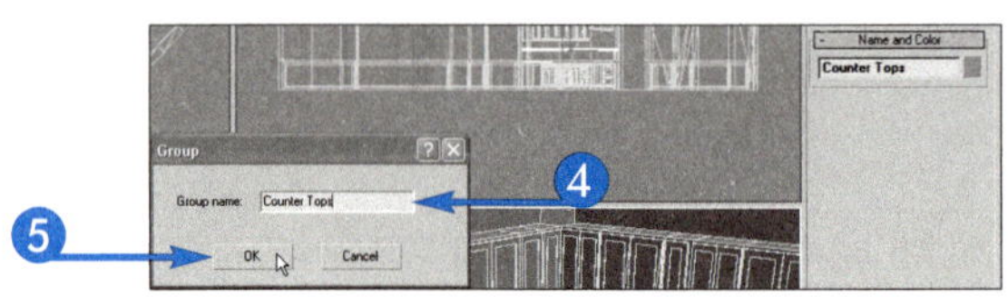

Ungroup Objects

6 Select a member of a group.

When you select a group, its name appears in the Name field in the Name and Color rollout.

7 Click Group.

8 Click Ungroup.

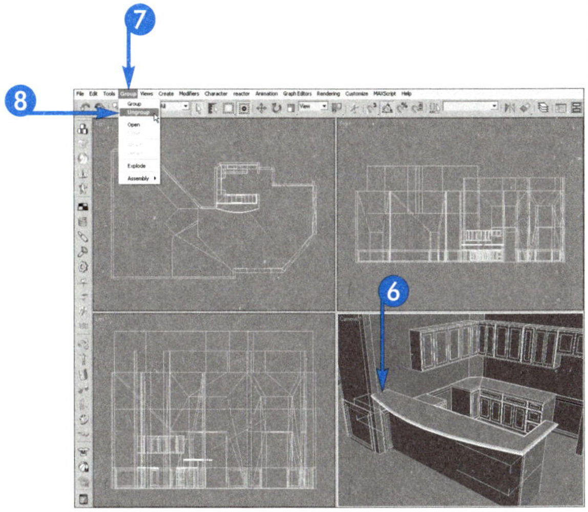

3ds Max ungroups the objects.

- The example shows that the group had two objects.

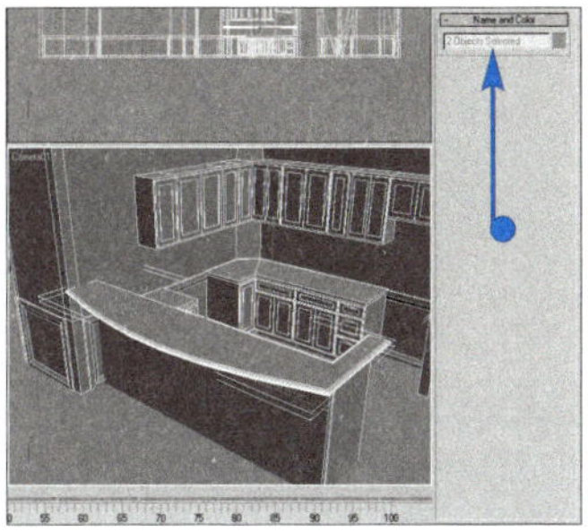

MASTER IT

What is the difference between ungrouping and exploding an object group?

3ds Max provides two commands for ungrouping a group of objects: Ungroup and Explode. The Ungroup command ungroups the objects back to the individual objects and nested groups that comprised the group. The Explode command ungroups the selected group and all nested groups within it. When you use either the Ungroup or Explode commands, 3ds Max removes all animation that you have applied to the group but not to individual objects.

What is the difference between a group and a selection set?

Objects in a group are treated as a single, larger object, while selection sets are a quick way to redundantly select objects. Modifiers that you apply to groups are applied to the group as a whole, rather than to each member object. Conversely, 3ds Max treats the objects in a selection set as individual items so that modifiers that you apply to selection sets affect each object individually. See the section "Create a Selection Set" for more information about selection sets.

How do I modify or transform individual objects in a group?

You can modify and transform individual objects in an object group by opening the group. To open a group, select the group, click Group in the main menu, and then click Open. Once the group is open, you can select an object and modify it. When you are done, click Group, and then click Close to close the group.

Attach and Detach an Object to and from a Group

You can add and remove objects and object groups to or from a group using the Attach and Detach commands. A group is comprised of objects and nested groups that you combine in a larger object. When you attach an object to an existing group, the selected object becomes part of the larger group object. Once it is attached, any modifications that you make to the group also affect the attached object; you can modify the object separately only after opening the group. See the section "Group and Ungroup Objects" for more information.

You can use the Detach command to remove an object from a group. To do so, you must first open the group so that you can select its member objects. After opening the group, you can select the objects that you want to remove from the group, and then use the Detach command. Once you remove the unwanted objects, you can close the group. For more information about selecting objects, see Chapter 2.

Note that it is often unwise to use groups in character animation because they create a hidden object that becomes the parent of the group's hierarchy. For this reason, consider setting up your own hierarchies with characters.

CD FILE: The Group2.max file is available on the CD-ROM for you to practice editing groups.

Attach and Detach an Object to and from a Group

Attach an Object

1. Select the object that you want to add to an existing group.
2. Click Group.
3. Click Attach.

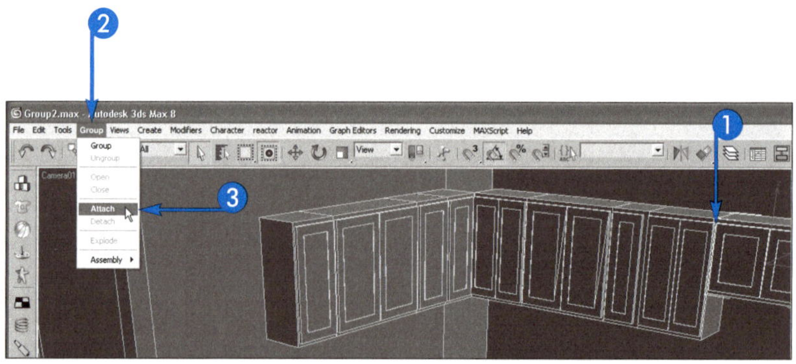

4. In the viewport, click a member of the group to which you want to attach the object.

   The selected object attaches to the group.

Detach an Object

1. Select a group.
2. Click Group.
3. Click Open.

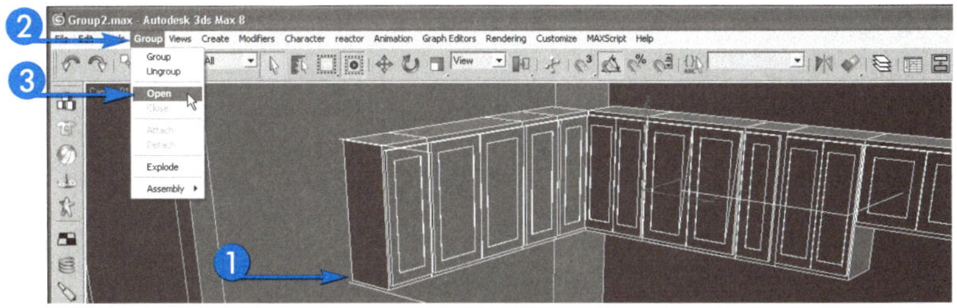

A pink bounding box appears around the objects in the group.

4. Select the object or nested group that you want to remove from the group.
5. Click Group.
6. Click Detach.

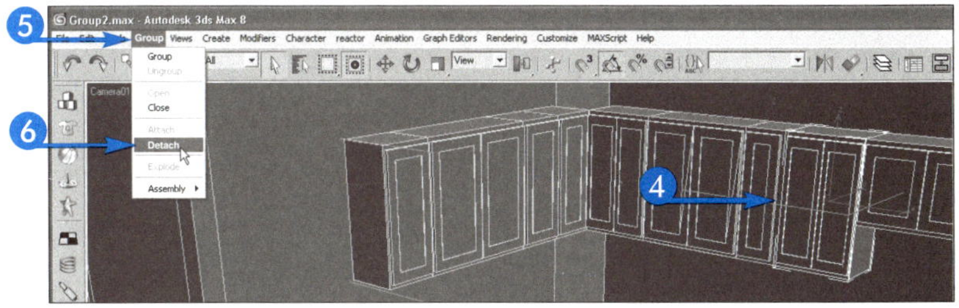

7. Select a member of the group.
8. Click Group.
9. Click Close.

The group closes.

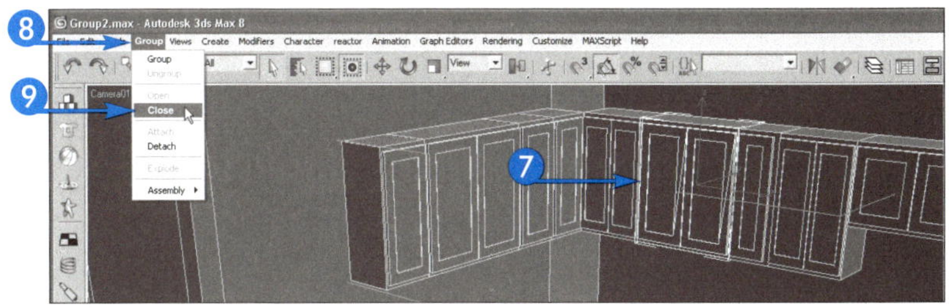

MASTER IT

Can I attach objects to an open group?

▼ Yes. This is another method that you can use to attach objects to a group. When the group is open, select any objects that you want to add to the group. Click Group from the main menu, click Attach, and then pick the pink bounding box of the open group to which you want to attach the objects. The selected objects are now members of the group.

How can I close all open groups?

▼ The Close command has no effect on non-group objects. Select everything in the scene, then click Group, and then click Close. All groups, even nested groups, are closed.

Can I remove items from a nested group?

▼ Yes. When a group object contains another group object, the attached group object is commonly referred to as the *nested* group. When you open an object group, the nested groups are not opened. If you want to remove items from a nested group, you must first click to select that group and then open it. Once the nested group is open, you can select the objects that you want to remove. When you are finished, you must close both group objects.

Merge Objects from Another File

The components of a 3ds Max scene are often created in separate 3ds Max files or by different artists. You can bring objects from another scene into your current project by merging the objects that you want into your scene. 3ds Max copies only the objects that you choose and places a copy of the objects in your scene. After merging the objects, you can freely modify the merged objects without affecting the objects in the original scene.

The Merge File dialog box displays a list of the objects and groups in the scene, with group names appearing in square brackets. If you have numerous objects in the scene, you can reduce the list by selecting the type of objects that you want to view in the List types area. You can then select the Display Subtree option to show hierarchies.

If the merged objects are created in a scene that uses different units, such as meters instead of inches, 3ds Max interprets the objects' dimensions and maintains them in the new scene. For example, an object with a 1.0-meter radius in a metric scene will have a 3'3.37" radius in a US Standard scene.

Merge Objects from Another File

1. Click File.
2. Click Merge.

The Merge File dialog box appears.

3. Select the file containing the objects that you want to merge into the current scene.
4. Click Open.

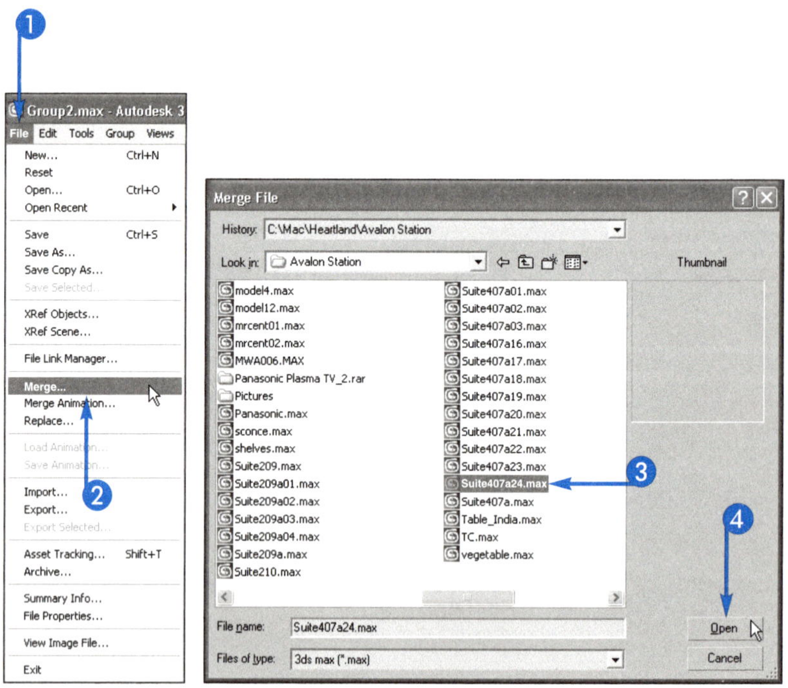

The Merge dialog box appears, displaying the objects and groups in the selected file.

5 Select the objects that you want to merge.

To select multiple objects, you can press and hold Ctrl or Shift while you click the additional objects.

6 Click OK.

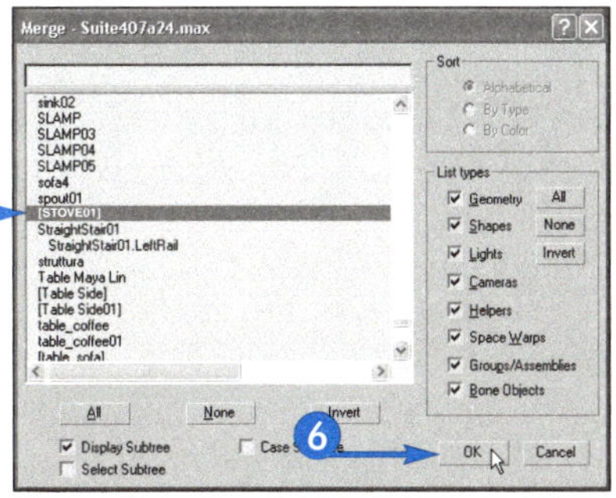

3ds Max merges the selected objects into your scene.

MASTER IT

How do I sort the list of merge objects by type?

When the Merge dialog box appears, the list of objects sorts alphabetically by name. If you select the Display Subtree option, the sort options on the right side of the screen are grayed out. If you want to sort objects by type or by color, and the options are grayed out, click Display Subtree to deselect it (☑ changes to ☐). When you click the By Type option (○ changes to ◉), the list sorts immediately by object type. Unchecking options in the List types area reduces the number and type of objects that appear in the list.

What happens if the objects that I am merging have the same names as some of the objects in my current scene?

When you merge objects into your scene, 3ds Max compares their names with the existing object names in the scene. If there are duplicate names, the Duplicate Name dialog box appears. You have the option of specifying a new name for the merged objects, skipping the merge, deleting the objects in the current scene and replacing them with the merged objects, or letting 3ds Max automatically rename the merged objects. You can either specify how to handle each duplicate object separately, or you can click the Apply to All Duplicates option to instruct 3ds Max to treat all duplicates in the same manner.

Replace Objects from Another File

With the Replace option, you can substitute objects in your current scene with identically named objects from another scene. This is a common technique in a production house so that animation work does not have to wait for props or sets to be completed. For example, the character animator can set up the fight sequences with low polygon substitutes for the weapons. The high polygon finished models replace the stand-ins for the final renderings.

When you select the replacement file, the Replace dialog box shows a list of the objects in the selected file that have the same name as objects in your current scene. This list only matches the objects by name, not by size or appearance; as a result, you can replace a pistol with a machine gun if you name both objects "gun."

3ds Max only replaces the geometry of the current object and its modifiers. It does not replace transforms, animation, space warp bindings, and hierarchy. The Merge command is the tool to use to bring an object, with all its features, into your current scene. See the section "Merge Objects from Another File" for more on merging.

The Replace1.max file is available on the CD-ROM for you to practice using the Replace tool.

Replace Objects from Another File

1. Click File.
2. Click Replace.

The Replace File dialog box appears, displaying a list of the objects that can be replaced.

3. Select the file that contains the objects that you want to replace.
4. Click Open.

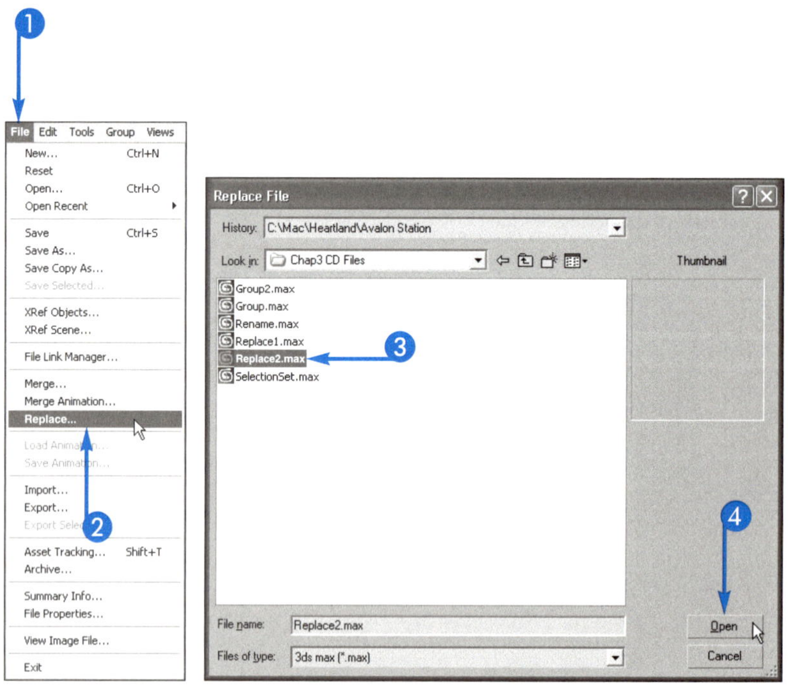

The Replace dialog box appears.

5 Select the objects that you want to replace.

To select multiple objects, you can press and hold Ctrl or Shift while you click additional objects.

- To replace all objects in the list, click All.

6 Click OK.

A dialog box appears, asking you to specify whether you want to replace materials.

7 Click Yes to use the replacement objects' materials.

- 3ds Max replaces the selected objects in the scene.

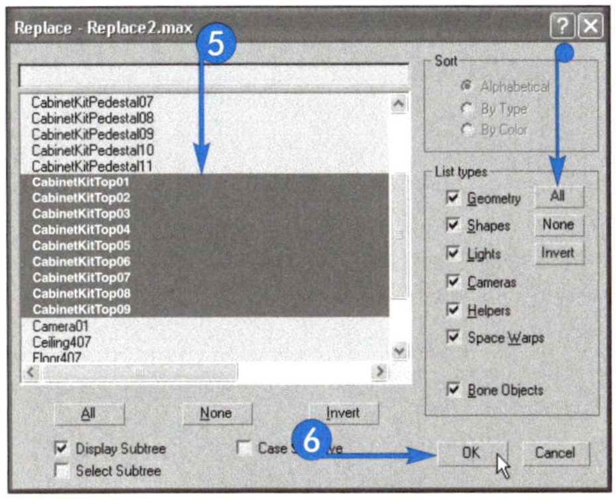

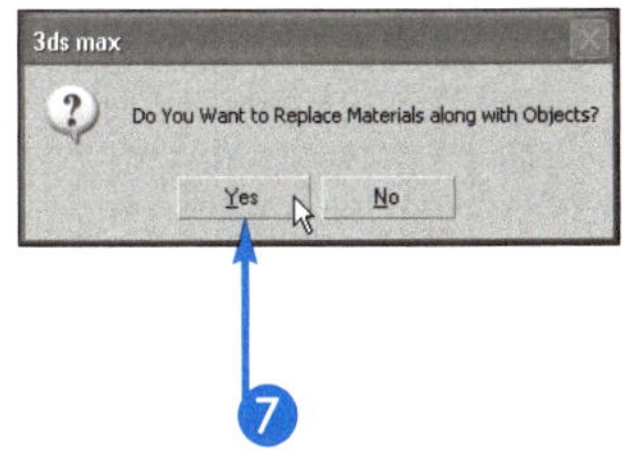

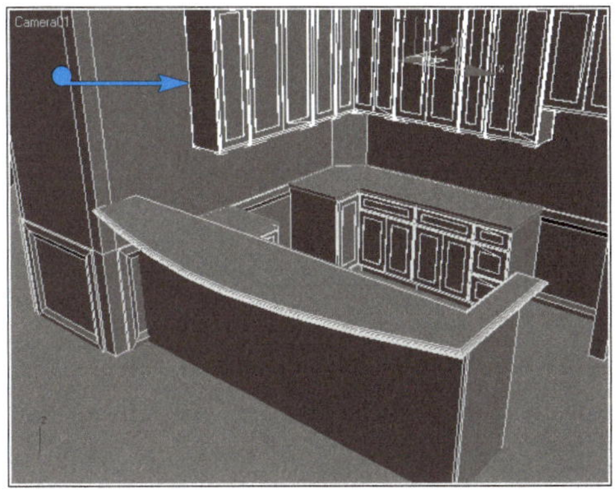

MASTER IT

Can I replace an object's materials as well as its geometry?

When you replace objects in your scene, you can opt to import the materials from the replacement objects into your scene. To do this, you simply click the appropriate response in the dialog box that appears after you perform step 6 in this section. If you select Yes, then 3ds Max replaces the objects, as well as the materials. Clicking No only replaces the objects. To reapply the materials that you had on the objects before you replaced them, you can use the Material Editor. For more information about applying materials, see Chapter 14.

Is this the only way to replace an object?

No. There is also a Replace modifier that you can apply to an object or objects. Using the Replace modifier, you can select objects within the current scene as replacement objects, or objects from another scene as externally referenced objects. Because it is in the Modifier Stack, you can eliminate the replace functionality by deleting the modifier, or by changing it in the modifier's Parameters rollout. For information on modifiers, see Chapter 6. See the section "Externally Reference Objects between Files" for more information on external references.

Externally Reference Objects between Files

If you intend to use the same objects in multiple scenes, or have multiple artists contributing to the same project, you can save time by sharing, or *externally referencing*, objects between files. When you externally reference a file, called an XRef, you create source objects in one file, which contain the features that you want, such as materials, animation, and modifiers. You then reference those objects in other files. When any file that contains an XRef is opened, 3ds Max inserts the externally referenced objects into it. Any changes you make to the source objects, in their independent files, are reflected the next time you open any scene that references them.

After creating the XRefs, you can specify how the cross-referenced objects are updated: automatically; when you make changes to the source object; or only when your scene is opened. You can also indicate whether the material is updated when you change it in the source object. If you want to change the material of the externally referenced object within your scene, select the Merge Materials option in the XRef Objects dialog box before you XRef the object.

CD FILE: The XRef.max file is available on the CD-ROM for you to practice using external references.

Externally Reference Objects between Files

1. Click File.
2. Click XRef Objects.

   The XRef Objects dialog box appears.
3. Click Create XRef Record from File (▣).

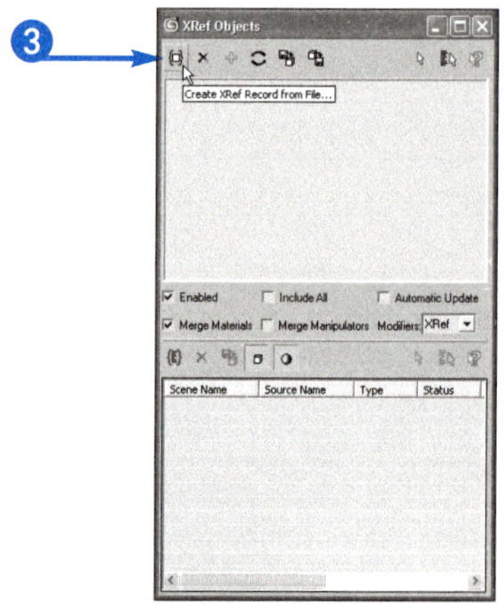

The Open File dialog box appears.

4. Click the file that contains the objects that you want to reference.
5. Click Open.

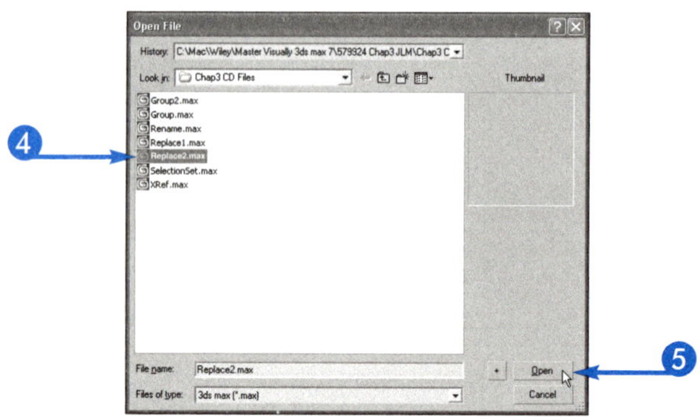

The XRef Merge dialog box appears.

6 Select the objects that you want to externally reference.

7 Click OK.

Note: *If a dialog box appears indicating duplicate material names, select how you want 3ds Max to handle the materials.*

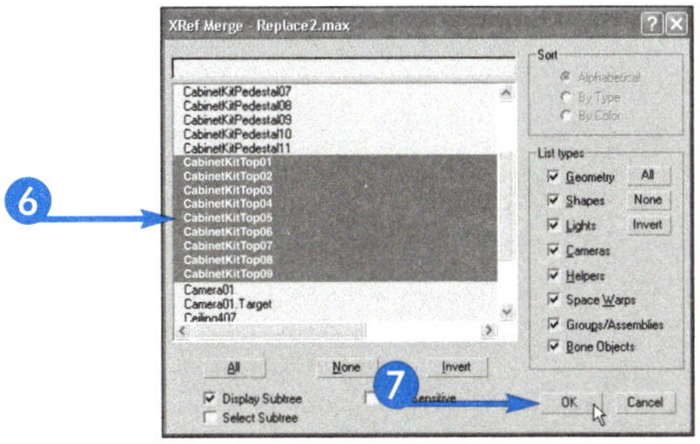

- 3ds Max adds the objects to your scene as external references.
- The XRef'd objects are listed in the bottom list box, and the filename appears in the top of the XRef Objects dialog box.

You may need to transform the object to match your scene.

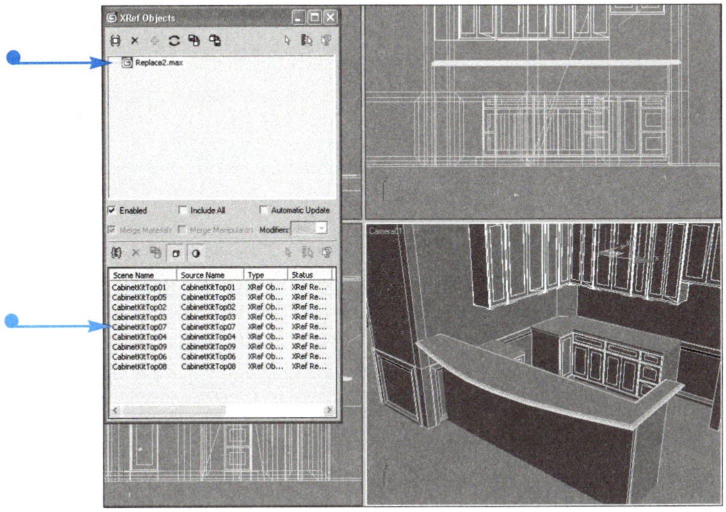

MASTER IT

What changes can I make to an externally referenced object?

▼ When you use an XRef object in your scene, you can animate it, add modifiers to it, transform it, and clone it. You can also create different modifications to distinct clones to produce different results in each clone. However, you cannot modify the basic structure of the object that uses the XRef. For example, you cannot change the number of segments in a sphere; you must make changes to the structure of the object in the source file. 3ds Max inserts XRefs into a scene at the same location that they reside in their source files, and you may need to move them.

What is a proxy object?

▼ If the externally referenced object has a high polygon count, then it may result in sluggish performance in your viewports. This performance may be made even slower when there are multiple instances of the XRef in the scene. A proxy object is a lower polygon object that acts as a stand-in for the XRefs in your viewports. It is usually a very low polygon version of the original object, created with the MultiRes modifier, that retains the basic size and shape of the original. Proxies display in the viewports while the original objects appears in the final renderings. For more information on the MultiRes modifier, see Chapter 6.

Work with the Layer Manager

Using Layer Manager, you can place your objects on different layers to organize them within your scenes. Consider populating each layer with objects that you want to view, hide, or freeze at the same time. For example, in a residential scene, you place the furniture, walls/windows/doors, and foliage on different layers. With Layer Manager, you can easily hide the building's structure and plants to clearly view and work on the furniture.

3ds Max uniquely names every layer and lists its contents upon expansion. In addition to hiding a layer's contents, you can set layer colors, freeze layers — making their member objects unselectable — turn off their ability to render or contribute to a radiosity solution, and even select objects based on their layer.

You can select any of the column names to organize the layers based on that feature. The Layer Manager is modeless, meaning that when it remains open, you can still interact with the objects in your scene.

The Layer Manager, inherited from Autodesk VIZ, mimics the Layer tools in AutoCAD and as such is not for the animator, but rather so CAD users could find a familiar set of tools in 3ds Max. For Layered animation, consider using the Motion Mixer under the Graph Editors menu.

A The Layer Manager Button

Clicking (icon) activates the Layer Manager.

B Layers Column

Lists all of the layers in your scene. Click the plus sign (⊞) to expand the layer. 3ds Max creates the default layer 0 for all scenes.

C Current Layer Column

3ds Max adds all new objects to the current layer. A check mark (☑) displays in this column next to the current layer. To switch current layers, click in this column across from another layer name.

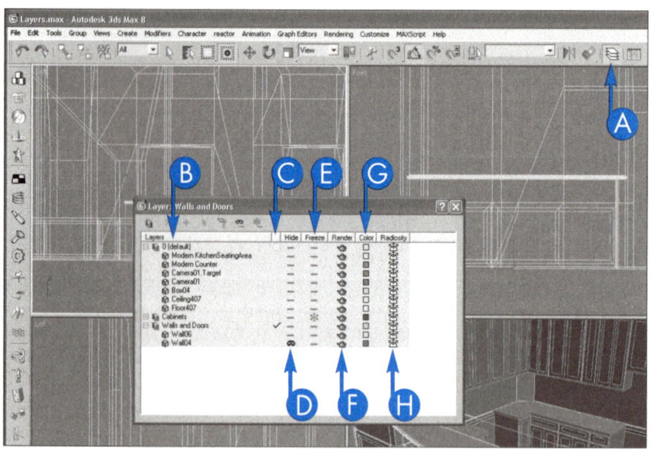

D Hide Column

Specifies which layers, along with their objects, are hidden. The Hidden icon (icon) indicates that the layer is hidden. You can toggle layers between hidden and unhidden using this column.

E Freeze Column

Specifies which layers, along with their objects, are frozen within your scene. The Freeze icon (icon) indicates a frozen layer whose objects you cannot select. You can toggle between frozen and unfrozen states using this column.

H Radiosity Column

The Radiosity icon (icon) indicates whether the layer's objects are calculated as part of a radiosity solution when Radiosity is used as the advanced lighting plugin.

G Color Column

Specifies the color associated with the layer. Click By Object to turn on By Layer in the Object Properties dialog box and set an object's color to the same color that the layer specifies.

F Render Column

The Render icon (icon) indicates that the objects on that layer will be rendered. If a layer is hidden, then its objects do not render, regardless of the setting in this column.

Controlling the Layer Manager

You can use the buttons on the Layer Manager toolbar to create, access, and manage the layers within your scene. Buttons that appear grayed out are unavailable on the toolbar or if the selected layer is empty but is the current layer. If the layer that you want to delete is the current layer, you must select a new current layer before deleting it.

Layer Manager Toolbar Buttons

Button	Button Name	Purpose
	Create New Layer	To create a new layer. 3ds Max creates layers with a default name of Layer, followed by a number, such as Layer01. When you select objects before clicking this button, 3ds Max adds them to the new layer.
	Delete Highlighted Empty Layers	To delete empty layers. You cannot delete a layer if it contains objects, if it is the current layer, or if it is layer 0. 3ds Max grays out this button to indicate when you cannot delete a selected layer.
	Add Selected Objects to Highlighted Layer	To add the objects that are selected in the scene to the currently selected layer. 3ds Max moves objects from their current layer into the new layer.
	Select Highlighted Objects and Layers	To select the objects in the current layer in your scene.
	Highlight Selected Objects' Layers	To highlight the layers in the Layer Manager that contain the objects that are selected in the scene. If you select objects from multiple layers, 3ds Max highlights all of the corresponding layers. When no objects are selected, this button appears as a question mark icon ( ).
	Hide/Unhide All Layers	To hide or unhide the contents of all layers. This does not override the hidden status of objects that are specifically hidden by the user. For more information on hiding objects, see Chapter 2.
	Freeze/Unfreeze All Layers	To freeze or unfreeze the contents of all layers. When you freeze objects within your scene, you cannot select them. For more information on freezing objects, see Chapter 2.

Layer and Object Rendering

Each layer has two states that it can hold in the Render column: Render and Don't Render. However, each object has three states: Render by Layer, Don't Render, and Render by Object. When the Layer is set to Render ( ), objects that are set to Render by Layer ( ) render, and objects that are set to Don't Render by Layer ( ) do not. When the layer is set to Don't Render ( ), the layer's objects that are set to either Render by Layer ( ) or Don't Render ( ) do not render. Objects that are set to Render by Object ( ) render based on the Renderable option (or) in the Object Properties dialog box. For more information about the Object Properties dialog box, see Chapter 2.

4 Create Objects Efficiently in 3ds Max

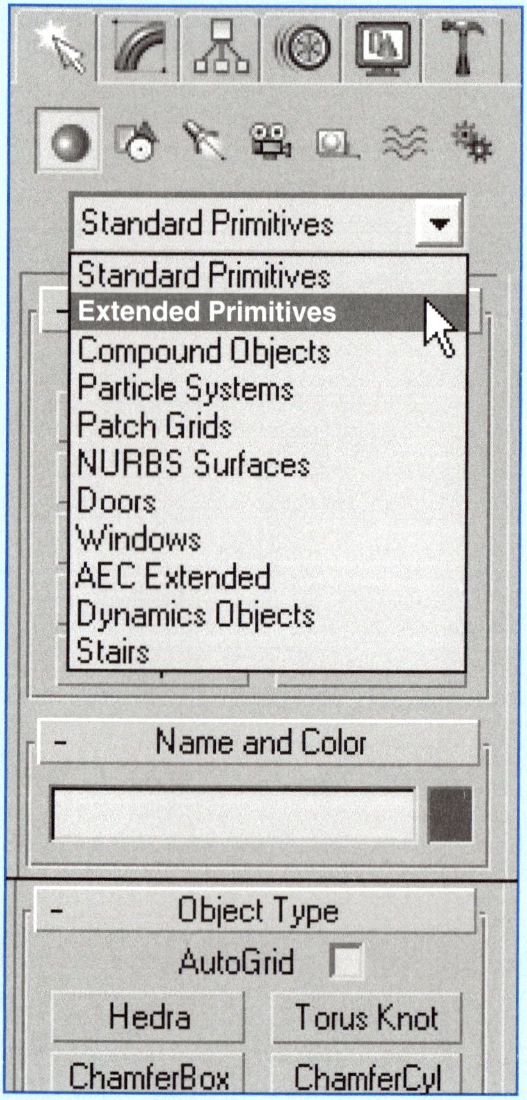

5 Modifying 2D Objects

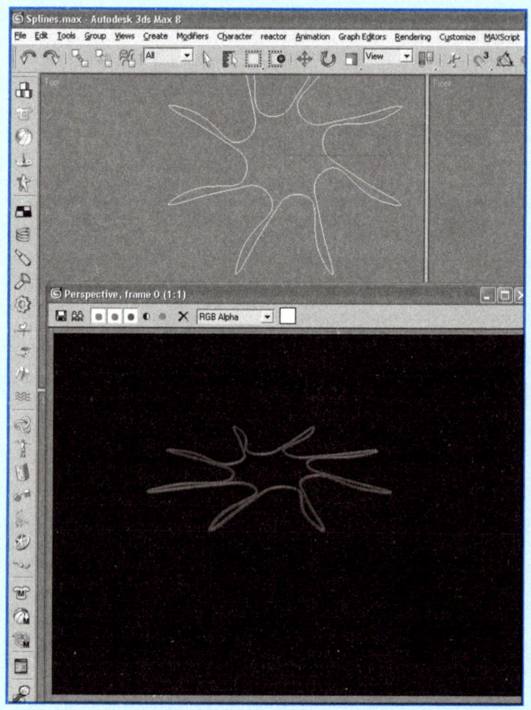

PART II
MODELING YOUR OBJECTS

6 Modifying 3D Objects

7 Creating Architectural Objects

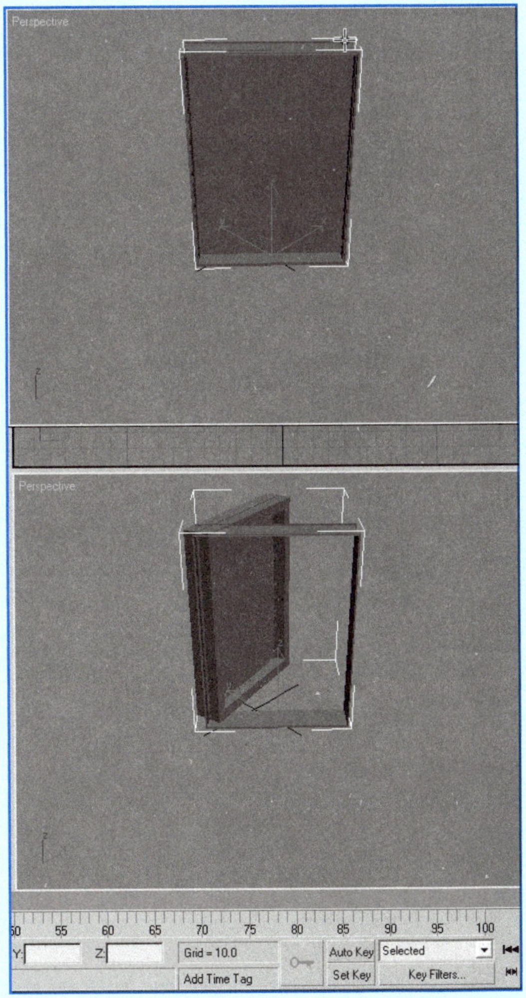

Understanding the Create Panel

You can use the Create panel, in the Command panel on the right side of the 3ds Max window, to generate objects in your scene including default objects, such as geometric primitives, lights, cameras, and even space warps and particle systems.

You create objects by specifying the object category, such as Geometry, Shapes, or Cameras. Some object categories have a subcategory list box to further define the objects. Below these categories are the *rollouts* — collapsible panel items that contain related controls. The Object Type, and Name and Color rollouts are standard throughout all of the object categories and subcategories, and additional object-specific rollouts appear when you create objects. The Creation Method, Keyboard Entry, and Parameters rollouts are available when you create most Geometry and Shape objects.

Once you create an object, you can immediately adjust its parameters in the Create panel. Remember that after you deselect the object, you must reselect it, and then open the Modify panel to change the available parameters. This is often the source of confusion for many novice users.

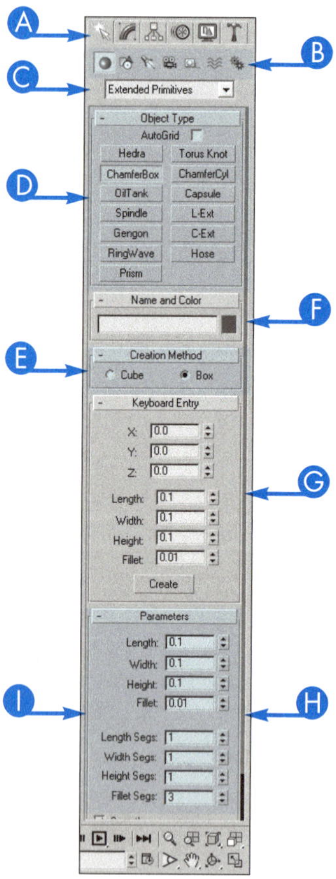

A Create Panel Tab

Click this tab ( ) to display the Create panel.

B Category Buttons

You can use these buttons to access seven categories of objects.

C Subcategory List Box

Displays the available object subcategories for the category that you select. Your subcategory selection changes the objects that appear in the Object Type rollout.

D Object Type Rollout

Contains buttons for each of the objects within the object category or subcategory that you select.

E Creation Method Rollout

Defines the procedure for creating objects with the mouse.

F Name and Color Rollout

Displays the name and color of an object. 3ds Max automatically assigns a default name and object color. For easy identification and object selection, the fields in this rollout display in all Command panels.

G Keyboard Entry Rollout

Provides parameters for creating a geometric or shape object using the keyboard.

H Panel Scrollbar

This small slider scrolls through the Create panel when it extends beyond the limits of your screen.

I Parameters Rollout

Adjusts the parameters for modifying the current object.

Object Categories

Button	Name	Description
	Geometry	Contains the subcategories Standard Primitives, Extended Primitives, Compound Objects, Particle Systems, Patch Grids, NURBS Surfaces, Doors, Windows AEC Extended, Dynamics Objects, and Stairs. 3ds Max includes anything that you create and expect to render in your scene under Geometry.
	Shapes	Contains 2D shapes, which you create with splines and NURBS curves. You can use shapes as components to create other objects or to create a motion trajectory.
	Lights	Contains different light objects that create illumination in your scene.
	Cameras	Contains camera objects, which have controls for viewing a scene.
	Helpers	Has objects that aid in scene animation, object positioning, and geometric measurement.
	Space Warps	Contains objects that you use with geometry objects and particle systems to distort the space around objects and, therefore, the objects themselves.
	Systems	Combines objects, controllers, and hierarchies to produce a desired, repetitive structure with a specific behavior. An example of a system is a Biped, which is a complete, linked structure for a bi-pedal character.

Creation Method Rollout

There is usually more than one method to create Geometry and Shape objects in 3ds Max. For example, when you create a sphere, you can either click to set the center and then drag to set the radius, or click to set one point on the sphere's perimeter and then drag to set the diameter. The first method, called Center, is the default, and the second method is called Edge. You set the procedure for creating objects in the Creation Method rollout. The creation method options vary, based on the object, and the rollout does not display for all geometry and shape objects.

Name and Color Rollout

The Name and Color rollout identifies a selected object's name and color. Although 3ds Max starts with default names and random colors for each newly created object, you can change these names in the Name and Color fields. Alternatively, you can rename objects in the Rename Objects dialog box. For more information about renaming an object, see Chapter 3.

To change an object's color, you can activate the color swatch to the right of the Name field. The Object Color dialog box appears, where you can select the object color that you want.

Create Objects with the Mouse

You can use your mouse to quickly create a new object. After you select the object type and a start location, you move the mouse to size the object. Some objects only require one click and drag, while other, more complicated objects, require more input. You can create objects using either the Geometry or Shapes category button in the Create panel. Each category has different subcategories that determine which objects display in the Object Type rollout.

Before you can create an object, you must specify a creation method in the Creation Method rollout. The *creation method* defines the procedure with which 3ds Max creates the object when you create it in the viewports. For example, when you create a box primitive, selecting the Box creation method produces a box with different length, width, and height dimensions based on where you click and drag. The Cube creation method produces a box with sides of equal length. See the section "Understanding the Create Panel" for more on creation methods.

You can tweak your object's size and location in the Parameters rollout by entering different values. Although you can quickly modify an object's parameters manually, if you prefer to create a more precise object, see the section "Create Objects with the Keyboard."

Create Objects with the Mouse

1. Click the Create Panel (▫) tab.

   The Create panel displays.

2. Click either the Geometry (▫) or Shapes (▫) Category button.

   The Geometry or Shapes controls appear.

3. Click here and select an object subcategory.

   The available object types display in the Object Type rollout.

4. Click the object type that you want to create.
5. Click the creation method that you want (○ changes to ◉).
6. In a viewport, click to define the location to begin the object's creation.
7. Drag and then release the mouse.

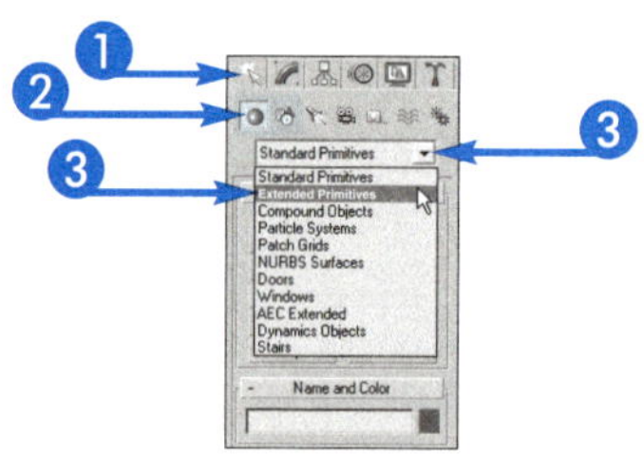

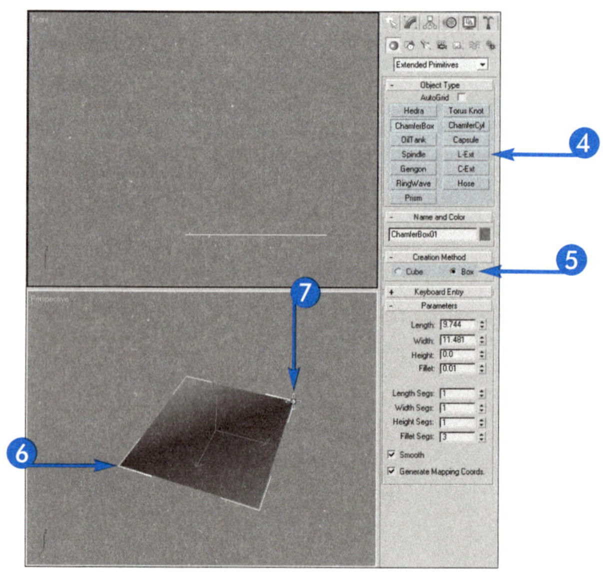

3ds Max defines the first object parameter.

8 If required, move, and then click the mouse to define additional parameters.

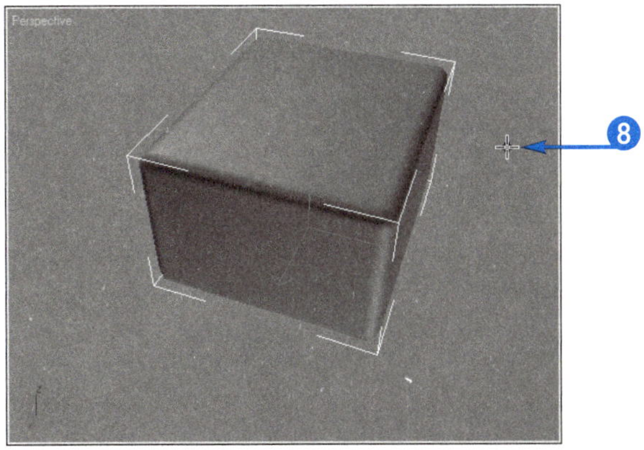

- 3ds Max creates the object in your viewport.
- You can type different values in the Parameters rollout to adjust the new object's proportions.

Note: *This is a general procedure and not suited to all objects. Some objects only require one click and drag, while others, such as Walls and Lines, have no limit to their creation steps.*

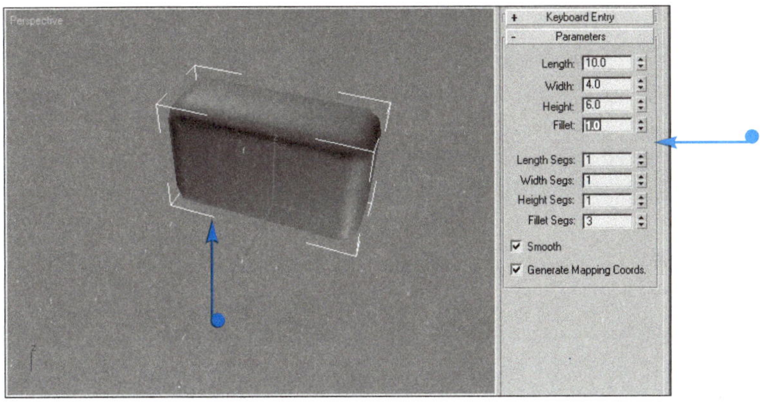

MASTER IT

How can I modify the object parameters after I create the object?

The Parameters rollout appears in the Create panel during object creation. When you select an existing or previously created object, the Parameters rollout is no longer available in the Create tab. You must then change an object's parameters in the Modify panel. Select the object in the viewport, and then click the Modify tab next to the Create tab in the Command panel. Type the modifications that you want in the Parameters rollout. You can change the object name in any Command panel, but, if you select multiple objects, you can only change the object color for all selected objects.

What are Primitive objects?

3ds Max provides a group of basic 3D objects, called *Primitives,* that you can use as starting points for more complex objects. These Primitives include basic geometric objects, such as boxes, spheres, and cones. 3ds Max has two different subcategories of Primitives: Standard for basic objects, and Extended for more complex objects, such as capsules or prisms.

How do I end object creation?

When you create a continuous object, such as a line or wall, each mouse click creates a new segment for the object. To stop creating segments, right-click in the viewport. The object will consist of the segments that you have already created. To discontinue the creation process of any simple object, right-click to stop and delete any existing partial objects.

Create Objects with the Keyboard

Instead of drawing an object using the mouse, you can create an object using the Keyboard Entry rollout to define the precise size and location of the object. This rollout contains different fields, based on the object type that you draw. For example, when you create a box, the Keyboard Entry fields allow you to specify the location of the pivot point on each axis — X, Y, Z — and values for the length, width, and height of the box. To quickly create an object where the exact dimensions do not immediately matter, or you intend to change dimensions later, see the section "Create Objects with the Mouse."

The Keyboard Entry rollout displays in the Create panel after you select the object type that you want to create. Because the options in the Creation Method rollout may affect the fields in the Keyboard Entry rollout, you should first select a creation method. For example, with a Box object, when you select the Cube creation method, and you enter a value for one dimension, the other dimensions change to match. See the section "Understanding the Create Panel" for more information about creation methods.

Create Objects with the Keyboard

1. Click [icon].
   The Create Panel appears.
2. Click either [icon] or [icon].
   The Geometry or Shapes controls appear.
3. Click here and select an object subcategory.
   The available object types display in the Object Type rollout.
4. Click an object type.
5. Click a creation method (○ changes to ◉).
6. Click the Plus sign ([+]).

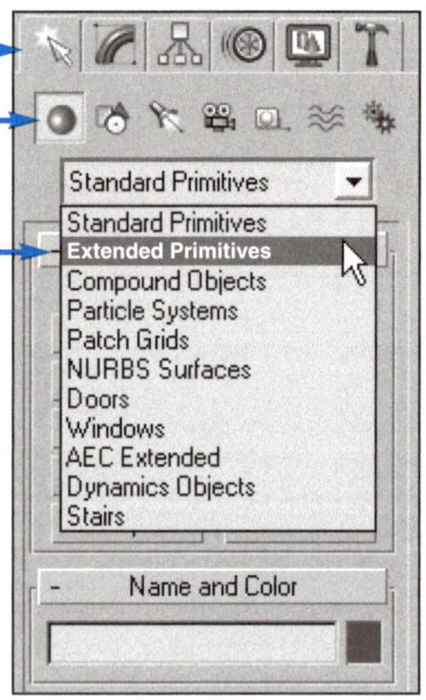

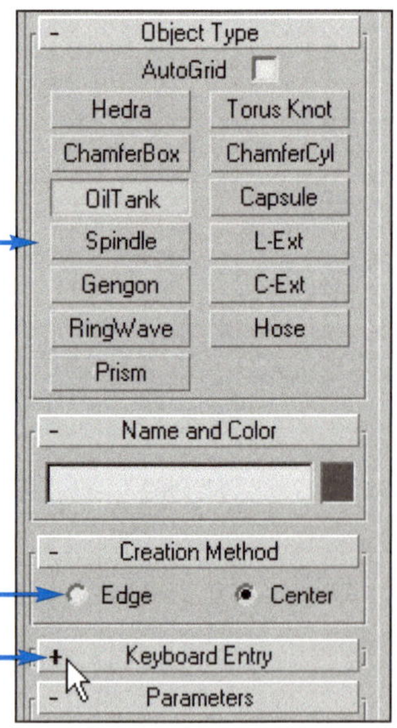

The Keyboard Entry rollout displays the fields for creating the selected object.

7 Type values for the object's location.

8 Type values for the object's parameters.

The fields vary, depending on the object type that you selected.

9 Click Create.

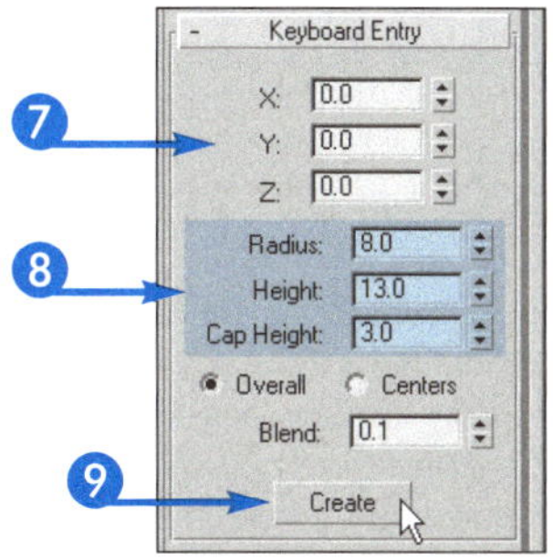

The object appears in the viewports with the parameters that you specified.

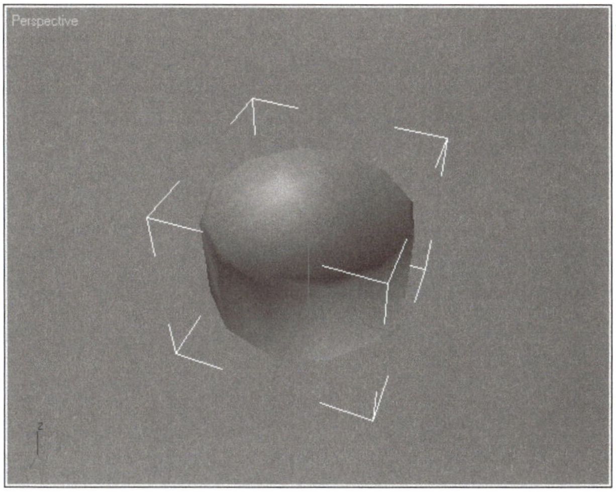

MASTER IT

What should I do if the Keyboard Entry rollout does not appear for the object type that I select?

Not all objects offer the Keyboard Entry rollout for object creation. If the Keyboard Entry rollout does not appear when you select an object, then you must use a combination of drawing and typing to define the object. To create an object without the Keyboard Entry rollout, first draw the object following the steps in the section "Create Objects with the Mouse." Next, type the dimensions that you want in the fields of the Parameters rollout.

Why does my box get wider instead of taller when I increase the Height value?

When you create a box with the mouse, the length and width create a base and are defined by the first click-drag-release that you perform. The height is determined by the distance that you move the mouse before clicking again, and is perpendicular to the base that you have already created. When you create a box in the Top or Perspective viewports, the base is in the XY plane and the height projects into the Z axis, as you would expect. However, if you create the box in the Front viewport, the base is in the XZ plane and the height projects into the Y axis.

Modify Object Parameters

Once you deselect an object, its parameters are no longer available in the Create panel. To update an object's parameters, such as its height, radius, or segmentation, you must select the object and then open the Modify panel in the Command panel area. The same Parameters rollout that appeared in the Create panel is now in the Modify panel.

To change the parameters of all instances of a cloned object, you must select and modify only one instance of the object. If you have modifiers applied on top of a primitive object, you must select the base level of the Modifier Stack to see the Parameters rollout for that primitive object. For more information on clones and Modifier Stacks, see Chapters 2 and 6, respectively.

MASTER IT

Why are all of my objects created with the same color?

▼ Under the default settings, 3ds Max assigns random colors to new objects. 3ds Max turns this off, but you can easily restore it. Select any object, and then click the color swatch to open the Object Color dialog box. Select the Assign Random Colors option (☐ changes to ☑) in the lower-left corner to turn the random color feature back on. Click OK. New objects are now created with random object colors.

Modify Object Parameters

1. Click .
2. Click to select the object that you want to modify.

Note: *For information and methods for selecting objects, see Chapter 2.*

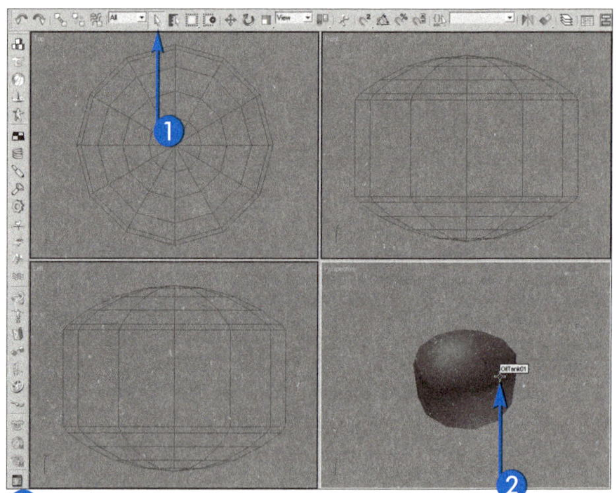

3. Click the Modify panel ().

   The Modify panel opens.

4. Type or select new values for the object's location and parameters.

   The changes are reflected in the viewports.

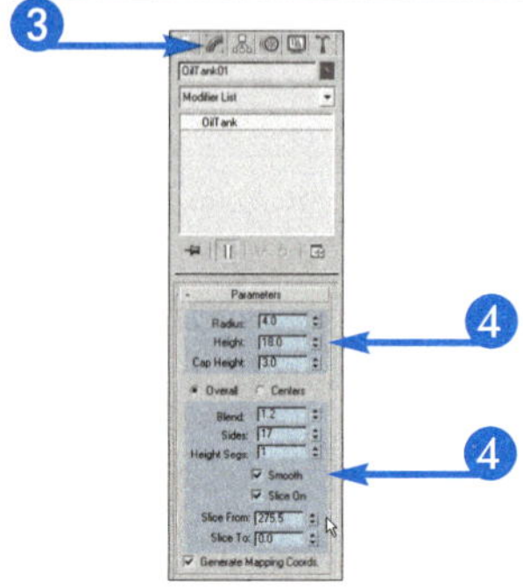

Convert Objects for Editing

Primitives are common elements in a scene and often need little or no alteration. You can use modifiers to add changes and qualities to the primitives that you cannot generate using the Parameters rollout. Once you take an object as far as you can with modifiers, you often need to continue modeling the object at its very basic level, that is, at the sub-objects that make up its structure. Depending on what the object is converted to, usually an editable mesh or editable poly, the sub-objects may consist of vertices, edges, faces, borders, polygons, and elements.

While it may seem counterintuitive to reduce a complex object to its basic components, converting — or *collapsing* — objects reduces the computer overhead required to maintain an intricate Modifier Stack. When you no longer need to alter the parameters of the entries in the Modifier Stack, you can convert the object to an editable mesh or an editable poly. If you want to maintain the parametric objects, you can apply an Edit Mesh or Edit Poly modifier instead of converting the object. This provides you with sub-object editing capability, but still gives you the freedom to change parameters. For more information on the Modifier Stack, see Chapter 6.

Convert Objects for Editing

1. Click [button].

Note: *See the section "Modify Object Parameters" for the location of this button.*

2. Click the object that you want to convert.
3. Right-click in the viewport.
4. In the quad menu, click Convert To.
5. Click Convert to Editable Poly.

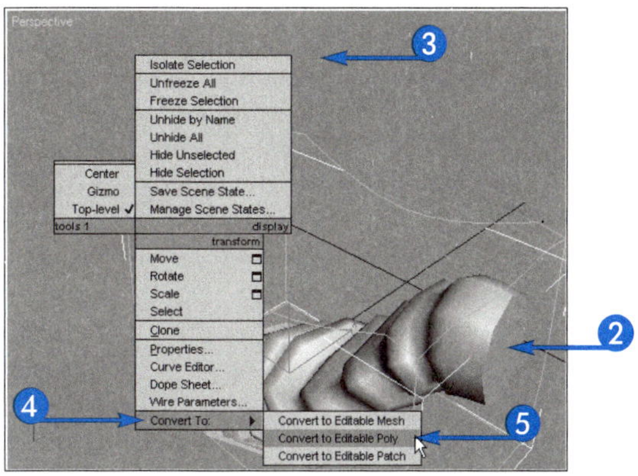

The object converts to an editable poly.

- The object's parameters are replaced with the editable poly controls.

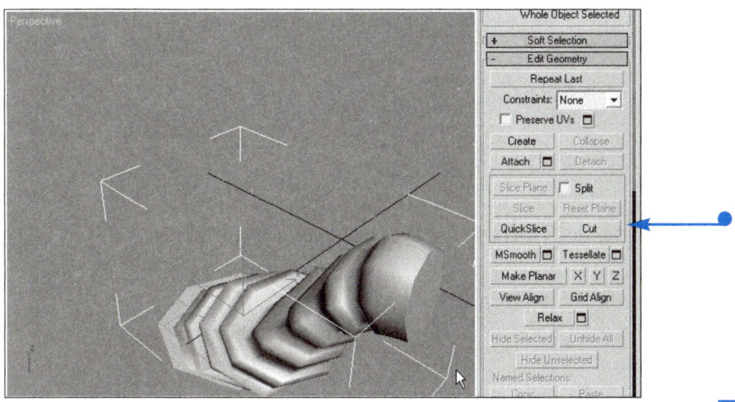

Understanding 2D Splines

You can use 2D objects as either a component to create 3D objects, or as a path for other objects to follow. Two-dimensional objects in 3ds Max come in two categories: Splines and NURBS curves. *Splines* are multi-segment curves with shapes that are defined by the location, type, and properties of the vertices located at the end of each segment. The number of steps that create each curved segment determine the smoothness of the segment. *NURBS*, or Non-Uniform Rational B-Splines, are mathematically generated curves that are based on their point locations. They are inherently smooth and do not need curvature added to their segments.

Parametric Spline Types

3ds Max has several parametric spline types and many common editable shapes that retain their original shape type when you modify parameter values. One exception is the Line object, a free-formed editable spline, which you modify by editing and transforming its sub-objects: Vertices, Edges, and Splines. Although 2D parametric shapes are great for creating splines, they lack the intricate shapes needed in a model or path. You control a parametric spline's sub-objects by converting the shape into an editable spline or adding the Edit Spline Modifier to it; you can only modify the parameters of a shape, but an editable spline allows you to add, move, rotate, and scale any selected sub-objects. While both options give you equal control, when you delete the Edit Spline Modifier, you leave the spline intact, while the editable spline option requires less memory to run. This chapter uses the editable spline option in its examples. For more about using the Modifier Stack, see Chapter 6.

Understanding Vertices

Vertices are points in space that terminate the ends of segments. There are four types: Bezier, Bezier Corner, Corner, and Smooth. Bezier and Bezier Corner have two tangent handles at each vertex, with handle length and location determining the curve's smoothness. Bezier handles are always a straight line; moving one handle causes the other to move reciprocally. You move the handles of the Bezier Corner independently. The Corner vertex type has no tangent handles, and the segments enter it as a straight line. The Smooth vertex type also has no tangent handles, and it creates a smooth transition of the segments through the vertex.

Understanding Segments

Segments are the portions of a spline that connect one vertex to the next. Steps make up each segment and they define how many straight lines create the segment. A 90-degree curve in a segment using one step creates a right angle, while three steps create a somewhat smoother transition.

Understanding Spline Sub-Objects

You can make a spline the sub-object of another spline. Spline sub-objects are contiguous segments that form an open or closed shape. A spline object can consist of one or more non-contiguous spline sub-objects. You can edit and transform the spline at the sub-object level. Depending on what sub-objects you modify, the editable spline option and Edit Spline Modifier display rollouts with paramenters. You select sub-objects with any of the selection methods, or with the Soft Selection option. Soft Selection creates an area of influence near any selected sub-objects, and applies, to a lesser degree, any transforms to the selected sub-objects.

Rollouts for 2D Spline Creation

You can use various rollouts in the Command panels to create splines.

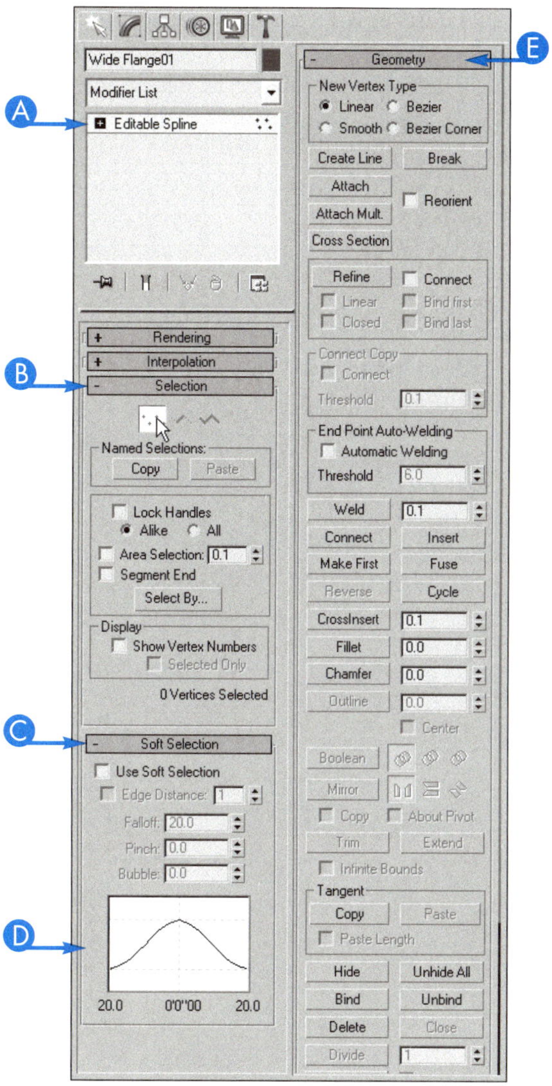

A Editable Spline

The type of object that is created when a parametric shape is converted into an editable spline. The icon for the selected sub-object, if any, displays to the right of the object name.

B Selection Rollout

Lets you select the part of the spline that you want to edit. You can use the three sub-object buttons – Vertex ( ), Segment ( ), and Spline ( ) – to select a sub-object to modify. Selected sub-objects appear in red, and unselected sub-objects in white. Selected sub-object information appears in the viewport and at the bottom of the Selection rollout.

C Soft Selection Rollout

The ìUse Soft Selectio n" option allows you to ease the effect of a transform that is applied to sub-objects that are near any selected sub-objects.

D Soft Selection Curve

A graphical representation of how the soft selection area of influence is applied to the shape.

E Geometry Rollout

This powerful rollout provides functions for editing splines, including adding, welding, breaking, and outlining splines. The rollout changes, depending on your sub-object selection.

Create a Parametric Spline

3ds Max has a library of parametric, two-dimensional shape objects that you can create with a series of mouse actions. You can immediately adjust each parametric object using the parameter fields in the object's Parameters rollout in the Create panel. However, once you deselect and then reselect the object, you must access the Parameters rollout through the Modify panel.

Splines are grouped into two categories, Splines and Extended Splines, which you can access in the Command panel. The Splines category contains common shapes such as circles, rectangles, and arcs, as well as less common but useful star shapes, multi-sided NGons, and the Helix shape, which extends a curve perpendicular to the plane in which it is created. The Extended Splines category contains design visualization shapes that correspond to the cross section of the steel components commonly found in construction projects. You can quickly create Columns, Angles, and Channel shapes by extruding Extended Splines shapes. See the section "Add Height to a Shape with the Extrude Modifier" for information on extrusions.

Create a Parametric Spline

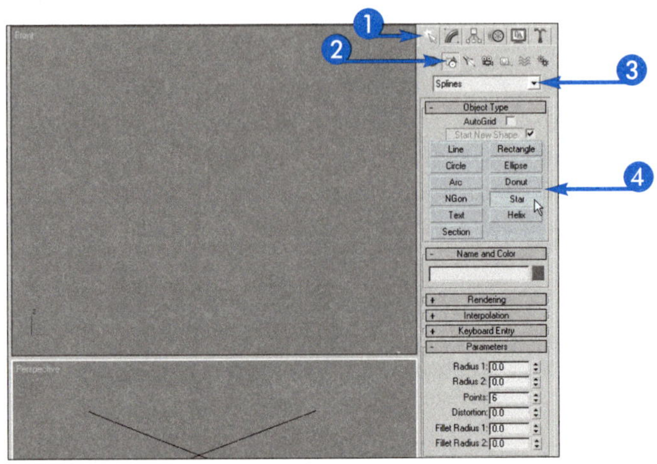

1. Click the Create panel tab ( ).

   The Create panel appears.

2. Click the Shapes button ( ).
3. Click here and select a spline category.

   The Object Type rollout displays the available object types.

4. Click an object type button.

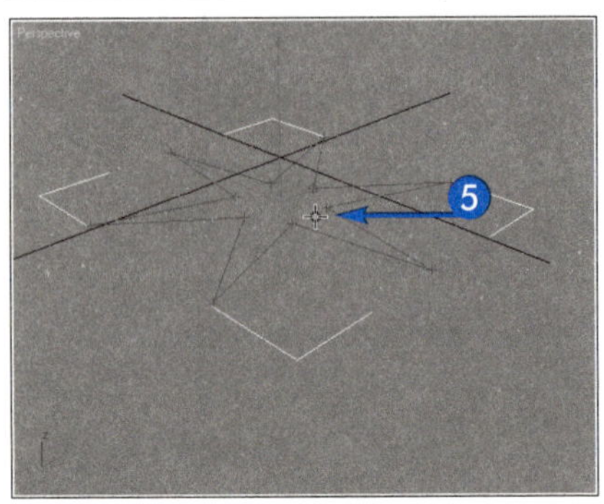

5. Click, drag, and then release the mouse in a viewport.

   If required, drag and then click to complete the object.

   The object is created in the viewport.

6 Type to change the values in the Parameters rollout.

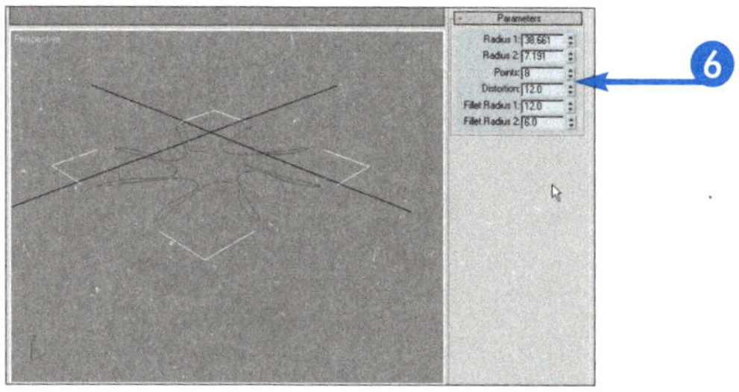

The object updates to reflect the changes.

7 To make the spline renderable, click the Plus sign (⊞) to expand the Rendering rollout.

8 Click the Enable In Renderer option (☐ changes to ☑).

9 Click the Quick Render button.

The 2D spline renders.

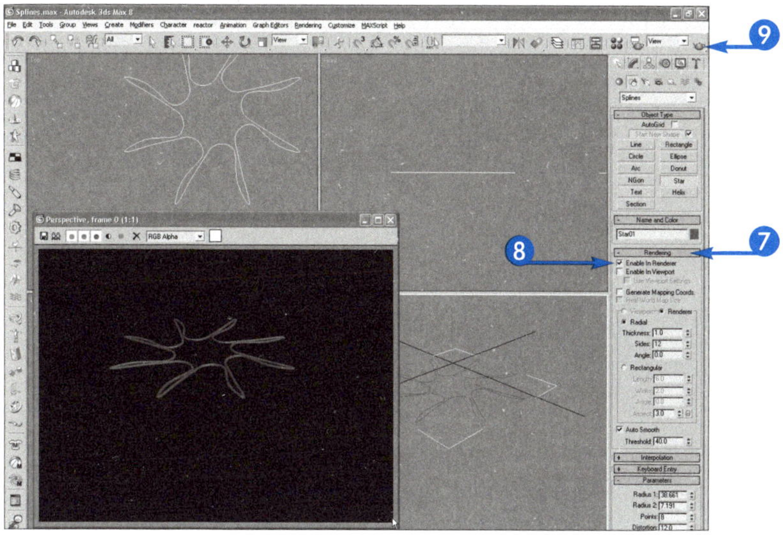

MASTER IT

Can I change the appearance of the rendered spline?

Yes. By default, the renderable splines appear as if they have a curved, tubular structure with a circular cross section. You can change the diameter and smoothness of the cross section by changing the Thickness and Angle values. Selecting Rectangular changes the cross section to a four-sided polygon with user-definable Length and Width values. Renderable splines can display mapped materials in the same way that true geometry objects do. Select the "Generate Mapping Coords." option to direct 3ds Max to spread a map once along the length of the spline and once along the cross section.

My curved shapes appear jagged. How can I fix this?

There are no truly curved shapes; all splines are made from straight line segments that connect vertices together. To give a more curvaceous appearance to your spline, you need to increase the number of segments, or steps, between each vertex. You can do this by expanding the Interpolation rollout and increasing the Steps value. The "Optimize" option in the Interpolation rollout causes 3ds Max to automatically remove unnecessary steps in straight segments. The Adaptive option sets the proper number of steps for the spline to result in smooth curves.

Create a Line Object

The parametric shapes available from the Object Type rollouts are not always acceptable for certain tasks. For example, there is no parametric shape available that represents the fluted cross section of a column, or a particular path that a roller coaster needs to follow. To create a free-form shape, you can use the Line tool located in the Object Type rollout.

Using the Line tool, you set the location of each vertex in the shape. You define the type of vertex by the type of click that sets each location; a simple click creates a Corner type vertex where the segments entering and exiting it are straight. A click, drag, and release creates a vertex with curved segments entering and exiting it. The farther you drag the mouse, the smoother the resultant curve. The settings in the Creation Method rollout define this behavior.

To create a closed spline, ensure that the last point clicked is at the same location as the first. When you click near the first vertex, a dialog box appears, asking if you want to close the spline. See the section "Edit an Existing Spline" for more information.

Create a Line Object

1. Click .

   The Create panel displays.

2. Click .
3. Click here and, if necessary, select Splines.

   The Object Type rollout displays the available object types.

4. Click Line.

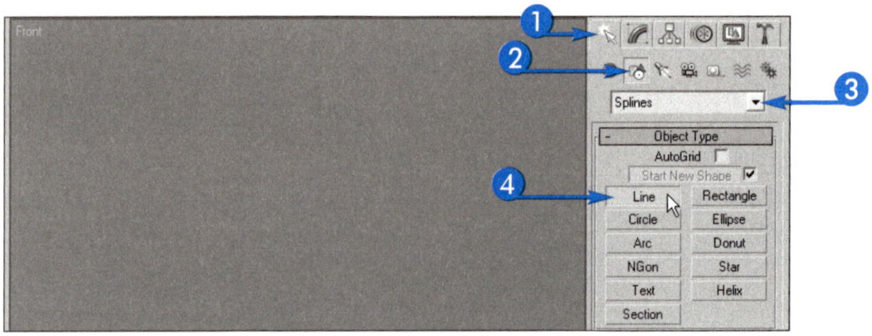

5. Without dragging, click in several places in a viewport to set the vertex locations.

   A line is created, with straight segments between the vertices.

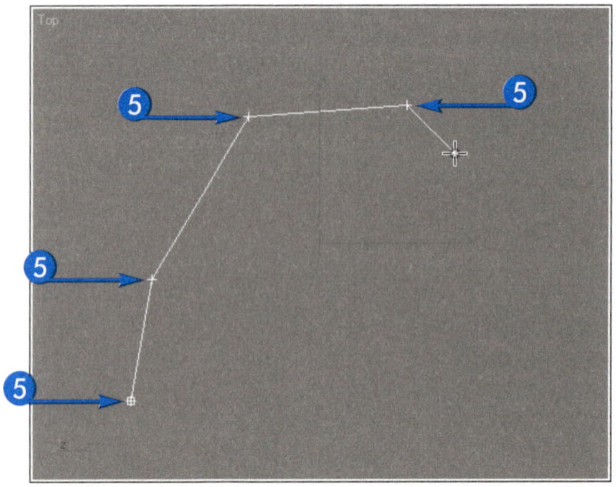

6 Continue clicking to create vertices, but drag and release after each click.

The line continues, but with curved segments between the vertices.

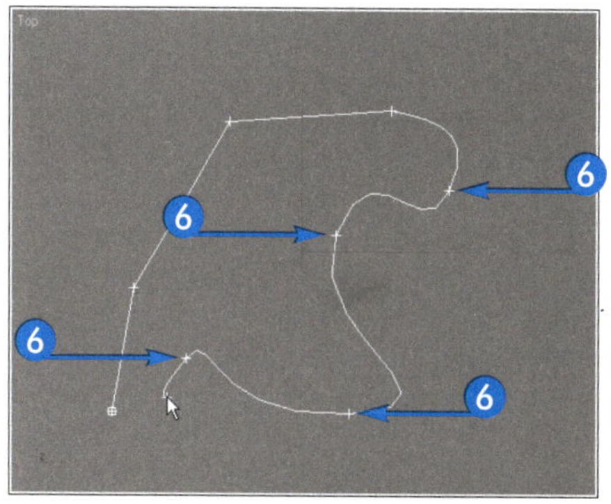

7 Click the first vertex that you created.

A dialog box appears, asking whether the spline should be closed.

8 Click Yes.

The spline closes.

The Line tool remains active and ready for you to draw another line.

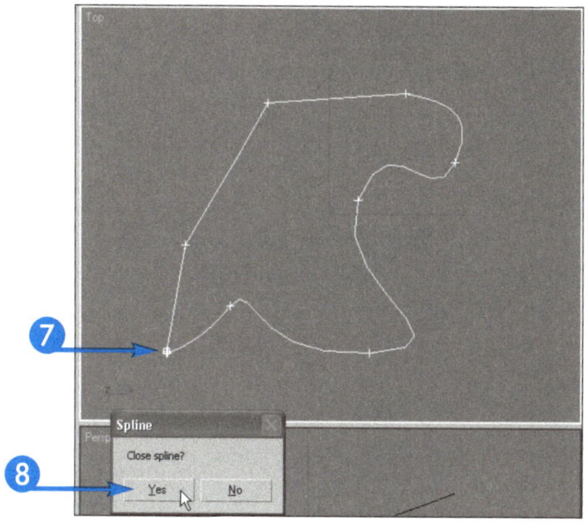

MASTER IT

How can I be more precise when I place my vertex locations?

▼ There are a couple of solutions for adding precision to your vertex locations. First, if the vertex locations are relative to objects in the scene, then you can turn on and then activate the object snaps. This causes the vertex to snap to certain object features, such as mid-points or face centers, when the cursor is in close proximity to them. You can draw lines with the Shift key held down to create straight lines in 90-degree increments. You can also enter coordinate values in the Keyboard Entry rollout, and then click Add Point to generate the vertices. You cannot switch between manual and keyboard entry methods when creating a single spline.

Can I change the types of vertices that are created when I click the mouse?

▼ Yes. By default, 3ds Max creates Corner vertices when you click, and Bezier curves when you click and drag, with the Line tool. You can change the default vertex types in the Creation Method rollout. With the Line tool active, click to expand the Creation Method rollout. In the Initial Type section, select Smooth to change the type of vertices that are created when you simply click in a vertex. Select Corner or Smooth in the Drag Type section to change the type of vertices that are created when you click and drag to create a vertex.

Edit an Existing Spline

Splines are 2D shape objects made up of vertices, segments, and spline sub-objects. You can use splines as components for building 3D objects or as animation paths for other objects. You use the tools for the sub-objects to make modifications to any spline object. For example, you may want to make an artistic "E" shape by moving and modifying the vertices of a parametric Text object. See the section "Understanding 2D Splines" for information about sub-objects.

You can use the Vertex option to move or change the vertices, or individual points, on your spline. The vertices appear as crosses on the object, while the spline's first vertex appears as a cross inside a box. Selected vertices are red, non-selected vertices are white, and information about the selected vertices displays at the bottom of the Selection rollout.

Depending on their type, you can modify the vertices of an editable spline by adjusting their tangent handles to control their shape, or move them within the scene. You can use a quad menu with the option to change the vertex type.

CD FILE: The EditSpline.max file is available on the CD-ROM for you to practice creating editable splines.

Edit an Existing Spline

Convert to an Editable Spline

1. Select a spline object.
2. Right-click to open the quad menu.
3. Click Convert To.
4. Click Convert to Editable Spline.

   The object is converted to an editable spline, and the editable spline rollouts appears in the Modify panel.

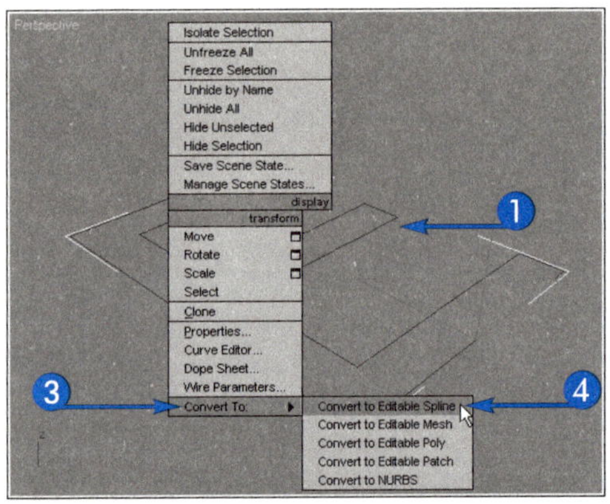

Move Vertices

5. Click the Vertex button ( ).
6. Select the vertices that you want to move.

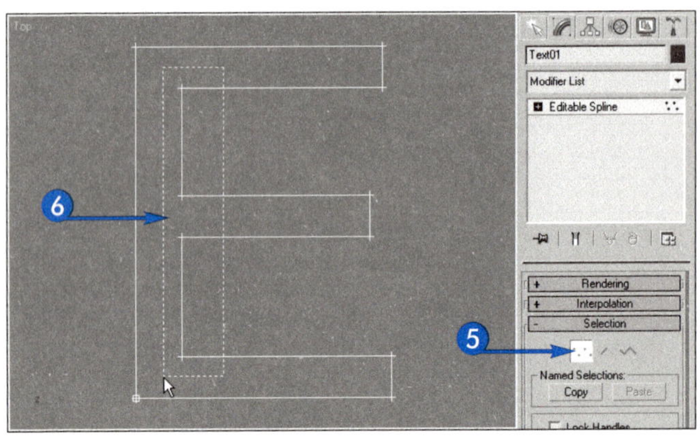

Selected vertices appear in red, and the number of selected vertices appears at the bottom of the Selection rollout.

7. Click the Select and Move button ( ).
8. Click and drag a vertex.

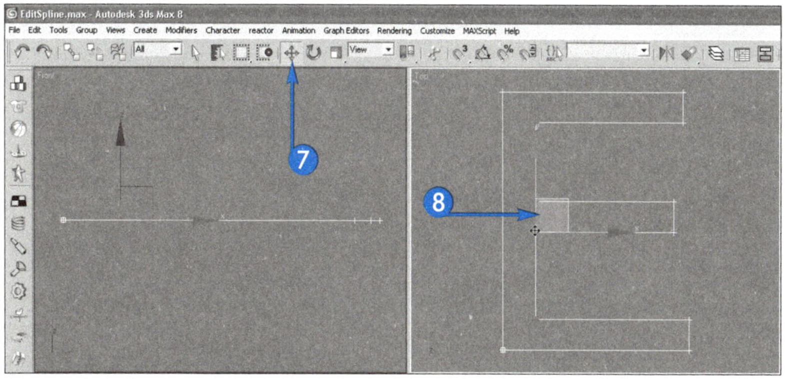

The selected vertices move.

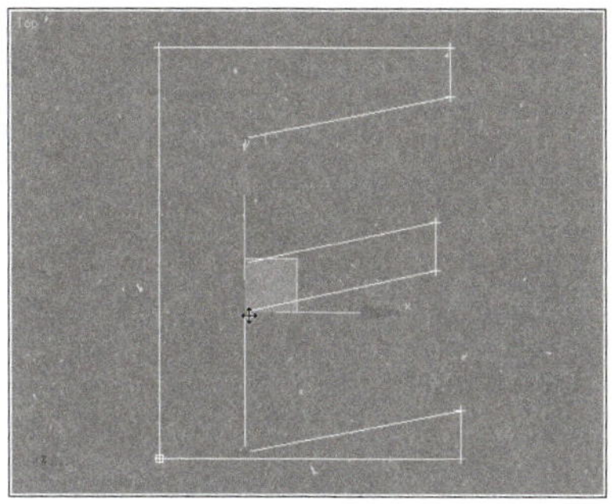

Can I change the vertex type?

▼ The type of vertex for a spline object depends on the object and how it was created. For example, while each vertex in a rectangle is a Bezier Corner, the vertices in an ellipse are all Bezier types. To change a vertex's type, select it and right-click to open the quad menu. In the quad menu that appears, select the vertex type to which you want to convert the selected vertices. You can select Bezier, Smooth, Corner, or Bezier Corner. The Bezier and Bezier Corner options have tangent handles to control the curvature of the segments entering the vertex. The Smooth and Corner options do not.

How do vertex handles work?

▼ Vertex handles appear as green lines, with boxes at the ends, that protrude from Bezier and Bezier Corner vertices. To make a vertex sharper, you move the handle ends closer to the vertex, and to make it smoother, you move the handles farther away. To change the angle of the segments entering the vertex, you move the handles perpendicular to the vertex. Bezier handles act as if they are a single object, and moving one perpendicularly moves the other in the opposite direction. Use the Shift key to move a single Bezier handle without affecting its corresponding handle on the other side of a vertex. Bezier Corner tangent handles can move independently of each other.

continued

Edit an Existing Spline

(Continued)

Instead of working with individual vertices, you can edit a segment or a spline sub-object. You generally work with spline segments when the vertex arrangement is correct but the segments themselves, and their associated vertices, need to be edited or you need to break a segment so that you can open a closed spline. You work with spline sub-objects when you must transform an entire spline or when you are creating compound shapes. The Geometry rollout is most often used with segment and spline sub-objects, and you can even add vertices to the shape at either sub-object level.

When you select the spline sub-object, your edits affect the entire spline. You can also select multiple splines at once and make changes that affect all of the splines.

At both the Segment and Spline sub-object level, you can detach a portion of the shape to become a separate shape object itself. At the Spline sub-object level, you can use the outline tool to create an offset version of a spline at a specific distance from the original. The new spline becomes another sub-object spline of the original shape.

CD FILE: The EditSpline.max file is available on the CD-ROM for you to practice creating editable splines.

Edit an Existing Spline *(continued)*

Break a Segment

1. Follow steps 1 to 4 in the subsection "Convert to an Editable Spline" on the previous page.
2. Click the Segment button ( ).
3. Click to select the segment that you want to break.

   The selected segment appears in red.
4. In the Geometry rollout, click Break.
5. Click at the point where you want to break the segment.

   A vertex is created.
6. Click .
7. Click and drag to move the new, broken segment to separate the vertices.

   The segment is broken.

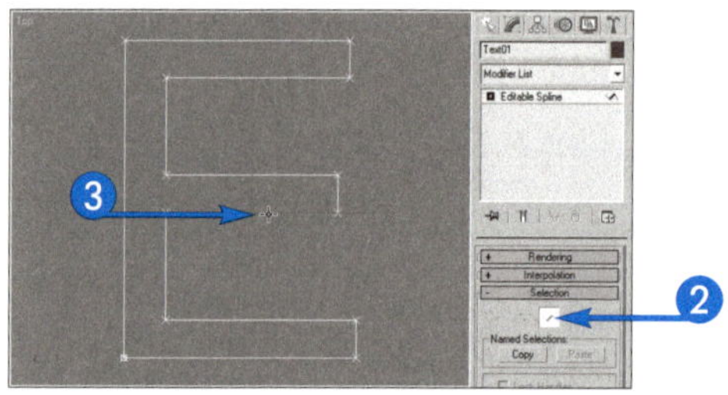

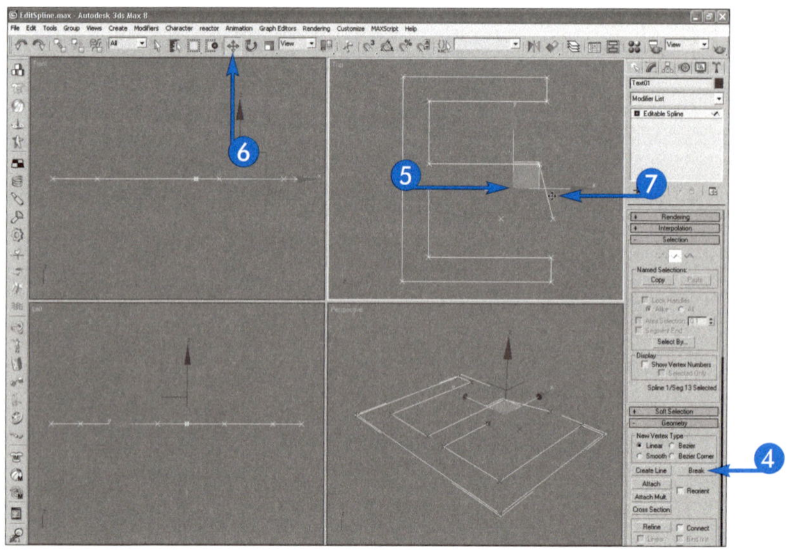

Outline a Spline

1. Follow steps 1 to 4 in the subsection "Convert to an Editable Spline" on the previous page.
2. Click the Spline button (![]).
3. Select the spline that you want to outline.

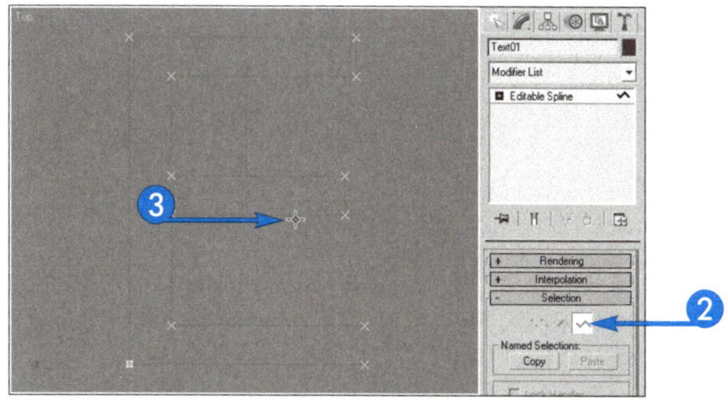

The selected spline displays in red.

4. In the Geometry rollout, click the Center option (☐ changes to ☑).
5. In the Outline field, specify the offset amount.

The outline spline is created with the specified offset amount.

The Center option replaces the original spline with the outline spline.

If you turn off Center, the original spline remains, and the outline is offset from it.

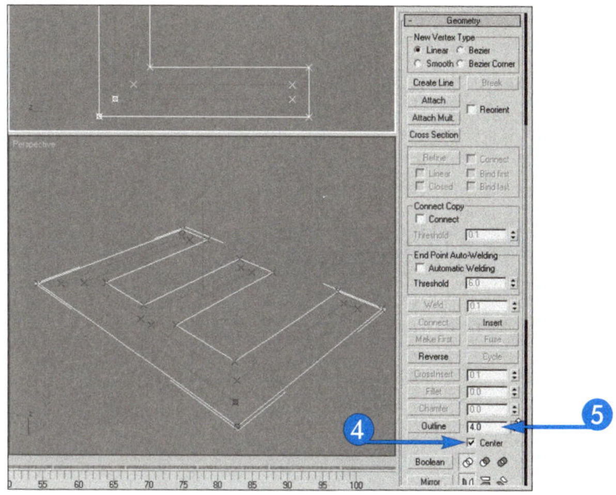

Can I combine splines to be one object?

▼ Yes, just as easily as you can detach a segment or spline from a spline object, you can attach one as well. With a spline selected, you can click Attach in the Geometry rollout, and then click any splines in the scene. Only splines can be attached in this manner. If you attach a spline that is still parametric, such as a Circle, then it loses all of its parametric controls. To pick the names of available splines from a list, click Attach Multiple to open the Attach Multiple dialog box.

How do I change the segment line type?

▼ When you select a segment, you can change the segment's type from a curve to a straight line, or vice versa. The segment type is based upon the initial spline object. For example, if you created an ellipse, then 3ds Max makes your segments curved. To change the line type, select the segment, right-click to display the quad menu, and then select Line. This creates a straight segment between the two vertices. You can also use the Curve and Line options with a spline to change all of the segments in the spline from lines to curves, or vice versa.

Create Multi-Spline Shapes

You can combine different spline objects together to create a single multi-spline shape object. This is ideal when you have multiple shapes that you want to treat as one object so that you can transform or modify them. A multiple-shaped object does not require that the shapes be adjacent or attached to each other. In fact, the various shapes can be located anywhere within your scene or nested within each other.

You can combine shapes together, either by creating new shape objects or by combining existing shapes. To add a new shape to an existing shape, you must deselect the Start New Shape option before you create the shape. By default, 3ds Max selects this option when you create a new shape. When you deselect the option, the new shape that you create becomes a part of a selected shape object.

You can combine existing shapes in your scene using the Modify panel. However, you must make the object to which you want to attach other objects into an editable spline, or you must apply the Edit Spline Modifier.

Create Multi-Spline Shapes

Add New Shapes as a Single Shape

1. Open the Object Type rollout in the Create panel.

Note: *To open the Object Type rollout, follow steps 1 to 3 in the section "Create a Line Object."*

2. Deselect the Start New Shape option (☑ changes to ☐).
3. Create a spline.
4. Create a second spline.

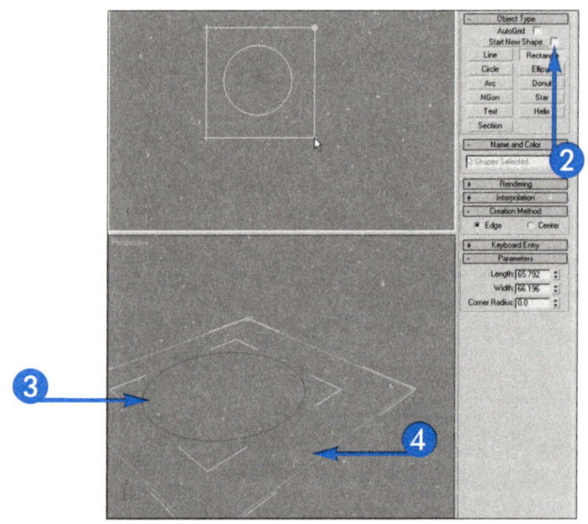

5. Click the Select Object button ( ) to terminate the command.
6. Click the Select By Name button ( ).

- The Select Objects dialog box opens to reveal that only one object was created and selected, using the first spline's name.

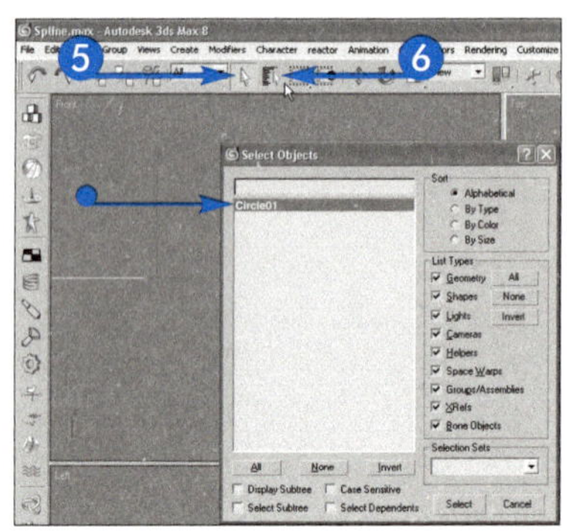

Combine Existing Shapes

1. Select a shape.
2. Right-click to open the quad menu.
3. Click Convert To.
4. Click Convert to Editable Spline.

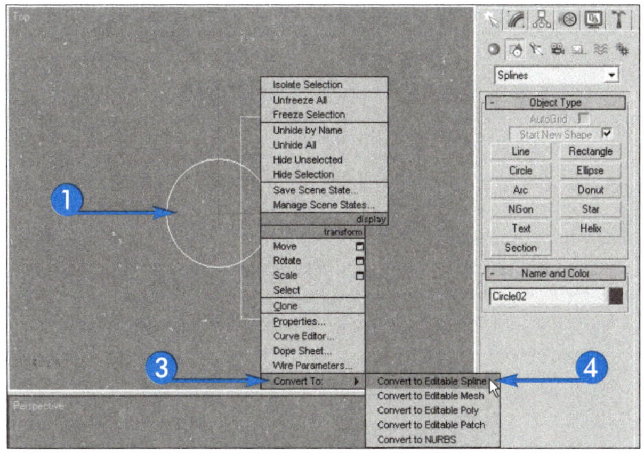

The Editable Spline rollouts appears in the Modify tab.

5. Click Attach in the Geometry rollout.
6. Click the spline that you want to attach.

The splines are attached and become a single spline.

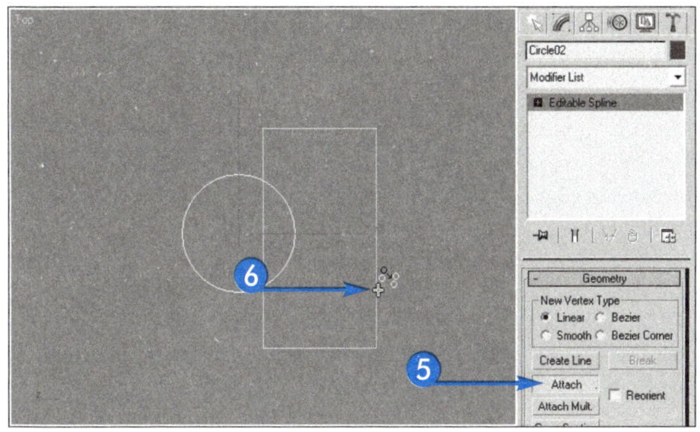

PART II

MASTER IT

What type of shape do I make when I create a multi-spline shape?

When you add a new shape to an existing shape from the Create panel, 3ds Max converts the combined shape into an editable spline. This occurs because the new shape that you create is no longer one of the spline objects; it is a combination of multiple spline objects and cannot be parametric. You can convert any spline object to an editable spline by right-clicking the object to display a quad menu. In the quad menu, click Convert To, and then click Convert to Editable Spline.

Can I separate splines from a multi-spline shape?

Yes. To separate a spline, select the multi-spline shape and then click the Modify Panel button ( ) to open the Modify panel. Click the Spline button ( ) to access the Spline sub-object level. Select the spline that you want to detach. Click Detach near the bottom of the Geometry rollout. In the Detach dialog box that opens, enter the name that you want your detached object to have. Click OK to detach the object, and then click the to exit the sub-object level.

Create Complex Shapes Using Spline Booleans

You can use the Line tool to create free-form spline shapes, and the Attach command to combine multiple splines into a single shape, but neither allows you to combine shapes into a single, contiguous spline. This is where Spline Booleans come in. Booleans are a set of functions that are used to trim, or combine, the areas of the distinct splines in a multi-spline shape.

There are three Spline Boolean functions: Union, Subtraction, and Intersection. Union combines two spline sub-objects and deletes any edges that were in contact with both splines. Subtraction deletes one spline and any area shared by both splines. The Intersection function retains the area shared by both objects and deletes any area and edges that are not shared. Spline Boolean functions can only be used at the Spline sub-object level of a multi-spline shape, and not with two separate spline objects.

See the section "Create Multi-Spline Shapes" for information on combining distinct splines into a single shape. For information on using the Boolean functions with geometry objects rather than splines see Chapter 6.

CD FILE: The SplineBoolean.max file is available on the CD-ROM for you to practice using Spline Booleans.

Create Complex Shapes Using Spline Booleans

Using the Boolean Union Function

1. After selecting the shape to which you want to apply the Boolean Union function, click the Spline button ( ) in the Selection rollout.

Note: *See the section "Edit an Existing Spline" for information on selecting sub-objects.*

2. Select one of the Splines to be united.
3. Click the Union button ( ).
4. Click Boolean.
5. Click the second spline to be united.

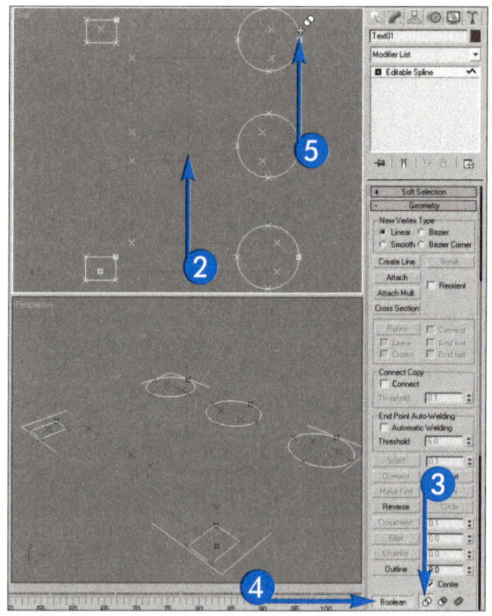

The splines are united, and the shared edges are deleted.

6. Repeat the command as required.

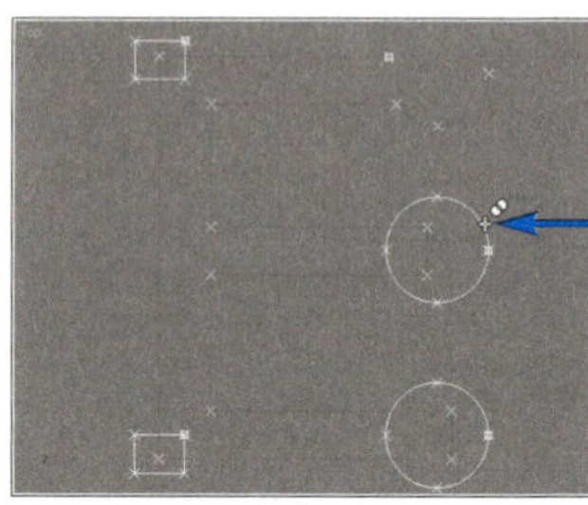

Using the Subtraction Function

1. After selecting the shape to which you want to apply the Boolean Union function, click in the Selection rollout.

Note: *See the section "Edit an Existing Spline" for information on selecting sub-objects.*

2. Select the Spline to be retained.
3. Click the Subtraction button ( ).
4. Click Boolean.
5. Click the spline to be subtracted.

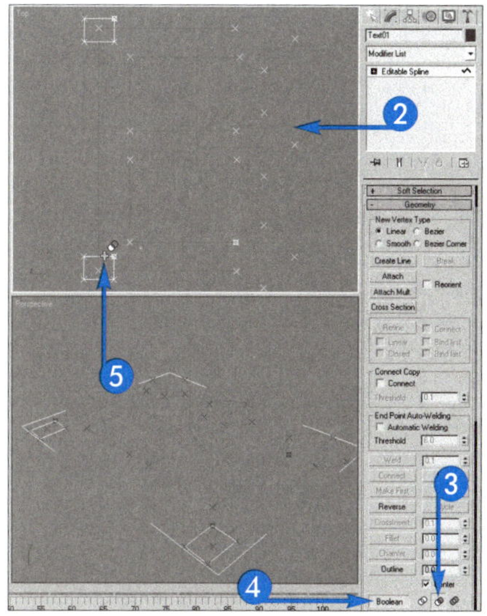

The second spline is deleted, along with any shared area.

6. Repeat steps 4 and 5 as required.

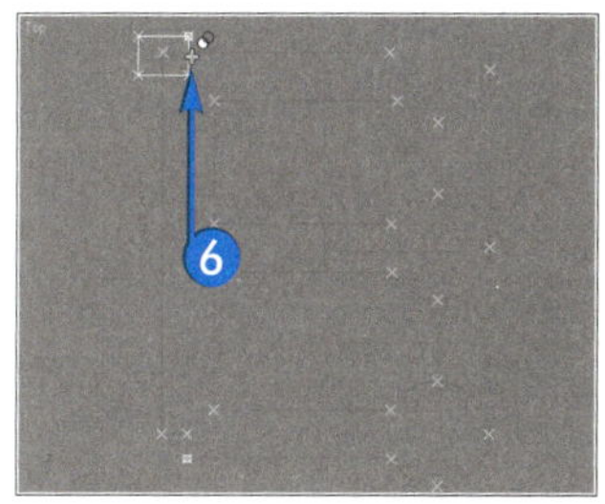

MASTER IT

My Boolean operations are not working. What is the problem?

- If you are working with a multi-spline shape, and not separate splines, then you may be working with open splines. 3ds Max requires that both of the splines you use with Boolean functions be closed so that they have an area with which to work. To quickly close a spline, go to the Spline sub-object level, expand the Geometry rollout if necessary, and then click Close. A new segment is added between the two end vertices.

My multi-spline shapes that I imported from another program appear messy. How can I clean them up?

- If you have spline-end vertices that stop short before they intersect an edge, then you can use the Extend command in the Geometry rollout to lengthen the segment until it does. If one spline's segment crosses over another, then you can use the Trim command to shorten it to the proper length. To introduce a curve or cant into a sharp intersection, enter values into the Fillet or Chamfer fields in the Geometry rollout. All of the solutions listed only work with sub-object splines.

Add Height to a Shape with the Extrude Modifier

You can use the Extrude modifier to turn any 2D shape into a 3D object. The Extrude modifier does this by giving the object height perpendicular to the orientation of the shape. To extrude the shape, 3ds Max creates a copy of the spline at the specified distance and then connects the two splines with faces.

You can modify your extruded figure in different ways. For example, specifying the number of segments that 3ds Max uses to define the object's height adds additional faces to the sides of the object.

When you extrude a shape that is open, meaning that the segments do not form a continuous path, the Extrude modifier creates an object with walls that have no thickness, and the ends of the object are not capped. When you close the shape, the ends are capped to form an object with volume. When there are closed spline sub-objects nested inside of one another, 3ds Max alternately caps every other spline. For example, if you extrude the letter "A," then the triangle at the top of the letter is a void.

CD FILE

The Extrude.max file is available on the CD-ROM for you to practice applying the Extrude modifier.

Add Height to a Shape with the Extrude Modifier

1. Select a shape.
2. Click the Modify panel button ( ).

   The Modify panel appears.
3. Click here and select Extrude.

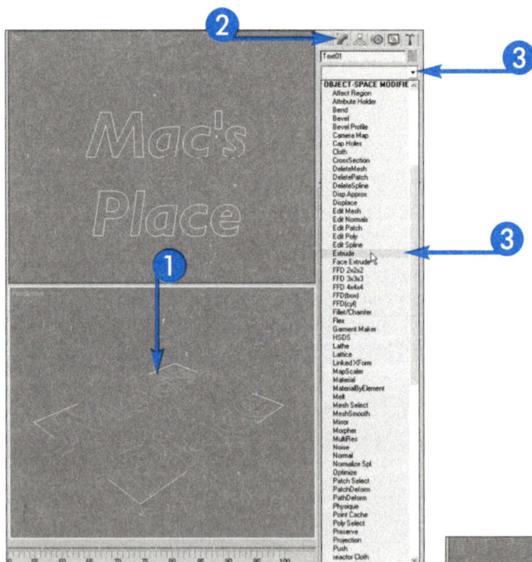

The Extrude Modifier rollouts appears on the Modify panel, and the object extrudes.

4. In the Amount field, type the number of units that you want to extrude the object.
   - The height changes to reflect the Amount value.

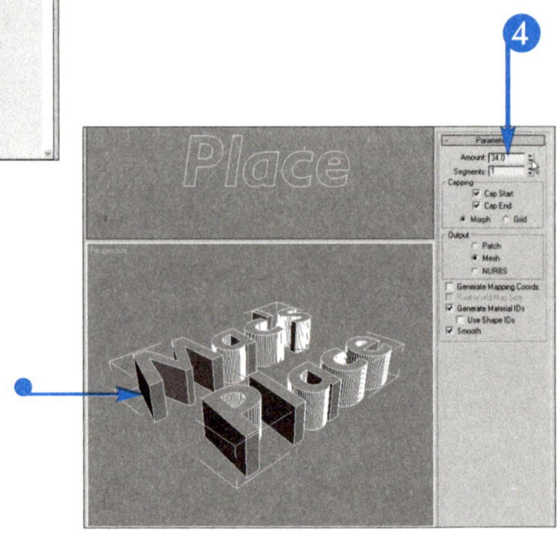

5 In the Segments field, type the number of segments that define the height.

- 3ds Max adds the specified number of segments.
- You can also deselect the Cap Start and Cap End options (☑ changes to ☐) to make the object hollow, with a 2-sided material applied.
- You can also click a different option in the Output section.

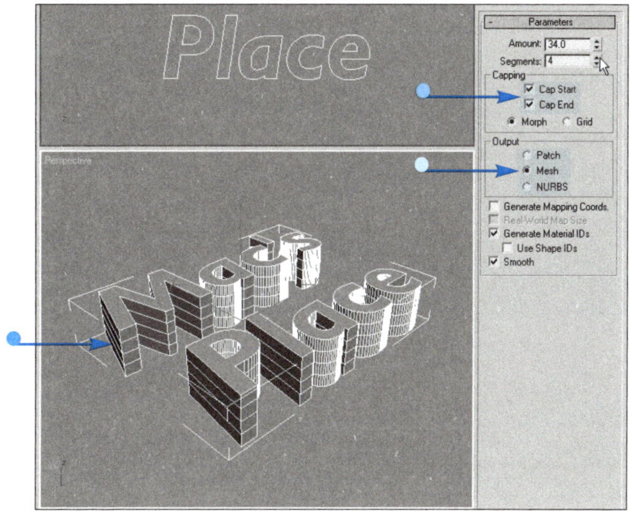

MASTER IT

Why does the back of my object disappear when I turn off the capping?

3ds Max objects are not solid — they are hollow. When you remove the caps on an extruded shape, you see the back faces of the newly exposed sides. By default, 3ds Max only renders one side of each face, as defined by a directional vector called the *face normal*. In the case of extruded splines and most other objects, the face normal is oriented outward from the center of the object. To see both sides of a face, you need to apply a 2-Sided material to the object. For information on the Material Editor, see Chapter 14.

What is the difference between the Extrude and Face Extrude Modifiers?

The Extrude Modifier works with 2D shapes to project their cross section and create a 3D object. You cannot use this modifier on objects that are already 3D. The Face Extrude Modifier is used to extrude a selection of faces perpendicular to the surface of a 3D object. This functionality also exists in the Edit Poly Modifier. However, if only a face extrusion is required, then the Face Extrude Modifier uses less memory to accomplish the task. For information about the Edit Poly Modifier, see Chapter 6.

Add Height to a Shape with the Bevel Modifier

You can use the Bevel modifier to convert a shape into a 3D object with beveled or chamfered edges. You most often use this effect to create extrusions with soft transitions between perpendicular faces.

You can bevel a shape upward, defining three different levels by height, each with its own Outline value. A positive value grows, while a negative value shrinks, the original shape. An Outline value of zero holds the shape's size constant, while a non-zero value causes it to transition from one level to the next. To create an object with short, beveled edges, use small Height values for Levels 1 and 3, and a larger value for Level 2. Level 1 should have a positive Outline value, to create the initial enlarging curve, and Level 3 should have a reciprocal negative Outline value to create symmetry.

By default, Bevel creates sharp-edged bevels. To round the bevel edges, you can apply the Smooth Across Levels option.

Avoid creating self-intersecting, and therefore invalid, shapes using the Outline values. When changing these values, watch for crossing splines that are formed through the Outline.

CD FILE: The Extrude.max file is available on the CD-ROM for you to practice using the Bevel modifier.

Add Height to a Shape with the Bevel Modifier

1. Select a shape.
2. Click .

   The Modify panel appears.
3. Click and select Bevel.

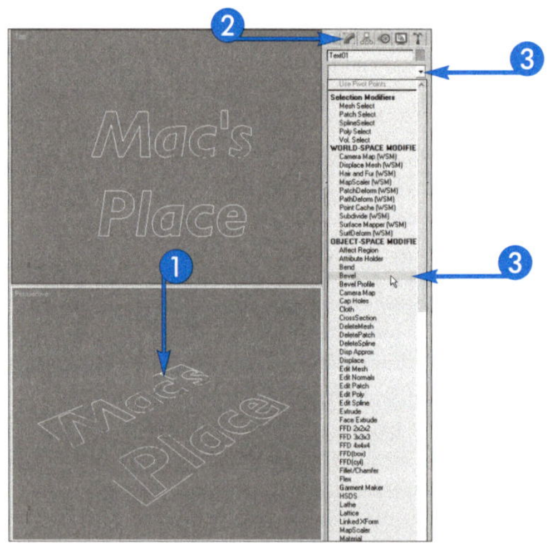

The Bevel modifier rollouts display in the Modify panel, and the object appears capped.

4. Type positive Height and Outline values for Level 1.
5. Click Level 2 and Level 3 (☐ changes to ☑).
6. Type a positive Height value for Level 2.
7. Type a positive Height and a negative Outline value for Level 3.

- The object reflects the Bevel settings.

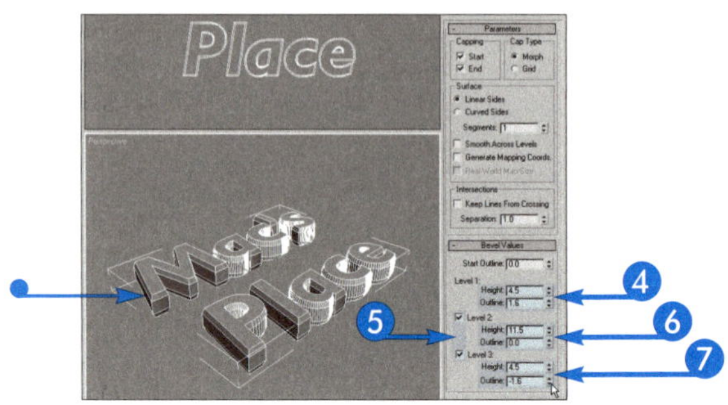

8 Click the Curved Sides option (○ changes to ◉).

9 Increase the Segments by typing a value to smooth each level.

10 Click the Smooth Across Levels option (☐ changes to ☑).

11 Click the Quick Render button (🫖).

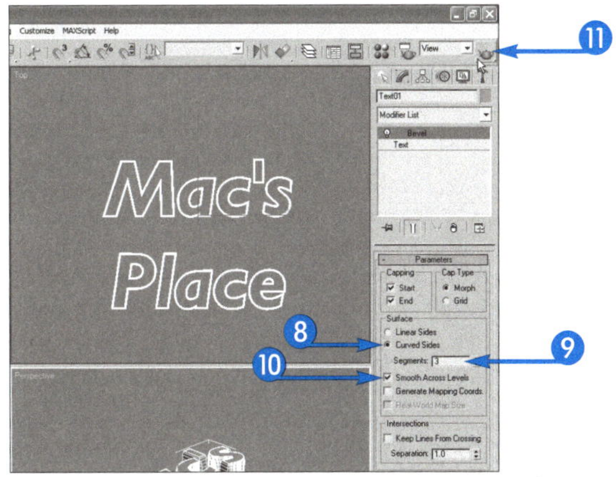

3ds Max renders the scene.

MASTER IT

Why do my edges appear to overlap, and why do some of my faces disappear?

The overlapping or missing faces can be caused by the bevels creating faces that are too large for narrow passages or loops in the shape. To avoid this condition, select the "Keep Lines From Crossing" option (☐ changes to ☑), located in the Parameters rollout. This option inserts extra vertices along the perimeter of the shape and substitutes straight segments for the sharp corners. Your edges may also overlap if they are too close together. You can avoid this by entering a value in the Separation field in the Parameters rollout.

How should I cap my beveled object?

You can place a cap at the start and/or end of your beveled object to terminate it with surfaces. The Morph Cap Type option (○ changes to ◉) creates faces that are designed to work well with the Morpher Modifier. The Grid Cap Type option (○ changes to ◉) creates cap faces in a matrix pattern that tend to render and deform better than faces created with the Morph option. Failing to create caps may result in apparently transparent faces. See the section "Add Height to a Shape with the Extrude Modifier" for an explanation of what is happening.

Create a Radial Object with the Lathe Modifier

You can use the Lathe Modifier to create a circular 3D object from any spline. When you lathe a spline, 3ds Max rotates the spline around a selected axis to create an object with a circular cross section. This allows you to create symmetrical objects, such as eggs, lamp shades, and baseball bats.

You can limit the degrees to which a spline rotates around the axis by specifying a value in the Degrees field. A value of 360 rotates the spline fully to create a complete object. Values of less than 360 degrees produce objects that do not completely rotate.

Lathed objects require you to specify a type of alignment for the rotation axis. For example, you can align the object to the Minimum, Maximum, or Center extents of the spline object's bounding box.

You can specify the type of object to which you want your lathed object to collapse by using the options in the Output section of the Parameters rollout. By default, 3ds Max converts all collapsed objects to an editable mesh. You can also collapse the object to a NURBS surface or an editable patch.

CD FILE The Lathe.max file is available on the CD-ROM for you to practice using the Lathe Modifier.

Create a Radial Object with the Lathe Modifier

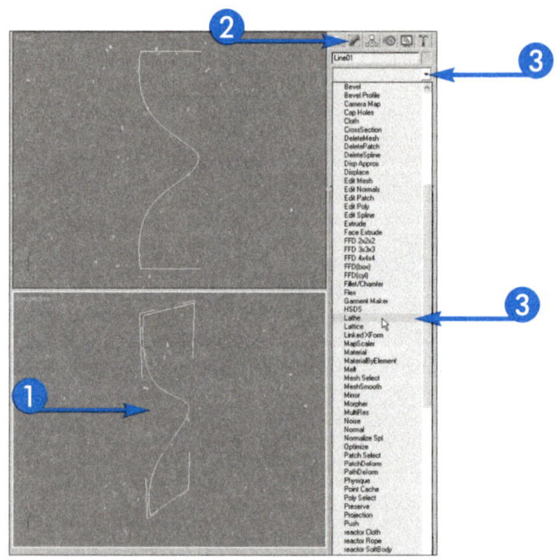

1. Select a shape.
2. Click .

   The Modify panel appears.
3. Click  and select Lathe.

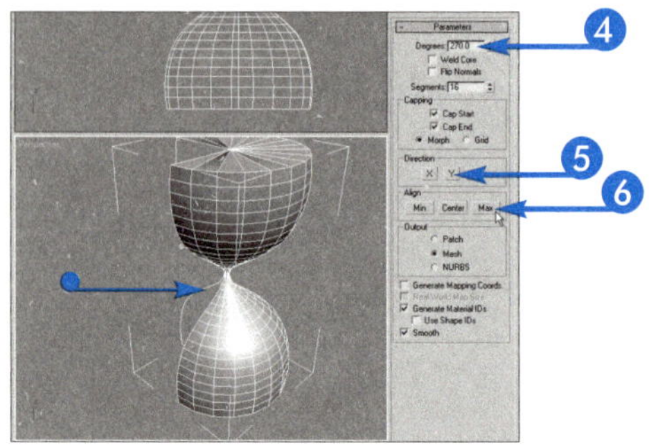

The Lathe Modifier rollouts appear in the Modify panel, and 3ds Max lathes the spline object using the default settings.

4. Type the degrees that you want the shape to rotate.
5. Click an axis around which you want the shape to rotate.
6. Click an alignment option.

In this example, the axis of revolution is aligned to the Maximum extents of the object.

7. Type a Segments value to increase the number of radial increments.

8. Click the Weld Core option (☐ changes to ☑) to eliminate co-located vertices along the rotation axis.

9. Click .

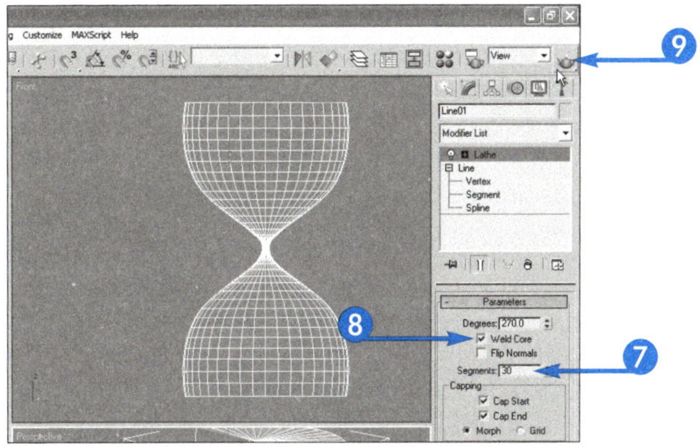

3ds Max renders the object.

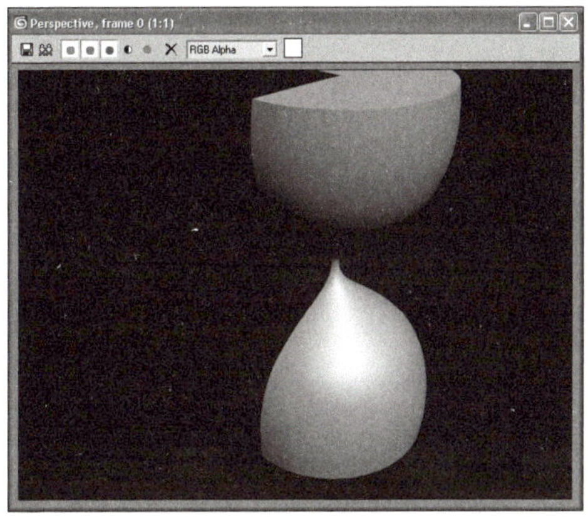

Why do I need to flip normals?

▼ By default, faces in 3ds Max have only one visible surface, defined by a vector called the *face normal*. When you lathe a 2D spline object, 3ds Max generally turns the normals outward so that the faces are visible to the viewer. If you prefer, 3ds Max has the option of reversing the orientation of the normals. By selecting the Flip Normals option (☐ changes to ☑), the normals flip outward, making the object appear as a solid shape, or as an inverted shape, if required.

What does the Generate Material IDs option do?

▼ Objects to which you have applied Multi/Sub-Object materials must have material IDs assigned that identify which faces receive which sub-materials. Selecting the Generate Material IDs option applies a material ID of 1 to the entire object when the Degrees value is set to 360. When Degrees is set to a value less than 360, then material IDs 2 and 3 are assigned to all of the faces on each of the capping surfaces that are created. See Chapter 16 for information on Multi/Sub-Object materials.

Create a Loft

Lofting is similar to extruding, except that the extrusion is along a spline, rather than perpendicular to the initial shape. When you create a loft in 3ds Max, you specify one spline object as the path and the other as the shape. The shape object is lofted along the path, thus maintaining a constant cross section, regardless of its orientation along the path.

A Loft object is actually a compound 3D object created from splines; although you must have at least two spline objects, you can use more than two objects to change the shape of the spline at specific distances along the path. The shape spline can be any spline in the scene, but the path spline must consist of only one continuous spline. For example, a Donut spline primitive can be the shape in a loft, but its two concentric circles prevent it from being the path.

See the section "Understanding 2D Splines" for more information about creating splines. See the section "Switch Between Shapes in a Loft" for information about changing the cross sections along the loft.

CD FILE: The Loft.max file is available on the CD-ROM for you to practice creating a Loft object.

Create a Loft

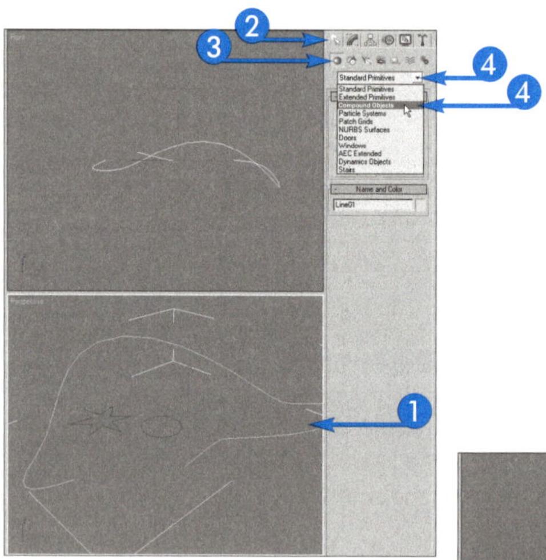

1. Select the shape that you want to be the path.
2. Click [icon].
3. Click [icon].
4. Click here and select Compound Objects.

   The available compound object types appear in the Command panel.

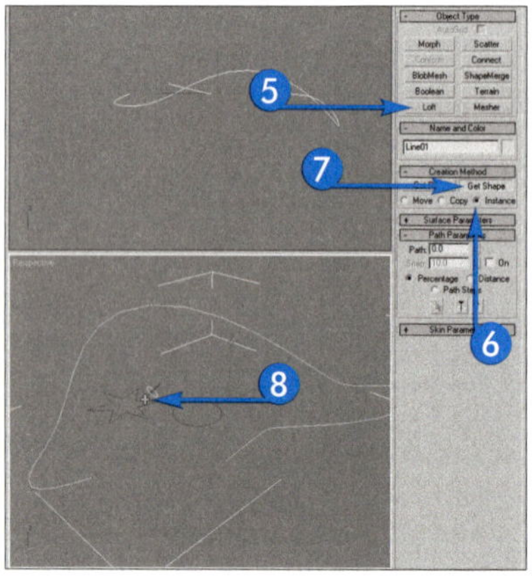

5. Click Loft.

   The Loft rollouts appear in the Command panel.
6. Click a creation method (○ changes to ◉).

   This example uses the Instance option.
7. Click Get Shape.
8. Click the shape object.

3ds Max creates the loft.

9. Select the Shape object.
10. Click [icon].
11. Modify the object.

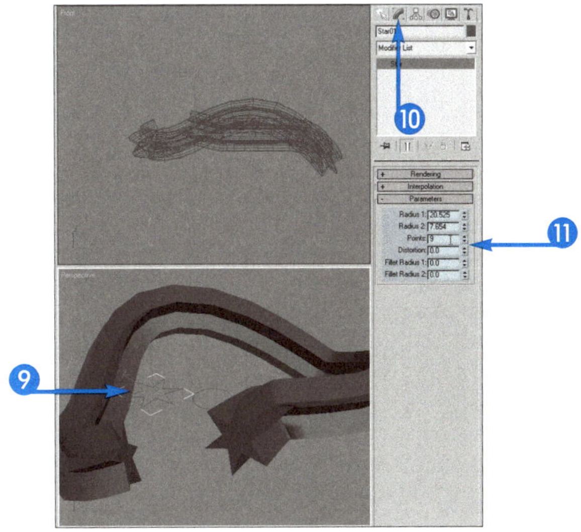

The loft updates to match the shape's changes.

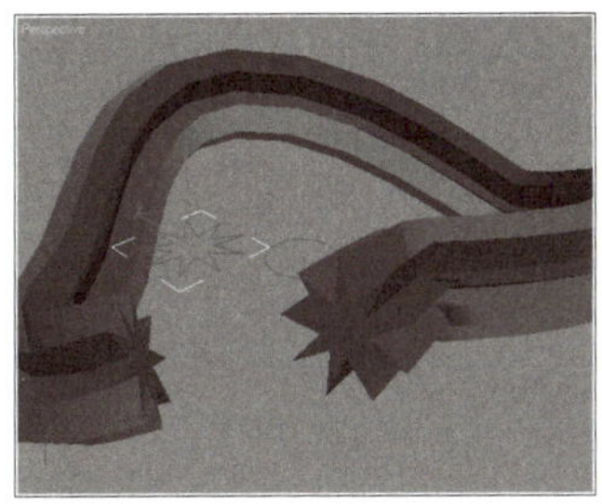

MASTER IT

What is the difference between the Move, Copy, and Instance creation methods?

- If you select the Move option (○ changes to ◉), then 3ds Max replaces splines with the Path object, and the initial Shape object with the Loft object. The Copy option leaves the original splines in the same location and creates the Loft object using copies of the objects. The Instance option is almost the same as the Copy option, the only difference being that the Loft object is an instance of those spline objects. If you alter the spline objects using the Instance option, the Loft object changes.

Why does my shape appear as a different size in the Loft?

- It has probably been scaled using the Scale transform. The Loft tool considers the parameters of an object that you select for a loft, but not any of its transforms. An object's location, rotation, or scale factor are irrelevant when it comes to lofting. A 4 unit-radius circle is different from an 8 unit-radius circle with a 50-percent scale factor applied. Although they appear the same size, 3ds Max uses the actual Radius value when creating the loft.

Switch between Shapes in a Loft

The cross-sectional shape of a Loft object is determined by the Shape object that you selected, as well as where along the path it is inserted. Once you select a shape, the Loft maintains that shape for the duration of the loft, or until you select another shape and insert it farther along the path.

The procedure to change the cross section of a loft is simple; just choose a location along the path for the new shape to be inserted, select the Get Shape button, and then select the new shape. 3ds Max automatically creates the transition between the two shapes. You can select the location as a percentage of the Path object or as a measured distance along the Path object using the Percentage or Distance options in the Path Parameters rollout. One restriction when switching between shapes is that you can only use single spline shapes. For example, you can switch between a circle and a star, but not between a circle and a donut. See the sections "Understanding 2D Splines" and "Create a Loft" for more information.

CD FILE The LoftChange.max file is available on the CD-ROM for you to practice changing the shapes in a Loft object.

Switch between Shapes in a Loft

1. Select the Loft object.
2. Select the Percentage or Distance option (○ changes to ◉).
3. Type a value along the path for the next shape in the Path field.

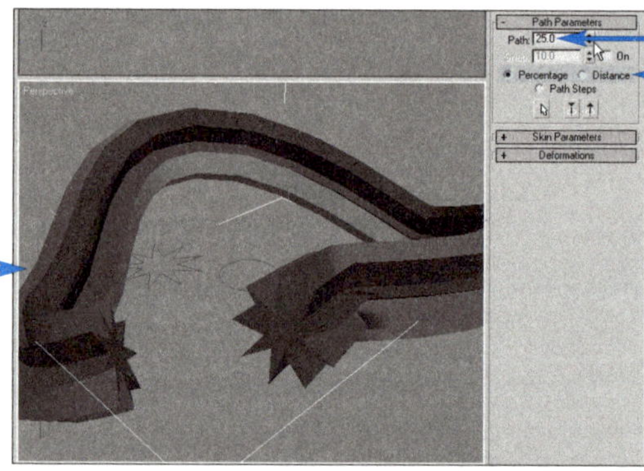

4. Click Get Shape.
5. Click the next shape object.

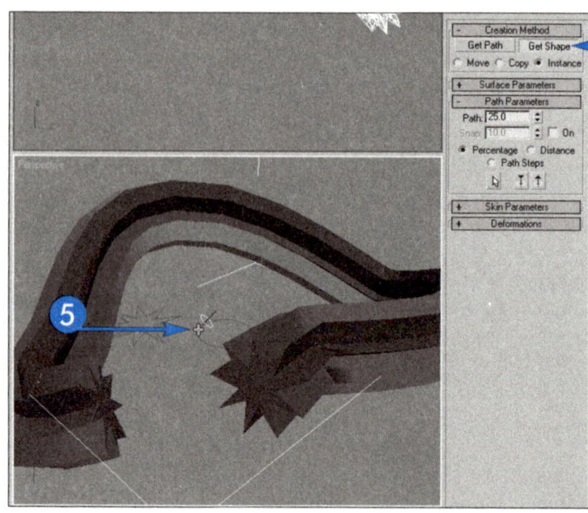

3ds Max inserts the next shape and continues it to the end of the path.

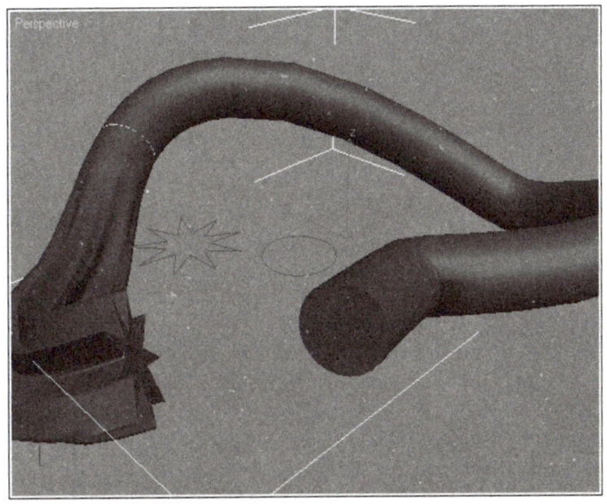

6 Repeat steps 2 to 5 to make additional changes.

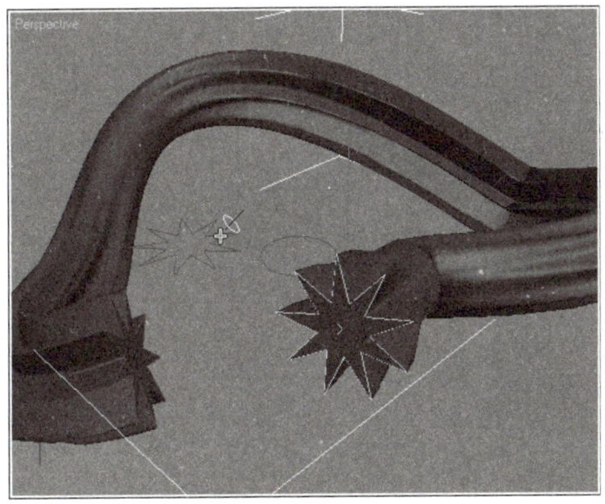

MASTER IT

What is the difference between the Sweep Modifier and the Loft compound object?

The Loft compound object and the Sweep Modifier both use two-dimensional shapes as cross sections for creating three-dimensional geometry. The Sweep Modifier can be more efficient in adjusting how the shape aligns with the path. Sweep also has a library of parametric shapes available and can use multi-spline shapes as path objects; although any shape can be used. Only the Loft compound object can change the cross-sectional shape along the path.

What is the difference between Shape Steps and Path Steps?

The Shape Steps and Path Steps parameters, both in the Skin Parameters rollout, define how much segmentation your Loft object is created with. Path Steps determines the number of steps, or divisions, that exist between each vertex in the shape object. The lower the Path Shapes value is, the less segmented the path will be. For example, a circular path, with Path Steps set to zero, results in a square-shaped Loft object. Shape Steps performs the same function regarding the Shape object of a Loft.

Understanding the Modifier Stack

Once you create an object in 3ds Max, you can continue to model the object as you desire. In 3ds Max, *modifiers* are parameter-driven tools that alter the shape or attributes of an object to achieve a specific effect. 3ds Max offers various types of modifiers that reshape the object, change its surface, and apply mapping coordinates.

Modifiers are additive, meaning that the appearance of an object changes as you place one modifier above another. Each modifier alters the result of the parameters or modifier located beneath it in the Modifier Stack. The Modifier Stack not only maintains the list of modifiers, but it also allows you to add, delete, and move modifiers to or from an object. You are not limited to only applying a modifier to an object; you can either apply them to a portion of an object, called a *sub-object*, or to any selection of objects.

Modifiers that you apply to a group of objects are called *Instanced Modifiers*. Similar to instanced objects, when you change the parameters of one modifier, the same parameters change in all instances of that modifier. For more on instanced objects, see Chapter 2. For more about creating objects, see Chapter 4. For information on the materials and mapping coordinates, see Chapters 14, 15, and 16.

A Modifier Stack

Lists the modifiers currently applied to the selected object. means there are sub-modifier levels. Light bulb icons (and) show that the modifier is turned on or off.

B Modifier List Box

Lists all of the modifiers that you can apply to the selected object(s). The opens the list.

C Pin Stack Button

Locks the Modifier Stack to the currently selected object. The Modifier Stack for that object appears even if you select another object.

D Show End Result On/Off Toggle Button

Displays the object with all applied modifiers. A deselected button () only displays the result up to the currently selected modifier in the stack.

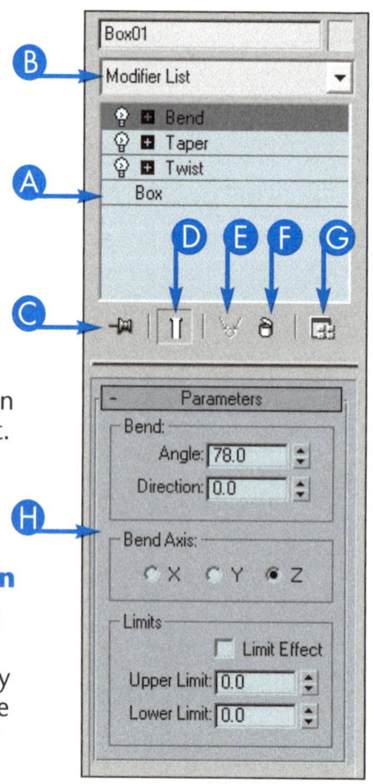

E Make Unique Button

Eliminates instance or reference links between modifiers and between objects. This is only active when you select a referenced or instanced modifier in the stack, or an instanced or referenced object.

F Remove Modifier from the Stack Button

Deletes the selected modifier from the stack, and removes the modifier's effects from the object.

G Configure Modifier Sets Button

Opens a menu with options for displaying a set of customizable modifier buttons, or for listing the modifiers in groups.

H Parameters Rollout

A Common rollout that displays the parameters that modify the selected object or modifier.

Modifier Stack Order

You can change the order 3ds Max applies modifiers to your object and thus affect an object's appearance. For example, a tall, thin object that you twist and then bend 180 degrees looks differently than the same object when you first bend and then twist it. Modifiers appear in the Modifier Stack in the order in which 3ds Max applies them to your object, with the base object's parameters always at the bottom of the stack. 3ds Max applies the modifiers starting with the lowest modifier in the stack and passes the result up to the next modifier higher in the stack.

You can change the order of the modifiers by moving them to new locations within the stack. If you do not select a modifier first, 3ds Max applies any new modifier to the top of the stack. If you select a modifier, 3ds Max applies any new modifiers directly above the selected modifier.

Modifier Types

Each modifier falls into one of three categories: Selection, Object-Space, and World-Space. Selection modifiers allow you to select a portion of your object, called a *sub-object selection*, so that modifiers that are passed to those selections only act upon the sub-objects. For example, selecting only the middle polygons of an object and applying the Twist modifier stabilizes the end polygons and makes the middle twist.

An Object-Space modifier affects the geometry of the object within its local space, thus affecting the local coordinates of the object's features. For example, the Bend modifier reshapes an object by bending it along one of its own axes. Similar to a space warp, World-Space modifiers affect the coordinates of the object within World space. *World space* is the position, rotation, and scale of the object within a scene; it is not local to the object itself. You can identify World-Space modifiers by the WSM acronym that appears in parentheses after each modifier name. For more on space warps, see Chapter 25.

Modifier Sub-Objects

Several modifiers give you access to an object's components, which are called sub-objects. The modifiers themselves may also have sub-objects. *Sub-objects* are portions of an object and can include its edges, faces, vertices, polygons, borders, and elements. For example, you can move individual vertices by selecting them at the sub-object level and using the Move transform tool.

When you select an object's sub-objects, a graphic appears next to the modifier in the stack to identify the selected sub-object type. 3ds Max continues to pass up the sub-object selection to the additional modifiers only until you clear the selection. You can clear the selection by placing one of the selection modifiers at the top of the stack without making any sub-object selections. See the section "Understanding Polygonal Mesh Objects" for more information on sub-objects.

Modifier-specific sub-objects can include the Center, which determines the point around which the effect orients, and the gizmo, which you use to visually manipulate the effect of the modifier. Modifier sub-objects do not render. You can view the available sub-objects when you click the Plus sign for a modifier in the stack. When you select a modifier's sub-object, it appears as a yellow object in the viewports.

Using the Modifier Stack

You can apply modifiers to selected objects using the drop-down list in the Modify panel. *Modifiers* alter an object to achieve a specific effect. They are also additive, meaning that a modifier applies its effect to the result of the modifier below it in the Modifier Stack.

As you add modifiers to an object, 3ds Max places them at the top of the stack or above the currently selected modifier. Only the parameters that define the current modifier appear in the Modify panel. These parameters vary, depending upon the modifier. As you adjust the modifier's values, 3ds Max displays the results in the viewports.

Once you apply and adjust the modifiers that you want, you can collapse the object. The result is an editable mesh or editable poly object, from which 3ds Max eliminates the modifiers and object parameters. It then converts the object into a polygonal mesh, retaining the shape that you created with the modifiers and parameters. To speed up viewport performance, you can transform and apply other modifiers to an editable mesh or editable poly object as you would any other object.

CD FILE: The Modifier01.max file is available on the CD-ROM for you to practice using the Modifier Stack.

Using the Modifier Stack

1. Select the object that you want to modify.

Note: *For more information on object selection, see Chapter 2.*

2. Click the Modify Panel button ( ).

   The Modify panel displays.

3. Click here to display a list of modifiers.
4. Click the modifier that you want.

   You can use the Scroll bar on the right side of the list to move through the list.

   - 3ds Max adds the modifier to the Modifier Stack above the object.

5. Type here to change the parameters for the modifier that you selected.

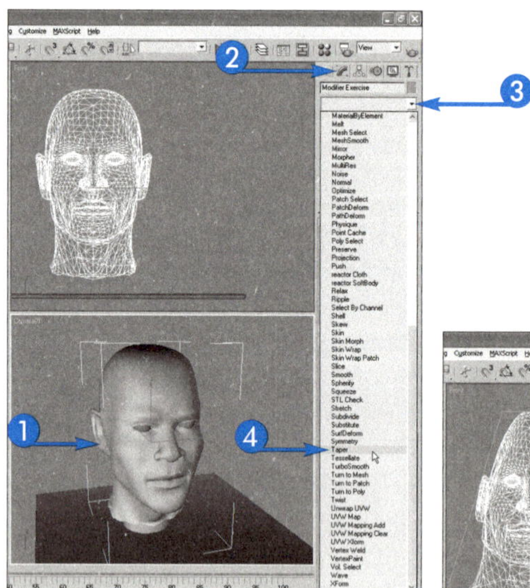

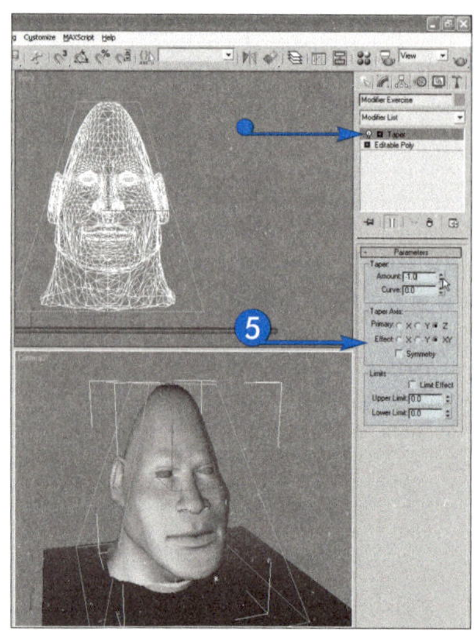

6. Repeat steps 3 to 5 to add another modifier.
7. Right-click the Modifier Stack.
8. Click Collapse All.

A Warning dialog box appears, confirming that you want to permanently apply the modifiers to the object.

9. Click Yes.

   - The object and modifiers are converted into an editable poly.

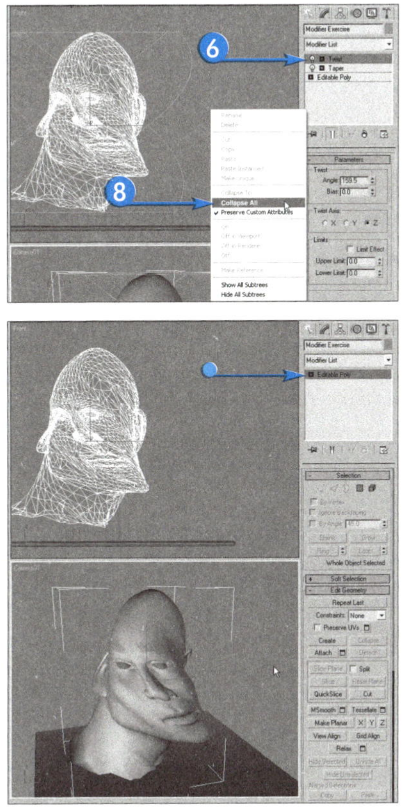

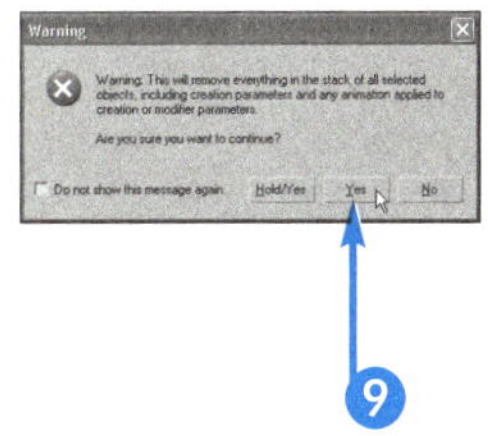

MASTER IT

What happens if I click Hold/Yes in the Warning dialog box when I collapse an object?

When you hold a scene, 3ds Max saves the current state into a file called maxhold.mx in the 3ds max/autobak folder. Whenever you collapse an object, or work with any commands that may achieve unexpected results, you should first either save the file or hold the file. When you click Hold/Yes, or click Edit and then click Hold from the Main menu, 3ds Max saves a copy of the scene before collapsing it. To restore the scene to its pre-collapsed state, you can click Edit, and then click Fetch. You cannot undo fetching a scene.

Can I apply a modifier to another object?

If you want to apply a copy of a modifier to another object in your scene, then you can click the modifier in the Modifier Stack and drag it to the other object. 3ds Max immediately applies it and then adds the modifier to the Modifier Stack for that object. To create an instance of a modifier, so that changes to one modifier's parameters affect all of the instanced modifiers, you can right-click the modifier and then select Copy from the pop-up menu. Select the target object, right-click the object or modifier in the Modifier Stack, right-click, and then select Paste Instanced.

Apply the Bend Modifier

You can use the Bend modifier to bend any 3D object along a specific local axis. For example, you can bend a tall cylinder into an arch shape for use as a handle on a tray cover. You can specify the angle of the bend and the axis upon which the bend occurs. You can also specify a direction to bend along the selected axis.

The bend of the object occurs from the axis center point and not the object's pivot point, which may be in a different location. You can change the center point to have the bend occur from a different point by moving the Center sub-object for the modifier. When you select the Center sub-object, the Move transform gizmo displays on the object and shows the current center point. For more information about the Move transform gizmo, see Chapter 2.

You can control the part of the object that bends by setting the Upper Limit and Lower Limit in the Parameters rollout. The limit value is measured from the bend center point. Any portion of the object outside the limit does not bend.

CD FILE: The Modifier01.max file is available on the CD-ROM for you to practice with the Bend modifier.

Apply the Bend Modifier

Bend the Object

1. Select the object that you want to bend.
2. Click .

   The Modify panel appears.
3. Click here and select Bend.

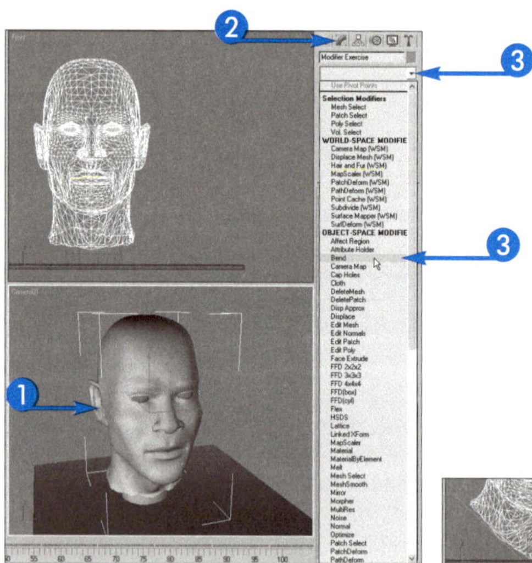

The Parameters rollout for the Bend Modifier appears in the Modify panel.

4. Click the axis around which you want the object to bend (○ changes to ◉).
5. Type an Angle value for the bend.

- The object bends around the selected axis.

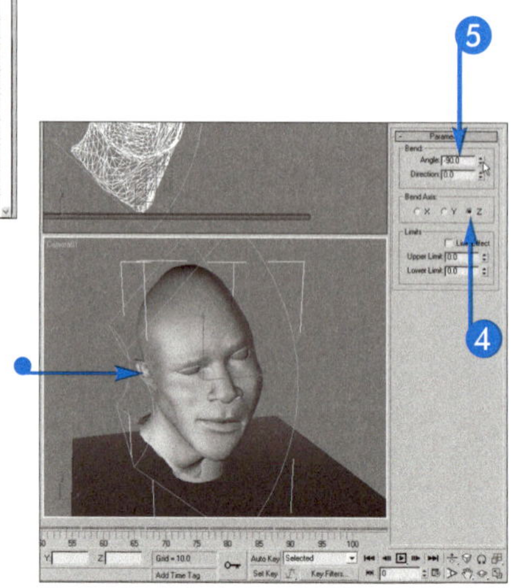

Change the Bend's Center Location with the Move Gizmo

6. Click the Plus sign (⊞) next to the Bend modifier to display the modifier sub-objects.
7. Click Center.

   The Move gizmo appears at the axis center with an outline of the current bend.
8. Click and drag the Move gizmo to adjust the center point for the axis.

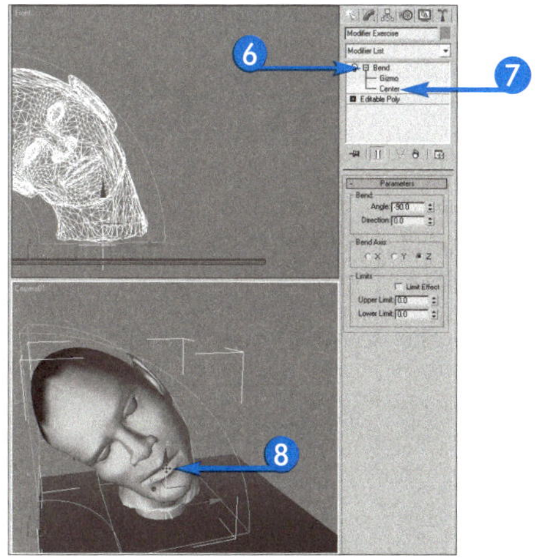

Change the Bend Location with the Limit Fields

9. Click the Limit Effect option (☐ changes to ☑).
10. Type the Upper and Lower Limits for the Bend modifier.

    - 3ds Max applies the bend within the limits that you specified.

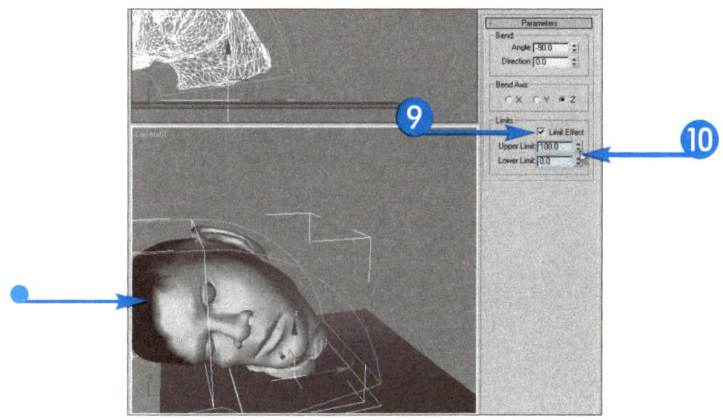

MASTER IT

Why does my bent object look jagged?

3ds Max bends your object by moving the object's vertices. If your object does not have enough vertices, then the bending action makes your object appear jagged or segmented. You can fix this problem by adding segments to the object. If the object is a primitive, then there is usually a Segments value that you can increase. To add segments to an editable poly, select the object in the Modifer Stack, click the Element sub-object, and then click Slice Plane. When you have positioned the gizmo where you want to create a segment, click Slice. See the section "Understanding Polygonal Mesh Objects" for more information about working with editable polys.

Why does the Lower Limit field change to zero when I type a value?

The limits are set as distances above and below the center point of the modifier. As a result, you must make the Upper Limit either a positive number or zero. The Lower Limit must be either a negative number or zero. If you type a positive value in the Lower Limit field, then 3ds Max changes it back to the nearest valid value, which is zero. If you move the center point of your object, then the limits remain the same. Depending upon where the center point is located, you may need to adjust the limit values.

Apply the Taper Modifier

You can use the Taper modifier to scale the ends of an object. This allows you to create an object, such as a candle or a spire that tapers at one end. The Taper modifier scales the ends of an object to a smaller or larger size based on the Amount value that you specify. Values between –10 and 10 are valid, with positive values increasing the tapered size of the object, and negative values decreasing the size. A Taper value of –1.0 tapers the object to a point at one end when the Center sub-object is at the other end.

The tapering occurs from the center point towards the end of the object, and you can move the Center sub-object to adjust where the tapering begins. You can do this by selecting the Center sub-object and using the Move transform gizmo. For more information about the Move transform gizmo, see Chapter 2.

You can also set limits to restrict the taper to a specific section of your object. 3ds Max only tapers the portion of the object that falls within these limits.

CD FILE: The Modifier01.max file is available on the CD-ROM for you to practice with the Taper modifier.

Apply the Taper Modifier

Taper the Object

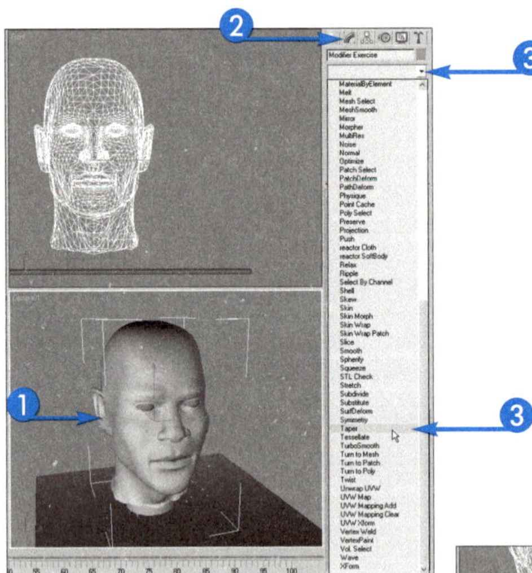

1. Select the object that you want to taper.

Note: *For more information on selecting objects, see Chapter 2.*

2. Click [Modify icon].

   The Modify panel appears.

3. Click here and select Taper.

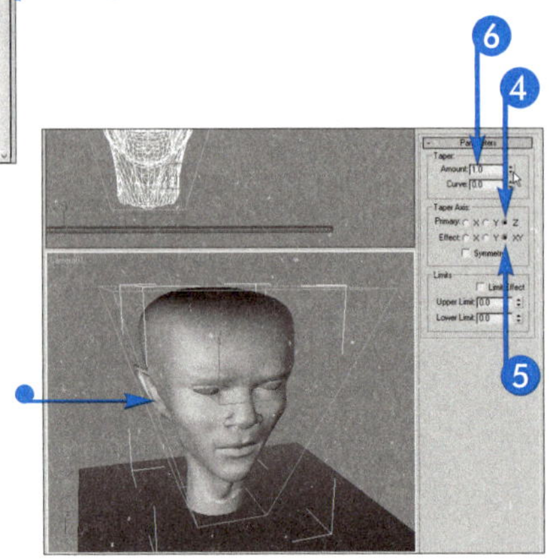

The Parameters rollout for the Taper Modifier appears in the Modify panel.

4. Click the Primary Axis along which you want the taper to occur (○ changes to ◉).

5. Click an axis or axes in which you want the effect to occur (○ changes to ◉).

6. Type a Taper Amount.

   - 3ds Max applies the tapering to the object.

Change the Taper's Center Location

7. Click ⊞ next to the Taper modifier to view the sub-objects.
8. Click Center.
9. Click and drag the Move transform gizmo to move the center point to a different location.

Note: *For more information on the Move transform gizmo, see Chapter 2.*

- The tapering adjusts to the new Center location.

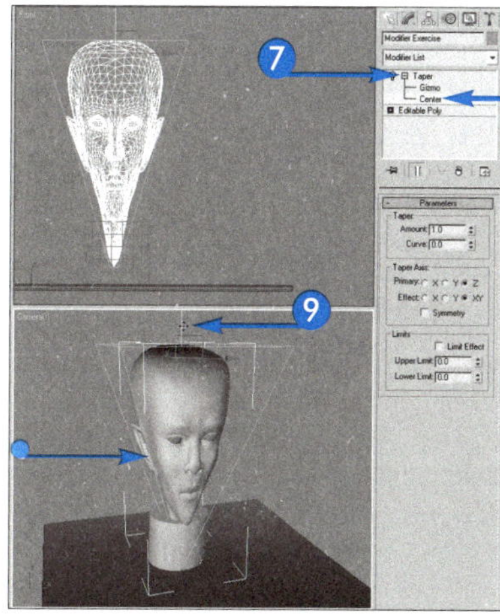

Change the Taper's Location with the Limit Fields

10. Click the Limit Effect option (☐ changes to ☑).
11. Type Upper and Lower Limit values.

- 3ds Max adjusts the tapering so that it only applies within the specified limits.

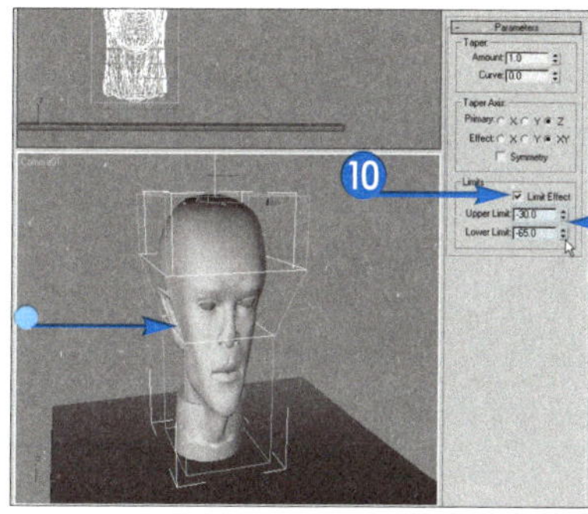

MASTER IT

What is the difference between the Primary axis and the Effect axis?

When you taper an object, you must specify both the Primary axis and the direction of the taper. The Primary axis is the center axis along which all tapering occurs. The Effect axis controls the direction of the tapering in relation to the Primary axis. When you select two Effect axes, the object tapers like a pyramid, but when you only select one, the object tapers like an extruded triangle. The available Effect axis options change, depending on the Primary axis that you select. For example, if your Primary axis is Z, then your Effect axis options are X, Y, and XY.

How can I make only one end of my object taper?

Tapering starts at the center point and tapers outward, based on the value that you type in the Amount field. If the selected center point is at the center of the Primary axis, then the object tapers on both sides, with one side tapering bigger and the other side tapering smaller. You can use the Limit Effect option to limit the effect for each side of the center point. If you do not want to taper the object on one end, then set that field to zero. The tapering starts at the center point and only tapers in one direction.

Apply the Twist Modifier

You can use the Twist modifier to coil an object around a specific local axis. This creates a twirling effect for an object such as an iron fence post.

When you apply the Twist modifier to an object, you must determine the axis around which you want to twist the object. By default, 3ds Max selects the Z-axis, although you can select either of the other two axes. You must also specify the rotation angle for the twist. A positive Angle value creates a clockwise twist, and a negative value produces a counterclockwise twist. You may need to add segmentation to the object to create a smooth twist effect.

The Bias value controls the uniformity of the twisting effect: A positive Bias value causes the twist to bunch up, away from the modifier's center; a negative value causes the twist to bunch up near the center; and a value of zero creates an even twist.

You can limit the part of the object that is twisted by setting upper and lower limits. 3ds Max only twists the section of the object within the limit range.

CD FILE: The Modifier01.max file is available on the CD-ROM for you to practice with the Twist modifier.

Apply the Twist Modifier

1. Click the object that you want to twist.

Note: *For more information on selecting objects, see Chapter 2.*

2. Click the Modify icon.

   The Modify panel appears.

3. Click here and select Twist.

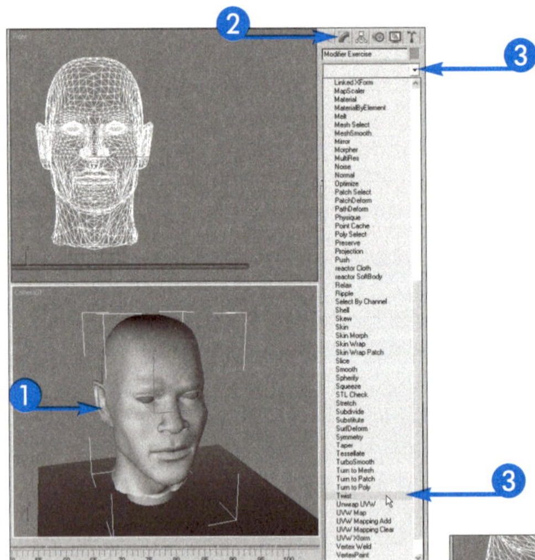

   The Parameters rollout for the Twist modifier appears in the Modify panel.

4. Click the axis around which you want to twist the object (○ changes to ◉).

5. Type a twist Angle value and an optional Bias value.

   You can specify a Bias value between –100 and 100.

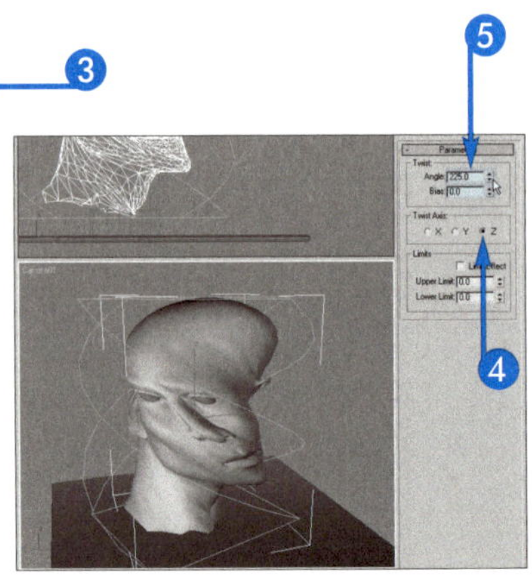

6 Click the Limit Effect option (☐ changes to ☑).

7 Type an Upper and Lower Limit for the twist.

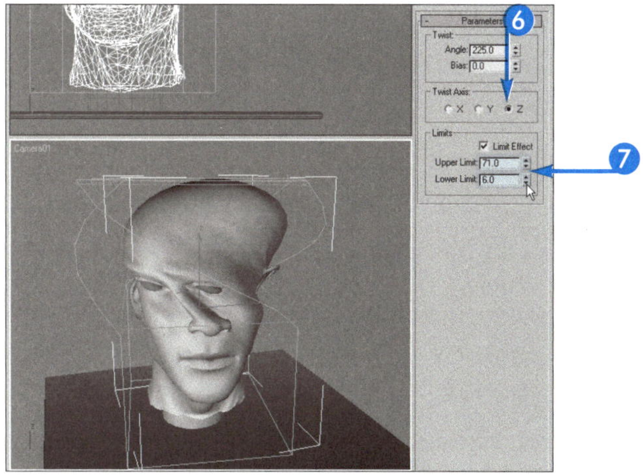

3ds Max applies the twist to the object within the specified limits.

- Horizontal orange planes indicate the limits.

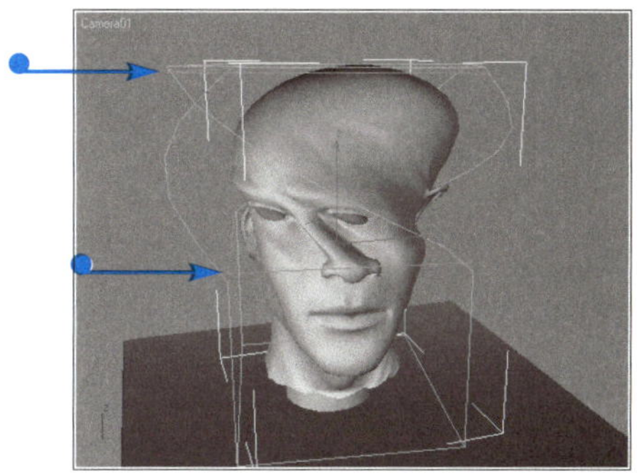

MASTER IT

What is the difference between a bold modifier and an italic modifier in the Modifier Stack?

Both a bold and an italic entry in the Modifier Stack indicate that an instance is involved. A bold modifier entry indicates that the object itself, along with any associated modifiers, is an instance clone of one or more other objects in the scene. Changing any parameters changes those parameters for all instanced objects. An italic modifier entry indicates that the modifier itself has been instance-cloned and applied to another object, but that the object itself may or may not be unique. You can apply instanced modifiers to completely dissimilar objects. Click the Make Unique button (icon) in the Modify panel to convert an instanced object or modifier into a distinct one.

How do I change the center point?

To change the point at which the twist begins, you can adjust the location of the center point of the Twist modifier that is applied to your object. To move the center point, click the Plus sign (icon) next to the Twist modifier in the stack, and then click Center. The Move transform gizmo appears at the location of the center point. By default, the center point of the Twist modifier is at the center point of the object, and not at the pivot point. To move the center point, click and drag the Move transform gizmo to the new location. For more information about the Transform gizmos, see Chapter 2.

Apply the Melt Modifier

You can use the Melt modifier to make an object appear as if it is melting and spreading out. For example, you can make a candle look as if the part near the flame is melting away. Although 3ds Max applies the melting to the center of the axis by default, you can adjust the melting by repositioning the Center sub-object.

You can select from four different predefined solidity substances: Ice, Glass, Jelly, and Plastic. These substances determine how your object melts. For example, if you select Ice, your object appears to melt along the edges in the same manner that ice does. You can also select Custom and specify a solidity value.

To customize your object's melt pattern, you must specify the Amount of melting that you want to apply to the object. You can specify a value between 0.0 and 1000, with higher values creating more of a melting effect. The % of Melt field controls the percentage that the object will spread as the amount of melting increases. For example, as ice melts, it appears to get wider as the ice cube flattens.

CD FILE: The Modifier01.max file is available on the CD-ROM for you to practice with the Melt modifier.

Apply the Melt Modifier

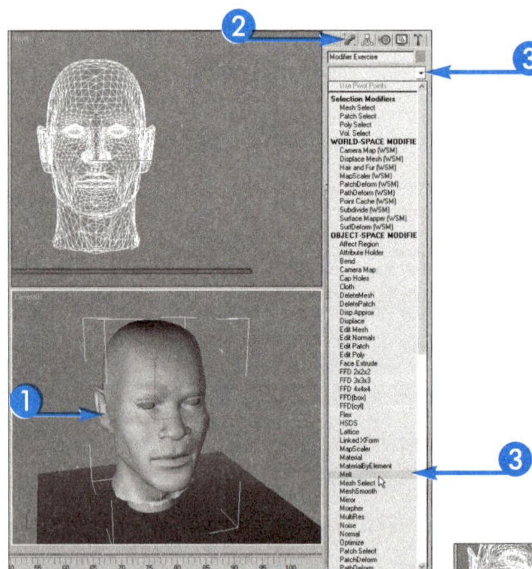

1. Select an object.

Note: *For more information about selecting objects, see Chapter 2.*

2. Click .

   The Modify panel displays.

3. Click here and select Melt.

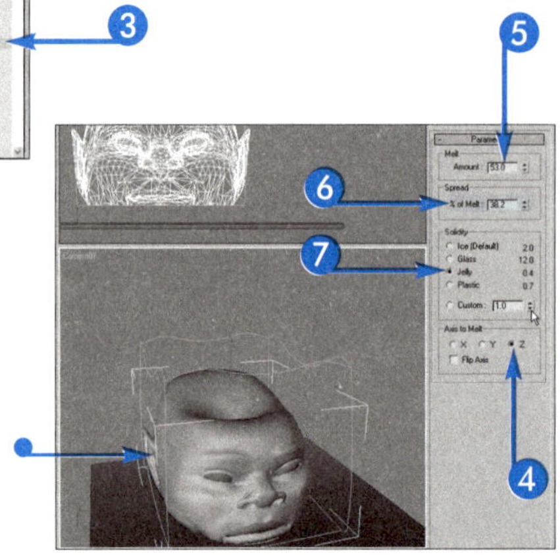

   The Melt modifier's Parameters rollout appears in the Modify panel.

4. Click an axis along which you want the melt to occur (○ changes to ◉).

5. Type a Melt Amount.

6. Type a % of Melt value.

7. Click to select a Solidity type (○ changes to ◉).

   3ds Max applies the parameters to the object.

Reduce Face Count with the MultiRes Modifier

The greatest factor in rendering time in a 3ds Max scene is the face count of the object. Although it is not the only determining factor, as a general rule, the greater the face count, the longer the expected rendering time will be.

You can apply the MultiRes modifier to your objects to reduce their face count while maintaining their general appearance. You can choose to vary the amount of reduction in faces with the object's proximity to the camera or the user's point of view. For example, an object that is seen close-up may have little or no reduction, while the same object may only require 20 percent of its faces when it is located in the distance and its features are less distinguishable.

You can determine the method of the reduction in face count by specifying either the actual number of vertices to use in the object, or the percentage of the original number to use.

CD FILE: The Modifier01.max file is available on the CD-ROM for you to practice with the MultiRes modifier.

Reduce Face Count with the MultiRes Modifier

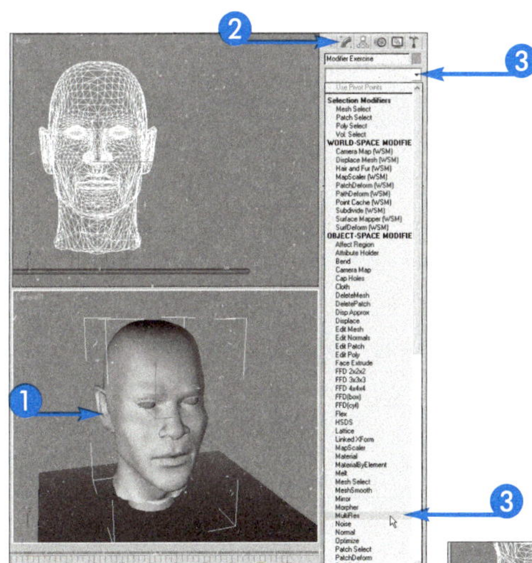

1. Select an object.

Note: *For more information about selecting objects, see Chapter 2.*

2. Click .

   The Modify panel displays.

3. Click here and select MultiRes.

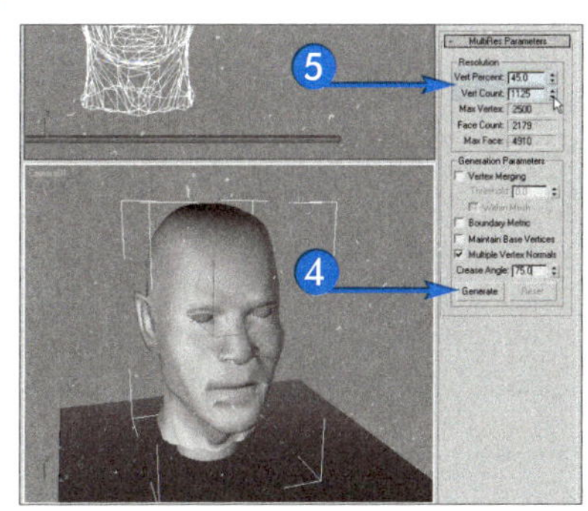

   The MultiRes modifier's Parameters rollout appears in the Modify panel.

4. Click Generate.
5. Type a Vert Percent or Vert Count value.

   3ds Max reduces the object's face count to reflect the modifier's parameters.

Add Randomness with the Noise Modifier

In computer graphics, it is very easy to create perfectly straight walls and lines, and perfectly smooth surfaces. Unfortunately, this is impractical for most real-world situations. Real objects, such as lawns, asteroids, shields, and faceplates, have imperfections in their surfaces that give them a sense of realism and personality.

In computer graphics, the term *noise* refers to randomness in an object, image, or motion. In 3ds Max, you can use the Noise modifier to disrupt the generally smooth surfaces that the program generates, and replace them with jagged or flowing surfaces.

The Noise modifier's Scale value may seem counterintuitive in that a smaller Scale value yields a greater effect on your object. This is because Scale refers to the size of the mathematical curve that distorts the object, rather than the amount of distortion itself. The Strength values are the parameters that determine the amount of distortion in each object.

You can apply standard noise or noise with a fractal algorithm by selecting the Fractal option. Fractal noise is more jagged and rough than standard noise and can distort your object much more.

CD FILE — The Modifier01.max file is available on the CD-ROM for you to practice with the Noise modifier.

Add Randomness with the Noise Modifier

1. Select an object.

Note: *For more information about selecting objects, see Chapter 2.*

2. Click .

   The Modify panel appears.

3. Click here and select Noise.

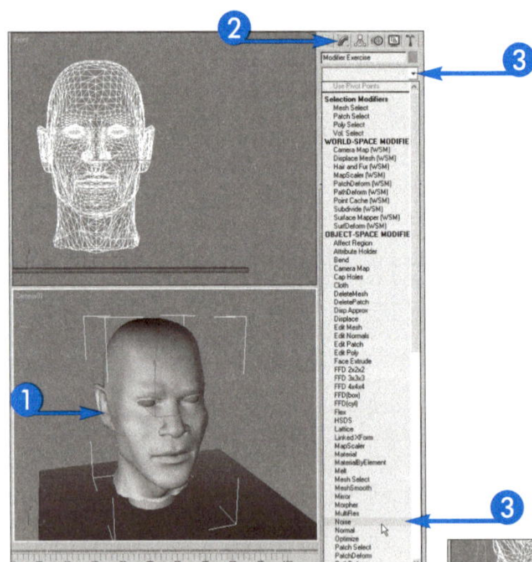

The Noise modifier's Parameters rollout appears in the Modify panel.

4. Type a Scale value.
5. Type X, Y, and Z Strength values.

   3ds Max alters the object's surfaces to reflect the modifier's parameters.

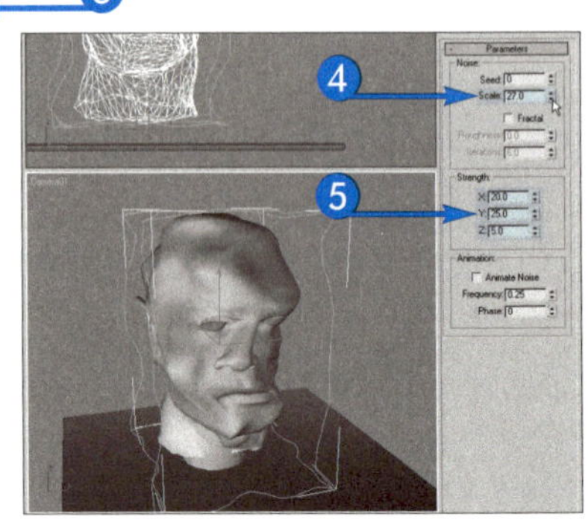

6. Click the Fractal option (☐ changes to ☑).
7. Type Roughness and Iterations values to alter the surface texture.

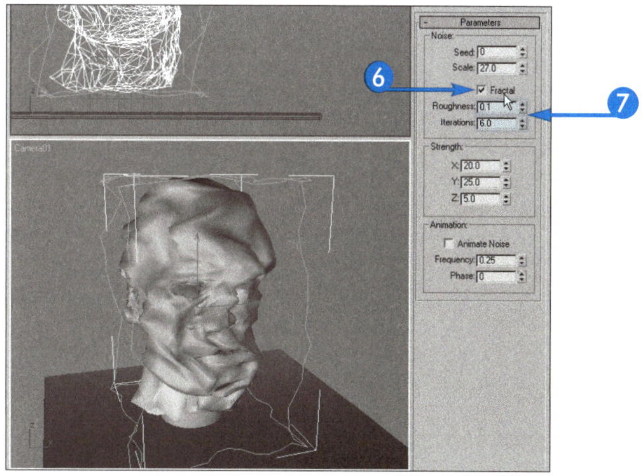

3ds Max creates a rougher surface with the Fractal option than with standard noise.

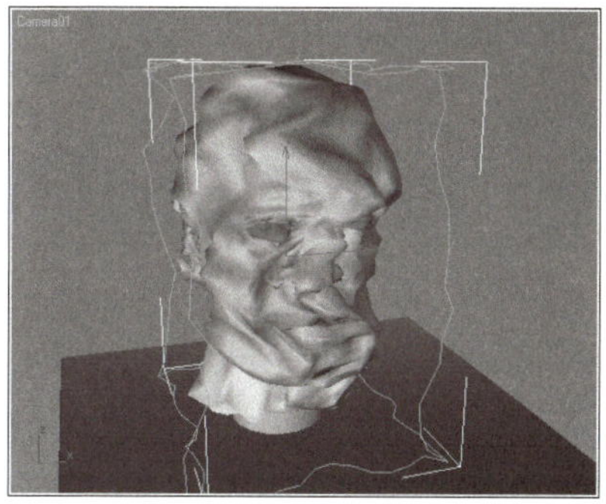

MASTER IT

Why are two keys created when I apply the Noise modifier?

When you apply the Noise modifier to an object, 3ds Max creates two animation keys in the Track bar at the bottom of the 3ds Max user interface. These keys create a default animation of the modifier's Phase value. To see the effect, select the Animate Noise option (☐ changes to ☑), and then click the Play animation button (▶) in the animation controls area. These default keys do not preclude you from editing, adding, or deleting Phase animation keys. You can also animate the other Noise parameters, but animation keys are not automatically generated for them. For more information on animation and animation keys, see Chapter 8.

Can I use noise to add randomness to an object's movements and materials?

Yes. As a controller, you can use noise to randomly add position, rotation, or scale variance to an object's transforms. For example, to achieve a random movement for an asteroid, it is easier to add a Noise controller to the asteroid's rotation, to give it a smooth and random tumble, than to create keys for every minor movement. You can also use noise in the Material Editor to add randomness to your materials. For example, a Noise map in the Opacity or Bump channels can cause your object to appear randomly transparent or with a random surface texture. For more on controllers and map channels, see Chapters 10 and 16, respectively.

Soften Edges with the Relax Modifier

The Relax modifier applies an opposite effect to the Noise modifier by reducing the angle between adjacent faces. You can use Relax to soften the edges of an object without increasing the face count. The Relax Value parameter determines the maximum amount that an object's vertices can move for each iteration increment. The larger the value, the greater the movement, based on the vertex's proximity to its neighboring vertices. Positive Relax Values result in smaller, smoother objects. Negative Relax Values create larger, jagged objects. The Iterations value determines how many times the Relax process repeats.

CD FILE: The Modifier02.max file is available on the CD-ROM for you to practice with the Relax modifier.

MASTER IT

What does the Keep Boundary Pts Fixed option do?

Objects, especially characters, commonly have openings such as eyes, a mouth, and nostrils. The "Keep Boundary Pts Fixed" option leaves the vertices around the perimeter of an object's opening in place. Regardless of the Relax Value and Iterations parameters, the vertices around an opening, and therefore the opening itself, remain in a fixed location and orientation. Deselecting this option (☑ changes to ☐) allows the opening perimeter vertices to react to the Relax modifier like all of the other vertices in the object.

Soften Edges with the Relax Modifier

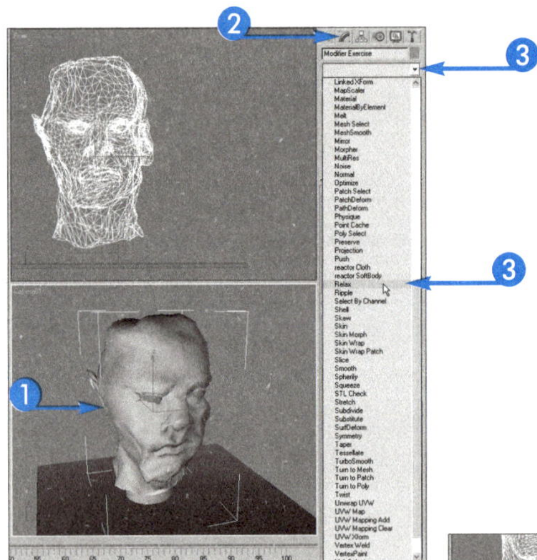

1. Select an object.

Note: *For more information about selecting objects, see Chapter 2.*

2. Click .

   The Modify panel appears.

3. Click here and select Relax.

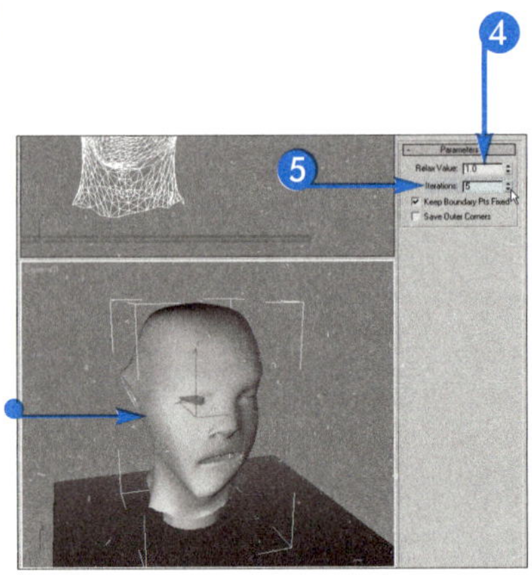

The Relax modifier's Parameters rollout appears in the Modify panel.

4. Type a positive Relax Value.
5. Type a larger value in the Iterations field.
   - 3ds Max smoothes the object to reflect the Relax modifier's parameters.

Smooth an Object with the TurboSmooth Modifier

The TurboSmooth modifier applies an opposite effect to that of the MultiRes modifier. TurboSmooth smoothes the surfaces of an object by subdividing its faces and averaging the angles between adjacent faces. The result is a smoother object without the reduction in size and possible distortion caused by the Relax modifier. The TurboSmooth modifier, a faster and simpler version of the MeshSmooth modifier, is often used to subdivide low polygon models, making them suitable for close-up viewing.

The main control parameter for the TurboSmooth modifier is the Iterations value. This value determines how many times the surfaces are subdivided. Each additional iteration exponentially increases the number of faces on the object. An object with 2,000 faces may increase to 12,000 with Iterations set to 1, and 50,000 with Iterations set to 2, depending on the shapes of the polygons that the faces comprise. Entering a large Iterations value, such as 8 or 10, can easily crash 3ds Max on most systems. However, you can safely increment the Iterations value by using the spinner arrows.

CD FILE: The Modifier03.max file is available on the CD-ROM for you to practice with the TurboSmooth modifier.

Smooth an Object with the TurboSmooth Modifier

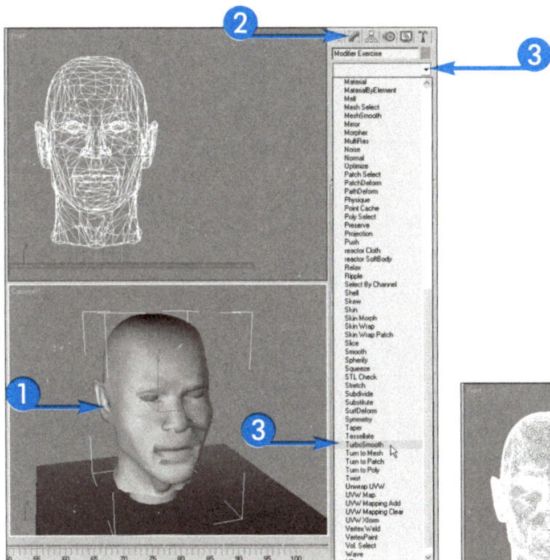

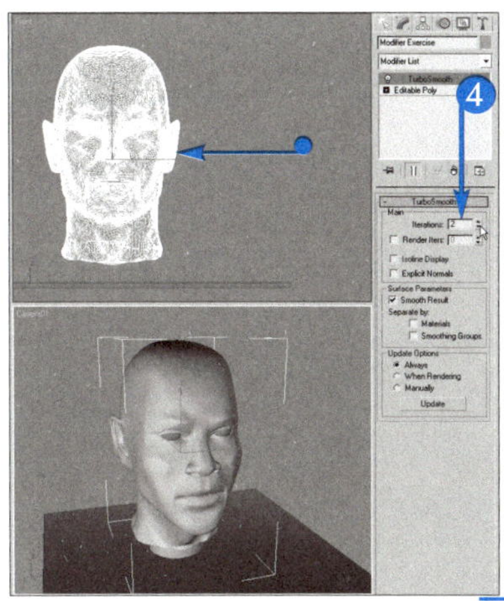

1. Select an object.

Note: *For more information about selecting objects, see Chapter 2.*

2. Click .

   The Modify panel appears.

3. Click here and select TurboSmooth.

   The TurboSmooth modifier's Parameters rollout appears in the Modify panel.

4. Type an Iterations value.

   - 3ds Max smoothes the object by subdividing its surfaces.

Add Thickness with the Shell Modifier

Unlike solids modelers, which add the elements of volume and mass, 3ds Max is a surface modeler that creates only surfaces for its objects; as a result, the objects are hollow. When these objects are closed, you do not know that they are hollow. However, these models often need to show an interior compartment, such as a car or airplane fuselage.

The Shell modifier solves this problem by creating a second, offset series of faces that are oriented in the opposite direction, and that match the configuration of the existing faces. The two sets of offset faces are then connected by additional faces along their perimeters to give the impression of thick walls.

An object that uses the Shell modifier does not need to be a complex, hollow model. For example, you can also use the Shell modifier to add depth to open shapes that you have extruded or lathed. For information on the Extrude and Lathe modifiers, see Chapter 5.

CD FILE: The Modifier04.max file is available on the CD-ROM for you to practice with the Shell modifier.

Add Thickness with the Shell Modifier

1. Select an object.

Note: *For more information about selecting objects, see Chapter 2.*

2. Click .

   The Modify panel appears.

3. Click here and select Shell.

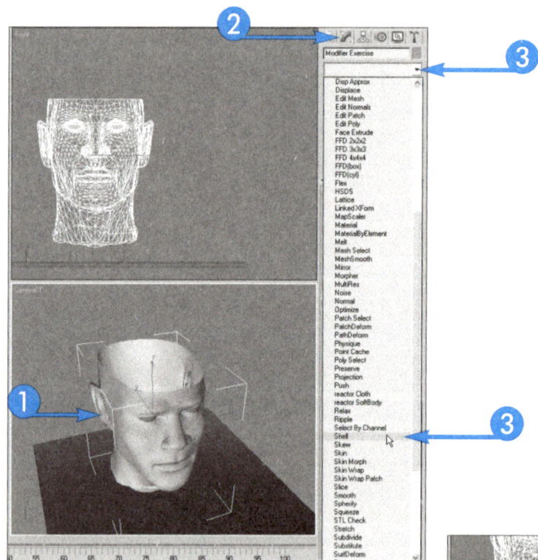

   The Shell modifier's Parameters rollout appears in the Modify panel.

4. Type an Inner and/or Outer Amount value.

   - 3ds Max adds thickness to the object's surfaces.

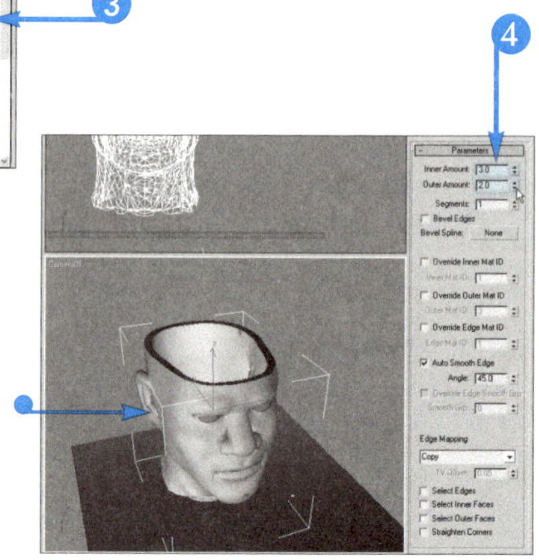

Model an Object with the Symmetry Modifier

An object is symmetrical when one side is a mirrored or balanced version of the other. Symmetry may occur along one or more of the object's axes, and most of the 3ds Max primitive objects begin in a symmetrical state. A box is symmetrical along all axes, while a pyramid is only symmetrical along two. A teapot is only symmetrical along its X-axis, which bisects the spout and handle.

The Symmetry modifier causes either one or two non-symmetrical sides to become symmetrical with their reciprocal side. You can use the Symmetry modifier to correct one side of a model that has become distorted, or to hasten the modeling process by allowing you to create only one half of a model and mirror its other side.

Keep in mind that true symmetry does not usually exist in real-world objects. In fact, classical animators avoid symmetry, which they refer to as "twinning." After applying the Symmetry modifier, you can collapse the Modifier Stack and then introduce imperfections into your model. See the section "Understanding the Modifier Stack" for information on collapsing an object.

CD FILE: The Modifier05.max file is available on the CD-ROM for you to practice with the Symmetry modifier.

Model an Object with the Symmetry Modifier

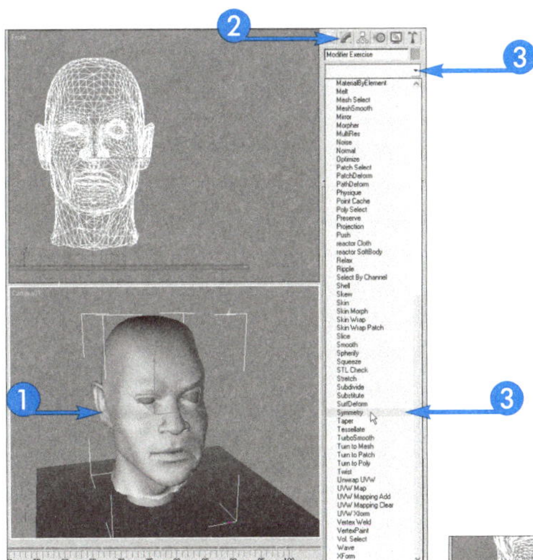

1. Select an object.

Note: *For more information about selecting objects, see Chapter 2.*

2. Click .

   The Modify panel appears.

3. Click here and select Symmetry.

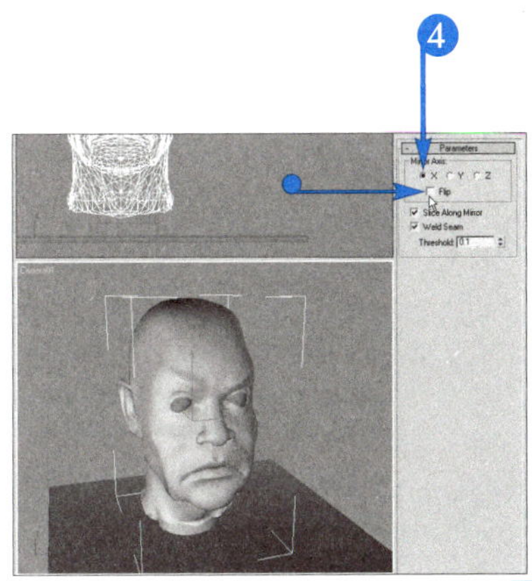

The Symmetry modifier's Parameters rollout appears in the Modify panel.

4. Select an axis around which you want to mirror the model (○ changes to ◉).

   3ds Max mirrors the positive side of the axis over to the negative side.

   - If necessary, you can select the Flip option (☐ changes to ☑) to reverse which side is mirrored over to the other.

Add Secondary Motion with the Flex Modifier

A common cartoon effect is to have a character stretch as it speeds away or shudder in a fluid manner as it comes to a sudden stop. The relocation of the object is called the primary motion, and the rubbery effect is called the secondary motion, or follow-through. This secondary motion gives the impression of great velocity and abrupt change. You can use the Flex modifier to add secondary motion to your animated objects without creating keys for every subtle movement.

The Flex modifier acts like a spring to control the movement that your objects gain. The Flex value determines how much animation occurs around each animation key, with higher values resulting in more animation. The Use Chase Springs option causes the object to resume its original shape after passing an animation key. When this option is active, the Strength and Sway values are available. The higher the Strength value, the stronger the chase springs are that allow the secondary motion. Higher Strength values result in less movement. The higher the Sway value, the longer it takes the object to resume its original shape.

CD FILE: The Modifier06.max file is available on the CD-ROM for you to practice with the Flex modifier.

Add Secondary Motion with the Flex Modifier

Add the Flex Modifier

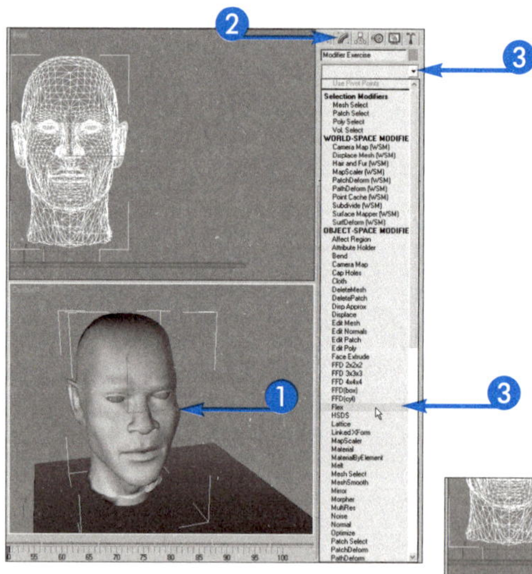

1. Select an animated object.

Note: *For more information about selecting objects, see Chapter 2.*

2. Click .

   The Modify panel appears.

3. Click here and select Flex.

   The Flex modifier's Parameters rollout appears in the Modify panel.

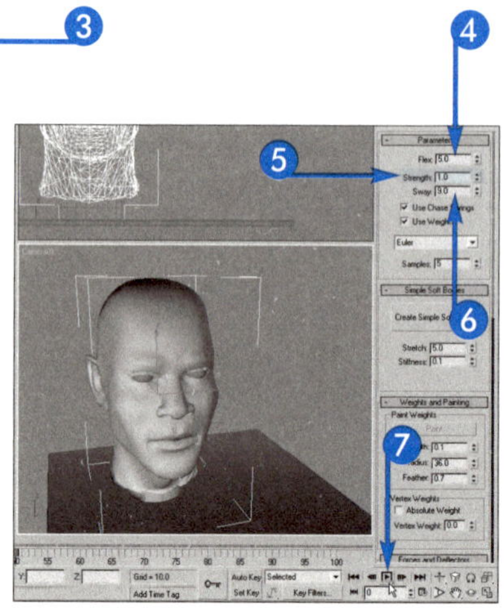

4. Type a Flex value.
5. Type a Strength value.
6. Type a Sway value.
7. Click the Play Animation button () to see the effect of the secondary motion.

   3ds Max plays the animation in the viewport. The flex occurs around the middle of the object.

Adjust the Center Sub-Object

8. Click ⊞ next to the Flex modifier.
9. Click the Center sub-object.

   The Move transform activates at the Center sub-object.

10. Click and drag the Move transform gizmo to the bottom of the object.
11. Click ▶ to see the effect of the secondary motion.

    3ds Max plays the animation in the viewport.

    The flex occurs around the middle of the object.

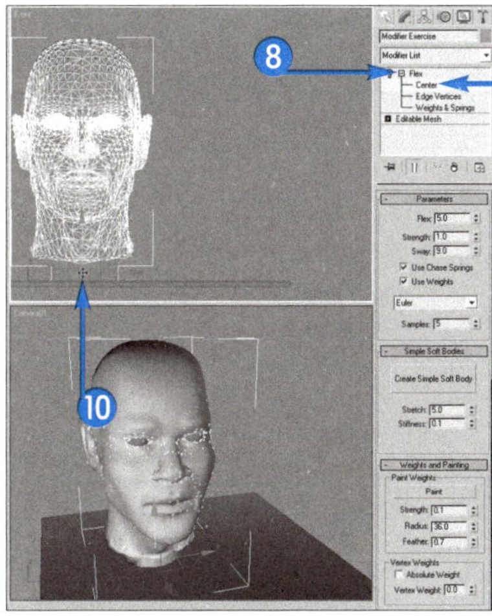

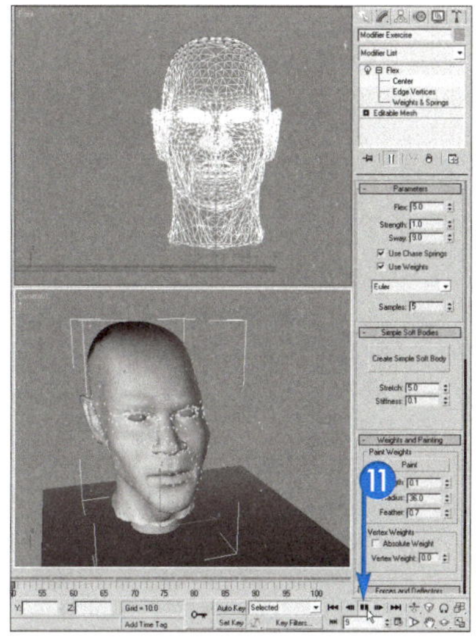

PART II

MASTER IT

What does the Samples setting do?

You can use the Samples value, along with the Solver Type drop-down list located above it, to specify how many times during every frame of animation 3ds Max calculates the secondary animation near the keys. A higher Samples value results in a more accurate flex simulation. However, a very high value may slow down your viewport playback without any visible increase in accuracy over lower values. The Solver Type is the algorithm used to calculate the object's secondary movement. The Euler solver is appropriate for most situations, but the Midpoint or Runge-Kutta4 solvers may be required if the object is complex or the Flex modifier yields unexpected results.

What does the Paint button do?

When the Flex modifier determines how much effect it has on a vertex, it does so based on the vertex's proximity to the modifier's Center sub-object. Objects that are closer receive more movement than those that are farther away. When you are at any of the Flex modifier's sub-object levels, you can click the Paint button, in the Weights and Painting rollout, to manually specify the flexibility of vertices. With Paint active, Type a value in the Radius field to specify the brush size. The Strength settings in the Paint Weights area determine how quickly the painted areas assume the Strength value set in the Parameters rollout. Click and drag the cursor over the object to adjust its vertices' flexibility.

Understanding Polygonal Mesh Objects

You commonly use polygonal mesh objects in most modeling tasks because they allow you to modify an object's sub-object components, such as the vertices, edges, and faces. An example is character modeling, where it is easier and more intuitive to select and move an object's vertices, to reshape its surface, than it is to apply a modifier or create a compound object to achieve the same result. Although they are the most widely used objects, you cannot use the Create panel to produce them; you can only create polygonal mesh objects by converting other objects.

3ds Max actually provides two different types of polygonal mesh objects: editable mesh and editable poly. Both object types allow you to transform your object by modifying the object at the sub-object level. Because the editable poly object has more capabilities, is more powerful, and has replaced the editable mesh object for most purposes in the 3D industries, it will be the only polygonal mesh type discussed here.

Understanding the Edit Poly Modifier

In addition to creating editable poly objects, you can also apply the Edit Poly Modifier to existing objects. This allows you to experiment with the polygon tools before committing to permanent changes in the object. If the Edit Poly Modifier yields acceptable results, then you can collapse the Modifier Stack and convert the object, along with the Edit Poly changes, into an editable poly object. If the Edit Poly Modifier does not yield the expected result, then you can simply delete the modifier from the stack. See the section "Using the Modifier Stack" for more information about applying modifiers and collapsing the stack.

Understanding the Editable Poly Object

The editable poly object allows you to model your object at the sub-object level. One of the major differences between an editable mesh and an editable poly is that editable polys are able to select and edit entire polygons, rather than being restricted to a mesh's triangular faces. The sub-objects of the editable poly are Vertex, Edge, Border, Polygon, and Element.

Anatomy of the Editable Poly Controls

Viewing an editable poly's controls in the Modify panel reveals several different rollouts that you can use to modify the object at the sub-object level. These rollouts are specific to the current sub-object level and are the same rollouts that display when you work with the Edit Poly Modifier. The rollouts that appear for an Editable Poly can include the Selection rollout, the Soft Selection rollout, the Edit (Sub-Object) rollout, the Edit Geometry rollout, the Subdivision Surface rollout, the Subdivision Displacement rollout, and the Paint Deformation rollout, as well as additional sub-object-specific rollouts. See the section "Select Sub-Objects of Polygonal Meshes" for more information about the Selection rollout.

A Editable Poly

When you convert an object to an editable poly, the object type and sub-objects appear in the Modifier Stack. A sub-object icon appears next to any selected sub-object level. When you apply the Edit Poly Modifier, the modifier appears above the object type in the stack.

B Selection Rollout

Contains controls for selecting editable poly sub-objects.

C Soft Selection Rollout

Contains tools for selecting sub-objects outside of the selected area, based on their proximity to the selected sub-objects.

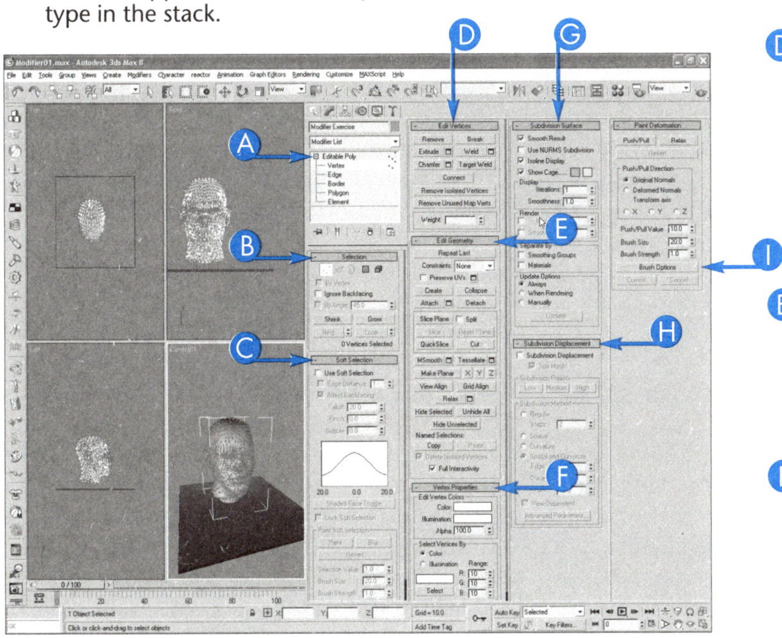

D Edit (Sub-Object) Rollout

Provides commands for editing at the sub-object level. This rollout is specific to the sub-object level that you have selected.

E Edit Geometry Rollout

Provides commands for editing the object, regardless of the sub-object level.

F (Sub-Object) Properties Rollout

Provides commands for customizing the appearance of the selected sub-object type in the viewports.

I Paint Deformation Rollout

Provides options for distorting sub-objects using a painting method. Strokes with a virtual brush effect displace the surfaces that it crosses.

H Subdivision Displacement Rollout

Provides options for determining how a surface is altered when you apply a Displacement map.

G Subdivision Surface Rollout

Provides options for altering the surface characteristics of the object.

Select Sub-Objects of Polygonal Meshes

When you select the components of editable poly objects, you can move, delete, weld, or otherwise edit these sections without affecting the sub-objects in the surrounding area. You can select the vertices, edges, polygons, a border around an opening, or an element, as well as the entire polygon. You can display an object's available sub-object levels by selecting it, opening the Modify panel, and then expanding the sub-object list in the Modifier Stack. You can also set the sub-object level using the appropriate button in the Selection rollout or by selecting an option from the quad menu.

Switching Sub-Object Levels with Keyboard Keys

The 1–5 keys along the top of the keyboard — not in the numeric keypad — switch 3ds Max to the same sub-object level as the button's location in the Selection rollout. For example, the 1 key switches to Vertex mode for editable polys and editable meshes, but the 3 key switches editable polys to Border mode and editable meshes to Face mode.

Selecting Editable Mesh or Editable Poly Components

You can select the components of an editable mesh or editable poly — called *sub-objects* — using most of the selection methods covered in Chapter 2, including selecting the sub-objects and using one of the selection region options located in the Main toolbar. The selection region options select all of the sub-objects entirely within, and those crossing the selection border also depend on whether the Crossing or Window option is active in the Main toolbar. Both of these options select sub-objects that are facing the current viewport as well as any sub-objects that are masked by the surfaces of the model and not currently visible. By selecting the Ignore Backfacing option in the Selection rollout, selection regions only select sub-objects that are facing the current viewport. For example, if a viewport displays the left side of a character's face and a rectangular selection region is created encompassing the entire head, only the vertices on the left side are selected. Vertices on the right side of the face, those that are oriented away from the viewport, are not selected.

Recalling Sub-Object Selections

It is common to recall a sub-object selection so that you can perform additional modifications on the same sub-objects. When you create a character model, you may need to repeatedly select the mouth, nostrils, or areas around the eyes to manipulate those areas. Just as they are used with geometry objects, you can use named selection sets with sub-object selections to quickly make redundant selections. You simply select the required sub-objects and then give a name for the set in the Named Selection Sets field in the Main toolbar. To recall the selection, you select it in the Named Selection Sets field. An object's sub-object named selection sets are only available when you are at a sub-object level for that object. See Chapter 3 for more information on named selection sets.

The Appearance of Selected Sub-Objects

When you select any sub-objects, your selections appear highlighted in red and any unselected sub-objects appear in blue. When sub-objects are selected using the Soft Selection option, their color is determined by their proximity to the truly selected sub-objects. See the section "Using Soft Selection to Transform Vertices" for more information on soft selections. You must exit any sub-object level in order to select another object in the scene.

Faces, and the Face Normal

Faces, both standalone and those that comprise polygons, have only one visible side by default. This side is determined by a vector called the *face normal* and you make this vector visible by selecting the Show Normals option in the Selection rollout. The normals, for any selected faces, appear as a blue line springing from the center of each face. Normals do not render and can assist in determining the cause of some rendering problems, including faces that appear to be absent. Applying a 2-Sided material overrides the visibility of the non-normal side of a face. See Chapters 14, 15, and 16 for information on materials.

The Selection Rollout

The following table and graphics list the buttons in the Selection rollout for both Editable Meshes and Editable Polys and illustrate exactly what you are selecting with each button.

Sub-Object Buttons in the Selection Rollout

Sub-object	Button	Definition
Vertex		A singular point in space defined by its X, Y, and Z coordinates in World space. Two edges that share a common endpoint can also share a vertex. Although vertices are usually found at the end of edges, they can also be isolated objects.
Edge		A linear feature that connects two vertices and forms the perimeter of faces and polygons. Visible edges are shown as solid lines in the viewports. Invisible edges, indicated by dotted lines, do not display in the viewport.
Border		In an Editable Poly object, this sub-object is comprised of the edges around the perimeter of a hole in an object.
Face		In an Editable Mesh object, this sub-object is a renderable object with three sides and three vertices. When co-planar faces exist within the same object, the faces form polygon sub-objects.
Polygon		Comprised of one or more co-planar faces that are bounded by visible edges. Polygons can have an unlimited number of edges and vertices.
Element		A collection of polygons within an editable mesh or editable poly object. You can select the element separately from an Editable Mesh object, even though the element typically comprises the entire object. Using the Attach command to attach one mesh to another causes each mesh to become an element of the new, greater mesh.

Create Editable Poly Objects

You can convert objects to editable poly objects to make sub-object edits, such as extruding a face or moving vertices. You can convert your object to either an editable mesh or an editable poly, and both object types allow you to work at the sub-object levels. However, because the editable poly's tools are more powerful, it is the focus of this section.

Once you create an editable poly, you cannot change the parameters of the original object, or any modifiers that were applied. For example, if you convert a twisted box to an editable poly, then you cannot change the segment parameters for the box, or the angle for the modifier.

3ds Max automatically converts most objects to editable meshes when you collapse the Modifier Stack. Some modifiers allow you to specify the type of object that you want to create before collapsing the stack, by selecting the object, and then selecting the object type from the quad menu.

See the sections "Understanding Polygonal Mesh Objects" and "Select Sub-Objects of Polygonal Meshes" for more information about polygonal mesh objects and sub-objects.

CD FILE: The Editable Poly.max file is available on the CD-ROM for you to practice creating Editable Poly objects.

Create Editable Poly Objects

Convert the Object from the Modifier Stack

1. Select an object to convert.
2. Right-click a blank area in the Modifier Stack.
3. Click Collapse All.

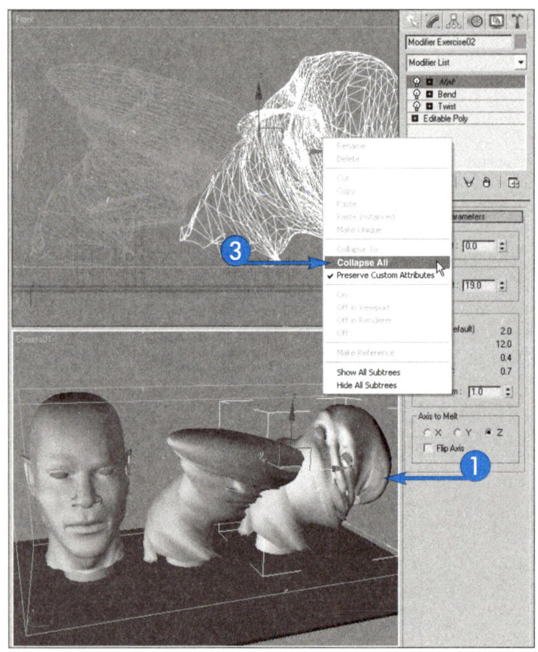

A Warning dialog box appears, indicating the loss of parameter control and animation.

4. Click Yes.

The selected object converts to an editable poly.

The object appears as an Editable Poly in the Modify panel.

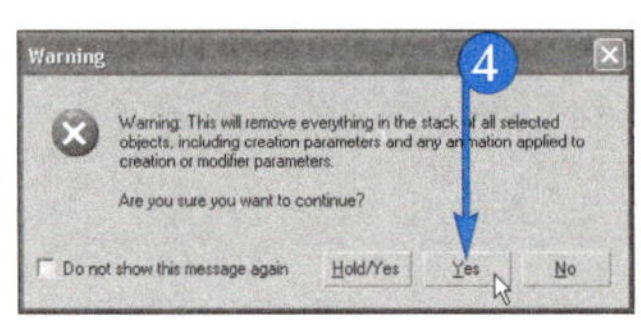

Convert the Object with the Quad Menu

1. Select an object to convert.
2. Right-click the object.
3. In the Quad menu, click Convert To.
4. Click Convert to Editable Poly.

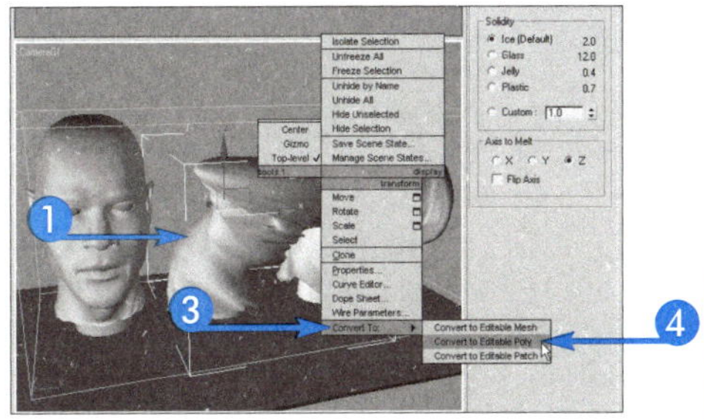

The selected object converts to an editable poly.

- The object appears as an Editable Poly in the Modify panel.

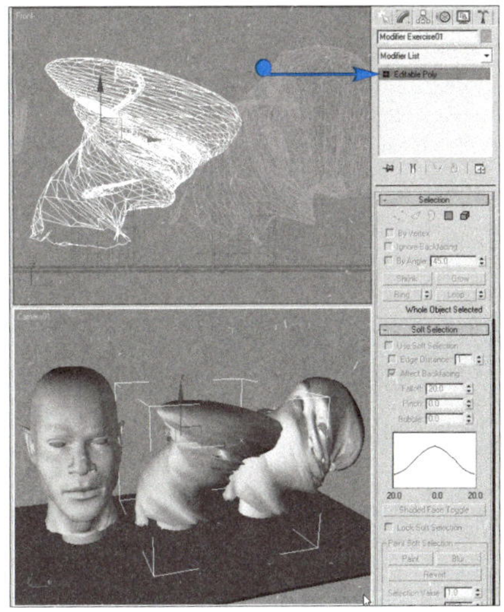

MASTER IT

When do I apply the Edit Poly Modifier instead of converting the object to an Editable Poly?

In most cases, converting an object to an editable poly is the preferred method. This is because changing the parameters in a modifier below the Edit Poly Modifier may yield unexpected results. When you select a modifier below Edit Poly, a dialog box appears to warn you of the unpredictable outcome. The Edit Poly Modifier is useful for experimenting with its tools on your object before collapsing the result into an editable poly object. Like any other modifier, you can disable or remove an Edit Poly from the object's Modifier Stack. See the section "Using the Modifier Stack" for more information on applying modifiers.

Can I convert a group or selection of objects to editable polys?

Yes. If you select several objects, you can right-click one of them, click Convert To, and then click Convert to Editable Poly from the quad menu. Each object is converted into a distinct editable poly. Because the Modifier Stack method is not available to convert multiple objects into editable polys, you must use the quad menu to do so. You can also use the quad menu to convert a selected group into editable polys. Each group member is converted and remains a member of the group. To convert an individual group member, you must open the group and then select the object before converting it. For more on groups, see Chapter 3.

Cut a Polygon

You can cut one polygon into two or more polygons using the Cut command in the Edit Geometry rollout. Cutting a polygon allows you to add visible edges so that you can transform only a part of the original polygon. For example, to create a recess in a wall, you can use the Cut command to create a door-sized polygon. You can then use commands such as Bevel and Offset to transform your new polygon to make it look more like a door.

You can begin your cut at any location on an existing edge. 3ds Max then adds a vertex where your cut begins. As you move the cursor to create an edge, 3ds Max automatically snaps, or extends, the end of the edge to the nearest vertex. Clicking your mouse creates additional vertices and edges between each subsequent vertex. You can right-click to terminate the Cut command. Keep in mind that you must select an existing vertex or edge as a starting point; you cannot create the first vertex in the center of a polygon. See the section "Understanding Polygonal Mesh Objects" for more information.

CD FILE: The Cut.max file is available on the CD-ROM for you to practice cutting polygons.

Cut a Polygon

1. Select an Editable Poly object to cut.

Note: *For more on creating an Editable Poly object, see the section "Create Editable Poly Objects."*

2. Click Cut.
3. Click where you want to create your first cut on the shape.

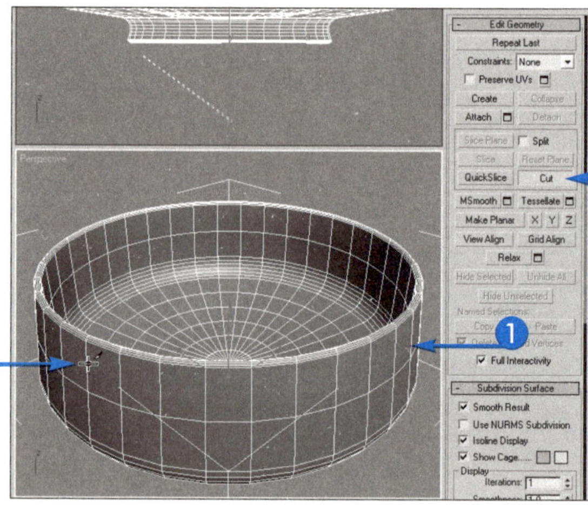

3ds Max creates the first vertex.

4. Move the cursor.
   - The edges that you are creating snap to the cursor location and the nearest vertex.
5. Click to create a vertex.

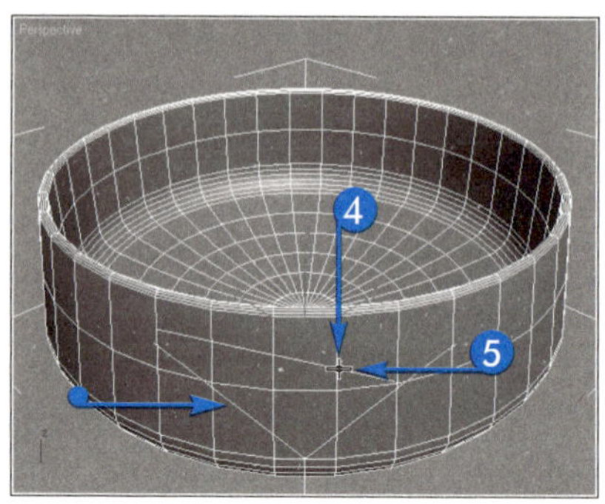

3ds Max creates another vertex and an edge between the two vertices.

6. Repeat steps 4 and 5 to create additional vertices.

7. Right-click to complete the cut.

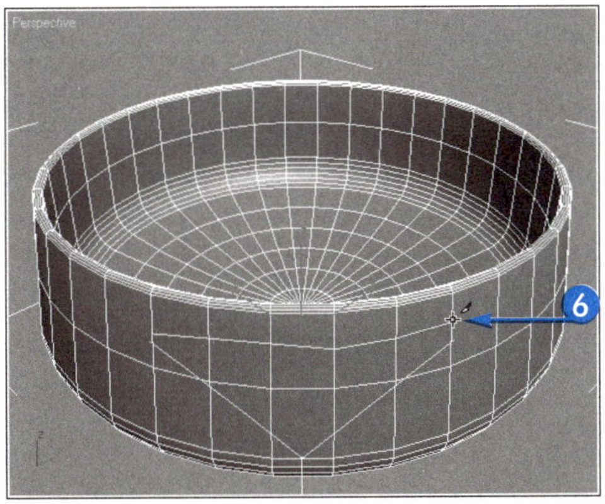

- 3ds Max creates the new polygons from the cut.

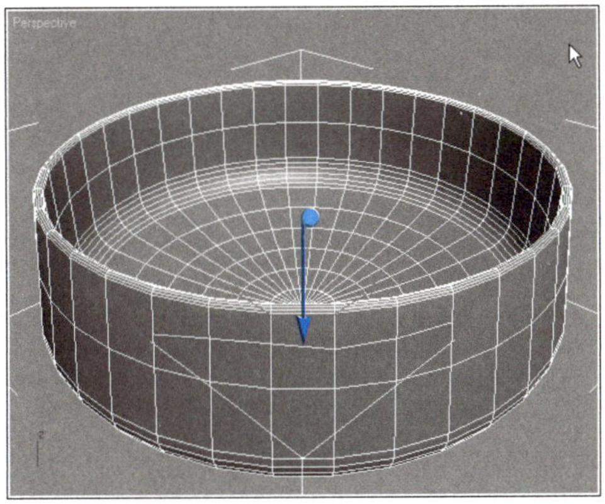

MASTER IT

How is the QuickSlice command different from the Cut command?

Although you can use the QuickSlice command to slice a polygon into two polygons, you do not have the same control as with the Cut command. When you use the QuickSlice command, it creates a slice plane between two edges that you select. This plane then projects through the entire object, cutting every polygon that it crosses. For example, if you QuickSlice across the front of a box, not only is the front polygon cut, but so are the back and two side polygons. The Cut tool, on the other hand, only cuts the surface on which you draw the edges. See the section "Select Sub-Objects of Polygonal Meshes" for more information about selecting sub-objects.

Why does the Cut command connect an edge to an existing vertex?

When you use the Cut command on an editable poly, by default, each vertex point that you create has one edge that snaps to a vertex or edge of the original shape. As you drag the mouse, the cut snaps to whichever vertex is closest. To cut a polygon in the center of another polygon, 3ds Max creates a visible edge to connect the new polygon to the old polygon. This is because, by definition, edges are the boundaries of faces or polygons, and it is impossible to terminate an edge in the middle of a face. Therefore, the Cut command snaps to a vertex, thus requiring you to create edges that form polygons.

Bevel and Extrude a Polygon

When you extrude a polygon, you are projecting it perpendicular to its surface and creating new edges and faces that connect the polygon's new location to its previous location. For example, you can create a cylinder when you extrude a circle. Beveling is similar to extruding, except that the extruded edges do not have to be parallel, and the polygon can become wider or narrower as it moves farther from its starting point. Bevels and extrusions can be either positive, away from your object, or negative, projecting into your object.

When you select a polygon sub-object, the Bevel command appears in the Edit Polygons rollout. You can create freehand bevels and extrusions by moving the mouse over the polygons, or you can use the Settings buttons, next to the appropriate tools, to create the features using dialog boxes.

When you bevel and extrude a polygon, 3ds Max limits your creation to one segmented level. To create multiple levels of beveling or extrusions, you must repeat the process. To make this easier, 3ds Max always leaves the original polygon selected after you conduct a bevel or extrusion operation.

The BevelExtrude.max file is available on the CD-ROM for you to practice beveling and extruding polygons.

Bevel and Extrude a Polygon

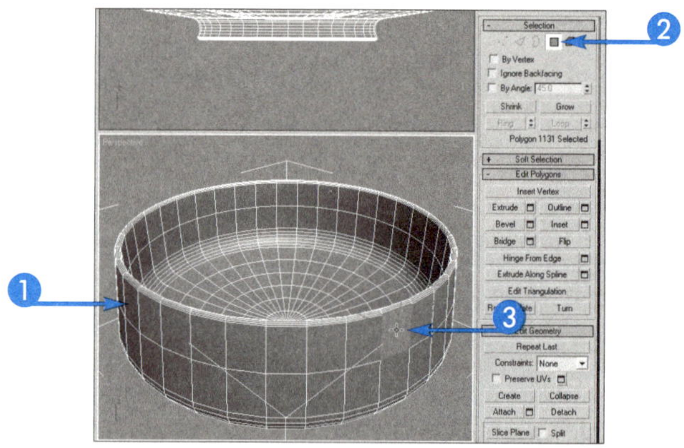

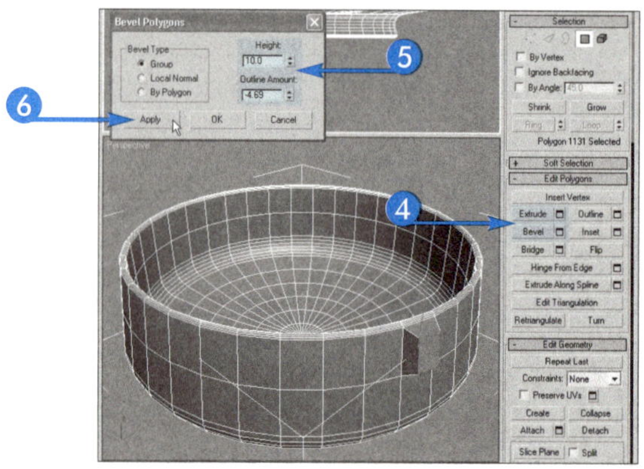

1 Select an Editable Poly object.

Note: *For more on creating an Editable Poly object, see the section "Create Editable Poly Objects."*

2 Click the Polygon button (▣).

3ds Max selects the polygon sub-object level.

3 Click the polygon that you want to bevel.

4 In the Edit Polygons rollout, click either Bevel or Extrude.

If the Edit Polygons rollout is not visible, then you can click and drag the Scroll bar to display it.

The Bevel or Extrude Polygons dialog box appears.

5 If you are creating a bevel, then type Height and Outline Amount values.

3ds Max previews the extruded or beveled polygons.

6 Click Apply.

- The command is executed and 3ds Max previews a repeat of the function.

7. Repeat steps 5 and 6 to create another bevel or extrusion.

8. Click OK to terminate the command and delete the preview.

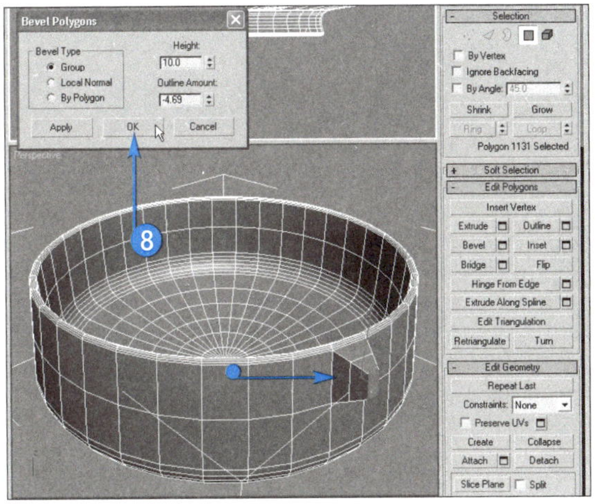

- 3ds Max creates the bevel or extrusion for the selected polygon.

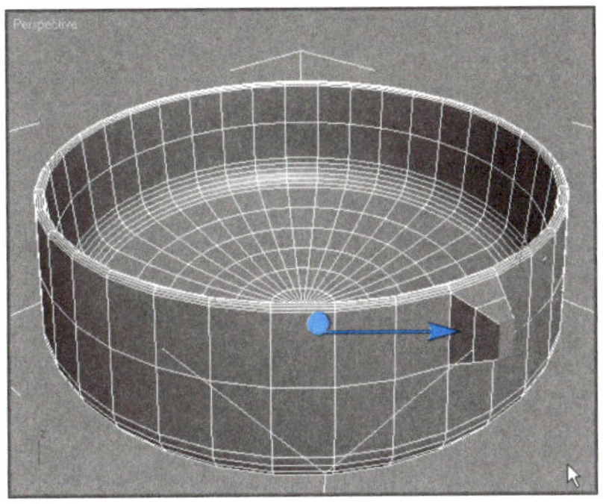

MASTER IT

What is a practical use of the Extrude or Bevel tool?

Many manufactured shapes have tapered sides. This is for aesthetics as well as function and ease of manufacturing. For example, to create a button on a console, you may begin with a small negative bevel that causes the polygon to taper as it recedes into the surface and creates the well into which a user can push the button. You can then use a positive bevel where the button again tapers inward, but this time, it projects above the surface of the console. This is the shaft of the button. Finally, a slight negative bevel forms a small depression on the top of the button that makes it comfortable to press.

Can I bevel and extrude other sub-object types?

Beveling is only available at the polygon sub-object level. However, you can use the Extrude tool with the other sub-objects types. When you extrude a sub-object, you move it away from or into the object, perpendicular to the sub-object's orientation. Any related sub-objects are altered to accommodate the extrusion that you perform. For example, if you extrude a vertex, then 3ds Max creates and adjusts the edges that are required to keep the vertex connected to the object.

Using Soft Selection to Transform Vertices

You can use soft selection to eliminate the jaggedness that occurs when you select and move vertices on an object. With soft selection, 3ds Max transforms the vertices near the selection to a lesser extent than the selected vertices themselves. This results in a smoother transition between edges. For example, if you move a vertex on a sphere without soft selection, then a sharp spike results. Moving the same vertex with soft selection creates a smooth-sided bulge.

You can control how the soft selection affects your object by defining the radius of the soft selection area, referred to as Falloff. The greater the Falloff, the more of the surrounding area is affected by the transformations. You can see the affected vertices and edges by selecting the vertices that you want to move. The soft selection areas are highlighted in different colors to show the degree to which those vertices are affected. Red vertices receive the full effect of a transform, while blue vertices are unaffected. The Pinch and Bubble values determine the amount of control that the transform has over the vertices that are not fully selected.

CD FILE: The Soft Selection.max file is available on the CD-ROM for you to practice using soft selections.

Using Soft Selection to Transform Vertices

1. Select an editable poly.

Note: *For more on creating an Editable Poly object, see the section "Create Editable Poly Objects."*

2. Click the Vertex button (▫).
3. Select the vertices that you want to transform.

Note: *For more information on selection methods, see Chapter 2.*

4. Click the Use Soft Selection option (☐ changes to ☑).

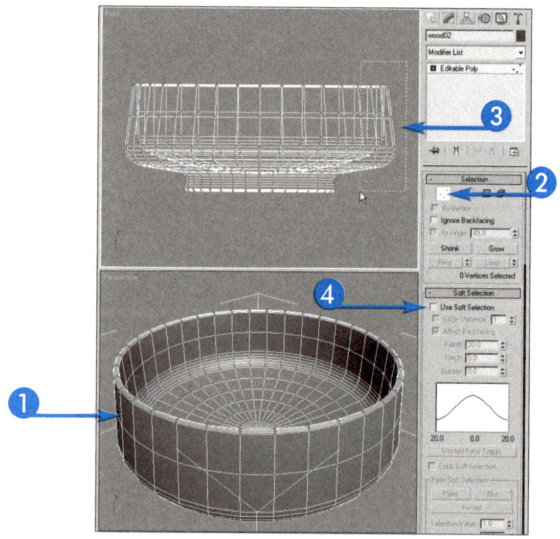

The default Falloff area is highlighted around the vertices that you selected.

5. Type a Falloff value.
   - If you want, you can also type Pinch and Bubble values.

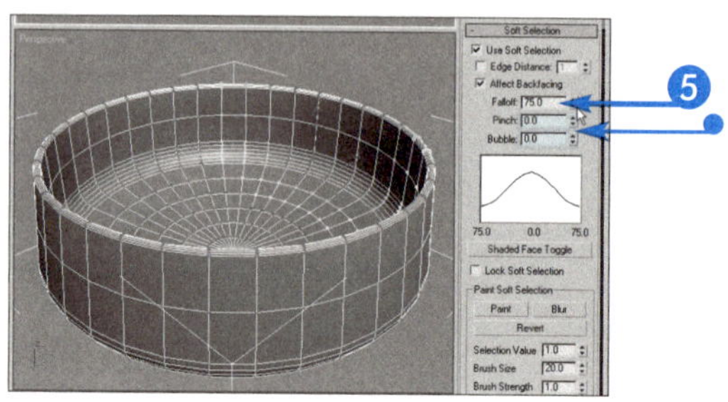

The Falloff area adjusts with the new settings.

- The Soft Selection Curve graphically displays the soft selection.

6 Click the Select and Move button (⊕).

7 Click and drag the selected vertices.

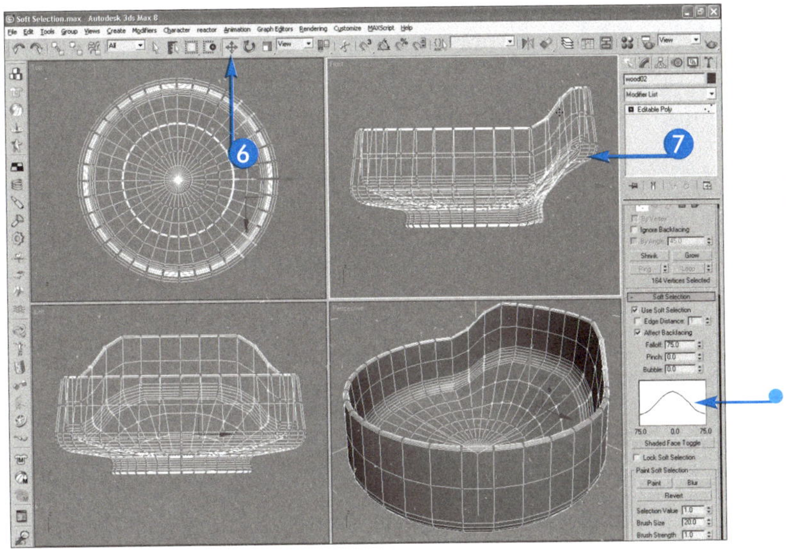

The surrounding vertices and edges adjust, based upon the soft selection settings.

The soft selection area adjusts as you move the selected vertex.

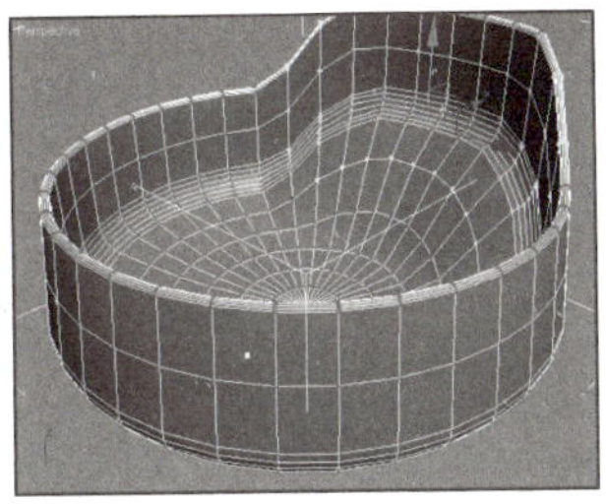

MASTER IT

Can I control the number of edges that I have in a selection?

▼ Yes. To select only the edges within a specific area of an object, click the Edge Distance option (☐ changes to ☑). In the Edge Distance field, type the maximum number of edges to include between the selected vertices or edges and the edge of the selection area. 3ds Max measures the number of edges on all sides of the selected vertices and combines the Edge Distance value with the specified Falloff value to determine the selection area's actual size. The area is not any larger than the number of edges that you specify, but the Falloff value may make the area smaller.

How can I preview the effect of my selection on the transformation?

▼ When you select edges or vertices on your object, 3ds Max displays the soft selection area using a gradient range of colors from red to blue. The vertices that you specifically select are red. The vertices and edges that are most affected by the soft selection are reddish-orange. The effect of the soft selection decreases, based on a sub-object's distance from the initial selection, and 3ds Max illustrates this decrease with a color change: Orange shows the next affected selections, followed by yellow-orange, yellow, yellow-green, green, and blue-green. Your transformation does not affect vertices and edges that 3ds Max displays in blue.

Simplify and Fix Geometry

You can remove edges and vertices using the Target Weld and Remove tools in the Edit Vertices rollout. This is a useful feature, as object modeling commonly results in the geometry of an object becoming too complex, so that the object contains unnecessary edges or vertices.

You can use the Target Weld tools to eliminate unwanted vertices that you may inadvertently create when you transform an object's geometry. You need to remove these unattached vertices because they can produce gaps within the surfaces of your geometry. The Target Weld tool welds the selected vertex to the vertex to which you drag it, thus allowing you to control where you want the weld to occur. Keep in mind that you can only weld a vertex to another vertex that is separated by a shared edge.

You can use the Remove tool to eliminate unwanted edges. For example, when you create multiple polygons on the side of a box object with the QuickSlice tool, you can simplify the object's surfaces by removing unnecessary edges and combining adjacent polygons into a single polygon.

The Weld.max file is available on the CD-ROM for you to practice welding vertices.

Simplify and Fix Geometry

Weld Vertices

1. Select an editable poly.

Note: *For more on creating an Editable Poly object, see the section "Create Editable Poly Objects."*

2. Click .
3. Click Target Weld in the Edit Vertices rollout.
4. Click and drag a vertex to the vertex to which you want to weld it.
   - To delete vertices, you can click Remove in the Edit Vertices rollout.

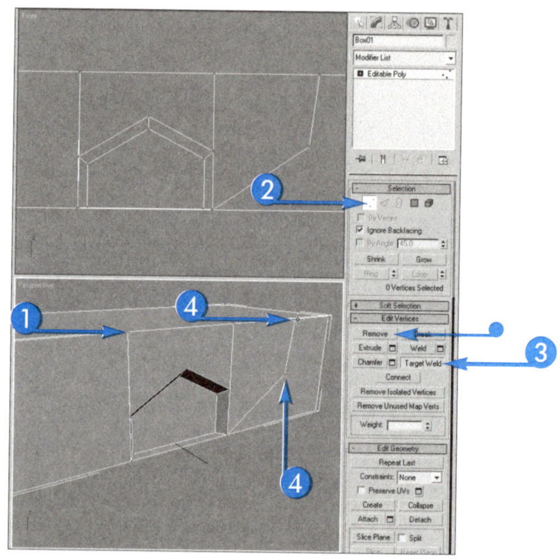

3ds Max welds the selected vertices together into one vertex.

You can repeat step 4 to weld additional vertices.

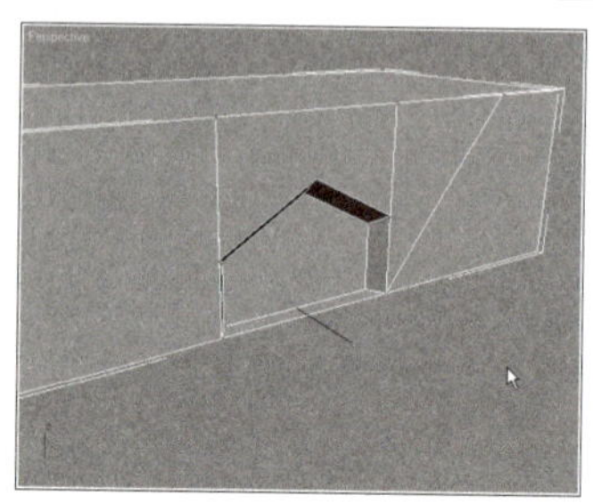

Remove Unwanted Edges

1. Click the Edge button (▢).
2. Click the edge that you want to remove.

   You can press and hold Ctrl to select multiple edges.
3. Click Remove in the Edit Edges rollout.

   If the Edit Edges rollout is not displayed, then you can click and drag the Scroll bar.

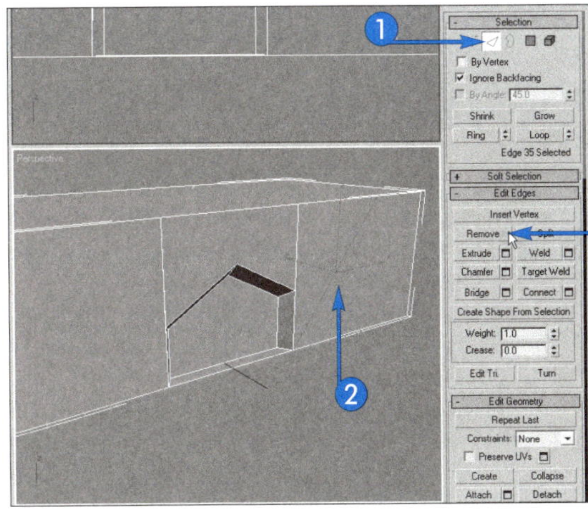

3ds Max removes the selected edges from the object.

MASTER IT

Can I quickly combine multiple vertices without clicking and dragging?

▼ Yes. You can use the Weld tool to quickly combine selected vertices, within a specific distance, into a single vertex. You can specify the range using the Weld Threshold field in the Weld Vertices dialog box, which you can display by clicking the Settings button (▣) next to the Weld button. The Weld Threshold value is the maximum distance within which 3ds Max welds all vertices together. 3ds Max creates the new vertex by averaging the original locations of the selected vertices. You can also use the Weld command to combine edges within a specific threshold. You can only weld edges with one polygon attached.

What happens when I use the Collapse tool on vertices?

▼ Located in the Edit Geometry rollout, the Collapse tool provides another method for combining vertices. It combines all of the selected vertices into one vertex and, unlike Weld, it does not use a threshold value to combine vertices within a certain range. Instead, it combines all vertices into a single vertex, regardless of the distance between the vertices. The new vertex location is an average of the distance between the selected vertices. Although clicking Collapse quickly combines vertices, it does not offer the control that is available with the Target Weld tool.

continued

Simplify and Fix Geometry *(Continued)*

As you adjust the vertices and edges of your geometry, you may inadvertently alter polygon faces. For example, after you make a transformation to an object, a polygon may no longer connect to the appropriate vertices — even though the vertices still exist — thus creating a gap in the surface. You can correct this problem by creating a new polygon face for your object. However, if the Cap command is not the best tool for the job, this may require that you delete an existing polygon so that you can create a new polygon to connect to the desired vertices.

You can use the Create command to create a new polygon for an editable poly object. This command selects all of the vertices in the selected object. You must select each of the vertices for your new polygon. You can create the new polygon by starting at one vertex and moving counterclockwise around the gap. Selected vertices are highlighted in red, indicating where 3ds Max will create the new polygon.

When you work with a polygon, you can select an unlimited number of vertices; however, the last vertex that you select must be the vertex where you started.

Simplify and Fix Geometry *(continued)*

Correct Polygon Edges

1. Select an editable poly.
2. Click .
3. Click the polygon that you want to remove.
4. Press Delete.

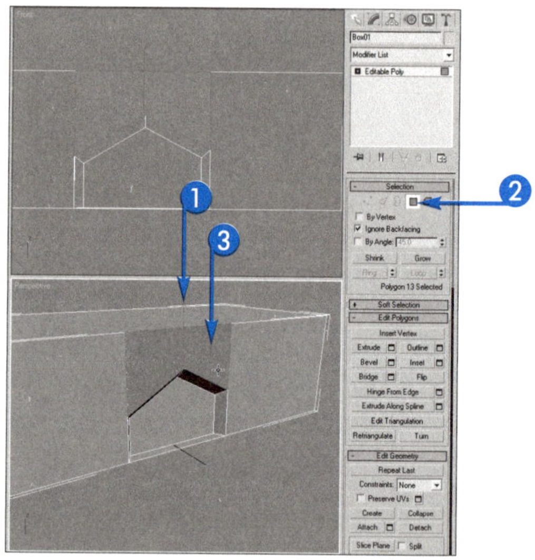

- 3ds Max removes the selected polygon from the object and creates a gap.

5. Click Create in the Edit Geometry rollout.
6. Click the first vertex.
7. Click and drag to the next vertex.

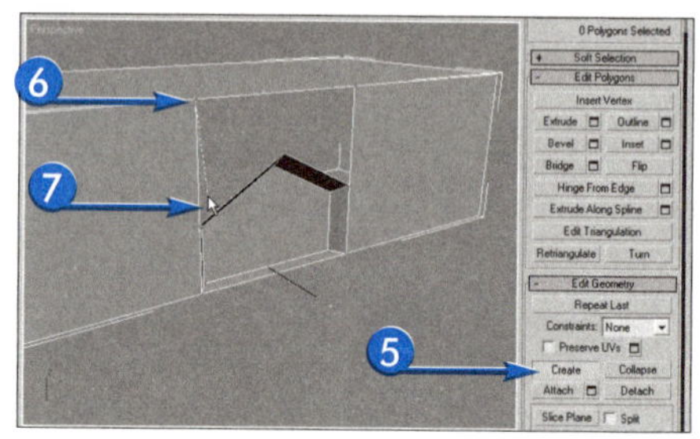

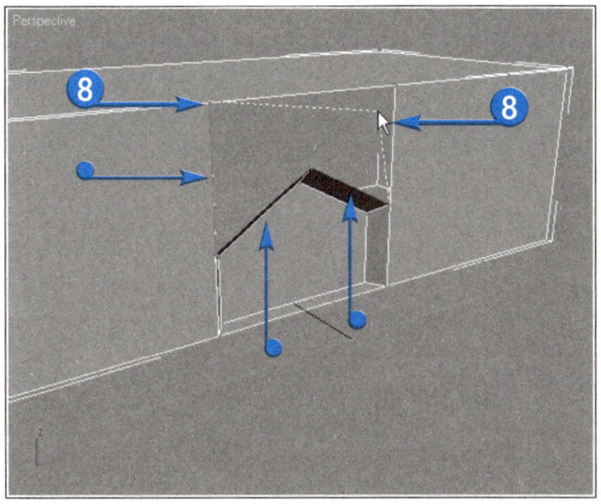

- The edge between the selected vertices is highlighted in red.

8 Continue clicking vertices until you click the original vertex.

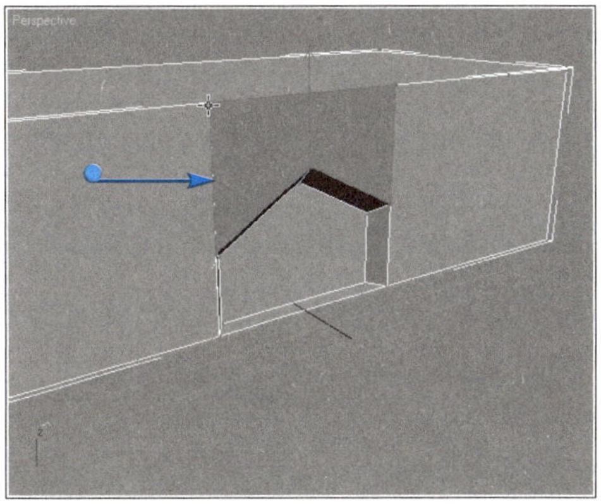

- 3ds Max creates a polygon that connects the selected vertices.

MASTER IT

Can I use the Cap command to fix a hole?

Yes. Depending on the geometry of your object, you may be able to fix a hole by replacing a polygon with the Cap command. To use the Cap command, click the Border button ( ) and then click an edge that surrounds the hole. 3ds Max automatically selects all of the edges in the hole's perimeter. To cap the hole, click Cap in the Edit Borders rollout. 3ds Max creates a polygon for the specified edges. The Cap tool may not be appropriate when you do not want to fill all of the edge borders with the same polygon, or if the hole's perimeter is jagged and uneven.

Can I add new vertices to the polygon?

Yes. When you use the Create command to create a polygon, you must click a vertex to create a polygon edge. If a vertex does not exist in the location that you want, you can create one by pressing and holding Shift while you click. You can create a new vertex along an existing edge, or within the hole that you are filling. The new vertices become a part of the geometry of the object. You can press Shift to create new vertices on both editable mesh and editable poly objects.

Create a Boolean Compound Object

Boolean compound objects create a single complex object by combining two simpler objects. You can create a Boolean compound object by performing one of three mathematical operations: Union, Intersection, or Subtraction. For example, you can remove a bite-shaped section of a sandwich by overlapping a closed-teeth-and-mouth object with the edge of the sandwich and then selecting the Subtract operation.

The objects with which you begin are referred to as *operands*, with the first selected object being Operand A and the second selected object being Operand B. The operands must be 3D objects and should have neither holes nor gaps in their geometry. If they have holes, then you may need to correct their geometry before performing a Boolean command. See the section "Add Thickness with the Shell Modifier" to see one repair method.

The Union operation combines the two operands together and removes the faces where the two operands overlap to create a new, clean surface. The Intersection operation does the exact opposite by combining the two operands only where they overlap and deleting the remaining geometry. The Subtraction operation is discussed in the next section.

CD FILE: The Boolean1.max file is available on the CD-ROM for you to practice creating Boolean compound objects.

Create a Boolean Compound Object

Perform a Union or Intersection Operation

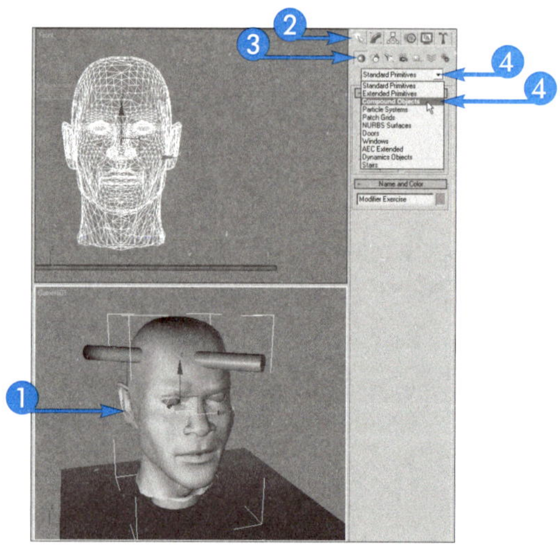

1. Select the first object that you want to combine.
2. Click the Create tab ( ).

   The Create panel appears.
3. Click the Geometry button ( ).
4. Click here and select Compound Objects.

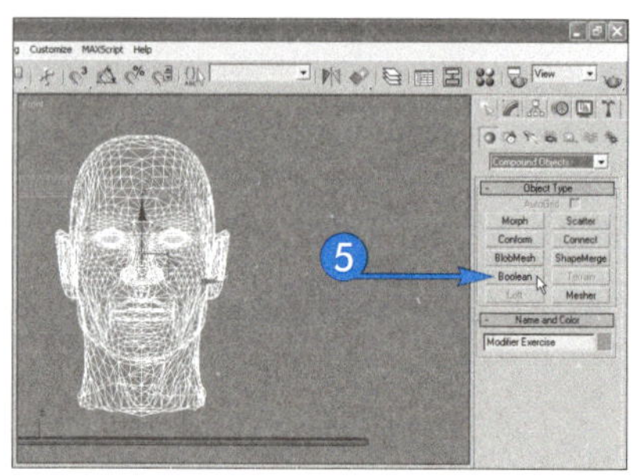

   The available compound object types appear in the Object Type rollout.
5. Click Boolean.

   If you have not selected a 3D object, then this option is unavailable.

The Boolean rollouts appear in the Create panel.

3ds Max lists the object that you selected as Operand A.

6 Click either the Union or Intersection option (◯ changes to ◉).

This example uses the Union operation.

7 Click Pick Operand B.

8 Select the object that you want to combine with the first object.

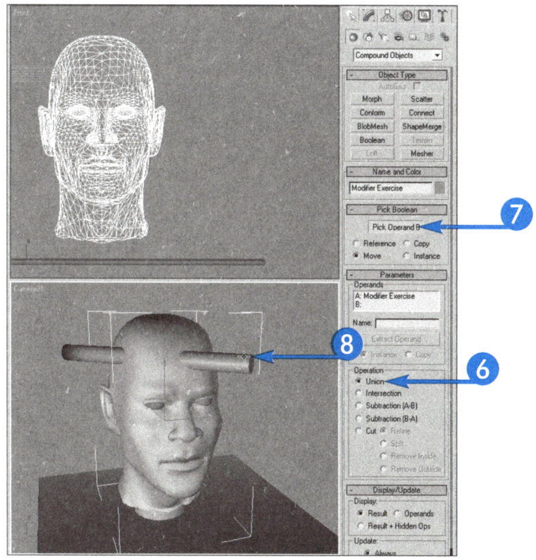

The two objects combine to create one Boolean object.

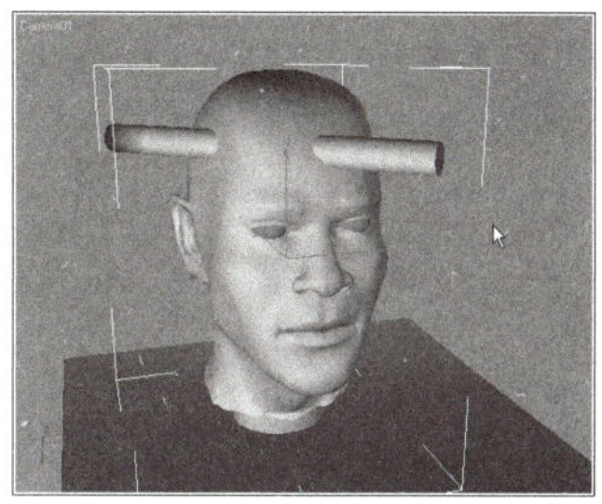

PART II

What happens to the materials that I have assigned to each object?

When you create a Boolean object from two objects that have assigned materials, 3ds Max allows you to address the material and mapping coordinates through the use of dialog boxes. If both objects have materials applied, 3ds Max prompts you for one of five choices for applying the materials and mapping coordinates. If only one object has a material, then 3ds Max asks whether the operand that does not have a material should inherit the material from the operand that does. For more information about mapping coordinates and applying materials to objects, see Chapters 14, 15, and 16.

Can I change the Boolean operation for an object?

Yes, when you create a Boolean compound object, 3ds Max stores the operands with the object as sub-objects. At any time, you can select a different Boolean function to perform in the Operation section of the Parameters rollout. 3ds Max uses the existing operands to execute the operation.

Does it matter if I select Copy or Move when I create a Boolean object?

The Pick Boolean rollout allows you either to move the Operand B or to create Instance, Reference, or Copy clones of the operand. If you do not want to maintain the original object, select the default Move option; 3ds Max combines Operand B with Operand A. To maintain the original copy of Operand B in the scene, select another option. This allows you to use the original object elsewhere.

continued

Create a Boolean Compound Object *(Continued)*

Another common operation to perform with the Boolean compound object is Subtraction. The operation subtracts the portion of the geometry that both operands share and retains the remaining part of one operand. For example, to create a porthole in a ship's hull, you can place a cylinder through the hull. Next, apply the Subtraction operation to subtract the cylinder and any volume that it shares with the hull. The result is the hull minus a hole where the cylinder was located.

The order in which you select your operands, and the specific Subtraction operation used, are important in the Subtraction operation and determine the result. For example, if Operand A is a box and Operand B is a cylinder protruding through the box, then subtracting B from A produces a box with a hole through it. Subtracting A from B produces the two parts of the cylinder that are outside the box. There are two Subtraction options available: A-B and B-A.

You can verify the operand order by referring to the Operands box in the Parameters rollout, and then selecting the corresponding Subtraction operation.

CD FILE: The Boolean1.max file is available on the CD-ROM for you to practice creating Boolean compound objects.

Create a Boolean Compound Object *(continued)*

Perform a Subtraction

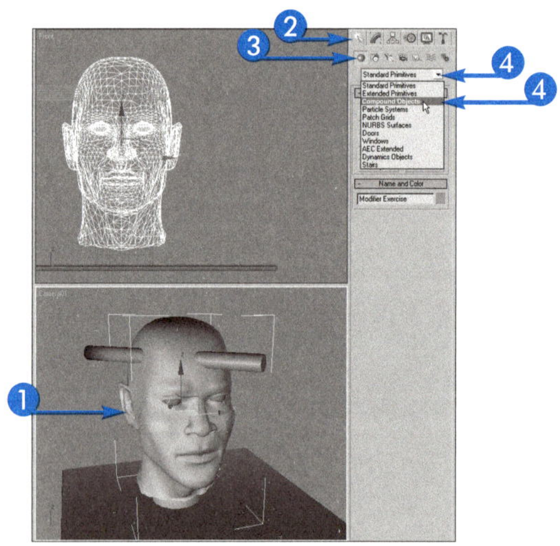

1. Select an object that you want to combine.
2. Click .

   The Create panel appears.
3. Click .
4. Click here and select Compound Objects.

   The available compound object types appear in the Object Type rollout.

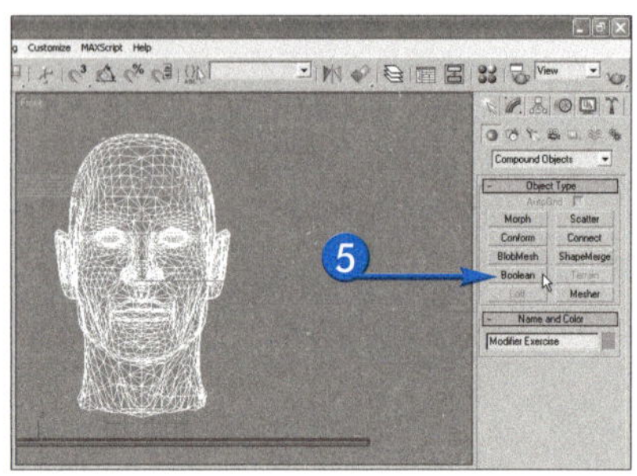

5. Click Boolean.

   If you have not selected a 3D object, then this option is unavailable.

The Boolean rollouts appear in the Create panel.

The object that you selected is listed as Operand A.

6 Click a "Subtraction" option (○ changes to ◉).

7 Click Pick Operand B.

8 Click the object that you want to subtract, or from which you want to subtract, depending on the option that you chose in step 6.

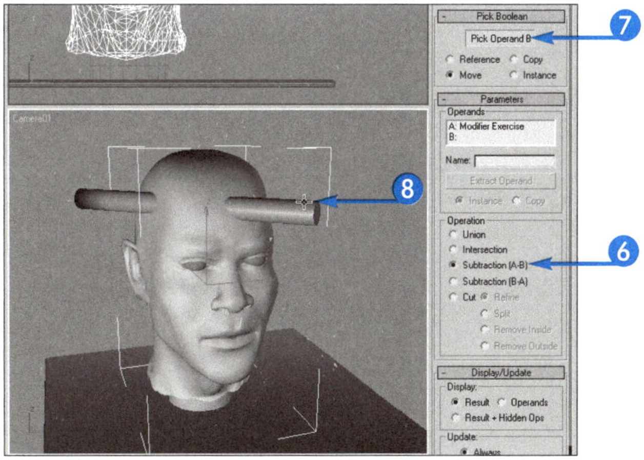

3ds Max subtracts one object from the other.

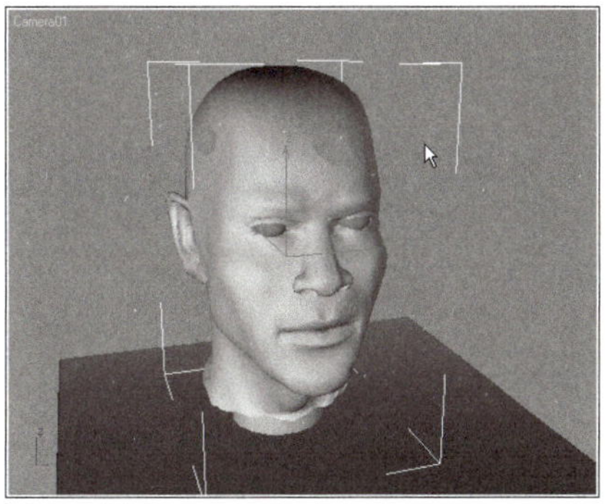

MASTER IT

Why did an object disappear when I performed another Boolean operation?

▼ Boolean operations are designed to work with only two operands. When you click Pick Operand B and then select a second Operand B, the first Operand B is deleted. There are two ways to subtract several objects from a single object with a Boolean operation. After creating a Boolean compound object, you can deselect it, then reselect it, and use the result of the previous Boolean as an operand in the new Boolean operation. This is called a *nested boolean*. A second method is to select one of the objects that will be a single element of a multi-element operand and attach the other operands to it. This creates a single operand comprised of several non-contiguous elements.

How can I view the original objects that created the Boolean object?

▼ When you create a Boolean object, 3ds Max maintains all information about the Boolean operation, including the operands. To view the operand objects, select the Boolean object and open the Modify panel by clicking . In the Display/Update rollout, click Operands to view the individual operands that you used to create the object, or click Result + Hidden Ops to view any invisible operands as wireframes. To reposition an operand, click next to Boolean in the Modifier Stack, and then choose Operands. Select an operand and then use any of the transforms to change its position, rotation, or scale.

Create a ShapeMerge Compound Object

You can use the ShapeMerge compound object to project the perimeter of a shape onto the surface of an object as new edges. The Merge option leaves the polygons that are created by these new edges intact so that they can then be deleted, extruded, or manipulated. The Cookie Cutter option deletes the new polygons.

To create a ShapeMerge compound object, your scene must contain both a 3D object and a 2D shape object. The shape is projected backward onto the surface, and so you must orient the shape to the object so that its local negative Z-axis faces the 3D object. For example, to create a cutout on a surface that is oriented toward the Front viewport, you can place your shape in front of the 3D object. For more information about creating and editing shapes, see Chapter 5. For information on rotating an object, see Chapter 2.

You can specify how to transfer the shape to the object by choosing the Move, Copy, Instance, or Reference options. See the section "Create a Boolean Compound Object" for more information about these options.

CD FILE The ShapeMerge.max file is available on the CD-ROM for you to practice creating ShapeMerge compound objects.

Create a ShapeMerge Compound Object

1. Select a 3D object.
2. Click .

   The Create panel appears.
3. Click .
4. Click here and select Compound Objects.

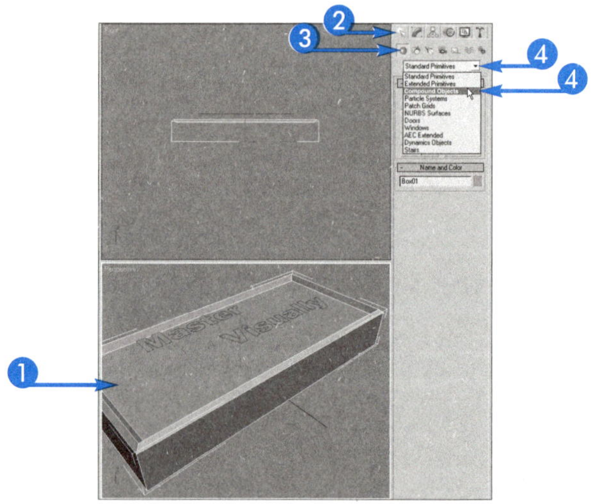

   The available compound object types appear in the Object Type rollout.
5. Click ShapeMerge.

   If you do not have a shape object that 3ds Max can combine with another object, then the ShapeMerge button is grayed-out.

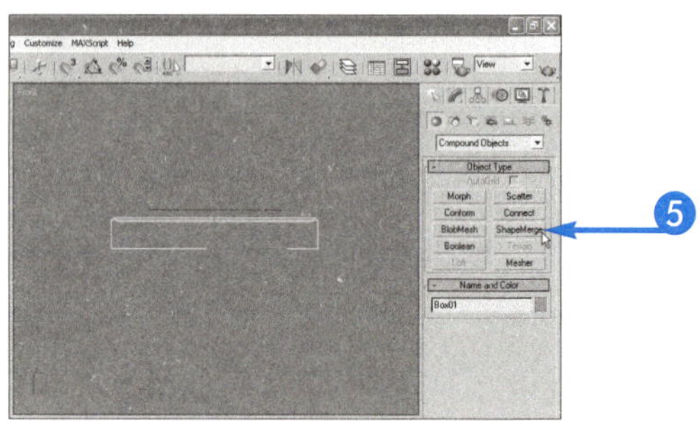

6. Click either the Cookie Cutter or Merge option (◯ changes to ◉).
7. Click a Move or Copy option (◯ changes to ◉).
8. Click Pick Shape.
9. Click the shape object.

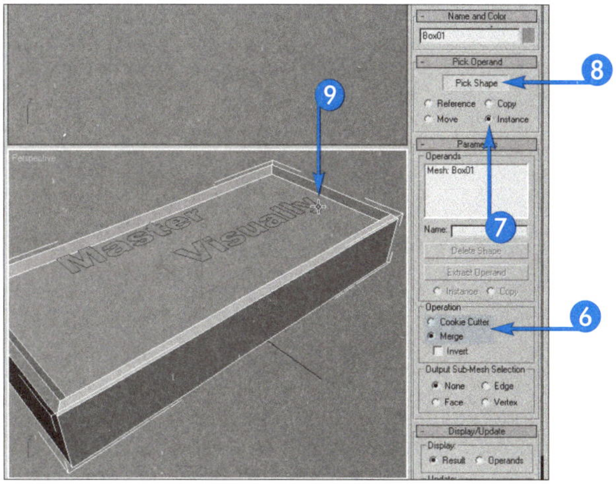

- 3ds Max adds the projected edges from the shape to the object.

Note: *You may need to turn on Edged Faces to see the new edges. For information on viewport rendering methods, see Chapter 1.*

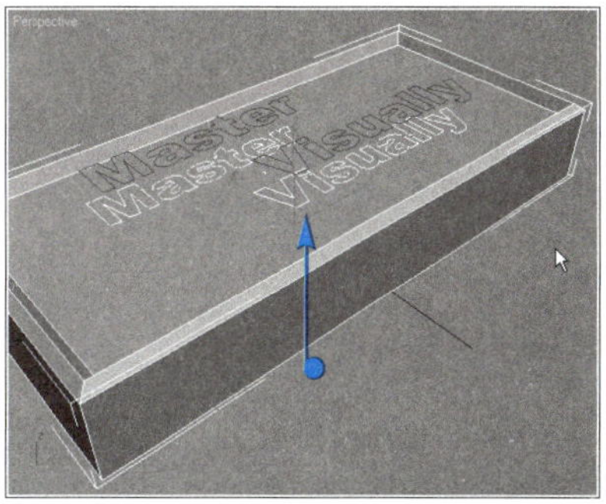

MASTER IT

How do I work with the edges or polygons of a merged shape?

When you merge a shape onto an object, 3ds Max projects the edges onto the object surface. To work with the edges, the best option is to convert the compound object to an editable poly object. You can convert the object by selecting it and then right-clicking to open the quad menu. Click Convert To, and then click Convert to Editable Poly — or Convert to Editable Mesh if you prefer — in the quad menu. Once you create an Editable Poly object, you can select the edges or polygons and use the available editing commands. For example, you can extrude the polygons from the object by selecting the Extrude command. See the section "Bevel and Extrude a Polygon" for more information.

Can I remove a shape that I have added to an object with ShapeMerge?

Yes. When you add a shape using either the Cookie Cutter or Merge operations, 3ds Max places it in the Operands list in the Parameters rollout. If you decide to remove the shape from your object, whether it was a Cookie Cutter or Merged shape, then you can do so. In the Operands list, click to select the name of the shape that you want to remove, and then click Delete Shape. 3ds Max removes the shape from your 3D object. If you want to make a copy of the shape, then click Extract Operand first to make a copy before clicking Delete Shape.

Create Walls

The major features that distinguish one architectural facility from another are the walls. Walls can form the perimeter of a structure, they can subdivide a large room into several smaller rooms, and they can act as partitions between spaces. Walls can reach from floor to ceiling, or they can terminate early, similar to the low walls that are used to guide foot traffic, or the partition walls around a cubicle.

The Wall objects in 3ds Max can help you create the kinds of walls that you need to build a structure in your scene. When you create a series of connected walls, 3ds Max considers them to be a single Wall object with several wall segments. As you create the wall segments, you can specify whether they are created to the left or right, or are centered on the cursor in the Justification area. When you place doors and windows in your walls, 3ds Max automatically creates the holes for them. If you relocate a door or window, then the hole moves with it. See the sections "Create Doors and Windows" and "Incorporate Doors and Windows into Walls" for more information.

Create Walls

Draw the Wall

1. Click the Create button ( ).
2. Click Geometry ( ).
3. Click here and select AEC Extended from the drop-down list.

   The AEC objects appear in the Object Type rollout.
4. Click Wall.

   The Wall parameters appear.
5. Set the Width and Height for the Wall.
6. Click to select an option for the Justification (○ changes to ◉).

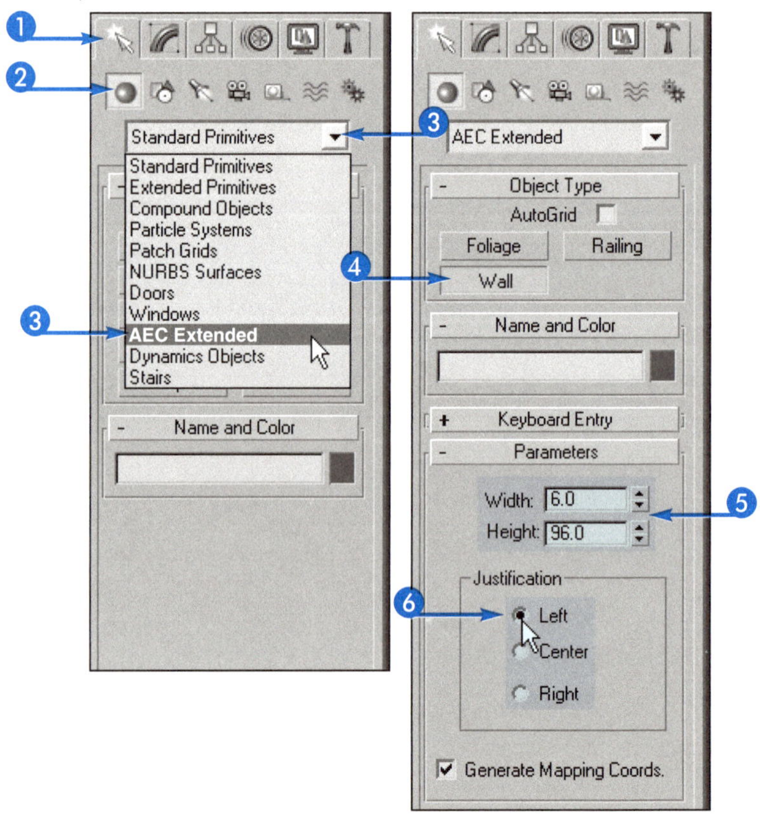

7. Click in the Top viewport to place the corners of the wall segments.
8. Click the first point that you clicked.

   The Weld Point dialog box appears.
9. Click Yes.

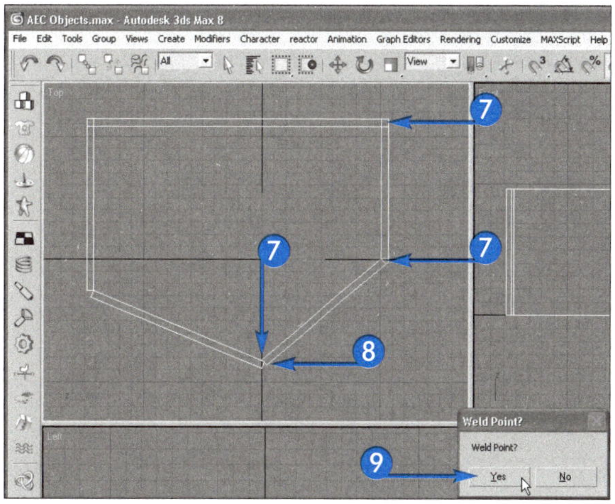

The start, and current, wall segments share a vertex.

You can right-click to discontinue creating wall segments.

Note: *When using radiosity, failing to weld the points may result in "light leaks" in the radiosity solution. See Chapter 18 for information on radiosity.*

MASTER IT

How can I keep my walls straight?

▼ When you pick the location for the corners of the walls, 3ds Max selects the precise point where the cursor is located. To force your cursor to a specfic point, and to help you keep your walls straight, click the 3D Snaps Toggle (▢) to turn the snaps on. Right-click ▢ to open the Grid and Snap Settings dialog box. In the dialog box, select Grid Points (☐ changes to ☑) and then close the dialog box. Now, whenever you move your cursor over the grid, it snaps to the grid points. For information on the Snap tools, see Chapter 2.

What does the Weld Point dialog box do?

▼ When you use Walls to create a closed room, you choose the first point selected to also be the last point selected. 3ds Max then terminates the wall at the same point that it began and opens the Weld Point dialog box. Clicking Yes in the dialog box instructs the program to use only one vertex, instead of two, to define the condition at that corner, and the overlapping geometry is deleted. This is the same condition at all of the other corners. If you click No, then two vertices define the corner, and you have the ability to open the walls by moving one of the vertices.

continued

Create Walls

(Continued)

Wall objects are easy to edit, and you can perform most edits at the sub-object level. Walls contain three types of sub-objects: vertices, segments, and profiles. Vertices are the points at the base of the Wall, at corners between Wall segments, and at the ends of Walls that terminate without forming a corner. You can reshape rooms by moving the vertices, and you can add more vertices at the Vertex or Segment sub-object level.

Segments are the sections of Walls between two vertices. Each segment can have its own parameters, distinct from the other segments in the Wall. At the Profile sub-object level, you can define the appearance of a wall segment's top and bottom edges. You can use the Profile tool to create walls that must follow a sloping roof or ground situation, or to meet gable roof conditions.

You can access the Wall sub-object levels via the Plus sign in the Modifier Stack to expand the list, and then by selecting the appropriate sub-object level. See the sections "Create Doors and Windows" and "Incorporate Doors and Windows into Walls" for more information on how to add Doors and Windows to your Wall objects.

Create Walls *(continued)*

Move a Vertex

10. Click the Modify Panel button ( ).
11. Click ⊞.

    The sub-object list expands.
12. Click Vertex.

    The Edit Vertex rollout appears.
13. Click the Select and Move button ( ).
14. Click to select a vertex.

    The Transform Gizmo appears on the vertex.
15. Click and drag the vertex to move it.

    The vertex and adjoining segments move.

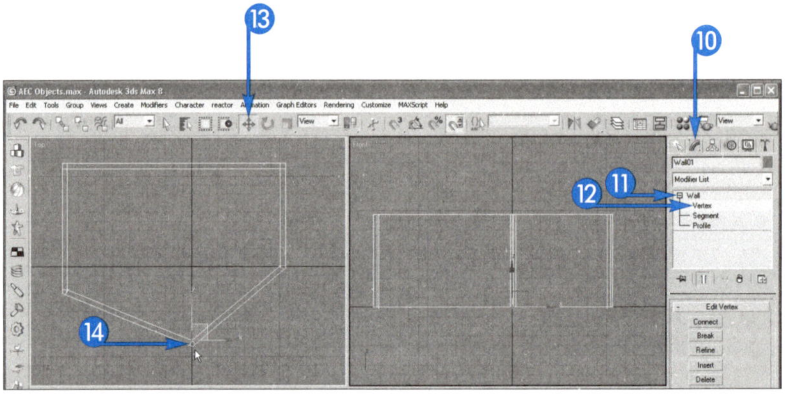

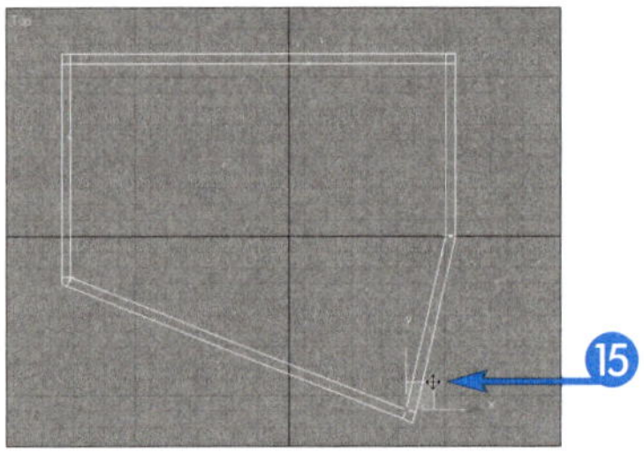

Adjust a Segment

16 Click Segment.

The Edit Segment rollout appears.

17 Click the Select Object button ( ).

18 Click to select a segment.

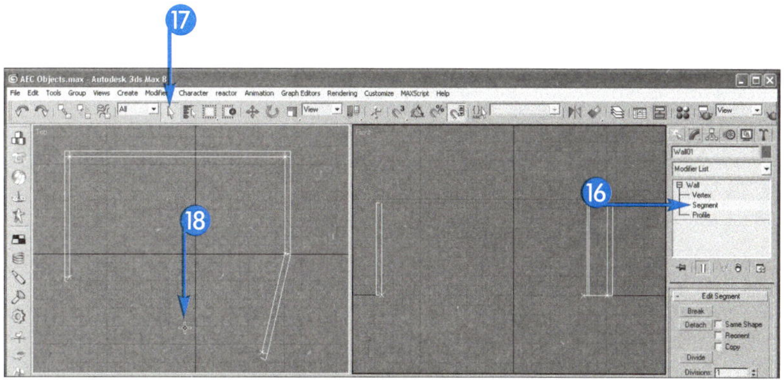

19 Type values to adjust the segment's Width, Height, or Bottom Offset parameters.

The parameter changes are reflected in the scene.

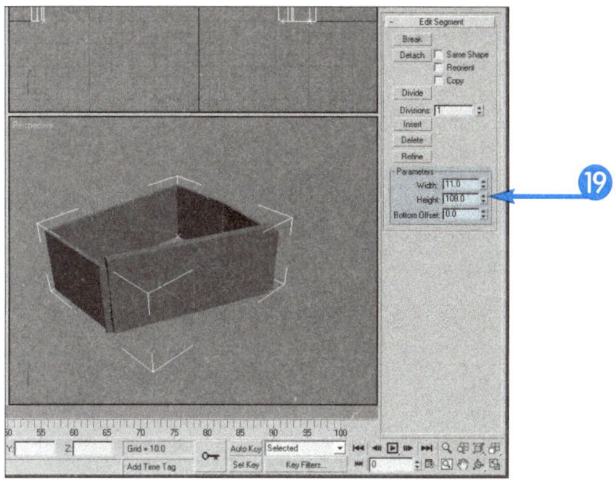

MASTER IT

How do I add vertices to a Wall?

▼ It is often easier to add vertices when working in Wireframe-shaded viewports. For more information on the viewport shading modes, see Chapter 1. You can add vertices to a Wall in either the Vertex or Segment sub-object level. While at either of those levels, click Insert in the Edit Segment rollout. In a viewport, click the bottom edge of a Wall segment where you want to add a vertex. Move the mouse and then click again to place the vertex where you want it. The adjoining Wall segments move to compensate for the new vertex. Right-click to stop creating vertices, or click another location to create a new one.

How do I change a segment's profile?

▼ With a Wall selected, click to open the Modify panel. Click the next to the Wall object in the Modifier Stack to expand the rollout, and then select Profile. Click in the Main toolbar and then select the section for which you want to change the profile. In the Edit Profile rollout, click Insert. Click along the top or bottom edge of the selected segment to create the profile vertex, and then drag and release to place the new vertex. To create a gable condition parametrically, select a segment, enter a Height value, and then click Create Gable.

Create Doors and Windows

3ds Max ships with a library of Door and Window objects that, when paired with Wall objects, can help you to quickly and accurately develop an architectural scene. There are three types of Door objects available: Pivot, Sliding, and BiFold. Pivot doors are the most common type and are simple doors that are hinged on one side or that you can customize to have two doors, each hinged at the door's frame. Sliding doors, commonly found on porches, elevators, and retail facilities, are included in the library, as well as BiFold as you may typically find in a closet. All of the Door types have many customizable parameters, including an Open value that you can use to specify the percent or angle at which the door is opened.

There are also six different Window types available. Each Window type creates a different style of window to fit most architectural needs. The windows are also fully customizable; you can modify the Windows' number and sizes, as well as the shape of their glass panes, mullions, and sills.

The methods for creating doors and windows are essentially the same. See the sections "Create Walls" and "Incorporate Doors and Windows into Walls" for more information.

Create Doors and Windows

1. Click the Create Panel button ( ).
2. Click .
3. Click here and select Doors or Windows.

   This example uses Windows.

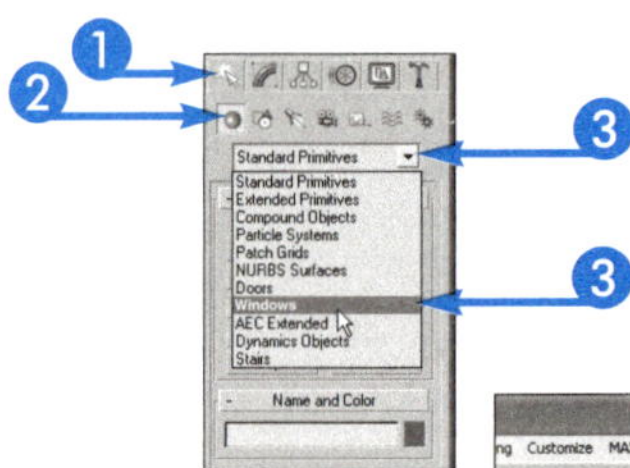

   The Window or Door buttons appear in the Object Type rollout.

4. Click a Window or Door type button.
5. In a viewport, click to place one corner.
6. Drag and release to set the width.
7. Move the cursor, and then click to set the depth.

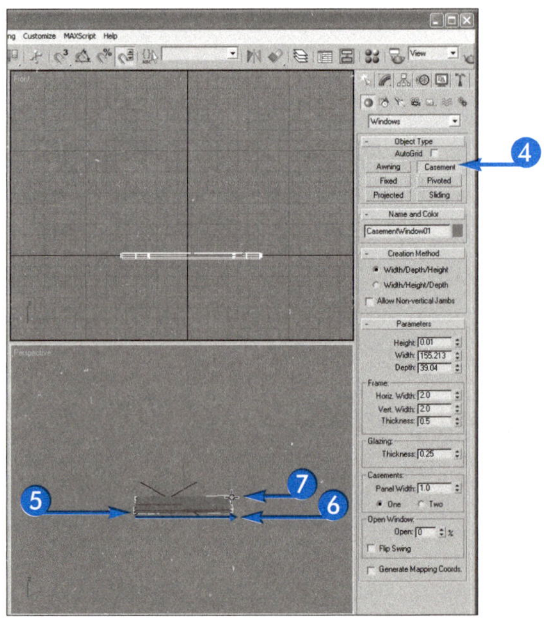

8 Move the cursor, and then click to set the height.

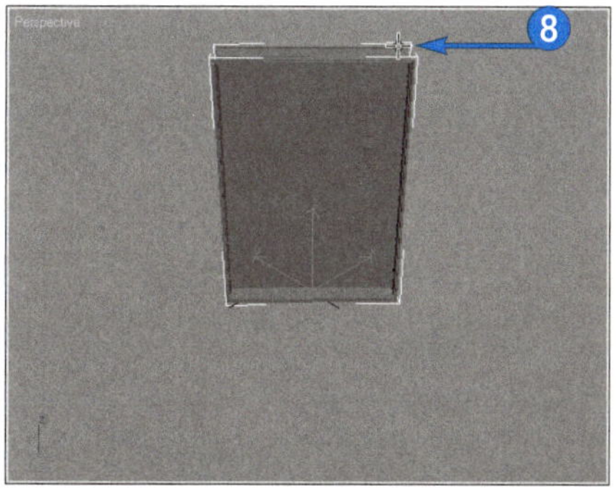

9 Adjust the parameters to achieve the look that you want.

The viewport updates to reflect your changes.

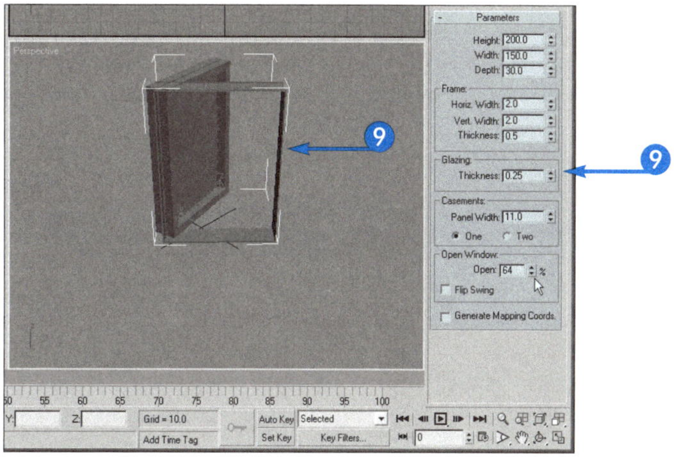

MASTER IT

I have linked a doorknob to my door, and so it moves with the door, but not when the door swings. Why?

This happens because 3ds Max considers the entire object — door, mullions, panels, and frame — to be a single object. When you linked the doorknob to the Door, you linked the doorknob to the Door's transforms. Swinging what 3ds Max refers to as the *Leaf* is a parameter change and not a Rotate transform usage. To situate the doorknob so that it moves, you need to use an Attachment controller for the doorknob's Position controller. For more information on controllers and constraints, see Chapter 10.

Do I have to rotate a window manually to match the pitch of a roof?

No. By default, 3ds Max requires that the width and depth of your Windows and Doors be parallel to the grid in which you created them, and that the height be perpendicular to the other two dimensions. You can override this relationship by clicking the "Allow Non-vertical Jambs" option (☐ changes to ☑) in the Creation Method rollout. With this option selected, you can create Doors and Windows at an angle for use as cellar doors or skylights. When using this method, you must use snaps to specify the corner locations of the objects. For more information about snaps, see Chapter 2.

Incorporate Doors and Windows into Walls

Walls, Doors, and Windows are integral parts of any architectural project, and you can incorporate the Windows and Doors into the Walls in one of two ways: using the Boolean Subtract function, or creating openings directly in the Walls. You must create an opening in a Wall for every Door or Window that is associated with that Wall. If you have not converted a Wall into an Editable Poly, or edited it with an Edit Poly Modifier, then you can use the Boolean Subtract function to create the opening, using the Wall and a box — similar in size to the Door or Window — as the operands. For information on Boolean operations, see Chapter 6.

If you have not converted the Wall, then you can easily create the Windows and Doors directly within the Wall. Using this method, when you relocate the Doors and Windows within the Wall, the opening moves with them. This method works best in a Wireframe-rendered viewport, with the Edge/Segment snap turned on. See Chapter 1 for information on viewport rendering modes, and Chapter 2 for more information on snaps.

CD FILE: The Wall.max file is available on the CD-ROM for you to practice incorporating Doors and Windows into Walls.

Incorporate Doors and Windows into Walls

1. Click the Snaps Toggle button () to turn it on.
2. Right-click the Snaps toggle.

   The Grid and Snap Settings dialog appears.
3. Click to select only the Edge/Segment option (☐ changes to ☑).
4. Click the Close button ().

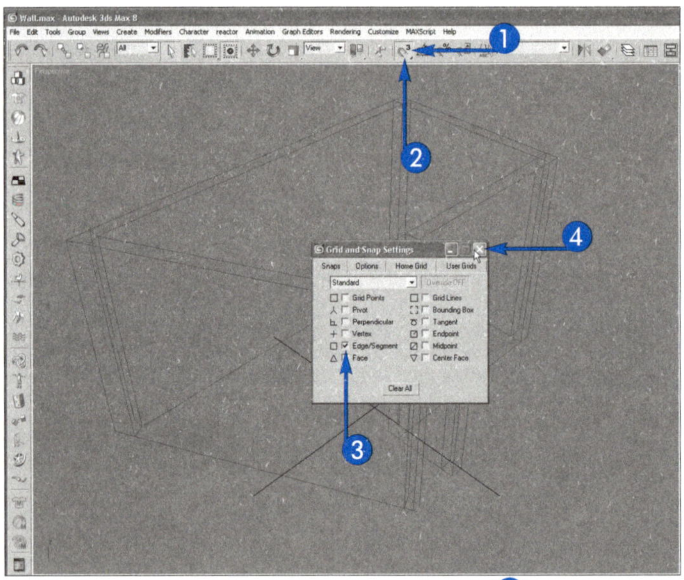

5. Click .
6. Click .
7. Click here and select Doors or Windows from the list.

   This example uses Windows.

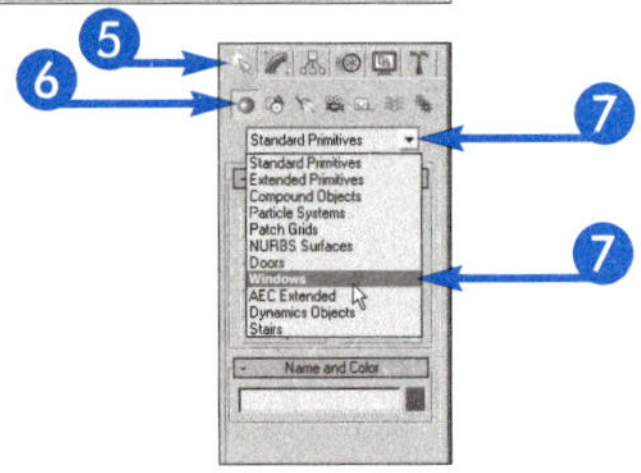

The Window or Door buttons appear in the Object Type rollout.

8. Click a Window or Door type button.
9. In a viewport, place the cursor over an edge of the Wall and click to place one corner.
10. Drag and release to set the width.
11. Move the cursor, and then click to set the depth.
12. Move the cursor, and then click to set the height.
13. Click [icon] to turn off the Snaps Toggle.
14. Click [icon].
15. Click and drag the object up or down, away from the edge.

The window moves to the new location that you specify and its opening moves with it.

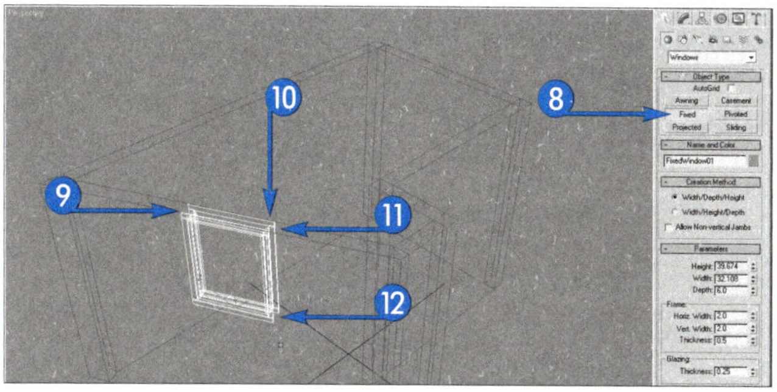

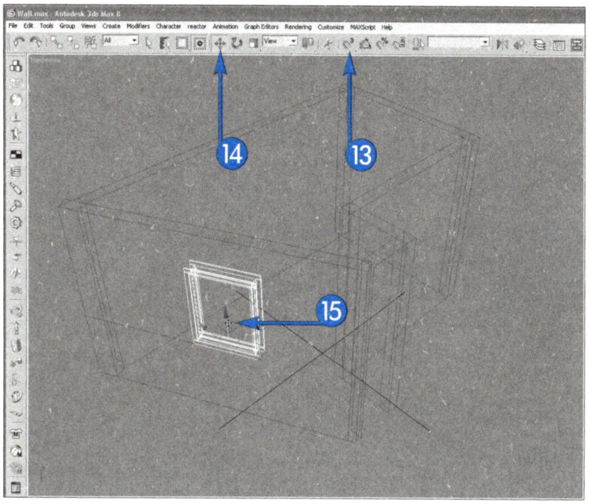

MASTER IT

I brought Windows in from another scene. Can I place them in a Wall?

Yes, you can. When you use the method described in this section, you are not only creating a Door or Window, but you are also creating a hierarchical linkage between the object and the Wall, with the Wall being the parent. You can manually position and orient a Window or Door so that it matches a Wall, then click [icon], click the Door or Window, and then drag and release it over the Wall. The Door or Window is now a child of the Wall, and the opening is created automatically. For information on working with hierarchies, see Chapter 13.

When I move a Door, why does the opening disappear?

Whenever you relocate a Door or Window within the boundaries of a Wall, the opening moves with it. If your opening disappears, then look at the scene from the Top viewport to see whether the object is still located inside the Wall segment. To ensure that your Door or Window does not move in front of, or behind, a Wall, make sure that the Move transform is using the Local Reference Coordinate System, especially if the Wall segment in question is at an angle. This ensures that the Door or Window moves relative to its own orientation in the scene. For information on reference coordinate systems, see Chapter 2.

Create Railings

Railings are commonly used to direct foot or vehicular traffic, as a safety precaution, and to create a queuing condition to control or direct people or vehicles in a waiting line. 3ds Max contains the tools that are necessary to create and modify many types of railing conditions and appearances, including Railing systems that contain more than one horizontal rail, and railings that are comprised of filled surfaces rather than a matrix of openings.

Within the Railing controls, you can determine the size, shape, and number of the structural pickets, as well as the intermediate posts and railings. Similar to Walls, you can create railings by picking the location points for each corner vertex. You can also create railings that follow the path of an existing open or closed spline in the scene. The selected splines should consist of a single spline shape, rather than more than one non-contiguous shape, such as a donut, to generate a predictable result.

See the section "Create Walls" for information on creating Wall objects.

The Railings.max file is available on the CD-ROM for you to practice creating Railing objects.

Create Railings

1. Click .
2. Click .
3. Click here and select AEC Extended.

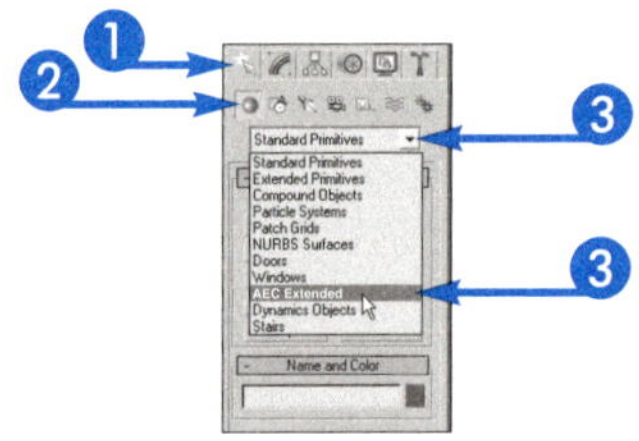

The AEC object buttons appear in the Object Type rollout.

4. Click Railing.

The Railing parameters rollout displays.

5. Click Pick Railing Path.
6. Click a spline in the scene.

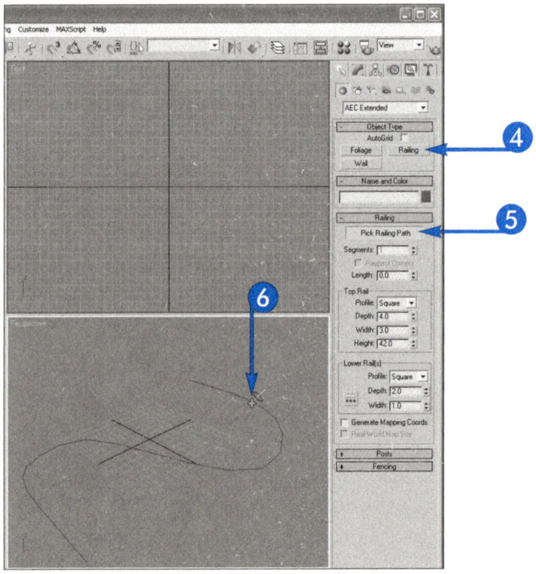

- The Railing appears on the spline path.

Because the Segments value is set to 1, the railing does not yet match the path.

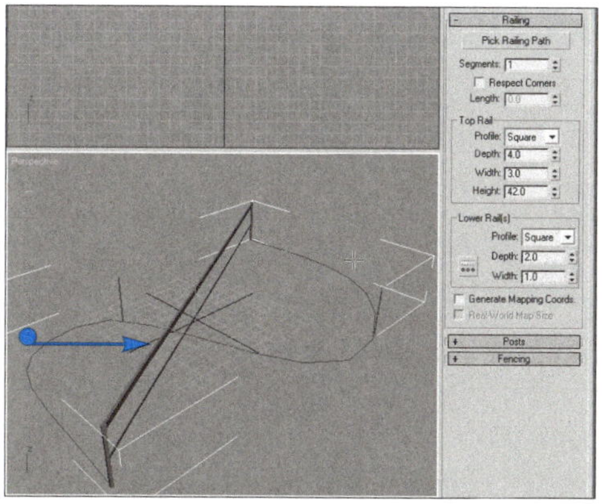

7 Type a higher number in the Segments field.

- When you have specified a sufficient number of segments applied, the railing matches the curvature of the path.

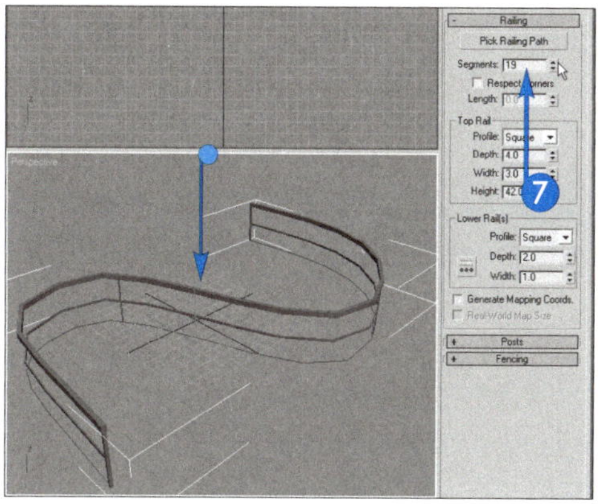

How do I control the number of vertical elements in my railing?

There are two vertical elements in a railing — pickets and posts — and they are both controlled with the same method. Pickets are structural members that hold your railing up, and posts are vertical members that partition your railing into several horizontal sections. The more posts that you have, the smoother a curved railing appears. To change the number of posts or pickets, click the Post Spacing button (▦) in the Posts or Fencing rollouts to open the Post Spacing or Picket Spacing dialog box. In the dialog box select either Count and type a quantity, or Spacing and type the distance between posts or pickets.

Does a railing path have to be simple?

No. Railing paths can be quite complicated and still remain valid. In fact, they do not even have to lie in a single plane. The spline can rise and fall with the ground, as well as bow outward and inward. You can even use a Helix spline primitive as a railing path to provide apparent safety or guidance around a spiraling path. Keep in mind that there is no error checking with a railing path; if you create a path that crosses itself, then the railing also crosses itself, regardless of the real-world feasibility.

Add Plants to Your Scenes with the Foliage Feature

Adding small, potted trees to a tiny, plain apartment can add life to the scene, just as placing large, old trees near a home can give the impression of stability and longevity. You can quickly create and modify a variety of trees in your scenes.

You can find trees in the Create menu in the Geometry tab, through the AEC Extended menu. The Foliage button activates a graphical menu, which shows typical images of the 12 trees in the tree library. You can simply drag a tree from the menu into your scene and start to modify it.

The Height parameter determines not only the height, but also the relative diameters of the trunk and branches. Density determines how many leaves are on each branch, while Pruning specifies how high or low on the trunk the branches start growing. Low Pruning values result in branches that are closer to the ground. Some tree types, like the Palm, do not let the branches get too close to the ground. You can choose to display the leaves, trunk, and branches of all trees, and some types also have flowers and roots that can display.

Add Plants to Your Scene with the Foliage Feature

1. Click .
2. Click .
3. Click here and select AEC Extended from the drop-down list.

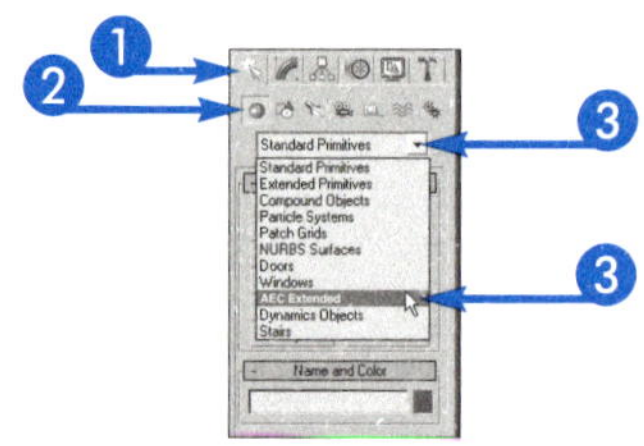

The AEC object buttons appear in the Object Type rollout.

4. Click Foliage.

The Foliage menu and rollouts appear.

5. Click a tree in the library and drag it into the scene.

3ds Max creates the tree.

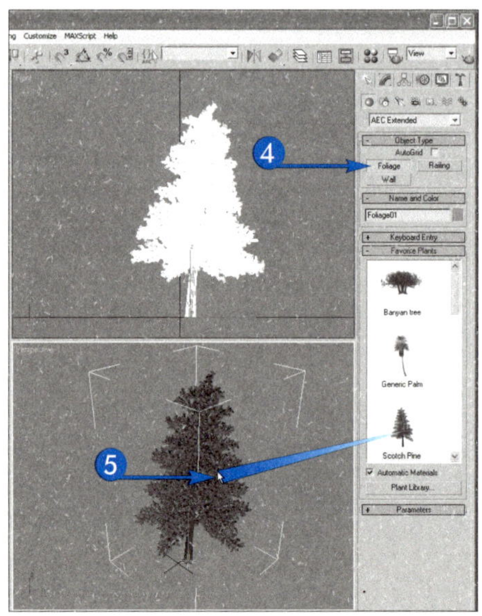

6 Click [+] to expand the Parameters rollout.

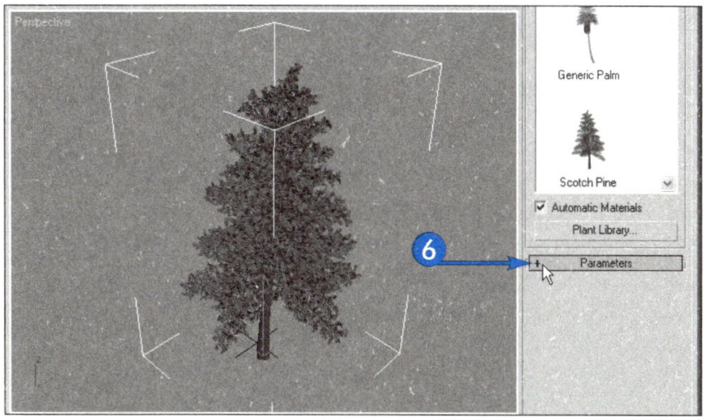

7 Type parameters to specify the tree you want.

The viewport updates to reflect your changes.

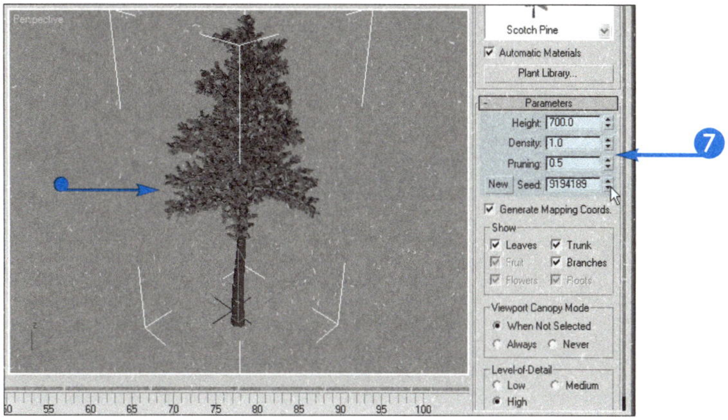

MASTER IT

If I add a lot of trees, my viewport movements slow to a crawl. How can I fix this?

▼ The default trees in the plant library each have anywhere from 2,100 to 100,000 faces. As you can imagine, it does not take a lot of trees to slow down even the fastest system, especially when it comes to viewport pans and zooms. To help overcome this, select the When Not Selected option (○ changes to ◉) in the Viewport Canopy Mode area of the Parameters rollout. This replaces the actual branches and leaves with a transparent bubble that represents them. This bubble refreshes much more quickly on the screen than the individual leaves when you render the scene.

Why do all of my trees look alike?

▼ When two or more trees share the exact same parameters, they produce identical foliage. To make similar but different trees, you can use the Seed parameter in the tree's Parameters rollout. The Seed value is an integer that is used as the base number for the algorithm that designs the trees. Two trees with identical parameters but different seed numbers have the same overall appearance, but there are differences in the angle of the trunks and locations of the branches and leaves. You can also reduce any appearance of copies by rotating some of the tree instances around their bases to display a different side of the tree.

Go to the Next Level with Stairs

To round out the Architectural, Engineering, and Construction tools available in 3ds Max, you can access tools to create an array of different stair types. You can build the very common straight stairs, or stairs that change directions in the shape of an L or a U — often called scissor stairs. You can even make a spiral staircase with just a few clicks, a task that is much easier than any of the previous methods that used copies, arrays, or snapshots. For more information on copying, as well as the Array and Snapshot tools, see Chapter 2.

The Stair tools are located in their own category in the Geometry tab. Like other elements in 3ds Max, Stairs are fully customizable, and nearly any stairway arrangement is possible. You can determine the length, width, and height of the stairs by clicking in the viewport and then fine-tuning the results in the Parameters rollout. Stairs can have handles on one or both sides, and the stairs can be open, with no risers, closed, or completely boxed in.

Go to the Next Level with Stairs

1. Click .
2. Click .
3. Click here and select Stairs.

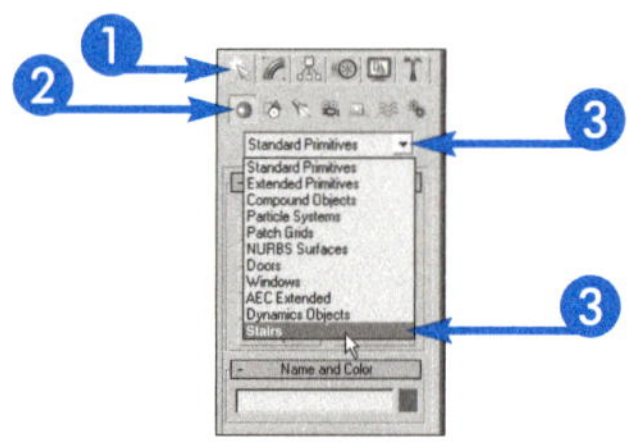

The Stair buttons appear in the Object Type rollout.

4. Click a stair type.
5. Click, drag, and release to set the footprint of the staircase.

Note: *The LTypeStair type requires an extra mouse click to set the footprint.*

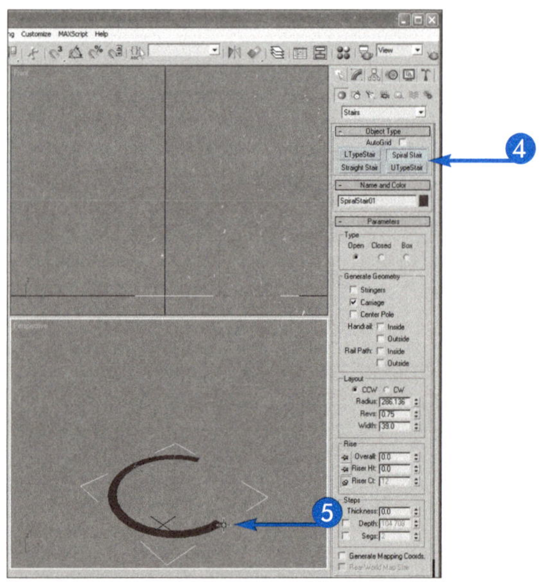

6 Move the mouse and then click to set the height of the stairs.

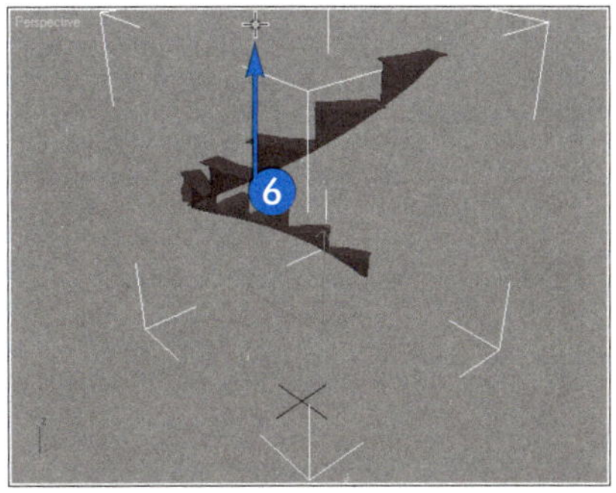

7 Click or type additional parameters that you want for the stairs.

The viewport updates to reflect your changes.

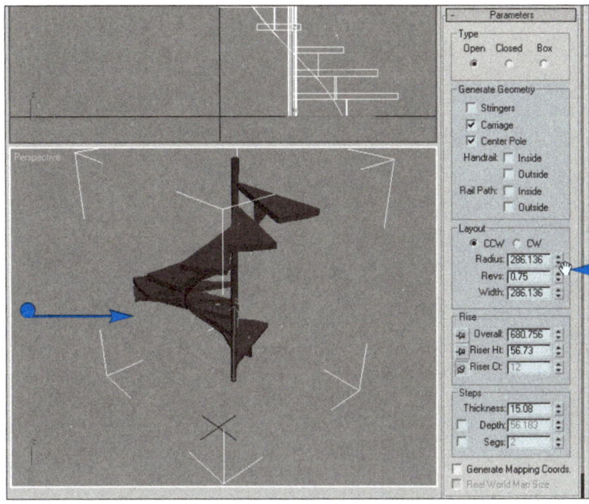

MASTER IT

Can I add a handrail to my stair?

Yes, you can use the Railing AEC objects in conjunction with the Stair objects. After you create the stair, click one, or both, of the Rail Path options in the Parameters rollout (☐ changes to ☑). This creates spline shapes that the railings can be constrained to as you create and modify them. In the Railings rollout, set the Height value to zero so that the rail paths follow the base of the stairs. Keep in mind that you may need to extend the railing posts downward to meet the stair. See the section "Create Railings" for more information on creating a railing that follows a path.

How do I set a specific number of stairs in a stairway?

The height of a stairway is determined by three factors, found in the Rise section of the Parameters rollout: Overall, Riser Height, and Riser Count. One of these parameters must be pinned ( ), while the other two remain unpinned ( ). The pinned value remains fixed, while the other two can be modified. To specify a certain number of stairs, unpin the Riser Count parameter, set the value, and then pin the parameter again. Changing the Overall or Riser Height values changes the height of the stairway, but not the number of stairs.

8 Control Animation Using Keyframes

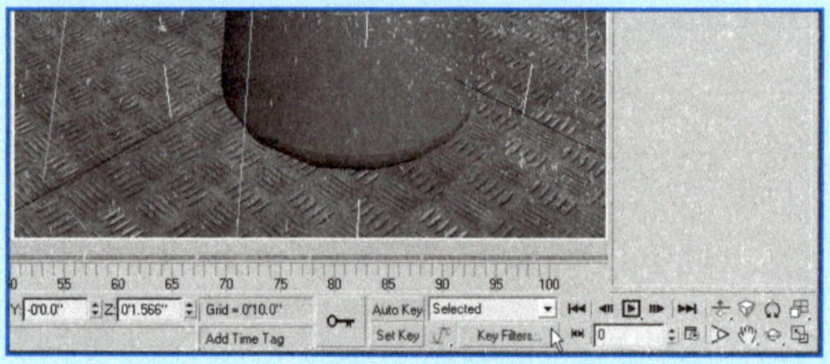

9 Working with the Track View

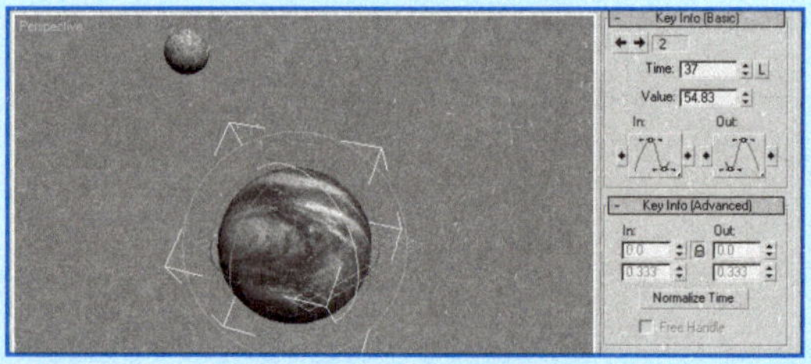

10 Working with Controllers and Constraints

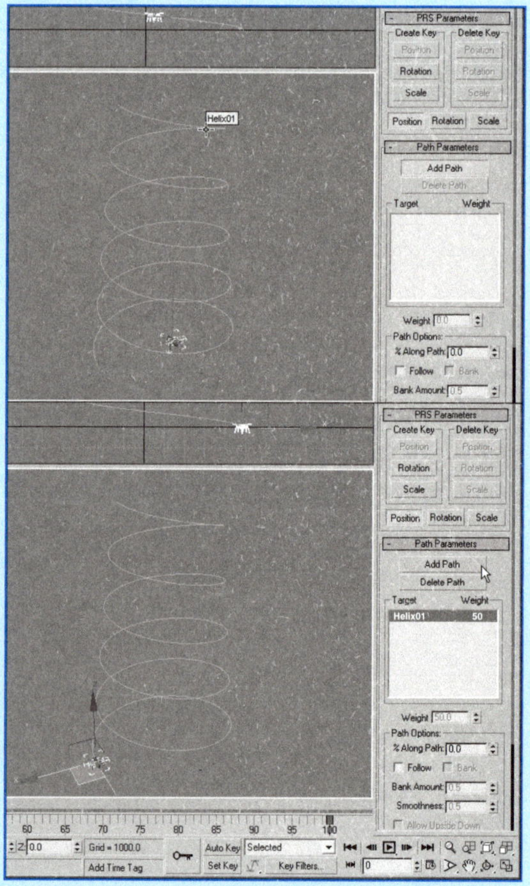

PART III
ANIMATING YOUR SCENE

11 Adjusting Animation with the Curve Editor

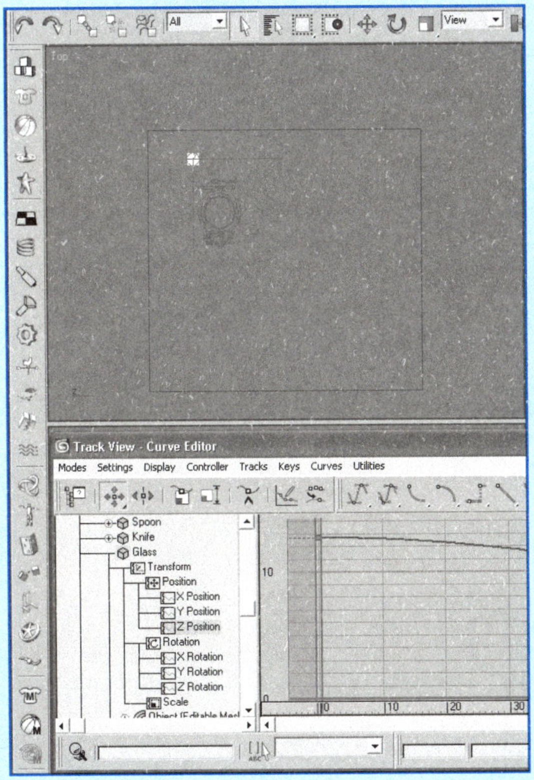

12 Working with the Dope Sheet Editor

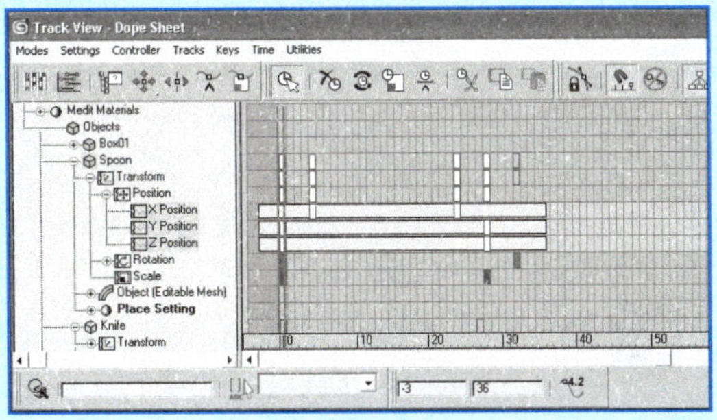

13 Working with Hierarchies

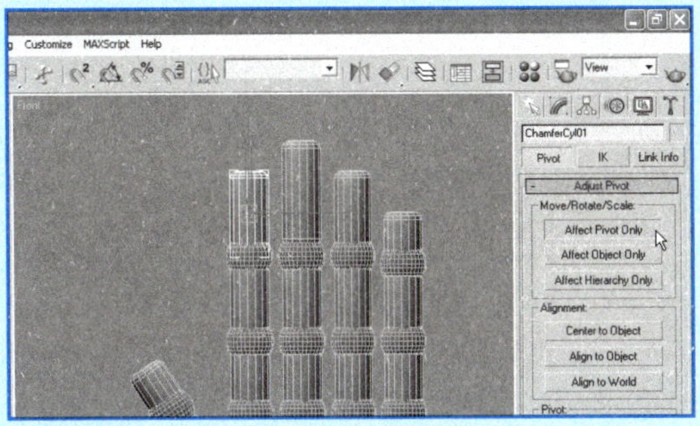

Understanding Animation

You can add *animation* — the illusion of change or movement over time — by repositioning, rotating, and scaling objects, and by changing modifier, material, light, or camera parameters at different times. 3ds Max animates by *keyframing*. Frames are particular points in time, with keyframes representing the most significant frames. Animation is like a series of pictures or storyboards, with keyframes representing the most important pictures.

This section identifies the various 3ds Max animation tools and lists buttons and features that create animation. You can animate nearly anything in a 3ds Max scene and, by using the tools effectively, you can create very convincing scenes.

3ds Max Animation Tools

3ds Max animation tools include the Track bar, the Time Slider, and the Auto Key button. 3ds Max color codes all keyframes in the Track bar with white selected keys, green Rotation keys, red Position keys, blue Scale keys, and all other key types in brown. For more on customizing colors, see Chapter 1.

A Time Slider

Shows the current frame for your scene. The Time Slider label shows the current frame number and the total number of frames.

B Time Controls

Allow you to play, stop, and review your animation, and set the animation length. Enter a number in the current frame field to jump to that frame.

C Animation Controls

Allow you to specify the method of creating keyframes.

D Default IN/OUT Tangents for New Keys Button

A flyout button to quickly set the default animation key tangents.

E Mini Curve Editor Button

Displays a Curve Editor with the same functionality as the Track View Curve Editor, through which you can view and edit the function curves for objects in your scene presentation.

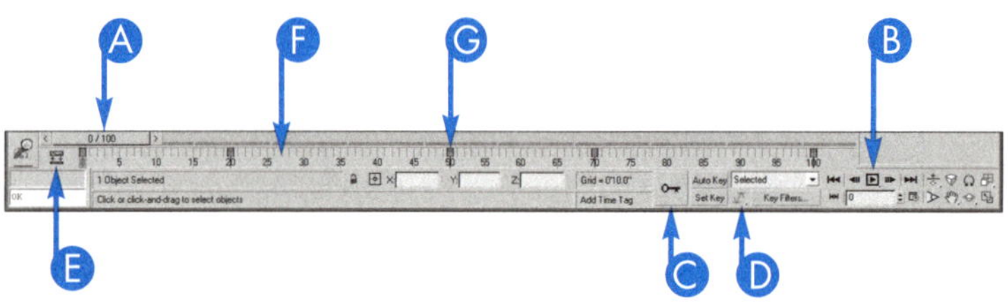

G Keyframe

A colored marker on the Track bar, which represents a specific state of an object or parameter, and which 3ds Max uses to interpolate your animation.

F Track Bar

The timeline for the animation, this bar shows frame numbers, including keyframes for the selected objects. The number of frames that appear depends on the length of the animation.

Keyframes and Interpolation

The difference between keys and keyframes can be a bit confusing. Any point where you set an animated value for a parameter is a key. The point in time that the change occurs is the keyframe. As a result, keys are the animated value, and keyframes are the point in time that the value occurs. An object can have multiple keys for different parameters at the same keyframe.

Remember that keys set for transforms are not absolute values but are relative to the previous coordinates. The transform's state at the first frame sets the stage for future transform keys. 3ds Max interpolates between the keyframes by calculating the state at any given point in time between each keyframe and inserting the appropriate parameters. As 3ds Max interpolates, it assigns values to create smooth transitions between the frames. However, the interpolated values may not always produce the animation results that you want. You customize the interpolation method by changing the tangent of the animation curve in the Curve Editor window. For more on working with curves and tangents, see Chapter 11.

Controlling Time

The Time Controls manage frame movement within the viewports. Pressing the different buttons moves the Time Slider to the corresponding frame. Within the Time Controls, you can also set the length of time that your scene occupies. For still images, this is irrelevant, but for animations, your scene length must be long enough to accommodate the animation. A 3ds Max scene can hold any number of frames, starting or ending at any point in time. A 3ds Max scene can have information from frame –100 to 1000, but the Active Time Segment may be set from frames 20 to 80. The Time Slider displays 20/80, and only that animation plays in the viewport.

Time Control Buttons

Name	Button	Description
Go to Start	(⏮)	Moves the animation to the first frame.
Previous Frame/Key	(◀II)/(I◀)	Either moves one frame back, or to the previous key, if you have selected the Key Mode Toggle button (⏮⏭).
Play Animation	(▶)	Plays through the animation frame by frame in the current viewport. When selected, ▶ becomes the Stop Animation button (II). The animation continues to loop until you click II.
Next Frame/Key	(II▶)/(▶I)	Either moves you one frame forward, or to the next keyframe, if you have selected ⏮⏭.
Go to End	⏭	Moves the animation to the last frame.
Key Mode Toggle	⏮⏭	Toggles between the key and frame modes. Selecting this button and then clicking I◀ and ▶I moves you back to the previous keyframe or forward to the next one, respectively. If deselected, clicking ◀II and II▶ moves you back or forward one frame at a time, respectively.
Current Frame Field	[52]	Shows the currently selected frame. Typing a value in the field moves you to a different frame.
Time Configuration	(icon)	Displays the Time Configuration dialog box, in which you can set animation length, time display, frame rate, and playback speed.

PART III

Animate Objects with Auto Key

You can use Auto Key mode to quickly animate an object. 3ds Max creates the keyframes for your animation whenever you change an object by transforming it or modifying any parameters.

When you activate Auto Key mode, the Auto Key button, Time Slider, and border of the current viewport turn red to remind you that 3ds Max is in animation mode. 3ds Max records changes to any parameters for the selected objects and creates keys at the current frame. If the current frame already has a key for a parameter and that parameter is changed, then 3ds Max updates the keyframe to reflect the new value. For example, if an object has keys at frames 0 and 50, setting the rotation from 30 to 45 degrees, and you activate Auto Key mode, go to frame 50, and then rotate the object 30 degrees, the object rotates from 30 to 75 degrees over 50 frames.

As you create new keyframes for your object, 3ds Max interpolates the values of the frames between the keyframes to create a smooth animation between the keyframes.

CD FILE The Keys.max file is available on the CD-ROM for you to practice with the Auto Key feature.

Animate Objects with Auto Key

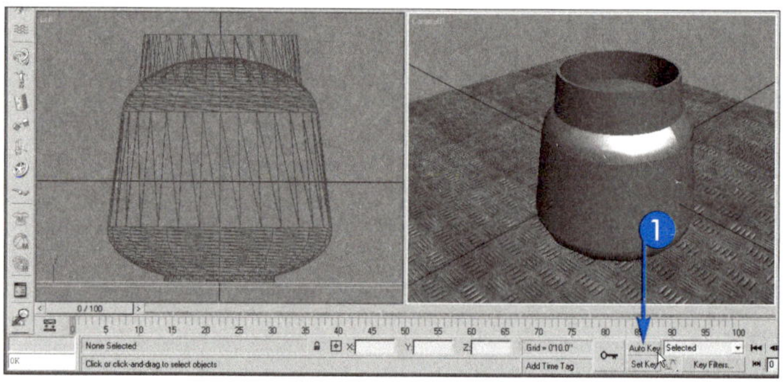

1 Click Auto Key.

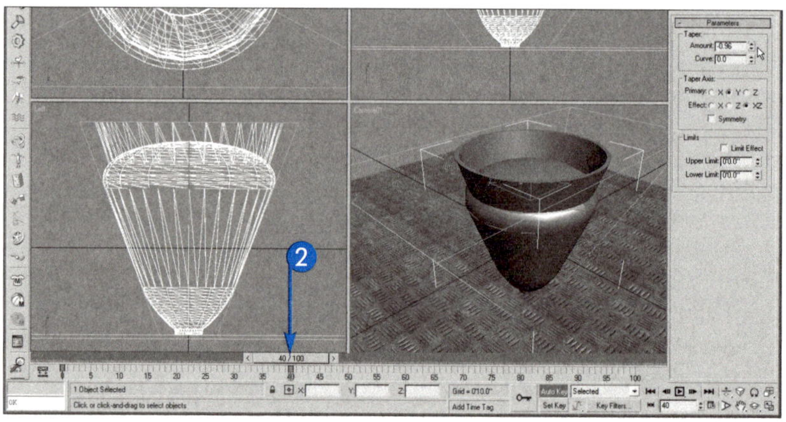

The current viewport border, Auto Key button, and Time Slider appear red.

2 Click and drag the Time Slider to the frame where you want to create a keyframe.

3 Modify the object.

A red border around a spinner indicates an animated parameter.

Note: *You can use one of the Transform options or the Modify panel to transform the object. For more information on transforming objects, see Chapter 2.*

- If this is the first keyframe created for this object, then 3ds Max creates a new key for the current frame and a key at frame 0.

4 Repeat steps 2 and 3 to create additional keyframes.

5 Click Auto Key to turn it off.

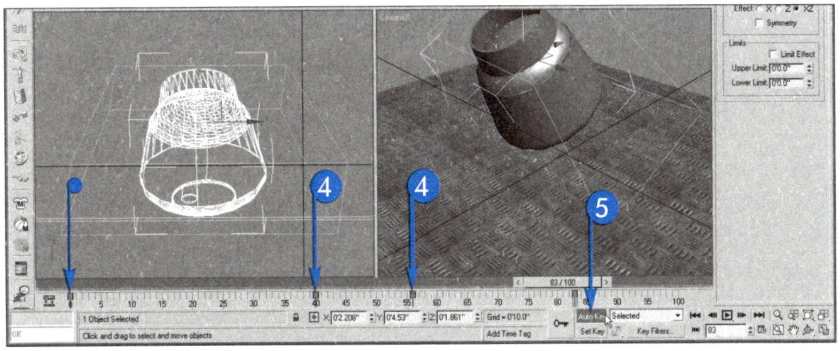

The current viewport border, Auto Key button, and Time Slider return to their default colors.

3ds Max creates keyframes for each change that you made.

- You can click the Play Animation button (▶) to view the animation in the current viewport.

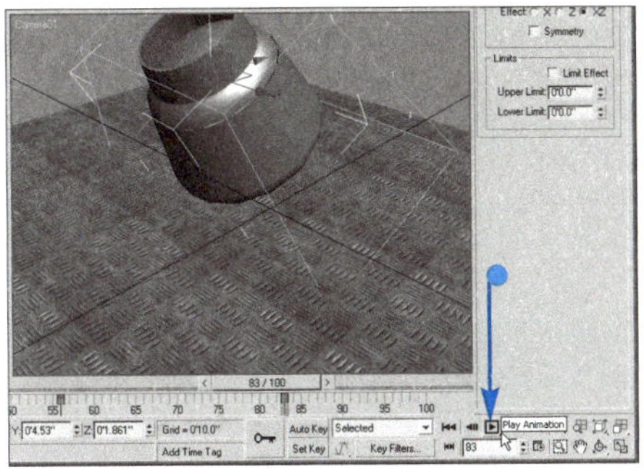

MASTER IT

What happens if I change an object after I animate it?

▼ After you animate an object with Auto Key, you can still modify it. If you change an object with the Auto Key mode off, then your changes to the object apply equally to all of the keys. For example, if you scale an object down 50 percent, then 3ds Max applies the scaling to all of the keyframes so that the object becomes 50 percent smaller. This eliminates the need to go to each keyframe and make the modifications when you decide to change an object. You simply transform it once, and the changes affect the entire animation.

What type of keys does Auto Key create?

▼ Auto Key creates the appropriate type of keys for the type of change that you make to an object. For example, if you scale the object, then 3ds Max creates a Scale key in the corresponding frame. If you scale and move the object, 3ds Max creates a Scale key along with Position keys for the X-, Y-, and Z-axes. The color of the keyframe on the Track bar indicates the type of key. If you have two types of keys, then the keyframe appears in two colors. For example, when you create both Position and Scale keys, the keyframe is red and blue. You can view and change key colors in the Customize User Interface dialog box.

Manually Animate Objects Using Set Key

You can manually control key creation for your animation using the Set Key mode. This mode allows you to modify an object and to specify when to create the key. When you use Set Key mode, 3ds Max creates one of each key type that you specify in the Set Key Filters dialog box. For example, if you select the default key filter's Position, Rotation, and Scale, and then activate the Set Key Mode button, then 3ds Max creates Position, Rotation, and Scale keys when you click the Set Keys button. Likewise, the Position filter creates X-Position, Y-Position, and Z-Position keys. Unlike Auto Key, Set Key does not automatically create a key at frame zero.

By modifying values in the Set Key Filters dialog box before creating your keys, you can control which key types appear, thus avoiding the creation of key types that you do not want to add to your animation. For example, if you have the Position filter turned off, you can move the object for a better view, rotate it, and then create the keys. 3ds Max creates a key for the rotation, but the move is discarded.

CD FILE: The Keys.max file is available on the CD-ROM for you to practice with the Set Key feature.

Manually Animate Objects Using Set Key

1. Select the object that you want to animate.
2. Click Key Filters.

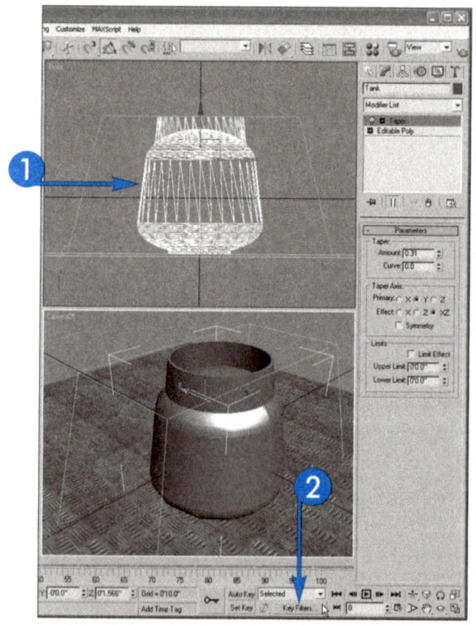

The Set Key Filters dialog box appears.

3. Click to select the types of keys that you want to create (☐ changes to ☑).

3ds Max creates the options that you select.

4. Click and drag the Time Slider to the frame where you want to create the first keys.

This is usually frame 0.

5. Click Set Key to turn on Set Key mode.
6. Click the Set Keys button (🔑) to set a key.

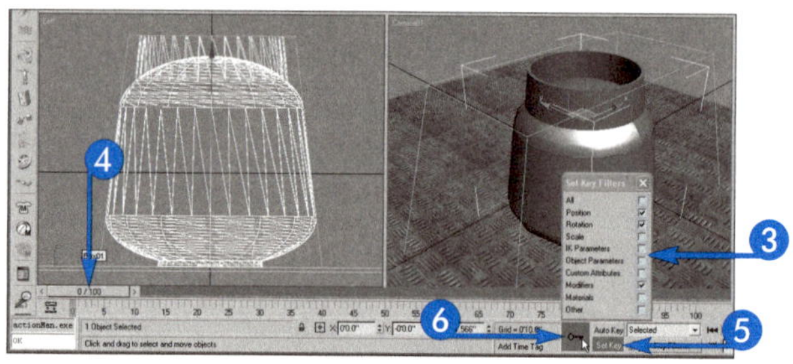

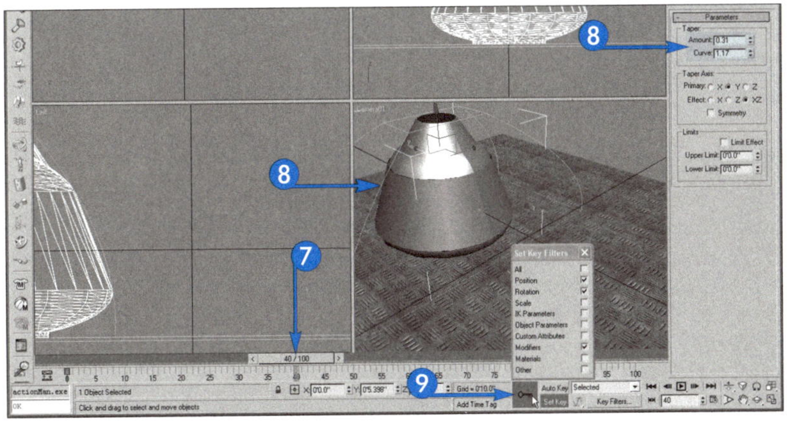

3ds Max creates the keys at the current frame.

7. Click and drag the Time Slider to the next frame in which you want to create keys.

8. Modify or transform the object.

Note: *For information on transforming objects, see Chapter 2.*

9. Click [key icon].

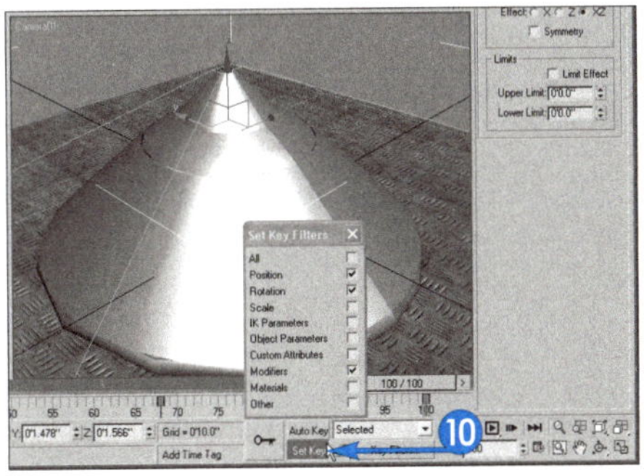

3ds Max creates a keyframe with the specified keys.

You can repeat steps 7 to 9 to create additional keys.

10. Click Set Key to turn off Set Key mode.

Master It

How can I view which keys I have created for a keyframe?

- Keyframes for an object display in the Track bar when you select the object. The color of the keyframe indicates the type of keys that you have created. See the section "Understanding Animation" to learn more about this color code. You can also view the type of keys in a keyframe by right-clicking the keyframe to display a menu listing all of the keys for the selected keyframe. To view the value of a key in the Key Info dialog box, click the key name in the menu. The Key Info dialog box appears and displays the frame number and key value. See the section "Adjusting Keyframes" for more information on modifying the values of a specific key.

What filter do I select to animate an object modifier?

- To animate an object modifier, you need to select the Modifiers filters in the Set Key Filters dialog box. Even if the transform filters are unchecked, transformation of a modifier's Gizmo or Center is keyed. See the section "Animate a Modifier" for more information.

Can I delete specific keys from a keyframe?

- You can eliminate unwanted keys from a keyframe by right-clicking the keyframe to display a menu. Click Delete Key to view a list of the current keys that you can delete, and then click the key that you want to delete. To delete all keys in a keyframe, select the keyframe, and then press the Delete key.

Adjusting Keyframes

After creating your keyframes for an object, you can modify either the entire keyframe or specific keys that are associated with the keyframe. For example, you can eliminate a keyframe entirely after previewing your animation, or you can change the rotation around the X-axis for the object.

To adjust the keyframe, you must select the object in a viewport. This displays the keyframes on the Track bar. If you delete a keyframe, then 3ds Max deletes all keys that are associated with that keyframe for the selected objects. After you delete the keyframe, 3ds Max re-interpolates the key values between the previous and next keyframes. You must have at least two keyframes for a parameter to have any animation.

You can also modify specific keys that are associated with the keyframe by displaying the Key Info dialog box for the selected key and then specifying a new value. You can move the key to a different keyframe by specifying the frame number in the Time field of the dialog box.

The Key Info dialog box also displays In and Out buttons for setting the curve tangent for the selected key.

CD FILE: The Adjust Keys.max file is available on the CD-ROM for you to practice with adjusting keyframes.

Adjusting Keyframes

Move a Key

1. Select the object that you want to modify.

   The keys for the object appear on the Track bar.

2. Click to select a key or keys.

   To select multiple keys, you can drag a selection rectangle around them in the Track bar.

   Alternatively, you can press the Ctrl and Alt keys to add and subtract from the selection.

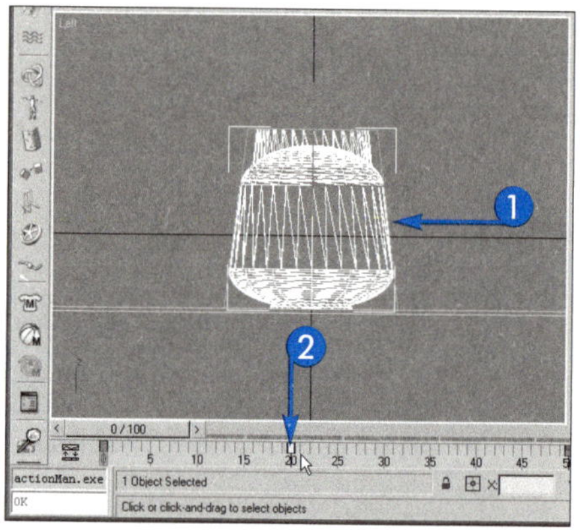

3. Click and drag the key to another location on the Track bar.

   3ds Max moves all of the keys associated with the keyframe to the new frame.

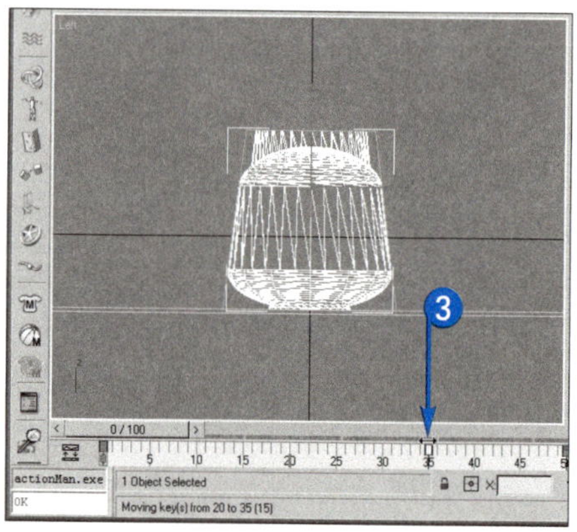

Change a Key Value

1. Click the object that you want to modify.

   The keyframes for the object display on the Track bar.

2. Right-click the keyframe that has the key that you want to modify.

3. In the menu that appears, click a key that you want to modify.

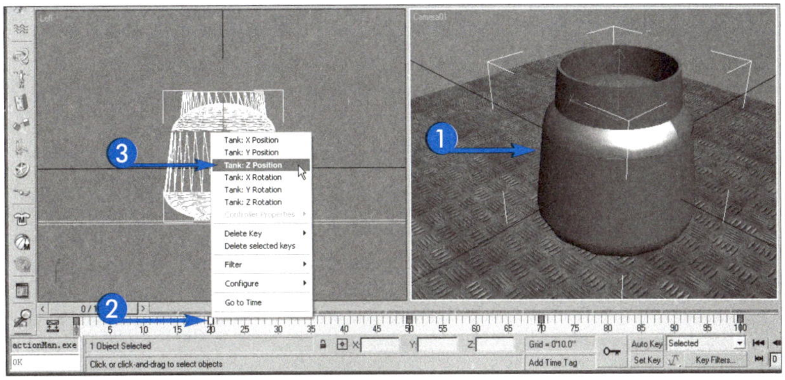

   The Key Info dialog box appears for the selected key.

4. Click and drag the Time Slider to the selected frame.

5. Type a new Value for the key or use the spinner arrows.

   - To move the key to a different frame, type a new Time value.

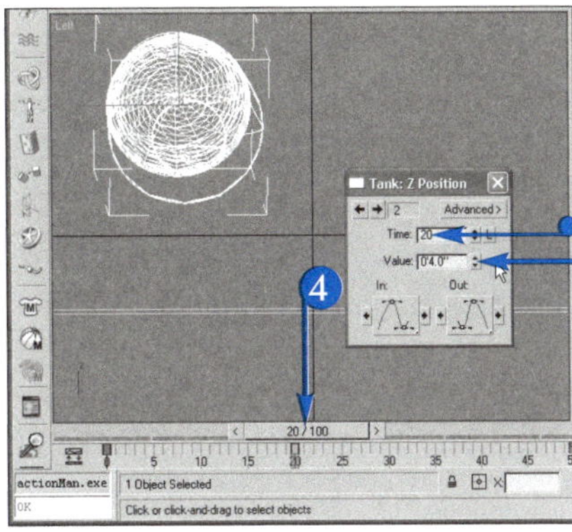

Can I make a copy of an existing keyframe?

▼ Yes. If a keyframe already exists with the values that you want to use, you can clone that keyframe. To clone a keyframe, press Shift and then click the keyframe on the Track bar. Drag the new keyframe to the location you want on the Track bar. 3ds Max duplicates all keys in the original keyframe. When you create or modify a keyframe, 3ds Max re-interpolates the values of the other frames. This ensures that animation remains smooth between all keyframes. To loop an animation, copy the keyframe from the first frame to the last.

How can I only loop one parameter and not all of them?

▼ If you want to use the Track bar to loop one key out of a keyframe that contains several keys, then you need to temporarily extract that key. For example, if you want to loop only the X Position, right-click the key at the first frame, and then select X Position from the menu that appears. In the Key Info dialog box, enter a Time value for a frame that has no keyframes. This extracts the X-Position key to that frame. Copy the new key to the final frame in the animation. Move the original key back to the first frame. The first and last keys now have the same X-Position value.

Change the Number of Frames in Your Scene

You can change an animation's length by adjusting the number of frames. Although, by default, an animation starts with 101 frames, numbered from 0 to 100, you can specify either new start and end times, or a new length. Specifying a different length changes the number of frames in the Track bar and Time Slider; 3ds Max automatically adjusts the End Time value. The number of frames in the Time Configuration dialog box is known as the Active Time Segment. Increasing the size of an animation by adding more frames causes existing keyframes to remain in the same location; 3ds Max adds new frames to the start or end of the animation. For example, if you increase the animation from 100 to 200 frames, 3ds Max adds the new frames at the end of the original 101 frames.

MASTER IT

Do I have to start my animation at frame zero?

▼ No, the scene can start at any frame, regardless of any existing animation. For example, your scene may start with a swinging door at frame zero, with the rest of the animation relying on this action. To add the time for an event to occur before the door opens, add frames to your scene by entering a negative number in the Start Time field.

Change the Number of Frames in Your Scene

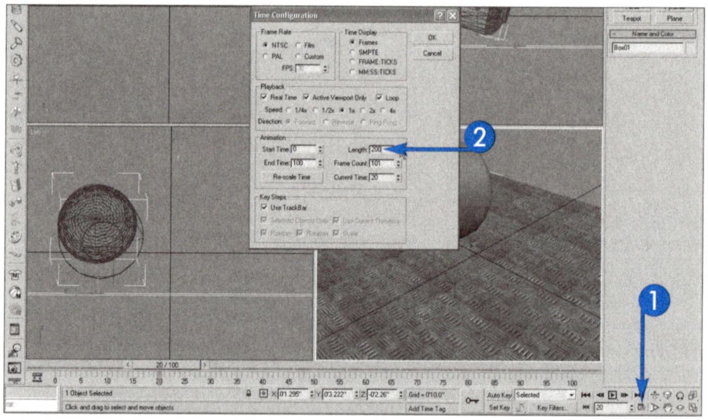

1. Click the Time Configuration button (⊡).

   The Time Configuration dialog box appears.

2. Type a new Length value.

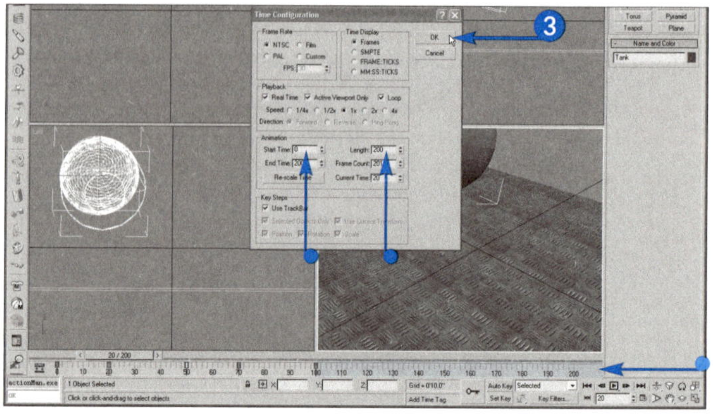

- The End Time and Frame Count values change to reflect the new length.
- The Track bar adjusts to show the new number of frames.

3. Click OK.

   The Time Configuration dialog box closes.

Change the Frame Rate

You can change the frame rate of the animation by changing the number of frames that appears each second. You sometimes need to change the frames per second (FPS) when you switch between different output formats. For example, to output for television broadcast, if you are located in most of North or South America or Japan, the default frame rate is 30 FPS. This means that 3ds Max produces 30 frames for every second of animation. To fill one minute of broadcast time, you would need 1800 frames of animation.

Switching the frame rate does not affect the timing of your animation. For example, if you switch your 30 FPS animation to a frame rate of 24 FPS, the animation still takes three seconds to view, and 3ds Max makes the animation 72 frames in length, instead of the original 90 frames.

If you have defined any keyframes for your animation, then 3ds Max adjusts the keyframes so that they still occur at the same time in the animation. 3ds Max does this by internally storing all keys with an internal precision of 1/4800 of a second. When you make changes to the frame rate, 3ds Max recalculates the timing for each key.

Change the Frame Rate

1. Click [icon].

   The Time Configuration dialog box appears.

2. Click a Frame Rate option (○ changes to ◉).

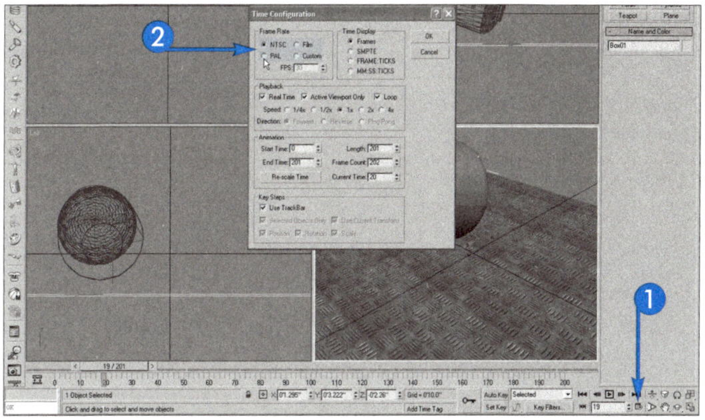

- The Length of the animation changes to reflect the new frame rate.
- The Track bar changes to the new animation length, and 3ds Max adjusts the existing keyframes to maintain the same timing.

3. Click OK.

   The Time Configuration dialog box closes.

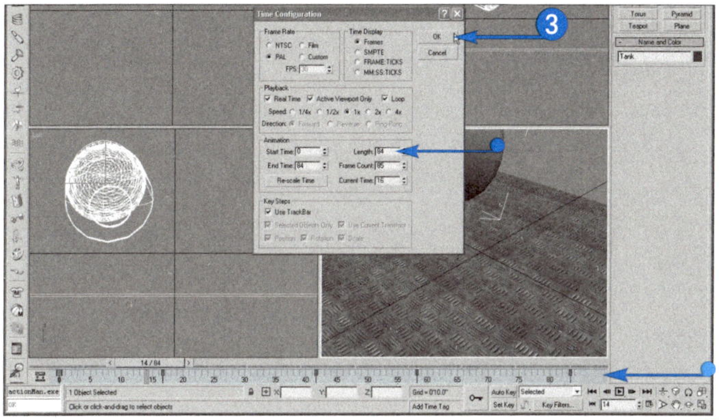

Animate a Modifier

You can animate the effects of modifiers to animate your object over time. For example, to make an object look as if it is bending back and forth, you can have 3ds Max gradually change the Angle parameter of the Bend Modifier. To animate it bending, you can animate the direction of the bend.

To animate a modifier, you must first select it in the Modifier Stack and set its initial parameters. 3ds Max adds a red border around the spinners — the up and down arrow buttons next to an input field — for any animated parameter that uses them.

You can animate a modifier's parameters using either Auto Key or Set Key mode. It is usually better to use Auto Key mode because 3ds Max only creates keys for the parameters of the modifier that you change. Using Set Key mode creates keys for all of the modifier's parameters, whether they are changed or not. If you want to use Set Key mode, then you must select the Modifier filters in the Set Key Filters dialog box.

CD FILE: The Modifier.max file is available on the CD-ROM for you to practice animating a modifier.

Animate a Modifier

1. Select the object with a modifier that you want to animate.
2. Click the Modify panel icon (Modify) to display the Modify panel.
3. Click Auto Key.

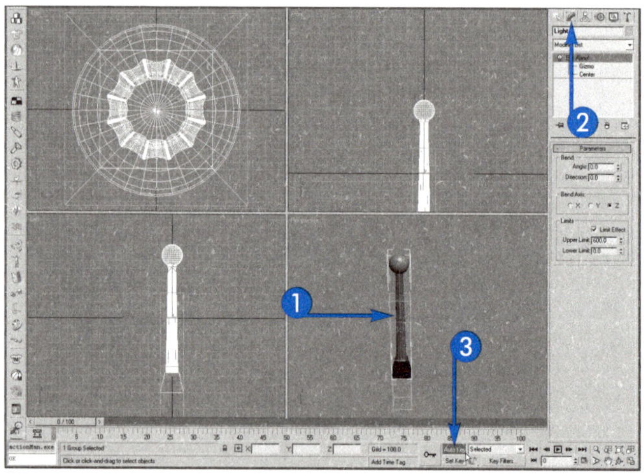

The Time Slider, Auto Key button, and current viewport frame appear red.

4. Click and drag the Time Slider to the frame at which you want to create a key.
5. Type the new parameter values in the Modify panel.

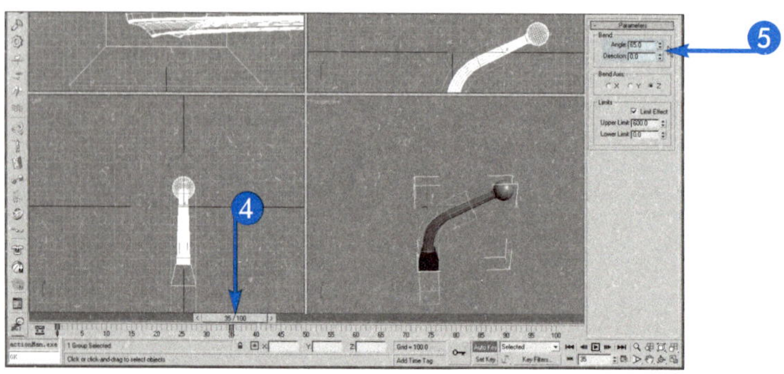

If the object has more than one modifier, you must select the modifier that you want to animate.

- 3ds Max creates a keyframe in frame zero with the original parameter values, and a keyframe at the current frame with the new parameter values.

6 Repeat steps 4 and 5 to create additional keyframes.

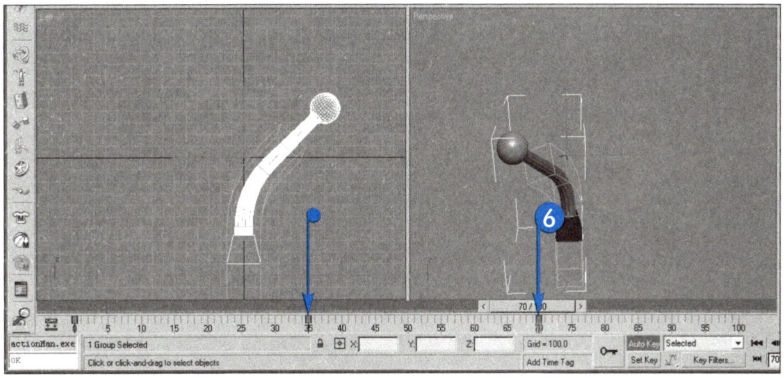

The keyframes display on the Track bar.

- You can click ▣ to play the animation in the current viewport.

Note: *See the section "Make a Preview Animation" for information on creating a preview animation.*

7 Click Auto Key to exit Auto Key mode.

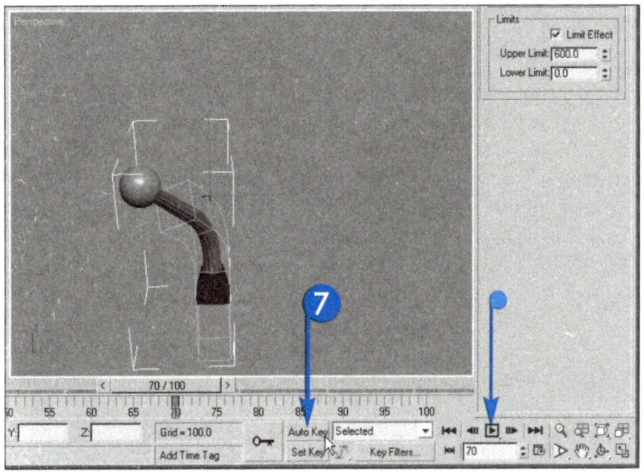

MASTER IT

How do I know which parameters have been modified?

▼ There are several ways to identify which objects and modifier parameters have keys. When you select an object and go to the Modify panel (click ▣), the animated parameters display red borders around their spinners. You can also drag the Time Slider and watch to see which parameter values change in the Modify panel. The Mini Curve Editor, found to the left of the Track bar, is a smaller version of the Track View Curve Editor. It displays the keys and function curves for the selected parameters. For more information on the Curve Editor, see Chapter 11.

Can I change the parameter values after creating the animation?

▼ Yes. In fact, you can do this without being in any animation mode. Right-click the keyframe to display a list of available keys. Select the key for the parameter that you want to change. The Key Info dialog box appears for that parameter. Type a new value in the Value field. The key updates to use the new value, and 3ds Max interpolates the new animation. If you prefer to work in an animation mode, then turn on Auto Key mode, move the Time Slider to the frame where the key exists, and then change the parameter. 3ds Max changes the existing key to the new parameter value.

Make a Preview Animation

You can create a preview animation of the current viewport to show an approximation of what the final rendering will look like. This is not intended to be the higher quality version or larger size of a final rendering, but a lower-quality version that you can use to check a scene's timing and composition and to look for unintended collisions or interpenetrations. The lower quality and size allow for a faster render time.

When you create a preview animation, 3ds Max generates an animation file, usually an AVI or MOV file, depending on your preference. After you create an AVI file, 3ds Max opens the file named _scene.avi and plays it in the Windows Media Player. When you save a preview in another file type, it is saved with a name that you specify, and you must open the associated application to view it.

When you create a preview animation, you can choose to render the entire scene or only a range of frames. You can also specify the quality of the rendering and whether 3ds Max only renders every second, third, fourth, and so on frame.

CD FILE: The Preview.max file is available on the CD-ROM for you to practice making a preview animation.

Make a Preview Animation

1. Click in the viewport for the preview animation.
2. Click Animation.
3. Click Make Preview.

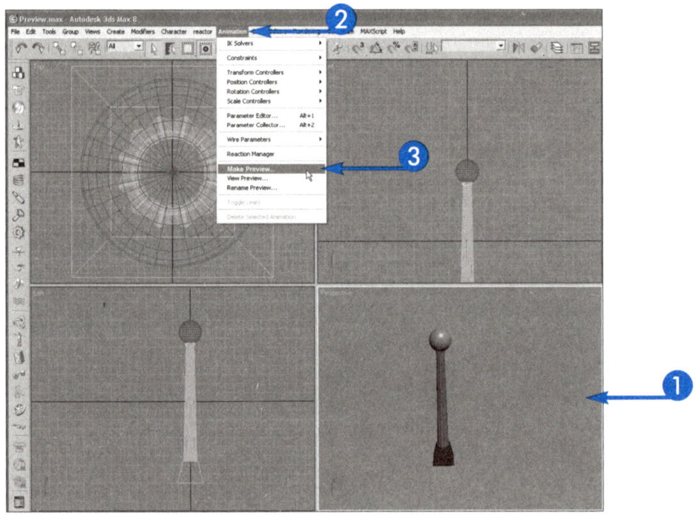

The Make Preview dialog box appears.

4. Click to select the Active Time Segment option (◯ changes to ◉).

- You can also select the Custom Range option (◯ changes to ◉) and type start and end frames to render only a block of frames.
- You can also change the output percent, specifying 100 percent of the animation at a resolution of 640 x 480.

5. Click Create.

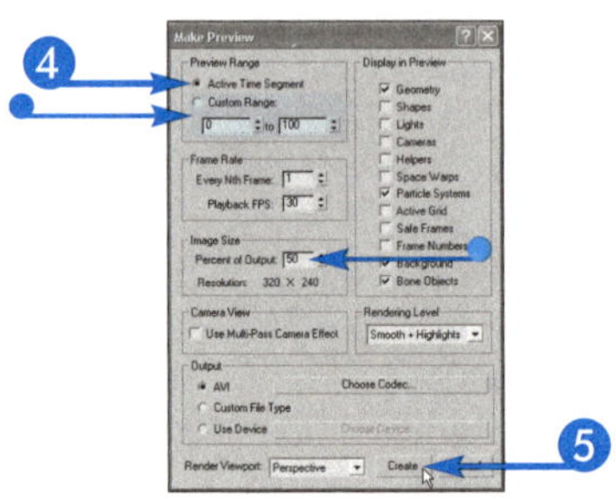

As the preview renders, the viewports are replaced with a single view, and the progress of the rendering creation appears at the bottom of the window.

- You can click Cancel to cancel the process.

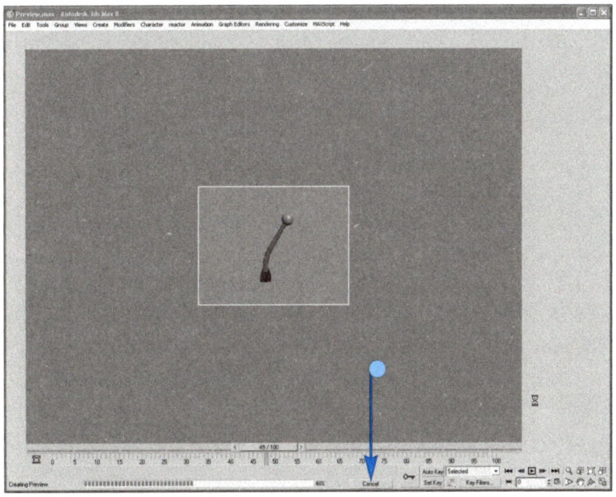

When the preview file is completed, the Windows Media Player opens and plays the file.

6 Click the Play button (▶) to view the animation again.

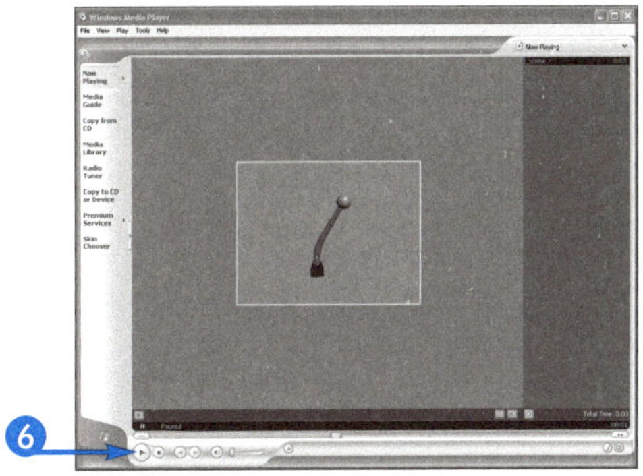

MASTER IT

I closed the Windows Media Player. How do I replay the preview animation?

▼ If you created a preview file using the default AVI settings, you can replay the preview by clicking Animation in the Main menu and then clicking View Preview. When you select View Preview, 3ds Max opens the latest version of the _scene.avi file and plays it in the Windows Media Player. If you created your preview file using a different format, you must open the program that supports that format and then open the corresponding preview file. The Make Preview feature overwrites an existing _scene.avi file. To save the current preview file, click Animation and then click Rename Preview.

How can I make my previews render faster?

▼ The Display in Preview section of the Make Preview dialog box allows you to select the options that you want to display in the preview. Geometry, Particle Systems, Background, and Bone Objects are the default selections, but you can uncheck (☑ changes to ☐) any options so that Make Preview ignores them. The Rendering Level list shows a list of rendering quality levels, identical to the viewport display quality levels. Select the minimum level that creates an adequate preview. If you are only looking at a scene's timing, the Facets level is adequate and Smooth + Highlight is overkill. For information on viewport display quality, see Chapter 1.

Understanding the Motion Panel

You can use the Motion panel to view, create, modify, and delete transform keys in your animation. A transform key determines the position, rotation, or scale of an object. You also assign *controllers* — tools that determine how 3ds Max interpolates animation from one key to the next — in this panel. For more on creating animations with 3D objects using keyframes, see Chapter 8. For more on selecting and applying controllers, see Chapter 10.

The Motion panel has two modes between which you can toggle, and which determine what rollouts appear: the Parameters mode and the Trajectories mode. In the Parameters mode, you can add new transform keys or edit the properties of existing keys for the selected object. For example, although you can add or modify a Rotation key, you cannot create additional non-transform keys, such as those that animate modifier parameters. To animate those values, you either use the Track view or the Modify panel. In Trajectories mode, you can view, add, move, or delete the position keys of your object to change its trajectory, which is the actual path that an object follows through virtual space. The object trajectory displays as a spline. Keyframes appear as white boxes, and interpolated frames appear as white dots. You can also convert an existing trajectory into a spline for use in your scene. For more on splines, see Chapter 5.

Trajectories Mode

A Selection Level

By clicking the Sub-Object button, you can select position keys for editing on the trajectory. You can also add, move, and delete keys from the trajectory. When Sub-Object is active, you cannot select any other object in the scene.

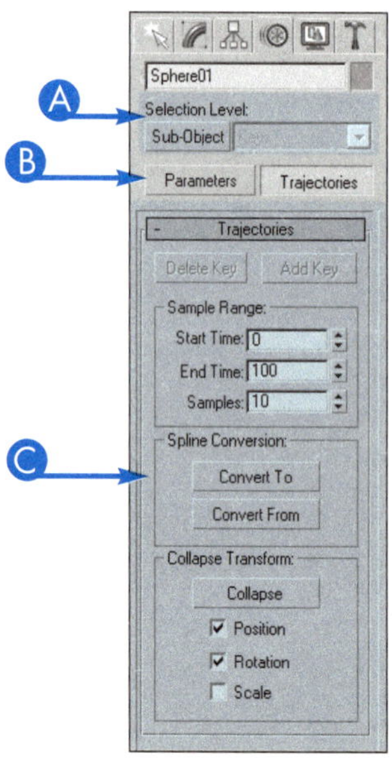

B Mode Buttons

Allow you to switch between the Parameters and Trajectories modes in the Motion panel.

C Trajectories Rollout

Contains options for adding and deleting keys to and from the trajectory. You can convert the current trajectory to a spline object. You can also convert any spline object to a trajectory for an object.

Parameters Mode

A Mode Buttons

Allow you to switch between the Parameters and Trajectories modes in the Motion panel.

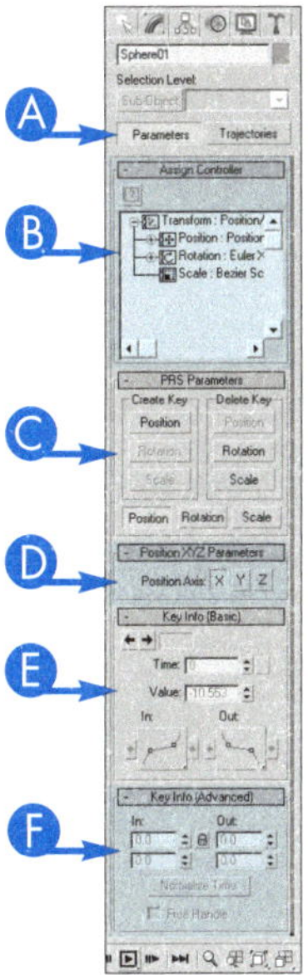

B Assign Controller Rollout

Displays and assigns the current transform controllers for the selected object.

C PRS Parameters Rollout

Contains options for creating or deleting Position, Rotation, and Scale keys, at the current frame, for the selected object. The buttons at the bottom of this rollout indicate which transforms are modified in the lower rollouts in the panel. 3ds Max grays out unavailable options.

D Controller-Specific Parameters Rollout

This rollout varies, depending on the controller that is assigned to the transform, and further specifies the controls that are available in the Key Info rollouts.

F Key Info (Advanced) Rollout

Contains options for controlling the speed of a parameter as it approaches and leaves the key. These fields are only active if you have specified a Custom tangent type.

E Key Info (Basic) Rollout

Contains options for changing the Time, Value, and tangent type for the selected key. By default, 3ds Max uses the Flat or Auto tangent type to interpolate the values between keys. You can select other tangent types using the corresponding In and Out buttons.

Create a Position Key in the Parameters Rollout

You can use the Parameters mode in the Motion panel to add a new Position key to a specific frame of your animation. Adding a key in the Modify panel changes an interpolated position into a keyed position that you can modify.

You can only have one Position key per frame. Therefore, to create a new Position key, you must move the Time Slider on a frame that has no Position key. You determine this by moving the Time Slider to a frame and looking at the Position button in the Create Key section of the PRS Parameters rollout; a grayed-out button indicates that the frame already has a Position key.

When you create a new Position key, 3ds Max adds separate keys for the X-, Y-, and Z-axes. It then assigns the object's current location values to each key. You can set new values for each key in the Key Info (Basic) rollout. The buttons in the Position XYZ Parameters rollout specify the axis with which you are working.

CD FILE: The Add Keys.max file is available on the CD-ROM for you to practice adding Position keys.

Create a Position Key in the Parameters Rollout

1. Select the object that you want to modify.
2. Click the Motion panel icon ( ).

   The Motion panel appears.
3. Click and drag the Time Slider to the frame where you want to create a Position key.
4. Click Position.

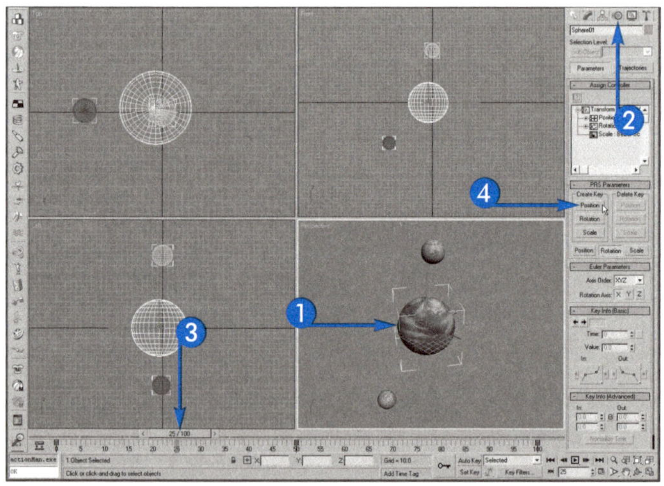

- 3ds Max creates a Position key at the current frame.

5. If it is not highlighted, click Position at the bottom of the PRS Parameters rollout.

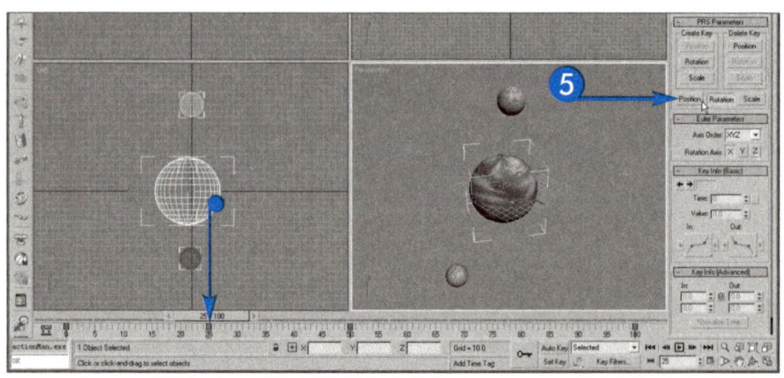

The Position XYZ Parameters rollout appears.

If you use a different Position controller, you see different rollouts.

6 Click the axis for which you want to change the key value.

7 Type a value to specify the position where you want the object to be in that axis.

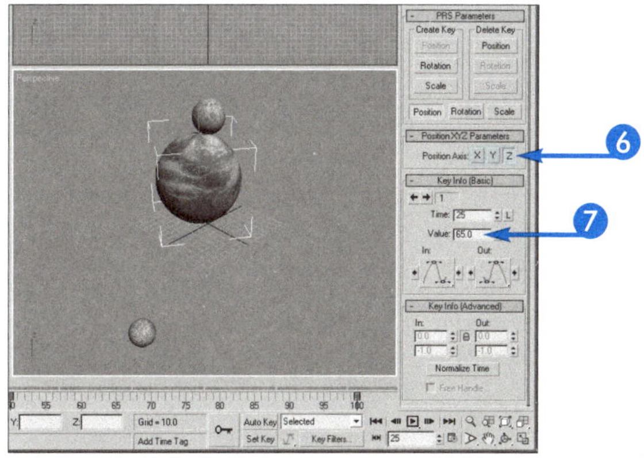

- The object's location updates in the viewports to reflect the Position key value.

8 Repeat steps 6 and 7 to modify the keys for the other axes.

9 Repeat steps 3 to 7 to add additional Position keys.

- You can click the Play Animation button (▶) to see the animation in the viewport.

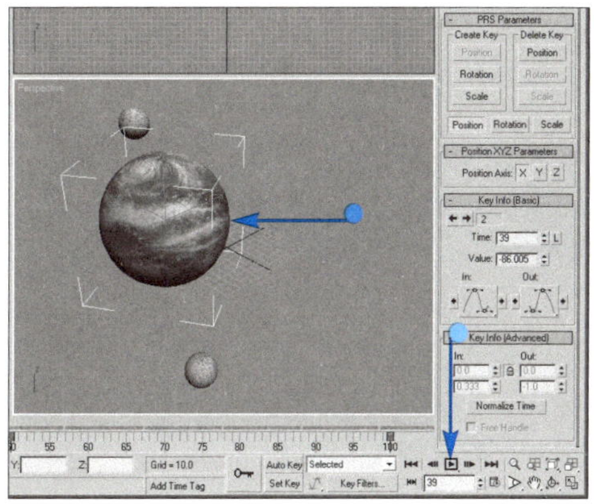

For the current frame, the Position key is grayed out, but I do not have a Position key in the frame. Why is this happening?

Some controllers do not allow you to set keys to determine the object's precise position. For example, if you have assigned a Noise controller to your object's position, then 3ds Max determines its random position based on the parameters that you have designated. As a result, the Position button under Create Keys remains grayed out for all frames. You can see the controllers that are assigned to your object by looking at the Assign Controller rollout. The default Position controller is the Position XYZ controller. It allows you to set key values for each axis.

How can I quickly change the Z-position values for only my object?

If you want to change just one axis of only the Position keys, you need to jump to only the frames that have Z-Position keys. First, click Position at the bottom of the PRS Parameters rollout to identify the type of key that you want to modify. Next, in the Position XYZ Parameters rollout, click the Z button to specify the axis. In the Key Info (Basic) rollout, click the right-facing arrow next to a grayed-out number in the top left corner. This moves the Time Slider to the next frame that has a Z-Position key, and other frames are ignored.

Create a Rotation Key in Parameters Mode

You can use the Parameters mode in the Motion panel to add a new Rotation key to a specific frame of your animation. Controllers determine how 3ds Max interpolates between keys and, depending upon the Rotation controller that is assigned to the object, you can set the rotation for each axis. The steps below describe how to create keys for the default Euler XYZ rotation controller.

To create a new Rotation key, the current frame must not have an existing Rotation key. You can quickly determine this by looking at the Rotation button in the Create Key section of the PRS Parameters rollout. If the button is grayed out, then the frame already has a Rotation key. See the section "Modify a Transform Key" for more information.

When you create a new Rotation key, 3ds Max creates a separate key for the X-, Y-, and Z-axes and assigns the current rotation values to each rotation key. You can change the value in the Key Info (Basic) rollout. The buttons in the Euler Parameters rollout allow you to switch between the three axes to set the appropriate values.

CD FILE The Add Keys.max file is available on the CD-ROM for you to practice adding Rotation keys.

Create a Rotation Key in Parameters Mode

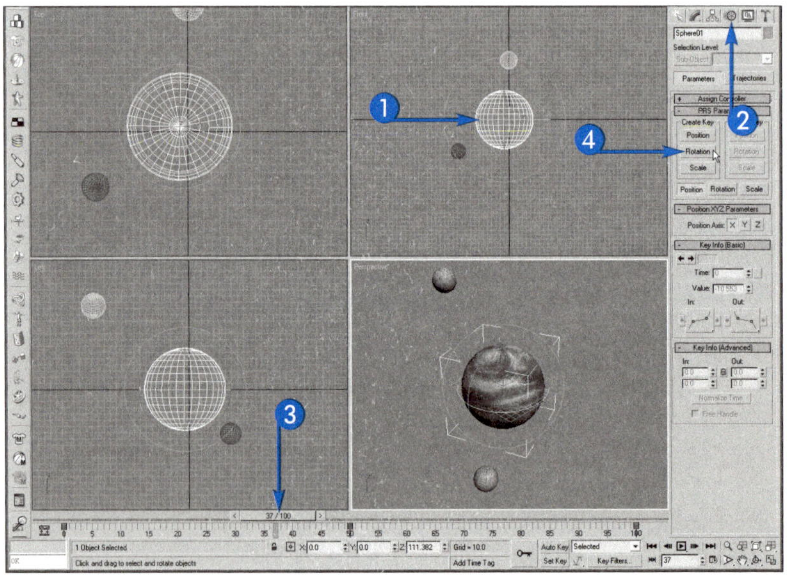

1. Select the object that you want to modify.
2. Click ⊚.

   The Motion panel appears.
3. Click and drag the Time Slider to the frame where you want to create a Rotation key.
4. Click Rotation.

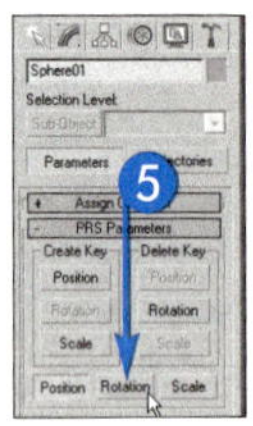

3ds Max creates a Rotation key.

5. Click Rotation at the bottom of the PRS Parameters rollout.

The Euler Parameters rollout displays.

6 Click the axis for which you want to set the key value.

7 Type a rotation value for the object in that axis.

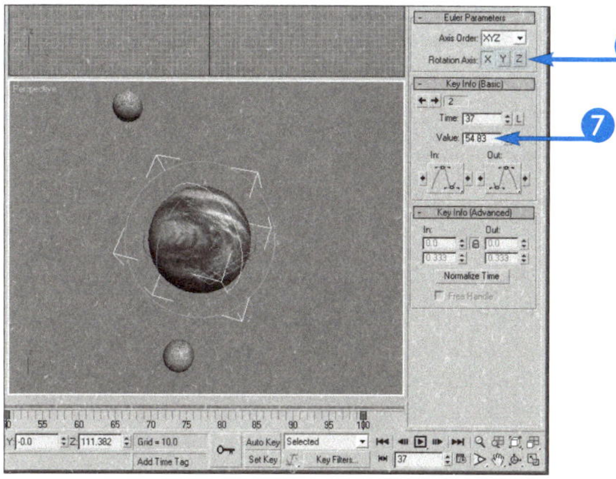

- The object's rotation updates in the viewports to reflect the Rotation key value.

8 Repeat steps 6 and 7 to modify the keys for the other axes.

9 Repeat steps 3 to 7 to add another Rotation key.

- You can click the Play Animation button (▶) to see the animation in the viewport.

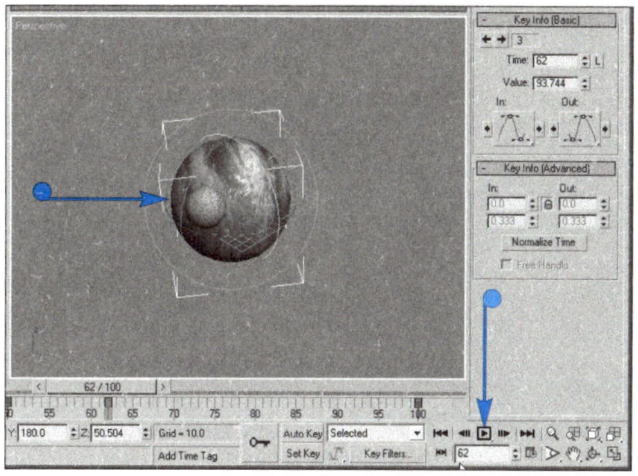

MASTER IT

Can I copy key values from one key to another?

Yes, you can copy key values from one key to another within the same object or between different objects. In the Key Info (Basic) rollout, highlight the Value or Time value that you want to copy, right-click in the field, and then select Copy from the pop-up menu. Navigate to the key to which you want to copy the value, highlight the current value, right-click in the field, and then select Paste. You must highlight the content of the target field because otherwise, when you paste the copied value, it appears in the field in addition to the existing value.

What is the purpose of the Axis Order field in the Euler Parameters rollout?

The Euler Parameters rollout opens when the default Euler XYZ controller is assigned as the rotation controller. This controller allows each axis to have its own, distinct controller for that axis's rotation. The object's final orientation may not be the sum of the three axes' rotations, but may be dependant on the order that the individual axis rotations occurs. The Axis Order specifies the sequence in which 3ds Max applies rotations to the axes. If you select an Axis Order of XYZ, then the X-axis rotates first, then the Y, and finally the Z. You can select the rotation order that produces the best effect for your animation.

Create a Scale Key

You can use the Parameters mode in the Motion panel to add a new Scale key to a specific frame of your animation. Controllers determine how 3ds Max interpolates between keys and, if you use the default Bezier Scale controller, then you can only create one Scale key that contains values for all three axes. Some of the other available controllers allow you to create separate keys for each axis. For more information on working with controllers, see Chapter 10.

To create a new Scale key, the current frame must not have a Scale key. You can quickly determine this by looking at the Scale button in the Create Key section of the PRS Parameters rollout. If the button is grayed out, then the selected frame already has a Scale key, and you can modify its values. See the section "Modify a Transform Key" for more information.

When you create a new Scale key, 3ds Max assigns the current interpolated values for each axis to the Scale key. You can set the new axis values in the Key Info (Basic) rollout.

CD FILE: The Add Keys.max file is available on the CD-ROM for you to practice adding Scale keys.

Create a Scale Key

1. Select the object that you want to modify.
2. Click [Motion panel icon].

   The Motion panel displays.
3. Click and drag the Time Slider to the frame where you want to create a Scale key.
4. Click Scale.

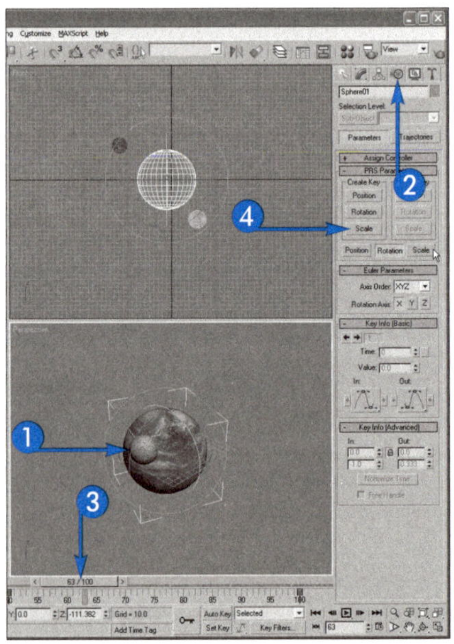

3ds Max creates a Scale key.

5. Click Scale at the bottom of the PRS Parameters rollout.

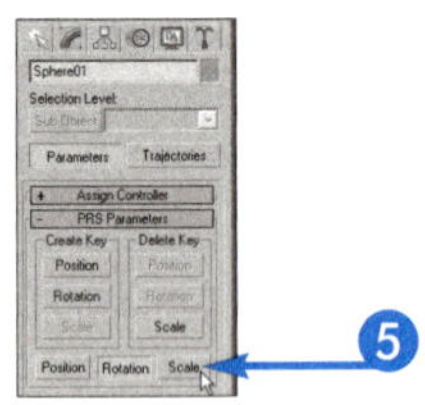

The Key Info (Basic) rollout changes to show the axis values for the current key.

6 Type new values for the X-, Y-, and Z-axes.

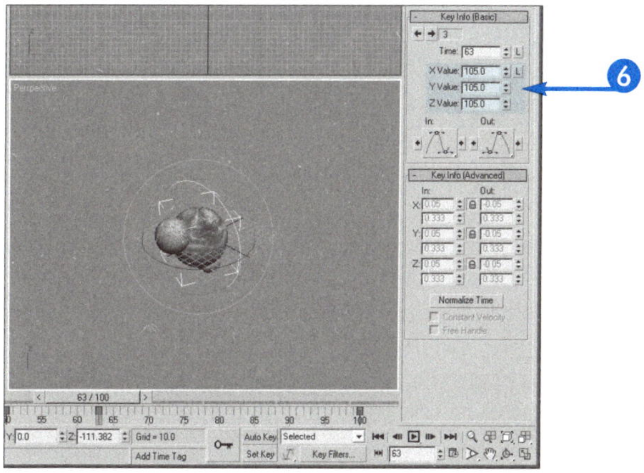

7 Repeat steps 3 to 6 to add another Scale key.

- The object scale updates in the viewports to reflect the Scale key values.
- You can click [Play] to see the animation in the viewport.

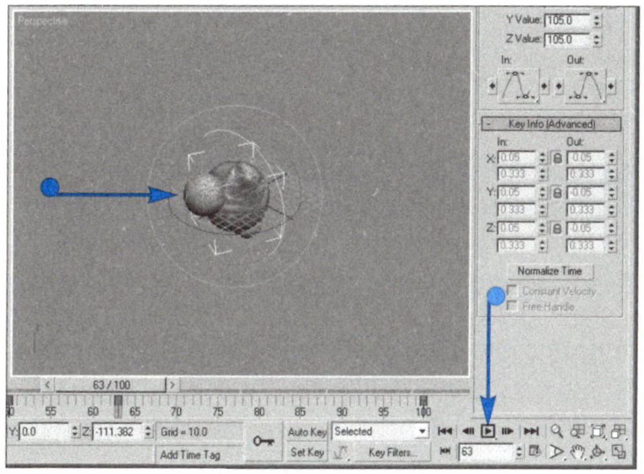

MASTER IT

What is the purpose of the "L" button that is located next to the Time field in the Key Info (Basic) rollout?

The Time Lock button ([L]) inhibits the movement of the current key and locks it to its present time. With the Time Lock button depressed, if you try to click and drag the key in the Track bar, then 3ds Max ignores your attemps to move it. Key movements are also stopped in the Curve Editor and Dope Sheet. The [L] is also available for Position and Rotation keys. For information on moving keys on the Track bar, see Chapter 8. For information on the Curve Editor and Dope Sheet, see Chapters 11 and 12.

What happens if I click the "L" button next to the X Value field in the Key Info (Basic) rollout?

If you want to apply the same scaling to all three axes, then you can click [L] to lock the three axis values to the value of the X-axis. This causes 3ds Max to ignore the values of the Y- and Z-axes. Whatever value you specify in the X-Value field, applies to all three axes. This works well when you have an object that you want to scale evenly on all axes. For example, to scale an object so that it doubles in size, click [L] and then type **200** in the X-Value field. The object scales to 200 percent on the Y- and Z-axes, as well.

Modify a Transform Key

Transform keys identify the Position, Rotation, and Scale values for an object at a particular point in time. You can use the Parameters mode in the Motion panel to change the value of any transform key for a selected object, or to delete transform keys.

You can modify a key's value by selecting the keyframe in the Track bar, and then looking at the PRS Parameters rollout to determine the types of keys that it contains. Existing transform key types are shown in the Delete Key section. If the frame contains a Position key, then 3ds Max grays out the Position button in the Create Key section and makes it available in the Delete Key section. When you delete a key, 3ds Max re-interpolates the animation between the remaining keys.

You specify the type of key to which to make modifications by selecting a transform button at the bottom of the PRS Parameters rollout. The subsequent rollouts adjust according to the type of transform. If no key exists for the transform type selected, then 3ds Max grays out the values in the Key Info (Basic) rollout.

CD FILE: The Add Keys.max file is available on the CD-ROM for you to practice modifying transform keys.

Modify a Transform Key

Change a Key Value

1. Select the object that you want to modify.
2. Click .

   The Motion panel appears.
3. Click and drag the Time Slider to the frame where you want to modify the values for a key.
4. Click the transform button that you want.

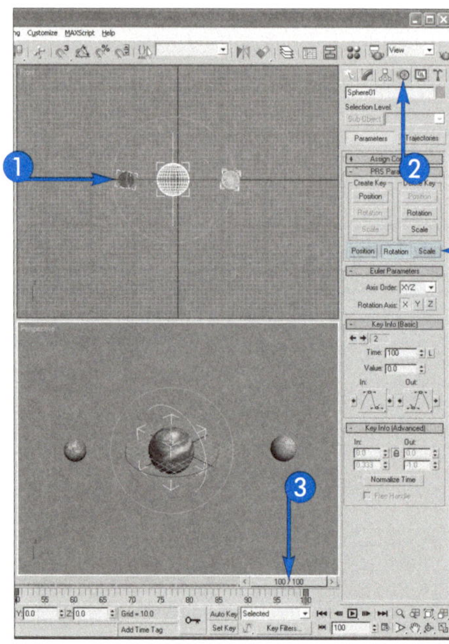

The rollouts change to reflect the transform selection.

5. If it is available, click the axis of the key that you want to modify.
6. Type the new key values.

   The object's transform updates in the viewports to reflect the new key values.

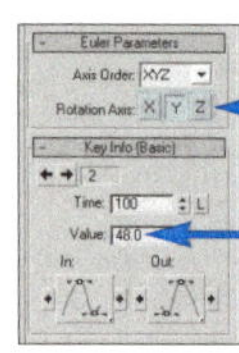

Delete a Key

1. In a viewport, click the object with the key that you want to delete.
2. Click [icon].

   The Motion panel appears.
3. Click and drag the Time Slider to the frame where you want to modify the value of a key.
4. In the Delete Key section, click the transform key type that you want to delete.

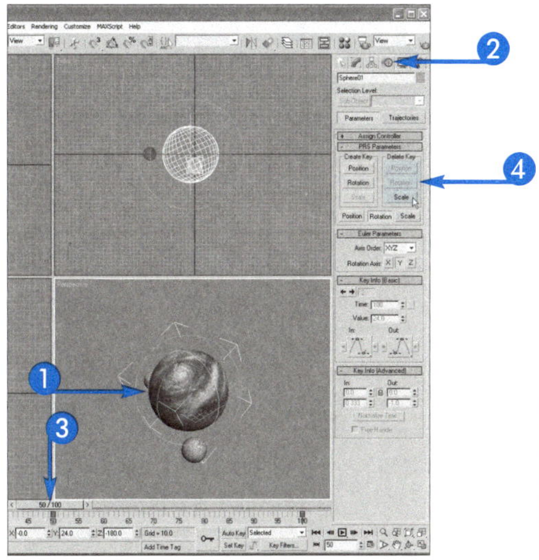

- 3ds Max removes the specified key from the selected frame.

If the frame has another type of key, then it still appears as a keyframe in the Track bar.

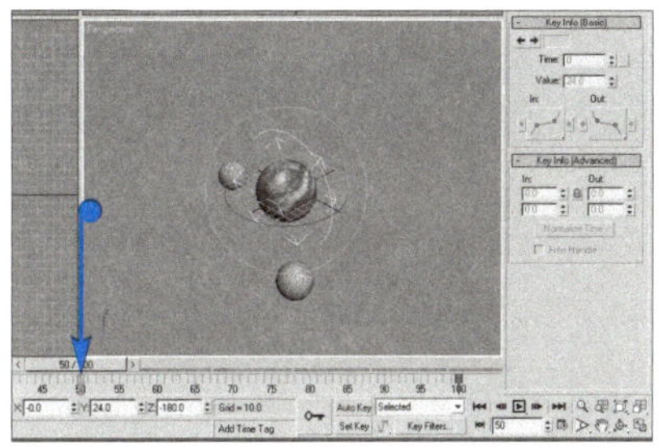

MASTER IT

How do I modify a keyframe that is not a transform key?

▼ The Motion panel is only for creating, modifying, and deleting transform keys that you have made for the position, rotation, and scale of an object. It does not allow you to modify animations that you created by changing the parameters of the object or a modifier. To modify a non-transform key, right-click the keyframe in the Track bar or Track view to display a list of the current keys. Click the key that you want. A Key Info dialog box appears, similar to the Key Info (Basic) rollout. Make the edits that you want to the key value. You can also use this method for transform key changes.

Why does 3ds Max place white brackets around my objects?

▼ When you move the Time Slider along the Track bar, 3ds Max displays white brackets around each object in your scene that has transform keys assigned at the current frame. For example, if you have two objects with transform keys that change their position at frame 50, when you select frame 50 in the Track bar, white brackets appear around each object. These brackets appear whether or not the object is selected. The white brackets only appear for transform keys; they do not appear for other types of keys, such as modifiers that are animated, and they only appear in Wireframe viewports.

Change the Trajectory of an Object

You can use the Trajectories mode in the Motion panel to view and modify the path along which an object moves within a scene. This provides a convenient method for controlling the movement of the object by allowing you to visually position the object, rather than entering numeric values.

An object's trajectory appears as a spline within the viewport, with each Position key represented as a white box. Interpolated frames appear as white dots on the spline. If you play the animation, the object moves along the trajectory path.

You can replace a portion of the current path of the object with a spline, to modify the object's trajectory. 3ds Max creates additional keys for the new path using the Start and End Time values, which define the frames in the animation that the new spline will occupy. It also creates a Sample value, which determines the number of new keys created on the path. For example, you can replace a section of the trajectory path between keys 25 and 50 by specifying 25 as the Start Time and 50 as the End Time.

CD FILE: The Trajectory.max file is available on the CD-ROM for you to practice changing an object's trajectory.

Change the Trajectory of an Object

1. In a viewport, click an object that you want to modify.
2. Click [Motion panel icon].

   The Motion panel appears.
3. Click Trajectories.

   The Trajectories rollout appears in the Motion panel.

   The current path appears for the object.
4. Type the frame where you want to insert the spline.
5. Type the frame where you want to end the spline.
6. Type the number of keys that you want to create on the spline.
7. Click Convert From.

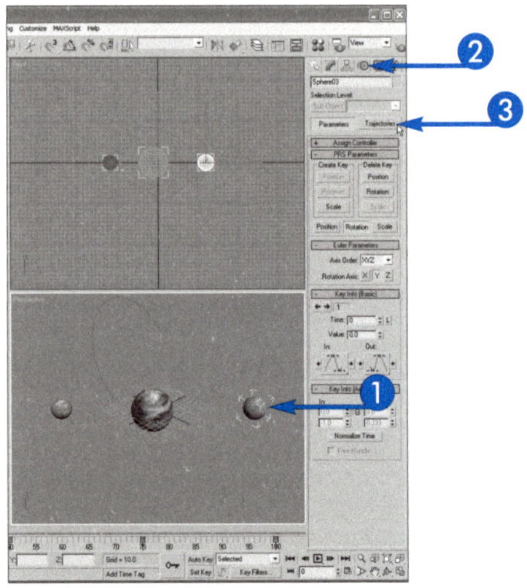

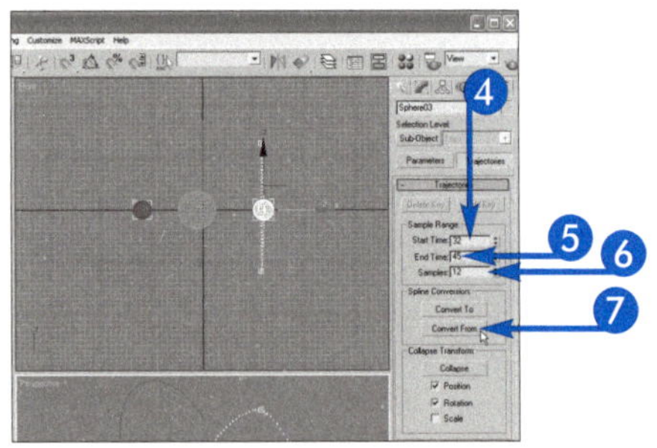

The Convert From button remains selected until you click a spline.

When you drag the cursor over a spline object, it changes to a cross cursor ( ).

8 Click a spline object.

Note: *For more information on creating and editing splines, see Chapters 4 and 5.*

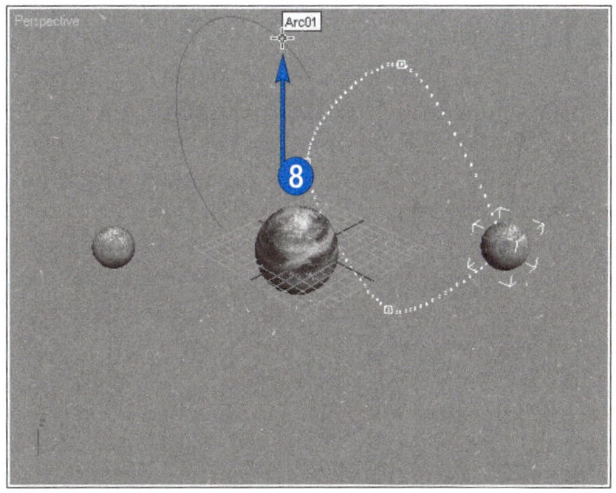

The trajectory of the object changes to include the new spline in the path.

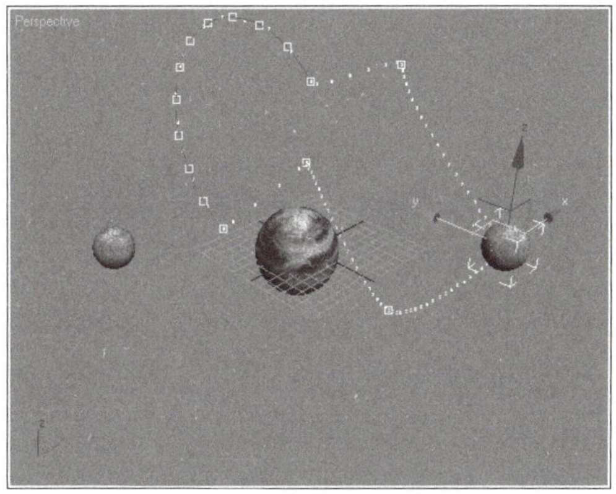

MASTER IT

Does it matter if the dots are not evenly spaced on the path?

Yes. The distance between the dots that represent each frame indicates the speed at which the object is moving. Because the amount of time between each frame is always constant, the greater the distance between dots, the farther the object has to travel between two frames. Therefore, a longer distance requires that the object move faster. You can adjust the distance between frames by moving keys, or creating new keys on your trajectory. Adding a Normalize Spline modifier evenly spaces the points on the path. See the section "Add and Move Position Keys" for more information on adding new keys to a trajectory.

Why does my object jump around after I add a path to the trajectory?

When you click Convert From, 3ds Max adds keys to represent the object's new location along the added spline, between the Start Time and End Time values. If a Position key already exists between those values, 3ds Max does not delete it, and it remains intact. 3ds Max interpolates the object's location, based on the existing key and the two new keys that are created before and after it. Regardless of the speed required, the movement of the object hits all position keys in the trajectory. See the section "Add and Move Position Keys" for information on deleting an unwanted key.

Add and Move Position Keys

You can use the Trajectories mode in the Motion panel to add and move keys on the animation path of your object. Adding new keys allows you to adjust the trajectory of the path. For example, you may want to make the trajectory more rounded. To do this, you can add additional keys and then move them to meet the trajectory that you want.

To move keys on the trajectory of an object, you must change the Selection Level to Keys. Within this mode, you can select individual or combinations of keys on the path in order to move or delete them. You can also click the path to create new keys.

When you add a key to the selected trajectory, 3ds Max creates a new position keyframe for the object on the Track bar. Although the new key has the position values of the selected frame, you can reposition it to adjust the values. Keep in mind that moving a key on the trajectory changes its values, not its frame. To move the key to a different frame, you need to move it on the Track bar.

The Trajectory.max file is available on the CD-ROM for you to practice adding and moving position keys.

Add and Move Position Keys

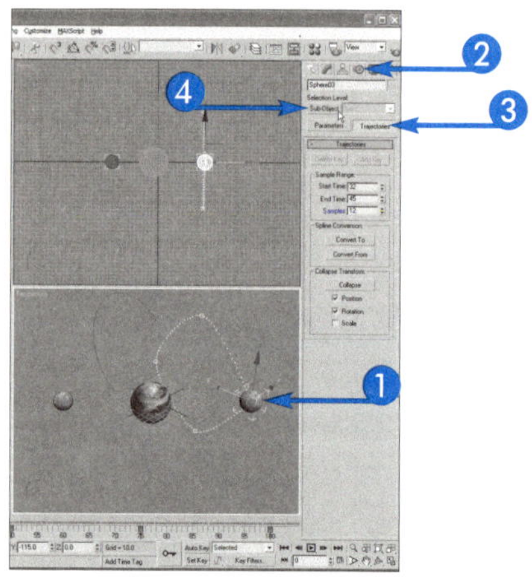

1. Select the object that you want to modify.
2. Click [icon].

   The Motion panel appears.
3. Click Trajectories.
4. Click Sub-Object.

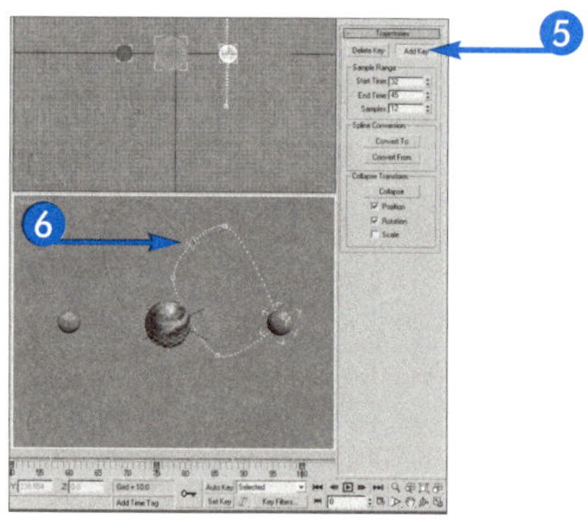

   Keys display in the Sub-Object field, indicating the selection level.
5. Click Add Key.
6. Click the trajectory path.

3ds Max creates a new key in the specified position.

7 Click Add Key.

3ds Max deselects the button.

8 Click the Select and Move button (✥).

9 Click and drag to position the new key.

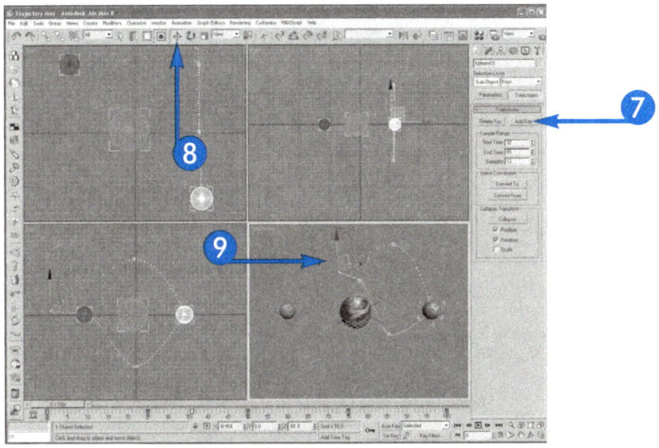

- The trajectory of the animation path changes to reflect the key movement.

10 Click Sub-Object to turn Sub-Object mode off.

You can repeat steps 5 and 6 to add additional keys.

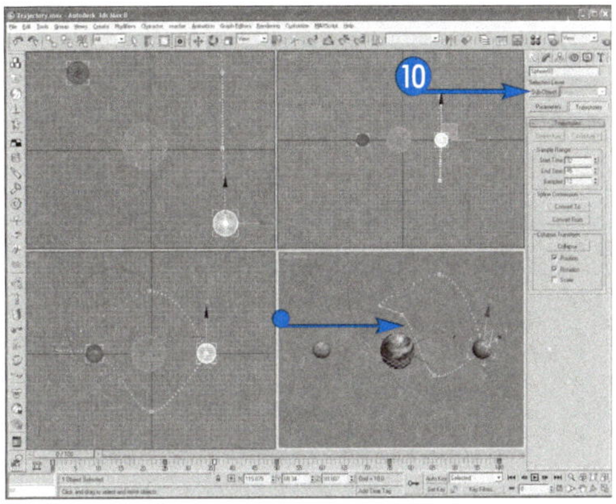

MASTER IT

How do I delete keys, and what happens when I do so?

▼ If you have keys on your animation path that you no longer need or want, you can remove them by activating the Keys Sub-Object level, selecting the key on the path, and then clicking Delete Key in the Trajectories rollout, or pressing Delete on the keyboard. 3ds Max removes the key from the Track bar as well as from the trajectory path. Because 3ds Max interpolates the keys between keyframes using keyframe values, when you delete a key, the trajectory of the path changes. This is because 3ds Max must recalculate the values in the remaining keys.

What happens if I collapse a transform?

▼ Controllers determine how 3ds Max interpolates the animated values for an object, including the transform key values. Somes of the controllers, such as the Noise controller and Path Constraint, do not use explicit values but, rather, parametric values based on user input parameters. These controllers do not generate transform keys. The Collapse button, in the Collapse Transform section of the Trajectories panel, converts the parametric values into explicit values, and creates keys that you can modify. At least one of the Position, Rotation, or Scale check boxes must be checked (☐ changes to ☑) in the Collapse Transform section for the Collapse button to be available. For more information on controllers and constraints, see Chapter 10.

Understanding Controllers and Constraints

All animation in 3ds Max is governed by the animation controller applied to an object track. While all objects have default transform controllers assigned to their transforms, and tracks also have controllers assigned automatically when you animate their parameters, these are often exchanged for controllers that are more appropriate for the type of animation. Controllers are divided into two categories: controllers and constraints.

What Is a Controller?

A controller stores and manages all key values for the animation of the selected track or parameter and interpolates the values of the frames between the keyframes. Controllers are self-contained and do not require one object to define their impact on another object.

What Is a Constraint?

If a controller requires the presences of another object in a scene to define the animation process, it is considered a constraint. You use constraints to control the position, rotation, or scale of an object, based on the relationship of that object to another object in a scene. For example, you can use a Path Constraint to animate an object that is moving along a specific spline object in your scene. This is an alternative method of path animation to the method outlined in Chapter 9.

Controllers, Constraints, and Keyframes

Controllers and constraints determine whether the animation uses keyframes. If there are keyframes, then 3ds Max determines how a transform or parameter is interpolated between frames, or how the entire animation length for that transform or parameter is addressed. Key tangency is used to control this interpolation. For example, the Bezier Position controller curves the path that an object follows, from one key to the next, so that the motion is curved and flowing, while a Linear Position controller moves an object in a straight line, at a constant velocity from key to key.

Controller Types

When you animate objects in 3ds Max using either Auto Key or Set Key, 3ds Max assigns default controllers. Because not all types of animation work well with the default controllers, you can assign other types of controllers to your animation to achieve different results. There are some controllers that produce animation without the need to create keyframes. For example, you can use the Noise controller to make an object move, scale, or rotate randomly. The animation controllers that are available in 3ds Max can be divided into six different categories, per the table on the following page.

Constraints

When you work with constraints, 3ds Max requires that you always have one object constrained to another object, which is the target object. The target object always imposes specific limits on the other object. 3ds Max provides seven different types of constraints that you can apply to objects in your scene. See the next page for the seven constraints types and their descriptions.

Controller Categories

Category	Description
Float	Animate parameters with a single floating-point value. For example, the Waveform controller allows you to create regular, periodic waveforms that you can use to control on/off-type motion such as blinking lights.
Point3	Animate three-component values such as the red, green, and blue color values or 3D points. For example, the Color RGB controller splits the R, G, and B components of a color into three tracks that you can control separately.
Position	Control the position coordinates of objects and selection sets through X-, Y-, and Z-position values. For example, the Position XYZ controller allows you to specify the key value of the object for each axis.
Rotation	Control the rotation coordinates of objects and selection sets through X-, Y-, and Z-rotation values. For example, the Euler XYZ controller allows you to specify the key rotation value of the object on each axis.
Scale	Control the scale values for objects by specifying a percentage value for each axis. For example, you can apply the Scale XYZ controller to an object to set separate scale keys for each axis.
Transform	Control all three types of transforms (position, rotation, and scale) with one controller. For example, 3ds Max applies the default controller Position/Rotation/Scale Transform to all object transforms. This controller includes the Position XYZ controller for the Position tracks, the Euler XYZ for the Rotation tracks, and the Bezier Scale controller for scaling.

Animation Constraints

Constraint	Description
Attachment	Attaches the position of an object to a specific face of another object. This causes the attached object to remain in contact with the other object throughout the animation sequence.
Link	Animates an object by linking it from one target object to the next. When you link an object, it inherits the position, rotation, and scale of the target object.
LookAt	Controls an object so that one axis is always oriented toward the target object. If the position of the target object changes, the LookAt constraint causes the other object to rotate until it is facing the target object.
Orientation	Causes the rotation of an object to always follow the rotation of the target object. If the target object rotates, then the other object matches its movement.
Path Constraint	Restricts the movement of an object to follow the path of a spline object. The object remains locked to the specified path and continues to follow the spline, even if you alter the spline object. More than one spline can affect the trajectory of an object.
Position	Causes an object to follow the position of a target object or the weighted position of several objects. If the target object moves, then the other object matches its movement.
Surface	Restricts the position of an object so that it remains on the surface of the target object. This allows you to restrict all movement of the object to remain on the surface of another object.

Assign a Path Constraint

You can restrict an object's motion so that it follows a specific path. For example, you can make a bee fly away from a flower along a specific path to a hive. To do this, you apply the Path Constraint to the object that you want to constrain and pick at least one spline, which serves as the path.

You can easily assign the Path Constraint using the Assign Controller rollout in the Motion panel. Assigning this controller allows you to apply the constraint to an object that does not have an assigned animation. If the object is already animated, then all other position information is discarded and replaced with a trajectory that follows the path.

In the Assign Controller rollout, you can select the Position track and then apply the Path Constraint. When you add a Path Constraint, the Path Parameters rollout appears in the Motion panel. You can use this rollout to select the paths for the object and specify how closely the object should follow the paths. By default, the object starts to follow the path at the first frame and reaches the end at the last frame.

CD FILE The Path.max file is available on the CD-ROM for you to practice assigning a Path Constraint.

Assign a Path Constraint

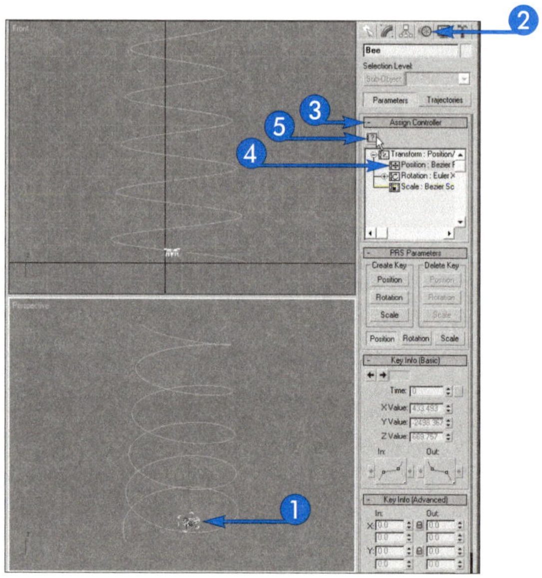

1. Select the object to animate along the path.
2. Click the Motion panel button (◎).
3. Click the Plus sign (⊞) to expand the Assign Controller rollout.
4. Click to highlight the Position track.

   If the Position track is not visible, then click ⊞ next to Transform.
5. Click the Assign Controller button (▣).

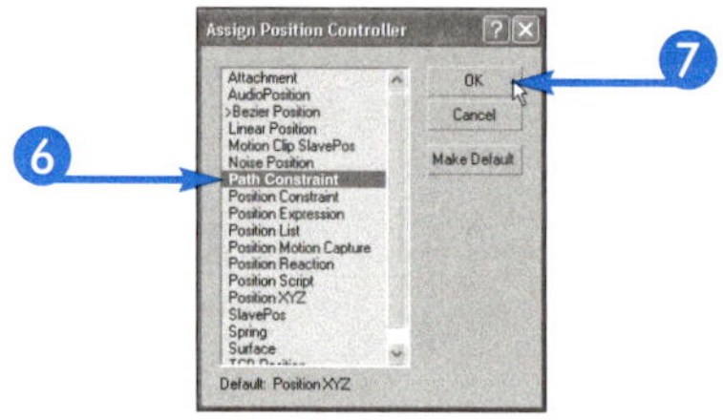

The Assign Position Controller dialog box appears.

6. Click Path Constraint.
7. Click OK.

3ds Max replaces the existing Position controller with the Path Constraint.

The Path Parameters rollout appears in the Motion panel.

8. Click Add Path.
9. Click the spline object.

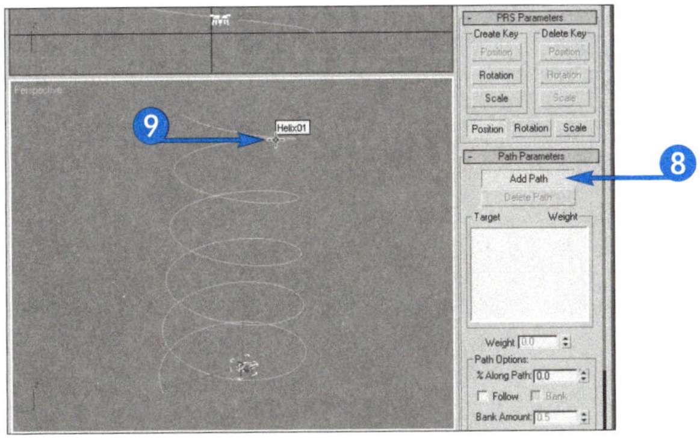

- The name of the spline object appears in the Target list box.
- You can click the Play Animation button (▶) to view the animation in the selected viewport.
- Click to select the Follow option if you want your object's orientation to follow the path's direction (☐ changes to ☑).

10. Click Add Path to discontinue selecting paths.

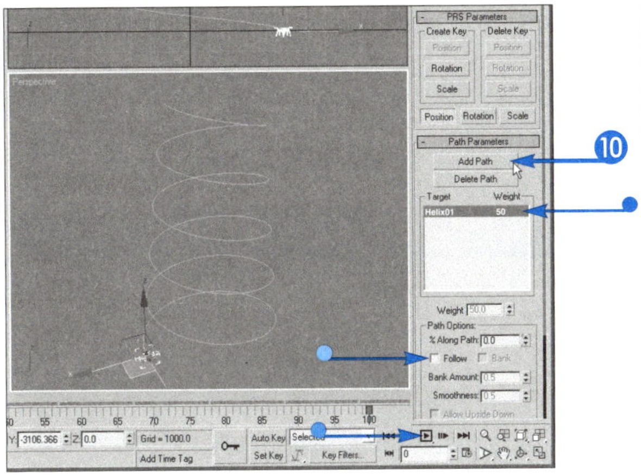

MASTER IT

Can I specify multiple paths for the object to follow?

Yes. You can use multiple spline objects to define the path that the object follows. You select each path by clicking Add Path and then selecting the desired spline object. By default, 3ds Max assigns each spline object a Weight value of 50. The Weight value, which you can adjust, determines the amount of influence the splines have on the object movement in relation to each other. The higher the Weight value, the more influence the spline has on the path of the object. For example, a spline with a Weight value of 60 has twice as much influence over an object that has a Weight value of 30.

In the Path Parameters rollout, what does the Path Options % Along Path field do?

The % Along Path field controls the amount, as a percent of the total path length, that the object has moved along the path at a specific frame. By default, the object moves an equal amount between each frame. For example, if you set your animation Active Time Segment at 100 frames, then the object moves one percent of the length of the spline object between each frame. To change the distance the object covers as it moves along the spline, you must create keyframes with the appropriate % Along Path value. For example, to move the object through 50 percent of the frames by frame 40, you must create a keyframe at frame 40 and type **50** in the % Along Path field.

Add Randomness with a Noise Controller

In computer graphics terminology, adding noise generally refers to adding randomness. You can apply noise as a modifier to randomly distort an object's appearance, in a material to randomly filter a map's effect on a material, or to randomly move, rotate, or scale an object. Manually adding Rotation keys to dozens of tumbling asteroids can be time-consuming, and you are not likely to see the random appearance that you are after. Assigning a Noise controller to the objects' rotation is a better solution.

After you apply the Noise controller, several settings determine how the object moves, rotates, or scales. In the Noise Controller dialog box, the X, Y, and Z Strength values determine how far or how much the controller affects the object, and the Frequency determines the rate at which the objects are affected. A higher Frequency causes a more jittery effect. An extremely low Frequency is often used for subtle effects. Selecting the Fractal Noise option causes additional spikes and valleys to appear in the Characteristic Graph, which is the visual interpretation of the Noise controller's effect on your object's transform.

CD FILE The Noise.max file is available on the CD-ROM for you to practice assigning a Noise controller.

Add Randomness with a Noise Controller

1. Select the object to which you want to add randomness.
2. Click the Motion panel button ( ).
3. Click ⊞ to expand the Assign Controller rollout.
4. Click to highlight a transform.

   If the transform tracks are not visible, click ⊞ next to Transform.
5. Click ▣.

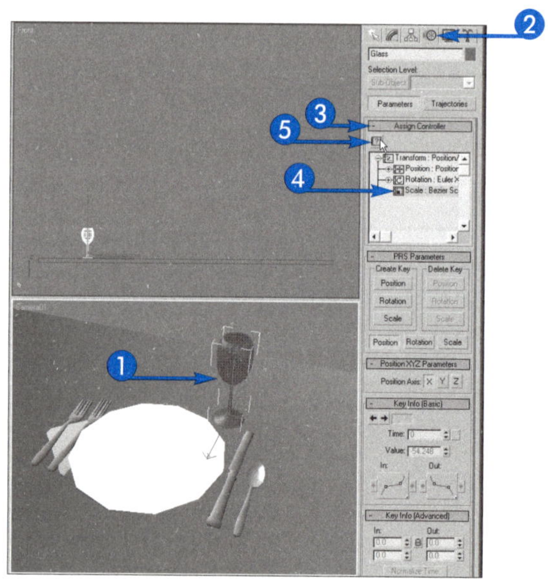

The Assign Scale Controller dialog box appears.

6. Click Noise Scale.
7. Click OK.

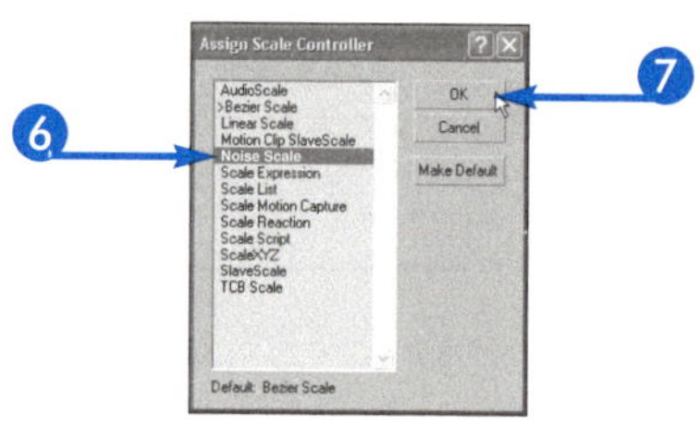

3ds Max replaces the existing transform's controller with the Noise controller.

The Noise Controller dialog box appears.

8 Type in these fields to adjust the values.

9 Click the Close button (☒) to close the dialog box.

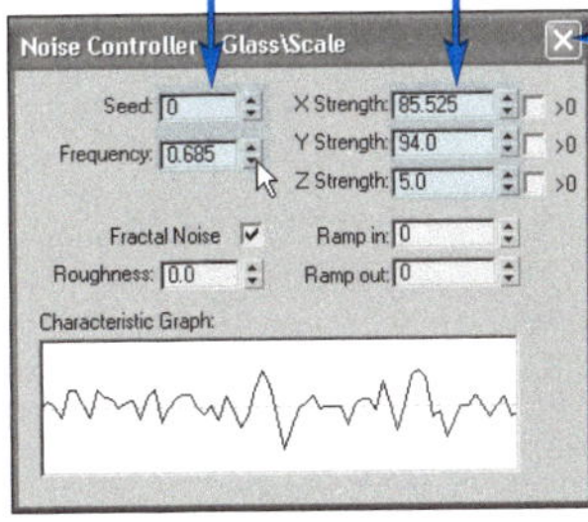

10 Click ▣ to see the animation.

- The object moves, rotates, or scales randomly.

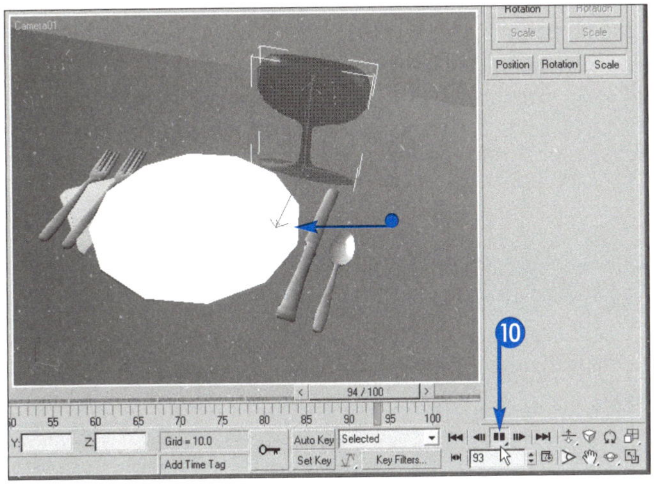

PART III

Can I use the Noise controller to add randomness to my scenes in other ways?

▼ Yes. In addition to being a modifier and a map type, the Noise controller can be assigned to almost any parameter in 3ds Max. For example, you can create a flickering light by assigning it to a Multiplier value of that light. Most modifiers can have a Noise controller assigned to their parameters to create a random application of that modifier. Applying a controller to a parameter, rather than a transform, is done through the Track View dialog boxes, rather than the Motion panel.

How can I change the Noise controller's parameters?

▼ Once you close the Noise Controller dialog box, you must reopen it to change the parameters. To do this, select and then right-click the controller in the Assign Controller rollout. Then select Properties from the dialog box.

What are the >0 check boxes for?

▼ The >0 options (☐ changes to ☑) in the Noise Controller dialog box cause each axis's Strength value to be greater than zero. For example, you use this option when you only want to randomly change an object's Height value using positive values. Negative values applied to a light's Multiplier cause it to cast darkness.

Stick to a Surface with a Surface Constraint

You can use the Surface constraint to place or move an object, called the *constrained object*, along the surface of another object, called the *surface object*. Actually, the pivot point of the constrained object is locked to the surface of the surface object. When you animate the position of the constrained object, it moves along the surface of the surface object. For example, you can use a Surface constraint to show a leech moving up a leg.

U, V, and W are axis directions that are similar to the X-, Y-, and Z-axes mentioned throughout this text. While X, Y, and Z represent fixed axes in space, U, V, and W represent axis directions relative to the orientation of an object. For example, if a character is facing the Front viewport, the world X direction is from its left to its right, and so is the U direction. If the character is facing the Left viewport, the world X direction is from front to back, but the U direction is still from left to right. The surface object has two axis controls to position the constrained object on the surface object.

The Surface.max file is available on the CD-ROM for you to practice assigning a Surface constraint.

Stick to a Surface with a Surface Constraint

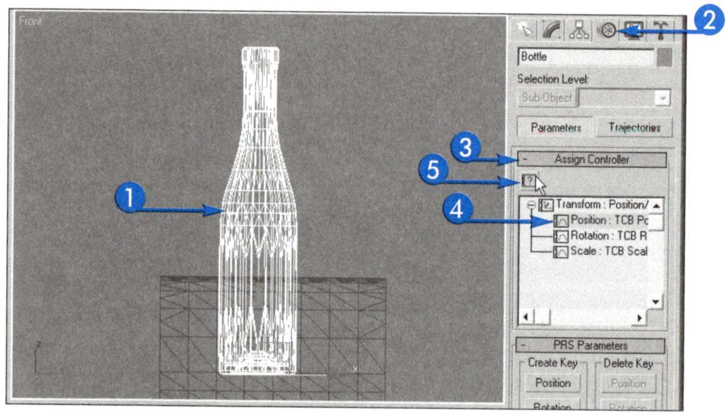

1. Select the object that you want to constrain.
2. Click [icon] to open the Motion panel.
3. Click [icon] to open the Assign Controller rollout.
4. Click to highlight the Position track.

   If the Position track is not visible, click [icon] next to Transform.
5. Click [icon].

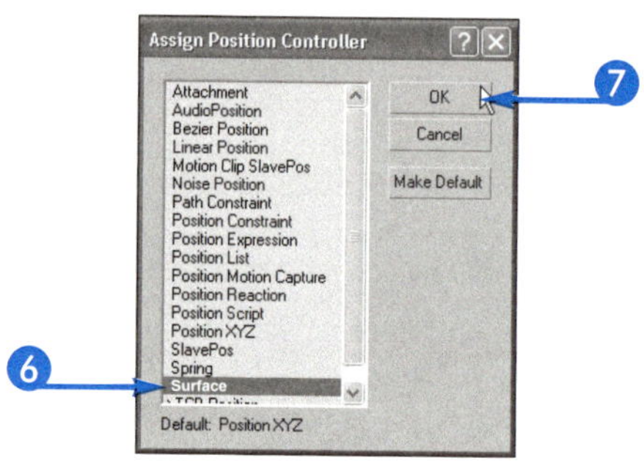

- The Assign Position Controller dialog box appears.

6. Click Surface.
7. Click OK.

3ds Max replaces the current Position controller with the Surface constraint.

The Surface Controller Parameters rollout appears in the Motion panel.

8 Click Pick Surface.

9 Click the surface object.

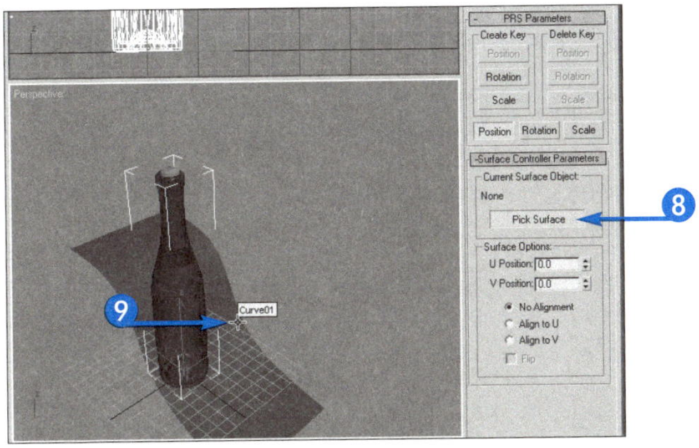

- The constrained object attaches to the surface object.

10 Type the V Position and U Position values for the initial location of the object.

The object moves to the specified position on the surface object.

11 Click to select either the Align to U option or the Align to V option to set the alignment of the objects (○ changes to ◉).

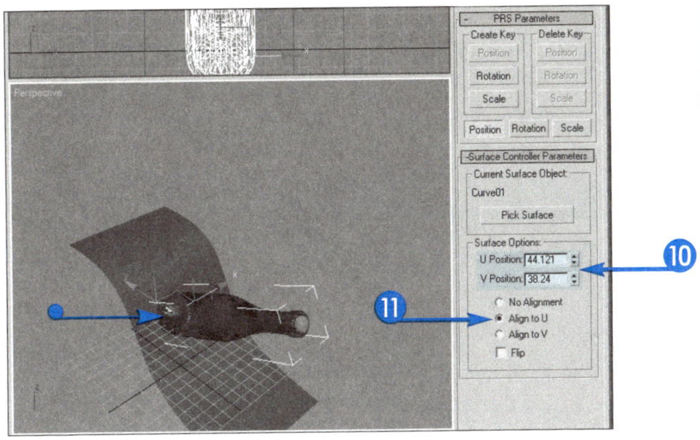

MASTER IT

I have an object that I want to use for my surface object. Why am I unable to select it?

▼ 3ds Max only allows you to select a parametric object as your surface object, which you can alter by changing the object's parameters. For example, to change the size of a sphere, you must adjust the Radius parameter. For this reason, you can apply the Surface constraint to the Sphere, as well as a Cone, Cylinder, Torus, single Quad Patches, loft, and NURBS objects, but not to editable meshes, editable polys, or any primitives not mentioned above. In addition, applying any modifiers to the surface object, such as applying a Bend modifier to a Cylinder, converts it to an editable mesh, thus prohibiting it from being the surface object.

What are the Alignment options for?

▼ When the Surface constraint constrains an object, it preserves the initial orientation of the object if you use the default No Alignment option (○ changes to ◉). For example, if you align a car to a hilly road, the car retains its horizontal posture, regardless of the hill's angle. Selecting the Align to U or Align to V option (○ changes to ◉) adapts the constrained object's orientation to match the face on the surface object on which it is currently resting. Clicking the Flip option (☐ changes to ☑) rotates the object 180 degrees around the U or V axis, depending on the axis to which the object is aligned.

Assign an Attachment Constraint

Similar to the Surface constraint, the Attachment constraint limits the position of a *source* object, so that it is fixed onto a specific face on a *target* object. You can hold the source object, such as a squirrel frantically holding on to a character's thrashing leg, in place using an Attachment constraint.

While the Surface constraint is limited to using only specific surface objects, the Attachment constraint can constrain your objects to the faces of any object. Most modifiers do not affect how the Attachment constraint holds one object to the face of another. In fact, the attachment controller is designed to hold an object in place on a surface that may be changing or flowing.

The basic procedure for attaching one object to another is to select your source object, and then change the Position controller to be the Attachment constraint. You then select the target object to attach to and then set the object's position on the new object. The source object's pivot point is fixed to the face over which it was positioned. For more information on pivot points, see Chapter 13.

CD FILE: The Attachment.max file is available on the CD-ROM for you to practice assigning an Attachment constraint.

Assign an Attachment Constraint

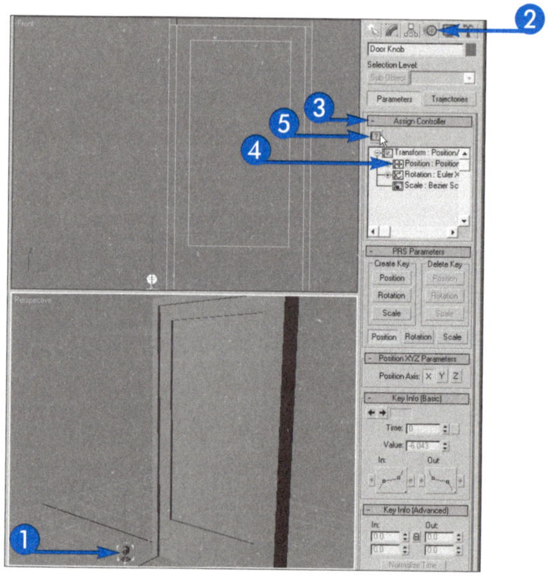

1. Select the object that you want to constrain.
2. Click to open the Motion panel.
3. Click to expand the Assign Controller rollout.
4. Click to highlight the Position track.

   If the Position track is not visible, click next to Transform.
5. Click .

- The Assign Position Controller dialog box appears.

6. Click Attachment.
7. Click OK.

3ds Max replaces the current Position controller with the Attachment constraint.

The Attachment Parameters rollout appears in the Motion panel.

8 Click Pick Object.

9 Click the Target object.

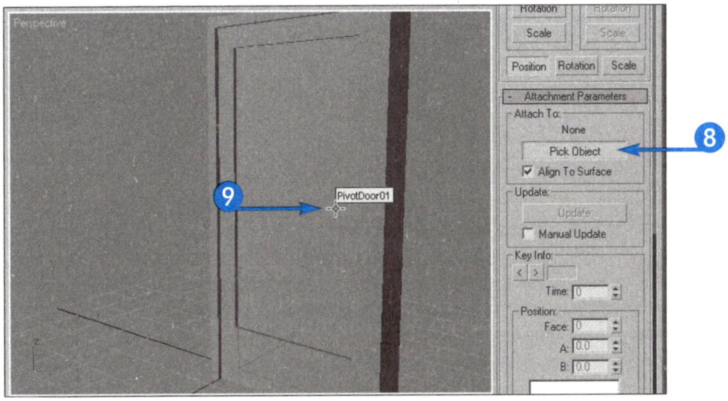

10 Click Set Position.

11 Click and drag over the surface of the target object.

When you release the mouse, the source object is fixed to the face over which you moved the cursor.

In the CD-ROM exercise, you can change the Open value for the door and watch the doorknob as the door opens.

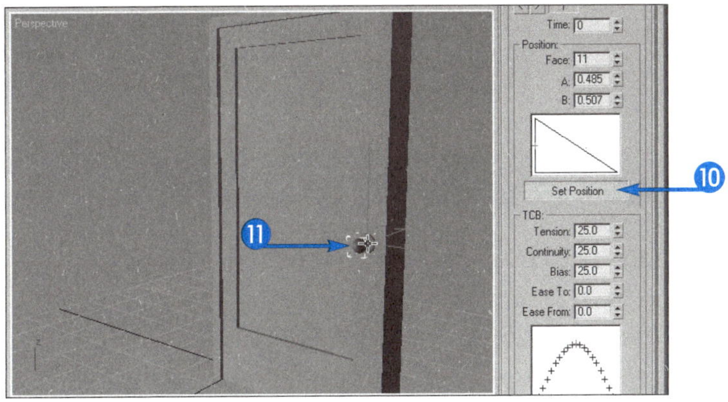

MASTER IT

When I use Edit Mesh, my source object moves around. Why?

3ds Max organizes all faces, edges, and vertices by assigning them a number. The Attachment constraint works by fixing an object's pivot point to a particular face on the source object. 3ds Max attaches the source object to a particular face by assigning it to that specific face number. For example, face #16 may be on the top of a box, but if you use the Edit Mesh modifier and then change the parameters, or do anything else that changes the number of faces, then the face numbers are redistributed. As a result, you do not know where face #16 will end up. If this happens, you can click Set Position and relocate your object.

Can I just link my object to the source object?

Yes. If neither object is going to move, or both objects are going to move together, then linking the objects together is a perfectly good solution. The Attachment constraint is designed for when the object's positions fluctuate. In the case of the 3ds Max door and window objects, the entire structure, including the frame, leaf, and panels, is considered one object. Linking a doorknob or handle to the door leaf or window panel does not change the object's location or orientation when the door or window opens or closes, only when the entire structure moves or rotates.

PART III

Control Orientation with a LookAt Constraint

A LookAt Constraint controls an object's orientation, based on the location of another object, called the *target* object, in a scene. You only apply the LookAt Constraint to the Rotation transform, and it replaces any existing transform. Once you apply it, you cannot use the Rotate tool to alter an object's orientation. For example, you can use the LookAt Constraint to force an anti-aircraft gun barrel to follow an incoming plane or to make a character's eyes follow the action in a scene.

When you assign the LookAt Constraint, by default, the local X-axis points toward the pivot point of the target object. If this is not the axis that you want to point at the target object, then you can select another axis in the Select LookAt Axis section of the Motion panel. If no specific axis should be oriented toward the target object, then you can use the Set Orientation button to set the object's initial orientation. With Set Orientation active, you can use the Rotate transform to align the object in the scene. For more information on rotating an object, see Chapter 2.

CD FILE The LookAt.max file is available on the CD-ROM for you to practice assigning a LookAt Constraint.

Control Orientation with a LookAt Constraint

1. Select the object that you want to constrain.
2. Click to open the Motion panel.
3. Click to open the Assign Controller rollout.
4. Click to highlight the Rotation track.

   If the Rotation track is not visible, click next to Transform.
5. Click .

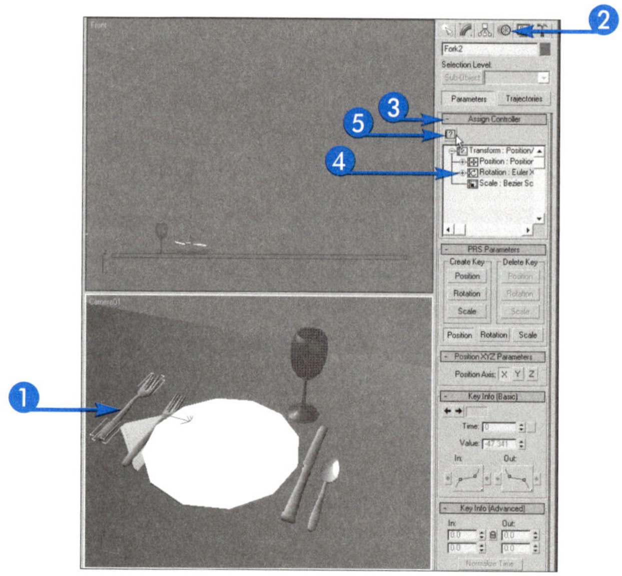

The Assign Rotation Controller dialog box appears.

6. Click LookAt Constraint.
7. Click OK.

3ds Max replaces the current Rotation controller with the LookAt constraint.

The LookAt Constraint rollout appears in the Motion panel.

8 Click Add LookAt Target.

9 Click the Target object.

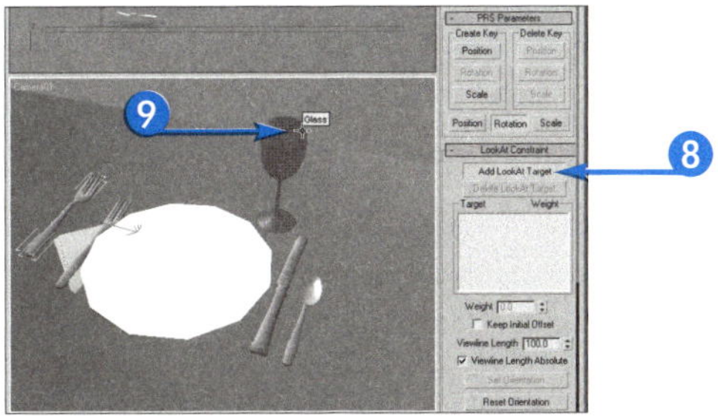

The target object's name appears in the Target list.

The object orients toward the target.

10 Click Add LookAt Target to turn it off.

11 Click Set Orientation.

12 Click the Select and Rotate button ( ).

13 Reorient your object.

14 Click Set Orientation to turn it off.

If you select and move the target object, your object's orientation follows it.

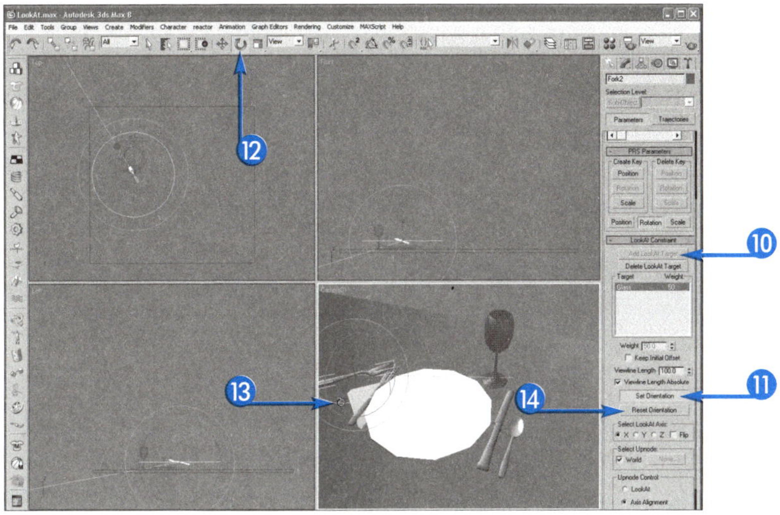

PART III

MASTER IT

How does adding more LookAt targets benefit me?

- The LookAt Constraint allows you to have several objects designated as LookAt targets. Each target is weighted in relation to the other targets, and the weight determines that object's influence in setting your object's orientation. For example, when you have several objects in a crowd, one object can dominate the focus of your object by having a Weight value higher than the others. Your object does not look directly at the heavily weighted object, but more toward it than any other object. The Weight field is available when more than one object is designated as a LookAt target.

Can I make my object stop looking at one object and start looking at another?

- Yes. There are two ways to accomplish this. First, you can shift your object's focus by using a Dummy as the target. A Dummy is a non-rendering helper object that you can use by selecting Create, and then selecting the Helpers menu. Moving the Dummy from the vicinity of one object to the vicinity of another appears to reorient your object's attention from one to another. You can also select both objects as target objects and give one an initial Weight value of zero. When you animate one object's weight ascending from zero and the other's decending to zero, your object's focus shifts from one object to the next.

Assign a Spring Controller

You can apply a Spring controller to make an object react with both primary and secondary motion to simulate fluid movement. The Spring controller works well when you want to animate objects that are linked together but that are all controlled by a *parent* object. For example, if the parent object is the top link of a chain, the links attached to the top link react to any motion that acts upon it. The attached links' movement is called *secondary motion,* or motion that occurs as a result of the first object's motion. 3ds Max also has the Reaction Manager available to create secondary motion.

To create secondary motion, you can apply the Spring controller to each of the objects that are linked to the parent object. 3ds Max now reflects any movement of the parent object on the child objects. You cannot apply the Spring controller to the parent object because it has other forces acting upon it.

You can animate the parent object using Auto Key to create keys that change the parent object's position. To make the entire set of objects react with secondary movement, you create keys that cause the master object to move back and forth.

CD FILE: The Spring.max file is available on the CD-ROM for you to practice assigning a Spring controller.

Assign a Spring Controller

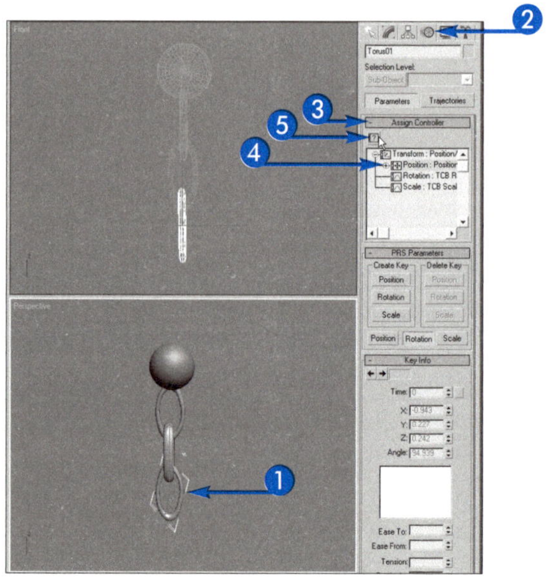

1. Select the first linked object.
2. Click to open the Motion panel.
3. Click to open the Assign Controller rollout.
4. Click to highlight the Position track.

   If the Position track is not visible, click next to Transform.

5. Click .

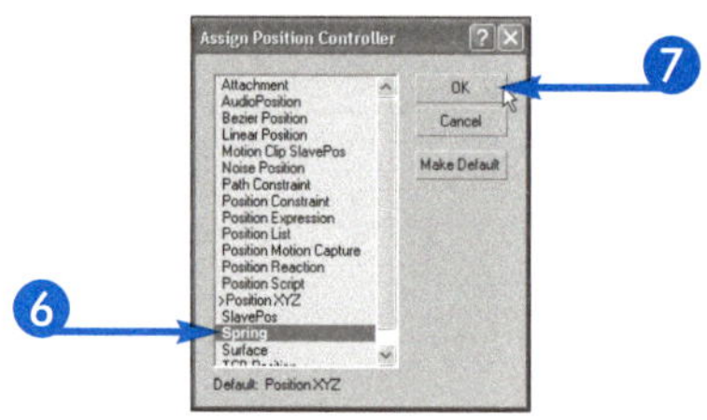

The Assign Position Controller dialog box appears.

6. Click Spring.
7. Click OK.

3ds Max adds the Spring Controller to the Position track.

The Spring Properties dialog box appears.

The rollouts on the dialog box also appear in the Motion panel.

8 Repeat steps 4 to 7 for each linked object.

9 Click the parent object.

10 Click Auto Key.

11 Drag the Time Slider to the frame where you want the animation to end.

12 Click the Select and Move button (✥).

13 Click and drag the parent object.

14 Click Auto Key to turn off the animation.

Note: *For more information on using Auto Key, see Chapter 8.*

- You can click ▶ to view the animation.

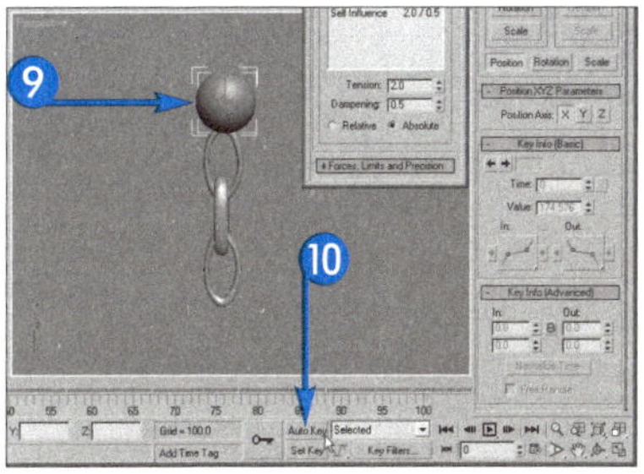

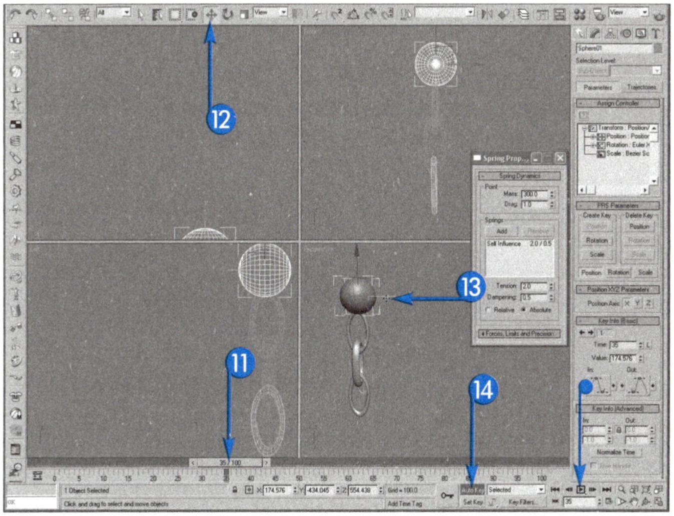

MASTER IT

Can I make one object react to another if they are not linked?

When an object is linked to another object, the spring effect occurs when the parent object moves. You do not have to specify the parent object to the spring object; that relationship is automatically created, as shown in the steps. If the objects are not linked, you need to specify the object to which you want the springs to react. In the Spring Dynamics rollout, click Add and then click the object that you want to be the spring object. The name of the object is added to the Springs list box.

Can my Spring controller object respond to external forces, such as wind?

You can specify external forces, such as wind and gravity, that affect the motion of your object. To select a force, you must already have that force active in the scene. You select the force in the Forces, Limits, and Precision rollout in the Motion panel. In the rollout, click Add and then click the force in a viewport. 3ds Max adds the name of the force to the External Forces list box. You can apply multiple forces to an object. For more information on using forces generated by space warps, see Chapter 25.

Understanding the Curve Editor

Although 3ds Max interpolates, or calculates, the values for the frames between the keyframes, it may not produce the results you desire. 3ds Max has two Track View Graph Editor modes that adjust the interpolation between keys: the Curve Editor, and the Dope Sheet Editor, discussed in Chapter 12.

The Curve Editor displays the parameters in your scene as *function curves*—editable splines that show animation changes over time. Adjusting the function curves modifies the animation. The Curve Editor has two panes: The left, called the Controller window, lists every object and parameter; the right, called the Key window, shows the selected parameter or transform as a curve, with keys appearing as boxes. A *track* is a single parameter that you can animate in your scene with each object's tracks distinct from those of every other object. Adding modifiers and their parameters can significantly increase the tracks, with complex scenes having thousands of tracks.

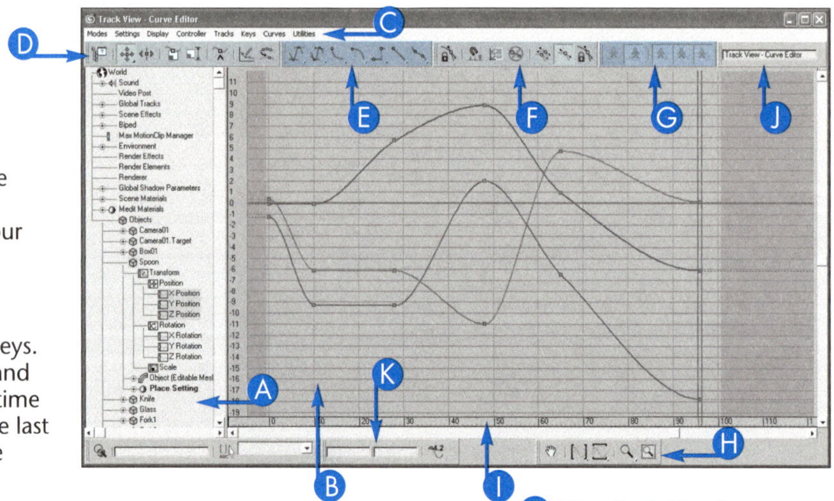

C Menu Bar

Contains the controls for editing the function curves; has many of the same commands as the Curve Editor toolbars.

D Keys Toolbar

Has options for adding and deleting keys, as well as for adjusting key locations.

E Key Tangents Toolbar

Contains tools for setting the tangency for selected keys. Select a default, or create your own custom tangency.

F Curves Toolbar

Controls the movement of keys. You can lock a key in place and define the animation when time exists beyond the time at the last key. You can also control the display of Tangent handles.

G Biped Toolbar

Has options for displaying the function curves for Biped objects. For information on Bipeds, see Chapter 27.

H Navigation Toolbar

Allows you to zoom and pan the display of the Key window.

B Key Window

Displays the function curves and keys for the selected tracks. The light-gray area represents the active time segment.

I Time Ruler

Measures time with settings you establish for the Track bar. For easy reference, you can move the Time Ruler from the bottom of the Key pane and align it with any track.

A Controller Window

Displays all tracks within the scene in a hierarchical tree. Tracks can have subtracks.

J Track Selection Toolbar

Has tools that quickly recall saved track selections.

K Key Stats Toolbar

Contains fields for adjusting the time and value for a selected key.

Understanding Tangents

Tangents interpolate values of animations between the keys that you specify. When you select a key on a curve in the Curve Editor, a tangent line appears with tangent handles on each end for adjusting the keyframe interpolation. The left handle adjusts the incoming tangent, or the angle at which the curve enters the key, and the right handle adjusts the outgoing tangent. Pulling the handle away from the curve flattens it; pulling toward the key sharpens it.

3ds Max has seven different tangent-type buttons that assign specific tangent styles to a key. While the Custom and Auto styles offer tangent handles, the other styles, such as Step or Smooth, do not. See the section "Understanding Tangent Types" for more on the available tangent types.

The function curve represents a change in the parameter over time. Vertical variation signifies changes in a parameters value in the curve, and the left-to-right flow of the curve represents the change in time. A flat curve entering or exiting a key, called the *incoming* or *outgoing* tangent, signifies a minor change in the parameter in the time near the key. A sharp angle entering and exiting a key means a parameter is quickly rising as it approaches the key and quickly decreasing as it leaves. Not all controller types have control handles to adjust the tangency of the curves.

A Tangent Line

Shows the tangency of the selected key. The type of tangent assigned to the key determines its appearance and visibility. Auto tangents display as dashed blue lines, and Custom tangents are solid black lines.

B Incoming Tangent Handle

Allows you to make custom adjustments to the incoming tangency of the key.

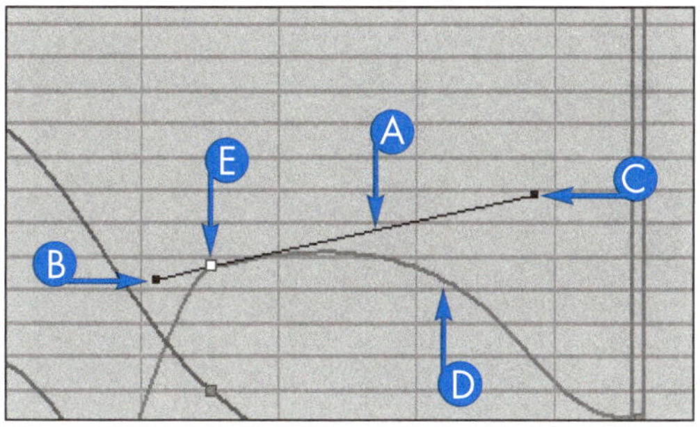

C Outgoing Tangent Handle

Allows you to make custom adjustments to the outgoing tangency of the key.

D Function Curve

Editable splines that show the change in values over time. Function curves for animated transforms display in different colors. X-axis curves are red, Y-axis curves are blue, and Z-axis curves are green.

E Key

Specifies an explicit parameter value at a specific point in time. Frames without keys are interpolated.

Understanding Tangent Types

The tangent type defines how quickly or smoothly a parameter value changes as it enters and exits a key. When you create an animation with Auto Key or Set Key, 3ds Max assigns an Auto Tangent value, which is an interpolation that produces a smooth curve entering and exiting each key. You replace the tangency by selecting one of the predefined tangent types on the Key Tangents toolbar, or by creating your own tangency for the selected key using the Set Tangents to Custom button.

You change tangent types via the Key Tangents toolbar, which has flyout buttons to set the incoming, outgoing, or both tangents of the selected keys. Incoming tangents define the interpolation before the key. Outgoing tangent defines the interpolation after the key. See the section "Understanding Tangents" for more on tangency. See the section "Set the Tangent Type" to change the tangent type. 3ds Max 8's new feature allows you to change the default tangent type using the Default In/Out Tangents for New Keys button at the bottom center of the user interface.

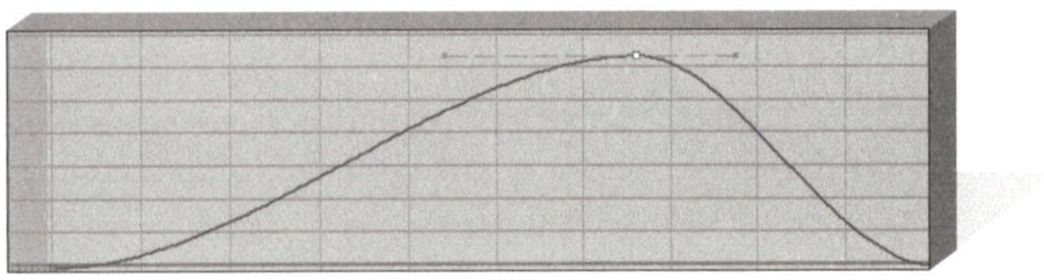

Auto Tangent ( )

The default tangent type of the Auto Key and Set Key, this tangent type creates a smooth Bezier curve entering and exiting a key. Sharp changes in the key values cause a Bezier curve to significantly overshoot a key, but the Auto tangent type prevents any overshooting when you apply it. Moving a tangent handle changes an Auto tangent to a Custom tangent.

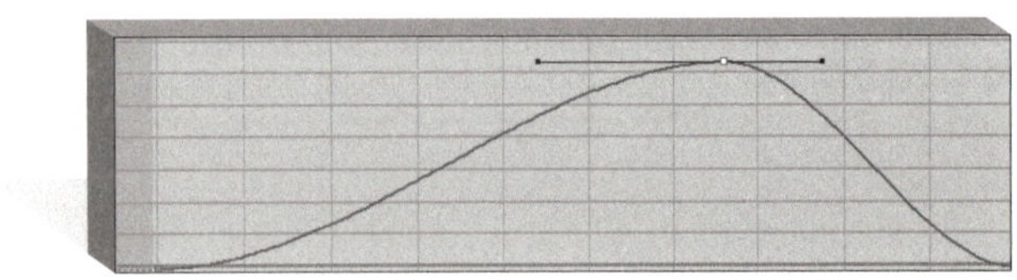

Custom Tangent ( )

This tangent type is a customizable curve that provides tangent handles for adjusting the angle at which the curve enters the key. Use the Move Keys button in the Keys toolbar to move the handle closer, to create an angle that is sharper or farther away, and to create a smoother angle. You can also move the handle up or down to change the direction of the curve.

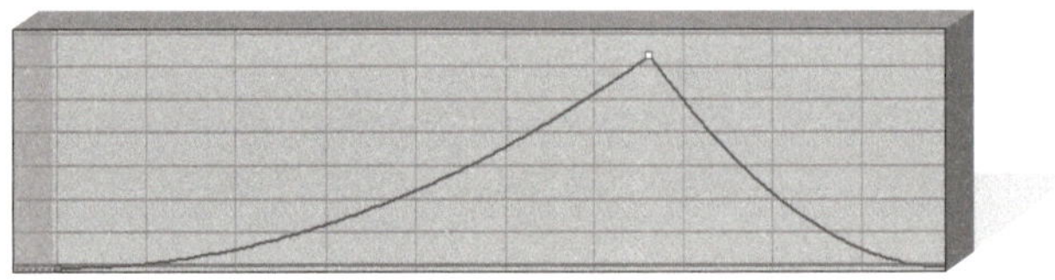

Fast Tangent ( )

This tangent type causes the interpolation rate to increase the parameter's rate of change as it approaches a key. Leaving the key, the interpolation rate decreases. The parameter appears to rush to change as it approaches the key, but then is reluctant to change once it leaves.

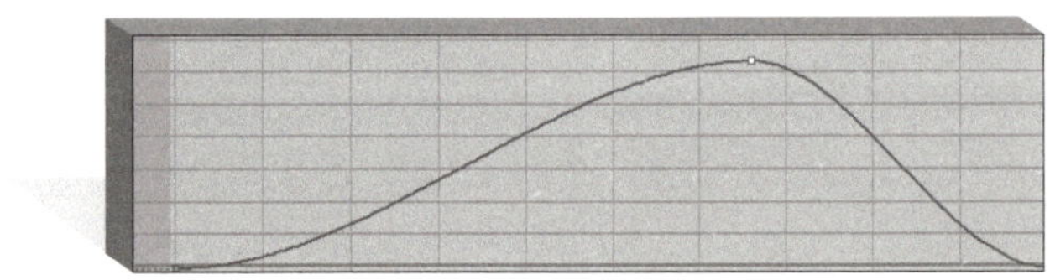

Slow Tangent ( )

The opposite of the Fast tangent type, this tangent type causes the interpolation rate to decrease the parameter's rate of change as it approaches a key. Leaving the key, the interpolation rate increases. For example, think of a balloon popping, where the expansion is slower at the end, but the decrease in size is very quick.

Step Tangent ( )

This produces an abrupt result that works best when you want the parameters to jump from one key to another, with no interpolation, in a jerky fashion. In traditional animation, this is called pose-to-pose animation. The first key's value remains constant until the tangent reaches the second key, where the value immediately changes to the second key's value. If an object has Step tangents that are selected for the Position tracks, then this causes the object to pop from one location to the next.

With this tangent type, you must have a matched set of tangents between two keys. For example, if one key has a Step Tangent for the outgoing tangent, the next key must have the Step Tangent for the incoming tangent. Fortunately, when you apply the Step Tangent to a key, 3ds Max automatically changes the tangent for the corresponding key.

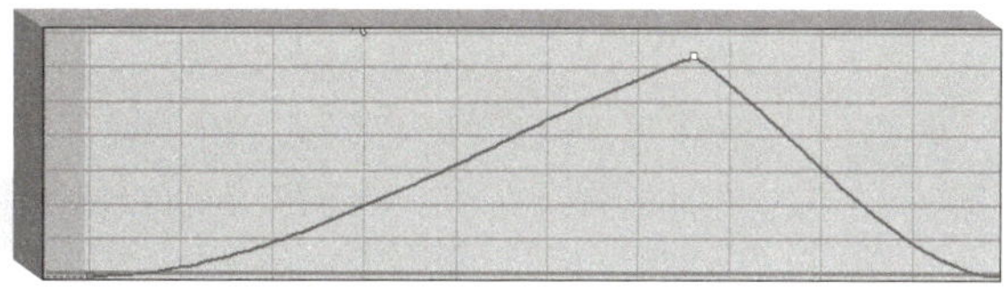

Linear Tangent ( )

The Linear tangent creates a linear, or straight, curve at the key. To obtain complete linear interpolation between two keys, you must set the outgoing tangent of the first key, and the incoming tangent of the second key, to Linear tangent. This type of transition works well for objects that do not change speed, such as the movement of an asteroid, or that have a jerky movement. The moving parts in an idling engine would have linear tangents, but the car's wheels, as it drives through town, would not.

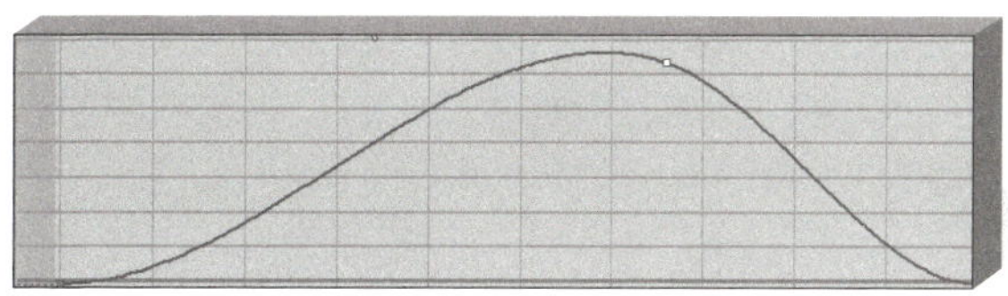

Smooth Tangent ( )

The Smooth tangent creates a smooth interpolation from one key through the next key. This type of curve makes your animation flow smoothly.

Change the Animation by Adding and Moving a Key Using the Curve Editor

You use the Curve Editor to add or move keys to refine your animation. This allows you to change the animation within your scene by altering the keys on the function curve, rather than by changing the object's parameters with Auto Key active. For example, using Auto Key, if your airplane needs to clear the mountain by a greater distance, you must select the object, move the Time Slider to the nearest keyframe, select the Move tool, turn on Auto Key, and then transform the object in the Z-axis. In the Curve Editor, you can select the Z-axis key nearest to the time when the plane is over the mountain and simply change the value.

Similarly, you can add keys in the Curve Editor without selecting and modifying the object in the viewports or Modify panel. When you select the Add Keys button, 3ds Max adds new keys at the location that you specify along the function curve of the selected track. You can move keys using the Move Keys button, which has flyout buttons available to lock the value or frame.

CD FILE The Key.max file is available on the CD-ROM for you to practice adding and moving keys with the Curve Editor.

Change the Animation by Adding and Moving a Key Using the Curve Editor

Add A Keyframe

1. Click the Curve Editor (Open) button ( ).

   The Curve Editor opens.

2. In the Controller window, click the track for the parameter in which you want to insert a key.

   The corresponding function curve displays in the Key window.

3. Click the Add Keys button ( ).

4. Click the location on the curve where you want to insert the key, and drag to place it.

   3ds Max adds a new key to the curve and interpolates its value between the two existing keys.

   - To avoid adding another key, click the Move Keys button ( ).
   - You can set the default tangent type for new keys with the Default In/Out Tangents for New Keys button at the bottom of the 3ds Max window.

3ds Max turns off the Add Keys mode.

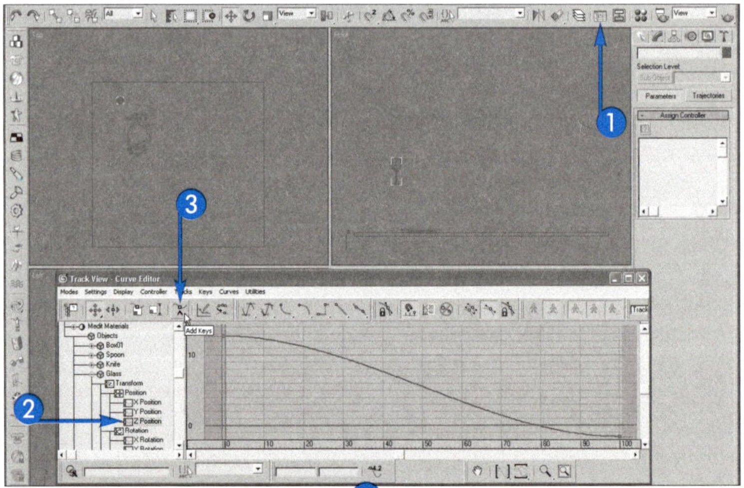

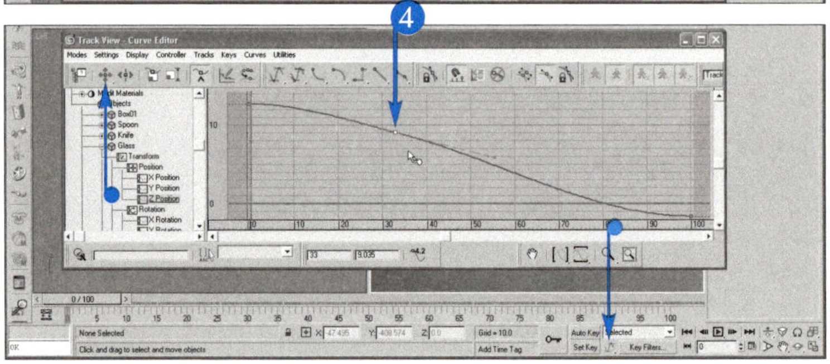

Move a Key

1. Click .
2. Click and drag the new key to the desired location.

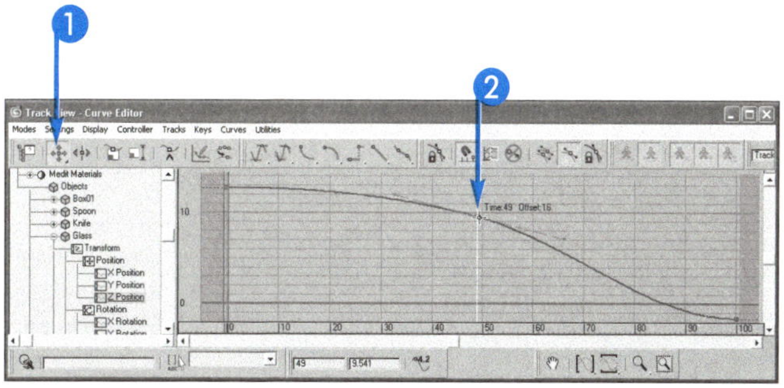

The selected key moves to a new frame, and the object reflects the change.

- You can drag the Time Sliders to preview the animation.

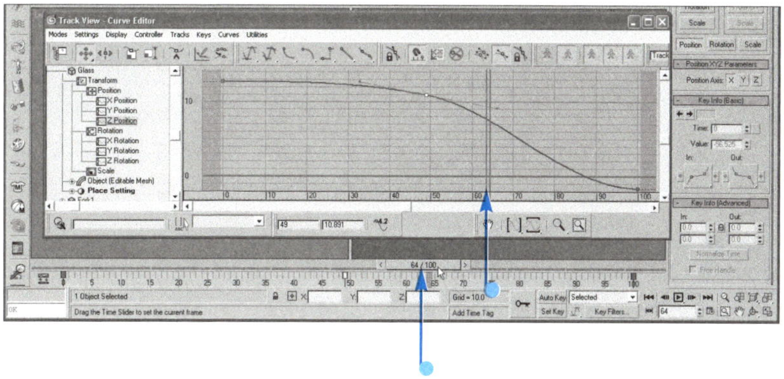

PART III

MASTER IT

Does the Snap Frames button have to be active to add or move keys?

No. A frame is not the smallest time increment available in 3ds Max, but it is a good tool to use when adjusting the timing of your animation. If the Snap Frames button ( ) is not active, you can place keys that do not fall exactly on frames, but, rather, between them. If precision is not a factor, then neither is Snap Frames, although it is probably a good idea to leave it on. If you need to place a key in close proximity to another key, to cause a very quick change in a parameter, then turn Snap Frames off when inserting or moving keys.

How can I easily move a key to the frame and value that I want?

3ds Max provides two fields for reading and manually entering precise values and frame numbers for a selected key. Located on the bottom edge of the Curve Editor, the docked Key Stats toolbar displays two fields for entering numeric data. With a single key selected, type a value in the second field to set the parameter's value for the key. Type a value in the first field to set the exact frame number for the key. If there are multiple keys selected, then only the second value field is available for input.

Set the Tangent Type

You can use the Curve Editor to change the tangent type for any keyframe in your animation to alter the flow of the animation. For example, instead of the smooth transition that 3ds Max creates between two keys using Auto tangent, you may want to create an abrupt transition where one key value remains unchanged until another key value displays.

You can quickly change the tangent type of a key by applying one of the seven default tangent types: Auto, Custom, Fast, Slow, Step, Linear, and Smooth. When you select one of these tangents, 3ds Max automatically changes the interpolation of the curve to reflect your selection. See the section "Understanding Tangent Types" for more information.

You can apply a different tangent type by selecting one of the buttons on the Key Tangents toolbar. The default buttons change the tangency for both the incoming and outgoing sides of the key. If you only want to change one side, you can use the corresponding flyout and select the incoming or outgoing button for the tangent type that you want to apply.

The Tangent.max file is available on the CD-ROM for you to practice with changing the tangent type.

Set the Tangent Type

1. Select the animated object that you want to change.
2. Click .

   The Curve Editor opens.
3. Click the Track that you want to change.

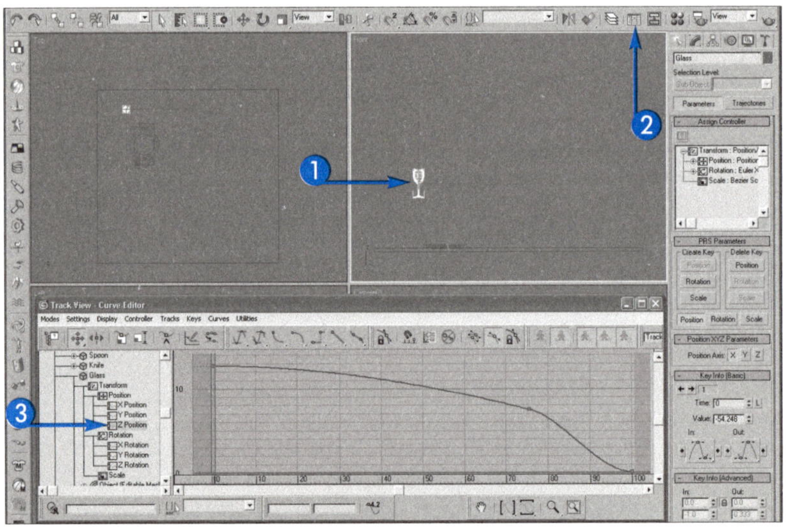

The Curve Editor displays with the function curve for the selected track.

4. Click the key that you want to change.

   3ds Max selects the key, and, if the key has Auto or Custom tangents, then the tangent handles display for the key.

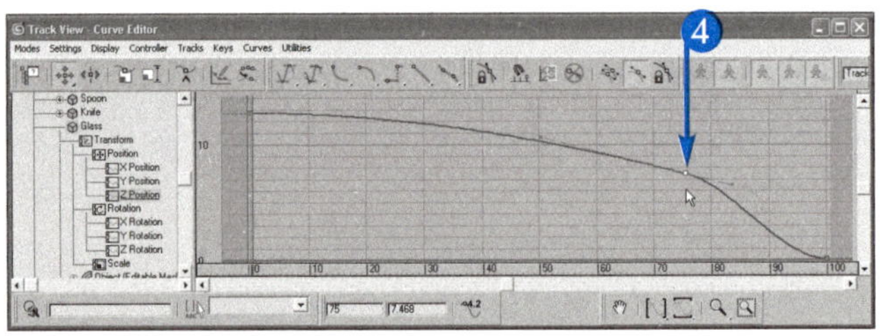

5 Click the desired Tangent key.

To set only the incoming tangent, click the Tangent flyout and then click the second button ( ).

To set the outgoing value, click the third button ( ).

- The tangency changes for the selected key.

You can repeat steps 4 and 5 to change the tangent type for additional keys.

- You can scrub the Time Sliders to preview the animation.
- You can set the default tangent type for new keys with the Default In/Out Tangents for New Keys button ( ) at the bottom of the 3ds Max window.

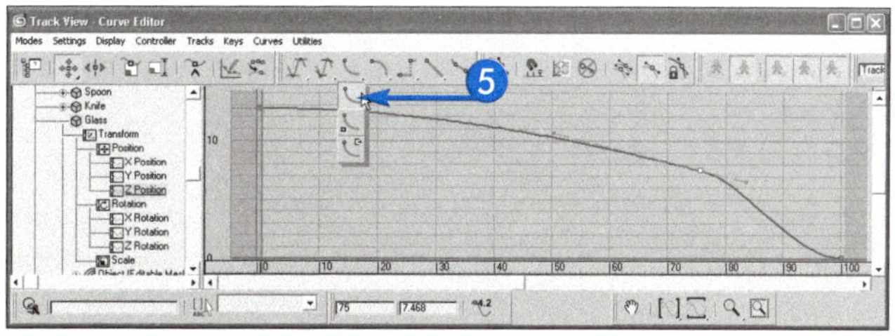

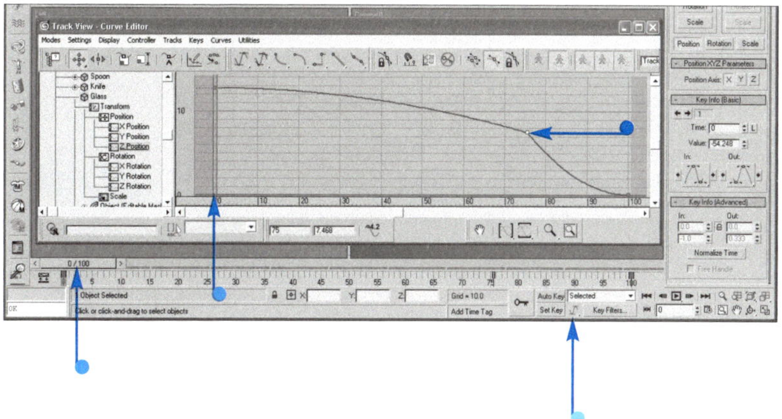

MASTER IT

How do I undo the tangent changes for a key?

▼ When you apply a different tangent type to a key, 3ds Max immediately applies the change to your animation. You can preview the animation in a viewport to ensure that you are happy with the results of the tangent selection. If not, then click Edit, and then click Undo to remove the tangent type change. If your last action was not to apply a tangent type to that key, then you cannot use the Undo command. One method to correct the problem is to apply the Set Tangents to Auto button ( ). This reapplies the default interpolation to the key.

How do I know what the tangent type is for a key?

▼ You can quickly see both the incoming and outgoing tangent types for any key by right-clicking the key. A Key Info dialog box shows all of the values for the selected key, including the current tangents, the frame time, and the value of the key. At the bottom of the dialog box, a button shows the current incoming Tangent value on the left and the outgoing Tangent value on the right. These button images correlate to the Tangent buttons on the Key Tangents toolbar. You can click a button and change tangents directly from this dialog box.

Create a Custom Tangent Type

You can create a custom tangent type for any key within the Curve Editor. This allows you to create a unique effect that you cannot achieve with any of the default tangent types.

When the selected key has a Custom tangent type, the tangent handles for the key display as solid black lines. This allows you to quickly identify a Custom tangent from an Auto tangent, which has blue dashed lines for tangent handles. When you select and move a handle of an Auto tangent, the key automatically changes to have Custom tangents.

The default button on the Key Tangents toolbar allows you to adjust both the incoming and outgoing tangent values simultaneously. As you move one handle vertically, the other handle moves in the opposite direction, maintaining a smooth transition through the key. To adjust each handle independently, you can unlock the handles by holding down the Shift key when moving one of them. Once they are unlocked, the handles for a key remain unlocked and you do not need to continue holding down the Shift key.

See the section "Understanding Tangent Types" for more information.

CD FILE: The Tangent.max file is available on the CD-ROM for you to practice with creating a Custom tangent type.

Create a Custom Tangent Type

1. Select the animated object that you want to change.
2. Click .

   The Curve Editor opens.
3. Click the Track that you want to change.

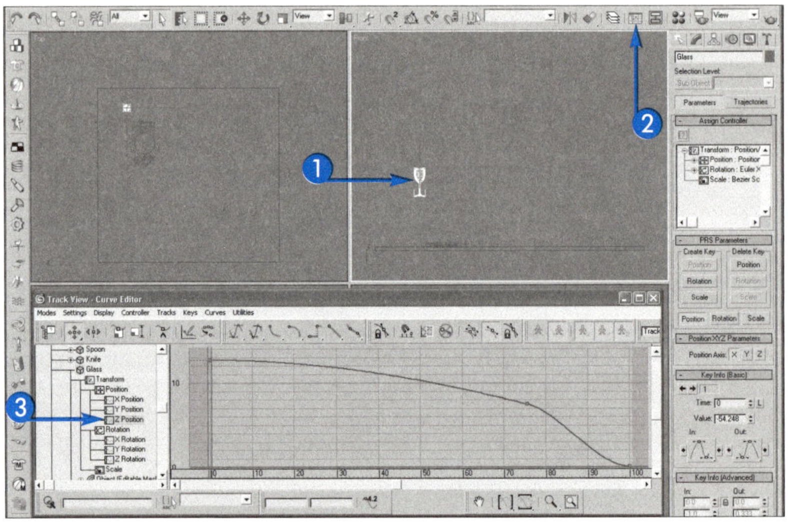

The Curve Editor displays the function curve for the selected object.

4. Click the key that you want to change.

   3ds Max selects the key, and, if the key has Auto tangents, then the tangent handles display for the curve.
5. Click the Set Tangents to Custom button ().

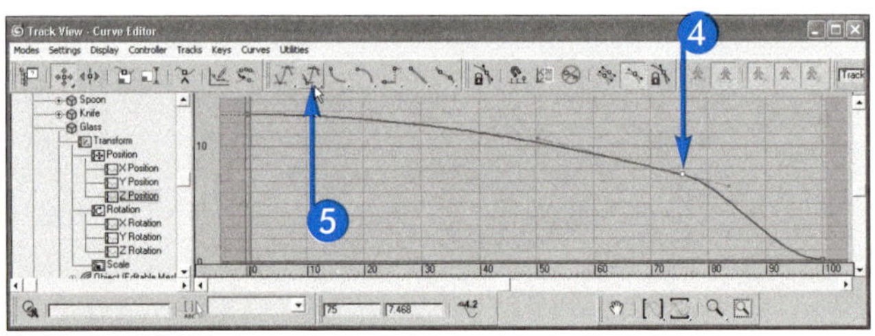

If the tangent handles exist for the key, then they change from blue dashed lines to solid black lines.

6. Press and hold the Shift key.
7. Click and drag the left handle to adjust the incoming tangent value for the key.

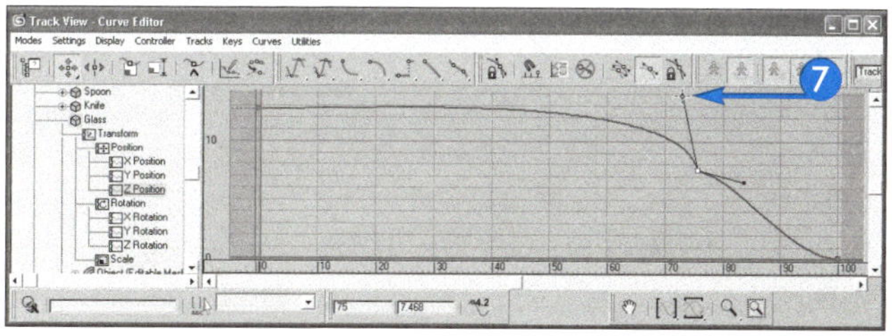

- To change the outgoing value, click and drag the right handle.

The curve adjusts to reflect the custom tangency of the key.

- You can drag the Time Sliders to preview the animation.

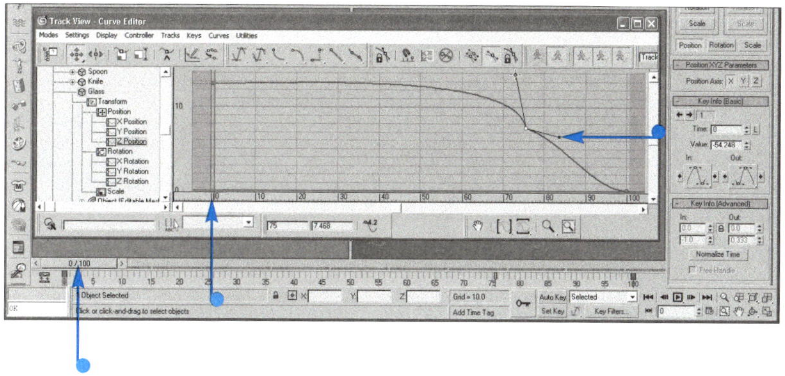

MASTER IT

Can I lock the tangent handles after I have unlocked them?

Yes. Once you have unlocked the tangent handles for a key, each time you move a handle, it moves independently of the other one. Once you have set a specific angle between the two handles, you can re-lock the handles again by clicking the Lock Tangents button (🔒) in the Curves toolbar. When you click this button, both the incoming and outgoing tangents of the selected key move simultaneously. You can also lock multiple keys together. By selecting multiple keys and then clicking 🔒, you can change the tangents of all selected keys that have tangents by dragging the tangent handle for one key. The Lock Tangents button is very similiar to the Lock Selection button 🔒 in the same toolbar.

Once I have keys selected, can I keep only those keys selected?

Yes. Because it is common for a curve to have many keys, it is often frustrating to try to reselect a specific key or keys when you are making modifications. You can restrict 3ds Max from deselecting a key or from selecting another key by locking the selection using the Lock Selection button (🔒) in the Curves toolbar. When Lock Selection is active, if you try to select other keys, then your attempts are ignored until you press 🔒 to deactivate it. When you activate Lock Selection with multiple keys selected, it locks all of the keys as a selection, although they can be moved independently.

Customize the Animation with a Freehand Curve

If you want the animation curve to have a specific shape, then instead of moving keys and changing tangent types, you can draw the curve within the Curve Editor. This allows you to create a curve with the exact shape you want by dragging the mouse in the Key window.

When you select the Draw Curves option, you can select an empty track and create the animation directly, or you can specify a track with an existing function curve and redraw all or a portion of it. 3ds Max automatically adds keys to the curve as you draw, and the speed at which you draw determines the number of keys that 3ds Max adds to the curve. If multiple tracks are selected in the Controller window, then Draw Curves simultaneously creates identical keys on all of the tracks.

In the Curve Editor, time flows from left to right. If you drag your curve from left to right, and then drag the cursor back to the left, then 3ds Max overwrites the existing keys with new ones.

The Tangent.max file is available on the CD-ROM for you to practice drawing a freehand curve.

Customize the Animation with a Freehand Curve

1. Select the animated object that you want to change.
2. Click ▦.

   The Curve Editor opens.
3. Click the Track that you want to change.

   The Curve Editor displays the function curve for the selected object.

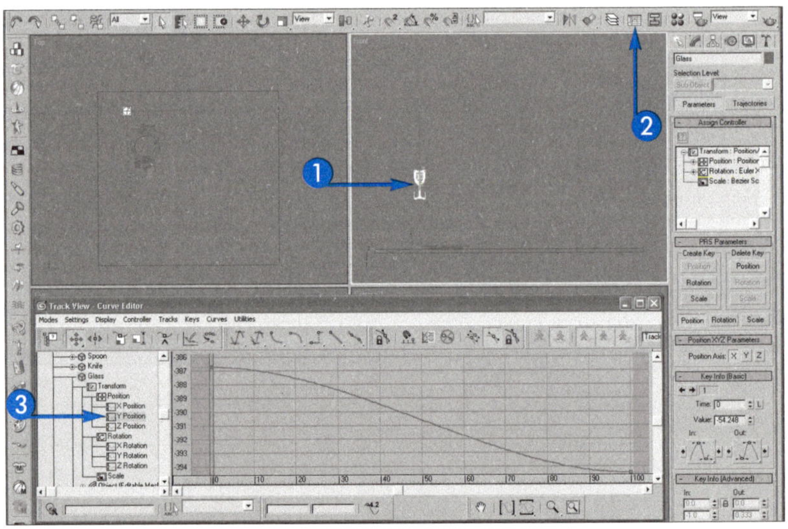

4. Click the Draw Curves button (⟋).

   The button highlights and the cursor changes to ✎.

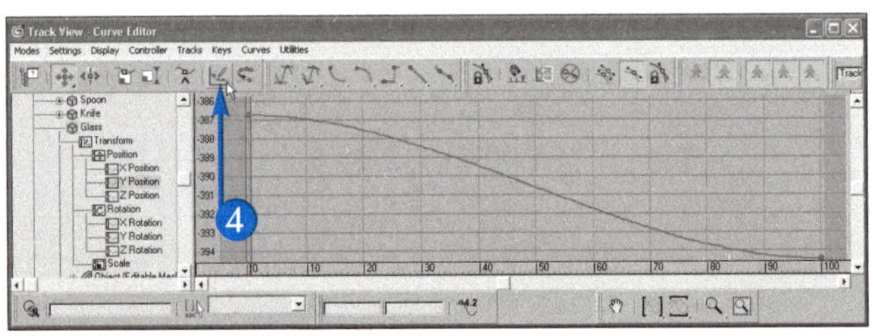

5 Click and drag to draw the curve in the Key window.

As you drag, new keys are created each time the curve changes.

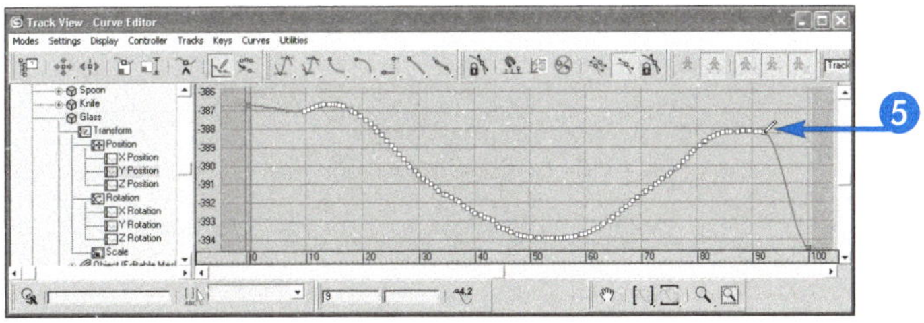

6 Click Move Keys to exit Draw Curves mode.

- You can scrub the Time Sliders to preview the animation.

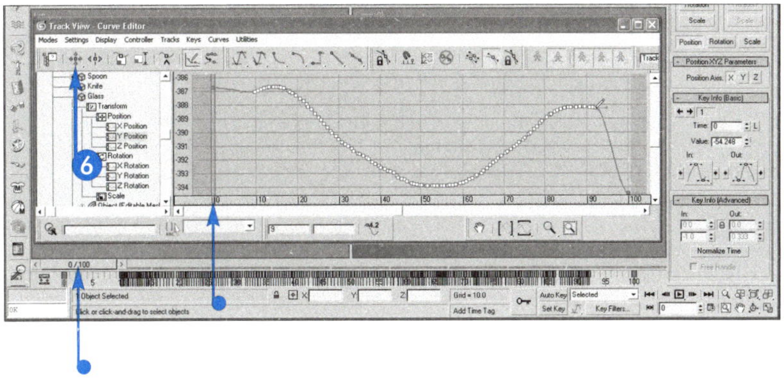

MASTER IT

The shape of my custom curve is correct, but the values do not change enough. Do I have to redraw the curve?

No. If the shape is acceptable, but the high values are not high enough and the low values are not low enough, then you can fix the problem. Select the keys that you want to fix, click the Scale Values button (), and then click and drag in the Key window. The values of the keys scale up or down, depending on the direction in which you drag. Similarly, you can click the Scale Keys button () to stretch or compress the amount of time that the selected keys occupy in your scene. Expanding the keys causes the animation to slow down and occur over a longer period of time.

What type of tangents are created for keys on a custom curve?

When you create a custom curve, 3ds Max assigns the Auto tangent to the incoming and outgoing sides of each key. This allows 3ds Max to automatically set tangents based on your curve. After you create the curve, you can customize the tangents of individual keys or selections of keys to control portions of the curve. You can do this by either applying one of the default tangent types or by creating a custom tangent. See the sections "Set the Tangent Type" for information on the tangent types, and "Create a Custom Tangent Type" for information on creating a custom tangent.

Reduce Animation Keys

To lower the number of keys on a curve, you can use the Reduce Keys tool, which decreases the number of keys while maintaining the overall shape of the curve and the appearance of the animation. This makes editing the curve much easier. You must select keys, either by clicking them or dragging a window around them, for Reduce Keys to have an effect.

The Reduce Keys button opens the Reduce Keys dialog box, where you input the Threshold value. This value determines the necessary difference between two adjacent keys to eliminate one of the keys. The higher the Threshold value, the more keys 3ds Max eliminates.

CD FILE: The Reduce Keys.max file is available on the CD-ROM for you to practice with reducing animation keys.

MASTER IT

What types of tangents are created when I reduce keys?

3ds Max tries to retain the same tangent type for the remaining keys that existed before you applied Reduce Keys. If all of the keys have the same tangents, this should not be a problem. However, if some of the keys have different tangent types, 3ds Max may delete these keys. If this occurs, simply select one of the remaining keys and change the tangent type.

Reduce Animation Keys

1. Follow steps 1 to 3 in the section "Customize the Animation with a Freehand Curve."

   The Curve Editor displays the curve for the selected object.

2. Click and drag a window around the keys that you want to reduce.

   The selected keys turn white.

3. Click the Reduce Keys button ( ).

   The Reduce Keys dialog box appears.

   - You can type a value in the Threshold field.

4. Click OK.

   3ds Max reduces the number of selected keys.

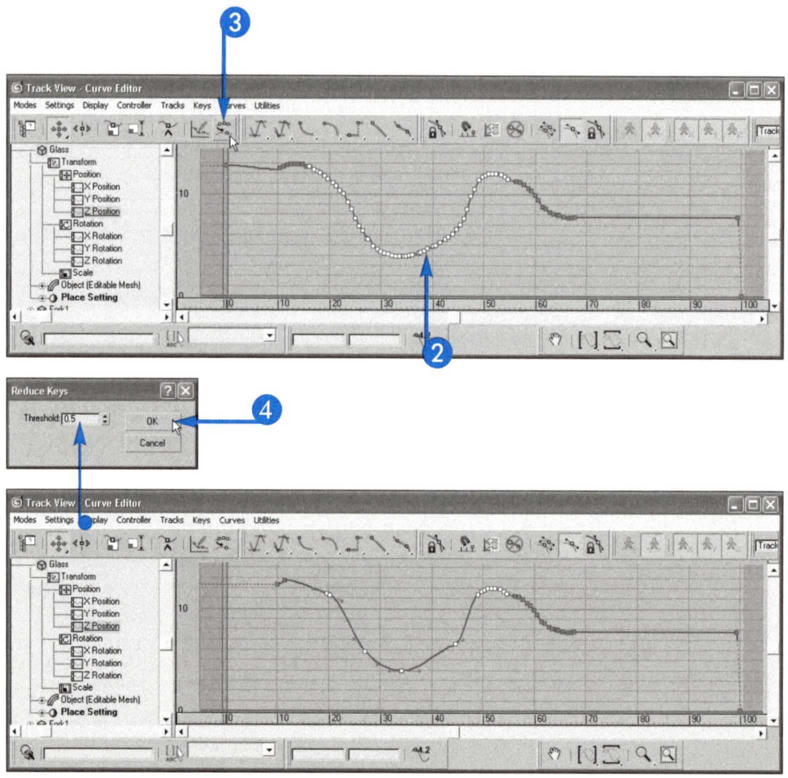

Control Visibility with a Visibility Track

You can determine at which frames an object is visible by controlling the keys on the object's Visibility track. You can use a Visibility track to create the effect of an object fading in or out of view by creating a curve with a value that rises or falls.

The only meaningful values for the keys on a Visibility track are those between zero and one. At a value of zero, the object is completely invisible, and at one it is completely visible. Values less than zero or greater than one do not affect the appearance of the object any more than values of zero or one do. Lower-visibility objects fade in the viewport as well, but they never completely disappear.

CD FILE: The Tangent.max file is available on the CD-ROM for you to practice with controlling a visibility track.

MASTER IT

How can I make my object flicker over a long period without making hundreds of keys?

▼ To create a random flicker of visibility for an object, you can add a Noise controller to the Visibility track of the object. If you want your object to be at least partially visible most of the time, select the >0 option (☐ changes to ☑) in the Noise Controller dialog box. If you want brief periods of total invisibility, leave this option unselected.

Control Visibility with a Visibility Track

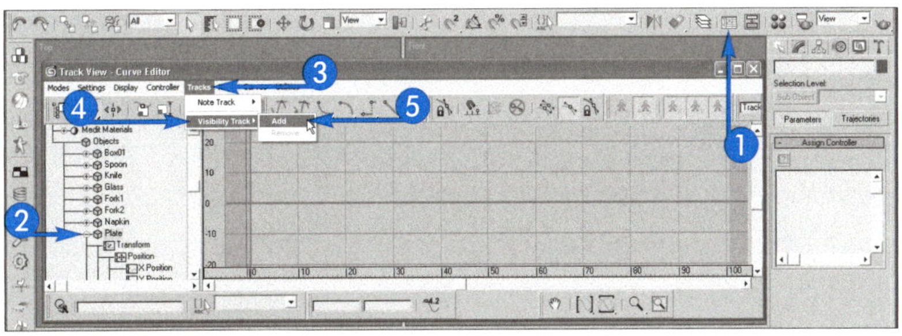

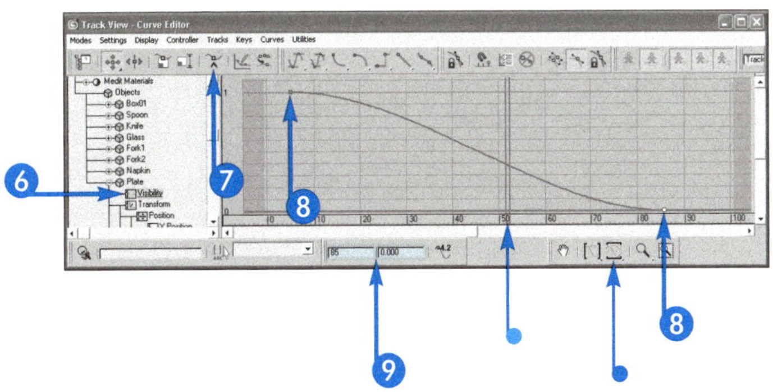

1. Click ▤.

   The Curve Editor opens.

2. Select the object to which you want to add a Visibility track.
3. Click Tracks.
4. Click Visibility Track.
5. Click Add.
6. Click the Visibility track.

   3ds Max displays the Visibility track as a dashed line in the Key window.

7. Click Add Keys (⊼).
8. Click the dashed line to add Visibility keys.
9. Type key values to set the visibility.

   - You can click Zoom Value Extents to see the curve more clearly.
   - You can scrub the Time Slider to preview the animation.

Assign a Controller in the Curve Editor

Controllers determine how the animation of an object is interpolated from one key to the next. Although Chapter 10 discussed assigning controllers and constraints to the transforms for an object, you use the Curve Editor, or Dope Sheet Editor to assign controllers to both transform and non-transform tracks.

Controllers handle interpolation, while Tangent buttons assign incoming and outgoing tangent styles, but only to those tracks with controllers whose interpolation you can adjust. For example, the Linear Float controller has keys, but the interpolation between the keys is constant and straight, regardless of any tangents that you assign. Some of the controllers, such as Noise Float or Waveform, do not even have keys.

The Bezier Float controller is the default controller for most tracks in 3ds Max. It provides a smooth transition between keys but is not appropriate for every situation. For example, to evenly twist an object back and forth, you must assign a Waveform controller to the Amount track of the object's Twist modifier. To twist the object based on the sound emitted by a WAV file, you must use an AudioFloat controller.

CD FILE: The Assign Controller.max file is available on the CD-ROM for you to practice with assigning a controller.

Assign a Controller in the Curve Editor

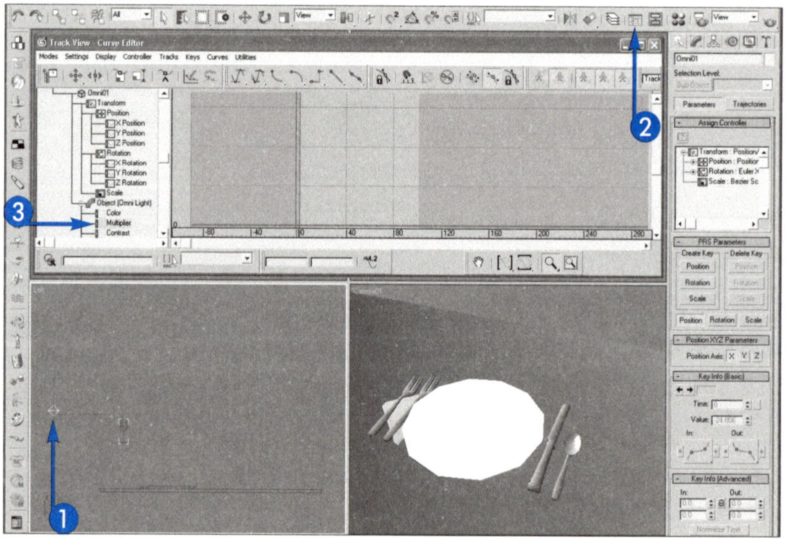

1. Select the animated object that you want to change.
2. Click (Curve Editor button).

   The Curve Editor opens.

3. Click the Track that you want to change.

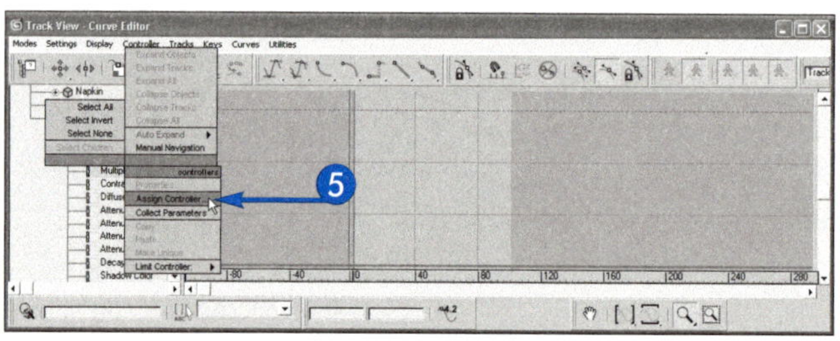

The Curve Editor displays the function curve for the selected object.

4. Right-click the selected track.
5. Click Assign Controller from the quad menu.

The Assign Float Controller dialog box appears.

6. Click the controller that you want to assign to the selected track.

7. Click OK.

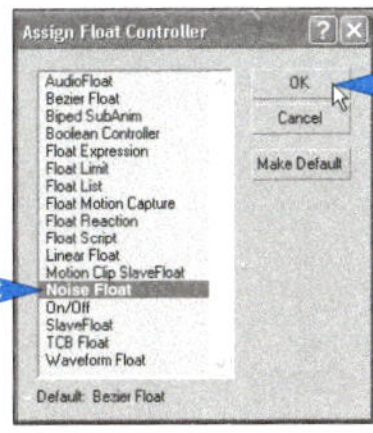

3ds Max replaces the existing controller with the new controller.

- Depending on the controller that you selected, a dialog box may open where you can input parameters to tweak the controller's effects.
- You can scrub the Time Slider to preview the animation.

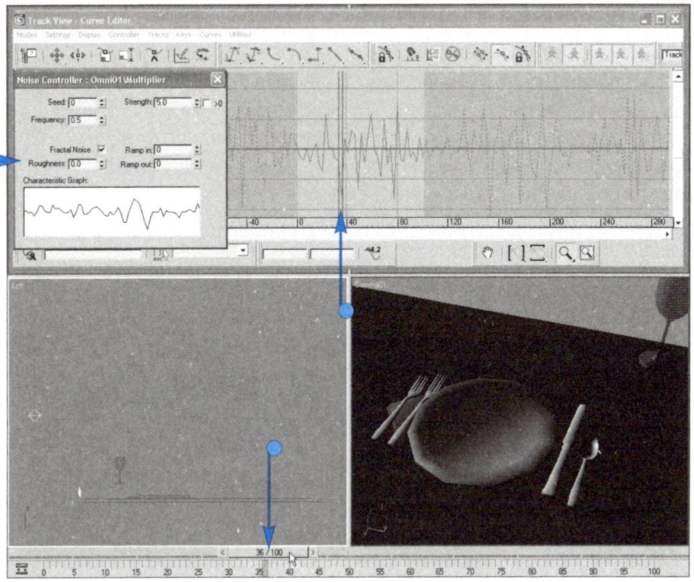

PART III

MASTER IT

How can I change the parameters that I set in a controller's dialog box after I close it?

When you assign certain controllers, such as Noise Float or AudioFloat, a dialog box opens for you to input parameter information that determines the controller's effect on the track. After you close the dialog box, you can reopen it by right-clicking the controller's track and then choosing Properties from the quad menu that appears. You can also reopen the dialog box by selecting the track, then clicking Controller on the Curve Editor menu bar, and then clicking Properties in the menu that appears.

How can I quickly return to a selected track after I close the Curve Editor?

If you find yourself returning to a specific track repeatedly, then you can save the Track view in its current state by turning it into a named Track view. To do this, simply type in the name that you want in the blank field at the right side of the Track View toolbar, and then close the Track view. The next time that you click the Track View button, a new Track view opens. To open the Track view that you named, click Graph Editors in the Main toolbar, then click Saved Track Views, and then click the name of the Track view that you saved.

Extend the Animation with Parameter Curve Out-of-Range Types

When you have a redundant animation, such as a wheel spinning or a machine cycling through a repetitive motion, you can instruct 3ds Max to repeat the animation sequence. The Parameter Curve Out-of-Range Type that you select determines how, if at all, the animation repeats. This can eliminate the need to create successive blocks of keys that replicate the same animation when the Active Time Segment is longer than the animation.

There are six Parameter Curve Out-of-Range Types, each of which has a different effect on how 3ds Max deals with the animation after the animation plays past the last key in a track. Constant holds a parameter's value steady. Cycle jumps from the last key value to the first. Loop is similar to Cycle, but it interpolates between the last and first keys. Ping Pong repeats the key pattern in the opposite manner, and Linear continues to change the parameter in the direction that it was moving. Relative Repeat repeats the animation with the last key as the base point for the next sequence.

The PCurve.max file is available on the CD-ROM for you to practice applying a Parameter Curve Out-of-Range Type.

Extend the Animation with Parameter Curve Out-of-Range Types

1. Select the animated object that you want to change.
2. Click .

   The Curve Editor opens.
3. Click the Track that want to extend.

   The Curve Editor displays the function curve for the selected object.
4. Click the Parameter Curve Out-of-Range Types button ( ).

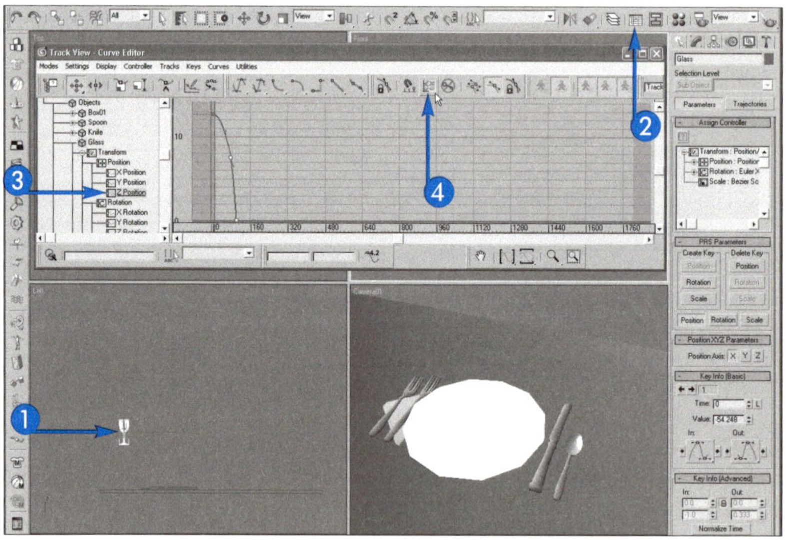

The Param Curve Out-of-Range Types dialog box appears.

5. Click the graphic for the type that you want to assign.
6. Click OK.

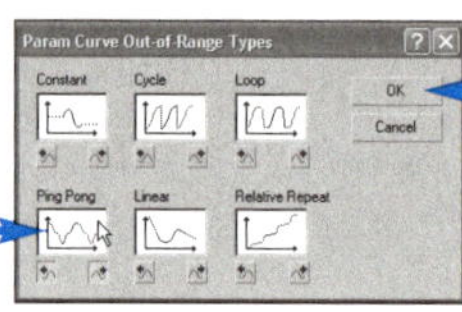

- 3ds Max displays the unkeyed Out-of-Range animation as blue dashed lines in the Key window.

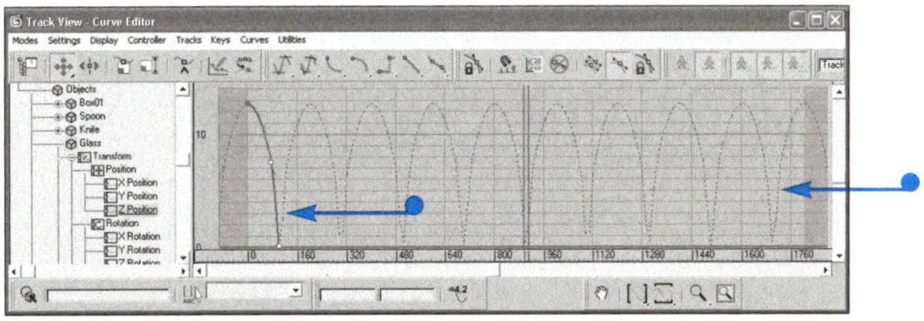

- You can scrub the Time Slider to preview the animation.

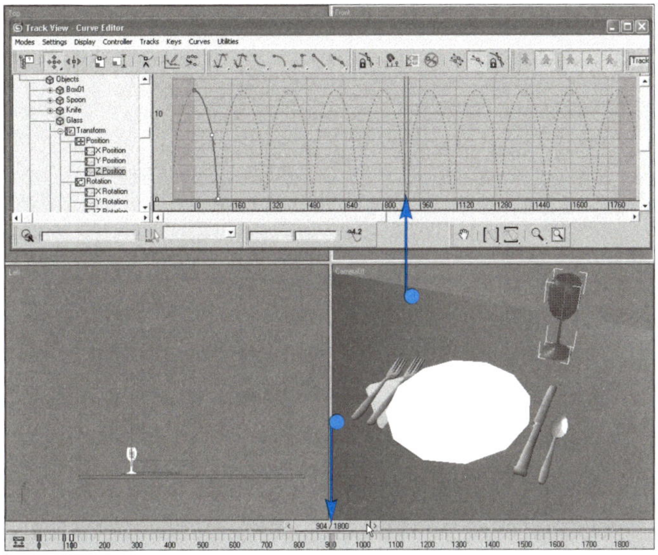

MASTER IT

What can I do if I want my object to not be animated for a period and then to repeat a motion after it starts?

▼ When you click a graphic in the Param Curve Out-of-Range Types dialog box, you assign that type to both the incoming animation, before the first key, and the outgoing animation, after the last key. The right and left arrows below the graphic allow you to assign a different Parameter Curve Out-of-Range Type to either the incoming or outgoing animation. To hold the object steady, use the Constant type for the incoming animation. Then use Cycle, Loop, or Relative Repeat on the outgoing side to repeat the sequence.

What is the quickest way to see the function curve for an object?

▼ The quickest way to see the function curves is through the quad menu. Select the object, right-click in a viewport and then select Track View from the quad menu. The Curve Editor opens and navigates to the selected object.

Can I change my looping animation into editable keys?

▼ Yes. In the Track View toolbar click Utilities, and then click Track View Utilities. Select Create Out of Range Keys in the Track View Utilities dialog box that opens. In the Create Out of Range Keys dialog box that opens, set the time range that keys will be created for and then click Apply.

Understanding the Dope Sheet

Similar to the Curve Editor mode in Chapter 11, the Track View Dope Sheet Editor allows you to view and edit all keyframe locations and all tracks for every object within a scene. While the Curve Editor shows the function curve for each selected track, the Dope Sheet Editor shows only the keys or *ranges*. This makes the Dope Sheet preferable over the Curve Editor when you like the action of the objects in the scene, but need to refine the timing.

The Dope Sheet has two panes: The Controller window lists every object and parameter; the Key window shows the keys or ranges as a horizontal graph on the curve.

The Dope Sheet has two different editing modes — the Edit Ranges mode and the Edit Keys mode. Both modes have the same toolbars and menu options.

The Edit Ranges mode shows each track only as a black range bar, with only the first and last keyframes showing as white boxes. Moving either of the white boxes condenses or expands the animation and moves the mid-range keys appropriately. Moving the bar itself simultaneously moves all of the keys an equal amount.

The default mode, Edit Keys, allows you to see all of the keyframes as individual boxes for the corresponding tracks, and you can move each key individually.

Edit Ranges Mode

A Key Window in Edit Ranges Mode

Displays track data as black bars that represent the entire length of the animation for the corresponding track. Boxes at either end of the black bar mark the animation's start and stop.

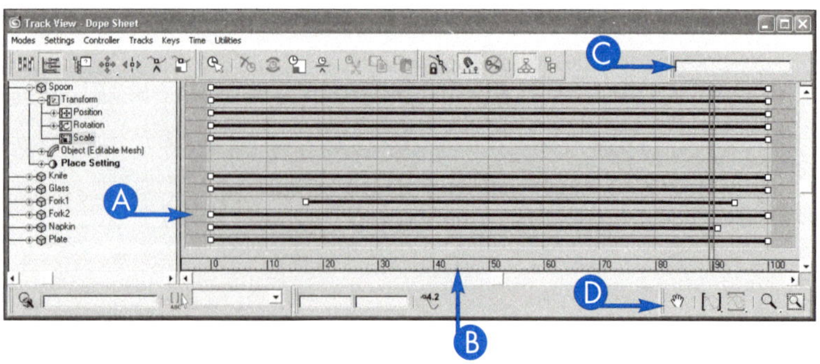

B Time Ruler

Measures time based using the current time settings established in the scene. Although the Time Ruler displays at the bottom of the Key pane, you can drag it up vertically and align it with any track.

D Navigation Toolbar

Provides options for zooming and panning the display of the keys and key ranges within the Key window.

C Name Toolbar

Displays the name of a named dope sheet.

Edit Keys Mode

A Controller Window

Displays all of the tracks within the scene in a hierarchical tree. Several types of default tracks display for every scene. By default, the animation tracks for the selected object display.

B Key Window in Edit Keys Mode

The default, this displays the animation in your scene as a series of boxes on a track and time grid. You can view and edit the animation timing for all tracks in a scene. Transform keys display in different colors to indicate each type of transform; Position transforms display in red, Rotation in green, and Scale in blue.

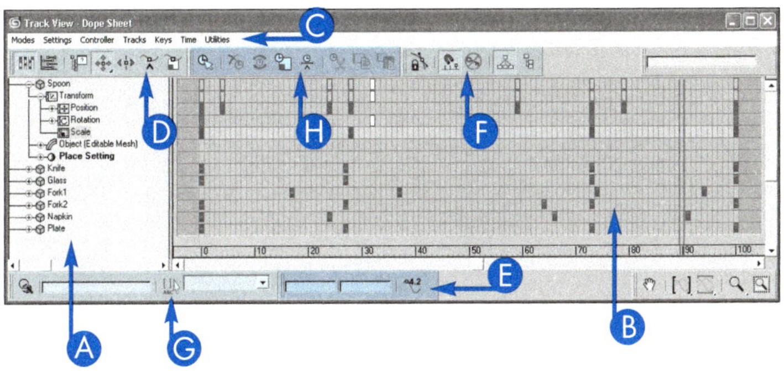

C Menu Bar

Contains options for controlling the animation timing of your objects. Has many of the same commands as the toolbars.

D Keys Toolbar

Provides options for adjusting the location of the keys as well as adding and deleting keys. Also provides buttons for switching between Edit Keys and Edit Ranges modes.

E Key Stats Toolbar

Shows the frame number and the value for the selected key. This only functions in Edit Keys mode.

F Display Toolbar

The options control the movement of keys. You can also control whether key manipulations affect tracks lower in the hierarchy in the Controller window.

G Track Selection Toolbar

Location for tools that are used to quickly recall saved track selections.

H Time Toolbar

Allows you to select and edit specific time ranges in your scene.

Add a Key Using the Dope Sheet

You can use the Dope Sheet to create additional keys for specific tracks in your scene. This is particularly useful when you have animated an object by changing its position and you want to create a keyframe for only one axis without affecting any other axes. For example, to create a position key for the X-axis, you can create, and change the value of, a key in the X Position track. This changes the interpolation of the X-axis without affecting the Y- and Z-axes.

Creating a new key at a specific time causes the value of the key to take on the current interpolated value. You can customize this key's Time and Value in the Key Info dialog box, which you can open by right-clicking the key. The upper-left corner of the Key Info dialog box also shows which key is selected sequentially for the current track. For example, if the selected key is the second key in the track, then the number is 2. You can also see and modify the Tangent values for the function curve.

The Dope Sheet.max file is available on the CD-ROM for you to practice adding keys with the Dope Sheet Editor.

Add a Key Using the Dope Sheet

Add a Keyframe

1. Click Graph Editors.
2. Click Track View – Dope Sheet.

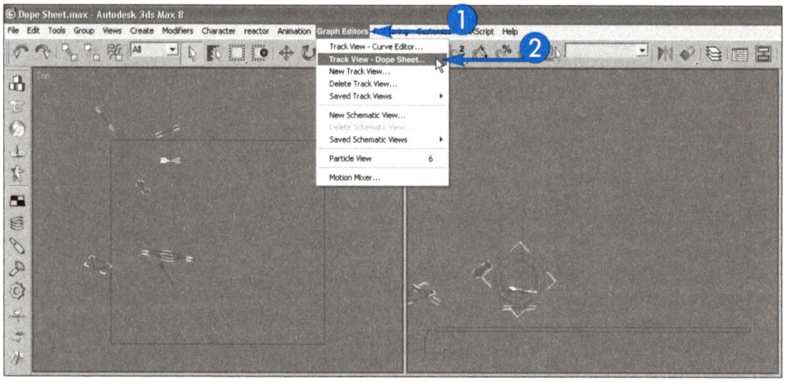

The Dope Sheet Editor opens.

3. Click the Add Keys button ( ).
4. In the Key window, click a track where you want to insert a key.

   3ds Max adds a new key to the animation for the specified track.

   You can repeat step 4 to create more keys.

5. To avoid adding another key, click to turn off the Add Keys button.

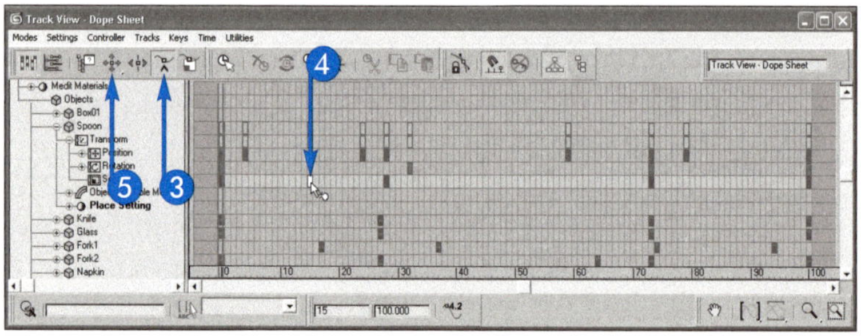

Set a Keyframe Value

6 Right-click the desired keyframe.

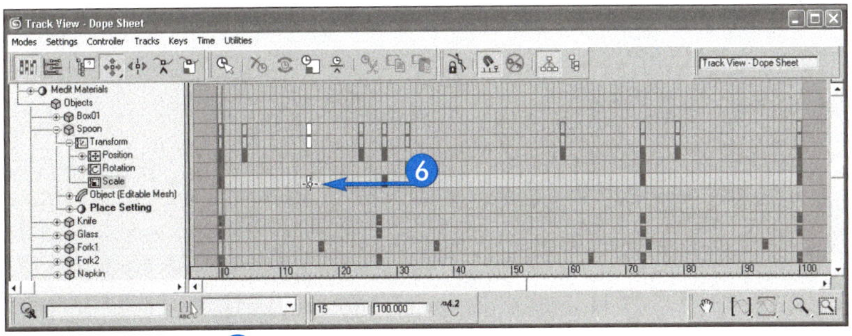

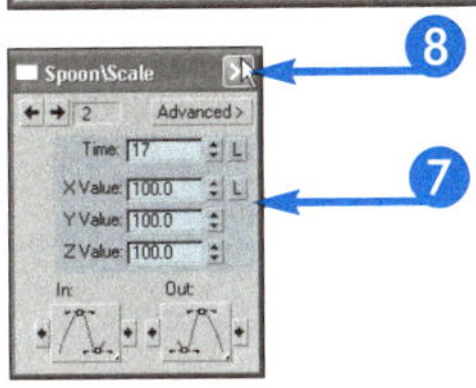

The Key Info dialog box displays the key number, Time, and Value of the selected key.

7 Type the desired values in the Time and Value fields.

8 Click the Close button (☒) to close the Key Info dialog box.

3ds Max applies the values.

MASTER IT

Can I create keyframes for all three axes?

▼ Yes. When you create new keyframes, you can either create the keyframes for the individual tracks, or for a series of tracks. For example, to create new position tracks, you can either create a new keyframe for each axis by clicking the X Position, Y Position, and Z Postion tracks individually, or you can create all three tracks by clicking Add Keys and then clicking the Position track, one level higher in the hierarchy. The Position track has no actual values, as it is only the parent of the lower keys; therefore, right-clicking its keys opens a quad menu, rather than the Key Info dialog box.

How can I tell which controller a parameter has assigned?

▼ Each transform and parameter has a controller assigned to it to define how the animation between keys is interpolated. Both the Dope Sheet and the Curve Editor can display the controllers in the Controller window. To see which controllers are assigned to each track, click the Filters button (Filters icon) in the Keys toolbar. In the Filter dialog box that appears, select the Controller Types option (☐ changes to ☑) in the Show section, and then click OK to close the dialog box. The controller types are now listed next to each parameter. For more information on controllers and constraints, see Chapter 10.

Change a Block of Time

You can use the Dope Sheet to modify the timing for a specific range of frames on selected tracks. This means that when you select and edit a segment of time, you may or may not affect the rest of the animation for that track. For example, when you select a block of time, that block can be scaled up or down. The time between keys within the selected block is condensed or expanded, but the keys beyond the block only shift in time; their spacing does not change. You can also delete or insert a block of time for a track.

A useful feature of the Dope Sheet is the ability to reverse a block of time. It is often easier to set the final condition of a scene and then animate its objects dispersing, than it is to animate the objects assembling properly. To animate a scene coming together, you can first set it properly, then animate the objects scattering, and then use the Dope Sheet's Reverse Time option to reverse a block of time so that the scene appears to converge, rather than diverge.

CD FILE The Dope Sheet.max file is available on the CD-ROM for you to practice changing a block of time.

Change a Block of Time

Select a Block of Time

1. Click Graph Editors.
2. Click Track View – Dope Sheet.

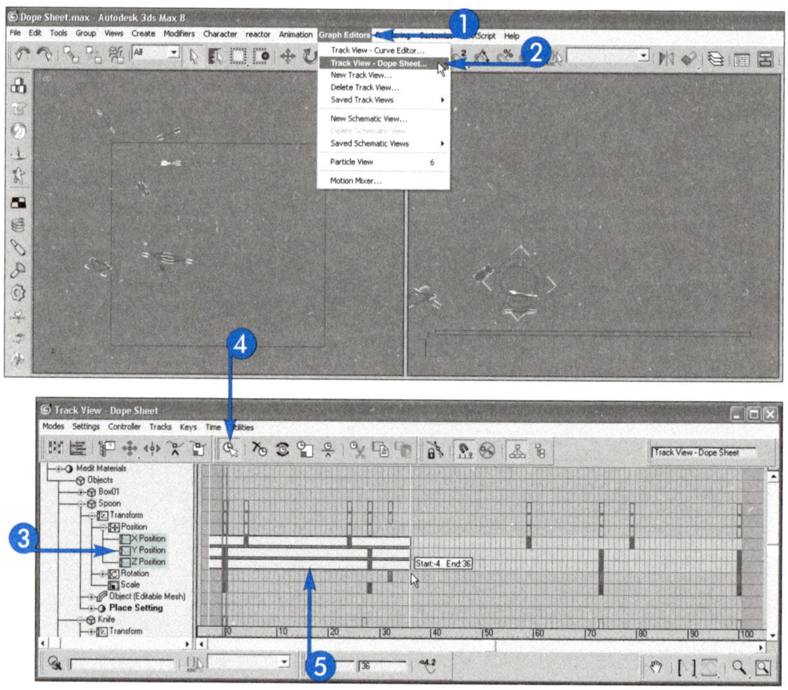

The Dope Sheet Editor opens.

3. In the Controller window, click the tracks that you want to edit.

   To select multiple tracks, press and hold Ctrl while you click.

4. Click the Select Time button (🔍).
5. Click and drag to select the block of time.

   Vertical yellow lines indicate the start and end of the selection.

   The start and end times are specified as you drag the selection.

Reverse a Block of Time

The selected time remains a tan color, and the selected keys turn white.

6. With a block of time selected, click Reverse Time ( ).

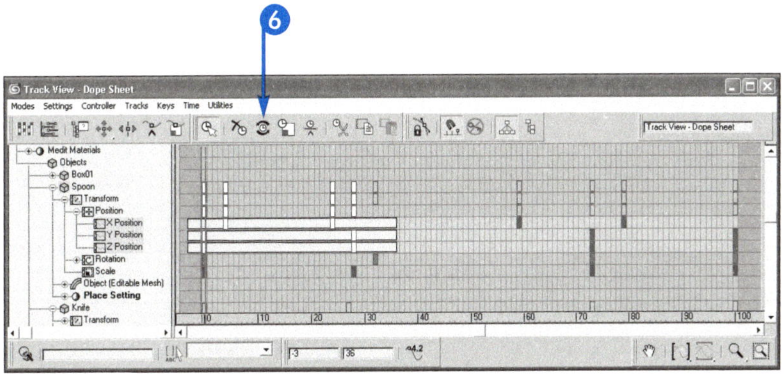

The keys in the selected block of time are mirrored.

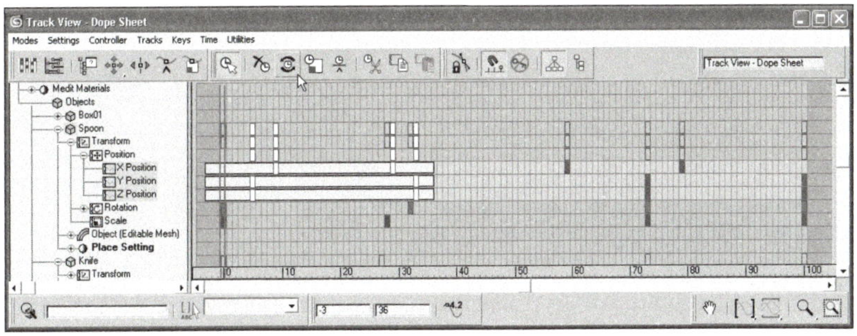

MASTER IT

What other options do I have to modify a selected block of time?

▼ There are several options on the Time toolbar that you can use to modify a block of time within your scene.

Button	Description
	Deletes the selected range of time.
	Scales the selected range of time.
	Inserts the specified amount of time into the selected tracks.
	Deletes the selected range of time and places it on the clipboard.
	Copies the selected range of time and places it on the clipboard.
	Pastes the range of time that was last cut or copied.

Why are some of the keys in the Controller window skinny?

▼ An object's keys do not need to be placed precisely at the point in time where a frame starts. For example, it is perfectly acceptable, and sometimes required, to place a key with a Time value of 30.5, rather than 30. 3ds Max identifies these non-frame keys by showing them as very thin keys in the Dope Sheet. By default, Snap Frames, in the Display toolbar, is turned on, thus locking key movements to full frame intervals. You can easily place keys at non-frame times using the left field found in the Key Stats toolbar. The right field controls the key's parameter value.

Edit Ranges

The Edit Ranges mode of the Dope Sheet allows you to move and scale an entire track of an animation without considering specific keys within that track. This mode is useful when you are more concerned about controlling the start and end of the animation, and not about specific keyframes.

In Edit Ranges mode, 3ds Max represents all tracks as black range bars, with a white box at each end to indicate the first and last keyframes. You can move your mouse to control how 3ds Max moves or scales the animation track. After selecting the black bar, using the Move Keys button, you can reposition the animation track. Selecting one of the white end boxes and moving it causes the animation to scale in the appropriate direction.

You can control a group of tracks or only individual tracks, depending upon where you click. For example, if you select the Position track, then you also control the subordinate X Position, Y Position, and Z Position tracks. If you select the X Position track, then you control only that track.

CD FILE: The Dope Sheet.max file is available on the CD-ROM for you to practice editing ranges.

Edit Ranges

Move a Range

1. Click Graph Editors.
2. Click Track View – Dope Sheet.

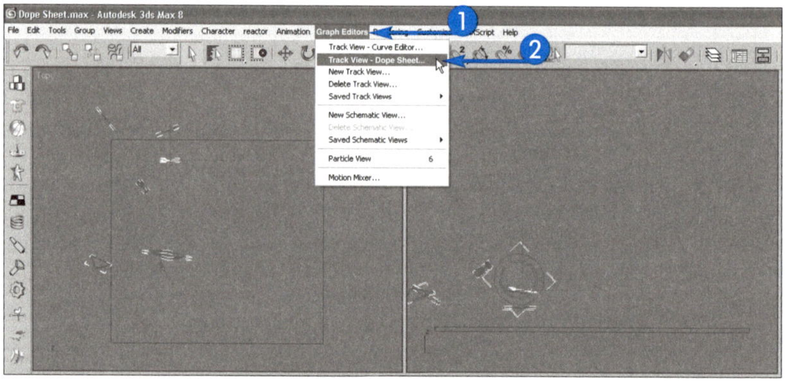

The Dope Sheet Editor opens.

3. On the Keys toolbar, click the Edit Ranges button (▤).

The Key window changes to show range bars that illustrate the start, end, and animation length for each track.

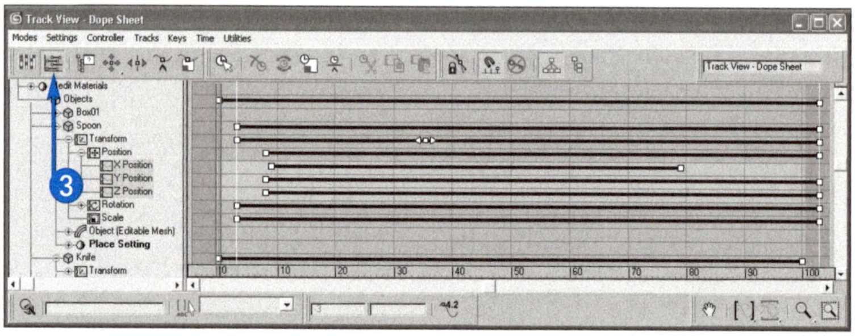

4 Click and drag the center of a range bar.

The cursor turns into a two-sided arrow, and the selected range moves.

If you selected a track with subordinate tracks, all subordinate ranges also move.

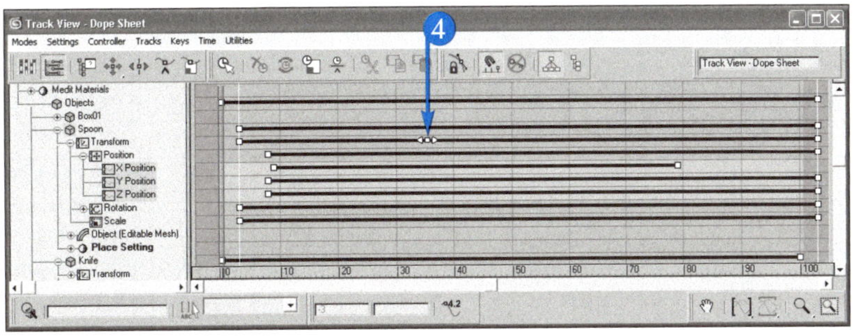

Scale a Range

5 Click and drag the box at the end of a range bar.

The cursor turns into a one-sided arrow, and the selected range scales.

If you selected a track with subordinate tracks, all subordinate ranges also scale.

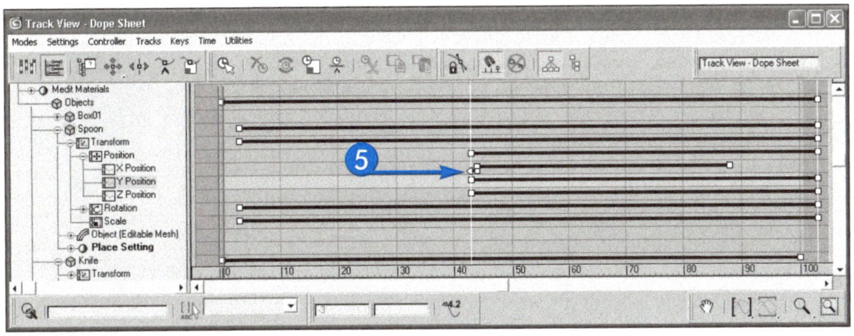

MASTER IT

What is the difference between scaling the range in Edit Ranges mode and scaling with Edit Keys mode?

In the Edit Ranges mode, all changes that you make to a track affect the entire track, and not just individual keys. Therefore, scaling a range scales the entire track. With the Edit Keys mode, you can select a specific block of frames that you want to scale. The scaling only affects the selected frames and the frames beyond it, but not the frames preceding it. See the section "Change a Block of Time" for more information on scaling a selection of frames.

Can I select a group of tracks to edit the range?

When working in the Edit Ranges mode, you can only make changes to a single track or a parent and its corresponding subordinate tracks. For example, this allows you to move the X Rotation, Y Rotation, and Z Rotation tracks simultaneously by selecting the Rotation parent track. However, you cannot select just the X Rotation and Y Rotation tracks. You need to move the two ranges separately; use the vertical yellow lines that appear when moving a range, to help line up each of the tracks that you move.

Add a Note Track and Notes

Games companies often use Note tracks when exporting 3ds Max files to their games engines. Exporters and converters can read the Note tracks and make decisions based on them.

You can create Note tracks under specific tracks in the Dope Sheet window to provide information about what different keys do. By creating notes about different keys, you can immediately spot the keys that perform specific types of animation. The notes that you specify only display when you view the Edit Keys mode of the Dope Sheet.

3ds Max creates the Note track under all selected tracks simultaneously, and each Note track becomes a subordinate track to the selected track.

When you create a Note track, it is initially empty, but you can easily add new notes to the track using the Add Keys option. When you create a new note, an icon appears in the corresponding frame. You can then specify the text that you want to describe the key in the Notes dialog box. The first line of text that you type displays as the title of the note in the Key window.

The Dope Sheet.max file is available on the CD-ROM for you to practice adding Note tracks.

Add a Note Track and Notes

1. In the Dope Sheet Controller window, click to select the track where you want to add a Note track.

   You can select multiple tracks, to create multiple Note tracks, by pressing and holding Ctrl as you click.

2. Click Tracks.
3. Click Note Track.
4. Click Add.

   The Note track appears as a subordinate track to the selected tracks.

5. Click to select the Note track.
6. Click .

   If Edit Ranges mode is active, then Edit Keys mode is turned on.

7. Click the frame where you want to create a note.

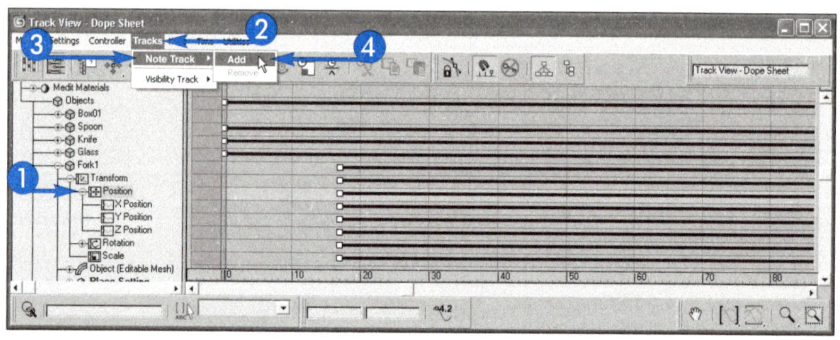

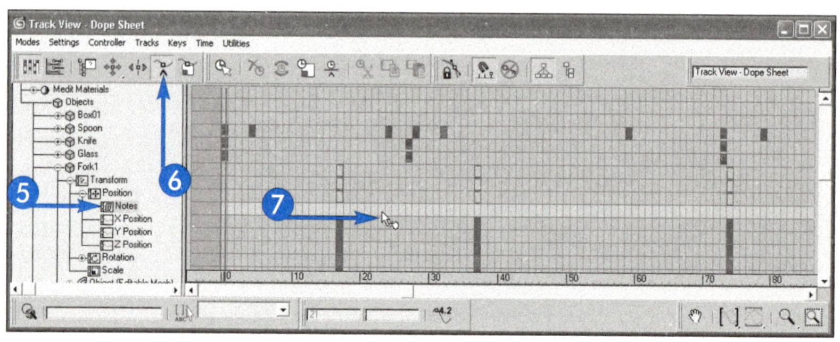

A note icon (▣) displays in the selected frame.

8 Right-click the note icon.

A Notes dialog box appears.

9 Type the note text that you want.

10 Click ☒ to close the Notes dialog box.

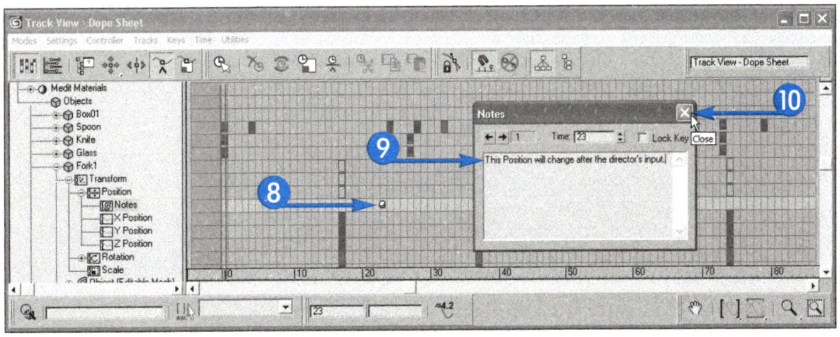

- The first line of your note displays to the right of the note icon.

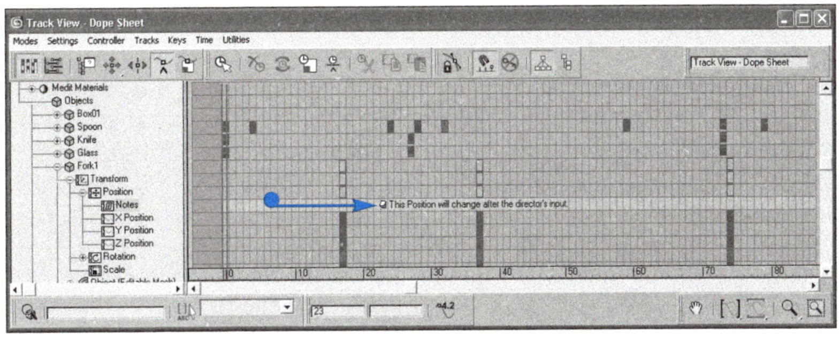

MASTER IT

What does the Lock Key option do?

▼ When you create note text, you can select the Lock Key option in the Notes dialog box. If you click Lock Key (☐ changes to ☑), the key is locked to that time on the Note track. This ensures that the Note key does not move if you use the Move, Slide, or Scale Keys options. If a Note is locked, the only way to change the time for the note is to right-click the note and then change the Time field in the Notes dialog box.

How do I keep the note text from overlapping?

▼ When you create a note, the first line of text that you type in the Notes dialog box displays next to the Note icon in the Note track. If you have multiple notes in the Note track, the text of one note may overlap the text of another note. To prevent this, you should keep the first line of text for the note short, and type a full description of your note in the other lines. Also, you can copy and paste the text in the Notes dialog box into other Notes dialog boxes by selecting the text and right-clicking it.

Understanding Hierarchies

To create complex animated systems, such as a moving car, a walking robot, or even a waving hand, you may need to associate different objects to each other. This association allows you to create animations that simulate the real thing by locking the transforms of one object to the transforms of another. For example, if you link the wheels to a car, then when you move the car, the wheels move with it. In 3ds Max, the process of connecting objects together is called *linking*, and a system of linked objects is a *hierarchy*. A hierarchy shows the relationship between the objects.

Parent/Child Relationships

As you link objects together, you create parent/child relationships. The *parent* object controls the child that is linked to it, and the child reacts to any transform that the parent object makes. Each child object can have only one parent, but one parent can have many children. A parent can also be a child for an object that is higher in the hierarchy.

To achieve the desired movement in an animation, you must develop the best hierarchy for your system of objects. You must link objects together in a logical progression from parent to child, and you should consider linking objects that maintain a constant proximity to each other. For example, if you link together the parts of a human arm, then you must first identify the parent of the chain, which is the shoulder. You then logically link the other parts, with the shoulder object being the parent of the upper arm, the upper arm being the parent of the forearm, the forearm being the parent of the hand, and so on through to the tips of the fingers.

Forward and Inverse Kinematics

The movement or animation of linked objects is referred to as *Kinematics*. There are two types of Kinematics in 3ds Max: Forward Kinematics and Inverse Kinematics.

Forward Kinematics, or FK, is the standard type of hierarchical animation. If you manipulate the top of the hierarchy, then the top's movement affects the chain of child objects or descendants. With Forward Kinematics, the child object inherits all transforms of the parent object. These include position, rotation, and scaling. When the parent object moves, all descendants in the hierarchy chain must follow. However, if a child object moves, then it has no effect on the movement of the parent object or any of its ancestor objects.

Inverse Kinematics, or IK, allows you to transform a parent object, based upon a child object's movement. For example, if you want to animate a person walking, you move the foot object; the ancestral objects, such as the shin and thigh, reposition to reflect the movement of the child. See the section "Apply Interactive Inverse Kinematics" for more information on animating with IK.

Linking Relationships and Pivot Points

A *pivot point* is the position in space that defines the location of your object. Extruded primitives, such as cylinders and boxes, have their pivot points at the center of their bases. Spherical objects, such as spheres and tori, have their pivot points at their geometric centers. When you move an object, you are actually moving the pivot point, and the geometry follows it. When you rotate an object, you are rotating the geometry around the pivot point, and when you perform a scale operation, the geometry is scaled toward or away from the pivot point. The pivot point is not in a fixed location; you can move it as you choose.

When you link two objects together at their pivot points, the link relationship between the two objects is determined by the position, rotation, and scale of each object when you originally link them. For example, if the parent and child objects are ten units apart when you link them, they remain at that distance when you make transforms to the parent object. If you move the parent object, the child object follows and maintains the same ten-unit distance.

The same relationship remains between the objects for any other types of transforms. For example, if you scale the parent object 200 percent, then the child object also scales 200 percent of its original size.

Keep in mind that with Forward Kinematics, these linking relationships only exist for transforms that you make to the parent object. Any transforms to the child object have no effect on the parent object.

3ds Max Hierarchy Terms

The relationship between linked objects in 3ds Max resembles the relationship between relatives on a family tree. In fact, 3ds Max uses similar terminology to refer to the relationships.

Hierarchy Terms

Term	*Description*
Ancestors	Identifies all of the parent objects of a selected object.
Branch	The path of objects that link an ancestor object to a specific child object.
Child	An object that is linked to another object. An object can be a child of one object and the parent of other objects.
Descendants	All child objects of a parent object and all of that parent's ancestors.
Hierarchy	A collection of parent and child objects linked together in a single structure.
Leaf	A child object that does not have a child object linked to it.
Link	Refers to the connection between a parent object and the child object. The link creates the relationship between the two objects by passing the transform information from the parent object.
Parent	An object that has linked child objects that it controls. Although a parent object can be a child of another object, each child object can only have one parent object.
Pivot Point	All objects are linked at the pivot points. The pivot point is the local center and coordinate system of an object. All transforms that you apply to an object affect the object from the pivot point.
Root	The parent object that is above all other child objects in a hierarchy. The root object is not linked to a parent.
Subtree	Refers to all descendants or child objects of a parent object.

Link and Unlink Objects

You can link two objects together to create a parent-and-child relationship within your scene. This creates a hierarchical relationship between the objects. The linked relationship remains in effect for the entire length of the scene.

The easiest method for linking objects is to use the Select and Link button on the Main toolbar. Using this option, you can link multiple child objects simultaneously to a parent object. You first select the objects that you want to link as children and then drag them to the desired parent object.

With hierarchical relationships, it is important to think about how you want to link your objects together so that you can obtain the appropriate results. See the section "Understanding Hierarchies" for more information on selecting the linking relationships.

The Unlink Selection option allows you to remove the link between a child object and its parent. When you remove links from selected objects, 3ds Max removes the link from the selected child object to its parent. Any child objects of the selected object are not affected.

CD FILE The Link.max file is available on the CD-ROM for you to practice with linking and unlinking objects.

Link and Unlink Objects

Link Objects

1. Click the Select and Link button ( ).
2. Select the object that you want as the child object.

Note: *For more information on selecting multiple objects, see Chapter 2.*

The cursor changes to the Link cursor ( ).

3. Click and drag from the child object to the desired parent object.

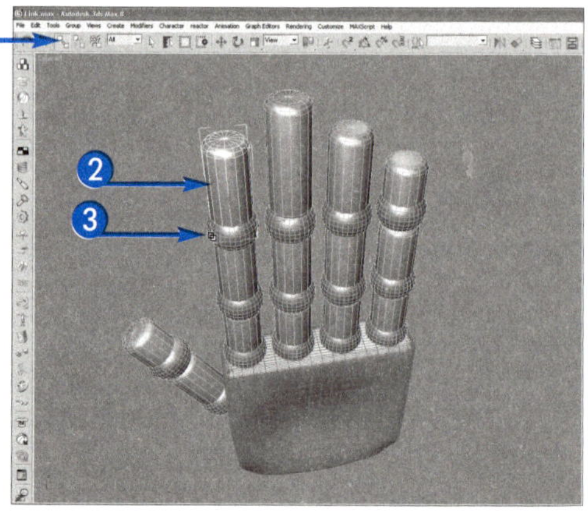

A dotted line connects the objects to show the relationship, and the cursor changes to another Link cursor ( ).

4. Release the mouse.
   - The parent blinks white briefly to signify the link.

To continue linking objects, repeat steps 2 to 4.

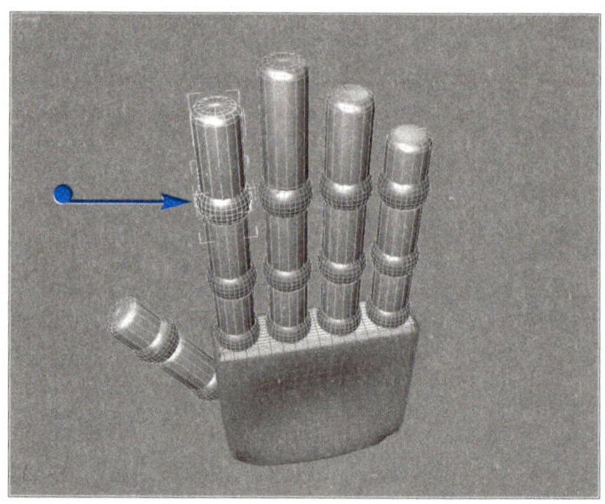

Unlink Objects

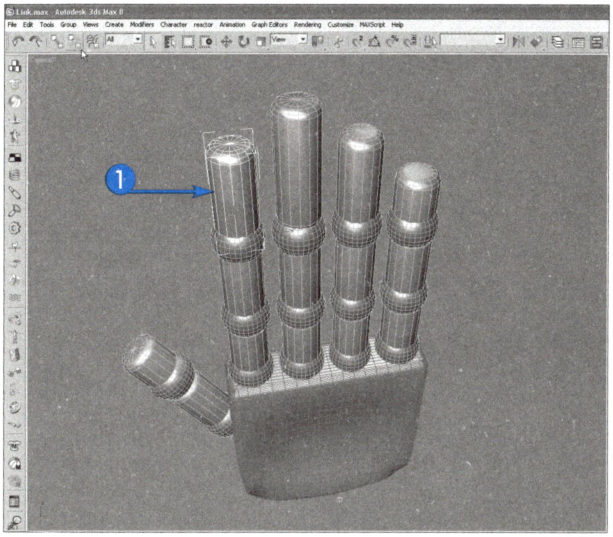

1. Select the object that you want to unlink from its parent.

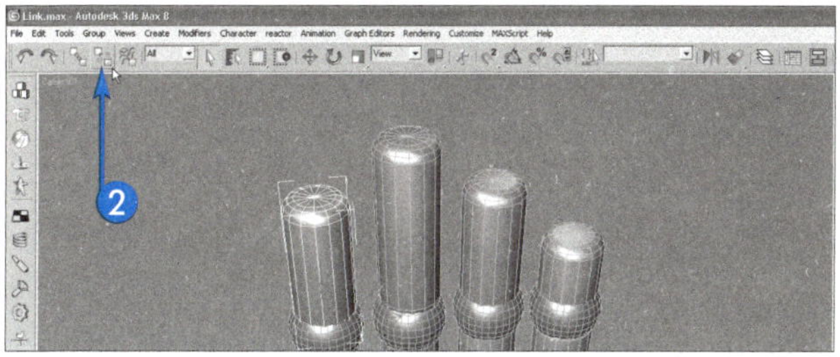

2. Click the Unlink Selection button (icon).

   The link between the parent and child objects is broken.

How do I know what the links are in my scene?

Although links between objects are not visible in the viewport, you can quickly see the links between objects by opening the Select Objects dialog box. To display the Select Objects dialog box, click the Select by Name button (icon). The Select Objects dialog box displays a list of the objects within the scene. To see a linked object, click the Display Subtree option (☐ changes to ☑). This displays the child objects indented under their parent objects in the subtree. The Select by Name button also opens the Select Parent dialog box, when the Select and Link button is active, to allow you to select a parent by name.

Can I animate the linking of objects?

You cannot animate the process of linking objects using the Select and Link button (icon). When you link objects in one frame, they remain linked for the entire animation. To create an animation where objects are only linked for part of it, use a Link controller from the Animation menu, or a Link constraint at the Transform level of the Assign Controller window, which allows you to link one object to another at a specific frame. You can change the link to specify a different object at a different frame. Remember to click (icon) to turn it off or the next time you select an object, you will link it instead. For more information on applying constraints to objects, see Chapter 10.

Move an Object's Pivot Point

A pivot point is a single point in space, with no dimensions, that is the reference point for an object. When a transform is applied to an object, that object reacts based on the location of the pivot point. For example, when you scale an object with the pivot point located at the base, it grows larger from the base upward, but the base itself is fixed. When you scale an object with the pivot point at its center, the object scales outward, in all directions.

When working with linked hierarchies, the pivot point is very important because the transform applied to a parent object is passed on to its children. If the pivot point is not located properly, the functionality of the movements will lose any credibility.

Using the transform tools, you can easily move or rotate the pivot point into place. You must be sure to turn off the Affect Pivot Only button, in the Hierarchy panel, after moving the pivot point; otherwise, the next commands that you issue are applied to that pivot point.

CD FILE: The Pivot.max file is available on the CD-ROM for you to practice with moving an object's pivot point.

Move an Object's Pivot Point

Set Pivot Points

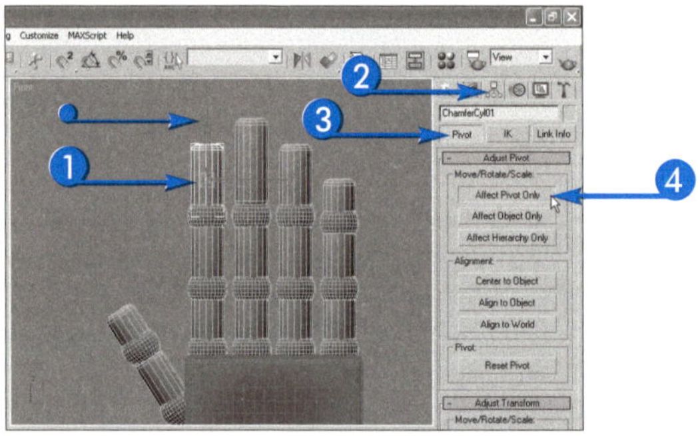

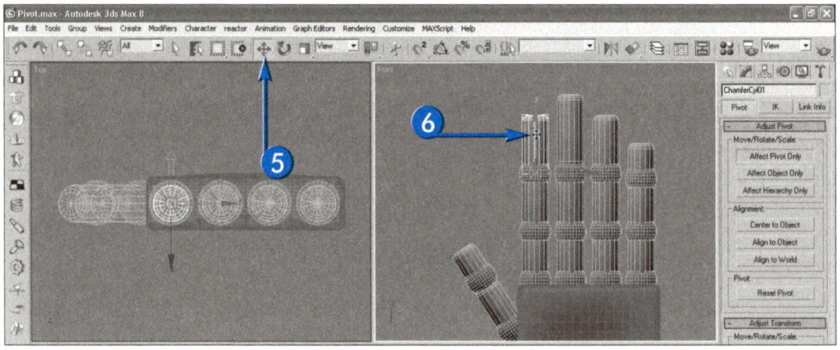

1. Select the object with the pivot point that you want to move.
2. Click the Hierarchy tab (icon).

   The Hierarchy panel opens.
3. Click Pivot.

   The Pivot panels open.
4. Click Affect Pivot Only.

   The axis tripod becomes the Pivot gizmo.
5. Click the Select and Move button (icon).
6. Click and drag the corresponding axis arrow of the Move gizmo to the desired location for the pivot point.

   The pivot point moves.

Note: *For more information on using the Move transform, see Chapter 2.*

7 Click Affect Pivot Only to turn off this feature.

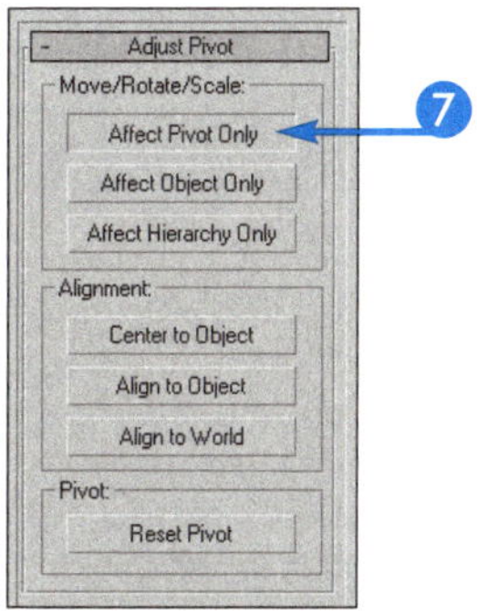

8 Rotate the selected object to test the new pivot point location.

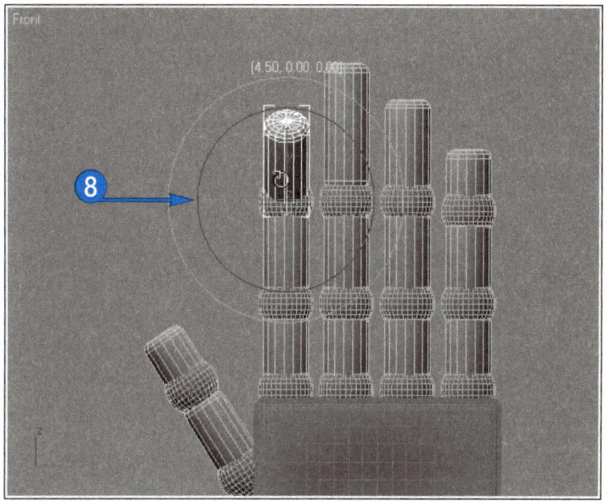

MASTER IT

Are there other ways to move the pivot point of an object?

▼ Yes. Rather than moving the pivot point, you can click the Affect Object Only button, which holds the pivot point steady but allows you to move the object around it instead. With Affect Pivot Only active, you can click any of the buttons in the Alignment section to align the pivot point using a variety of methods. You can use the Center to Object option to quickly move the pivot point to the center of the object's bounding box. The Reset Pivot button moves and reorients the pivot to the state that it was in when you created the object.

I want to arrange clones of an object in a circle. Can moving the pivot help me?

▼ Yes, it certainly can. To arrange your objects in a circular pattern, start by moving the original object's pivot point to the center of the pattern. Turn on the Angle Snap Toggle, ( ) in the Main toolbar, and set the Angle value to any value that is evenly divisible into 360 (degees), for example, 30. Press and hold the Shift key and then rotate the object one increment of the angle snap. In the Clone Objects dialog box, select a clone type and type a Number of Copies value that fills in the circle with objects. For this example, the number is 11 — one original plus 11 copies equals 12, and 12 objects at 30-degree increments equals 360 degrees.

Understanding the Schematic View

The Schematic view window offers an alternative method for viewing and modifying the hierarchies within your scene. Not only can you view the hierarchical relationships between objects, but you can also access the other object relationships, such as object properties, materials, controllers, constraints, and modifiers.

The Schematic view displays everything as a rectangular box or node on a flow chart. The nodes, which contain information about the object or modifier, are connected on the chart to show the relationships between them. 3ds Max uses different coloring for each type of node on the chart, with the default color for an object node being blue.

You can design and save specific Schematic views that you can access anytime, thus saving you time as you work on a project. By default, 3ds Max names the Schematic view, Schematic View 1. It then increases the number for each Schematic view that you save, although you can also customize these names.

A Toolbar

Contains options for linking and unlinking objects, deleting objects, copying modifiers and materials, and changing the layout of the Schematic view.

B Display Floater

Designates the categories of information that display in the Schematic view window. You can select the specific relationships and entities that display by clicking the names or corresponding buttons.

C Nodes

Rectangular boxes that display for each entity in the scene. Nodes display in different colors to indicate the type of nodes. You control which nodes display by the selections on the Display Floater.

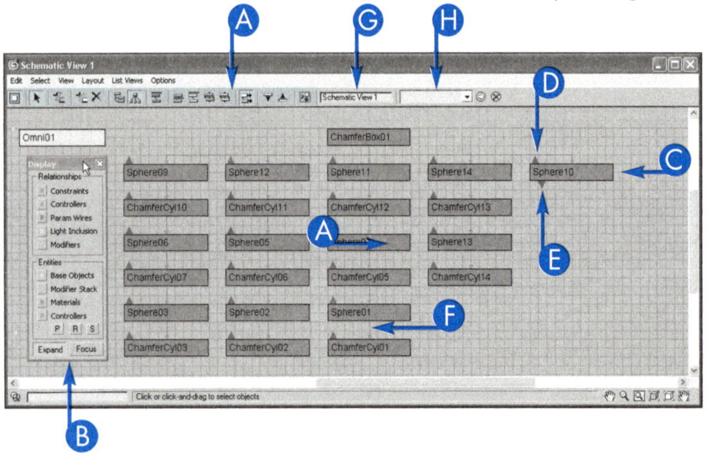

D Up Arrow

Indicates that the entity has parent entities. Clicking the arrow collapses the entity so that children are hidden under the parent node.

E Down Arrow

Indicates that the entity has collapsed child entities. Clicking the arrow opens the next level of child entities.

H Bookmark Name Field

Displays the name of the current bookmark. Bookmarks allow you to mark selections of entities that you want to quickly locate in the Schematic view. Typing a new name and pressing Enter creates a new bookmark.

G Schematic View Name Field

Shows the name of the current Schematic view. Typing a new name and pressing Enter creates a new, saved Schematic view.

F Hierarchical Relationship

A green line shows the hierarchical relationship between objects in the scene. Unconnected objects do not have a hierarchical relationship.

Schematic View Toolbar

Located at the top of the Schematic view window, the toolbar gives you access to a variety of options. Most of the buttons change the layout of the Schematic view graph. Layout changes only affect the Schematic view; they do not affect the objects in your scene.

You also have options for changing the links between objects and object properties, as well as for removing objects, and these changes affect your scene. See the section "Link and Unlink Objects in Schematic View" for more information.

Schematic View Toolbar Buttons

Button	*Description*
	Opens the Display Floater window, where you select which entity nodes you want to be visible in the Schematic view.
	Allows you to click and select nodes within the Schematic view. Selected nodes are white.
	Creates links between parent and child objects. This button also copies modifiers and materials between objects.
	Removes the parental link from a selected object. This action does not affect an object's child links.
	Deletes the selection by removing it from the Schematic view, as well as from the scene.
	Indents the child objects under their parent objects to create a hierarchical view of the scene.
	Shows all associations between objects, as well as their references and instances. This action indents object modifiers and materials under the object.
	Automatically arranges the nodes, based on default settings. Changes that you made to the layout of the Schematic view are lost.
	Automatically arranges the child nodes of a selected parent node.
	Automatically arranges the selected nodes within the Schematic view.
	Frees all nodes for repositioning within the Schematic view, regardless of any organizational settings.
	Frees the selected nodes for repositioning within the Schematic view.
	Moves a node's children whenever you move the node. The child nodes maintain their proximity to their parent.
	Displays all of the child nodes of the selected parent node.
	Collapses all of the child nodes of the selected parent node, which remains visible.
	Displays the Schematic View Preferences dialog box, where you control what displays in the Schematic view.
	Zooms and pans the Schematic view window to view the bookmark shown in the Bookmark Name field.
	Removes the bookmark that displays in the Bookmark Name field.

Link and Unlink Objects in Schematic View

You can use the Schematic view to link and unlink objects in your scene to simulate realistic movement in your animation. Linking objects creates a hierarchical relationship. This produces parent-and-child relationships between objects, with the *parent objects* controlling the children linked to them, and the *child objects* reacting to the transforms of the parent objects. Changes in the Schematic view affect the objects within the viewports, although the effect may not be visible. Hierarchical relationships require that you think about how to link your objects together so that you can achieve appropriate results from your animation. See the section "Understanding Hierarchies" for more information.

A link between objects does not need to be a permanent relationship. For example, you may want to link the wheels to a car to place it in your scene, but unlink them when you are going to stack them in the corner. The Unlink Selected option allows you to remove the link between a child object and its parent. Any child objects of the selected object are not affected.

The Schematic View.max file is available on the CD-ROM for you to practice with linking and unlinking objects in the Schematic view.

Link and Unlink Objects in Schematic View

Link Objects

1. Click Schematic view (Open) ( ).

   The Schematic view window opens.

2. Click the Connect button ( ).
3. Click the desired child node.

   To link multiple children objects, you can click and drag around the object nodes to select them.

4. Drag the child objects to the desired parent node.

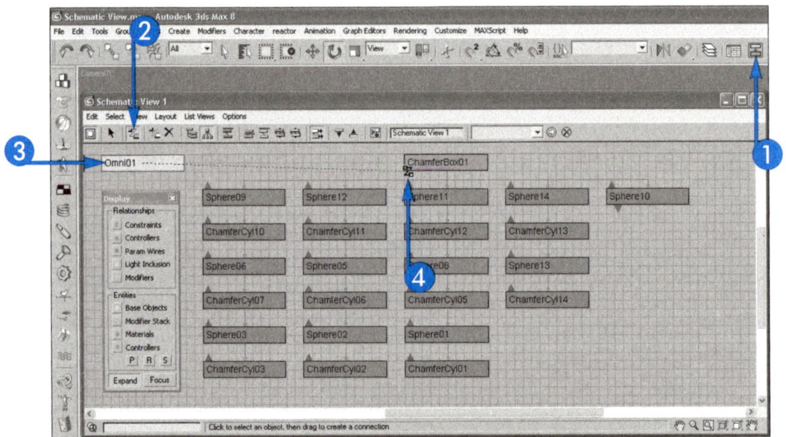

The selected object node links to the parent object node that you specify.

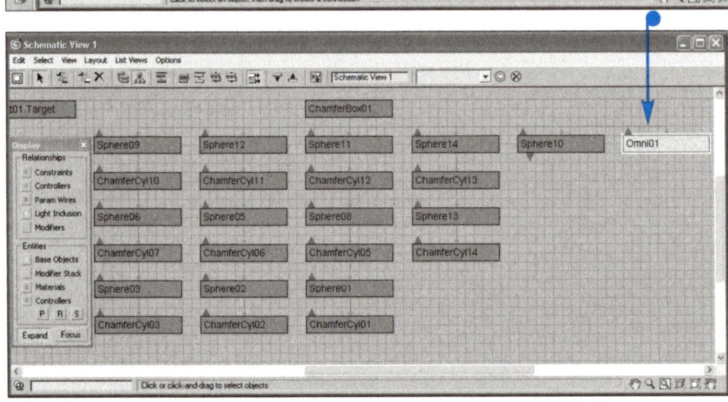

- A green line shows the hierarchical relationship between the objects.

Unlink Objects

1. Click [select icon].
2. Click the node of the object that you want to unlink from its parent.

   To select multiple object nodes, you can click and drag a selection box around the children nodes.
3. Click the Unlink Selected button ([unlink icon]).

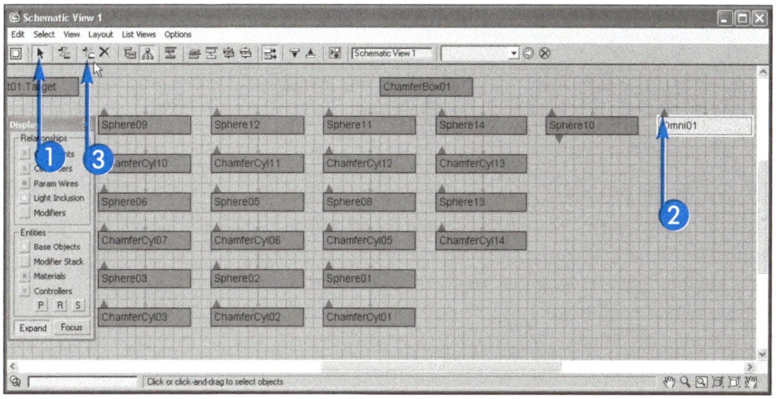

- The selected objects are unlinked from their parent objects.

All existing attached child links remain.

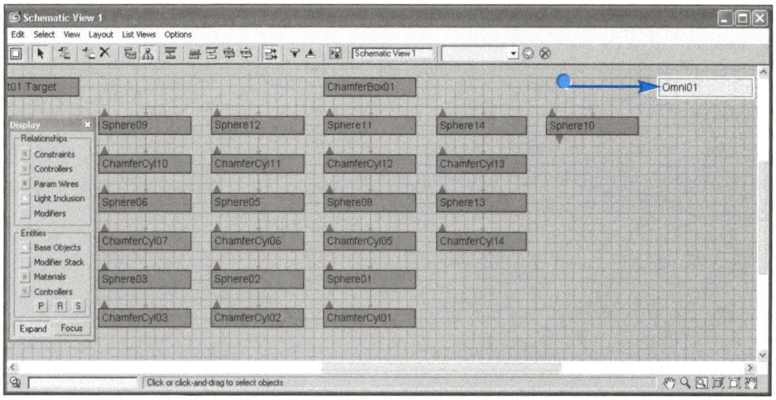

MASTER IT

How do I get back to a specific Schematic view display that I liked?

For large scenes, the Schematic view can be extensive and complicated. Once you have a view of the nodes that you anticipate returning to, you can create a bookmark for that view. To do this, first click in the Bookmark Name field in the Schematic view toolbar. Then type a name for your bookmark and press Enter. After you have zoomed or panned to change your view of the Schematic view, click the down arrow next to the Bookmark Name field and then select a bookmark from the list. Click the Go to Bookmark button to return to the bookmarked view.

How do I copy modifiers between objects in the Schematic view?

To copy a modifier, click the Connect button ([connect icon]), then click the modifier node in the Schematic view window, and then drag it to an object. The Attach Modifer dialog box opens with options for connecting the modifier. Selecting Copy applies an exact copy of the modifier, with all of its current settings, to the selected object. Any future modifications do not affect the copy. The Move command moves the modifier to the selected object. Selecting Instance copies the modifier, and any changes that you make to either modifier node is also made to the other. For information on modifiers, see Chapters 5 and 6.

Apply Interactive Inverse Kinematics

You can use Inverse Kinematics, or IK, for more complex animations where you want the movement of the child object to affect its parent, or ancestor object. For example, if you make the child object a foot, and the parent object a shin, then you can use IK to cause the foot's movement to affect the shin.

With IK animation, the parent-child hierarchy that you created remains intact, but 3ds Max calculates the appropriate position for the ancestor objects when the child object transforms. This involves at least the following steps: creating a linked system of objects, positioning pivot points, setting the system terminator, and defining joint constraints.

To apply IK, you must have a linked system of at least three objects, and they must be linked to form a chain of child and parent relationships. Next, you must determine the pivot point for each object. All motion between the objects occurs around the pivot point. In the foot example, you set the pivot point at the ankle so that it is positioned between the foot object and the lower leg object.

CD FILE The IK.max file is available on the CD-ROM for you to practice with IK.

Apply Inverse Kinematics

Set Terminator

1. Click the Hierarchy tab (the Hierarchy tab icon).

   The Hierarchy panel opens.

2. Click IK.

   The rollouts on the Hierarchy panel change.

3. Select the object where you want the animation to terminate.

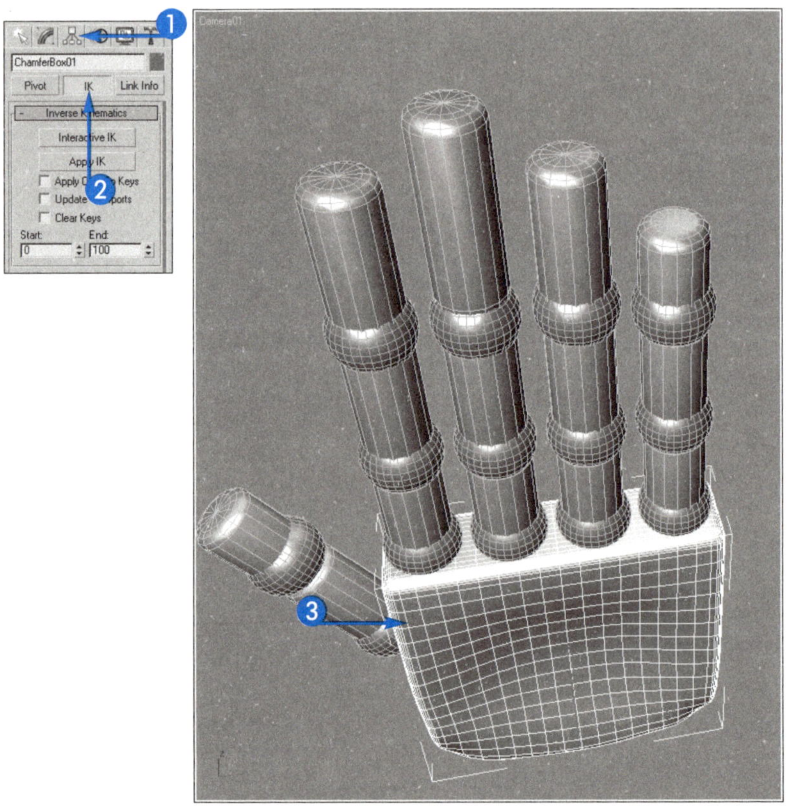

4. Click the Terminator option in the Object Parameters rollout (☐ changes to ☑).

The selected object is set as the terminator for any motion that occurs in the descendant objects.

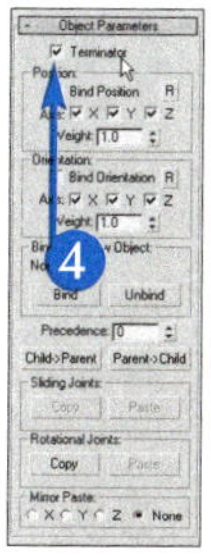

5. Drag the scroll bar down in the Hierarchy panel to display the Rotational Joints rollout.

The Rotational Joints rollout displays options for setting constraints on each axis.

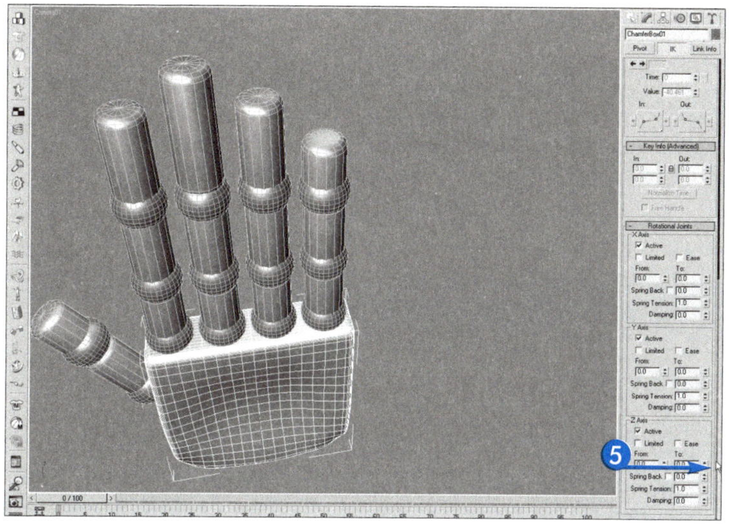

How do the options on the Auto Termination rollout work?

▼ The Terminator option sets the selected object as the termination point for IK animation in its decendants. Any animation that occurs stops at the selected object. The Auto Termination rollout works with Interactive IK and allows you to set different Terminator objects, depending upon the selected object. For example, you may want to terminate the animation three objects above the current object. To do this, select a value of 3 in the # of Links Up field in the Auto Termination rollout. The settings affect all objects in your chain. As a result, if you move a different object, then the animation terminates three objects above.

If I use IK, can I move other objects in the chain?

▼ Yes. When you apply Interactive IK to a hierarchical chain of objects, the parent-and-child relationships remain intact. The object maintains not only the new IK settings, but also the original Forward Kinematic settings. This allows you to transform any object in the chain and have the children and parents react. For example, if you move the lower leg, then the foot follows, based on the FK settings, and the upper leg moves using the IK settings.

continued

Apply Interactive Inverse Kinematics *(Continued)*

To control the movement of each object at the joint or pivot points, specify the joint constraints in the Rotational Joints rollout. By limiting the joint movement along an axis, you can control the amount of movement that can occur in each direction.

The Rotational Joints rollout enables you to control the joint movement on each of the three axes. For example, a knee normally bends back at about 90 degrees but not forward. By limiting the movement on the Z-axis between -90 and 0, you ensure that the knee does not bend forward. Because the knee has limited movement in other directions, you allow very limited movement on the X- and Y-axes. You should set movement limits on the axes for all objects in the chain.

After setting the limits for each joint, you must test your IK system. To see the movement, you must activate IK with the appropriate button at the top of the Hierarchy panel in the Inverse Kinematics rollout. You can then move the last object in the chain to see whether your settings are correct. As you move or rotate that object, 3ds Max calculates the movement that the parent object is required to make.

Apply Inverse Kinematics *(continued)*

Set Joint Constraints

6. Select the first object to constrain.
7. Click Limited (☐ changes to ☑).
8. Type the beginning constraint angle.
9. Type the ending constraint angle.
10. Repeat steps 7 to 9 for the Y- and Z-axes.

    The joint constraints are set for each axis.

11. Repeat steps 6 to 10 for each remaining object in the chain.

    You do not need to set constraints for the Terminator object.

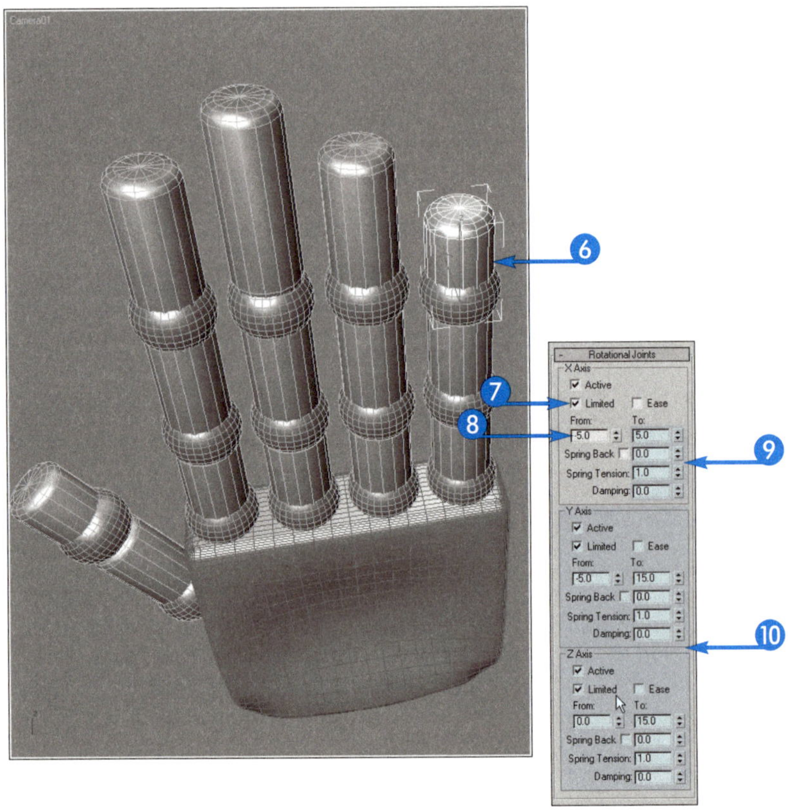

Animate the Object

12 Drag the scroll bar up to the top of the Hierarchy panel.

The Inverse Kinematics rollout becomes visible.

13 Click Interactive IK.

14 Click [icon].

15 Click and drag an object in the chain.

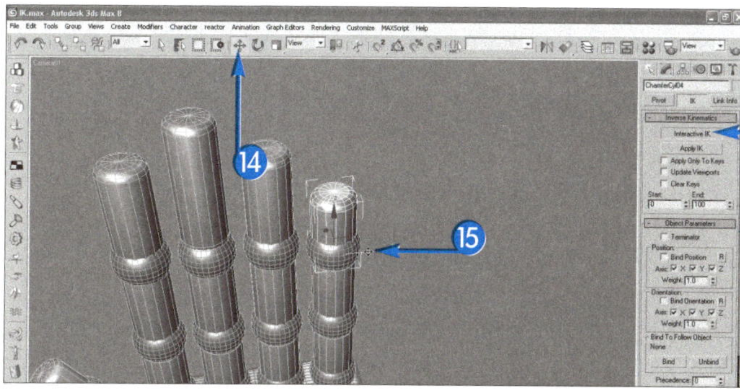

The ancestor objects in the chain follow the movement.

The terminated object remains unmoved.

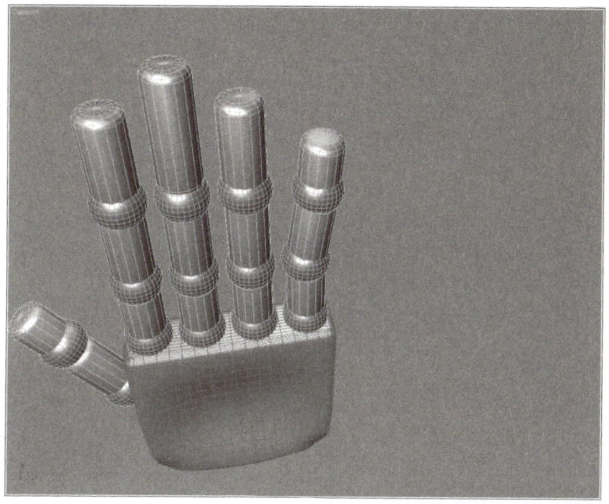

MASTER IT

How do I know what limits to set in the Rotational Joints rollout?

- When you set limits for an object in the Rotational Joints rollout, you should ensure that you have the appropriate limits. There are two methods for viewing the effect of the limits. If you use the spinners in the From and To field, then each time you click a spinner arrow, the object moves or rotates to that limit value. You can also see the effect of a limit by clicking the From and To labels for an axis. When you click a label, the object moves to that limit until you release the mouse.

How do I animate my Interactive IK scene objects?

- You can use the Auto Key button with Interactive IK to create animation for your scene. To create the animation, click Interactive IK, and then click Auto Key. Drag the Time Slider to the desired keyframe. Click the end object and drag it to the desired location. 3ds Max calculates the required movement for the other objects and creates the keyframe. Continue the process to create additional keyframes. For more information on animating with Auto Key, see Chapter 8.

Maintain Consistency with Parameter Wiring

In addition to linking one object to another, so that the parent object's transforms pass down to the child, you can also *wire* one object's parameters to another object. When the parameter of one object is changed, the wired parameter of the second object also changes. Unlike instanced objects, the parameters are not required to represent the same property in identical objects. For example, you can wire the Height parameter of a Box primitive to the Radius 1 parameter of a Tube primitive so that the Box always fits inside the tube. Only the values of the parameters are passed between wired objects, and not the parameters themselves.

Wiring does not require that one object's parameters must control the parameters of the other object. Wiring can be unidirectional — with one object's changes driving the changes in the other object — or bidirectional — with either object's changes modifying the other. See the section "Link and Unlink Objects" for more information on linking objects.

CD FILE: The Wire.max file is available on the CD-ROM for you to practice with linking and unlinking objects.

Maintain Consistency with Parameter Wiring

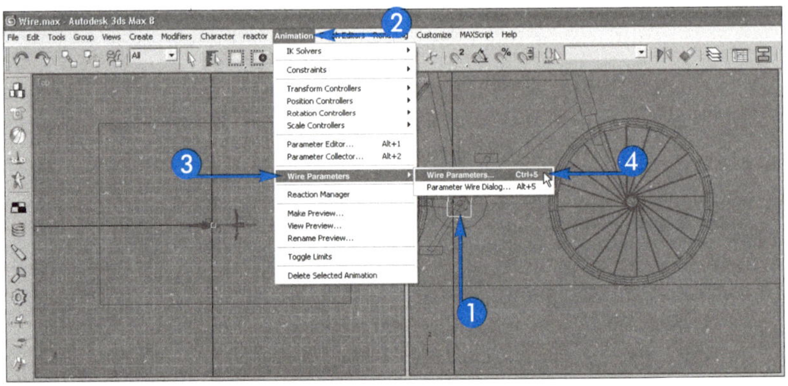

1. Select one of the objects that you want to wire.
2. Click Animation.
3. Click Wire Parameters.
4. Click Wire Parameters.

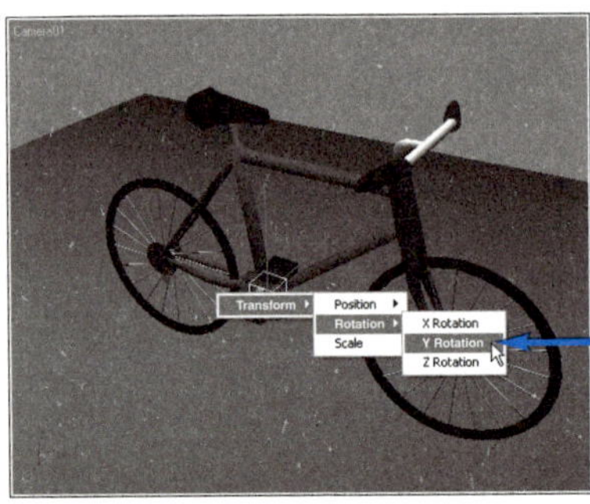

A contextual menu opens.

5. Navigate to, and click, the parameter that you want to wire.

This example selects the Y Rotation parameter.

A rubber band line attaches to your cursor.

6. Click the object with the parameter to which you want to wire.

7. In the contextual menu, navigate to and click the parameter that you want to wire.

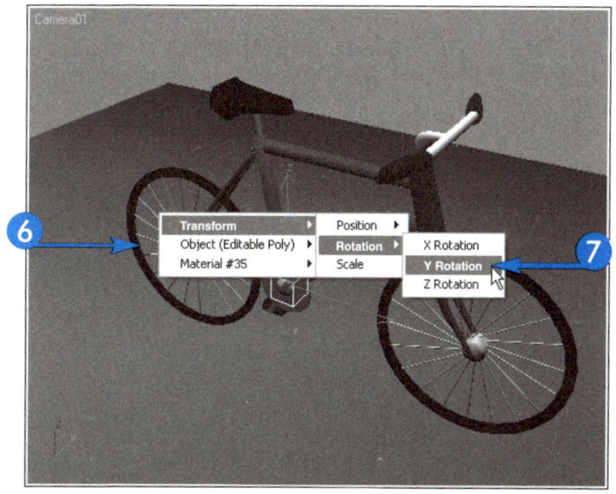

The Parameter Wiring dialog box appears.

8. Click a control direction button.

9. Click Connect.

The object's parameters are wired. Changing the control object's parameters affects the other object.

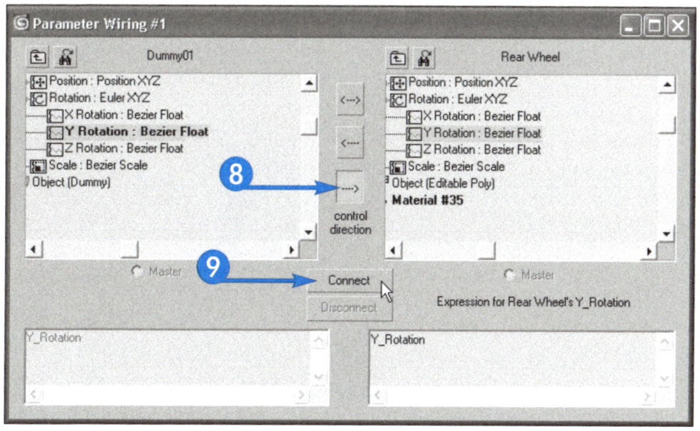

Can I modify the number that is being wired to a parameter?

Yes. The number being wired is actually an expression that details the value of the source parameter, and you can alter this number mathematically. For example, if the Radius1 value of a Tube is wired to be the same as the Height value of a Box, then the expression, in the white field at the bottom of the Parameter Wiring dialog box, is Height. To make the Radius1 parameter maintain a value that is twice the Height of the Box, change the expression to "Height * 2." To make the Radius1 parameter maintain a value that is half the Height of the Box, change the expression to "Height / 2." See the 3ds Max User Reference for a list of valid mathematical operators.

My wired objects are hard to see. How can I select them more easily?

Selecting them may not be the best solution, especially if they are difficult to effectively transform. You can use a Manipulator object, by clicking Create, then clicking Helpers, and then clicking Manipulators. Manipulators are gizmos that are always visible in the current viewport. They come in three styles: Cone Angle, Plane Angle, and Slider. Simply wire the parameter of your choice to the Value parameter of the manipulator, and then set the control direction so that the manipulator controls the object. Any changes made to the manipulator are reflected in your scene. You can adjust manipulator values with the Select and Manipulate tool ().

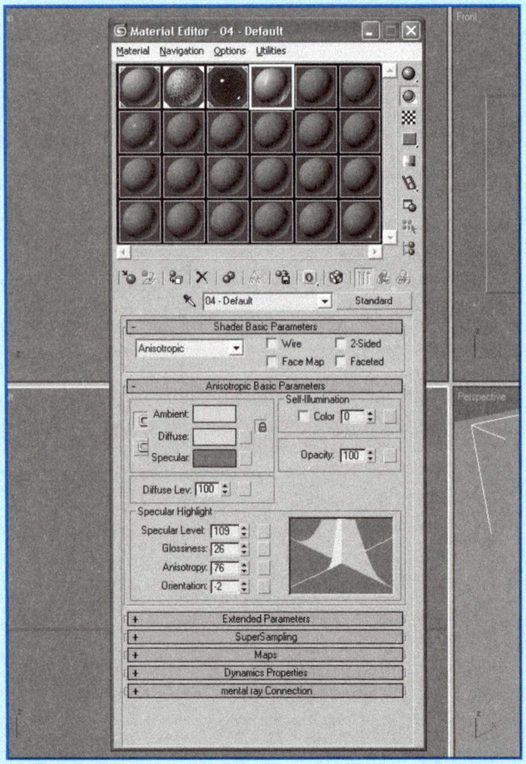

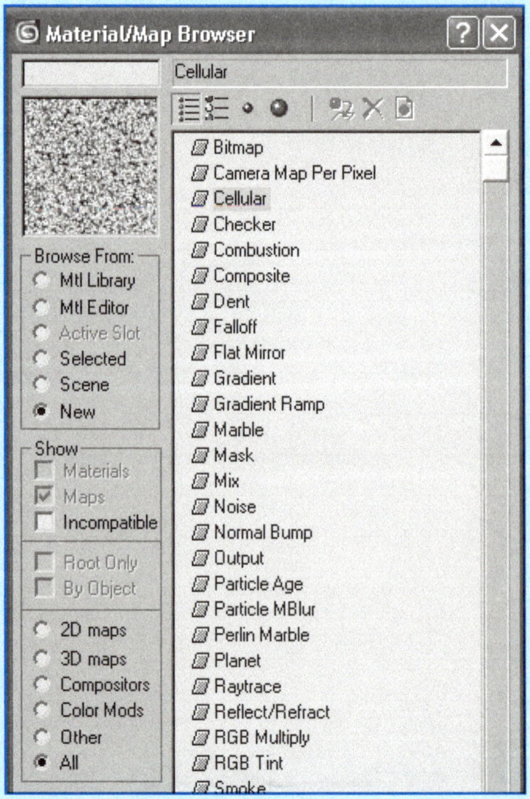

Material/Map Browser
Cellular
Browse From:
Mtl Library
Mtl Editor
Active Slot
Selected
Scene
New
Show
Materials
Maps
Incompatible
Root Only
By Object
2D maps
3D maps
Compositors
Color Mods
Other
All
Bitmap
Camera Map Per Pixel
Cellular
Checker
Combustion
Composite
Dent
Falloff
Flat Mirror
Gradient
Gradient Ramp
Marble
Mask
Mix
Noise
Normal Bump
Output
Particle Age
Particle MBlur
Perlin Marble
Planet
Raytrace
Reflect/Refract
RGB Multiply
RGB Tint

PART IV WORKING WITH MATERIALS AND MAPS

16 Using Material and Channel Types

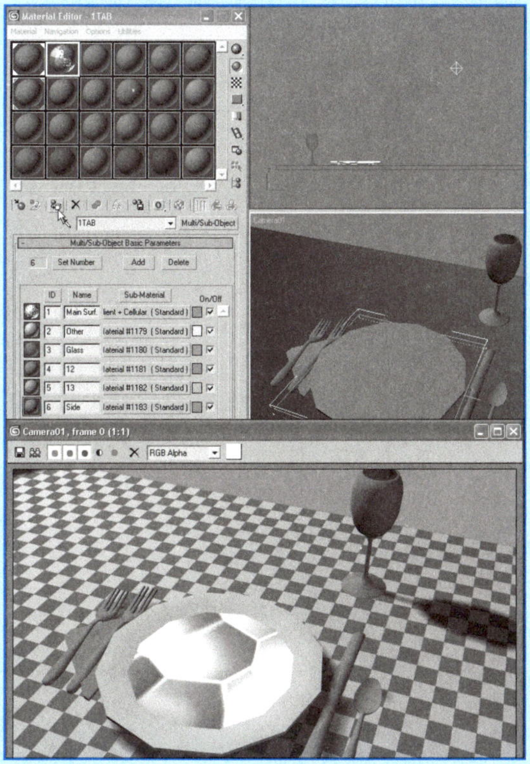

Understanding the Material Editor

With the Material Editor, you can make the objects in your scene look like almost anything. You can change the appearance of your scene's materials to appear as rough stone, polished glass, or fluffy smoke, depending on the applied material. A *material* describes how an object's surface appears when rendered, and includes such properties as color, texture, opacity, and shininess. The material can describe a simple color or it can contain maps, which are image files that define a material's components. For example, to make an object look like bricks, you use a *diffuse color map*, which causes the surface pixels. Using the same image as a *bump map* adds a textured appearance.

Although you can have any number of materials in a scene, the Material Editor can display up to 24 sample slots. As you make changes to the material through the rollouts in the Material Editor, the sample slots update to preview the effects. The Material Editor's Menu bar, and horizontal and a vertical toolbars contain tools that control the sample slot's appearance, material application and selection, and access to material-related utilities.

Rollouts, which are specific to the components for a selected material type, have controls that modify the characteristics of your materials so you can further define your material.

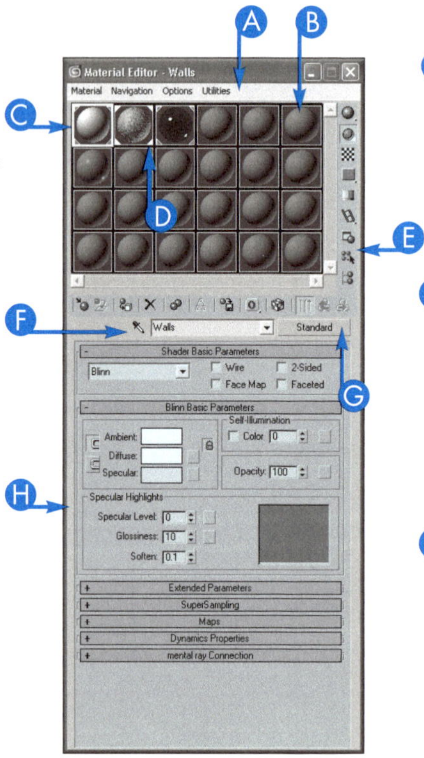

Ⓐ Material Editor Menu

Has the most commonly used tools, many of which are also available in the toolbar buttons.

Ⓑ Sample Slots

Showcase the designing materials you can add to your scene. By default the sample objects appear as spheres.

Ⓒ Selected Material

A white box displays around the currently selected material in the sample slot. The rollouts change to reflect the selection.

Ⓓ Hot Material

When you apply a material to an object in your scene, 3ds Max marks the material's corners with white bordered triangles. When the object in the scene is selected, the triangles are filled in with white.

Ⓔ Toolbars

The Material Editor window has both a vertical and horizontal toolbar with tools for managing and modifying materials for your scene.

Ⓕ Material Name

Displays the name of the currently selected material, sub-material, or map in the sample slot. 3ds Max uses the default names until they are changed by the user.

Ⓖ Material Type

Indicates the type of material or map that you have selected. You can change the material type by clicking the button to display the Material/Map Browser and selecting a different type. See Chapter 15 for more information on the Material/Map Browser.

Ⓗ Rollouts

Allow you to change the parameters of the selected material. The rollouts change, based on the material or map type.

Sample Slots

There are 24 sample slots in the Material Editor, and you can view 6, 15, or all 24 at one time. You set the number of slots to display via the Options button (▣) and then select a configuration in the Material Editor Options dialog box. You can modify the material in the selected sample slot by using the options in the rollouts. For example, you can change the color of the material by adjusting the Diffuse color in the Basic Parameters rollout.

Each sample slot initially uses a sphere as the sample object to preview the material. You can change the sample object via the Sample Type flyout button (▣) and selecting a new type.

Standard Material Color Components

The way that you see objects in the real world, and the way that 3ds Max mimics the process, is when your eyes catch the light that bounces off surfaces. When you see color, you see the light that hits the surfaces, and then diffuses in all directions; the rays that hit your eyes define the object's color. Light also reflects off surfaces and directly into your eyes, creating a glint, or specular highlight. In 3ds Max, the materials that you apply, along with the lights in your scene, determine how objects appear when rendered.

To create a realistic object, you must consider how the object's appearance changes, based on how it reflects light. You specify how a material reflects light by setting the different color component values — *Diffuse, Ambient,* and *Specular* — in the Basic Parameters rollout in the Material Editor. The default material type in 3ds Max is the Standard material, which provides a single, uniform color for the surface of an object.

You set the values for a color component by selecting the color swatch next to the corresponding component. This opens the Color Selector dialog box, where you select colors based on their RGB (Red, Green, Blue) or HSV (Hue, Saturation, Value) components, or by picking the color from a graphic and adjusting the Whiteness and Blackness values.

Color Components

Component	*Description*
Ambient	The object's color when it is in shadow. The object color is illuminated with indirect light instead of direct light.
Diffuse	The object's color under direct lighting. The diffuse color is normally the color used to describe an object. When rendered, this color may appear different, depending on the hue of the light that illuminates it.
Specular	The highlight color on a shiny surface. This typically matches the color of the primary light source. For example, to simulate bright sunlight, you can use a specular color of very pale yellow. The Specular Level value determines the brightness of the Specular highlight.
Opacity	The amount of light that is unable to pass through an object. Use the Opacity field to control the transparency of an object.
Self-Illumination	The color that apparently illuminates the surface of the object. As you increase the Self-Illumination value, both the shadows on the object and the surface texture are reduced. Self-illumination does not illuminate other objects and does not add light energy to the scene.
Filter	The color of the surface of an object that is visible through a transparent object. This parameter is set in the Extended Parameters rollout.

continued

Understanding the Material Editor *(Continued)*

Material Editor Tools

The Material Editor provides two different toolbars that contain buttons to control the materials and maps that you assign to each sample slot. The buttons are divided into a horizontal and a vertical toolbar. Some of the buttons on these toolbars are on flyouts that provide additional button options.

Vertical Toolbar Buttons

Button Name	*Image*	*Description*
Sample Type		Determines the shape of the object that displays in the sample slot. By default, the shape is a Sphere. To select a different shape, click and hold the button and then select another shape from the flyout button options. You can also choose a custom sample object in the Material Editor Options dialog box.
Backlight		Toggles a second light on and off, which originates behind the object in the sample slot.
Background		Displays a checkered background in the sample slot to make it easier to see the effects of the Opacity settings. You can also add custom background images for the sample slots.
Sample UV Tiling		Adjusts the tiling of a mapped material on the object in the sample slot. The default option has no tiling. This does not affect how the map applies to an object. To add tiling, click and hold the button, and then select the appropriate button from the flyout menu. For example, the 2x2 button displays the map four times — twice in the U dimension and twice in the V dimension. For more information on using maps in materials, see Chapter 15.
Video Color Check		Checks the selected material to ensure that it does not contain any colors that are not supported by the NTSC and PAL formats. These are the standard formats used to display broadcast television images.
Make Preview		Creates a preview of an animated material. Flyout options allow you to play and save the preview.
Options		Displays the Material Editor Options dialog box, where you can control how maps and materials display in the sample slots. The dialog box includes options for selecting both a custom background image and a sample object.
Select by Material		Selects all objects in the scene using the material in the currently selected sample slot.
Material/Map Navigator		Displays a dialog box where you can view a tree containing the different sub-materials or map channels for the selected material. Selecting a sub-material or map causes the sample slot to show the settings for that sub-material or map.

Horizontal Toolbar Buttons		
Button Name	**Image**	**Description**
Get Material		Opens the Material/Map Browser, which has different material and map types and sources that you can add to a material or sample slot. For more information on using the Material/Map Browser, see Chapter 15.
Put Material to Scene		Replaces the material on all objects in the scene where it is applied. The new material is given a duplicate name.
Assign Material to Selection		Applies a material to all objects that you have selected in the scene. See the section "Apply a Material to an Object" for more information on applying materials.
Reset Map/Mtl to Default		Resets the current material back to the default values. This can apply to either the material in the sample slot or the scene, or both.
Make Material Copy		Makes the selected hot material cool by eliminating the links to objects in the scene. However, the material is still applied to the objects. After you select this button, the changes that you make to the material in the sample slot do not affect the material applied to the objects in the scene.
Make Unique		Converts an instanced copy of a sub-material or map into a unique material or map.
Put to Library		Adds the selected material to the current material library. See the section "Save a Material to a Library" for more on saving materials.
Material Effects Channel		Creates a unique channel ID for applying post-processing effects. To set the channel ID, click and hold the button to view 15 additional channels.
Show Map in Viewport		Displays the map on the surfaces of the objects in your Smooth + Highlights rendered viewport. For more on the different viewport rendering options, see Chapter 1.
Show End Result		When toggled on, the material displays in the sample slot with all maps applied. When toggled off (), the sample slot displays the material or map at the current level only.
Go to Parent		Moves you up one level when working with maps or compound materials. For example, when you work at the Diffuse Color map level for a Standard material, this button moves you back up to the top level of the material.
Go to Sibling		When you work with maps or compound materials, this moves to the next map or material at the same level. For example, at the Diffuse Color map level for a Standard material, this button moves you to the next map level that contains a map.
Pick Material from Object		Click this button, and then click an object to fill the current sample slot with the material from that object.

Understanding the Material Shaders

You can use the Material shader to change the appearance of a standard object. A shader defines how the material reacts to light that hits its surfaces. The Standard material includes eight different shaders, each with its own algorithm that defines the transitions between light and dark object areas. The Shader Basic Parameters rollout controls how 3ds Max shades the object. The eight shaders are Anisotropic, Blinn, Metal, Multi-Layer, Oren-Nayar-Blinn, Phong, Strauss, and Translucent Shader. By default, all Standard material uses the Blinn shader.

When you select a shader, a shader-specific rollout appears under the Shader Basic Parameters rollout. You use this rollout to set the color component parameters — Ambient, Diffuse, Filter, Opacity, and Self-Illumination — for the selected shader. You can also control a shader's specular highlight brightness using the Specular Level and glossiness values. See the section "Understanding the Material Editor" for more on component parameters. You can also lock some color components together so that changing one component automatically changes another. A small blank button on the right side of most parameters has maps for this color component value.

This section first reviews the Shader Basic Parameters rollout and its options. It then presents the components common to all eight shaders and then discusses each of the eight shader-specific rollouts.

The Shader Basic Parameters Rollout

A Shader Drop-Down List Box

Shows the eight available shaders, each of which you can use to define your material. The Blinn shader is the default.

B Wire

Creates a wireframe surface when the object is rendered with the specified shader parameters. The edges of the objects are shown as lines and the surfaces are not displayed.

C 2-Sided

Applies the material to both sides of each surface.This is especially useful when you are working with transparent materials, such as glass or objects with openings.

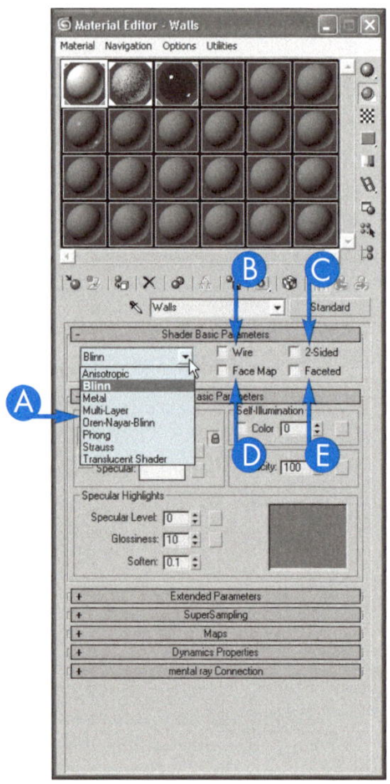

D Face Map

Applies the material to each face of the object. If the material includes a map, the map is applied to each face separately. See the section ìU nderstanding the Material Editor" for an explanation of maps.

E Faceted

Causes 3ds Max to ignore any smoothing of the object surface, thus making the object faceted. Use this option to make your objects appear to be made of flat, rather than curved, surfaces.

Components Common to All Shaders

A Color Components

Show the Hue or settings for each of the material's color components. The color displays on the color swatch next to the parameter. For more on the Standard Material color components, see the section "Understanding the Material Editor."

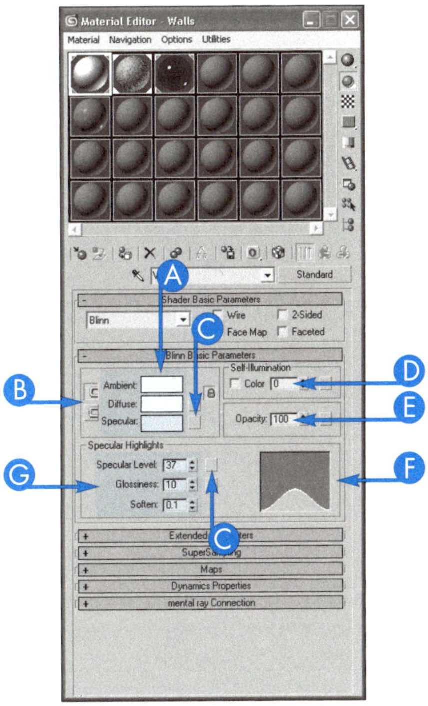

B Color Locks

Locks two color components together so that changes made to one component are reflected in the other.

C Component Map Button

If blank, it launches the Material/Map Browser, where you can select a map for the component. When a component uses a map, an M displays on the button. Clicking the M button takes you to the controls for that map.

D Self-Illumination

The amount that an object's surfaces appear to glow. The Self-Illumination color value fades any shadows or textures on the object as you increase the value.

E Opacity

Determines the transparency of the material. At 100 the object is 100 percent opaque, and at zero it is 100 percent transparent. Transparent objects can still display specular highlights.

F Highlight Graph

Illustrates the effects of the Specular Highlight values. The Glossiness value affects the curve's width and the highlight's size. The Specular Level affects the curve's height and the highlight's intensity. The Anisotropy and Orientation values, where available, adjusts how oblong the highlight is and the direction that it points.

G Specular Highlight Settings

Control the size and shape of highlights. Parameter values vary, based on the selected shader. Chrome spheres have bright, small specular highlights, and bowling balls have dimmer, larger highlights.

continued

Understanding the Material Shaders *(Continued)*

Anisotropic Shader

This creates long, elliptical highlights to simulate realistic materials for glass bottles or textured metal surfaces. The Anisotropy value controls the shape of the highlight by increasing or decreasing the highlight size in one of the two axis directions. The higher the Anisotropy value, the more elliptical the highlights are; a value of zero creates circular highlights. Changing the Orientation value changes the highlight direction. For this shader, you can specify the component colors for Ambient, Diffuse, Specular, and Self-Illumination in the Anisotropic Basic Parameters rollout. You can also change the Opacity and Diffuse Level values.

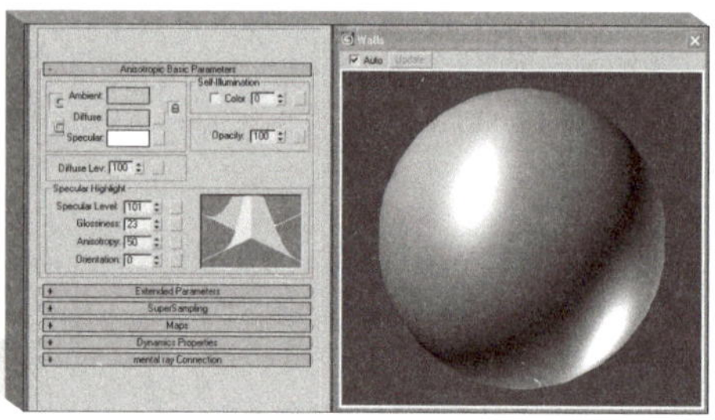

Blinn Shader

The default shader for all Standard materials, this is a good, general-purpose shader that produces soft, round Specular highlights. You can specify the component colors for Ambient, Diffuse, Specular, and Self-Illumination in the Blinn Basic Parameters rollout. You can also specify the Opacity level for the object surface. The Blinn shader is similar to the Phong shader, with the Blinn shader producing rounder highlights with the same parameter values.

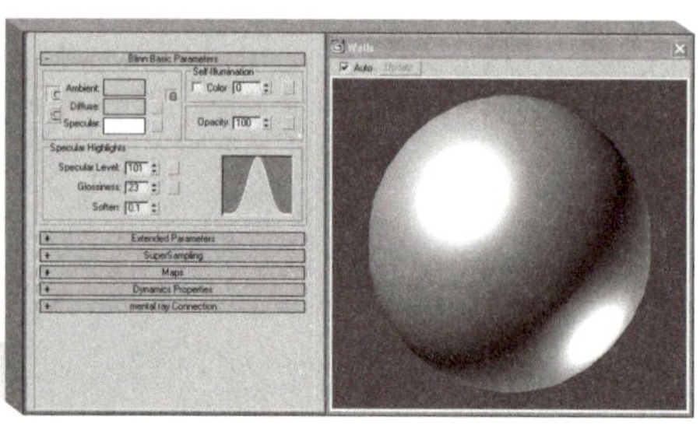

Metal Shader

This simulates metallic surfaces, determining the Specular color as a value between the Diffuse color and the color of the light. With the Metal shader, the Glossiness spinner allows you to control the size and shape of the specular areas. With this shader, you can specify the component colors for Ambient, Diffuse, and Self-Illumination, as well as the Opacity level. However, you cannot specify a Specular color.

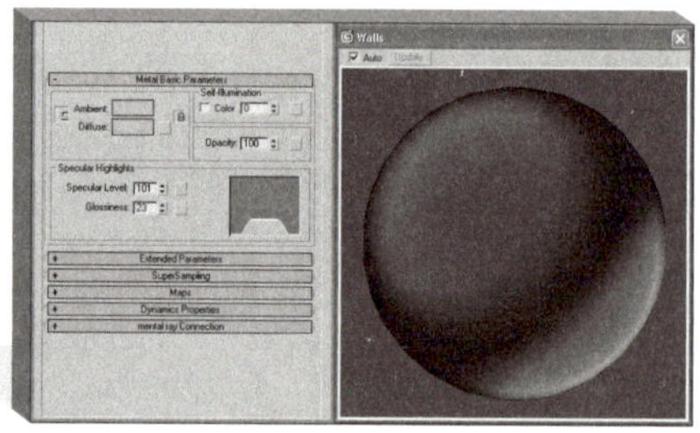

Multi-Layer Shader

This shader creates two different anisotropic highlights in your material and is useful when you have complex, highly polished surfaces similar to that of a new car. When the highlight layers cross, the colors of the two shaders blend together. Each highlight has its own Specular layer — which you adjust by specifying the Color, Level, Glossiness, Anisotropy, and Orientation values — and its own highlight graph. You can make the highlights on a layer more circular by setting the value of the Anisotropy parameter closer to zero.

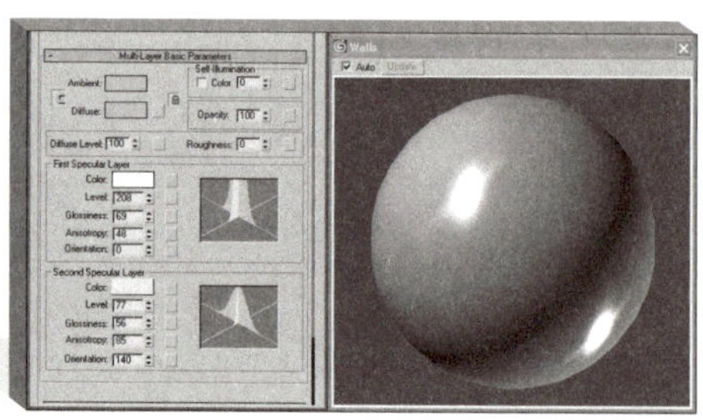

Oren-Nayar-Blinn Shader

This shader creates material with a matte finish, and with more subtle highlights. You can also apply the shader to surfaces such as textiles, carpet, and even skin. This shader has the same color component parameters as the Blinn shader, as well as additional parameters for setting the Diffuse Level and Roughness.

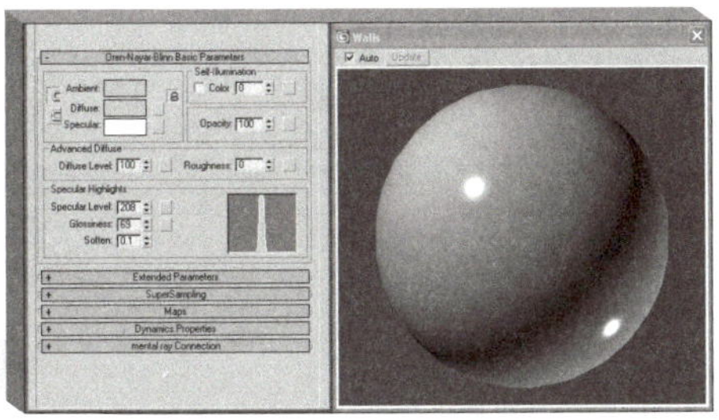

Phong Shader

This is another general-purpose shader that creates soft, round highlights just like the Blinn shader. In fact, both shaders provide the same parameters for setting the color component values. Phong was actually the default shader before Blinn came along, but its highlights are not as soft or round as the Blinn shader. With the Phong shader, you can specify the component colors for Ambient, Diffuse, Specular, and Self-Illumination. You also specify the Opacity level for the object surface.

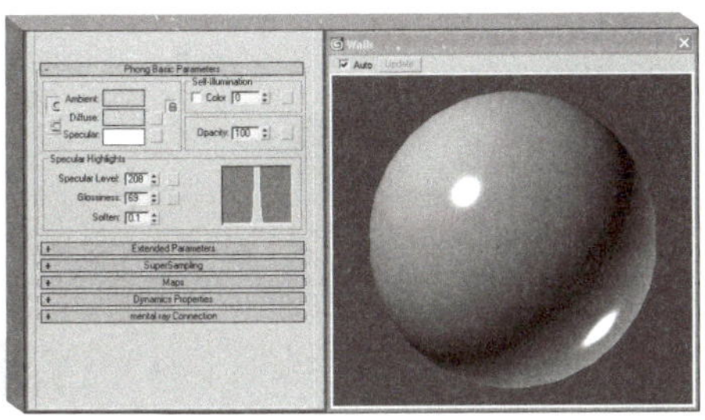

Strauss Shader

This shader offers another method for applying a metallic appearance to materials. Because the Strauss shader has only four parameter values, you may find it easier to work with than the Metal shader. However, the Strauss shader does not have the same level of control as the Metal shader. With this shader, you select the Color, Glossiness, Metalness, and Opacity. To create a more metallic appearance, increase the Glossiness value to create more visible highlights. You can also increase the Metalness parameter to make the highlights appear more focused.

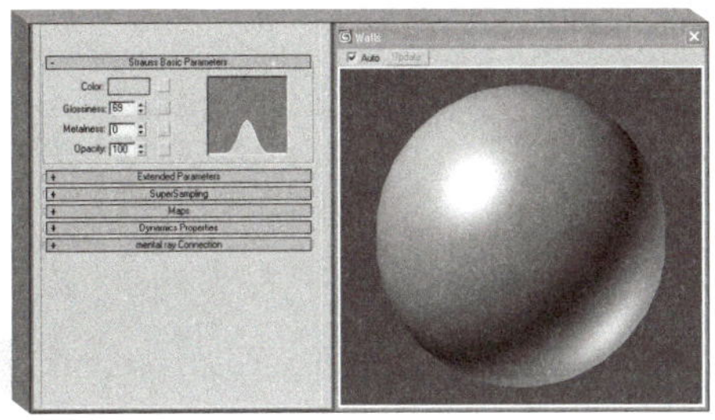

Translucent Shader

You use this shader to create a material through which light can pass. This works well when you want to create a semi-transparent material, such as frosted glass, where it appears to have illumination from behind. In addition to using all the same parameters as the Blinn shader, the Translucent shader also has Transparency settings for specifying the Translucent color that illuminates from within the object.

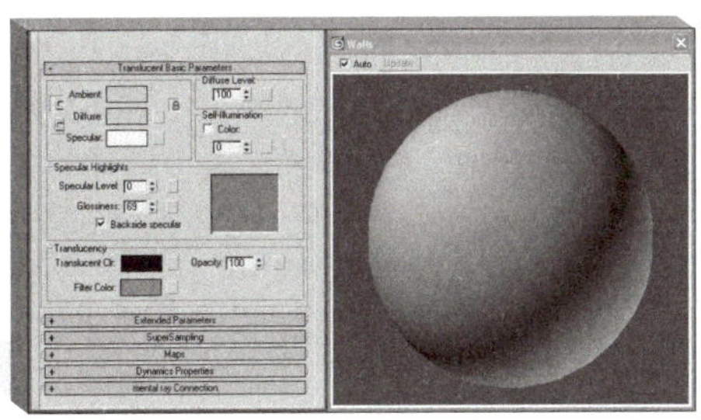

Create a Standard Material

You can create new materials for objects in your scene in the Material Editor, for example, to make your object look like metal or glass. Once you create a material, you can apply it to objects in your scene.

By default, all of the sample slots contain materials with the Standard material type and Blinn shader. You can modify any one of the default slots to create your new material by selecting a sample slot at the top of the Material Editor. The slot becomes both the current slot and the location where 3ds Max stores the new material. As you modify the material parameters, 3ds Max updates the results on the sample object.

With the Standard material type, you can design materials with a single color or Diffuse Color map. You adjust the material's appearance by first selecting a shader and then adjusting the values for each parameter, as described in the section "Understanding the Material Shaders."

To modify the material type of the object, you select any of the other available material types. Because 3ds Max has a wide range of materials in libraries, you do not have to design all the materials yourself. For more on material libraries, see the section "Save a Material to a Library." For more about selecting a material type in the Material/Map Browser, see Chapter 15.

Create a Standard Material

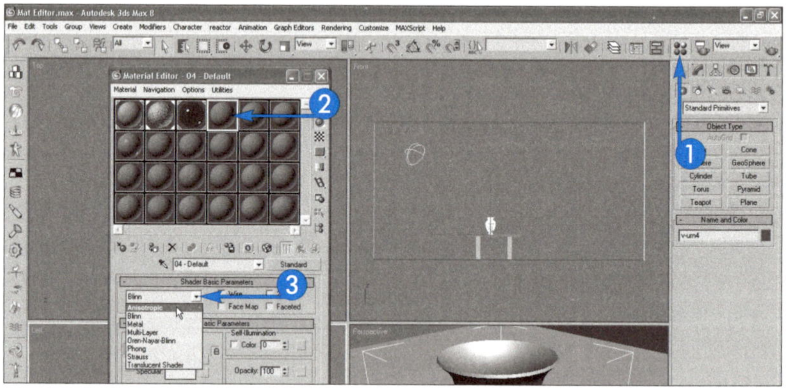

1 Click the Material Editor button (▦).

The Material Editor opens.

2 Click a sample slot for the new material.

3 Click here and select the desired shader.

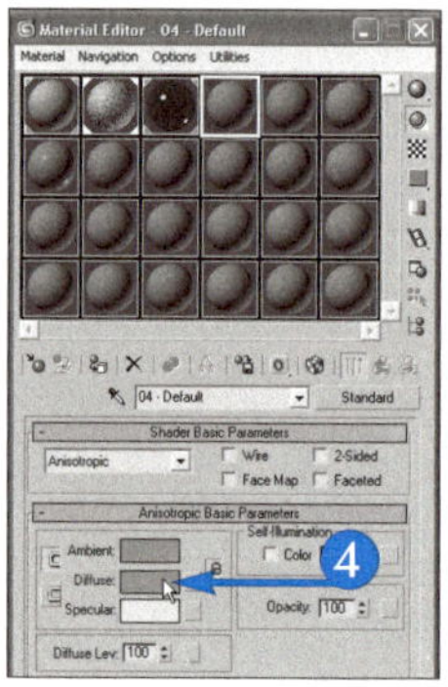

The Shader Basic Parameters rollout reflects the shader selection.

4 Click one of the color swatches.

The Color Selector dialog box appears.

5 Adjust the color by clicking and dragging the sliders.

You can adjust sliders for: Red, Green, and Blue; Hue, Saturation, and Value; or Hue, Whiteness, and Blackness.

You can use any combination of sliders to adjust your color. All the sliders are interdependent.

6 Click Close.

The color is added to the selected color swatch, and the sample material is updated.

7 Repeat steps 4 to 6 for the other color components.

You can unlock the Ambient and Diffuse colors by clicking if you want.

8 Type a value in the Specular Level field.

9 Type a value in the Glossiness field.

If available, specify other parameters.

The material updates to reflect the parameter settings.

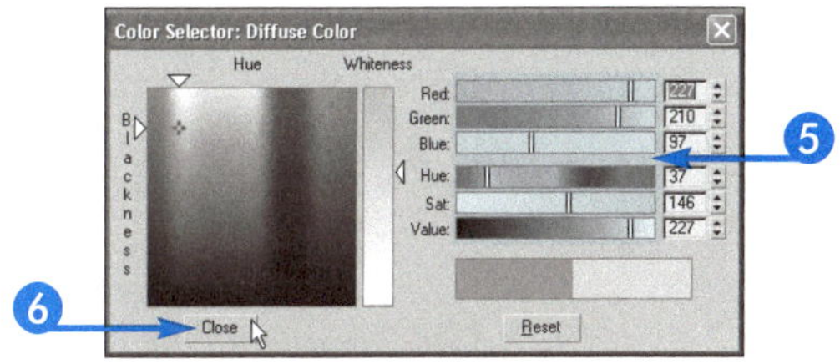

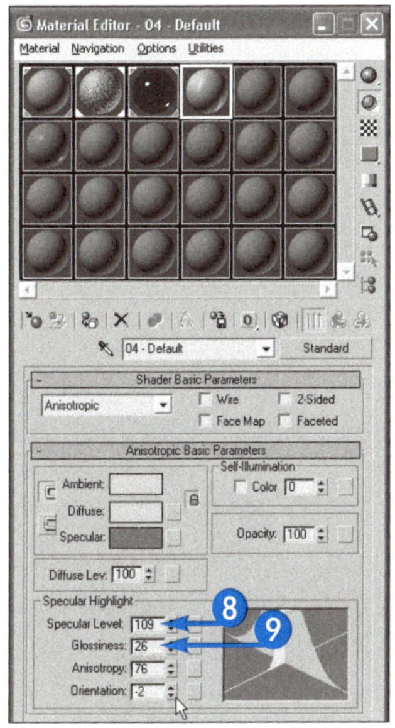

MASTER IT

What happens if I apply a map to a color component?

This depends on the component to which you apply it. For example, the Diffuse Color map applies the image to the surface of the object, while the other map channels determine how much the related settings affect the material. You can assign a map to the parameters that are followed by a small blank button. When you click the button, the Material/Map Browser opens, and you can select the map for the component. When you select a map, an M displays on the button to indicate that the parameter is using a map. Clicking an M button displays the parameter rollouts for modifying the corresponding map. You can also assign maps in the Maps rollout.

Can I use a different sample object to view my material?

Yes, you can create a custom object that you can load and use in a sample slot. To load a sample object, you must first create a .max file that contains a single object that can fit inside a 100-by-100-unit cube. This is the object size that you use for sample objects. Load the sample object into your project by clicking the Options button ( ) to display the Material Editor Options dialog box. Click File Name and select your file. In the Sample Type flyout, click Custom. Your custom object displays in the selected sample slot.

Apply a Material to an Object

You can apply previously created materials that are in the sample slots to objects in your scene. 3ds Max refers to the applied material as *hot,* meaning that any changes that you make to that material automatically apply to the objects that have that material assigned to them. 3ds Max marks the sample slot with triangles in each corner to indicate that the material is hot.

You can apply a material either by dragging it from the viewport and dropping in onto an object, or by using the Assign Material to Selection button in the horizontal toolbar. If you use the Assign Material to Selection button, 3ds Max applies the selected material to all selected objects in the scene.

If you drag and drop the material onto a selection of objects, 3ds Max gives you the option of either applying the material to all the selected objects, or only to the object on which you dropped it. You can also drag the material onto an object that is not selected in the viewports. You can even drag and drop materials onto sub-object selection sets of faces or polygons.

Apply a Material to an Object

Using the Assign Material to Selection Button

1. Select the objects to which you want to apply the material.

2. In the Material Editor, click the sample slot containing the material.

Note: *For information on selecting objects, see Chapter 2. See the section "Create a Standard Material" for more on the Material Editor.*

3. Click the Assign Material to Selection button ().

   3ds Max applies the material to the selected objects.

   - 3ds Max marks the sample slot with triangles in the corners to indicate that the material is hot.

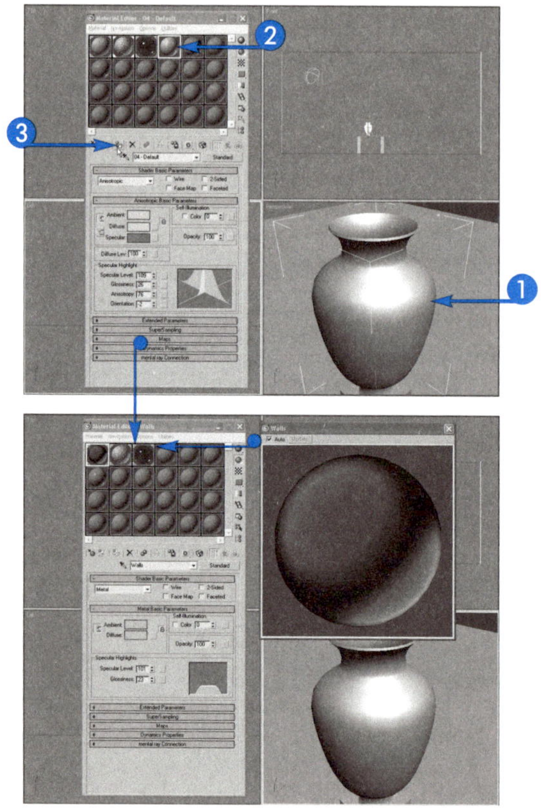

Drag Material onto an Object

1. In the Material Editor, click the sample slot that contains the material that you want to apply.

Note: *See the section "Create a Standard Material" for more on the Material Editor.*

2. Click and drag the material onto an object in a viewport.
3. Release the mouse.

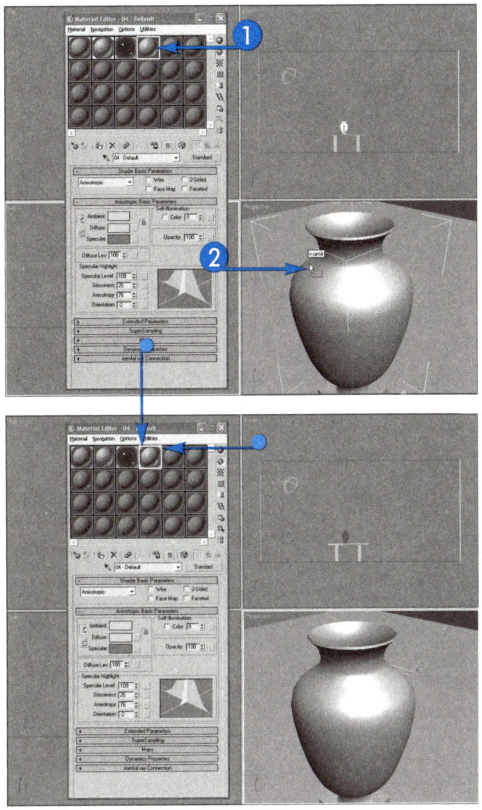

3ds Max applies the material to the selected object.

- 3ds Max marks the sample slot with triangles in the corners to indicate that the material is hot.

MASTER IT

How do I keep from changing an object when I modify a material?

When you assign a material to an object in a scene, 3ds Max marks the material as hot. This means that any changes that you make to this material immediately apply to the object in the scene. If you want to break the link between the material and the object, then you must make the material cool by removing all links. This allows you to modify the material without affecting any objects in your scene. To cool a material, select the sample slot containing the material and then click the Make Material Copy button (). This copies the material within the sample slot while maintaining its properties and name but removing all links to objects.

How do I know which objects are using what material in my scene?

You can select all the objects in your scene that are using a specific material, as long as that material is hot. To select the objects, click the sample slot containing the material in the Material Editor, and then click the Select by Material button (). The Select Objects dialog box appears with names of all the objects in the scene. The objects using that material are highlighted. To select all those objects, click Select. Only the objects that are highlighted in the Select Objects dialog box are selected in your scene.

Save a Material to a Library

When you create materials in the Material Editor, you can place them on the objects in your scene, or you can store them in a material library. Storing materials in a material library is a simple way to maintain them outside the Material Editor.

3ds Max maintains a default material library, and several specialized libraries, that contain different materials that you can use in any scene. By saving the material in a library, you and anyone with access to your files, can access your material. You may also want to create your own library with materials that are specific to your needs. By saving the material to the material library, you can reload it into the Material Editor at any time.

When you save a material, it is a good idea to give it a descriptive material name. The Put To Library dialog box shows the current name of the material, but you can assign any name. You should select a name that you can use to easily identify that material. After saving the material, you can load it into the Material Editor for any scene from the Material/Map Browser. For more information on loading a material from a library, see Chapter 15.

Save a Material to a Library

1. Click [icon] to display the Material Editor.
2. Click the sample slot containing the material that you want to save.

Note: *See the section "Create a Standard Material" for more on the Material Editor.*

3. Click the Put to Library button ([icon]).

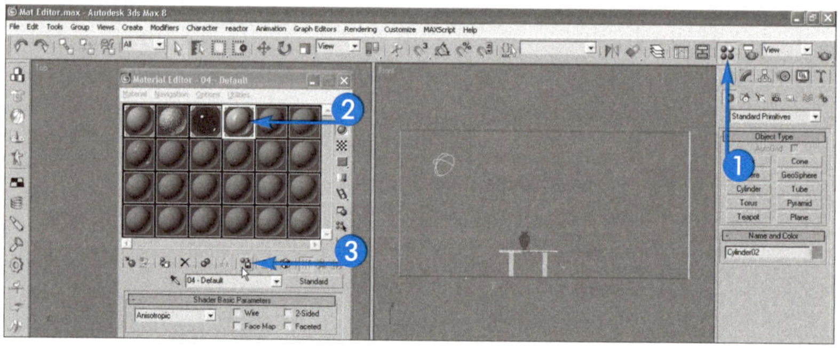

The Put To Library dialog box appears with the current material name.

4. Type the name that you want to use to identify the material.
5. Click OK.

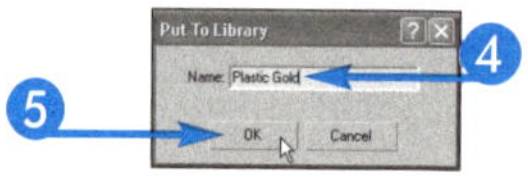

3ds Max saves the material in the current material library.

Load a Material from an Object

You can load into the Material Editor any material from any object that has an assigned material. This allows you to modify the material.

You can retrieve the material from an object using the Pick Material from Object button. Selecting this button changes the cursor to an empty eyedropper. As the cursor moves over an object with a material, it changes to a full cursor, and the name of that object displays in a tooltip next to the cursor. When you select the material, it loads into the current sample slot in the Material Editor and replaces any existing material. All of the material properties are loaded from the object, including the original material name.

When the material is loaded into the sample slot, it becomes hot. Any changes that you make to the material in the Material Editor are immediately updated on the object.

If you use the material that you load on multiple objects in your scene, 3ds Max links the material to all of those objects. Any changes that you make to the material affect not only the object that you originally selected, but all other objects with that material.

Load a Material from an Object

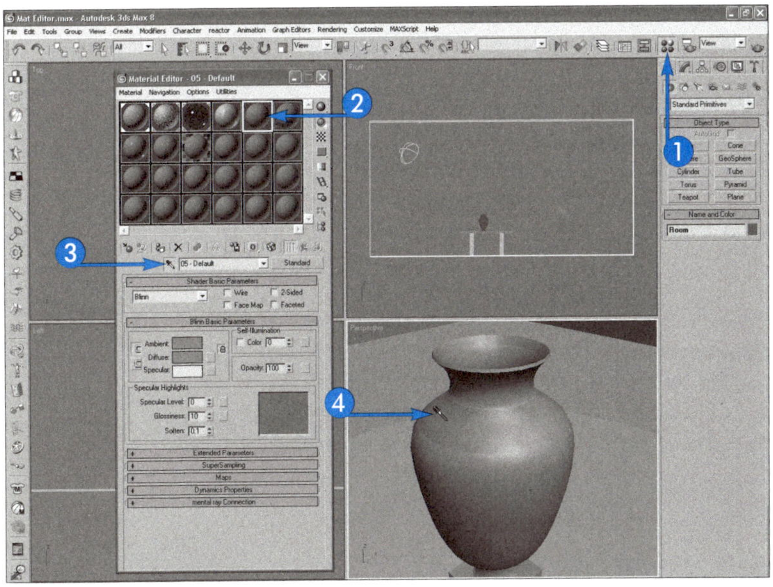

1. Click the Material Editor button to display the Material Editor.
2. Click the sample slot where you want to load the material.
3. Click the Pick Material from Object button (eyedropper).
4. Click the object in the scene with the material that you want to load.

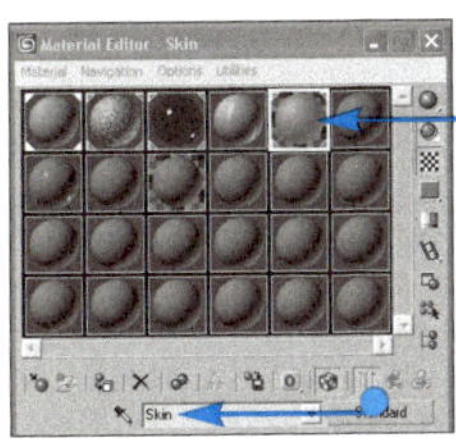

- 3ds Max loads the material into the sample slot.
- The material name changes to reflect the name of the material that was applied to the object.

Understanding Material Types

3ds Max has several different material types that you can use to create realistic materials in your scenes. You can create many different effects with the parameter options that are available for the default Standard material. However, if you want to create specific types of materials, then you may find it easier to select one of the other available material types. For example, to create the appearance of glass, you can use the Architectural material type and then select the Glass-Clear template. This allows you to quickly create a material that looks like clear glass on your object when it is rendered.

Some of the material types allow you to create compound materials that combine two or more materials together. For example, with the Blend material type, you can mix two materials on one object.

Selecting and Identifying Material Types

The available material types appear in the Material/Map Browser. Although 3ds Max provides several common material types that are always available with the Default Scanline Renderer, you can add other material types to the list, based on the selected renderer.

3ds Max uses different-colored sphere icons to identify the source of a material. Blue sphere icons indicate the common material types that are always available. If your renderer has additional material types, 3ds Max places a yellow sphere icon next to them. A material type with a pink icon allows you to create materials specific to your display driver. For example, if you use the Direct3D display driver, then the DirectX 9 material type becomes available.

Advanced Lighting Override Material

You can select the Advanced Lighting Override material to directly control the radiosity properties of a material. The effects of this material are only evident when it is used with the Radiosity or Light Tracer advanced lighting plug-ins.

Architectural Material

You can select the Architectural material to create realistic architectural materials, such as glass, metal, or painted surfaces. To create an Architectural material, you select one of the available material templates and then adjust the parameters for that template. For more information about using the Architectural material, see Chapter 16. To achieve the best effects with these materials, consider using photometric lights in your scene; you cannot achieve the desired results with standard lights.

Blend Material

The Blend material allows you to create a compound material consisting of two separate materials that are blended together on a single surface. You can control the way the materials are blended by setting the values for the Mixing Curve or by using a map to mask one of the materials. You can use the Blend material to make one surface appear to have been scraped off to expose the surface below it.

Composite Material

The Composite material allows you to create a compound material by mixing up to ten different materials together. You combine the materials by adding, subtracting, or mixing the opacity of each material. You can set the influence of one component material to dominate the material by increasing its Amount spinner; you can animate this effect to change a material's appearance.

Double-Sided Material

This material is a compound material that consists of different materials that are placed on the front and back sides of an object's faces. This material allows a 2D object to have one material on each side.

Ink 'n Paint Material

The Ink 'n Paint material allows you to create 2D cartoon-type effects. This material has flat shading with inked borders. You can set the border width or choose to have the ink appear with a varied width.

Lightscape Mtl Material

This material allows you to control how radiosity affects a material for an object by controlling the Brightness, Contrast, Ambient Light, and Bump Amount. Use this material with Autodesk's Lightscape product and not with the advanced lighting plug-ins that ship with 3ds Max.

Matte/Shadow Material

The Matte/Shadow material allows you to create a compound material to make portions of a scene invisible. This allows you to create an object that blocks geometry behind it in the scene. Even though they do not render, objects with Matte/Shadow materials can still cast and receive shadows. You can use a Matte/Shadow material to make it appear as if objects in your scene cast shadows onto surfaces that only exist in a background image.

Morpher Material

This material allows you to change the materials on an object as it morphs into a morph target. To use this material, you must associate it with an object that has the Morpher modifier applied to it. The material channels correlate with the channels included with the Morpher modifier.

Multi/Sub-Object Material

Each object can only have one material applied to it. To make it appear as if several materials are applied to a single object, you need to use the Multi/Sub-Object material. This material is composed of sub-materials that are applied to the object based on the material ID number of each face. Faces with a material ID number of one are assigned sub-material number one, and so on.

Raytrace Material

The Raytrace material allows you to create surfaces with reflections and refractions to produce realistic shiny and transparent materials in your scenes. Raytracing can add a significant amount of time to your renderings.

Shell Material

The Shell material uses a texture map when rendered using a process called "texture baking." This process combines all the textures into a single new one. You can use a Shell material to display surface texture and shadows without having lights affect the object. This can significantly decrease the amount of time required to render a scene and is especially useful in video game production.

Shellac Material

This material is a compound material that combines two materials by placing one on top of the other. The colors from the top "shellac" material are mixed with the base material colors, and you control the amount of color blending between the two materials. The Shellac material gives the effect that one material is coating the other, similar to a thin coat of paint or gloss.

Top/Bottom

The Top/Bottom material is a compound material that assigns different materials to the top and bottom of an object. You define how much the two materials are blended together at the position where they meet and the position where the two materials are blended. For example, a pole can appear dark and wet near the water from which it extends, and light and dry near the top.

Change the Material Type

You can change the material type for any material in the sample slots in the Material Editor. This allows you to select a material type that creates the most realistic material for your scene. For example, if you want to create an architectural product, such as glass, you can select an Architectural material type. To combine materials, you need to create one of the compound material types, such as the Blend.

You can select a new material type from the Material/Map Browser, which lists all the available material types. The material types may change, depending upon the Renderer that you have selected, and your video display driver. See the section "Understanding Material Types" for more information.

If you select a compound material type, then 3ds Max prompts you to either keep the existing material as a sub-material or to discard it. When you select the material type, the name of the material type appears on the Material Type button. This allows you to see which material type you have selected. The rollouts on the Material Editor change to reflect the controls that are available for the selected material type.

Change the Material Type

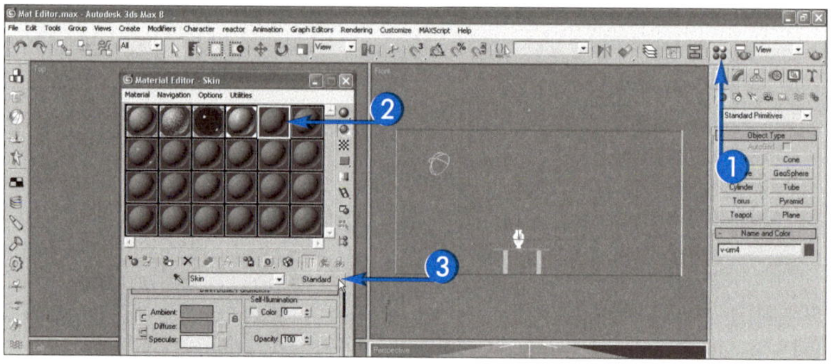

1. Click to open the Material Editor.
2. Click the sample slot where you want to create the material.
3. Click the Material Type button.

Note: *See the section "Create a Standard Material" for more information on the Material Editor.*

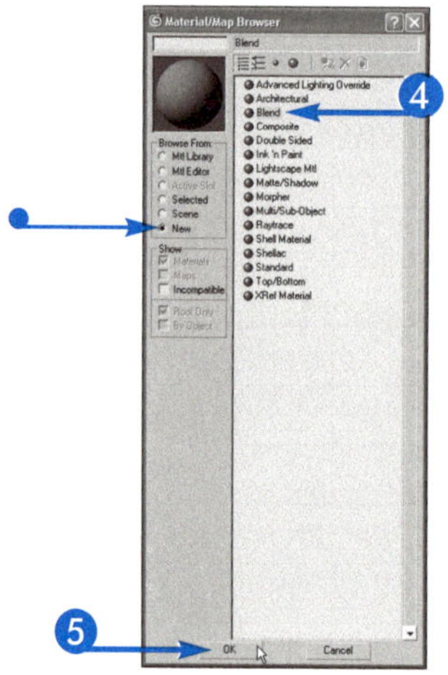

The Material/Map Browser displays a list of the available material types.

- If the list is not displayed, then click the New option (○ changes to ◉) in the Browse From group.

4. Click a material type.
5. Click OK.

If you selected a compound material, the Replace Material dialog box appears.

6. Click the "Keep old material as sub-material?" option to keep the old material (○ changes to ◉).

- To completely replace the existing material, you can click the "Discard old material?" option (○ changes to ◉).

7. Click OK.

- The rollouts on the Material Editor change to reflect your selection.

The material sample changes to reflect the selection.

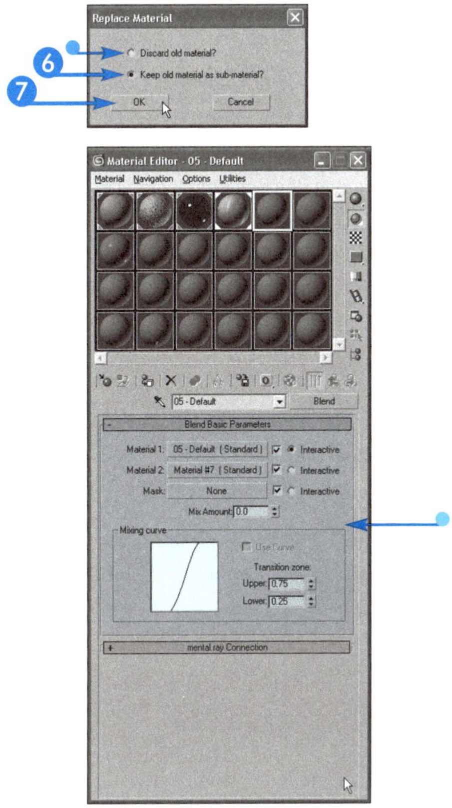

What happens to a hot material when I change the material type?

▼ If you have a material that is hot because it is linked to one or more objects in your scene, then the objects remain linked to that material, even when you change the material type. This means that the new material type is immediately applied to the linked objects. If you do not want the material type to change for objects in your scene, then you need to remove the linking by changing the material to make it cool. To cool the material, click the Make Material Copy button (▣) to copy that material into the selected sample slot. You can also click Reset Map/Mtl to Default Settings (☒) to clear the material from the slot.

Can I undo the material type change?

▼ No, when you select a new material type, you cannot undo that action. The reason is that the parameters of the original material type are lost. If you have applied the material to any objects in your scene, the changes are lost for those objects as well. If you want to use that material again, you should save it to a material library. That way, you can reload the material type at any time. See the section "Save a Material to a Library" for more information on saving materials.

Animate a Material

You can animate materials using the Auto Key button in the same way that you animate an object's parameters. 3ds Max allows you to animate almost all of the parameter values of a material. For example, you can animate the color of an object by changing the Diffuse color between different frames. When you do this, 3ds Max animates the color change by fading from one color to the next between the keys. You create the animation by creating keyframes when you want the animation to occur, and then by changing the parameters of the material at that time.

As with object animation, 3ds Max interpolates the values for each frame between the keys that you specify. Animated parameters for a material are marked with red brackets in the Material Editor so that you can quickly identify which parameters change over time.

A material's animation tracks are separate from the animation tracks of the object in the Curve Editor and Dope Sheet Editor. If you view keys for each frame, you can see that separate keys exist for the animation changes. For information on the Curve Editor and Dope Sheet Editor, see Chapters 11 and 12.

Animate a Material

1. Click [icon] to open the Material Editor.
2. Select the material that you want to animate.
3. Click the Auto Key button.

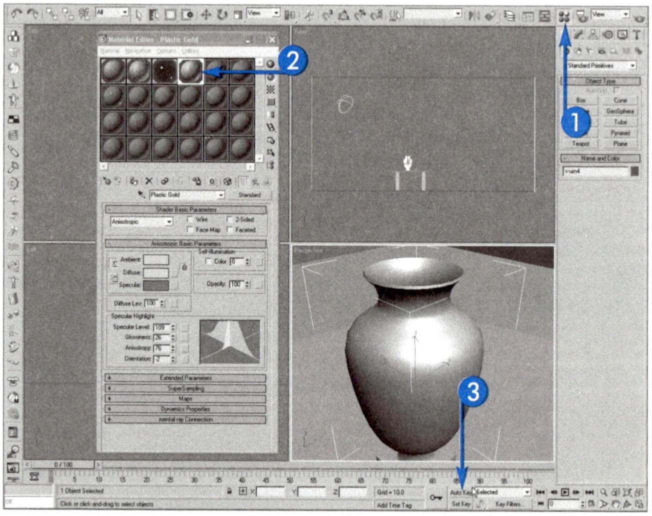

The borders around the sample slot, Auto Key button, and Time Slider bar display in red.

4. Click and drag the Time Slider to the location on the Timeline where you want the material to change.
5. Modify the material by typing to change any of its parameters.

The material changes in the sample slot.

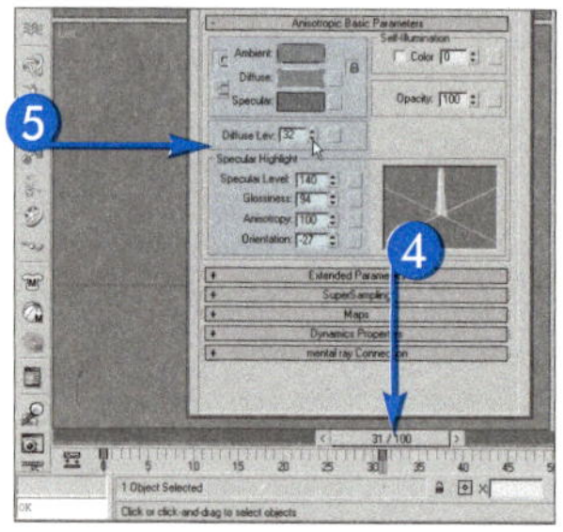

6. Repeat steps 4 and 5 to add additional keyframes.
7. Click Auto Key to turn it off.

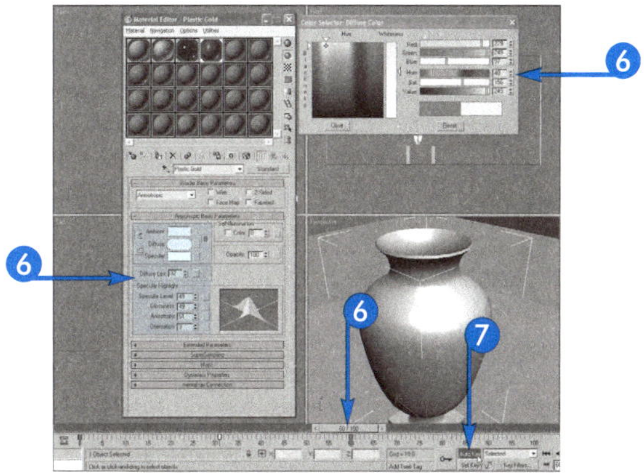

- You can drag the Time Slider to see the material change in the sample slot.

Note: *See the section "Apply Material to an Object" for information on applying the material to objects in a scene.*

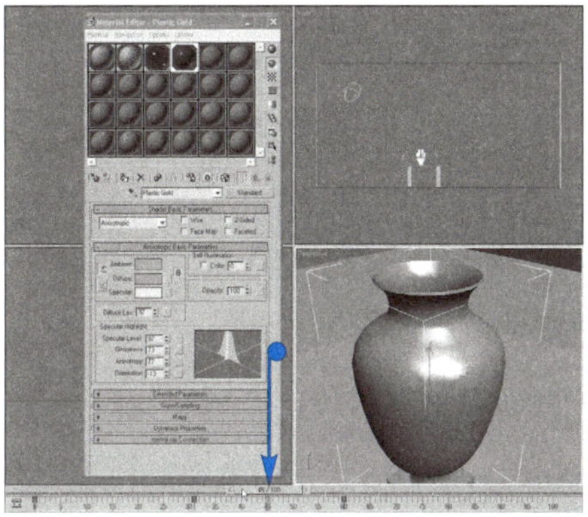

MASTER IT

Can I switch material types during an animation?

Yes and no. You cannot change the actual material type during an animation. To create the effect of switching material types, you need to use one of the compound materials — such as Blend — and then animate the parameters related to each sub-material. For example, with the Blend material, the Mix Amount parameter indicates the amount of each sub-material that is mixed into the material. If you set a Mix Amount of zero in the first frame, then you can see 100 percent of the first sub-material. If you set the Mix Amount to 100, then you can see all of the second material. By animating the Mix Amount, you can animate a change between the two materials.

Can I use animation files as maps in my materials?

Yes, you can use either AVI or MOV files as maps in your materials. You can use the Time rollout, located at the bottom of the Material Editor when modifying a map's parameters, to control the animation of the map. This allows you to specify the frame where you want the animation to begin, as well as the playback speed. To specify the start of the animation, type a frame number in the Start Frame field. To control the speed at which the animation occurs on the material, specify the Playback Rate. A Playback Rate value of one plays the material animation at one animation frame per one scene frame. To play it faster, increase the number.

Preview a Material

You can preview an animated material before you apply it to an object. This is especially useful when you want to see how the animation will look, but you do not want to go through the long process of rendering.

You can specify the parameters that create the preview by using the Create Material Preview dialog box, which you access through the Make Preview button. For example, although 3ds Max creates the material animation for the entire range of frames by default, you may only want to preview part of the animation. Select the Custom Range option to preview only specific frames in the Active Time Segment.

You can also control the playback rate of the animation using two options. The Every Nth Frame field allows you to sample the frames. If you specify a value of five, then you see every fifth frame of the animation. You can change the playback rate by specifying the number of frames per second to play in the Playback FPS field. The other option that you can control is the resolution of the playback. The default image size is 100, which is equal to a resolution of 101 by 99 pixels.

Preview a Material

1. Click to open the Material Editor.
2. Select the sample slot that you want to preview.

Note: *See the section "Animate a Material" for more information.*

3. Click the Make Preview button ( ).

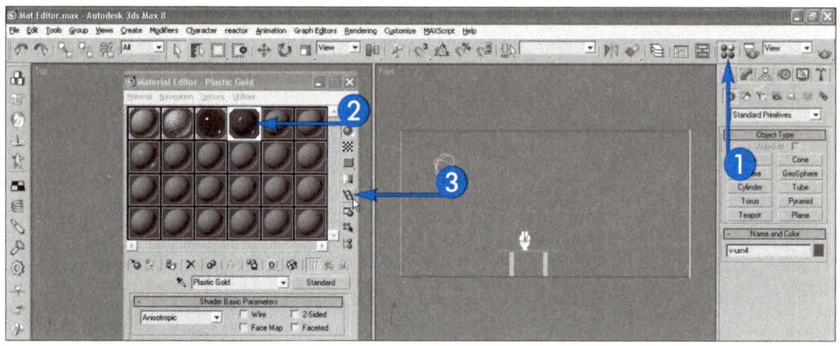

The Create Material Preview dialog box appears.

4. Select a Preview Range (○ changes to ◉).

   You can click Active Time Segment to preview the entire animation.

   You can click Custom Range and specify the range of frames for the animation.

   - If desired, you can type a different value in the Every Nth Frame, Playback FPS, and Percent of Output fields.

5. Click OK.

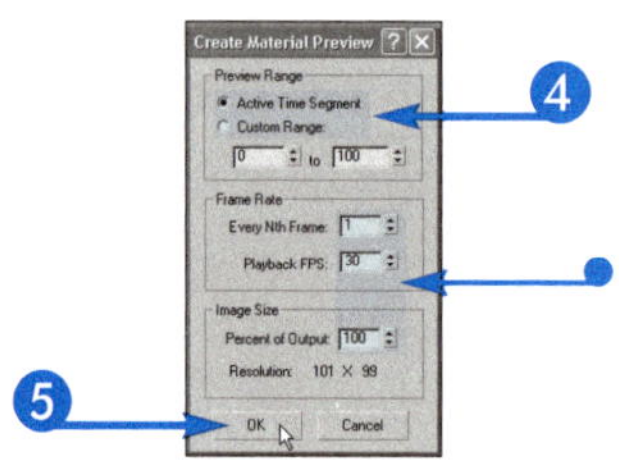

- As the preview renders, the viewports display the current scene, and the Creating Material Preview progress bar displays at the bottom.
- To cancel the process, you can click Cancel.

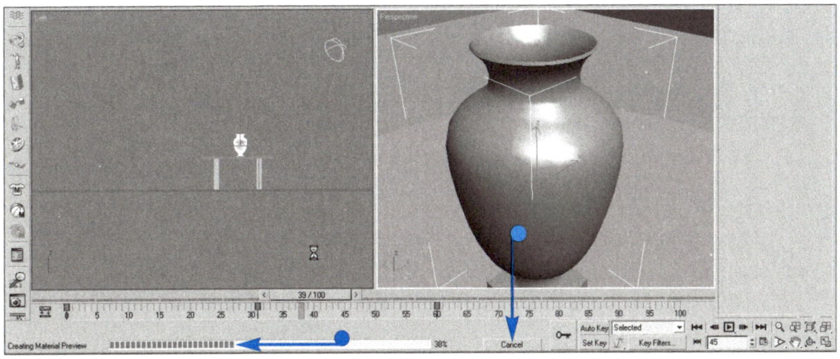

When the preview file is created, the Windows Media Player opens and plays the animation.

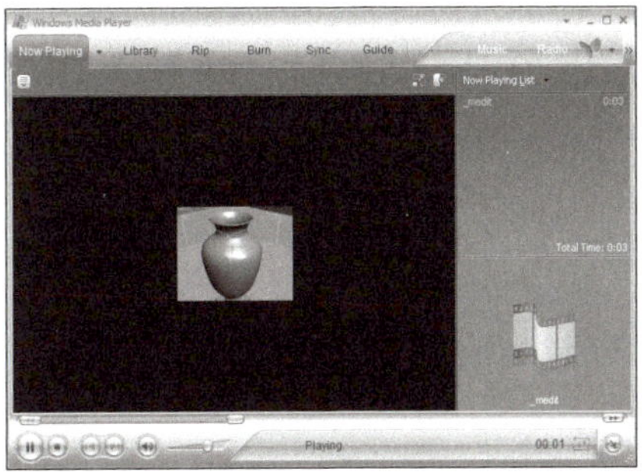

MASTER IT

I closed the Windows Media Player. How do I replay the preview animation of the material that I created?

▼ When you create a preview of an animated material, 3ds Max creates an AVI file containing the animation and stores it in the \previews subdirectory of your 3ds Max program files folder. The default name assigned to the animation file is _medit.avi. 3ds Max replays the file each time you generate a new preview animation. You can replay the last animation that you created by clicking the Play Preview button ( ) on the Preview flyout. 3ds Max automatically loads the last animated material file in the Windows Media Player so that you can replay it.

How do I save a preview?

▼ The Play Preview option only replays the last animated material preview that you created. If you want to be able to replay a preview after rendering other previews, without re-rendering it, then you can save it under a different name. To save the current preview, click the Save Preview button ( ) on the Preview flyout. This displays the Save Preview As dialog box. Navigate to the folder where you want to save the preview. Type the name that you want to use to save the file in the File name field and then click Save.

Create a Multi/Sub-Object Material

You can apply different materials to different portions of an object by using the sub-object levels of the object to specify where you want to place these materials. For example, you may want the cushion of a chair to be a different material than the chair arms. When you apply the materials to an object in this manner, you create a Multi/Sub-Object material.

If you are working with an Editable Poly, you can select the Polygon sub-object and apply materials to a selection of polygons. To select the different sub-object levels, you must display the Modify panel for the selected object. If the object is an Editable Mesh or Editable Poly, you can select the sub-object level that you want to use. If the object is not a polygonal mesh object, you must convert it or apply an Edit Mesh or Edit Poly modifier to it in order to gain access to the sub-object levels.

After selecting the sub-object level, you can select the portion of the object where you want to apply one material. When you assign the material, it is only applied to the selected faces of the object.

Create a Multi/Sub-Object Material

1. Select an Editable Poly object to which you want to apply the materials.
2. Click the Modify panel tab ( ).

   The Modify panel opens.
3. Click the Material Editor button ( ).

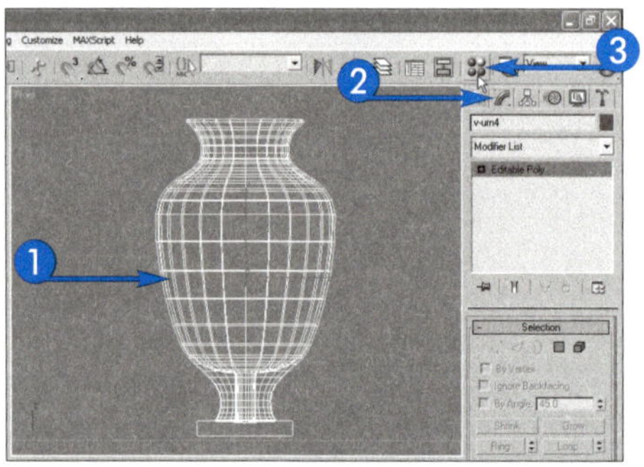

   The Material Editor appears.
4. Click the sub-object level that you want to use to add materials to the object.
5. Select the portion of the object where you want to apply the first material.

   To select multiple portions, press and hold Ctrl while you select them.
6. In the Material Editor, click a sample slot and drag it to the selected part of the object.

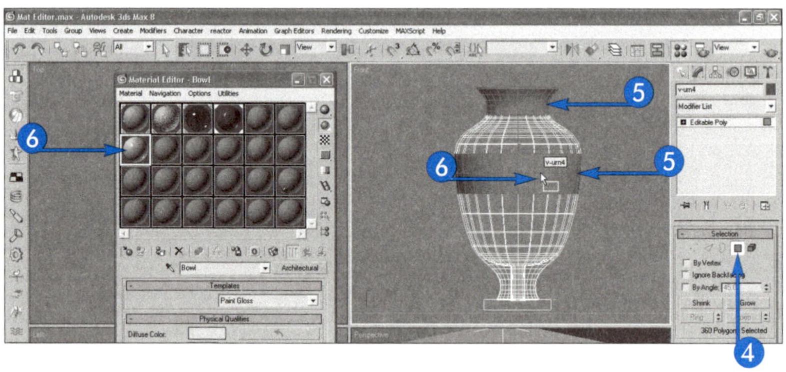

3ds Max adds the material to the selected portions of the object.

7. Repeat steps 4 to 6 for each additional sub-material.
8. Click here to exit any sub-object mode.
9. Select an unused sample slot.
10. Click the Get Material button ( ).
11. Click the Selected option in the Browse From section (○ changes to ◉).
12. Double-click the material in the list.

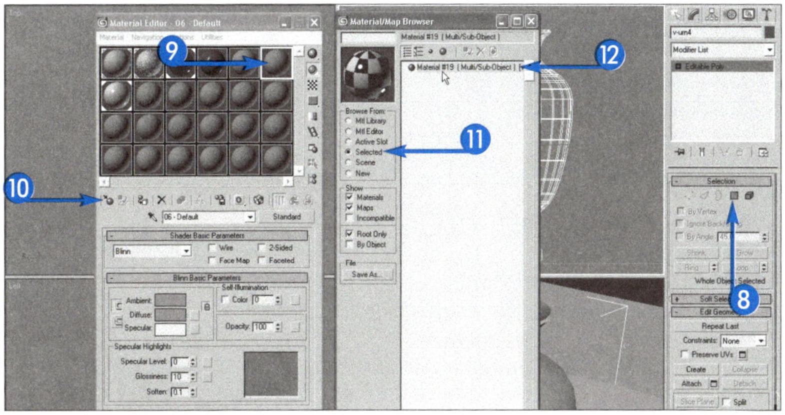

- The Multi/Sub-Object material appears in the sample slot.

The object now contains multiple materials.

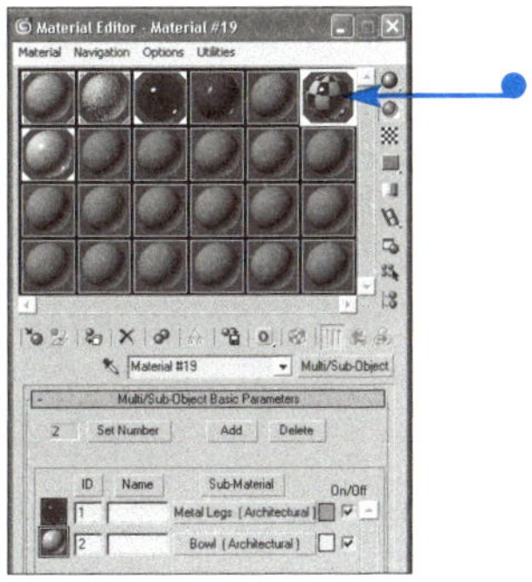

MASTER IT

Can I use the Material IDs to apply different materials?

▼ Yes, another method for applying multiple materials to an object is to use the Material IDs that are assigned to an object when it is created. For example, when you create a Primitive object, Material IDs are created for the object. In most cases, the Material IDs are set to one. To change the Material ID for a sub-object, select the sub-objects and change the Set ID value in the *sub-object* Properties rollout in the Modify panel, where *sub-object* is one of several sub-object names. To assign different materials to the material IDs of an object, you need to create a Multi/Sub-Object material. With this material type, you can specify the material that you want to apply to each Material ID on your object.

What is the best way to duplicate colors between color swatches?

▼ If you want to copy a color — for example, from the Diffuse to the Specular color swatch — you can click the Diffuse swatch and then drag it to the Specular swatch. A dialog box appears, asking whether you want to Swap, Copy, or Instance the colors. When you select Instance, changes made to one color are reflected in the other color. To copy a color from one material to another, right-click the color swatch of the first material and then select Copy from the pop-up menu. Open the other material, right-click the color swatch, and select Paste. There is also a utility called Color Clipboard that allows you to create a Floater to copy and paste colors.

Understanding the Material/Map Browser

Regardless of an object's shape, you can use a material to define an object's surface appearance, making it look like glass, plastic, stone, or smoke. Maps are image files, such as TIFFs and JPEGs, that alter the look of the material. For example, Diffuse Color maps place the image onto the object's surface, while Bump maps make the surface look like a raised texture. The Material/Map Browser contains all available materials and maps for objects in your scenes. You can select them from a variety of sources, apply them to the selected sample slot in the Material Editor, and then customize them in the rollouts.

You access the Material/Map Browser through the Material Type button near the top of the Material Editor, through any map button in the Maps rollout or the shader's Basic Parameters rollout, or through the Get Material button in the horizontal toolbar of the Material Editor. The material list that displays in the Material/Map Browser varies, depending on the option that opened it. For example, the Material Type button opens the list of available material types for creating new materials.

Icons differentiate the materials and the maps in the Material/Map Browser. Materials display with a sphere icon, blue for standard and yellow for mental ray. Maps display parallelogram icons.

Anatomy of the Material/Map Browser

A Toolbar

Changes the way the materials appear in the Material/Map list. You can view materials by name, or select differently sized icon views. Also has options for loading and updating materials, deleting unwanted materials, and clearing all materials from a library.

B Material/Map List

Lists all of the materials and maps based on the selected Browse From and Show options. A Material icon ( ) appears next to each material. A Map icon ( ) appears next to each map.

C Browse From Group

Determines where 3ds Max gets the list of materials to display in the Material/Map list.

D Sample Slot

Previews the material or map selected.

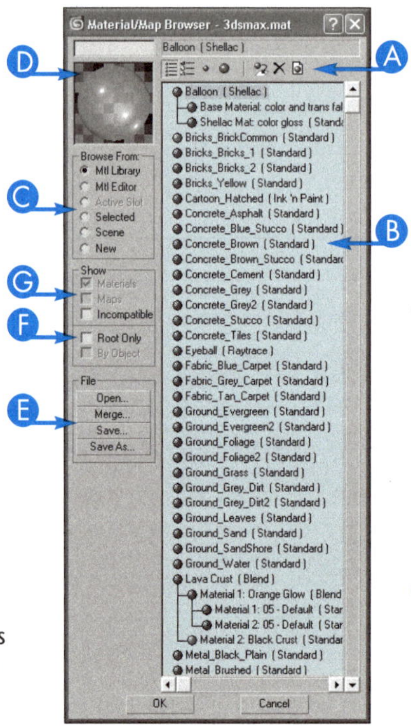

E File Group

When the Mtl Library option is selected in the Browse From section, this group displays options for opening or saving a material library for merging two libraries, or for saving the current library.

F Root Only Group

Available for all Browse From options except New. When unchecked, all maps and sub-materials contained within materials appear subordinate to those materials.

G Show Group

Filters the list to display only maps or materials. Option availability depends on the Browse From group selection. The Incompatible option displays materials, shown in gray, that are incompatible with the current renderer.

Browsing with the Material/Map Browser

The Material/Map Browser helps you quickly list or locate materials and maps. You can then use these materials to create new materials, or use materials from a specific library, the Material Editor, a particular sample slot in the Material Editor, or from an object in the scene. What displays depends on what you select in the Browse From section. For example, to view the materials and maps in the current material library, you select the Mtl Library option. 3ds Max has six different browse sources from which you can select in the Browse From section. The following table shows all six browse sources and their descriptions.

Browse Sources

Source	Description
Mtl Library	Displays the contents of the currently loaded material library. The default material library is named 3dsmax.mat. You can view the other available libraries, including the materials and maps, or create new libraries. See the section "Open a Material Library" for more information.
Mtl Editor	Displays the contents of all 24 sample slots in the Material Editor. If you have not assigned new materials, the sample slots display the default Standard material. For more on the sample slots, see Chapter 14.
Active Slot	Shows the contents of the currently selected sample slot in the Material Editor. If the current material has sub-materials, the complete hierarchy displays for the material. You can click different materials within the hierarchy to view them in the Material Editor.
Selected	Displays the materials and maps applied to the currently selected objects in the scene.
Scene	Displays all materials and maps applied to objects within the scene.
New	Displays the list of material types that you can use to create new materials in the Material Editor. You can create new materials using material types other than the default Standard material type, or you can use an existing material as a sub-material in a new compound material. The different materials display when you click the Material Type button (Standard) in the Material Editor. For more on the available material types, see Chapter 14.

Visible Material/Map Browser Contents

The contents of the Material/Map Browser display differently, depending on how you open the browser. For example, if you open the Material/Map Browser by clicking a map button, only map types display, and not material types. How you launch the Material/Map Browser determines what 3ds Max displays in order to save you time in locating what you want. The following table summarizes what you can view, depending on how you launch the Material/Map Browser. For more on opening the Material Editor, see Chapter 14. You can also control what displays by selecting different options in the Show section. For example, selecting the Incompatible option displays the available materials that do not work properly with the current renderer.

How You Open the Browser	What You See
Using the Get Material button ( )	The materials and maps in the currently selected Browse From option.
Using the Material Type button (Standard)	The compatible material types for the current renderer.
Clicking a map button for a parameter	The maps available in the currently selected Browse From option.

PART IV

Open a Material Library

You can quickly open the additional material libraries that contain materials and maps not found in the default 3dsmax.mat library, or that you have created yourself. This gives you greater flexibility in selecting the material or map that best suits your object or animation. You open a new library using the Open button in the File section that becomes available when you select the Mtl Library Browse From option.

When you open a new library, 3ds Max replaces what is currently open in the Material/Map Browser with the contents of the new library and displays its name at the top of the browser window. Opening a new library does not affect the materials and maps that you are currently using. However, 3ds Max adds any new materials that you save in the Material Editor to the open material library.

When you select the Open command, 3ds Max opens the default material library folder, which is named matlibs and is located in the root 3ds Max folder. You can see all of the existing libraries, identified by a .mat extension, in that folder. You can open one of these material libraries, or you can open a material library in another location.

Open a Material Library

1. Click the Material Editor button ().
2. In the Material Editor, click the Get Material button ().
3. In the Material/Map Browser dialog box, click Open.
   - If Open is not visible, then click the Mtl Library Browse From option (○ changes to ◉).
4. In the Open Material Library dialog box, select the library that you want to open.
5. Click Open.

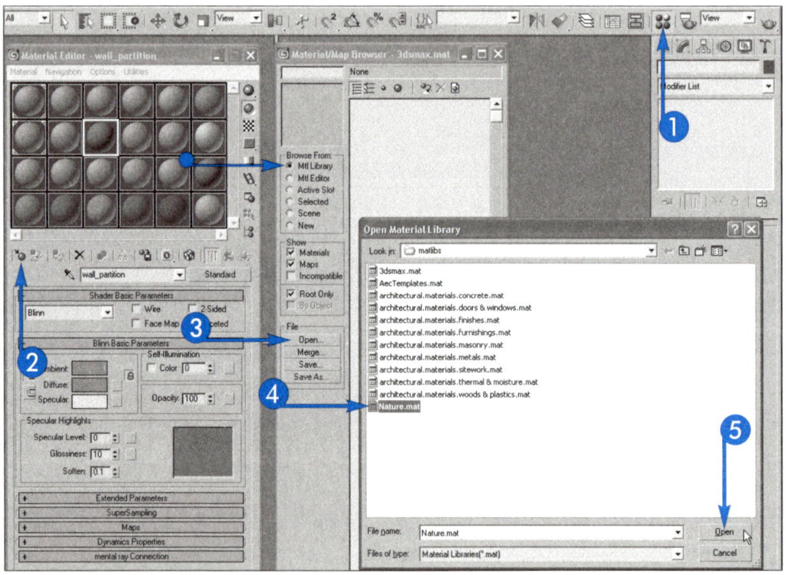

The contents of the selected library display in the Material/Map Browser, and the name appears in the Title bar.

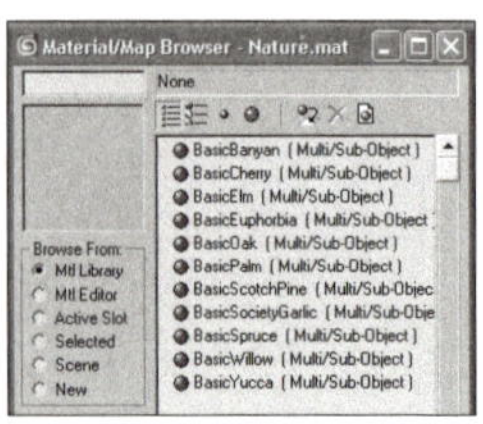

Delete a Material from a Material Library

You can remove any map or material that you no longer want from the currently selected material library. When you remove a material or map from the library, 3ds Max removes it only from the list that currently displays in the Material/Map Browser, and not from the saved version of the library. This safeguard ensures that you do not accidentally delete a material or map that you need. The deletions that you make to a library do not become part of the library until you save the library, after which 3ds Max permanently deletes the material, and you cannot reload it.

MASTER IT

How do I retrieve a material that I accidentally deleted?

▼ 3ds Max only removes deleted materials from the visible Material/Map Browser and they remain in the library until you save it. If you delete the wrong material, and do not save the library, you can retrieve the material or map by opening that material library again. However, when you reopen the library, 3ds Max deletes all materials or maps not saved to the library. See the section "Open a Material Library" for more information.

PART IV

Delete a Material from a Material Library

1. Click .

   The Material Editor opens.

2. Click .

   The Material/Map Browser dialog box appears.

3. In the Material/Map Browser, click the material or map that you want to delete.

4. Click the Delete From Library button ().

   3ds Max removes the material from the list.

Note: *You cannot undo the next step.*

5. Click Save.

   The material library file updates by removing the deleted material or map.

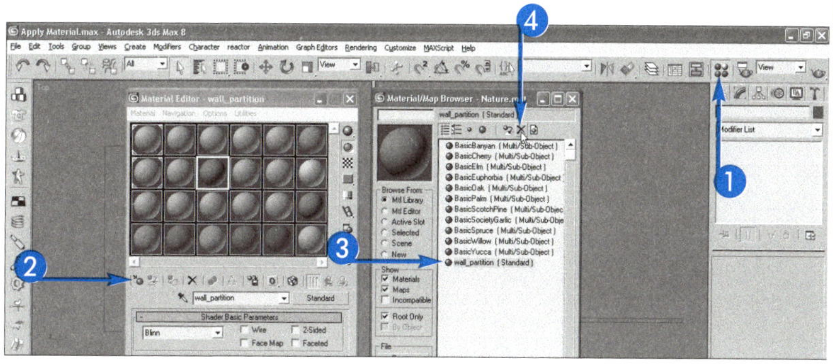

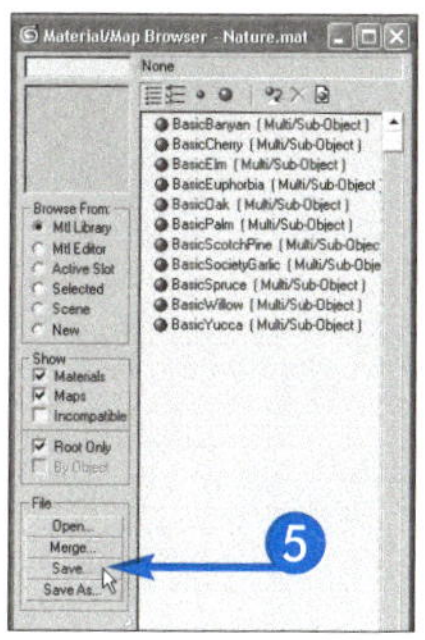

Apply a Material from the Material Library

You can select and apply any material in a material library to objects in your scene. By using an existing material, you do not have to create the material that you want to use with the existing material types. For example, if you want to create a material that looks like blue carpet, you can select the Fabric_Blue_Carpet material from the default library. Once a material is in the Material Editor, you can make any necessary changes, which do not affect the material in the library.

You must place a material listed in the Material/Map Browser into a sample slot in the Material Editor before you modify or apply it. Once the material is there, you can modify and apply it in the same fashion as the materials that you create. This allows you to modify the material by changing its parameters or maps. For example, to use a material that creates a metallic look with a different Diffuse color, you can change those properties of the material in the Material Editor. For more information on working with the Material Editor, see Chapters 14 and 16.

Apply a Material from the Material Library

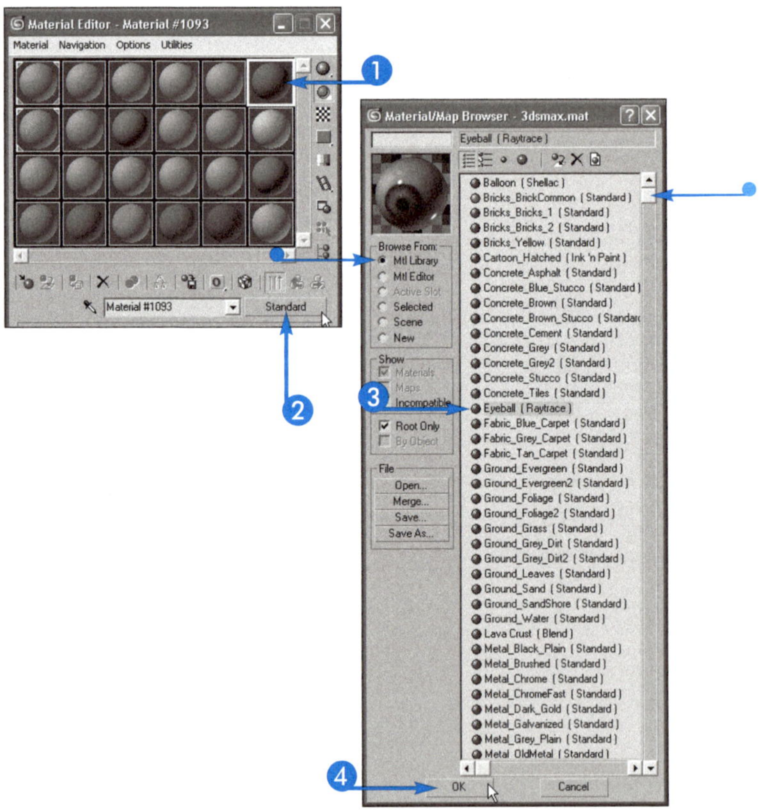

1. In the Material Editor, click in the sample slot where you want to place the material.

Note: *To open the Material Editor, see the section "Open a Material Library."*

2. Click the Material Type button.

   The Material/Map Browser dialog box appears, displaying a list of the available materials in the current material library.

   - If the list of materials in the material library does not display, click the Mtl Library option (○ changes to ⦿).
   - You can drag the Scroll bar to see the complete list of materials.

3. Click a material in the list.

   The selected material displays in the sample slot.

4. Click OK.

3ds Max adds the material to the sample slot in the Material Editor.

If the original material in that sample slot was hot, then the material updates in the viewports.

- The parameters and maps for the selected material display in the Material Editor.

You can adjust any of the parameters.

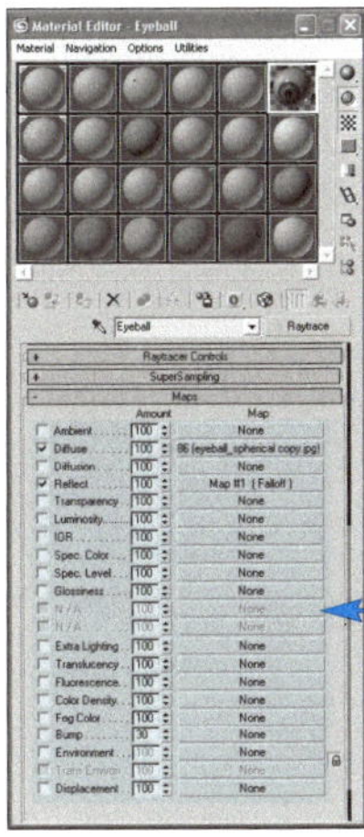

5 Select an object.

6 Click the Assign Material to Selection button ( ).

3ds Max assigns the material to the object.

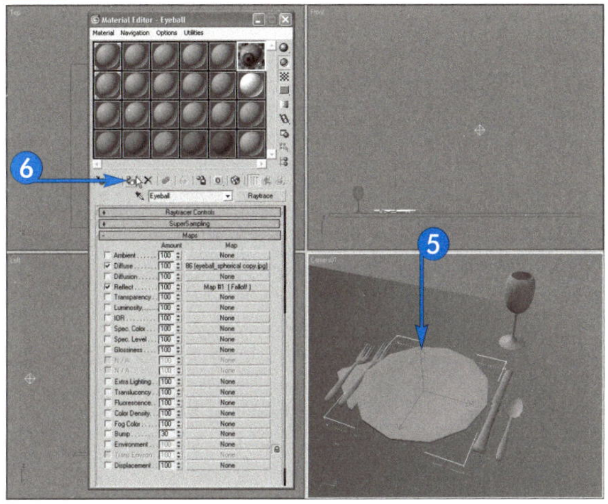

MASTER IT

Can I apply a material in the Material/Map Browser directly to an object in a scene?

Yes. Click and drag the material onto an object in a viewport. 3ds Max applies the material with its current parameters. Because you apply the material directly to the object, you do not see 3ds Max adding it to a sample slot in the Material Editor. To add the material to multiple objects, drag and drop it on each object. To add a material from an object to a sample slot, select the object and then activate the Selected option (○ changes to ◉) in the Browse From section in the Material/Map Browser. The material list displays the material from the selected object. Select the material from the list, and click OK.

I cannot find the OK or Cancel buttons in the Material/Map Browser. Why not?

When the Material/Map Browser displays, its layout changes, depending on how you launched it. If you open it by clicking the Material Type button, as described in the steps, then the OK and Cancel buttons appear at the bottom of the dialog box. Opening it by clicking the Get Material button ( ) in the Material Editor's horizontal toolbar prevents the OK and Cancel buttons from appearing. You can still select materials, but you must drag and drop them onto the desired sample slot in the Material Editor, or you can double-click the material name in the list to copy it to a sample slot.

Merge Material Libraries

You can merge the materials from any two libraries to create a single library containing both sets of materials. This gives you a central location for the materials and can provide easy access to the tools that you need to create a scene.

To start the merge process, you open the library into which you want to merge everything. You then use the Merge Material Library dialog box to select the material library containing the materials that you want to merge into the open library. 3ds Max then opens the Merge dialog box, where you have the options of merging either the entire library or individual materials. 3ds Max merges only the materials that you select into the current material library. After merging is complete, you must save the open material library to save any changes that you made. If you do not, then when you switch libraries and re-open the library where you merged everything, the merged materials no longer appear.

During the merge process, 3ds Max copies, rather than moves, the contents of the second library, and its original materials remain intact. This allows you to change the merge materials without affecting the original materials.

Merge Material Libraries

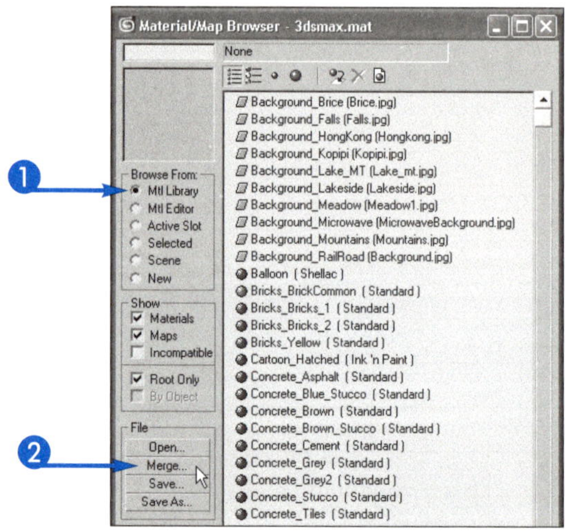

1. Open the material library where you want to merge the other materials.

Note: *See the section "Open a Material Library" for more information.*

2. Click Merge.

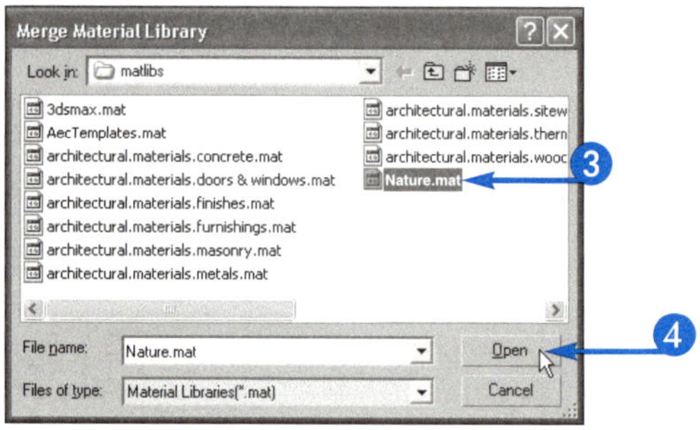

The Merge Material Library dialog box appears.

3. Select the library containing the materials that you want to merge into your open library.
4. Click Open.

The Merge dialog box appears.

5. Select the materials that you want to merge.
   - You can click All to merge all materials into the current material library.

   To select specific materials, you can press and hold Ctrl and click each material name.

6. Click OK.

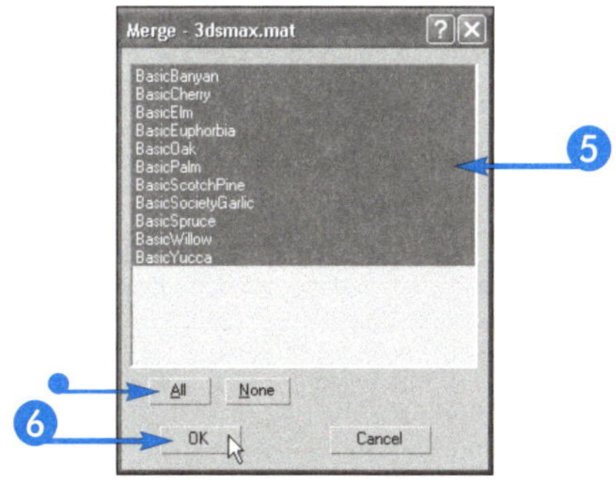

The selected materials merge into the current library.

7. Click Save.

The new materials are saved to the material library.

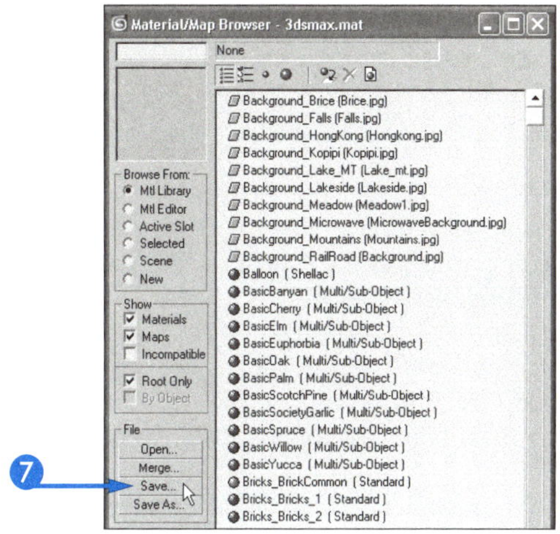

PART IV

MASTER IT

Can I merge materials into a library from another scene?

▼ Yes. Not only can you merge materials from a material library, but you can also merge them from any scene file. This allows you to build a library containing custom materials that you have created for other scenes. To merge materials from a scene, click Merge to open the the Merge Material Library dialog box, then click ▾ next to Files of type, and then select 3ds Max (*.max, *.chr). Locate the 3ds Max scene file from which you want to get the materials, and click Open. In the Merge dialog box, select the materials that you want to merge.

What if there is already a material in the open library with the same name as a material that I am merging into the library?

▼ Each material in a scene or in a library must have a unique name. When you merge materials into a material library, 3ds Max checks for materials with duplicate names. If they are detected, a warning appears and gives you three options for dealing with the duplicates: Skip, Delete Old, and Auto-Rename. If you do not want to merge the duplicate materials, then click Skip so that 3ds Max does not merge them. To replace the merged material in the current material library, click Delete Old. If you want both materials, click Auto-Rename so that 3ds Max can rename the merged materials.

Understanding Maps

Maps help you to create more realistic materials by replacing simple colors on your objects' surface with complex images and textures. Maps also control the location of Specular highlights, opacity, self-illumination, and several other material properties. A *map* is simply an image file that you apply to a feature of a material and it can consist of photographs, patterns, or any other type of design that creates the effect you want. Maps can be external files, with extensions such as .tif and .jpg. 3ds Max can also internally generate what it calls *procedural maps*, which have patterns created purely with mathematics.

Whether you import or generate a map, you apply it to a material by selecting it from the Material/Map Browser. All maps are listed with a parallelogram icon next to them, and all are grouped into basic categories, with each category creating different types of effects. Maps fall into five categories: 2D maps, 3D maps, Compositors, Color Modifiers, and Other.

2D Maps

2D maps are image files that may have originated as digital photographs, scans, or files created in, or edited by, image-editing software such as Adobe Photoshop. 3ds Max also has a variety of 2D maps that it can generate procedurally, which you can modify by altering any of the parameters that vary for each map type. Because two-dimensional objects have no depth, you apply 2D maps to the surface of an object. Two-dimensional maps are ideal for applying a real-world substance, such as brick or carpet, onto an object in 3ds Max that represents a surface made of the same substance. The following table lists the different types of 2D maps that you are likely to encounter.

2D Map Types

Map Type	*Description*
Bitmap	For importing a still-image file, such as a TIFF or JPEG file, or an animation file such as an AVI or MOV file, that you can apply to the surface of the object. You can import 18 different graphic and animation file types into any of the map channels. For information on map channels, see Chapter 16.
Checker	Creates a checker pattern out of two different colors that you specify. You can also specify a map as the value for either color parameter.
Combustion	Interfaces with Autodesk's Combustion software to create Combustion-produced effects for the material. You can only use the Combustion map if you have the Combustion software program loaded on your system.
Gradient	Uses two or three different colors to create either a linear or radial gradient image. Gradients are useful for varying the opacity or color of a surface over distance.
Gradient Ramp	Similar to the Gradient map but more powerful, with additional gradient styles to choose from and the ability to add several more color choices in a single gradient pattern.
Swirl	Combines two different colors to create a swirled pattern. You specify the amount and intensity of the swirling and, like the other map types, you can animate all the parameters.
Tiles	Creates a material with several pattern styles similar to bricks or stacked tiles. You can use one of the available patterns or create your own custom patterns.

3D Maps

Three-dimensional maps are generated procedurally, meaning that they are only mathematically generated, based on the values of their parameters and not an image file. 3ds Max creates these maps at render time to produce patterns in all three dimensions. This allows you to create a textured pattern on the object. For example, you can apply the Wood map to produce a material with the texture of wood grain. If you extrude any of the surfaces, the wood grain matches the extruded surface to the existing surfaces. You can use Noise and Smoke as Diffuse Color or Opacity maps to randomly vary the surface color and opacity of an object. 3ds Max provides several different 3D map types.

3D Map Types

Map Type	Description
Cellular	Creates a pattern of connected lumps that work well for objects with an uneven but smooth surface.
Dent	Creates indentations on the surface of the object using a random pattern.
Falloff	Creates a grayscale image based upon the angular falloff direction of the surface normals. For example, the default setup creates white faces that point outward from, and black faces that are parallel to, the current view. Using a Falloff map, in conjunction with a bitmap in the Bump map channel, you can make the texture appear more realistic as the distance increases. For more on the different map channels, see Chapter 16.
Marble	When you select a base and vein color, 3ds Max generates a third color as a vein and creates a marble-like pattern with colored veins.
Noise	When you select two colors, 3ds Max creates a random pattern on the surface of the material in one of three Noise types: Regular, Fractal, and Turbulence. Noise is a common map type that is used to add randomness to a material.
Particle Age	When used with Particle Systems, this changes the color of the particles over their lifespan.
Particle MBlur	When used with Particle Systems, this blurs particles based on their velocity.
Perlin Marble	Creates more complex marble patterns than the Marble map.
Planet	Creates land and water masses to simulate a planet's surface. You should only use this map as a Diffuse map. For information on the different map channels, see Chapter 16.
Smoke	Similar to the Noise map type, Smoke creates the effect of a flowing, wispy pattern. You typically assign Smoke to the Opacity parameter and you animate it.
Speckle	Creates a speckled surface that works well for making patterns on rocks or organic surfaces.
Splat	Creates an uneven, two-color pattern similar to splattered paint.
Stucco	Creates a random stucco-surface pattern. This map works well as both a Diffuse Color and a Bump map.
Waves	Creates surface patterns similar to a churning water surface. You can control the appearance of the turbulence by defining the number of waves, their size, and their height. This map works well as either a Bump or Diffuse Color map.
Wood	Creates the pattern of wood grain using two colors that you specify.

continued

Understanding Maps *(Continued)*

Compositor Maps

The Compositor map types combine other maps and colors to create a combined map. You can use these maps to apply labels to surfaces or to superimpose one map over another so that two maps can occupy a single parameter.

Compositor Map Types

Map Type	*Description*
Composite	Combines two or more image files together to form a single image for use in a single material parameter. Composite uses the alpha channel of each image file to determine which parts of each contributing image are visible.
Mask	Allows you to determine which parts of a map are visible by using a second map called a *mask* that is placed above it. The white portions of the mask allow you to see the map below it, and the black portions of the mask hide the map and allow you to see the surface of the objects.
Mix	Merges two maps or colors on the surface of the object. The Mix Amount controls how much of each map or color is displayed.
RGB Multiply	When used as a Bump map, this type generates significant surface changes by multiplying the RGB values of two maps to create a new map.

Color Modifier Maps

The Color Modifier allows you to alter the color of different types of maps, such as changing the map tinting to achieve a different color appearance or inverting a map's output to change the direction of a bump pattern.

Color Modifier Types

Map Type	*Description*
Output	Adds the functionality found in the bitmap map type, to procedural maps to control the final color output of the map.
RGB Tint	Allows you to change the color of an object's material by altering the RGB, or red, green, and blue, values of a map.
Vertex Color	Allows you to make the vertex coloring visible after rendering on an editable mesh, editable poly, or editable patch object.

Other Map Types

3ds Max provides additional map types in the Other category. These maps include Reflection and Refraction maps as well as mental ray shaders, Normal Bitmap maps, and Camera Per-Pixel Projection maps.

If you have selected the mental ray renderer, you can select additional mental ray shader maps that control how the surface of the object responds to light. The mental ray shader maps display in the Material/Map Browser with a yellow parallelogram.

The Texture Baking (Render to Texture) feature places the rendered look of shadows and textures as an image directly on an object's surface. Texture baking is used in the video game industry to show the effect of light on a surface without actually having to calculate it at every frame. You can use the Normal Bump map to apply texture-baking to the Bump or Displacement parameters. Use the Camera Map Per-Pixel map to project a map from the direction of a specific camera.

The Reflection and Refraction maps provide four different types of maps for creating reflection and refraction properties on your objects.

Reflection and Refraction Maps Types

Map Type	*Description*
Flat Mirror	Creates a reflection on the flat surfaces of the object only. You assign the map to coplanar faces, instead of the entire object.
Raytrace	An alternative to the Raytrace material, the Raytrace map produces the most accurate reflections and refractions on objects, but it is also much slower to render than the Reflect/Refract map. You normally assign the Raytrace map to the Reflection or Refraction material parameters.
Reflect/Refract	Produces both reflections and refractions on the object surface.
Thin Wall Refraction	Simulates the refraction created by viewing the object through a refractive substance such as a glass plate or a thick gloss coating.

Mapping Coordinates

When you use several types of maps, especially 2D maps, you must specify how they display on the object surface by using mapping coordinates. 3ds Max uses a spatial coordinate system, UVW, which is similar to the XYZ coordinate system used for 3D objects. The "U" dimension represents the width of the 2D image map, the "V" represents the image height, and the "W" measures the distance away from the object's surface, perpendicular to the object faces. The "W" dimension usually defines the axis around which a map is rotated. By setting the UVW coordinates, you control the placement of the map on the object surface. You can control Mapping Coordinates by adding mapping modifiers, such as UVW Map or MapScaler, to the object's Modifier Stack.

Material/Map Hierarchy

Each material can have a hierarchical tree of materials with sub-materials and maps. A sub-material having its own sub-materials and maps can be a composite of two or more other maps. You can move through the tree using the buttons and options listed in the following table. The Material/Map Navigator is also useful for navigating through complex material and map hierarchies.

Button/Option	*Location*	*What It Does*
Go To Parent button	Material Editor	Moves up one level in the hierarchy.
Go to Sibling button	Material Editor	Moves laterally within the hierarchy to a material or occupied map channel.
Scene option	Material/Map Browser	Shows the hierarchy of the materials in the current scene. Sub-materials are indented under the corresponding parent materials.

Add a Map to a Material

You can apply maps to most parameters of a material in order to assign images and patterns instead of just color values. For example, to display a speckled pattern across the surface of an egg, you apply a Speckle map to the Diffuse Color channel of the egg object's material.

You apply maps to material parameters in the Maps rollout in the Material Editor. The Maps rollout lists all the map channels for the selected material, and this list varies, depending on the material type. When you select a map, the Material Editor displays the controls for that map, which is one level lower in the material's hierarchy. You can use the Go to Parent button to go back to the material's top level.

If a map is assigned, the name of the map appears on the map's button in the Maps rollout; "None" indicates no map assignment. You control the intensity of the map for each parameter by setting the Amount value in the Maps rollout. See the section "Understanding the Material/Map Browser" for more information. See the section "Understanding Maps" for more information on the various types of available maps.

Add a Map to a Material

1. Click .

   The Material Editor opens.

2. Select a sample slot.
3. Drag the Scroll bar to display the Maps rollout.
4. Click one of the map buttons labeled None.

   You can apply a map to any of the parameters listed in the Maps rollout.

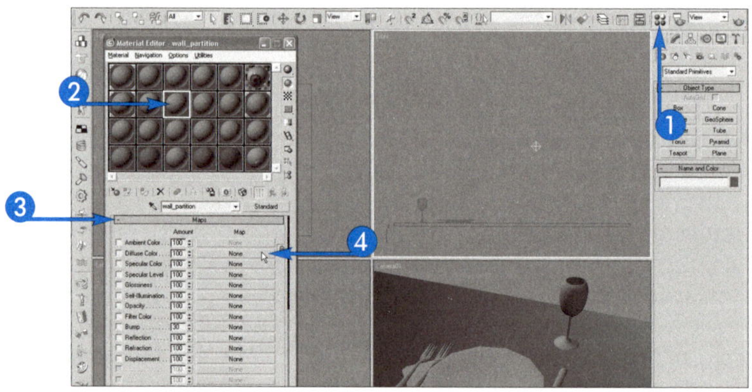

   The Material/Map Browser dialog box appears, displaying a list of map types.

5. Click a map type.
6. Click OK.

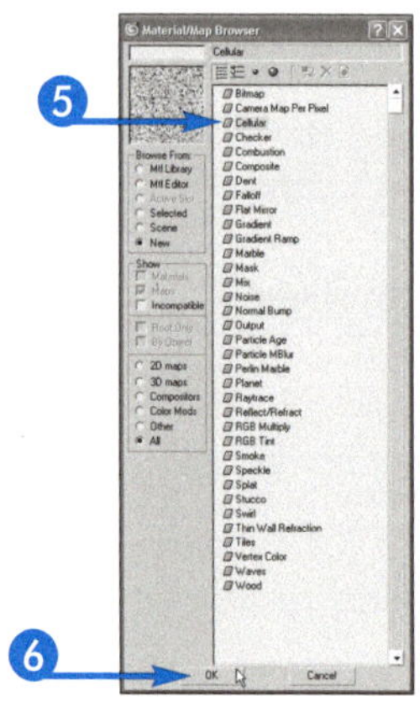

The parameters for the selected map display in the Material Editor.

The material updates to show the selected map.

- You can adjust the map's parameters.

7 Click the Go to Parent button ( ).

The parent material parameters display in the Material Editor.

- If you want, you can type a different value in the Amount field to reduce the intensity of the map.

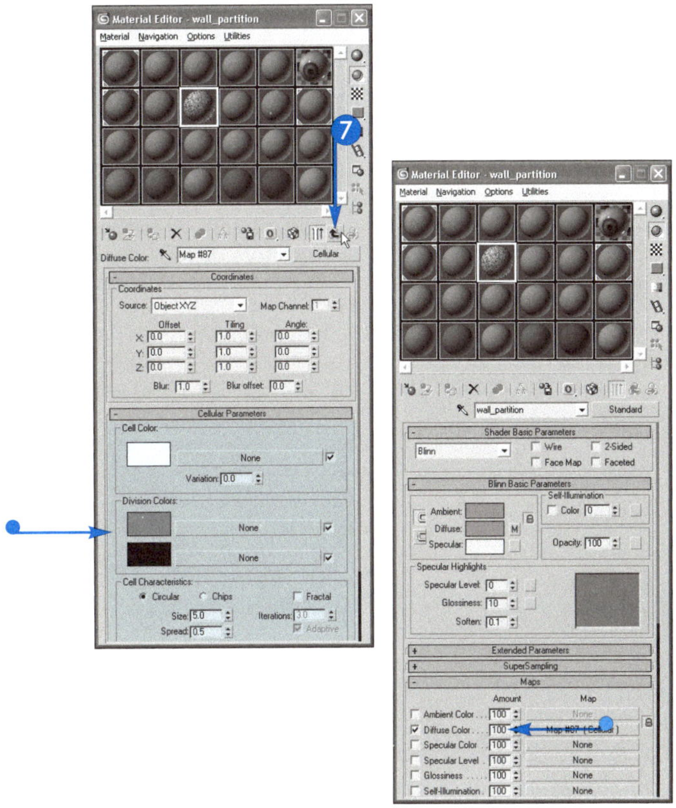

MASTER IT

Can I add the same map to more than one material parameter?

Yes, it is a common practice to add the same map to multiple map channels. To clone a map from one parameter to another, simply click the map's button in the Maps rollout, and then drag and drop it onto another button. A Copy (Instance) Map dialog box appears, prompting you to decide if the map should be a copy or an instance, or whether the two map buttons should swap their maps. Copied maps allow you to change one map's parameters without affecting the other, while instanced maps maintain identical parameters, regardless of which map you change.

How do I remove a map from a material?

There are a few ways to do this. If you want to see the result of the material without the map, but are not sure that you want to delete it yet, you can deselect the check box to the left of the map channel name in the Maps rollout (☑ changes to ☐). This disables the map without deleting it. Setting the Amount value to zero has the same effect. To completely remove a map from a material, right-click the map button, in the Maps rollout or the shader's Basic Parameters rollout, and then select Clear from the pop-up menu. You can also drag the "None" label from another map slot onto the field with the map name to achieve the same result.

Add an Image to an Object's Surface

You can use a bitmap to apply an image file to any material channel to display the map on the surface of an object. For example, you can place a bitmap in the Diffuse Color channel to show a picture of your yacht on the label of a bottle, or your kids in a portrait on the wall.

The process for applying a bitmap image is simple: You first select the material into which you want to place the object. Next, in the Maps rollout, you select the material parameter to which you want to assign the image. The Diffuse Color and Ambient map channels use the full color of your image and apply it to the surfaces of the object, while the other map channels use a grayscale equivalent version of the image to determine that parameter's effect on the material. Finally, you locate and select the image that you want to place on the object.

Once you apply a bitmap to a material, 3ds Max continues to open that same image file using the same file location whenever you render the scene.

CD FILE The Material.max file is available on the CD-ROM for you to practice applying a Diffuse Color map.

Add an Image to an Object's Surface

Apply Bitmapped Material

1. Click the Material Editor button ( ).

   The Material Editor opens.

2. Click the sample slot of the material to which you want to add a bitmap.

3. In the Maps rollout, click the map button (None) next to Diffuse Color.

   You can apply a bitmap to another parameter by clicking the corresponding parameter button.

   The Material/Map Browser appears.

4. Click Bitmap at the top of the list.

5. Click OK.

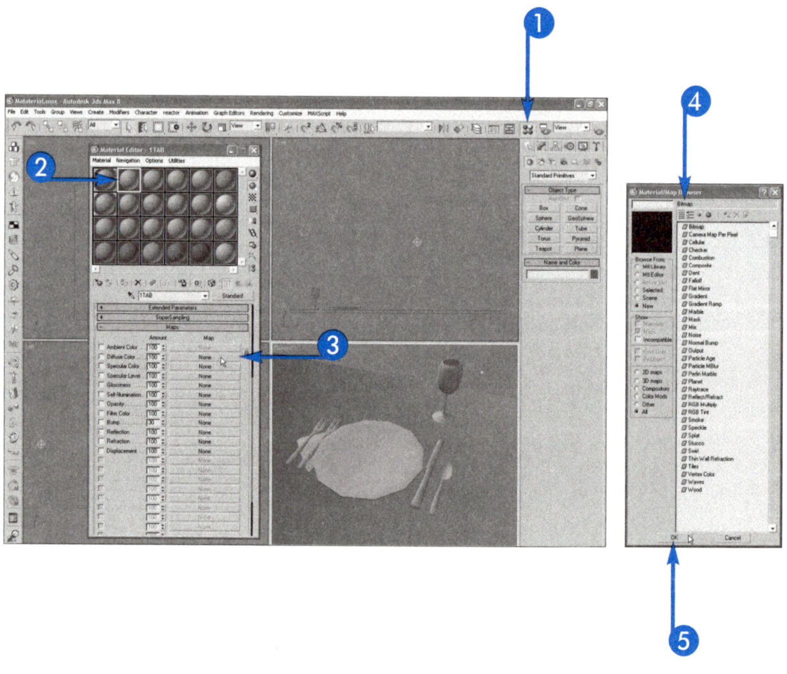

The Select Bitmap Image File dialog box appears.

6. Locate and select the image file that you want to apply to the material.
7. Click Open.

   3ds Max applies the selected image file to the material as a bitmap map.

8. Click the Assign Material to Selection button (icon) to assign the mapped material to the selection in the scene.
9. Click the Show Map in Viewport button (icon) to see the map on the object.

Note: *Use Show Map in Viewport sparingly. With several maps in use, it can slow down your system.*

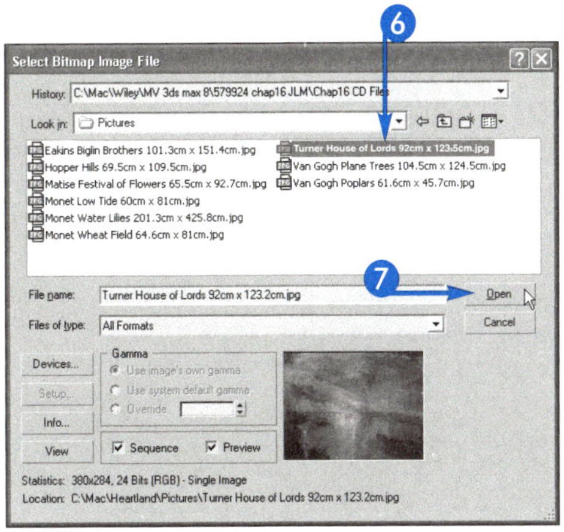

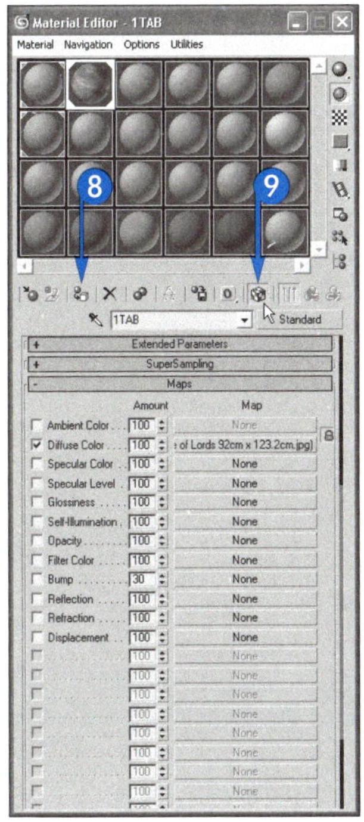

MASTER IT

What types of image files can I use with the bitmap map?

▼ 3ds Max allows you to apply both still-image and animated files as bitmap maps. 3ds Max supports the most common file formats for both file types. To apply a still image, you can use image files with the following file extensions: .bmp, .cin, .dds, .gif, .jpeg, .png, .psd, .rgb, .rpf, .tga, .tiff, .hdr, .pic, .rgbe, and .yuv. To create a bitmap map that includes an animation file or a sequence of still images, you can use files with the following extensions: .avi, .flc, .ifl, .mov, and .mpeg.

How do I apply the mapped material to a part of an object?

▼ You can apply materials to an entire object, or to specific parts of the object. If your object is an editable poly or editable mesh, or it has an Edit Poly or Edit Mesh modifier applied, then you can use the Modify panel to select the specific part of the object where you want to apply the material. You can also use the UVW Mapping coordinates to adjust the placement of a material on an object. See the section "Adjust Materials on an Object Using the UVW Map Modifier" for more information. See the section "Using the Multi/Sub-Object Material" for more information on applying multiple materials to an object. For information about selecting sub-objects of polygonal mesh objects, see Chapter 6.

continued

Add an Image to an Object's Surface *(Continued)*

A button at the top of the Bitmap Parameters rollout shows the image file's name and path. You can use this button to change the image file. You can use the Reload button to retrieve the file from its source and reload it into 3ds Max. This technique is useful when you are making changes to the file in an image-editing program and you want to see the result in 3ds Max. You must save the file in the other application before reloading it.

To specify the portion of a bitmap that the material should use, you can adjust the parameters in the Cropping/Placement section of the Bitmap Parameters rollout. To crop an image, you can specify U, V, W, and H values manually, but it is much easier to click the View Image button and use the cropping handles to crop the image. Only the area inside the cropping perimeter is used by the material, and the image file itself is not altered.

You can select the Apply option to use your cropping or placement changes, and deselect the Apply option to undo the changes.

The Material.max file is available on the CD-ROM for you to practice applying a Diffuse Color map.

Add an Image to an Object's Surface *(continued)*

Crop a Bitmap Map

The mapped material is visible on the selected object.

10 In the Bitmap Parameters rollout, click the Crop option (○ changes to ◉).

11 Click View Image.

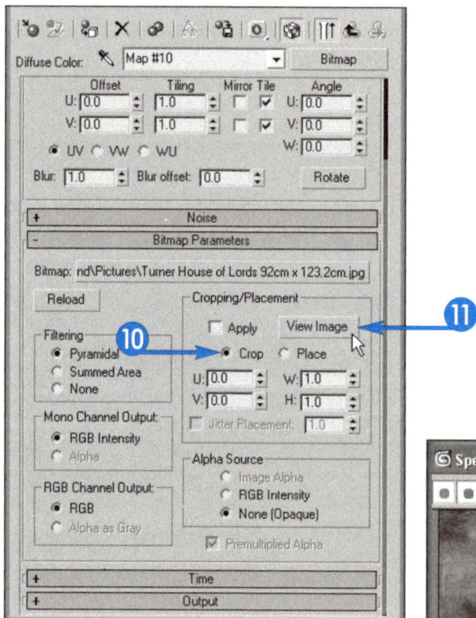

The Specify Cropping/Placement window appears.

12 Click and drag the handles on the edges to create cropping borders.

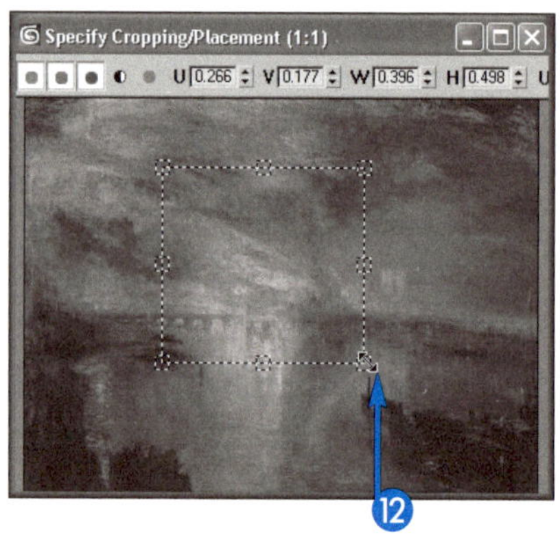

- The U, V, W, and H parameter values update for the bitmap image.

13 Click the Apply option (☐ changes to ☑).

The bitmap map updates in the material and on the objects in the scene.

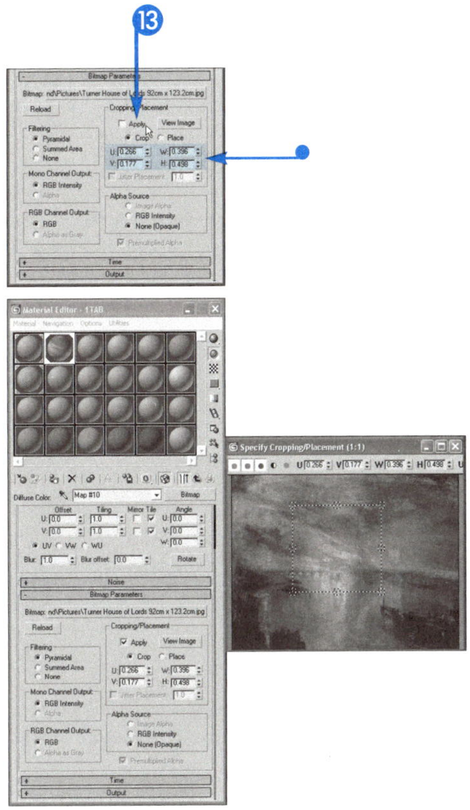

MASTER IT

Which filtering option should I select for my map?

▼ Antialiasing is a method of blurring adjacent pixels to give a smoother appearance to objects and mapped materials. The Filtering options allow you to select which type of antialiasing 3ds Max applies to image maps. You have three options: Pyramidal, Summed Area, or None. The default filtering method, Pyramidal, requires the least amount of memory and works well for most images. The Summed Area filter produces the best results but requires much more memory than the Pyramidal filter. Use the Summed Area filter with smaller maps and on maps that are on objects on which the viewer will focus. Use Pyramidal in all other situations. If you select None, then no filtering is applied.

Can I resize the image?

▼ Yes. You can use the options in the Cropping/Placement section of the Bitmap Parameters rollout to resize the image without cropping it. To resize an image, you can click the Place option (○ changes to ◉) in the Cropping/Placement section. Click View Image to see the image in the Specify Cropping/Placement window. The image displays with a selection marquee in the window. Click and drag the handles on the sides and corners of the window to resize it. You can drag the handles toward the center of the object to reduce the size, or away from the center to increase the size. You can also click and drag the image to move it within the window.

Add Texture with a Bump Map

In 3ds Max, you can create the appearance of raised or embossed texture to an object using the Bump channel of the object's material, with a technique called *bump mapping*. Bump mapping adds a shadow map, created by 3ds Max during rendering, that simulates texture by adding shadows where they normally fall if the object's faces were not flat. For example, a brick wall looks flat and unconvincing if you only use the image of a real wall in the Diffuse Color channel and nothing in the Bump channel. Copying the same map into the Bump channel creates the effect of surface texture.

Bump mapping creates texturing on the surface of an object using the color intensity of the map. Black areas of the map do not affect the material, and white areas appear to protrude. Gray areas vary, depending on their intensity, and when you use a color map, the grayscale equivalent of the color determines the bump. You set the height of the apparent bump using the Amount field next to the Bump channel in the Maps rollout.

CD FILE: The Bump.max file is available on the CD-ROM for you to practice applying a bump map.

Add Texture with a Bump Map

1. Open the Material Editor.

Note: *For more on opening the Material Editor, see the section "Add an Image to an Object's Surface."*

2. Select the material to which you want to add a bump map.
3. In the Maps rollout, click the None button for the Bump channel.

   The Material/Map Browser appears.

4. Click a map that you want to use for texture.

   This example uses the Cellular map.

5. Click OK.

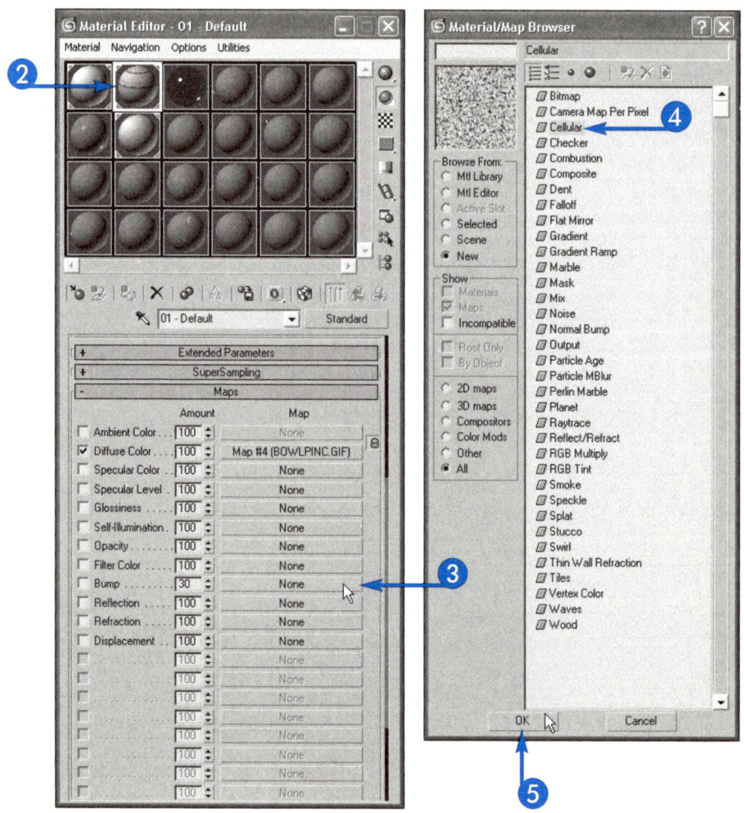

The map's parameters display in the Material Editor.

6 Adjust the map's parameters to fit your needs.

7 Click the Go to Parent button ().

- The Bump channel is selected in the Maps rollout.
- The map's effect displays in the sample slot.
- If you want, you can change the value in the Amount field.
- If required, you can select an object and click to assign the material to the object.

8 Click the Quick Render button ().

The image renders with the specified bump settings.

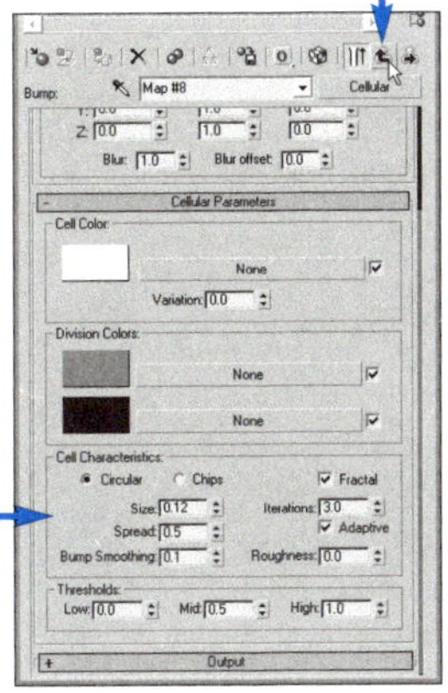

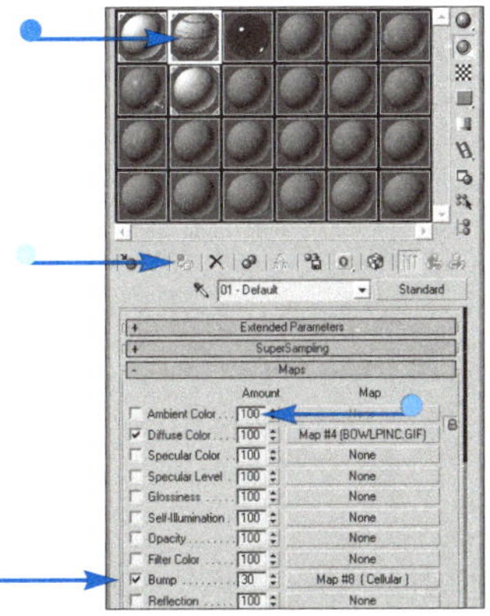

Can I use a bitmap image for bump mapping?

▼ Yes. You can use any of the map types for bump mapping. If you select a bitmap image, then you should use one that has a good contrast between the dark and light areas to create a better texture. If you are trying to match the Bump to the Diffuse Color channel, then consider taking a copy of the Diffuse Color map into an image-editing program and increasing the contrast before using it as a bump map. If you use a bitmap to create your bump mapping, then ensure that the bitmap image is always available when you open the scene file. See the section "Add an Image to an Object's Surface" for more information.

The bump mapping does not display in the viewport. How do I view it?

▼ Bump mapping is only visible when you render the object. This is because the renderer must generate the apparent shadows using the map that you assign to the Bump channel. Any changes that you make to the bump map are not visible in the viewport unless the viewport render mode is set to Smooth + Highlights, and the Show Map in Viewport button () is selected in the Material Editor's horizontal toolbar. This shows where the map is applied, but not the bump effect that it yields when rendered. You can quickly render the object to see the effect of your bump mapping by clicking . For more information on rendering, see Chapter 20.

Define Transparency with an Opacity Map

You can create a void effect by using a map in a material's Opacity channel. For example, you can define an area that has been cut out of a thin-walled object without creating more complex geometry. Using a Noise map in the Opacity channel can generate random areas of opacity to create an eerie or murky effect.

Opacity mapping defines the opacity of the material based on the color intensity of the map. Black areas of the map are 100 percent transparent, while white areas are 100 percent opaque. Gray areas vary, depending on their intensity, and color maps use the grayscale equivalent of the colors in the map. You can limit the opacity using the Amount field in the Maps rollout. When the Amount is set to 50, even areas of the Opacity map that are black only appear as 50 percent transparent.

By default, 3ds Max only displays and renders one side of each face. Using opacity with hollow objects allows you to see through to the non-rendering faces. You can select the 2-Sided option for the material so that both sides of each face render.

CD FILE: The Opacity.max file is available on the CD-ROM for you to practice applying an Opacity map.

Define Transparency with an Opacity Map

1. Open the Material Editor.

Note: *For more on opening the Material Editor, see the section "Add an Image to an Object's Surface."*

2. Select the material to which you want to add an opacity map.
3. In the Maps rollout, click the None button for the Opacity channel.

   The Material/Map Browser appears.

4. Click a map with which you want to define the opacity.

   This example uses the Checker map.

5. Click OK.

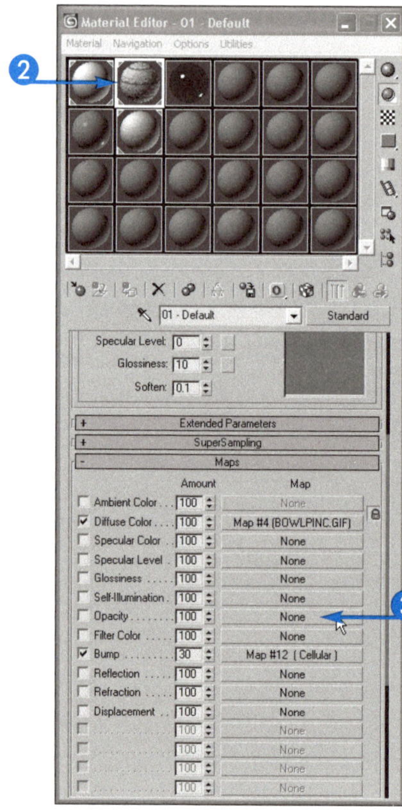

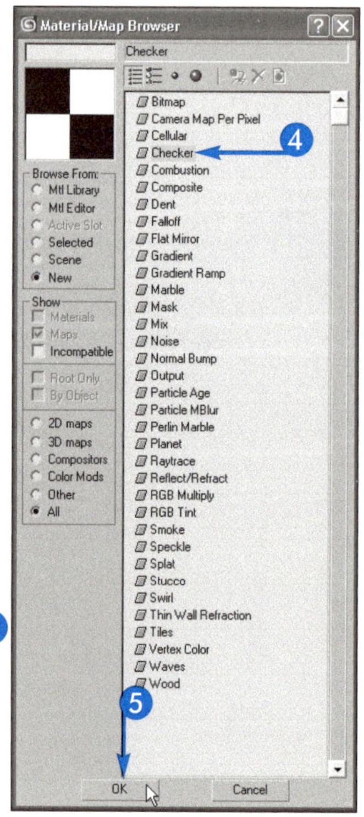

The map's parameters display in the Material Editor.

6. Adjust the map's parameters to fit your needs.
7. Click .
   - The Opacity channel is selected in the Maps rollout.
   - The map's effect displays in the sample slot.
   - If you want, you can change the value in the Amount field.
8. Click the 2-Sided option (☐ changes to ☑).
   - If required, you can select an object and click to assign the material to it.
9. Click .

   The image renders with the specified opacity settings.

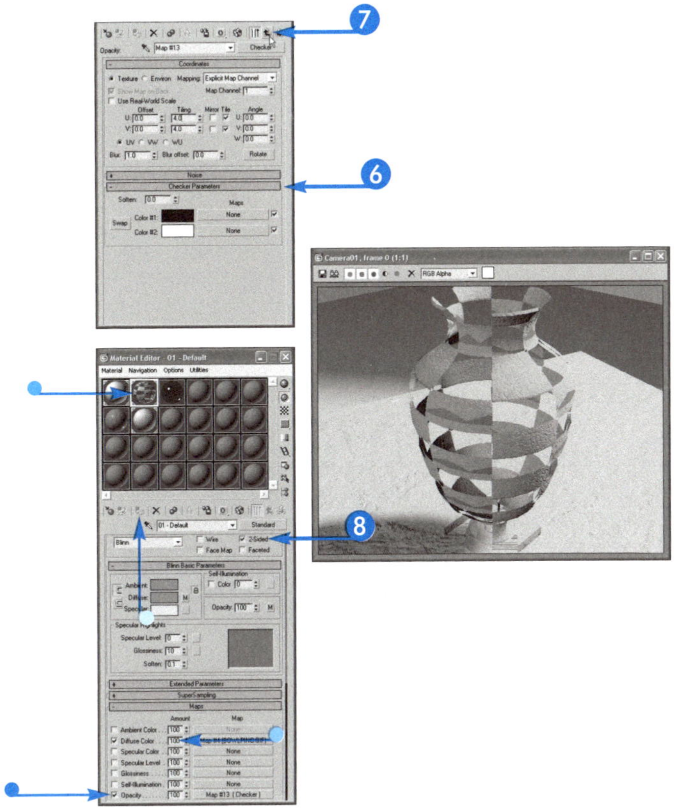

Master It

If my object is transparent, then why does it show a Specular highlight?

The dark areas of an opacity map determine where you can see through an object's surfaces and not whether the surface exists or not. The Specular highlights appear, even where the object appears transparent, because there is still a surface there to reflect the light. In the case of a glass portion of an object, you want the Specular highlight to display to give the object a sense of density and smoothness. See the section "Limit Specularity with a Specular Map" for information on defining the Specular locations with a material.

Why do the edges look wrong where the opacity starts?

When you apply an opacity map, especially one with a good amount of contrast, the faces of an object can appear to come to an abrupt end and seem to float in space, detached from any object. This may become more pronounced when you view the object from a sharp angle. For these reasons, you may often find it appropriate to add a transition between the contrasting colors when the created void areas are bound by opaque areas resulting in a short, gradiated edge to the visible faces. You can do this in an imaging editing program or with Gradient maps inside 3ds Max.

Limit Specularity with a Specular Map

After color, the parameters that most identify a material are the size, shape, and intensity of its Specular highlight. A small, bright Specular highlight indicates a smooth, glossy material, and a larger, less intense highlight makes the material look smooth, but not very glossy. An example of the former is a brand new billiard ball, while the latter is an older billiard ball that has been in use for a long time. The absence of a Specular highlight indicates a surface that diffuses all light, such as rough brick or tree bark.

The controls in the Specular Highlights section of the shader's Basic Parameters rollout determine the highlight's size, shape, and intensity. You can place a map in the Specular Highlight channel of the material to control where on the object the Specular highlight appears.

Map areas that are black do not display Specular highlights, while white areas display highlights with the settings specified in the Specular Highlights section. Gray areas vary, depending on their intensity, and color maps use the grayscale equivalent of their colors. You can limit the specularity by using the Amount field.

CD FILE: The Specular.max file is available on the CD-ROM for you to practice with a Specular map.

Limit Specularity with a Specular Map

1. Open the Material Editor.

Note: *For more on opening the Material Editor, see the section "Add an Image to an Object's Surface."*

2. Click the material to which you want to add an opacity map.
3. In the Maps rollout, click the None button for the Specular Level channel.

   The Material/Map Browser appears.
4. Click a map with which you want to define the specularity.

   This example uses the Checker map.
5. Click OK.

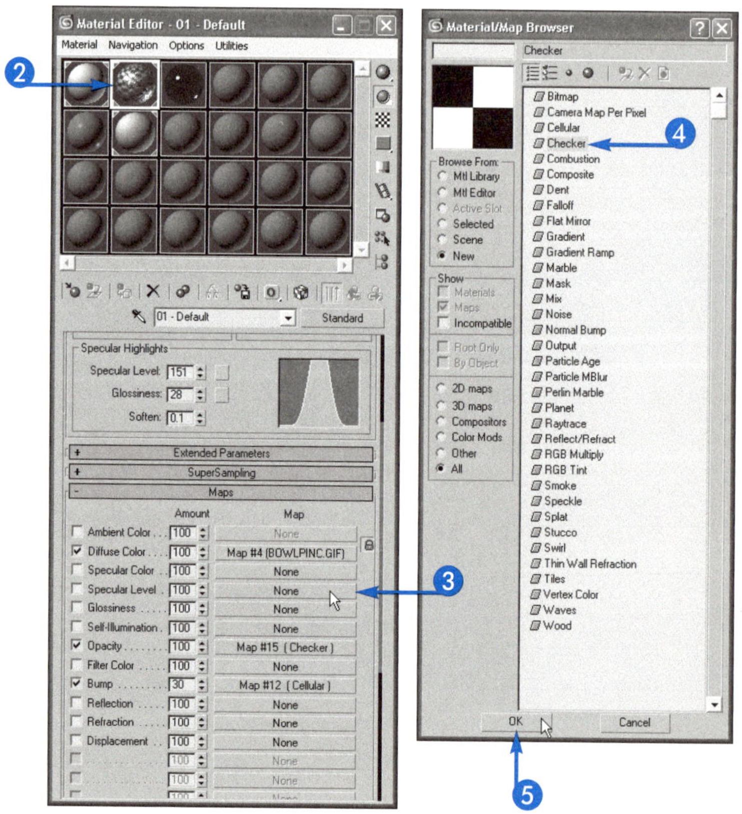

The map's parameters display in the Material Editor.

6 Adjust the map's parameters as required.

This example sets the Checker parameters to match the parameters for the Opacity channel.

7 Click .

The Specular Level channel is selected in the Maps rollout.

- The map's effect displays in the sample slot.
- If you want, you can change the value in the Amount field.
- If required, you can select an object and click to assign the material to it.

8 Click .

The image renders with the specular area restricted by the map.

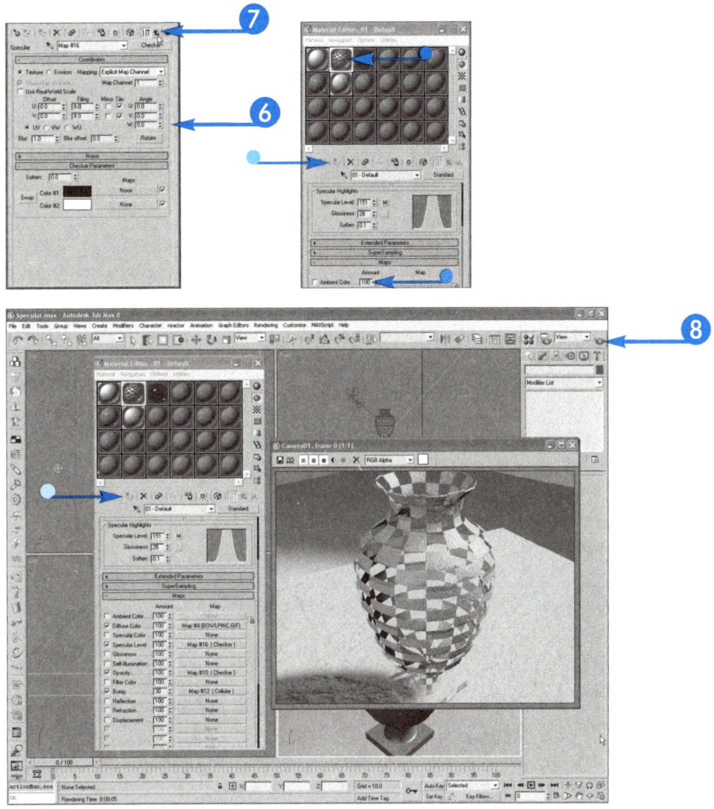

MASTER IT

What is the difference between the Specular Level map and the Glossiness map?

Both of these map channels affect the appearance of Specular highlight of a material and they are somewhat interdependant. The Specular Level map defines where and how intense a Specular highlight can appear on an object. The Glossiness map defines the size and sharpness the Specular highlight. If there is no Specular highlight, caused by an all white Specular Level map or a Specular Level value of zero in the Basic Parameters rollout, then the Glossiness map has no affect.

Can I use the same map for a Specular Level map as I do for another map channel?

Absolutely. It is a common practice to copy maps from one channel to another. In the steps in this section, you may find it faster to simply drag the Opacity map button to the Specular highlight map button. Once you do this, a pop-up menu appears, asking if you want to make the map an independent copy of the original or an instance, or whether you want the two maps to swap locations in the Maps rollout. When maps are instanced, changes to one map's parameters also affect the other map.

Create a Raytrace Metal Material

You can create realistic reflective materials using the Raytrace material. Raytracing produces the most realistic reflections and refractions on materials by tracing the light rays throughout the scene. You typically apply a Raytrace material to a shiny surface to show the reflections of other objects in the scene or the refractions as light passes through transparent materials.

You can customize your Raytrace material by using the rollouts in the Material Editor. The Raytrace-specific controls are located in the Raytrace Basic Parameters rollout. By default, 3ds Max applies the Phong shader to the Raytraced material, but there are several other choices.

You can determine the size, shape, and intensity of a shiny surface's highlights by adjusting the values in the Specular Highlight section of the Raytrace Basic Parameters rollout.

When using a transparent material, you need to adjust the *Index of Refraction*, or IOR, which determines how the material distorts light that passes through it. A low IOR results in less distortion. Most real-world materials have an IOR between 1.0 and 3.5, and glass has an IOR between 1.5 and 1.7.

CD FILE: The Material.max file is available on the CD-ROM for you to practice creating a Raytrace metal material.

Create a Raytrace Metal Material

1. In the Material Editor, click the sample slot for the new material.

Note: *For more on opening the Material Editor, see the section "Add an Image to an Object's Surface."*

2. Click the Material Type button.

   The Material/Map Browser appears, displaying the available material types.

3. Click Raytrace.
4. Click OK.

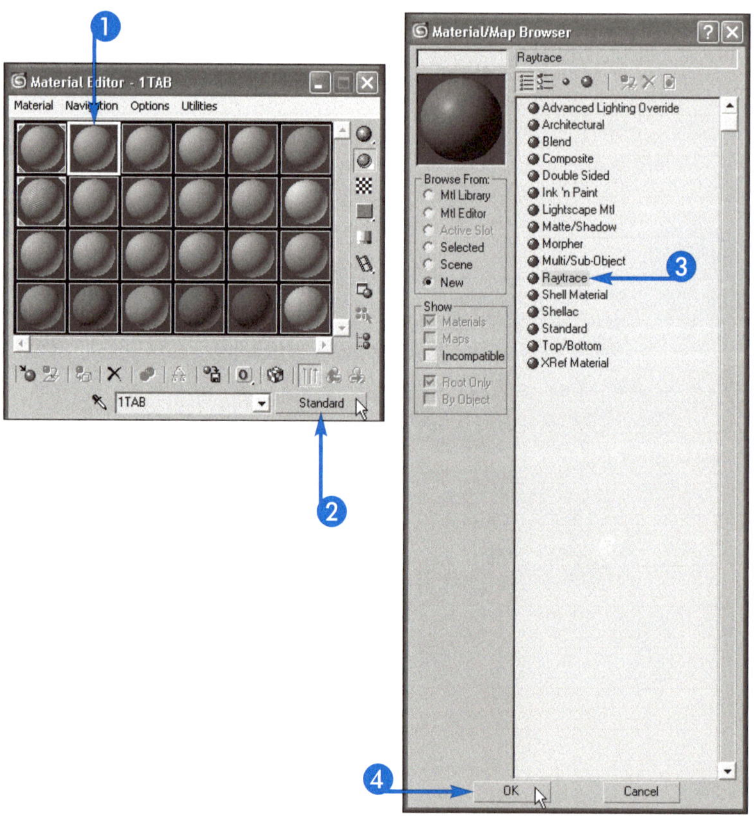

- 3ds Max creates the Raytraced material in the selected sample slot.
- You can click here and select another shader if you want.

5 Click the Diffuse color swatch and set the color for the material.

6 Type **169** for Specular Level, type **60** for Glossiness, and type **0.6** for Soften.

The values above are a good starting point for metallic highlights.

7 Click the Map button ( ) for the Reflect parameter.

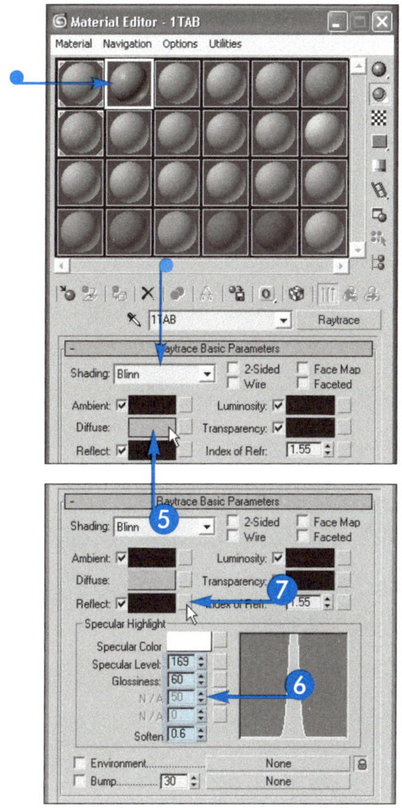

MASTER IT

How do I select the Diffuse color for my Raytraced material?

The color that you apply to the Diffuse parameter for a Raytraced material determines both the surface color and how the material reflects light. The darker the Diffuse color, the more light the material reflects. The Diffuse color is still the color that the object reflects, but the Reflection and Transparency effects are layered on top of the Diffuse color. As a result, the Diffuse color is only visible where the object is not reflecting its surroundings. When an object is partially reflecting its surroundings, the Diffuse color shows through the reflections.

What is the difference between the Raytrace material and a Raytrace map?

The main difference between the two is that you can apply a Raytrace map to a specific map channel of any Standard material. For example, when you apply a Raytrace map to the Reflection parameter in the Maps rollout, the object accurately reflects its surroundings without the need for 3ds Max to calculate the other, more intricate, parameters of a Raytrace material. Raytrace materials are more complex and accurate, but Standard materials with Raytrace maps render more quickly.

continued

Create a Raytrace Metal Material *(Continued)*

You can control surface reflectance of the Raytrace material that you are creating. In the real world, surfaces reflect light differently, based on the viewing angle of the object. For example, if you look directly through a window, the transparent state of the window's glass allows you to clearly see what is on the other side of the window. However, looking through the window at an angle creates a reflection on the window's surface. This reflection is called the *Fresnel Effect*.

You can apply the Fresnel Effect to your Raytrace material by setting a Falloff map for the Reflect parameter of the material. You can then select Fresnel as the Falloff Type for the map. You must also deselect the Override Material IOR option in the Falloff Parameters rollout to ensure that 3ds Max applies the correct IOR value to your material.

When you apply the Raytrace material to an object, you do not see its full effect until you render the object. To quickly determine how the Raytrace material appears on an object, you can select the Quick Render option. For more information on rendering, see Chapter 20.

Create a Raytrace Metal Material *(continued)*

The Material/Map Browser displays a list of available maps.

8 Click Falloff.

9 Click OK.

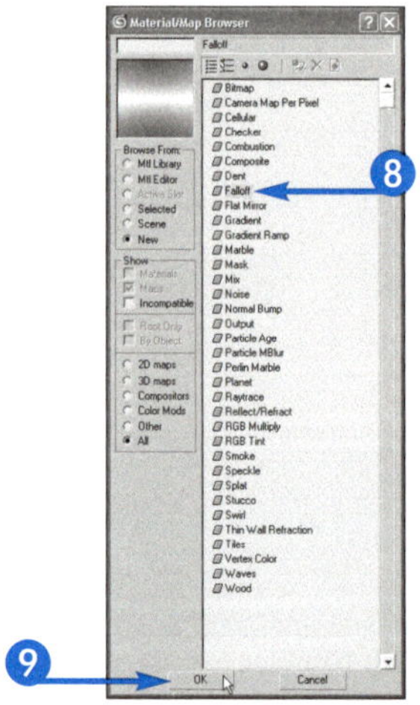

The Falloff Parameters rollout appears in the Material Editor.

10 Click here and then select a Falloff Type.

This example uses Fresnel.

The results of the Falloff type differ, depending on the viewing angle to the object.

11 Click to deselect the Override Material IOR option (☑ changes to ☐).

12 Click and drag the material to the object in the viewport.

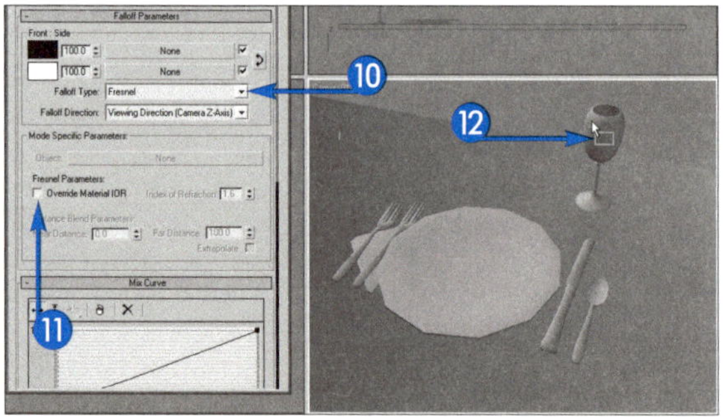

- 3ds Max adds the Raytrace material to the object.

⑬ Click [icon].

3ds Max renders the scene in the viewport to show the Raytrace material.

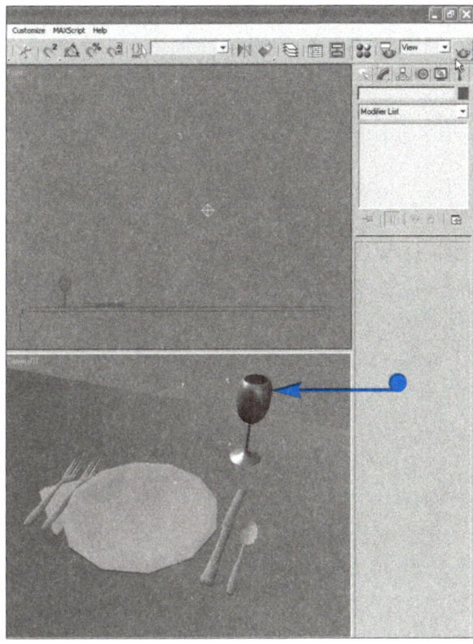

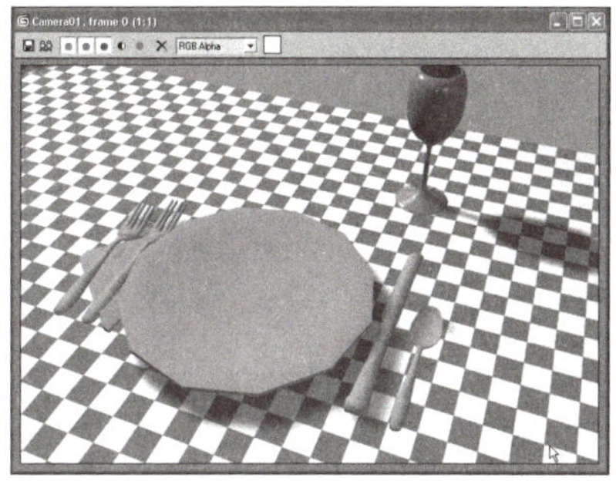

MASTER IT

How do I create a realistic glass object using a Raytrace material?

For glass objects, you need to change how the light refracts by setting the Index of Refraction value between 1.5 and 1.7. The higher the value, the more the material distorts the images behind it. You also need to make the material transparent. You can do this by clicking the Transparency color swatch in the Raytrace Basic Parameters rollout and selecting a color close to white, or by deselecting the Transparency option (☑ changes to ☐) and then typing a value near 100 in the field that replaces the color swatch.

Do I need special lighting with a Raytrace material?

No, you do not need to add special lighting to your scene. In fact, you can use any type of lighting with Raytrace materials. The Raytracer traces the light rays of whatever lighting you use in your scene and uses this information to determine the reflection and refraction values for your objects. For example, if you want to produce shadows for your objects, as shown in these steps, then you need to apply lighting to the objects. When you apply Raytrace materials to the objects, they also show a reflection of the light, based upon the light placement. For more information on adding lighting to a scene, see Chapter 17.

Using the Multi/Sub-Object Material

When an object is made of several different components, each with its own material features, then you need to apply a Multi/Sub-Object material to address the different components. A Multi/Sub-Object material contains different sub-materials that have their own distinct qualities. When you apply the material to an object, the different sub-materials apply to the sub-object areas of the object, based on the Material IDs that you assign. For example, when you create a television, you assign different Material IDs to the screen, case, and controls. Each numbered sub-material is applied to the faces of the object with the corresponding Material IDs. When you drag and drop separate materials onto sub-object selections of Editable Mesh or Editable Poly objects, 3ds Max automatically creates a Multi/Sub-Object material.

By default, the Material Editor lists ten sub-materials, each displaying a preview sample sphere, a Name field, a Material button, a Color swatch, and an Enable check box. You change the number of sub-materials via the Set Number button in the Material Editor. You should have one sub-material for each set of correspondingly numbered faces on the object to which the material is applied.

CD FILE: The Sub-Material.max file is available on the CD-ROM for you to practice creating Multi/Sub-Object materials.

Using the Multi/Sub-Object Material

1. In the Material Editor, click the sample slot for the new material.

Note: For more on opening the Material Editor, see the section "Add an Image to an Object's Surface."

2. Click the Material Type button.

   The Material/Map Browser appears.

3. Click Multi/Sub-Object.
4. Click OK.
5. Click OK in the Replace Material dialog box that appears.

   3ds Max creates the Multi/Sub-Object material.

   The Multi/Sub-Object Basic Parameters rollout displays in the Material Editor, with the default number of sub-materials.

6. In the Material Editor, click Set Number.

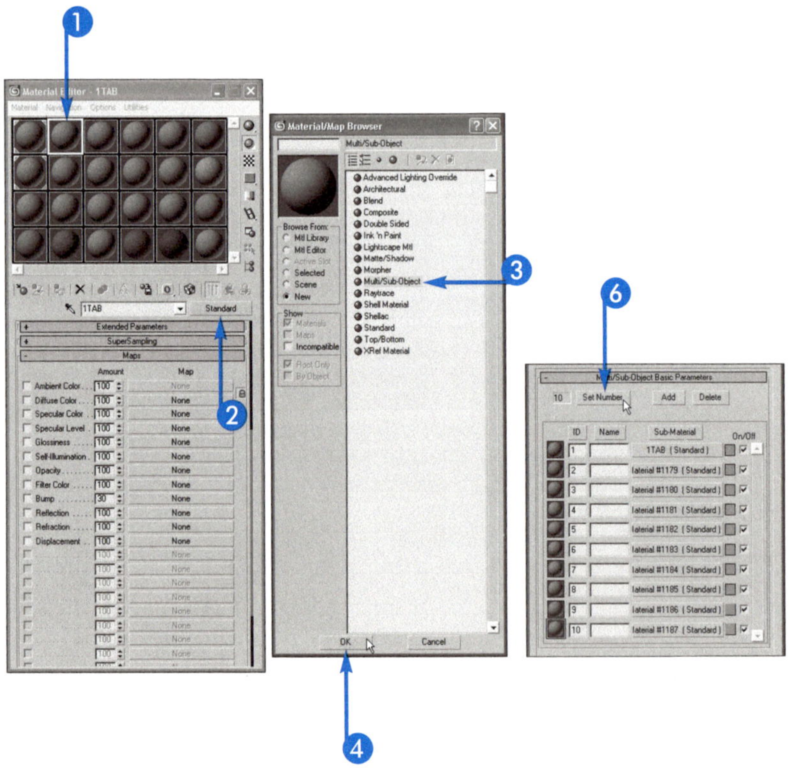

The Set Number of Materials dialog box appears.

7. Type the number of sub-materials that you want the material to contain.
8. Click OK.

The Multi/Sub-Object Basic Parameters rollout updates to display the specified number of materials.

9. Click the Material button for the first sub-material.

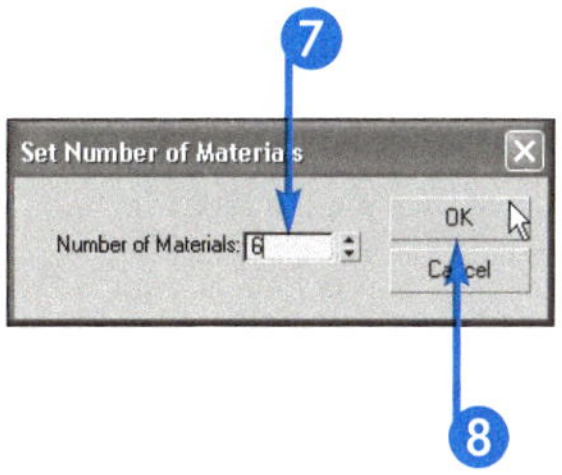

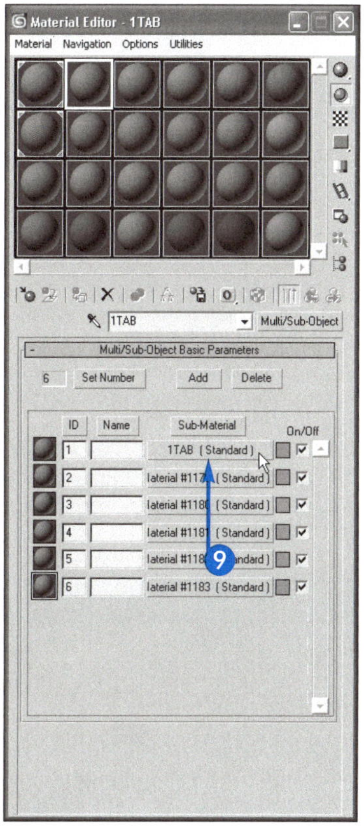

MASTER IT

Do I need to create a custom material for each sub-material?

▼ No. When you create a Multi/Sub-Object material, 3ds Max automatically creates materials for each sub-material in the list. The default materials are the Standard material type with the default color components. If you only want to change the material color, then you can click the Color swatch next to the Material Type button and select the material color that you want in the Color Selector dialog box. You can click the Color swatch to change the color of any material type that you have created for a sub-material. For information on Color swatches and using the Color Selector, see Chapter 14.

How do I set the Material IDs for the faces on my object?

▼ The Material IDs are set at the Face, Polygon, or Element sub-object level of an editable poly or editable mesh, or of an object with an Edit Poly or Edit Mesh modifier applied. Select the sub-objects for which you want to set the Material ID, and then expand the Polygon Properties or Surface Properties rollout, depending on the object or modifier that you are altering. Enter the Material ID that you want to assign to the selected face in the Set ID field. For more information on the Editable Poly object and the Edit Poly modifier, see Chapter 6.

continued

Using the Multi/Sub-Object Material *(Continued)*

You can create custom materials for every sub-material in the Multi/Sub-Object Material Parameters rollout. These materials can use any 3ds Max material type or map, and you can define each sub-material independently in the Material Editor. The sub-material parameters display when you select the corresponding material button. You can use the Go to Parent button to move to the top of the material hierarchy, or the Go to Sibling button to move to the next sub-material.

Each sub-material displays in a separate area on the object in the sample slot. For example, with four sub-materials, this object is divided into four sections.

When you assign a Multi/Sub-Object material to an object, 3ds Max looks for Material IDs on the sub-object surfaces that match the number for each sub-material. If a sub-material does not have a correspondingly numbered sub-object on the object that the material is assigned to, then that sub-material is ignored. For example, when you apply a material with three sub-materials to an object that uses only Material ID numbers 1 and 2, then sub-material number 3 does not show on the object.

The Sub-Material.max file is available on the CD-ROM for you to practice creating Multi/Sub-Object materials.

Using the Multi/Sub-Object Material *(continued)*

The selected sub-material displays in the Material Editor.

⑩ Create the sub-material that you want by adjusting the material's parameters, such as the shader color components and maps.

Note: *For more information on creating materials, see Chapter 14.*

⑪ Click the Go to Parent button ( ) to return to the Multi/Sub-Object material.

- The changes to the sub-material display in the list and the sample slot.
- It is a good idea to name your sub-materials in the Name field.

⑫ Repeat steps 9 to 11 to create additional sub-materials.

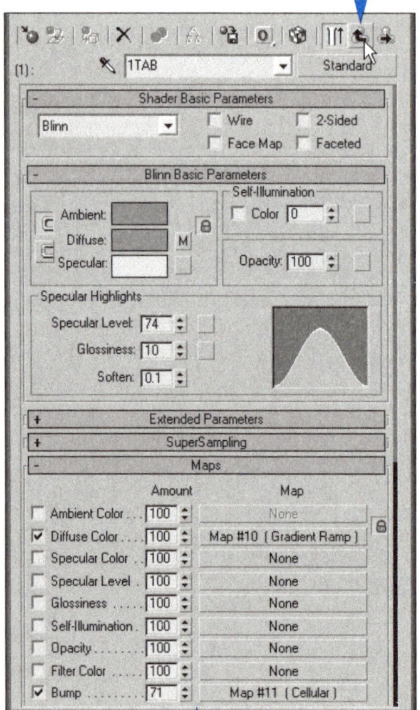

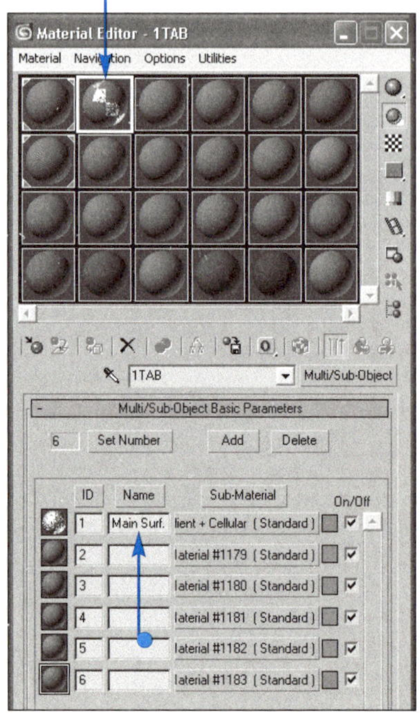

The material in the sample slot displays all the sub-materials.

13. Select an object.
14. Click .
15. Click .

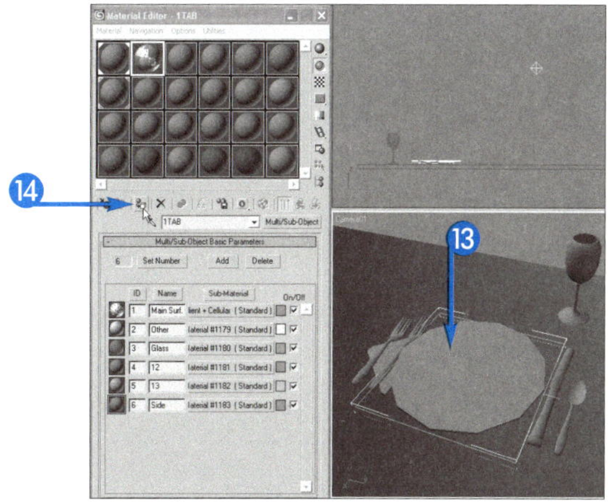

3ds Max renders the scene with the Multi/Sub-Object material applied to your object.

Can I remove specific sub-materials?

- Yes. Instead of using the Set Number button to reduce the number of materials in the list, you can manually remove specific materials from the list by clicking the small sample sphere of the sub-material and then clicking Delete in the Multi/Sub-Object Basic Parameters rollout. When you remove a sub-material, the Material IDs do not change for the remaining materials. For example, if you have four materials and you delete the sub-material with an ID of 3, then three sub-materials remain with IDs of 1, 2, and 4. You can manually type a new ID for any sub-material in the ID field.

Can I sort the list of sub-materials?

- Yes, you can sort the list of sub-materials for the Multi/Sub-Object material by ID, Name, or Sub-Material. This is especially helpful when your list is too long to fit in the rollout. When you sort by ID, 3ds Max sorts the list in ascending numerical order. This is the default sorting method, with the material assigned ID 1 appearing at the top of the list. If you have assigned names to the materials, then you can click Name to sort them alphabetically. You can also sort the materials alphabetically by clicking Sub-Material.

Create an Architectural Material

Architectural materials are specialty materials that are designed for use with photometric lights and the Radiosity advanced lighting plug-in. When used in conjunction with these features, Architectural materials yield technically accurate results. You cannot achieve the same accuracy when using Standard lights without radiosity. For information on setting up lights in 3ds Max, see Chapters 17 and 18.

You can use the Architectural material type to create several different types of construction materials, including glass, wood flooring, and painted walls. You can also easily create custom scene materials from the included templates by specifying the necessary parameter values.

The default template loads with parameters for setting the properties of an architectural material. You can then use the parameters to create a custom material, or you can load one of the pre-defined templates, such as Clear Glass, from the Templates rollout.

When you select a template, the parameter values in the Physical Qualities rollout change to display the appropriate values for the selection. For example, selecting the Glass-Clear template sets the Transparency value to 100, making the material completely transparent.

CD FILE — The ArchGlass.max file is available on the CD-ROM for you to practice creating Architectural materials.

Create an Architectural Material

1. In the Material Editor, select the sample slot where you want to create the material.
2. Click the Material Type button.

   The Material/Map Browser appears.
3. Click Architectural.
4. Click OK.

   The Architectural material templates load in the Material Editor.
5. Click here and select Glass-Clear.

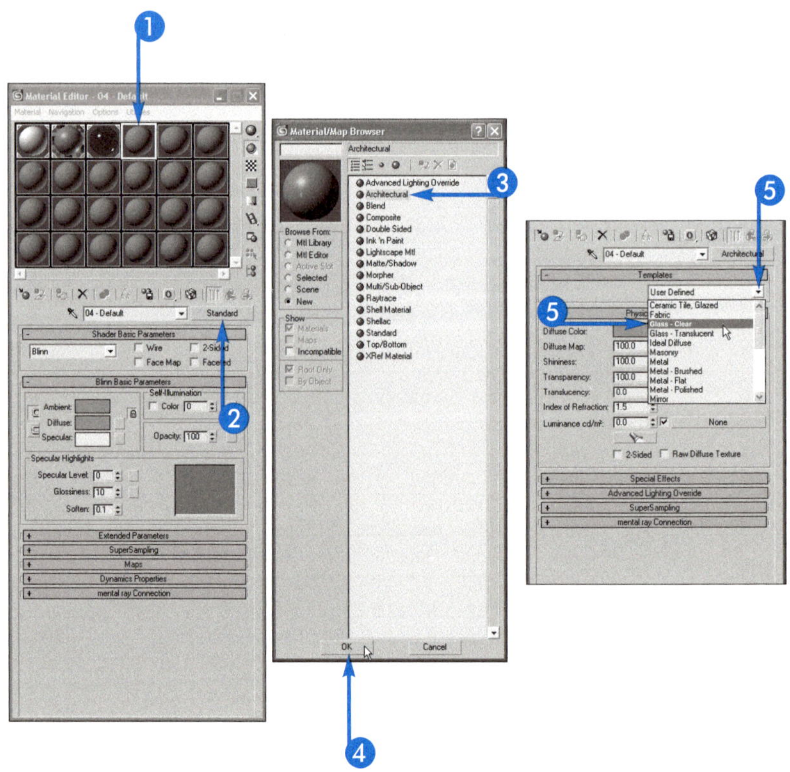

The parameter settings load for the selected template.

6 Adjust the material's parameters as required.

7 Select an object and click [icon] to apply the material to it.

8 Recalculate the radiosity solution.

Note: *For information on radiosity, see Chapter 18.*

9 Click Render.

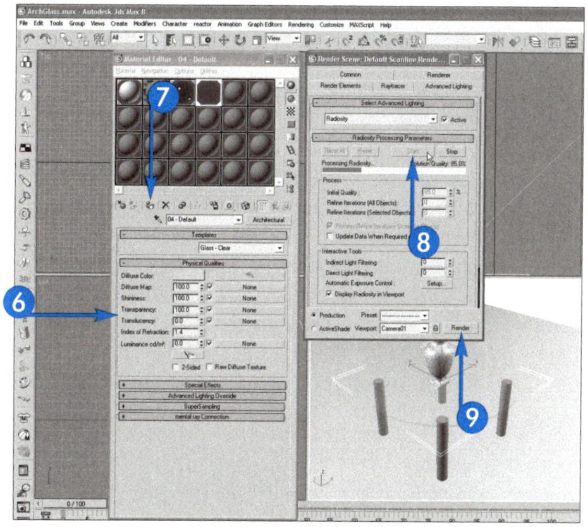

3ds Max renders the scene with the Architectural material.

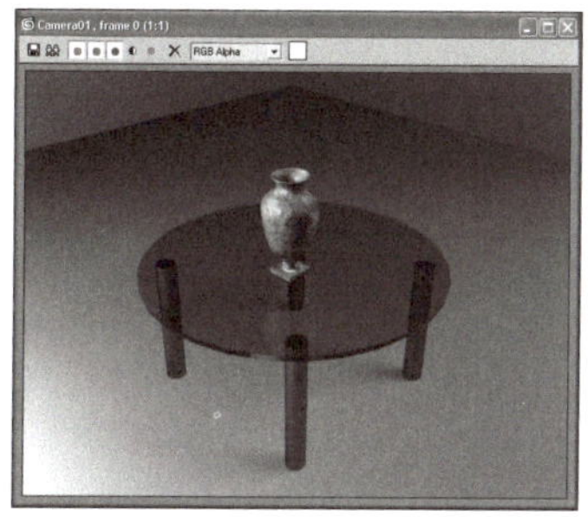

MASTER IT

What materials can I create with the Architectural material type?

▼ The Architectural material type provides templates for creating ceramic tile, fabric, glass, masonry, paper, plastic, stone, water, wood, several different metals, and mirrored and painted surfaces. Keep in mind that the template that you select only loads the parameter values to create a starting point for the material. You can adjust those parameter settings to achieve the results that fit your scene. This includes not only setting the Diffuse color for the material, but also applying maps to different parameters. For example, you can add a pattern to your Glass material by loading a map for the Diffuse Map parameter.

Should I use mental ray with Architectural materials?

▼ Architectural materials work best with the Default Scanline Renderer. Although the mental ray Renderer can be used with the Architectural materials, there are some restrictions on what you can do. Consult any third-party renderer's documentation before using any Architectural materials in a scene with those renderers. The mental ray Renderer ignores the illumination from the material's Luminance setting, which normally adds to the light in the scene. The mental ray renderer also controls the antialiasing of maps internally and does not adhere to any of the Architectural material's sampling settings.

Create an Ink 'n Paint Material

Many of the concepts and tools used in animation today are based on the tools used in early cartoon animation. The Material Editor has come full circle by providing a material that mimics the hand-drawn and inked look of cartoons. The Ink 'n Paint material displays perimeter edges as solid lines and uses a limited number of color changes across the faces of the object with the material applied.

Ink 'n Paint material controls are broken into two separate features: those that affect the ink, which is drawn around the perimeters, and those that affect the paint that fills in the surfaces. The Paint Levels parameter, in the Paint Controls rollout, determines the number of color shifts that the paint can have over a surface. The Lighted color is the diffuse color for the object, and the Shaded and Highlight colors determine the object's ambient and Specular colors.

In the Ink Controls rollout, you can set the minimum and maximum ink width and whether the width can vary, to create a more hand-drawn appearance in the material.

CD FILE The Ink_n_Paint.max file is available on the CD-ROM for you to practice creating Ink 'n Paint materials.

Create an Ink 'n Paint Material

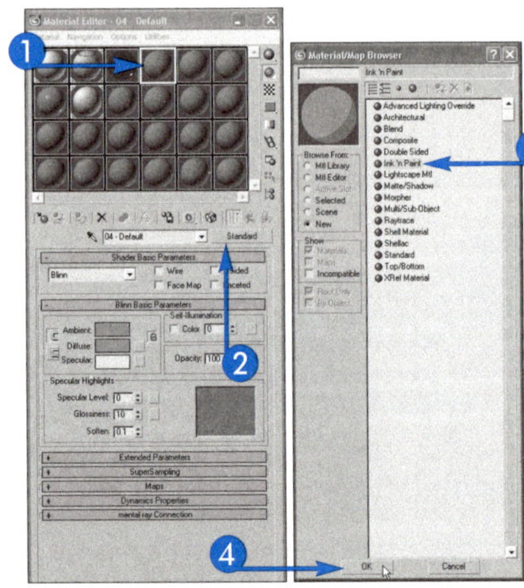

1. In the Material Editor, select the sample slot where you want to create the material.
2. Click the Material Type button.

   The Material/Map Browser appears.
3. Click Ink 'n Paint.
4. Click OK.

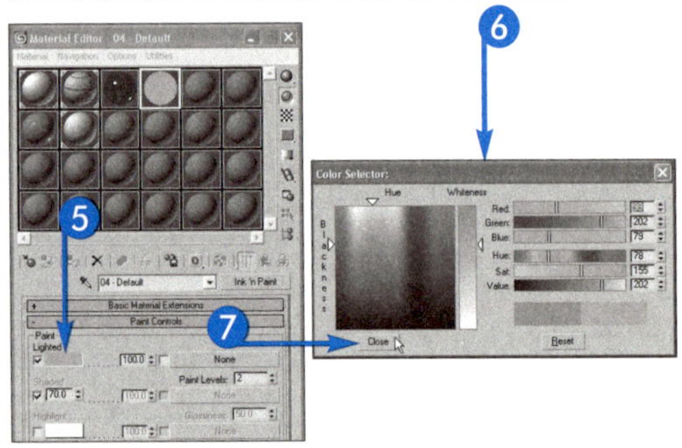

The Ink 'n Paint material rollouts display in the Material Editor.

5. Click the Lighted Color swatch.

   The Color Selector dialog box appears.
6. Use the sliders and spinners to specify the color for the material.
7. Click Close.

The new color displays in the sample slot.

8. Type a higher number in the Paint Levels field.
9. Click the Variable Width option (☐ becomes ☑).
10. Select an object and click to apply the material to it.
11. Click .

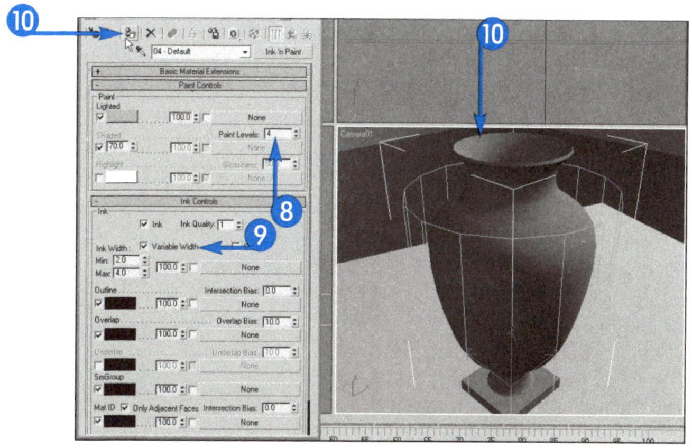

3ds Max renders the scene with the Ink 'n Paint material that you created.

Why does the Shaded parameter show up as a number, rather than a color?

▼ The Shaded parameter sets the color for the unlit faces of the object with the Ink 'n Paint material applied. By default, this is a numeric value that determines the color based on a percentage of the Lighted color. A value of 100 is the same as the Lighted color, and a value of zero is black. You can set a distinct color for the Shaded parameter by deselecting the Shaded check box (☑ changes to ☐) to display a Color swatch. Click the Color swatch to open the Color Selector, where you can set the Shaded color.

What are all of the Color swatches for in the Ink Controls rollout?

▼ The Color swatches determine the colors for the five possible ink conditions, and the check box next to each Color swatch turns the feature on and off. The Outline parameter creates ink lines around the outermost perimeter of the object. The Overlap and Underlap parameters control the ink when one portion of the object is placed in front of another. The SmGroup parameter places ink lines between surfaces that belong to different smoothing groups, and the Mat ID parameter draws ink lines between surfaces with different material ID numbers. All ink conditions are turned on by default, except Underlap. See the section "Using the Multi/Sub-Object Material" for information on Material IDs.

Adjust Materials on an Object Using the UVW Map Modifier

An object's mapping coordinates instruct 3ds Max on how to place a material's maps onto the object's surfaces. For example, you may want to place the image as if it were flat and projecting onto the object, or wrapped around the object spherically or cylindrically. Procedural maps, such as Cellular and Noise, do not need mapping coordinates.

Primitive and compound objects have default mapping coordinates assigned, but these coordinates are lost when you convert an object to an editable poly. To apply mapping coordinates to an editable poly, or to override existing mapping coordinates, you must apply the UVW Map modifier.

Using the UVW Map modifier, the maps are projected from a gizmo onto the surfaces of the object. You typically use Planar mapping to project the map from a rectangle-shaped gizmo onto a flat object. Each mapping type projects the map using a different method. The U, V, and W axes of a map relate to its width, height, and depth. You can control the repeating of the map with the U, V, and W Tile values.

CD FILE The UVW.max file is available on the CD-ROM for you to practice applying the UVW Map modifier.

Adjust Materials on an Object Using the UVW Map Modifier

1. Select an object.
2. Apply a mapped material to the object.

Note: *For information on applying materials, see Chapter 14.*

3. Click the Modify Panel icon ( ).

   The Modify panel appears.

4. Click ▾ and select UVW Map.

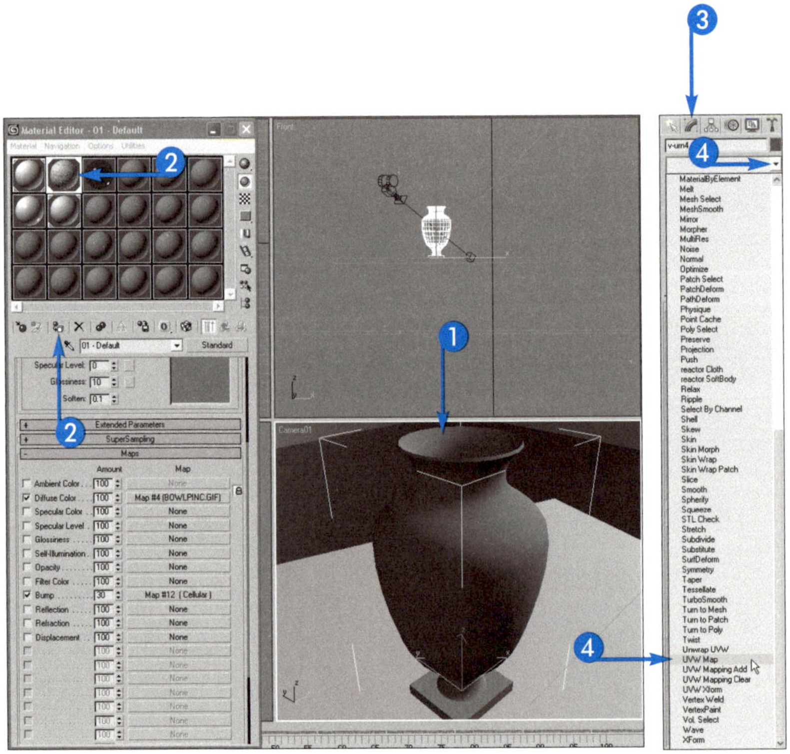

The UVW Map modifier's parameters display in the Modify panel.

The default Planar mapping type is assigned.

5 Click the mapping parameter that fits your object's shape (○ changes to ◉).

The mapping changes on the object.

- You can enter values to adjust the U, V, and W tiling across the surface of your object.

6 Click .

3ds Max renders the scene with the assigned mapping coordinates.

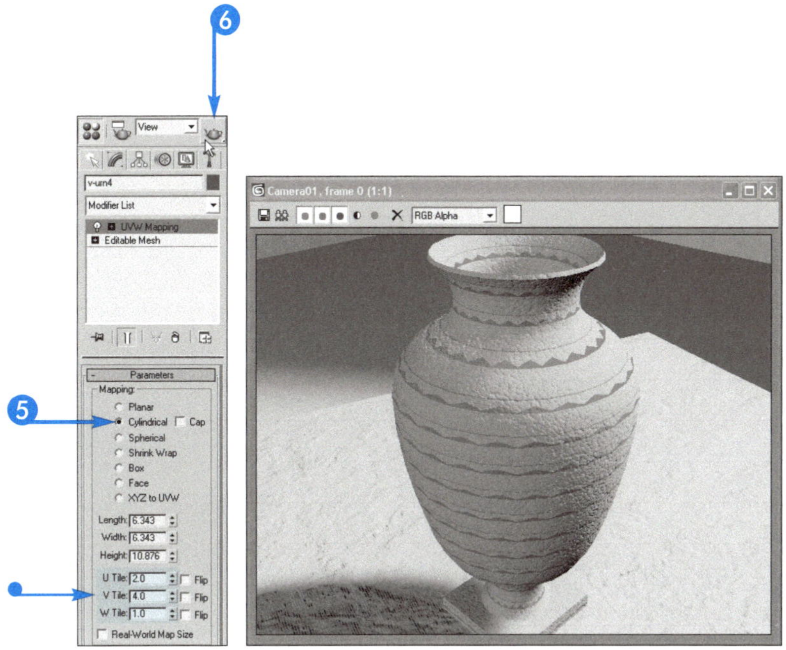

MASTER IT

What are the Length, Width, and Height fields for?

As with several other modifiers that you can apply to an object, the UVW Map modifier has a gizmo that you can use to control the placement of the map on the object. Changing the values of the Length, Width, and Height fields, in the Parameters rollout, changes the size of the UVW Map gizmo. This, in turn, can alter the location and size of the map on the object. You can also change the positioning of the map by expanding the modifier in the Modifier Stack, selecting Gizmo, and then using the Transform tools to move, scale, or rotate the gizmo. For more information about the Transform gizmos, see Chapter 2.

Why do I see an error message about the UVW Map modifier when I try to render my mapped object?

The fastest way to know whether an object needs mapping coordinates and the UVW Map modifier is to render your scene. A Missing Map Coordinates dialog box appears if you attempt to render an object with a material that contains a bitmap that does not have mapping coordinates. For example, the message [UVW 1]; vase, means that the UVW mapping coordinates are missing for the object named vase. The message displays because 3ds Max does not know how to apply the mapped material to the object, as it does not have mapping coordinates. If you see an error message like this, you can correct it by applying the UVW Map modifier to the specified object.

17 Using Standard Lights

18 Using Advanced Lighting

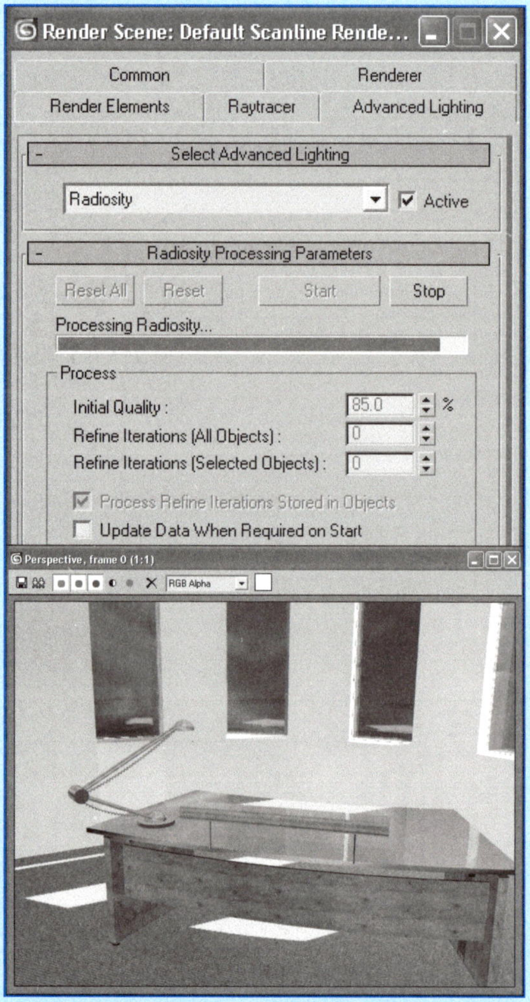

PART V

ADDING LIGHTS AND CAMERAS

19 Using Cameras

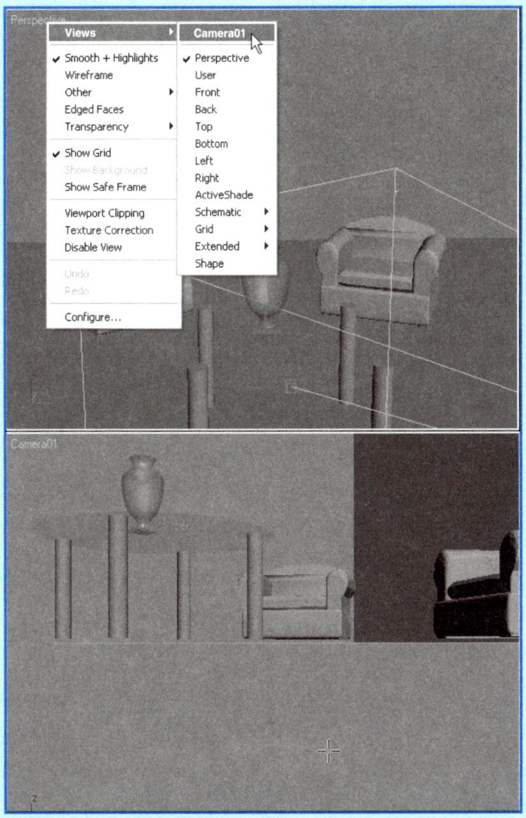

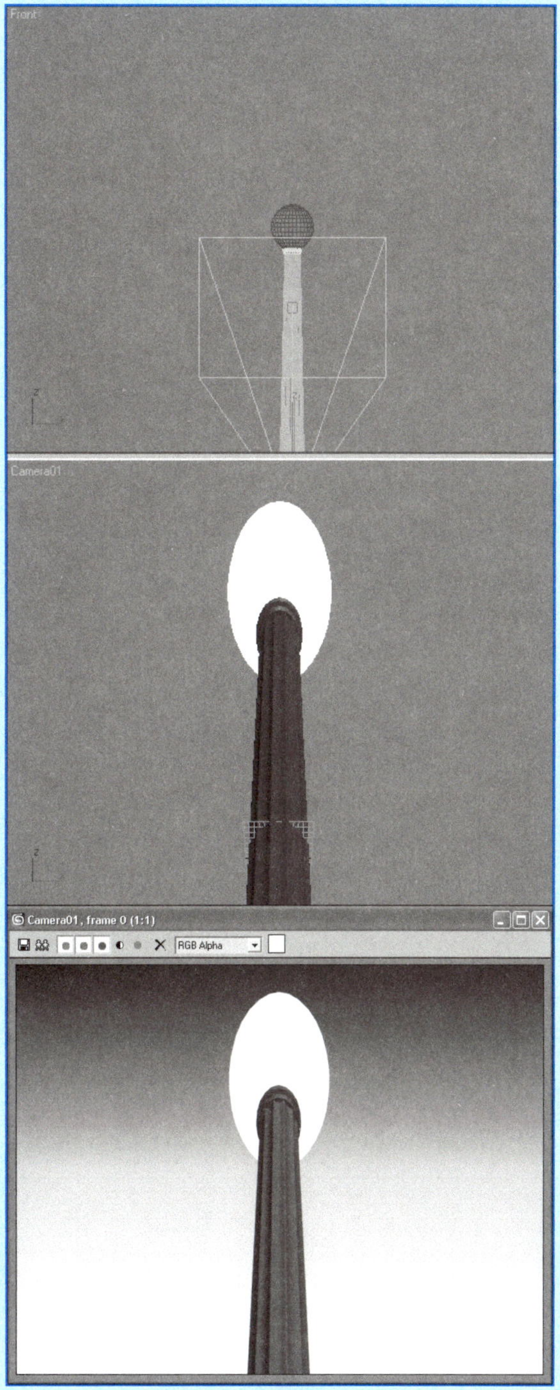

Understanding Standard Lights

You can use lighting, a critical element in the creation of any 3ds Max project, to properly view objects, to enhance the look and feel of your scene, and to help the viewer to focus on specific objects. Every scene must have some type of lighting 3ds Max automatically adds two non-editable default lights to every new scene and positions them above the scene on the left side and at the bottom-right side.

This default lighting is only meant to illuminate the objects, and is often ineffective. Placing any new light in your scene automatically deletes the default lighting. 3ds Max provides two different lighting categories for your use, Standard and Photometric. Photometric lights are designed for use with the Radiosity lighting plug-in that is discussed in Chapter 18. You use Standard lighting in scenes that do not use a lighting plug-in.

You can select your lighting options via the Lights button in the Create panel.

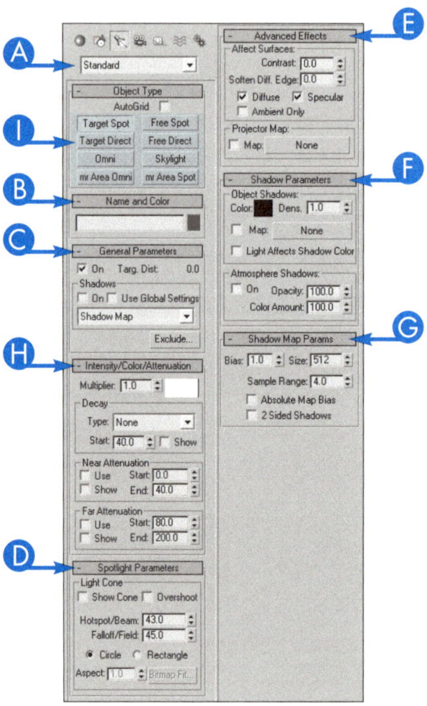

A Light Category List Box

Switches between Standard and Photometric lights. The Object Type rollout buttons reflects the Light type that you select.

B Name and Color Rollout

Displays the name and color of the selected light.

C General Parameters Rollout

Turns the light on or off and activates the light's shadows. You select the shadow type, and you can choose which objects are affected by the light.

D Spotlight Parameters Rollout

Displays with Spotlight light types. You can specify the angular distances for both the Hotspot and Falloff cones. When a Directional light is selected, the Directional Parameters rollout displays with the same controls.

E Advanced Effects Rollout

Controls how the light interacts with the surface of objects.

F Shadow Parameters Rollout

Specifies a color and density for the shadows. You also can set whether the light affects shadow color and other shadow parameters

G Shadow Map Params Rollout

Customizes the Shadow Maps selected in the General Parameters rollout including the size of the bitmap used for a shadow.

H Intensity/Color/ Attenuation Rollout

Controls the brightness and color of the illumination that the light emits. You can also specify the attenuation and decay of the light, which determine how the light diminishes over distance.

I Object Type Buttons

Allow you to create one of eight different Standard lights.

Standard versus Photometric Lights

3ds Max provides two different categories of lighting for your scene — Standard and Photometric. Each category has different types of lights that you can apply, depending upon the method that you use to light your scene. Both categories of lighting allow you to light both the entire scene and individual objects. The difference between the lighting categories is in the type of lighting effects that you can create.

Because they are easier to work with than Photometric lights, you commonly use Standard lights in 3ds Max to simulate artificial lighting, such as household lamps, office lighting, and stage lighting. You can also use Standard lights to simulate the sun, although you cannot control the physical intensity of the sunlight as you can with Photometric lighting.

Because Photometric lights are based upon physical parameters such as brightness, intensity, color temperature, and light distribution, these lights produce more accurate lighting and are commonly used in architectural renderings. Photometric lighting is measured using real-world measurement values, with light intensity in lumens, and light temperatures in degrees Kelvin. Because Photometric lights depend on the scene scale being correct, using Photometric lights in a physically large scene produces dark results. Photometric lights not only calculate the illumination from the lights themselves, but also the light that bounces off the objects in the scene.

Standard Light Object Types

3ds Max has eight different types of lights. Because each type of light produces different effects, you can use any combination of lighting types to achieve the result that you want. Once you select a light type, you can customize the parameters for the light using the rollouts in the Create panel. You can also modify the position and orientation for the light using the Transform tools.

Standard Light Object Types

Type	*Description*
Target Spot	Creates a light with all illumination emitting from a single point in the shape of a cone. The light's orientation is locked toward its Target object. To change the orientation of the light, you move the target.
Free Spot	The same as the Target Spot, but with no Target object. You can change the orientation of the Free Spotlight using the Rotate Transform tool.
Target Direct	Creates a light with all illumination emitting in parallel rays from a circular plane in the shape of a cylinder. The light's orientation is locked toward its Target object. To change the orientation of the light, you move the target.
Free Direct	The same as the Target Direct, but with no Target object. You can change the orientation of the Free Direct light using the Rotate Transform tool.
Omni	Creates a light that casts light rays in all directions equally. The two default lights that 3ds Max adds to a scene are Omni lights.
Skylight	Creates a controllable ambient light object that you can add to your scenes. The location of the light does not matter. The Skylight is designed to model daylight and is meant to be used with the Light Tracer.
mr Area Omni	Designed for use with the mental ray Renderer, this object type creates a light object that emits light in all directions from either a spherical or cylindrical area. If you render the scene with the Default Scanline Renderer, then the light is treated as a standard Omni light object.
mr Area Spot	Designed for use with the mental ray Renderer, this object type creates a light object that emits a focused beam from a rectangular or disc-shaped area. If rendered with the Default Scanline Renderer, then the light is treated as a standard Free Spotlight object.

Create Standard Light Objects

You can use any combination of lights to illuminate your scene. Typically, a scene has more than one light source, which helps to create a sense of depth. Lighting a scene in 3ds Max is similar to setting up lighting for a camera shoot. Lights are strategically placed in the scene to achieve specific results. A good lighting method consists of three different types of lights: a key light, fill lights, and a backlight.

You can use the key light as the main light that focuses on the subject of your scene. A key light is positioned in front of and above the subject, and it should also be positioned slightly to the side. You may want to turn on the light's shadows so that they are cast in the scene by the key light. A spotlight is often used as the key light.

To position light objects, you can use the Transform tools. Use the Move tool to adjust the position of the light, or its target in the viewports. Use the Rotate tool to orient free lights to point them at the subject of the scene.

CD FILE: The CreateLights.max file is available on the CD-ROM for you to practice creating Standard lights.

Create Standard Light Objects

Create a Key Light

1. Click the Create Panel button ( ).
2. Click the Lights button ( ) to create light objects.

   The Standard light types display by default.

   If the Photometric lights are shown, click ▾ to display the Standard light types.
3. Click Target Spot.

   The Target Spot parameters display.
4. Click the On option (☐ changes to ☑) in the Shadows section.
5. Click to place the light object in front of the subject.
6. Drag and release to set the target location.

   3ds Max creates a light and deletes the default lights.
7. Click the Select and Move button ( ).
8. Click and drag to position the light.

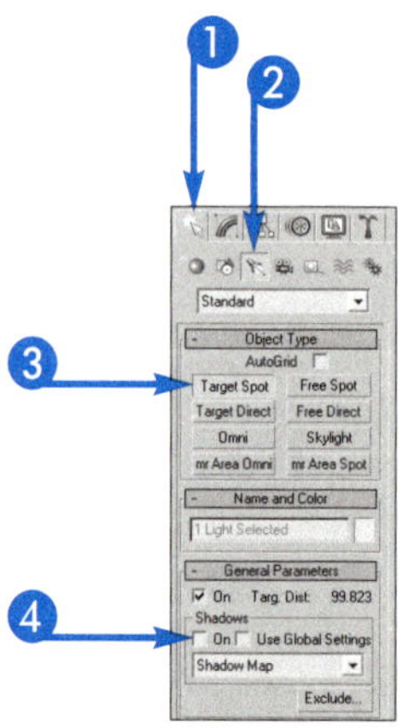

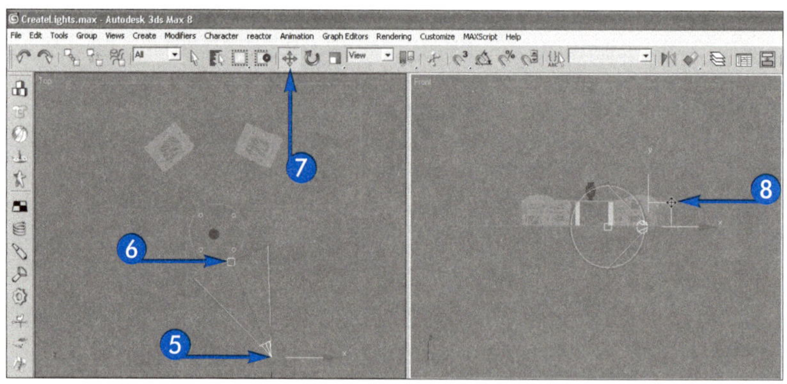

The light moves to the new position. The target remains unchanged.

9 Click and drag the target to move it.

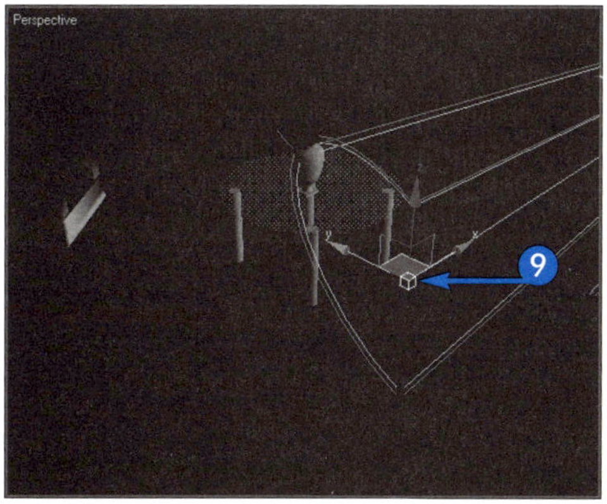

The light reorients itself to focus on the target.

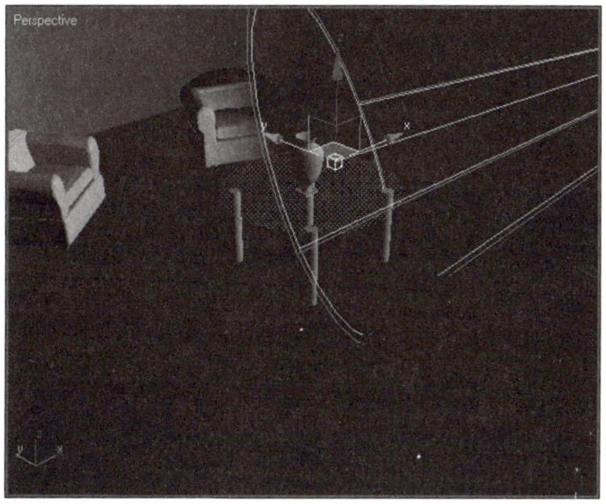

MASTER IT

Why should the key light cast shadows?

In real life, if you look at most objects, you see that they cast shadows that are created by the areas of the object where the light is obscured. Shadows are normally caused by the main light source. To specify that 3ds Max creates shadows in your scene, you must activate the Shadows On option (☐ changes to ☑), in the General Parameters rollout, for the key light. This causes shadowing to occur when rendering in the areas that are obscured from the key light. 3ds Max actually provides different types of shadows that you can select. See the sections "Apply Shadow Maps to a Light" and "Apply Ray Traced Shadows to a Light" for more information about working with shadows.

What is the difference between using a Free Spot and a Target Spot as a key light?

The only difference between these two lights is the target. With a Target Spot light, you have an explicit target object that you can select and move to reorient the light. When you move the light itself, it remains oriented toward the target at all times. With the Free Spot light, you change the orientation of the light by using the Rotate transform. Be sure to change the Rotate transform's Reference Coordinate System to Local to more easily control the rotations. For information on the Reference Coordinate Systems, see Chapter 2.

continued

Create Standard Light Objects *(Continued)*

To enhance the lighting in your scene, you can add fill lights and backlights. 3ds Max's Standard lights do not calculate bounced illumination and these lights are intended to represent bounced light and other additional light sources.

There is no limit to the amount of fill and back lights that you can add to your scene, but the fewer that you can get away with, the better. The larger the scene, the more lights you may need. It is a good idea to start with one fill light, typically below and to the opposite side of the key light, and then to add additional lights as required. Non-shadow-casting Omnis are a good choice because they cast light in all directions.

The back light serves the purpose of helping to frame your subject against the background. An Omni light also works well as a back light.

Because both lighting types are meant to fill in the gaps in a scene, you want them to be less bright than your key light. To do this, you reduce the Multiplier value in the Intensity/Color/Attenuation rollout.

The CreateFillLights.max file is available on the CD-ROM for you to practice adding fill and backlights.

Create Standard Light Objects *(continued)*

Create Fill and Back Lights

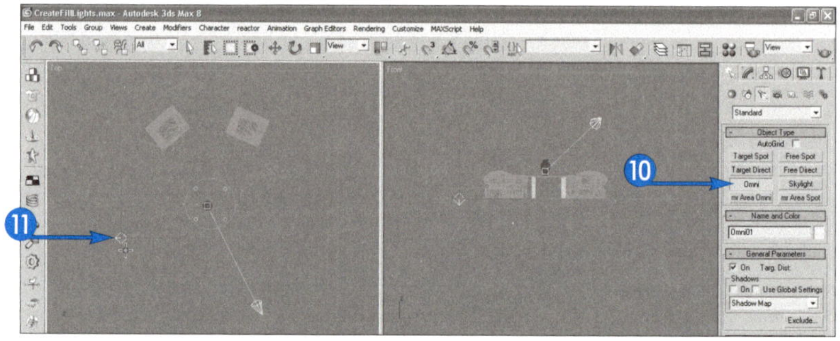

10. In the Create panel, click Omni.

    The Omni light parameters display in the Create panel.

11. Click in the Top viewport to add the fill light to your scene.

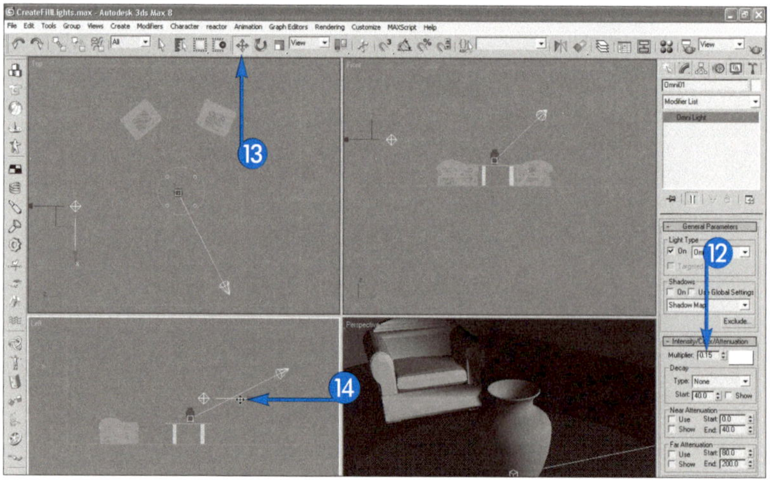

    3ds Max creates the Omni light in your scene.

12. Lower the Multiplier value.

Note: *See the section "Adjust the Brightness of a Light" for more information about the Multiplier field.*

13. Click ⊕.

14. Click and drag to move the light.

Create a Backlight

15. In the Create panel, click Omni.

    The Omni object light parameters display in the Create panel.

16. In the viewports, click to add the backlight object behind the objects in your scene.

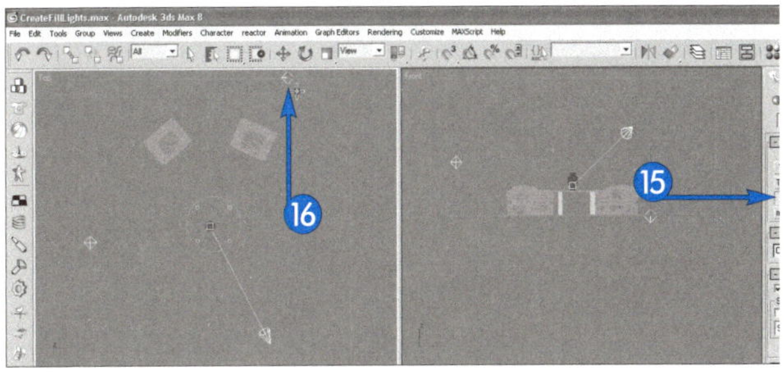

- 3ds Max creates the Omni light object in your scene.

17. Adjust the Multiplier value if required.

18. Click the Quick Render button ( ).

    3ds Max renders the current viewport with the new lighting.

How do I control which objects are affected by the light?

3ds Max allows you to select objects that you do not want to be affected by the light and to exclude them from the light's effect. When you do this, the rendering is adjusted so that it does not calculate those objects in the light's illumination. Keep in mind that other lights in the scene may still cast light on those objects. You can exclude objects by clicking the Exclude button in the General Parameters rollout. See the section "Include and Exclude Objects from a Light's Effects" for more information about excluding objects.

What does the Multiplier field do?

Located in the Intensity/Color/Attenuation rollout, the Multiplier field controls the intensity of the light. The default value of the Multiplier is 1. If you want to make the light brighter, then you can increase this value. For example, a value of 2.0 makes the light twice as bright, while a value of 0.5 reduces the light intensity by half. Keep in mind that when you work with secondary lights and backlights, you want to reduce the intensity of these lights compared to the key light. See the section "Adjust the Brightness of a Light" for more information about the Multiplier.

Adjust the Color of a Light

You can use the color of light to change the mood of a scene. 3ds Max allows you to select a light color for any light object. By changing the color of light, you change the color that it projects onto the objects in your scene.

As a default, 3ds Max assigns the color white to all lights that you create. However, in reality most light sources are not truly white. For example, in early morning or evening, the sun casts a yellow, orange, or even red tint. At midday the sunlight has a whiter color, with a blue ambient tint from the sky. When working with outdoor lighting, the angle and color of the light help to determine the time of day. Light colors change indoors, depending upon the amount of natural lighting versus artificial lighting, and the colors of the objects in the scene.

As with any other object, to make modifications to a light, you use the Modify panel. You specify the color that you want for lighting in the Color Selector dialog box, which you can access through the Intensity/Color/Attenuation rollout.

The LightColor.max file is available on the CD-ROM for you to practice adjusting a light's color.

Adjust the Color of a Light

1. Select the light that you want to modify.
2. Click the Modify panel button ().

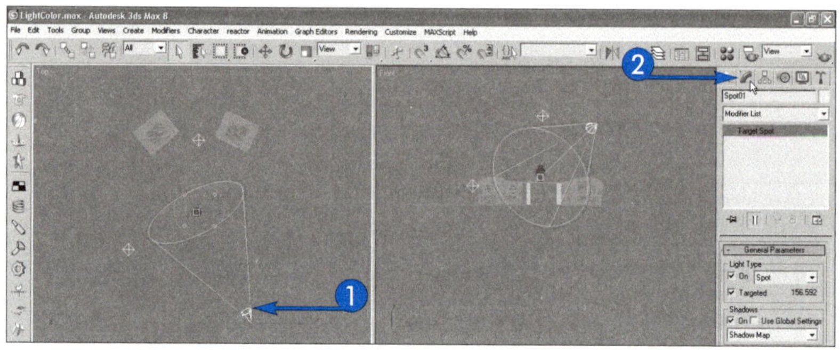

The parameters display for the selected light in the Modify panel.

3. Click the Intensity/Color/Attenuation rollout to expand it.
4. Click the Color Swatch.

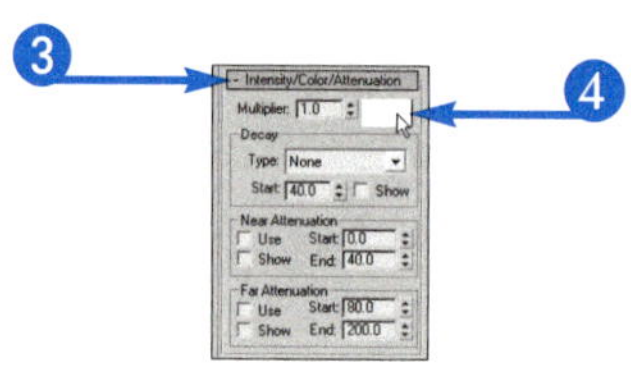

The Color Selector dialog box appears.

5 Click in the large Hue field to select the color that you want.

6 Click and drag the Blackness slider up or down to select the amount of black that is added to the color.

7 Click and drag the Whiteness slider to change the saturation of the color.

You can also specify the color using the sliders on the right side of the dialog box.

8 Click Close.

The color of the light changes for the light object.

9 Click the Quick Render button (icon) to render the scene with the new lighting.

3ds Max renders the scene.

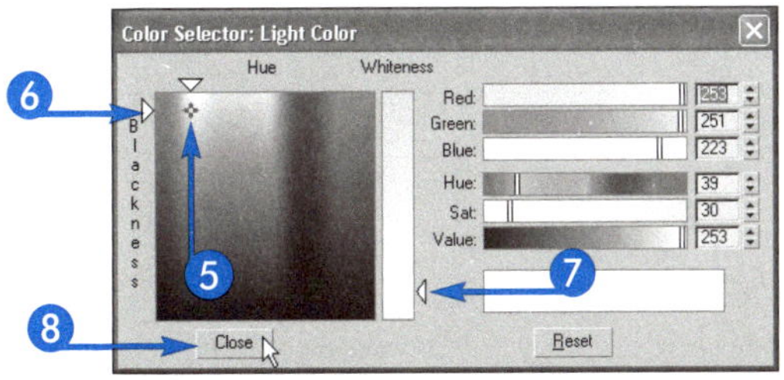

What color should I use for secondary lighting?

▼ Secondary lighting represents either reflected light or another light source, and so the placement of secondary lighting dictates the color that you should use. If the light represents moonlight, then it should have a pale-blue hue to it. If the subject of your rendering is in a room or near a large, colorful object, then the fill or back light's colors should shift slightly toward the color of the walls or the object. If a true light source — such as a lamp or an illuminated sign — is creating the secondary light source, then that source's color dictates the color of your light. By using light colors that match the surroundings, you emphasize the surrounding objects, and not the lights.

Can I control the shadow color?

▼ Yes, you can change the color of the shadows in your scene. Changing the shadow colors allows you to create interesting effects. Keep in mind that the shadow color changes for all objects that the light affects. You set the shadow color in the Shadow Parameters rollout. The Color Selector dialog box also allows you to control the density of the shadows. See the sections "Apply Shadow Maps to a Light" and "Apply Ray Traced Shadows to a Light" for more information on working with shadows.

Adjust the Brightness of a Light

You can control the brightness, or how much energy is emitted, for each light in a scene. This brightness affects the appearance of the objects in the scene. For example, when the light is too bright, it causes the objects to appear washed out. In contrast, if the light is dim, then the scene appears dark, and the details and colors of the objects are difficult to see.

Many factors influence the brightness of the light, such as the placement of objects and other lights in the scene. You can control the brightness of each light using the Multiplier field in the Intensity/Color/Attenuation rollout.

The first light that you create has a default Multiplier value of 1.0. Once you adjust the Multiplier of a light, the next light that you create adopts a default Multiplier with the same value. You can increase the intensity to make it brighter by entering a value over 1.0. Be careful when increasing the Multiplier, as you may overly light a scene by making a light too bright. Instead, consider using multiple lights with lower multipliers to more evenly illuminate your scene.

CD FILE: The LightBrightness.max file is available on the CD-ROM for you to practice adjusting a light's intensity.

Adjust the Brightness of a Light

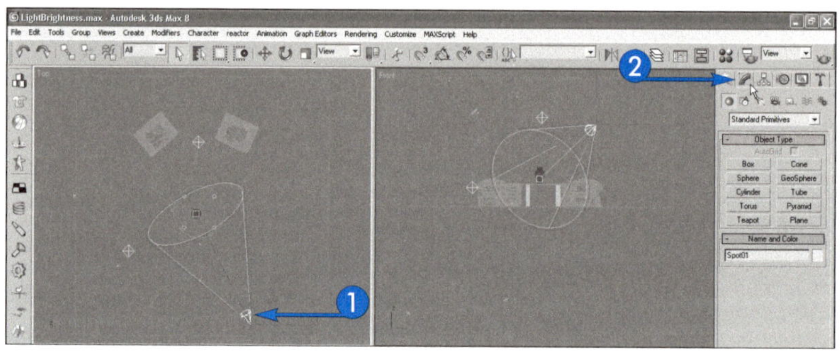

1. Select the light that you want to modify.
2. Click .

The parameters display for the selected light in the Modify panel.

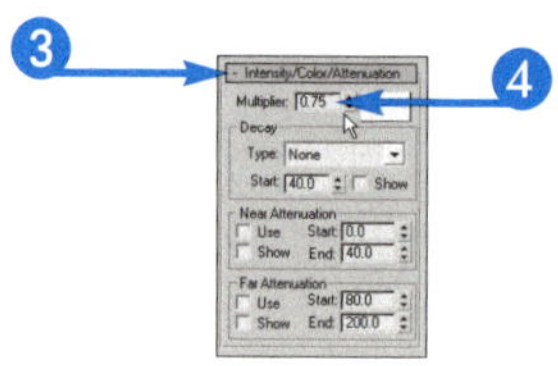

3. Click the Intensity/Color/Attenuation rollout to expand it.
4. Type a value in the Multiplier field.

A value under 1.0 decreases the brightness, while a value above 1.0 increases the brightness.

This example uses a value of 0.75, which gives 75% of normal brightness.

The brightness changes in the viewports.

5 Right-click in a viewport that you want to render.

6 Click to render the scene.

The scene renders using the light's Multiplier value that you specified.

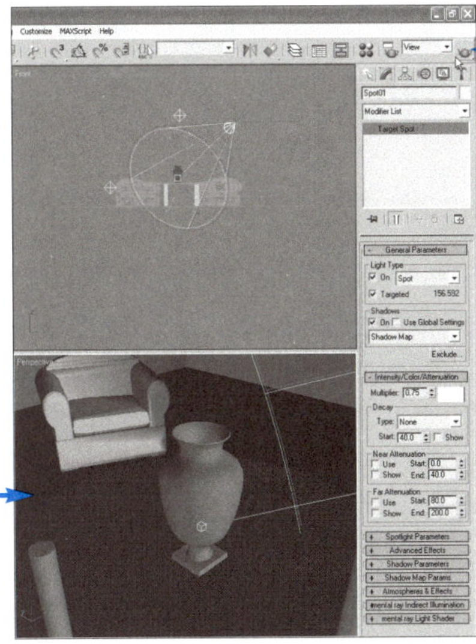

I increased the light intensity, but now my light color is not apparent. What happened?

- Increasing the intensity of any light by specifying a Multiplier value over 1.0 causes the light to become whiter in appearance, no matter what color you have specified in the Color Selector dialog box. The color becomes washed out because the color of the light approaches white. Keep in mind that the Multiplier only affects the intensity of the light within the hotspot, and that it does not affect the Falloff. Even if the Multiplier is high, the light color is still visible in the Falloff. See the section "Adjust the Hotspot of a Light" for more information about the hotspot.

What happens if I specify a Multiplier value that is negative?

- 3ds Max allows you to specify a negative number in the Multiplier field. Specifying a negative Multiplier value creates negative light. When you have a negative light object, you are actually removing light from the scene instead of adding light. For example, if you want to make the back corner of your scene dark, you can create a negative light. A negative light affects more than the light that is emitted from other lights; it also affects the light color. If you apply a negative light to a colored light, the color of the light approaches the complementary color.

Adjust the Hotspot of a Light

You can adjust the size of the hotspot for Spotlight and Directional lights in your scene. The hotspot is the bright circle of light in the center of a Spotlight or Directional light's cone. All light within the hotspot has the full intensity set by the light's Multiplier value. The hotspot is surrounded by another circle of light called the Falloff, which transitions the hotspot to the surrounding darkness.

The hotspot of a light is always smaller than the Falloff. The greater the difference in size between the hotspot and the Falloff, the softer the edges of the Falloff. See the section "Adjust the Falloff of a Light" for more information.

You can adjust the hotspot of a light by using the light controls while viewing the scene through the light, or by using the Hotspot/Beam field in the Spotlight or Directional Parameters rollout. You can use the first method for any spotlight or directional light, whether selected or not, and it accurately shows where the light will be cast. The second method is faster but requires that the light be selected.

The LightHotspot.max file is available on the CD-ROM for you to practice adjusting a light's hotspot.

Adjust the Hotspot of a Light

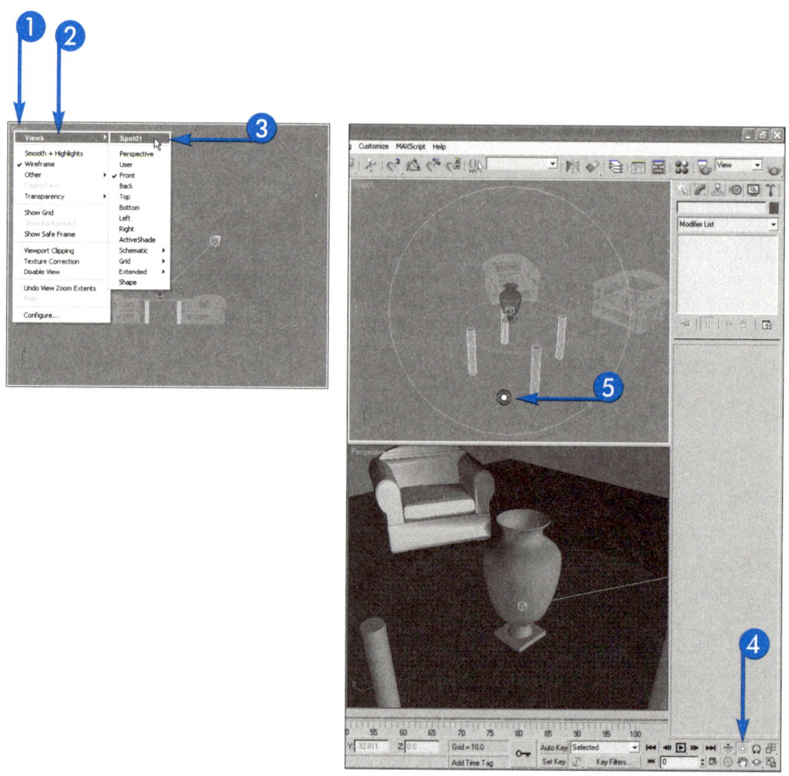

1. Right-click the name of a viewport.
2. Click Views.
3. Click the name of a light through which you want to view the scene.

   This example uses a light object called Spot01.

   The viewport changes to show the view from the selected light.

   The hotspot displays as a light-blue circle, and the Falloff displays as a dark-blue circle.
4. Click the Light Hotspot button ( ).
5. Click and drag to increase or decrease the size of the hotspot.

   Press and hold the Shift key down to increase the Falloff when the hotspot value approaches it.

The size of the hotspot changes in the viewports.

6. Select the viewport to render.
7. Click .

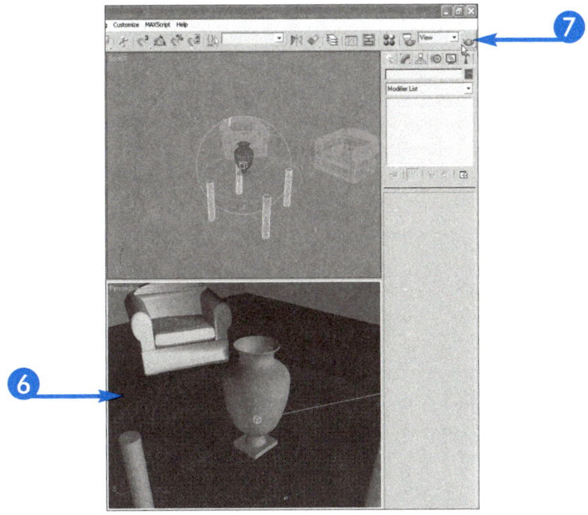

- The scene renders so that you can view the adjustments to the hotspot for the selected light.

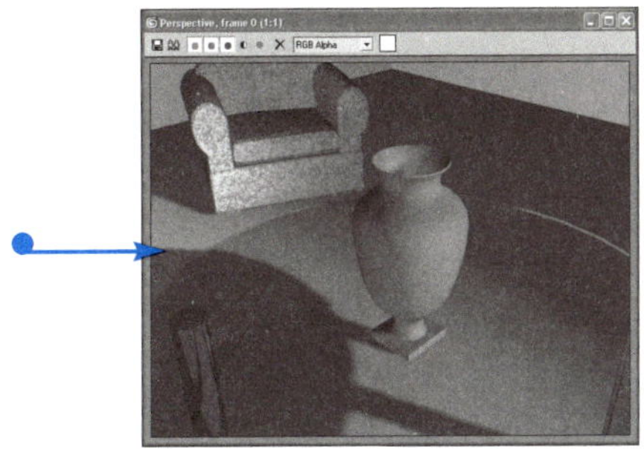

MASTER IT

What do the control buttons do in a Light viewport?

▼ When you select a Light viewport, the View Navigation buttons in the lower-right corner of the 3ds Max window change to Light Navigation buttons, as described in the table below.

Light Navigation Buttons

Button	Description
	The Dolly flyout provides buttons for moving the light, target, or both. The light and target move along the axis that connects them.
	Adjusts the hotspot of the light by resizing the light-blue hotspot circle.
	Rotates the light around its Z-axis.
	Changes the Falloff angle of the light by resizing the dark-blue Falloff circle.
	Moves the light perpendicular to the line of sight.
	Rotates the target around the light.
	Rotates the light around the target.

Adjust the Falloff of a Light

You can adjust the size of the Falloff for Spotlight and Directional lights in your scene. By adjusting the size of the Falloff, you can increase or decrease the amount of light around the hotspot.

The *Falloff* is the area where the light transitions from the hotspot into the surrounding scene. The Falloff area surrounds the hotspot part of the light and is always larger than the hotspot. The greater the difference in size between the hotspot and the Falloff, the softer the edges are around the Falloff. The default difference between the hotspot and Falloff is very small.

You can adjust the Falloff of a light using the light controls while viewing the scene through the light, or by using the Falloff/Field field in the Spotlight or Directional Parameters rollout. When you use the first method for any spotlight or directional light, whether selected or not, it provides accurate feedback regarding where the Falloff will extend. The second method is faster, but it requires that the light be selected.

The LightHotspot.max file is available on the CD-ROM for you to practice adjusting a light's Falloff.

Adjust the Falloff of a Light

1. Right-click the name of a viewport.
2. Click Views.
3. Click the name of a light through which you want to view the scene.

   This example uses a light object called Spot01.

   The viewport changes to show the view from the selected light.

   The Falloff displays as a dark blue-gray circle around the hotspot circle.
4. Click the Light Falloff button (◎).
5. Click and drag to change the size of the Falloff.

   Hold the Shift key down to decrease the hotspot when the Falloff value approaches it.

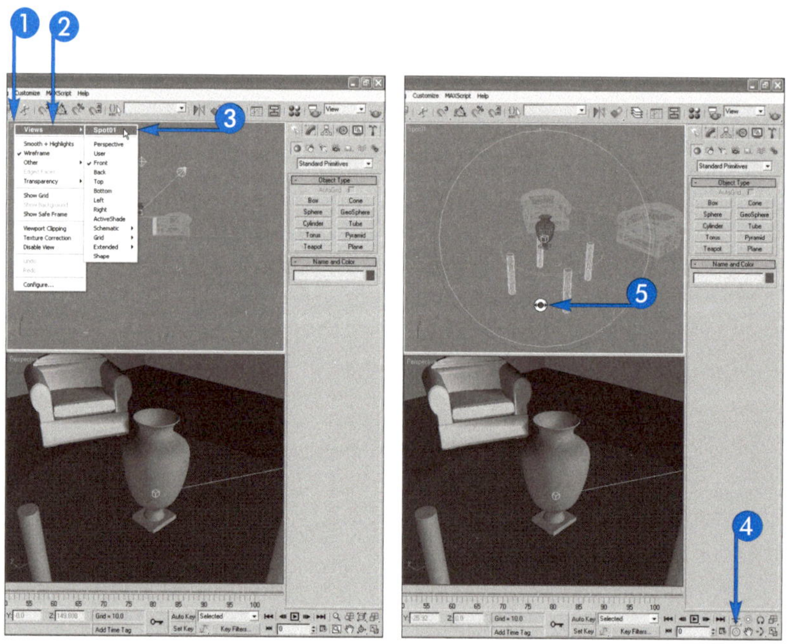

The size of the Falloff adjusts in the viewports.

6 Right-click in the viewport that you want to render.

7 Click .

3ds Max renders the scene.

The Falloff is the gradient area around the bright white area.

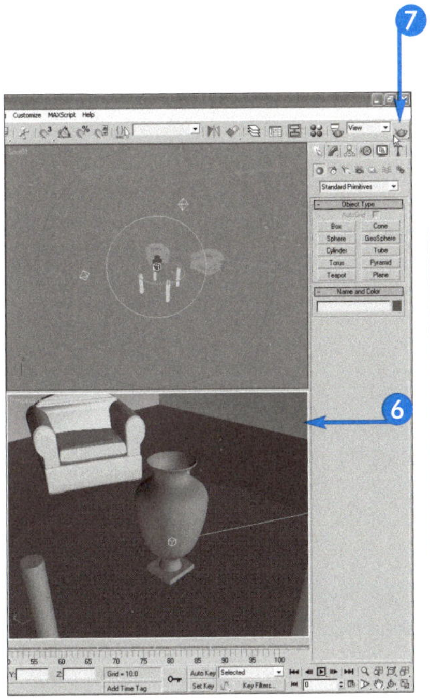

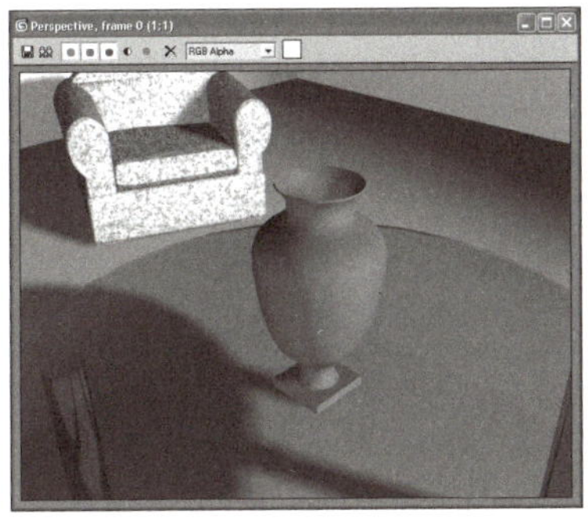

MASTER IT

Can I adjust the hotspot and Falloff simultaneously for a light?

Yes, 3ds Max allows you to control both the hotspot and Falloff at the same time. To do this, after clicking , hold down the Ctrl key while you resize the hotspot. As you resize it, 3ds Max maintains the distance between the hotspot and Falloff, causing each one to resize simultaneously. Keep in mind that you can do the same thing by selecting the Light Falloff button (). See the section "Adjust the Falloff of a Light" for more information about working with light Falloff.

Can I change the shape of the Falloff?

Yes. 3ds Max allows you to use two different shapes for both the Falloff and hotspot of a light. You can use either a circle or a rectangle. Keep in mind that 3ds Max applies the same shape to both the Falloff and hotspot. You set the shape of the Falloff and hotspot in the Spotlight Parameters rollout for spotlights and in the Directional Parameters rollout for directional lights. You can click either the Circle or Rectangle option (○ changes to ◉) to show your selection. When Rectangle is selected, you can change the value in the Aspect field to change the shape of the rectangle.

Adjust the Attenuation of a Light

The energy emitted by real-world lights decreases over distance and you can use the Attenuation controls to make your lights behave in the same way. For example, the farther away you are from a lamp, the less light that shines from it. If you do not use Attenuation, then Standard lights in 3ds Max shine the same amount of light on all objects.

The Far Attenuation controls the distance from the source at which the light no longer casts illumination. Between the source and the Start distance, the light is at full intensity. Between the Start and End distances, the light fades from full to zero intensity. No light is cast beyond the End distance.

In order to use Attenuation, you must select the Use option. When you activate Attenuation, either two disks appear in the cone of a spotlight or directional light, or two spheres appear around an Omni light. The tan disk or sphere indicates the Start distance, and the brown disk or sphere indicates the End distance. Even if you are using a Decay option, the light does not project beyond the End distance.

CD FILE: The LightHotspot.max file is available on the CD-ROM for you to practice adjusting a light's attenuation.

Adjust the Attenuation of a Light

1. Select the light that you want modify.
2. Click .
3. In the Intensity/Color/Attenuation rollout, click the Use in the Far Attenuation group (☐ changes to ☑).

   The Far Attenuation discs or spheres display in the viewport.
4. Type a value in the Start field.
5. Type a value in the End field.

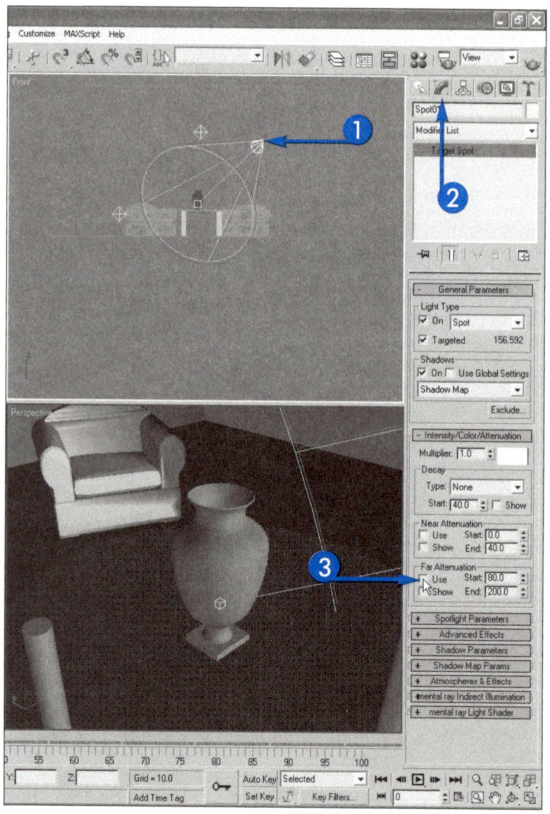

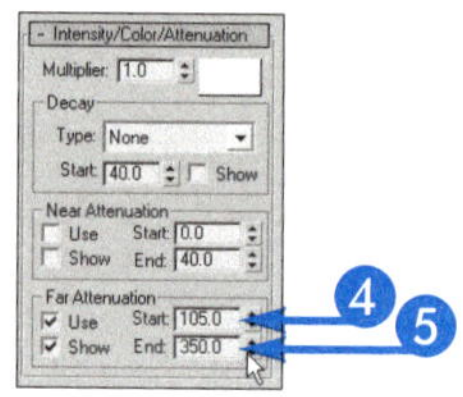

6 Repeat steps 1 to 5 for the other lights in your scene.

7 Right-click in the viewport to render the scene.

8 Click .

The scene renders with the new attenuation values applied.

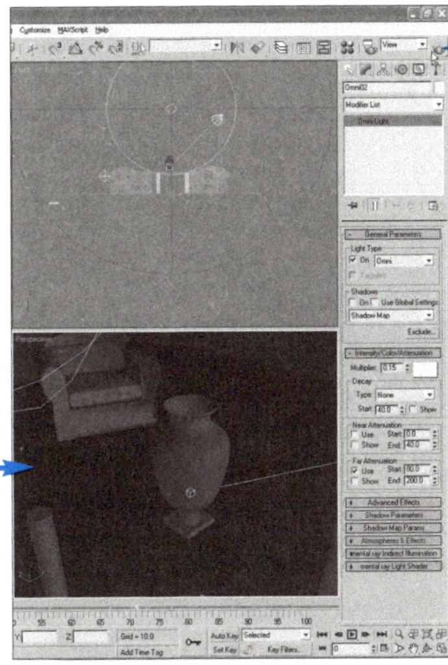

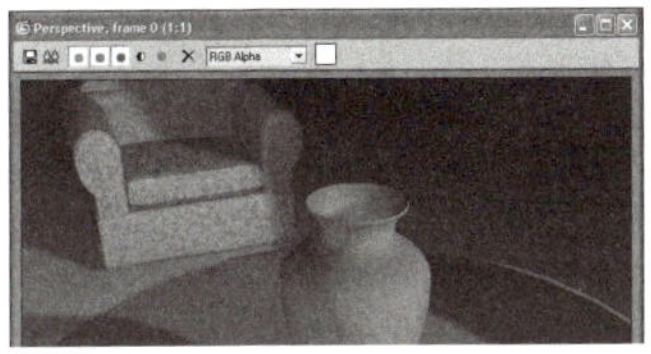

PART V

MASTER IT

How does the Decay parameter affect light attenuation?

▼ Decay is another method that you can use to fade out light. Instead of using different Attenuation distances, Decay uses a mathematical formula to determine how to reduce the intensity of the light over distance. There are three Decay choices: None, the default, applies no decay to the light; Inverse, which uses the Inverse Decay formula; and Inverse Square, which actually models the "real-world" decay of light. Regardless of the decay model that you select, no light is cast beyond the End of Far Attenuation parameter.

What is Near Attenuation?

▼ Near Attenuation works in the opposite way to Far Attenuation. Rather than determining where a light stops casting light, it determines where a light starts casting light. Between the source and the Start distance, no light is cast. Between the Start distance and the End distance, the light grows from zero light to full intensity. Unless Far Attenuation or Decay is also in use, the light remains at full intensity for an unlimited distance. If you have set Near Attenuation, then the Decay calculations start at the End value for the Near Attenuation. If you do not use Near Attenuation, then the light begins to fade or decay at the light source.

Include and Exclude Objects from a Light's Effects

You can prevent certain objects in your scene from being affected by a specific light. Although light exclusion does not reflect "real-world" light conditions, it can be helpful when laying out your scene. You can selectively exclude objects from a light to balance your scene or to allow light to penetrate a wall or obstruction in order to represent bounced light.

When you exclude objects from a light, you can use one of three options, shadow casting, illumination, or both. If you want the object to be illuminated, but not to cast shadows onto other objects, then you can select the Shadow Casting option. The Illumination option excludes the object from being illuminated, but it still casts shadows, and the Both option causes the light to ignore the object entirely.

Keep in mind that the light exclusion list is specific to each light. If there are multiple, non-instanced lights in your scene, then an object can be excluded from one light, and still be lit by another light.

CD FILE: The LightHotspot.max file is available on the CD-ROM for you to practice adjusting a light's attenuation.

Include and Exclude Objects from a Light's Effects

1. Select a light.
2. Click .
3. In the General Parameters rollout, click Exclude.

   The Exclude/Include dialog box appears.

4. Select the objects that you want to exclude.
5. Click the double-right arrow button (»).

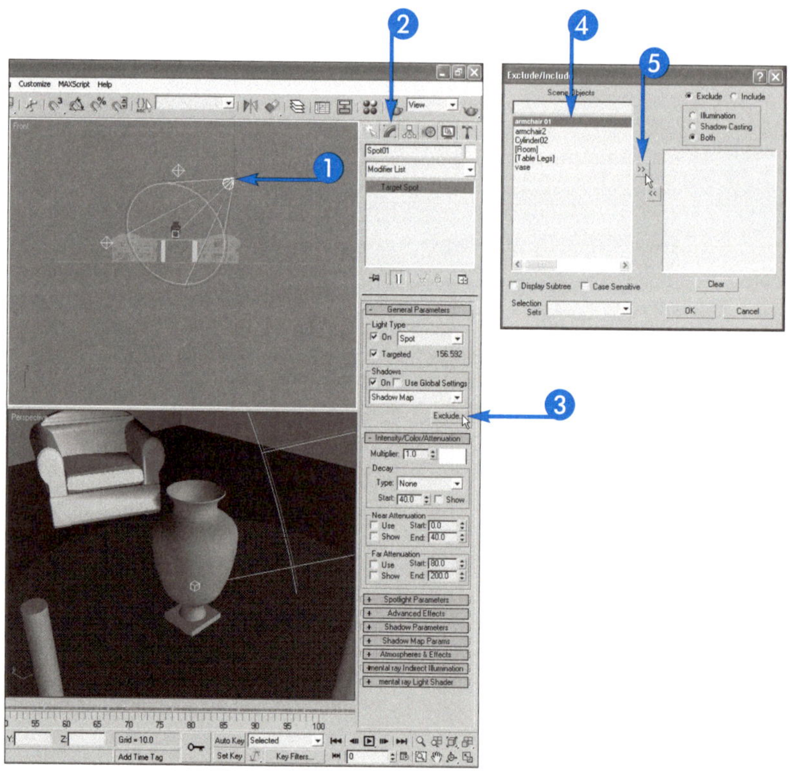

3ds Max moves the selected objects to the Exclude list.

6. Click the Both option to exclude objects from illumination and shadow casting (○ changes to ◉).

7. Click OK.

8. Click .

The scene renders with the specified objects excluded from the light.

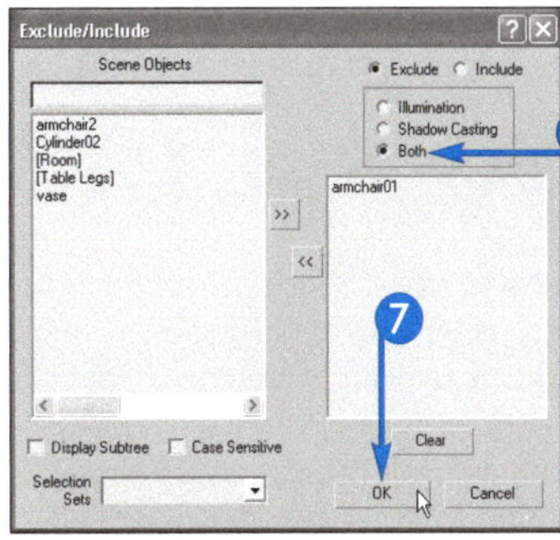

MASTER IT

What happens if I click the Include option in the Exclude/Include dialog box?

The Exclude/Include dialog box actually allows you to specify a list of objects to either exclude from the light or include in the light. You toggle between the two options by clicking either the Exclude or Include option (○ charges to ◉) at the top-right corner of the dialog box. By default, when you click Exclude for a light object, the list box on the right side of the dialog box lists all of the objects that will be excluded from the corresponding light. If you click Include, then all of the objects in the box on the right side will be included in the light, and the unselected objects on the left will be excluded.

How do I exclude specific objects inside a group?

Like the rest of 3ds Max, the Exclude/Include dialog box treats a group of objects as a single object. Groups are identified in the list with square brackets ([ ]) around the group name. You cannot exclude individual objects from the group; you can only exclude the entire group. Even when a group is open, and you move the group member to the exclusion list, it is still affected by the light. If you want to exclude specific objects, you need to ungroup the objects in the group before opening the Exclude/Include dialog box. For more information about grouping and ungrouping objects, see Chapter 3.

Apply Shadow Maps to a Light

Opaque, real-world objects obscure light and cast shadows onto other objects. To make your 3D scenes look more realistic, you can apply shadows as part of your lighting scheme. Shadows can be turned on or off for each light, and 3ds Max provides different shadow types that you can select. The Shadow Map type works well for creating shadows in most scenes, and it renders more quickly than the other types. The Shadow Map type actually creates a bitmap image of the shadow that is added to your scene at rendering time.

When you use shadows, you can specify the shadow color and density in the Shadow Parameters rollout. The default density is 1.0. If you want darker shadows, then you can increase the density.

The Shadow Map Params rollout allows you to control the resolution and blur factor of a shadow. The Size field specifies the resolution of the shadow; higher Size values result in less jagged shadow perimeters. The Sample Range field controls the softening of the shadow edges. Specifying a higher value, such as 10, creates soft, blurred edges on the shadow.

CD FILE The ShadowLight.max file is available on the CD-ROM for you to practice applying Shadow Map shadows.

Apply Shadow Maps to a Light

1. Select the light with which you want to apply shadows.
2. Click .
3. In the Shadows area of the General Parameters rollout, click the On option (☐ changes to ☑).
4. Click ▾ and select Shadow Map.

   3ds Max displays the Shadow Parameters rollout.
5. In the Object Shadows area, type a shadow density in the Dens. field.
   - If you want, you can click the color swatch and change the shadow color.

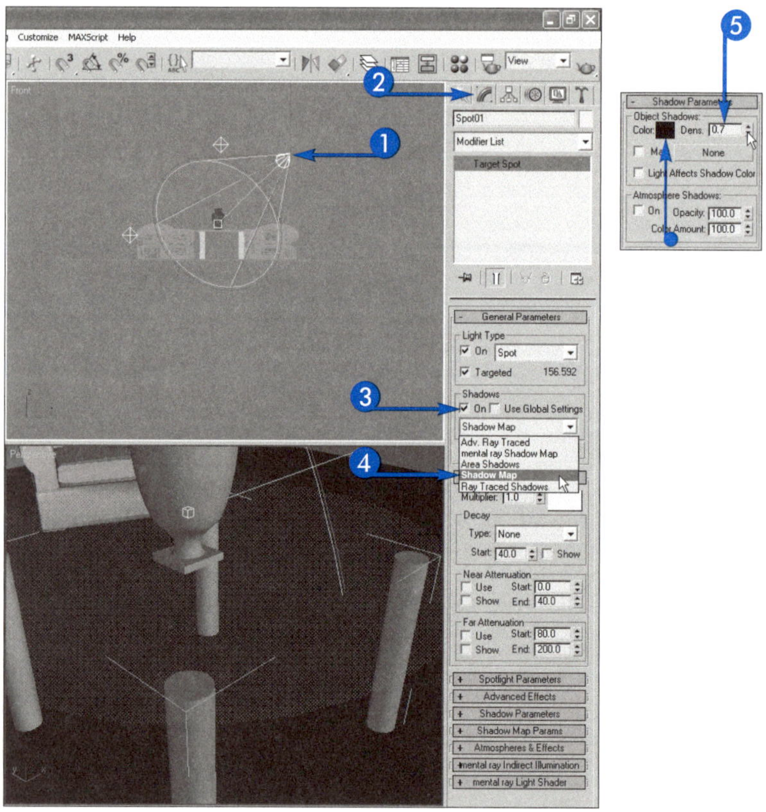

6. In the Shadow Map Params rollout, type a value for the size of the shadow map in pixels squared.

   This example uses a value of 1024, for crisper shadows.

7. In the Sample Range field, type a value to specify the softness of the shadow edges.

   This example uses 10.0 for softer edges.

8. Right-click in the viewport to render.

9. Click [icon].

   The scene renders, with soft shadows created for each object.

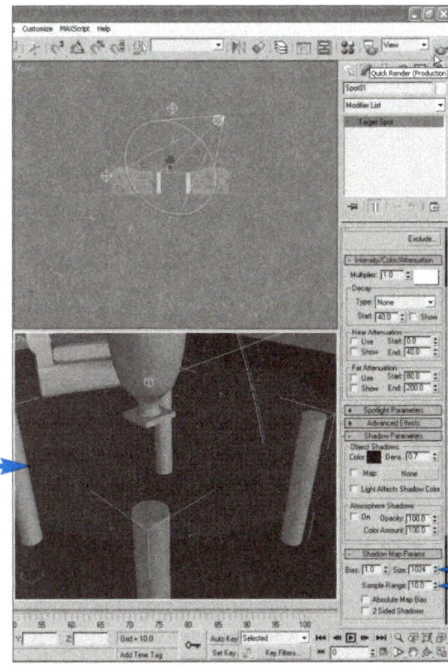

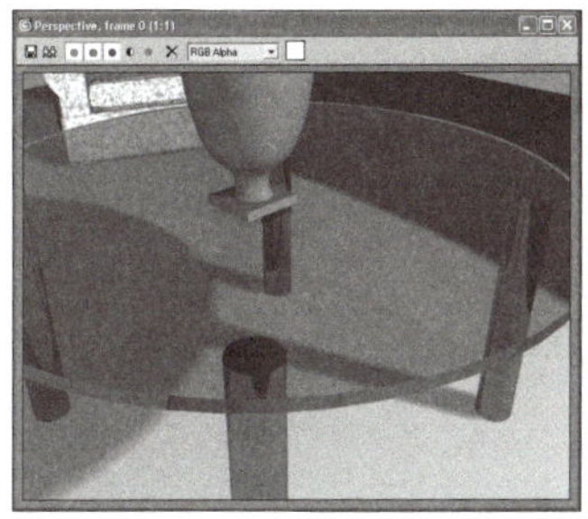

MASTER IT

How do I keep an object from casting a shadow?

When you turn on shadows for a light, the shadows apply to all objects in the scene that are affected by the light. If you do not want an object to cast a shadow from a specific light, then you need to exclude that object from shadow casting by using the Exclude/Include dialog box that displays when you click the Exclude button. See the section "Include and Exclude Objects from a Light's Effects" for more information on excluding objects. To restrict an object from casting a shadow from all current and future lights, select the object, right-click, and then select Properties from the quad menu. Deselect the Cast Shadows option in the Rendering Control section of the Object Properties dialog box that appears.

Can I change the proximity of the shadow to the object?

Yes. By default, when you turn on shadows, 3ds Max automatically specifies that the shadows fall away from the light source connected to the object. If you need to adjust the shadows so that they fall farther away from the object, then you need to change the value in the Bias field. The Bias field is located in the Shadow Map Params rollout. The default Bias value is 1.0. Increasing the Bias value moves the shadow farther from the object that is casting the shadow. You can decrease the Bias value to pull the shadow back toward the object. Adjusting the map Bias is common when objects are very close together or when an object casts shadows onto itself.

Apply Ray Traced Shadows to a Light

You can use Ray Traced Shadows in scenes where the shadow needs to respect the opacity of the objects. This is a common solution when your scene has transparent objects, such as glass.

The default Shadow Map shadows do not recognize object transparency when you are creating shadows. By not recognizing the transparency, the Shadow Map shadows are all one shade of gray. With the Ray Traced Shadows, the transparency of the objects is recognized, creating shadows that are different shades, based upon the object transparency.

Ray Traced Shadows are very crisp shadows but, unlike the Shadow Map shadows, they do not provide the option to soften the edges of the shadows. To make a shadow less harsh, you can reduce the density of the shadow in the Shadow Parameters rollout.

You can control the Bias value of the Ray Traced Shadows in the Ray Traced Shadow Params rollout. By increasing the Bias value, you move the shadow away from the object that is casting it. This adjustment is normally used to control shadows that are casting onto the wrong surfaces.

CD FILE: The ShadowLight.max file is available on the CD-ROM for you to practice applying Ray Traced Shadows.

Apply Ray Traced Shadows to a Light

1. Select the light with which you want to apply shadows.
2. Click ▨.
3. In the Shadows area of the General Parameters rollout, click the On option (☐ changes to ☑).
4. Click ▾ and select Ray Traced Shadows.

   The Shadow Parameters rollout displays.
5. Type a value for the shadow density in the Dens. field.

   This example uses a value of 0.5.

   - If you want, you can click the color swatch to change the shadow color.

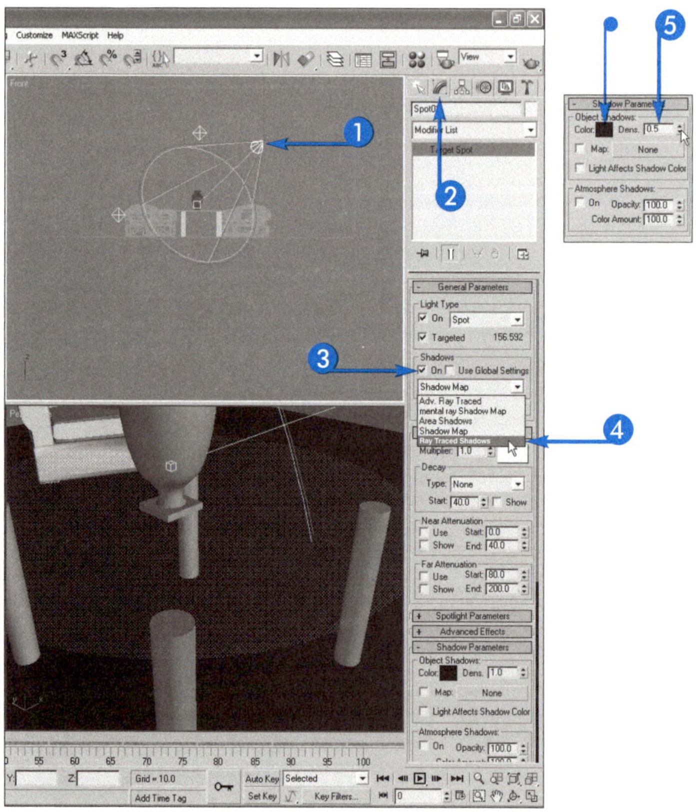

6 In the Ray Traced Shadow Params rollout, type a value in the Ray Bias field.

This example uses a value of 2.0.

7 Right-click the viewport that you want to render.

8 Click .

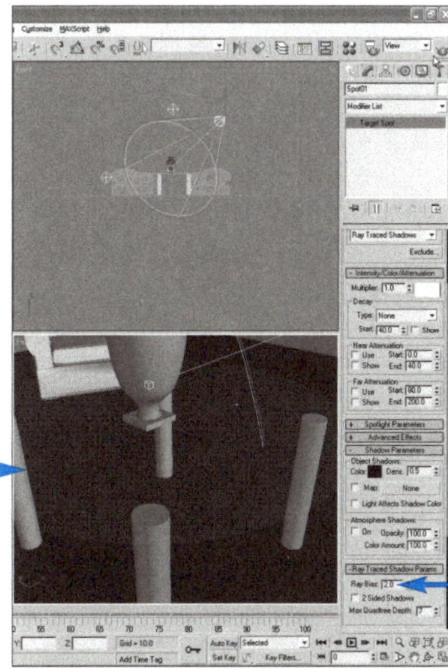

- The scene renders to show different shades of shadows, based upon the transparency of the objects.

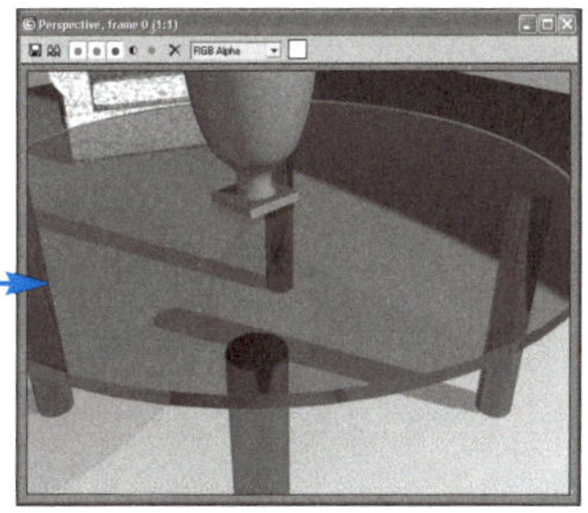

MASTER IT

How do maps affect the shadows?

You can use maps to change the appearance of the shadows that are cast by the selected light. If you apply a map, the shadows cast by the objects include the pattern from the selected map. You can apply a map to the shadows of a light by clicking the Map option (☐ changes to ☑) in the Shadow Parameters rollout. When you click the button, the Material/Map Browser displays a list of the available maps. The name of the selected map displays on the Map button. If you want to remove the effect of the map, simply click the Map option to deselect it (☐ changes to ☑). For more information about working with the Material/Map Browser, see Chapter 15.

Why does the Ray Traced Shadow not maintain the color of my transparent object?

Ray Traced Shadows can match their color to the color of the transparent object through which the light passes, but this is a function of the material as well as the light. Open the Material Editor and select the sample slot containing the object's material. Open the shader-specific Basic Parameters rollout and the Extended Parameters rollout. The Filter color is the color that Ray Traced Shadows will become. Click and drag the Diffuse color swatch onto the Filter color swatch and select Copy in the dialog box that appears. The Ray Traced Shadows now respect the Diffuse color that is copied into the Filter swatch.

Represent the Sun with a Sunlight System

The main light in most outdoor daytime scenes is the sun. 3ds Max contains the Sunlight system for quickly creating a sun to accurately illuminate your scene. Architects and planners can use this system to create time-accurate light-shadow studies that are relevant to the location of the modeled structure or facility anywhere in the world. It is a common practice to animate the sun's position to display the locations of the sun's light and shadows on a facility over time.

Because it is more than simply a light, the Sunlight system is accessed with the Systems button in the Create panel, rather than the Lights button. Sunlight systems are composed of two components, a compass rose and a directional light. The compass rose — a diagrammatical representation of the four cardinal directions, North, South, East, and West — is used to orient the scene to the direction that it would face if the scene were in the real world. The directional light is a typical light, with shadows turned on and the Ray Traced Shadows type selected.

CD FILE: The SunLight.max file is available on the CD-ROM for you to practice creating a Sunlight system.

Represent the Sun with a Sunlight System

Create a Sunlight System

1. Click the Create Panel button ( ).
2. Click the Systems button ( ).
3. Click Sunlight.

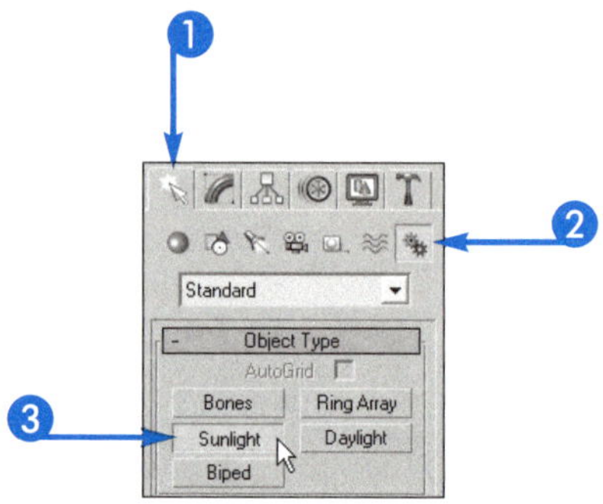

The Control Parameters rollout appears.

4. Click and drag in the Top viewport to create the compass rose.

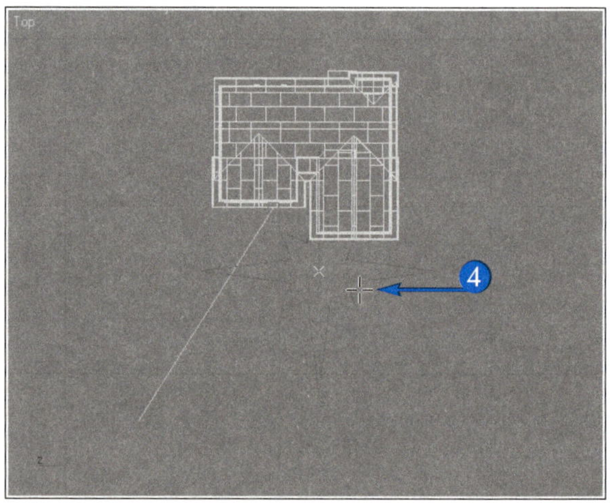

5. Move the mouse and then click to set the location of the sun.

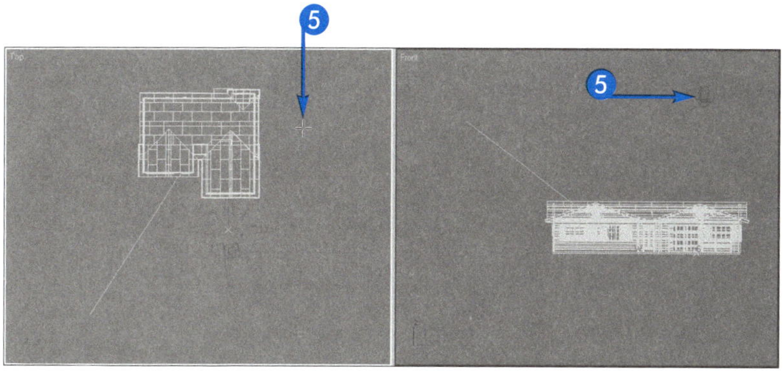

6. To change the distance from the Sun light to the compass rose, increase the Orbital Scale value.

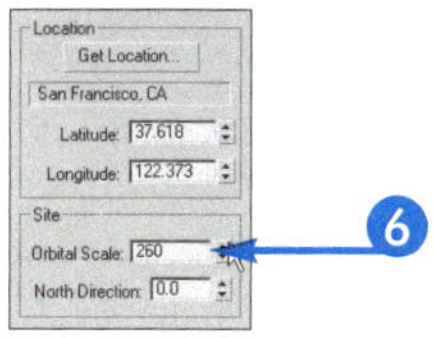

MASTER IT

What is the difference between a Sunlight system and a Daylight system?

▼ The Sunlight system and Daylight system are virtually the same in the way they are created and controlled. The difference is that the Sunlight system uses a single Standard Directional Light for illumination. The Daylight system uses either a Standard Directional light or an IES Sun light in conjunction with either a Standard Skylight or an IES Sky light. The IES Sun light and the IES Sky light are photometric lights and are intended for use with the Radiosity lighting plug-in. For information on the advanced lighting options in 3ds Max, see Chapter 18.

Not everything in my scene casts shadows from the Sun light. Why is this?

▼ A Spotlight and Directional light are best described as simply a portion of an Omni light that has been allowed to cast light. For example, if you painted an incandescent bulb, except for a small area, then you would create a Spotlight from an Omni light. In the Spotlight Parameters and Directional Parameters rollouts, there is an Overshoot option. When it is On — the default for the Sun light in a Sunlight system — the Directional light casts illumination in all directions, as if it were an Omni, but it only casts shadows in the same areas that it would if Overshoot were not turned on.

continued

Represent the Sun with a Sunlight System *(Continued)*

You can position the Sunlight system to locate and orient the Sun light to represent the sun at any location on Earth and at any time or date. You start the process by using the Rotate transform to rotate the compass rose until its North arrow points in the same direction that North is represented in your scene. Be sure to only rotate it around the Z-axis; otherwise, it tilts in your scene, and the Sun does not move properly.

The time and location for your scene must be entered to properly locate the Sun light in relation to your scene object's virtual location. With the light selected, the Sun light's location and time are entered in the Control Parameters rollout in the Motion panel. You enter the time, date, and whether the scene uses Daylight Saving Time. You then specify the scene's world location, and 3ds Max moves and orients the light accordingly. There is an extensive list of worldwide locations from which you can choose and, if accuracy is extremely important, then you can input the latitude and longitude coordinates for your scene's location.

CD FILE: The SunLight.max file is available on the CD-ROM for you to practice creating a Sunlight system.

Represent the Sun with a Sunlight System *(continued)*

Orient the Compass Rose

7. Click the Select and Rotate button ( ).
8. Select the compass rose.
9. Click and drag the Z-axis to rotate the compass rose.

   For information on the Rotate transform, see Chapter 2.

Set the Time and Location

The compass and light rotate.

10. Select the Sun light.
11. Click the Motion button ( ).

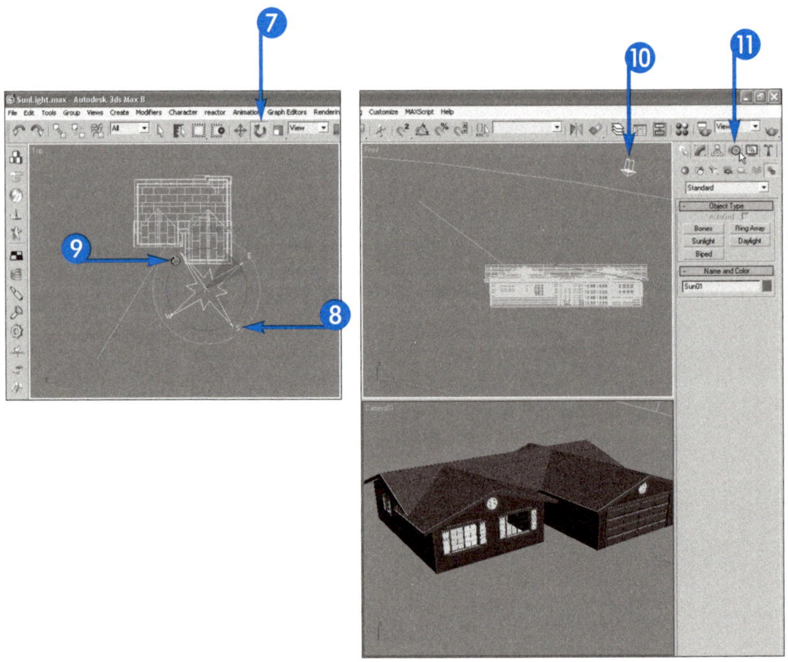

The Control Parameters rollout appears.

⑫ Set the date and time that you want to be represented in the scene.

⑬ Click Get Location.

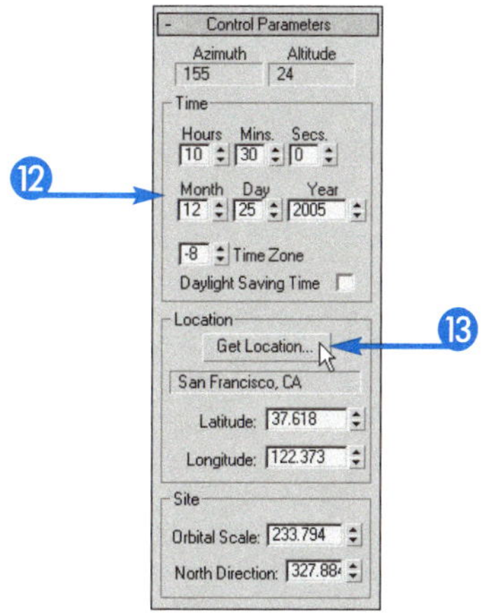

The Geographic Location dialog box appears.

⑭ Select the location for your scene.

⑮ Click OK.

The light moves to represent the sun at the time and location that you specified.

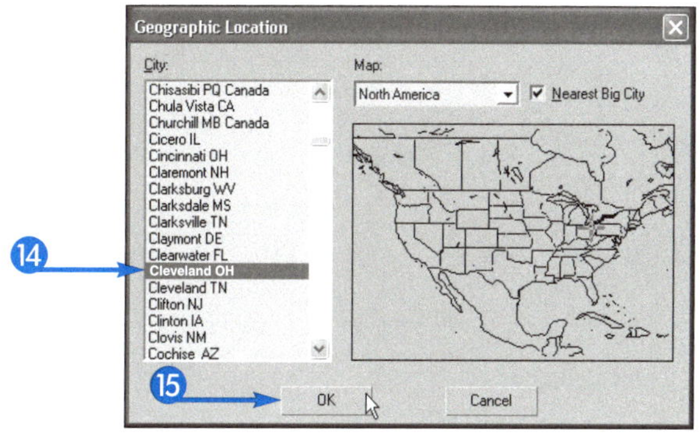

MASTER IT

Can I choose a location that is not in North America?

▼ Yes, you can choose a location for your scene from anywhere in the world. To select a location that is not in North America, select the light, click the Motion tab, and then click Get Location. When the Geographical Location dialog box appears, click ▾ at the top of the dialog box and choose a region from the list. The graphic and list of city names change to reflect the region that you select. Deselect the Nearest Big City option (☐ changes to ☑) to visually select a specific location on the map rather than allowing 3ds Max to assume that you are attempting to pick one of the cities in the list.

Can I change the parameters of a Sunlight?

▼ Yes. The light that represents the sun is just a Directional light contained in an orientation system. You can change the parameters by selecting the light and then clicking the Modify panel button (). The default shadow type for the light is Ray Traced Shadows, but this may be more effective with the Shadow Map option when representing a cloudy day. Changing the light's color is common, but it is not recommended that you activate the light's attenuation, this would be an unrealistic representation of the sun's effect.

Understanding Photometric Lights

3ds Max offers a category of lights called Photometric lights that are based on real-world lighting data. Unlike Standard lights, the Photometric lights base their light measurements on values such as Kelvin for light temperature, and lumens or candelas for light intensity.

You can create Photometric lights by clicking the Lights button in the Create panel and then selecting the Photometric light category. 3ds Max displays the different Photometric light types that are available. When you select a Photometric light type, the rollouts in the Create panel display the parameters for that light type.

Photometric Light Types

Type	*Description*
Target Point	Creates a Point light object that emits illumination from a single source that is then directed at a specific target in your scene. Similar to the Target Spotlights and Target Directional lights in the Standard category, a Target Point light's orientation is determined by the target object that it continually faces. The Target Point light object has three different methods for specifying how the light distributes within the scene: Isotropic, Spotlight, and Web distribution. For information on Standard lights, see Chapter 17.
Free Point	The same as the Target Point without a target object. You control the light's orientation with the Rotate transform.
Target Linear	Creates a light object that emits illumination, from a straight line extending from the light icon, perpendicular toward a target object. The target object toward which the Target Linear light continually emits its illumination determines the direction of the linear light. Linear lights work well for creating long lights, such as fluorescent tubes or light coves. With a Target Linear light object, you can select either Web or Diffuse distribution.
Free Linear	The same as the Target Linear without a target object. You can control the light's orientation with the Rotate transform.
Target Area	Creates an Area light object that emits illumination from a rectangular region toward a specific target in your scene. The target object toward which the Target Area light continually emits its illumination determines the direction of the target area light. Area lights work well for creating light that comes through windows or overhead lighting. With a Target Area light object, you can select either Web or Diffuse distribution.
Free Area	The same as the Target Area without a target object. You control the light's orientation with the Rotate transform.
IES Sun	Creates a light object that simulates the bright, outdoor light that comes from the sun. The light object can have a Light Intensity value of 50 billion lux, creating a very powerful light. You can combine the IES Sunlight object with a Daylight System so that you can base the values of the light on geographical location, date, and time.
IES Sky	Creates a light object that simulates the ambient light component of a sky. You can specify whether the sky is clear, partly cloudy, or cloudy. You can use this light object with the Daylight System.

Photometric Light Colors

When you work with Photometric lights, the color of the light, also called the color temperature, is based upon real-world light colors. 3ds Max provides three methods for setting the light color: light type, Kelvin measurement, or Filter color. You select the light color in the Intensity/Color/Distribution rollout.

You can choose from a list of real-world lighting types, and 3ds Max sets the lighting color temperature based on your selection. You can select default colors that correspond to real-world lighting types. For example, when you select Fluorescent lighting, it creates a light color that is yellow-white.

If you choose to set the color by a Kelvin degree measurement, as you change the number of degrees, the corresponding color value displays in the corresponding Color swatch.

With both light type and Kelvin measurement, you can also apply a filter to the light to change the lighting color. When you select a color through the Filter Color swatch, 3ds Max acts as if a colored filter, or gel, has been placed over the light source.

Photometric Light Type Colors

Light Type	*Color*
Cool White	Yellow-white
Custom	Any custom color
D65White	White
Daylight Fluorescent	White with a gray tint
Fluorescent	Yellow-white
Halogen	Beige-white
High Pressure Solution	Tan
Incandescent	Beige-white
Low Pressure Solution	Light orange
Mercury	Green-white
Metal Halide	Yellow-white
Phosphor Mercury	Light green
Quartz	Yellow-white
White Fluorescent	Yellow-white
Xenon	White

Light Distribution Methods

With each Photometric light that you create, you must specify the light distribution method. This determines how the light spreads within the scene. There are four distribution methods: Isotropic, Diffuse, Spotlight, and Web. Not all distribution methods are available with each light type. For example, an Area light can only use either Web or Diffuse distribution.

The Isotropic method emits omni-directional illumination, which distributes light equally in all directions within your scene. The Diffuse method is similar to the Isotropic, except that the light that is emitted perpendicular to the light source is more intense than light that is emitted at angles less than or greater than 90 degrees.

The Spotlight distribution method creates a beam of light that is focused in one direction in the shape of a cone. With a Spotlight method, the intensity falls off with distance, as well as the light rays' proximity to the angular limits of the cone.

The Web distribution method is a custom method that allows you to describe the distribution pattern of the light. You can either specify the X-, Y-, and Z-axis rotation values, or load a file that describes the pattern. Lighting manufacturers routinely make these files available through their Web sites.

Create Photometric Preset Lights

You can add real-world lighting to your scene by selecting one of the preset lights that are available in 3ds Max. Preset lights are Photometric lights that have parameter values that match the correct light settings for common real-world lights. For example, when you select the Generic 60W Bulb setting, 3ds Max creates a light with the correct intensity, lighting, and distribution settings for a 60-watt incandescent light bulb.

To place a preset light, you select it from the Create menu. When you select a specific preset light, the parameters for that light load in the Create panel. All of the preset lights are created by using the standard Photometric light objects.

For example, when you select the Generic 100W Bulb preset, you are actually creating a Free Point light object with parameter values set to match those of a 100-watt incandescent light bulb.

You can modify the parameter values for the light in the Create panel before adding it to your scene. For example, you can have the light cast shadows on your objects. For more information about setting values for shadows, see Chapter 17.

CD FILE: The Lights.max file is available on the CD-ROM for you to practice creating light presets.

Create Photometric Preset Lights

1. Click Create.
2. Click Lights.
3. Click Photometric Lights.
4. Click Presets.
5. Click a preset.

   This example uses the 60W Bulb preset.

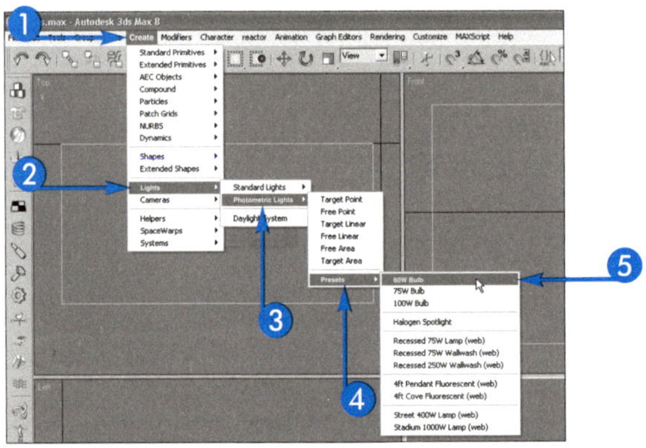

The Create panel displays the parameters for the light type that you selected.

- You can click the On option to cast shadows onto the objects in the scene (☐ changes to ☑).

6. Click in a viewport.

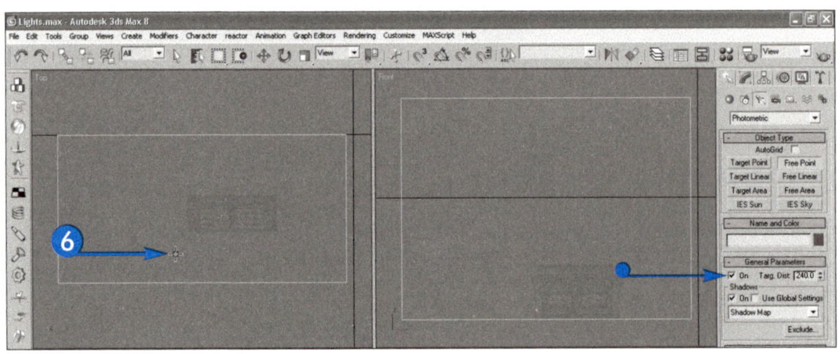

3ds Max creates the light in your scene.

7. Click .

8. Click and drag the Move gizmo to reposition the light.

   If necessary, you can use to rotate the light.

9. Select the viewport that you want to render, and then click .

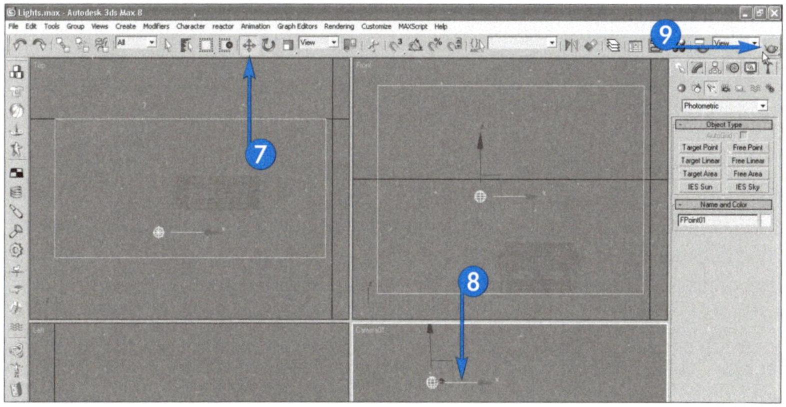

The scene renders, adding the illumination from the Photometric light.

MASTER IT

I added a Photometric light to my scene, but it is barely visible. How do I correct this problem?

▼ When you use Photometric lighting in your scenes, you need to keep in mind that the lighting is based on real-world measurements. For example, if you select a generic 60W Bulb setting, it creates a light object that emits the equivalent of a 60-watt light bulb. The amount of light that actually emits in your scene is determined by the area that a 60-watt bulb would illuminate. The preset measurements are based upon current units of measurement. Make sure that your scene is not scaled too large.

Can I still use Photometric lights with a scene that is not at "real-world" scale?

▼ Yes, you can use Photometric or Standard lighting in any scene. If your scene is not scaled appropriately for real-world measurements, then you should increase the intensity of the Photometric lights to ensure that they are adequate. Keep in mind that this reduces the accuracy of the light presets. You set the intensity of a light with the Multiplier field in the Intensity/Color/Distribution rollout. Increasing the Multiplier value increases the light intensity. For example, if the Multiplier is set to 200 percent, then the intensity of the light is twice the baseline value of 100 percent.

Using the Light Tracer

You can use the Light Tracer advanced lighting plug-in — available only when using the Default Scanline renderer — with a Skylight object to create realistic outdoor lighting. For example, you can create diffuse shading and reflections in your scene. The Light Tracer creates the diffuse shading and reflections by calculating how the light in the scene bounces off different object surfaces. The Light Tracer works with all types of materials, including reflective materials such as Raytrace materials and maps.

In the Advanced Lighting tab of the Render Scene dialog box, you can specify Multiplier values for the Light Tracer and Sky Light, as well as the other parameters. For example, you may need to reduce the brightness of the Skylight object to work with the Light Tracer.

The Bounces parameter controls the number of times that light rays bounce off each surface. The higher the value, the more ambient light appears on the object at the expense of more time required to render your scene. You can also control how much color bleeds from one object to another with the Color Bleed parameter.

CD FILE: The LightTracer.max file is available on the CD-ROM for you to practice using the Light Tracer.

Using The Light Tracer

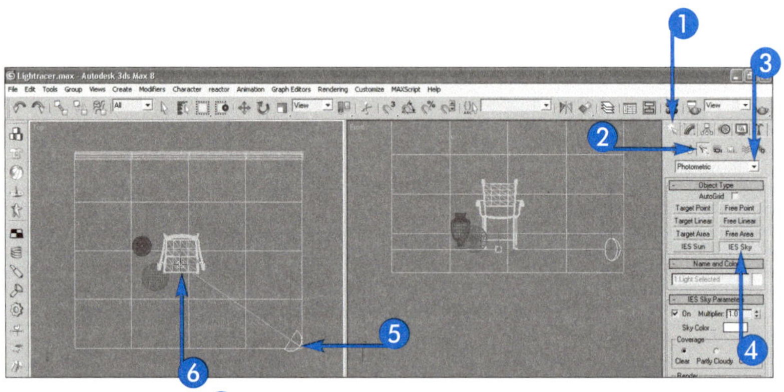

1. Click the Create Panel button ( ).
2. Click the Lights button ( ).
3. Click here and select Photometric.
4. Click IES Sky.
5. Click in the viewport to place the light.
6. Drag and release to set the target location.

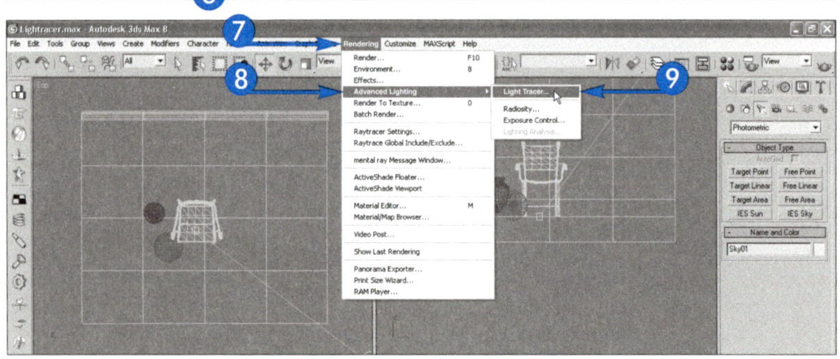

3ds Max creates the Skylight object with the specified target.

You can move the light and target as required to a new location.

Note: *For information on moving objects, see Chapter 2.*

7. Click Rendering.
8. Click Advanced Lighting.
9. Click Light Tracer.

The Render Scene dialog box appears.

10 Type a Sky Lights value for the light's intensity.

This example uses a value of 0.2.

11 Type the number of times that you want the light to bounce.

12 Type the amount of color bleeding that you want to allow.

13 Select the viewport that you want to render, and then click Render.

The scene renders, using the specified Light Tracer values.

Diffuse shadows and reflections are created.

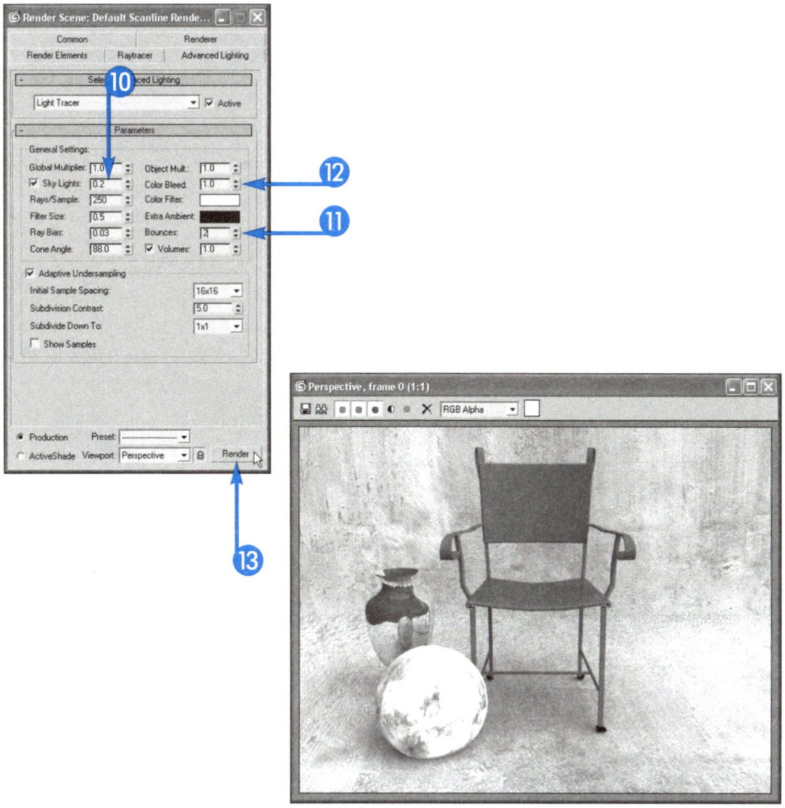

Which parameters should I set for the Light Tracer?

The Light Tracer includes several different parameters that you can use to control its effects.

Light Tracer Parameters

Parameter	Description
Global Multiplier	Controls the overall effect of the Light Tracer.
Object Mult.	Controls the amount of light reflected by objects in the scene.
Sky Light	Controls the brightness of the skylights.
Color Bleed	Adjusts the amount of color bleed in the scene.
Rays/Sample	Indicates the number of light rays that are cast for every sample point.
Color Filter	Tints the light colors in the scene.
Ray Bias	Moves the location of the Light Tracer effects toward the object surfaces.
Bounces	Sets the number of times that each light ray bounces off a surface before terminating. The maximum number of bounces is ten.
Cone Angle	The initial angular limitation for the light rays that are cast.
Volumes	Increases or decreases the amount of illumination that a volumetric light contributes to a scene.

Create a Visible Light Source

You can create an object in your scene that looks like the bright surface of a light source. For example, you can create the bulb for a lamp or even the headlights of a car.

When you add a light to a scene, the actual object that creates the illumination is not visible when you render the scene. In order to make objects in your scene look like visible light sources, you can create an object with a self-illuminated material applied and then place a light inside of it.

You create self-illuminated materials in the Material Editor by setting the Self-Illumination value to 100. Setting Self-Illumination creates the illusion that the material is emitting light, although no illumination is added to the scene. With a high Self-Illumination value, all of the shadows are replaced with the Diffuse color, and other lights have no effect on the illumination of the object. Because self-illumination can cause an object to look flat with no contours, it should be used sparingly. See Chapter 23 for information on volumetric lights: the process of making the light rays themselves visible.

CD FILE The VisibleLight.max file is available on the CD-ROM for you to practice creating a visible light source.

Create a Visible Light Source

Create a Self-illuminating Object

1. Click [icon].
2. Click the geometry button ([icon]) .
3. Click an object type button.
4. Click and drag in a viewport to create the object.

Note: *For information on creating objects, see Chapter 4.*

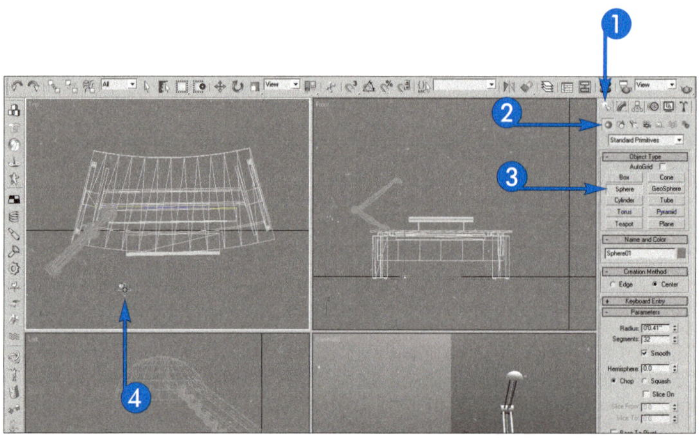

5. Click [icon].
6. Click and drag to position the object.
7. Click the Material Editor button ([icon]).

Note: *For information on moving objects, see Chapter 2.*

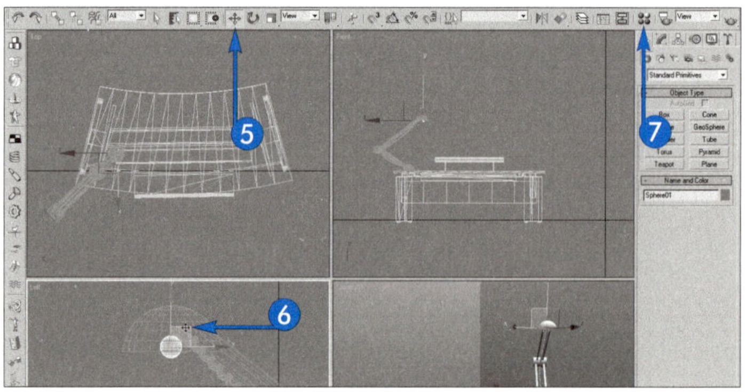

The Material Editor opens.

8. Click a sample slot.
9. Click the Diffuse color swatch.

   The Color Selector dialog box appears.

10. Click and drag the Whiteness slider to the bottom.

    3ds Max updates the Diffuse color.

11. Click Close.
12. In the Color field of the Self-Illumination area, type **100**.
13. Click the Assign Material to Selection button (icon).

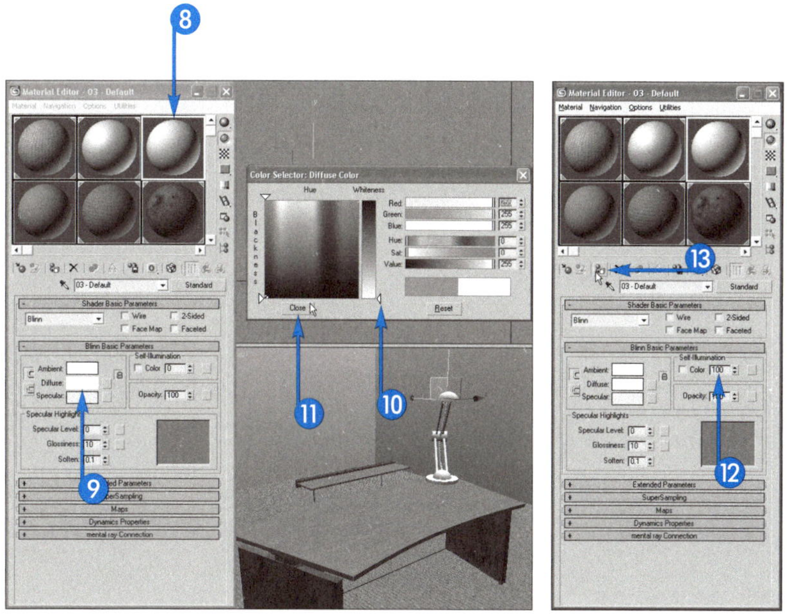

MASTER IT

Can I apply a map as the Self-Illumination value?

- Absolutely. As with any other color component of a material, you can also assign a map to the Self-Illumination Color value by clicking the Map button next to the Self-Illumination spinner buttons. When you apply a map, it determines the parts of the material that are self-illuminated. All white areas of the mapped material are fully self-illuminated. Black areas of the mapped material have no self-illumination, and the colored areas between black and white have various degrees of self-illumination, based upon the corresponding grayscale value.

Should I change the Opacity value for a self-illuminated material?

- If you want, you can reduce the Opacity value of the material from 100, which is fully opaque. When creating a self-illuminated material, you typically want the material to be fairly opaque so that it can stand out in your scene. Keep in mind that if you reduce the opacity of the material too much, it may not be visible in the scene. To resolve this problem, you want both a transparent and self-illuminated material. In the Extended Parameters rollout, select the Additive option. This adds the Diffuse color of the material to the color of the objects that are behind it.

continued

Create a Visible Light Source *(Continued)*

You can create any type of light object to cast light from inside a self-illuminated object. However, you should select a light type that corresponds to the type of lighting that you want the object to emit. For example, if you are creating a small desk lamp, then you would probably select a Target Spot light to cast light on the desk. Creating a street lamp would work well with an Omni light.

To create the light, click or click and drag in the Top viewport. You can use the Move and Rotate tools to position the light so that it is located within the part of the light surface object that you created.

When you create the light object, you can specify the appropriate parameter values, including the exclusion of the light surface object from the light's shadow casting. When you create light objects in a scene, such as a lamp, these types of objects typically cast shadows. You should turn on shadows and select a shadow type for generating the shadows. For more information about setting light parameter values and working with shadows, see Chapter 17.

Create a Visible Light Source *(continued)*

Apply Light to an Object

The material is applied to the selected object.

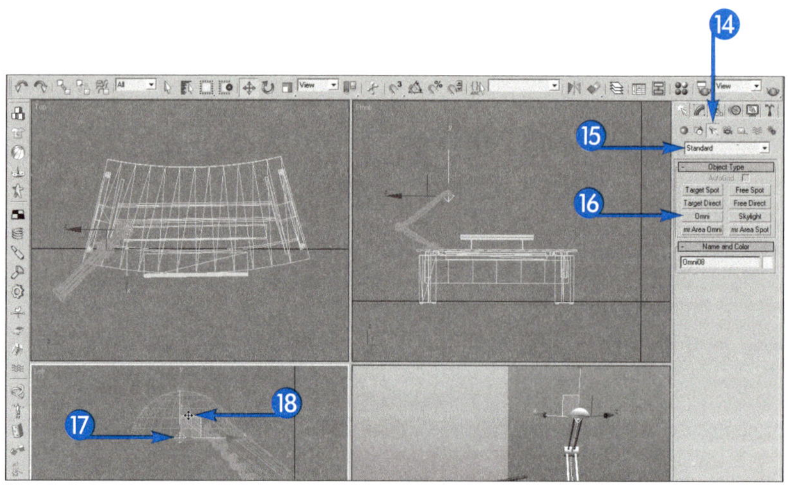

14 Click .

15 Click ▾ and select Standard.

16 Click a light type.

This example uses an Omni light.

17 Click to create the light.

18 Move the light inside the visible light object.

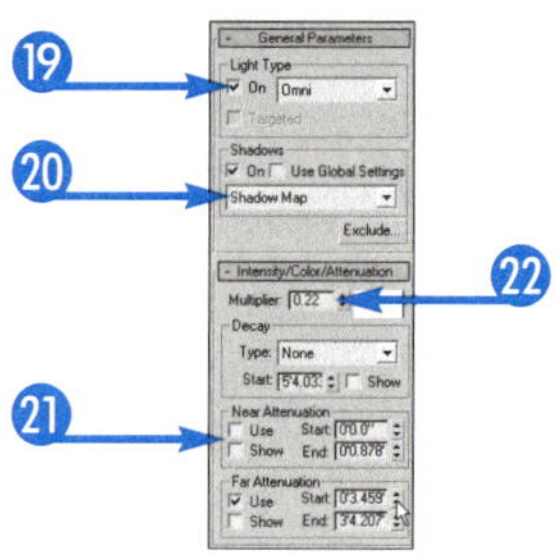

19 Click the On option in the Shadows section (☐ changes to ☑).

20 Click ▾ and select a shadow type.

21 Set Attenuation values if necessary.

22 Type a Multiplier value for light brightness.

Note: *For more information about setting Attenuation, see Chapter 17.*

You can also set other parameter values for the light object.

23 Click Exclude.

The Exclude/Include dialog box appears.

24 Select the visible light object, and then click » to exclude it.

25 Ensure that the Exclude and Both options are selected, and then click OK.

Note: *For more information about excluding objects, see Chapter 17.*

26 Click [icon].

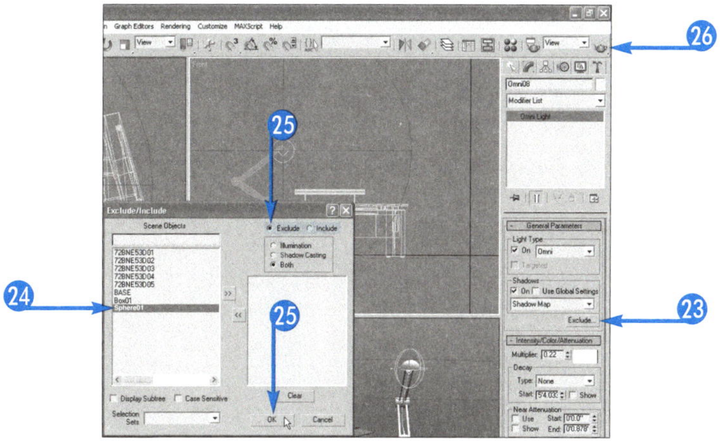

3ds Max renders the scene, creating a visible light object.

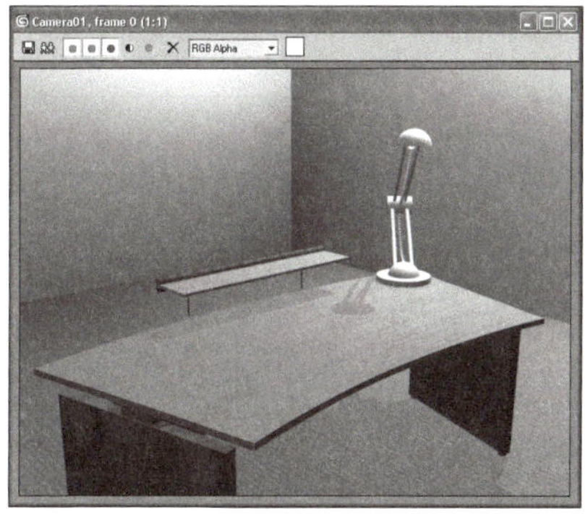

Master It

Can I use a Target light to create the visible light object?

Yes. You can use a Free, Target, or Omni light with your visible light object. If you use a Target light, then set the target for where you want the light to fall in the scene. For example, if you are creating a search light, then your target may be the side of a building. This ensures that the light hits the building to show that the light is on. You can also target any Free Spotlight or Directional light by selecting the Targeted option in the General Parameters rollout for the selected light. When a light is targeted, you cannot type the target distance.

How do I make the actual light emitted from the lamp visible?

When you create a visible light object, as described in this section, the actual light emitted from the lamp is not visible. If you want to make it visible, you have two different options: You can apply either a lens flare or a volume light. The lens flare creates flare effects around the light object. The volume light creates visible light rays for the light object. For more information about creating a Volume Light effect, see Chapter 23. See the section "Apply a Lens Effect to a Light" for information about using a lens flare.

Apply a Lens Effect to a Light

Lens Effects are a family of effects that change the appearance of lights or objects when they are rendered. There are several Lens Effects available, including a starburst and lens flare, and the ability to make lights and objects glow. Lens Effects are found in the Environment and Effects dialog box, and additional rendering effects are discussed in Chapter 21.

When you create a Lens Effect, there are actually several different types that you can select. The Ray effect works well when you create light objects, such as lamps, because it creates bright rays of light that radiate from the center of the light object. When you select a specific Lens Effect, the rollouts change to display parameters for that selected effect. For example, selecting Ray displays the Ray Element rollout. Lens effects that are added after the scene is rendered and do not add more illumination to the scene.

To create a Lens Effect for a specific light, you need to select that light both in your scene and in the Lights drop-down list in the Environment and Effects dialog box.

CD FILE The LensEffect.max file is available on the CD-ROM for you to practice adding a Lens Effect.

Apply a Lens Effect to a Light

1. Click Rendering.
2. Click Effects.

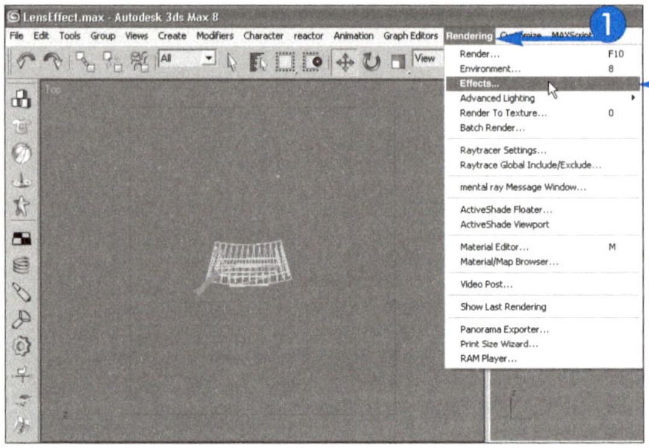

The Environment and Effects dialog box appears, displaying the Effects tab.

3. Click Add.

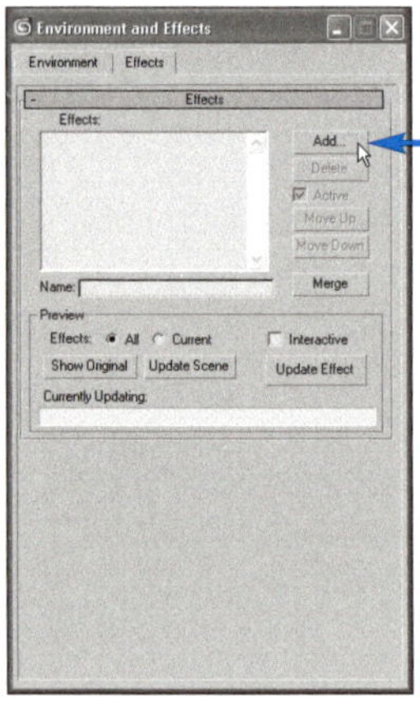

The Add Effect dialog box appears.

4. Click Lens Effects.

5. Click OK.

3ds Max adds the Lens Effect to the Effects list. Additional rollouts are added to the dialog box, with parameters for setting a Lens Effect.

6. In the Lens Effects Parameters rollout, click Ray.

7. Click the single arrow button (>).

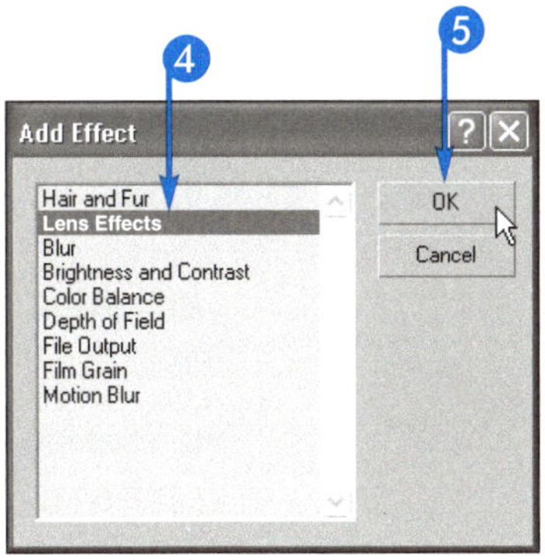

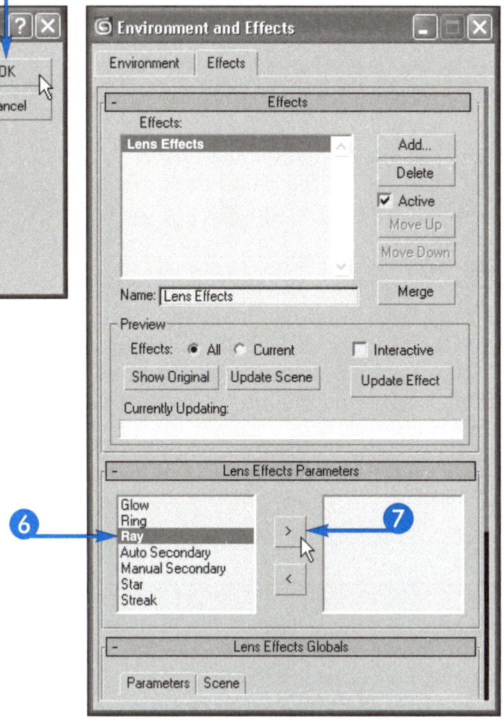

MASTER IT

Is there another method for selecting a light if it is not visible in the viewport?

▼ Yes. If the light to which you want to apply the Lens Effect is not visible in the viewport, or is difficult to select by clicking, then you can select it from the Select Objects dialog box. To display the Select Objects dialog box, click the Select by Name button in the Main toolbar or press the H key on the keyboard. When the Select Objects dialog box appears, select the name of the light, and then click Select. The name is added to the Lights drop-down list box in the Parameters section of the Lens Effects Globals rollout.

Can I select a different Lens Effect?

▼ You can use any of the effects listed in the Lens Effects Parameters rollout. Each effect creates a different appearance for a light.

Lens Effects

Effect	*Description*
Glow	Creates a circular, glowing aura around the light object. This effect works well for creating neon lights or visible light sources.
Ring	Creates a ring that surrounds the light object.
Ray	Creates bright rays that emit from the light object in all directions.
Auto Secondary	Creates a camera-lens flare effect that creates small, bright circles near the light object.
Manual Secondary	Creates additional camera-lens flares that you can add manually.
Star	Similar to a Ray Lens Effect, but wider and with additional controls.
Streak	Creates a horizontal band of light through the center of the light object.

PART V

continued

Apply a Lens Effect to a Light *(Continued)*

After you apply the Ray Lens Effect to the light, you can specify the parameters that control the appearance of the effect in the Ray Element rollout.

You need to specify a size for the rays that are emitted, in the Size field, to determine the overall length of the rays. You can also specify the actual number of rays by entering a number in the Num field. The specified number of rays are randomly positioned around the light object. The Sharp parameter controls how crisp and clear the rays appear. The value of this parameter can be between zero and ten. The Intensity parameter controls the overall brightness of the rays. Increasing the Intensity value makes rays brighter and more opaque.

Lens Effects can take a good amount of time to add to a rendering and may need to be rendered repeatedly to achieve the desired effect. To hasten this process, you can render the effect once and then update the effect in the Rendered Frame Window. When you update the effect, the entire scene is not rendered again — only the effect is updated.

Apply a Lens Effect to a Light *(continued)*

Ray is added to the right field as a Lens Effect in the scene.

8. Click Pick Light.
9. Click to select the light.

   The name of the selected light appears in the Lights field.

10. Type a number in the Size field for the length of the rays.
11. Type a number in the Num field for the number of rays.
12. Type a number in the Sharp field to set the sharpness of the rays.
13. Type a number in the Intensity field for the brightness of the effect.

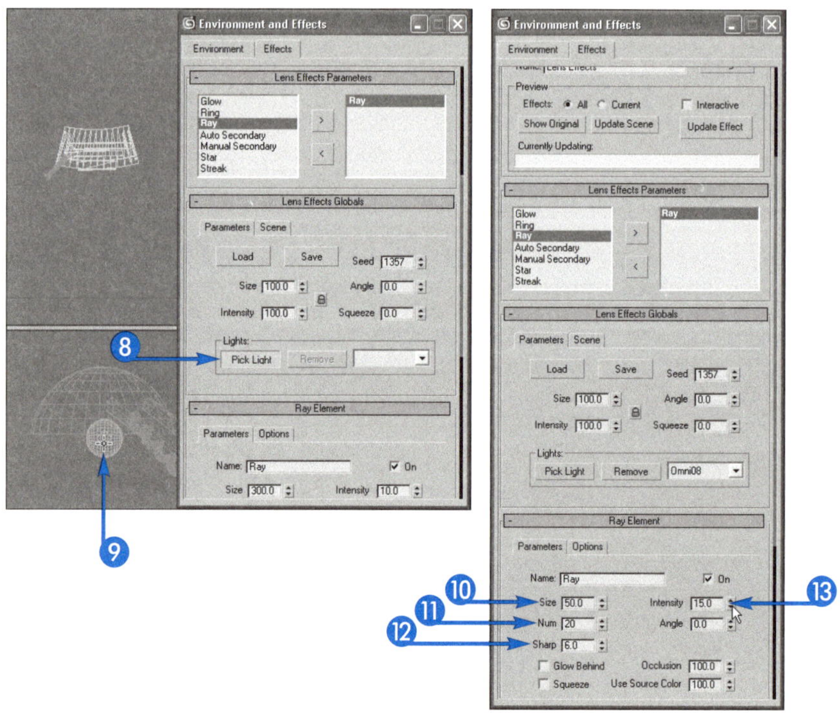

14 In the Effects rollout, click Update Scene.

3ds Max renders the scene and then adds the effect.

You can change the values that you entered in steps 10 to 13 and then click Update Effect after each modification.

3ds Max updates the effect without re-rendering the scene.

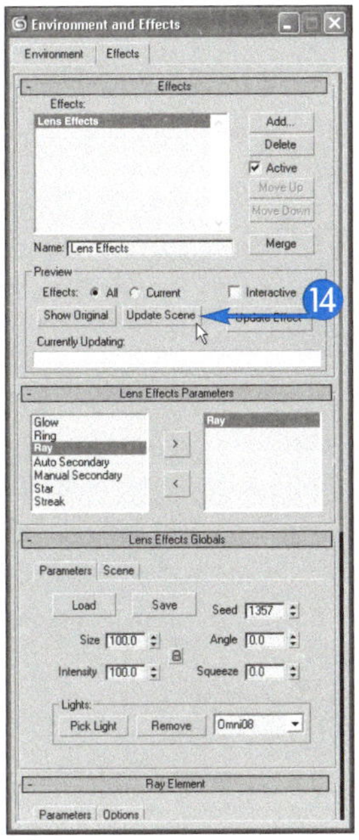

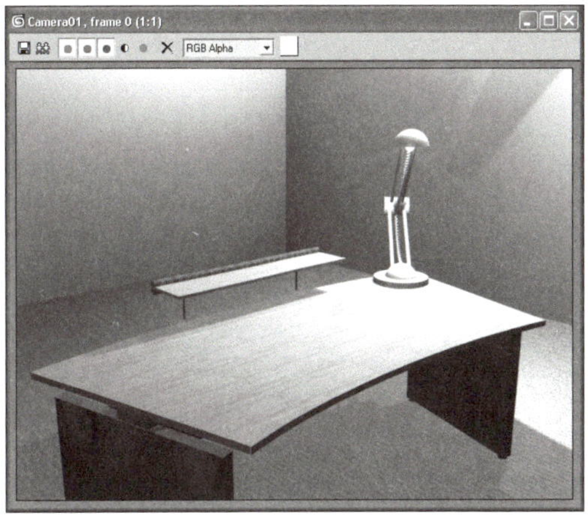

Should I use the Interactive option?

- Probably not. The Interactive option (☐ changes to ☑) in the Preview section of the Effects rollout causes the Lens Effect to be updated in the Rendered Frame Window each time a parameter changes. This can result in a significant reduction in productivity while the effect is continually updated. This is especially true when you use the spinner buttons to change the parameter values. You should only use the Interactive option when entering the parameters from the keyboard and when immediate feedback for each parameter change is required.

Can I add the Lens Effect directly to the light?

- Yes. When you create or modify a light, you can add a Lens Effect in the Atmospheres & Effects rollout in the Modify panel for that light. To add the Lens Effect to the selected light, click Add to display the Add Atmosphere or Effect dialog box. Click Lens Effects. The Lens Effect appears in the list box in the Atmospheres & Effects rollout. To specify the settings for the effect, select the Lens Effect in the list box and then click Setup. In the Environment and Effects dialog box that appears, you can specify all of the settings as described in the steps.

Using Exposure Control

You can use exposure control to control the overall brightness, contrast, and color levels in your scene. You can set exposure control for any scene that contains lighting, to make a dark scene brighter or to dim an overly bright scene.

Exposure control is an environmental setting that you can set in the Environment tab of the Environment and Effects dialog box, which you can access from the Rendering menu. By default, exposure control is not applied to a scene. Although you can select any of the available exposure control options, if you are working with Photometric lights, Radiosity, or other advanced lighting features, you should almost always use the Logarithmic exposure control option.

When you set the exposure control for your scene, you can use the Render Preview button to preview the scene in the dialog box. If you do not like the results, you can use the parameters in the Exposure Control Parameters rollout to change the settings.

The rollout includes options for controlling the Brightness, Contrast, Mid Tones, and Physical Scale values. You can also apply a specific color correction.

CD FILE: The Exposure.max file is available on the CD-ROM for you to practice using exposure control.

Using Exposure Control

1. Click Rendering.
2. Click Environment.

   The Environment and Effects dialog box appears, displaying the Environment tab.

3. Click ▾ and then click an Exposure Control option.

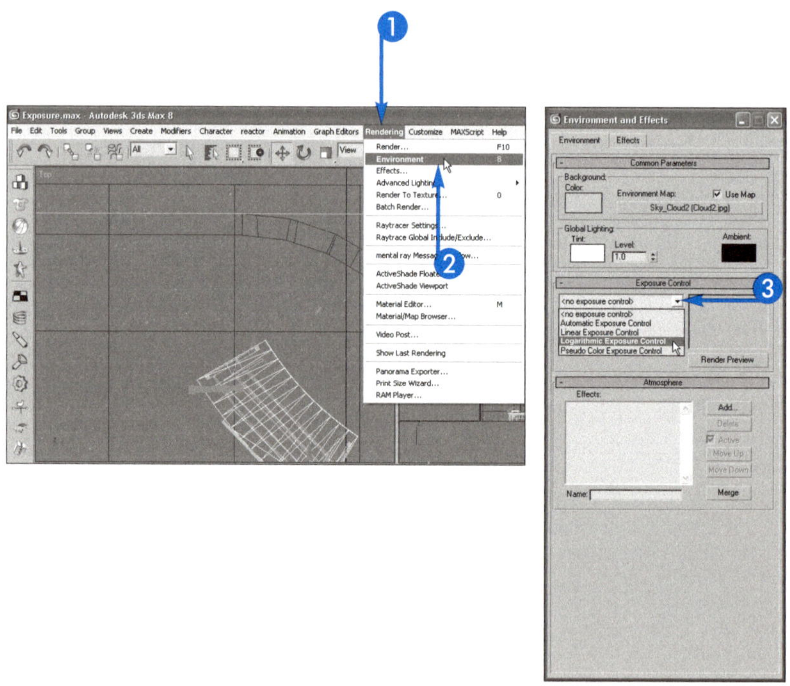

The parameters display for the exposure control that you selected.

4. Click Render Preview to see how the control affects lighting in your scene.

   The preview displays in the dialog box.

5. Type different values in the Brightness and Contrast fields if required.

6. Click .

   3ds Max renders the scene with the exposure control settings that you specified.

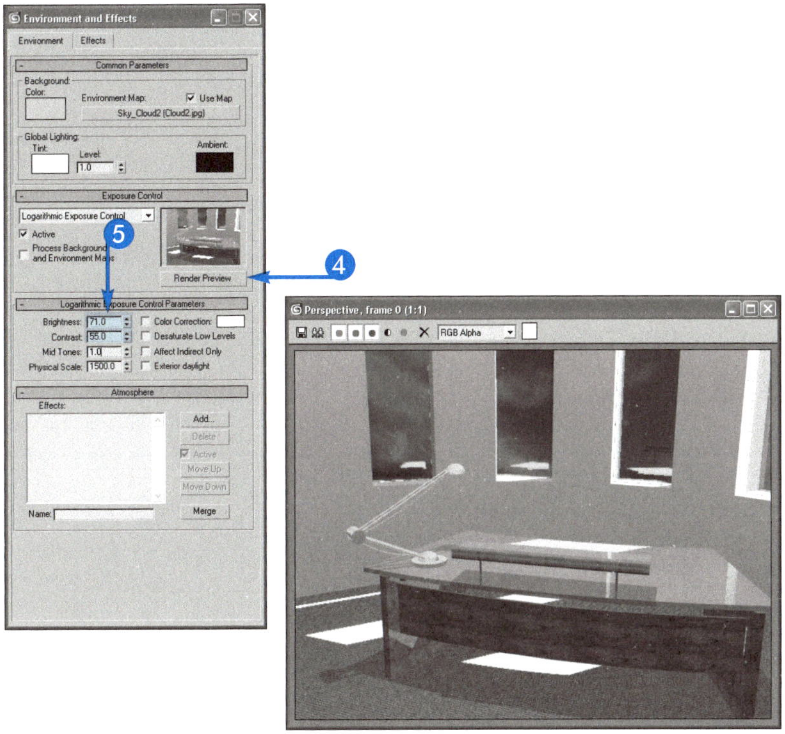

MASTER IT

What does the Physical Scale value control?

- The Physical Scale value changes the intensity of the light that is emitted by Standard lights. By multiplying the Physical Scale value by the Multiplier for each Standard light, 3ds Max converts the light intensity value for the light object. For example, if the Multiplier of a Standard light is 1 and the Physical Scale value is 1500.0, then the light has an intensity value of 1500.0 candelas. The Physical Scale value only works with Standard lights. Any Photometric lights in your scene are not affected.

When should I use the "Affect Indirect Only" option?

- You can use the "Affect Indirect Only" option (☐ changes to ☑) if your scene includes only Standard lights as your primary light source with radiosity. When you select it, the Logarithmic exposure control is applied only to the areas of the scene that have indirect lighting.

When should I use the "Exterior daylight" option (☐ changes to ☑)?

- If you are creating an outdoor scene with the IES Sun light object, then you can select the Exterior Daylight settings to adjust the scene for the brightness that the light creates.

Understanding Radiosity

Radiosity is a popular method for creating diffused shadows and reflections through the Default Scanline Renderer. Your rendering becomes a two-step process that first creates a radiosity solution for your scene by calculating how the light bounces around the environment and distributes its energy. Once the radiosity solution is created, it is saved with your scene. When you render the scene, the radiosity solution is used by the renderer. You only have to re-create the radiosity solution if the geometry, lighting, or materials in the scene change. See the section "Using Radiosity in a Scene" for more information.

Radiosity is a lighting plug-in that is only used with the Default Scanline Renderer. You can turn on Radiosity and control the parameters in the Advanced Lighting panel of the Render Scene dialog box. When you select Radiosity, several rollouts display to allow you to customize the parameter values. These rollouts are shown in the following illustrations.

Radiosity is designed to work with real-world measurements. This is why it works best with Photometric lights that are based on real-world light settings. When you apply Radiosity, you must size objects in your scene properly to achieve the correct results. For example, a door should be 36 inches wide and not 36 feet or 36 meters.

B Radiosity Processing Parameters Rollout

Contains the controls for creating the Radiosity solution for the selected scene. The Initial Quality value determines the accuracy of the energy distribution for the radiosity solution.

C Radiosity Meshing Parameters Rollout

Subdivides the models in the scene into polygon meshes. The size of the meshes is defined by the user. When you create more polygons in the scene, there are more surfaces to accurately reflect the diffused light in the scene.

D Select Advanced Lighting Rollout

Identifies the advanced lighting method that is currently selected for the scene. You can select from either of the listed plug-ins: Radiosity or Light Tracer. To disable the current lighting method, click the Active option (☑ changes to ☐).

A Rendering Options

Contains controls for selecting the renderer that you use to render the current scene. You can also select the viewport that you want to render.

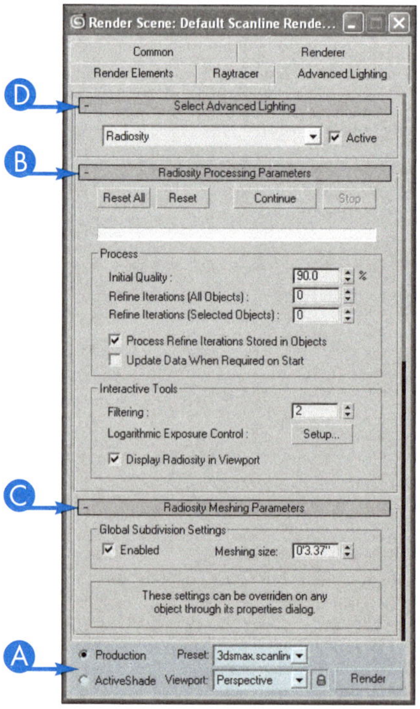

E Light Painting Rollout

Allows you to add and remove illumination to and from surfaces of objects by using the illumination tools. You can make the adjustments without having to reprocess Radiosity.

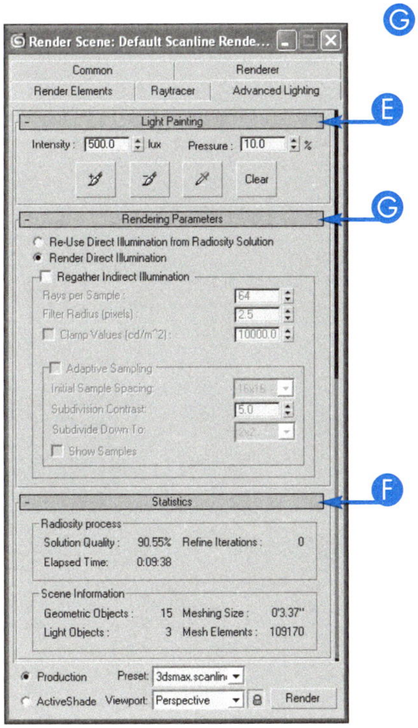

F Statistics Rollout

Provides information about the most recent creation of the Radiosity solution. This includes specifying the Solution Quality value, number of Refine Iterations, and amount of time required to create the solution.

G Rendering Parameters Rollout

Allows you to control how the Radiosity is rendered in the scene. When you render with a Radiosity solution, 3ds Max renders the lights in the scene to create the shadows and then adds the ambient light in the Radiosity solution.

To use the direct illumination that was rendered by Radiosity, click the ìRe-Use Di rect Illumination from Radiosity Solution" option (○ changes to ◉). Click the "Render Direct Illumination" option (○ changes to ◉) to render direct illumination with the Default Scanline Renderer.

You can use the same light-gathering options used by the Radiosity plug-in to capture the indirect lighting of each pixel. This feature improves the accuracy of the images, but requires a lot more time to render.

Using Radiosity in a Scene

You can simulate realistic diffused illumination and shadowing in your scene using Radiosity. Radiosity determines the diffused shadows and lighting by calculating the way light bounces around the environment.

Radiosity is one of the Advanced Lighting plug-ins available in the Render Scene dialog box and is only available with the Default Scanline Renderer. The different rollouts that display in the Advanced Lighting panel allow you to customize the Radiosity parameters for the scene. For example, you can set the initial quality of the Radiosity solution. See the section "Understanding Radiosity" for more information.

When you render your scene using Radiosity, it is a two-step process. You need to first create the Radiosity solution, which defines the energy distribution in your scene. Then, once the Radiosity solution is created, you render the scene.

When you generate a Radiosity solution, 3ds Max stores it with the scene and applies it each time you render. Once the Radiosity solution is created, you only have to re-create it if you make changes to the scene's objects, lights, or materials. This shortens the time required to render the scene.

CD FILE The Radiosity.max file is available on the CD-ROM for you to practice using Radiosity.

Using Radiosity in a Scene

1. Click Rendering.
2. Click Advanced Lighting.
3. Click Radiosity.

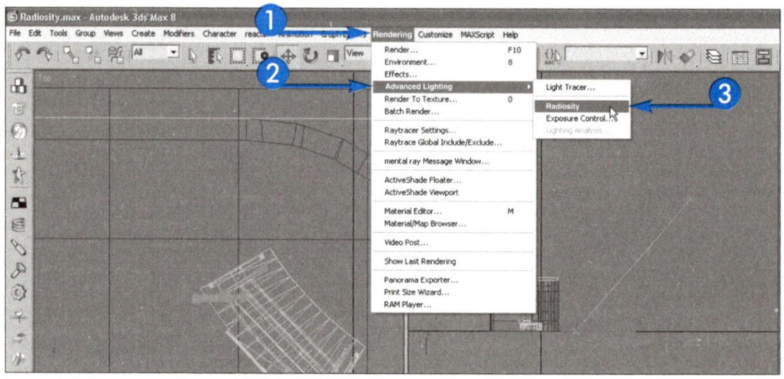

The Render Scene dialog box appears, with Radiosity selected as the Advanced Lighting plug-in.

You can modify the parameter values in the rollouts.

Note: *See the section "Understanding Radiosity" for more information about the settings.*

4. Click Start.

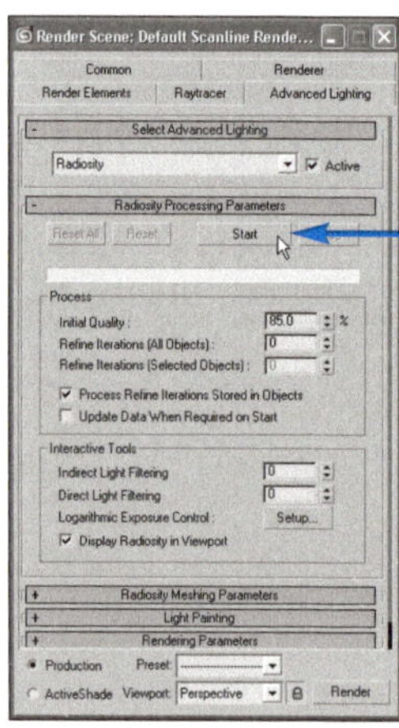

3ds Max generates the Radiosity solution for the scene.

- You can click Stop to stop the process.

5 After 3ds Max generates the Radiosity solution, click Render.

The scene renders using the Radiosity solution that 3ds Max generated.

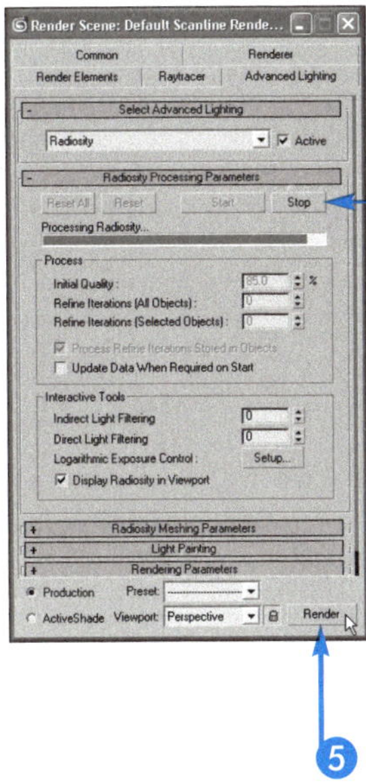

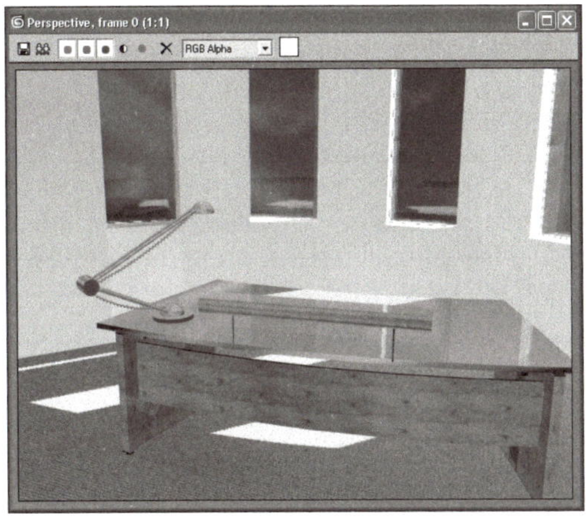

My scene seems too bright. How do I reduce the brightness?

▼ You can control the brightness of a scene with exposure control. When working with Radiosity, you should almost always use the Logarithmic exposure control. This control is automatically assigned when you select Radiosity. You can customize the exposure control settings by clicking Setup in the Interactive Tools section of the Radiosity Processing Parameters rollout. In the Environment & Effects dialog box that appears, you can customize the settings of the exposure control. See the section "Using Exposure Control" for more information about setting the values.

My scene does not have any diffused lighting after creating a Radiosity solution. What is the problem?

▼ In order for Radiosity to work correctly, your scene must include models with polygon meshes on their surface. This creates multiple surfaces for the light to reflect and diffuse within the scene. If you have a lot of flat surfaces, where light cannot bounce from one surface to another, then you will not see the results that you want. To correct this problem, you can enable meshing in the Radiosity Meshing Parameters rollout. This creates polygon meshing at the specified size throughout the scene. The smaller the mesh, the more lighting detail that is created. This also means that the rendering time is increased, with more surfaces to diffuse light.

About Cameras

Cameras are objects that you can place anywhere in your scene in order to create and preserve a different viewpoint.

As with all object types, you can create camera objects in the Create panel. There are only two types of cameras: Free and Target. You can adjust the orientation of a Free camera by rotating the camera with the Rotate transform. A Target camera is always oriented toward its associated Target object, and so you can adjust the orientation of the Target camera by moving the Target object. You can alternate between camera types by selecting an option in the Type drop-down list in the Modify panel. Cameras differ from Perspective views in that they can be animated.

After you place a camera, you can view your scene from the viewpoint of the camera by switching a viewport to a Camera view. In a Camera view, you can see the scene as if you are looking through the lens of the camera. For more information about switching viewport views, see Chapter 1.

Camera Components

A camera is comprised of up to three components — the camera itself, a field-of-view cone, and, if applicable, a target object.

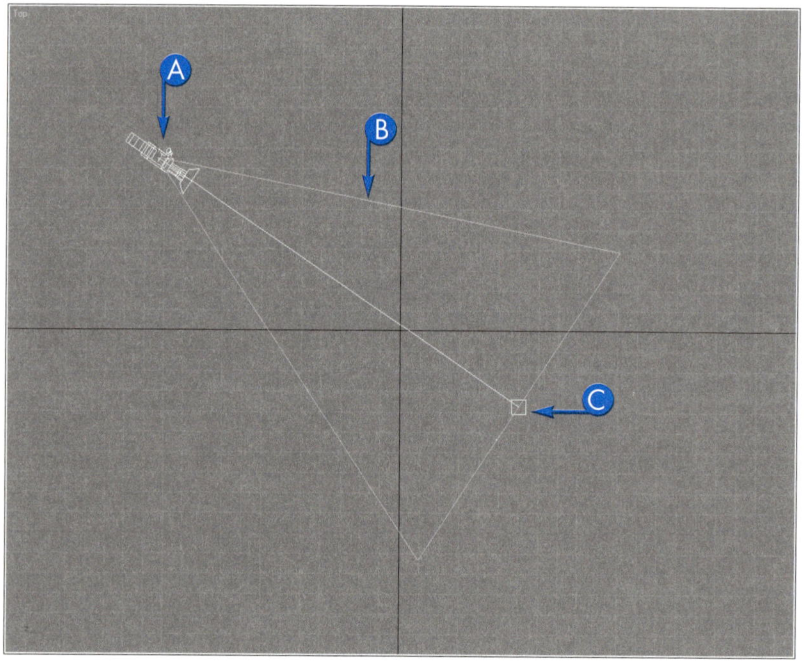

A Camera

Provides a specific point of view in the scene.

B Field-of-View Cone

Shows the field-of-view limits for the camera. Only the objects within the camera's field of view are visible in the Camera viewport and renderings.

C Camera Target

Object to which a Target camera always points, regardless of where the camera is located.

Camera Parameters

When you create a camera, the Parameters rollout displays all the parameter values that you can set for the camera. The Parameter values are the same for both the Free and Target cameras.

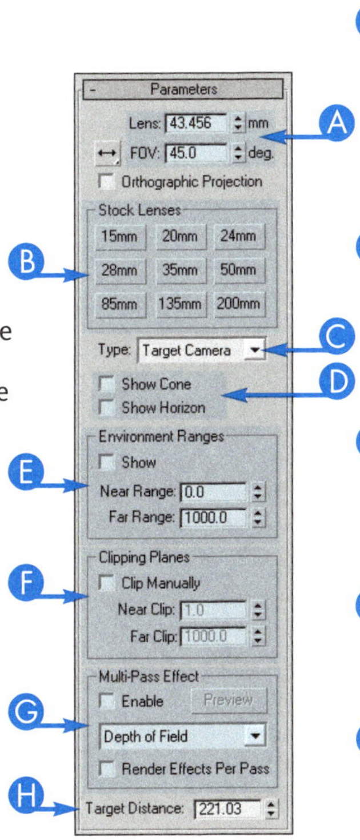

A Lens/FOV Fields

The Lens field corresponds to a standard camera's lens length, which is used to identify the focal length. Specified in millimeters, this measurement indicates the distance from the front of the lens to the light-sensitive surface.

The field-of-view (FOV) for the lens is measured in degrees. You can indicate the measurement horizontally, vertically, or diagonally by clicking the corresponding direction button next to the field.

B Stock Lenses

Select one of the stock lens settings to adjust the values in the Lens and FOV fields in order to help match real-world camera settings.

C Type Field

Indicates whether the selected camera is a Free or Target camera.

D Show Cone/Horizon

When checked, Show Cone displays the camera's FOV cone, even when the camera is not selected. Show Horizon displays the horizon line in the camera's viewport.

E Environment Ranges

Indicate the near- and far-range limits where the atmospheric effects display in renderings of the Camera viewports.

F Clipping Planes

Creates a near and far limitation between which the scene's faces will be displayed.

G Multi-Pass Effect

Creates a motion blur or depth-of-field rendering effect.

H Target Distance

Indicates the distance between the camera and the target. With a Free camera, this is determined by an implied target centered at the end of the FOV cone.

Create a Camera

You can create a camera that gives you a custom view of your scene. When you use the Camera view, you can see what is visible from the viewpoint of the camera. For example, if you point a camera at a table and then switch a viewport to the Camera view, you can see the table. The camera's location, Lens length, and FOV determine how the object appears.

You add a camera object to your scene via the Cameras button in the Create panel. You can create either a Target camera or Free camera, and the camera's initial orientation is based upon the type of camera that you create.

To create a Target camera, you click to place the camera and then drag and release to place the target. The camera is oriented to face the target. When you create a Free camera, you click in a viewport, and the camera is oriented away from the viewport or toward the World negative Z-axis.

You can switch any viewport to a camera's view by right-clicking a viewport's label and selecting the camera name from the pop-up menu.

CD FILE: The Camera.max file is available on the CD-ROM for you to practice creating cameras.

Create a Camera

1. Click the Create panel button ( ).
2. Click the Cameras button ( ).

   The camera type buttons display in the Object Type rollout.

3. Click Target.

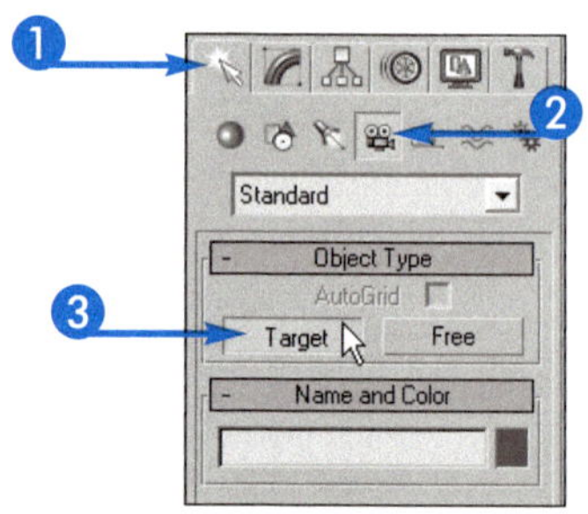

   The camera parameters display in the Create panel.

4. Click in a viewport to place the camera.
5. Drag and release to place the camera's target.

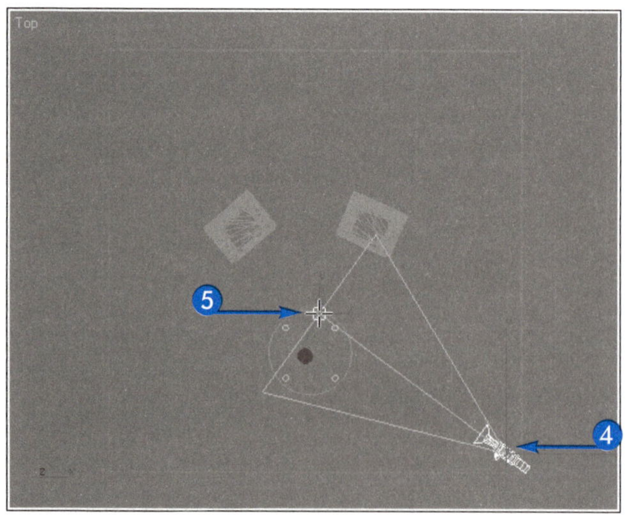

3ds Max creates a camera in the viewports.

6 Right-click a viewport title.

7 Click Views.

8 Click a camera's name.

This example uses Camera01.

The viewport changes to show the scene from the camera's point-of-view.

- You can right-click a viewport title and then click Smooth + Highlights to see the surfaces and highlights of the objects.

MASTER IT

In which viewport should I click to create a Free camera?

When you create a Free camera, it is often easier to create it in the Top viewport because the orientation of the camera is set by the viewport where you click. Because 3ds Max always positions the camera along the negative Z-axis of the viewport, it points away from the spot where you click, or the World negative Z-axis when it is created in a Perspective or Camera viewport. When you rotate a Free camera to change its orientation, always change the Rotate transform's Reference Coordinate System to Local to better control the rotation. You can also create and orient a Target camera and then change it into a Free camera. For information on Reference Coordinate Systems, see Chapter 2.

Can I hide the cameras in the viewports?

Yes, you can hide cameras so that they are not visible in any viewports. To hide a specific camera, select it, then right-click and select Hide Selection from the quad menu. 3ds Max also allows you to hide specific categories of objects, such as cameras or lights. You can select the category that you want to hide in the Display panel. In the Display panel, locate the Hide by Category rollout and expand it if necessary. Click Cameras (☐ changes to ☑). All camera objects in the scene are now hidden. You can unhide the camera objects by clicking Cameras again to deselect this option. Even when cameras are hidden, you can still view the scene through a Camera viewport.

Adjust a Camera's Position

You can use the Transform tools to move or rotate a camera or target object in your scene. This allows you to orient the camera in the direction that you want. For information on the Transform tools, see Chapter 2.

When you add a Target camera to your scene, it is oriented toward its target. A Free camera, which has no target, is oriented toward the negative Z-axis of the viewport where you created it, or the World negative Z-axis. For example, a camera that you create in the Top viewport points downward. If you want to have immediate orientation feedback when you transform a camera, then switch a viewport to the camera's view.

You can use the Rotate transform to change the direction in which a Free camera is pointing. Change the Rotate transform's Reference Coordinate System to Local so that the rotations are around the camera's local axes rather than the World X-, Y-, and Z-axes. You can only rotate a Target camera so that the camera rolls in place; you must move the target to change the camera's orientation.

CD FILE: The TransformCamera.max file is available on the CD-ROM for you to practice transforming cameras.

Adjust a Camera's Position

Move a Camera

1. Click the Select and Move button (✥).
2. Click and drag a camera in a viewport.

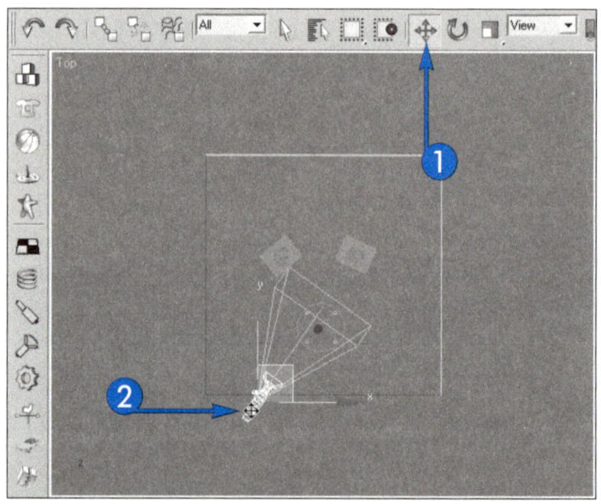

The camera position changes to reflect the movement.

If the camera is a Target camera, then it rotates to maintain its orientation toward the target object.

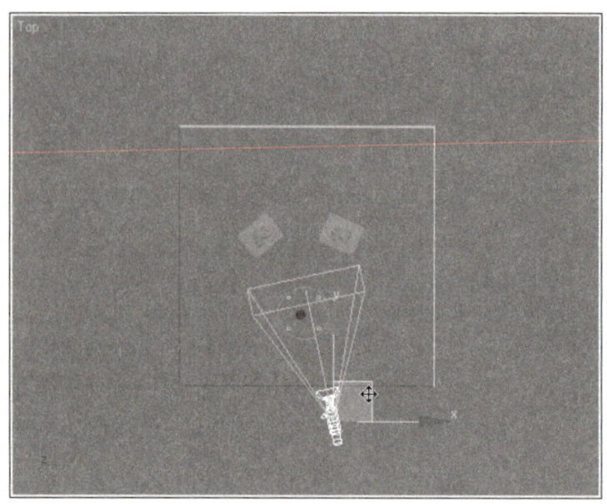

Rotate a Camera

3 Click the Select and Rotate button ().

4 Click here and select Local.

5 Select a Free camera.

6 Click and drag a Rotate gizmo axis.

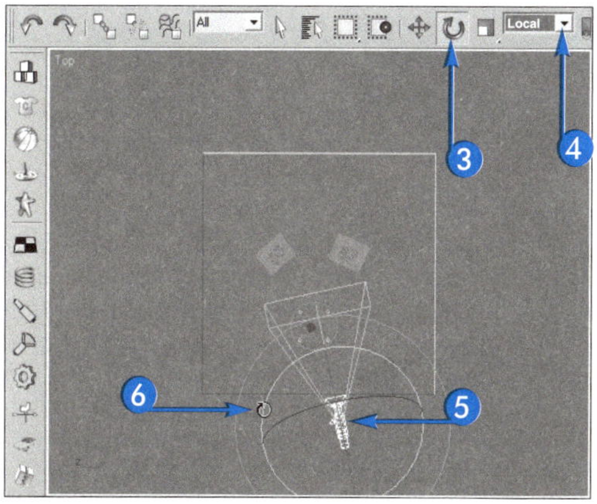

The camera rotates within the scene.

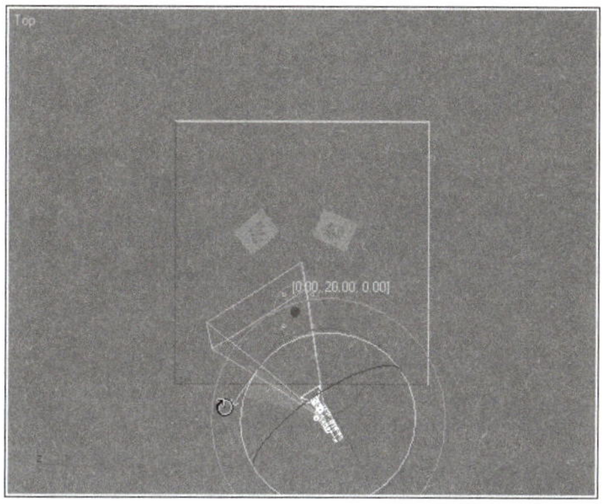

MASTER IT

What is the difference between using the Transform tools and using the Camera Navigation controls?

The Transform tools allow you to move and rotate all objects, including cameras. In non-camera viewports, they are the only tools available for changing the location and orientation of the camera. When you add a camera to your scene, you should use the Select and Move () and the Select and Rotate () buttons to set the initial position of the camera. You can then fine-tune the camera in the Camera viewport with the Camera Navigation controls, located in the bottom-right corner of the user interface. The Camera Navigation controls display only when a Camera viewport is active. Using the Camera Navigation controls, you can move, rotate, orbit, and change the field-of-view of a camera by dragging in the Camera viewport.

How do I display the gizmos when I move or rotate a camera?

The Transform gizmos display by default when you move, rotate, or scale an object. They help to control the transformations of objects by allowing you to restrict movement to one axis, or along all axes. You can control the display of the gizmos in the Views menu. To turn the gizmos on, the default state for all transforms, click Views, and then click Show Transform Gizmo. If gizmos are turned on, then a check mark displays next to the Show Transform Gizmo option in the Views menu. You can also click the X shortcut key to toggle the Transform gizmos on and off. Use the minus and equal keys to decrease or increase the gizmos' sizes.

Adjust a Camera's Lens Settings

You can adjust a camera's Lens and FOV (Field-of-View) settings to change the view from the camera to mimic real-world cameras or to achieve a certain effect. The Lens and FOV parameters are interdependent; when you adjust one, the other adjusts accordingly.

When you adjust the Lens parameter, you change the settings for the focal length of the lens. The focal length value is measured in millimeters; a smaller focal length displays more of the scene. This mimics the focal length of a lens in a real-world camera, where the focal length is a measurement from the lens to the light-sensitive surface inside the camera. Extremely low Lens, or high FOV, values can cause significant distortion in the Camera viewport. The FOV measures the angular limitation, measured in degrees, that is viewable from the camera. The FOV can be measured horizontally, vertically, or diagonally.

You can use an assortment of stock lenses that display in the Parameters rollout as starting points for a camera. When you select a stock lens, the Lens and FOV parameter values are set, although you can adjust these values.

CD FILE

The LensCamera.max file is available on the CD-ROM for you to practice adjusting a camera's lens.

Adjust a Camera's Lens Setting

1. In a viewport, select the camera.
2. Click the Modify panel button ().

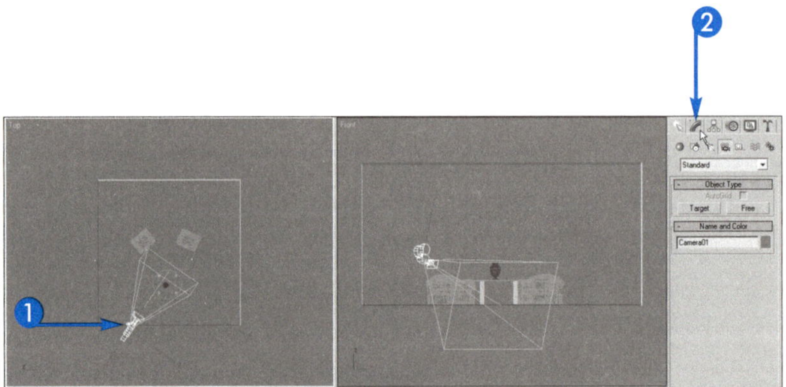

The parameters display for the selected camera in the Modify panel.

3. Right-click a viewport title.
4. Click Views.
5. Select a camera.

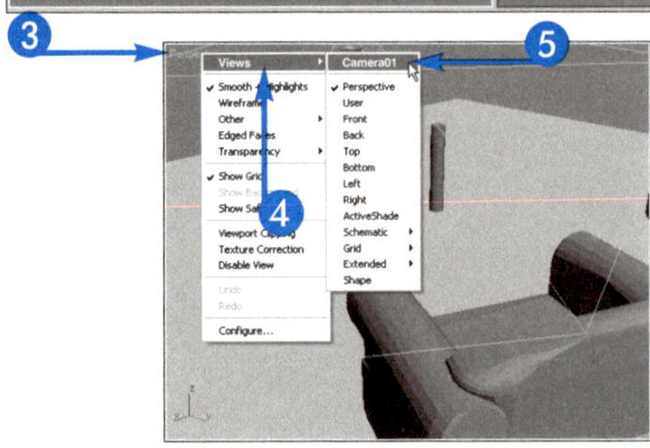

The viewport displays the view from the camera that you selected.

6. Click a Stock Lenses button.

7. Click here to change the Lens and FOV parameters to the setting you want.

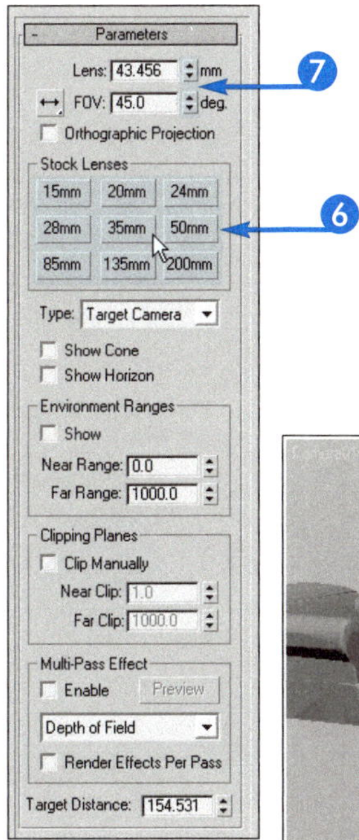

The Camera view changes to show the new lens settings.

MASTER IT

What does the Show Horizon option do?

▼ The Show Horizon option (☐ changes to ☑), in a camera's Parameters rollout, displays a line in your camera viewports that identifies where the virtual horizon is in your scene. This can assist you in matching scene objects to an image used as a background in the scene. When the camera is parallel to the World XY plane, the horizon line is at the same height as the camera and centered vertically in the viewport. When the camera rotates upward or downward, the horizon line moves in the opposite direction in the viewport. The horizon line does not render.

Why does the FOV value change when I change the Lens value?

▼ The FOV value is directly linked to the Lens value, and so changing one value inversly affects the other. In a real-world camera, imagine placing a cone that extends out of the camera's lens that touches the perimeter of the lens and then tapers down to a point where it touches the light-sensitive surface. Shortening the distance from the lens to the point of the cone (Lens) increases the angle from the point to the edge of the lens (FOV). You can adjust the FOV value based on a horizontal, vertical, or diagonal measurement. To change the FOV measurement method, click the FOV Direction flyout, to the left of the FOV field, and click the button indicating the measurement direction that you want.

Using the Dolly Camera Control

You can move the camera, target, or both, along the camera's current line-of-sight using the Dolly buttons. These buttons are available as a flyout in the viewport controls for a Camera view. Using the Dolly button allows you to create smooth forward or backward camera movements without changing the orientation of the camera. With a Free camera, you can only dolly the camera itself.

When you dolly a camera, the camera moves back and forth along the main axis, which runs perpendicular to the camera target, or implied target for a Free camera. As the camera moves closer to the target, you create the effect of zooming in on the target, which causes the objects in the camera to appear larger.

When you dolly the target of the camera, you move the target either closer to or farther from the camera along the main axis.

When you dolly both the camera and target, the distance remains the same between them, and you move along the main axis of the camera.

CD FILE: The DollyCamera.max file is available on the CD-ROM for you to practice dollying a camera.

Using the Dolly Camera Control

Dolly the Camera

1. Select the Camera view viewport.

Note: *See the section "Create a Camera" for information about setting the Camera view.*

2. Click the Dolly Camera button ( ).
3. Click and drag downward in the viewport to dolly the camera away from the target.

   You can also click and drag up to dolly the camera forward.

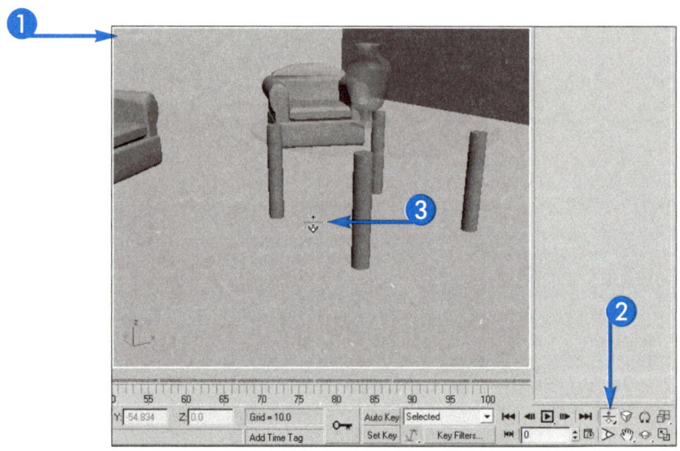

- The camera moves away from the target, making the objects in the Camera view appear farther from the camera.

Dolly the Target

1. Select the Camera viewport.
2. Click and hold to display the Dolly flyout menu.
3. Click the Dolly Target button ( ).

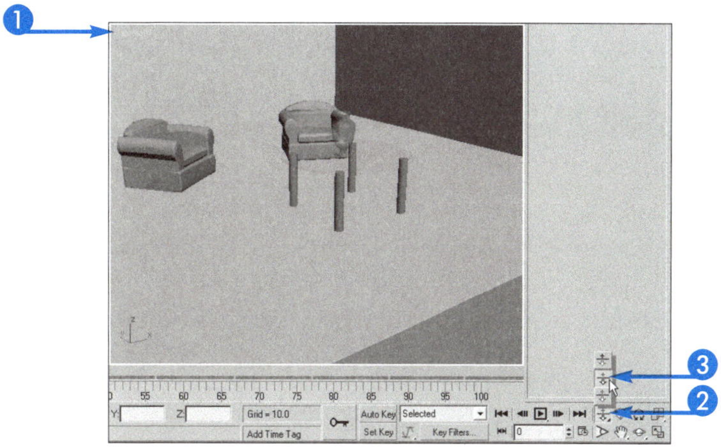

4. Click in the Camera viewport and drag downward to dolly the target toward the camera.

   The camera target moves toward the camera.

   You can drag upward to dolly the target away from the camera.

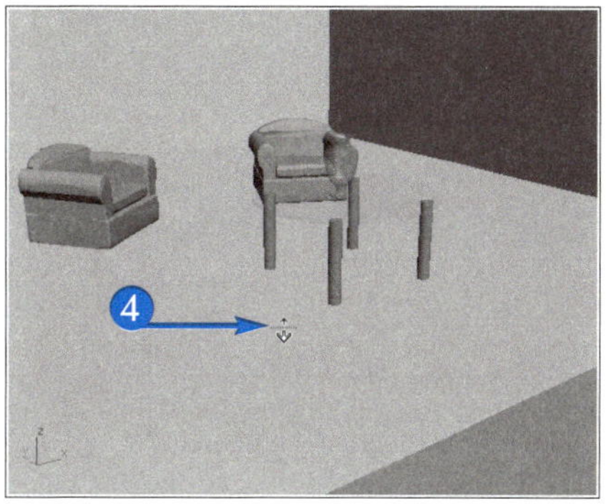

MASTER IT

How do I distinguish between the three Dolly buttons in the flyout menu?

▼ The images on these three buttons are very similar, with a slight variation in the colors of the images. The easiest way to distinguish between the buttons is in the order in which they appear in the flyout. The top button ( ) is the Dolly Camera button. This button only moves the camera. The middle button ( ) is the Dolly Target button, which only moves the camera target. The bottom button ( ), called the Dolly + Camera button, moves both the camera and the target.

Why do I not see a change in the scene when I use the Dolly Target button?

▼ When you dolly the target, you do not change the Camera view at all. Clicking and dragging in the viewport only moves the target along the main axis, perpendicular to the camera. This action changes the location of the camera target, which affects how other camera viewport control buttons work, such as the Orbit Camera button ( ). For example, if you move the camera target, then clicking causes the camera to orbit around a different location in the scene. See the section "Using the Orbit Camera Control" for more information.

Using the Orbit Camera Control

You can use the Orbit Camera control to rotate a camera around a target in a scene. This control allows you to focus on one area of your scene and view it from any angle.

When you orbit a Target camera, the camera rotates around that target, maintaining the same distance between the target and the camera. If you rotate a Free camera, the camera uses an implied target that is located at the center of the camera's cone.

You can freely rotate the camera around the target along the X- and Y-axes by using your mouse. Horizontal mouse movements rotate the camera horizontally, and vertical mouse movements rotate the camera vertically. You can restrict the movement explicitly to either the X- or Y-axis by pressing the Shift key as you drag vertically or horizontally. This keeps the camera movement confined to the axis where you start the rotation.

Keep in mind that orbiting the camera in your scene does not change the focal length of the camera.

The DollyCamera.max file is available on the CD-ROM for you to practice orbiting a camera.

Using the Orbit Camera Control

1. Select a Camera viewport.

Note: *See the section "Create a Camera" for information about setting the Camera view.*

2. Click the Orbit Camera button ( ).

   If is not visible, then you can click and hold to display the flyout menu, and select the top button.

3. Press Shift.

4. Click and drag in the viewport to the right or left.

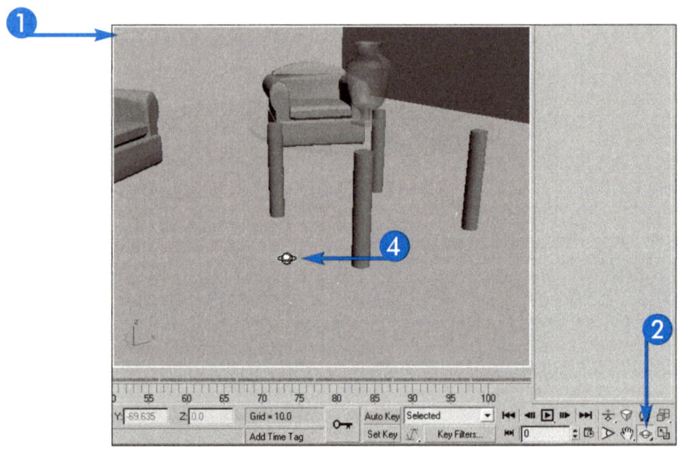

The camera rotates horizontally, showing a different viewpoint of the target.

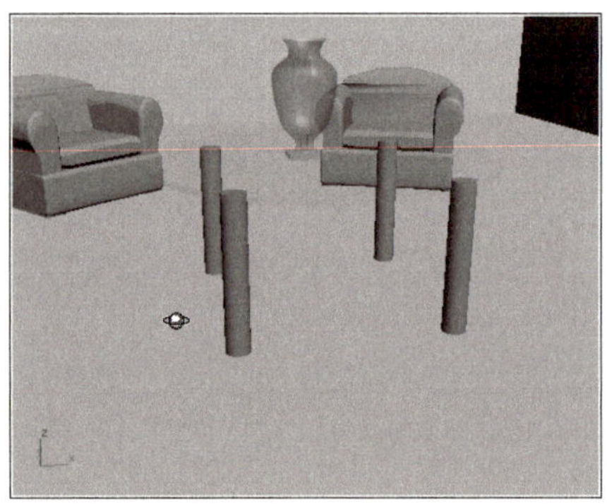

Using the Pan Camera Control

You can use the Pan Camera control to rotate the target around the camera, which remains in a fixed location. This control allows you to view any area of the scene from a single location.

When you use the Pan Camera control, the camera rotates vertically or horizontally to follow the target. If you pan with a Target camera, then the camera follows the camera target, maintaining the same distance between the target and the camera. If you pan with a Free camera, then the camera uses an implied target at the specified target distance and follows the target's movement.

You can freely rotate the target around the camera along the X- and Y-axes by dragging with your mouse. Left and right mouse movements rotate the target horizontally, while forward and backward mouse movements rotate the target vertically. You can restrict the rotation to either the X- or Y-axis by pressing the Shift key as you drag the mouse. This confines the target movement to the axis where you start the rotation.

Keep in mind that panning the camera does not change its focal length.

CD FILE: The DollyCamera.max file is available on the CD-ROM for you to practice panning a camera.

Using the Pan Camera Control

1. Select a Camera viewport.

Note: *See the section "Create a Camera" for information about setting the Camera view.*

2. Click [Pan Camera button].

If [Pan Camera button] is not visible, then you can click and hold [flyout button] to display the flyout menu, and click the bottom button.

3. Press Shift.

4. Click and drag upward in the viewport.

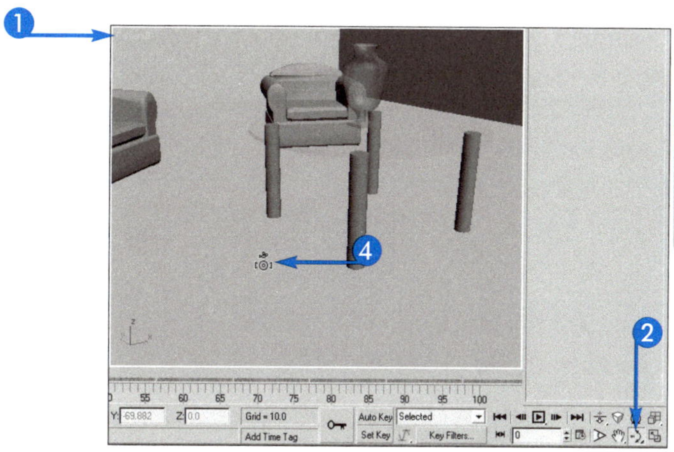

- The camera target rotates vertically, and the objects in the scene also appear to rotate.

Using the Roll Camera Control

You can use the Roll Camera control to rotate the camera around its local Z-axis. Rolling the camera makes the scene appear to spin in a circle. A camera roll is commonly used in film to create the effect of a spinning object — such as a downed airplane — and you can animate a camera roll in 3ds Max to create this effect.

When you roll the camera, it remains in the same location in your scene and simply rotates around while maintaining the same target distance. There is no difference between rolling a Target or Free camera; they both roll around the local Z-axis of the camera. When you roll the camera, the focal length of the camera remains the same.

You can roll the camera by dragging the mouse horizontally across the screen. When you move your mouse to the right, you create a clockwise roll of the camera, which makes the objects in the scene appear to spin counterclockwise. When you move your mouse to the left, it has the opposite effect.

CD FILE: The DollyCamera.max file is available on the CD-ROM for you to practice adjusting a camera's roll.

Using the Roll Camera Control

1. Select the Camera viewport.

Note: *See the section "Create a Camera" for information about setting the Camera view.*

2. Click the Roll Camera button ().
3. Click and drag across the screen.

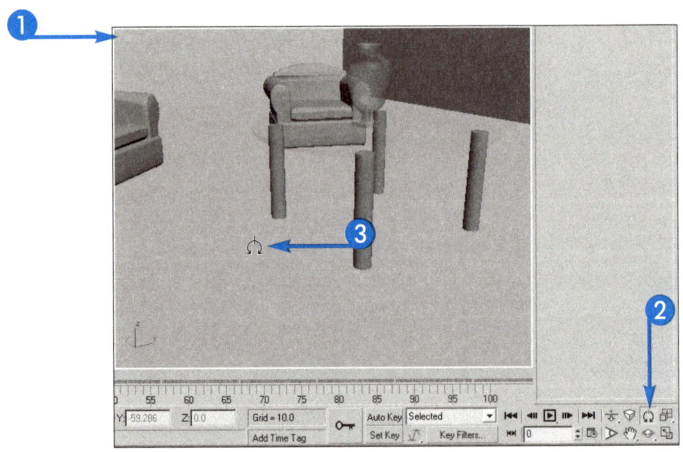

- The camera rolls around the Z-axis, making the objects in view appear to spin.
- This is the same result as if you used the Rotate transform to rotate the camera around its local Z-axis.

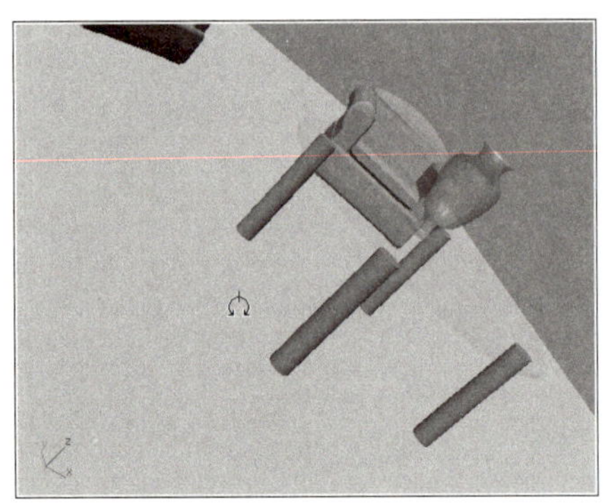

Using the Truck Camera Control

You can use the Truck Camera control to move the camera perpendicular to its line of sight. This allows you to move the camera so that another part of the scene is visible within the camera, while remaining the same distance from its target. Trucking the camera has no effect on the field of view or lens length.

You can truck the camera in your scene by dragging the mouse either left and right or forward and backward, to create horizontal or vertical camera movement.

When you truck a Target camera, the target moves with the camera. 3ds Max maintains the distance between the camera and the target.

CD FILE: The DollyCamera.max file is available on the CD-ROM for you to practice trucking a camera.

MASTER IT

Can I truck the camera in only one direction?

Yes. Use the Shift key to constrain the camera along a single axis. By doing so, you can only truck the camera along the first axis that you use. For example, to truck a camera horizontally, hold down the Shift key and drag either left or right. Once you drag horizontally, you cannot move vertically until you release the mouse button and click again.

Using the Truck Camera Control

1. Select a Camera viewport.

Note: *See the section "Create a Camera" for information about setting the Camera view.*

2. Click the Truck Camera button ( ).

   If is not visible, then click and hold to display the flyout menu.

3. Click and drag across the screen.

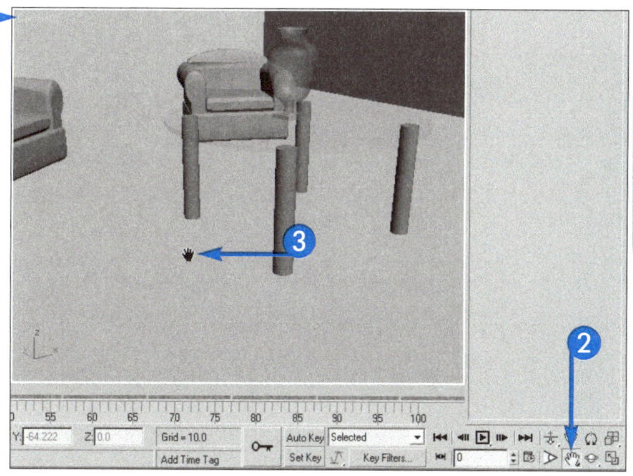

The camera moves horizontally.

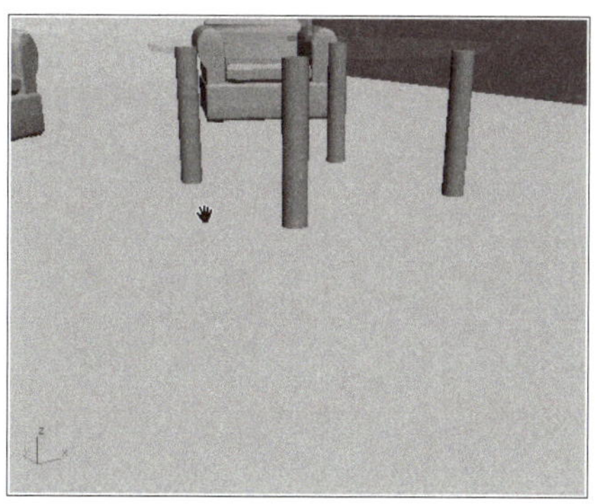

PART V

Using the Field-of-View Control

You can use the Field-of-View control to adjust the viewable angle of a camera without changing its location in the scene. When you use the Field-of-View control, the results resemble those of the Zoom tool that is available with the standard viewports. The Field-of-View control is similar to the Dolly Camera control, except that the camera's perspective changes as you increase or decrease the Field-of-View angle, but not when you use the Dolly Camera control. See the section "Using the Dolly Camera Control" for information about dollying the camera, target, or both.

The field of view is actually an angle, the apex of the angle is the camera, and the lines of the angles are the visible sides of the view, which are indicated by the camera's cone. For example, as you decrease the field of view, you are able to see less of the scene. You can control this by using the FOV field in the camera's Parameters rollout in the Modify panel. Keep in mind that large field-of-view angles can result in significant perspective distortion in the viewport.

The DollyCamera.max file is available on the CD-ROM for you to practice using the FOV control.

Using the Field-of-View Control

1. Select a Camera viewport.

Note: *See the section "Create a Camera" for information about setting the Camera view.*

2. Click the Field-of-View button (▷).
3. Click and drag upward to decrease the field of view.

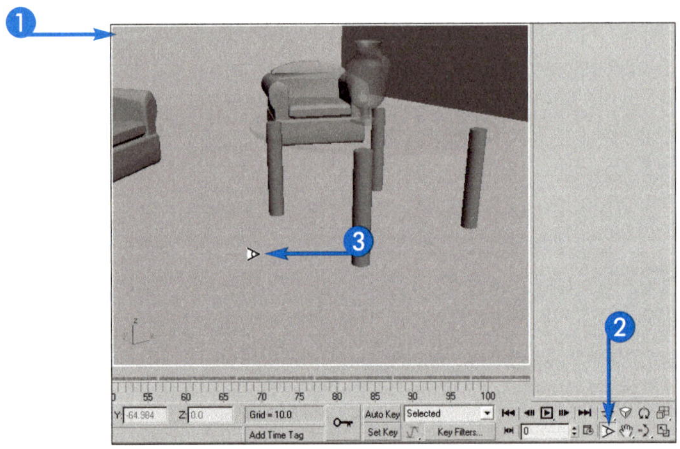

The field of view decreases as you zoom toward the scene.

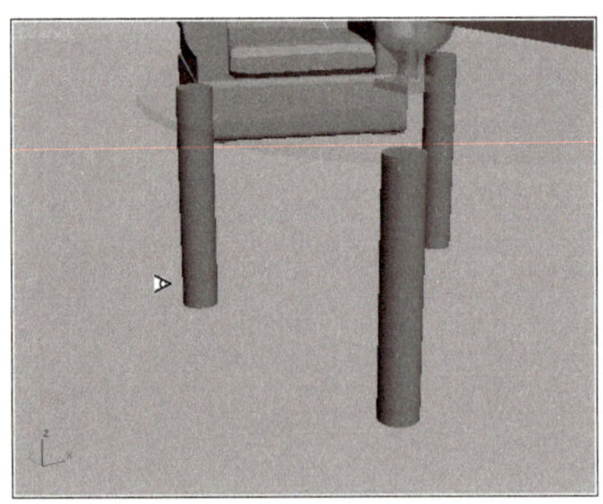

Using the Perspective Camera Control

You can use the Perspective control to adjust the camera's field-of-view while simultaneously dollying the camera. This creates an effect, usually to show a character's anxiety, where the character remains focused and fixed in size, while objects in the foreground and background leave the frame or become distorted. This technique was made famous in Alfred Hitchcock's movie *Vertigo* and is usually animated. See the section "Using the Dolly Camera Control" for information on dollying the camera, target, or both, and the section "Using the Field-of-View Control" for information on adjusting a camera's field of view.

As the camera moves closer to the target, the field of view widens and the perspective increases. Moving the camera away from the target reduces the field of view for the camera and decreases the perspective flare. The maximum Field-of-View value is 175 degrees, which occurs when the camera is nearly touching the camera target.

You can increase the speed of the Perspective control in the viewport by holding down the Ctrl key when you drag the cursor.

CD FILE: The DollyCamera.max file is available on the CD-ROM for you to practice using the Perspective camera control.

Using the Perspective Camera Control

1. Select a Camera viewport.

Note: *See the section "Create a Camera" for information about setting the Camera view.*

2. Click .
3. Click and drag upward.

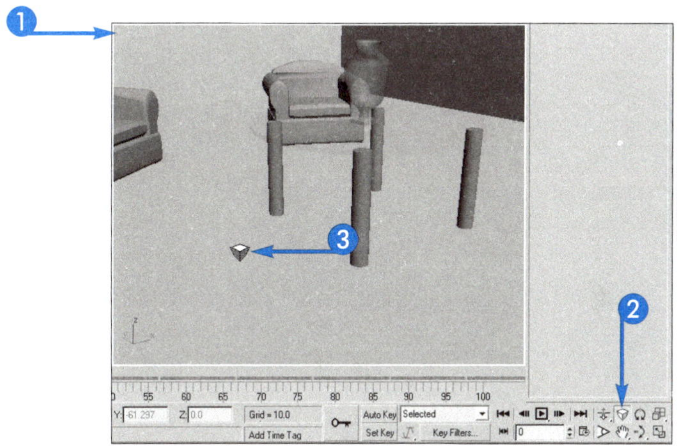

The field of view widens, and the perspective distortion increases for the camera.

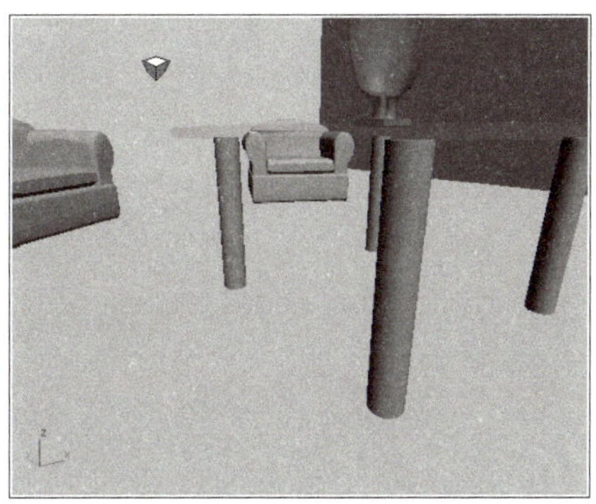

Apply a Camera Correction Modifier

You can apply a Camera Correction modifier to a camera to create a two-point perspective for the Camera's viewport. This allows you to change the way the vertical lines on an object appear to converge as they get taller, which makes a straight object appear slanted. In traditional photography, this is called *keystoning*.

Although the Camera Correction modifier allows you to modify a camera object, you cannot access this feature from the Modify panel. You add the modifier from the quad menu that displays when you right-click in a viewport or from the Modifiers menu. Once you select the modifier, it is added to the Modifier Stack for the camera object.

When you apply the Camera Correction modifier, you can set two parameter values, Amount and Direction. The Amount value indicates the amount of perspective correction that you want to make. The Direction value indicates the direction in which the correction should be made. The default value for the Direction field is 90. A value greater than 90 corrects the perspective to the left, while a value less than 90 corrects it to the right.

CD FILE: The CorrectCamera.max file is available on the CD-ROM for you to practice using the Camera Correction modifier.

Apply a Camera Correction Modifier

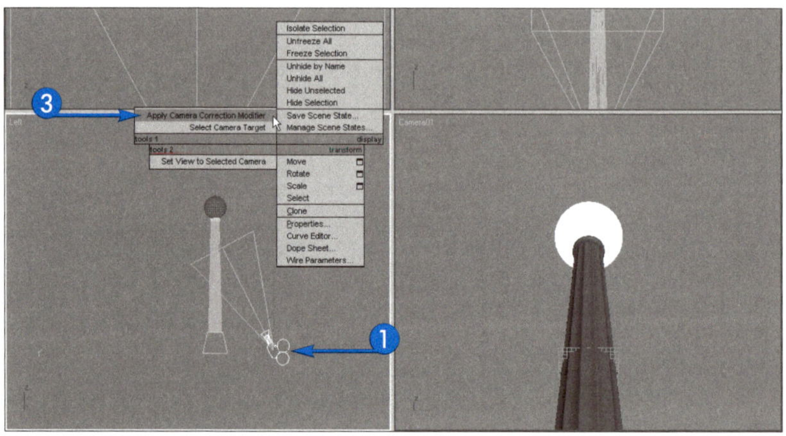

1. Select the camera.
2. Right-click the viewport to display the quad menu.
3. Click Apply Camera Correction Modifier.

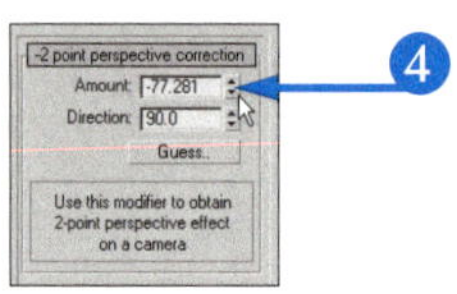

The Camera Correction modifier is applied to the camera.

The parameters display in the Modify panel, with an initial correction for the modifier.

4. Type new Amount and Direction values, if necessary.

The Camera view adjusts to reflect the settings.

5. Click the Camera viewport to make it active.
6. Click the Quick Render button ( ).

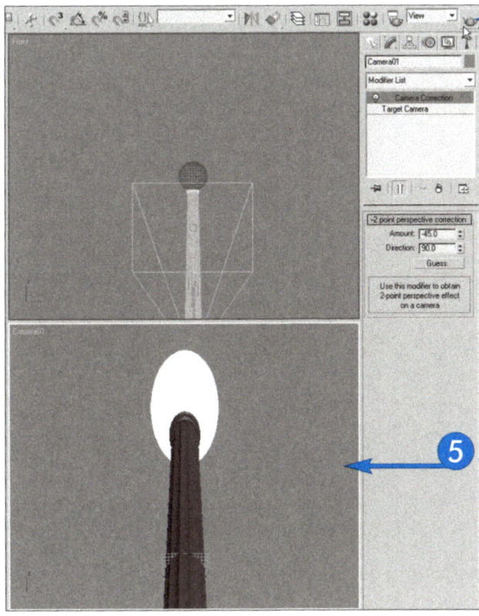

The Camera view renders, showing the application of the Camera Correction modifier.

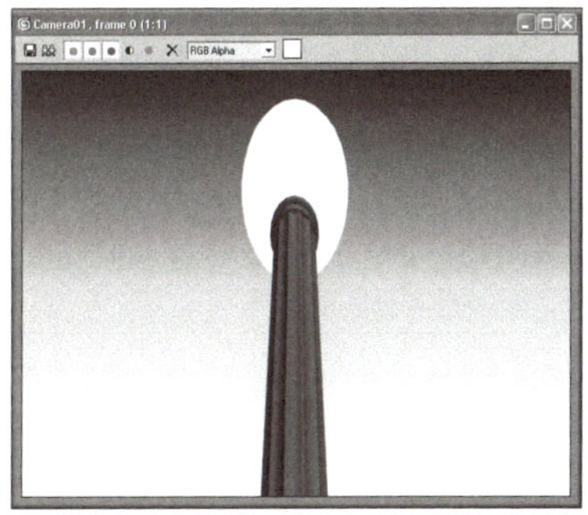

MASTER IT

What happens to the camera when I apply the Camera Correction modifier?

When you use the Camera Correction modifier, 3ds Max evaluates your Camera view and determines initial values for the Amount and Direction fields in order to create the two-point perspective correction. Initial correction values display in the fields. If, after making modifications to the values, you want to return to the default settings for the modifier, then click Guess. When you use the modifier, you are distorting the field of view for the camera to make the vertical lines look straighter. The more the Amount value changes, the more distorted the field of view appears for the camera.

How do I turn off the Camera Correction modifier?

As with any other modifier, the Camera Correction modifier can be controlled from the Modifier Stack in the Modify panel. In the Modify panel, you can change the modifiers that are listed in the modifier values, disable them, and remove them. To disable the modifier, click the light bulb icon ( ) next to the modifier name in the Modifier Stack. When the modifier is disabled, you can see the view from the camera before 3ds Max applied the modifier. Click off the light bulb icon ( ) to activate the modifier again. For more information about working with the Modifier Stack, see Chapter 6.

Apply Depth of Field

You can create a depth-of-field effect in your scene using a camera. This effect makes the objects in the distance appear out of focus or slightly blurred. The depth-of-field effect imitates the effect achieved with a real-world camera when you focus on objects close to the camera.

In order to create a depth-of-field effect, you need to select the camera and then choose the Depth of Field Multi-Pass effect in the Parameters rollout. You can use either the Target Distance of the camera or the Focal Depth field to specify the distance at which the objects should be in focus. Any objects outside that distance are blurred.

3ds Max creates this effect using multiple renderings of the same scene. The camera is moved slightly between each rendering. This camera movement creates the blurred effect for objects outside the specified focal depth.

You can test the Depth-of-Field settings in the Camera view without rendering by using the Preview button in the Multi-Pass Effect section. This allows you to quickly determine whether you have specified the correct distance for the focal depth.

CD FILE: The DepthCamera.max file is available on the CD-ROM for you to practice creating a depth-of-field effect.

Apply Depth of Field

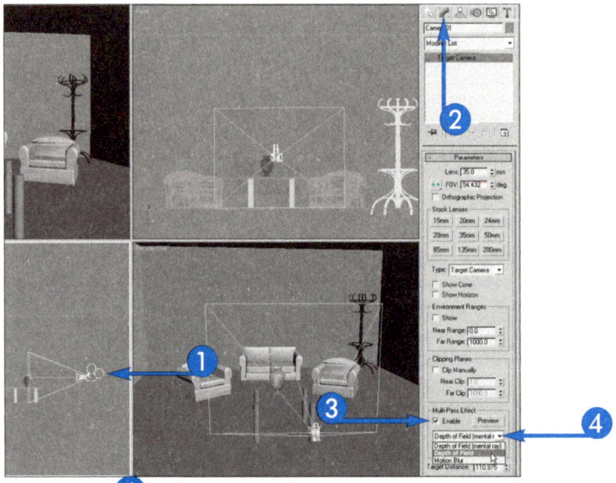

1. Select the camera.
2. Click .
3. In the Multi-Pass Effect section, click the Enable option (☐ changes to ☑).
4. Click here and select Depth of Field.

   You need to ensure that one viewport displays the Camera view.

Note: *See the section "Create a Camera" for more information.*

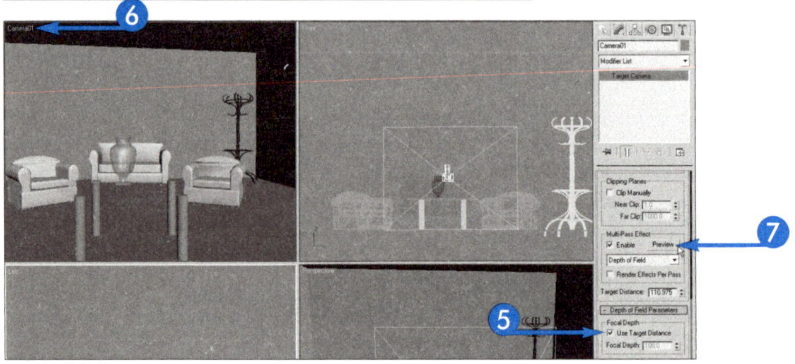

The Depth of Field Parameters rollout appears.

5. Click the Use Target Distance option (☐ changes to ☑).

   To specify a different offset value, deselect the Target Distance option, and type a value in the Focal Depth field.

6. Make the Camera viewport active.
7. Click Preview.

- A preview of the depth-of-field effect displays in the Camera viewport.

8 Click [icon].

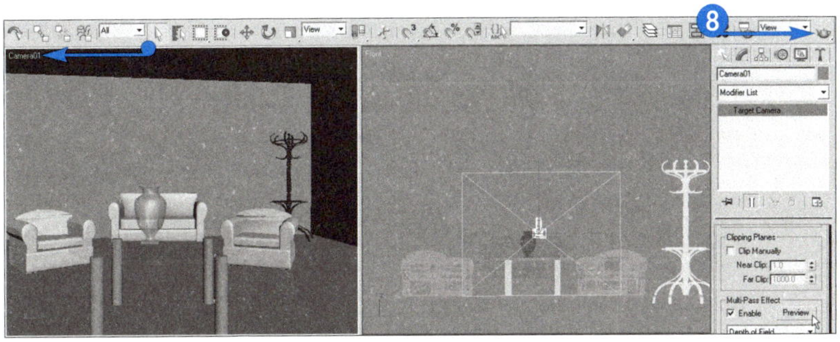

3ds Max renders the scene with the depth-of-field effect.

MASTER IT

Can I create a depth-of-field effect for the Mental Ray renderer?

▼ Yes. To do this, the Mental Ray renderer must use the Depth of Field (mental ray) Multi-Pass Effect. The Depth of Field Multi-Pass effect only works with the Default Scanline renderer. If you select the Depth of Field (mental ray) effect, the Depth of Field Parameters rollout displays one parameter, f-Stop, with a default value of 2.0. You can change the depth of field by changing the f-Stop value. Increasing the f-Stop value narrows the depth of field, while decreasing the f-Stop value broadens the depth of field.

How do I control the amount of blurring used to create the depth-of-field effect?

▼ You can blur the objects outside the focal depth by rendering several different samples of the same frame. The Sampling section in the Depth of Field Parameters rollout specifies the number of rendering passes used to create the effect. The default number is 12, which means that the scene is rendered 12 times with a slight movement of the camera. You can increase the number to improve the effect, although this also slows down the rendering process. The Sample Radius field indicates the amount of shifting that is applied to each rendering. Increase this value to create more blurring.

20 Using the Render Tools

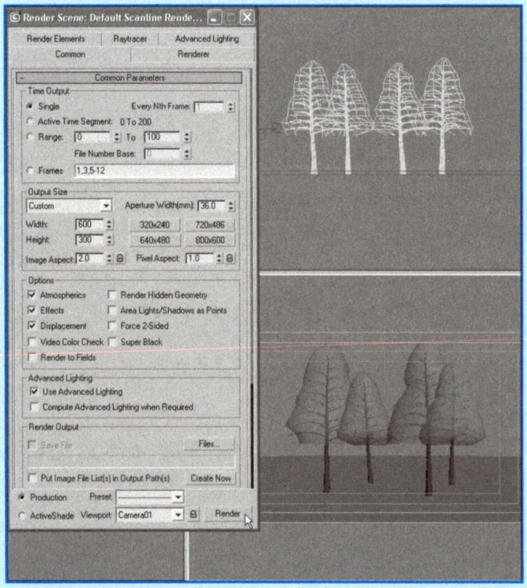

21 Using the Render Scene Dialog Box

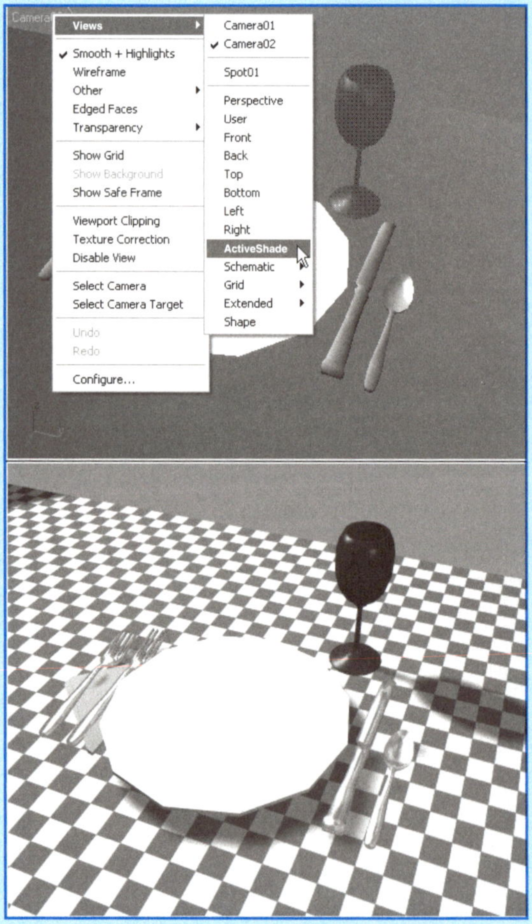

PART VI PERFORMING QUALITY RENDERING

22 Apply Rendering Effects

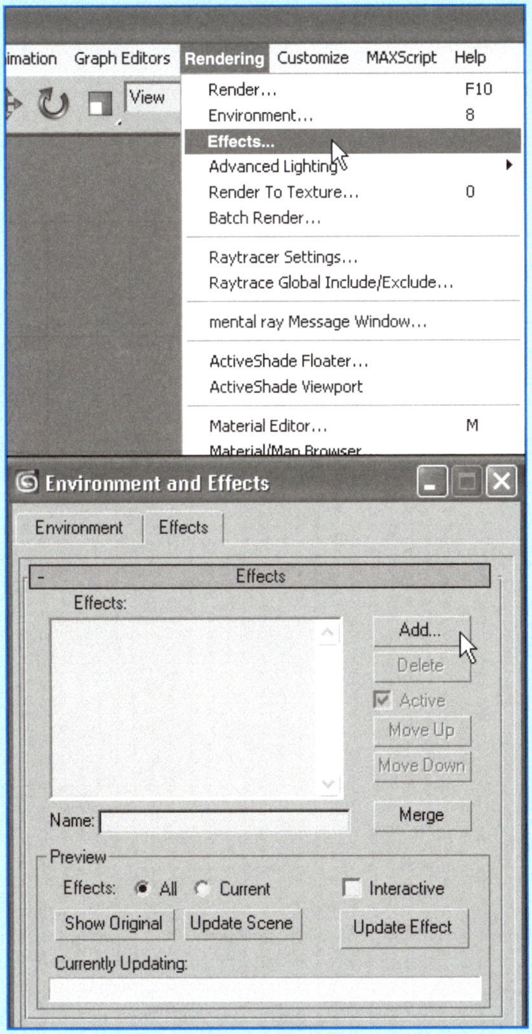

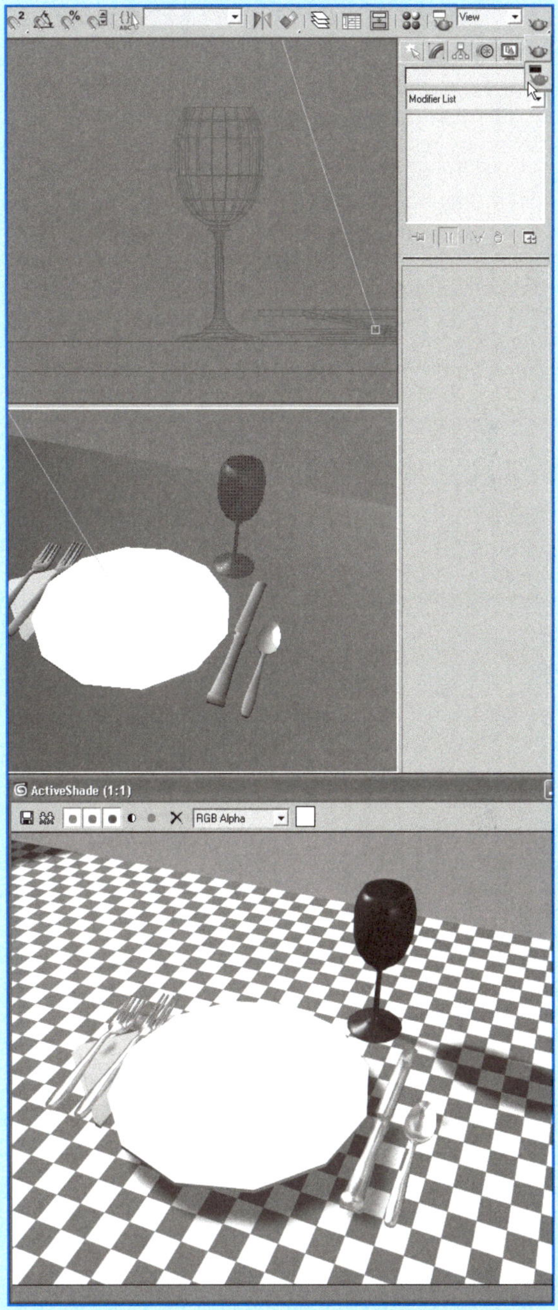

Render Your Scenes

With the Render Scene dialog box, you can customize your settings for both final production rendering and ActiveShade rendering by selecting the renderer that you want; specifying the output resolution, output location, and special rendering effects, such as radiosity; and specifying settings that determine the quality and features of your rendering. The Render Scene dialog box has different panels that control rendering options. Three standard panels display for all renderers: Common, Renderer, and Render Elements. Additional custom panels display for each renderer. For information on ActiveShade, see Chapter 21.

In 3ds Max, *rendering* involves calculating all of the objects and materials in your scene, along with lights, atmospheres, and effects, and creating an image from those calculations. A *renderer*, also called a *render engine*, is the code or program that controls how a scene renders given your specified quality settings, specific options and materials. 3ds Max has three renderers, the Default Scanline Renderer, the mental ray Renderer, and the seldom-used, ASCII-generating VUE File Renderer. Only the Default Scanline Renderer is available as the renderer for ActiveShade windows. You can also add several third-party renderers, which are available as plug-ins. See the section "3ds Max Renderers" for more on 3ds Max renderers.

A Common Panel

Includes three different rollouts: Common Parameters, Email Notifications, and Assign Renderer where you can set the time segment to render, output size, output options, and output location; send an e-mail when the rendering is complete, or if it fails; and specify the renderer that you want to use.

B Renderer Panel

Contains the main controls for the active renderer. This rollout contains parameters for controlling options such as antialiasing and motion blurs.

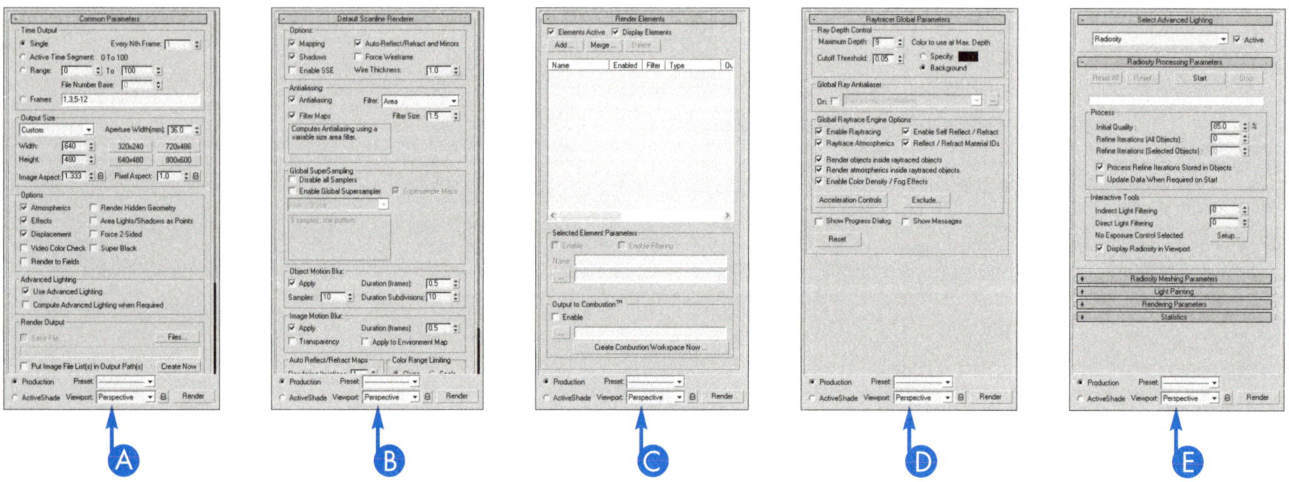

C Render Elements Panel

Here, you create separate rendered files for your scene elements, such as shadows and reflections. You can use individual image files with either image-processing or compositing software, such as Autodesk Combustion.

D Raytracer Panel

Available with the Default Scanline Renderer, this panel controls the output of raytraced scene elements.

E Advanced Lighting Panel

Available with the Default Scanline Renderer. In this panel, you can specify an advanced lighting plug-in and its settings.

3ds Max Renderers

When you render your scene, 3ds Max allows you to select the renderer that you want to use. Because different renderers produce different types of results, the renderer that you use is an important factor in the appearance of your scene. Although 3ds Max initially assigns the Default Scanline Renderer to all of the scenes that you create, you can choose any one of the three renderers that ship with 3ds Max to render your scene.

You can select the renderer that you want to use in the Assign Renderer rollout of the Common panel in the Render Scene dialog box. You can also set the renderer that 3ds Max uses for Production rendering, Material Editor, and ActiveShade.

Available Renderers

Renderer	*Description*
Default Scanline Renderer	The default renderer that ships with 3ds Max. The Default Scanline Renderer renders the scene as a series of horizontal lines. This renderer provides several advanced rendering options, including raytracing, radiosity, and the Light Tracer. You can also use the Render to Texture option — from the Render menu — to bake complex textures into objects. This is a technique that is frequently used by game developers, to speed up real-time rendering within the videogame.
mental ray Renderer	A Production renderer created by Mental Images for creating physically correct simulations of lighting effects. The mental ray Renderer allows you to create physically correct global illumination in your scene. The mental ray Renderer works best for rendering photometric lights. You can also use it to produce Caustics, which is the reflection and refraction of light through an object, such as water or glass.
VUE File Renderer	Produces an ASCII text file that contains a script describing camera movements in relation to the objects in the scene. The VUE File Renderer saves the output to a file that you specify in the Renderer panel.

Render Controls

Located at the bottom of the Render Scene dialog box, you use these controls to select either a Production or ActiveShade render, as well as a render preset, and the viewport that you want to render. The Lock Viewpoint button (🔒), locks the Viewport field so that the same viewpoint always renders.

Understanding Render Presets

3ds Max allows you to use presets that specify a custom set of rendering parameters, including the renderer that you want to use. 3ds Max provides several default presets, although you can also create and save your own presets. For example, the 3dsmax.scanline.radiosity.high preset includes settings for the Default Scanline Renderer, Environment, Advanced Lighting, and Raytracer. When you load a preset, it loads all of the rendering parameter values that were saved with the preset. For example, with the 3dsmax.scanline.radiosity.high preset, the Advanced Lighting panel parameters are set for the Radiosity plug-in.

You can select the preset that you want to load in the Preset list box in the Render Controls area of the Render Scene dialog box. Selecting a preset may change the renderer that is assigned to your scene in the Assign Renderer rollout. To specify a preset for the Production renderer, you need to select the Production option, in the Render Controls area, before changing the Preset value. You can also set the Preset value for the ActiveShade renderer. See the sections "Create a Render Preset" and "Load a Render Preset" for more information on Render Presets.

Image Resolution

One of the most important factors of any rendering is the output size of the image that you want to create. *Resolution* is the actual number of pixels that make up the width and height of the image. A 640 x 480 image comprises a grid of 640 columns of pixels and 480 rows of pixels. *Aspect ratio* refers to the proportion of image width to height. You can find it by dividing the image width by the image height: 640/480 = 1.33.

You may have heard the term aspect ratio used in relation to television screens, where a standard television in Japan and North and South America has an aspect ratio of 1.33. If the National Television Standards Committee, or NTSC, conpliant TV displays images at 720 x 486, then why is the aspect ratio 1.48, rather than 1.33? You must also consider the aspect ratio of non-square pixels such as the NTSC standard pixel aspect ratio of 0.9: (720/486)/(1/0.9)=1.33. The output size is specified in the Output Size section of the Common Parameters rollout in the Common panel.

A Output Size List Box

Provides a list of common standard formats for film and video resolutions and aspect ratios. For example, if you are creating an animation to play on television, then you can select the NTSC DV option. The resolution and image aspect settings then load in the Output Size section.

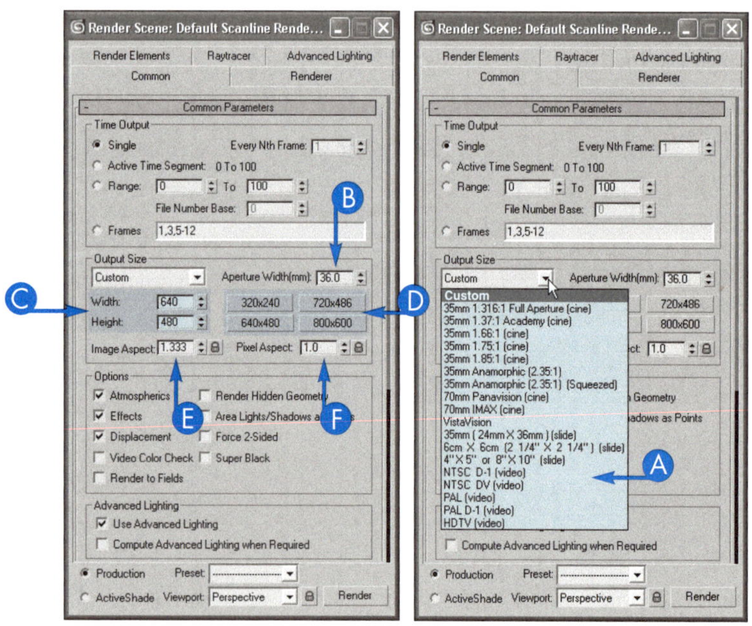

B Aperture Width Field

Allows you to set the aperture width of the virtual camera that is creating the rendered output. Changing this value affects the relationship between the FOV and Lens values of the camera, but does not change the view of the scene.

C Width/Height Fields

Allow you to set the resolution of the image by specifying the width and height values for the rendered output. The values are specified in pixels.

D Preset Resolution Buttons

Buttons that display common resolution sizes for the selected format.

E Image Aspect Field

Changes the aspect ratio of the image. You can only change the aspect ratio for the Custom format. Changing the aspect ratio alters the Height value.

F Pixel Aspect Field

Sets the shape of the pixel in the rendered image. Some video formats require a pixel that is taller than it is wide, such as NTSC D-1, which has a value of 0.9.

Standard Output Formats

When you select one of the standard output formats provided with 3ds Max, the parameters in the Output Size section change to reflect the selection. When you select a standard output format, the only changes that you can make are to adjust the Width and Height values. Any adjustment to the Width value changes the Height value, and vice versa. The reason is that the aspect ratio for the format must be maintained.

Standard Output Formats

Format	Image Aspect	Pixel Aspect	Aperture Width
35mm 1.316:1 Full Aperture (cine)	1.32	1.0	24
35mm 1.37:1 Academy (cine)	1.37	1.0	20.955
35mm 1.66:1 (cine)	1.66667	1.0	20.955
35mm 1.75:1 (cine)	1.75	1.0	20.955
35mm 1.85:1 (cine)	1.85	1.0	20.955
35mm Anamorphic (2.35:1)	2.35	1.0	42.57
35mm Anamorphic (2.35:1) (Squeezed)	2.35	2.0	42.57
70mm Panavision (cine)	2.2	1.0	48.59
70mm IMAX (cine)	1.3642	1.0	48.59
VistaVision	1.5	1.0	37.719
35mm (24mm x 36mm) (slide)	1.5	1.0	34.20
6cm x 6cm (2 1/4" x 2 1/4") (slide)	1.0	1.0	51.60
4" x 5" or 8" x 10" (slide)	1.33333	1.0	88.90
NTSC D-1 (video)	1.33333	0.9	20.12
NTSC DV (video)	1.35	0.9	20.12
PAL (video)	1.33333	1.0	20.12
PAL DV (video)	1.33333	1.06667	20.12
HDTV (video)	1.77778	1.0	20.12

Understanding Safe Frames

When you render a scene that you intend to broadcast, what you see on your computer screen and in the Rendered Frame window may not be what you see on a television screen. You can resize your viewport to any type of proportion, but this does not affect the proportions of your rendering. Televisions also tend to overscan the input and clip off the edges of the images that they display resulting in your output images being cropped on all sides. For more on the Rendered Frame window, see Chapter 21.

You can use Safe Frames to show you both the proportions of your rendered image and what portions of your image are in areas that are safe from cropping. The Aspect Ratio setting, which you specify in the Common panel, determines the shape of the Safe Frames, which are centered in the viewports. You activate Show Safe Frames in the menu that appears when you right-click a viewport's label. See the section "Resolution and Image Aspect Ratio Sizes" for more information.

The Safe Frame option consists of four different frames. You should keep all of these frames in mind when setting up your scene for rendering, usually through a camera.

A Live Area

The area of the scene that will actually be rendered. This is based on the Output Size Height and Width settings in the Render Scene dialog box, and not the shape of the viewport.

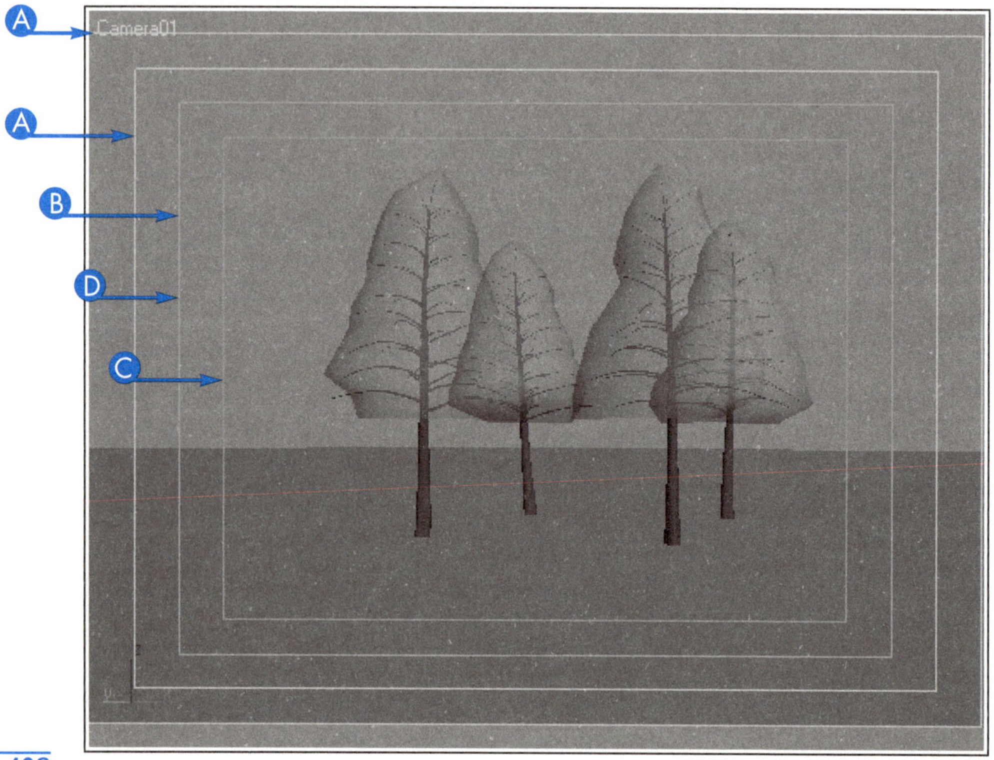

B Action Safe Area

The part of the rendered image or animation is not trimmed when viewed on a television screen or projected in a theater.

C User Safe Area

An optional frame that you can use to create custom requirements for your rendering. You can activate this feature in the Customize Viewports dialog box.

D Title Safe Area

The area of the image where it is safe for you to add text.

View Safe Frames

You can view the Safe Frames in any viewport. This allows you to see how your scene will render, based upon the aspect ratio settings. For example, if you specify a video format, such as HDTV, then 3ds Max crops the view to show how it will appear on a widescreen television.

You can display or hide the Safe Frames for each viewport by toggling the Show Safe Frame option on and off in the menu that displays when you right-click the viewport title. You typically only need to view the Safe Frames in the viewport that you intend to render, normally a Camera viewport.

MASTER IT

Do Safe Frames control what I render?

No. Rendering specifications are controlled by the Render Scene dialog box. Safe Frames help you to compose your objects and cameras in the safest way possible. Televisions are not standardized to the point where each one crops every image by the same amount. As a result, an object that is placed between the Action Safe area and the Live area may appear on one television but not on another. Although you should never count on objects that are outside the Action Safe frame being visible onscreen, they may still appear.

View Safe Frames

1. In the viewport, right-click the viewport title.
2. Click Show Safe Frame.

The Safe Frames display for the viewport, based upon the current aspect ratio and Safe Frame settings.

Customize Safe Frames

You can customize how Safe Frames display in your viewport. This specifies which frames display, and their sizes, when you activate the Safe Frame option. You can customize Safe Frame sizes to fit your intended output device if you know what it will be.

When you render a scene, the full render size is called the *live area*. Although you can see all of this area on your computer screen, it is cropped when viewed on a television or projected in a theater. The Action Safe frame identifies the probable visible area. The Title Safe frame identifies where the text titles can safely appear without distortion due to screen curvature.

You specify the Safe Frame settings in the Safe Frame panel of the Viewport Configuration dialog box, by specifying which frames are to appear in the viewport. You also control the sizing of each frame. By default, the Action Safe frame is 10 percent smaller than the Live Area, the Title Safe frame is 20 percent smaller, and the User Safe frame is 30 percent smaller. You can adjust the sizing by changing the value of the Both field or unlocking the frame and specifying different percentages for the Horizontal and Vertical values.

Customize Safe Frames

1 Right-click a viewport title.

2 Click Configure.

The Viewport Configuration dialog box appears.

3 Click the Live Area option (☐ changes to ☑) to turn any safe frame on or off.

4 In the Both field, type a percent reduction for all sides of a frame.

You can click the Lock option (☐ changes to ☑) to deselect it, and type custom values for Horizontal and Vertical sides.

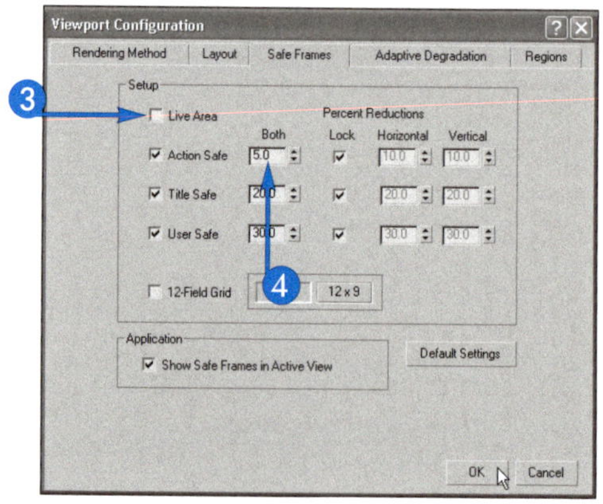

5 Select the "Show Safe Frames in Active View" option (☐ changes to ☑).

6 Click OK.

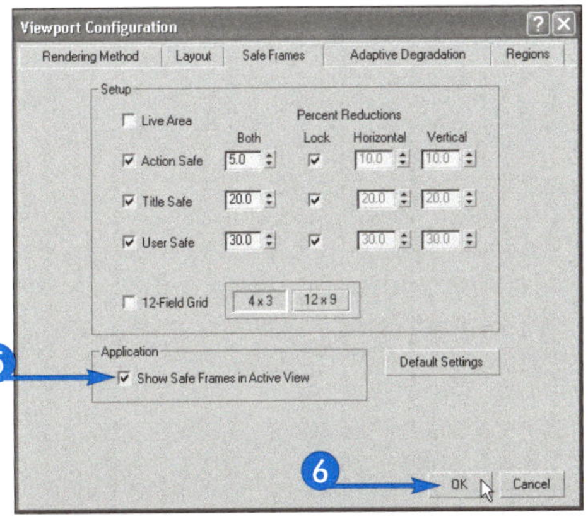

The Safe Frames display in the selected viewport.

How do I see what is being cropped out of the view?

One advantage of using Safe Frames is that the contents of the viewport are cropped to match the renderable size of the output. However, because 3ds Max crops the view, you do not see what has been cropped out. 3ds Max allows you to change your settings so that you can see what is being cropped. To do this, deselect the "Mask Viewport to Safe Region" option (☐ changes to ☑) in the Viewports panel of the Preference Settings dialog box. The dialog box opens when you click Customize, and then click Preferences. When you deselect this option, the viewport area is marked by the yellow Live Area frame, and everything outside this frame is no longer cropped in the viewport.

Do I need to use the 12-Field Grid?

No. The 12-Field Grid is another option (☐ changes to ☑) that allows you to see how the scene appears. This is a common tool used by video directors to specify which areas of the scene need to be adjusted. You can adjust the location of objects in your scene by moving them within the grid. You can designate a grid of 12 fields by selecting 4 x 3, or a grid of 108 fields by selecting 12 x 9. Keep in mind that if you turn the grid on, then it displays whenever you view the Safe Frames. If you want to deactivate the grid, then you need to deselect the 12-Field Grid option in the Viewport Configuration dialog box.

Set a Custom Output Size

You can specify the output size for the rendering of your scene in 3ds Max. The output size is important for two reasons: First, it affects the size at which your rendering displays; second, the larger the size, the longer it takes to render the scene. When you specify the output size, you can select from the predefined formats or you can create your own custom output size.

When you select the Custom option in the Output Size list box, all of the fields in the Output Size section are available for editing. When you use any of the preset formats, you can only change the values of the Width and Height fields.

When you change either the Width or Height values, the Image Aspect value also changes. The reason is that the Image Aspect value is calculated by dividing the Width by the Height. Conversely, any changes to the Image Aspect value cause the Height value to change. The Pixel Aspect, which indicates the proportions of each pixel in the rendered image, also affects the value in the Image Aspect field. See the section "Resolution and Image Aspect Ratio Sizes" for more information on aspect sizes.

Set a Custom Output Size

1. Select the viewport that you want to render.
2. Click Rendering.
3. Click Render.
   - You can also click the Render Scene button ().

The Render Scene dialog box appears.

4. In the Output Size section, click ▾.
5. Click Custom.

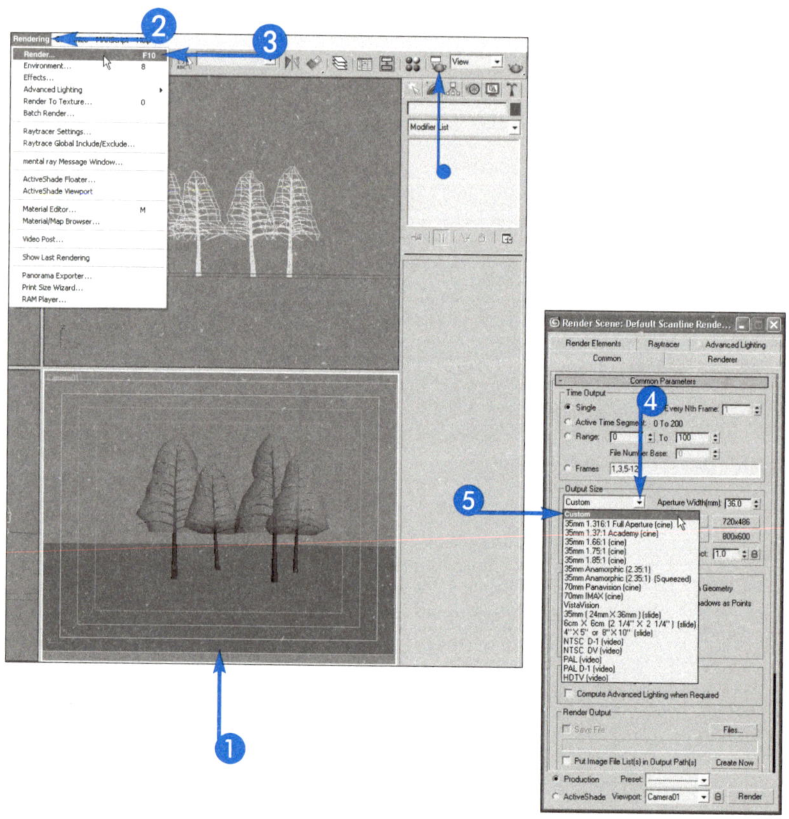

6 In the Width field, type a width, in pixels, for the output image.

7 In the Height field, type a height, in pixels, for the output image.

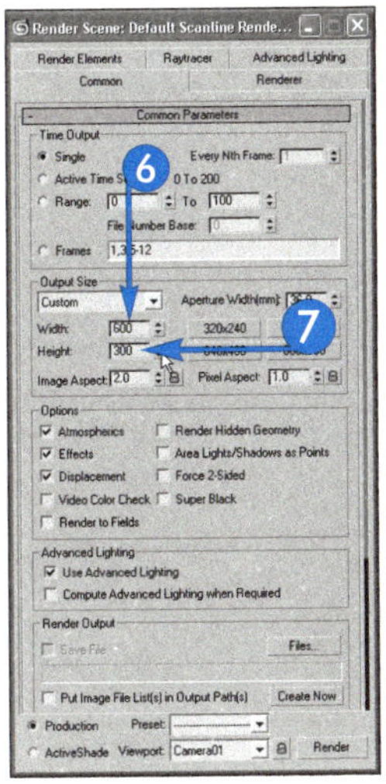

- The Aspect Ratio value changes to match the height and width.
- If Show Safe Frame is active, then the viewport crops to show the part of the scene that 3ds Max will output.

Note: *See the section "Customize Safe Frames" for information on Safe Frames.*

If you want, you can click the Render button to render the scene.

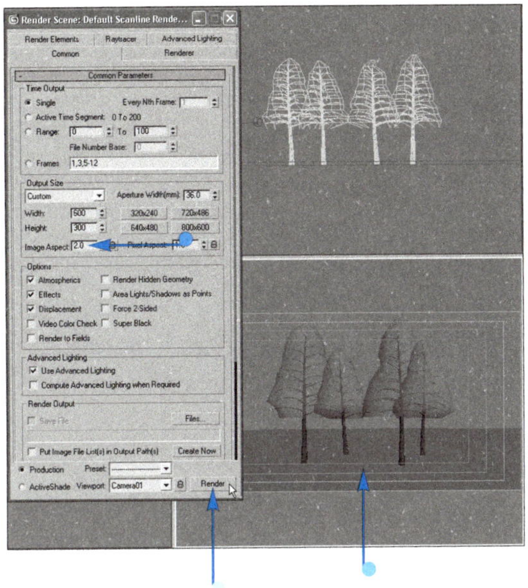

MASTER IT

Can I save my custom resolution settings?

Yes. You can create a preset resolution that displays on one of the four Preset Resolution buttons. To modify a Preset Resolution button, right-click one of the four Preset Resolution buttons to display the Configure Preset dialog box. To create a Preset button using the current Width, Height, and Pixel Aspect values, click Get Current Settings. You can also type values for each parameter in the corresponding fields. When you click OK, the Preset Resolution button changes to the new settings. If you create a Render Preset, the Resolution Preset buttons are saved with that Render Preset. See the section "Create a Render Preset" for more information.

Why does the image looked stretched when I reduce the Pixel Aspect value?

The Pixel Aspect value indicates the shape of the pixel when the image is rendered. If you are rendering for digital video formats, such as NTSC DV or NTSC D-1, then the Pixel Aspect value is 0.9, which creates a rectangular-shaped pixel. As a result, this makes your objects appear stretched when you view your scene on a computer monitor. This occurs because computer monitors can only display square pixels. Keep in mind that the stretching only appears on a computer monitor; it will appear normal when viewed on a video output source that displays rectangular pixels.

Understanding Antialiasing

Antialiasing is a process that smoothes the edges of objects in your images so that they do not appear jagged. Jagged lines can occur in 3ds Max renderings, as well as any computer graphics, because the images that 3ds Max creates are based upon a grid of individual pixels. Because each pixel can be a different color, any border between foreground and background objects, which consists of curved or diagonal lines, appears jagged when rendered. This jagged effect is referred to as *aliasing*.

To soften the jagged edges, antialiasing applies a blurring effect to the edge pixels. The antialiasing process adds or changes pixels around the edges that are a similar color to the foreground and background objects' colors.

To create the best antialiasing effect in your image, you can apply a specific antialiasing filter to the scene. Each of the available filters uses a different process for applying the antialiasing effect.

You can select an antialiasing filter for the Default Scanline Renderer in the Renderer panel of the Render Scene dialog box. The mental ray Renderer uses sampling as an antialiasing method, and you can also control this in the Renderer panel when mental ray is the current renderer.

The Default Scanline Renderer Rollout

This rollout contains controls that turn autoaliasing on and off, that let you select filters, and more.

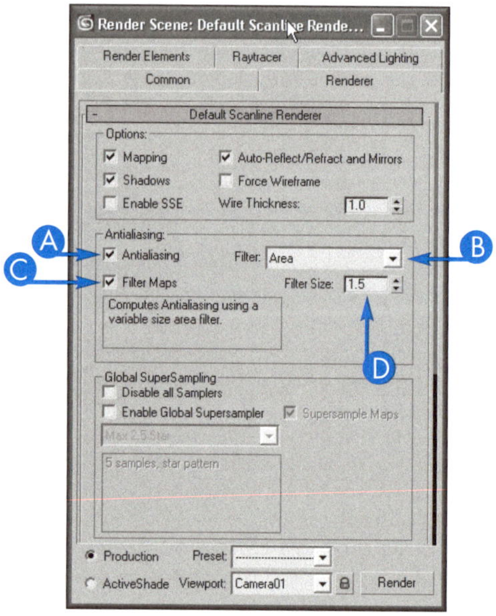

A Antialiasing Option

Indicates whether antialiasing is active. You can turn off antialiasing to speed up the rendering time when you render test images.

B Filter List Box

Allows you to select one of the available antialiasing filters that ship with 3ds Max. Some filters cause additional fields to display in the Antialiasing section.

C Filter Maps Option

Specifies whether to apply antialiasing to mapped materials during rendering.

D Filter Size Field

Allows you to set the amount of blurring that 3ds Max applies to the image with the selected filter. This field is unavailable for some filters.

Antialiasing Filters

3ds Max provides several different filters that you can use to specify the antialiasing effect for the rendered image. Each filter type requires specific parameter values. Although the Filter Size field displays for all of the filter types, you can only specify the value for certain filter types.

Antialiasing Filter Types

Filter Type	*Description*
Area	The default antialiasing filter for the Scanline renderer. The Area filter uses the specified Filter Size value to determine the amount of antialiasing that is applied to the image.
Blackman	Sharpens the image edges by using a 25-pixel area to compare colors. The Blackman filter provides no edge enhancements.
Blend	Applies a blend of a sharp and coarse filter using values that are specified for the Filter Size and Blend parameters.
Catmull-Rom	Sharpens the image using a 25-pixel filter that provides edge enhancements. This is a popular filter for architectural visualizations.
Cook Variable	Allows you the flexibility to produce a sharp-edged result when the Filter Size value is small, or a blurred image when the Filter Size value is larger than 2.5.
Cubic	Creates a blurring effect based upon the cubic-spline curves.
Mitchell-Netravali	Filters the image using the Blur and Ringing parameter values that you specify. This filter allows you to control the edge enhancement and blurring effects. Specifying a Ringing value above 0.5 can affect the background and alpha channel colors.
Plate Match/MAX R2	Useful when you need to match the material map on an object to a background image. With this filter, the mapped texture of the object is not affected by the antialiasing of the edges.
Quadratic	Applies a 9-pixel-area blurring effect, based upon a quadratic spline.
Sharp Quadratic	Applies a 9-pixel-area sharpening effect.
Soften	Creates a soft blurring effect using the specified Filter Size value.
Video	Blurs the image using a 25-pixel filter that is optimized for use with NTSC or PAL video.

Using the Cook Variable Antialiasing Filter

You can apply antialiasing to your rendering to eliminate the jagged edges that can appear with curves. By default, when you render with the Default Scanline Renderer, 3ds Max applies the Area filter for antialiasing your scene, although you can select another filter.

To make the edges of your objects appear either sharper or softer, you can use the Cook Variable as a general-purpose antialiasing filter with the Default Scanline Renderer. The Cook Variable filter is easy to use because you only have to adjust one parameter value, the Filter Size. This value allows you to adjust the edges or objects, from sharp and crisp, to softer and blurred.

You can select the filter type in the Renderer panel's Antialiasing section. 3ds Max provides several different filters that you can apply during rendering. Each render type provides a different method of antialiasing your scene.

To change the appearance of the objects' edges, you can change the value of the Filter Size parameter. Values between 1.0 and 2.5 produce sharp edges within the image, while values greater than 2.5 make the edges softer.

CD FILE: The Antialiasing.max file is available on the CD-ROM for you to practice with applying antialiasing filters.

Using the Cook Variable Antialiasing Filter

1. Click to select the viewport that you want to render.
2. Click Rendering.
3. Click Render.
   - You can also click (Render Scene icon) to display the Render Scene dialog box.

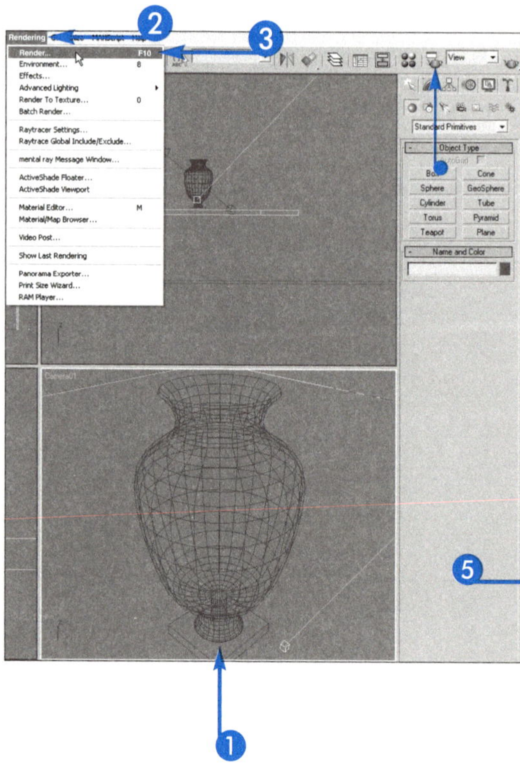

The Render Scene dialog box appears.

4. Click the Renderer tab to display the Renderer panel.
5. Click to select the Antialiasing option (☐ changes to ☑).
6. Click ▾ to display a list of filters.
7. Click Cook Variable.

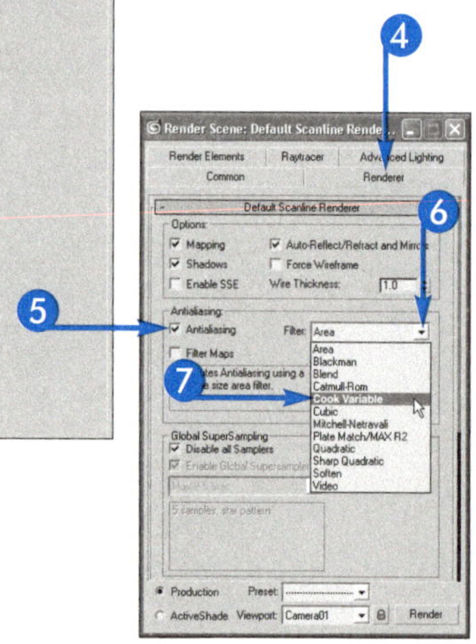

The parameter fields update for the selected filter.

8 Type a Filter Size for the Cook Variable filter.

9 Click Render.

As the scene renders, 3ds Max applies the antialiasing filter to the objects in the scene.

You can repeat the steps in this exercise to practice applying the other antialiasing filters.

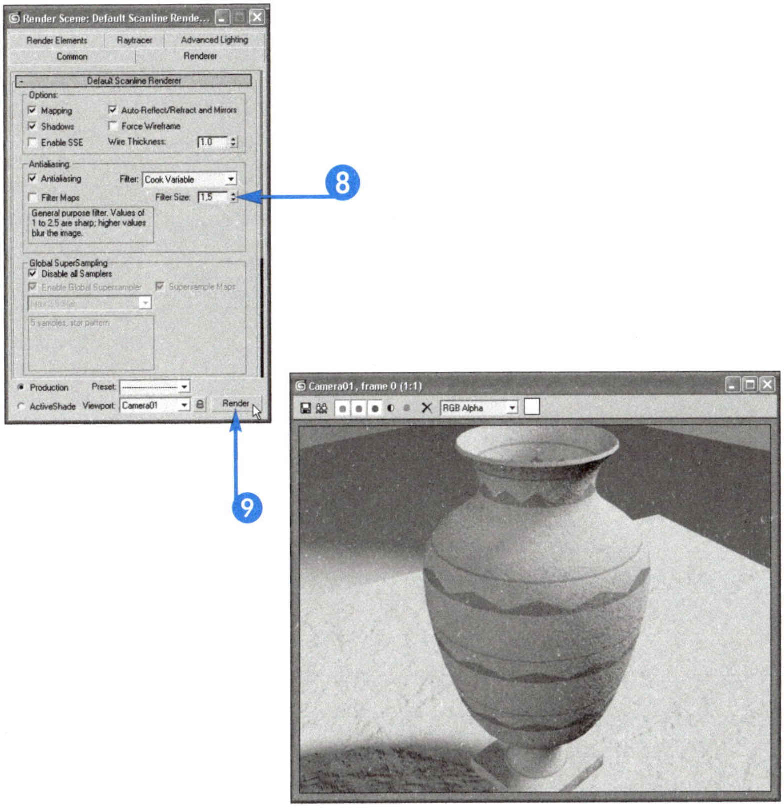

MASTER IT

How does the selected renderer affect the antialiasing options?

▼ The Antialiasing section displays in the Renderer tab when you select the Default Scanline Renderer. It allows you to select the antialiasing that occurs only with that renderer. If you select another renderer, then you may not see the option to set the antialiasing filter. You can specify the renderer that 3ds Max uses to render your scene for production, the Material Editor's sample slots, and the ActiveShade window in the Assign Renderer section in the Common panel of the Render Scene dialog box. See the section "Assign a Renderer" for more information on setting the renderer.

Can I antialias objects that have a background image?

▼ Yes. By default, 3ds Max does not apply an antialias filter to any images that you have applied to the background of your scene. If you want to apply the antialiasing that you have specified for your scene to the scene's background image, then you must change the Filter Background setting in the Preference Settings dialog box. To do so, click Customize, then click Preferences, and then click the Rendering tab in the Preference Settings dialog box. Select the Filter Background option (☐ changes to ☑) in the Background section. For more information on applying a background image to a scene, see Chapter 22.

Create a Render Preset

In 3ds Max, you can save as a Render Preset rendering settings that you often use. By creating a Render Preset, you eliminate the need to redefine your rendering preferences with each scene that you render, or to re-create the settings for final and preview renderings. Once you save a preset, you can reload it in any scene to apply exactly the same rendering settings each time.

To create a Render Preset using the current Render Scene dialog box settings, you first define the name of your Render Preset file. 3ds Max allows you to use any unique name. However, you should create a descriptive name that allows you to easily identify the type of rendering settings that are defined by the preset file.

After defining the preset file name, you need to specify the settings that you want to save in the preset file in the Select Preset Categories dialog box. Only the categories that you create and that are highlighted will be defined in the Render Preset. 3ds Max lists the renderer as a special category that you can select separately, and you can also select your environment and effects settings separately as part of the preset file.

Create a Render Preset

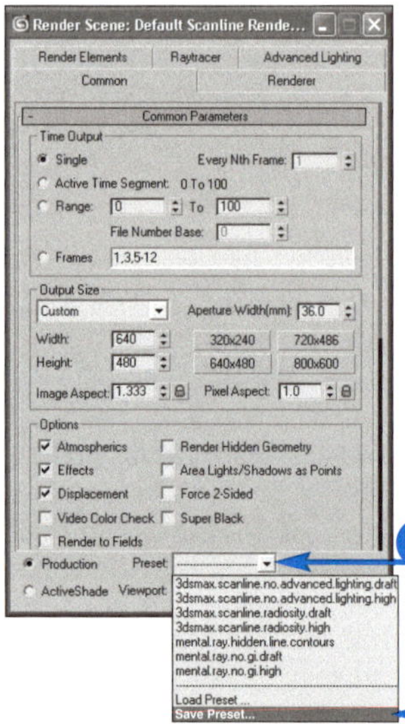

1. Open the Render Scene dialog box.

Note: *To open this dialog box, see the section "Using the Cook Variable Antialiasing Filter."*

2. Click ▾ in the Preset list box.
3. Click Save Preset.

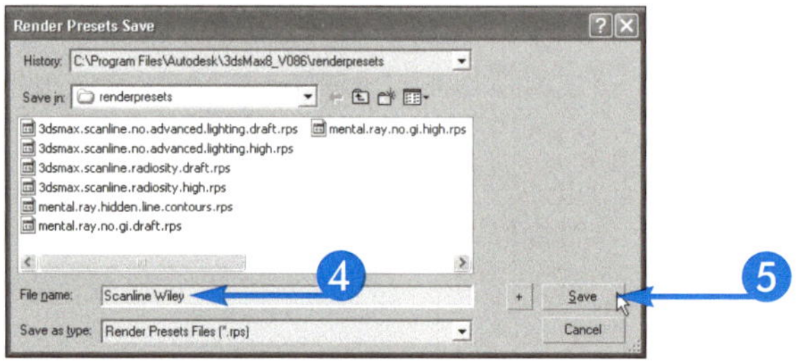

The Render Presets Save dialog box appears.

4. Type a unique name for the preset in the File name field.
5. Click Save.

The Select Preset Categories dialog box appears.

6 Press and hold down Ctrl.

7 Click a category to deselect or select it.

By default, all categories are selected when the dialog box appears.

8 Click Save.

- 3ds Max saves the new preset and loads it in the Preset field.

You can click Render to render your scene with the specified Preset.

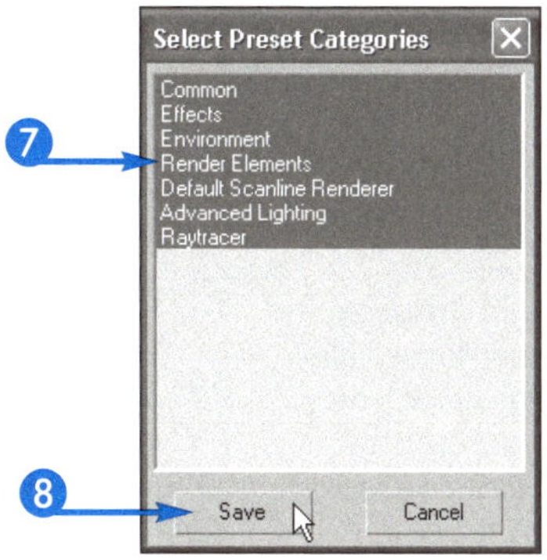

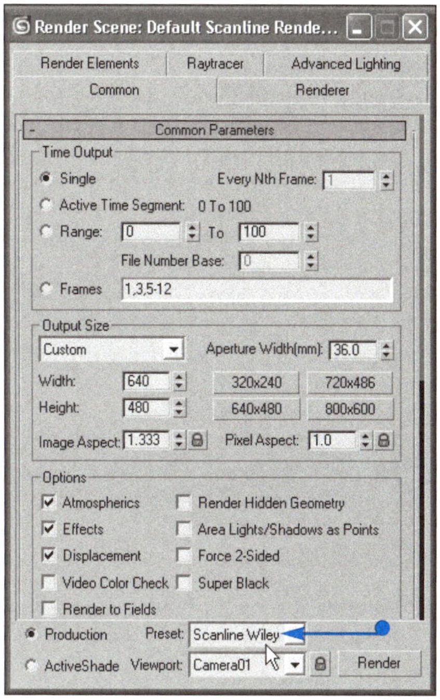

MASTER IT

Why do I need to select the renderer separately from the Common panel?

When you select the categories that you want to save as part of your Render Preset file, you must select the renderer category separately, even though the renderer is actually selected in the Common panel of the Render Scene dialog box. If you do not select the renderer category, then your Render Preset file does not contain that renderer, even though you may have selected it in the Common panel. By listing the renderer separately in the category list, you can select other panels without selecting the Common panel, and still select the renderer.

What presets does 3ds Max provide?

3ds Max provides seven different rendering presets that you can select from the Preset field at the bottom of the Render Scene dialog box. There are four presets for the Scanline renderer and three presets for the mental ray Renderer. Each preset name identifies the settings that have been applied to that preset. For example, the 3dsmax.scanline.no.advanced.lighting.draft preset loads the Default Scanline Renderer, with no advanced lighting options loaded in the Advanced Lighting panel. The mental ray presets provide a good starting point when experimenting with the mental ray Renderer's settings.

Load a Render Preset

A Render Preset file allows you to maintain consistency between your renderings in 3ds Max. For example, you may have one Render Preset file that contains the rendering settings for all scenes that you print out onto 11x17-inch media, and another preset for previewing scenes that will eventually be broadcast. You can load a Render Preset file to apply a custom set of rendering parameters to a current scene.

When you load 3ds Max, there are several default Render Presets that you can use to obtain specific rendering options, such as using the mental ray Renderer with no global illumination. You can load any of the default Render Presets, or you can load a custom Render Preset file that you have created. See the section "Create a Render Preset" for more information on saving a Render Preset file.

When you load a Render Preset, you can decide which of the render categories in the Render Preset file are loaded in the Select Preset Categories dialog box. The Select Preset Categories dialog box displays only the categories that were saved with the Render Preset file. You can select all the categories, or only load specific ones.

Load a Render Preset

1. Open the Render Scene dialog box.

Note: *To open this dialog box, see the section "Using the Cook Variable Antialiasing Filter."*

2. Click ▾ to expand the Preset list box.
3. Click Load Preset.

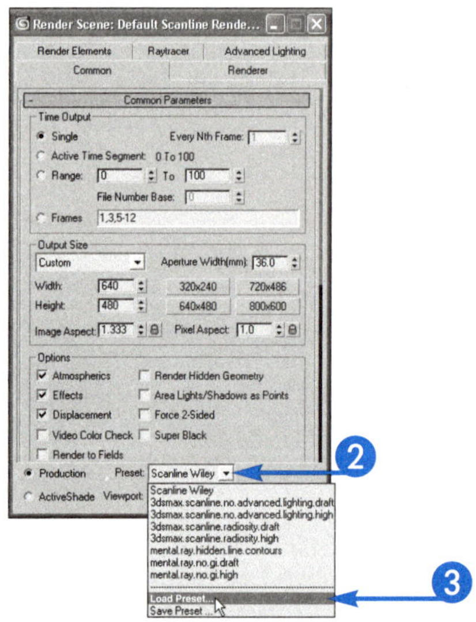

The Render Presets Load dialog box appears.

4. Click to select the Render Preset file that you want to load.
5. Click Open.

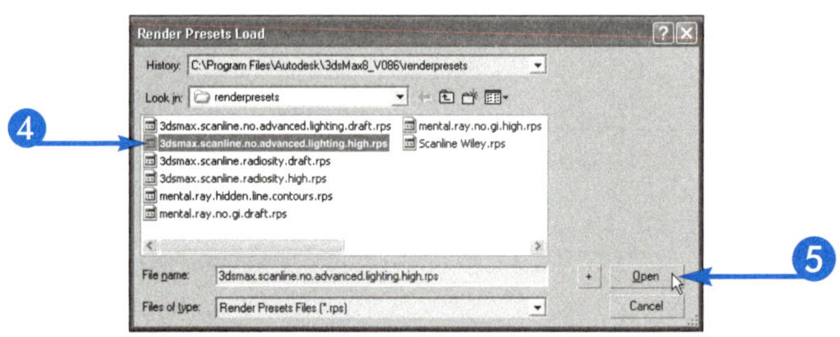

The Select Preset Categories dialog box appears.

6 Press and hold down Ctrl.

7 Click a category to deselect or select it.

By default, all categories are selected when the dialog box appears.

8 Click Load.

- The selected preset appears in the Preset field.

You can click Render to render the scene with the selected preset.

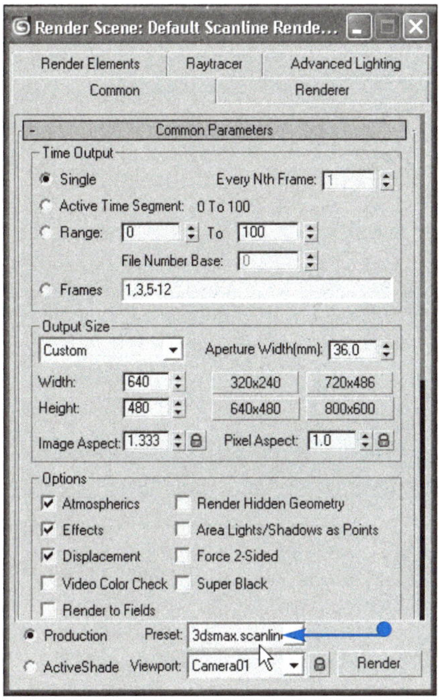

Can I load a preset from the Preset list box?

Yes. You can load a preset from either the drop-down list or the Render Presets Load dialog box. The drop-down list only displays the last ten presets that have been used. As a result, if you use a preset more than once, it appears multiple times on the list, and all of the available presets may not display. If you select a preset from the drop-down list, the Select Preset Categories dialog box appears so that you can select the categories that you want to load. By using the Render Presets Load dialog box, you can see all the available Render Presets.

Why does my ActiveShade viewport revert to a standard viewport when I load a preset?

Any available renderer can be used to create a rendering in the Rendered Frame window, but only the Default Scanline Renderer can be used to render to an ActiveShade viewport. When you load a Render Preset that specifies a renderer that is incompatible with ActiveShade, such as the mental ray Renderer, 3ds Max evaluates this and then switches the viewport rendering mode to its pre-ActiveShade condition. The viewport can be switched back to an ActiveShade viewport after the preset has been loaded. For information on ActiveShade and the Rendered Frame window, see Chapter 21.

Set Render Output Options

When you render your scene as an animation, a series of images, or a single image, you can specify the various output options. This allows you to stipulate whether the scene is simply rendered to the Rendered Frame window or is saved in a file that you can view inside or outside 3ds Max.

When you decide to render your scene to a file, you need to specify the output file type in the Render Output File dialog box. 3ds Max allows you to create several different types of image and animation files in the Save as type field, but you must select a file type from that field, before clicking the Save button.

Once you specify a file type and filename, you can determine whether the output is saved to a file by selecting the Save File option. This allows you to save the output to a file when you are satisfied with the rendering results. You can also specify whether the output displays in the Rendered Frame window after it is rendered. Even though 3ds Max displays the Rendered Frame window by default, you can turn this option off to gain a small increase in speed.

Set Render Output Options

1. Open the Render Scene dialog box.

Note: *To open this dialog box, see the section "Using the Cook Variable Antialiasing Filter."*

2. Click Files.

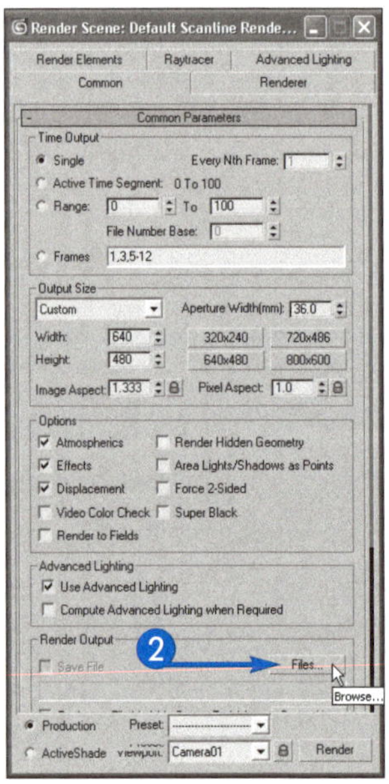

The Render Output File dialog box appears.

3. Type the output file name in the File name field.
4. Click ▾ to display a list of file types.
5. Click a file type.
6. Click Save.

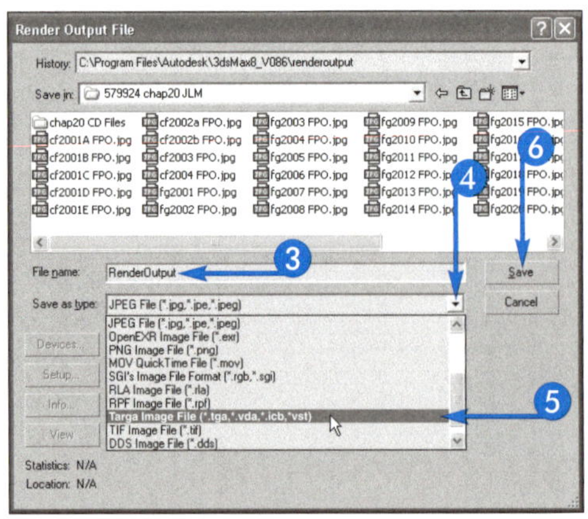

A dialog box may appear, with specific settings for the selected output file type.

7 Type or click options to specify the output settings that you want.

8 Click OK.

- The Save File option is selected in the Render Output section.

You can turn off file rendering by clicking the Save File option (☑ changes to ☐).

- The name of the output file displays.

9 Click Render.

The files are rendered.

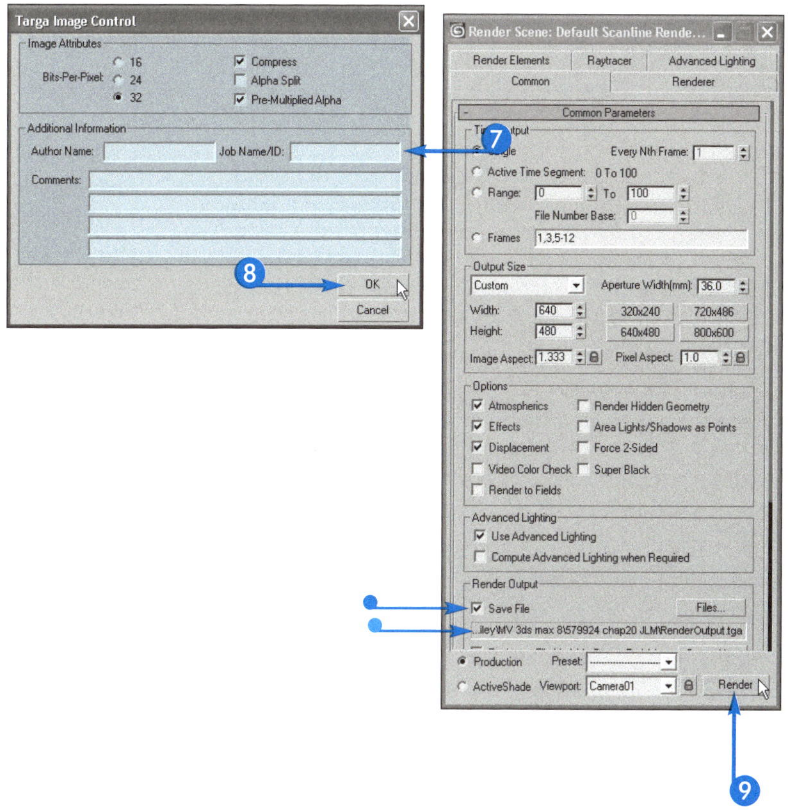

MASTER IT

What does the Net Render option do?

This option (☐ changes to ☑), found in the Render Output section of the Render Scene dialog box's Common tab, enables 3ds Max to use multiple computers on a network to complete an animation rendering task. All the systems must have 3ds Max installed, but these installations can be from the same single purchased copy of the program. As long as the additional copies are not authorized, they will not function as anything but rendering stations. This is an acceptable use of the program in accordance with the End User License Agreement. Look for information on Backburner in the 3ds Max help files for information on network rendering.

What does the Render to Fields option do?

Most production-level animation is rendered to sequential images that are composited together, rather than to a single animation file. A field consists of every other horizontal row, either odd or even, of pixels in an image. Render to Fields (☐ changes to ☑) causes 3ds Max to break a rendered image into fields and to add the field information to the image file. Rather than displaying one image per frame, at 1/30 or 1/25 of a second, depending on the regional standard that you are using, one field can be displayed every half-frame. This results in a smoother animation. Fields make animation look better on "interlaced" display devices like televisions. However, fields are not appropriate for computer media animation files, such as AVI or MOV.

Assign a Renderer

You assign the renderer that you want to use for Production, ActiveShade, and the Material Editor in the Common panel of the Render Scene dialog box. When you assign a renderer, 3ds Max uses it for all renderings for both the current project and new projects. Changing the renderer does not alter the renderer that is used in existing projects.

You change the renderer in the Assign Renderer rollout of the Render Scene dialog box. There is a separate field for each area — Production, Material Editor, and ActiveShade — where you can assign a renderer. The Production renderer is used if you are not rendering with ActiveShade. ActiveShade can only use the Default Scanline Renderer from the list of renderers that ship with 3ds Max.

The Choose Renderer dialog box displays a list of the available renderers. By default, 3ds Max provides three different renderers — the Default Scanline Renderer, mental ray Renderer, and VUE File Renderer — but the list can also contain other third-party renderers that you have installed. See the section "Render Your Scenes with the Render Scene Dialog Box" for more information on the default renderers that are provided with 3ds Max.

Assign a Renderer

1. Click .

   The Render Scene dialog box appears.

2. Click to expand the Assign Renderer rollout.

   If necessary, drag the Scroll bar down to locate the Assign Renderer rollout.

3. Click the Choose Renderer button (...) for the type of renderer that you want to set.

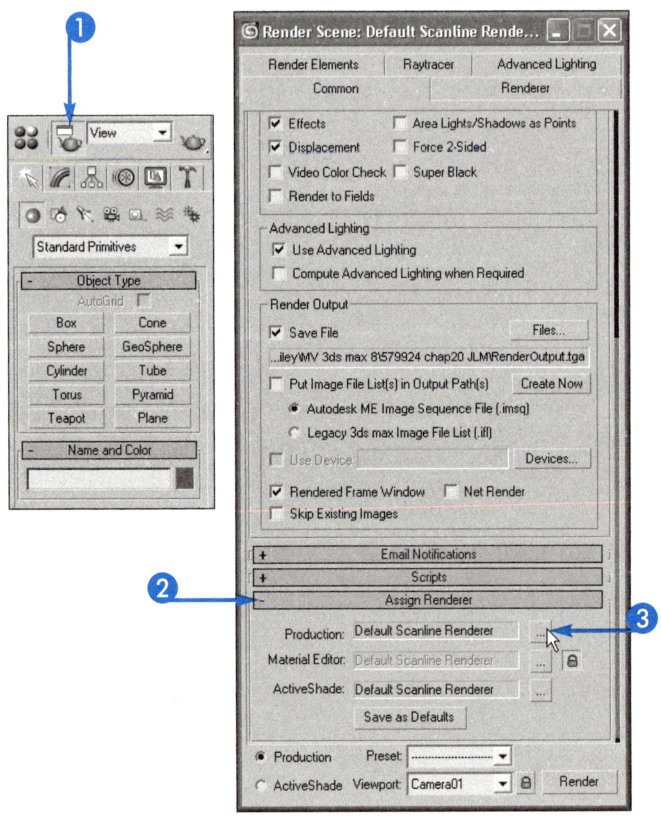

The Choose Renderer dialog box appears.

4. Click to select the renderer that you want to use.
5. Click OK.

- The selected renderer changes.

The panels in the Render Scene dialog box change to reflect the renderer that you have selected.

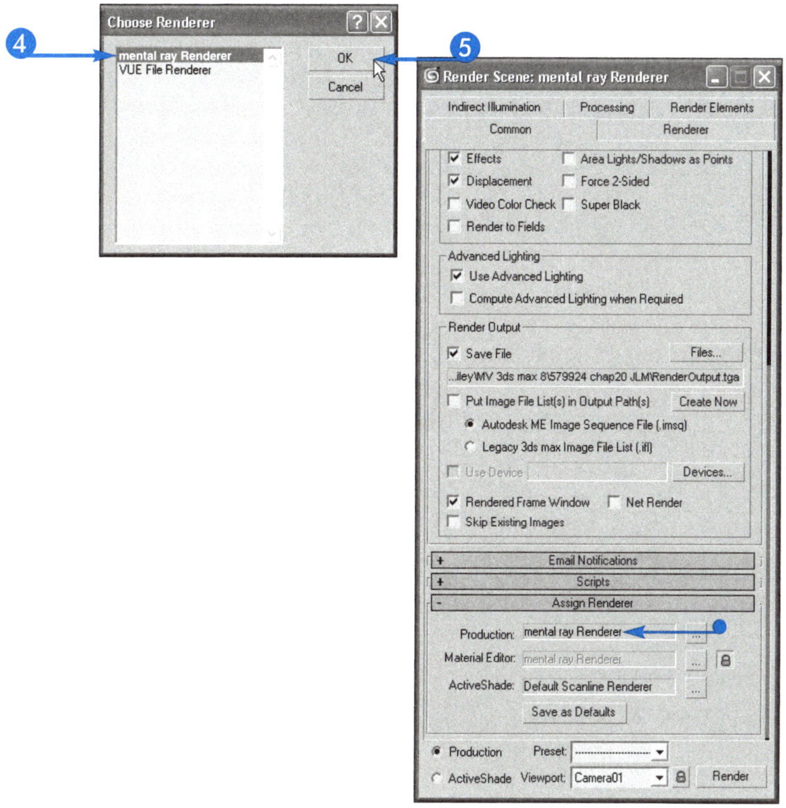

MASTER IT

Why is the renderer locked for the Material Editor?

▼ By default, the Material Editor uses the same renderer as the Production renderer to render material samples that display in the sample slots. This allows you to preview the materials consistently in the Material Editor. The Lock to Current Renderer button (🔒) locks the Material Editor's renderer to be the same as the Production renderer. To change the Material Editor's renderer, click 🔒 — the button changes to 🔓 — and then follow the procedure outlined in this exercise. Any changes to the Production renderer do not affect the Material Editor's renderer.

How do I change the default rendering?

▼ By default, 3ds Max uses the Default Scanline Renderer as the default renderer for all three rendering types: Production, Material Editor, and ActiveShade. These defaults are set each time you open 3ds Max. If you want to use different renderers as your default renderers, then you can click the Save as Defaults button at the bottom of the Assign Renderer rollout. When you select Save as Defaults, whichever renderers are specified for Production, Material Editor, and ActiveShade become the new defaults.

Render with the Raytracer

You can use the Raytracer panel in the Render Scene dialog box to control rendering of raytraced materials, maps, and shadows using the Default Scanline Renderer. For example, you can speed up the rendering of the scene by deactivating the raytracer.

The Raytracer panel allows you to specify whether raytracer is active and how the light rays travel between objects. You can use the Ray Depth Control section to specify how light travels between objects that create a mirror effect. The Maximum Depth field indicates the maximum number of times that light rays can bounce between objects; values between 0 and 100 are valid. The Cutoff Threshold field indicates the percentage that the ray affects a pixel color before the ray is stopped and no longer affects the scene, even if it is below the Maximum Depth value.

With the Raytracer panel, you can select the objects that you want to be raytraced in the Exclude/Include dialog box. If you exclude objects that have shiny raytraced materials, then they still have the same shiny, reflective material, but they do not produce reflections on surrounding objects.

CD FILE: The Raytrace.max file is available on the CD-ROM for you to practice rendering with the raytracer.

Render with the Raytracer

1. Open the Render Scene dialog box.

Note: *To open this dialog box, see the section "Using the Cook Variable Antialiasing Filter."*

2. Click the Raytracer tab.
3. Click to select the Enable Raytracing option (☐ changes to ☑).
4. In the Maximum Depth field, type a number between 0 and 100.

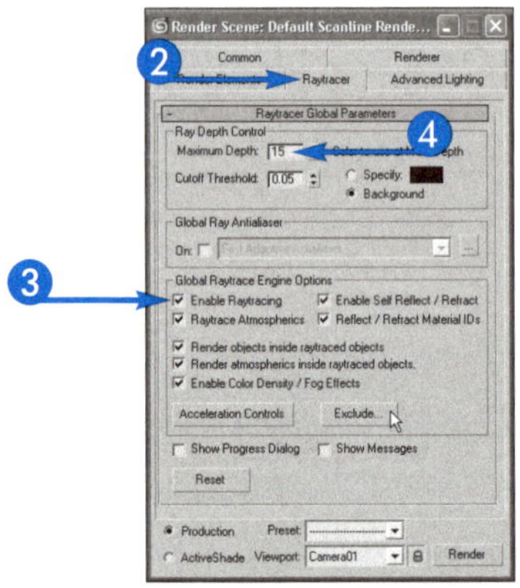

5. Type a Cutoff Threshold value.
6. Click Exclude.

   The Exclude/Include dialog box appears.

7. Ctrl + Click to select the objects that you want to exclude from raytracing.
8. Click ».

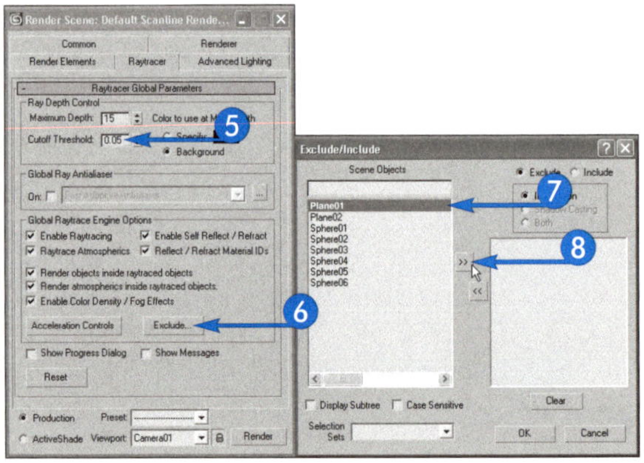

3ds Max adds the selected objects to the Exclude list.

9. Click OK.

The Exclude/Include dialog box closes.

10. Click Render.

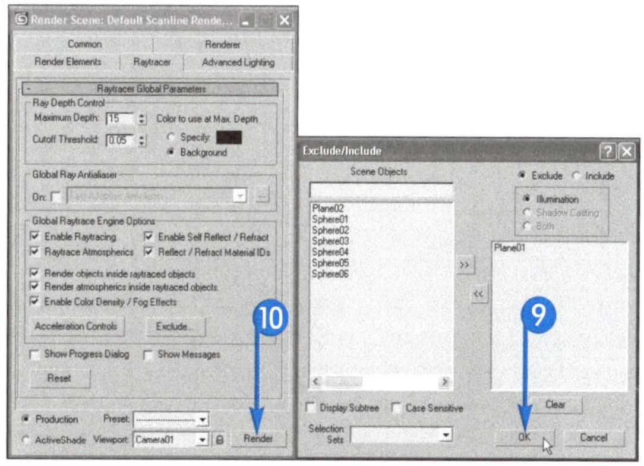

The scene renders with the specified raytracer options.

The excluded objects do not produce raytraced reflections on other objects.

MASTER IT

When do I need to use antialiasing?

3ds Max provides two different types of antialiasing, at the material level and at the render level. Normally, if the "Use Global Settings" (☐ changes to ☑) option is selected in the SuperSampling rollout for the Raytrace Material in the Material Editor, then you do not need to apply a render-level antialasing filter to your scene. This is a default setting for all Raytrace materials. The only time that you may want to use an antialiasing filter with the raytracer is to add blurring or defocusing to the raytracing in your scene. For more information on working with the Material Editor, see Chapter 14. See the section "Understanding Antialising" for more information on antialiasing.

What is the difference between blurring and defocusing?

Both blurring and defocusing create a blur effect for the reflections and refractions in the scene. The difference is in how they manage the distance between the object surfaces. If you apply blurring, you are able to blur the refractions and reflections that are produced in the scene. The blurring is not affected by distance between objects in the scene. If you apply defocusing, the blurring is applied, based upon the distance from the surface of the object; the farther away the object is, the more blurring occurs.

Understanding Caustics

You can use Caustics to simulate the effect of light hitting a surface after it is transmitted through transparent and reflective materials. You should consider using Caustics when the reflections and refractions are extremely important and the additional rendering time required is acceptable. For example, Caustics are useful when working with glass or liquids, such as water. They create realistic-looking surfaces, because they accurately calculate how the light reacts when it strikes each surface.

Caustics are generated by tracing the photons that are emitted from a light and mapping how these photons reflect or refract off each surface in the scene until their energy is completely dispersed. Because caustic generation requires extensive calculations, you specify each object in the scene that generates caustics individually. By default, all objects receive Caustics, but you can choose to turn this feature off for any object.

Caustics are only available with the mental ray Renderer. You can control how Caustics generate in your scene by setting parameters in the Caustics and Global Illumination rollout of the Indirect Illumination panel.

A Enable Option

Activates the calculation of Caustics.

B Maximum Num. Photons per Sample

Indicates the number of photons used to calculate the intensity of each Caustic. Increase the number to reduce noise by making the Caustics blurrier.

C Maximum Sampling Radius

Sets the size of each photon in the scene. The default value creates photons that are 1/100 of the radius of the scene. Increasing the size creates smoothing between overlapping photons.

D Filter

Specifies the filter that is used to sharpen the Caustics. You can select Box, Cone, or Gauss.

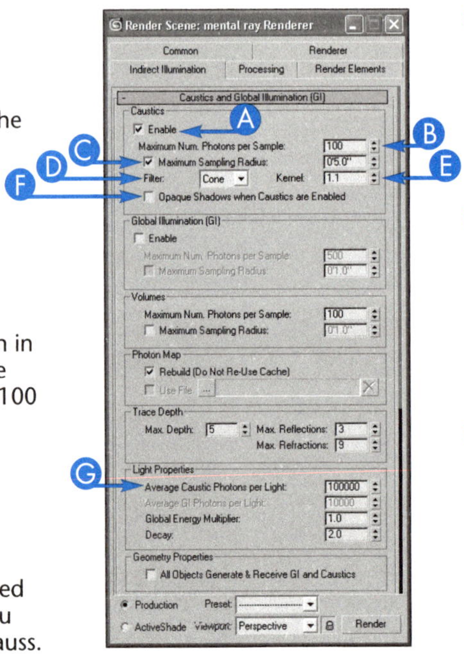

E Kernel

Controls the sharpness of Caustics when the Cone filter is selected. The value must be greater than 1.0.

F Opaque Shadows When Caustics Are Enabled Option

When selected, shadows are opaque instead of transparent.

G Average Caustic Photons per Light

Indicates the number of photons emitted by each light to create Caustics. Increasing the number makes the Caustics more accurate, but also increases render time.

Caustic Requirements

Because Caustics require so much processing power, using Caustics requires more than just enabling this feature in the Indirect Illumination panel of the Render Scene dialog box. You also need to specify the objects that generate the Caustics in your scene.

In order to use Caustics, your scene must include at least one light and one object to generate them. You must also have at least one object that receives Caustics. If you do not have these elements, then you receive an error message when you attempt to render the scene.

By default, the option to receive Caustics is selected for all objects that you create in 3ds Max. However, you must specify the objects that generate Caustics. You can specify how an object handles Caustics in the Object Properties dialog box. See the section "Using Caustics to Simulate Light Transmission" for more information on setting objects to generate Caustics.

Photon Map

When you generate Caustics in your scene, the mental ray Renderer calculates the effect using a technique called *photon mapping.* A photon map is a procedure that determines the indirect illumination effects of Caustics and global illumination on each surface in your scene. Photon mapping traces the photons that are emitted from each light as they are reflected or refracted off or through each object until they strike a surface, where they are diffused.

When working with Caustics, photon mapping keeps track of each surface that the photon strikes, until the object surface has been specified to receive Caustics. The number of photons emitted by each light in your scene is controlled by the Average Caustic Photons per Light setting. The number that you specify in this field is used by the photon map to trace the Caustics. Although the default is 100,000, you may want to increase this number to improve the accuracy of the Caustics.

Caustic Filters

The mental ray Renderer provides three different filters that you can use when generating Caustics: Box, Cone, and Gauss. The filter that you select controls how sharp the Caustic effects appear in your scene.

The Box filter is the default filter that is applied when you enable Caustics in your scene. This filter requires less rendering time, although the Caustic effects are not as sharp.

The Cone filter is a popular filter because it creates sharper Caustics than the Box filter. You can control how sharp the Caustics are by changing the value in the Kernel field. If you increase the value in the Kernel field, the Caustics become blurrier. The Gauss filter creates smoother Caustics than the Cone filter.

Using Caustics to Simulate Light Transmission

You can use Caustics to simulate light transmission through a transparent or reflective material, such as glass or liquids. This allows you to create realistic transparent surfaces, as well as the light's effect on secondary surfaces that it contacts.

To use Caustics, you must use the mental ray Renderer. The mental ray Renderer traces the emission of photons from lights and through other objects and defines how they strike each surface. You must have at least one object that generates Caustics, one object that receives Caustics, and a light source to generate the photons that pass through the object.

Caustics require a lot of calculations, and so they are only applied to the objects that you specify to produce Caustics. For example, if you have a drinking glass in your scene, then you need to select that glass object and specify in the Object Properties dialog box that it generate Caustics.

Caustics are an option in the Caustics and Global Illumination rollout of the Indirect Illumination panel of the Render Scene dialog box. You can modify the default parameter values to adjust the photon size and transmission.

CD FILE: The Caustics.max file is available on the CD-ROM for you to practice using Caustics.

Using Caustics to Simulate Light Transmission

Set Caustic Generation for an Object

1. Select the object that will generate Caustics.
2. Right-click the object.

   The quad menu appears.
3. Click Properties.

   The Object Properties dialog box appears.
4. Click the mental ray tab.
5. Click the Generate Caustics option (☐ changes to ☑).
6. Click OK.

   You can repeat steps 1 to 5 for each object that you want to generate Caustics.

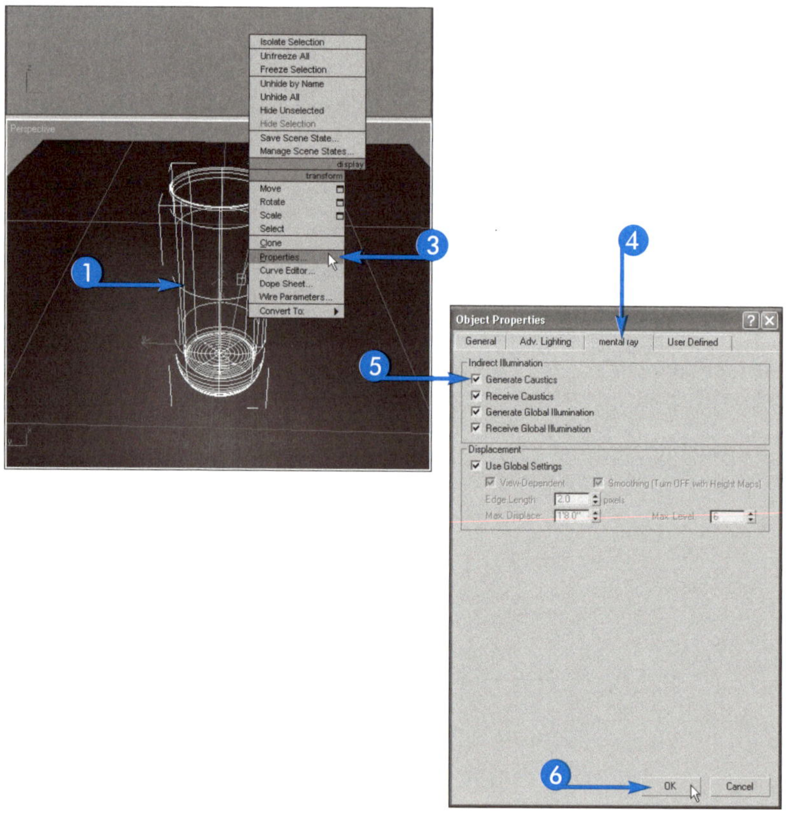

Render with Caustics

7. Click the Render Scene button (▣).

   The Render Scene dialog box appears.

8. Click the Indirect Illumination tab.

Note: *See the section "Assign a Renderer" for information on setting mental ray as the renderer.*

9. Click the Enable option in the Caustics section (☐ changes to ☑).

10. Click Render.

    The scene renders, producing Caustics for the selected objects.

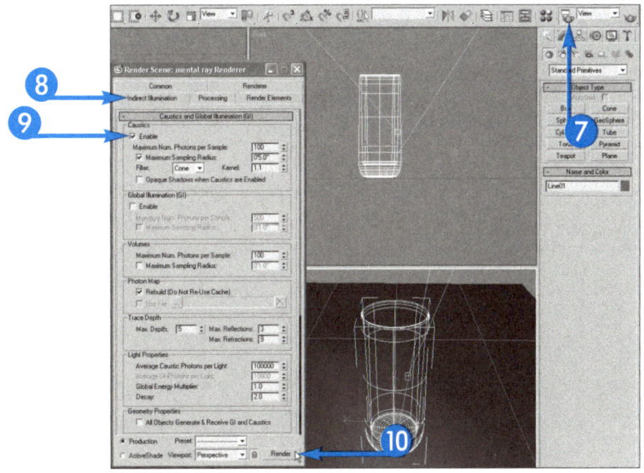

Why are there so many spots in my rendered image?

▼ When you render your scene with Caustics, the size of the photons determines how the reflections and refactions of the light appear on the surfaces that receive the Caustics. When the photons overlap on a surface, they are blended together to create smoother effects. If the photons are too small, then they do not overlap, and instead produce several small spots of light. To increase the photon size, you need to increase the value in the Maximum Sampling Radius field. If this option is deselected, then the default value for the photon size is 1/100 of the radius of the scene. You can specify any value to increase or decrease the size.

Does 3ds Max need to rebuild the photon map with each render?

▼ No. You can specify that 3ds Max saves the photon map to a file that can be used each time you render a specific scene. This is especially useful when rendering animations or sequential files. When you save the photon map to a file, 3ds Max creates a PMAP file for your scene. To save the photon map to a file, click the Rebuild option in the Photon Map section to deselect it (☑ changes to ☐). Click ▭ and then name the file in the Save As dialog box that appears. To discontinue using the photon file, click Use File.

Selective Rendering Tools

You can perform the process of rendering your scene to create an image or images of the objects. 3ds Max combines the geometry in your scene with all of the other elements, including lights, materials, and environment settings, to create the desired output as images or animations.

3ds Max applies different rendering types, depending upon your output requirements. These rendering types include the viewports and ActiveShade window, as well as Production, which acts as a high-quality preview in the Rendered Frame window. The results of each rendering type are a trade-off between speed and quality. For example, the rendering that displays in each viewport is optimized for speed, while the production output is optimized for quality. Both the viewports and production rendering have settings to further customize their respective rendering speed and quality.

Viewport Rendering

Because viewport rendering is designed for speed and to change quickly as you alter your object in the scene, the standard viewports do not display all lighting and environmental effects results. You can specify different rendering levels for each viewport to control the redraw speed of the scene and thus how objects in your scene appear in the viewport as you make changes. For example, you can view all objects as wireframe, or you can set viewports to show the objects with the materials applied by selecting the Smooth + Highlights option. You adjust the rendering level for each viewport in the Viewport Configuration dialog box, or by right-clicking a viewport label to display the quad menu.

ActiveShade

ActiveShade is the next level of rendering above viewport rendering. ActiveShade displays an interactive preview of the final rendering without completely rendering the entire scene. ActiveShade interactively updates as you alter the lights and materials in your scene. Because ActiveShade does not completely render the scene, the appearance of the lighting and material is not as precise as in the production rendering. When you move objects or modify the object geometry, these changes do not interactively update in the ActiveShade window. To see these effects, you must re-render the scene.

The ActiveShade rendering of your scene can appear in two locations: either in a floating window or in a viewport. You can only have one ActiveShade window open. See the section "Preview Your Scene with ActiveShade" for more information.

By default, ActiveShade uses the 3ds Max Default Scanline Renderer to create the preview of the rendered scene. If you are using a different renderer for your Production rendering, you may want to change the ActiveShade renderer.

Production Rendering

The Production rendering of your scene produces the highest-quality result, but it is also the most time-consuming of the three rendering types. Because all settings in your scene are applied during this process, the Production rendering can take anywhere from several minutes to several hours to complete.

You can control how the renderer, or render engine, creates the scene. To do this, you select a renderer and then specify the settings for that renderer in the Render Scene dialog box. By default, 3ds Max uses the Default Scanline Renderer for all rendering, but you can select another renderer, such as the mental ray Renderer or a number of third-party renderers that are also available.

Rendered Frame Window

The Rendered Frame window displays the rendered output for the production rendering. The controls that appear on the toolbar at the top of the window allow you to change the output or clone the window itself. The Rendered Frame window overwrites itself each time; creating a clone allows you to save a copy of the Rendered Frame window to compare with subsequent renderings.

A Save Bitmap Button

Saves the rendered image that displays in the window. This button displays the Browse Images for Output dialog box, where you specify the name and file format for saving the image.

B Clone Rendered Frame Window Button

Creates another Rendered Frame window that contains the same rendered output.

C Enable RGB Channel Buttons

Enables or disables the Red, Green, and Blue channels in the displayed image.

D Monochrome Button

Displays a monochrome version of the rendered image.

E Display Alpha Channel Button

Displays the Alpha channel for the image.

F Clear Button

Removes the image from the Rendered Frame window.

G Channel Display List

Allows you to select from the different channels that are rendered with the image. For most images, only the RGB Alpha channel is available.

H Color Swatch

Displays the color of the last pixel that you right-clicked in the window. You can click the Color swatch to open a Color Selector or right-click it to copy the color to the Clipboard.

Preview Your Scene with ActiveShade

You can use ActiveShade to preview the rendering of your scene. Because ActiveShade is interactive, it allows you to quickly see how the changes that you make to materials and lights affect your scene. For example, when you apply a material to an object, it automatically updates in the ActiveShade window. For slower renderings, a thin yellow line descends along the right edge of the ActiveShade window to indicate its progress.

3ds Max places the ActiveShade either in a floating window or directly in the selected viewport. If you want to use ActiveShade interactively while you modify your scene, then you should consider placing it in a viewport to eliminate an extra window on your screen while working in the other viewports.

When you place an ActiveShade in a viewport, it replaces the previous view, and the viewport title does not display in the corner of the ActiveShade view. You can control ActiveShade through the quad menu that displays when you right-click the ActiveShade viewport, which includes an option for closing ActiveShade.

The Rendering.max file is available on the CD-ROM for you to practice using ActiveShade.

Preview Your Scene with ActiveShade

Add ActiveShade to a Viewport

1. Right-click the title of the viewport that you want to view in ActiveShade.
2. Click Views.
3. Click ActiveShade.

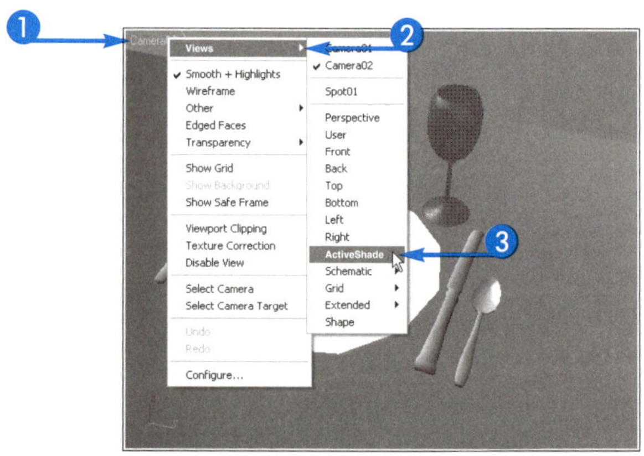

ActiveShade renders the view in the selected viewport.

To create a floating ActiveShade window, click Rendering, and then click ActiveShade Floater.

Remove ActiveShade from a Viewport

1. Right-click in the ActiveShade viewport to display a quad menu.
2. Click Close.

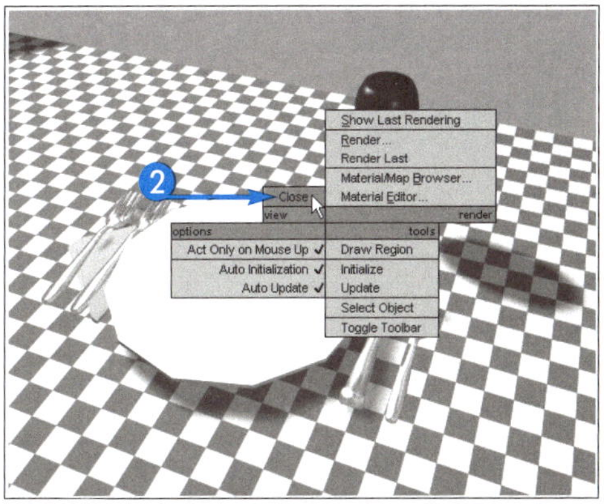

The view in the viewport changes back to the original view.

MASTER IT

Can I control how often the ActiveShade viewport updates?

Yes, you can control how your ActiveShade viewport updates by selecting the appropriate options in the ActiveShade quad menu. There are three options that you can set for auto-updating. These options are all selected by default. The Act Only on Mouse Up option: When setting a value, 3ds Max waits for the mouse to be released before updating the ActiveShade window or viewport. The Auto Initialization option: Changes made to mapped materials cause ActiveShade to update. The Auto Update option: Changes made to lighting and non-mapped materials are automatically updated in the ActiveShade window.

Can I just update a section of the window?

If you are making changes to just one section of your scene, then you can use the Draw Region option in the quad menu. When you select this option, you can draw a box around a section of the scene so that only that part updates as you make changes. Once the Draw Region is active, it remains active until you turn it off by clicking outside the region. When you turn it off, the entire scene updates, based upon the update options that you have selected.

Render Using the Quick Render Tool

You can quickly render a view in any viewport using the Quick Render tool, which is available on the Main toolbar. When you use the Quick Render tool, 3ds Max renders the current viewport using the current render settings. Quick Render works well for re-rendering your scene once you establish your render settings. See the section "Using the Render Region Option" for more information on setting rendering options using the Render Scene dialog box.

You can use Quick Render to display either a Production render or ActiveShade render. You can switch between the two options using the Quick Render flyout menu. Both types of rendering use the render settings that are specified in the Render Scene dialog box. For example, if the current Production renderer is set to the mental ray Renderer, then when you select the Quick Render (Production) button, 3ds Max renders the view using the mental ray Renderer.

To render the entire view of the current viewport, select View in the Render Type list box. When you select either Quick Render button, the selected view renders and displays in the Rendered Frame window.

The Rendering.max file is available on the CD-ROM for you to practice using Quick Render.

Render Using the Quick Render Tool

Render a View with the Production Render Engine

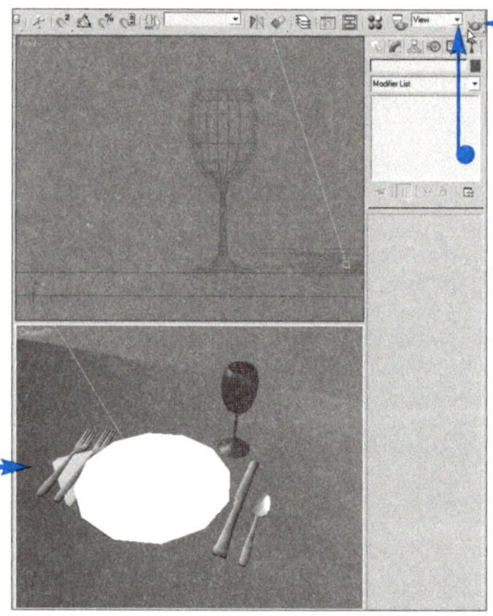

1. Click to select the viewport view that you want to render.
   - If it is not selected, then click here and select View.
2. Click the Quick Render button ( ).

The selected view renders in the Rendered Frame window.

Render a View with ActiveShade

1. Click to select the viewport view that you want to render.
   - If it is not selected, then click here and select View.
2. Click and hold until the flyout buttons appear.
3. Click the Quick Render (ActiveShade) button ().

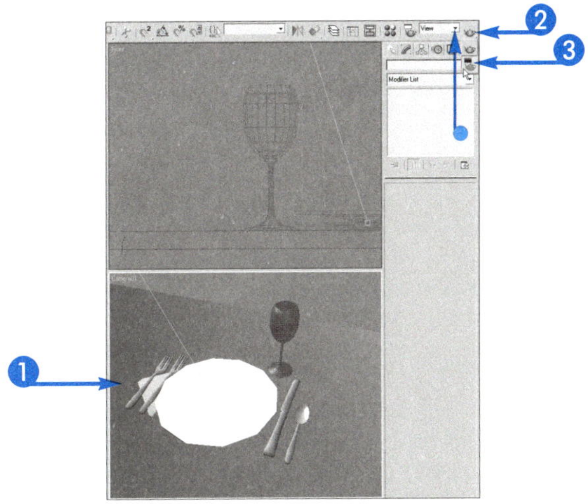

The selected view renders in an ActiveShade floating window.

MASTER IT

I selected a viewport before clicking the Quick Render button. Why does the view from another viewport render?

When you specify your render settings in the Render Scene dialog box, you can specify that the scene render in a particular viewport, such as a Perspective viewport. You do this by locking the viewport. If the viewport is locked, then this viewport is rendered when you use Quick Render, regardless of the viewport that you select. To render a different viewport, you need to unlock the viewport in the Render Scene dialog box by deselecting the Lock View button () at the bottom of the dialog box. See the section "Using the Render Selected Option" for more information about the Render Scene dialog box.

Why does an error message display when I click the Quick Render button?

ActiveShade allows you to have only one ActiveShade window open at a time. If you click the Quick Render (ActiveShade) button () while ActiveShade is open in either a viewport or a floating window, then a message box appears, indicating that an ActiveShade window is already open. You can click OK to close the current ActiveShade window and open a new one. To preserve your existing ActiveShade window, clone it by clicking the Clone Rendered Frame window button () in the ActiveShade toolbar. This creates a clone of the ActiveShade window and allows you to create a new, original ActiveShade.

Using the Render Selected Option

You can choose to render only specific objects in your scene with the Render Type list box. This allows you to see how specific objects in your scene will appear, without rendering the entire view. This is useful when you make changes to an object's materials or modifiers and want to see only how they affect that object. To render only certain objects, you need to select those objects using any of the 3ds Max selection options.

To render only the selected objects, choose Selected in the Render Type list box. When you click Quick Render, only the selected objects render, but the objects render in the same location that they occupy in the current viewport.

For example, if a desk is located on the right side of the viewport, then it is positioned on the right side of the Rendered Frame window.

Keep in mind that the selection made in the Render Type list box also affects renderings that are generated by the Render Scene dialog box. See the section "Selective Rendering Tools" for more information on the Rendered Frame window.

The Rendering.max file is available on the CD-ROM for you to practice using the Render Selected option.

Using the Render Selected Option

1 Select the objects that you want to render.

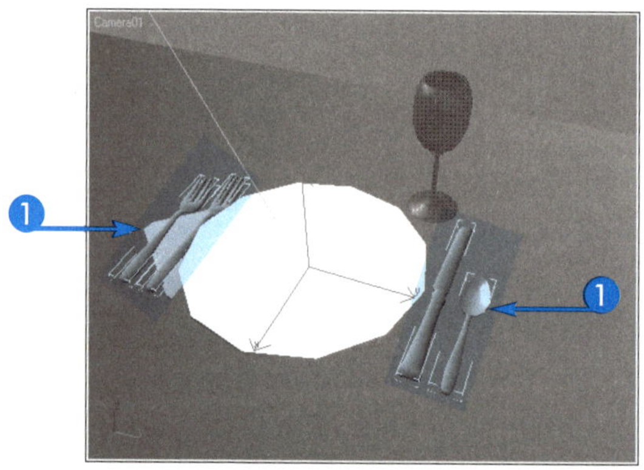

2 Click here and select Selected.

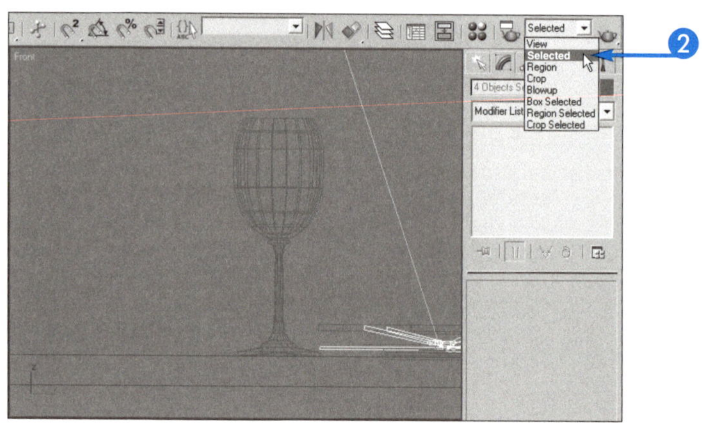

3 Click .

The selected objects render in the Rendered Frame window.

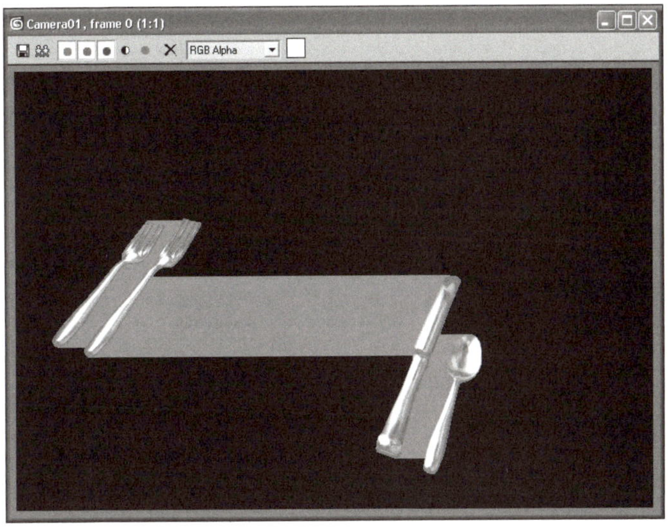

MASTER IT

Why does the Rendered Frame window still show my last render?

When you render only selected objects or portions of your scene, 3ds Max does not clear the Rendered Frame window before rendering your selection. As a result, you can still see the areas of the Rendered Frame window that were not overwritten with your last rendering. The selected objects are rendered and placed on top of the previous render. If you only want to see the selected objects, then you need to clear the Rendered Frame window and re-render your object selection. To do this, click the Clear button (X) in the Rendered Frame window's toolbar, and then click again; the selected objects re-render.

Can I render selected objects with ActiveShade?

No. When you select , 3ds Max does not render only the selected objects in the scene. Even when you have selected specific objects, 3ds Max renders the entire view in an ActiveShade floating window. If you only want to use ActiveShade, then you must use the Draw Region option, found in the quad menu that displays when you right-click in the viewport. This allows you to draw a box around the objects that you want to update. See the section "Preview Your Scene with ActiveShade" for more information on working with ActiveShade.

Using the Render Region Option

You can render only a part of your scene by using the Render Region option. When you render a region of your scene, 3ds Max renders only the part of the scene that is within a rectangular region that you designate. For example, if you are adjusting the lighting and materials in one area of the scene, then you can use this tool to see how well your adjustments work without rendering the entire scene.

In order to render a part of the scene, you need to select the Region option in the Render Type list box. When you select Quick Render (Production), a dashed box displays in the center of the selected viewport. You can use this box to specify the part of the scene that you want to render. You can move the entire box or resize it by using the handles on the sides and corners. The selected region of the scene renders in the Rendered Frame window. The region appears in the same location as if the entire scene were visible.

CD FILE: The Rendering.max file is available on the CD-ROM for you to practice using the Render Region option.

Using the Render Region Option

1. Click to select a viewport.
2. Click here and select Region.

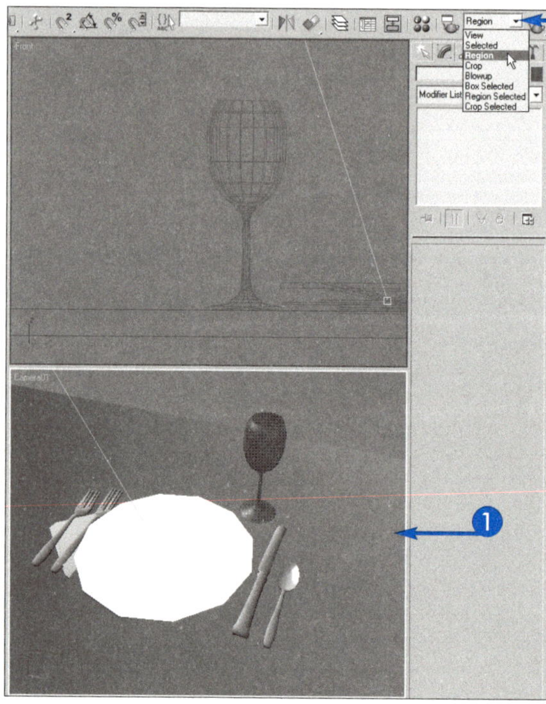

3. Click the Quick Render icon.

A box displays in the current viewport.

4 Click and drag a handle to resize the box.

You can click and drag in the middle of the box to move it.

5 Click OK.

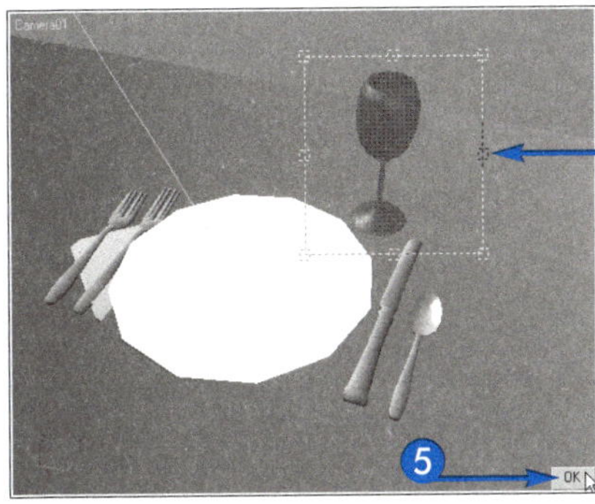

3ds Max renders the selected part of the scene. If you rendered previously, the non-region area may appear in the Rendered Frame window.

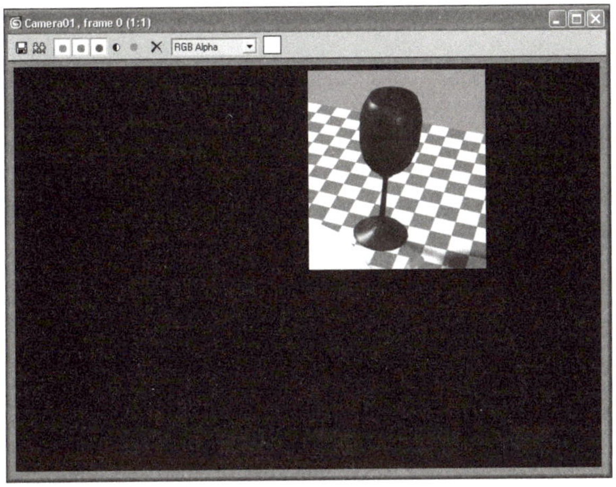

MASTER IT

How can I compare different renderings?

- Each time you render your scene, 3ds Max stores that rendering in memory until you render the scene again. In order to keep a rendering for comparison, you need to copy it. You can do this by copying a rendering from the Rendered Frame window. If you want to compare one rendering to another, then with the first rendering open in the Rendered Frame window, click the Clone button (). This creates a copy of the rendering in another Rendered Frame window. Keep the windows open and re-render your scene. The new rendering appears in the original window so that you can compare the renderings.

What is the difference between the Region and Region Selected options?

- The Region option renders only the part of the scene that you indicate by dragging a rectangular region in the viewport. If only a part of an object is inside the region, then only that part of the object renders. The Rendered Frame window's rendered area remains the same size, and any area that falls outside the region does not update in the Rendered Frame window. The Region Selected option renders all the selected objects and the parts of the other objects in the scene that are within the bounding boxes of the selected objects. This includes all objects that are located in front of or behind the selected objects in the scene.

Using the Render Crop Option

You can render only a portion of your scene by using the Render Crop option. This is useful when you want to render a part of the scene, but you want to render at the resolution of the full View rendering. For example, if your scene is set to render at 640 x 480 and you specify an area that consists of the top-right quadrant of the viewport, then you will render an image that is 320 x 240.

The Rendered Frame window resizes to match the proportions of the selection. This differs from the Region option because, under the same circumstances, the Region option would render a 640 x 480 image, but only the top-right quadrant would be filled with pixels that show your scene.

To crop the scene to render only a part of it, you can select the Crop option in the Render Type list box. A dashed box appears in the current viewport. You can select the part that you want to crop by either moving the box or resizing it by using the handles on the sides and corners.

CD FILE — The Rendering.max file is available on the CD-ROM for you to practice using the Render Crop option.

Using the Render Crop Option

1. Click to select a viewport.
2. Click here and select Crop.

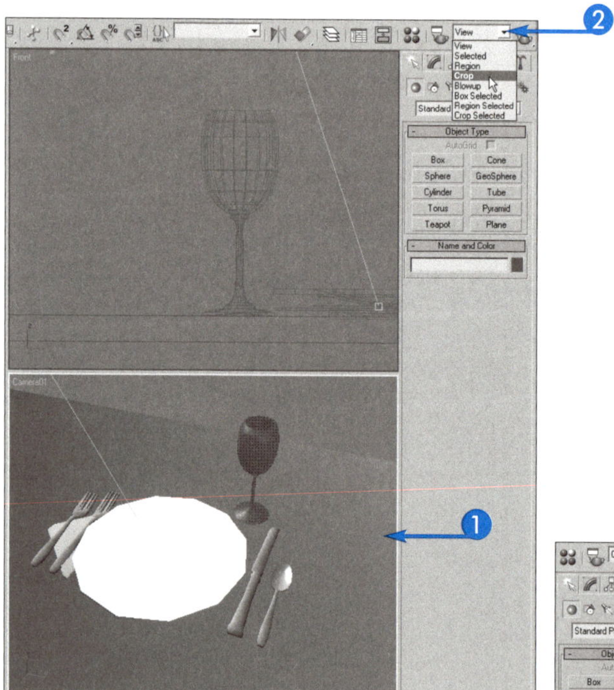

3. Click .

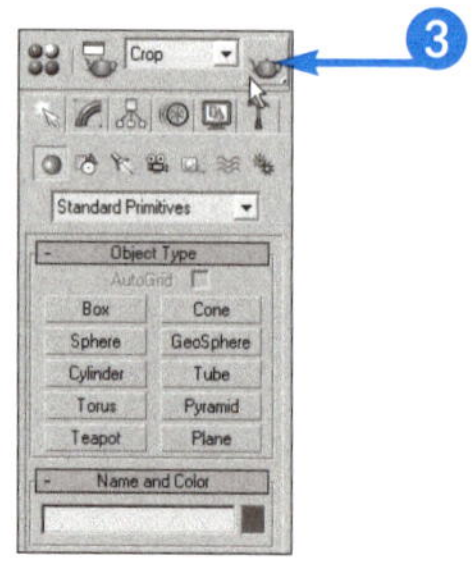

A box displays in the current viewport.

4. Click and drag the handles to resize the box and mark the area that you want to crop.

   You can click and drag in the middle of the box to move it.

5. Click OK.

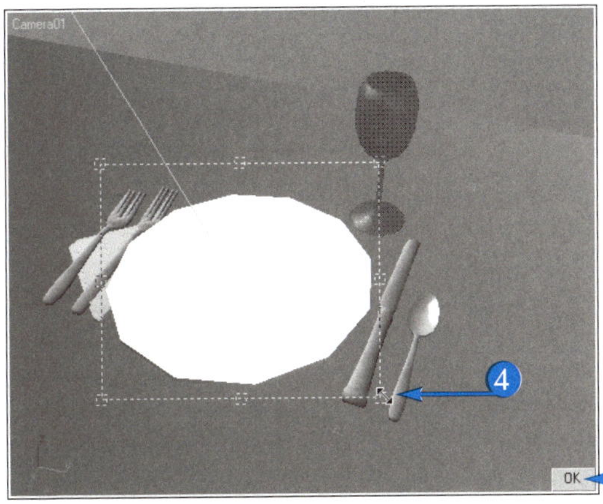

3ds Max renders the cropped part of the scene.

MASTER IT

How do I change the resolution of my rendering?

You set the resolution for the rendering in the Render Scene dialog box. These settings affect all renderings of your scene using either of the Quick Render options. 3ds Max allows you to select from preset resolution sizes or specify your own custom resolution. The larger the resolution, the longer it takes to render your scene. It is a good idea to use a lower resolution to render while you are creating your scene, and then select your final resolution when you are ready to create the final rendering. For more information on setting the resolution for rendering, see Chapter 20.

What is the difference between the Crop and Crop Selected options?

The Crop option renders only the part of the scene that you indicate by dragging a rectangular region in the viewport. If only a part of an object is inside the region, then only that part of the object is rendered. The Rendered Frame window's rendered area is reduced to fit the region selected. The Crop Selected option also reduces the size of the Rendered Frame window to match the region, but renders all the selected objects and the parts of the other objects in the scene that are within the bounding boxes of the selected objects. This includes all objects that are located in front of or behind the selected objects in the scene.

Using the Render Blowup Option

You can use the Render Blowup option to zoom in on and render a part of the scene, filling the entire Rendered Frame window. This is useful when you want to blow up a part of the scene to ensure that you will achieve the desired results during final rendering.

In order to blow up and render a part of the scene, select the Blowup option in the Render Type list box. This option displays a dashed box in the current viewport. You can select the part that you want to blow up, either by moving the box or by resizing it with the handles on the sides and corners.

Only the selected part of the scene is rendered. This selected part resizes to fit the current resolution settings, which match the render output settings for the Rendered Frame window. For example, if you set your rendering output at 640 x 480 in the Render Scene dialog box and you blow up a part of the scene, then that part resizes to 640 x 480.

The Rendering.max file is available on the CD-ROM for you to practice using the Render Blowup option.

Using the Render Blowup Option

1. Click to select a viewport.
2. Click here and select Blowup.

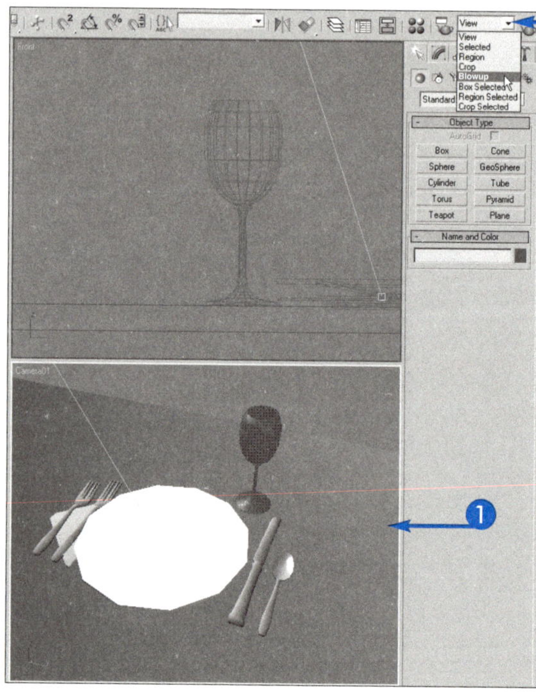

3. Click .

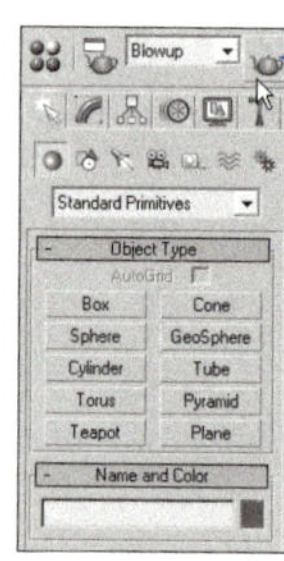

A box displays in the current viewport.

4 Click and drag the handles to resize the box and mark the area to blow up.

You can click and drag in the middle of the box to move it.

5 Click OK.

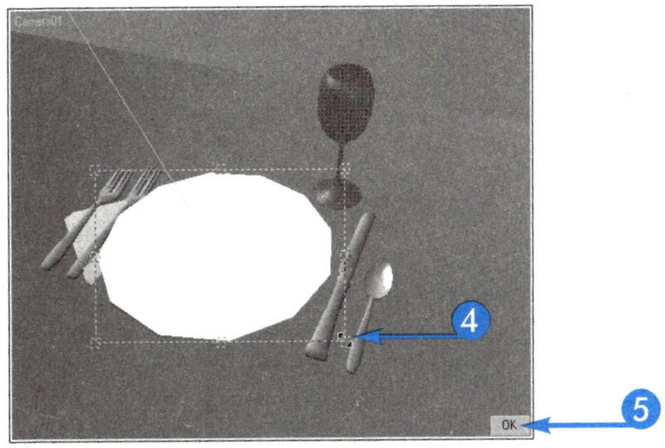

3ds Max blows up the selected part of the scene to fit the Rendered Frame window.

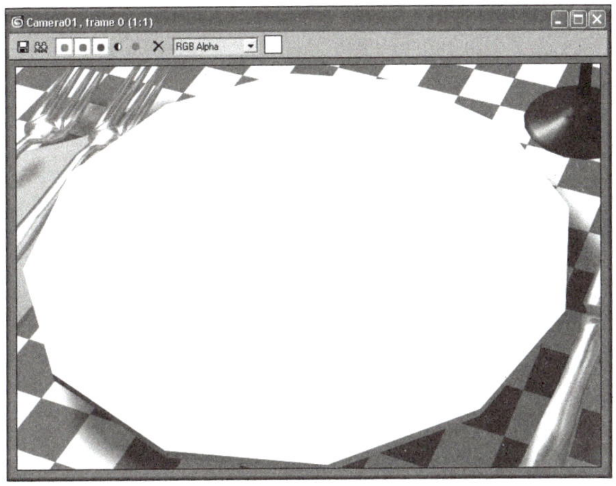

MASTER IT

What is the difference between the Region, Crop, and Blowup options?

You can use all three options to render only a specific part of your scene; the difference is in the appearance of the rendering in the Rendered Frame window. Both the Region and Crop options maintain the same size of the selected region when it is rendered. With the Region option, the selected region displays in a window that is sized to the current resolution, with the unrendered part appearing black. With the Crop option, the window size matches that of the rendered region. The Blowup option increases the size of the selected region to fit the current resolution. As a result, the objects in the selected region appear larger.

Can I save the contents of the Rendered Frame window?

You can save the Rendered Frame window's contents to any graphic format that is supported by 3ds Max. For example, you can create a JPEG file for use in Web pages, or a TIFF file for printing. The Rendered Frame Window saves the image exactly as you see it. For example, if you use the Region option, your saved output includes the areas that were not rendered. To save the contents of the Rendered Frame window, click the Save Bitmap button (💾). The Browse Images for Output dialog box appears. Type the name for the file in the File Name field and select the file format in the Save as Type field. Click Save.

Compare Renderings with the RAM Player

You can quickly compare any two images or animations that you have rendered in 3ds Max by using the RAM Player. This tool is useful when you are trying to refine settings for lighting and materials in your scene. You can load two renderings, with different scene settings, into the RAM Player in order to compare them.

The RAM Player contains two different channels that you can use to load images or animations. You load the first image in Channel A and the second image in Channel B. You can load an image from the last rendering, or from a saved file.

To compare two renderings of the same scene, you can create the first rendering and load it in Channel A of the RAM Player. You can then create the second rendering with the new settings, and load it in Channel B of the RAM Player. When both channels are loaded, they both display in the window, with half of each rendering being visible. You can use the slider at the top of the window to control how much of each image dominates the RAM window, and compare the two renderings. You can also use the RAM Player for processing still image sequences into movies at varying levels of compression and resolution.

Compare Renderings with the RAM Player

1. Click Rendering.
2. Click RAM Player.

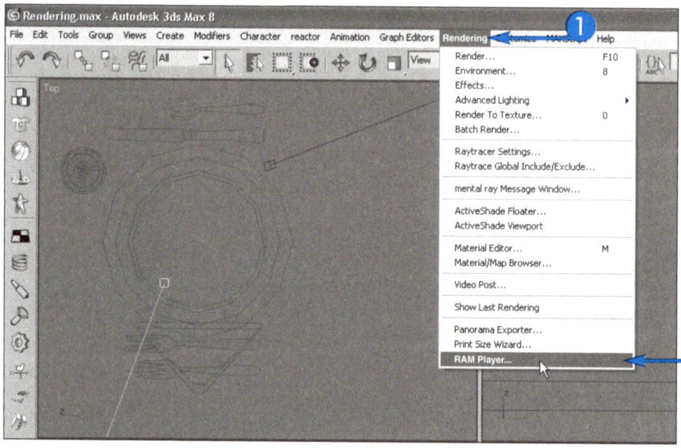

The RAM Player opens.

3. Click the Open Last Rendered Image in Channel A button ().
   - You can also click the Open Channel A button () to display a dialog box that allows you to open an existing image file instead.

The RAM Player Configuration dialog box appears.

4. Click OK.

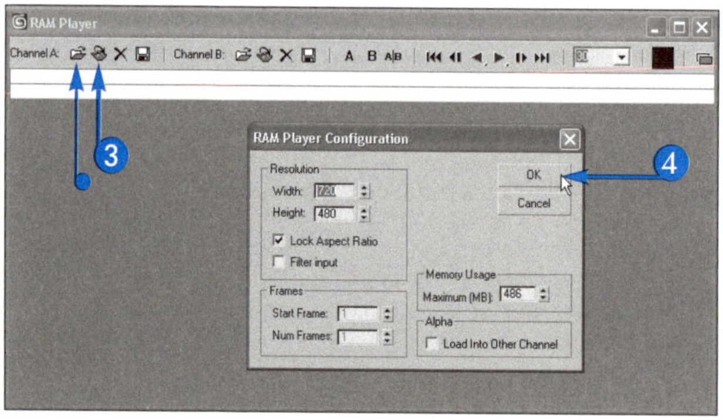

- The last rendered scene loads in Channel A.

You can make changes to your scene and re-render it.

5. Repeat steps 3 and 4 for Channel B.

3ds Max loads the latest rendering of the scene.

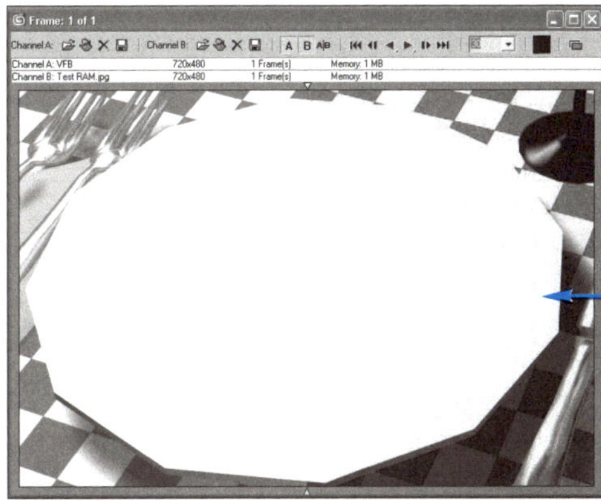

- You can drag the slider to compare the difference between the two renderings.

MASTER IT

Can I load the image at a different resolution?

Yes. When you load an image into each channel, the RAM Player Configuration dialog box allows you to specify the resolution that you want for the image or animation that you are loading. To compare images, you should specify the same resolution for both channels. If you do not remember the resolution for each channel, then you can verify the resolution by looking at the table under the RAM Player toolbar. This table also specifies whether the channel contains an animation or image by indicating the number of frames.

Is there another method that I can use to compare two images?

Yes. You can also view the images with a horizontal split screen that allows you to move the slider up and down. To create a horizontal split screen, click the Horizontal/Vertical Split Screen button (A|B). The split now runs horizontally, with the image in Channel A at the top and the image in Channel B at the bottom. You can click the button again to switch back to the vertical split-screen window, with the Channel A image on the left and the Channel B image on the right.

Change the Background Color

You can set the color of the background that displays when your scene is rendered in 3ds Max. This allows you to specify a color other than the default black that displays in any areas where you do not have objects.

The background color of your scene is controlled by the environment settings in the Environment and Effects dialog box. The background can consist of either a specific color or an image map. See the section "Apply a Picture to the Background" for more information on using an image map for the background.

To set the environmental background color, you need to use the Background Color swatch to open the Color Selector dialog box. You can adjust the sliders in the Hue and Blackness field to set the hue and darkness levels. You can control how saturated the color is by adjusting the Whiteness slider. You can also set the color using the Red, Green, Blue, Hue, Saturation, and Value fields. The color swatches above the Reset button show the before and after colors.

Change the Background Color

1. Click Rendering.
2. Click Environment.

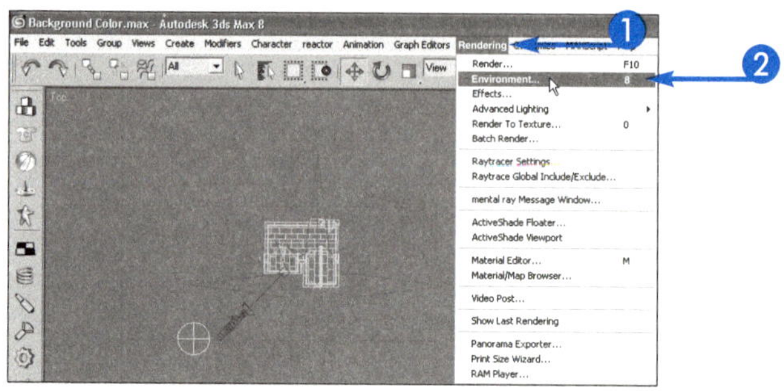

The Environment and Effects dialog box appears, displaying the Environment tab.

3. Click the Background Color swatch.

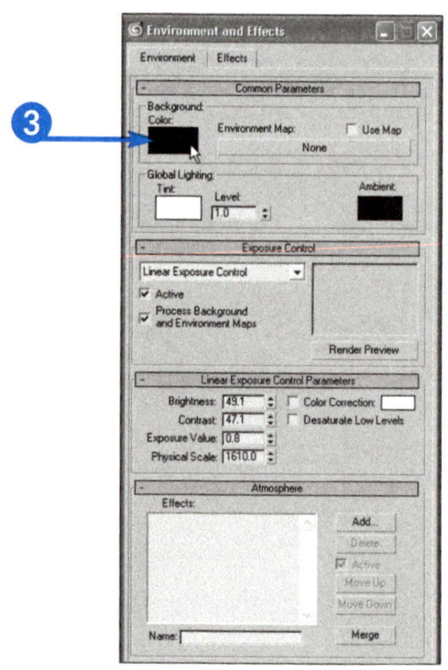

The Color Selector dialog box appears.

4. Click and drag the Hue slider to select the color that you want.
5. Click and drag the Blackness slider to lighten or darken the shade.
6. Click and drag the Whiteness slider to select the saturation of the color.
7. Click Close.

   The Background Color swatch updates to show the new background color selection.

8. Click the Quick Render button ( ).

   The scene renders using the new background color.

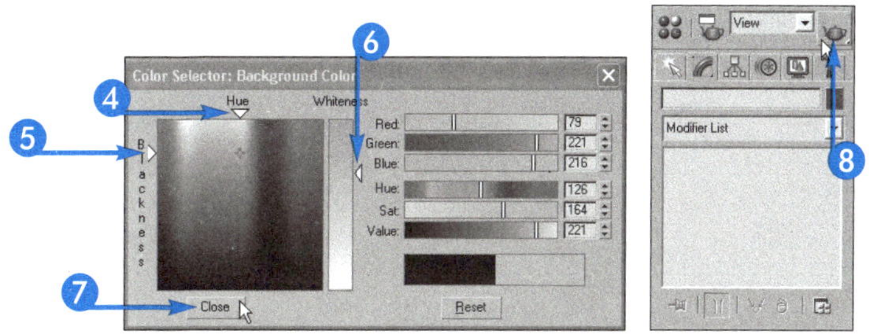

Can I save the Environment settings to use with other scenes?

Yes. 3ds Max allows you to save any environmental settings and effects that you create as part of a Render Preset file so that you can load them with any scene. You create a Render Preset file from the Render Scene dialog box by selecting Save Preset in the Preset drop-down list at the bottom of the dialog box. You can also select the specific rendering settings that you want to save. To save settings related to the environment, such as the background color or map, you need to select the Environment category in the Select Preset Categories dialog box. For more information on creating a Render Preset, see Chapter 20.

Can I animate the background color?

Yes. You can animate the background color in a scene. For example, you may want to change the background color from black to white during an animation of your scene. To animate the background color, you turn on Auto Key, drag the Time Slider to the frame by which you want the color to change, and then change the color. The colors gradually transition from one to the other. You are only limited in the number of color changes by the number of frames in the scene. For more information on using Auto Key, see Chapter 8.

Apply a Picture to the Background

You can set the background of your scene to use a picture or any other available map in 3ds Max. For example, you may want to add a picture of a beach in the background. Adding a picture or map to the background creates an *environment map*.

You can load a picture into the background in the Environment tab of the Environment and Effects dialog box. You can select either an image or a map. The image can exist anywhere on your system, and the map can come from the current scene, a material library, or a slot in the Material Editor. Selecting the Environment Map button brings up the Material/Map Browser that you can use to browse for and select the map.

When you load a map from the Material Library, the name of the selected map displays on the Environment Map button. If you select the Use Map option, the map loads in the background when the scene renders, and 3ds Max ignores the Background color. For more information on the Material/Map Browser, see Chapter 15. For information on rendering scenes, see Chapter 21.

Apply a Picture to the Background

1. Click Rendering.
2. Click Environment.

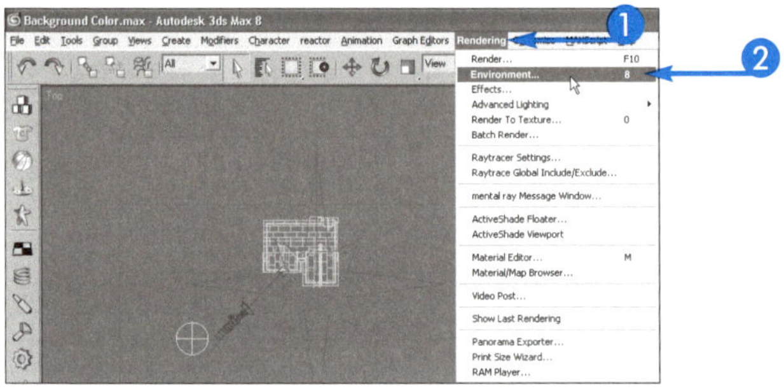

The Environment and Effects dialog box appears.

3. Click the Environment Map button.

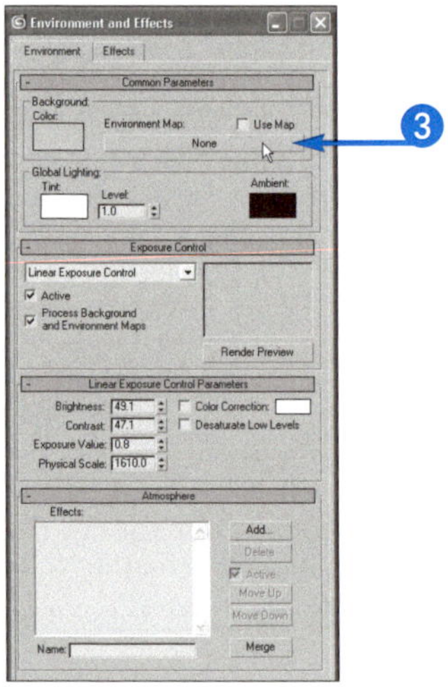

The Material/Map Browser dialog box appears.

4 Click to select the map that you want.

Note: *For information on using the Material/Map Browser, see Chapter 15.*

5 Click OK.

The name of the selected map displays on the Environment Map button.

3ds Max activates the Use Map option (☐ changes to ☑).

6 Click the render button.

The scene renders, and the selected map displays in the background.

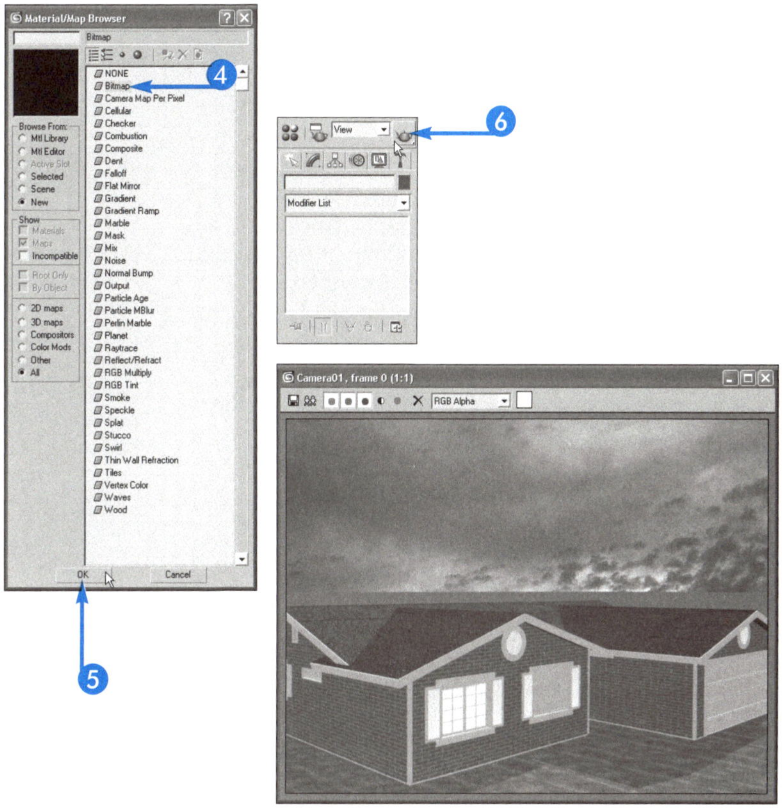

MASTER IT

How do I modify a material that I have specified as the environment map?

▼ You can modify any environment map in the Material Editor. In order to modify an environment map, click the Material Editor button to open the Material Editor. Click the Environment Map button in the Environment and Effects dialog box, and drag the Environment Map button to an empty slot in the Material Editor. A dialog box appears, asking if you want to create an instance or copy of the selected map. Select the Instance option, and click OK. Any changes that you make to the material in the Material Editor update as the environment map. For more information on using the Material Editor, see Chapter 14.

How do I load a picture on my computer as the environment map for the scene?

▼ To load a picture that is not in the Material Editor or in a material library, use the Bitmap map type, which appears in the list when you click the New option (○ changes to ◉) in the Browse From section of the Material/Map Browser. When you select Bitmap, a Select Bitmap Image File dialog box appears. Locate the desired file and click Open. The selected file loads into your scene as the environment map, and the filename displays on the Environment Map button. To make your background move with the camera movement, map the bitmap image to a sphere with its normals flipped instead of using an environment map. Your camera movement then appears correctly.

Apply a Film Grain Effect

You can apply a Film Grain effect to any rendered scene to make it appear as if the scene were scanned from a film or photograph. This effect can also help your scene to match the grain in your background when your background image source is a scanned image.

You can apply a film grain to a scene in the Effects panel of the Environment and Effects dialog box. All of the effects that you add using the Effects panel are applied to your scene in post-production. As a result, 3ds Max applies the effects on top of the rendered scene. Because 3ds Max applies the Film Grain effect in post-production, you can actually apply it interactively. This allows you to change the grain value and instantly see the results without having to re-render the scene.

When you select the Film Grain effect, the Film Grain Parameters rollout displays in the Effects panel. The rollout contains two parameters for the effect: Grain and Ignore Background. The Grain parameter indicates the size of the grain that you want to apply. You can specify a value between 0 and 10.0. The Ignore Background option prevents 3ds Max from applying the effect to the background.

Apply a Film Grain Effect

1. Click Rendering.
2. Click Effects.

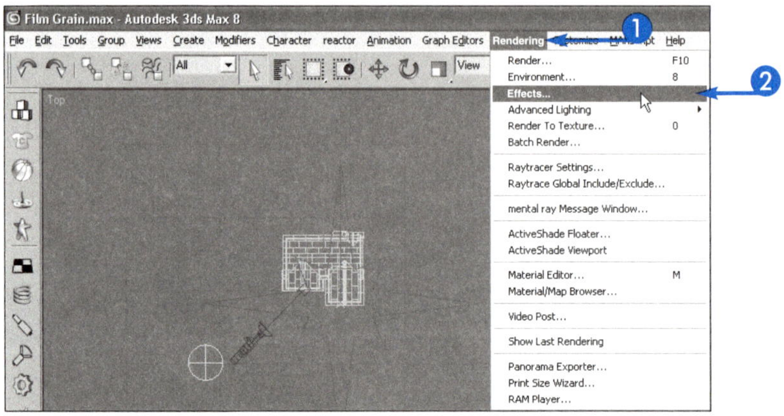

The Environment and Effects dialog box appears, displaying the Effects panel.

3. Click Add.

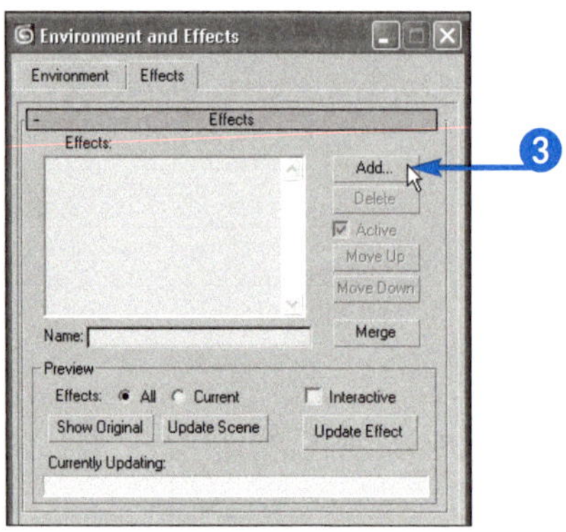

The Add Effect dialog box appears.

4. Click Film Grain.
5. Click OK.

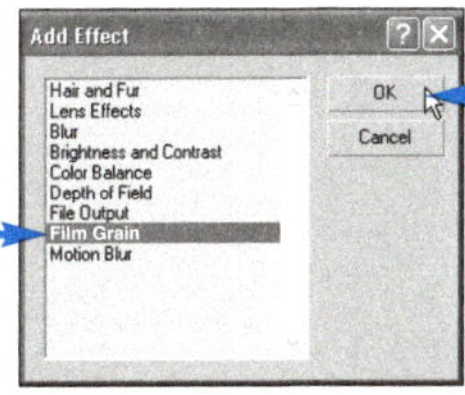

The Film Grain effect appears in the Effects list.

6. Click the Interactive option (☐ changes to ☑).

   The scene renders.

7. Type the amount of film grain that you want.

   The rendering of the scene updates to show the Film Grain effect.

MASTER IT

Can I apply multiple effects to my scene?

▼ Yes. You can apply any combination of effects that appear in the list in the Add Effect dialog box. When you add multiple effects to the scene, their order in the Effects list box determines the order in which 3ds Max adds them to your scene. For example, if you have two effects, the top effect is added first, followed by the effect that appears next in the list. The order in which 3ds Max adds the effects can change the appearance of your scene. You can reorder the list of effects using the Move Up and Move Down buttons to move a selected effect.

How do I use effects that I applied to another scene?

▼ You can merge effects from another scene that you have created. This allows you to apply the same effect values to both scenes. To merge effects from another scene, click Merge in the Effects panel. The Open dialog box appears. Locate and select the scene file that contains the effects that you want to use, and click Open. In the Merge Rendering Effects dialog box, click to select the effects that you want to merge into the current scene, and then click OK. The selected effects are added to the list of effects for your current scene.

Apply a Color Balance Effect

You can apply a Color Balance effect to correct a color cast in your scene. For example, you can add a specific color tint to the scene by using the different color channels.

You can apply a Color Balance effect in the Effects panel of the Environment and Effects dialog box. 3ds Max applies all of the effects that you add using the Effects panel to your scene in post-production. As a result, 3ds Max applies the effects on top of the rendered scene allowing you to employ the effect interactively and instantly see the results as you move the color sliders to change the color tint, without having to re-render the scene.

When you select a Color Balance effect, the Color Balance Parameters rollout displays in the Effects panel. The rollout contains sliders for setting the Cyan-Red, Magenta-Green, and Yellow-Blue color channels. When you drag the slider toward a side, 3ds Max tints the scene with the corresponding color. The Preserve Luminosity option maintains the luminosity of the scene while applying the specified color tint. The Ignore Background option prevents 3ds Max from applying the effect to the background.

Apply a Color Balance Effect

1. Click Rendering.
2. Click Effects.

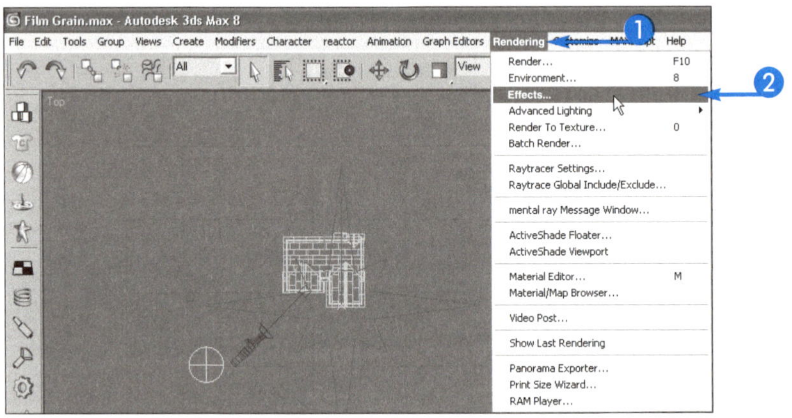

The Environment and Effects dialog box appears, displaying the Effects panel.

3. Click Add.

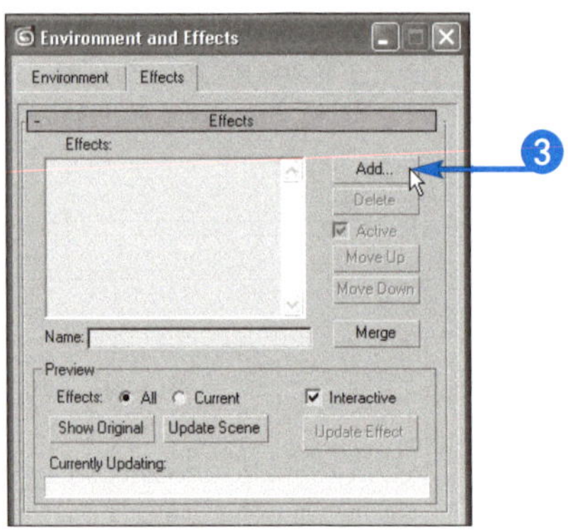

The Add Effect dialog box appears.

4 Click Color Balance.

5 Click OK.

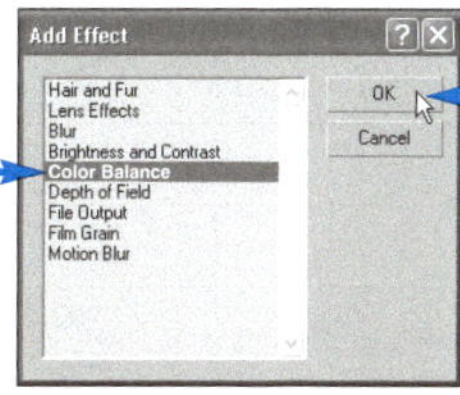

The Color Balance effect appears in the Effects list.

6 Click the Interactive option (☐ changes to ☑).

The scene renders.

7 Click and drag the color sliders to adjust the color channel of the rendered scene.

8 Click the Preserve Luminosity option (☐ changes to ☑).

The rendering of the scene updates to show the Color Balance effect.

How do I compare the effect to the original rendered scene?

Because the effects that you apply from the Effects panel are all applied after rendering is complete, you can switch the view in the Rendered Frame window to show the rendered scene either with or without the effects. To view the scene without the effects, click the Show Original button in the Effects rollout. When you click this button, 3ds Max temporarily removes the effects from the rendering, but the effect settings remain in the Effects panel. To once again view the scene with the effects, click Show Effects button in the same location that Show Original was.

What is the purpose of the Name field in the Effects rollout?

The Name field allows you to change the name of a selected effect. This is useful if you want to apply the same effect to your rendered scene multiple times. For example, you may want to use the Color Balance effect once to tint the entire scene, including the background, and another time to tint only the geometry in the scene. To change the name of an effect, select the effect in the Effects list box so that the name of the selected effect displays in the Name field. When you type a new name in the field, it is automatically updated.

Apply a Blur Effect

You can apply a Blur effect to any rendered scene to soften the appearance of the objects in the scene. For example, you may want to use this effect to create the illusion of fast camera movement.

You can apply a Blur effect to a scene in the Effects panel of the Environment and Effects dialog box. All of the effects that you add using the Effects panel are applied to your scene in post-production. As a result, 3ds Max applies the effects on top of the rendered scene. This actually allows you to employ the effect interactively and to instantly see the results as you change the blur parameters in the Effects panel, without having to re-render the scene.

When you select the Blur effect, the Blur Parameters rollout appears in the Effects panel. The rollout contains three different blurring methods: Uniform, Directional, and Radial. The Uniform blur effect applies an even blur across the entire scene, and the Directional blur effect allows you to blur along a certain direction. The Radial blur effect applies a blur from a user-defined central point in the image.

Apply a Blur Effect

1. Click Rendering.
2. Click Effects.

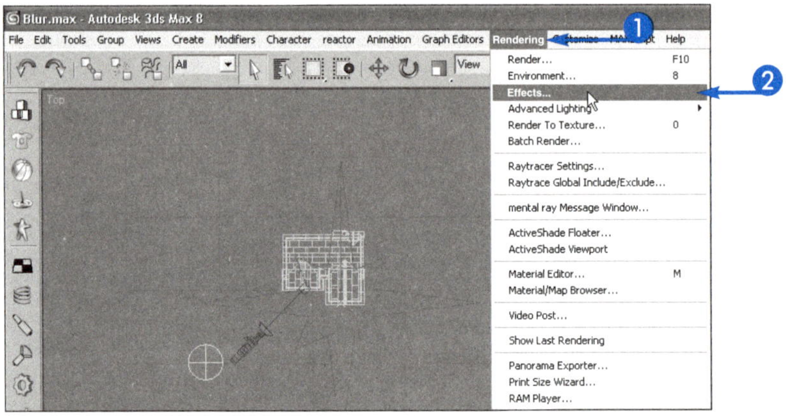

The Environment and Effects dialog box appears, displaying the Effects panel.

3. Click Add.

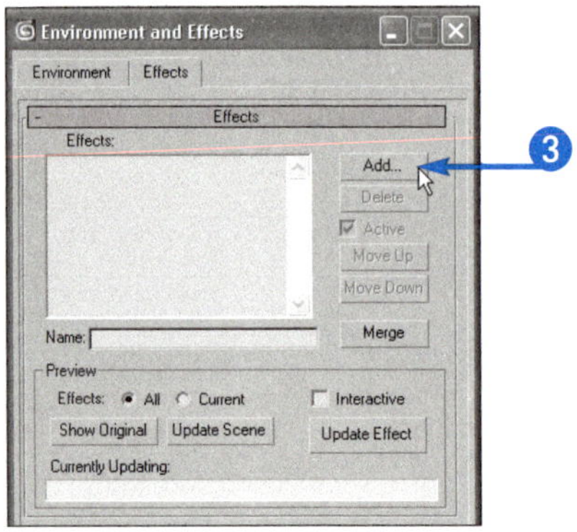

The Add Effect dialog box appears.

4 Click Blur.

5 Click OK.

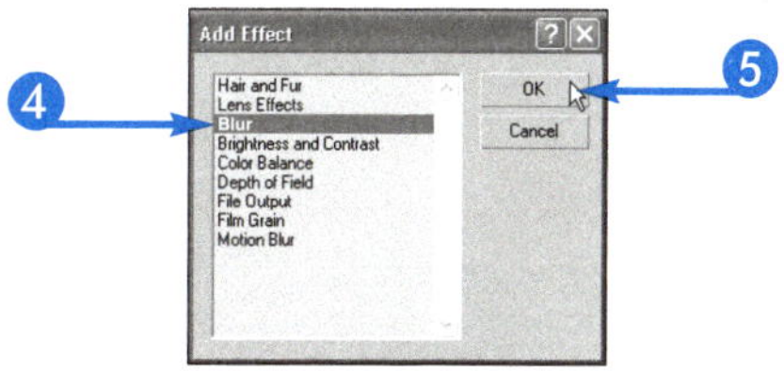

The Blur effect appears in the Effects list.

6 Click the Interactive option (☐ changes to ☑).

The scene renders.

7 Click a Blur type (○ changes to ◉).

8 Type a Pixel Radius percent.

If you want, you can specify other parameter values for the selected Blur effect.

3ds Max updates the rendering of the scene to show the Blur effect.

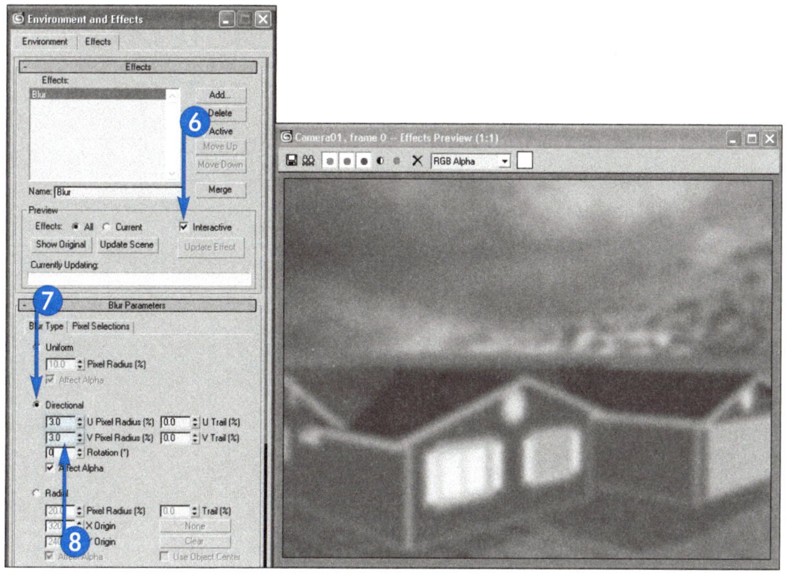

Do I have to blur the entire rendered scene?

▼ No. You can select parts of the scene to blur in the Pixel Selections tab in the Blur Parameters rollout. When you select this tab, you can specify that the blurring apply to only a part of the rendered scene. The Whole Image option blurs everything in the scene. The Non-Background option blurs everything but the background. The Luminance option blurs objects with the specified amount of luminance. The Map Mask option blurs by using a mask that you apply with the Material/Map Browser. The Object ID option blurs the objects with the specified object ID, and the Material ID option blurs the materials with the specified material ID.

What do the Trail [%] parameters do for the Directional and Radial blur methods?

▼ The Trail [%] parameters allow you to create a blur direction within your rendered scene. Setting a value for the Trail [%] parameter creates the illusion that the camera is moving in that direction by tapering off the Blur effect over distance. With the Directional method, you can specify either a U Trail [%] value to make the blur appear horizontally, or a V Trail [%] value to make the blur appear vertically. The Trail [%] value for the Radial blur causes the blur to appear as if the camera is moving toward the specified center of the blur.

23 Create Atmospheric Effects

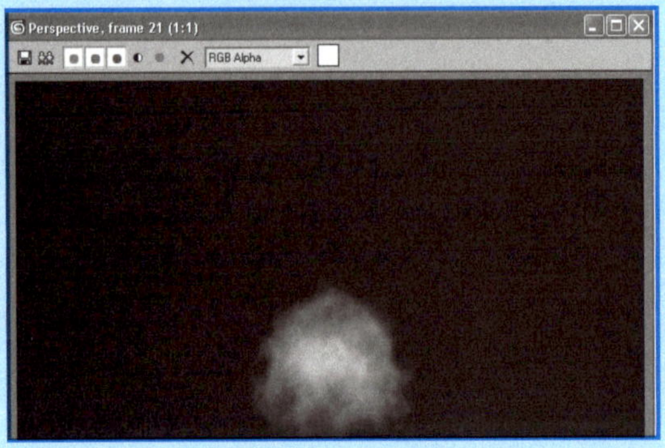

24 Working with Particle Systems

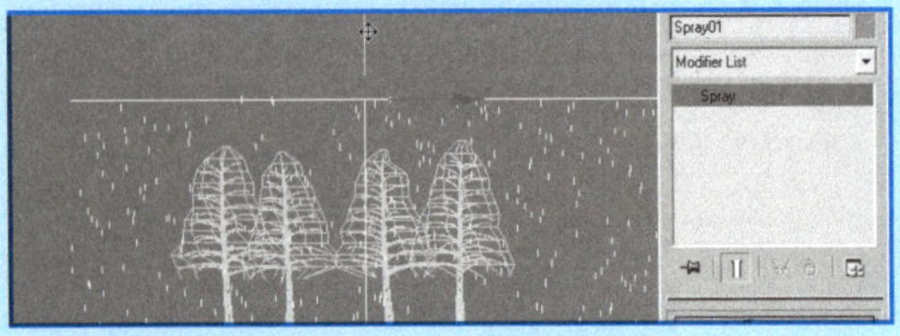

25 Using Space Warps

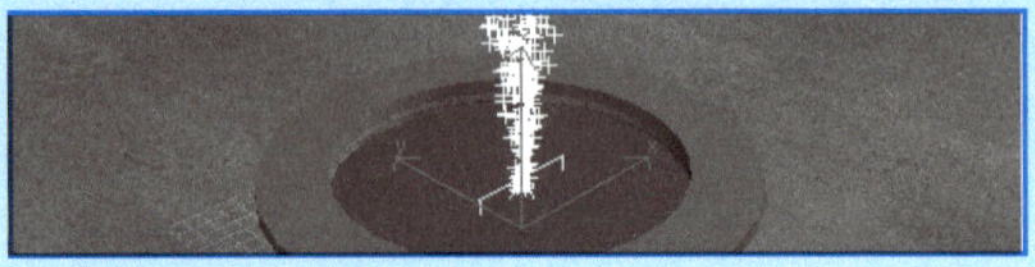

26 Working with the Reactor

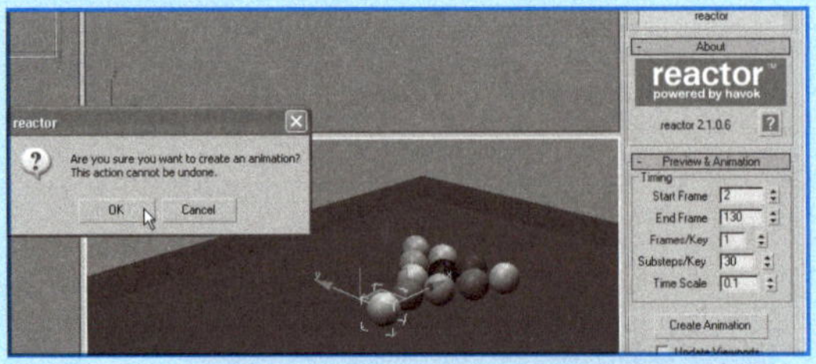

PART VII APPLY EFFECTS FOR SUPER RESULTS

27 Controlling a Character with Character Studio

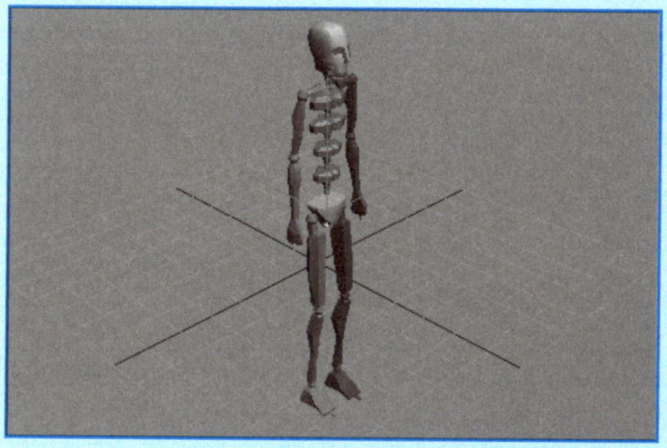

28 Adding Cloth to Your Scenes

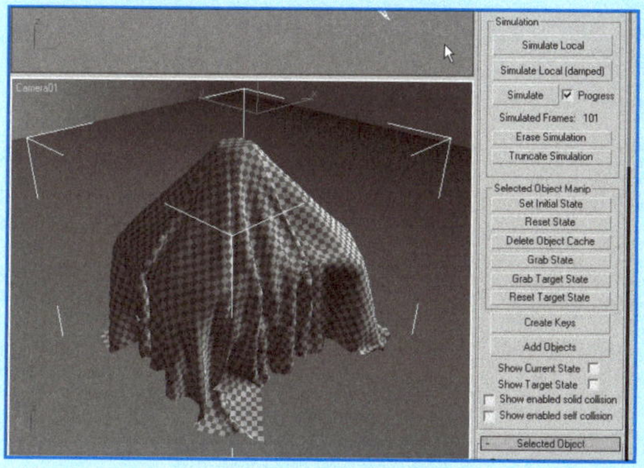

29 Adding Hair and Fur to Your Objects

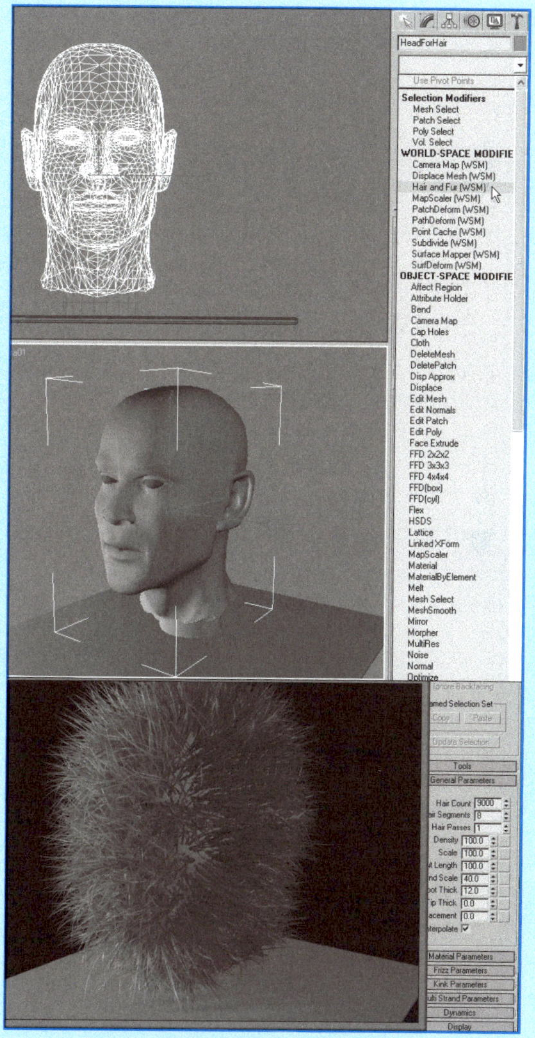

Understanding Atmospheric Effects

3ds Max provides four different atmospheric effects for creating 3D volumetric elements in your scene. These atmospheric effects allow you to create a three-dimensional appearance for fire, fog, and airborne particles in the path of a light.

You can add atmospheric effects to your scene using the Atmosphere rollout in the Environment tab of the Environment and Effects dialog box. When you select an effect, an additional effect-specific rollout appears where you can specify the parameters for the selected effect.

Although they exist in your scene just like other objects, atmospheric effects are not visible within the viewport. 3ds Max actually creates the effects during the rendering process.

All of the effects, except for the Fog effect, must be linked to another type of object in order to work. The Fire Effect and Volume Fog are linked to Helper objects called Atmospheric Apparatuses, and the Volume Light is linked to a light object.

3ds Max Atmospheric Effects

Effect	*Description*
Fire Effect	Creates a fire, smoke, or explosion effect that can be animated in your scene. You must use the Fire Effect with an Atmospheric Apparatus that defines the extents of the Fire Effect.
Fog	Creates a fog or haze effect throughout the entire scene. You can create either Standard fog, which has no upper or lower constraints, or Layered fog, which is limited to a user-defined upper and lower Z dimension in your scene.
Volume Fog	Creates a fog or haze effect that only exists within a specified part of the scene. You can create an Atmospheric Apparatus to define the extents of the Volume Fog within the scene.
Volume Light	Creates the effect of a beam of light piercing through a haze or fog from a specified light object in your scene. With the Volume Light effect, you must specify the light object or objects that produce the effect.

Atmospheric Apparatus

3ds Max provides three different Atmospheric Apparatuses, also called gizmos, which you can use to create atmospheric effects in your scene. You must use one of these gizmos when creating a Fire Effect or Volume Fog.

An Atmospheric Apparatus is one of several 3ds Max Helper object types. You can create an Atmospheric Apparatus from the Create panel using the Helper category button () and then selecting the Atmospheric Apparatus from the subcategory drop-down list. The Atmospheric Apparatus subcategory displays the buttons for the three different gizmo types. When you select one, an additional Parameter rollout appears with controls for customizing the gizmo in your scene.

You can add gizmos to the scene by clicking and dragging in a viewport. Although these gizmos appear in the viewports as wireframe objects, they do not render in the scene.

You can transform Atmospheric Apparatuses in your scene by using the Move, Rotate, and Scale tools, just like a geometry object. For more on using the transform tools, see Chapter 2.

Ⓐ Helpers Category Button

Displays the Helpers rollouts, where you can create helpers in your scene. Helpers are non-rendering objects that help you to perform different tasks. When working with an atmospheric effect, a helper localizes the effect.

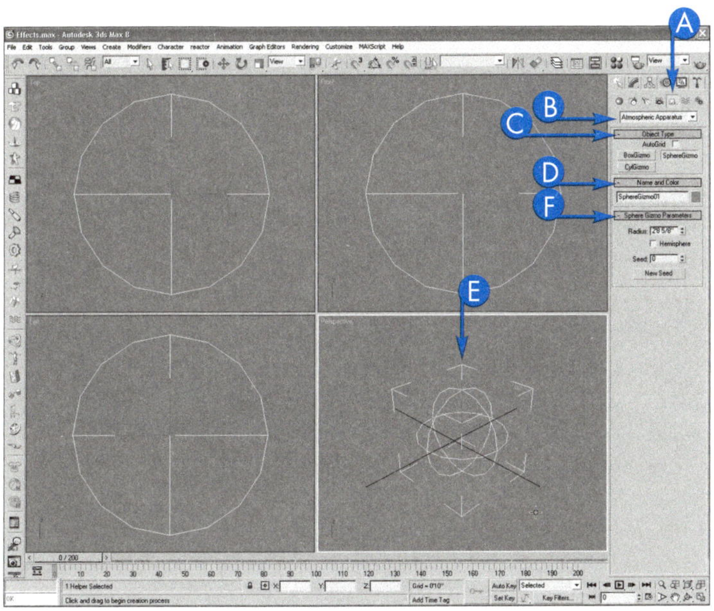

Ⓕ Gizmo Parameters Rollout

Each Atmospheric Apparatus type has a Parameters rollout where you can specify the size of the apparatus and the Seed value for calculating the atmospheric effect.

If you have multiple gizmos with the same atmospheric effect assigned, then the Seed value should be different so that the effects have a distinct appearance.

The SphereGizmo allows you to create a hemisphere shape where the bottom of the gizmo is flat.

Ⓑ Helper Subcategory List

Displays a list of helper subcategories that you can use to create helpers that are designed to work either as standalone devices or with a variety of 3ds Max tools.

Ⓒ Object Type Rollout

Displays the buttons for creating the three types of Atmospheric Apparatuses: BoxGizmo, SphereGizmo, and CylGizmo.

Ⓓ Name And Color Rollout

Indicates the name of a gizmo and its object color when it displays in the viewports.

Ⓔ Atmospheric Apparatus/Gizmo

A wireframe object that only displays in the viewports. The associated atmospheric effect displays within the confines of the gizmo when 3ds Max renders the scene.

Apply a Fire Effect

You can use the Fire Effect to create burning flames or smoke that is confined to a specific area in your scene. In order to create a Fire Effect in your scene, you must first create an Atmospheric Apparatus, or gizmo, that contains the entire Fire Effect.

You can create an Atmospheric Apparatus in the Create panel when you select the Helpers category. The Atmospheric Apparatus gizmo objects are part of the Atmospheric Apparatus subcategory.

You can use any of the three possible gizmos to create the Fire Effect by selecting the gizmo shape that best matches the shape of the effect that you want to create. For example, in most cases, the SphereGizmo works best for a typical fire. Because you can shape the SphereGizmo into a hemisphere, you can restrict the Fire Effect so that it is flat on the bottom.

When creating a gizmo for your effect, you can use the transform tools to scale, move, and rotate the gizmo. For example, with a Fire Effect, the fire is wider than it is tall, and so you can scale the gizmo to be longer or taller along the Z-axis.

Apply a Fire Effect

Create an Atmospheric Apparatus Gizmo

1. Click the Create Panel button ( ).
2. In the Create panel, click the Helpers button ( ).
3. Click here and select Atmospheric Apparatus.

   The Atmospheric Apparatus gizmo buttons display in the Object Type rollout.
4. Click SphereGizmo.
5. Click the Hemisphere option (☐ changes to ☑).
6. Click and drag in the Perspective viewport to create the gizmo.

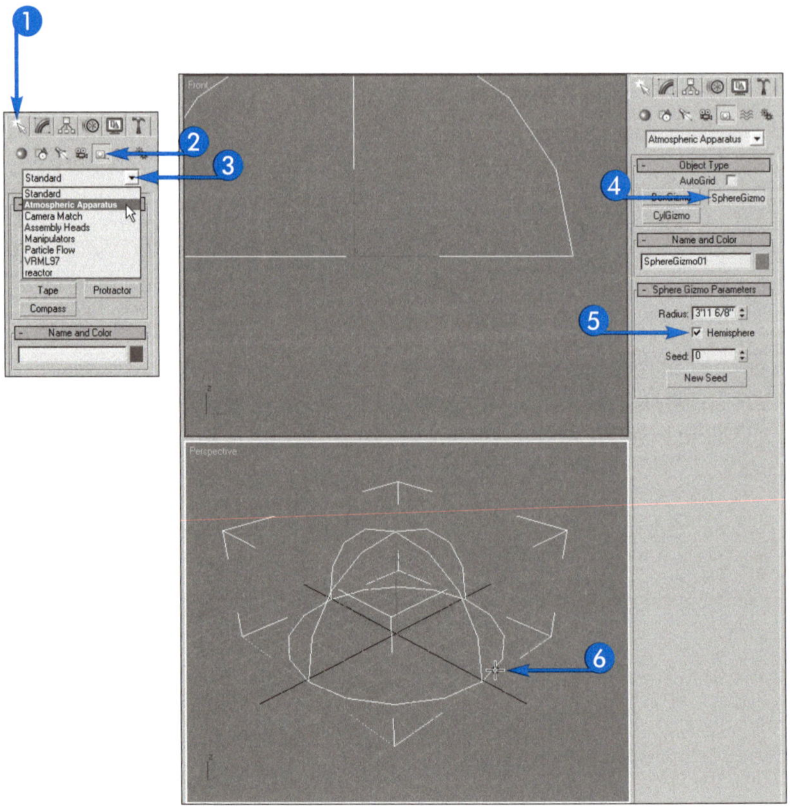

The Wireframe, hemisphere-shaped gizmo appears.

7. Click ▣.
8. Click and drag to scale the gizmo on the Z-axis.

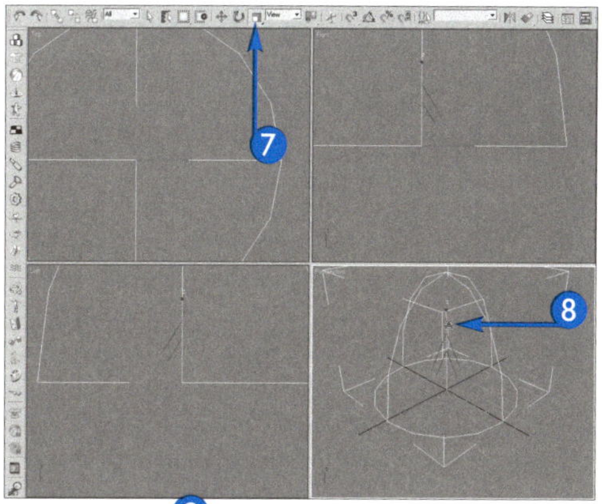

The gizmo appears taller to allow for higher flames.

9. Click the Modify panel button (◩).

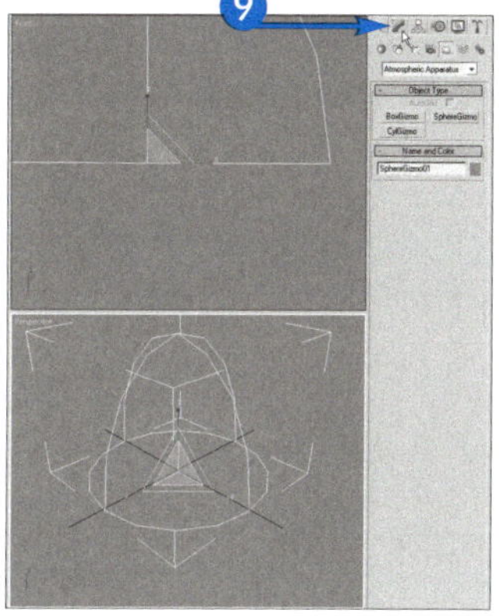

MASTER IT

What is the Seed parameter used for?

▼ The Seed parameter sets the base value that 3ds Max uses to mathematically calculate the appearance of the atmospheric effect that is associated with a particular Atmospheric Apparatus gizmo. The default value for this parameter is zero. If you are using multiple occurrences of the same effect in your scene, such as multiple camp fires or clouds, then assign a different Seed value to each instance. This ensures that each effect has a different appearance. You can assign a different Seed value either by typing a number in the field or by clicking New Seed. If you click New Seed, 3ds Max generates a random number and places it in the Seed field.

Can the Fire Effect illuminate a scene?

▼ No. 3ds Max adds the Fire Effect after it renders the scene, and so it does not add illumination or cast shadows in your scene. If you want to create a fire that appears to illuminate your scene, then you need to add lights to the scene and place them within the Atmospheric Apparatus objects. If you want the Fire Effect to cast shadows, then you need to enable the Shadow-casting parameter for the lights. For information on adding light objects to your scene, see Chapter 17.

continued

Apply a Fire Effect *(Continued)*

After creating the Atmospheric Apparatus to define the location of the effect, you must assign the Fire Effect to the gizmo in the Modify panel. This allows you to define which atmospheric effect displays within the boundaries of the gizmo.

When you click Add in the Atmospheres & Effects rollout, the Add Atmosphere dialog box only displays the Fire Effect and Volume Fog effect. The reason is that these are the only atmospheric effects that work with a gizmo.

After you assign the effect, you must set the parameter values in the Environment and Effects dialog box that appears. The Fire Effect Parameters rollout displays the settings for the effect, including the parameter values for the color, shape, and characteristics of the fire. These three groups of parameters control the appearance of the Fire Effect.

By default, the dialog box displays three colors that are commonly used to create the inner and outer flame colors and the smoke, although you can select any colors you want. You can also select one of two flame types: The Tendril type produces long flames, similar to what you see when you build a fire with a fixed base; the Fireball type creates rounder, more equally distributed flames.

Apply a Fire Effect *(continued)*

Create a Fire Effect

The Modify panel displays two rollouts for modifying the selected gizmo.

10 Click Add.

The Add Atmosphere dialog box appears.

11 Click Fire Effect.

12 Click OK.

The Fire Effect option displays in the list box in the Atmospheres & Effects rollout.

13 Click to select the effect.

14 Click Setup.

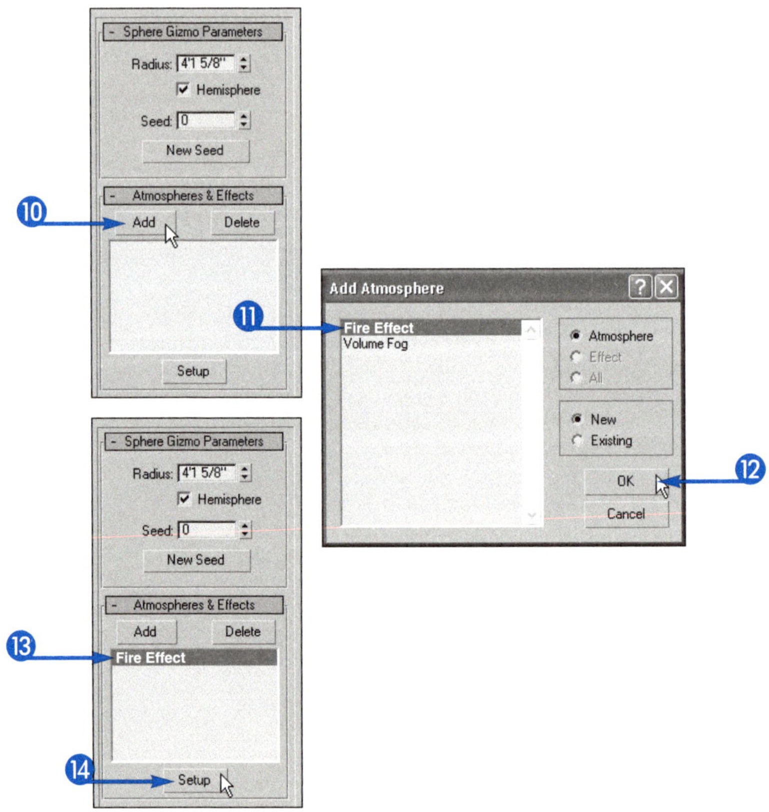

The Environment and Effects dialog box appears, displaying the Environment tab and the Fire Effect Parameters rollout.

15 Click to select the Tendril option (○ changes to ◉).

16 Type an amount in the Stretch field.

This example uses a value of 0.8.

17 Type a value in the Flame Size field.

This example uses a value of 18.0.

18 Click the Quick Render button (🫖).

Atmospheric effects only render in Camera or Perspective viewports.

The scene renders, creating the Fire Effect in the location that you specified.

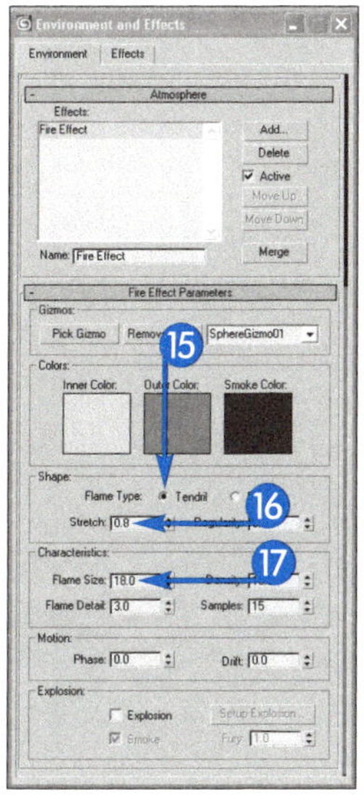

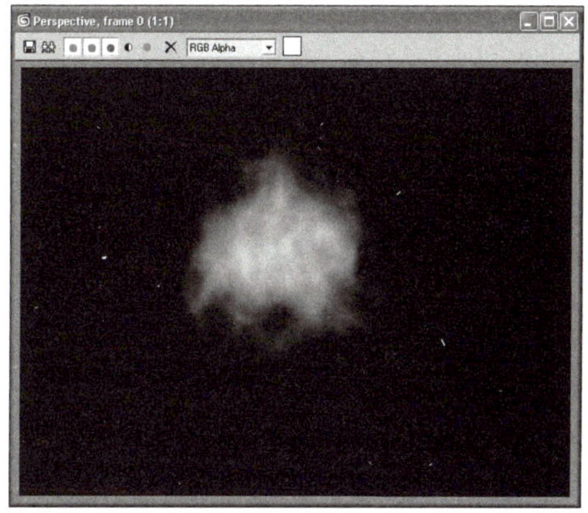

What parameter values should I set for the Fire Effect?

▼ 3ds Max assigns default values for the Fire Effect in each field in the Shape and Characteristics sections of the Environment and Effects dialog box. You can change the values of these parameter fields to change the appearance of the effect.

Parameter	*Description*
Stretch	Use with the "Tendril" flames option to control the length of the flames. Values greater than 1.0 create elongated and skinny flames, while values less than 1.0 create shorter and wider flames.
Regularity	Indicates the degree to which the gizmo is filled with the flame. Values can be between 0 and 1.0, with a value of 1.0 filling the gizmo entirely.
Flame Size	Determines the overall size of each flame. Values between 15.0 and 30.0 work best, with higher numbers used with fireballs and lower numbers with tendrils.
Density	Sets the density of the flames at the center. The higher the Density value, the brighter the flames are at the center.
Flame Detail	Determines the level of color change and the sharpness of each flame. Higher values produce sharper flames and longer render times.
Samples	Indicates how often the effect is calculated during rendering. When you specify a higher Samples value, 3ds Max creates more detail in the effect but requires longer render times.

Animate a Fire Effect

All of the parameter values that you create for a Fire Effect can change over time. When you animate these values and render the scene as an animation file, the Fire Effect resembles a burning fire when you play the animation.

To animate the Fire Effect, you need to create keyframes for the parameters in the Motion section of the Fire Effect Parameters rollout in the Environment and Effects dialog box. One method for animating the values is to activate Auto Key mode, drag the Time Slider to the end of the Active Time Segment, and then change the values.

There are two values in the Motion section: The Phase parameter specifies how wildly the fire burns; the Drift parameter controls how high the flames rise in the Z-axis. A high Drift value creates high-burning, hot flames. A low value creates a lower, slow-burning fire.

After specifying these values, you can render the scene to an animation file using the Render Scene dialog box. You must select the Active Time Segment option to render the entire animation sequence.

CD FILE: The Fire Effect.max file is available on the CD-ROM for you to practice animating a Fire Effect.

Animate a Fire Effect

1. Select the Atmospheric Apparatus gizmo in a Perspective or Camera viewport.
2. Click .
3. In the Modify panel, click Fire Effect in the list box in the Atmospheres & Effects rollout.
4. Click Setup.

   The Environment and Effects dialog box appears, displaying the Environment tab.

5. Click Auto Key.

   The Auto Key button, Time Slider, and viewport border turn red.

6. Click and drag the Time Slider to the end of the current time segment.
7. Type a value in the Phase field.
8. Type a value in the Drift field.

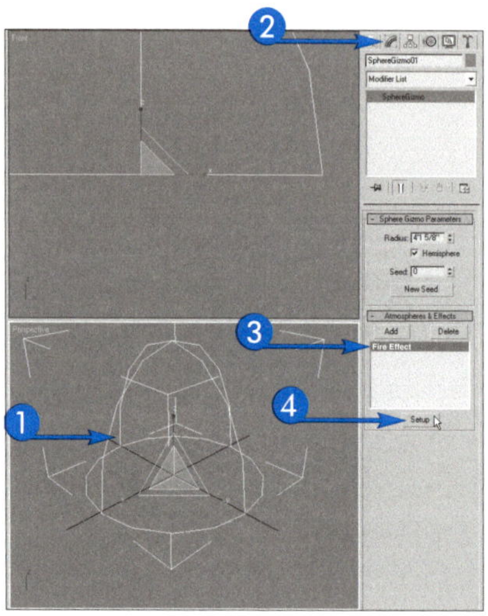

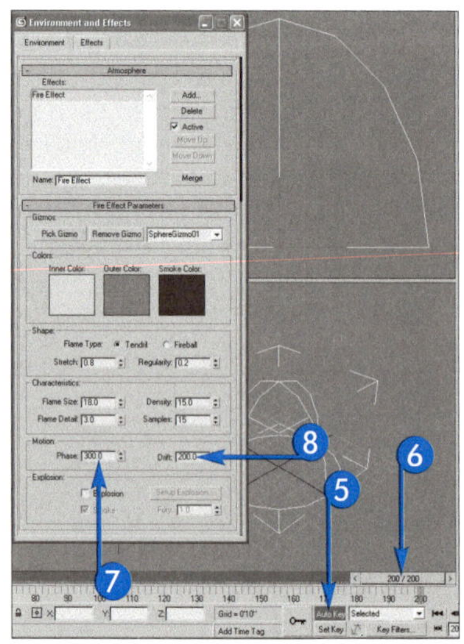

9. Repeat step 5 to deactivate the Auto Key.
10. Click the Render Scene button ( ).

    The Render Scene dialog box appears.
11. Click the Active Time Segment option (○ changes to ◉).
12. Click the Save File option (☐ changes to ☑).
    - If you have not specified a file name, then click Files and specify a name for the animation file that you want to create.

Note: *For more information on rendering, see Chapter 21.*

13. Click Render.

    3ds Max renders the animation frames.

    When the rendering process is complete, you can open and view the newly created animation file by clicking File and then clicking View Image File.

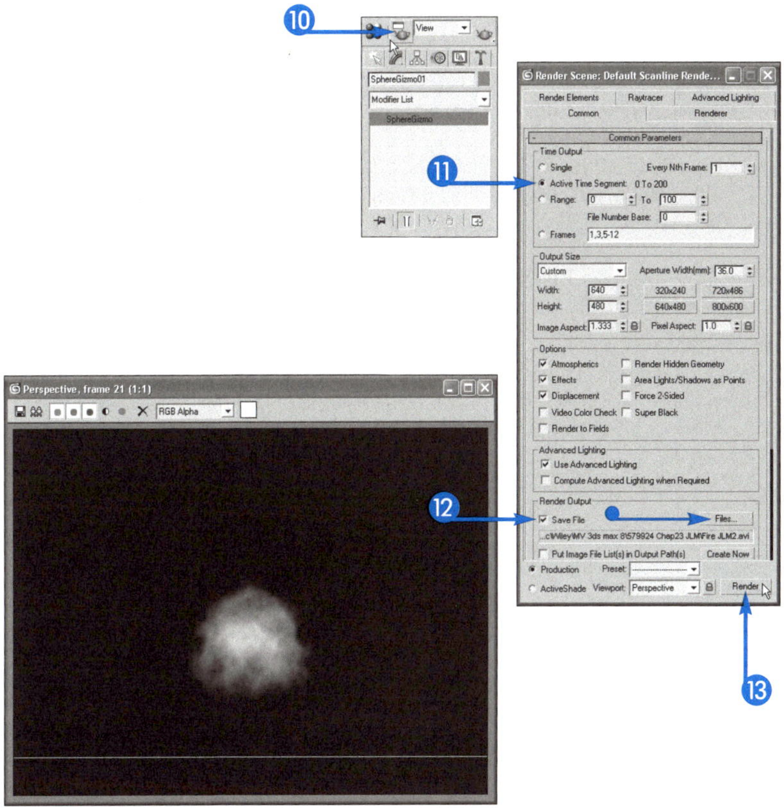

MASTER IT

Why do the flames in the fire get faster and then slow down?

▼ When you animate a parameter value, 3ds Max automatically assigns an Auto function curve to the animation to create a smooth transition between key values. With an Auto curve, the values appear to start off slow, speed up, and then slow down again before the next key. This technique prevents you from overshooting the key value. However, when creating a Fire Effect, this type of animation is not realistic. You can replace the Auto curve in the Curve Editor. You need to set the Phase and Drift curves under the Environment, Fire Effect tracks to Linear curves by clicking the Set Tangents to Linear button ( ). See Chapter 11 for information on the Curve Editor.

Can I use the Preview Animation option to see how the Fire Effect will look?

▼ No. The Preview Animation option — which you can access by clicking Animation and then clicking Make Preview — does not generate atmospheric effects. In order to view an animation that you have created for an atmospheric effect, you must render the scene to a file using the Render Scene dialog box. When you render to a file, 3ds Max creates an animation file that contains the specified frames. You can select either the entire active time segment or a specific range of frames. For more information on using the Render Scene dialog box to render to a file, see Chapter 21.

Apply a Fog Effect

You can create a Fog effect that obscures the objects and background by adding a hazy appearance to your scene. When you apply the Fog effect, 3ds Max applies it to the entire scene using the parameters that you specify in the Fog Parameters rollout in the Environment and Effects dialog box.

There are two types of Fog effect that you can create: Standard or Layered. The Standard type applies the fog to the entire scene. You can control the density of Standard fog by entering a Far percent value, and the density of Layered fog by entering a Density value. The Layered type controls the Fog effects vertically in your scene; you can specify a Top and Bottom value to control the maximum and minimum Z-axis range for the fog. You can also create tiers of fog by adding multiple Fog effects and then specifying different Top and Bottom values to indicate the location and size of each layer.

You must render the scene in a Perspective or Camera viewport in order to see the Fog effect because the other viewports cannot display it.

CD FILE: The FogEffect.max file is available on the CD-ROM for you to practice creating a Fog effect.

Apply a Fog Effect

1. Click Rendering.
2. Click Environment.

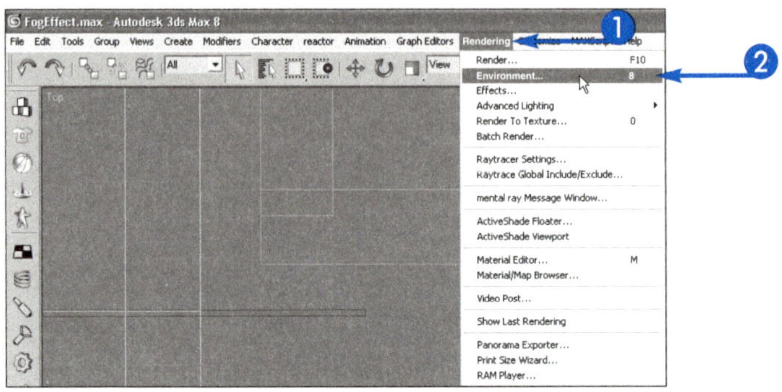

The Environment and Effects dialog box appears, displaying the Environment tab.

3. Click Add.

The Add Atmospheric Effect dialog box appears.

4. Click Fog.
5. Click OK.

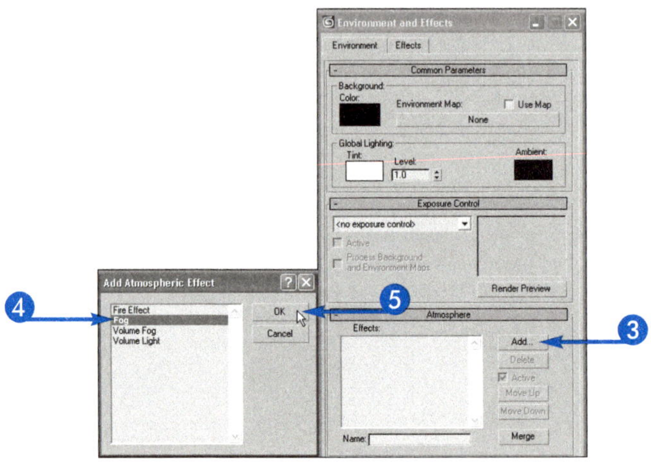

3ds Max adds the Fog effect to the list box.

6. Click the Layered option (○ changes to ◉) or click the Standard option to create a standard Fog effect.
7. Type a Top and Bottom value.
8. Type a Density value for the fog.
9. Click the Horizon Noise option (☐ changes to ☑).
10. Click [Render button].

3ds Max renders the scene, and applies a Fog effect using the parameter values that you specified.

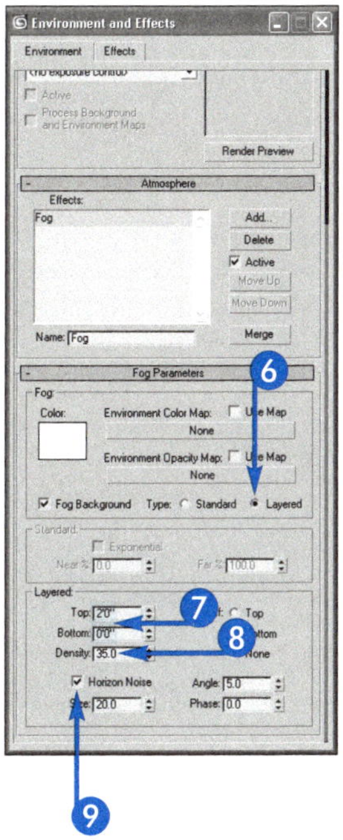

MASTER IT

Should I change the fog color?

▼ It depends upon the type of effect that you are trying to create in your scene. By default, 3ds Max uses white as the fog color, and the scene's background color tends to bleed through. The degree of the fog color that 3ds Max applies is determined by the density of the fog. You can change the fog color by clicking the Color swatch and selecting a different color in the Color Selector dialog box. For example, you can select green or purple for an eerie effect or a pale blue to imply a colder environment.

What do the Map buttons do?

▼ The two Map buttons allow you to use image maps to control the color and density of the fog in your scene. When you click a Map button, the Material/Map Browser appears and allows you to select a map to use. With the Environment Color Map button, you select a map to use as the color for the fog. With the Environment Opacity Map button, you select a map to use to determine the fog density. The Smoke and Noise maps work well for creating fog effects in your scene. For information on Noise and other map types, see Chapters 14, 15, and 16.

Animate a Fog Effect

You can animate a Fog effect to add movement to the fog in your scene. For example, you can create the effect of fog rolling in at dusk.

To animate a Fog effect, you can create keyframes that contain different values for the fog parameters. You can animate all of the parameters for both types of fog. For example, with the Standard fog type, you can change the values of the Near % or Far % parameters to change the density of the fog in the scene. With Layered fog, you can change the parameter values to move or expand the fog tiers.

You can use Auto Key to create keyframes for your animation. You can click and drag the Time Slider to the frame where you want to create the keyframe and then specify the parameter values that you want. Keep in mind that when you animate environmental effects, the keys do not display on the Track bar.

Once you set the animation length in the Render Scene dialog box, you can render the scene to an animated file format or to sequential still frames.

CD FILE: The FogEffectAnimate.max file is available on the CD-ROM for you to practice animating a Fog effect.

Animate a Fog Effect

1. In the Environment and Effects dialog box, click Fog.

   Note: *To display the Environment and Effects dialog box, click Rendering, and then click Environment.*

2. Click Auto Key.
3. Click and drag the Time Slider to the end of the Active Time Segment.
4. Type the new parameter values for the new keyframe.

   3ds Max displays red brackets around the spinners for each animated parameter.

5. Repeat step 2 to deactivate Auto Key mode.
6. Click [icon].

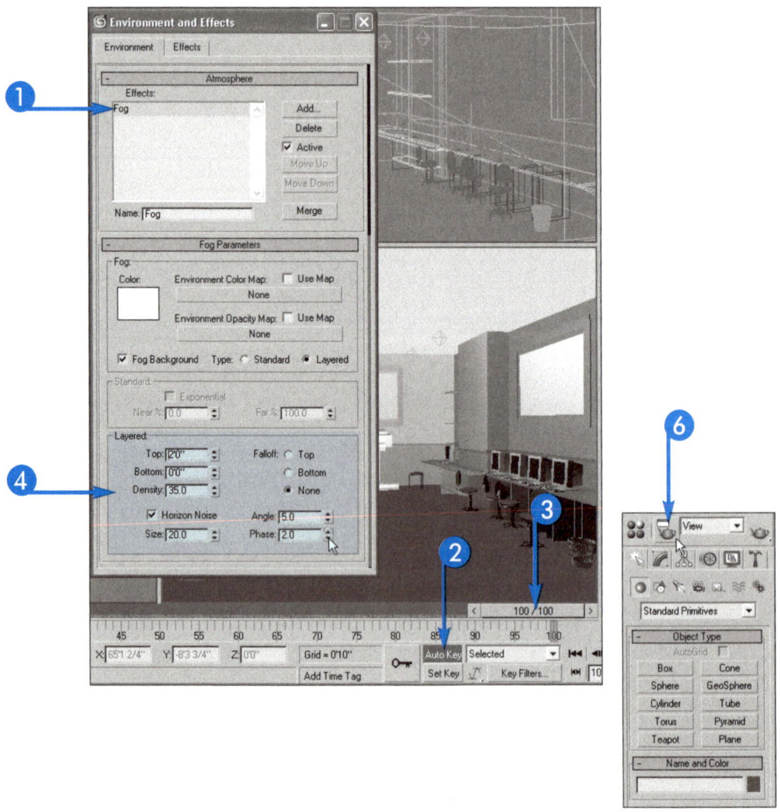

The Render Scene dialog box appears.

7. Click the Active Time Segment option (○ changes to ◉).
8. Click the Save File option (☐ changes to ☑).
   - If you have not specified a filename, then click Files and specify a name for the animation file that you want to create.
9. Click Render.

3ds Max renders the animation frames.

When the rendering process is complete, you can open and view the newly created animation file by clicking File and then clicking View Image File.

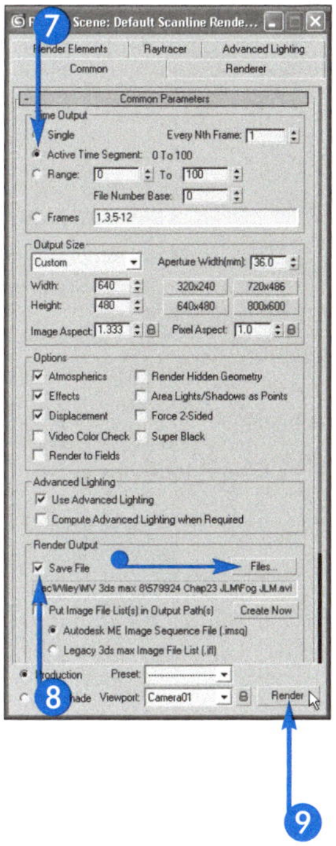

MASTER IT

If my animation is not visible as keys in the Track bar how do I know that my effect is animated?

▼ You can see the Fog effect parameters that have been animated in the Environment and Effects dialog box. When you view the parameters of an environmental effect that has been modified, red brackets appear around the spinners for the parameters that are animated. You can see the parameter values change at each frame by dragging, or scrubbing, the Time Slider. As you drag the Time Slider, the animated values change. For more information on animating parameter values, see Chapter 8.

Why does the entire scene have fog when I have specified the Top and Bottom values for the Layered fog type?

▼ You can use the layered Fog effect when your camera or point of view is located either above or below the fog tier. If your camera is inside the fog bank, then the fog obscures the entire screen. To determine the elevation of your camera, select it, click the Move transform, and then read the Z-axis value in the Transform Type-Ins. If the value is between the Top and Bottom values of the layered fog, then your camera is in the fog bank. For information on the the Move transform and the Transform Type-Ins, see Chapter 2.

Apply a Volume Light Effect

You can use a Volume Light effect to simulate the appearance of a beam of light, such as from a flashlight or headlight, reflecting off particulate matter in the air.

You can create a Volume Light effect in the Environment tab of the Environment and Effects dialog box. In order to use a Volume Light effect, you must associate it with a light that is producing illumination in the scene. Although you can associate a Volume Light to any light, Volume Light normally works best with a Spot or Directional light that focuses the illumination in a single direction.

3ds Max uses the settings for the light to create the Volume Light effect. For example, the Volume Light boundaries are based on the cone size settings for the light object. For more information, see Chapter 17.

You can use the fields in the Volume Light Parameters rollout to specify the volume, attenuation, and noise settings for the light. For example, the Density field adjusts the density of the light beams; the higher the density, the brighter and less opaque the beams appear.

The VolumeLight.max file is available on the CD-ROM for you to practice creating Volume Light effects.

Apply a Volume Light Effect

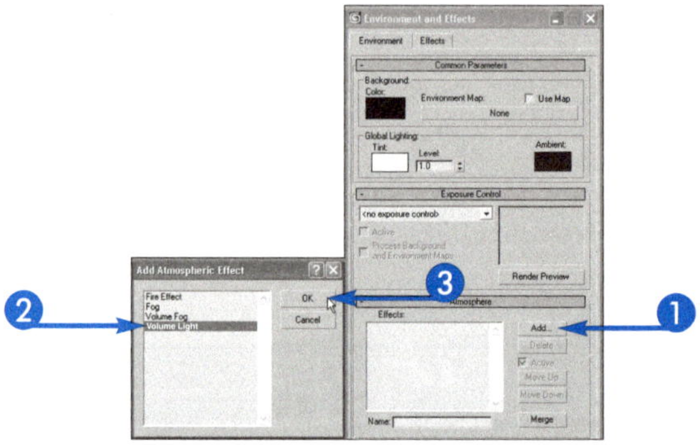

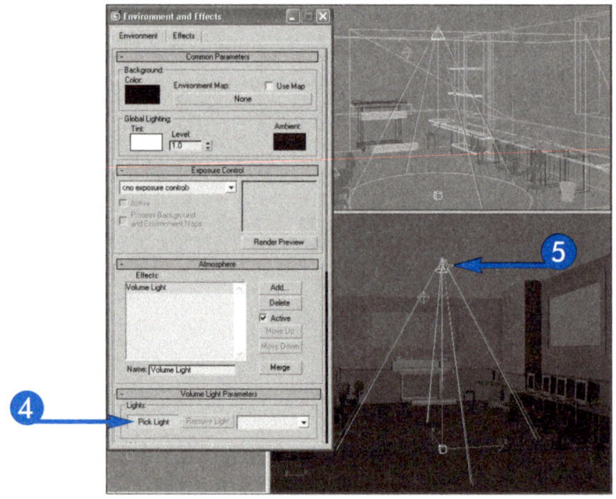

1. Click Add in the Environment tab of the Environment and Effects dialog box.

Note: *To display the Environment and Effects dialog box, click Rendering, and then click Environment.*

The Add Atmospheric Effect dialog box appears.

2. Click Volume Light.
3. Click OK.

The Volume Light effect appears in the list box.

4. Click Pick Light.
5. Click to select the light in the scene.

- The name of the associated light displays in the Lights field.

6 Type a value in the Density field to determine how much of the background is obscured by the effect.

If you want, you can specify other parameter values.

7 Click .

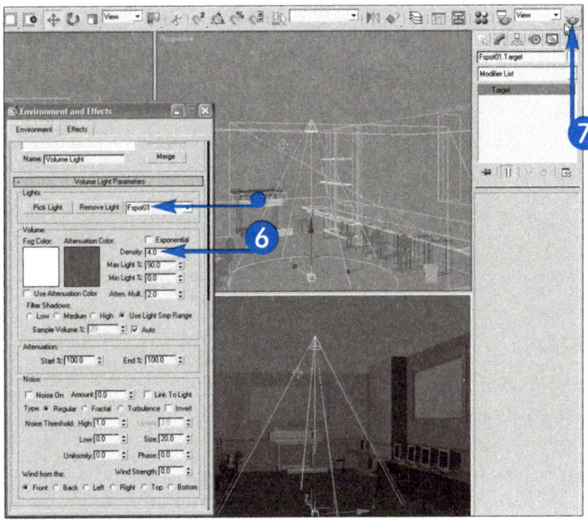

The scene renders, creating the Volume Light effect for the selected light object.

MASTER IT

Should I change the Fog Color and Attenuation Color parameters?

▼ Yes, if you want to change the appearance of your light beam. You can change both colors in the Color Selector by clicking a Color swatch. 3ds Max adds the fog color to the existing light color in order to produce the light beams in your scene. The attenuation color is the color of the light beam at a distance from the light source. To add the attenuation color to the rendered scene, you can select the Use Attenuation Color option (☐ changes to ☑). Attenuation must also be active for the light in order to work with the Volume Light effect.

Can I also add the Volume Light effect to a light from the Modify panel?

▼ Yes. You can assign a Volume Light effect to a light, either in the Environment and Effects dialog box, as described in these steps, or in the Modify panel. To use the Modify panel, you must first select the light. In the Modify panel, expand the Atmospheres & Effects rollout and click Add. In the Add Atmosphere or Effect dialog box, click Volume Light, and then click OK. If you want to modify the Volume Light effect, click the Setup button in the Atmospheres & Effects rollout or select the effect in the Environment and Effects dialog box.

Animate a Volume Light Effect

You can animate a Volume Light effect to show disturbances in the air, such as fog and wind. For example, you can create wispy light beams from a light source. In the real world, although the light beam may not move, atmospheric disturbances cause the particulate matter that is diffusing the light to move through it.

Although all of the parameters of the Volume Light effect can be animated, the parameters in the Noise section are used to create the light's random effects. To create movement within your effect, you can usually just animate the Phase parameter that affects the wind movement.

To create the animation, you can use Auto Key to create keyframes. You click and drag the Time Slider to the frame where you want to create the keyframe and then change the Phase value. Keep in mind that when you animate environmental effects, the keys do not display on the Track bar.

Once you set the animation, you must render the scene to an animated file format. You specify the file output in the Render scene dialog box.

The VolumeLightAnimate.max file is available on the CD-ROM for you to practice animating a Volume Light effect.

Animate a Volume Light Effect

1 Click Volume Light in the list box of the Environment and Effects dialog box.

Note: *To display this dialog box, click Rendering, and then click Environment.*

2 Click to select the Noise On option (☐ changes to ☑).

3 Click Auto Key.

4 Click and drag the Time Slider to the end of the Active Time Segment.

5 Type a Phase value at the current frame.

You can change other parameter values.

3ds Max displays red brackets around the spinners for the modified parameter.

6 Repeat step 3 to deactivate Auto Key mode.

7 Click .

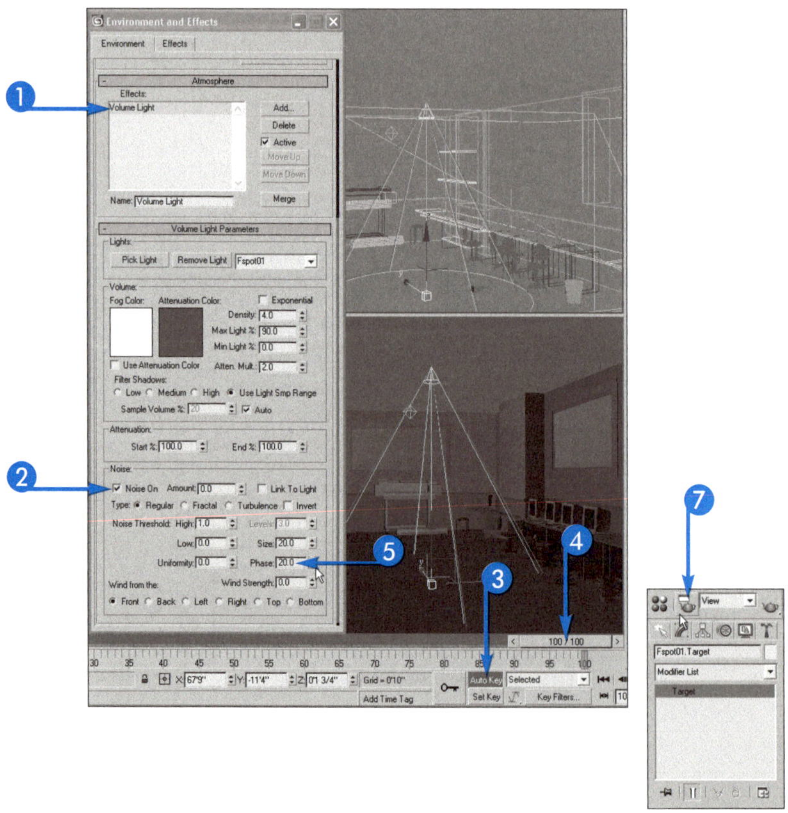

The Render Scene dialog box appears.

8. Click the Active Time Segment option (○ changes to ◉).

9. Click the Save File option (☐ changes to ☑).

- If you have not specified a filename, then click Files and specify a name for the animation file that you want to create.

10. Click Render.

3ds Max renders the animation frames.

When the rendering process is complete, you can open and view the newly created animation file.

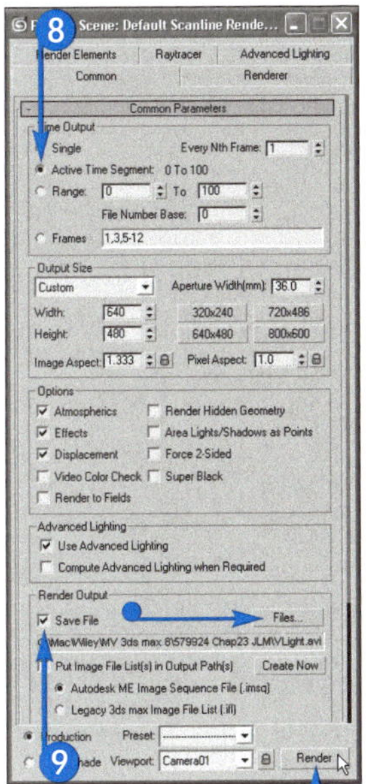

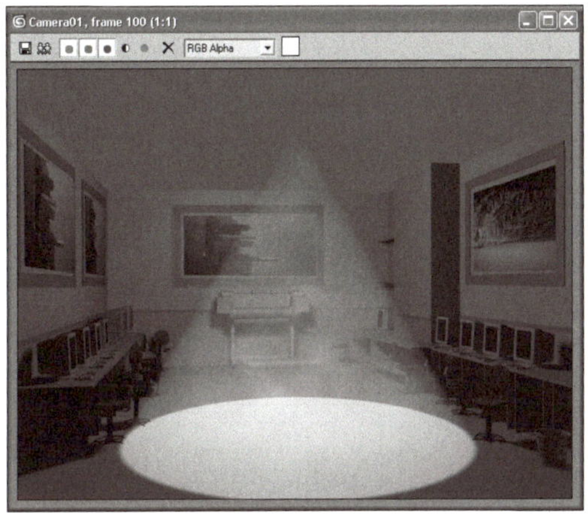

Is there a limit to the possible number of atmospheric effects in a scene?

▼ There is no numerical limit, but you may be limited by the power of your system. Atmospheric effects are computationally intensive and can slow down your system significantly. If some of the effects in your scene are in the distance, then consider substituting geometry in your scene for the effects. For example, track lights at the far end of a long corridor can use a transparent cone primitive rather than a volume light. Similarly,you can use pyramids with animated Noise modifier rather than the Fire Effect to simulate fires in distant campgrounds.

How do I remove animated parameter values from an environmental effect?

▼ Once you have animated a Volume Light parameter, you need to use the Curve Editor to remove the animation. To display the Curve Editor, click Graph Editors, and then click Track View – Curve Editor. In the Curve Editor, locate the parameter or track values that you want to remove. You can locate the parameter curves under Environment, Volume Light. An icon appears next to each track that is animated. Display the parameter curve. Click to select a key and press Delete to remove it. For more information on the Curve Editor, see Chapter 11.

Understanding Particle Systems

You can use particle systems to create natural phenomena such as rain, snow, spraying water, and smoke. A particle system is a tool that allows you to create and animate a large number of small, simple objects in order to create a fluid mass of objects. You control the objects within the system with an *emitter*, which determines the origin and movement direction of the particles and is the object that you select when you need to modify any of the particle system's parameters. The emitter is not visible when you render your 3ds Max scene.

3ds Max includes several different types of particles that can vary, based on shape, texture, color, and motion. Particle systems are treated as single objects that you create from the Create panel's Geometry tab. As with other object types, once you create a particle system, you can change it in the Modify panel by selecting the emitter in the viewports.

Although each particle system type displays different rollouts, each type requires the same basic information for determining the particle size and number, particle shape, animation timing, and emitter size.

A Object Type Rollout

Displays a list of the seven different types of particle systems that you can create in 3ds Max.

Each particle system has an emitter that controls particle discharge within your scene.

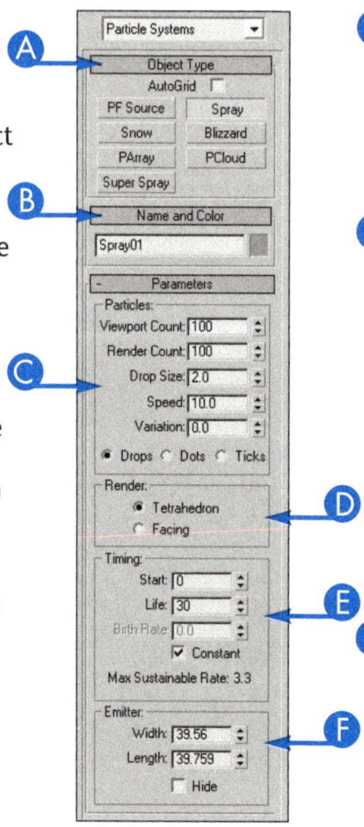

B Name and Color Rollout

Indicates the name of the particle system, as well as the color that 3ds Max uses to display the emitter object in the scene.

If you have not assigned a material, then 3ds Max applies this color to the generated particles.

C Particles Section

Allows you to specify the number of particles that are created, the particle size, the speed of particle movement from the emitter, and the variation in direction of movement for particles.

You can specify the maximum number of particles that display both in the viewports and in renderings. You can also choose whether the particles display as drops, dots, or ticks in the viewports.

D Render Section

Allows you to select how the particles display when they are rendered.

E Timing Section

Allows you to control the life cycle of the particles by indicating the frame where the particle emission starts, and the number of frames in which each particle should exist.

You can also indicate the number of new particles that should be created in each frame.

F Emitter Section

Indicates the size of the emitter in the scene.

Particle System Types

3ds Max has two different categories of particle systems — event-driven and non-event-driven. Event-driven particle systems use the results of test conditions to determine what action to perform on the particles. For example, you can create an event that changes the color of particles that are ten frames old. You create event-driven particle systems using the Particle Flow, or PF, Source type. The remaining particle systems are non-event-driven systems and use the same properties for handling the particles throughout the entire animation. 3ds Max has six different types of non-event-driven particle systems that you can select from the Create panel.

Non-Event-Driven Particle System Types

Type	*Description*
Spray	The most basic particle system. The particles travel in a straight line from the emitter surface, unless acted upon by a space warp. Useful for creating rain or a fountain.
Snow	Creates a particle system that simulates the falling of snow, or even confetti, by providing parameters to make the particles tumble as they fall from the emitter.
Blizzard	Provides an advanced version of the Snow particle system. With the Blizzard particle system type, you can use different mesh objects, including MetaParticles that can merge and separate, or instanced objects as the particles.
PArray	Allows you to select an object as the object emitter. This is the location from where all particles originate, even though the scene may contain a separate emitter object. You can also use the PArray type to create a particle system that consists of the fragmented pieces of an object.
PCloud	Creates a particle system that is confined to the volume of the PCloud emitter. Useful for particles that you want to confine to a specific volume, such as a cloud in the sky.
Super Spray	Provides an advanced version of the Spray particle system. With the Super Spray particle system type, you can use different mesh objects, including MetaParticles that can merge and separate, or instanced objects as the particles. More control is given over the particle motion than with the other non-event-driven particle systems.

Emitters

Each particle system type that you create adds an emitter object to the scene. The emitter is responsible for defining the direction of the particle travel and the area that the particles will cover. With most types of particle systems, the particles are emitted directly from the emitter object. This is true with the Spray, Snow, Super Spray, and Blizzard types. With the PArray and PCloud types, the emitter is actually a placeholder, with the particles coming from the associated object.

With particle systems that use the emitter as the creation point for the particles, you position the emitter object so that it is aligned and oriented correctly, based upon the direction of flow that you want for the particles. You also need to size it to indicate the amount of the scene that you want to cover with particles. You can use the Transform tools to move and rotate the emitter object.

A Emitter Size

You can size the emitter within the viewport to cover the part of the scene where the particles should flow.

B Emitter Vector

You can position the emitter in the scene so that the associated vector points in the direction for the particle flow.

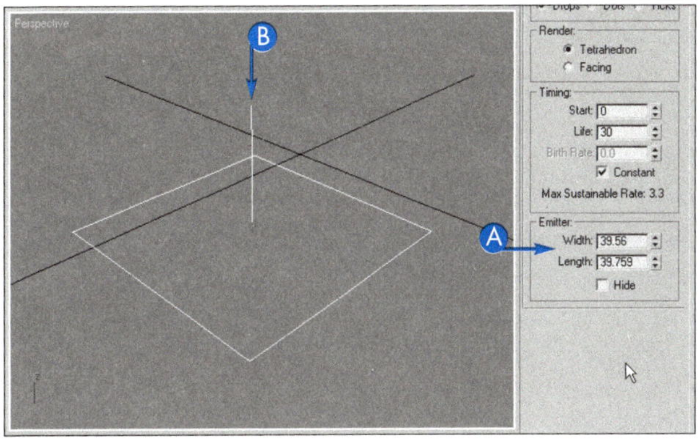

PART VII

Using Spray Particles

You can use the Spray particle system type to create a system that simulates the vertical movement of particles. This is useful when you want to simulate falling water drops, such as rain.

You can create a Spray particle system by selecting the Spray button in the Create panel when you select Particle Systems as the subcategory. The emitter is created with the vector pointing away from you in most viewports, and downward in a Perspective or Camera viewport. You can click and drag to create the emitter object, and you can also specify the emitter size in the emitter section parameters rollout. You need to use the Transform tools if you want to move or rotate the emitter in your scene.

You can adjust the parameter values as required. The Render Count indicates the maximum number of particles that display in a rendered frame. You can specify the size of each particle in the Drop Size field. Keep in mind that increasing the Birth Rate beyond the Maximum Sustainable Rate causes the particles to be emitted in bursts.

The Spray.max file is available on the CD-ROM for you to practice creating Spray particle systems.

Using Spray Particles

1. Click the Create Panel tab ( ) and then click the Geometry button ( ).
2. Click here and select Particle Systems.

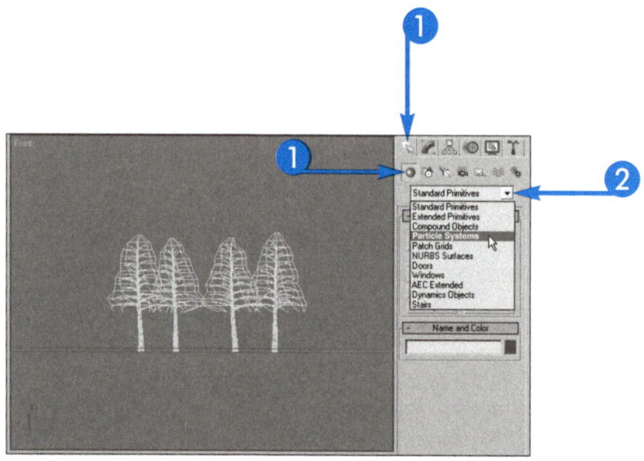

The particle system types are listed in the Object Type rollout.

3. Click Spray.
4. Click and drag in the Top viewport to create the Spray emitter.

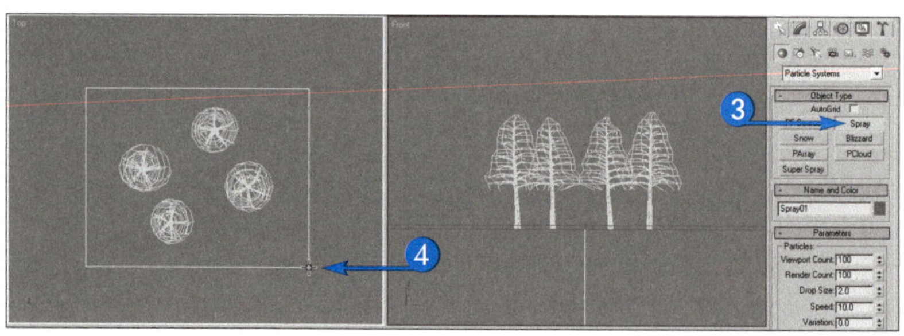

3ds Max creates and orients the emitter.

5. In the Viewport Count and Render Count fields, type the maximum number of particles to display.
6. Type the Drop Size.
7. Click the Tetrahedron option to create teardrop-shaped particles (○ changes to ◉).
8. Type the frame number when particles should first be created.
9. Type the number of frames that each particle should live.
10. Click the Select and Move button (✥).
11. Drag the emitter object up above the other objects in the scene.
12. Click the Material Editor button (⁘).

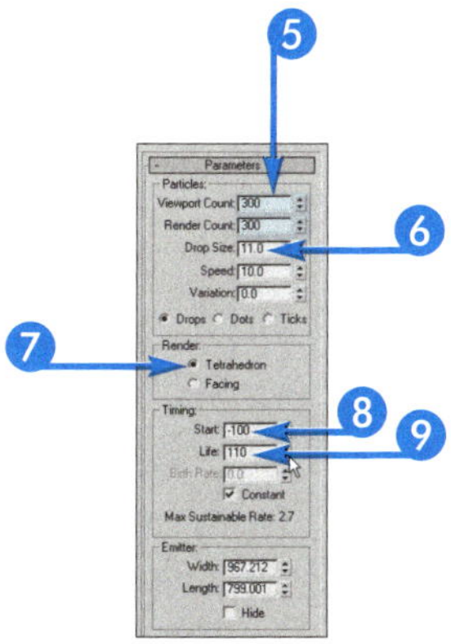

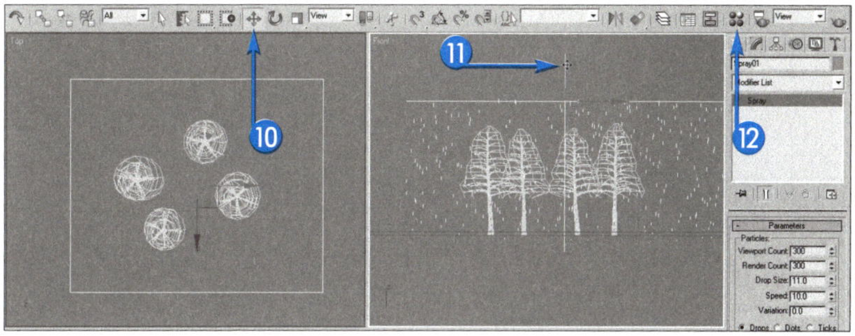

MASTER IT

Do I need to specify a viewport count?

No. The Viewport Count field indicates the number of particles that display when you view your scene in the viewports. The number of particles is also used when you create a preview of the animation by clicking Animation and then clicking Make Preview. The Viewport Count field has no effect on the final rendered scene. You can control the number of particles in your rendered scene with the Render Count field. The viewport count is generally equal to or lower than the render count to prevent your system from slowing down. For more information on previewing animations in 3ds Max, see Chapter 8.

When would I use the Facing particle shape?

The Facing particle shape creates a rectangular object for each particle. The rectangular object is always facing the viewport that is being rendered, such as toward the Camera or Perspective viewport. Each particle has a width and height that is equal to the specified Drop Size value. You can use this particle type to assign a material to the particle system that contains the opacity and diffuse maps needed to give the particles the appearance that you want, such as smoke or dust, without creating an extremely dense particle system. You can only render particles with the Facing render type in Perspective or Camera views.

continued

Using Spray Particles *(Continued)*

You need to assign the material that you want the Spray particles in your scene to use. As with any other object, you can create the material that you want to use in the Material Editor. With the Tetrahedron shape, because the particles in a spray system are typically quite small, you only usually need to set the Diffuse color to create the material effect. However, you can also adjust the Self-Illumination and other properties to control how the particles display in the scene.

Once you set up your particle system, you must render it using the Render Scene dialog box. You typically use particle systems in animations, and so you should render the Active Time Segment or a range of time in order to see the particle motion within the scene. Keep in mind that the particle creation does not start until the frame that you specify in the Start field.

To see the full effect of the particles, you must then render the animation to a file. For more information on rendering with the Render Scene dialog box, see Chapter 20.

Using Spray Particles *(continued)*

The Material Editor appears.

13 Create a material for the particles.

Note: *For more information on creating a material, see Chapters 14, 15, and 16.*

14 Click .

3ds Max applies the material to the particles.

15 Click the Render Scene button ().

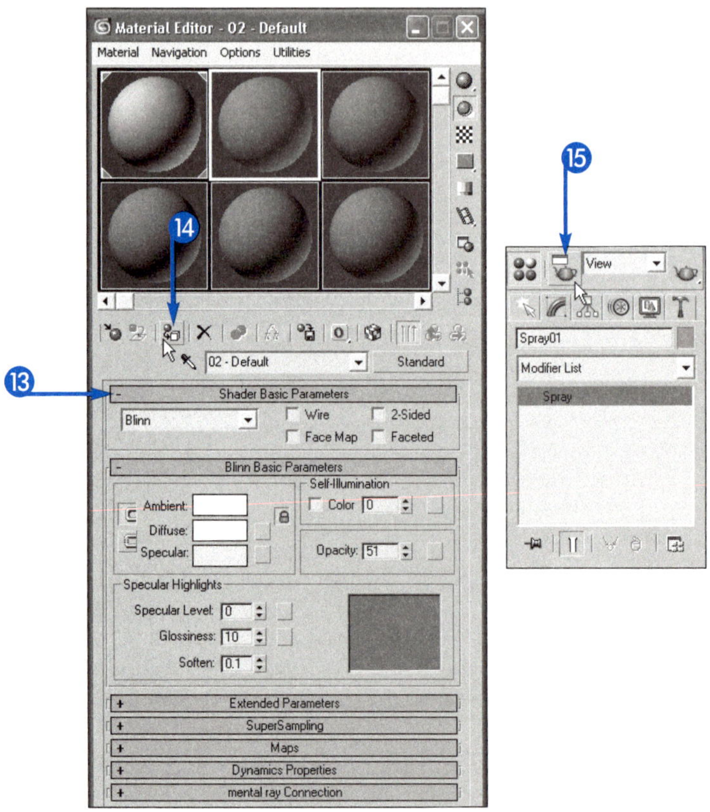

The Render Scene dialog box appears.

16 Click the Active Time Segment option (○ changes to ◉).

17 Click the Save File option (☐ changes to ☑).

- If you have not specified a file name, then click Files and specify an animation file to create.

18 Click Render.

3ds Max renders the animation frames.

When the rendering process is complete, you can open and view the animation file.

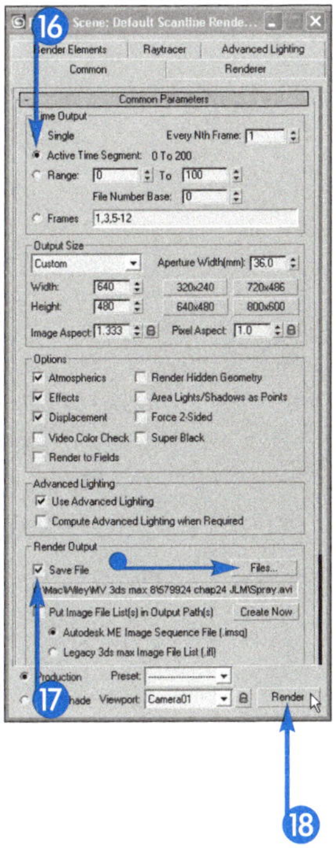

Can I use the Preview Animation to view the particle system animation in my scene?

Yes, but you will not see the same results as when you render the scene. When you preview the animation by clicking Animation and then clicking Make Preview, the preview only displays particles using the particle shape specified for display in the viewport. For a Spray particle system, the particles display as either Drops, Dots, or Ticks, depending upon the selection. Also, when you select the Make Preview option, the emitter object displays in the preview, rather than being hidden as it is in a true rendering. For more information on previewing animations, see Chapter 8.

Why do I not see the particles when I render one frame?

The parameters listed in the Timing section in the Parameters rollout determine the frames where particles display in the scene. The Start field indicates the first frame where particles are emitted. If the value in the Start field is zero, then particle emission starts in the first frame. However, if you render only that frame, then you may not see any particles. If you want the particles to exist as a stream at frame zero, then you can set the Start value to -10 or some other negative number. This begins the emission prior to frame zero. Also check to make sure that the Drop Size is not too small to display in the rendering.

Using Snow Particles

You can use the Snow particle system type to create particles that rotate randomly. This is useful for simulating falling snow or confetti.

To create a Snow particle system, you can select the Snow button in the Create panel when you select Particle Systems as the subcategory. You should create the Snow particle system emitter in the Top viewport. The emitter should also be large enough to emit particles through the viewed portion of the scene. When you create the emitter in the Top viewport, the particles fall in the negative Z direction. You can use the Transform tools to position the emitter at the top of your scene.

You can specify several parameter values for the particle system. The Render Count indicates the maximum number of particles that display in a rendered frame at one time, and you can specify the size of each particle in the Drop Size field. The Tumble parameters allow you to specify how much you want the particles to rotate; the Tumble field indicates the amount of rotation, and the Tumble Rate field indicates the particles' rotation speed.

CD FILE: The Snow.max file is available on the CD-ROM for you to practice creating Snow particle systems.

Using Snow Particles

1. Click and then click .
2. Click here and select Particle Systems.

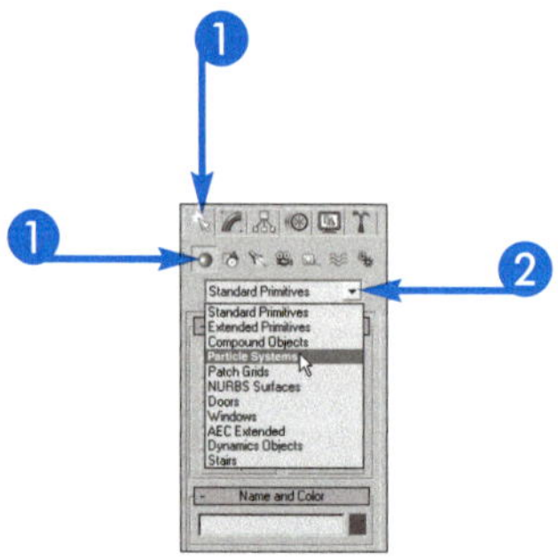

- The available particle system types appear in the Object Type rollout.

3. Click Snow.
4. Click and drag in the Top viewport to create the Snow emitter.

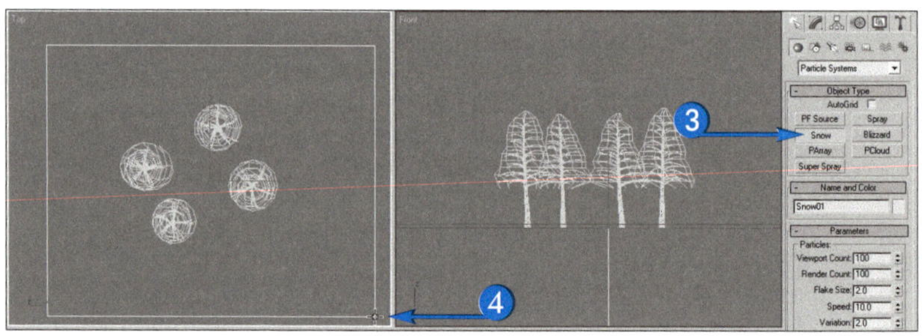

The emitter aligns with the Z-axis.

5. Type the maximum number of particles to display in a frame.
6. Type a particle size in the Flake Size field, and a value between 0 and 1 in the Tumble field.
7. Type a rotation speed in the Tumble Rate field.
8. Type the first frame number where particles should be created, and the number of frames that each particle should last.
9. Click .
10. Move the emitter object up above the other objects in the scene.
11. Click .

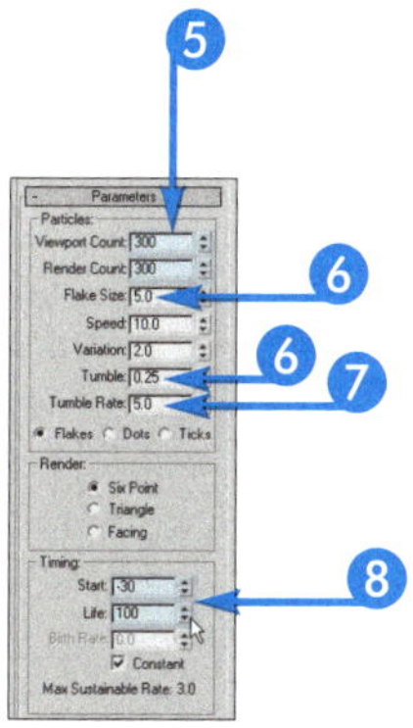

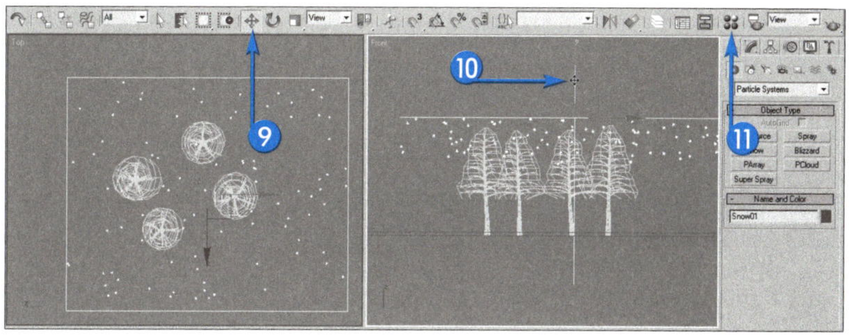

MASTER IT

What does the Birth Rate field do?

▼ The Birth Rate field allows you to specify the number of new particles that are created in each frame. This field is not available if you select the Constant option. If you select Constant, then 3ds Max determines the number of new particles to create by dividing the total number of particles in the Render Count field by the lifespan of the particles. To specify the number of particles that you want to create in each frame, click the Constant option to deselect it (☑ changes to ☐). Then type the number of particles that you want to create in the Birth Rate field. Specifying a number higher than the Constant Sustainable Rate leads to pauses in the emission of particles.

Do I need to specify values for both the Tumble and Tumble Rate parameters?

▼ No, although both parameters are related. The Tumble parameter specifies the amount of rotation that a particle makes as it falls. You can specify a value between zero and one, with zero indicating that the particles have no rotation. Each particle rotates around a randomly generated axis. The Tumble Rate parameter specifies the speed at which each particle rotates within the animation. The higher the value, the faster the particles rotate. Keep in mind that this value does not affect the falling speed of the particle, only the speed at which it revolves around the axis. If you set Tumble to zero, then the Tumble Rate parameter value is ignored.

continued

Using Snow Particles *(Continued)*

You need to assign the material that you want to use for creation of the Snow particles in your scene. If you do not assign a material, the scene renders using the object color. You can create the material for the particles in the Material Editor, using any of the available material options, including Opacity and Self-Illumination.

Once you have set up your particle system, you need to render it using the Render Scene dialog box. Particle systems are typically used in animations, and so you should render the Active Time Segment or a range of frames in order to see the particles being created. Keep in mind that the particle creation does not start until the frame specified in the Start field.

You then need to render the animation to a file or a sequence of still images. For more information on rendering with the Render Scene dialog box, see Chapter 20.

Once you create your animation file, you can view it by opening the file and playing it in the appropriate player.

Using Snow Particles *(continued)*

The Material Editor appears.

12. Create a material for the particles.

Note: *For more information on creating a material, see Chapters 14, 15, and 16.*

13. Click .

3ds Max applies the material to the particles.

14. Click .

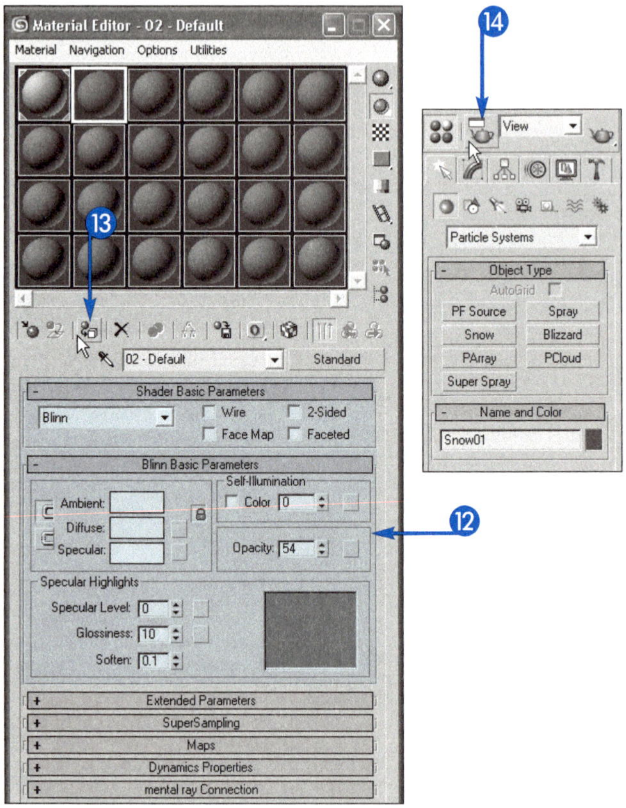

The Render Scene dialog box appears.

15 Click the Active Time Segment option (○ changes to ◉).

16 Click the Save File option (☐ changes to ☑).

- If you have not specified a file name, then click Files and specify an animation file to create.

17 Click Render.

3ds Max renders the animation frames.

When the rendering process is complete, you can open and view the animation file with the Spray particle system.

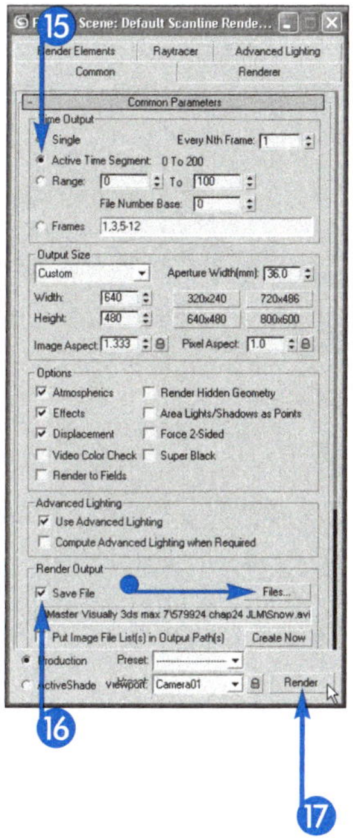

How do I change the size and creation rate of particles during the animation?

▼ The parameter values for the particle system can be animated. This allows you to change the values of different parameters during the animation. For example, you may want to change the Birth Rate value to increase the number of particles that are being produced, or you may want to increase the particle size. In order to animate any of the particle parameter values, you need to create keys for these values. The easiest method is to turn on Auto Key, move the Time Slider to the frames that you want for the keys, and then change the value. For more information on creating keys, see Chapter 8.

How do I create different-colored particles?

▼ In order to create particles that are rendered in different colors, you need to apply a Multi/Sub-Object material type to the particle system. By applying the Multi/Sub-Object material, you are using a single material that consists of several distinct sub-materials. When your scene is rendered, 3ds Max randomly applies a sub-material to each particle. This allows you to have one particle system emitting particles that are several different colors. Each sub-material can also have its own properties, such as Opacity or Self-Illumination. For more information on creating a Multi/Sub-Object material, see Chapter 16.

Using PArray Particles to Fragment an Object

You can use a PArray particle system to create particles that emit from an object's surface or contain fragmented chunks of the object. For example, you may want to make an object look like it has exploded into several pieces.

When you apply a PArray particle system to your scene, you associate the particle system directly to an object in the scene. All particle emission is generated from the surface of this object.

To create a PArray particle system, select Particle Systems as the subcategory, and then select the PArray button in the Create panel. Because the emitter is just a placeholder in your scene, it does not matter where it is created. After creating the emitter, you can associate it to the object that will emit the particles.

To create particles that consist of fragments of the object, you need to select Object Fragments as the particle type. This creates fragments that consist of the faces of the object. You can set the Thickness to give the fragments depth as they break away from the object. Fragments with a Thickness of zero are single-sided polygons.

CD FILE: The PArray.max file is available on the CD-ROM for you to practice creating PArray particle systems.

Using PArray Particles to Fragment an Object

1. Click and then click .
2. Click here and select Particle Systems.

   The available particle system types appear in the Object Type rollout.
3. Click PArray.
4. Click and drag in a viewport to create the PArray emitter.

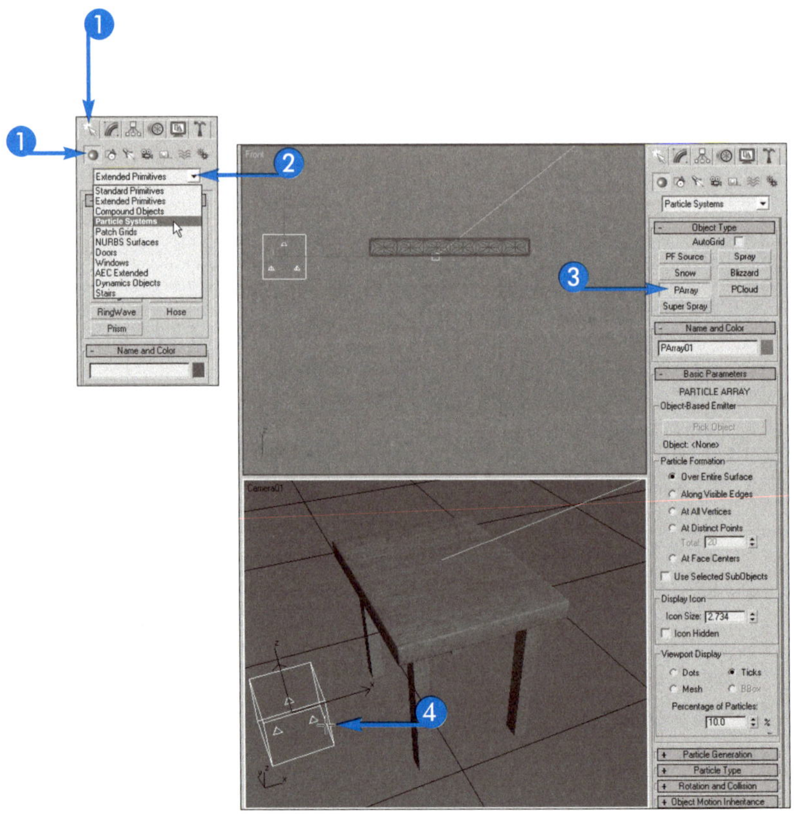

5 Click Pick Object.

6 Click the object in the scene that you want to emit the particles.

The object blinks briefly to acknowledge the association.

The particle icons display on the surface of the selected object.

7 In the Particle Type rollout, click the Object Fragments option (○ changes to ◉).

8 Type a value in the Thickness field.

9 Click .

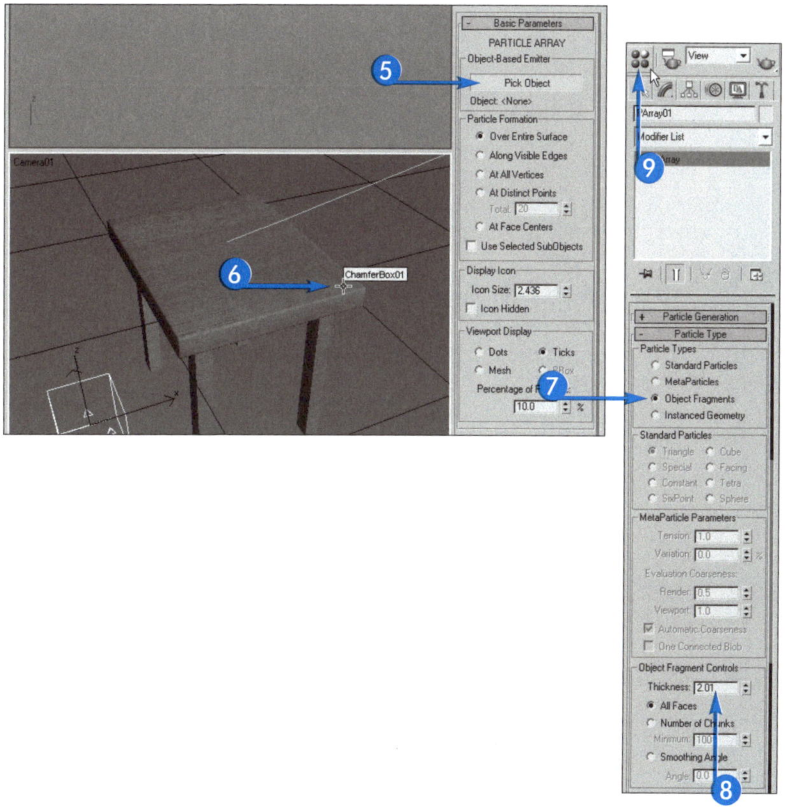

Can I delay the start of the object breaking into fragments?

Yes. As with the other non-event-driven particle systems, the start of the PArray particle creation is controlled by specific parameter values. With the PArray type, the Emit Start parameter indicates the frame where the particle generation begins. If you have selected the Object Fragments option for the PArray particle type, this is the frame where the particles that form the fragments of the object start to break apart. You can also specify when particles are removed from the scene by specifying a frame number in the Display Until field. When the animation reaches the specified frame, all particles are removed from the scene.

What are MetaParticles?

The MetaParticles are a particle type where the individual particles blend together when they get close to each other, to form blobs or streams of particles. This particle type works well when you want to simulate water, mercury, or other liquids with the particle system. When you select this particle type, you need to specify a Tension value. This value determines how easily the particles blend with one another. The higher the value, the fewer particles that blend together.

The MetaParticles particle type is available with the PArray, PCloud, Super Spray, and Blizzard particle systems. You can also consider using the BlobMesh compound object as instanced geometry to achieve an effect similar to MetaParticles.

continued

Using PArray Particles to Fragment an Object *(Continued)*

You can apply the same material to the PArray particle system that you applied to the selected object, to create the illusion that the object is breaking apart.

When you use any of the PArray particle types, the object remains in place as the emitter of the particles. Because you are creating the appearance of the object's breaking up, you want to hide the object in the scene. You do this by setting the Visibility of the object to zero in the Object Properties dialog box. If you do not do this, the particles fragment, but the object remains unaffected. Select the object, right-click, and then choose Properties to open the Object Properties dialog box.

Once you set up your particle system, you need to render it. Particle systems are typically used in animations, and so you should render the Active Time Segment or a range of frames to see the effect of the particles. For more information on rendering, see Chapter 20.

Once you create your animation file, you can view it by opening the file in the appropriate animation player.

Using PArray Particles to Fragment an Object *(continued)*

The Material Editor appears.

10 Select the material that you used for the emitter object.

11 Click .

The material is applied to the particles.

12 Select the emitter object, the table top in this example.

13 Right-click in the viewport to display a quad menu.

14 Click Properties.

The Object Properties dialog box appears.

15 In the General panel, type **0.0** in the Visibility field.

16 Click OK.

17 Click .

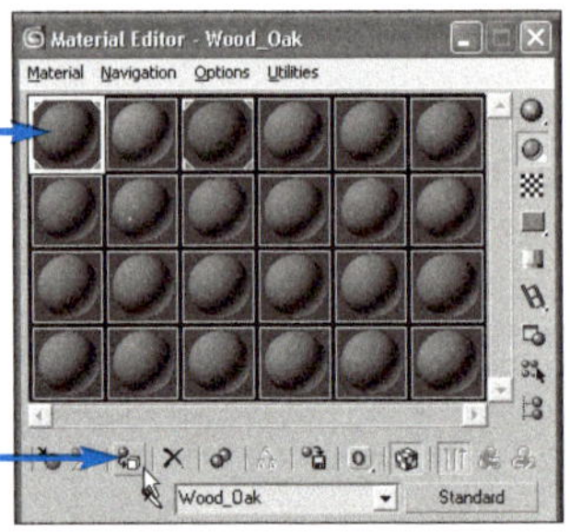

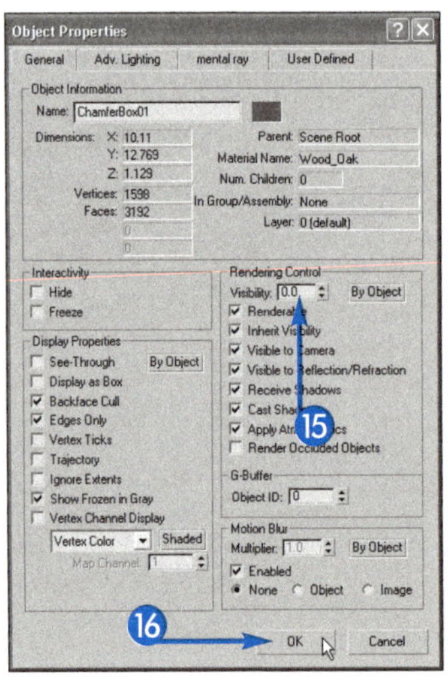

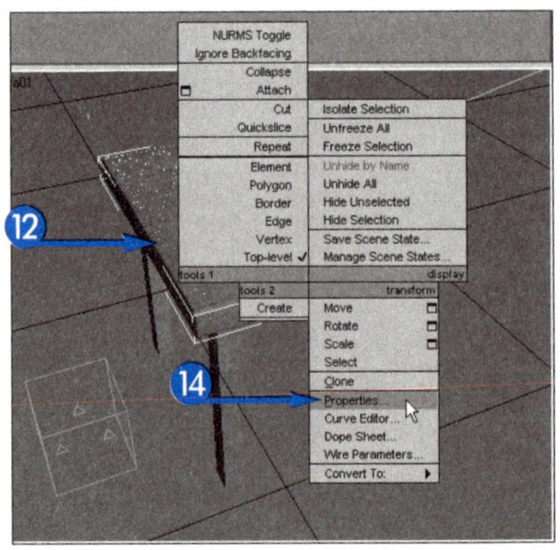

The Render Scene dialog box appears.

18 Click the Active Time Segment option (○ changes to ◉).

19 Click the Save File option (☐ changes to ☑).

- If you have not specified a file name, then click Files and specify an animation file to create.

20 Click Render.

3ds Max renders the animation frames.

When the rendering process is complete, you can open and view the animation file with the PArray particle system.

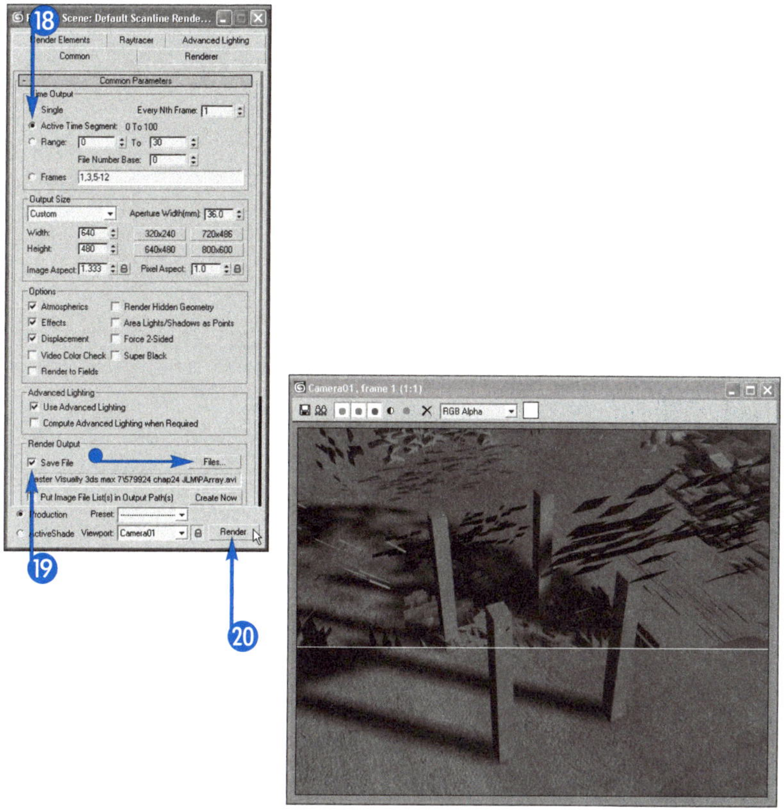

Can I animate the visibility change of the object?

▼ Yes. In fact, if you do not start the fragmenting of the object in the first frame, then you should wait to change the visibility of the object until the frame where the animation starts. To do this, click Auto Key to activate animation for the scene. Move to the frame where the PArray begins fragmenting the object, and change the Visibility value to 0.0, as shown in the steps. Now, move to the previous frame and set the Visibility to 1. If you do not set both keyframes, the visibility of the object will gradually fade. By making the change between two frames, you make the transition instant.

How do I make the particles look more like the object is exploding?

▼ You can apply a PBomb space warp to create the effect of an explosion in your scene. The PBomb space warp is specifically designed to work with a particle system. When you apply a PBomb space warp, it creates a wave at the specified scene that blows up the associated particle system. 3ds Max provides several different types of space warps, and many of them can be applied to particle systems including Gravity and Deflectors. For more information on working with space warps, see Chapter 25.

Understanding Particle Flow

You can use Particle Flow to control particle movement, based upon specific events and tests. For example, you can create an event that changes the size of the particles after they are ten frames old.

To create and maintain a Particle Flow system, 3ds Max provides the Particle View window. Working in Particle View, you can lay out the Particle Flow system by creating a particle flow diagram, similar to a flow chart. Each Particle Flow system consists of at least one event that contains a list of actions for the event. Multiple events are wired together to show the flow of the particle system and to identify which tests control which events. The actions that make up each event are either operators or tests.

A Event Display

Provides a particle diagram of the Particle Flow system. The particle diagram displays one or more events that are wired together to show the event flow.

B Menu Bar

Provides options for modifying, selecting, and analyzing the particle system.

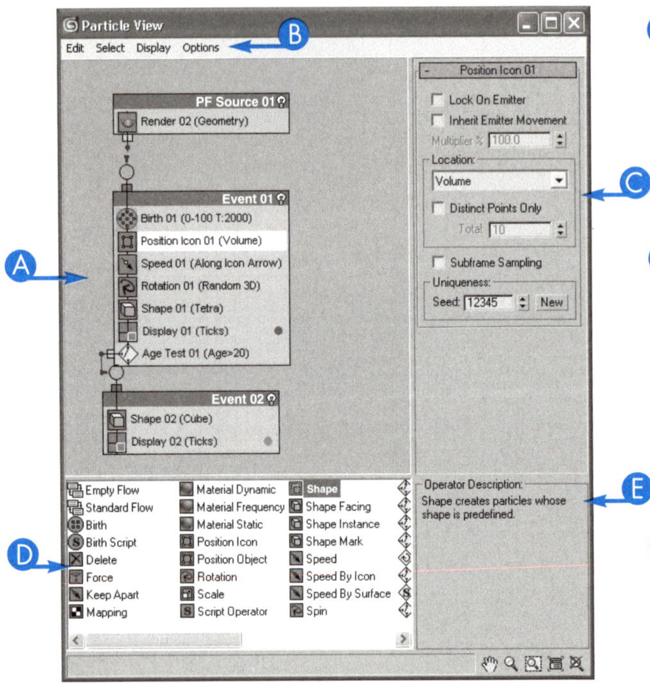

C Parameters Panel

Provides rollouts containing the parameters that are associated with the selected action in the particle diagram.

D Depot

Contains a list of the available operators and tests that you can add to the Particle Flow system.

You can add operators and tests to existing events, or you can create new events.

E Operator Description Panel

Provides a description of the operator or event selected in the Depot.

Events

Each Particle Flow system consists of one or more events that are wired together to show the relationship between the events. The first event in the system is the Global Event. The Global Event contains the operators that affect the entire particle system. For example, by default, the Global Event contains a Render operator that indicates how particles will be rendered for the scene.

The next event in the Particle Flow system is the Birth event. This event always contains the Birth operator so that the system can generate particles. The Birth event also contains other operators that define the initial parameter values for the Particle Flow system. 3ds Max assigns a default name of Event 01 to the Birth event. Each new event is named incrementally; as a result, the next event is Event 02. You can also apply custom names to each event. Each event can be comprised of multiple operators and tests.

Tests

Tests determine when the particles in the event move to another event in the Particle Flow system. Tests check to determine whether specific conditions are satisfied. When the condition of the test is satisfied, the result of the test is True. A True test passes the associated particles to the event that is wired to the test. Particles that do not satisfy the conditions of the test are not passed to the next event, but do continue down the list in the event and may pass a subsequent test that is listed.

You can add tests to an event from the Depot. Tests should be placed at the end of the event so that the operators in the event can be applied. You can add multiple tests to an event. The first test is applied to all particles in the event, with additional tests applied only to the particles that remain.

Particle Flow Tests

Test	Description
Age Test	Checks to see if a specific amount of time has passed. The test is based upon the age of the particles, duration of the animation, or duration of the event.
Collision	Checks for particles that collide with a Deflector space warp. A collision also tests to determine whether particle speed has changed. The DynaFlect deflectors are ignored by the Collision test.
Collision Spawn	Creates new particles when a particle collides with Deflector space warps. The DynaFlect deflectors are ignored by the Collision test.
Find Target	Sends the particles toward a specified object. You can either use the target icon created by the test or send the particles to an object.
Go To Rotation	Causes the particles to achieve a specific orientation.
Scale Test	Allows you to check the particle size before or after scaling.
Script Test	Allows you to test the particle condition by writing a script using MAXScript.
Send Out	Sends all particles to the wired event without meeting any stipulations.
Spawn	Creates new particles from each existing particle. The new particles are sent to the wired event.
Speed Test	Tests for the linear or radial speed of a particle or its acceleration.
Split Amount	Sends a portion of the particles to the wired event. The portion can be a percentage of particles or a specific number.
Split Selected	Sends only selected particles to the wired event.
Split Source	Splits the particle stream, based upon the event where the particles were created.

continued

Understanding Particle Flow *(Continued)*

Operators

Operators are the main element in each event and define the characteristics of the particles during that event. For example, the operators can specify the speed, direction, or shape of the particles.

The available operators are listed in the Depot that appears at the bottom of the Particle View window. Each operator has an illustrative icon with either a green or blue background.

The available operators can be divided into six different categories that describe how the operators affect the particle flow: Birth and Death, Transforms, Speed, Shape, Material and Mapping, and Utility.

One thing to keep in mind is that while materials can be applied to particles in events, those materials do not follow the particles that move to other events. As a result, if you want to use specific materials, you need to assign them to the particles in each event. If you want the materials to be applied to all particles, you can apply a material operator to the Global event.

Birth and Death Operators

Operator	*Description*
Birth	The first operator in the event that follows the Global event. This operator enables the creation of particles within your particle system.
Birth Script	Can be used in place of the Birth operator. The Birth Script operator uses a MAXScript script to create particles in your scene. You can modify the script by clicking the Edit Script button.
Delete	Removes particles from the particle system, based upon the parameters that you specify.

Transforms Operators

Operator	*Description*
Position Icon	Controls the location where particles are emitted from the emitter.
Position Object	Allows you to select an object in your scene as the particle emitter.
Rotation	Allows you to animate the orientation of the particles within the corresponding event.
Scale	Allows you to change the particle size by scaling.
Spin	Spins each particle in the event by the specified amount.

Shape Operators

Operator	Description
Shape	Defines the shape used to display particles when the scene is rendered.
Shape Facing	Creates a rectangular particle that always faces the camera, an object, or a specific direction. Use this operator to create particles for effects such as fire, smoke, water, or bubbles, and apply an appropriate material to set the appearance of the particles.
Shape Instance	Creates particles that are instance copies of the specified object in the scene. Any changes that you make to the original object geometry affect the particles in the particle system.
Shape Mark	Replaces particles with either a rectangle or box cut out of a specific object in the scene. This operator works well for leaving marks in your scenes after particles impact objects.

Material and Mapping Operators

Operator	Description
Material Static	Allows you to assign a material for the particles that display during the corresponding event.
Material Frequency	Allows you to assign a material that uses sub-materials to the event. You can specify the frequency with which each sub-material appears on particles during that event.
Material Dynamic	Allows you to assign material IDs to the particles with the ability to randomly change those IDs during the event. This allows you to assign materials to each particle, based upon the particle's material ID.
Mapping	Allows you to assign UVW mapping coordinates to the surface of each particle in the event. Use this operator when you have assigned a map using one of the Material operators in the same event.

Speed Operators

Operator	Description
Speed	Sets the basic speed and direction of the particles. By default, the Speed operator is added to the first event in each new Particle Flow system.
Speed By Icon	Sets the particles to follow the motion designated by the Speed By Icon operator that is created in your scene. The icon is not rendered.
Speed By Surface	Sets the particles in the particle system to follow the speed and direction of any object in the scene.
Keep Apart	Uses the applied forces to minimize the collisions between particles in the system.

Utility Operators

Operator	Description
Cache	Used with complex particle systems to store the particle states in memory. This improves the performance of the particle system when the scene is played back in the viewports.
Display	Allows you to specify how particles display in the viewports. To view the actual shapes that will be rendered, select the Geometry option.
Force	Allows you to select a space warp object that has been applied to the scene as an influence on the particles in the current event.
Notes	Allows you to add comments about the event. The notes do not affect how the particle system renders.
Render	Allows you to specify the form that the rendered particles take.
Script Operator	Allows you to create a MAXScript script that controls many aspects of the particles within the current event.

Create a Particle Flow Source

You can use the PF Source particle system option to create an event-driven particle system. This allows you to create complex particle systems that are controlled by both events that occur and tests that are passed. For example, you can change the shape of the particles in the system when they are of a certain age.

You can add a Particle Flow system to your scene from the Create panel by placing the emitter icon in your scene. As with other particle systems, you can use the Transform tools to position and orient the emitter icon in your scene.

After you create the Particle Flow Source icon, the Particle Flow system is designed using the Particle View window. When you first open the window, you see the two default events created by 3ds Max. The operators in the events allow you to set most of the common parameter values. The Birth operator controls the creation of the particles and has parameters for setting the frame where the particle creation starts and ends, as well as the total number of particles that are created.

Create a Particle Flow Source

Create Particle Flow

1. Click and then click .
2. Click to display a list of Geometry types.
3. Click Particle Systems.

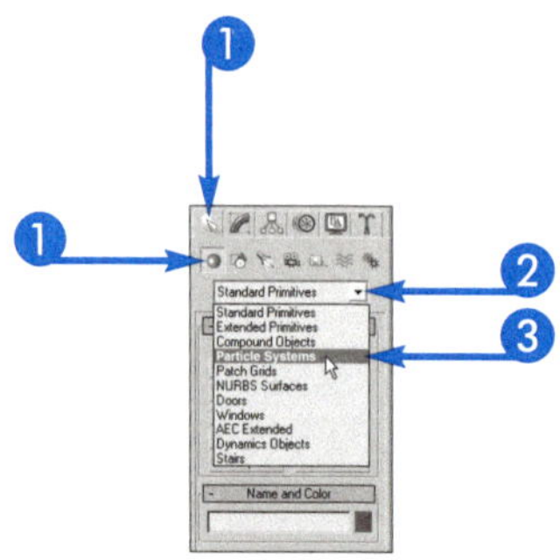

The available particle system types appear in the Object Type rollout.

4. Click PF Source.
5. Click and drag in a viewport to create the emitter icon.

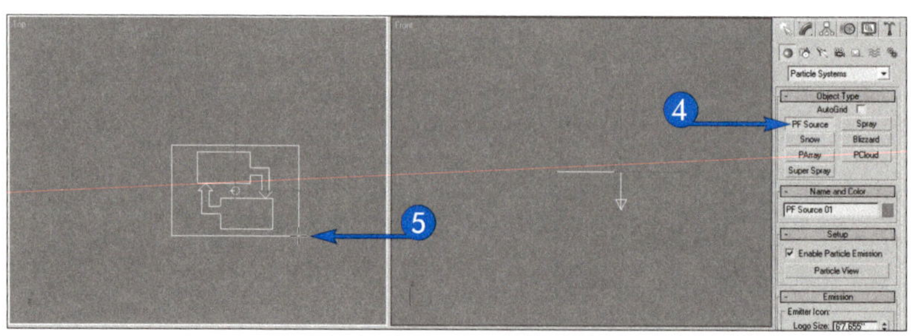

The newly created emitter icon is oriented toward the negative Z-axis.

6. Click ![icon].

7. Click Particle View.

   The Particle View window appears.

8. Click the Birth operator in Event 01 to display its parameters.

9. Type the number of the frame in which you want to start particle creation.

10. Type the number of the frame in which you want to end particle creation.

11. Type the total number of particles that you want to create.

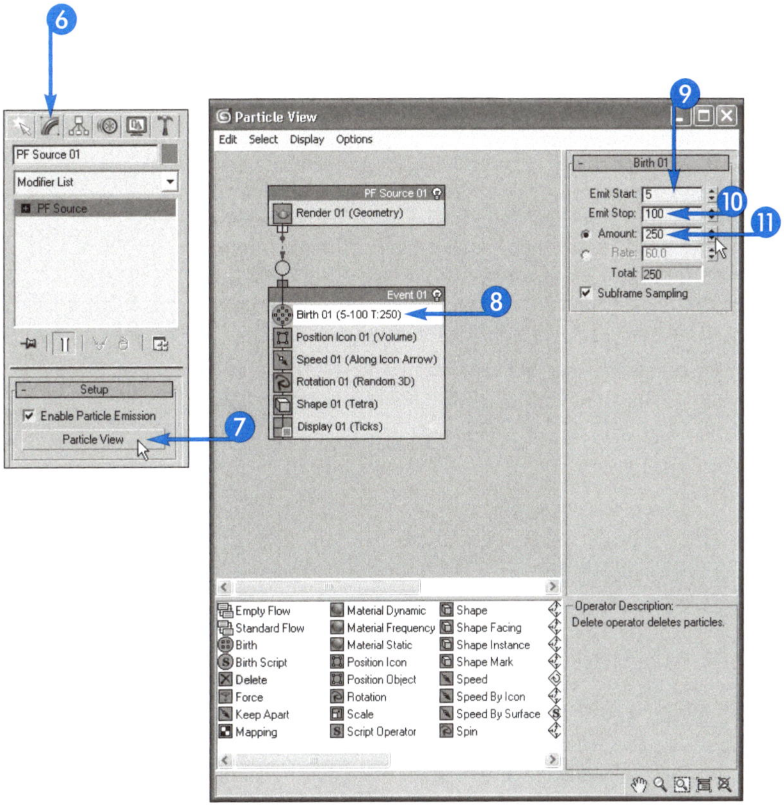

Master It

What if I want a different-shaped emitter icon?

▼ When you create the Particle Flow Source icon in the viewport, the default Icon Type is Rectangle. You can set the initial size of the icon by dragging in the viewport, or by setting the size of an existing icon by changing the Length and Width parameters in the Emission rollout. You can also set the size of the logo that displays in the center of the emitter icon. If you are emitting particles from the Particle Flow Source, then you can also select one of the other available Types: Box, Circle, or Sphere. You can set the icon shape in the Icon Type field of the Emission rollout.

What if I want the Particle Flow system to be emitted from an object in my scene?

▼ In order to emit particles from an object instead of the Particle Flow Source icon, you must associate the object in the Particle View window. To link to an object, add the Position Object operator to the first event. In the Parameters panel, click Add and then click the object in your scene that you want to use as the emitter. The name of the selected object appears in the Emitter Objects list box. You can also select the object by clicking By List and then selecting it by name in the Select Emitter Objects dialog box.

continued

Create a Particle Flow Source *(Continued)*

To move particles between events, there must be a test to determine which particles should move to the event. For example, if you want to change the shape of the particles after they have been in the scene for 20 frames, then you would perform an Age Test. Only the particles that test True for the Age Test — meaning that they are 20 frames old — move to the next event.

You should place the test to check the particles at the end of the event. This ensures that all the actions prior to that test are performed. When the test is encountered, only the particles that test True move on to the new event. You can add a Delete operator after the test, if required, to remove any particles from the scene that do not past the test.

You can create a new event by dragging an operator or test from the Depot into the empty space of the Event Display. After creating a new event, you must wire a test from one event to the input of another event. When you do this, 3ds Max knows which event to send the particles to when the test value is True.

Create a Particle Flow Source *(continued)*

Add a Particle Flow Test and Event

⑫ Click a test in the Depot and drag it into an event.

⑬ Release the mouse button.

The test is added to the event at the cursor location where you released the mouse button.

⑭ Click to select an operator.

⑮ Drag an operator from the Depot to the Event Display.

⑯ Set test parameters in the Parameters panel.

A new event is created for the operator.

⑰ Click the blue dot next to the test and drag to the new event.

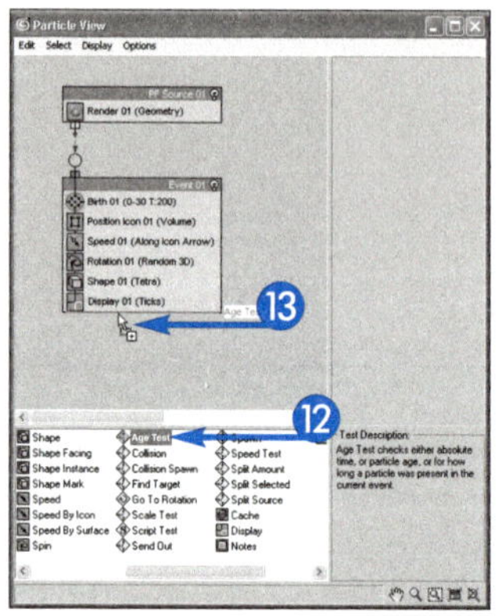

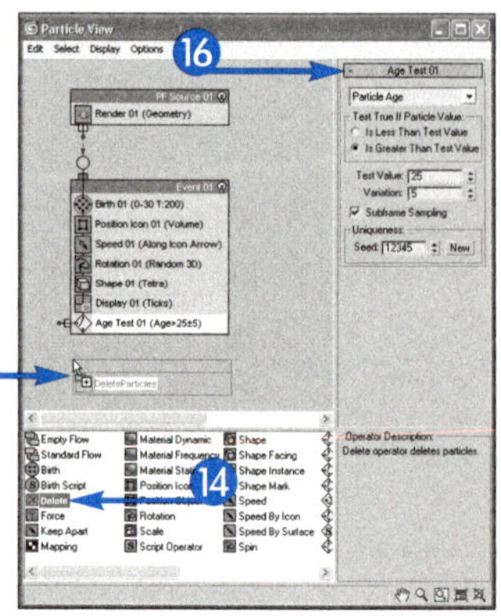

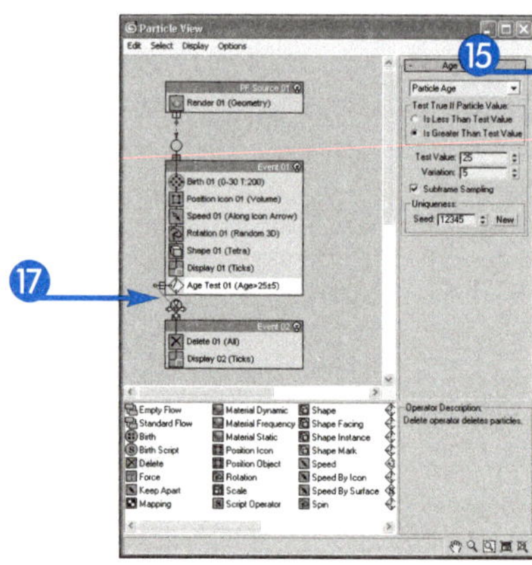

The two events are wired together at the test.

18 Click the operator.

19 Set the parameter values in the Parameters section.

20 Click [icon] to render the scene with the Particle Flow system.

Note: *For information on rendering to an output file, see Chapter 20.*

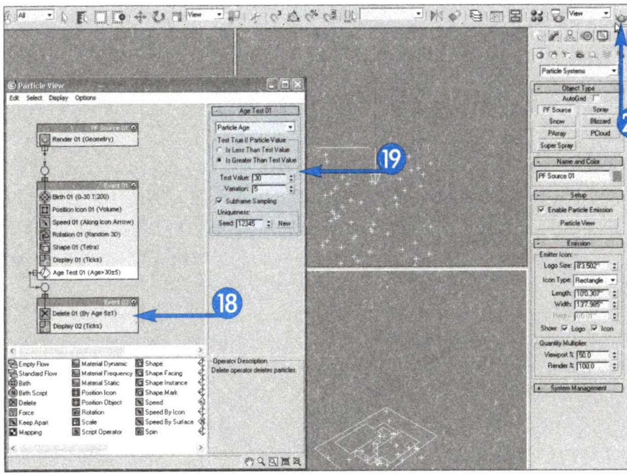

The events created in the Particle View window occur when 3ds Max renders the scene.

Can I test the particle system in the viewport?

Yes. You can test it by dragging the Time Slider along the Timeline. The particles that display in the viewports are controlled by the Display operator that is created in each event that you create. The default Particle Display icon is Ticks, which display as a Plus sign (+) for each particle. You can select from other icon types, including the image that will be rendered. To change the Particle Display to show the rendered image, click [icon] next to the Type field and select Geometry. You must do this for each event.

How do I simulate the effects of different forces on the particle system?

You can simulate different forces, such as wind or gravity, by using the Force operator and then selecting the space warp object that affects the particle system. The selected space warp only affects the particle system within the event. In order to add the influence of a space warp, you must click Add in the Force rollout. Click to select the space warp icon from your scene. 3ds Max allows you to apply the Displace, Drag, Gravity, Motor, PBomb, Push, Vortex, and Wind space warps to a Particle Flow system. For more information on working with space warps, see Chapter 25.

Understanding Space Warps

You can apply space warps, which are objects that apply a specific type of force, to control the movement or shape of selected objects in your scene. For example, a Gravity space warp creates a natural gravity force to cause particles in a particle system to move in a specified direction. You can use the Gravity space warp to cause the water shooting out from a fountain to fall toward the ground. A Ripple space warp bends the space around it into a ripple shape, and any objects that are bound to that space warp will also deform when they are in close proximity to it.

A space warp object is non-renderable, which means that it is only visible in the viewport as a gizmo. This gizmo represents the type of space warp that you have applied, as well as the direction, if there is one, associated with the source. A space warp only affects the objects that are bound to it. You can bind several objects to the same space warp, and you can also bind multiple space warps to the same object. When an object is initially bound to a space warp, it briefly turns white and blinks to indicate that the binding was successful. To discontinue a space warp's effect on an object, either turn off the Light Bulb icon next to the binding in the Modifier Stack, or delete the Modifier Stack entry altogether.

3ds Max provides four different categories of space warps that you can select from the Create panel. Each category contains specific types of space warps to which the objects in your scene can be bound. The six types of space warps are: Forces, Deflectors, Geometric/Deformable, Modifier-Based, Particles & Dynamics, and reactor. Particles & Dynamics and reactor space warps are not covered in this chapter.

Forces Space Warps

The Forces space warps are typically applied to particle systems and dynamic simulations. When used with a particle system, the space warp is bound to the space warp's emitter gizmo.

Forces Space Warp Types

Type	*Description*
Motor	Employs a rotational spin, around the Motor icon, to the particles or bound objects.
Push	Applies a constant, directional force to the particles from a bound particle system. The particles are thrust in the direction in which the Push gizmo is pointing, when it maintains a positive value.
Vortex	Creates a whirlpool effect on the particles so that they spin around and then downward in a spiral. This space warp is useful for creating whirlpools, tornados, or other funnel-like conditions.
Drag	Reduces the velocity of the particle system, within a specific range, of your scene.
Path Follow	Forces particles to follow a path that is defined by a spline object in your scene.
PBomb	Designed for use with the PArray particle system to simulate the blowing up of an object into fragments.
Displace	Pushes objects and particles to change their surface structure. You can define the strength and effect of the displacement with the Strength and Decay parameter values.
Gravity	Adds the effect of gravity to a scene by applying a constant, direct acceleration force to a particle system.
Wind	Applies a directional force to simulate wind, thus affecting the movement of particles. The Turbulence and Frequency settings can add randomness to the space warp's effect.

Deflector Space Warps

The Deflector space warps, also called deflectors, provide several different methods of repelling particles. Particles that come in contact with deflectors bounce off as if they have struck a solid object.

Deflector Space Warps

Type	Description
POmniFlect	A plane-shaped deflector.
PDynaFlect	A plane-shaped deflector. The particles can also affect the objects that they strike when used in dynamics simulations.
SOmniFlect	A sphere-shaped deflector.
SDynaFlect	A sphere-shaped deflector. The particles can also affect the objects that they strike when used in dynamics simulations.
UOmniFlect	Allows you to designate any geometric object in the scene as a deflector.
UDynaFlect	Allows you to select any geometric object as a deflector. The object can react to the particles' impact in dynamics simulations.
SDeflector	A simplified version of the SOmniFlect deflector.
UDeflector	A simplified version of the UOmniFlect deflector.
Deflector	A simplified version of the POmniFlect deflector.

Geometric/Deformable Space Warp

The Geometric/Deformable space warps deform the geometry of the associated object. Unlike modifiers, which some of these space warps mimic, the space itself is being deformed, not the object, and the bound objects must approach the space warps to be affected.

Geometric/Deformable Space Warps

Type	Description
FFD (Box)	A box-shaped space warp containing control points that are used to deform the bound object. Even if the object is bound to the space warp, it must be within the space warp's volume to be deformed.
FFD (Cyl)	A cylinder-shaped space warp containing control points that are used to deform the bound object. Even if the object is bound to the space warp, it must be within the space warp's volume to be deformed.
Wave	A linear wave-shaped space warp. The bound objects do not have to be near the gizmo to be affected; the space warp's effects project infinitely beyond the gizmo unless the Decay value is set.
Ripple	A radial wave-shaped space warp. The bound objects do not have to be near the gizmo to be affected; the space warp's effects project infinitely beyond the gizmo unless the Decay value is set.
Displace	Displace pushes objects and particles to change their surface structure. You can define the effect of the displacement with the Strength and Decay parameters.
Conform	Moves the vertices of the bound objects in the gizmo-specified direction until they come in contact with a target object or move a certain distance from their original position.
Bomb	Causes an object to explode to its individual faces. Adjust the Strength parameter to specify how far the faces travel. This space warp does not generally produce results suitable for up-close viewing.

Modifier-Based Space Warps

You use these space warps to apply common modifier effects to several objects simultaneously, with each object sharing the gizmo's center point for the effect.

Modifier-Based Space Warps

Type	Description
Bend	Bends the bound objects around a specified axis.
Noise	Creates random surface patterns in the bound objects.
Skew	Offsets the geometry of the selected objects along the selected axis.
Taper	Tapers the selected objects by scaling each end of the objects.
Twist	Creates a twirling effect in the bound objects.
Stretch	Scales the bound objects up in one axis and down in the other two axes to maintain a constant volume.

Simulate Gravity with a Gravity Space Warp

You can use the Gravity space warp to add the effect of gravity to the particles in a particle system. For example, you can control a water fountain so that the water particles fall back down toward the ground.

You add a Gravity space warp to your scene from the Create panel's Space Warps tab. You can add the Gravity space warp anywhere in your scene; it is not necessary to place it near the particle system. The Gravity is initially oriented toward the negative Z-axis of the viewport where you created it, but you can alter it using the Rotate transform tool.

After adding the Gravity, you must bind the particle system to it. As soon as you bind the particle system to the Gravity, the effect of the Gravity appears in the viewports. Depending upon the speed of your particles, they fall toward the ground.

You can adjust the Gravity's effect on the bound objects by changing the value of the Strength parameter from its default value of 1.0. Increase the value to apply more gravity, or decrease it for less.

CD FILE: The Gravity.max file is available on the CD-ROM for you to practice applying a Gravity space warp.

Simulate Gravity with a Gravity Space Warp

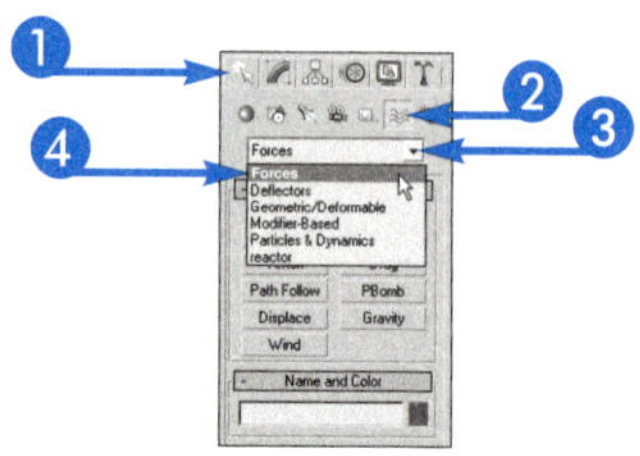

1. Click the Create Panel tab ( ).
2. Click the Space Warps button ( ).
3. Click ▾ to display a list of space warp types.
4. Click Forces.

   The available Forces space warp buttons display.

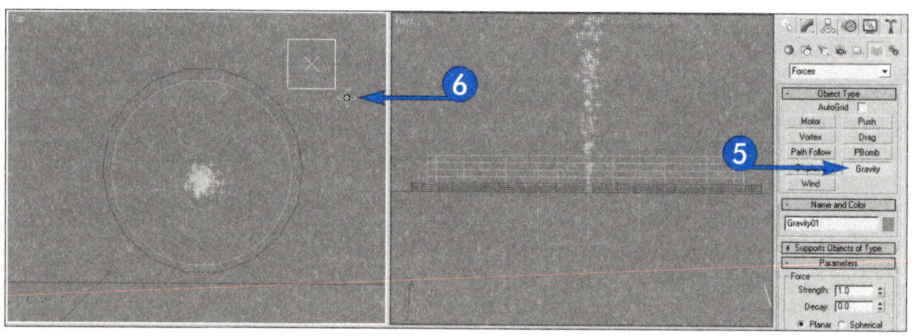

5. Click Gravity.
6. Click and drag in the Top viewport to create the Gravity gizmo.

3ds Max creates the Gravity gizmo.

7 Click the Bind to Space Warp button (▧).

8 Click the particle system and drag it to the Gravity gizmo.

You can click any particle or the particle emitter itself.

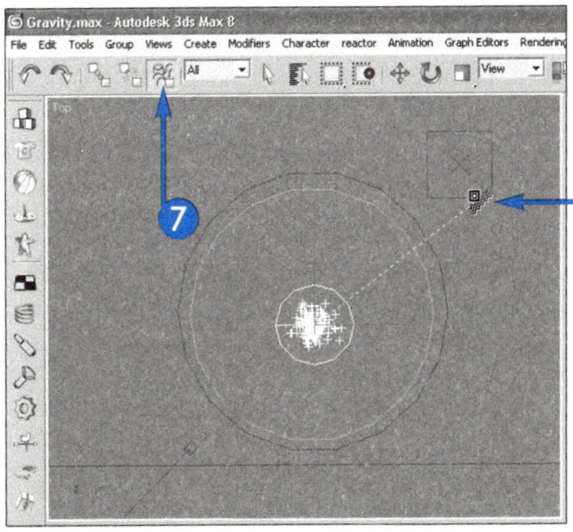

- The particles adjust to the Gravity's force.
- You can click ▣ to preview your animation.

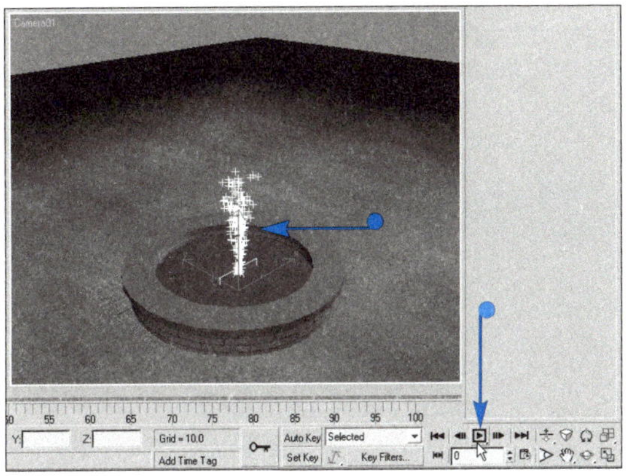

My particles are not emitting high enough when I apply Gravity. What should I do?

When you add a Gravity space warp object, you are applying a force that simulates the natural force of gravity. This causes particles moving against the force to decelerate and then to move in the direction of the gravity. When you apply a Gravity force to a particle system, the speed of the particle system determines how it reacts with the gravity. If the particle system is shooting straight up, you may need to increase the Speed parameter of the particles to achieve the results that you want. Although you can also decrease the Strength parameter for the Gravity force, this reduces the force that is pulling the particles back down.

What does the Decay parameter do?

The Decay parameter controls the strength of the Gravity force within the scene. If the Decay parameter value is 0.0, then the Gravity force is the same strength through the entire scene. If you increase the Decay value, the gravity's strength diminishes the farther your objects are from the Gravity object. If you increase the Decay value, you can select the Range Indicators option to see the location in the scene where the gravity force is half of the maximum value. 3ds Max displays two planes if you have selected Planar gravity, or a double-hooped sphere for Spherical gravity.

Simulate Wind with a Wind Space Warp

Similar to Gravity, the Wind space warp adds a directional force that you can apply to a particle system. For example, to add the effect of wind blowing on a stream of water, you can animate the rotation of a Wind space warp.

You add a Wind space warp to your scene from the Create panel's Space Warps tab; it is not necessary to place the gizmo near the particle system. The Wind is initially oriented toward the negative Z-axis of the viewport where you created it, but you can alter it using the Rotate transform tool.

After adding the Wind, you must bind the particle system to it. As soon as it is bound, the effect of the Wind is visible in the viewports. The particles move away from the particle system, in the direction that the Wind gizmo is oriented.

You can adjust the Wind's effect by changing the value of its Strength parameter, from its default value of 1.0. Change the Turbulence value to add randomness to the Wind's effect on the particles.

CD FILE: The Wind.max file is available on the CD-ROM for you to practice applying a Wind space warp.

Simulate Wind with a Wind Space Warp

1. Click .
2. Click .
3. Click ▾ to display a list of space warp types.
4. Click Forces.

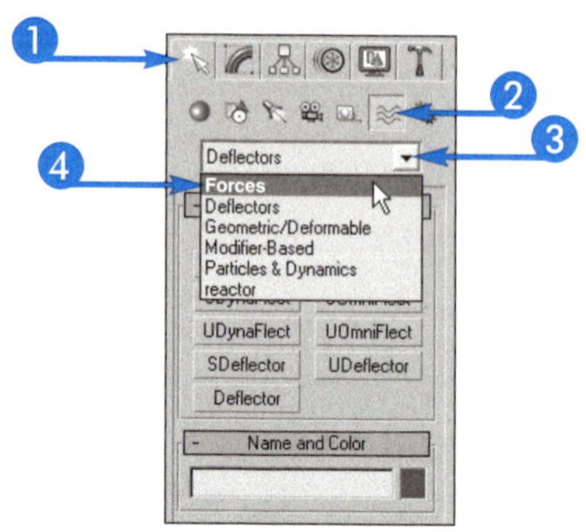

- The available Forces space warp buttons display.

5. Click Wind.
6. Click and drag in the Front viewport to create the Wind gizmo.

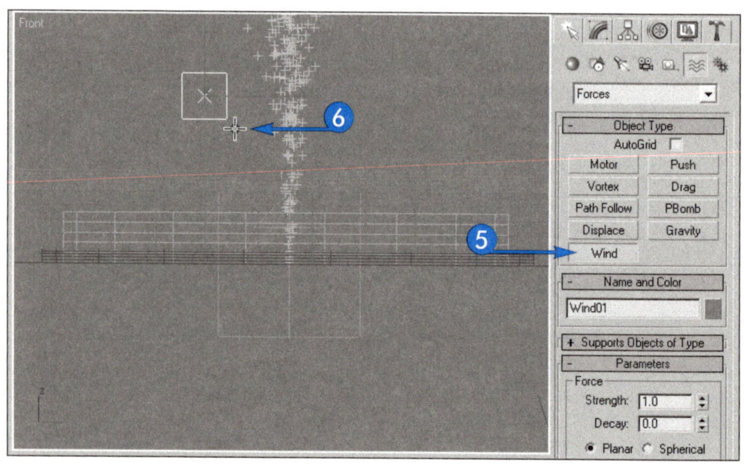

3ds Max creates the Wind gizmo.

7 Click .

8 Click the particle system and drag to the Wind gizmo.

You can click any particle or the particle emitter itself.

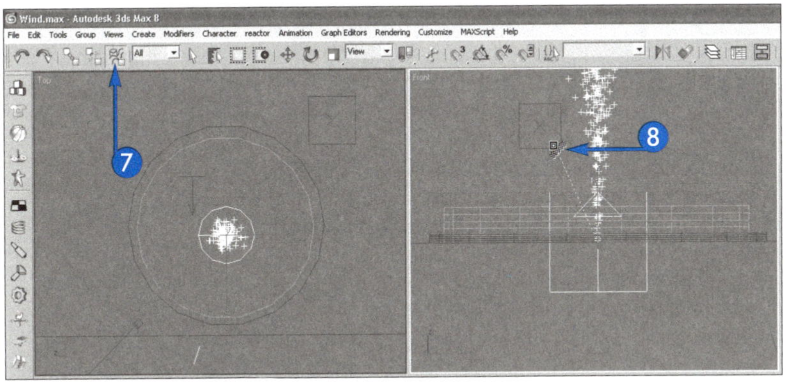

- The particles adjust to the Wind's force.

You can select the Wind and then click to change the Wind's parameters.

- You can click to preview your animation.

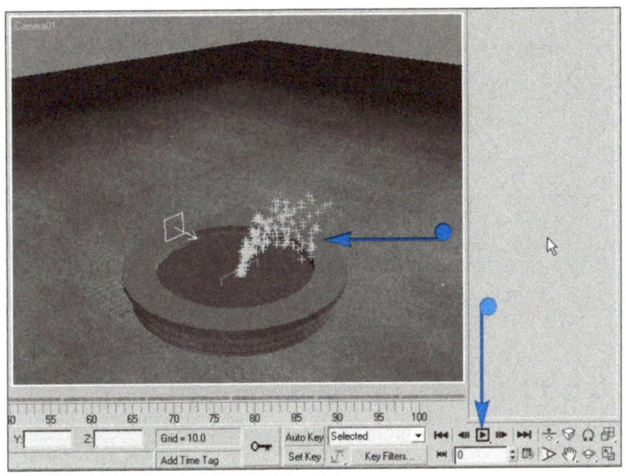

MASTER IT

How can I stop the Wind from affecting some of my particle systems but not all of them?

A single space warp can have several objects bound to it. In the case of the Wind space warp, this ensures that the Wind's effects are consistent throughout the scene. To temporarily prevent a space warp from affecting an object or particle system, select the bound object and then open the Modify tab. Click the light bulb icon next to the space warp's binding in the Modifier Stack to activate its effect. To remove the space warp from the object entirely, right-click the space warp's binding in the Modifier Stack and then select Delete from the pop-up menu. For information on the Modifier Stack, see Chapter 6.

What does the Scale parameter do?

The force that the Wind space warp applies to a particle system is constant and evenly distributed, and so it may not create the realistic effect that you want. To add randomness to the effect, you can increase the Turbulence value from its default of 0.0. The larger the Turbulence value, the greater the randomness of each particle's movement. The Scale parameter determines how smoothly the Turbulence alters the paths of the particles. Lower Scale values result in smoother particle movements, and higher Scale values cause the particles' movements to be more radical.

Blow Stuff Up with the PBomb Space Warp

You can use the PBomb space warp in your scene to create the effect of one or more objects exploding and fragmenting. For example, you may want projectiles in your scene to blow up when they impact their target, and then fall to the ground. When used in conjunction with the PArray particle system, the PBomb space warp breaks objects into chunks, but the effect may not be suitable for viewing in high detail.

You can add a PBomb space warp to your scene from the Create panel's Space Warps tab. When the explosion occurs, the fragments of the bound objects move away from the location of the PBomb gizmo. The closer the object is to the bomb, the more the explosion affects it. After adding the PBomb gizmo, you need to bind it to the PArray particle system.

You adjust the effects of the PBomb space warp by selecting the gizmo and then opening the Modify panel. The Basic Parameters rollout displays the controls to set the strength and direction of the explosion, and the start time.

The PBomb.max file is available on the CD-ROM for you to practice using the PBomb space warp.

Blow Stuff Up with the PBomb Space Warp

1. Click .
2. Click .
3. Click to display a list of space warp types.
4. Click Forces.

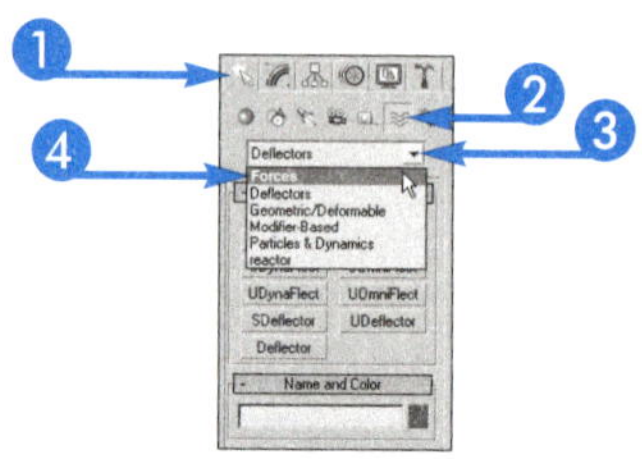

The available Forces space warp buttons display.

5. Click PBomb.
6. Click and drag in a viewport to create the PBomb gizmo.

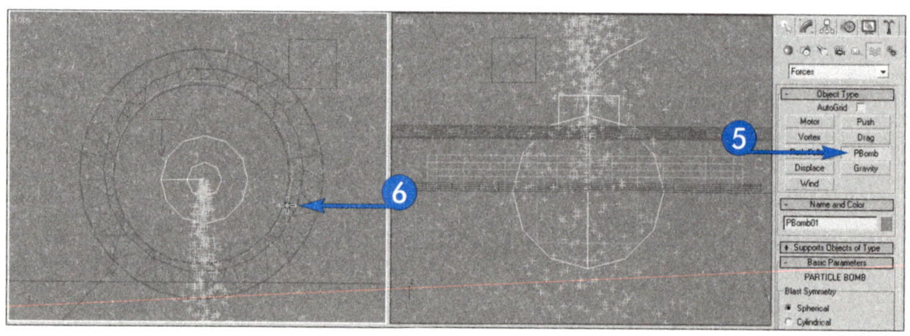

3ds Max creates the PBomb gizmo.

7. Click [icon].

8. Click the PBomb gizmo and drag to the PArray gizmo.

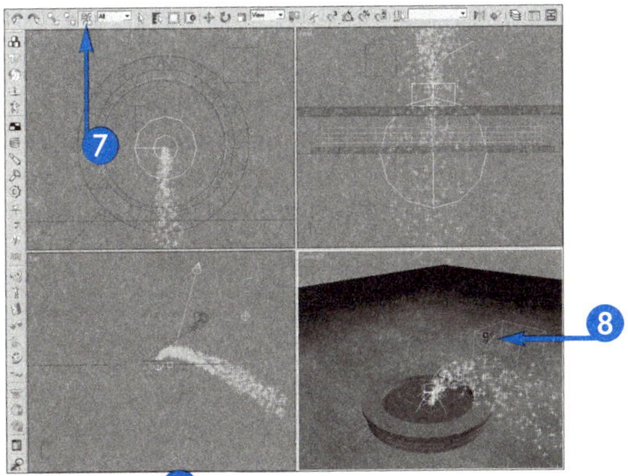

The PArray gizmo flashes briefly to indicate a successful binding.

9. Click [icon].

The parameters for the PBomb space warp display in the Modify panel.

10. Type the parameter values that you want.

- You can click [icon] to preview the animation.

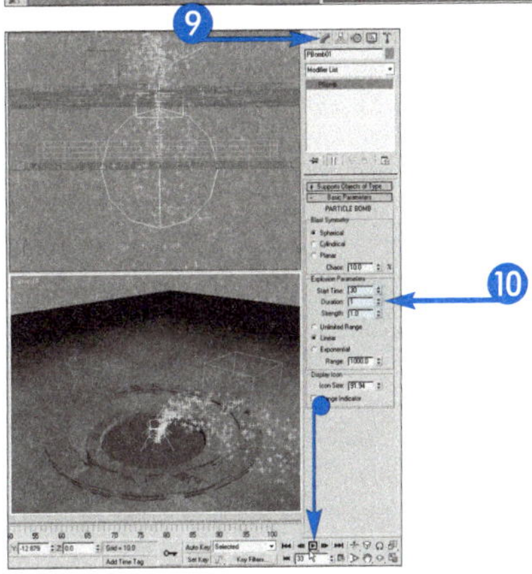

MASTER IT

My explosion looks too even and consistent, even at a distance. How can I fix this?

The PBomb space warp has a few controls and techniques that can add some randomness to the explosion. You can raise the Chaos parameter's value to increase the number of directions in which the fragments move, although they still generally move away from the PBomb gizmo and downward with gravity. You can also animate the Spin parameter's value so that the spin rate, in rotations per second, decreases with time. If there is more than one bomb going off in the scene, you can bind one object to multiple bombs. The forces emitted from each space warp affect the object from different directions and different intensities if you use different Strength parameters.

Can I use the Bomb space warp to create explosions?

The Bomb space warp simply disintegrates the bound objects to their individual faces. It is less computationally expensive than the other fragmenting space warps, but at a cost of a simpler fragmenting pattern. This results in several triangular, often equally sized, objects being projected from the bomb site. This is an unrealistic condition and is rarely an adequate effect in a scene that requires an explosion. However, if the explosion is in the distance, and not a focus of the viewer's attention, the Bomb space warp's effect may be passable.

Apply the Ripple Space Warp

You can apply a Ripple space warp to your scene to create the effect of a radial wave that is emitted from a central point on an object. For example, you may want to make a body of water look as if waves are generated after an object is dropped into it.

You can add a Ripple space warp to your scene from the Create panel's Space Warps tab. You can place the Ripple gizmo anywhere around or inside the object that you want to ripple. Creating the Ripple gizmo is a three-step process: First, you click to locate and create the gizmo. Second, you drag and release to set the radius. Third, you move your mouse and click to set the amplitude, or height, of the wave. After adding the Ripple gizmo, you must bind the objects that you want to ripple in your scene to it. You can bind any object to the Ripple gizmo.

You can adjust the effects of the Ripple space warp in the Modify panel. The Modify panel displays the Ripple Parameters rollout, where you can control the ripple appearance.

CD FILE The Ripple.max file is available on the CD-ROM for you to practice applying a Ripple space warp.

Apply the Ripple Space Warp

1. Click .
2. Click .
3. Click to display a list of space warp types.
4. Click Geometric/Deformable.

   The available Geometric/Deformable space warp buttons display.

5. Click Ripple.
6. Click, drag, and release in the Top viewport to create the Ripple gizmo.
7. Click, drag, and release to set the initial amplitude for the ripple.

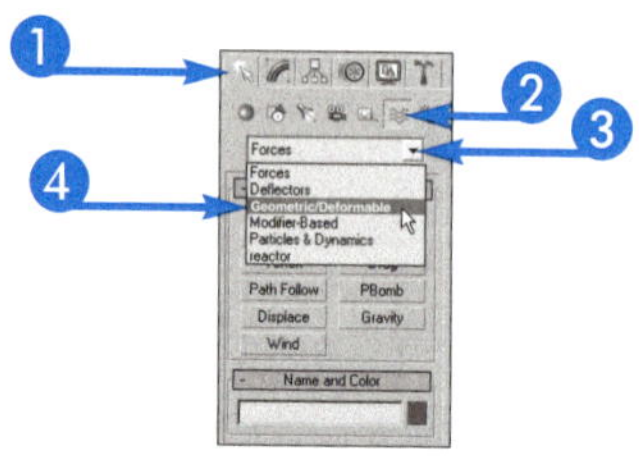

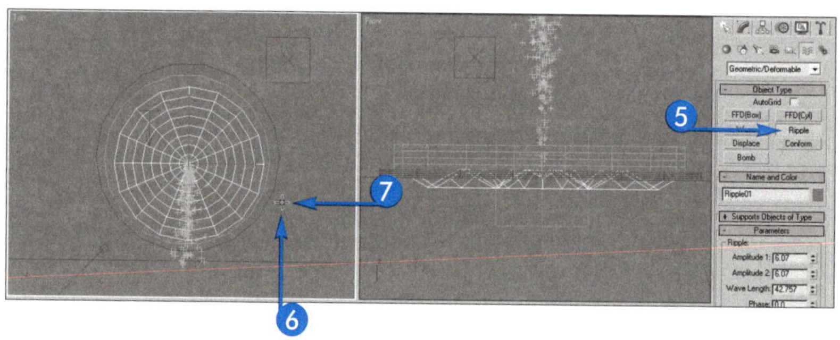

3ds Max creates the Ripple gizmo.

8 Specify the parameter values that you want for the ripple.

9 Click .

In a cluttered scene, use the Select by Name button ( ) to select an object from a list.

10 Click the object and drag to bind it to the Ripple gizmo.

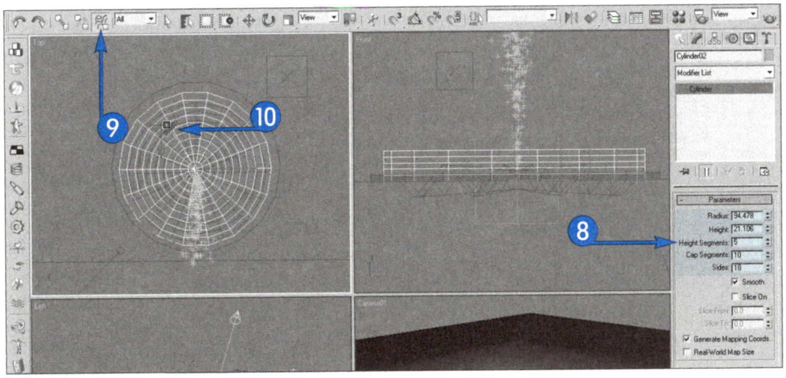

3ds Max applies the Ripple effect to the selected object.

You can see the effect in the viewports.

MASTER IT

How do I animate the Ripple space warp in my scene?

Unlike some of the other space warps, Ripple does not automatically animate in your scene. To animate the Ripple effect, you must create keyframes for the parameter values. For more information on creating animation with keyframes, see Chapter 8. Although you can animate all of the parameter values, the Phase parameter is designed to move the crest of the wave from the center of the gizmo. To animate it, activate Auto Key and drag the Time Slider to the frame where you want the new parameter values to occur. Every increase of 1.0 in the Phase parameter adds one more cycle to the ripple.

If I use the Ripple space warp for multiple objects, can I adjust the effect on a specific object?

Yes. 3ds Max provides a separate parameter value that you can set for each bound object. This value controls the amount of flexibility for that object. By adjusting the parameter value, you can adjust the amount of the Ripple effect that is visible on that object. To adjust the value, select the bound object and then click the Modify Panel button ( ) to view the Modify panel. In the Modifier Stack, select the Ripple Binding (WSM) entry. The Flexibility parameter displays in the Parameters rollout. To increase the Ripple effect, increase the value. Type a value less than 1.0 to reduce the effect.

Apply a Twist Space Warp

You can use the Twist space warp to twirl objects, in a specific axis, around the Twist gizmo. This effect is similar to the Twist modifier that you apply to individual objects. The advantage to using the Twist space warp is that each object twists around the gizmo relative to its location in space, rather than around its own gizmo's pivot point.

You can add a Twist space warp, which resembles a box, to your scene from the Create panel's Space Warps tab. You must then bind the objects that you want to twist simultaneously to the gizmo.

You can adjust the parameter values for the Twist space warp in the Modify panel. These values display in two rollouts, which allow you to control the size of the gizmo, amount of twist, twist axis, and limits. By default, the Z-axis is selected as the axis to twist around, but you can select either of the other two axes.

You can specify a rotation angle for the twist. Positive Angle values create clockwise twists, and negative Angle values produce counter-clockwise twists.

CD FILE: The Twist.max file is available on the CD-ROM for you to practice applying the Twist space warp.

Apply a Twist Space Warp

1. Click .
2. Click .
3. Click to display a list of space warp types.
4. Click Modifier-Based.

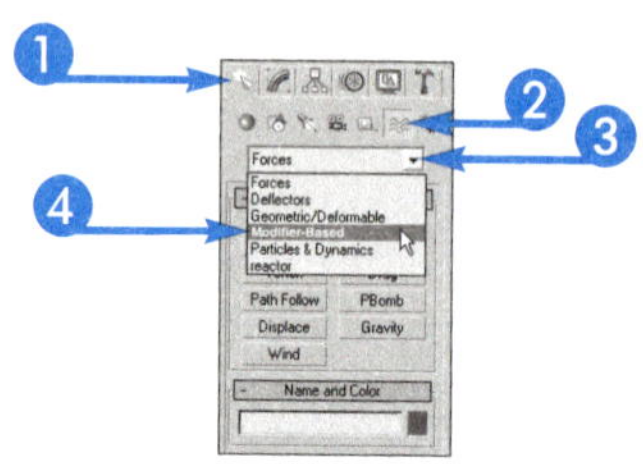

The available Modifier-Based space warp buttons display in the Object Type rollout.

5. Click Twist.
6. Click, drag, and release in a viewport to create the base of the Twist gizmo.
7. Click, drag, and release to set the Height of the gizmo.

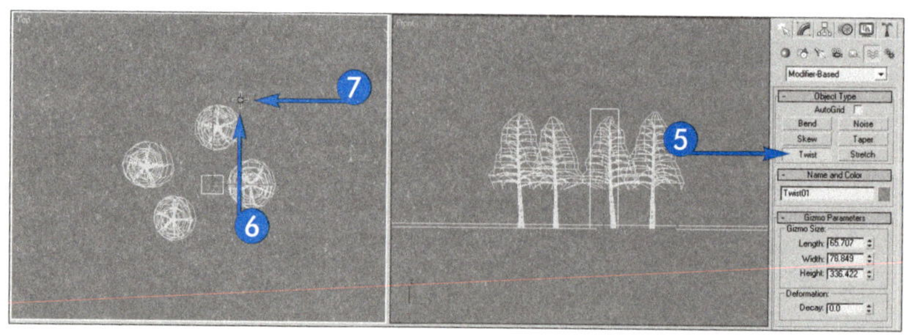

3ds Max creates the Twist gizmo.

8 Select all of the objects that you want to bind.

9 Click .

10 Click one object and drag to the Twist gizmo.

11 Select the Twist gizmo and then click .

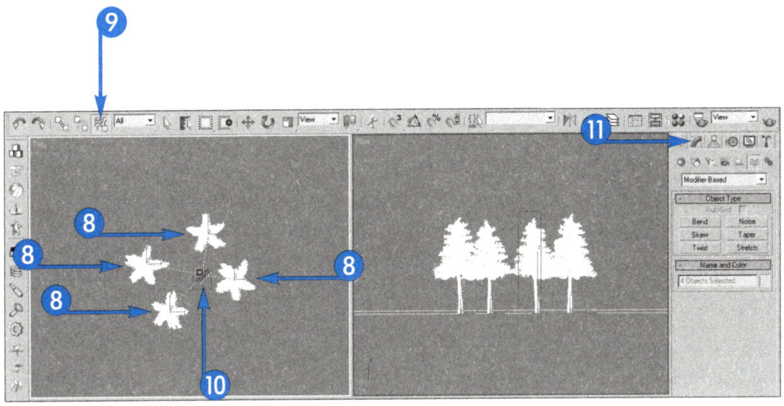

The parameters for the Twist space warp display in the Modify panel.

12 Type a twist value in the Angle field.

3ds Max twists all the bound objects simultaneously.

You can click the Quick Render button ( ) to render a viewport.

MASTER IT

Do I need to adjust the Bias?

- No, this is not necessary. You can specify a Bias value to control the uniformity of the twisting in the scene. If you specify a Bias value of 0 (zero), which is the default, the twisting is even across the length of each object in your scene. Using a negative value causes the twisting to bunch up near the center point of each object. Depending on the Twist Axis that you select, when you type a positive Bias value, the base of the object remains straight, and then the twisting bunches up near the opposite end.

How do I limit the Twist effect?

- You can limit the part of each object that is twisted by setting the Upper Limit and Lower Limit values. The limit range is a distance, rather than a percentage of the objects' heights. When you specify limits, only the part of the object within the limit range is twisted. For example, you may only want to twist a 50-unit-long object for its last 15 units. To do this, you would set 35 as the Lower Limit and 50 as the Upper Limit before adjusting the other parameter values. Keep in mind that you must select the Limit Effect option (☐ changes to ☑) in order for the limits to be active.

Follow a Path with the Path Follow Space Warp

The Path Follow space warp directs a particle system's stream of particles to follow a designated path. With a creative use of visual effects, MetaParticles, or substituted geometry, a simple piece of text can be brought to life in a visually pleasing manner.

The path can be any open or closed 2D shape object. When a complex shape — consisting of more than one non-contiguous spline sub-object — is used as the target spline, only one of the spline sub-objects is followed by the particles.

Using the Path Follow space warp requires that there be two existing objects in the scene: a spline and a particle system. Only the particle system is bound to the space warp; the target spline is indicated in the Path Follow's Modify panel parameters. The Start Frame and Travel Time parameters are also located in the Modify panel. Start Frame designates when the particles begin to travel down the spline, and Travel Time is the number of frames it takes for the particles to reach the end. For information on particle systems, see Chapter 24.

CD FILE

The Path Follow.max file is available on the CD-ROM for you to practice with the Path Follow space warp.

Follow a Path with the Path Follow Space Warp

1. Click .
2. Click .
3. Click to display a list of space warp types.
4. Click Forces.

   The available Forces space warp buttons display in the Object Type rollout.
5. Click Path Follow.
6. Click and drag in a viewport.

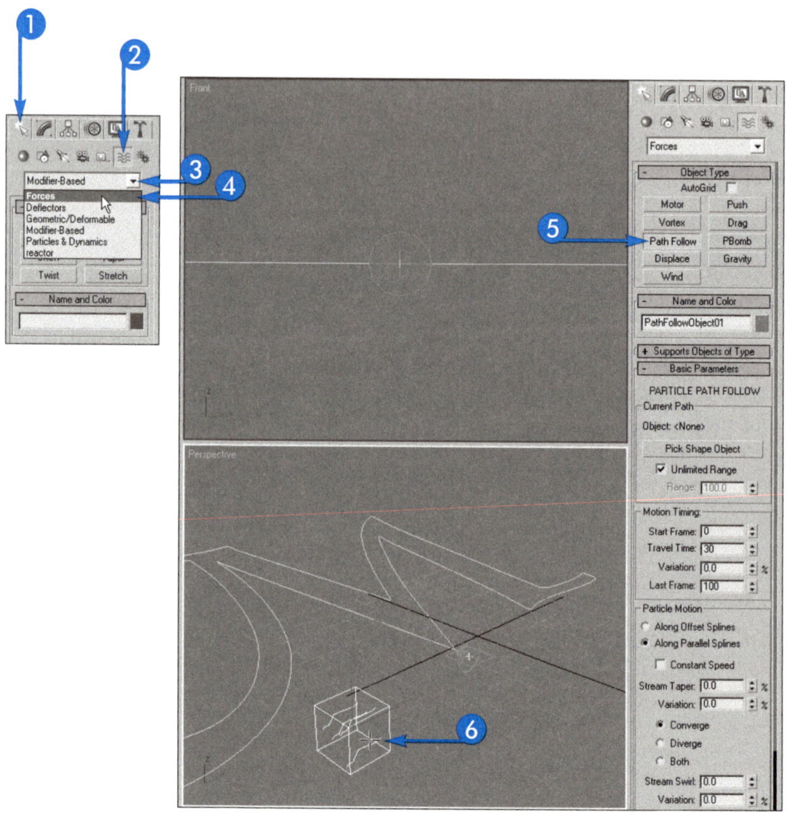

3ds Max creates the Path Follow gizmo.

7. Type Start Frame and Travel Time values.
8. Click Pick Shape Object.
9. Click a shape.

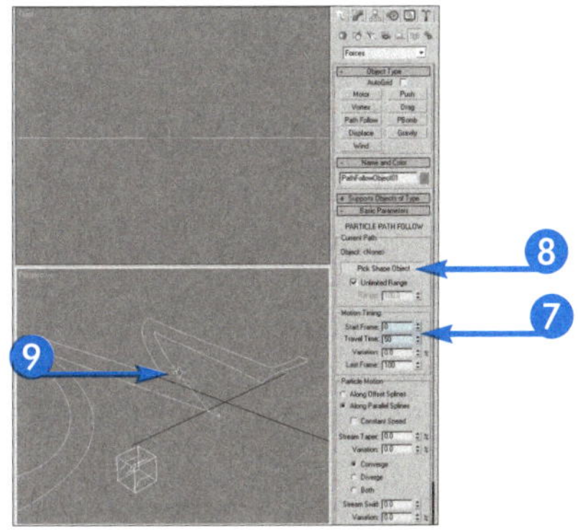

The shape name appears in the Modify panel.

10. Click .
11. Click the particle system and drag to the Path Follow gizmo.

    The particle system is bound to the space warp.

- You can click to preview the animation.

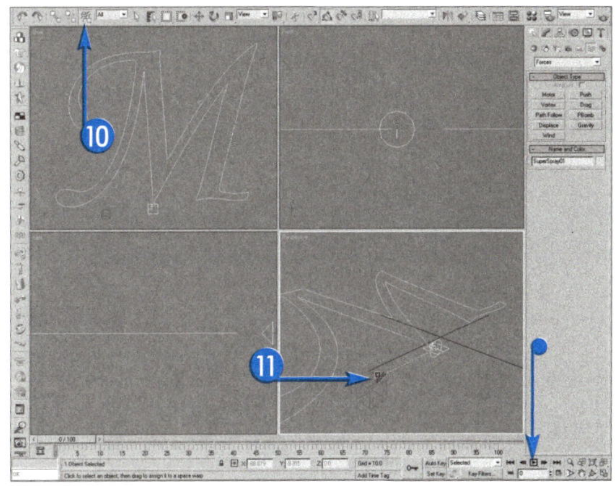

MASTER IT

Why is the Pick Shape Object button not available?

There are a couple of reasons why this may happen. When you create the Path Follow space warp, Pick Shape Object is immediately available. However, if you click Undo and then click Redo, the Pick Shape Object button becomes grayed out. Go to the Modify panel, instead of the Create panel, to access the button. After you create the space warp, select another object, and then reselect the space warp, almost all of the rollouts disappear. In this case, go to the Modify panel to access the controls, including Pick Shape Object. For a list of possible shapes in the scene, click when is active.

Why do my particles disappear before they reach the end of the shape?

The Start Frame and Travel Time settings in the Path Follow's parameters determine when the particles start, and how long it takes to follow the path. However, the particle system's parameters must also meet the criteria required to allow the particles to reach the end of the path. If the particle system's Life value is too short, the particles will die before reaching the end. If the Emit Stop or Display Until values are too low, then the particle system stops emitting or displaying the particles before the path is completed. For more information on particle systems, see Chapter 24.

Change Particle Directions with Deflectors

Deflectors cause particles that come in contact with them to bounce as if they are hitting a solid object. For example, deflectors can make bullets bounce off your hero, or broken glass stop when it hits the floor. Deflectors can also be used in conjunction with other space warps such as Gravity and PBomb.

Deflectors come in two basic shapes, planes and spheres, and these can be adapted to fit many situations. However, you can use a UOmniFlect deflector, which uses the surface of any geometry object in your scene, to deflect particles. Even animated objects can be used with the UOmniFlect deflector.

Most of the deflector types have several controls that determine how and when particles bounce off them. The Bounce value is a multiplier that determines the speed at which a particle leaves the deflector after hitting it. A value of 1.0 causes the particle to ricochet off at the same speed as its approach. Use a low Bounce value, with a Gravity space warp, to represent particles hitting a softer surface, such as a curtain, and falling away.

CD FILE: The Deflectors.max file is available on the CD-ROM for you to practice using deflectors.

Change Particle Directions with Deflectors

Using a POmniFlect Deflector

1. Click .
2. Click .
3. Click to display a list of space warp types.
4. Click Deflectors.

   The available Deflector space warp buttons display in the Object Type rollout.

5. Click POmniFlect.
6. Click and drag in a viewport.

   3ds Max creates the POmniFlect gizmo.

   - Type values to adjust any parameters, if necessary.

   The Time On and Time Off fields identify when the deflector is active.

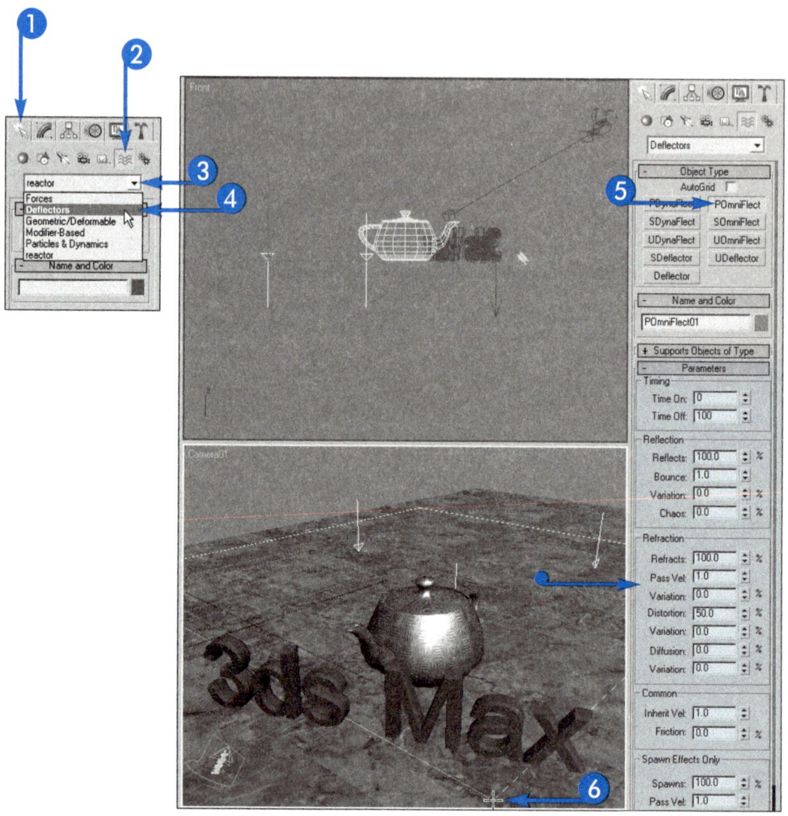

7 Click [icon].

8 Click the particle system and drag to the deflector.

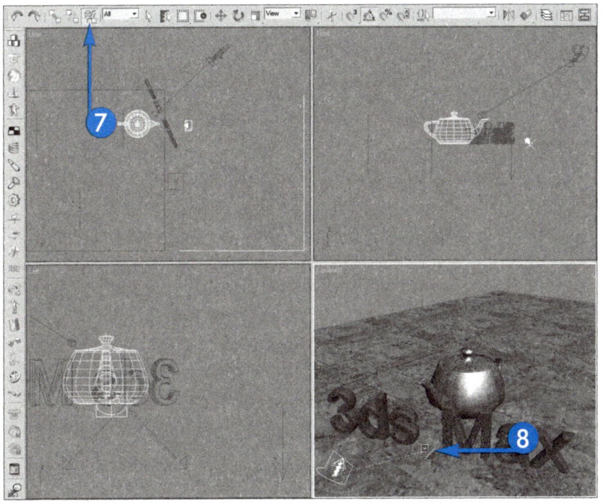

The particle system flashes to indicate that it is bound to the space warp.

- You may need to click and drag the Time Slider forward to see the effect of the deflector.
- You can click [icon] to preview the animation.

MASTER IT

Why do my particles stop bouncing off the deflectors?

There could be a few reasons for this. Unlike the Gravity and Ripple space warps, deflectors must be located in the stream of particles to have any effect. Determine whether the deflector has moved or turned so that the particles no longer impact it. Also, deflectors are only operational as long as the current scene time is within the range that you specified in the Time On and Time Off parameters in the Deflector's Modify panel. If the deflector is completely unresponsive, select the particle system to ensure that the binding is still present in the Modifier Stack and that it is not turned off.

PART VII

continued

Change Particle Directions with Deflectors *(Continued)*

Particles in a scene can be acted upon by several forces that dictate changes to their direction and speed. The Gravity and Wind space warps, for example, can work in tandem to distribute the particles throughout the scene. This results in an often unpredictable spread of particles. When the scene does not exist with a single, flat object to represent the ground plane, which is more common than not, the particles may need to bounce off several objects to keep their trajectories true and realistic. For example, the ejected shell casings from a machine gun may need to bounce off a window frame and a boot before coming to rest on the floor. Fortunately, there is no limit to the number of deflectors that you can bind a particle system to.

Planes and spheres are easily represented by the available planar and spherical deflectors, but, there are occasions where an odd-shaped object is required to deflect particles. These are the situations that the UOmniFlect deflector was designed for. The UOmniFlect deflector uses a selected geometry object as the deflector while the UOmniFlect gizmo remains in the scene as the selectable link to its parameter.

Change Particle Directions with Deflectors *(continued)*

Using a UOmniFlect Deflector

1. Click .
2. Click .
3. Click to display a list of space warp types.
4. Click Deflectors.

   The available Deflector space warp buttons display in the Object Type rollout.
5. Click UOmniFlect.
6. Click and drag in a viewport.

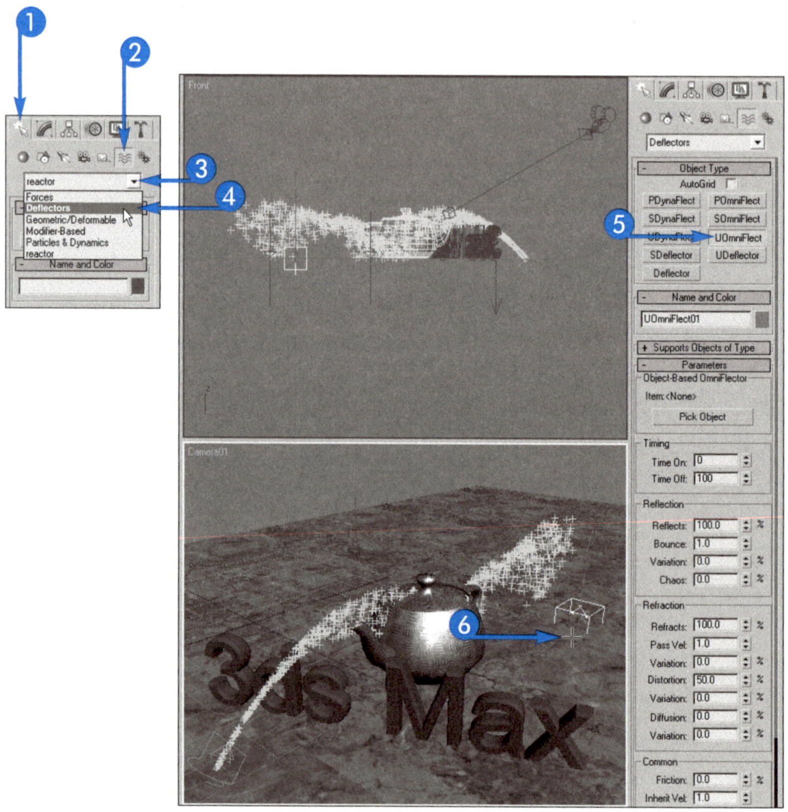

3ds Max creates the UOmniFlect gizmo.

The location of the space warp does not matter.

7. Adjust any parameter values if necessary.

The Time On and Time Off fields identify when the deflector is active.

8. Click Pick Object.

9. Click the object that you want to use as a deflector.

10. Click .

11. Click the particle system and drag to the deflector.

The particle system is bound to the space warp, and the object deflects the particles.

- You may need to click and drag the Time Slider forward to see the effect of the deflector.
- You can click to preview the animation.

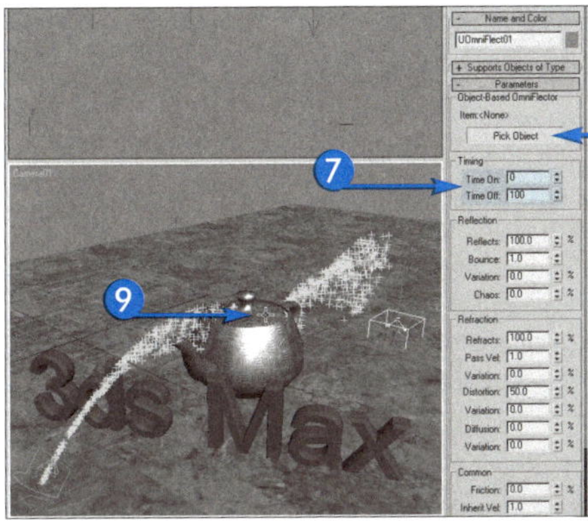

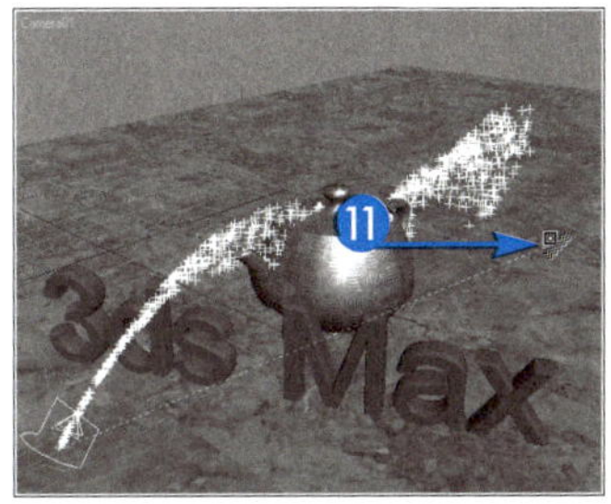

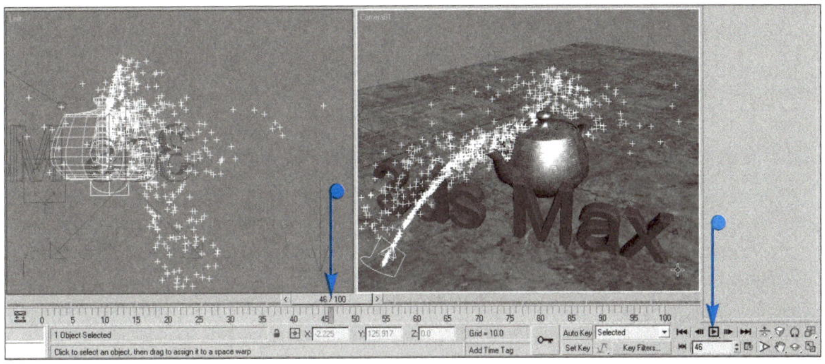

MASTER IT

Why do some particles get past my deflectors?

Deflectors can be set to allow a percentage of particles through. Check to ensure that the Reflects value is set to 100 percent. If the Reflects value is at 100 percent, then you are encountering a phenomenon called particle leakage. This occurs most often when the deflector is moving, or when an object that is used as a deflector is deforming. The particles are moving from one side of the deflector to the other without enough time to sample the particle's location and cause the deflection. This can usually be solved by increasing the particle system's Subframe Sampling value, by slowing down the particles, or by adding additional deflectors.

Understanding Reactor

You can use reactor to create complex simulations of interactions between objects in your scene. Formerly a third-party plug-in, reactor is an integrated physics engine in 3ds Max. Reactor's features are available from the Utilities panel, the reactor menu, and the reactor toolbar.

Reactor uses the laws and principles of physics to calculate how objects react when they collide in your scene and interact with your scene's properties, such as wind and gravity. The collisions are based upon the properties of the objects, which in turn are based upon the objects' collection types.

You can define an object collection type by selecting the appropriate button on the reactor toolbar from the reactor menu. You can use the reactor rollouts that display in the Utilities panel to set the properties for the collection objects.

A Utilities Rollout

Lists the utilities that you can use with 3ds Max. You can access additional utilities by clicking More.

B About Rollout

Indicates the version of reactor that is installed, and identifies the company that developed reactor.

C Preview & Animation Rollout

Defines the frames that are used to create the reactor simulation. Also provides buttons for previewing the simulation in the reactor Real-Time Preview window. The Create Animation button generates the required keyframes to simulate the object interactions.

D Reactor Toolbar

Assigns the functionality of reactor to objects in your scene. You can define collections, modifiers, and constraints.

E World Rollout

Controls parameters related to the scene, such as the strength and direction of gravity.

F Collisions Rollout

Controls collisions between objects. You can disable collision detection between specific objects as required.

G Properties Rollout

Sets the physical properties of the selected objects using the Mass, Elasticity, and Friction values, as well as the shape for the simulation. You can set the properties for any object that has been assigned a collection.

H Utils Rollout

Provides utilities for analyzing and optimizing the simulation.

I Display Rollout

Controls the display of the simulation in the reactor Real-Time Preview window.

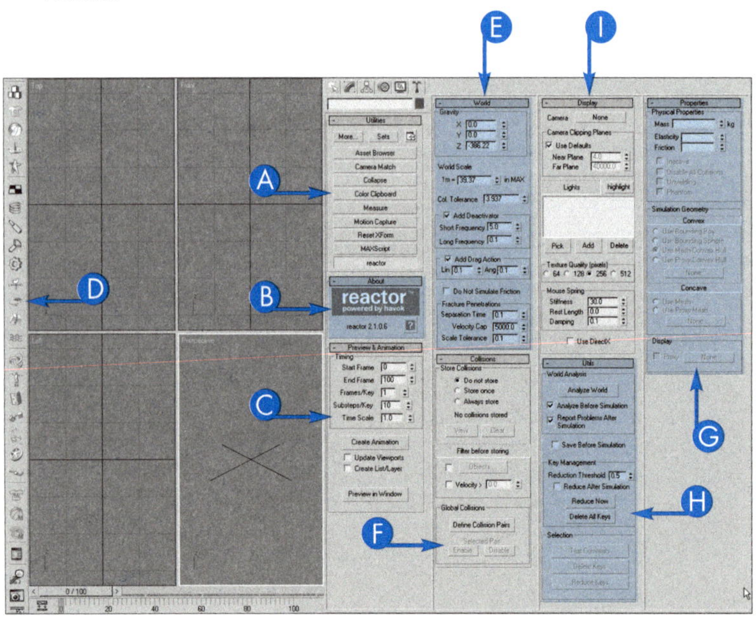

Collections

When you use reactor to create simulations, you must first create a collection to which each object in the simulation belongs. The collection defines how each object reacts during collisions. For example, a bowling ball and the pins are affected by a collision, whereas the alley is not.

You can define the reaction of the object by assigning it to a reactor collection. There are five different reactor collection types: Rigid Body, Soft Body, Cloth, Rope, and Deforming Mesh. You must include all objects in a reactor simulation in one of these collections or they will be ignored. The reactor toolbar contains buttons for each of these collection types.

Keep in mind that reactor objects actually fall into two categories, Rigid Body and Soft Body. The Rigid Body objects are those whose geometry does not change over time when affected by collisions with other objects or forces. The Soft Body objects, which are themselves broken into four collections, are those objects whose geometry is affected by collisions and forces such as wind.

Reactor Collection Types

Button	Type	Description
	Rigid Body	All objects that do not change shape as a result of an interaction with other objects.
	Soft Body	3D objects that change shape over time as a result of an interaction with other objects.
	Cloth	2D objects that change shape over time as a result of an interaction with other objects.
	Rope	Linear objects that change shape over time as a result of an interaction with other objects.
	Deforming Mesh	A mesh object with vertices that have already been animated.

When you add a collection to your scene, a non-rendering collection icon displays in the viewports. When you select the collection icon, you can make modifications that affect the objects in that collection.

Modifiers

Modifiers are used to define Deformable Body objects before they can be added to collections. The modifier specifies the type of simulations that can be performed with the object. Reactor provides three different modifiers: Cloth, Soft Body, and Rope.

Reactor Modifier Types

Button	Type	Description
	Cloth	Turns any object into a deformable mesh. Apply this modifier to objects that you want to use as flags, clothing, curtains, or any other type of loose fabric.
	Soft Body	Turns any rigid object into a flexible object that can be transformed to change its overall appearance during a simulation, such as a pillow being hit by a heavy object. You can control how flexible the object is by adjusting the Stiffness, Mass, and Friction parameter values.
	Rope	Turns a spline object into a Rope object. You can use Rope objects to simulate ropes, hair, chains, or any other rope-like object.

PART VII

continued

Understanding Reactor *(Continued)*

Constraints

Reactor uses constraints to restrict the movement of rigid body objects in a simulation. You can use constraints to ensure that an object reacts correctly during a collision. For example, pushing on a door should cause it to swing open, and not fall over. This motion can be controlled with a Hinge constraint.

The constraints that are available with reactor fall into two categories, Simple and Cooperative. You can add the Simple constraints directly to the rigid bodies in the scene. The Cooperative constraints are more complex and require the use of a Constraint Solver to calculate all the constraints needed for the simulation.

Reactor Constraint Types

Button	*Type*	*Description*
	Spring	A simple constraint that creates an elastic effect between two rigid body objects. The Spring constraint reacts in a similar manner to a real-world spring by working to maintain its resting length and therefore returning the attached objects to their original positions.
	Linear Dashpot	A simple constraint that constrains two rigid body objects together, like a very strong Spring constraint. It can also constrain a rigid body object to a precise location in the scene.
	Angular Dashpot	A simple constraint that constrains the rotation between two rigid body objects. You can also use it to constrain the rotation of one rigid body object to a specific orientation.
	Constraint Solver	Used to hold — and perform the required calculations for — cooperative constraints for rigid body collections. Without a Constraint Solver, the cooperative constraints do not react properly.
	Rag Doll	A cooperative constraint that simulates the behavior of body joints such as ankles, shoulders, and hips. You can specify the range of movement for each constraint.
	Hinge	A cooperative constraint that simulates the movement between two objects with a shared, specified pivot location.
	Point-to-Point	A cooperative constraint that creates an attachment point between two rigid body objects, or one object and a point in World space. Each object can transform independently while maintaining the connection point.
	Prismatic	A cooperative constraint that connects two rigid body objects, or one object to a point in space. The movement of the objects is restricted to one axis and there is no rotation permitted.
	Car-Wheel	A cooperative constraint that allows you to attach a wheel to another rigid body object. You can rotate the wheel around a specific axis.
	Point-Path	A cooperative constraint that attaches two rigid body objects together to form a hierarchy. The child object can move along a path relative to the parent object.

Water

Reactor includes a Water object to simulate the behavior of water or any other liquid surface. Reactor objects can interact with the Water object to create physically accurate effects, such as waves and ripples in the water. When an object hits the surface of the water, reactor calculates the mass of the object to determine its buoyancy value. This calculation determines whether the object floats on the surface of the water, how high it floats, or whether it sinks. You can change the density of the Water object to simulate the density of other liquids.

The reactor Water object is actually a space warp that simulates the water surface. You can add a Water object either by clicking the Create Water button ( ) in the reactor toolbar, or by selecting the Water space warp under the reactor category of the space warps in the Create panel. Both options produce the same result. Like any other space warp, a Water object does not render. Therefore, to make its effects visible, you must bind it to another object that displays as the rendered water. See the section "Simulate a Water Surface" for more information on rendering realistic water surfaces with reactor. For information on space warps, see Chapter 25.

Wind

Like gravity, wind is a natural force that affects the physical reactions of objects in real life. Reactor provides a Wind object ( ) that allows you to introduce wind effects to your scene. When you add wind to your scene, you can control the speed, gusts, and direction of the effect. The parameters can be animated to make the effects change over time.

Real-Time Preview

When working with reactor, you can preview your simulation at any time by clicking the Preview in Window button in the Preview & Animation rollout in the Utilities panel, or the Preview Animation button ( ) in the reactor toolbar. The Real-Time Preview window allows you to interact with the objects in your simulation using the mouse buttons.

The Real-Time Preview window displays only if you have the OpenGL or Direct3D display drivers loaded.

To interact with objects in the simulation, right-click the objects and drag to move them. If you drag with the left mouse button, then you can rotate the scene.

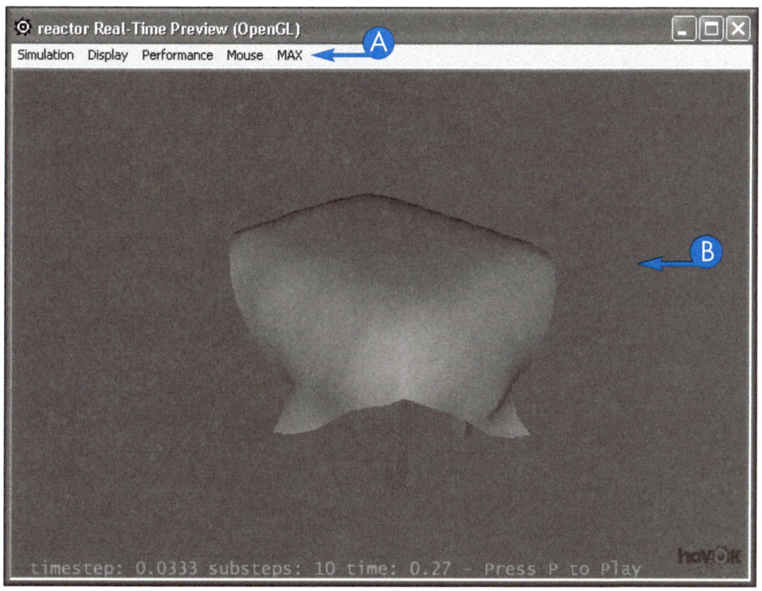

A Preview Toolbar

Controls the reactor simulation. You can adjust the camera, the display settings, and the performance of the simulation. Any changes that you make in the Preview window can also be updated in your reactor settings in 3ds Max.

B Real-Time Preview Interactive Display

Displays the reactor simulation. You can play the simulation by pressing P on the keyboard. As the simulation plays, the bottom of the window provides the Timing information that is used to create the simulation.

Create a Rigid Body Simulation

You can use reactor Rigid Body Collections to simulate the reactions that occur when solid objects collide. This animation works well with objects that do not change shape when they come into contact with other objects. For example, if two pool balls collide, they remain the same shape, but the speed at which they collide determines how the objects react after they collide.

Creating a rigid body simulation involves identifying the objects that are affected, setting object parameters and initial animation, and then rendering the results. The first step is to select the objects that make up the effect and assign them to a Rigid Body Collection that contains all objects that interact. For example, if the objects are rolling across a flat plane, you must include that plane because its parameters affect the entire animation.

When you add a Rigid Body Collection to your scene, 3ds Max creates an icon to represent it. Any objects that are selected when you create the collection are added to it, and additional objects can be added from the RB Collection Properties rollout.

CD FILE: The RigidBody.max file is available on the CD-ROM for you to practice creating rigid body simulations.

Create a Rigid Body Simulation

Create a Rigid Body Collection

1. Click the Create Rigid Body Collection button ( ).
2. Click in a viewport.

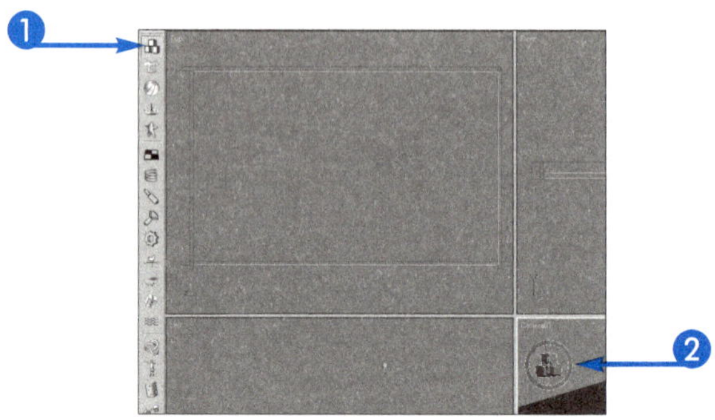

- The Rigid Body Collection icon displays.

The Create panel displays the properties for the Rigid Body Collection object.

3. In the RB Collection Properties rollout, click Add.

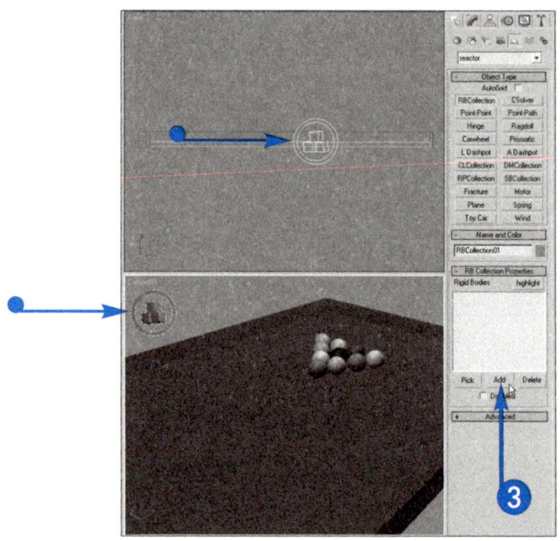

The Select rigid bodies dialog box appears.

4 Click All to select all objects in the scene.

To select individual objects, you can hold down the Ctrl key and click each object.

5 Click Select.

3ds Max adds the selected objects in the scene to the Rigid Body Collection.

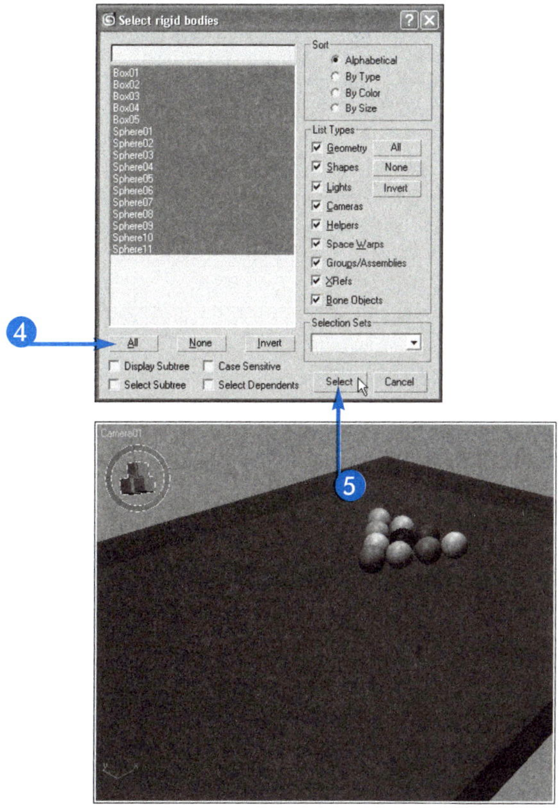

What is the ODE Solver?

▼ The Ordinary Differential Equation, or ODE, solver, in the Advanced rollout, is used by reactor to calculate the reactions between rigid body objects. There are two different solver options, Euler and Runge-Kutta. The Euler solver is the default solver. It is also the faster of the two, and typically provides very good results. The Runge-Kutta solver requires more time to calculate, but it also produces more physically accurate results. You should always select the Runge-Kutta solver when you have objects in the Rigid Body Collection that are connected using Spring, Linear Dashpot, or Angular Dashpot constraints.

Can I add and remove objects to and from the Rigid Body Collection?

▼ Yes. As with other objects that you create in 3ds Max, a Rigid Body Collection can also be modified. To make modifications, you need to select the Rigid Body Collection icon in a viewport and then click to display the Modify panel. To remove objects from the list, select the object name in the list box and then click Delete. Keep in mind that the object is no longer used in the animation. To add objects, click Pick and then click an object in the scene to select it, or click Add to select it from a dialog box. When you select a new object, it is added to the list box.

continued

Create a Rigid Body Simulation *(Continued)*

You can set the properties for each object so that reactor knows how to treat them in the simulation. For example, an object with a larger mass reacts differently than a lower-mass object under the same conditions. You can set object properties, such as the mass, friction, and elasticity, in the Rigid Body Properties dialog box.

The Mass property, which indicates the density and volume of the object, controls how it interacts with other objects. For example, if the Mass value is zero, the object remains in a fixed location throughout the animation.

The Friction property controls how smoothly two objects move when in contact with each other. The Friction values of both objects combine to determine how the objects interact. You can use values between zero and five, although zero to one produce the most realistic results.

The Elasticity property controls how bouncy the object is when an object collides with it. As with the Friction property, the Elasticity of the two objects is combined to calculate the effect. You can use values between zero and five, although zero to one produce the most realistic results.

Create a Rigid Body Simulation *(continued)*

Set Object Properties

6. Select an object in the scene.
7. Click the Open Property Editor button ( ).

The Rigid Body Properties dialog box appears.

8. Enter a value in the Mass field.
9. Enter a value for the object friction in the Friction field.
10. Enter a value to indicate how the object bounces in the Elasticity field.

If the object should not react to a collision, click Unyielding (☐ changes to ☑).

11. Repeat steps 6 to 10 for each Rigid Body object.

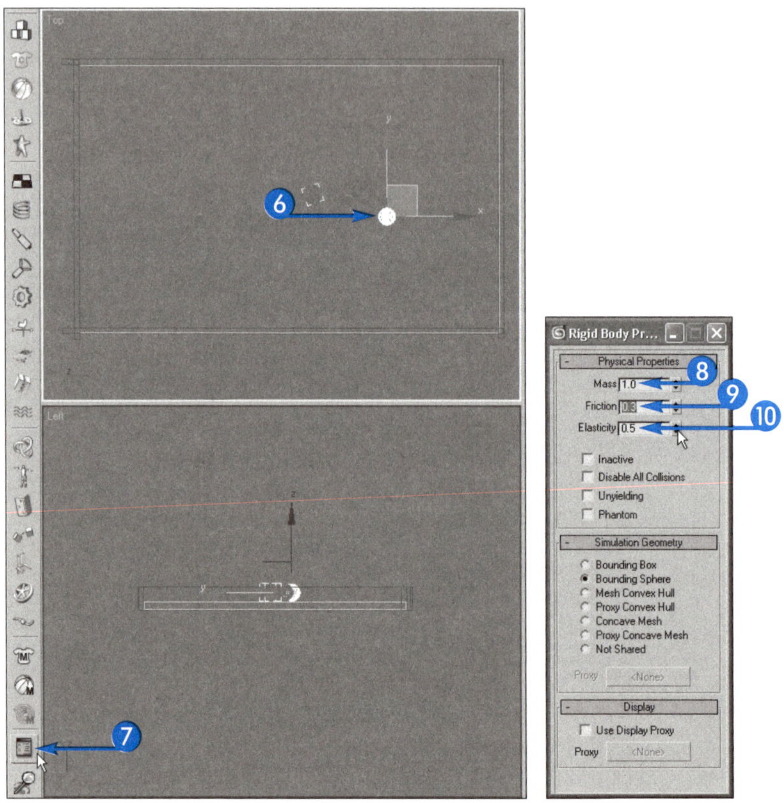

Create an Initial Animation

12. Click Auto Key.

Note: *For more information on animating objects with Auto Key, see Chapter 8.*

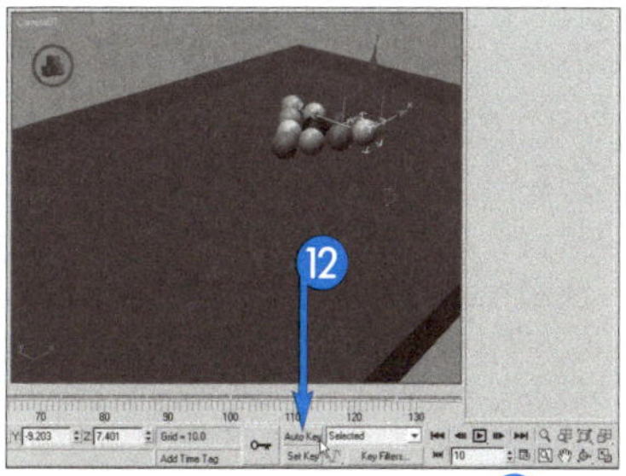

The Auto Key button, Timeline, and viewport border are highlighted in red.

13. Click and drag the Time Slider to a non-zero frame.

14. Click [move icon].

You can use any of the transform tools.

Note: *For more information on transforming objects, see Chapter 2.*

15. Click the object that you want to animate, and drag to move it.

16. Click Auto Key to turn it off.

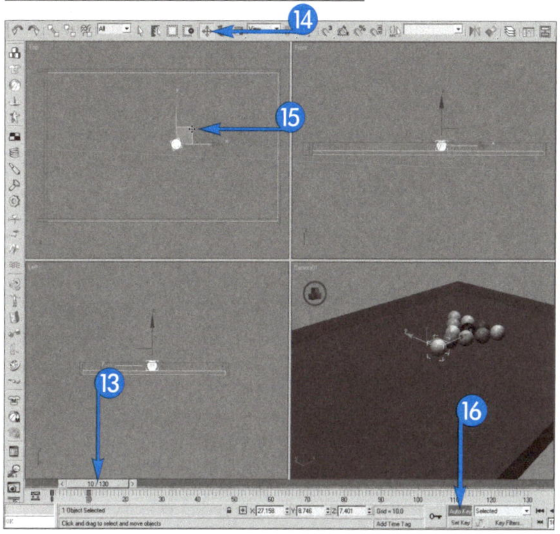

MASTER IT

When would I select the Inactive or Disable All Collisions options?

- These are two of the four property options that you can set for each object to control how they respond to other objects. If you set an object as Inactive, it does not affect the animation until another object interacts with it. If you select Disable All Collisions, the object is not affected by collisions with other objects. Select Unyielding if you have an object, such as a wall, that should not move when an object interacts with it. The Phantom option is the same as Disable All Collisions, but it can be used to trigger another event.

Do I need to set the Simulation Geometry for each object?

- When reactor creates the simulations, it uses objects with simple geometry to calculate the reactions when the objects collide. These Simulation Geometries, or proxies, are used because it simplifies the necessary calculations. By replacing a complex object with a simple geometric shape, such as a sphere or a box, the calculations required are simplified, thus making the calculation faster. By default, reactor selects the Simulation Geometry that it uses in the calculation, although you can select a different geometry. You can see the applied Simulation Geometry for each object in the Real-Time Preview window by clicking Display, and then clicking Sim Edges.

Create a Rigid Body Simulation *(Continued)*

After you have set the properties for the animation, you can preview it to see the results. Previewing is essential because it allows you to quickly see how the simulation will be animated in your rendered scene. The Real-Time Preview window creates a simulation using the initial animation that you created.

Before viewing the preview of the simulation, you should specify the timing parameter values. You can specify the time parameters in the Preview & Animation rollout in the Utilities panel.

You need to specify the animation frames in your scene that you want to use to calculate the simulation. You can specify the first frame to use in the Start Frame field and the last frame in the End Frame field. For example, you may want to start your scene at frame 5 and end it at frame 90, after the simulation no longer yields any productive results.

The Real-Time Preview window displays a simulation of the animation that is created with reactor. Although the Real-Time Preview displays the objects as solid objects, it does not display any materials that you have applied to the objects.

Create a Rigid Body Simulation *(continued)*

Set Animation Parameters

17 Click the Utilities panel icon (T).

18 Click reactor.

The reactor rollouts display in the Utilities panel.

19 Click to expand the Preview & Animation rollout.

20 Type the frame number where you want to start the reactor simulation.

21 Type the frame number where you want to end the reactor simulation.

22 Click Preview in Window.

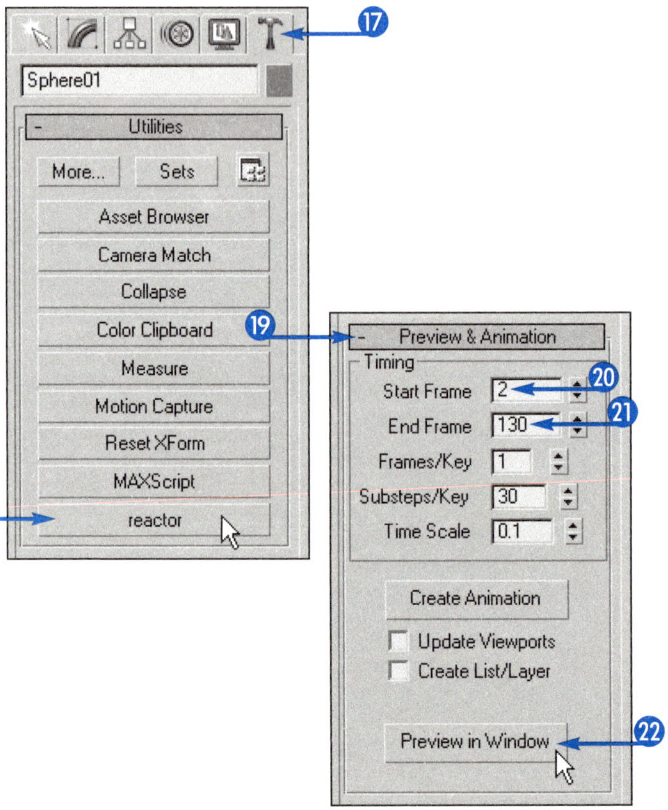

Preview the Animation

The Real-Time Preview window appears.

23 Press P.

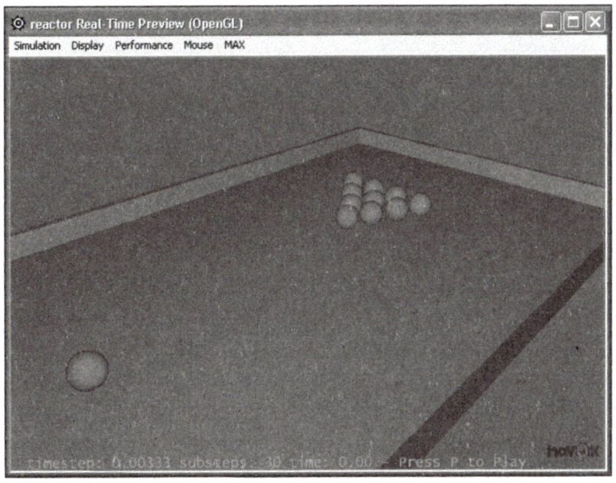

The reactor simulation plays in the window.

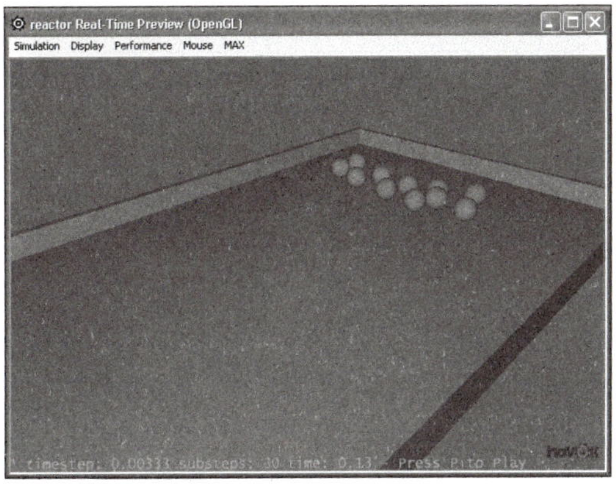

MASTER IT

How do I make an object's movement constant?

▼ By default, when you create animation in 3ds Max, the animation effects are based on keys that fall along a Bezier curve. This causes the animation to start out slow and gradually increase between keyframes. As each keyframe approaches, the speed of the animation decreases to ensure that the transition through the key is smooth. In some animations, such as a rolling ball, this is not desirable. You can adjust the curve of the animation using the Curve Editor. To open the Curve Editor, click Graph Editors, and then click Track View-Curve Editor. Select the keys and set the tangents to Linear. This creates animation that flows at a constant speed. For information on the Curve Editor, see Chapter 11.

Why does reactor display an error message when I use a Plane primitive object in a collection?

▼ Reactor requires objects with depth to compute the effects of collisions within a scene. However, Plane objects are two-dimensional. You can use one of two options to replace a Plane object: You can either create a flat Box object, or you can use the Plane object provided by reactor. To create a reactor Plane object in your scene, click the Create Plane button (). The reactor plane is a fixed, infinite plane that can be moved and rotated using the Transform options. For more information on transforming objects, see Chapter 2.

Render a Reactor Simulation

You can render any scene that contains a simulation created by reactor. This allows you to create an animation file, such as an AVI or MOV, that you can view inside or outside 3ds Max. In order to render the simulation, you must first create the animation keyframes. The keyframes contain object movements in the scene as calculated by reactor.

You can specify the settings for creating the keyframes in the Preview & Animation rollout. You can specify the number of frames for every keyframe that you want to create for the simulation in the Frames/Key field. By default, reactor creates one keyframe for every frame in the animation. This produces the most accurate animation but requires more time to calculate. You can increase this number to reduce the number of keyframes.

When you click the Create Animation button, reactor displays a warning that you cannot undo the creation of keyframes. After the keyframes are created, you can use the Render Scene dialog box to render the Active Time Segment. For more information on using the Render Scene dialog box, see Chapter 20.

CD FILE: The RigidBodyComplete.max file is available on the CD-ROM for you to practice rendering a reactor simulation.

Render a Reactor Simulation

1. Click the Utilities panel icon ( ).
2. Click reactor.
3. Click Preview & Animation to open the rollout.
4. Type the frame numbers to start and end the reactor simulation, as well as the number of frames for every keyframe.
5. Click Create Animation.

   A reactor dialog box appears to verify your selection.
6. Click OK.

   Reactor creates keyframes for the objects that are affected.
7. Click the Render Scene button ( ).

Note: *For information on rendering with the Render Scene dialog box, see Chapter 20.*

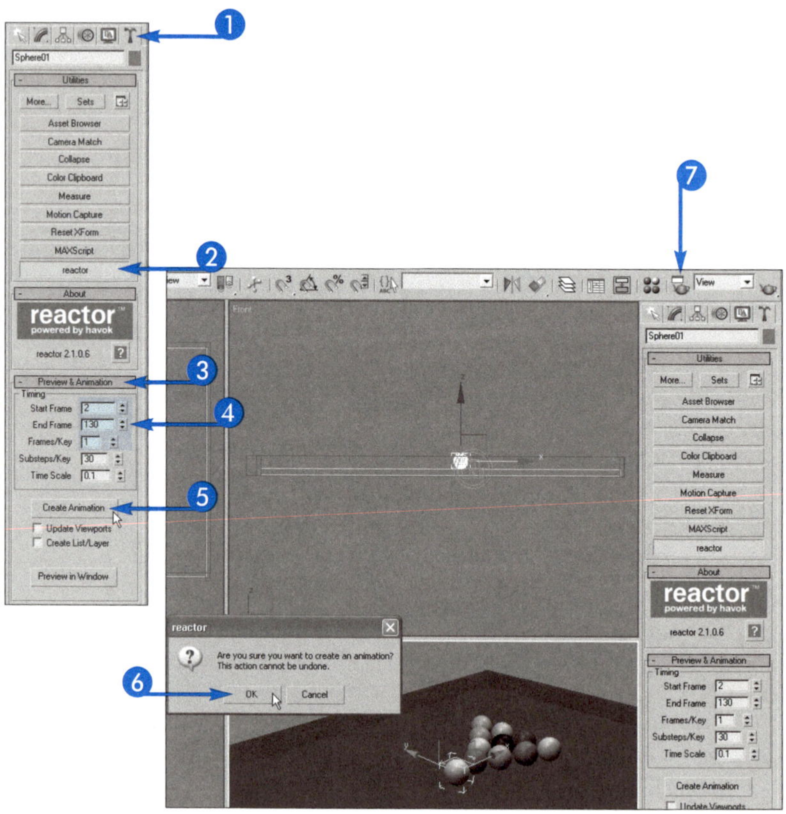

The Render Scene dialog box appears.

8 Click the Active Time Segment option (◯ changes to ◉).

9 Click the Save File option (☐ changes to ☑).

- If you have not specified a file name, click Files and specify an animation file to create.

10 Click Render.

3ds Max renders the entire scene to create an animation file that includes the simulation created by reactor.

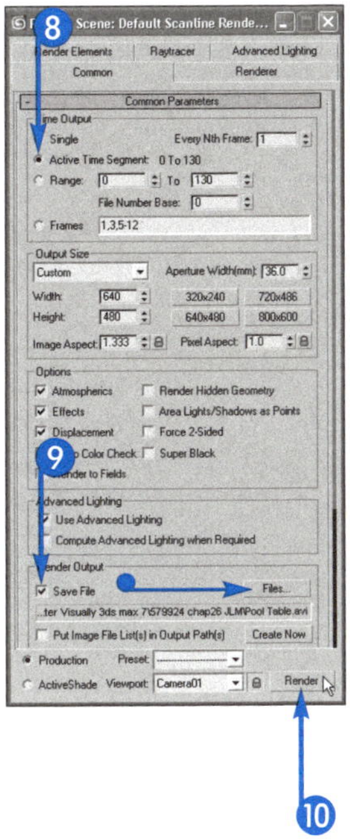

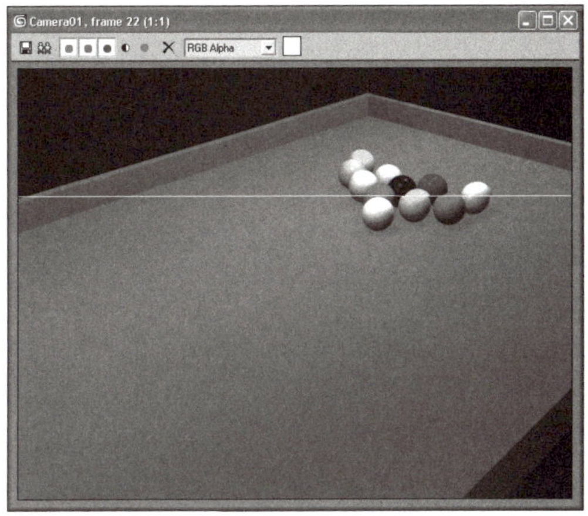

MASTER IT

What does the Time Scale do?

▼ You can use the Time Scale to change the scale of time between reactor and 3ds Max by adjusting the Time Scale value in the Preview & Animation rollout. A value of 1 maintains a constant time value. To create a slow-motion animation, specify a value less than 1. To increase the speed of the animation, specify a value greater than 1.

Can I use the Make Preview feature to see the animation?

▼ Yes, after reactor creates the keyframes, you can preview the animation before rendering by clicking Animation and then clicking Make Preview. 3ds Max creates a preview AVI file and opens it in the Windows Media Player.

How do I undo the keyframes created by reactor?

▼ You cannot undo the creation of keyframes by reactor. As a result, a warning dialog box displays whenever you click Create Animation. However, 3ds Max provides another method using the Hold and Fetch commands. Before clicking Create Animation, click Edit, and then click Hold. This creates a copy of the current scene. After creating the keyframes, if you are unhappy with the results, you can click Edit and then click Fetch to return the scene to the state before reactor created the keyframes. You can also select the objects in the scene and then delete the keys in the Track bar.

Create a Cloth Object Collection

You can create a Cloth object that reacts with the same properties as real cloth when it collides with other objects in the scene. Creating this type of object allows you to simulate the effects of fabric, sheets, flags, banners, and even clothing.

You can create a Cloth object with reactor in a two-step process. You must first apply the Cloth modifier to the object in your scene that you want to use as a Cloth object. The Cloth modifier sets the specific cloth properties for the object. The Mass property indicates the mass of the object in kilograms. You can adjust the other properties to control how stiff the cloth is when it drapes.

After setting the Cloth modifier properties, you must assign the Cloth object to a Cloth Collection. All Cloth objects must be added to the Cloth Collection before they are used by reactor.

You can preview the Cloth object in the Real-Time Preview window. This allows you to see how the Cloth object reacts when it comes in contact with other reactor objects. 3ds Max 8 also ships with a Cloth modifier that is covered in Chapter 28.

CD FILE: The Cloth.max file is available on the CD-ROM for you to practice creating a Cloth Collection.

Create a Cloth Object Collection

1. Select the animated object that you want to make into a Cloth object.

Note: *For more information on animating objects, see Chapter 8.*

2. Click the Apply Cloth Modifier button ( ).

   3ds Max adds the reactor Cloth modifier to the object. The parameters for the modifier display in the Modify panel.

3. Type a Mass value, and any other required values, for the Cloth object.

4. Click the Create Cloth Collection button ( ).

   3ds Max creates a Cloth Collection and adds the selected object.

   The contents of the collection display in the Cloth Entities list box.

5. Click the Utilities panel icon ( ).

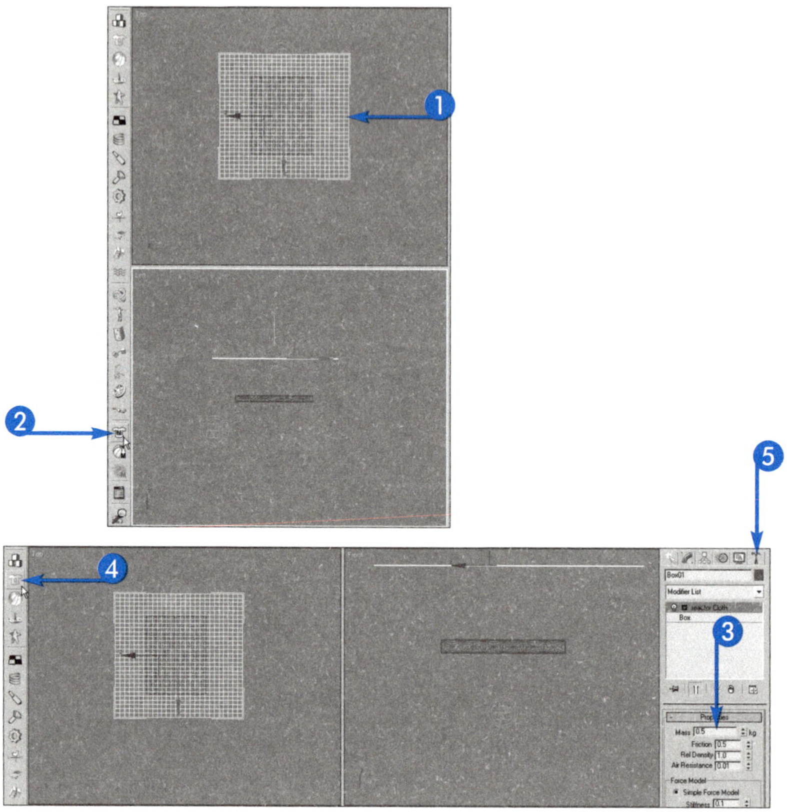

6 Click to select reactor.

7 Click to expand the Preview & Animation rollout.

8 Type the frame number where you want to start, and then type the last frame that you want to use in the simulation.

9 Click Preview in Window.

The Real-Time Preview window appears.

10 Press P to preview the reactor simulation.

Note: *See the section "Render a Reactor Simulation" for information on rendering the Cloth object.*

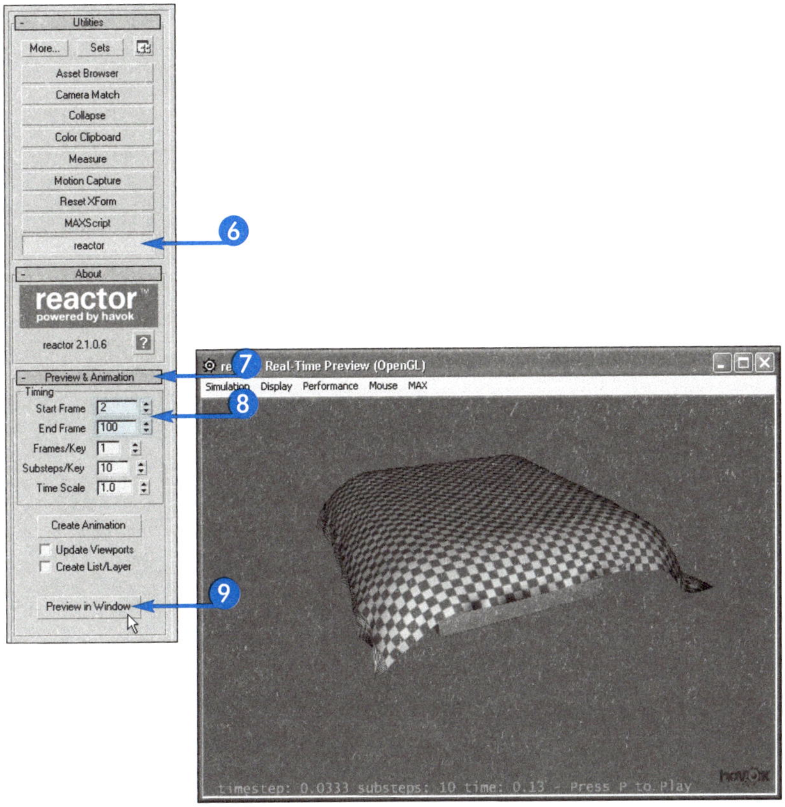

Why does the draping of my Cloth object look jagged?

When a Cloth object deforms, it folds along the contiguous edges. If the object is not very complex, the folding and draping of the object is not very realistic. To correct the problem, you must increase the complexity of the object. For example, if the Cloth object is a Plane, then you can increase the values of the Length Segs and Width Segs of the Plane's parameters. If an object is an editable poly, then the Tessellate tool may be the best option. For more information on working with objects in 3ds Max, see Chapters 4 and 6.

Why does the Cloth object ignore other objects in my scene?

When you create a scene that calculates interactions between objects using reactor, every object involved must be part of a reactor collection. Therefore, if the Cloth object interacts with other objects in the scene, the objects must be defined in a reactor collection. For example, if the cloth drapes over a solid object, then that object must be part of a Rigid Body Collection. Objects can be in any one of the four reactor collections. See the section "Understanding Reactor" for more information on collections.

Simulate a Flag with Wind

You can use reactor to simulate wind affecting a Cloth object, such as a flag blowing in the wind. In order to create a Flag simulation, you must use three different reactor components: a Cloth object, a Rigid Body object, and wind. You need a Rigid Body object to which you can attach the Cloth object. To attach the Cloth object, you must create a constraint that allows you to attach a deformable body to a particular point in World space to constrain its movement. For example, when creating a flag, you would create a constraint that attaches it to a pole.

In order to attach the Cloth object to the Rigid Body object, you must define the locations or vertices that should be attached. To do this, you must select Vertex as the sub-object of the Cloth object, which allows you to select the individual vertices of the Cloth object to attach to the Rigid body. The Attach to Rigid Body constraint indicates that you want to attach the selected vertices to a Rigid Body object. When you select that object, 3ds Max creates the connection.

CD FILE: The Wind.max file is available on the CD-ROM for you to practice simulating the Wind effect.

Simulate a Flag with Wind

Create a Cloth constraint

1. Select the flag Cloth object.

***Note:** See the section "Create a Cloth Object Collection" for more information on creating a Cloth object.*

2. Click to display the Modify panel.
3. Click next to reactor Cloth in the Modifier Stack.

The Vertex sub-object option displays in the Modifier Stack.

4. Click Vertex.
5. Select the points on the Cloth object that you want to attach.

You can hold down Ctrl to select multiple points.

6. In the Constraints rollout, click Attach To Rigid Body.

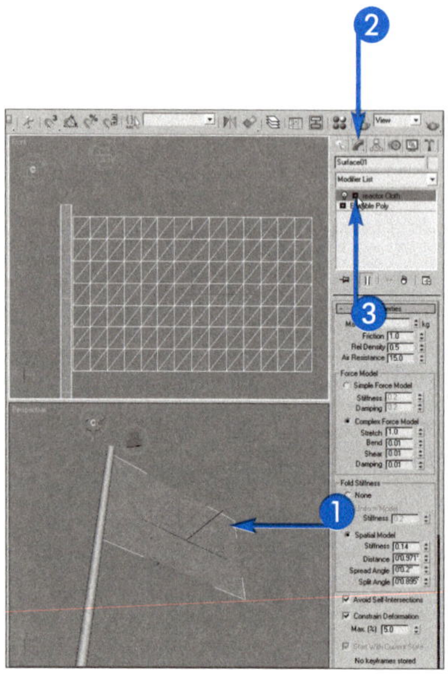

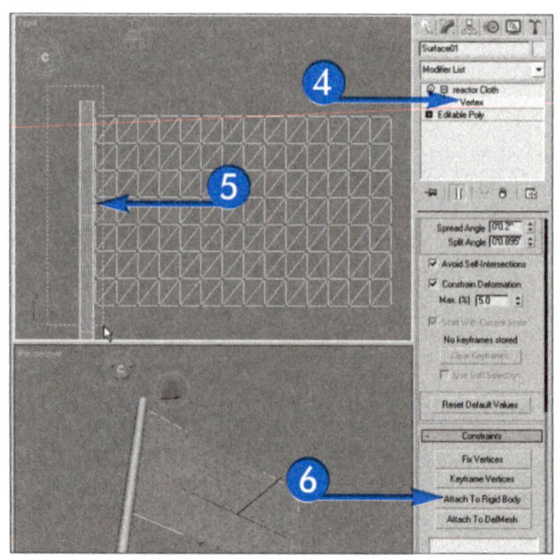

3ds Max creates the Attach To RigidBody constraint.

7. Click the Attach To RigidBody constraint.

   The constraint highlights.

8. In the Attach to RigidBody rollout, click None.

9. Click the Rigid Body object to which you want to constrain the Cloth object.

Note: *See the section "Create a Rigid Body Simulation" for more information on defining Rigid Body objects.*

- The name of the Rigid Body object displays on the button.

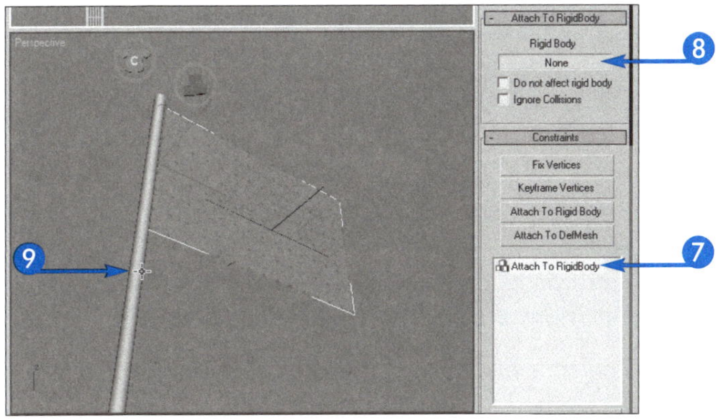

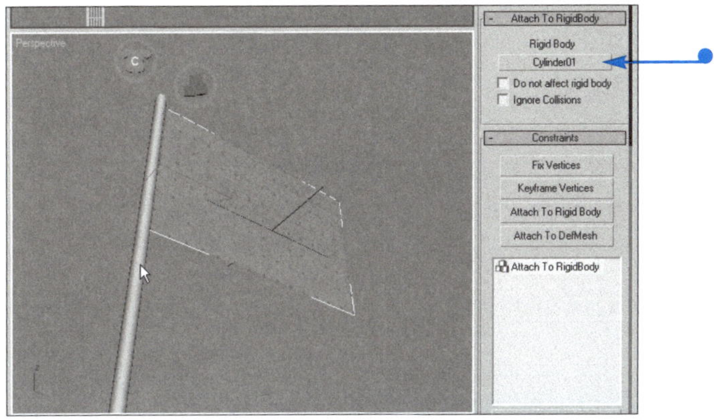

What Cloth properties should I set when creating a flag?

▼ Cloth properties are based on flag size and the amount of wind that affects the flag. By default, the mass is at 1 kilogram, but you typically want to reduce this value; a 0.5 value makes the flag lighter so it blows better in the wind. You can also adjust the Air Resistance, which controls how the Cloth object loses energy as it moves in the wind. Selecting the Avoid Self-Intersections option near the bottom of the Properties rollout ensures that the flag will blow without its surfaces crossing each other.

What other constraints can I make with deformable objects?

▼ There are actually four different constraints that you can apply to Deformable Body objects in order to constrain their movement.

Constraint	Description
Fix Vertices	Fixes the selected vertices to their current position in World space.
Keyframe Vertices	Fixes the selected vertices to a location, based upon the current animation. This allows you to reposition the selected vertices by creating keyframes.
Attach to RigidBody	Attaches the selected vertices to a Rigid Body object in the scene.
Attach to DefMesh	Attaches the selected vertices to a deforming mesh object.

continued

Simulate a Flag with Wind *(Continued)*

You can create the effect of blowing wind in your scene. This allows you to create the effect of a flag blowing in the breeze.

When you add wind, 3ds Max creates a Wind icon containing a weathervane arrow that points in the direction in which the wind blows. As a result, it is important to orient the Wind icon correctly to produce the results you want.

You can also specify the wind speed. The higher the value, the stronger the wind strength appears in your scene.

When working with Cloth objects, you should select the Ripple option to create the ripples in the cloth that are typical in the real world. You can select the type of ripples that you want to create in the Cloth objects. For example, Left/Right creates ripples from left to right.

Because wind can often swirl around in the real world, thus causing rippling effects both left to right and up and down, you may want to create a second Wind helper from a different angle. This can help to balance the motion of the flag.

Simulate a Flag with Wind *(continued)*

Create the Wind effect

10 Click .

11 Click in the viewport to position the Wind icon.

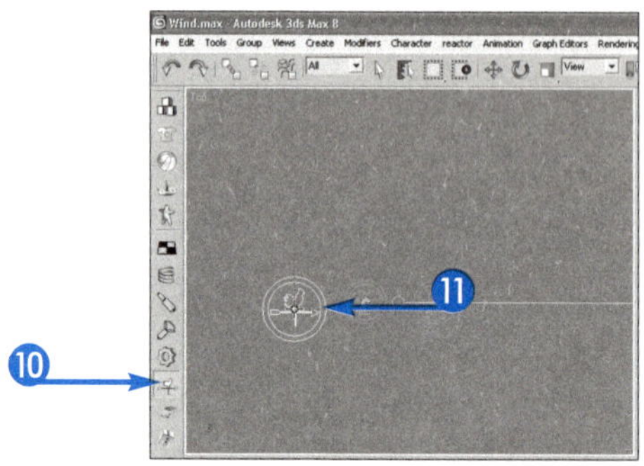

3ds Max creates a Wind icon in the viewport.

12 Click .

13 Click and drag the Rotate transform gizmo to rotate it so that the arrow points in the direction that you want.

Note: *For more information on rotating objects, see Chapter 2.*

If necessary, you can click and move the Wind icon.

14 Click .

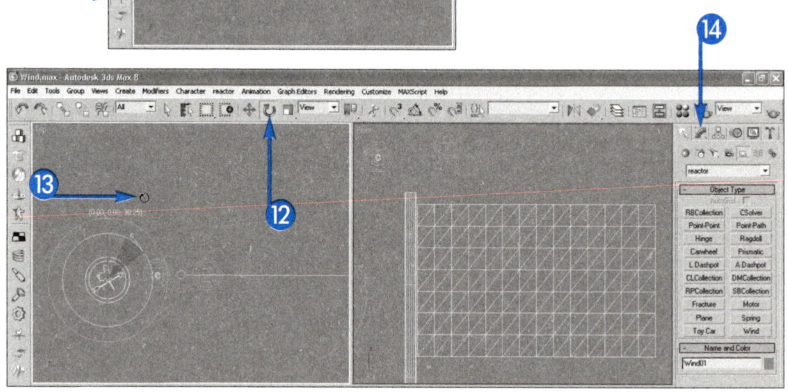

The Modify panel displays the Wind parameters.

15 Enter a value in the Wind Speed field.

16 Click Ripple (☐ changes to ☑).

17 Click Back/Forward (○ changes to ◉).

You can repeat steps 9 to 16 to create a second wind that ripples the Cloth object from left to right. Click Left/Right (○ changes to ◉) in the Ripple section.

18 Click 🔨.

The Utilities panel appears.

19 Click reactor.

20 Click to display the Preview & Animation rollout.

21 Click Preview in Window.

The Real-Time Preview window appears.

22 Press P to preview the flag simulation.

Note: *See the section "Render a Reactor Simulation" for information on rendering the flag.*

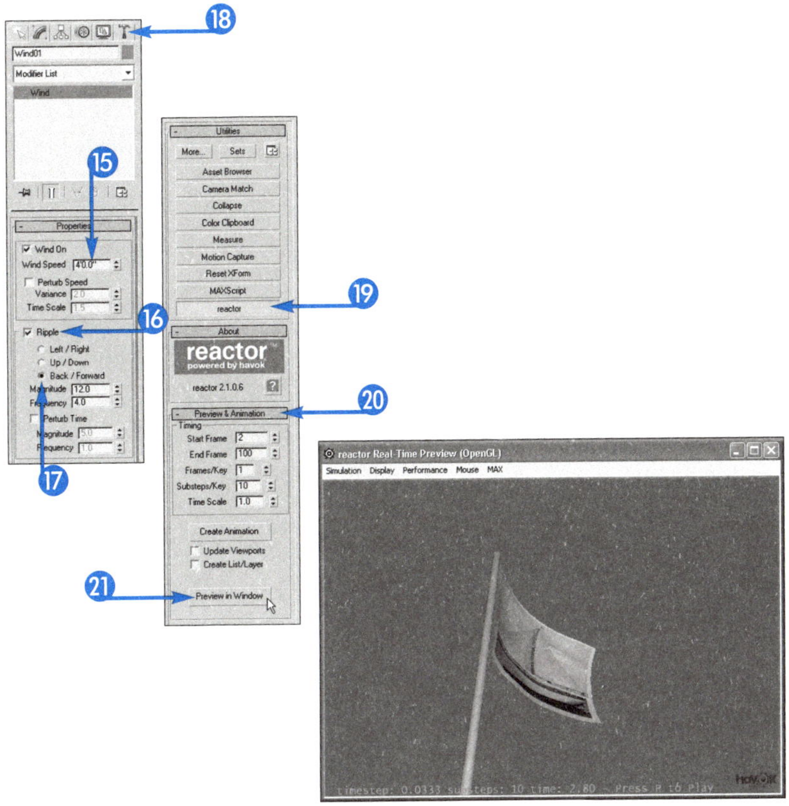

Do I need to animate the wind?

▼ No. The Wind helper automatically creates a wind force that animates the reactor Deformable Body objects in the scene. However, you can animate the parameter values associated with the Wind helper to change the Wind effect over time. For example, you can animate the Wind On parameter to control when the Wind effect is active in your scene. You can animate the following Wind parameters: Wind On, Wind Speed, Ripple, Enable Shelter, and Use Range.

What does Perturb Speed do?

▼ The Perturb Speed option allows you to change wind strength over time. Using Perturb Speed allows reactor to animate the strength of the wind instead of manually animating wind speed. If you select Perturb Speed, you need to specify values for the two associated parameters. The Variance field indicates the amount of variance that you want in the wind speed. The Time Scale field indicates how quickly the wind speed should change. Increase the value to produce a rapid change in the wind speed.

Simulate a Water Surface

You can use the reactor Water effect to simulate a liquid surface in your scene. This allows you to create a surface that reacts in a similar way to water in the real world by using the masses of Rigid Body objects to determine the effects of ripples in the water. The masses of the objects also determine whether the objects float on the surface or sink to the bottom.

When you use the Water effect in reactor, you are actually creating a space warp. Because the Water object is a space warp, it does not display when rendered in your scene and, in order to see the effect, you must bind an object that represents the water to the Water space warp.

When you create the Water effect, you can set the properties that control the amount of rippling that occurs when objects hit the surface. The Wave Speed properties control the speed at which the waves move across the surface of the water. The Min Ripple and Max Ripple properties control the size of the waves generated in the water.

Simulate a Water Surface

1. Click the Create Water button ( ).
2. Click and drag in a viewport to create a Water space warp that matches the size of your Water object.

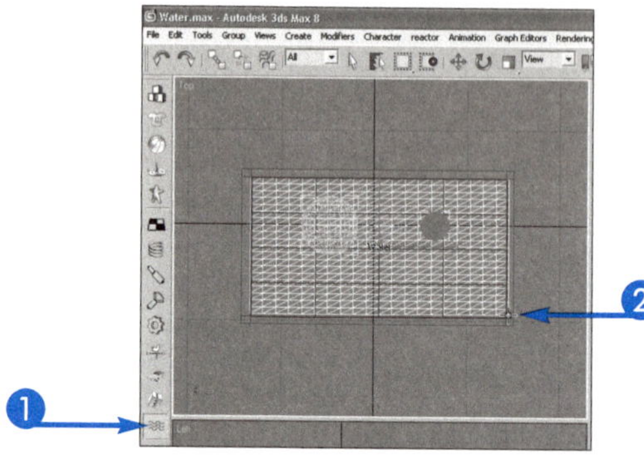

The space warp appears in the scene, labeled Water.

3. Click .
4. Click the Water space warp and drag to the Water object.

   The Water space warp is bound to the object.

5. Click .

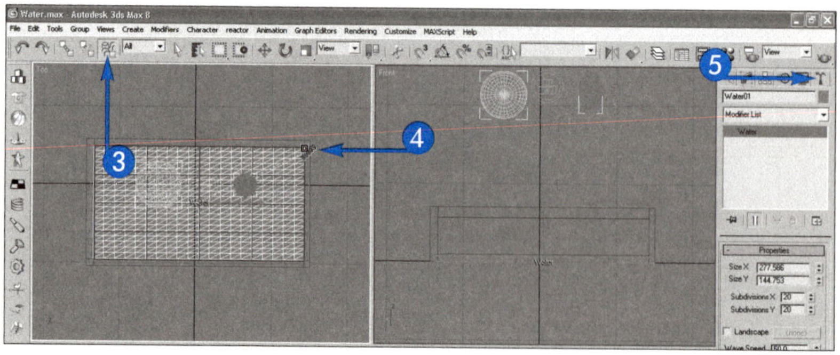

The Utilities panel appears.

6. Click reactor.
7. Click to display the Preview & Animation rollout.
8. Click Preview in Window.

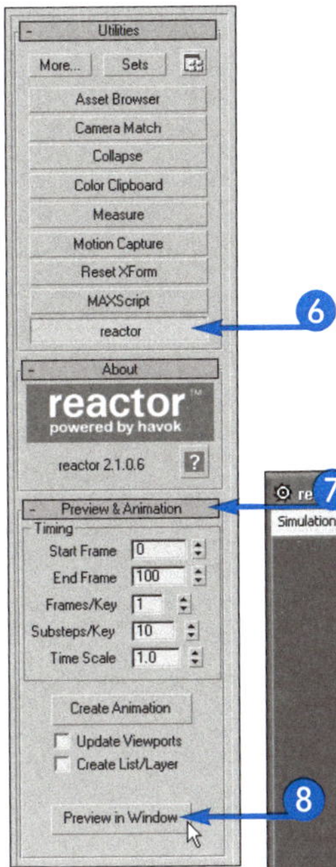

The Real-Time Preview window appears.

9. Press P to preview the Water simulation.

Note: See the section "Render a Reactor Simulation" for more information.

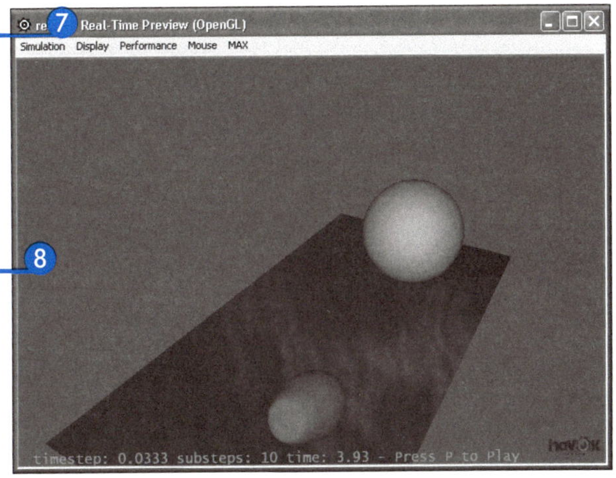

MASTER IT

Why does the water surface in my scene appear solid?

When you use the Water space warp with reactor, it must be surrounded by Rigid Body objects. Each side of the water must be a separate Rigid Body object so that reactor can compute the physical properties of the objects, based upon their reactions with the Water space warp. If you try to place the water in a compound object, or an object with one side, like a cylinder, then reactor cannot compute the values, and the water surface appears solid. The best method is to use objects, such as boxes, to create your sides. Ensure that you set the mass of the objects to zero so that they are not affected by the water or gravity.

What causes objects that fall in the water to float or sink?

The way in which objects and water interact is based upon two values: the density of the water and the mass of the object hitting the water surface. By default, the water has a density of 1.0, similar to real-world water. If you are creating liquids that are denser than water, then you may want to increase that value. The mass of the object controls whether it floats or sinks. Objects with a low mass-to-volume ratio normally float, while objects with a high mass-to-volume ratio sink.

Create a Biped

An important component in Character Studio is the biped, a pre-built, modifiable character rig that you can use to create character animation. Hands, feet, two segment arms and legs, hip, torsos, and even tails and ponytails are available as Biped sub-objects that you can fit to an existing 3D model. With a biped, you can quickly create a bone structure that is used to drive the animation of a bipedal, or two-footed, character. However, not only humanoid characters can be created with the biped feature; you can just as easily use the biped system to create the rig for an ape, a dinosaur, or even a bird or insect. You can also use bipeds to animate four-legged creatures.

A biped is a system, similar to the Sunlight system, and so it is located under the Systems category. Simply use the Biped button and drag in a viewport to set the biped's height; the other structural parameters of the system are created proportional to the height. The Root Name parameter determines the name of the biped's root and the prefix of all of its child objects. See the section "Add the Biped to Your Model" for information on the Physique modifier.

Create a Biped

1. Click the Create panel tab ( ).
2. Click the Systems button ( ).
3. Click Biped.

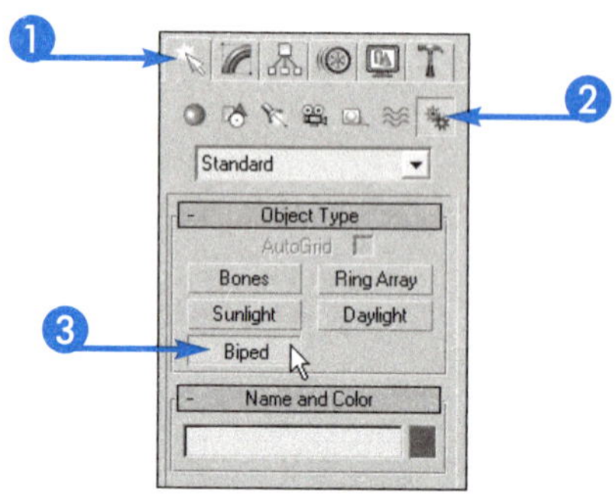

The biped rollouts appear in the Command panel.

4. Click and drag in a viewport.

3ds Max creates the biped.

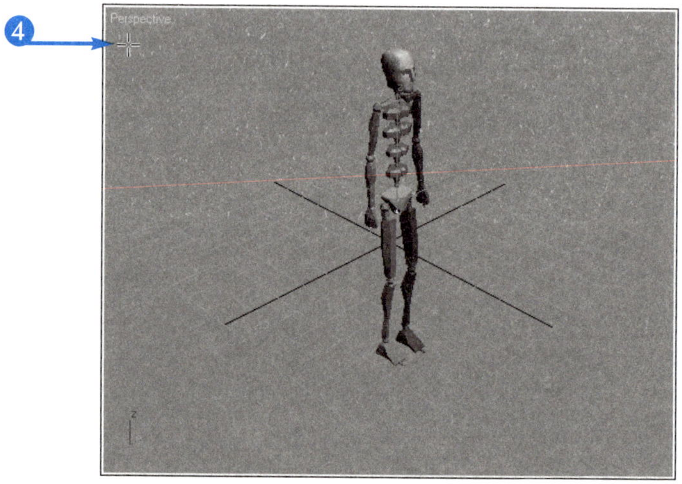

5 Type a Root Name.

6 Click ▾.

7 Select a Body Type for the biped.

8 Click the Select by Name button (▦).

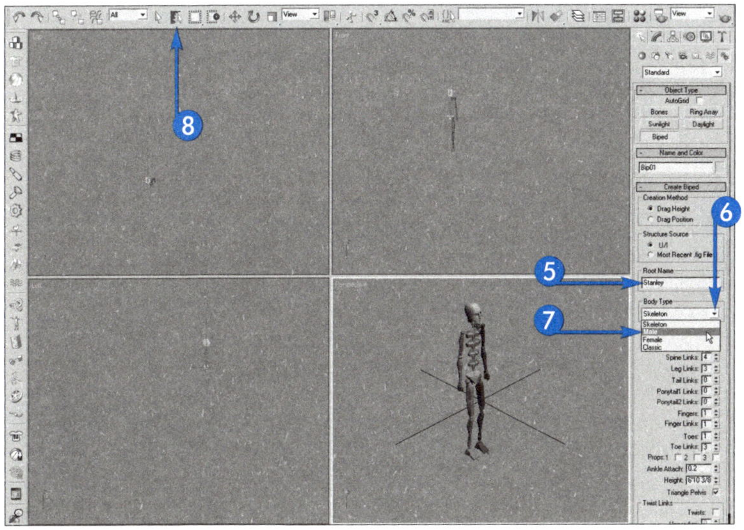

The Select Objects dialog box appears, where you can verify the object naming convention.

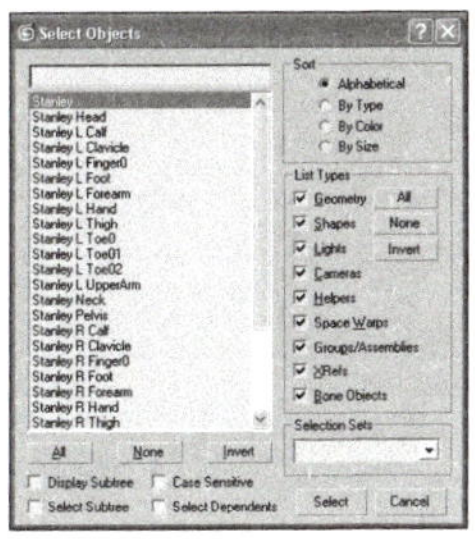

MASTER IT

What is the difference between Drag Height and Drag Position?

As shown in the exercise, you create a biped by dragging in the viewport. With the default Drag Height option selected, dragging the mouse determines the height of the biped. With the Drag Position option selected, dragging the mouse only controls where you create the biped The height is set by the option that you select in the Structure Source section. The U/I option (○ changes to ◉) tells 3ds Max to use the height from the parameters set in the last biped that you created, and the "Most Recent .fig File" option (○ changes to ◉) uses the height of the last biped structure that you saved as a FIG file.

What is the root object?

A biped is a relatively complex hierarchy system. Each object is designated as a child object and is linked to another object, which is referred to as its parent object. Any transforms that you apply to a parent are also transferred to the child. As a result, an object can be both a child and a parent. For example, a hand is the parent of the fingers, but a child of the forearm. The root object is the diamond-shaped object that is located inside the pelvis, at the top of the hierarchy. All objects are children or descendants of the Root object. For more information on hierarchies, see Chapter 13.

Modify a Biped's Structure

Any primitive or system that you create in 3ds Max is rarely in its final configuration from the start. For example, with a Light object, you may need to adjust its attenuation or select its shadow type. Bipeds are no different, and there are several parameters available to modify the structure of your biped, such as its height or number of fingers. Like everything else that you create in 3ds Max, you can immediately adjust many of the biped's parameters in the Create panel. However, unlike other objects, once you reselect a biped, its parameters do not appear in the Modify panel.

Because bipeds are specifically designed for animation, their parameters appear in the Motion panel. You modify and animate biped movements in Footstep mode. You modify their appearance in Figure mode, through the Structure rollout, which displays the biped's structural parameters. You can select any one of the objects in a biped, and then click the Motion button, to access the tools that control the entire system.

The Stanley.max file is available on the CD-ROM for you to practice modifying a biped's structure.

Modify a Biped's Structure

1. Select any biped object.
2. Click the Motion button ().
3. Click the Figure mode button ().

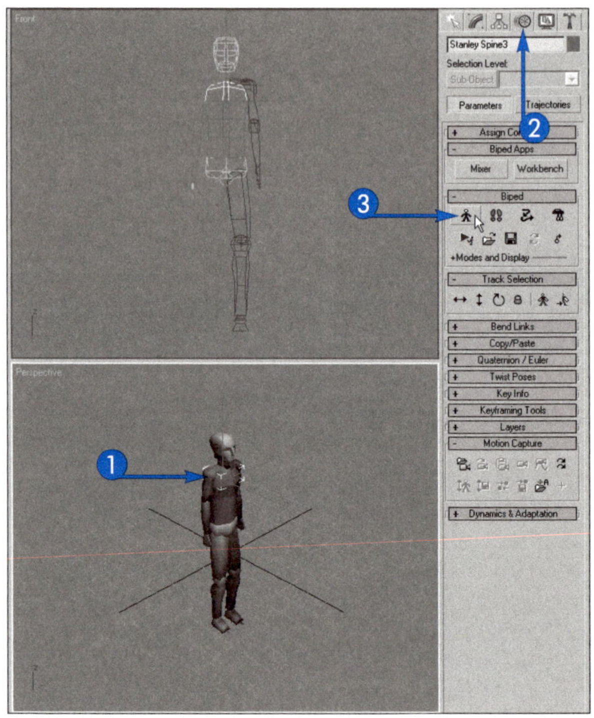

The rollouts appear for Figure mode.

4. Click + to expand the Structure rollout.

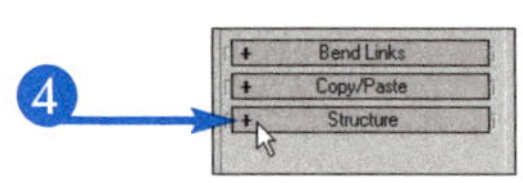

5. Type a larger number in the Height field.
6. Type a larger number in the Fingers field.
7. Type larger numbers in the Tail Links and Ponytail1 Links fields.
8. Click ▾ and select a different Body Type.

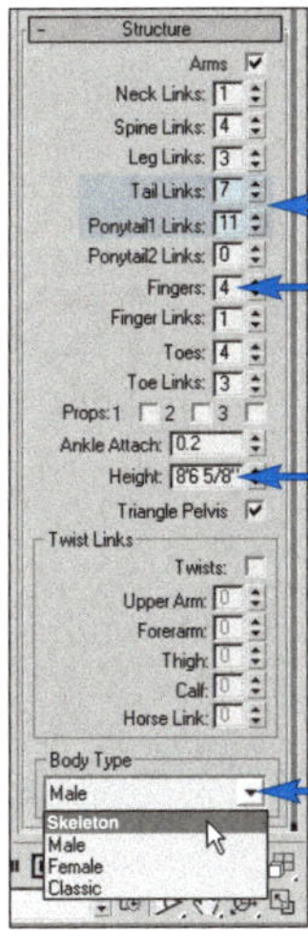

3ds Max updates the biped body type and structure.

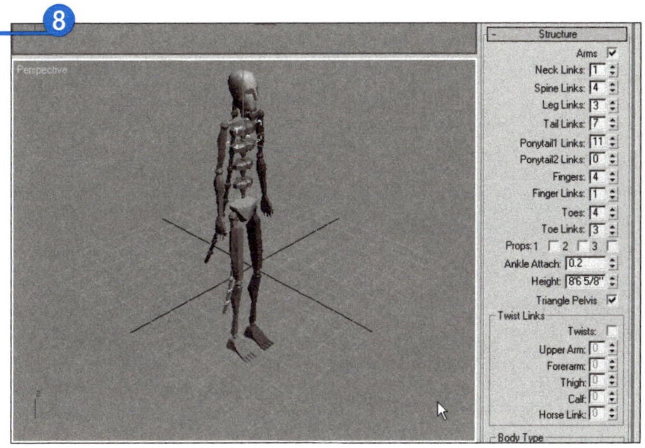

MASTER IT

Why is there an option to create a biped without arms?

▼ You can remove the arms from a biped by deselecting the Arms option (☑ changes to ☐) in the Structure rollout. This option is useful when what would be considered a character's arms are better controlled by the torso. For example, when a barnyard contains a few roaming chickens, it may be better to control the chickens' wings with the torso of the biped rather than the arms. However, if the chickens need to spread and flap their wings, then the arms would be required.

If the biped is supposed to be buried inside a mesh, why does the body type matter?

▼ The biped should be structured so that it fits as closely to the mesh as possible to give the most accurate control to the Physique or Skin modifier. The different Body Type options are meant to provide you with the closest possible starting point for the biped. The broader shoulders for the male and wider hips and breasts for the female are designed to fit their respective character types. You can adjust any body type to fit a model — the Body Type options just start you in the right direction. See the section "Modify a Biped's Bones" for information on fine-tuning a biped.

Modify a Biped's Bones

When you make a biped, 3ds Max creates the individual objects in the hierarchy in proportion to the height that you specify by either dragging the mouse or by setting the Height parameter. The proportions, which are similar to the proportions found in an adult human, may be acceptable but rarely match the final proportions that you will need. You can modify the biped's bones to change their size to match, as closely as possible, the model that you are animating. For example, a basketball player may need longer arms and legs than normal, or an obese character may need thicker and wider biped bones, but not necessarily longer ones. When considering aliens or animals, the appearance of the bones can be in nearly any configuration.

You can control the shape of the bones by using the Scale transform. All Scale transforms must be performed using the Local transform coordinate system so that the transformations are relative to the object's orientation, rather than to the World space. For information about transform coordinate systems, see Chapter 2.

The Stanley.max file is available on the CD-ROM for you to practice modifying a biped's bones.

Modify a Biped's Bones

Scale Bones

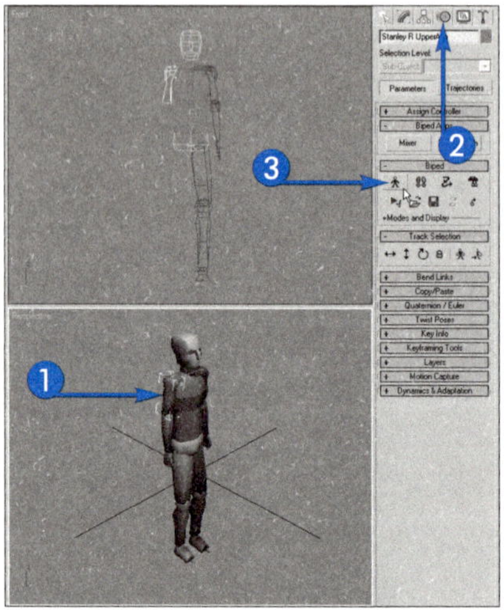

1. Select a biped object.
2. Click .
3. Click the Biped button ( ).

The rollouts appear for Figure mode.

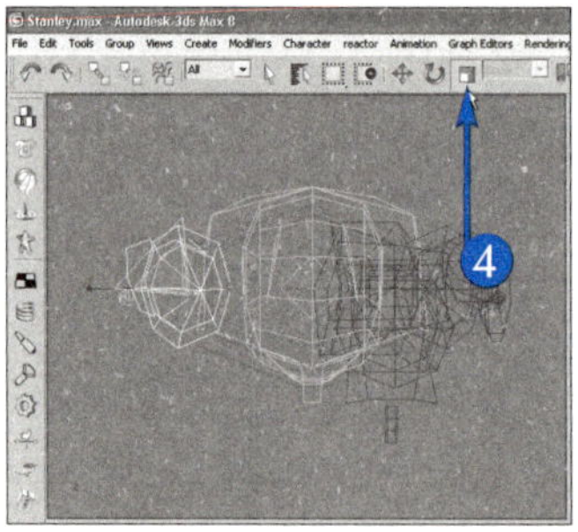

4. Click the Uniform Scale button ( ).

The Scale transform gizmo appears, and the Local transform coordinate system is activated and then grayed out.

5 Click and drag the Y-axis handle to lengthen the object.

The bone appears longer.

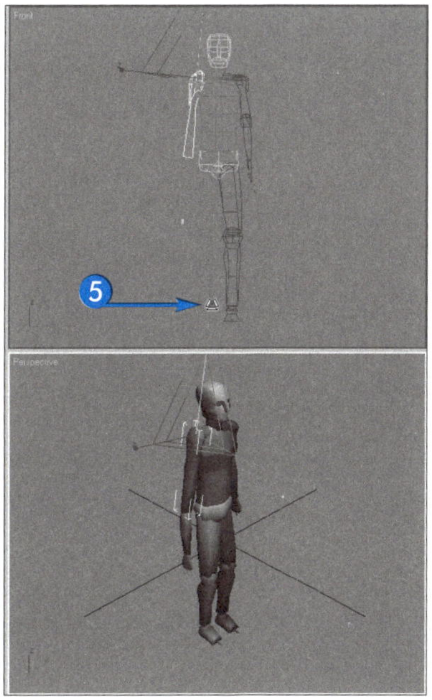

6 Click and drag the X- or Z-axis handle.

The biped object gets thicker or narrower.

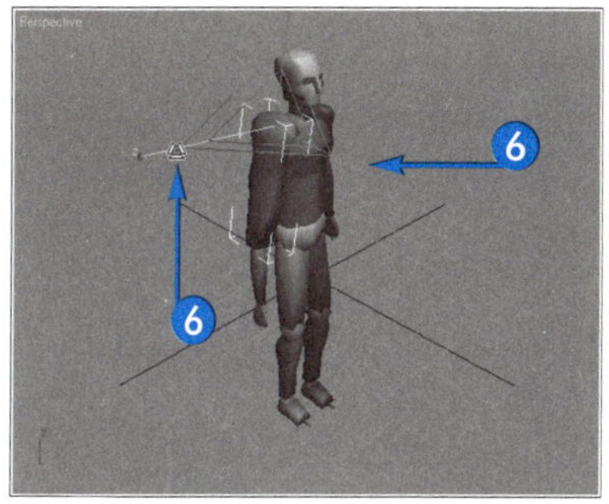

MASTER IT

If I make a biped that I like, can I duplicate it?

▼ Yes. As with other objects, you can hold down the Shift key and then move the biped to create a clone of the biped. You can also save the biped's structure and bone information as a FIG file that you can apply to any biped in any file. To do this, click the Save button (💾) in Figure mode. In the Save As dialog box that appears, give the FIG file a name and then click Save. Select another biped and then click the Open button (📂) to apply the settings to the biped.

After I clone a biped, it jumps to a new location when I try to change its structure. Why does this happen?

▼ You are probably trying to modify the biped's structure after using the Shift and Move command to clone it. You can only modify a biped's structural information, including position and orientation, in Figure mode. When you make changes to a biped outside of Figure mode, these changes are lost the next time you return to Figure mode or transform the object. When you click (Figure mode button), 3ds Max enters Figure mode, and your biped moves back to its original location, which is the same location as the biped from which it was cloned.

continued

Modify a Biped's Bones *(Continued)*

The purpose of a biped is to create a bone structure that is easy to animate. This animation drives the movement of a model that surrounds it. It is a common practice to model a character in what is called the Reference position, or the Da Vinci pose. In this position, the character's feet are about shoulder width apart, with the feet facing forward. The arms extend laterally from the body, with the palms facing downward. This pose allows you to place the biped within the model, with a clean view of the model in at least two viewports.

To match the pose of your model, you need to rotate your biped's objects with the Rotate transform. The Rotate transform is the transform that you use most often when animating your bipeds. You should perform most rotations with the Local transform coordinate system, although it is not required as it is with the Scale transform. See the section "Make your Biped Dance" for information on animating a biped. For information on transform coordinate systems, see Chapter 2.

CD FILE: The Stanley.max file is available on the CD-ROM for you to practice modifying a biped's bones.

Modify a Biped's Bones *(continued)*

Pose the Biped

1. Select a biped object.
2. Click .
3. Click .

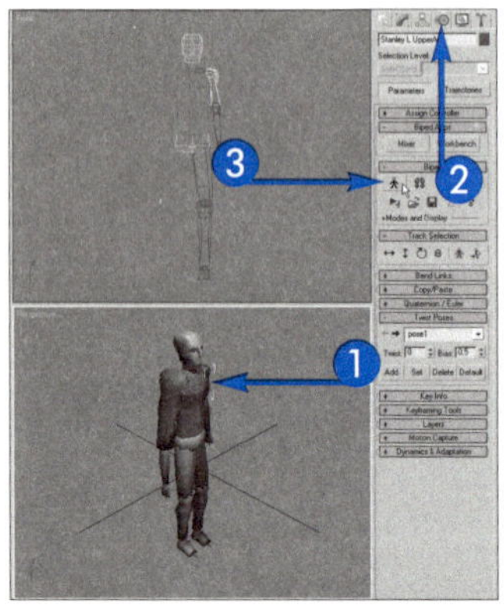

The rollouts appear for the Figure mode.

4. Click the Select and Rotate button ( ).

   The Rotate transform gizmo appears.

5. Click here and select Local.
6. Click and drag an axis handle to rotate the object.

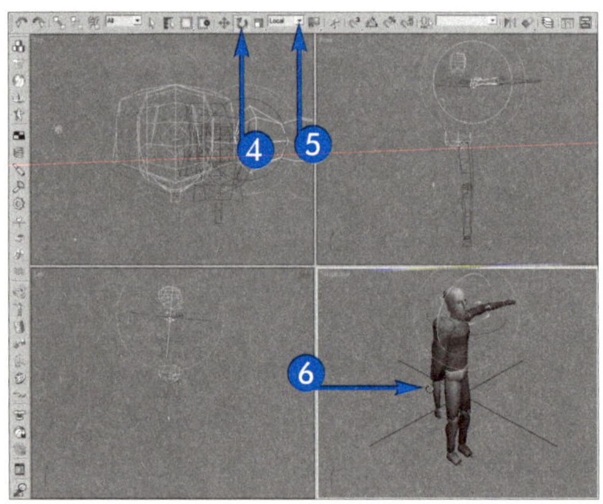

Copy and Paste the Pose

7. Click [+] to expand the Copy/Paste rollout.
8. Click the Create Collection button ( )
9. Click the Copy Posture button ( ).
10. Select the reciprocal object on the other side of the biped.

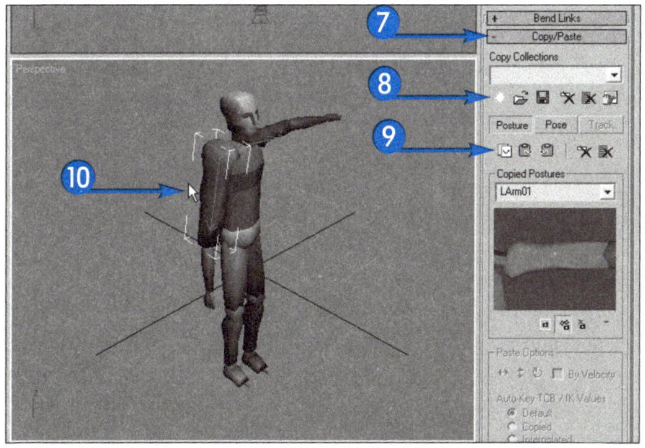

11. Click the Paste Posture Opposite button ( ).

    3ds Max copies the orientation and structure of the first object to the object on the other side.

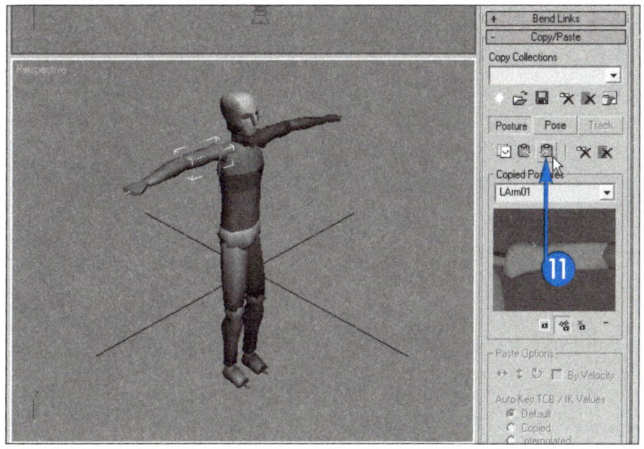

MASTER IT

Can I change the color of my biped's objects?

▼ Yes, although it may not be a good idea. By default, the objects on the biped's left side are green, and on the right side, they are blue. This is to help you to quickly distinguish which objects you have selected. 3ds Max carries this color scheme through the biped's footsteps and the biped's tracks in the Track View dialog box. You can change an object's color by selecting the object, then clicking the Color swatch in the Name and Color rollout, and then selecting a different color.

Can I change the name of my biped objects?

▼ Yes, you can. To change a single object's name, select the object and then type a new name in the Name field of the Name and Color rollout. This only changes the name of the selected object. To change the prefix name of all objects in a biped, select the biped, open the Motion panel, and then expand the Biped rollout. If necessary, expand the Modes and Display section. In the Name field, type the name for the root object, which becomes the prefix for all other objects.

Make Your Biped Dance

You can add motion to a biped by using footsteps. Footsteps are Biped sub-objects that define when and where each of the biped's feet will land. For example, when you first create footsteps, they alternate between the left and right foot and are at a constant speed and in a straight line. You create footsteps in Footstep mode and then associate them with the biped. If the biped already has footsteps assigned to it, then your new footsteps are appended to the existing steps.

When you assign footsteps to a biped, one of the true strengths of Character Studio becomes evident. You can create hundreds, even thousands, of keys with just a single mouse-click. With each step, 3ds Max sets keys for every movement of every applicable joint, including the arm swings, knee and ankle rotations, and hip pivots. Even a back-and-forth sway of a tail or ponytail is automatically keyed.

If you are a professional animator, you do not need to use footsteps; instead, you can use freeform animation. Freeform animation offers very powerful tools that extend the workflow of traditional skeleton animation techniques.

CD FILE The Stanley2.max file is available on the CD-ROM for you to practice assigning footsteps to a biped.

Make Your Biped Dance

Add Footsteps

1. Select a biped object.
2. Click .
3. Click the Footstep mode button ( ).

   Rollouts appear for the Footstep mode.
4. In the expanded Footstep Creation rollout, click the Walk button ( ).
5. Click the Create Multiple Footsteps button ( ).

   The Create Multiple Footsteps dialog box appears.
6. Type the number of footsteps that you want to create.
7. Click OK.

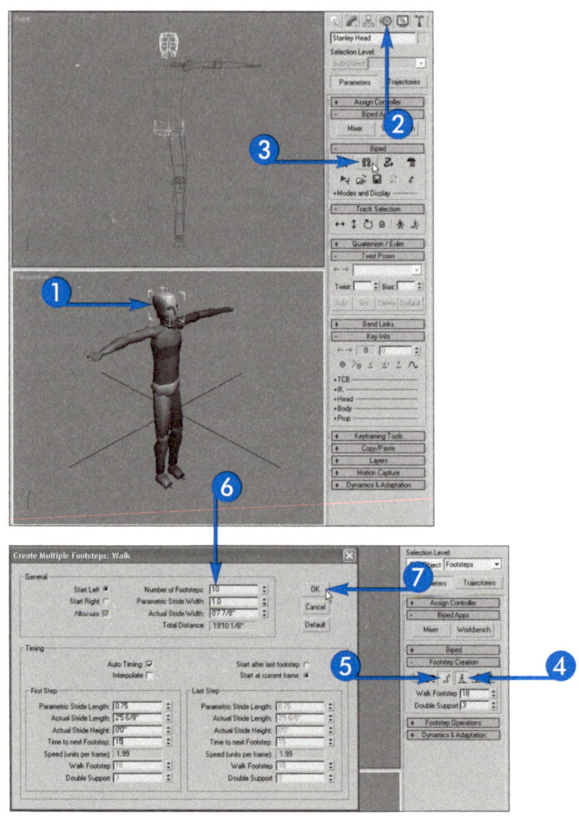

The footsteps appear in the viewports.

8 Click the ⊞ to expand the Footstep Operations rollout.

9 Click the Create the Keys for Inactive Footsteps button ( ).

- The biped object displays a white highlight to indicate the presence of keys.

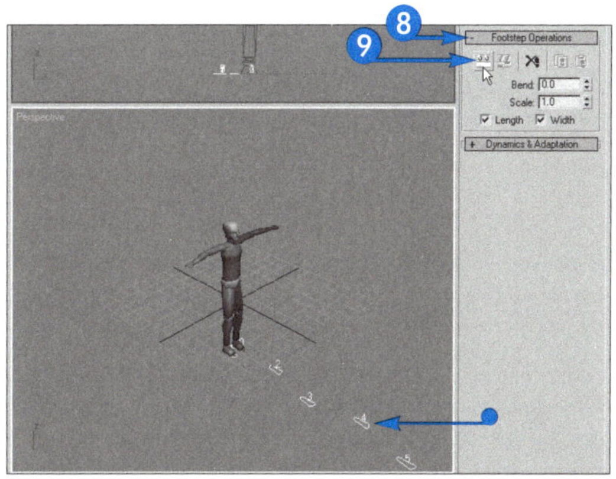

10 Click the Play Animation button ( ).

- The biped walks along the footstep path.

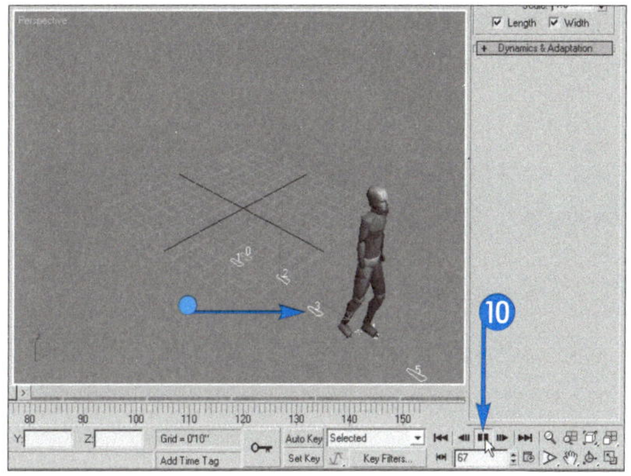

MASTER IT

What is the difference between choosing the Walk , Run , or Jump button in the Footstep Creation rollout?

▼ These options determine the number of feet that are touching the ground at any given time. When you select Walk, the biped either has one foot on the ground or two feet on the ground at any time during its walk cycle. During a Run cycle, it has either one foot on the ground or no feet on the ground when it is bounding from one step to the next. Whe you choose Jump, either both of the biped's feet are on the ground — at the beginning or end of the jump — or neither foot is on the ground.

What do the Walk Footstep and Double Support fields control?

▼ Located in the Footstep Creation rollout, these fields determine how fast the biped walks. The Walk Footstep field sets the number of frames that a foot is in contact with the ground, from when the heel plants until the toes rise. The Double Support field sets how many frames exist in each cycle when both feet are on the ground. When you select the Run or Jump cycles, 3ds Max also displays similar fields that allow you to control step time and airborne time.

continued

Make Your Biped Dance *(Continued)*

In the first part of this exercise, the biped walks the length of a footstep path that you create. However, the walk is stiff and lacks any flair or individuality. For example, there is little swivel to the hips, and the head never looks right or left.

You can use Auto Key mode to overwrite or augment the biped's default animation using additional keys. With the Auto Key active, 3ds Max saves any changes that you make to the biped as animation keys. Keep in mind that when you place a new key between existing keys, 3ds Max does not change the object's state at those keys. For example, if a biped's arm is down and forward at frame 30 and down and backwards at frame 45, then adding a keyframe at frame 38, with the arm raised, causes the biped's arm to snap up and down in one-half second. However, deleting, or spreading out, the frames on either side of frame 38 would slow down the motion and make it more realistic.

The Stanley Dance.max file is available on the CD-ROM for you to practice moving a biped's footsteps and bones. Stanley Dance.avi and Stanley Dance Complete.max are available on the CD as examples of Stanley's dancing ability.

Make Your Biped Dance *(continued)*

Move the Footsteps

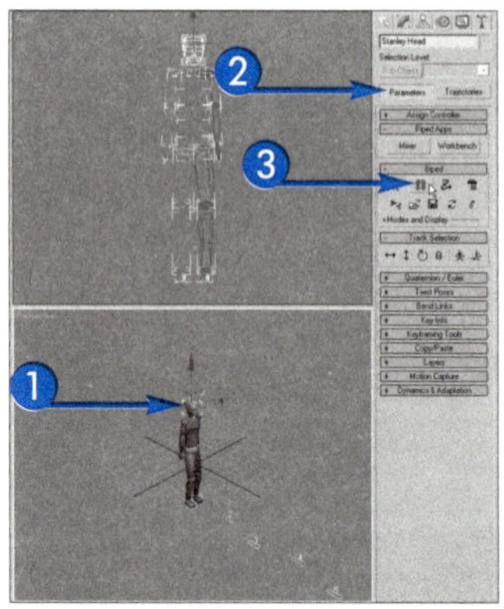

1. Select the biped object.
2. Click Parameters.
3. Click .

Rollouts appear for the Footstep mode.

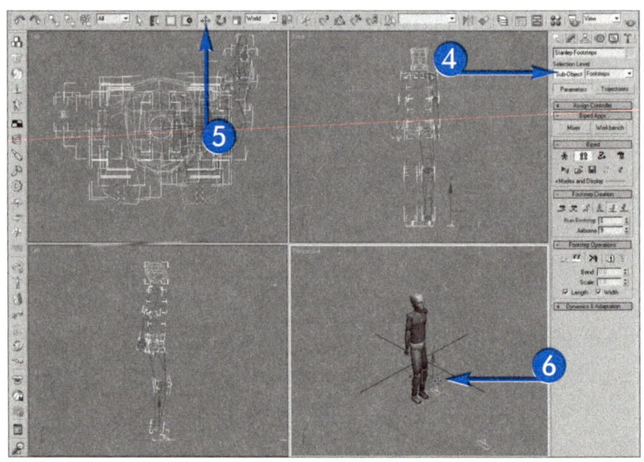

4. Click Sub-Object to select the Footsteps sub-object mode.
5. Click the Select and Move button ( ).
6. Select and move a footstep using the Move transform.

   You can also click and rotate the footstep.
7. Repeat steps 5 and 6 for the other footsteps.

Add Animation Keys using Freeform Mode

8 Click [icon] to exit Footstep mode.

9 Select a body part.

The keys appear in the Track bar for the object you selected.

10 Drag the Time Slider to the time at which you want to add a key.

11 Click Auto Key.

12 Click and drag the Rotate gizmo to rotate the object.

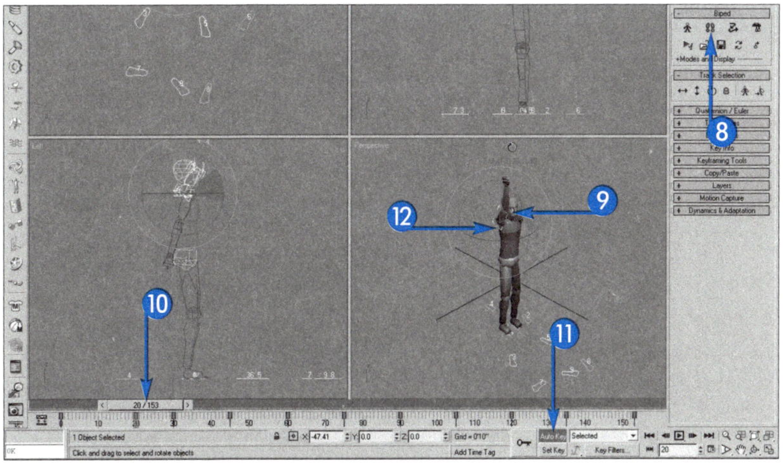

3ds Max creates a new key for the transformed object.

13 Repeat steps 9 to 12 to transform the other body parts and delete any existing keys.

14 Click Auto Key to turn off Auto Key mode.

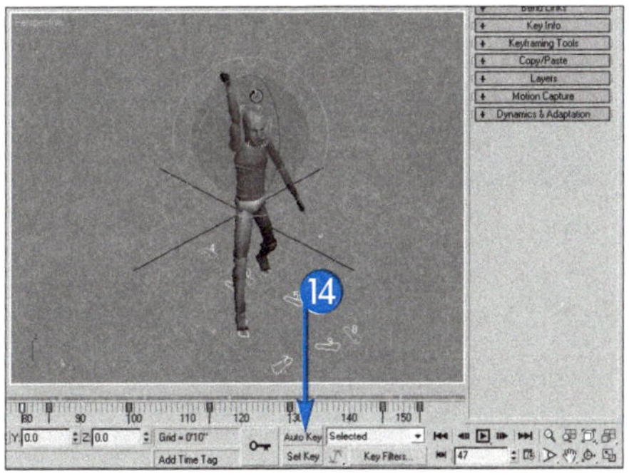

MASTER IT

I want to rotate both of the biped's arms identically. How can I do this?

You can simply select both arms before you apply the Rotate transform. 3ds Max has special selection tools just for doing this with bipeds. Select the objects on one side that you want to transform. In the Track Selection rollout, click the Symmetrical button ([icon]). The same bones are also selected on the biped's opposite side. With bones selected on one side, you can also click the Opposite button ([icon]) to deselect the current objects and then select the same objects on the opposite side.

Can I hide the footstep numbers and still show the footsteps?

Yes. In the Biped rollout, expand the Modes and Display section if necessary. In the Display area, click the Preferences button ([icon]) to open the Display Preferences dialog box. In the Footsteps area, click the Hide All Numbers button and then click OK. To display the numbers again, Click the Show All Numbers button. In this dialog box, you can also show or hide the footsteps themselves and change the footstep colors.

Add the Biped to Your Model

After the biped, the second major feature in Character Studio is the Physique modifier. The Physique modifier is the link between the biped and your model, and it defines which biped component controls which vertices of that model.

Once you create a biped, and adjust its bones to match the proportions of the model, you can select all the objects that comprise the model and then apply the Physique modifier to them. After you click the Attach to Node button, you select the root object of the biped. 3ds Max pauses for a few moments, and the cursor changes to a coffee cup to signify that the action is proceeding, as it associates each vertex with the nearest biped component. This may take a while, depending on the complexity of the biped and the model. Once completed, any animations that you have applied to the biped are reflected in the model.

See the sections "Modify a Biped's Bones," "Make Your Biped Dance," and "Create a Biped" for more information.

CD FILE The Man1.max file is available on the CD-ROM for you to practice applying the Physique modifier to a model.

Add the Biped to Your Model

1. Create a biped.
2. Adjust the pose and bones of the biped so that it is contained within the model.

Note: *See the sections "Create a Biped" and "Modifying a Biped's Bones" for information on creating and adjusting a biped.*

Note: *It is a common practice to freeze the model while adjusting the biped to prevent the model from being selected. See Chapter 2 for information on freezing objects.*

3. Select all the components of the model.
4. Click the Modify panel button ( ).
5. Click .
6. Click Physique.

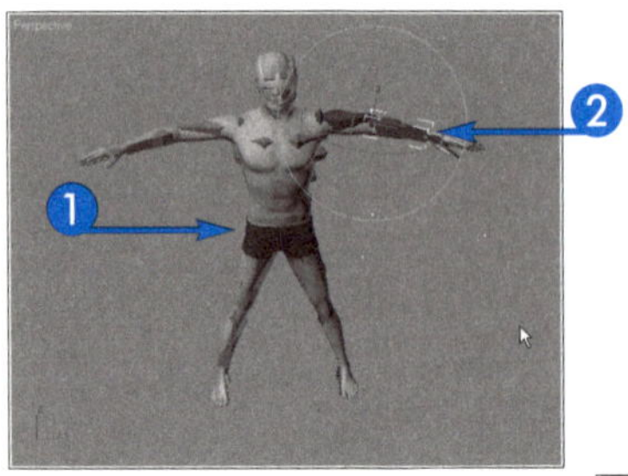

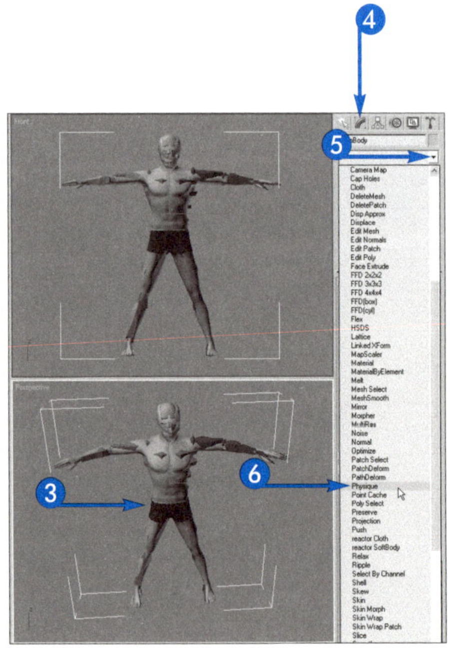

The Physique rollouts appear.

7. Click the Attach to Node button ( ).

8. Select the root object.

   You can press the H key to select it by name in the Pick Object dialog box.

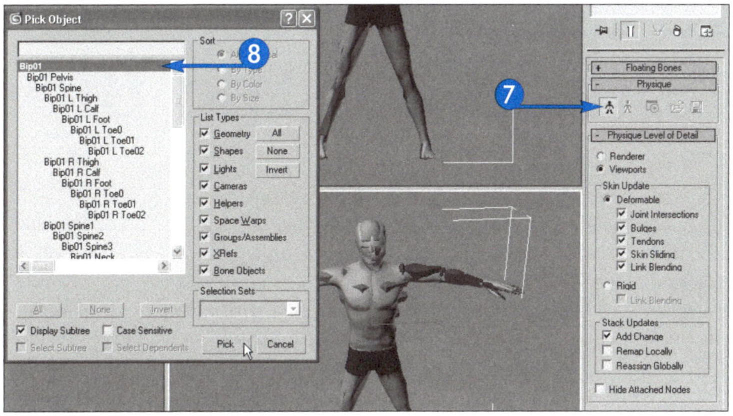

The Physique Initialization dialog box appears.

9. Click Initialize.

   3ds Max associates the biped with the model. Any animations that are added to the biped will be reflected in the model.

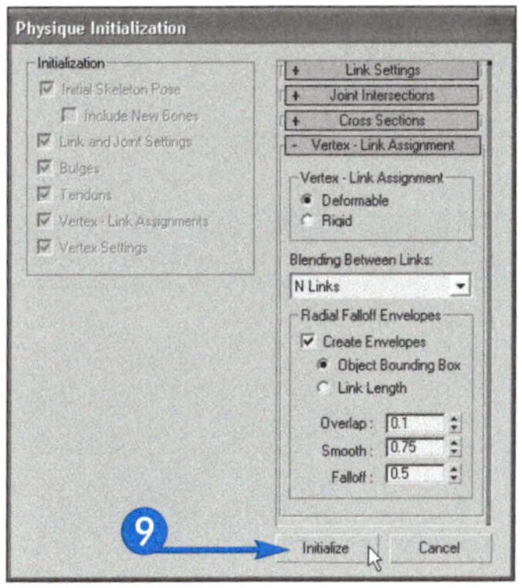

MASTER IT

When I play the animation, my biped walks off the screen. How can I prevent this from happening?

▼ If your biped's walk cycle is too long to see in the viewports, then you can use In Place mode to review the animation. In Place mode pans the viewport laterally with the biped's movements, to keep the biped centered on the screen. In the Biped rollout, expand the Modes and Display section. In the Modes area, click the In Place mode button ( ). Then click the Play Animation button ( ) to view the corrected animation. Keep in mind that In Place mode does not work in Camera viewports.

What is the difference between Physique and Skin?

▼ Physique and Skin are both modifiers that associate a model with an underlying bone structure. Skin — which is the more recent and preferred method — has better controls for refining how bones affect the model's vertices. Physique, which has improved in recent releases of Character Studio, may sometimes be faster when working with a biped as the bone structure. Some character animators use one or the other, or even both, on a single rig to define the animation restriction for their models.

Adjust the Areas of the Model That the Biped Affects

The biped's animation is what drives the movements of a model. Each one of the biped's components has an area of influence around it that dictates which of the model's vertices is controlled by that component. 3ds Max refers to these areas as envelopes. If these envelopes are not sized appropriately, the model may not animate properly. However, you can correct this.

Each bone has two envelopes: an inner and an outer envelope. Vertices that are inside a bone's inner envelope are entirely controlled by that bone. Any motion performed by that bone is translated directly to the vertices. Any vertices that are outside the outer envelope are not controlled by the bone. Vertices that are located between the envelopes are controlled, to a varying degree, based on their proximity to either envelope.

The size and shape of the envelopes are controlled at the Envelope sub-object level of the Physique modifier. The radius of the inner, outer, or both envelopes can be set, as well as the amount the envelopes for the selected bone can overlap its parent or child bones. Vertices can be influenced by more than one bone's envelopes.

The Envelopes.max file is available on the CD-ROM for you to practice adjusting the Physique modifier's envelopes.

Adjust the Areas of the Model That the Biped Affects

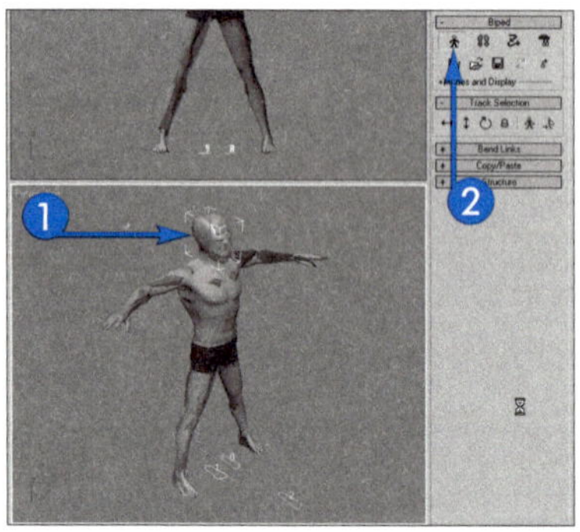

1. Select a biped whose fingertips do not behave correctly.
2. Click .

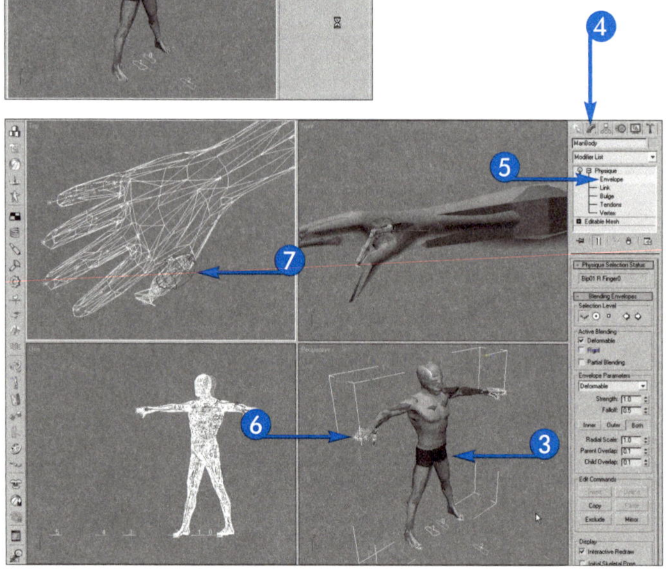

3. Select the mesh.
4. Click .
5. Expand the Physique modifier; then select the Envelope sub-object.
6. Zoom in on the bone that needs its envelopes adjusted.
7. Select the yellow line at the center of the bone to display the envelopes.

Note: *In the situation shown here, the best course of action may be to relocate the thumb links better.*

8. Type to set the Radial Scale, Parent, and Child Overlap values until the model's vertices are inside the envelopes.

9. Repeat steps 6 and 8 for other bones as required.

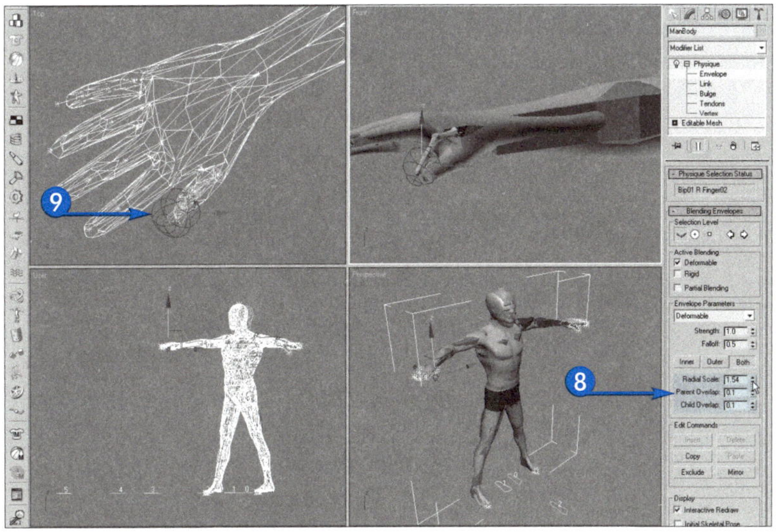

10. Exit Envelope sub-object mode, select the biped, and exit Figure mode.

   Repeat the process if the offending vertices are not repaired.

MASTER IT

Can I change footsteps into keyed animation?

Yes. If you have created footstep animation for your biped, you can convert all of the footstep driven animation into individual keys. This is often done for easier modification and addition of subtle adjustments to the characters walk. To convert to freeform animation, first select your biped and ensure that your are not in Footstep or Figure mode. In the Biped rollout click the Convert button to open the Convert to freeform dialog box. Click OK to convert the footsteps into freeform animation.

Simulate a Cloth Sheet

3ds Max 8 now uses the Cloth modifier to simulate the behavior of cloth. This allows artists to quickly create cloth-based simulations such as table cloths, flags, curtains, and, best of all, clothes for their characters. Using the Cloth modifier, you can assign the specific properties to your Cloth objects to cause them to react as they would in a real-world situation. For example, a pair of denim pants hanging on a clothesline reacts to wind differently than a silk blouse or a flannel shirt.

You can apply the Cloth modifier to the objects that you want to react like cloth. However, within the modifier's parameters, you must identify which objects the Cloth object is to react with when 3ds Max calculates the cloth's simulation. Objects are categorized as Cloth, Collision Objects, and Inactive. Inactive objects are objects that are normally part of the simulation but that are temporarily exempt, usually for debugging purposes.

For information on applying modifiers and the Modifier Stack, see Chapter 6.

CD FILE: The Tablecloth.max file is available on the CD-ROM for you to practice applying the Cloth modifier to objects in your scene.

Simulate a Cloth Sheet

Apply the Cloth Modifier

1. Select the object that you want to behave as cloth.
2. Click the Modify panel button ().
3. Click ▾ and select Cloth.

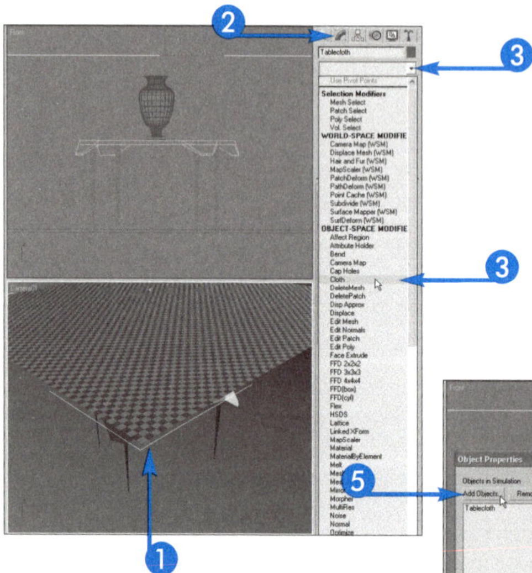

Select the Simulation Objects

The Cloth modifier rollouts appear in the Command panel.

4. Click Object Properties.

   The Object Properties dialog box appears.

5. Click Add Objects.

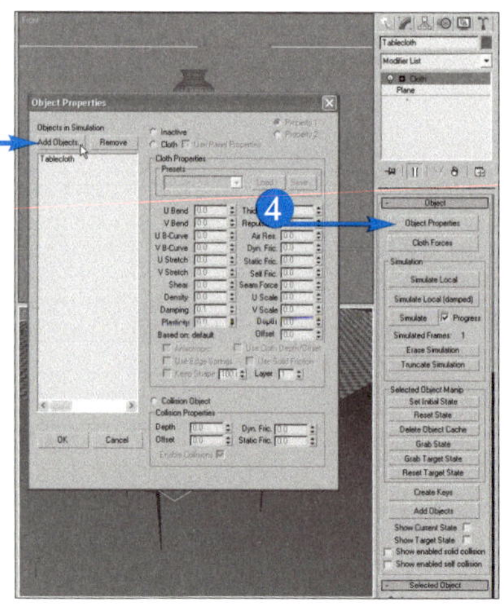

The Add Objects to Cloth Simulation dialog box appears.

6. Select the objects that you want to be in the simulation with the Cloth object.
7. Click Add.

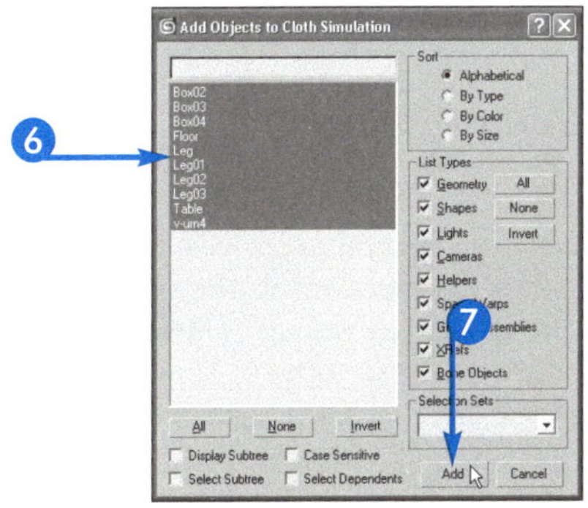

The added objects appear highlighted in the Objects in Simulation list.

8. Select the Collision Object option (○ changes to ◉).
9. Select the Cloth object and then click the Cloth option (○ changes to ◉).

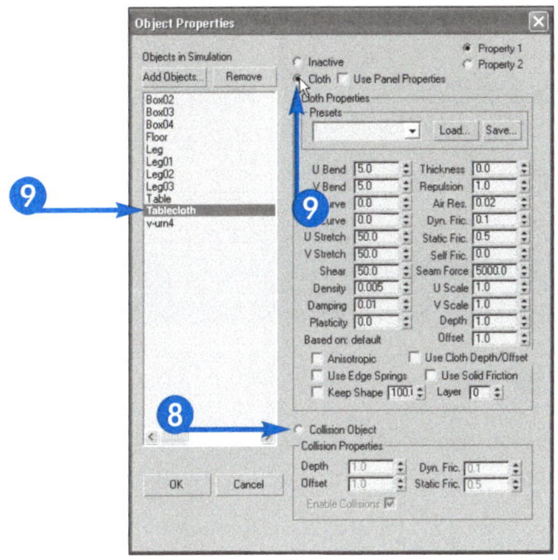

Do I need to add all of the objects in my scene to the simulation?

No. 3ds Max considers all of the objects that are included in the Objects in Simulation list when it calculates each frame of a simulation. Adding unnecessary objects slows down the simulation without any benefit to your scene. If you suspect that an object in the list is not affected by the Cloth object, then set it as Inactive and rerun the simulation. If it does not need to be included, then select it and click Remove.

Will Stitch be upgraded?

It is unlikely that Stitch, a cloth simulation plug-in for previous versions of 3ds Max, will be upgraded any further. Stitch became clothfx for release 7 of 3ds Max and is now included in the base package of 3ds Max 8 as the Cloth and Garment Maker modifiers. If you are looking for information or support for Stitch or clothfx, then contact the developer, Size8 Software at www.size8software.com, or the distributer, Turbosquid at www.turbosquid.com.

continued

Simulate a Cloth Sheet *(Continued)*

There are several properties that determine how a Cloth object reacts to the other objects in the simulation, as well as to itself. The first property to consider is the mesh density, or the quantity of edges and vertices of the object that represents the cloth.

The cloth simulation can only bend the Cloth object along the existing edges, which requires that the object have a substantial number of edges along which it can bend. The more edges that are available, the more accurate the simulation will be. If your object has Segments settings, then you can use them to increase the number of edges, although this often results in perpendicular edges that may not simulate realistically. You can add the Tessellate modifier to any geometry object to increase its density, with edges that are not perpendicular to each other.

There is a point of diminishing returns where additional edges no longer produce visible results. Do not create more edges than you need to when setting up your scene. For information on animating parameters and transforms, see Chapter 8. For information on setting an object's parameters, see Chapter 4.

Simulate a Cloth Sheet *(continued)*

Subdivide the Mesh

10. With the Cloth object selected, click the object level in the Modifier Stack.

    A Warning dialog box appears.

11. Click Yes.

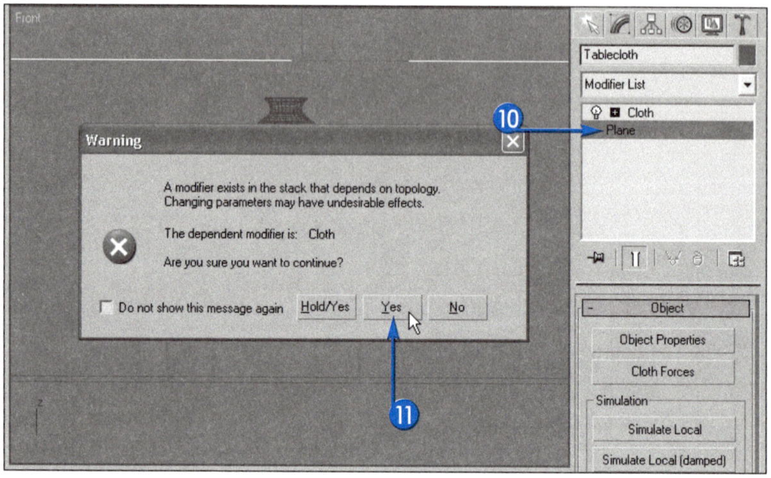

The object's Parameters rollout appears.

12. Type in higher Segments values for the object.

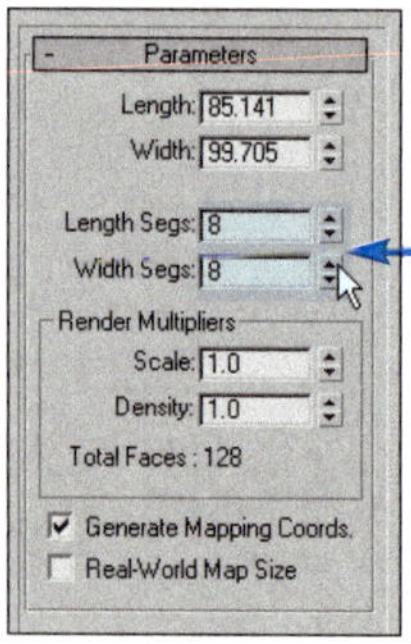

⓭ Click ▾ and then click Tessellate.

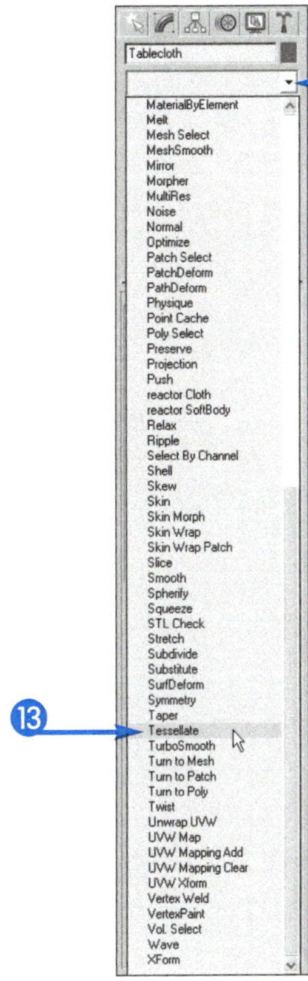

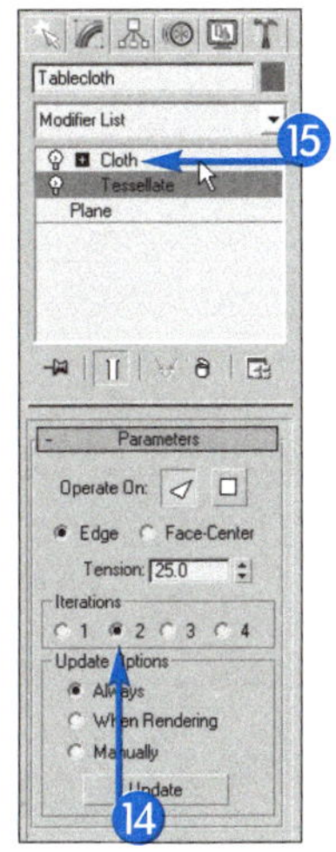

The Tessellate parameters appear.

⓮ Select an Iterations value to subdivide your mesh (○ changes to ◉).

This example uses a value of 2.

⓯ Click Cloth to return to the top of the Modifier Stack.

MASTER IT

Are there other ways to subdivide the mesh?

▼ Yes. If your object is an editable poly, then enter the Polygon sub-object level, select the polygons to be subdivided, and then click the Tessellate or Tessellate Settings buttons. Both methods subdivide the selected polygons. You can also apply the MeshSmooth or TurboSmooth modifier to your object, although these modifiers tend to retain the perpendicularity of the edges. When you use a modifier to subdivide your mesh, be sure to place it below the Cloth modifier in the Modifier Stack.

Can I apply the Cloth modifier to anything?

▼ No. You can only apply the Cloth modifier to a Mesh object, although any Mesh object can be treated like cloth. For example, if you want to deflate an inflatable character, then you can apply the Cloth modifier to it and then run the simulation. Be sure to add the floor, or any furniture, to the simulation as Collision Objects so that the character does not fall through the floor. Depending on the Cloth settings when you run the simulation, your character should deflate nicely.

continued

Simulate a Cloth Sheet *(Continued)*

The Cloth modifier not only sets the objects and parameters for a cloth simulation but also controls the creation of the simulation itself. The simulation calculates when and where the vertices of the Cloth object are with regard to any collision objects or any external forces.

Once you run the simulation, even if you delete or move the collision objects, the Cloth object transforms exactly as it did when the simulation was created. Because of this, the simulation must be run, or rerun, after you modify any objects in the Objects in Simulation list, or any objects that might come in contact with the cloth.

For a simulation to be recalculated, you must delete the existing simulation using the Erase Simulation button in the Object rollout. Erasing a simulation is not an action that you can undo. A simulation may only be required for a certain number of frames, such as curtains rustling when a door opens. To delete a part of a simulation after a specific frame, you can move the Time Slider to that frame and then click Truncate Simulation.

CD FILE The Tablecloth2.max file is available on the CD-ROM for you to practice running a cloth simulation.

Simulate a Cloth Sheet *(continued)*

Run the Simulation

16 Click Simulate.

The Cloth dialog box appears, displaying the progress of the simulation.

17 Click Cancel if you need to make parameter changes.

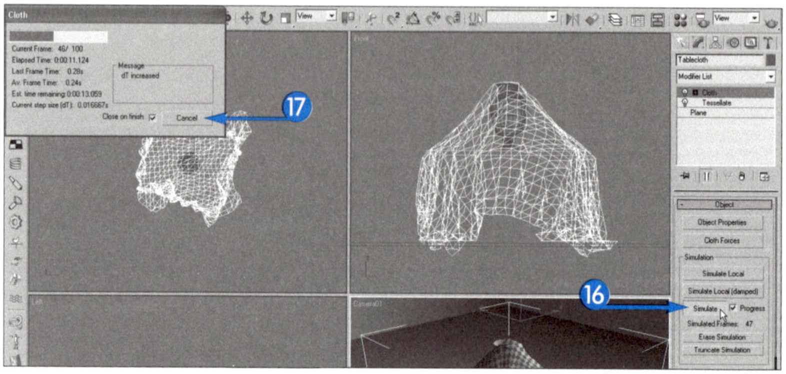

In this example, some of the Collision objects poke through the cloth.

18 Click Erase Simulation.

The simulation resets.

19 Click Object Properties.

20 In the Object Properties dialog box, click the Cloth object.

21 Type to specify a higher Shear value.

22 Click OK.

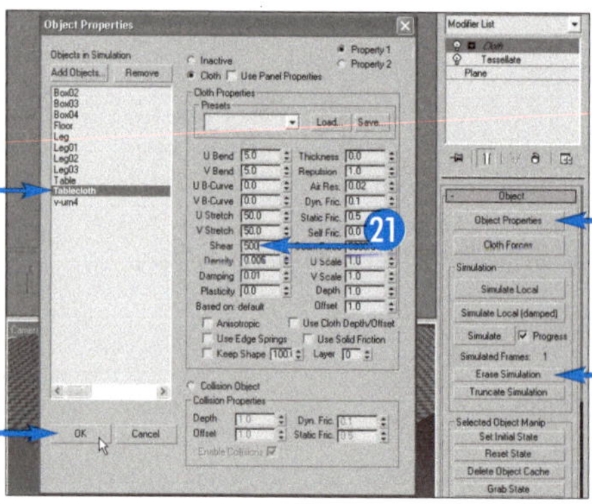

23 Return to the Tesselate Level of the Modifier Stack.

24 Click to select a higher Iterations number (○ changes to ◉).

25 Click Cloth to return to the Cloth level.

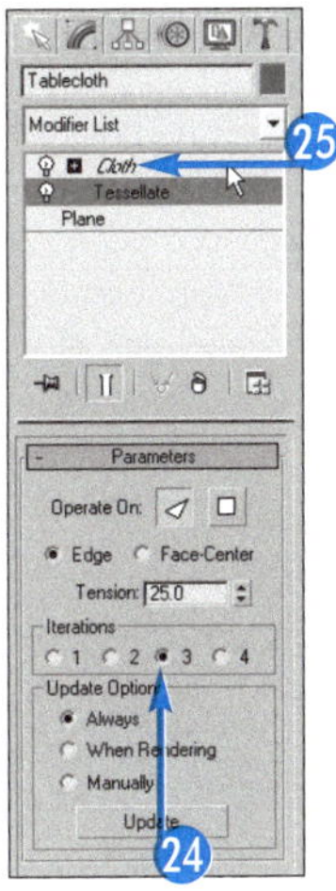

26 In the Object rollout, click Simulate to rerun the simulation.

Although the simulation takes longer this time, there are no objects poking through the Cloth object.

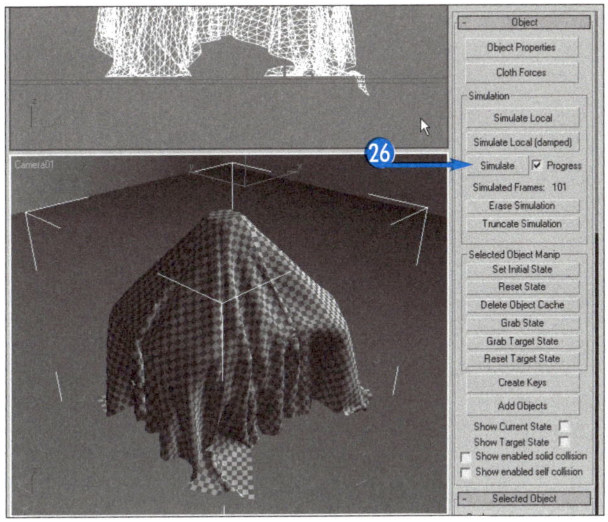

MASTER IT

What is the difference between Simulate and Simulate Local?

▼ When you use the Simulate button, the cloth reacts to the objects in the Objects in Simulation list over the length of the Active Time Segment. As a result, the simulation exists as an animation from its beginning state until its ending state. Simulate Local runs the cloth simulation without creating any animation. If you drag the Time Slider to the left after a local simulation, the cloth does not return to its initial state as it would after a simulation.

Should I use Cloth or reactor for cloth simulations?

▼ This depends on your goal. The Cloth modifier has controls for specifying the type of cloth that you want to simulate, as well as its properties regarding how it reacts with itself and other objects. For example, you can specify the cloth to be leather or denim. A Cloth Collection, which is created with reactor, may be better at reacting with other objects, but it is not as accurate regarding the material's properties.

Modify a Simulation with Space Warps

In a cloth simulation, the objects controlled by the Cloth modifier can also react to external forces such as the Wind space warp. Wind can add a sense of randomness to your scene while at the same time adding the feeling of size to the viewer's perception. After you add a space warp to the scene, it must also be added to the cloth simulation in the Forces dialog box or the simulation ignores it.

Although it is true that only 3D objects can have the Cloth modifier applied to them, there is a method for making 2D objects into cloth-ready 3D meshes. With a closed spline selected, you can add the Garment Maker modifier. This creates a well-tessellated mesh that is ready for the Cloth modifier. If a spline is not closed, then a warning dialog box appears to let you know, but the modifier still appears at the top of the Modifier Stack. You can use the Density value to determine the amount of tessellation.

For information on adding and modifying Wind and other space warps, see Chapter 25.

CD FILE: The Banner.max file is available on the CD-ROM for you to practice adding space warps to the cloth simulation.

Modify a Simulation with Space Warps

1. Select a closed spline to which you want to apply the Garment Maker modifier.
2. Click .
3. Click and then select Garment Maker.

The object tessellates.

4. Click and then click Cloth.

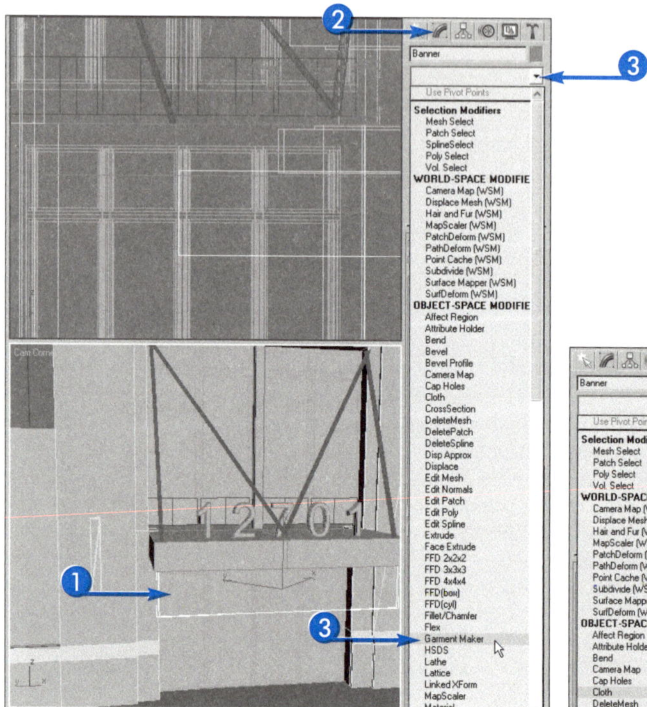

The Cloth modifier appears at the top of the Modifier Stack.

5. Click Object Properties.

   The Object Properties dialog box appears.

6. Click Add Objects.

   The Add Objects to Cloth Simulation dialog box appears.

7. Select the objects that you want to add to the simulation.
8. Click Add.
9. Select the Cloth object and then select the Cloth option (○ changes to ◉) in the Object Properties rollout.
10. Select the other object.
11. Select the Collision Object option (○ changes to ◉).

Note: *See the section "Simulate a Cloth Sheet" for information on Cloth and Collision objects.*

12. Click OK.

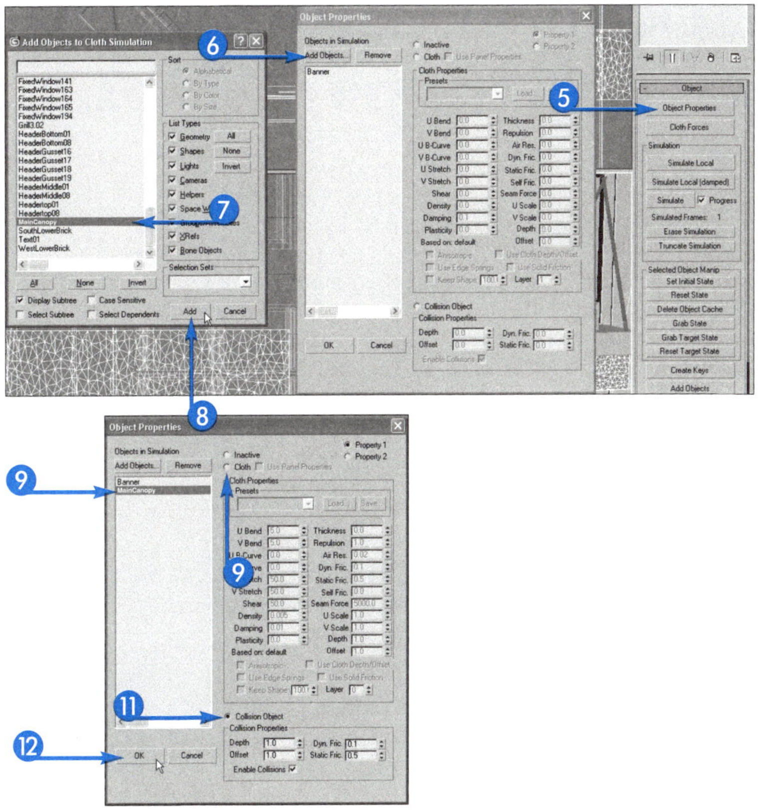

MASTER IT

Why do my rectangular-shaped meshes have rounded corners?

When you apply the Garment Maker modifier to a closed, single spline, rectangle shape primitive, this always causes the corners to curve. To prevent this, first convert the rectangle into an editable spline. Go to the Vertex sub-object level, and then select all the vertices. In the Geometry rollout, click the Break button. This turns each edge into a separate spline sub-object. When you reapply the Garment Maker modifier, the corners are crisp.

continued

Modify a Simulation with Space Warps *(Continued)*

You can pin portions of Cloth objects to other objects in the scene to fix them in place. For example, a curtain can be pinned to a curtain rod so that the top edge stays in place while the rest of the surface is allowed to billow in the wind. In order to pin portions of the cloth, you must select specific vertices and assign them to other objects that are included in the simulation as Collision objects.

Pinning an object also allows you to keep the Floor object in the scene but out of the simulation. The Collision objects that you select are not required to remain motionless. For example, if you assign groups of vertices along the top edge of a curtain to objects that represent the curtain rings, then moving the rings to one side has the effect of opening the curtain during the simulation.

For information on selecting and manipulating sub-objects, see Chapter 6.

CD FILE: The Banner2.max file is available on the CD-ROM for you to practice adding space warps to the cloth simulation.

Modify a Simulation with Space Warps *(continued)*

13. Select the Cloth object.
14. Click the Plus sign (⊞) to expand the Cloth modifier, and then click Group.
15. Select the vertices that you want to remain in place.
16. Click Make Group.
17. In the Make Group dialog box that appears, type a name.
18. Click OK.

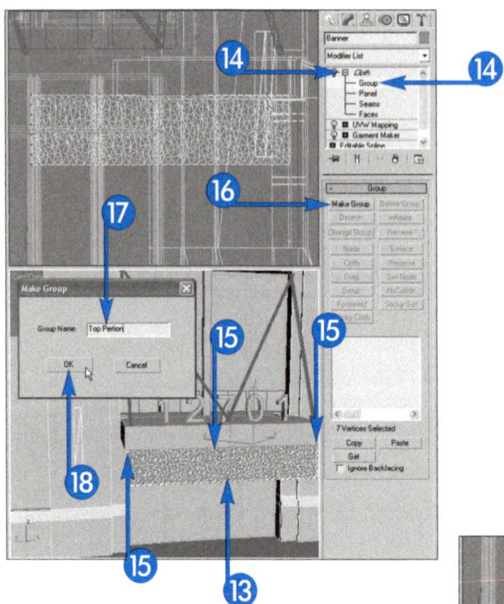

The group name appears in the Group field.

19. Click Sim Node.
20. Click the object to which you want to assign the group.

The group is assigned.

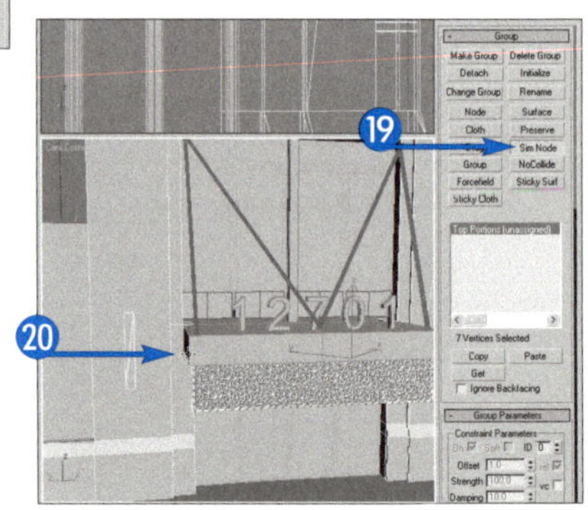

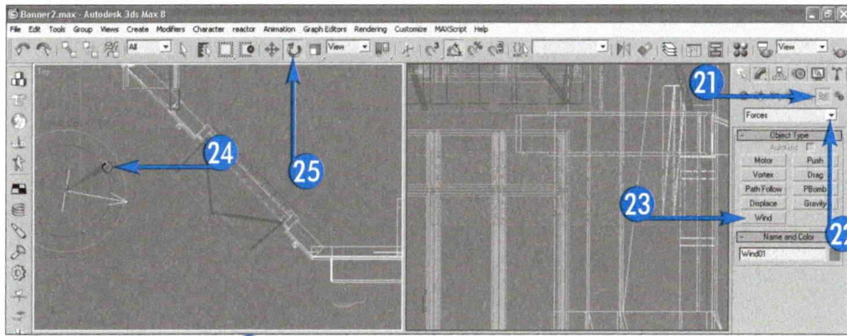

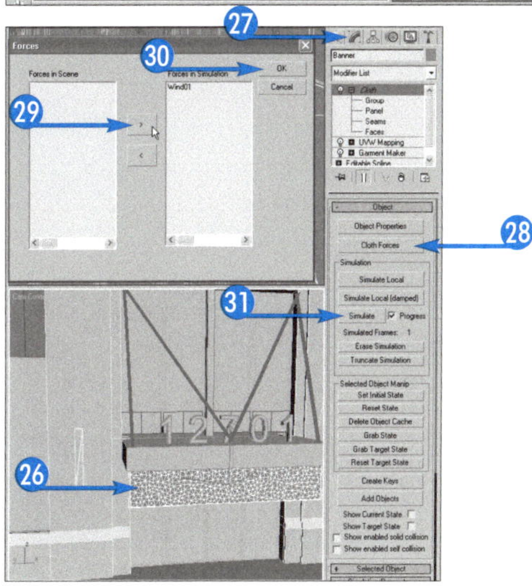

The Cloth modifier appears at the top of the Modifier Stack.

21 In the Create Panel, click .

22 Click and choose Forces.

23 Click Wind.

24 Click and drag in the Top viewport to create the Wind space warp.

25 Click the Select and Rotate button () and then orient the space warp.

26 Set the Cloth object.

27 Click .

28 Click Cloth Forces.

29 In the Forces dialog box that appears, click the right arrow button ().

30 Click OK.

31 Click Simulate to run the simulation.

The Cloth object billows in the wind, while the vertex group remains in place.

MASTER IT

I have a mapped material applied to my spline. Why does it not appear properly?

- A mapped material requires mapping coordinates to properly appear when rendered. You can apply the UVW Map modifier to your object, but you must apply it above the Garment Maker modifier and below the Cloth modifier. If it is applied to the spline, then Garment Maker is not available in the drop-down list. If UVW Map is above the Cloth modifier, then it is applied to the result of the simulation, rather than to the object's initial state.

Add Hair to an Object

3ds Max 8 now allows you to place hair and fur on your objects and characters. You can use this feature to create head and facial hair for a character, fur or feathers for an animal or alien, or even to populate a lawn with hundreds of thousands of blades of grass. Rather than creating potentially millions of polygons, which could slow down a scene's performance and workflow, you can apply hair as a rendering effect instead of as individual strands of geometry.

Hair only appears in a rendering, and is rendered in two separate passes — one for shadows and one for the hair itself — in the Rendered Frame window. In the viewports, only red guides appear to display the length and location of the hair that will be rendered, and a small amount — two percent by default — of the rendering hairs are represented by the guides.

For information on rendering, see Chapters 20 and 21. For more information on adding rendering effects, see Chapter 22.

CD FILE The Hair.max file is available on the CD-ROM for you to practice adding hair to an object.

Add Hair to an Object

Add the Hair and Fur Effect

1. Click Rendering.
2. Click Effects.

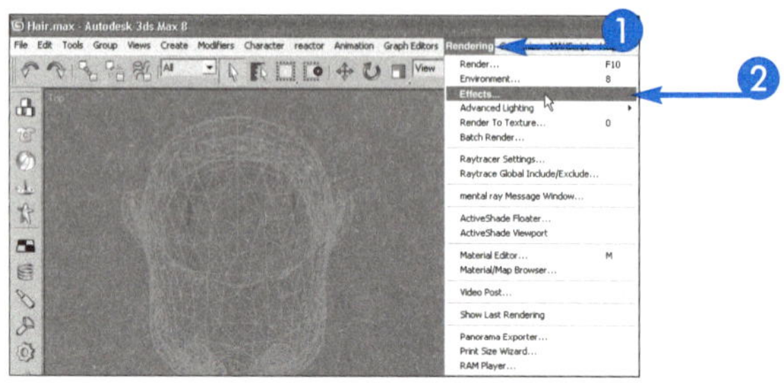

The Environment and Effects dialog box appears, displaying the Effects tab.

3. Click Add.

The Add Effect dialog box appears.

4. Click Hair and Fur.
5. Click OK.

The Hair and Fur effect is added.

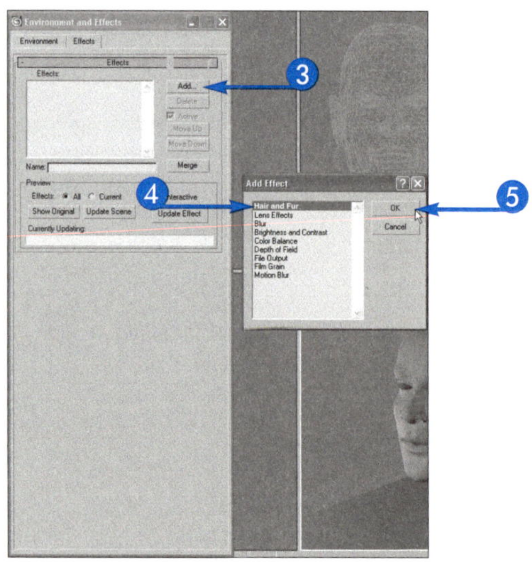

Add the Hair and Fur Modifier

6. Select an object.
7. Click the Modify panel button (icon).
8. Click ▾ and then select Hair and Fur (WSM).

The guides appear in the viewports.

9. Click the Quick Render button (icon).
   - The scene renders in three passes, displaying the hair.

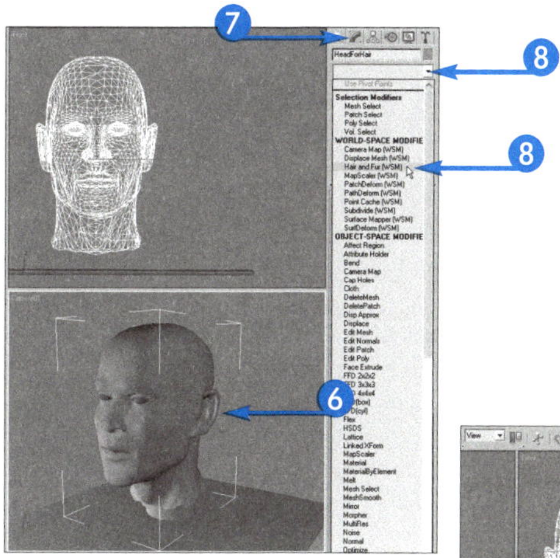

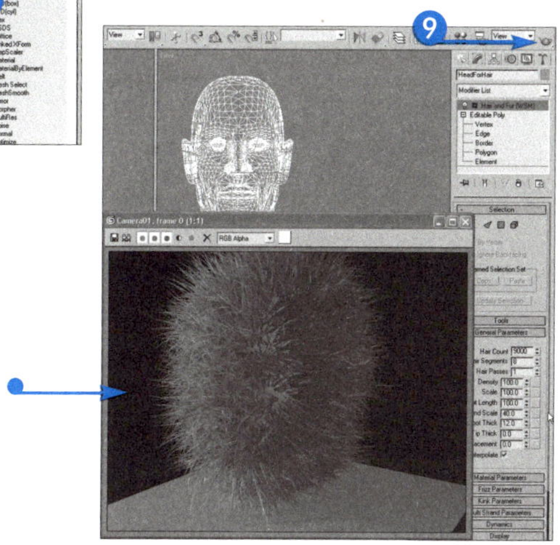

MASTER IT

Why does my hair not render?

There can be a couple of reasons why your hair does not render. First, the Hair and Fur effect can only be rendered in perspective views such as cameras, and not in orthographic views such as Top or User. You should receive a warning when you initiate a rendering in an incompatible viewport. Next, ensure that the Active option is checked (☐ changes to ☑) when Hair and Fur is selected in the Effects rollout of the Environment and Effects dialog box. If this option is not selected, then the effect has been temporarily toggled off.

Why am I unable to use Interactive with Hair and Fur?

The Interactive option, in the Environment and Effects dialog box, displays instant updates to effects in the Rendered Frame window. While this may be fine for the Blur or Lens Effects effects, it is not compatible with Hair and Fur, which may take a long time to update for every parameter change. To use Interactive with the other effects, without seeing a warning dialog box regarding Hair and Fur, select the Current option (○ becomes ◉) in the Preview section. Only the selected effect updates in the Rendered Frame window. You still need to disable the Interactive option when working with Hair and Fur.

Restrict Hair to Specific Locations

A kiwi fruit or a fuzzy alien pod may be completely covered with hair or fur, but it is less likely that most other objects or characters will have a perfect coat. Even dogs and cats have hair-free areas on their feet, nose, and lips. The Hair and Fur modifier has three sub-object modes available to help you choose the specific faces, polygons, or elements of the object to which the modifier is applied. With a sub-object mode selected, you can use any of the 3ds Max selection tools to select the areas to which you want to apply the Hair effect. Toggle on the Ignore Backfacing option to select only the sub-objects, with normals facing the selection tool. For information on the selection tools, see Chapter 2.

See the section "Add Hair to an Object" for more information on adding the Hair and Fur effect.

CD FILE The HairSpecific.max file is available on the CD-ROM for you to practice restricting the location of hair. The Hair and Fur effect has already been added in this file.

Restrict Hair to Specific Locations

1. Select an object.
2. Click [icon].
3. Click [▾] and then select Hair and Fur (WSM).

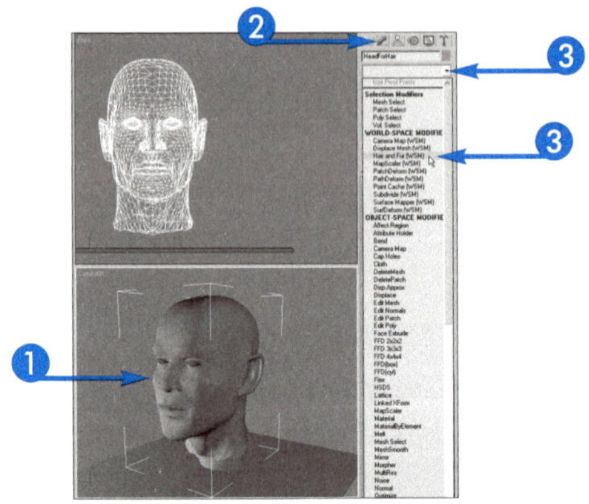

The guides appear in the viewports.

4. Click the Polygon sub-object button ([icon]).
5. Click the Select Object button ([icon]).
6. Select the polygons to which you want to apply hair.

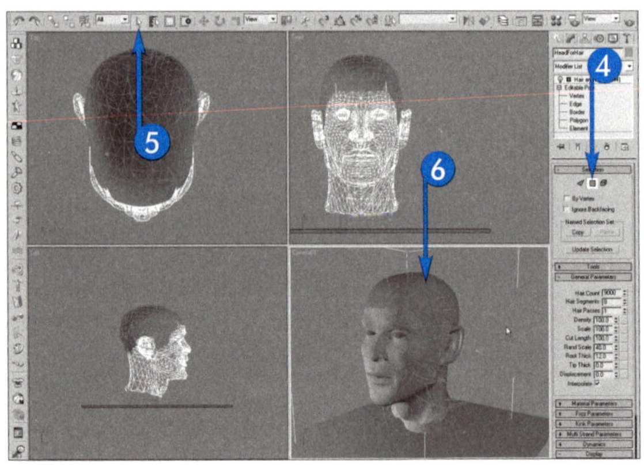

7 Click Update Selection.

The guides restrict to the selected polygons.

8 Click .

The scene renders with the hair restricted to the selected polygons.

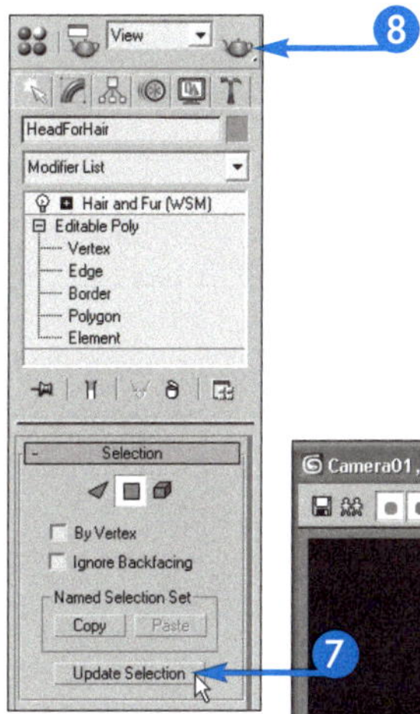

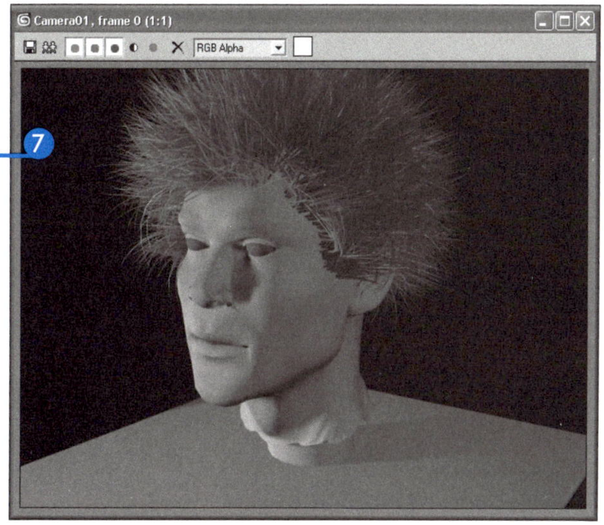

MASTER IT

Why does my hair not cast shadows?

- If spotlights are absent from your scene, then the Hair and Fur effect uses its own default Omni light to illuminate and cast shadows. If a spotlight exists, even if it is not oriented toward the hair, then the default Omni is ignored. Ensure that at least one of the spotlights that illuminate the hair has Shadows turned on in the General Parameters rollout. Shadow Maps work best with Hair and Fur, and mental ray lights do not cast shadows. For more information on lights and shadows, see Chapter 17.

My hair appears over-illuminated. How can I reduce this effect without changing the overall lighting in my scene?

- By default, the Hair and Fur effects use all spotlights to illuminate hair. To only use specific lights, deselect the "Use all lights at render time" (☐ changes to ☑) option at the bottom of the Environment and Effects dialog box. Next, select the lights that you want the effect to use, and then click the Add Hair Properties button at the bottom of the dialog box. This adds a Hair Light Attr rollout to each of the selected lights, with controls for specifying the shadow resolution, fuzz factor, and a toggle for the light's effect on the hair.

Modify the Hair Parameters

The default Hair and Fur settings tend to have the appearance of a long, unkempt mane that is in desperate need of a combing. The Hair and Fur modifier has many controls for changing the appearance of the hair, including its length, density, thickness, and actual hair count.

There are several controls available that you can use to select and adjust the hair's material, including root and tip color, specularity, and glossiness. Most of the parameters, located in the Material Parameters rollout, can be further clarified using an image map in their map channels. You can access the map channels by clicking any of the gray boxes to the right of the parameter spinners or fields. For information on material and map properties and application, see Chapters 14, 15, and 16.

See the section "Comb Your Hair" for information on styling hair. See the section "Add Hair to an Object" for information on adding the Hair and Fur effect.

CD FILE The HairParameters.max file is available onthe CD-ROM for you to practice changing hair parameters. The Hair and Fur effect has already been added in this file.

Modify the Hair Parameters

1. Select the object with hair.
2. Click .
3. Click the Plus icons (+) to expand the General Parameters and Material Parameters rollouts.

- You can type a higher Hair Count value to make the hair coverage thicker.
- You can type a lower Scale value to shorten the hair.
- You can type a lower Root Thick value to make each hair finer.

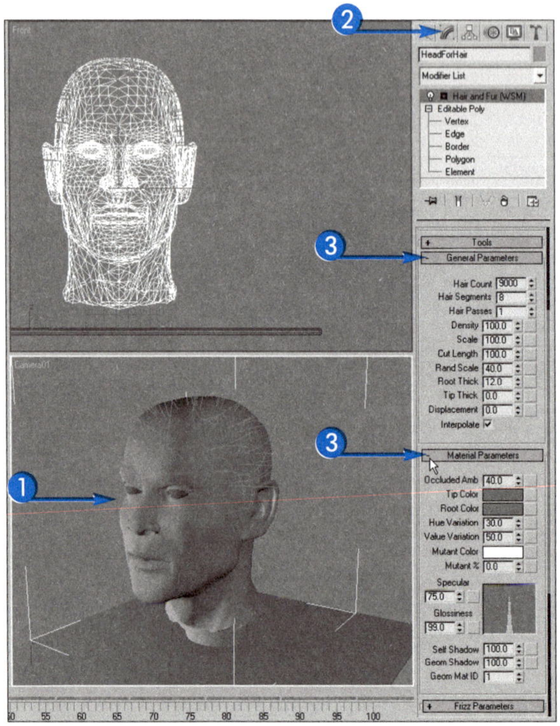

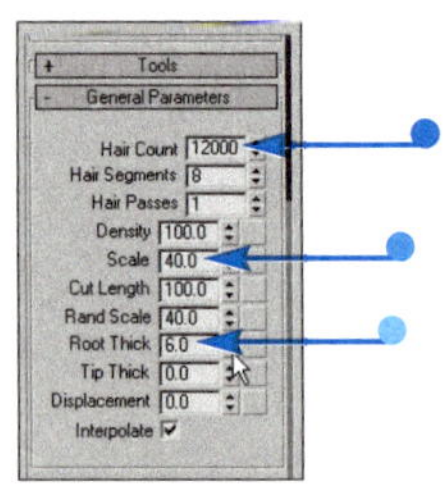

4 Click the Tip Color swatch.

The Color Selector dialog box appears.

5 Click a color to set the color for the hair tips.

You can use the spinners and sliders to adjust the color values.

6 Repeat steps 4 and 5 for the root color.

7 Click [button].

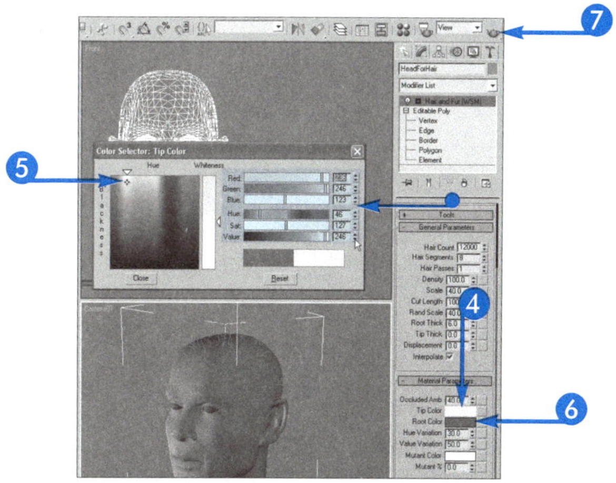

3ds Max renders the scene with the new parameters.

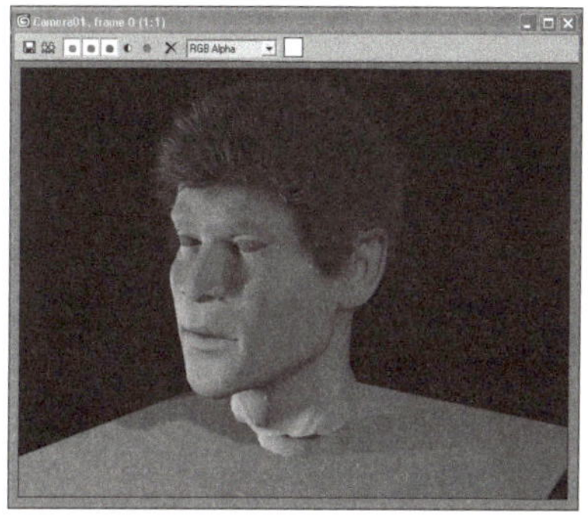

MASTER IT

What is the difference between the Cut Length and Scale parameters?

The Cut Length parameter defines the length of the hair as a percentage of the Scale value. Animating the Cut Length value causes the hair to appear to grow or fade. The Scale parameter changes the overall scale, length, and thickness of the hair to any value below its default value of 100. Both the Scale and Cut Length parameters can be controlled using an image map. Any area defined as white contains hairs at the parameter's fully-defined length. As the colors shift towards black, the length and scale diminish.

I want to modify the area of my model that contains hair, but I do not want to start the selection over. How can I do this?

Once you make a sub-object selection, you can store it in the file by entering a name in the Named Selection Sets field in the Main toolbar. Any time you need to make that same selection, click [button] next to the Named Selection Sets field and choose the name from the list. The name of a Named Selection Set for an object's sub-object is only available when you are at that sub-object level for the specified object. If no sub-object level is accessed, then the list displays Named Selection Sets for the scene's objects.

Comb Your Hair

The appearance of the hair and fur generated by 3ds Max at render time is based on the guides that are created by the Hair and Fur modifier. The guides always extend outward, perpendicular to the surface of the face from which they spring. See the section "Modify the Hair Parameters" for more information.

The Style window, which you can access through the Tools rollout, contains the tools for combing, cutting, and otherwise modifying the guides. Using a hairbrush analogy, you can simply comb the guides until they form the desired shape. You can define whether the brush affects the tip, root, or entire hair, and change the size of the brush by holding down the B key and dragging in the Style dialog box window. After you exit the dialog box and render your scene, the hair follows the newly shaped guides.

See the section "Add Hair to an Object" for information on adding the Hair and Fur effect.

The HairParameters.max file is available on the CD-ROM for you to practice changing hair parameters. The Hair and Fur effect has already been added in this file.

Comb Your Hair

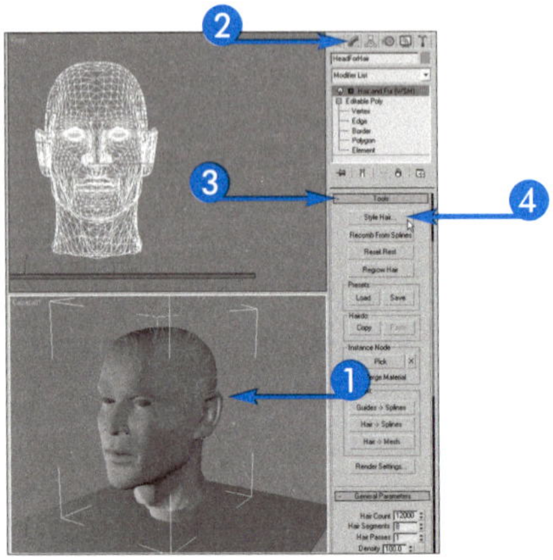

1. Select the object with hair.
2. Click .
3. Click the Plus icon (+) to expand the Tools rollout.
4. Click Style Hair.

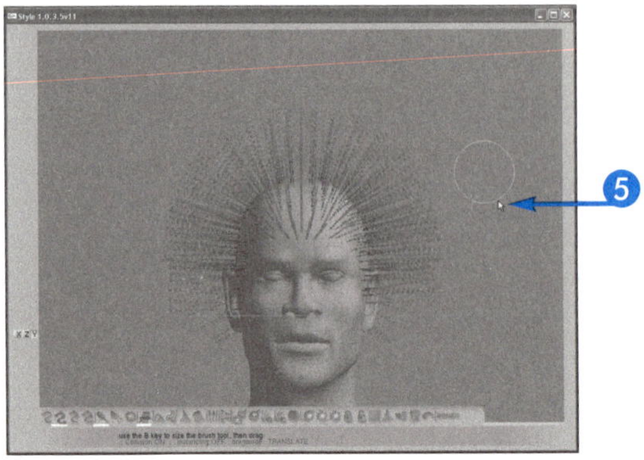

The Style window appears.

5. Press the B key and then drag your cursor to size the brush.

The brush size changes.

6. Click the Select the Whole Strand button (icon).
7. Click the Brush Mode button (icon).
8. Drag the brush over the hairs.
9. Repeat step 5 to 8 until you have created the hairstyle that you want.
10. Click the X, Z, and Y buttons to change the view.
11. Click Done when you are finished.

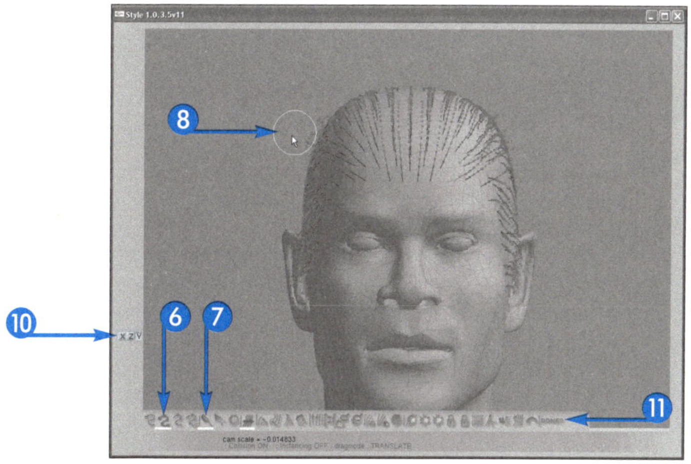

12. Click (icon).

    The scene renders with the new hairstyle.

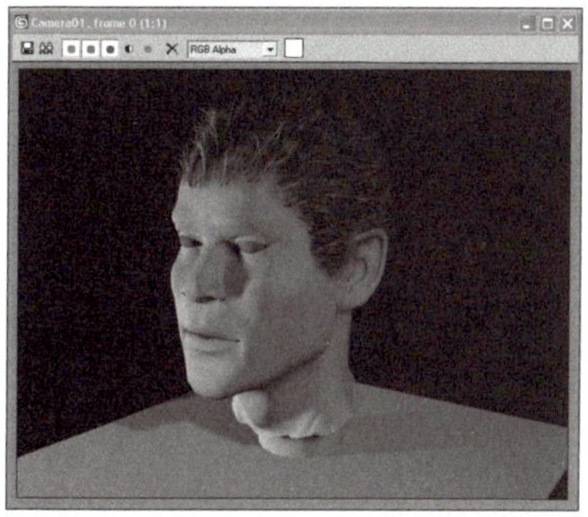

MASTER IT

I have created a Blur effect, but the hair is not blurring. Why?

▼ All of the rendering effects listed in the Effects tab of the Environment and Effects dialog box are applied to the rendered scene in order, from top to bottom. Your Blur effect is probably located above the Hair and Fur effect, causing the scene to be blurred first, followed by the hair's being generated. To fix this problem, select the Blur effect in the Effects field, and then click the Move Down button until it is below the Hair and Fur effect.

Can I have hair that varies in color?

▼ Yes. The Tip Color and Root Color swatches, in the Material Parameters rollout, both allow an image map to determine the color of the hair. Click the gray button to the left of the swatch, and then, in the Material/Map Browser dialog box, select Bitmap. Navigate to and select the bitmap that you want to use to set the hair color, and then click Open. To use the same map to set the color for the other hair Color parameter, click and drag the first parameter's map button, which now displays an M, to the other map button and choose Instance in the dialog box that appears.

Load and Save a Hair Preset

3ds Max ships with several hair presets that have many of the parameters set to popular and commonly used values. By loading a hair preset, you can quickly achieve the look of platinum blond hair, an Afro, or a well-fertilized lawn. Because the parameters are not fixed, they can be used as a starting point for any look that you are trying to achieve. For example, if the platnumblond preset is close to what you need, but the color is off, then you can load the preset and change the Tip Color and Root Color parameters. If you create a Hair or Fur effect that you may want to apply to objects in another scene, then you can save it as a preset. All parameters for the Hair and Fur are saved in the preset, except for display information and any changes that were made in the Style dialog box.

See the section "Add Hair to an Object" for information on adding the Hair and Fur effect.

CD FILE — The HairComb.max file is available on the CD-ROM for you to practice loading and saving hair parameters. The Hair and Fur effect has already been added in this file.

Load and Save a Hair Preset

Save a Hair Preset

1. Select the object with hair.
2. Click .
3. Click the Plus icon (+) to expand the Tools rollout.
4. Click Save.

   The Type a preset name dialog box appears.
5. Type a preset name.
6. Click OK.

   An indicator at the bottom of the screen indicates that a swatch is being rendered.

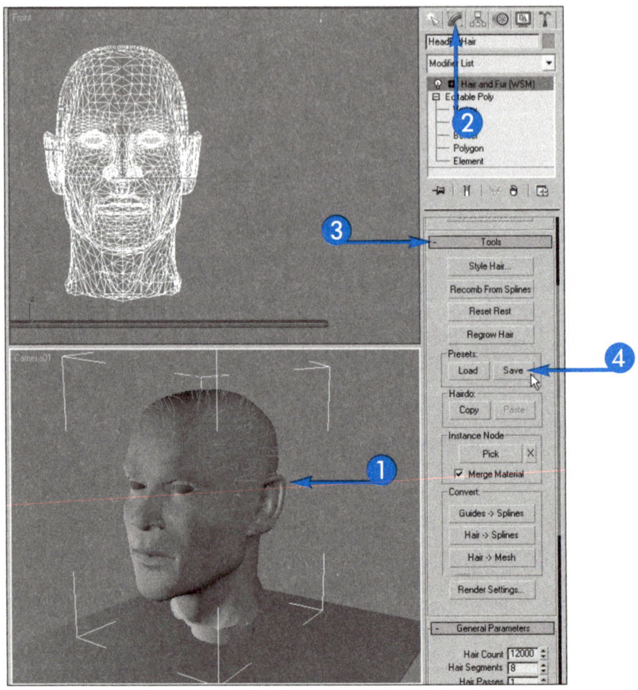

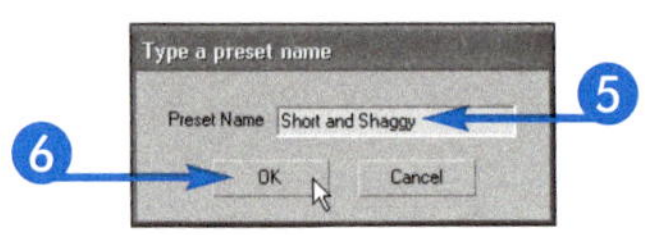

Load a Hair Preset

1 Click Load.

The Hair and Fur presets dialog box appears.

2 Double-click the preset swatch that you want to load.

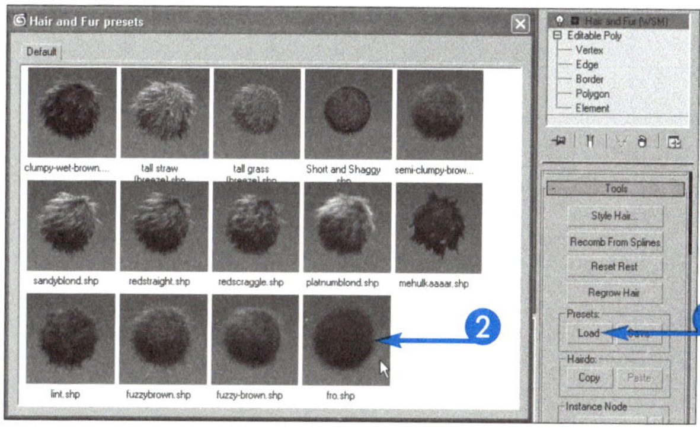

The dialog box closes, and the preset parameters are applied.

3 Click .

The scene is rendered with the new hair preset.

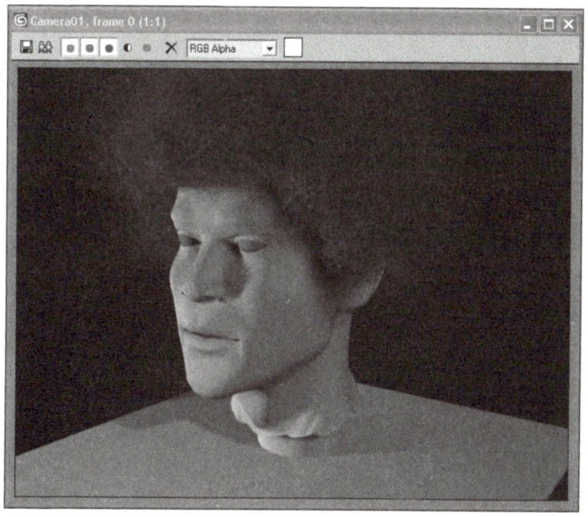

MASTER IT

I have applied Hair to a spline but no hair is rendered. Why?

- The Hair and Fur modifier can create hair on both geometry objects and spline objects. When using splines, the shape that the hair sprouts from must be comprised of more than one spline sub-object. The hairs' roots are located near the spline's first vertex. The numerically sequential splines act as guides for the hair emitted from the splines. Because of this, each spline sub-object must be adjacent to its numerically adjacent component. For example, the spline sub-object number two should be physically located between sub-objects number one and three. The spline sub-object number displays at the bottom of the Selection rollout when the sub-object is selected.

What are mutant hairs?

- Mutant hairs are indiscriminately chosen hairs that do not display the same material colors that the other hairs do. This can provide a bit of randomness to the hair color and show a character that is starting to go gray. The percent of hairs to be designated as mutant hairs is set in the Mutant % field in the Material Parameters rollout. The color for the mutant hairs is established in the Color Selector that opens when you click on the Mutant Color color swatch.

Appendix

MASTER
VISUALLY®
3ds Max® 8
The Complete Visual R
by Jon
trademarks or registered trademarks of John Wiley & Sons, Inc. and/or
affiliates. 3ds max is a registered trademark of Autodesk, Inc. All
other trademarks are property of their respective owners.
Part #0555028402
CD ID #MD02056A

Camera01, frame 0 (1:1)
RGB Alpha

PART VIII APPENDIX

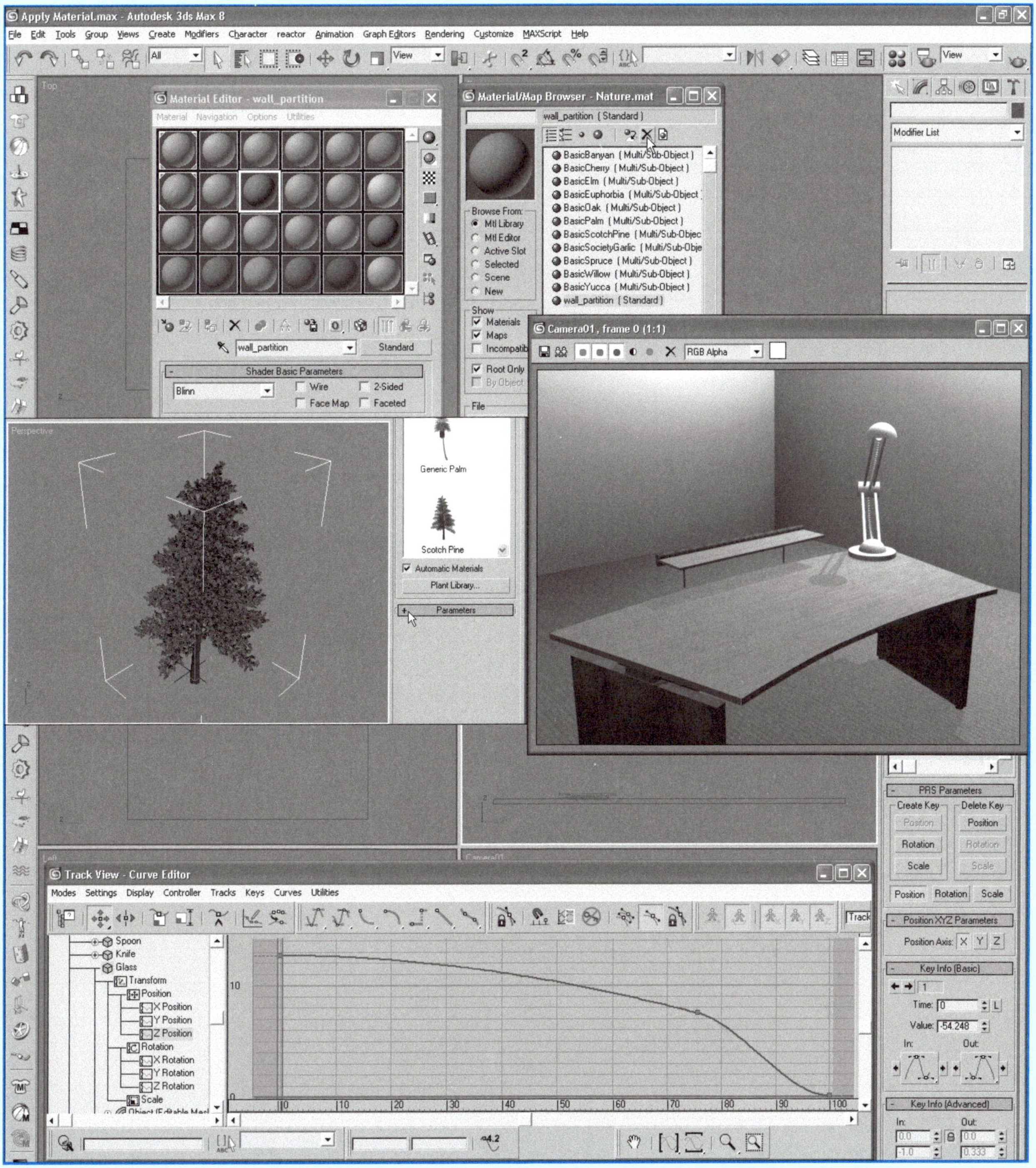

What's on the CD-ROM

You can use the CD-ROM included in this book to access many useful files and programs. Before installing any of the programs on the disc, you should check that you do not already have a newer version of the program already installed on your computer. To install different versions of the same program, you should contact the program's manufacturer. For the latest and greatest information, please refer to the ReadMe file located at the root level of the CD-ROM.

System Requirements

To use the contents of the CD-ROM, your computer must have the following hardware and software. The following requirements are for Windows 2000 (with SP4 or later) or Windows XP:

Hardware:

- PC with a Pentium III processor or AMD processor running at 500 Mhz or faster (dual Intel)
- Xeon or dual AMD Athlon or Opteron 32-bit system recommended)
- At least 512 MB of total RAM installed on your computer; for best performance, we recommend at least 1 GB
- 500 MB swap space (2 GB recommended)
- Graphics card supporting 1024x768x16-bit color with 64 MB RAM
- (OpenGL and Direct3D hardware acceleration supported; 3D graphics accelerator 1280x1024x32-bit color with 256 MB RAM recommended)
- Microsoft Windows–compliant pointing device (optimized for Microsoft IntelliMouse)
- Wacom(tm) Intuos or similar pressure-sensitive tablet recommended for vertex paint
- DVD-ROM drive
- Optional: sound card and speakers, cabling for TCP/IP-compliant network, 3D hardware graphics acceleration, video input and output devices, joystick, MIDI instruments, three-button mouse

Software:

- Microsoft Windows XP Professional SP2 (recommended), Windows XP Home Edition SP2, or Windows 2000 SP4.
- Microsoft Internet Explorer 6
- DirectX 9.0c (required), OpenGL (optional)

Author's Files

You can use these files to follow along the step-by-step instructions in the various sections in this book. In this manner, you can read the steps as you see the actual results in 3ds Max. When a particular section has a file that you can follow on the CD-ROM, you see the following icon:

Simply open 3ds Max 8, open the file that is indicated next to the CD icon, and then follow the steps in the section. You can browse the files directly from the CD-ROM, or you can copy them to your hard drive and use them as the basis for your own projects. To find the files on the CD-ROM, open the Samples folder on the CD drive.

3ds Max 8, Trial Version: Installing and Using the Software

For Windows 2000 and XP. Freeware.

Autodesk 3ds Max 8 is a state-of-the-art tool to create 3d animation for game development, design visualization, visual effects, and education. For more information about 3ds Max, visit their Web site at usa.autodesk.com/adsk/servlet/index?id=5659302&siteID=123112 .

Troubleshooting

The programs on the CD-ROM should work on computers with the minimum of system requirements. However, some programs may not work properly.

The two most likely problems for the programs not working properly include not having enough memory (RAM) for the programs you want to use, or having other programs running that affect the installation or running of a program. If you receive error messages, try one or more of the methods below and then try using the software again:

- Turn off any anti-virus software
- Close all running programs
- In Windows, close the CD-ROM interface and run demos or installations directly from Windows Explorer
- Have your local computer store add more RAM to your computer

Customer Care

If you have trouble with the CD-ROM, please call the Wiley Product Technical Support phone number at (800) 762-2974. Outside the United States, call 1(317) 572-3994. You can also contact Wiley Product Technical Support at http://support.wiley.com. John Wiley & Sons will provide technical support only for installation and other general quality control items. For technical support on the applications themselves, consult the program's vendor or author. To place additional orders or to request information about other Wiley products, please call (877) 762-2974.

Wiley Publishing, Inc. End-User License Agreement

READ THIS. You should carefully read these terms and conditions before opening the software packet(s) included with *Master VISUALLY 3ds Max 8*. This is a license agreement ("Agreement") between you and Wiley Publishing, Inc. ("WPI"). By opening the accompanying software packet(s), you acknowledge that you have read and accept the following terms and conditions. If you do not agree and do not want to be bound by such terms and conditions, promptly return the Book and the unopened software packet(s) to the place you obtained them from for a full refund.

1. **License Grant.** WPI grants to you (either an individual or entity) a nonexclusive license to use one copy of the enclosed software program(s) (collectively, the "Software") solely for your own personal or business purposes on a single computer (whether a standard computer or a workstation component of a multi-user network). The Software is in use on a computer when it is loaded into temporary memory (RAM) or installed into permanent memory (hard disc, CD-ROM, or other storage device). WPI reserves all rights not expressly granted herein.

2. **Ownership.** WPI is the owner of all right, title, and interest, including copyright, in and to the compilation of the Software recorded on the disc(s) or CD-ROM ("Software Media"). Copyright to the individual programs recorded on the Software Media is owned by the author, or other authorized copyright owner of each program. Ownership of the Software and all proprietary rights relating thereto remain with WPI and its licensers.

3. **Restrictions on Use and Transfer.**

   (a) You may only (i) make one copy of the Software for backup or archival purposes, or (ii) transfer the Software to a single hard disc, provided that you keep the original for backup or archival purposes. You may not (i) rent or lease the Software, (ii) copy or reproduce the Software through a LAN or other network system or through any computer subscriber system or bulletin-board system, or (iii) modify, adapt, or create derivative works based on the Software.

   (b) You may not reverse engineer, decompile, or disassemble the Software. You may transfer the Software and user documentation on a permanent basis, provided that the transferee agrees to accept the terms and conditions of this Agreement and you retain no copies. If the Software is an update or has been updated, any transfer must include the most recent update and all prior versions.

4. **Restrictions on Use of Individual Programs.** You must follow the individual requirements and restrictions detailed for each individual program in Appendix D of this Book. These limitations are also contained in the individual license agreements recorded on the Software Media. These limitations may include a requirement that after using the program for a specified period of time, the user must pay a registration fee or discontinue use. By opening the Software packet(s), you will be agreeing to abide by the licenses and restrictions for these individual programs that are detailed in Appendix D and on the Software Media. None of the material on this Software Media or listed in this Book may ever be redistributed, in original or modified form, for commercial purposes.

5. **Limited Warranty.**

(a) WPI warrants that the Software and Software Media are free from defects in materials and workmanship under normal use for a period of sixty (60) days from the date of purchase of this Book. If WPI receives notification within the warranty period of defects in materials or workmanship, WPI will replace the defective Software Media.

(b) **WPI AND THE AUTHOR OF THE BOOK DISCLAIM ALL OTHER WARRANTIES, EXPRESS OR IMPLIED, INCLUDING WITHOUT LIMITATION IMPLIED WARRANTIES OF MERCHANTABILITY AND FITNESS FOR A PARTICULAR PURPOSE, WITH RESPECT TO THE SOFTWARE, THE PROGRAMS, THE SOURCE CODE CONTAINED THEREIN, AND/OR THE TECHNIQUES DESCRIBED IN THIS BOOK. WPI DOES NOT WARRANT THAT THE FUNCTIONS CONTAINED IN THE SOFTWARE WILL MEET YOUR REQUIREMENTS OR THAT THE OPERATION OF THE SOFTWARE WILL BE ERROR FREE.**

(c) This limited warranty gives you specific legal rights, and you may have other rights that vary from jurisdiction to jurisdiction.

6. **Remedies.**

(a) WPI's entire liability and your exclusive remedy for defects in materials and workmanship shall be limited to replacement of the Software Media, which may be returned to WPI with a copy of your receipt at the following address: Software Media Fulfillment Department, Attn.: *Master VISUALLY 3ds Max*, Wiley Publishing, Inc., 10475 Crosspoint Blvd., Indianapolis, IN 46256, or call 1-800-762-2974. Please allow four to six weeks for delivery. This Limited Warranty is void if failure of the Software Media has resulted from accident, abuse, or misapplication. Any replacement Software Media will be warranted for the remainder of the original warranty period or thirty (30) days, whichever is longer.

(b) In no event shall WPI or the author be liable for any damages whatsoever (including without limitation damages for loss of business profits, business interruption, loss of business information, or any other pecuniary loss) arising from the use of or inability to use the Book or the Software, even if WPI has been advised of the possibility of such damages.

(c) Because some jurisdictions do not allow the exclusion or limitation of liability for consequential or incidental damages, the above limitation or exclusion may not apply to you.

7. **U.S. Government Restricted Rights.** Use, duplication, or disclosure of the Software for or on behalf of the United States of America, its agencies and/or instrumentalities (the "U.S. Government") is subject to restrictions as stated in paragraph (c)(1)(ii) of the Rights in Technical Data and Computer Software clause of DFARS 252.227-7013, or subparagraphs (c) (1) and (2) of the Commercial Computer Software - Restricted Rights clause at FAR 52.227-19, and in similar clauses in the NASA FAR supplement, as applicable.

8. **General.** This Agreement constitutes the entire understanding of the parties and revokes and supersedes all prior agreements, oral or written, between them and may not be modified or amended except in a writing signed by both parties hereto that specifically refers to this Agreement. This Agreement shall take precedence over any other documents that may be in conflict herewith. If any one or more provisions contained in this Agreement are held by any court or tribunal to be invalid, illegal, or otherwise unenforceable, each and every other provision shall remain in full force and effect.

Numbers

INDEX

continued

continued

D

continued

continued

N

O

P

continued

Q

R

continued

continued

continued

U

V